lonely planet

Alaska

Jim DuFresne
Greg Benchwick, Catherine Bodry

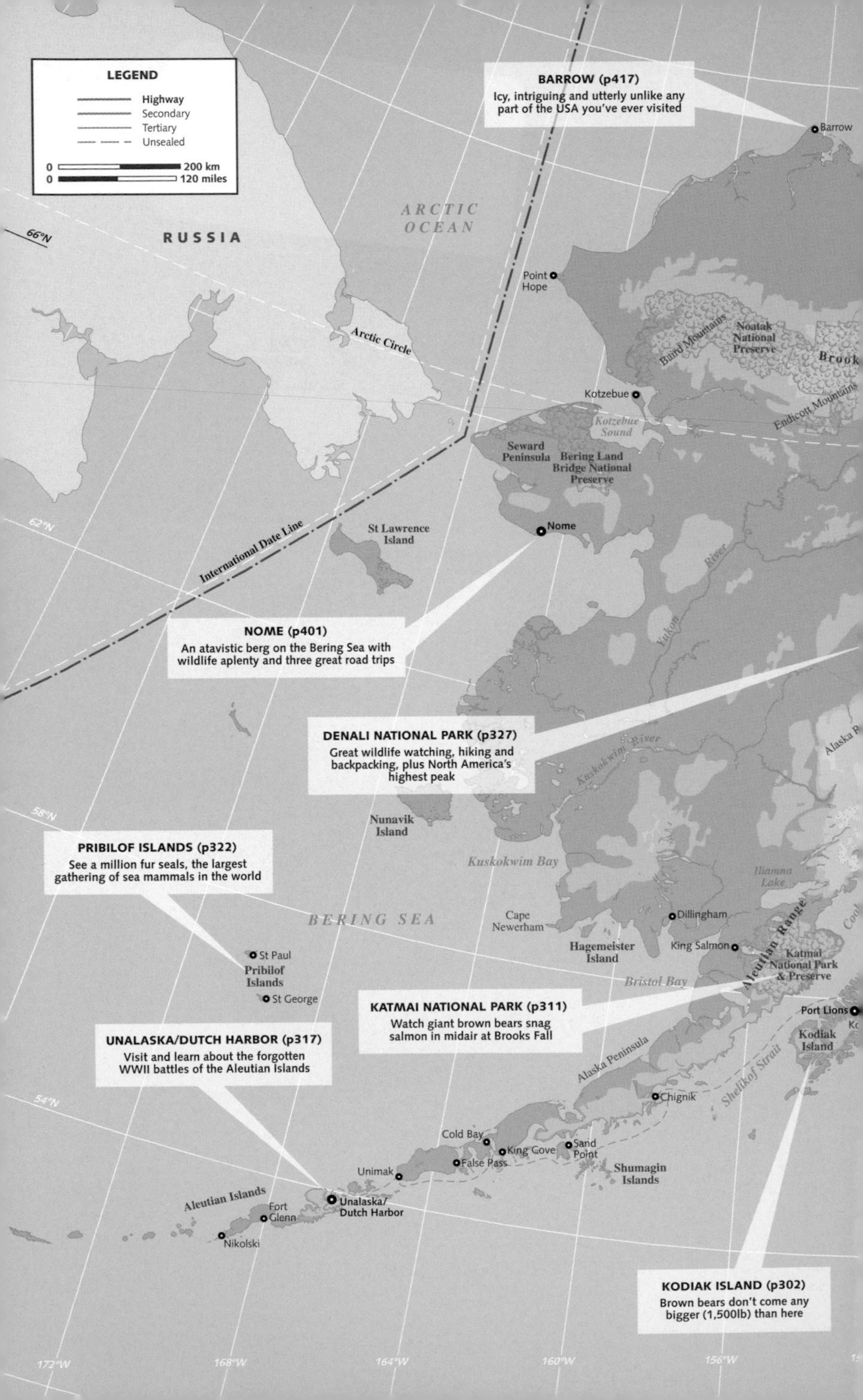

LEGEND
Highway
Secondary
Tertiary
Unsealed
0 200 km
0 120 miles
BARROW (p417)
Icy, intriguing and utterly unlike any part of the USA you've ever visited
Barrow
ARCTIC OCEAN
RUSSIA
66°N
Point Hope
Arctic Circle
Noatak National Preserve
Baird Mountains
Brook
Kotzebue
Endicott Mountains
Kotzebue Sound
Seward Peninsula
Bering Land Bridge National Preserve
62°N
Nome
St Lawrence Island
International Date Line
River
Yukon
NOME (p401)
An atavistic berg on the Bering Sea with wildlife aplenty and three great road trips
DENALI NATIONAL PARK (p327)
Great wildlife watching, hiking and backpacking, plus North America's highest peak
Kuskokwim River
Alaska R
58°N
Nunavik Island
PRIBILOF ISLANDS (p322)
See a million fur seals, the largest gathering of sea mammals in the world
Kuskokwim Bay
Iliamna Lake
BERING SEA
Cape Newerham
Dillingham
Aleutian Range
St Paul
Pribilof Islands
St George
Hagemeister Island
King Salmon
Katmai National Park & Preserve
Bristol Bay
KATMAI NATIONAL PARK (p311)
Watch giant brown bears snag salmon in midair at Brooks Fall
Port Lions
Kodiak Island
UNALASKA/DUTCH HARBOR (p317)
Visit and learn about the forgotten WWII battles of the Aleutian Islands
Alaska Peninsula
Shelikof Strait
54°N
Chignik
Cold Bay
King Cove
Sand Point
False Pass
Shumagin Islands
Unimak
Aleutian Islands
Fort Glenn
Unalaska/ Dutch Harbor
Nikolski
KODIAK ISLAND (p302)
Brown bears don't come any bigger (1,500lb) than here
172°W
168°W
164°W
160°W
156°W

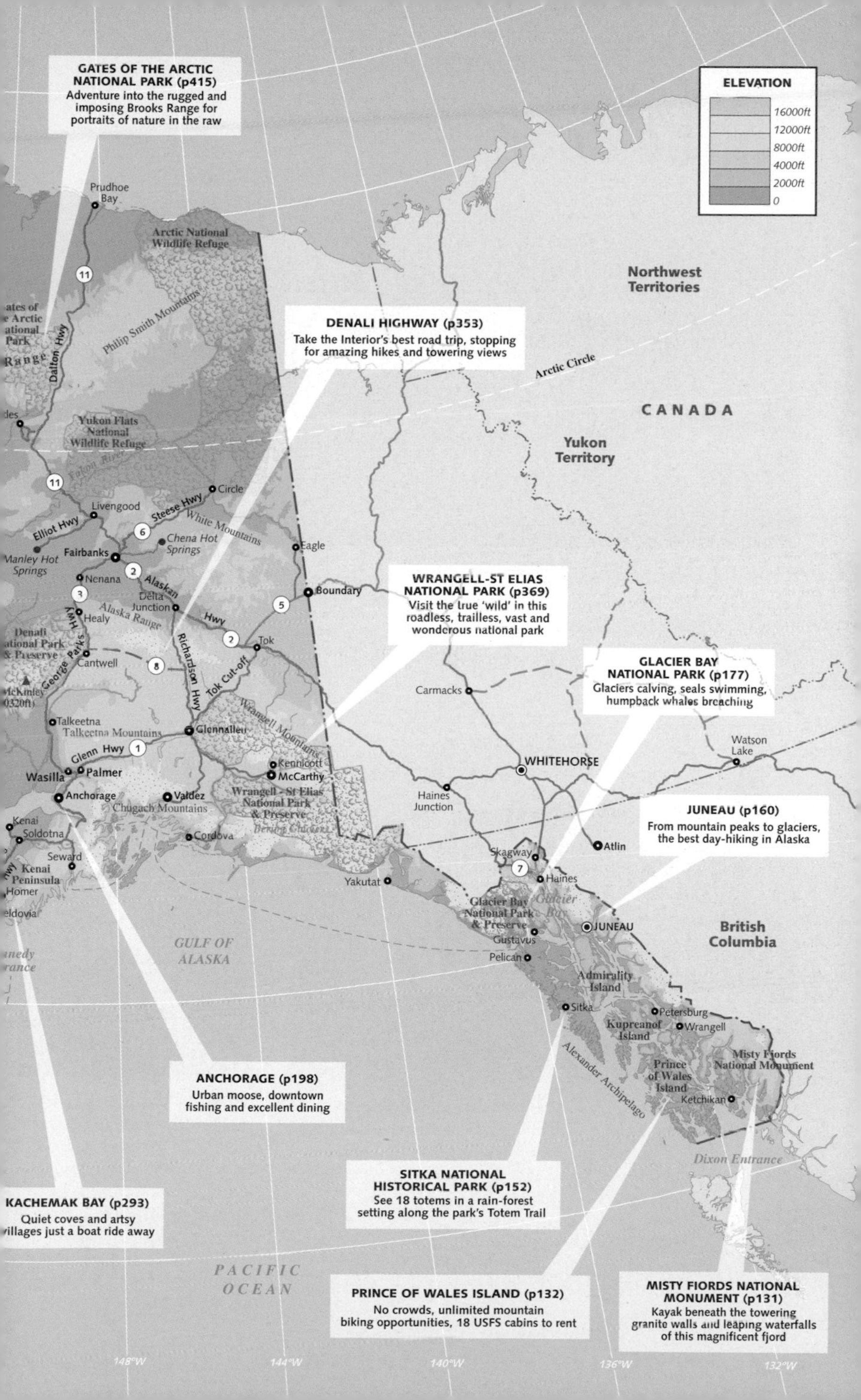
GATES OF THE ARCTIC NATIONAL PARK (p415)
Adventure into the rugged and imposing Brooks Range for portraits of nature in the raw
ELEVATION
16000ft
12000ft
8000ft
4000ft
2000ft
0
Prudhoe Bay
Arctic National Wildlife Refuge
Philip Smith Mountains
Dalton Hwy
Northwest Territories
DENALI HIGHWAY (p353)
Take the Interior's best road trip, stopping for amazing hikes and towering views
Arctic Circle
CANADA
Yukon Territory
Yukon Flats National Wildlife Refuge
Yukon River
Circle
Livengood
Steese Hwy
Elliot Hwy
White Mountains
Chena Hot Springs
Manley Hot Springs
Fairbanks
Eagle
Nenana
Alaskan
Hwy
Delta Junction
Healy
Alaska Range
Boundary
WRANGELL-ST ELIAS NATIONAL PARK (p369)
Visit the true 'wild' in this roadless, trailless, vast and wonderous national park
Tok
Cantwell
George Parks
Richardson Hwy
Tok Cut-off
GLACIER BAY NATIONAL PARK (p177)
Glaciers calving, seals swimming, humpback whales breaching
Carmacks
Talkeetna
Talkeetna Mountains
Wrangell Mountains
Glennallen
Glenn Hwy
Wasilla
Palmer
Kennicott
McCarthy
WHITEHORSE
Watson Lake
Anchorage
Valdez
Chugach Mountains
Wrangell - St Elias National Park & Preserve
Bering Glacier
Haines Junction
Kenai
Soldotna
Cordova
Seward
Kenai Peninsula
Homer
JUNEAU (p160)
From mountain peaks to glaciers, the best day-hiking in Alaska
Atlin
Skagway
Haines
Yakutat
Glacier Bay National Park & Preserve
Glacier Bay
Gustavus
JUNEAU
British Columbia
GULF OF ALASKA
Pelican
Admiralty Island
Sitka
Petersburg
Kupreanof Island
Wrangell
Alexander Archipelago
Prince of Wales Island
Misty Fiords National Monument
Ketchikan
ANCHORAGE (p198)
Urban moose, downtown fishing and excellent dining
Dixon Entrance
SITKA NATIONAL HISTORICAL PARK (p152)
See 18 totems in a rain-forest setting along the park's Totem Trail
KACHEMAK BAY (p293)
Quiet coves and artsy villages just a boat ride away
PACIFIC OCEAN
PRINCE OF WALES ISLAND (p132)
No crowds, unlimited mountain biking opportunities, 18 USFS cabins to rent
MISTY FIORDS NATIONAL MONUMENT (p131)
Kayak beneath the towering granite walls and leaping waterfalls of this magnificent fjord
148°W
144°W
140°W
136°W
132°W

On the Road

JIM DUFRESNE Coordinating Author

Unalaska/Dutch Harbor's (p317) finest hotel smelled like a fish market because out front a crew was unrolling 300yd of dragnet still containing small bits of trapped pollack. Almost immediately 50 bald eagles descended on it, some feeding only 10ft away from me. Only in a place called Unalaska.

CATHERINE BODRY After several weeks in nothing but mountains, I was totally unprepared for the mountains to take a giant step back and make room for the sky when I drove down the Copper River Hwy (p248). I turned my music up and enjoyed the very open road.

GREG BENCHWICK Sometimes you just have to head out into the field to test the hiking sections of the book. It's a tough job, but somebody's got to do it. Here I am road-testing our Denali National Park hiking section (p335). My favorite part about hiking in Denali: no people, no trails.

For full author biographies see p448.

Alaska Highlights

Alaska's top adventures and experiences? They're on every page of this book. But for the best of the best we recruited seasoned Lonely Planet authors, staff and readers for their thoughts on what they think are the essential things to see, do and taste in the Final Frontier. Enjoy their colorful journey through the following pages.

Anything missing? Let us know! Visit www.lonelyplanet.com and pass along your own favorite Alaskan highlights.

PETER PTSCHELINZEW

1 GLACIER HIKES

On a summer day, you still need to bundle up before hiking onto the foot of a glacier (p76). Make sure you put on a pair of gloves. If you try to climb with sneakers you may fall flat on your face. Climb a little farther up and you start wondering if a crack will suddenly form and send you tumbling in. Up farther still you start to experience the magnitude. Then, interestingly, it starts to get a bit mundane. Miles and miles of flat white ice.

Todd Sotkiewicz, Lonely Planet staff

KAYAKING THE KENAI PENINSULA

We paddled silently across the glassy surface trying not to disturb the sea otters and to get a closer look. One quickly dove underwater and resurfaced really close, nearly capsizing a startled kayaker. It was a beautiful sunny day in early fall. Unfortunately no puffin, whale or sea lion sightings but we had the ocean and a deserted island lunch to ourselves. It seemed like most of Alaska had already closed in preparation for winter but the quieter time of year was an amazing way to experience the last frontier…far from the cruise-ship and peak-season crowds (p74).

Jessica Rose, Lonely Planet staff

2

JESSICA

THE 'TOUR' IN DENALI NATIONAL PARK

Probably the best wildlife watching in all of Alaska, the Denali National Park bus trip (p332) takes you past rushing arctic rivers, vast arching mountain vistas, including Mt McKinley (North America's tallest peak), and more than 70 miles of dusty wonder-world road not open to private vehicles most of the year. Along the way, you are almost ensured close encounters with grizzly, moose, caribou and more. But there are no cash-back guarantees. With a few more days, you can actually touch nature as you trundle out to remote lakes, rivers and land few eyes will ever see.

Greg Benchwick, Lonely Planet author

NPS PHOTO/KENT MILLER

3

LEE F

4

THE YUKON RAILWAY

Ride the amazing White Pass & Yukon Route railway (p196) from Skagway to Whitehorse for fantastic mountainous scenery. Hike to one of the small lakes above the town, or visit the site where the infamous Soapy Smith was shot. Skagway was a gold rush jumping-off point.

Whitefox, traveler

ANCHORAGE

With Denali's peaks less than 200 miles away, it's easy to skip Anchorage (p198) and head for the wilderness. But stroll Native dwellings at the Alaska Native Heritage Center (p203), take a bike ride along the Tony Knowles Coastal Trail (p206) to Earthquake Park (p205) or share a beer with locals at 'Koots' (p214) and you'll find yourself at home in this down-to-earth city.

Heather Dickson, Lonely Planet staff

5

BRENT WINEBRENNER

FRESH WILD SALMON

The color is bright, and the meat rich and oily. Grilled to perfection, with just some lemon, garlic and butter, there is nothing more satisfying than a fresh fillet of king salmon (p87).

Catherine Bodry, Lonely Planet author

6

JERRY ALEXANDER

KENT MILLER

7 ZIPLINING IN KETCHIKAN

We loved the zipline (p80). We were strapped to the line with a harness. You stand up, lift your legs and off you go. When you need to put on the brakes you just apply pressure to the lowest line above. If you don't make it to the next platform, you have to pull your way up.

Kent Miller, traveler, Michigan

MIDNIGHT SUN

If you're in Fairbanks at the end of June, check out the Midnight Sun Baseball Game (p386). Only in Alaska…

Greg Benchwick, Lonely Planet author

8

PHOTOLIB

JIM DUF

9 THE MT ROBERTS TRAMWAY

The climb to the summit of Mt Roberts is not overly hard but it is steady. Within an hour most people break out of the trees where at their feet are stunning views of the towns of Juneau and Douglas with the Gastineau Channel between them. Even better is the nearby station of the Mt Roberts Tramway (p163), a great place to stop at after an afternoon of alpine scrambling. For the price of a cold beer – and who couldn't use one after climbing a mountain? – you receive a complimentary ride back to Juneau on the tramway.

Jim DuFresne, Lonely Planet author

THE NORTHERN LIGHTS

One of the best places to see the Aurora is Fairbanks (p391) – you have a clear view of it and Fairbanks is accessible. Stretch out on the grass and watch the lights dancing across the sky, intertwining, separating and changing color.

Carmenng, traveler

10

CHRIS MADELEY/PHOTOLIBRARY

JUNEAU

Juneau (p160) is the kind of place where you suddenly feel compelled to buy a souvenir bear in a knitted sweater, it's just so darn pretty! My favorite day in Juneau would be a brisk morning walk alongside the Mendenhall Glacier, followed by a warming ale behind the swinging doors of the Red Dog Saloon.

Heather Dickson, Lonely Planet staff

11

JESSICA

JIM DUFRESNE

THE MILLION DOLLAR BRIDGE

Standing on the single-lane bridge on the Copper River Hwy (p248), you're sandwiched between two massive glaciers: Childs and Mears. Icebergs from Mears float under your feet to join those released from Childs, and, between these two ancient slabs of ice, you feel very, very small.

Catherine Bodry, Lonely Planet author

13

CATHERINE

12

FINE DINING IN HAINES

Handbills plastered around town announced Dungeness crab would be for sale in Haines' Harbor (p185). So a line of hungry campers and locals were waiting when the fishing boat tied up. For $5 they received a crab so alive they had to keep an eye on its pinchers. The campers headed back to their sites with fresh crab and cold beer for a seafood feast with plastic forks, a newspaper tablecloth on a picnic table and views of mountainous Lynn Canal. It's the best outdoor dining Alaska has to offer.

Jim DuFresne, Lonely Planet author

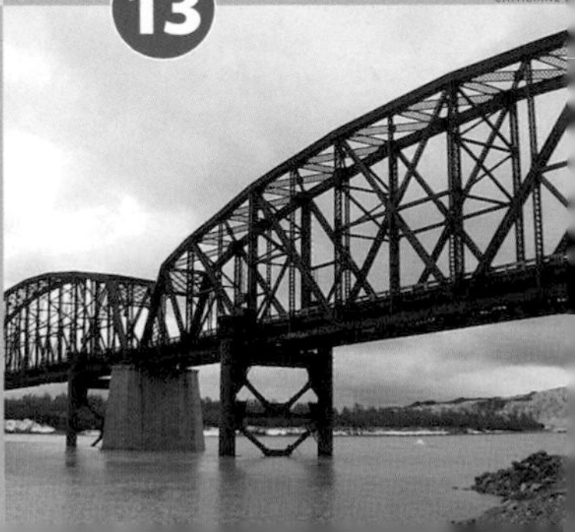

ALASKA STOCK LLC / ALAMY

14 THE NORTHERNMOST CITY IN THE USA

While a visit to Barrow (p417) is prohibitively expensive for most independent travelers, it may just be worth the splurge. After all, this is the northernmost settlement in the USA and the largest Iñupiat community in Alaska. It's also kind of stark. But therein lies its ethereal beauty: an arctic ghetto sitting on the edge of the imposing frozen ocean, a blip of human existence in an otherwise desolate land. Head out from town to look for polar bears – there's an amazing selection of migrating birds, too – or stay nearby to uncover the traditions of the Iñupiat.

Greg Benchwick, Lonely Planet author

BRENT WINEBRENNER

15 CHATTING UP THE LOCALS

Perhaps it's the solitude. Perhaps it's the dark winter nights or endless summer days. Whatever the reason, the characters who call Alaska home can be strange and kooky but oh-so-interesting. Start up a conversation with the friendly locals and you'll soon be reminded that there are many different ways to view the world (p53).

Lou LaGrange, Lonely Planet staff

JON

16 SPOTTING YOUR FIRST URBAN MOOSE

The moose (p83) never fails to cause a scene, calmly chewing someone's flowers while locals and tourists hover with cameras. Their legs always seem to be taller than a car, and though they nonchalantly meander away with a slow gait, the informal crowd of paparazzi shoulders after them.

Catherine Bodry, Lonely Planet Author

JON ARNOLD IMAGES LTD / A

17 THE END OF THE ROAD

Life begins at the end of the road in Alaska. And no community better embodies the spirit of off-the-grid Alaska than McCarthy (p370). This gold-rush town sits within the borders of Wrangell-St Elias National Park, the largest in the USA, and maintains the spirited energy of the bygone days of frontiersmanship and rugged individualism. You can also jet off for flightseeing or amazing backcountry adventures from this magical little village. For travelers on a budget, there are always day-hikes to the Kennicott Glacier, paddles down the Nizina, Chitina and Kennicott Rivers or open-mic night at the town's historic saloon.

Greg Benchwick, Lonely Planet author

THE SEWARD HIGHWAY

With tight curves and massive peaks, the bore tide and mountain passes, it's tempting to pull over and gawk at every turn. Why not? At only 126 miles, you can make a day of the trip from Anchorage to Seward (p218), appreciating the freedom of an open road in a very large land.

Catherine Bodry, Lonely Planet author

18

RICHARD CUMMINS

MT MCKINLEY

If you're lucky enough to catch a glimpse of 'the Great One' on a clear day, the sheer size of this monster mountain (p40) is impressive. The effect can be truly awe-inspiring and humbling.

Lou LaGrange, Lonely Planet staff

19

LEE F

ALASKA'S INSIDE PASSAGE

Whether you're cruising liner style or by Alaska State Ferry, you'll be cooing at the views and sunsets just the same as you make your way up (or down) the Inside Passage (p38). Two of the best stop-offs are Wrangell (p137; check out Petroglyph Beach) and Sitka (p149), the old capital of Russian America.

Heather Dickson, Lonely Planet staff

20

EMILY RIDDELL

ANDY

21

THE BEARS AT FISH CREEK

The best reason to take the out-of-the-way side trip to Hyder is finding your way to Fish Creek (p133), 6 miles north of this Southeast Alaska hamlet. From late July to September, you can watch brown and black bears feed on chum salmon from observation decks that put you less than 40ft away. Watching a brown bear chasing down a salmon is Alaska wildlife viewing at its most exciting.

Jim DuFresne, Lonely Planet author

KAYAKING THE COLUMBIA GLACIER

I've made many trips to Alaska and have always tried to stay off the beaten path. I love little towns like McCarthy (or even Elfin Cove!). Recently I treated myself for a day on Prince William Sound from Valdez. I joined Pangaea Adventures (p238) for a day of sea kayaking at Columbia Glacier (p238). Yes, it was a guided trip, but we all had an amazing day.

Outsiding, traveler

22

MARK NEWMAN

MANLEY HOT SPRINGS

This is an amazing hot springs (p397), in a small friendly town, off the beaten path, 90 miles north of Fairbanks. The hot spring itself is in a large greenhouse draped with tropical flowers and grapevines. You rent the entire greenhouse for $5 a person.

Missworldly, traveler

23

DENNIS FRATES / ALAMY

JIM DUF

24 THE TOP OF MT BALLYHOO

It's not easy to reach Dutch Harbor – it's a long ferry ride out to the Aleutian Islands or an expensive flight – nor is it easy to reach the top of Mt Ballyhoo (p319). The route to the flattish peak is along a winding, narrow dirt road with no guardrails. But once there, you're surrounded by the military remains of one of the fiercest campaigns of WWII. Only now the explosions and sirens of battle have been replaced by the quiet, tranquil world of a mountain where you can stand on the edge and watch eagles soar beneath you.

Jim DuFresne, Lonely Planet author

PHOTOLI

25 THE MT MARATHON RACE IN SEWARD

The gun goes off and the runners breeze by…and then up. You follow them as they form a single-file line up a near-vertical trail. Once they reach the top, they fly back down. Hitting the street, legs wobbling and often muddy or bloody, every runner is welcomed by a cheering crowd lining the streets. This is how Fourth of July is celebrated in Alaska (p260).

Catherine Bodry, Lonely Planet author

Contents

Regional Map Contents

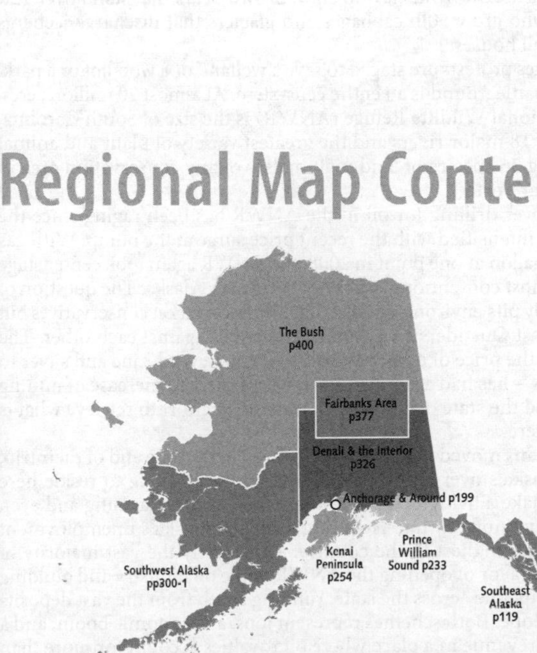

Destination Alaska

The seven kayakers following the Savonoski Loop in Katmai National Park were settled in for the evening, sipping mugs of hot tea, when across the Grosvenor River a brown bear appeared. It was a young male, maybe 200lb, 300lb tops. He followed the bank for a short spell and then splashed across the river and came within 30yd of their four Kleppers, folding kayaks composed of a light wooden frame and a rubberized canvas hull that a brown bear, even a small one, could mangle in minutes. The kayakers stood in unison, grabbed pots and pans and banged them while chanting 'hey bear, whoa bear!' For a brief moment everybody stared nervously at each other, acknowledging the other's existence, then the young bear decided that whatever the kayakers were selling, he didn't want and scrambled off into the woods.

FAST FACTS

Population: 676,987

Gross domestic product: $43.8 billion

Highest point: Mt McKinley (20,320ft)

Land mass: 586,400 sq miles

Number of Rhode Islands that could fit into Alaska: 425

Proportion of Alaska that lies within the Arctic Circle: 30%

Wild salmon harvested in Alaska: 137 million pounds or 90% of the USA's total

Most cruise ship passengers: Juneau (985,000 annually)

Days without the sun in Barrow: 84

Distance from Russia: 55 miles

Alaska is where human beings stand on an equal footing with nature. Nowhere else in the USA is there such an undeveloped, unpopulated and untrampled place.

Tourists who make the long journey north solely to discover the unspoiled character of this 'final frontier' are still often stunned by the grandeur of what they see. There are mountains, glaciers and rivers in other parts of North America, but few are on the same scale as those in Alaska. This state has the third longest river in the USA, 17 of the country's 20 highest peaks and 5000 glaciers, including one larger than Switzerland. The Arctic winters are one long night and Arctic summers one long day. In Alaska, there are king crabs that measure 3ft from claw to claw, brown bears that stand over 12ft tall, farmers who grow 90lb cabbages and glaciers that discharge icebergs the size of small houses.

In other states protests are staged to save a wetland or a woodlot or a park. In Alaska the battleground is an entire ecosystem. At almost 20 million acres, the Arctic National Wildlife Refuge (ANWR) is the size of South Carolina, encompassing 18 major rivers and the greatest variety of plant and animal life – including 36 species of land mammals – of any conservation area in the circumpolar north.

The battle over drilling for oil in the ANWR has been raging since the 1980s, but has intensified with the recent price surge at the pump. With gas breaking $4 a gallon at one point in 2008, the ANWR again took center stage as one of the most contentious issues hovering over Alaska. The question of drilling not only pits environmentalists against free-market conservatives but Alaskans against Outsiders and even Native tribes against each other. The sudden rise in the price of other resources – copper, gold, zinc and silver to name but a few – has had a similar effect, with a marked increase of mining projects around the state delving into nature in an effort to retrieve what is needed elsewhere.

Many Alaskans moved here, or simply stayed here at the end of their trip, because of Alaska's overwhelming beauty. But in choosing to reside here they have to make a living in a place where there is little farming and even less industrial manufacturing. Hovering near 7%, Alaska's unemployment rate is one of the highest in the country. This is why the vast majority of Alaskans are in favor of opening the ANWR to the oil industry and building a natural gas pipeline across the state, running south from the vast deposits in the North Slope. Both schemes represent jobs, an economic boom, and a new source of revenue in a place where oil royalties account for more than 80% of the state treasury.

The burden of unemployment also accounts for why the majority of Alaskans are in favor of their beleaguered 'bridges to nowhere' – huge, costly spans across the Knik Arm north of Anchorage and from Ketchikan to the lightly populated Gravina Island in the Southeast. To the rest of the country these projects represent pork-barrel politicking (spending designed to win votes) at its worst, but to locals they are avenues to expansion, offering flat land on which to farm, develop light industries and build affordable housing.

New road construction is also a contentious issue within the state, particularly the ongoing saga of building a 51-mile road north from Juneau to Skagway, where roads connect to Canada and eventually to the Alaska Hwy. The price tag stands at $400 million – a small price to pay, say many Alaskans, to help an isolated city where declines in logging and fishing have driven workers away and where the proposal to move the state capital to a more central location is almost constantly under consideration. But moving the capital is not the heart of the issue – it's really about expansion and confronting nature in a state where less than 1% of the land is developed. It's about making a year-round living, even when the cruise ships aren't in port.

Alaskans are acutely aware of the issues, both local and global, that they face. They are aware that their state is at a historic crossroad. Few question global warming in Alaska. Melting glaciers, grasshoppers in the Mat-Su Valley and Native villages slipping into the sea because of the disappearance of Arctic ice quickly ends any debate about climate change in the Far North. Alaska is known for its abundance of wildlife, yet in 2008 the polar bear was listed as a threatened species by the US Department of the Interior. The numbers of Cook Inlet beluga whales have decreased so dramatically in recent years that they are being considered for listing under the Endangered Species Act, and the king salmon run was so weak up the Yukon River in 2008 that even residents with subsistence rights were restricted from filling their quotas.

Alaskans also realize they face a changing of the guard in Washington DC. They may have disdain for the nation's capital, seeing it as an Outsider intruder, but the reality is they have reaped the benefits of pork-barrel funding thanks to their elder statesmen, Congressman Don Young and former US Senator Ted Stevens. Stevens is already gone, voted out in late 2008, and Young is also climbing in age. Stevens was found guilty of political misdeeds and Young is also under federal investigation. It's obvious in Alaska that new faces are just around the corner and when they arrive the state's time at the funding trough may be sharply limited.

In the end, however, Alaskans will prevail. They are a hardworking breed, ingenious at surviving in one of the harshest climates in the world. Rugged and individual, they can endure the coldest winters, the worst earthquakes and even summers when the rivers aren't choking with salmon. They will prevail because, like every tourist who steps off the boat, they also have been overwhelmed by the nature they've witnessed and, affected strongly by this incredible land, they have chosen to stay.

Getting Started

You can't see all of Alaska in a summer and you can't plan an Alaskan trip in a week. This is no quickie getaway. For most travelers the 49th state is a big land that's far away. Its size means visitors need to focus on the regions that interest them the most, while its short, but busy, summer season almost demands advance planning. The less time and the tighter the budget you have, the more you'll want to plan the trip and have reservations in place when you arrive. It's easy to travel in Alaska but not at the last minute.

WHEN TO GO

The traditional season for heading to Alaska is June through August when the weather is at its best, the days are long and everybody – tourists and locals alike – are outside playing. Summers in Alaska are a beautiful mixture of long days and short nights, climaxing on summer solstice (June 21) when Anchorage enjoys more than 19 hours of sunlight and Fairbanks almost 22 hours. Along with the sunshine, the average summer temperatures in the Interior range from 55°F to 75°F, with a brief period in July to August when they top 80°F or even 90°F. Anchorage averages 60°F to 70°F in the summer while the Southeast and Prince William Sound are cooler and wetter. The Bush, north of the Arctic Circle, is cool for most of the summer, with temperatures around 45°F.

See climate charts (p423) for more information.

July and August are also the period of high prices, 'No Vacancy' signs and a Disneyland-like atmosphere at the entrance of Denali National Park. Consider beginning or ending your trip during the shoulder seasons of May or September. Alpine trails are still snow-covered in May and the Southeast can be a rainy place in late September, but the demand for lodging is down, most outdoor activities are still possible and prices are easier to stomach.

Arriving in Alaska in April is possible in the Southeast and the Kenai Peninsula, but much of the state will be enduring spring breakup – when warm weather 'breaks up' ice – a time of slush and mud. Stay during October and you're guaranteed rain most of the time in the Southeast and Southcentral regions and snow in the Interior and Fairbanks. Arriving in Alaska during the winter and traveling outside the major cities is possible but requires special planning as many of the accommodations, forms of transportation and attractions will either be closed or greatly reduced. For information on what is open during the winter months see the **Alaska Travel Industry Association** (www.winterinalaska.com).

DON'T LEAVE HOME WITHOUT...

- Protection – a hat, a fleece and rain gear – against Alaska's climate (p423).
- Cell phone – network coverage is amazing, even in the remote corners of Alaska (p430).
- Hiking equipment – a pack, boots, water bottle, etc. Avoid having to purchase this equipment at exorbitant Alaskan prices.
- Checking the visa situation, as US entrance requirements have changed dramatically in recent years (p431).
- Casual clothes – the number of upscale restaurants with a dress code is limited to a handful in Anchorage. Leave the black tie at home.
- Extra cash and time to enjoy a great outdoor adventure.

COSTS & MONEY

Alaska is traditionally known for having the highest cost of living in the country due in the most part to the high cost of fuel needed to transport everything long distances north and the high cost of labor. It's one thing to live in Alaska – it's another to travel there. Because tourism in Alaska is basically a three-month season, the summer prices are inflated to cover the other nine months when many restaurants and motels are barely scraping by.

There is nothing you can do about the cost of fuel, so if you're on a tight budget, try to avoid the labor cost. Use public transport, stay in campgrounds or hostels and enjoy your favorite brew around a campfire at night. Restaurants, bars, hotels and taxi companies, with their inflated peak-season prices, will quickly drain your funds. A rule of thumb for Alaskan prices is that they're most affordable in Anchorage and Fairbanks, and increase the further you are from these cities. The Southeast is generally cheaper than the Interior, and places like Haines are a bargain in terms of Alaskan tourism. When traveling in the Bush be prepared for anything, even $200-a-night rooms with paper-thin walls and cigarette burns in the carpet.

A budget traveler who camps and stays in hostels, cooks two meals a day and participates in low-cost activities such as hiking can travel in Alaska for $60 to $70 a day. A family of four, staying in motels, eating twice a day in restaurants and renting a car, should expect daily expenses of $300 or higher. Because they provide your transportation, lodging and food, large cruise ships are often a bargain in Alaskan travel, particularly for families. For more money-saving tips with the kids see the Alaska for Families chapter (p39). At the other end of the travel spectrum are upscale lodges and remote wilderness camps (p24) where daily expenses could be $400 to $500 per person for accommodations, meals and activities.

HIGH COST OF FUEL

The spiraling cost of oil in 2008 had a profound effect on Alaskan tourism. Many tour operators had already set their ticket prices when oil broke $140 a barrel and were expected to be forced to raise them considerably in 2009 to make up for the losses. Also be prepared for fuel surcharges, an additional fee to the published fare. In 2008 some were as high as 41%.

TRAVELING RESPONSIBLY

The Alaskan environment is delicate and to protect it we as tourists need to tread lightly, travel responsibly and enjoy this incredible land without adversely impacting its natural wonders or Native culture. Global warming in particular has affected Alaska greater than any other region of the USA, so reducing your carbon footprint is critical to this state and the Arctic as a whole. This includes bypassing a rental vehicle when there is public transportation, not always an easy thing to do in Alaska. In roadless areas like the Southeast, travel on the Alaska Marine Hwy leaves a far smaller footprint than if two or three people charter a bush plane to the same destination.

In many secluded communities trash is a costly concern and a major headache, so it's imperative that travelers try to reduce their own. Avoid buying bottled water if at all possible, simply refill at the tap, and say no to plastic bags at supermarkets as they often end up in the trees on the edge of town. In parks and campgrounds take your trash out with you, even if there's a litter barrel nearby.

Be conscious of the wilderness and wildlife. Practice low-impact camping and hiking, and when traveling beyond the road do so in small numbers. Choose outfitters and guides that do the same, particularly those specializing in bear watching. Mobs of people watching bears at close range is never a healthy thing for the bruins.

Support Native culture and the arts. Avoid purchasing illegal ivory or other crafts by always looking for the Silver Hand symbol for authenticity (p429). Patronize the lodges, tours and other businesses that are eco-friendly, of which many are highlighted in the regional chapters. Organizations to help you travel responsibly include:

HOW MUCH?

Mountain bike rental $25-35 per day

Two-hour raft trip $70-80

One-hour flightseeing tour $200

1lb of king crab $15-20

Whale watching cruise $130

TOP PICKS

Wildlife Viewing Spots

For many, the highlight of a trip to Alaska is the wildlife. Here are the best places to see something wild.

- Brooks Falls (Katmai National Park, p312) Bears, bears and more brown bears!
- Denali Park Rd (Denali National Park, p334) Mountain sheep, moose, caribou and brown bears
- St Paul Island (Pribilof Islands, p322) Seabirds and fur seals
- Kenai Fjords National Park (Seward, p266) Whales, sea lions and seals
- Expedition Park (Dutch Harbor, p319) Bald eagles
- Fish Creek Bridge (Hyder, p133) Black and brown bears
- Arctic Ocean (Barrow, p419) Polar bears
- Stephens Passage (Juneau, p166) Humpback whales
- Fort Abercrombie State Historical Park (Kodiak, p304) Tidal pool marine life
- Ship Creek (Anchorage p202, or practically any stream in July) Salmon

Only in Alaska

Welcome to Alaska! Only in this unusual state can you…

- Pan for gold on a beach (Nome, p405)
- Walk on a glacier without first climbing a mountain (Matanuska Glacier, p367)
- Zipline down a mountain to a creek full of bears feasting on salmon (Ketchikan, p126)
- Play golf at 2am (Fairbanks, p386)
- Hook a 200lb halibut (Homer, p285)
- Take a sled-dog ride across an ice field (Juneau, p167)
- See a radish the size of a softball (Palmer, p228)
- Tan in the midnight sun (Barrow, p417)

Best Eco-Friendly Wilderness Lodges

These remote resorts are not cheap but their settings are truly on the edge of the wilderness.

- Sadie Cove Wilderness Lodge – kayaks and hot tubs in Kachemak Bay (p294)
- Camp Denali – at the end of the road in Denali National Park (p341)
- Hallo Bay Bear Camp – watching bears on the Katmai coast (p313)
- Island Lodge – an island retreat in the middle of Lake Clark National Park (p315)
- Tolovana Hot Springs – rustic cabins and hot springs reached by an 11-mile hike (p397)

Alaska BnBscape (www.bnbscape.com/alaska/alaska.htm) An online guide to eco-friendly B&Bs and inns.

Alaska Conservation Solutions (www.alaskaconservationsolutions.com) Dedicated to drawing attention to the devastating consequences of global warming in Alaska, this site includes tips on being an 'Alaska Carbon Reducer' when traveling.

Alaska Wilderness Recreation & Tourism Association (www.awrta.org) Tour companies and outfitters committed to responsible tourism and minimizing visitor impact.

Sustainable Travel International (www.sustainabletravelinternational.org) Has an 'eco-directory' that lets you search for green lodges and tour operators in Alaska as well as around the world.

TRAVEL LITERATURE

Alaska's wild nature has inspired a lot of authors throughout the years, both homegrown and international.

Coming into the Country (1977) by John McPhee is arguably the best portrait of Alaska ever written. McPhee shifts from wilderness settings to the urban environment, from Eagle to Juneau, as he follows Alaska's emergence into statehood during the 1970s. A timeless classic.

A National Book Award winner, *Arctic Dreams* (2001) is a compelling look at the Far North and author Barry Lopez' personal journey to a land of stunted trees and endless days.

Jon Krakauer's bestseller *Into the Wild* (1997) recounts why a young man from a well-to-do family abandons civilization and walks alone into the Denali wilderness. The book is as much about what he was seeking as it is about why he died, and you might as well read it – now that the movie is out, everybody else is!

One Man's Wilderness: An Alaskan Odyssey (1999) by Sam Keith chronicles Dick Proenneke's dream of building a cabin in the wilderness near Lake Clark in 1968 and why he stayed there to become a self-sufficient hermit for 31 years. Alaskans consider this a far more interesting read than Krakauer's tale.

Ordinary Wolves (2005) is the critically acclaimed novel by Seth Kantner. Born and raised in Alaska's Interior, Kantner draws on personal experience to weave a tale about a boy growing up white in Bush Alaska and his struggle to be accepted by the village Iñupiat. As true an account of village life as there is.

Spike Walker details the rich rewards – a deckhand could earn $100,000 in four months – and high risks of king crabbing in the Bering Sea during the boom years of the 1980s in *Working on the Edge* (1993).

From Tlingit myths and Robert Service poetry to Art Davison's account of climbing Mt McKinley in the winter, *The Last New Land: Stories of Alaska Past and Present* (1996) is a comprehensive anthology of writings on the Far North.

INTERNET RESOURCES

Highly computer literate and extremely remote, Alaska was made for the internet.

Alaska Magazine (www.alaskamagazine.com) The online edition of this statewide magazine is loaded with articles on Alaska and links for travelers.

Alaska Public Lands Information Centers (www.nps.gov/aplic/center) Before you hit the trail, head here for information on national parks, state parks and other public land.

Alaska Travel Industry Association (www.travelalaska.com) The official tourism marketing arm for the state has its vacation planner online along with listings of B&Bs, motels, tours and more.

Explore North (www.explorenorth.com) A site dedicated to Alaska and the circumpolar north with articles, travel tips and links to lodges and operators.

Lonely Planet (www.lonelyplanet.com) Travel news and summaries, the Thorn Tree bulletin board and links to more web resources.

Events Calendar

Alaskan summers are short so locals pack them with festivals and celebrations. Two of the liveliest are Independence Day and summer solstice. Stop in the small towns (Skagway, McCarthy, Eagle) on July 4 for the best festivals and head as far north as you can on June 21 to celebrate the longest day of the year.

APRIL & MAY

GARNET FESTIVAL late Apr

Celebrate the arrival of spring in Wrangell with the largest springtime concentration of bald eagles in North America (www.wrangellchamber.org; p141).

ALASKA FOLK FESTIVAL mid-Apr

Musicians from across Alaska and the Yukon descend on Juneau for a week of music and dancing. Who cares if it rains every day? (www.akfolkfest.org; p168)

COPPER RIVER DELTA SHOREBIRD FESTIVAL early May

Birds and birders invade Cordova for some of the greatest migrations in Alaska (www.cordovachamber.com).

KACHEMAK BAY SHOREBIRD FESTIVAL early May

If the birders aren't gathering in Cordova then they're nesting in Homer, enjoying workshops, field trips and birding presentations (www.homeralaska.org).

LITTLE NORWAY FESTIVAL mid-May

Be a Viking for a day in Petersburg and feast on seafood at night at one of Southeast Alaska's oldest festivals (www.petersburg.org; p147).

JUNEAU JAZZ & CLASSICS mid-May

Jazz and blues fills the air for 10 days in Alaska's beautiful capital city (www.jazzandclassics.org; p168).

KODIAK CRAB FESTIVAL late May

Cheer on the survival-suit racers then grab a plate and dig into all the king crab you can eat (www.kodiak.org; p306).

JUNE

SUMMER MUSIC FESTIVAL throughout Jun

Chamber music, concerts and lots of culture by the sea in beautiful Sitka. Book tickets in advance (www.sitkamusicfestival.org; p155).

COLONY DAYS mid-Jun

A parade and other activities, including a bed race down Main St, in honor of the first farmers arriving in Palmer (www.palmerchamber.org).

MOOSE PASS SUMMER SOLSTICE FESTIVAL near Jun 21

Small-town fun and games, not to mention a short parade, in the Kenai Peninsula (www.moosepass.net; p258).

MIDNIGHT SUN FESTIVAL Jun 21

Celebrate summer solstice in Fairbanks with music from 40 banks on three stages, the Yukon 800 Power Boat Races and a baseball game that starts at midnight but doesn't need any lights (www.explorefairbanks.com).

MAYOR'S MIDNIGHT SUN MARATHON Jun 21

On the longest day of the year there's more than enough time to join 3500 other runners for a 26.2-mile race in and around Anchorage (www.mayorsmarathon.com).

MIDNIGHT SUN FESTIVAL near Jun 21

With 22-hour days, this Nome festival can pack a lot in: a parade, street dance, BBQ chicken feed, softball tournament and Folk Fest, among other activities (www.nomealaska.org).

NALUKATAQ (WHALING FESTIVAL) late Jun

Join Barrow residents to celebrate another successful whaling season with dancing, blanket tosses and a taste of *muktuk* (whale blubber) (www.cityofbarrow.org; p419).

POLAR BEAR SWIM late Jun

The water's fine in Nome if the frozen Bering Sea ice has broken up by then! Submersion of the entire body earns you to a certificate you can hang on the wall (www.nomealaska.org).

GOLD RUSH DAYS late Jun
A family affair with logging events, mining competition and a whole lot food vendors (www.traveljuneau.com; p168).

JULY

INDEPENDENCE DAY PARADE Jul 4
Soapy Smith, Alaska's most lovable scoundrel, rode at the head of Skagway's first parade in 1898, and this small town has been staging a great one ever since (www.skagway.com; p193).

MT MARATHON RACE Jul 4
An exhausting 3.1-mile run up a 3022ft-high peak. The record is around 43 minutes (p264).

NENANA RIVER WILDWATER FESTIVAL mid-Jul
Two days of kayak and raft races through the whitewater that flows past Denali National Park (www.nenanawildwater.org).

BEAR PAW FESTIVAL mid-Jul
Home of the Slippery Salmon Olympics, where teams of two race with a dead fish through Eagle River (www.cer.org).

GOLDEN DAYS mid-Jul
A midsummer festival when Fairbanks cheers on the hairiest legs and the biggest moustaches in town (www.explorefairbanks.com; p386).

MOOSE DROPPING FESTIVAL mid-Jul
Talkeetna is invaded by Mountain Mothers to the delight of men everywhere and everybody takes a turn tossing a moose nugget (www.talkeetnachamber.org).

SOUTHEAST ALASKA STATE FAIR late Jul
The Fiddler Contest is lively and the Most Lovable Dog Competition is cute but by all means don't miss the pig races (www.seakfair.org; p184).

AUGUST

BLUEBERRY FESTIVAL early Aug
A celebration of art, food, songs and foot races of Ketchikan's favorite wild berry (www.visit-ketchikan.com; p127).

TALKEETNA BLUEGRASS & MUSIC FESTIVAL early Aug
The best campout music festival in Alaska, when more than 30 bluegrass bands jam for 20 hours (www.talkeetnabluegrass.com).

TANANA VALLEY FAIR early Aug
Nine days of big veggies, midway rides and a truck mud bog competition in Fairbanks (www.tananavalleyfair.org).

FIRE TIRE FESTIVAL early Aug
Grab your mountain bike and ride the road to McCarthy. Lots of families ride the scenic, 60-mile route (wwwarcticbike.org).

GOLD RUSH DAYS early Aug
Five days of bed races, dances and fish feeds in Valdez. Oh, and a little gold rush history, too (www.valdezalaska.org).

ALASKA STATE FAIR late Aug
Palmer's Showcase for 100lb cabbages and the best Spam recipes in the state (www.alaskastatefair.org; p228).

SEPTEMBER & OCTOBER

KODIAK STATE FAIR & RODEO Labor Day
Breakin' broncos and wrestling steers in Kodiak. For the noncowboys there are pie-eating and halibut-cleaning contests (www.kodiak.org; p306)

SEWARD MUSIC & ARTS FESTIVAL late Sep
Artists and more than 20 musical acts and theatrical companies gather on the shores of Resurrection Bay in Seward (www.sewardak.org; p264).

BLUEBERRY BASH late Sep
Alaska's largest wild blueberries are found in Unalaska, which is why this bake-off and festival sends everybody home with blue teeth and purple tongues (wwwunalaska.info).

GREAT ALASKA BEER TRAIN early Oct
All aboard! The *Microbrew Express* is a special run of the Alaska Railroad from Anchorage to Portage loaded with happy passengers sipping the best beer made in Alaska (www.alaskarailroad.com).

ALASKA DAY CELEBRATION mid-Oct
Sitka dresses the part in celebrating the actual transfer ceremony when the United States purchased Alaska from Russia in 1867 (www.sitka.org; p155).

NOVEMBER

WHALEFEST! early Nov
Whales galore in Sitka, so many you don't even need a boat to view them (www.sitkawhalefest.org; p155).

Itineraries

CLASSIC ROUTES

THE GREAT ALCAN

One to Two Months

The Alcan is the wilderness version of Route 66, a classic American road trip. Mile 1 of the Alaska Hwy is Dawson Creek and it's a 1390-mile, five-day drive to **Delta Junction** (p358). Collect your certificate for having survived the Alcan and push on to **Fairbanks** (p378). Recover with a soak in **Chena Hot Springs** (p393).

Follow the George Parks Hwy south for wildlife watching at **Denali National Park** (p327), and a day at Talkeetna for a flightseeing tour of **Mt McKinley** (p348). Treat yourself to a fine meal in **Anchorage** (p211) and check out the **Anchorage Museum of History & Art** (p202).

Go to Whittier to board the **Alaska Marine Highway ferry** (p36) for a two-day cruise to **Juneau** (p160). See salmon and bears at **Mendenhall Glacier** (p174) and climb **Mt Roberts** (p165). Jump back on the ferry to reach beautiful **Sitka** (p149) and then on to Ketchikan for a boat tour of the stunning **Misty Fiords National Monument** (p107). Finally head to Bellingham, WA, to end an odyssey that involved 2000 miles on the road and seven days on the ferry.

The great wilderness road trip since the 1950s: driving to Alaska. It's almost 2000 miles on the road beginning with the Alcan in Canada and then seven days on the Alaska Marine Highway ferry. In between lies a whole lot of spectacular scenery.

CRUISING SOUTHEAST ALASKA

Two Weeks

This is an easy-to-plan trip to a scenic region of Alaska, although you should reserve space on the **Alaska Marine Highway ferry** (p36) if you want a cabin. Board the ferry in Bellingham, WA, and enjoy the coastal scenery for a couple of days before disembarking for two days at **Ketchikan** (p121). If it's not raining spend a day climbing **Deer Mountain** (p125) and enjoy lunch on the peak with panoramic views of the Inside Passage. Head out to **Totem Bight State Park** (p131) to see totems and a colorful community house.

Catch the ferry to **Wrangell** (p137) and take a wild jet-boat tour up the **Stikine River** (p140), North America's fastest navigable river. Continue to Sitka on the ferry for an afternoon at **Sitka National Historical Park** (p152) and another on a **whale watching cruise** (p154).

Head to Juneau and sign up for a walk across the beautiful ice of **Mendenhall Glacier** (p174). Top that off the next day by climbing Mt Roberts and then having a beer (or two) before taking the **Mt Roberts tramway** (p163) back to the city. In the evening enjoy one of the city's **salmon bakes** (p169).

Climb aboard the high-speed catamaran, **MV Fairweather** (p173), for two days in Skagway, the historic start of the Klondike Gold Rush. Board the **White Pass & Yukon Route Railroad** (p192) for a day trip to Lake Bennett and in the evening catch the rollicking **Days of '98 Show** (p195). Backtrack to Juneau and spend your final day flying through the rainforest like an eagle on one of the city's two **ziplines** (p167). Fly home from Juneau or extend your trip and take the state ferry back.

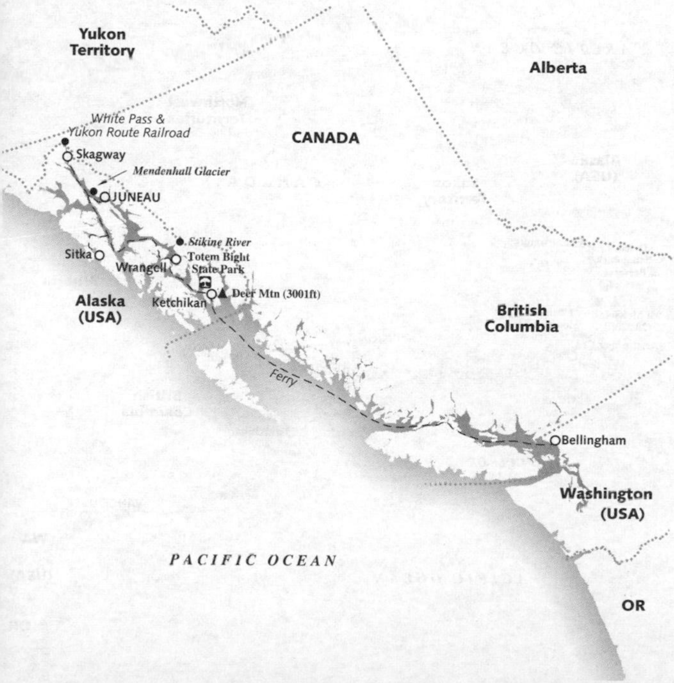

Spent too much time behind the wheel? Hop on a ferry in Bellingham and cruise through the most interesting slice of Alaska, the practically road-less Southeast. A vehicle is not needed, but boots are a necessity as there are great trails at every port.

AN ALASKAN FAMILY ADVENTURE **Two Weeks**

Cruising can be an affordable way for a family to see a watery chunk of Alaska. Combine shipboard life with an overland extension that you've plotted yourself and the trip is even more satisfying, as every day isn't spent with the cruise-ship group.

Fly to Fairbanks from Anchorage and take in some great family sights such as **Pioneer Park** (p382).

Hop on the **Alaska Railroad** (p441), because kids love trains, the following morning for Denali National Park and visit the **Murie Science & Learning Center** (p331) at the park entrance. Put aside another day to take the **shuttle bus** (p332) to look for wildlife along Park Rd. Hop back on the Alaska Railroad for Anchorage and spend a day in Alaska's largest city at the **Alaska Zoo** (p207) or hiking **Flattop Mountain** (p206).

Jump on the Alaska Railroad one last time and head for Whittier. Book a seven-day **cruise** (p35) that begins in Whittier and ends in Vancouver or Seattle. Depending when the ship departs, you might have time for a half-day trip with **Prince William Sound Cruises & Tour** (p251) to see marine wildlife and watch Surprise Glacier discharging huge icebergs.

Board your cruise ship for Southeast Alaska. The ports of call differ slightly from one vessel to the next, but almost all of them stop at Skagway, Juneau and Ketchikan. In Skagway your kids will enjoy a trip to **Liarsville Gold Rush Trail Camp** (p193), where they can try their hands at panning for gold. In Juneau head to **Macauley Salmon Hatchery** (p167) for seawater aquariums, touch tanks and viewing windows that allow visitors to see thousands of salmon spawning. In Ketchikan, splurge on the **Bering Sea Crab Fishermen's Tour** (p127) to watch a commercial fishing crew catch giant king crabs.

Take your family on a wild Alaskan adventure by combining the Alaska Railroad with a cruise-ship jaunt. Stop at Denali National Park and hike Flattop Mountain. On the cruise, check out the gold rush days in Skagway and spawning salmon in Juneau.

RV SOUTHCENTRAL

10 Days

This trip could easily be done in a rental vehicle but Alaska is the dream of every RVer and you can be a road hog even if you don't own one. Fly into **Anchorage** (p198) and rent a recreation vehicle (RV) for 10 days (make sure you book well in advance). Stop at one of the city's large supermarkets, pack your RV with groceries and the local brew and then beat it out of town.

Head 45 miles north and spend the afternoon exploring **Hatcher Pass** (p230) and pitch camp in **Palmer** (p226). Follow the Glenn Hwy east, stopping to go on a wild raft trip down the **Matanuska River** (p367) complete with Class IV rapids. Spend the night at the first state campground that appeals to you before reaching **Glennallen** (p365).

Travel south on the Richardson Hwy and follow the McCarthy Rd east to the Kennicott River, 127 miles from Glennallen. Spend the next day exploring the quaint village of McCarthy and the amazing mining ruins at **Kennecott** (p371). Return to Richardson Hwy and head south. Check out **Worthington Glacier** (p374) and then spend the night camping in the alps at **Blueberry Lake State Recreation Site** (p375).

Continue west into Valdez and stay an extra day to splurge on a **Columbia Glacier cruise** (p238). Load your RV on the **Alaska Marine Highway ferry** (reserve this in advance; p240) and sail across Prince William Sound to **Whittier** (p247). On the same day drive 90 miles south to Seward, passing through scenic Turnagain Pass. Perhaps stay two days in **Seward** (p259); book a halibut charter or kayak in Resurrection Bay, but on the afternoon of the second day hightail it back to **Anchorage** (127 miles; p198) to turn in the RV before the dealer closes.

Be a road hog! Rent an RV in Anchorage and tackle this 650-mile drive in 10 days. Along the way explore the alpine mining ruins in Hatcher Pass, cruise past Columbia Glacier on a state ferry and hook a halibut in Seward.

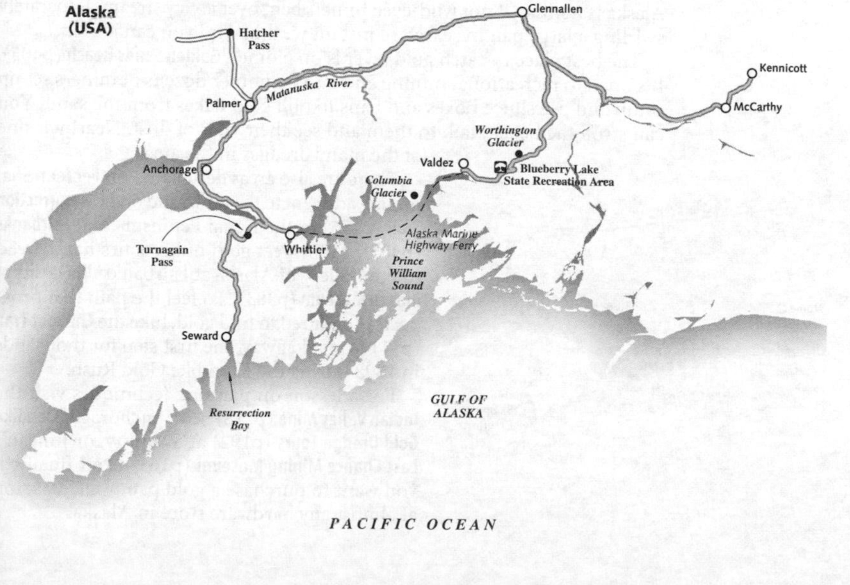

TAILORED TRIPS

ALASKA RAILROADING

Alaska doesn't have a lot of railroads, but those it does have pass through some of the most amazing scenery in the country. For history buffs, the **White Pass & Yukon Route Railroad** (p192) is a must on any itinerary. The narrow-gauge line was built in 1900 during the height of the Klondike Gold Rush, putting the Chilkoot Trail out of business. From Skagway the train climbs steeply to 2885ft through the mountains until it reaches White Pass and then chugs along to serene Lake Bennett.

The most popular ticket is the Alaska Railroad's **Denali Star Train** (p441) from Anchorage to Fairbanks, stopping at Denali National Park along the way. But board the **Coastal Classic Train** (p441) for the most scenic rail route – the 114-mile run from Anchorage to Seward. The train ride begins by skirting Turnagain Arm and then climbs an alpine pass and comes within view of three glaciers before reaching Seward on Resurrection Bay.

For a uniquely Alaskan experience, join the locals on the Alaska Railroad's Hurricane Turn in **Talkeetna** (p350). This small train offers one of the country's last flag-stop services as it journeys through the Susitna River wilderness to Hurricane. Or hop on the **Great Alaska Beer Train** (p27) in early October for a special one-day run from Anchorage to Portage that is loaded with Alaskan microbrews and happy passengers.

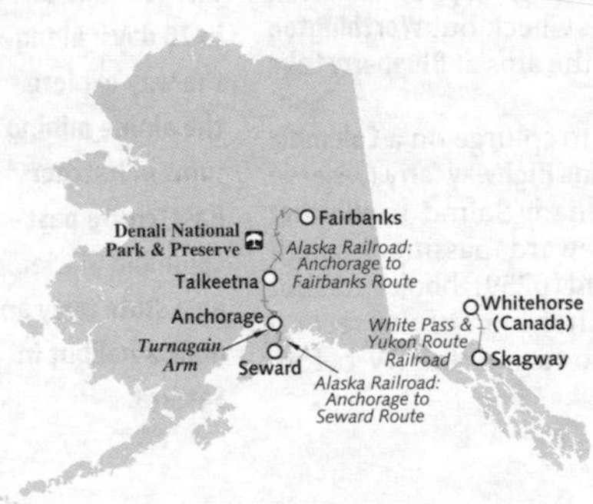

GOLD FEVER

Alaska is nothing if not wild-eyed miners bent over an icy stream desperately swirling a large pan in search of instant wealth. And you can join in.

The best place to catch gold fever is on Nome's **Golden Sands Beach** (p405). It's open to recreational mining and every summer dozens of miners set up camp and use sluice boxes and pans to pull gold flakes from the sand. You can stroll the beach, talk to them and see their vials of dust. Nearby is one of the many dredges in the area.

There are also areas designated for recreational mining adjacent to the north end of the **Resurrection Trail** (p256) in the Kenai Peninsula and **Fairbanks** (p385). To inspect gold nuggets firsthand, head to the Gallery of Alaska at Fairbanks' **University of Alaska Museum** (p383). To feel the pain that prospectors endured to find gold, hike the **Chilkoot Trail** (p91) from Skagway, the first step for thousands in 1898 during the Klondike Gold Rush.

For a lesson on panning techniques visit the **Indian Valley Mine** (p218) near Anchorage, **Klondike Gold Dredge Tours** (p192) at Skagway, or Juneau's **Last Chance Mining Museum** (p163). And finally, if you want to purchase a gold pan, well, just stop at almost any hardware store in Alaska.

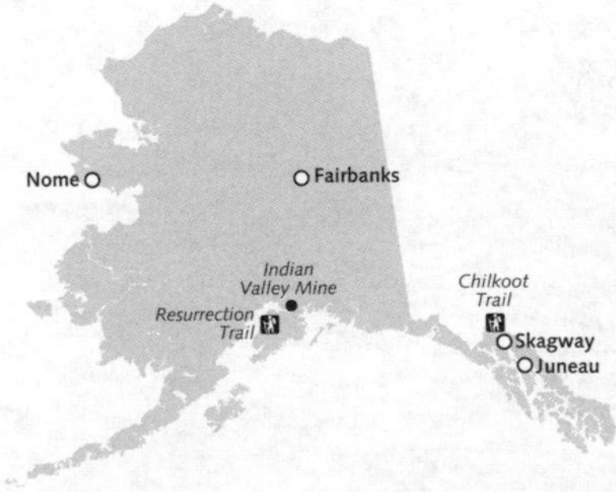

HOT SPRINGS

Even if it's not winter, hot springs can offer welcome relief after a long day on the road. Fairbanks is the access point for several that are reached by road, one – **Chena Hot Springs** (p393) – even by a paved road. These springs are by far the most developed in the area and include a bar that serves cold beer for when you're done soaking in the 110°F hot tub. The more intrepid follow the Elliot Hwy 152 miles to **Manley Hot Springs** (p397), where bathing takes place in a huge, thermal-heated greenhouse that's a veritable Babylonian garden of grapes, Asian pears and hibiscus flowers.

One of the most remote springs in Alaska is **Pilgrim Hot Springs** (p409), a 50-mile road trip from Nome.

In Southeast Alaska, the public bathhouse at tiny **Tenakee Springs** (p158), where the water bubbles out of the ground at 108°F, is the best-known hot springs but it's hardly the only one. Boat tours up the Stikine River out of Wrangell often stop for a soak at the two bathhouses at **Chief Shakes Hot Springs** (p140). The most adventurous soak is at **White Sulphur Springs Cabin** (p155), which most people access from Sitka via a floatplane. Reserve this USFS cabin, pack in a good bottle of wine and in the evening you'll be sipping and soaking.

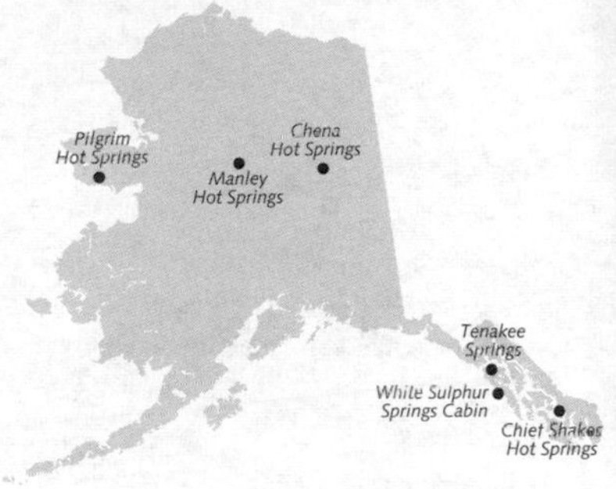

LOOKING FOR BEARS

One of the fastest growing activities in Alaska is bear watching. There are no shortages of bears in the 49th State, nor tourists wanting to see one – preferably catching and devouring a salmon. Two of the most famous bear viewing sites are Brooks Falls in **Katmai National Park** (p312) and on the shuttle buses in **Denali National Park** (p332). To see the largest brown bears, bruins that often tip the scales at 1000lb or more, you need to visit **Kodiak National Wildlife Refuge** (p310). To spend a week viewing bears, book a cot at **Hallo Bay Bear Camp** (p313) on a remote stretch of coast along the Alaska Peninsula.

The most affordable bear watching is found in Southeast Alaska. Hyder may be hard to reach but once there, it is free to spend an afternoon at **Fish Creek Bridge** (p133) watching brown bears. It's even easier and cheaper to see the brown and black bears feasting on salmon at Juneau's **Steep Creek** (p174) near the Mendenhall Glacier. At **Anan Creek** (p139) near Wrangell you can rent a USFS cabin for $35 a night that comes with four bear-watching permits to the stream where brown and black bears come in July and August.

To see a polar bear head either to **Point Barrow** (p418) at the top of the world…or to the **Alaska Zoo** (p207).

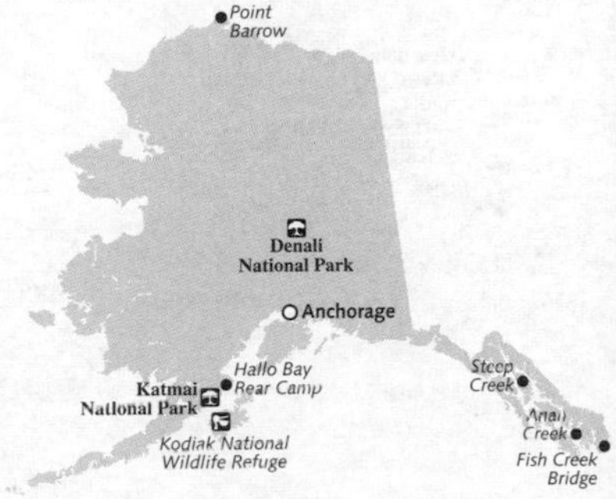

FERRIES, TRAILS & CABINS

The **Alaska Marine Hwy** (p36) snakes through the channels and passages of Southeast Alaska, providing transport to thousands of tourists every summer, many of whom like to hike. With advance planning you could easily put together a trip in which at every port you could hike to a free-use shelter or a US Forest Service cabin that rents for $35 to $45 a night.

Begin in Ketchikan and head downtown to pick up the **Deer Mountain Trail** (p102). This 3-mile hike leads you to the summit and a free-use shelter above the treeline nearby. Just to the north is Petersburg, where you can jump off the ferry and tackle the 4-mile **Raven Trail** (p145), reaching the USFS Raven Roost Cabin by nightfall.

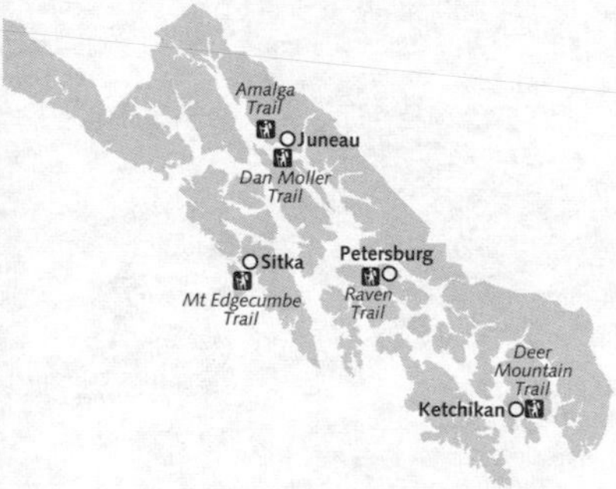

Juneau has five hike-in USFS cabins. North of the ferry terminal is the **Amalga Trail** (p166), a 7.5-mile hike that ends at Eagle Glacier Cabin near the glacier itself. For the best alpine cabin head downtown and hike the **Dan Moller Trail** (p165) 3 miles to the Dan Moller Cabin.

One of the most unusual cabin hikes in Southeast is Sitka's **Mt Edgecumbe Trail** (p153). After arriving, you'll need to arrange a water taxi to Kruzof Island where the 6.7-mile route to the top of the extinct volcano is located. At the start of the trail is a USFS cabin and halfway up is a free-use shelter. How convenient!

THE ULTIMATE BUSH EXPLORER

While it isn't cheap, exploring Alaska's mythic Bush is well worth the hefty price tag. Start your Bush adventure with a flight to **Bettles** (p417). You'll probably end up spending a day or so in this friendly community before taking another flight out to your 'drop spot.' One of the best river trips is along the **Upper Noatak River** (p416). This five- to seven-day journey takes you from Portage Creek to a riverside lake near Kacachurak Creek. You'll need to fly back from there, or you can continue the trip for another two weeks down through the **Gates of the Arctic National Park** (p415) and the **Noatak National Preserve** (p401) to the indigenous stronghold of **Kotzebue** (p410). Ultimate Bush explorers could then fly from Kotzebue to **Nome** (p401). This remote town definitely warrants around three days of exploration, one for each of its amazing roads, which take you to hot springs, small Bush communities or ruined gold rush areas. Big spenders could also pony up for a flight from Anchorage to **Barrow** (p417), where you'll get a chance to spot polar bears and some 185 species of migrating birds. But the real exploration begins when you put the guidebook aside (p420) and head into the vast wilderness that defines this frontier state.

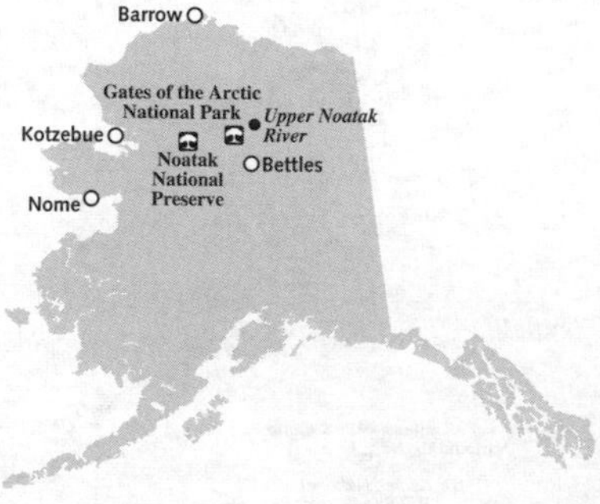

Cruising in Alaska

While many independent travelers will find the strictures of 'cruise life' a bit stifling, there are plenty of reasons to take an Alaskan cruise, namely the two 'Cs': comfort and convenience. And in a state that could take months, if not years, to thoroughly explore, you get a chance to see many of the top sights in one convenient, all-inclusive package.

Most days, you'll get a chance to disembark in port for anywhere from four to eight hours, where you can bop around town, take in a hike or an excursion (which will cost you extra, of course), or even a longer trip inland to Denali National Park, Talkeetna or Eagle. You also get to sit on deck and spot bald eagles hunting, humpback whales breaching and glaciers calving: not a bad little bit of sight-seeing. On the smaller lines, you'll get more wildlife excursions and more stops. And backpackers, independent travelers and spendthrifts can always hop on the Alaska Marine Highway ferry. You see the same sights, but you don't get a casino, heated pool, hot-tub, B-team comedian, all-you-can-eat buffet or cruise director.

Cruises run May through September. For the best weather, try going in July and August, but for a bit less traffic and cheaper tickets, consider taking a cruise in shoulder season, early May and late September.

PICKING YOUR SHIP

Cruise Ships

For the comfort of a floating all-inclusive hotel, you can't beat a large cruise ship. These resorts on the sea do have their limitations. You won't be able to stop in as many places as you can on a small ship, and you'll be sharing your Alaska 'wilderness' experience with around 3000 other vacationers. Most large cruises stop only in the major ports of call, and generally start from Vancouver or Seattle. Excursions range from heli-seeing trips and zipline tours to guided hikes, kayaks and day trips to Denali National Park. Cruises cost around $120 a night, but that does not include your flight to the port of embarkation. You can save money (sometimes up to 50%) by hopping on a 'repositioning' cruise, which takes the boat back to its homeport.

Whale baleen was the plastic of its day and was used in the 19th century to make parasol ribs and bodices.

Here's how they break down:

Carnival (☎ 888-227-64825; www.carnival.com) Young people rule on these ships.
Celebrity (☎ 877-202-4345; www.celebritycruises.com) Family friendly and laid back.
Holland America (☎ 877-932-4259; www.hollandamerica.com) A bit more classy.
Norwegian (☎ 866-234-7350; www.ncl.com) Works well for the older crowd.
Princess (☎ 800-774-62377; www.princess.com) Nonroyalty need not apply.
Royal Caribbean (☎ 866-562-7625; www.royalcaribbean.com) Despite the name, it offers more than 50 voyages to Alaska each summer.

Small Ships

Just 3% of Alaskan cruisers take a small-ship voyage. And while you'll have tighter quarters, bumpier seas and less entertainment options than on the big boys, these vessels offer better chances at seeing wildlife, more land and kayak excursions, onboard naturalists (most of the time), generally better food, a more casual atmosphere (you can leave that blue sports coat at the office where it belongs), and a more intimate portrait of Alaska.

These boats sleep anywhere from eight to 100 and are more likely to depart from Alaska. While this is probably your best bet if you are looking to match

ALASKA MARINE HIGHWAY: THE INDEPENDENT TRAVELER'S CRUISE *Jim DuFresne*

Travel on the state ferries is a leisurely and delightful experience. The midnight sun is warm, the scenery stunning and the possibility of sighting whales, bald eagles or sea lions keeps most travelers at the side of the ship.

Alaska Marine Highway (☎ 465-3941, 800-642-0066; www.ferryalaska.com) runs ferries equipped with observation decks, food services, lounges and solariums with deck chairs. You can rent a stateroom for overnight trips – these aren't as 'stately' as they may sound, and are downright spartan compared with what you'll get on a cruise liner – but many travelers head straight for the solarium and unroll their sleeping bags on deck chairs. You can find information on specific ports of call and rates in the Southeast (p118), Southwest (p298) and Prince William Sound (p232) chapters.

The ferries have cafeterias or snack bars, and a few have sit-down restaurants, but budget travelers can save money by bringing their own food and cooking it on board the ship. There are microwaves on every ship. Most ships have onboard naturalists who give a running commentary of the trip. Bring your headphones, warm clothes, some extra snacks and a good book.

Ferry schedules change almost annually but in 2008 one vessel departed from Bellingham, WA, and three from Prince Rupert, BC, for Alaska, first port being Ketchikan. Most ferries then depart for Wrangell, Petersburg, Sitka, Juneau, Haines and Skagway before heading back. From Haines you can drive north and within a couple of hours pick up the Alcan. A trip from Bellingham to Juneau takes 2½ to four days, depending on the route.

Nine ships ply the waters of Southeast Alaska and once a month the MV *Kennicott* makes a special run from Southeast Alaska across the Gulf of Alaska to Whittier. This links the Southeast routes of the Alaska Marine Highway ferries to the Southcentral portion that includes such ports as Homer, Kodiak, Valdez and Cordova. This sailing is extremely popular because it allows travelers to skip the long haul over the Alcan. Book it long before you arrive in Alaska.

Along with the Southeast, the Alaska Marine Highway services Southcentral and Southwest Alaska. Three ferries, including the high-speed catamaran MV *Chenega* connect 16 communities, including Cordova, Valdez, Whittier, Homer and Kodiak.

Once a month from May through September the MV *Tustumena* makes a special run along the Alaska Peninsula to Aleutian Islands (p308).

If the Alaska Marine Highway ferries are full in Bellingham, head to Port Hardy at the north end of Vancouver Island, where **BC Ferries** (☎ 250-386-3431, 888-223-3779; www.bcferries.com) leave for Prince Rupert, BC. From this Canadian city, you can transfer to the Alaska Marine Highway and continue to Southeast Alaska on ferries not as heavily in demand as those in Bellingham.

Reservations

The ferries are extremely popular during the peak season (June to August). If boarding in Bellingham, you absolutely need reservations for a cabin or vehicle space, and just to be safe you should probably have one even if you're just a walk-on passenger.

The summer sailing schedule comes out in December and can be seen online. Reservations can be done online or by calling the Alaska Marine Highway. When reserving space, you must know the ports you want to visit along the route, with exact dates. Stopovers are not free; rather, tickets are priced on a port-to-port basis.

All fares listed in this book are for adults (aged 12 and older) but do not include a fuel surcharge, generally around 10%, but that could change in these times of erratic diesel prices. A ticket from Bellingham to Juneau runs about $330 per person; a two-berth cabin will cost you an extra $300 or so.

comfort with quality and authentic experience, it does come with a steeper price tag: anywhere from $400 to $1200 a night.

SMALL-SHIP CRUISES

Each small cruise ship is different. Here's a breakdown of some of our favorites:

Adventure Life Voyages (☎ 800-244-6118; www.alvoyages.com; maximum passengers 62-128; per person $7599-19,349) Has top-end trips out to the Aleutians, King Island, around the 'Ring of Fire,' through the Northwest Passage, and over to Russia.

our pick **AdventureSmith Explorations** (☎ 800-728-7825; www.adventuresmithexplorations.com; maximum passengers 12-102; per person $1390-4500) This company offsets its carbon emissions and focuses on learning and adventure cruises in Southeast Alaska aboard its fleet of small boats, which range from intimate charters (accommodating just 12 people) to larger cruisers that can take around 100 people. The boats have kayaks and small skiffs for the numerous excursions that include everything from kayaking in Glacier Bay National Park to wildlife watching near Tracy Arm, the ABC Islands, Icy Straight, Misty Fjords and Frederick Sound. Most trips depart from Juneau.

America Safari Cruises (☎ 888-862-8881; www.amsafari.com; maximum passengers 12-36; per person $4395-7995) Offers themed cruises that focus on whale watching, Glacier Bay, wildlife watching or adventure travel. The small boats have modern, elegant staterooms, and a naturalist is on board to teach you the ways of the Alaska wilderness. Most trips depart from Juneau, but they have one trip that leaves from Seattle.

Cruise West (☎ 888-851-8133; www.cruisewest.com; maximum passengers 102; per person $3999-18,499) It does cruises up to the Bering Sea, passing Kodiak, Katmai National Park, the Shumagin Islands, Dutch Harbor, the Pribilof Islands, on up to Nome.

Discovery Voyages (☎ 800-324-7602; www.discoveryvoyages.com; maximum passengers 12, cabins 6; per person $3650-15,850) While the quarters are tight on this small boat, Discovery Voyages offer some interesting five- to eight-day options, with trips focusing on whale watching, hiking and kayaking, photography, or wildlife exploration. It also offsets its carbon emissions.

Lindblad Expeditions (☎ 800-397 3348; www.expeditions.com; maximum passengers 62, cabins 31; per person from $7500) Offers kayaking, wilderness walks, onboard naturalists and Zodiac excursions during eight-day cruises in the Southeast. Many trips include the airfare from

The PBS series 'American Experience' did a documentary on *Building the Alaska Highway*, which includes interesting anecdotes from an all-black troop that was integral in the highway's construction.

Visit www.responsibletravel.com for the low-down on the environmental and cultural impact of cruises.

TO CRUISE OR NOT TO CRUISE?

Travelers on a tight schedule (or budget, or both) may find a cruise is the best option for seeing Alaska. But opponents to this form of travel argue that mainstream cruises offer little or no interaction with the locals, have a negative impact on the environment, and are changing the face of coastal Alaska one T-shirt shop at a time. If you are on the fence about taking a cruise, it's worth examining the issue a bit more closely.

The million or so yearly cruise visitors do bring money into the state: a couple hundred million dollars a year. That means jobs, better schools, bigger museums and cultural centers, and more infrastructure. But at what cost? Some towns see up to five cruise ships a day. That's around 15,000 people that come to port, storm through the downtown, then hop back on the ship without having given or received anything from the local community aside from maybe a commemorative spoon. This deluge of tourists does bring money in and create jobs, but it also dilutes the local culture and causes noisome overcrowding. And, as of late, some local tour operators are exclusively working with the ships, meaning that independent travelers won't get a chance to go to a salmon-bake on a private island or take a spin on the 'world's longest zipline' near Hoonah.

There's also the environmental impact of cruising. A large cruise liner like the *Queen Mary* emits 0.43kg of carbon dioxide per mile, while a long-haul flight releases about 25kg. In Alaska, an 11-day cruise from Seattle to Juneau on a small boat with around 100 guests will burn about 71 gallons of fuel per passenger, releasing some 0.77 tons of carbon into the air per passenger. The flight from Seattle to Juneau releases some 0.17 tons of carbon per passenger. Cruise ships also release around 17% of total worldwide nitrogen oxide emissions, and create around 50 tons of garbage and a million tons of wastewater on a one-week voyage. We all knew that flying was bad for the environment, but, if you do the math, it seems cruising is much more harmful. Where's Al Gore when you need him?

Seattle, and take visitors from Juneau through the Inside Passage, past Tracy Arm, Petersburg, Frederick Sound, Chatham Strait, Glacier Bay National Park, Point Adolphus and Inian Pass.

Yukon Queen II (☎ 867-993-5599, 800-544-2206; www.hollandamerica.com; one way $90) This 110-passenger tour boat plies the mighty Yukon between Eagle and Dawson City.

The IMAX film *Alaska: Spirit of the Wild* brings the wilds of Alaska into your home. Charlton Heston did the narration, but never mentioned his 'cold, dead hands.'

PICKING YOUR CRUISE ROUTE

Inside Passage

This is the classic. You sail from Seattle or Vancouver up through the Inside Passage. The 'great land' coastal views don't start until Prince Rupert Island. Most trips will stop in Ketchikan, which has just about as many bars as people and some very fine totem poles. They then continue to the state capital in Juneau, home to a lovely glacier and some nice heli-seeing tours; Skagway, a gold-rush port with some nice hiking not far out of town; and the granddaddy attraction of Alaska cruises, Glacier Bay, where you'll see 11 tidewater glaciers spilling their icy wears into the sea.

Ann Vipond's book *Alaska by Cruise Ship* provides port-by-port information on cruising in Alaska.

Gulf of Alaska

This trip includes the Inside Passage, but then continues to the Gulf of Alaska, with stops in Seward, the Hubbard Glacier and Prince William Sound. While you get a broader picture of coastal Alaska on this one-way cruise, it also comes at a price, as you'll generally need to arrange for flights from separate ports.

Bering Sea

These trips are more expensive and generally focus on natural and cultural history. Folks that enjoy learning on their vacations will like this trip, with stops in the Pribilof Islands, Nome and, on the really expensive cruises, King Island.

Nome probably got its odd moniker when a mapmaker confused a British officer's notes. The officer didn't know Nome's name, so he penned '?Name,' which eventually morphed on maps to Nome.

'Cruisetours'

These trips give you the chance to get off the boat for about half of your trip. Most begin with the Inside Passage cruise, then head out on a tour bus, with stops in Talkeetna, Denali National Park, Fairbanks, Eagle or the Copper River. Most cruise companies have all-inclusive hotels in these destinations (basically cruise ships without the rocking).

Alaska for Families

Everybody is a kid in Alaska. Whether it's a stream choking with bright red salmon or a bald eagle winging its way across an open sky, nature's wonders captivate five-year-olds just as much as their parents. A fourth grader might not fully appreciate, or even endure, a visit to Wall Street like Dad, but both will be equally stunned when they see the 8-mile-wide face of Hubbard Glacier from the deck of a cruise ship.

The best that Alaska has to offer is not stuffy museums or amusement parks filled with heart-pounding rides. It's outdoor adventure, wildlife and scenery on a grand scale, attractions and activities that will intrigue the entire family.

Whether you're a kid or not.

Going Places: Alaska and the Yukon for Families (2005) by Nancy Thalia Reynolds is a handy guide offering hundreds of tips on where to take your kids in Alaska and what to do once you get there.

PRACTICALITIES

The Basics

Although it's more associated with senior citizens heading up the Alcan in a monster RV, Alaska welcomes families and is well suited to serve them. Alaska is a young state – the median age is 33 – and very family orientated, so infant needs, such as disposable diapers and formula, are widely available in most cities, towns and villages. Diaper-changing facilities are often found in major transportation centers including airports and ferry terminals. Breast-feeding in public is practiced in large cities but not always tolerated in small rural towns.

The chain motels in Alaska, such as **Super 8 Motel** (☎ 800-800-8000; www.super8.com), **Travelodge** (☎ 800-578-7878; www.travelodge.com) and **Comfort Inn** (☎ 877-424-6423; www.comfortinn.com) have roll-away beds for children and cribs for toddlers. You'll find that many independently owned accommodations and lodges in small towns won't offer such amenities. If you absolutely need a crib at night either check your lodging in advance or bring along a travel crib.

Alaska has more earthquakes than any other state. Visit earthquake.usgs.gov/learning/kids to learn more and even enjoy earthquake puzzles and cartoons.

The same is true for car seats. **Budget Rent A Car** (☎ 800-248-0150; www.budgetalaskaonline.com), **Avis** (☎ 800-331-1212; www.avis.com) and many national companies have safety seats for toddlers and young children. The cost is around $10 a day and you should try to reserve them in advance. Unfortunately the smaller, independent agencies away from the airports, which generally offer better rental rates, often do not have car seats.

Licensed daycare is available in the cities and often in the major towns throughout Alaska. Most will accept drop-ins for a day during the summer if you want to climb a mountain without having to deal with an infant or toddler. The cost ranges from $30 to $50 a day and it usually needs to be set up in advance.

TOP PICKS: ALASKAN ADVENTURES FOR CHILDREN

Ride the Alyeska tram Reach the alpine region above Girdwood's Alyeska Resort (p220) the easy way and then explore it by hiking the Alyeska Glacier View Trail.

Paddle Orcas Cove Join a guided kayak trip to Orcas Cove (p125) that begins with a boat ride from Ketchikan and includes looking for sea lions, seals and, yes, orcas.

Walk on a glacier A self-guided trail at Matanuska Glacier leads families 200 yards onto the ice itself (p367).

Rent a wilderness cabin There are 190 USFS cabins in Southeast Alaska and Prince William Sound, and most of them are reached via floatplane (p73). How exciting is that?

Take a train to Spencer Glacier Board the Alaska Railroad's Spencer Whistle Stop (p221) for a night camping in front of Spencer Glacier.

Accepting drop-ins in Fairbanks is **Kids N' Round** (☎ 907-456-5436) and in Juneau **Gold Creek Child Development** (☎ 907-586-6085). In Anchorage, contact **Child Care Connection** (☎ 907-563-1966; www.childcareconnection.org), which has an online child-care referrals page to assist in finding a day-care service in Alaska's largest city.

Imaginarium (p208) is Anchorage's wondrous and whimsical science center, ideal for a family on a rainy afternoon.

Like elsewhere in the USA, most Alaskan restaurants welcome families and tend to cater to children with high chairs, kids menus of smaller sizes and reduced prices, and waitresses quick with a rag when somebody spills their drink. Upscale places where an infant would be frowned upon are limited to a handful in Anchorage. One of the best places to take children for dinner is to a salmon bake, an outdoor affair that is lively and colorful and where no one will care if junior drops a glass of milk on the ground.

Transportation

One of the best ways to see Alaska with toddlers or young children is on a cruise ship (p35). The larger the ship, the more family amenities and activities it will offer. **Carnival Cruises** (www.carnival.com) offers Camp Carnival, an activity-based program for children ages two through 14, and in-cabin babysitting services for those who are younger. Other cruise ship companies have similar programs.

You're in Alaska and your kids want to see where Santa Claus lives – head to the North Pole near Fairbanks (p394).

Smaller cruise ships, those that hold fewer than 200, do not work as well with children as their accommodations and activities – such as kayaking, wilderness walks and Zodiac excursions – are usually geared more towards adventurous couples. But the **Alaska Marine Highway System** (www.ferryalaska.com; p437) is well suited for families. Children have the space to move around, and large ferries like the MV *Columbia*, MV *Kennicott*, MV *Malaspina* and MV *Matanuska* feature both current movies and ranger programs on marine life, birds and glaciers.

Children also do well on the **Alaska Railroad** (www.akrr.com; p441) as they can walk between passenger carriages and spend time taking in the scenery from special domed viewing cars. You could avoid long drives by flying in and out of Anchorage and Fairbanks and taking the Alaska Railroad from one

MY FIRST VIEW OF MT MCKINLEY *Meg Spenchian*

We were late as usual. Once my parents, two brothers and I had finally reached the Denali Park bus station, we discovered we had missed our 6am bus ride. So typical for my family. But after we managed to claim seats on the 7am shuttle ride, the day was anything but typical. We had no more than sat down when the glistening sun broke out and the indigo sky outlined the incredible surroundings that is Denali National Park.

For almost four hours our bus jostled along the edge of extensive cliffs, which my older brother, Greg, anxiously scanned for anything that moved. We bumped our way along the Park Rd, catching snapshots of various wildlife, taking in the beautiful sights of the natural world and then, at Mile 10, we caught our first view of the mountain itself. By the time we arrived at Eielson Visitor Center at Mile 66, my entire family was overwhelmed by the overpowering size of Mt McKinley. The sheer beauty of North America's highest peak magnifies our personal love and respect for the natural world in which we live. My mom, being her usual self, broke down into tears just from being enveloped in the moment. Usually my two brothers and I would roll our eyes in unison and crack a joke or two, but this time we only leaned back and nodded in understanding.

When you see Mt McKinley, you see a world untouched by the claws of humanity. You gaze upon a massive mountain outlined in crystal, ice-blue skies, and you feel a sense of hope. Hope that there you can still, and always will be able to, experience nature's most spectacular moments. For me seeing Mt McKinley was one of those moments, that in this pure and untrampled world that is Alaska, I found a real sense of peace.

Meg Spenchian is a 14-year-old from Michigan who traveled to Alaska in 2008 with her family.

city to the other, stopping along the way at such popular places as Talkeetna or Denali National Park.

Discounts

In Alaska families with young children can look forward to a wide range of discounts. Kids aged two through 11 receive a 50% discount on the Alaska Marine Hwy, and infants travel free. The same discount and age limits apply to children riding the Alaska Railroad. City bus systems also discount heavily for children. Anchorage's **People Mover** (www.peoplemover.org; p217), the state's largest, offers kids aged five to 18 years a 40% discount and no charge for those who are younger.

Attractions and tours will also have special entry fees for children. Museums offer some of the largest discounts, often 50% to 75%, with children under the age of six or seven free. Many tour operators also offer reduced kids rates; the popular **White Pass & Yukon Railroad** (www.whitepassrailroad.com; p192) in Skagway offers a 50% discount to kids three to 12 years old, as does Seward's **Kenai Fjords Tours** (www.kenaifjords.com; p268) on its wildlife boat tours in Kenai Fjords National Park. If more than one company is offering a particular bus or boat tour, it pays to look around in order to secure the best rate for children.

It's a long flight to Alaska but www.flyingwithkids.com will help you and your kids get through it.

HEADING OUTDOORS

If your family enjoys the outdoors, Alaska can be a relatively affordable place once you've arrived. A campsite is cheap compared to a motel room, and hiking, backpacking and wildlife watching are free. Even fishing is free for children, as Alaska does not require anglers under the age of 16 to have a fishing license.

For general information and great tips about traveling with your children anywhere in the world, even Alaska, read Lonely Planet's *Travel with Children*.

Hiking & Backpacking

The key to any Alaskan adventure is to match the hike to your child's ability and level of endurance. Children lacking outdoor experience or in poor walking shape will have a tough time on the Flattop Mountain Trail (p206), Anchorage's most popular family day hike. On the other hand, a four-day hike along the Resurrection Pass Trail (p94) can be handled by children as young as six if their packs are light and the pace is relaxed. You have to decide where to go based on what they can do.

With children in tow, it's equally important to select a hike that has an interesting aspect to it – a glacier, gold mine ruins, waterfalls or a remote cabin to stop for lunch. It is always a highlight for children to spot wildlife while hiking, but it's impossible to know when a moose will pop out of the woods or a handful of Dall sheep will wander over a ridge. In July and August, however, you can count on seeing a lot of fish in a salmon stream, a wide variety of marine life in tidal pools, and bald eagles where the birds are known to congregate to feed, such as Chilkat River in Haines. Everybody just has to keep their eyes open.

When backpacking with children, make sure their pack will hold up in Alaska's weather. This is particularly true with their rain gear, both parka and rain pants. If you're wearing a fleece jersey and a Gore-Tex shell, why shouldn't they? It is also important to pack enough food. After a full day of hiking parents are always shocked to see their children consume twice as much as they would at home. And if there is a battle over the last spoonful of macaroni and cheese, a hungry child will always win.

Six national parks in Alaska – Denali, Gates of the Arctic, Glacier Bay, Sitka, Klondike and Wrangell-St Elias – have Junior Ranger programs (www.nps.gov/learn/juniorranger.htm) for children.

Kayaking & Canoeing

Paddling with children involves a greater risk than hiking due to the frigid temperature of most fjords, rivers and lakes in Alaska. You simply don't want to tip at any cost. You need to judge how much paddling experience your

HOW OLD DO I HAVE TO BE TO...

Climb Flattop Mountain This is the first summit for more kids in Alaska than any other peak. However, parts of the ascent are steep and the path is rocky. Children should be at least five or six before attempting this Anchorage trail.

Go glacier trekking Most outfitters say a child needs to be at least 12 to join a regular guided glacier trek. Families with children aged eight to 11 years can often book a private outing so that the trek is customized for the abilities of the youngest child.

Paddle a kayak By utilizing a double kayak, companies will take children as young as six on paddles in well-protected areas. But be aware: parents do the bulk of the paddling, with kids under the age of ten in the front.

Pan for gold Children as young as three or four will try their hand panning for gold but can get bored quickly and end up just throwing rocks in the stream. By the time they turn seven, many kids have gold fever and will pan all afternoon if you let them.

Dig for a clam If you can squat, you can dig into the muck for a clam. You'll see kids two or three years old out on the tidal flats with mud on their hands, elbows and faces.

Fly in a floatplane Any age. Infants are held on the lap of a parent and car seats are used for toddlers.

Join a whitewater raft trip For serious whitewater (Class III-IV), outfitters prefer children to be at least 10 years old if a guide is rowing the raft and 14 if it's a paddle raft. For Class II whitewater, children as young as seven can participate on a float.

Ride a Denali shuttle bus For children under the age of four, you must bring a car seat to ride a shuttle bus along the Denali Park Rd. Children under the age of 13 are free!

Join mom or dad on a halibut charter Children as young as five will often join a parent on a halibut charter and do well because they don't have to constantly hold the rod (that's what rod holders are for). If they hook an 80-pounder, or basically a fish bigger than they are, parents or the captain can help them reel it in. On many charters children under the age of 12 are free.

Billy and his family struggle along the Chilkoot Trail during the Klondike Gold Rush in *The Gold Rush Kid* (2008) by Mary Waldorf, a historical novel for young teens.

child has – and, for that matter, you as well – when considering kayaking and canoeing adventures.

Flat, calm water should be the rule with young children. Choose a place like Auke Bay (p166) near Juneau where you can rent double kayaks to team up a parent with a child and then spend an afternoon paddling around the small islands in the protective bay. Another excellent choice for a flat-water paddle is to rent canoes at Nancy Lake State Recreation Area (p345), while the Chena River (p115) in the heart of Fairbanks can be paddled upstream almost as easily as downstream. Needless to say all rentals should come with paddles and lifejackets that fit your child.

Wilderness Cabins

For toddlers and children younger than five years, the best way to escape into the wilderness is to rent a backcountry cabin in Tongass or Chugach National Forests or other parks in Alaska (see p73). Most cabins are reached by floatplane, an exciting start to any adventure for a child, allowing you to bypass long hikes with heavy backpacks into the area. The rustic cabins offer secure lodging in a remote place where children often have a good chance to see wildlife or catch fish.

Wildlife Watching

Sea Life Discovery Tours in Sitka (p154) uses a glass-bottomed boat that lets children enjoy sea life without getting wet.

Children marvel at seeing wildlife in its natural habitat but may not always have the patience for a long wait before something pops out of the woods. The shuttle buses that travel the Denali National Park Rd (p332) offer one of Alaska's best wildlife viewing opportunities, but the entire trip to Wonder Lake and back is an extremely long day with few opportunities to get out of your seat. With most children it's better to ride only to Eielson Visitor Center, leave the bus for a short hike in the area and then head back.

Marine wildlife boat tours work out better because, let's face it, a boat trip is a lot more fun than a bus ride. There are extensive opportunities for this in Southeast Alaska where whale-watching tours are very popular in towns such as Petersburg, Sitka and Juneau. Nature tours that are done in vans are also ideal for children as they stop often and usually include short walks. An excellent one for families is offered by Alaska Nature Tours (p183) in Haines, which heads out in the evening along the Chilkoot River to look for eagles, mountain goats and brown bears feeding on salmon.

The State of Alaska's website for kids, www.state.ak.us/local/kids, features great videos of Alaskan wildlife.

History

Alaska made it to 50, celebrating in 2009 the 50th anniversary of President Dwight Eisenhower's official welcome into the Union. It's been a long, strange road, from being labeled a frozen wasteland to the discovery of the country's largest oil reservoir and from the persecution of Native Alaskans to creating Native corporations and granting them land, money and subsistence rights that are the envy of other indigenous peoples today. Like everything else about Alaska, its history is uniquely its own.

EARLY ALASKANS

A track from a three-toed, meat-eating dinosaur, dating back 70 million years, was discovered in Denali National Park in 2005.

It is believed that the first Alaskans migrated from Asia to North America between 15,000 and 30,000 years ago, during an ice age that lowered the sea level and created a 900-mile land bridge linking Siberia and Alaska. The nomadic groups who crossed the bridge were not bent on exploration but on following the animal herds that provided them with food and clothing.

The first major invasion, which came across the land bridge from Asia, was by the Tlingits and the Haidas, who settled throughout the Southeast and British Columbia, and the Athabascans, a nomadic tribe that settled in the Interior. The other two major groups were the Iñupiat, who settled the north coast of Alaska and Canada (where they are known as Inuit), and the Yupik, who settled southwest Alaska. The smallest group of Alaska Natives to arrive was the Aleuts of the Aleutian Islands. The Iñupiat, Yupik and Aleuts are believed to have migrated 3000 years ago and were well established by the time the Europeans arrived.

The Tlingit and Haida cultures were advanced; the tribes had permanent settlements, including large clan dwellings that housed related families. These tribes were noted for their excellent wood carving, especially carved poles, called totems, which can still be seen today in the Totem Heritage Center (p124) in Ketchikan, Sitka National Historical Park (p152) and many other places in the Southeast. The Tlingits were spread across the Southeast in large numbers and occasionally went as far south as Seattle in their huge dugout canoes. Both groups had few problems gathering food, as fish and game were plentiful in the Southeast.

John Smelcer's *The Raven and the Totem* (1992) is a collection of 60 traditional Native myths and legends offering a fascinating view of Alaska before the Europeans arrived.

Life was not so easy for the Aleuts, Iñupiat and Yupik. With much colder winters and cooler summers, these people had to develop a highly effective sea-hunting culture to sustain life in the harsh regions of Alaska. This was especially true for the Iñupiat, who could not have survived the winters without their skilled ice-hunting techniques. In spring, armed only with jade-tipped harpoons, the Iñupiat, in skin-covered kayaks called *bidarkas* and *umiaks,* stalked and killed 60-ton bowhead whales. Though motorized

TIMELINE

28,000–13,000 BC

The first Alaskans arrive, migrating across a 900-mile land bridge from Asia to North America and eventually settling throughout the state in tribal groups with distinct cultures.

AD 1741

Danish explorer Vitus Bering, employed by Peter the Great for the service of Russia, makes his third trip to North America and becomes the first European to set foot on Alaska.

1784

Russian Grigorii Shelikhov establishes the first permanent European settlement at Three Saints Bay on Kodiak Island. Eight years later he is granted a monopoly on furs as head of the Russian-American Company.

boats replaced the kayaks and modern harpoons the jade-tipped spears, the whaling tradition still lives on in places such as Barrow.

The indigenous people, despite their harsh environment, were numerous until non-Natives, particularly fur traders and whalers, brought guns, alcohol and disease that destroyed the Alaska Natives' delicate relationship with nature and wiped out whole communities. At one time an estimated 20,000 Aleuts lived throughout the Aleutian Islands. In only 50 years the Russians reduced the Aleut population to less than 2000. The whalers who arrived at Iñupiat villages in the mid-19th century were similarly destructive, introducing alcohol that devastated the lifestyles of entire villages. When the 50th anniversary of the Alaska Highway was celebrated in 1992, many Alaska Natives and Canadians called the event a 'commemoration' not a 'celebration,' due to the destructive forces that the link to Canada and the rest of the USA brought, including disease, alcohol and a cash economy.

Looking for a long-lost relative in Alaska? Check out the Yukon & Alaska Genealogy Centre at yukonalaska.com/pathfinder/gen for help.

AGE OF EXPLORATION

Thanks to the cold and stormy North Pacific, Alaska was one of the last places in the world to be mapped by Europeans. Because of this, explorers from several countries attempted to lay claim to the land and its resources by establishing a fort or two.

Spanish Admiral Bartholeme de Fonte is credited by many with making the first European trip into Alaskan waters in 1640, but the first written record of the state was made by Vitus Bering, a Danish navigator sailing for the Russian tsar. In 1728 Bering's explorations demonstrated that America and Asia were two separate continents. Thirteen years later, commanding the *St Peter*, he went ashore near Cordova, becoming the first European to set foot in Alaska. Bering and many of his crew died from scurvy during that journey, but his lieutenant survived to return to Europe with fur pelts and tales of fabulous seal and otter colonies, and Alaska's first boom was under way. Russian fur merchants wasted little time in overrunning the Aleutian Islands and quickly established a settlement at Unalaska and then Kodiak Island. Chaos followed, as bands of Russian hunters robbed and murdered each other for furs, while the peaceful Aleuts, living near the hunting grounds, were almost annihilated through massacres and forced labor. By the 1790s Russia had organized the Russian-American Company to regulate the fur trade and ease the violent competition.

Alaska in the Wake of the North Star (2005) by Loel Shuler is an account of a coastline trip from Sitka to Barrow in 1949, just before WWII modernization overwhelmed ancient cultures.

The British arrived when Captain James Cook began searching the area for the Northwest Passage. Cook sailed north from Vancouver Island to Southcentral Alaska in 1778, anchoring at what is now Cook Inlet for a spell before continuing on to the Aleutian Islands, Bering Sea and Arctic Ocean. The French sent Jean-François Galaup, comte de La Pérouse, who in 1786 made it as far as Lituya Bay, now part of Glacier Bay National Park. The wicked tides within the long, narrow bay caught the exploration party off guard, capsizing three longboats, killing 21 sailors and discouraging the French from colonizing the area.

The last shot of the Civil War was fired in the Bering Sea by the CSS *Shenandoah* on June 22, 1865, 74 days after Appomattox.

1804

With four war ships, Aleksandr Baranov defeats the Tlingit at Sitka and then establishes New Archangel as the new capital of the Russian-American Company.

1867

Secretary of State William H Seward negotiates the US purchase of Alaska from Russia for $7.2 million. It takes six months for Congress to approve the treaty.

1878

Ten years after a salmon saltery is opened in Klawock on Prince of Wales Island, a San Francisco company builds the first salmon cannery in Alaska.

FIVE WHO SHAPED ALASKA

William H Seward, Sr (1801–72) Seward was secretary of state under President Andrew Johnson when he staged an all-night session with a Russian minister, negotiating the sale of Alaska to the USA. The men emerged at 4am on March 30, 1867, agreeing on a price tag of $7.2 million or $98 million in 2008 dollars. Despite never having been to Alaska and being mocked in the media, Seward lobbied for the congressional approval of the treaty and paid for a public education campaign himself. Today Alaskans celebrate the event on Seward's Day, the last Monday of March.

James Wickersham (1857–1939) Wickersham didn't arrive in Alaska until he was 42 but went on to become one of the most influential Alaskans in the early 20th century. In 1900, Wickersham was sent to Eagle City as a newly appointed judge, the only one in a judicial district that stretched 300,000 sq miles from the Arctic to the tip of the Aleutians. For the next 30 years he provided justice in an often lawless place and then served as congressional delegate. He introduced the first Alaskan statehood bill in 1916, put together the first serious attempt to climb Mt McKinley and played a key role in establishing what is now Denali National Park.

William Egan (1914–84) Egan was born in Valdez where he worked as a miner, grocer and cannery worker before being elected to six terms in the territorial legislature. While in Juneau he lobbied hard for statehood and served as president of the state constitutional convention. After Alaska became the 49th state of the Union, Egan was elected as its first governor in 1959 and re-elected in 1962 and 1970. He is the only Alaskan governor born and educated in Alaska.

Jay Hammond (1922–2005) Hammond was a pilot, trapper, hunting guide, commercial fisherman and, from 1975 to 1982, governor of Alaska. He was elected on a platform of permanently saving a portion of the oil money that was about to gush down the Trans-Alaska Pipeline, and while in office worked tirelessly for the creation of the Permanent Fund. Today this wildly popular program pays every man, woman and child in Alaska an annual share of the state's oil wealth just for living there.

Jimmy Carter (1924–) Carter was on the eve of leaving the presidency in 1980 when he signed the Alaska National Interest Lands Conservation Act (ANILCA), knowing incoming President Ronald Reagan had promised to veto the bill. Often called the most significant land conservation measure in the history of the USA, the statute protected 106 million acres of federal lands in Alaska, doubling the size of the country's national park and refuge system and tripling the amount of land designated as wilderness. ANILCA expanded the national park system in Alaska by over 43 million acres and created 10 new national parks.

Having depleted the fur colonies in the Aleutians, Aleksandr Baranov, who headed the Russian-American Company, moved his territorial capital from Kodiak to Sitka in the Southeast, where he built a stunning city, dubbed 'an American Paris in Alaska.' At one point, Baranov oversaw (some would say ruled) an immensely profitable fur empire that stretched from Bristol Bay to Northern California. When the British began pushing north into Southeast Alaska, he built a second fort near the mouth of the Stikine River in 1834. That fort, which was named St Dionysius at the time, evolved into the small lumbering and fishing town of Wrangell.

View the actual canceled check and receipt for the purchase of Alaska from Russia in 1867 at www.archives.gov/education/lessons/alaska/cancelled-check.html.

SEWARD'S FOLLY

By the 1860s Russian control of Alaska had become problematic. The Russians found themselves badly overextended: their involvement in Napoleon's

1880

Led by Tlingit Chief Kowee, Richard Harris and Joe Juneau discover gold from a creek in Silver Bow Basin. The next year miners rename their tent city from Harrisburg to Juneau.

1882

A US Navy cutter shells Angoon in a retaliation for an uprising and then sends a landing party to loot and burn the rest of the Native village.

1887

The Sheldon Jackson Museum is established in Sitka as Alaska's first museum with artifacts collected by Reverend Sheldon Jackson during his travels through rural Alaska.

European wars, a declining fur industry and the long lines of shipping between Sitka and the heartland of Russia were draining their national treasury. The country made several overtures to the USA to purchase Alaska but it wasn't until 1867 that Secretary of State William H Seward, with extremely keen foresight, signed a treaty to purchase the state for $7.2 million – less than 2¢ an acre.

By then the US public was in an uproar over the purchase of 'Seward's Ice Box' or 'Walrussia,' and, on the Senate floor, the battle to ratify the treaty lasted six months before the sale was finally approved. On October 18, 1867, the formal transfer of Alaska to the Americans took place in Sitka. Alaska remained a lawless, unorganized territory for the next 20 years, with the US Army in charge at one point and the US Navy at another.

This great land, remote and inaccessible to all but a few hardy settlers, stayed a dark, frozen mystery to most people. Eventually its riches were uncovered. First whaling began, then the phenomenal salmon runs, with the first canneries built in 1878 at Klawock on Prince of Wales Island.

Good Time Girls of the Alaska-Yukon Gold Rush (2003) by Lael Morgan covers the women who followed the stampeders north, including one prostitute who married the mayor of Fairbanks and hosted President Warren Harding.

THE ALASKAN GOLD RUSH

What truly brought Alaska into the world limelight, however, was gold. The promise of quick riches and frontier adventures was the most effective lure Alaska has ever had and, to some degree, still has today. Gold was discovered in the Gastineau Channel in the 1880s, and the towns of Juneau and Douglas sprang up overnight. Circle City, in the Interior, emerged in 1893, when gold was discovered in Birch Creek. Three years later, one of the world's most colorful gold rushes took place in the Klondike region of Canada's Yukon Territory.

Often called 'the last grand adventure,' the Klondike Gold Rush occurred when the country and much of the world was suffering a severe recession. When the banner headline of the *Seattle Post-Intelligencer* bellowed 'GOLD! GOLD! GOLD! GOLD!' on July 17, 1897, thousands of people quit their jobs and sold their homes to finance a trip through Southeast Alaska to the newly created boomtown of Skagway. From this tent city almost 30,000 prospectors tackled the steep Chilkoot Trail (p91) to Lake Bennett, where they built crude rafts to float the rest of the way to the goldfields. An equal number of people returned home along the same route, broke and disillusioned.

The number of miners who made fortunes was small, but the tales and legends that emerged were endless. The Klondike stampede, though it only lasted from 1896 to the early 1900s, was Alaska's most colorful era and forever earned the state the reputation of being the country's last frontier.

Within three years of the Klondike stampede Alaska's population doubled to 63,592, including more than 30,000 non-Native people. Nome, another gold boomtown, was the largest city in the territory, with 12,000 residents, while gold prompted the capital to be moved from Sitka to Juneau.

To enter Canada on the Chilkoot Trail, miners were required to carry a year's supply of food, including 400lb of flour and 200lb of bacon.

Discover the Alaska State Library's catalogue of gold rush photos from 1893–1916 at library.state.ak.us/hist/goldrush/table.html.

1898

Klondike Gold Rush turns Skagway into Alaska's largest city, with a population of 10,000. Canadian Mounties describe the lawless town as 'little better than a hell on earth.'

1913

Walter Harper, an Alaska Native, becomes the first person to summit Mt McKinley, the highest peak in North America. He is joined by Harry Karstens, who later becomes the first superintendent of Denali National Park.

1915

Anchorage is founded when Ship Creek is chosen as a survey camp to build the Alaska Railroad and by the end of a year is a tent city of 2000.

BUILDING THE ALCAN

A land link between Alaska and the rest of the USA was envisioned as early as 1930, but it took WWII to turn the nation's attention north to embark on one of the greatest engineering feats of the 20th century: constructing a 1390-mile road through remote wilderness.

Deemed a military necessity and authorized by President Franklin Roosevelt only two months after the attack on Pearl Harbor, the Alcan was designed to be an overland route far enough inland to be out of range of airplanes transported on Japanese aircraft carriers. The exact route followed old winter roads, trap lines and pack trails, and by March 9, 1942, construction had begun. Within three months, more than 10,000 troops, most of them from the US Army Corps of Engineers, were in the Canadian wilderness. The soldiers felled trees, put down gravel, struggled with permafrost and built pontoon bridges, all at a breakneck pace. They endured temperatures of -30°F in April, snowfalls in June and swarms of mosquitoes and gnats for most of the summer. They worked 16-hour days, spent nights in pup tents and went weeks without hearing from commanders in base camps, much less from their families.

Despite the harsh conditions, the speed with which the Alcan was built is astounding. With most crews working out of two main camps, Whitehorse and Fort St John, a regiment from the west met a regiment from the east on September 23 at Contact Creek, today Mile 588 of the highway. When a final link was completed near Kluane Lake in late October, the Alcan was open, having been built in only eight months and 12 days.

The official dedication of the Alcan took place on November 20, 1942, at Soldier's Summit near Kluane Lake, at which time an army truck departed from the ceremony and arrived at Fairbanks the next day. It became the first vehicle to travel the entire highway but has since been followed by thousands more, many of them with travelers looking for adventure and grandeur on North America's great wilderness road trip.

WORLD WAR II

In June 1942, only six months after their attack on Pearl Harbor, the Japanese opened their Aleutian Islands campaign by bombing Dutch Harbor for two days and then taking Attu and Kiska Islands. Other than Guam, it was the only foreign invasion of US soil during WWII and is often dubbed 'the Forgotten War' because most Americans are unaware of what took place in Alaska. The battle to retake Attu Island was a bloody one. After 19 days and landing more than 15,000 troops, US forces recaptured the plot of barren land, but only after suffering 3929 casualties including 549 deaths. Of the more than 2300 Japanese on Attu, fewer than 30 surrendered, with many taking their own lives.

What had quickly become apparent to both sides was the role the capricious Aleutian weather played in the campaign. Soldiers shot their own troops in the fog; unable to penetrate fog and clouds, ships were thrown against rocks and sunk in heavy seas; and pilots met the sides of mountains in low overcast skies. Bad weather literally saved Kodiak, keeping Japanese pilots at bay the night they planned to bomb it.

The Japanese invasion of the Aleutian Islands in 1942 was the first time that an enemy had occupied American soil since the War of 1812.

For details of the 'Forgotten War' of the Aleutian Islands during WWII, visit the National Park Service at www.nps.gov/aleu.

1923

President Warren Harding comes to Alaska to drive in the golden spike and celebrate the completion of the Alaska Railroad. The first president to visit Alaska dies within two weeks of his trip.

1935

The first of 200 Depression-era families from Minnesota, Wisconsin and Michigan arrive in the Matanuska Valley to begin farming as part of the 'New Deal' experiment and Palmer is established.

1942

Japan bombs Dutch Harbor for two days during WWII and then invades the remote Aleutian Islands of Attu and Kiska. Americans build the Alcan (Alaska Hwy).

THE ALCAN & STATEHOOD

Following the Japanese attack on the Aleutian Islands in 1942, Congress panicked and rushed to protect the rest of Alaska. Large army and air-force bases were set up at Anchorage, Fairbanks, Sitka and Whittier, and thousands of military personnel were stationed in Alaska. But it was the famous Alcan (also known as the Alaska Hwy) that was the single most important project of the military expansion. The road was built by the military, but Alaska's residents benefited, as the Alcan aided their ability to access and make use of Alaska's natural resources.

The Alaska Statehood Commission website at www.gov.state.ak.us/ASCC covers the history and events of Alaskan statehood in photos, videos and articles.

In 1916 Alaska's territorial legislature submitted its first statehood bill. The effort was first quashed by the Seattle-based canned-salmon industry, who wanted to prevent local control of Alaska's resources, then the stock market crash of 1929 and WWII kept Congress occupied with more demanding issues. But the growth brought on by the Alcan, and to a lesser degree the new military bases, pushed Alaska firmly into the 20th century and renewed its drive for statehood. When the US Senate passed the Alaska statehood bill on June 30, 1958, Alaska had made it into the Union and was officially proclaimed the country's 49th state by President Dwight Eisenhower that January.

The Thousand Mile War: World War II in Alaska and the Aleutians (1988) by Brian Garfield is the best book ever written about the 'Forgotten War' in the Aleutian Islands.

Alaska entered the 1960s full of promise when disaster struck: the most powerful earthquake ever recorded in North America (registering 9.2 on the Richter scale) hit Southcentral Alaska on Good Friday morning in 1964. More than 100 lives were lost, and damage was estimated at $500 million. In Anchorage office buildings sank 10ft into the ground, and houses slid more than 1200ft off a bluff into Knik Arm. A tidal wave virtually obliterated the community of Valdez. In Kodiak and Seward, 32ft of the coastline slipped into the Gulf of Alaska, and Cordova lost its entire harbor as the sea rose 16ft.

THE ALASKAN BLACK-GOLD RUSH

The devastating 1964 earthquake left the newborn state in a shambles, but a more pleasant gift from nature soon rushed Alaska to recovery and beyond. In 1968 Atlantic Richfield discovered massive oil deposits underneath Prudhoe Bay in the Arctic Ocean. The value of the oil doubled after the Arab oil embargo of 1973. However, it couldn't be tapped until there was a pipeline to transport it to the warm-water port of Valdez and the pipeline couldn't be built until the US Congress, which still administered most of the land, settled the intense controversy among industry, environmentalists and Alaska Natives over historical claims to the land.

Fairbanks journalist Dermot Cole recalls the best of the pipeline tales he heard during the three-year boom that engulfed his city in *Amazing Pipeline Stories* (1997).

The Alaska Native Claims Settlement Act of 1971 was an unprecedented piece of legislation that opened the way for a consortium of oil companies to undertake the construction of the 789-mile pipeline. The Trans-Alaska Pipeline took three years to build, cost more than $8 billion – in 1977 dollars – and, at the time, was the most expensive private construction project ever

1959

Alaska officially becomes the 49th state when President Dwight Eisenhower signs the statehood declaration on January 3. William A Egan is sworn in as the first governor.

1964

North America's worst earthquake, 9.2 on the Richter scale, takes place on Good Friday, devastating Anchorage and Southcentral Alaska, with 131 people losing their lives.

1968

Oil and natural gas are discovered at Prudhoe Bay on the North Slope by Atlantic Richfield Company and Exxon. The next year the state of Alaska stages a $900 million North Slope oil lease sale.

DRILLING FOR OIL IN THE LAST GREAT WILDERNESS

Alaska is a battleground for environmental issues, but none tugs more at the nation's conscience than the push to drill for oil in the Arctic National Wildlife Refuge (ANWR). Yellowstone National Park sees more visitors in a weekend than this refuge does in a year, yet the battle over oil has turned ANWR into a sacred icon: America's last great wilderness.

The refuge was created under President Dwight D Eisenhower in the 1950s and expanded to 19.6 million acres by President Jimmy Carter in 1980. It's often labeled by environmentalists as America's Serengeti, a pristine wilderness inhabited by 45 species of mammals, including grizzly bears, polar bears and wolves. Millions of migratory birds use the refuge to nest, and every spring the country's second-largest caribou herd, 150,000 strong, gives birth to 40,000 calves there.

But there is also oil in the refuge, concentrated in its fragile coastal plains that span 1.5 million acres along the Beaufort Sea. Geologists believe the ANWR has the largest untapped reserve in the country, rivaling the massive Prudhoe Bay fields to the west when they were first explored. The US Geological Survey has estimated the amount of recoverable oil at between 5.6 billion and 16 billion barrels.

The oil industry, salivating over such a large field, contends only 8% of the refuge would be affected by its infrastructure. Environmentalists contend that the refuge would never quench more than 2% of the US' thirst for oil and would not put the country on a course of 'energy independence.' A majority of Alaskans are eager to drill, while Native tribes who live in and around ANWR are split over the issue.

Politically the battle has raged since the earliest days of President Ronald Reagan in the 1980s. In 1996 President Bill Clinton vetoed pro-drilling legislation passed by the Republican-controlled Congress and in 2005 only a successful Democratic filibuster prevented Alaskan Senator Ted Stevens from attaching a drilling amendment to a defense appropriations bill.

Throughout the controversy public opinion outside of Alaska has been steadily against an industrial invasion of ANWR. However, in 2008 the sudden escalation of the price of gas to above $4 a gallon quickly reversed those sentiments and for the first time a Pew Research Poll showed a majority of Americans were in favor of drilling. With oil bouncing between $70 and $100 a barrel and the public in favor of drilling, ANWR's days as an untouched wilderness may be over.

From pump station No 1 to Valdez, the Trans-Alaska Pipeline crosses three mountain ranges, 34 major rivers and 500 streams.

undertaken. At the peak of construction, the pipeline employed 28,000 people, doing '7-12s' (seven 12-hour shifts a week).

The oil began to flow on June 20, 1977, and for a decade oil gave Alaska an economic base that was the envy of every other state, accounting for as much as 80% of state government revenue. In the explosive growth period of the mid-1980s, Alaskans enjoyed the highest per-capita income in the country. The state's budget was in the billions. Legislators in Juneau transformed Anchorage into a stunning city, with sports arenas, libraries and performing-arts centers, and provided virtually every bush town with a million-dollar school. From 1980 to 1986 this state of only half a million residents generated revenue of $26 billion.

1971

President Richard Nixon signs the Alaska Native Claims Settlement Act to pave the way for the Trans-Alaska Pipeline. Native Alaskans give up claims in return for nearly $1 billion and 44 million acres.

1973

The first Iditarod Trail Sled Dog Race is held on an old dog team mail route blazed in 1910. The winner covers the 1150-mile race between Wasilla and Nome in 20 days.

1980

President Jimmy Carter signs the Alaska National Interests Lands Conservation Act (ANILCA), preserving 79.54 million acres of wilderness and creating or enlarging 15 national parks.

DISASTER AT VALDEZ

For most Alaskans, the abundant oil made it hard to see beyond the gleam of the oil dollar. Reality hit hard in 1989, when the *Exxon Valdez,* a 987ft Exxon oil supertanker, rammed Bligh Reef a few hours out of the port of Valdez. The ship spilled almost 11 million gallons of North Slope crude into the bountiful waters of Prince William Sound. Alaskans and the rest of the country watched in horror as the oil spill quickly became far too large for booms to contain, spreading 600 miles from the grounding site. State residents were shocked as oil began to appear from the glacier-carved cliffs of Kenai Fjords to the bird rookeries of Katmai National Park. The spill eventually contaminated 1567 miles of shoreline and killed an estimated 645,000 birds and 5000 sea otters.

Out of the Channel: the Exxon Valdez Oil Spill in Prince William Sound (1999) by John Keeble is an in-depth account of Exxon's response and cover-up, which the author contends did more damage than the original spill.

Today the oil, like other resources exploited in the past, is simply running out. That pot of gold called Prudhoe Bay began its decline in 1988 and now produces less than half of its 1987 peak of two million barrels a day. The end of the Cold War and the subsequent downsizing of the US military in the early 1990s was more bad economic news for Alaska. Alaskan state revenues, once the envy of every other state governor in the country, went tumbling along with the declining oil royalties. With more than 80% of its state budget derived from oil revenue, Alaska was awash with red ink from the early 1990s until 2004, managing a balanced budget only twice.

A NEW ALASKA

Alaska was at a low point both financially and politically in 2006 when Sarah Palin, a self-described 'hockey mom' and former mayor of Wasilla, ran for governor. At the time, three former state legislators had been arrested on public corruption charges, while in Washington, DC, longtime Senator Ted Stevens and Representative Don Young were under federal investigation for bribery. Palin stunned the political world when she crushed incumbent Governor Frank Murkowski in the Republican primary by almost two-to-one. She was then handed the keys to the governor's mansion in the general election by voters tired of their state being dominated by career politicians. In 2008 she stunned the political world even more when presidential candidate John McCain named Palin his running mate on the Republican ticket. McCain lost the historic election to Barack Obama but the campaign vaulted Palin onto the national stage as.

In 1980, flushed with oil revenue, the Alaska legislature repealed the state income tax in a special session and approved refunding 1979 income tax payments.

In her first year as governor, Palin worked with legislators to dramatically increase Alaska's share of royalties from oil production. When oil began its meteoric rise in price on the world markets, topping $140 a barrel in 2008, Alaska was carried along for the ride. Oil revenue pumped almost $7 billion into the state treasury that year, giving Alaska a $5 billion surplus during a time when many states couldn't make ends meet.

But the rising price of oil was a double-edged sword for Alaska. The state still has an unemployment rate hovering near 7%, one of the highest in the

1985

Libby Riddles of Teller gambles by departing in a blizzard when no other musher would and becomes the first woman to win the Iditarod Trail Sled Dog Race.

1989

The *Exxon Valdez* runs aground on Bligh Reef and spills 11 million gallons of oil into Prince William Sound, becoming the worst man-made environmental disaster to occur at sea.

1994

Alaskan Tommy Moe becomes the first American male skier to win two medals in a single Winter Olympics after capturing the gold for downhill and the silver for Super G at Lillehammer, Norway.

UNCLE TED

Ted Stevens was already a decorated WWII pilot and Harvard Law School graduate when in 1953, after accepting a position in Fairbanks, he moved to Alaska with his wife by driving the Alaska Hwy in the dead of winter. A mere six months later Stevens was appointed the US attorney for Fairbanks and was eventually elected as a state representative. In 1968 Stevens was appointed US senator for Alaska and has held onto that position ever since, never receiving less than 66% of the vote after his first election in 1970.

Such longevity allowed Stevens to break Strom Thurmond's record as the longest-serving Republican senator in 2007 with 38 years and three months of continual service. For the majority of Alaskans, Stevens has always been their senator, the reason many have dubbed him 'senator for life.'

Citizens Against Government Waste, America's top non-profit government watchdog, have kept tabs on 'Uncle Ted' since they started tracking congressional spending in 2000. The senator has been duly noted for his ability to bring home the 'pork.' In 2008 the Feds returned $295 per Alaskan citizen in local projects. Per capita that's the highest in the country by far, with other states averaging only $34 per person. In 2005 Stevens was ridiculed by the national media when in a speech from the Senate floor he angrily opposed diverting the Bridge to Nowhere funds (p124) to help New Orleans recover from Hurricane Katrina. Congress dropped the specific allocation for the bridge, but Alaska still received the money and simply spent it elsewhere.

Stevens was good at what he did but his legendary tenure in the US Senate came to an end in 2009. The previous year, a jury found him found guilty of federal corruption – failing to report tens of thousands of dollars in gifts and services he had received from friends – and convicted of him seven felony charges. Stevens vowed to appeal the decision but in November Alaskans had had enough and narrowly voted him out of office in his bid for an eighth term. In recent years Alaskans have shown a distaste for tainted career politicians. The question now is, can they live without the pork?

Visit the Alaska Historical Society at www.alaskahistoricalsociety.org – a great site for history buffs with articles, timelines and links to museums around the state.

country, and the high cost of fuel was devastating rural communities where everything has to be shipped in, often by costly air freight. The short-term solution was the state issuing every resident a $1200 energy check along with the annual Permanent Fund check. Between the two, a family of four picked up $13,076 in 2008 for simply living in Alaska.

But many Alaskans believe the long-term solution lies in opening up the Arctic National Wildlife Refuge (ANWR) to drilling, the construction of a natural gas line from the North Slope to the Lower 48, opening new mines, and other major projects designed to extract valuable minerals. Thus the greatest challenge facing Alaskans in the 21st century is convincing a nation, and more importantly Washington, DC, they have a right to make a living from an economy based on removing natural resources from the country's great wilderness areas. With a sky-rocketing price of gas at the pump, it might not be a hard argument to win.

2006

Sarah Palin, former mayor of Wasilla, stuns the political world by beating the incumbent governor to become Alaska's first female governor, and at 42, also its youngest.

2008

Largest check in the 28-year history of the Permanent Fund Dividend is sent out. Every man, woman and child who has lived in Alaska for six months or longer receives $2069.

2009

On January 3 Alaskans celebrate the 50th anniversary of their state officially being admitted to the Union, the first new state to be included since Arizona was admitted in 1912.

The Culture

The state is young: Alaska just turned 50, and its residents are new, the majority having moved here from somewhere else. Yet thanks to its isolation, its spectacular scenery and, yes, its long, dark winters, Alaska has a culture that is vibrant and rich, and a northern lifestyle that is thoroughly unique: whether its Alaska Natives celebrating a successful whale hunt in Barrow; or residents of Juneau staging a folk music festival to help pass an April of daily rain.

REGIONAL IDENTITY

The stereotypical Alaskan is a sourdough miner, hunched over an icy stream in an attempt to find that golden nugget that will send him home rich. There are still independent miners in Alaska – especially now that gold is hovering around $800 per ounce – and you certainly don't want to wander on their claim.

Whatever Alaskan town you're headed to, the Community Photo Library (www.dced.state.ak.us/dca/photos/comm_list.cfm) can provide a glimpse of everyday life in it.

But while most of Alaska is made up of rural, road-less areas collectively known as the Bush, most Alaskans are urban. Almost 60% of the residents live in the three largest cities: Anchorage, Fairbanks and Juneau. There are also Alaskans maintaining a subsistence lifestyle, gathering and hunting the majority of their food and living in small villages that can only be reached by boat, plane or, in the winter, snowmobile in the winter. But the majority live in urban neighborhoods, work a nine-to-five job and head to the supermarket when their cupboards are bare.

And most Alaskans are newcomers. Only 30% of the state's population was born in Alaska, the rest moved there, including all but one of its eight elected governors. Such a transient population creates a melting pot of ideas, philosophies and priorities. What they usually have in common is an interest in the great outdoors: they were lured here to either exploit it or enjoy it, and many residents do a little of both.

Thus debates in Alaska usually center on land, resources and, in particular, locking up the wilderness. Alaskans consider themselves good guardians of the Final Frontier, but the majority have few problems with drilling in the Arctic National Wildlife Refuge (ANWR) or clear-cutting Tongass National Forest. There are some liberal bastions of environmentalism, Juneau and Homer being the best known, but over the years Alaskans have moved to the Right, voting for Republican presidents, fighting tax increases and becoming one of the first states to pass a constitutional amendment banning same-sex marriages.

Tourists come to visit and marvel at the grand scenery. But Alaskans are here to stay, so they need to make a living in their chosen home, a land where there is little industry or farming. They regard trees, oil and fish as an opportunity to do that. To many Alaskans that's not exploitation, it's how you survive a winter when the sun never shines.

The furthest north supermarket in the USA is in Barrow, a $4 million store constructed on stilts to prevent central heating from thawing the permafrost.

LIFESTYLE

In Anchorage, residents can shop at enclosed malls, spend an afternoon at one of 162 parks, go in-line skating along 122 miles of paved bike paths, or get in their car and drive to another town. The median household income is almost $60,000, unemployment is less than 6% and if you get sick, there are six major hospitals to choose from.

Some 400 miles west of Anchorage is Nunapitchuk, a village of 545 residents, located on the swampy tundra of the Yukon-Kuskokwim Delta. There are no roads to or within Nunapitchuk; homes and buildings are connected by

A SWEET END TO HONEY BUCKETS

Alaska has the lowest percentage of indoor plumbing of any state in the country, but that's changing, one honey bucket at a time.

A honey bucket is traditionally a 5-gallon plastic pail that replaces a flush toilet in communities lacking a sewage system. The bucket sits within a wooden frame affixed with a toilet seat lid, and when filled is hauled by hand – carefully – to a community disposal site. It's estimated that 15,000 rural Alaskans live in communities without running water where homes, local government offices and even medical clinics, use honey buckets.

Nunapitchuk, located 22 miles northwest of Bethel, was one of those communities. But thanks to state grants and an innovative 'Flush Tank and Haul System' designed specifically for rural Alaska, the village of 545 residents slowly but steadily eliminated honey buckets. The final one was removed in 2007. It was such a monumental occasion that residents staged a No More Bucket Festival, to celebrate the end of hauling waste by hand, a day highlighted by music, a potluck dinner and a spirited 'fill-the-bucket' relay race.

a network of boardwalks. There is one store in town, and a health clinic. Most residents practice subsistence fishing and hunting. The median household income is $29,000, unemployment is 17% and a quart of boxed milk (you can't buy fresh here) is $4.

Lifestyles in Alaska are as diverse as the state is big. Rural or urban, Alaskans tend to be individualistic, following few outside trends and, instead, adhering to what their harsh environment dictates. Mother Nature and those -30°F winter days, not California, are responsible for the Alaskan dress code, even in Anchorage's finest restaurants. In the summer, Alaskans play because the weather is nice and the days are long. In the winter, they linger at the office because the temperature is often below 0°F.

According to a marketing research firm, Anchorage has three coffee shops per 10,000 residents, beating out even Seattle, and making it, per capita, the country's mocha mecca.

In many ways Alaska is progressive. Women are seen as equals in most places, thanks in part to Susan Butcher beating her male counterparts to win the Iditarod Trail Sled Dog Race four times from 1986 to 1990. Alaska women also do well economically, with among the highest median earnings in the country and a poverty rate that's only lower in Minnesota, Maryland and New Hampshire. On the other hand, Alaska is not as tolerant of gays and lesbians as most other states, particularly outside the major cities.

Visitors may find most of the locals they meet in towns and cities have lifestyles similar to their own. They work, they love their weekends, they live in a variety of homes big and small, and they participate in double coupon days at supermarkets. Even in remote villages there are satellite TV dishes, the latest hip-hop CDs and internet access to the rest of the world.

But Alaska also has social ills, spurred on in a large measure by the environment. The isolation of small towns and the darkness of winter has contributed to Alaska being one of the top 10 states for binge and heavy drinking, and sixth overall for the amount of alcohol sold per capita. Since the 1980s, Alaska has seen some of the highest per capita use of controlled drugs in the country, while it is second only to Nevada for suicides among women.

To survive this climate and to avoid those demons, you have to possess a passion for the land and an individualistic approach to a lifestyle that few, other than Alaskans, would choose.

Women won the 1150-mile Iditarod Trail Sled Dog Race five out of six years from 1985 to 1990, and finished second the one year they didn't win it.

POPULATION

Alaska is by far the largest state in the USA but has the fourth-smallest population, making it the most sparse. Lots of land but few people, with a density of 1.2 persons per sq mile. In the rest of the country it's 80 persons per sq mile, and in Manhattan it's more than 70,000. As late as the mid-

1980s Alaska had the fewest residents of any state in the country. Now it has surpassed Wyoming, Vermont and North Dakota.

Alaskans are overwhelmingly urban (74%) and white (70%), with 42% of them living in one city, Anchorage. But they are four years younger than the national average: the median age is 33. And along with Nevada, Alaska is still the only other state that has more men (almost 51%) than women. That leads to the most popular saying among Alaskan women: 'the odds are good but the goods are odd.'

MULTICULTURALISM

Military bases and the construction of the Alaska Hwy during WWII spurred Alaska's most rapid period of growth, creating a society that in the 1950s was largely a mix of Alaska Natives and military-minded whites. Since then the percentages of both indigenous people (see the boxed text, p56) and especially the military, due to base closures, have drastically decreased.

Three times a week listeners of KMXT Public Radio in Kodiak can tune into *The Alutiiq Word of the Week*, a feature designed to teach the Alutiiq language.

Alaska is still predominantly white (70%), with Alaska Natives now representing less than 16% and African Americans less than 4% of the population. The most significant immigration growth in Alaska has been Asians, now making up 4.2% of the population. This is particularly true in communities connected to the commercial fishing industry; in Unalaska and Dutch Harbor, Asians represent 30% of the residents and outnumber Alaska Natives.

But Alaska's cultural tensions generally aren't between races, or even sourdoughs (old-timers) and cheechakos (newcomers). Tension is often found between rural and urban, and in particular Alaska Natives and the rest of the state. Sensitive issues such as subsistence rights can bring on spirited debates, but rarely more than that.

RELIGION

Every religion that mainstream America practices in the Lower 48 can be found in Alaska, but the state's oldest and most enduring is Russian Orthodox. In 1794, after Russian merchants and traders had decimated indigenous populations, particularly the Aleuts, missionaries arrived. The priests not only converted the indigenous people of Southwest, Southcentral and Southeast Alaska to a new religious belief, but also managed to provide Alaska Natives basic privileges, including education and wages.

Ironically, a period that started with brutal hostility ended with a legacy still evident today through Russian family names and active Russian Orthodox congregations in 80 Alaskan communities. The familiar domes of their churches can be seen in Juneau, Sitka, Kodiak and Unalaska, while the Museum of the Aleutians (p318) devotes a good portion of its exhibits to the close relationship between the Aleuts and the Russian Orthodox religion.

ECONOMY

Since the early 1980s, Alaska's economy has been fueled by oil. Nearly 90% of the state's general fund revenue comes from taxes on oil and gas production. When the price of a barrel is up, as it was in the early 1980s and again in 2008, Alaska is flushed with cash. When it isn't, such as the mid-1990s, there are serious budget problems in Juneau because Alaska has the lowest individual tax burden in the country. Thanks to oil, residents do not pay state taxes on income, sales or inheritance.

The War Journal of Lila Ann Smith (2007), by Irving Warner, is a moving historical novel, based on the invasion of Attu by the Japanese in WWII, and the Aleuts who became prisoners of war.

But the greater problem with such a narrow economy based on mineral extraction is when the minerals begin to run out. Prudhoe Bay, the largest oil field in North America, is drying up and today its production is less than 50% of its peak in the mid-1980s. That's why the vast majority of Alaskans are in favor of drilling in the ANWR and the state is pushing

ALASKA NATIVES

Long before Western colonization, Alaska Natives had established a thriving culture and lifestyle in one of the world's harshest environments. Although they traded and even fought with each other, the tribes inhabited separate regions. The Aleuts and Alutiiqs lived from Prince William Sound to the end of the Aleutian Islands; the Iñupiat and Yupik lived on Alaska's northern and western coasts; the Athabascan populated the Interior; and the Tlingit, Haida and Tsimshian lived along the coasts of Southeast Alaska. Today the ethnic and territorial distinctions have blurred, especially with the growing number of Alaska Natives moving to urban areas. But for the most part, the lines have been maintained and their culture has survived the onslaught of Western civilization because the majority of Alaska Natives still live on their traditional homeland.

More than 118,000 indigenous people, half of whom are Iñupiat, live in Alaska but the percentage of the population that is Alaska Native has greatly decreased. Prior to 1940 they were the majority. During WWII they became a minority, and today they represent less than 16%. Even more dramatic has been the shift to the cities. Alaska Natives living in the large urban areas increased from 17% in 1970 to 45% today, and the largest center of indigenous people in Alaska isn't Barrow, but Anchorage, home to 27,000 Alaska Natives.

In the rural Bush, Alaska Natives today face a multitude of challenges. Alcohol abuse is perhaps the most serious problem, leading to elevated levels of domestic violence, crime and suicides. Alaska Natives account for almost 40% of all suicides in the state, and toxicology results show that in rural Alaska alcohol was present in 70% of cases. Since 1980 the state has allowed local control of alcohol and 120 villages now have some form of prohibition: either totally dry; damp (you can drink but not purchase alcohol); or restrictive wet (the community controls the liquor store). But such restrictions lead to rampant and extremely profitable bootlegging; a fifth of whiskey that sells for $10 in Anchorage could fetch $150 in an isolated village.

Other problems that villagers face range from a higher rate of sexual assault to an inability to recruit sufficient numbers of teachers, police officers and medical professionals to the Bush. It's estimated that only 29% of Alaska Native children (and even fewer adults) have access to dental care resulting in 2½ times the number of cavities of the average American child.

Many Alaska Native leaders believe that the solution is preserving and practicing their culture, particularly their languages. Only 36% of Alaska Natives still use their native language, and among those living in Anchorage and Fairbanks it's only 17%. Such statistics led to the creation of Bethel's Ayaprum Elitnaurvik, a Yupik immersion school where studies and classes are divided between English and Yupik. Because of the decreasing number of residents who could speak Iñupiaq fluently, in the Northwest Arctic, Alaska Native leaders approached Rosetta Stone, a language-learning company, who then released, in 2007, *Iñupiaq Coastal Language*, a software program that teaches by immersion rather than by translation.

Most travelers to Alaska will be unlikely to hear a Native language spoken and will usually only encounter indigenous culture at museums such as the Alaska Native Heritage Center (p203) in Anchorage or Ketchikan's Totem Heritage Center (p124). To experience the rich culture and the subsistent way of life of Native villages you need to travel to one, and for the vast majority of visitors that means a package tour to Barrow. To travel to small, remote villages you either have to have a contact there or travel with somebody who does, such as an outfitter. That's because tourist facilities – lodges and restaurants – are nonexistent in many places. Nor should you just set up camp on the edge of town. Often the land around a village is owned by one of the 13 Native corporations created by the Alaska Native Claims Settlement Act in 1971. More times than not, the land is open to public use but you will need to arrange permission in advance and possibly pay a fee.

hard to get a gas pipeline built from the North Slope oilfields to markets in the Lower 48. There is 36 trillion cubic feet of natural gas on the North Slope, making it one of the world's largest proven reserves, and the reason Alaska provided $500 million in seed money to TransCanada Corp in 2008 to pursue the project. When completed, the proposed gas pipeline would top the Trans-Alaska Pipeline, stretching 1715 miles to Calgary in Alberta and costing between $26 billion and $30 billion.

Many mining projects are also in the works. The proposed Pebble Mine in the Alaska Peninsula may have environmentalists up in arms, but it rates as one of the top metal reserves in the world, with staggering amounts of gold, copper and molybdenum waiting to be extracted. Hard-rock mining for gold is also accelerating on the Seward Peninsula, near Nome, while in the Southeast new mines or the expansion of existing ones have been proposed from Prince of Wales Island to Juneau.

For Alaskans it's almost impossible to diversify beyond this boom-and-bust economy based on natural resources. Alaska unfortunately is at the end of an economic highway; raw materials leave the state, finished products come back. Government officials have long argued for in-state processing of raw materials – oil, timber, fish – as a way to stabilize the economy. But this has never been feasible due to high salaries, costly transportation and expensive-to-build infrastructure such as plants and mills.

Commercial fishing, rebuilt on the bottom fishery of Pollack and the marketing of wild salmon, is a renewable resource that has rebounded recently. In 2006, Alaska totaled 5.4 billion lb, or 56% of the country's catch, valued at $1.3 billion. That includes 90% of the country's wild salmon harvest, making commercial fishing Alaska's largest private sector employer, providing 40,000 jobs. But the industry's contribution of $100 million into the state treasury is a distant second to the oil and gas industry's almost $7 billion in 2008.

In *Catch and Release: The Insiders Guide to Alaska Men* (1997), by Jane Haigh, Kelly Hegarty-Lammers and Patricia Walsh, three lifelong Alaskans dispel the myth of the 'Alaska Man' in a fun and witty style.

SPORTS

The state sport of Alaska, officially adopted in 1972, is dog mushing, and its Super Bowl, the biggest spectator sport in the state, is the Iditarod (see the boxed text, p58). But there are other spectator sports in Alaska that you don't have to bundle up to watch, including the great American pastime: baseball. The **Alaska Baseball League** (www.alaskabaseballleague.org) is made up of six semipro teams of highly regarded college players eyeing the major leagues. Teams include Fairbanks' **Alaska Goldpanners** (www.goldpanners.com) and the **Anchorage Bucs** (www.anchoragebucs.com), and among the major leaguers who have played in Alaska are sluggers Barry Bonds and Mark McGwire.

The state's most unusual sporting event is the **World Eskimo-Indian Olympics** (www.weio.org) in July, when several hundred athletes converge on Fairbanks. For four days Alaska Natives compete in greased pole walking, seal skinning, blanket toss and other events that display the skills traditionally needed for survival in a harsh environment.

ALASKA'S PERMANENT FUND

Travelers pay a lot to see Alaska, but Alaskans are paid for simply living here. Permanent Fund Dividends (PFDs) are annual checks that began in 1980 when Alaskans approved to set aside a quarter of all mineral-lease royalties, but particularly those from Prudhoe Bay, in a constitutionally protected 'Alaska Permanent Fund.' At the urging of then-governor Jay Hammond, the state legislature created the PFD payment program and in 1982 began handing out the interest from the fund: $1000 to every Alaskan resident, including children. In 2008 the PFD was a record $2069, and for people who have lived in Alaska since 1982, the PFD has padded their bank accounts by $29,605.

The Permanent Fund now contains $40 billion and earns more revenue for the state than Prudhoe Bay. The arrival of the checks every October is known as 'Dividend Days,' a time when kids skip school, long lines form at the banks and villages empty out because suddenly there is almost $1 billion to spend on airline tickets. The checks are so beloved that when asked in 1999 to sacrifice just a small portion of the PFD to ease the state's growing budget deficit, 83% of Alaskans voted 'no.'

There are no professional sports teams in Alaska, but even the smallest towns have a sports bar with a wide-screen TV and patrons cheering on Alaska's adopted home teams: Seattle Mariners, Seattle Seahawks and other pro clubs based in the US Northwest.

The University of Alaska website www.buyalaska.com allows Alaskans and visitors to search for in-state products and services before buying Outside.

MEDIA

A good read before your trip is **Alaska Magazine** (www.alaskamagazine.com), which has the state's best writers – Nick Jans, Sherry Simpson and Ned Rozell – as regular contributors. The **Anchorage Daily News** (www.adn.com) is Alaska's largest newspaper and a top-rated publication that won the Pulitzer Prize in the 1970s for stories on the Trans-Alaska Pipeline.

Radio stations are widespread in Alaska. There are more than 20 stations in the Anchorage area alone, broadcasting everything from jazz to religion. In smaller towns, public radio is a particularly important outlet for news and entertainment. **Alaska Public Radio Network** (www.akradio.org) has 18 stations in communities as far-flung as Barrow and Fort Yukon.

Tom Bodett, a carpenter living in Homer, and spokesman for Motel 6, uses his self-deprecating humor to pen his best essays about Alaska in *As Far as You Can Go Without a Passport* (1992).

ARTS

The winters are long and the scenery is spectacular. This more than anything else has been the basis for the arts in Alaska. The cultural scene in the Far North has a long tradition, beginning with Alaska Natives and continuing today in places such as Homer, Girdwood and Haines.

Native Arts & Crafts

Alaska's first artists, its indigenous people, still create some of the state's most impressive work. Alaska Natives are renowned for their ingenious use

THE IDITAROD

In 1948 Joe Redington Sr arrived in Alaska with just $18 in his pocket, and used $13 of it to cover a filing fee for a 101-acre homestead in Knik. By accident – some say fate – Redington's homestead was located only a few hundred feet from the historic Iditarod Trail, an old dogsled mail route from Seward to Nome. Redington was fascinated by the Iditarod Trail and the famous 'serum run' that saved the town of Nome from diphtheria in 1925, when mushers used the trail to relay medical supplies across Alaska.

Worried that snowmobiles might replace sled dogs, Redington proposed an Anchorage–Nome race along the historic trail, and then worked tirelessly to stage the first 1100-mile Iditarod in 1973. Alaska's 'Last Great Race,' the world's longest sled dog event, was born.

Despite some rocky times, the Iditarod has endured. It's held in early March, when the temperatures are usually in the low teens and the snow coverage is good. Most visitors to Alaska catch the race at the start – 4th Ave and E St in Anchorage – but that is strictly ceremonial. The mushers run their teams for only a few miles and then truck them up to Wasilla or Willow for a restart of the event.

From there they follow one of two routes of the historic trail, crossing two mountain ranges, following a frozen Yukon River for 150 miles, and passing through dozens of small native villages before arriving to cheering crowds in Nome. The race has drawn criticism from some animal rights groups, who have protested nationally against the event, arguing that such distances are cruel. Supporters, however, contend that these sled dogs are the canine equivalents of magnificent, well-trained athletes. In 2008, a record 95 teams entered the race, with 78 reaching Nome and the winner, Lance Mackey, covering 1161 miles in nine days and 11 hours to win $69,000.

A trip to Anchorage to witness more than 1000 dogs take to the starting line for the Iditarod is an eye-opening experience. But even if a midwinter trip to Alaska is out of the question you can still watch the famous race. Every year a number of mushers are equipped with special tracking devices on their sleds so fans can watch their progress in real time by logging on to www.iditarod.com and clicking 'Iditarod Tracker.'

of natural materials that were at hand, from roots and ivory tusks to birch bark and grasses. Aleuts in Alaska's Southwest villages decorate some of their baskets with seal intestine.

Traditionally, Native artisans gathered their materials in the fall and began carving and weaving in December, when cold weather forced them to remain inside. But, thanks in part to the marketing by Native corporations to an increasing number of tourists, Alaska Native arts have become an important slice of the economy in many Bush communities, and are practiced throughout the year.

Alaska Native Arts, a nonprofit that educates, promotes and sells traditional and contemporary Native artwork, has an excellent website (www.alaskanativearts.org).

The Iñupiat and Yupik, having the fewest resources to work with, traditionally made their objects out of sea-mammal parts; their scrimshaw work, also known as 'engraved ivory,' is incredibly detailed etching often presenting a vignette of daily life on a whale bone or walrus tusk. They made *mukluks* (knee-high boots) out of sealskin and parkas out of the skins of caribou or ground squirrels.

Athabascans of the Interior had mastered the art of porcupine-quill weaving and embroidery in the 19th century when beads were introduced to Alaska's indigenous peoples by Russian traders, whalers and agents of the Hudson Bay Company. Athabascans quickly adopted these shiny and colorful ornaments to adorn clothing and footwear, and today are renowned for their intricate bead embroidery.

But perhaps no single item represents indigenous art better than Alaskan basketry. Each group produces stunning baskets in very distinctive styles, made solely from materials at hand. Athabascans weave baskets from alder, willow roots and birch bark; the Tlingits use cedar bark and spruce root; the Iñupiat use grasses and baleen, a glossy, hard material that hangs from the jaws of whales; the Yupik often decorate their baskets with sea lion whiskers and feathers.

A 6- or 8-inch-long ivory carving can easily cost between $300 and $600 depending on the amount of detail involved and the Alaska Native who carved it.

The Aleuts are perhaps the most renowned basket weavers. Using rye grass, which grows abundantly in the Aleutian Islands, they are able to work the pliable but very tough material into tiny, intricately woven baskets. The three styles of Aleut baskets (Attu, Atka and Unalaska) carry a steep price in shops, but can be viewed at several Southwest cultural centers, including the Alutiiq Museum (p304) in Kodiak, and the Museum of the Aleutians (p318) in Dutch Harbor.

Literature

Two of the best-known writers identified with Alaska were not native to the land nor did they spend much time there, but Jack London and Robert Service witnessed Alaska's greatest adventure and turned the experience into literary careers.

Kodiak's Alutiiq Museum (www.alutiiqmuseum.org) is both a physical and online home for information about the Alutiiq people and their culture.

London, an American, departed for the Klondike Gold Rush in 1897, hoping to get rich panning gold (see the boxed text, p60). Service, a Canadian bank teller, was transferred to Dawson City in 1902 and then wrote his first book of verse, *The Spell of the Yukon*. The work was an immediate success, and contained his best-known ballads, 'The Shooting of Dan McGrew' and 'The Cremation of Sam McGee.' Both portray the hardship and violence of life during the gold rush and are recited not just in the Yukon, but probably more often on stages and certainly more often in bars across Alaska.

Today's contemporary standouts of Alaskan literature are not memorized nearly as much as Service's, but are no less elegant in capturing the spirit of the Far North. Kotzebue author Seth Kantner followed his critically acclaimed first novel, *Ordinary Wolves*, with the equally intriguing *Shopping for Porcupine*, a series of short stories about growing up in the Alaska wilderness. One of the best Alaska Native novels is *Two Old Women* by Velma Wallis, an Athabascan born in Fort Yukon. This moving tale covers the saga of two elderly women abandoned by their migrating tribe during a harsh winter.

Other Alaskans who have captured the soul of the Far North include Nick Jans, whose *The Last Light Breaking* is considered a classic on life among the Iñupiat, and Sherry Simpson, who chronicles living in Fairbanks in the series of wonderful stories, *The Way Winter Comes.* For entertaining fiction using Alaska's commercial fishing as a stage, there's Bill McCloskey, whose three novels have characters ranging from the greenhorn fisherman to the hardnose cannery manager, leaping from one to the next. His first, *Highliners*, is still his best.

Not Really An Alaskan Mountain Man (2004), by Doug Fine, is the humorous true story of an East Coast, big-city guy who moves to rural Alaska and discovers he's not a 'mountain man.'

Small cabins and long winter nights filled with sinister thoughts have also given rise to Alaska's share of mystery writers. Dean of the Alaskan whodunit is *New York Times* bestseller Dana Stanebow, whose ex-DA investigator Kate Shugak has appeared in 15 novels, the latest *A Deeper Sleep*. Sue Henry is equally prolific with musher-turned-crime-solver Jessie Arnold in novels like *Murder on the Iditarod Trail* and *Cold Company.*

Michael Chabon, the Pulitzer Prize–winning author of *The Yiddish Policemen's Union* (2008), isn't an Alaskan, but his murder mystery/love story is an entertaining whodunit that takes place in Sitka.

Theater & Dance

For many visitors, theater in Alaska is a group of actors who first serve the local salmon bake and then perform a tongue-in-cheek, melodramatic play. But the 49th state also has a committed – though small – theatrical community that writes, produces and performs plays. The best-known stage in Alaska is Juneau's Perseverance Theatre (p172). Founded in 1979, the company presents classic and original plays, and has become the state's flagship professional theater in fostering work by Alaskan writers. That includes *How I Learned to Drive,* which premiered at the Perseverance Theatre in 1996 and won playwright Paula Vogel a Pulitzer Prize in 1998.

Serious theater can be found in several other Alaskan communities: Anchorage has a number of performing groups, including the Alaska Dance Theatre and the Eccentric Theatre Company (p215); in Homer there's Pier One Theater (p289); and to the north, the Fairbanks Shakespeare Theatre

JACK LONDON'S ALASKA

Raised by his mother in Oakland, California, Jack London quit school at 14 to seek adventures that included trying his hand as an oyster pirate and riding the rails throughout the USA as a hobo. In 1897 he dropped out of the University of California at Berkeley to seek his fortune in the Klondike Gold Rush. He endured the Chilkoot Trail, reached the Yukon goldfields and staked a claim that November. But the following spring London developed a severe case of scurvy and eventually used a small boat to float 1500 miles down the Yukon River to St Michael where he sailed to California. He stayed in the Far North only a year and, like most miners, returned home penniless, but with a head full of stories and tales.

His first book, *The Son of the Wolf,* appeared in 1900 and his two classics followed shortly after that: *Call of the Wild* (1903) and *White Fang* (1906). The central characters of London's best-known novels are dogs. Buck is stolen to be a sled dog in Alaska in *Call of the Wild,* while White Fang, half-dog, half-wolf, curbs his natural hostility and learns to love after a new world is opened up to him. Using the colorful Klondike as a backdrop, London's classics focus on the struggles between man and nature, and learning to survive in the harsh Alaskan wilderness.

Strikingly handsome and full of laughter, London was one of the most romantic figures of his time, and his books were huge bestsellers. The first printing of *Call of the Wild,* 10,000 books, sold out in 24 hours. He went on to produce 50 books of fiction and nonfiction in only 17 years and became the country's highest-paid writer of the day. He is also one of the most extensively translated American authors. Despite his success, London led a tumultuous life that included financial problems and disparaging reviews. He was only 40 when he died in 1916.

(p389). For more on Alaskan theaters contact the **Alaska State Council of the Arts** (☎ 907-269-6610; www.eed.state.ak.us/aksca).

Music

Anchorage has the population and the pull to host well-known artists and bands, with most of them playing at Atwood Concert Hall, Sullivan Sports Arena or even Chilkoot Charlie's (p214). If they're in town, **Center-Tix** (☎ 907-263-2787; www.centertix.net) will sell you the ticket. You can also catch nationally known acts, particularly country bands, at the Alaska State Fair Borealis Theatre in Palmer and Fairbanks' Carlson Center. Beyond that a band has to be on the downside of its career before it arrives in towns such as Juneau, Ketchikan or Kodiak.

The website www.mosquitonet.com/%7Egcn is a comprehensive site that covers Alaskan folk musicians and festivals.

Homegrown artists, and we're not talking Jewel here, make up an important segment of the Alaskan music scene and are the reason for the state's numerous music festivals. Among the best in the Southeast are the Alaska Folk Festival (p168), which has been held in Juneau for more than 30 years, and the Sitka Summer Music Festival (p155). They're also strumming guitars all across the Interior from the Talkeetna Bluegrass Festival to the Fairbanks Summer Folk Fest (p352).

Architecture

Most Outsiders associate Alaska architecture with an igloo, a structure that isn't built much anymore and is gone by summer. But thanks to old-style pork-barrel politics and a new gush of oil revenue, Alaska, and Anchorage in particular, is raising some eyebrows architecturally.

The Museum of the North at the University of Alaska Fairbanks (p383) was boxy and mundane until it was transformed by a $42 million expansion in 2006. The result was a stunning showcase whose striking exterior was inspired by mountains and glaciers, while inside a soaring lobby and walls of windows treat visitors to views of the Alaska Range, including Mt McKinley.

The website www.museums.state.ak.us/list.html reviews the museums and their exhibits in almost 40 Alaskan villages and cities from tiny Anaktuvuk Pass to Anchorage.

Fairbanks' arch-rival will surely have an equally impressive cultural center when the Anchorage Museum of History & Art (p202) opens its $106 million expansion due in the summer of 2009 at the time of writing. Glass walls housing exhibits, large windows framing views of Anchorage and an observation area where Mt McKinley will also be visible on a clear day, will make the museum both 'transparent and translucent.' Inside you will experience the grandeur of Alaska that surrounds Anchorage. Outside you will get a sense, before you even enter, of the treasures waiting to be explored.

Cinema & TV

Hollywood is Hollywood and Alaska is Alaska but the two do occasionally mix, especially in Hyder. This tiny, isolated town in Southeast Alaska (pop 83) has been the setting for five Hollywood films. The most recent was *Insomnia* (2002), in which Al Pacino plays a police officer sent to a small Alaskan town to investigate a killer played by Robin Williams. But there was also *Bear Island* (1978), loaded with stars – Donald Sutherland, Vanessa Redgrave, Lloyd Bridges, Christopher Lee – and *Ice Man* (1984), about a team of scientists who find a frozen prehistoric man and bring him back to life. The 49th state has also been the backdrop for TV, including an episode of *Baywatch* and the Emmy Award–winning series *Northern Exposure* in the mid-1990s. But reality TV is where Alaska has hit the motherlode. Tough men in tough jobs are seen on *Tougher in Alaska*, while ordinary people must live off the land in *The Alaska Experiment*. The most popular, however, is the *Deadliest Catch*, focusing on the dangerous king crab fishery in the Bering Sea.

Alaska Magazine Television is a half-hour TV show, based on a popular magazine focusing on travel and lifestyle, aired 52 times a year on public TV stations throughout the country.

Food & Drink

One of the most popular bumper stickers in Alaska, seen from Ketchikan to Dutch Harbor, says 'Friends Don't Let Friends Eat Farmed Fish.' Alaska's cuisine is all about seafood. Not fish raised in overcrowded pens, but real seafood that lives wild in the oceans and is hooked or netted. Practically everything in a supermarket is shipped here from somewhere else, often far away – but not the crab, salmon, halibut and shrimp. It's not cheap – nothing on the menu is in Alaska – but the seafood is fresh, abundant and, like everything else in this state, served in huge portions.

What Real Alaskans Eat (2003), by Stephen Lay, is a tongue-in-cheek history of why Alaskans eat what they do. Mixed into the text are recipes for everything from roasted beaver tail to bear-fat biscuits.

STAPLES & SPECIALTIES

Wild seafood is so important to Alaskans that the state has a law banning salmon farming. When fish farms from Norway, Chile and Scotland flooded the market with salmon, Alaskans quickly realized they could not compete with the cheap prices. So the state took a hint from organic farmers in pitching their product: wild salmon tastes better, is better for you and is well worth the extra cost. You'll see a range of seafood on every menu, and in some supermarkets the display cases of wild seafood – king crab legs ($18 per pound), sockeye salmon steaks ($10 per pound), halibut ($16 per pound) – rival those filled with steaks and chops.

Away from the sea, sourdough is one of Alaska's best-known specialties. Turn-of-the-century prospectors were dependent on the yeasty starter to make their breads and hotcakes rise. Because the sourdough supply is replenished with additional flour and water after each use, it would remain active and fresh, well, indefinitely. Today there's hardly a restaurant in Alaska that doesn't serve sourdough pancakes, along with the usual eggs, omelettes and sausage, for breakfast. Some chefs, with a wink of their eye, claim their sourdough dates back to the Klondike Gold Rush. The ultimate treat in the morning is sourdough pancakes riddled with fresh blueberries and smothered in maple syrup. This legendary but affordable Alaskan cuisine makes breakfast the best-value meal in this land of high prices.

Alaska accounts for almost half of the world's and 90% of North America's harvest of wild salmon; in 2007 that amounted to 137 million fish.

Seafood & Shellfish

Menus at restaurants are dominated by seafood. The traditional main used to be the 'Captain's Platter,' a plate heaped with a deep-fried offering of halibut, shrimp and clams. But in recent years Alaskans have become health-conscious, and much more creative. It's no longer shocking to see smoked salmon pizza at the local pizzeria, a crab-and-avocado sandwich at the deli or seared wild salmon, topped off with rhubarb-ginger chutney, at the upscale restaurant in town.

Halibut and three species of salmon – king, coho (silver) and sockeye (red) – are the most commonly served fish. But other types can also be enjoyed, including rockfish, sablefish (black cod), pollack and sole. Shellfish – clams, oysters, mussels and scallops (with giant ones coming from the Bering Sea) – are also very common, as are snow and Dungeness crabs and a variety of shrimps and prawns.

The Alaska Seafood Marketing Institute's website (www.alaskaseafood.org) is loaded with recipes, seafood facts and nutritional information.

The ultimate feast for many, however, is a pound of steamed king crab legs, which effectively replaces lobster in the Far North, dipped in drawn butter. Such a treat will set you back $30 to $50 depending on the restaurant, but fresh king crab is so good it's why some visitors end up as Alaskans.

Seafood also makes an appearance at lunchtime. Every café that serves a hamburger also offers a salmon burger, but many Alaskans are happy with just a bowl of seafood chowder: thick, creamy and loaded with everything from clams and shrimps to crab, salmon and halibut. If it's served in a sourdough bread bowl, you're set for the rest of the day.

Game

Alaskans adore their wild game. But unless you hunt or know somebody who does, there isn't really much opportunity for the average visitor to indulge in tasting such local favorites as mountain goat, caribou and deer. Moose is such prized game that state troopers maintain lists of residents who are ready at a minute's notice to chainsaw one killed in a car crash. It's much too valuable and much too enormous to leave as roadkill.

About 15 million acres of soil in Alaska is suitable for farming but only a million acres of it is currently being farmed.

Most 'game' seen in restaurants is either Alaska-bred buffalo or reindeer. Buffalo burgers, a healthy alternative to beef burgers, are available throughout the state. Even more popular is reindeer sausage, a spicy mix of ground reindeer and pork. It accompanies eggs on the breakfast menu, and can be found grilling on almost every hot-dog cart in Alaska. With a heap of sauerkraut and a squeeze of spicy brown mustard, it's the quickest lunch in the state.

Ethnic Food

An influx of Asians migrating to Alaska has resulted in most towns having at least one ethnic restaurant. Chinese restaurants are widespread throughout the state, even in remote communities such as Nome and Unalaska. Many offer what Alaskans love most: all-you-can-eat lunch and dinner buffets, featuring a dozen mains, fried rice, spring rolls, egg-drop soup and unlimited trips. With lunch priced around $9 to $11, and dinner $12 to $15, these are among Alaska's best-value eating options. Many supermarkets maintain Asian food counters, where a main and fried rice is $6 to $8.

Sushi bars are also on the rise and, with the state's abundance of fresh seafood, can be especially good, even in out-of-the-way places such as Kodiak. Thai, Vietnamese and Korean restaurants can already be found in Anchorage, and it won't be long before they carve a niche in other Alaskan cities.

The dessert 'Baked Alaska' is claimed to have originated at Delmonico's Restaurant in New York City in 1876, and was created in honor of the newly acquired territory of Alaska.

DRINKS

Whatever you prefer to sip, varieties are brewed and fermented in Alaska. Alaskans even make wine; not out of grapes of course, because they don't have the climate to grow them, but a handful of wineries in Anchorage and Haines, among other places, are making it out of rhubarb, strawberries, blueberries and fireweed flower.

Coffee

The coffee craze that began in Seattle has hit Alaska with full force. Espresso shops are everywhere: even in small towns such as McCarthy, you can find somebody with an espresso machine. Anchorage has dozens of espresso

ALASKAN SALMON BAKES

One popular eating event during summer in much of the state, but especially in the Southeast, is the salmon bake. This is an outdoor affair, set up next to a gurgling stream, with locally caught salmon that is grilled, smothered with somebody's homemade barbecue sauce and served all-you-can-eat style. A dinner costs $20 to $27, is strictly something tourists do, but is often the dining highlight of a trip to Alaska. One of the most adventurous salmon bakes is at Taku Glacier Lodge (p170), which begins with a 15-minute floatplane flight from Juneau and includes flying over a glacier.

shops, including drive-throughs where off-to-work employees line up every morning for a quick caffeine hit.

Alcohol

The legal drinking age in Alaska is 21. Except for in the 70 Alaska Native towns that are dry (alcohol is prohibited) or damp (the sale of alcohol is prohibited), finding an open bar or liquor store is never very difficult; in fact, only the churches outnumber the bars. The abundance of drinking establishments and the long, dark winters go toward explaining why Alaska has the highest alcoholism rate in the USA.

Bars in the larger cities vary in their decor, and many offer music and dancing. The bars in smaller towns are good places to have a brew and mingle with commercial fishermen, loggers or other locals. Bar hours vary, but there are always a few places that open their doors at 9am and don't close until 5am.

The online edition of the *Anchorage Press* (www.anchoragepress.com) has reviews of restaurants, microbrew beers and clubs in Alaska's largest city.

The usual US beer (Miller, Budweiser etc) is served, but Alaska's microbreweries are growing and it's unusual if a bar doesn't have at least one microbrew on tap. Alaska's largest brewery is Juneau's Alaskan Brewing Company (p174), and its Alaska Amber is a staple throughout the state, and even as far away as California and Arizona. In bars a pint of microbrew is $5 to $6, in stores a six-pack is $8 to $10. Beer lovers who want to try a broad range of the state's microbrews should head to Haines for the Great Alaska Craft Beer & Home Brew Festival (p184) in May.

CELEBRATIONS

Even when the festival isn't about food, food is always a big part of Alaskan celebrations. Petersburg's Little Norway Festival (p147), in May, celebrates Norwegian Independence Day, but is best known for the seafood and shrimp feeds staged at night. Alaska's oldest food celebration is the Kodiak Crab Festival (p306). This weeklong event was first held in 1958 and today still features lots of cooked king crab. The most unusual gastronomic event is the Great Alaska Beer Train (p27). On a special run in early October, the Alaska Railroad departs Anchorage for Portage, loaded with Alaskan microbrews and people anxious to try them.

Alaskans love Spam, that chopped-ham-in-a-can. On a per-capita basis, only Hawaiians eat more Spam in the USA.

WHERE TO EAT & DRINK

The mainstay of Alaskan restaurants, particularly in small towns, is the main-street café. It opens early in the morning (sometimes at 4am if it's catering to charter-fishing captains) serving eggs, bacon, pancakes and oatmeal, and con-

TASTY TRAVEL

You know you're in Alaska if you're eating…

Birch syrup Tapped from paper birch trees, it's lighter and not as sweet as maple syrup but has its own distinct flavor. Look for it in Haines, home of Birchboy Products (www.birchboy.com).

Squaw candy This is salmon jerky, fillets that have been dried or smoked and are very chewy. Although it's a staple for rural Alaskans in winter, you can purchase it in gift shops.

Halibut beer bits These small chunks of halibut are soaked in beer, lightly coated and deep fried. Fish and chips were never so good and you'll find the best bits in Petersburg (see Coastal Cold Storage, p148).

Spam Alaskans love that chopped-ham-in-a-can because it (seemingly) keeps forever. See chefs trot out Spam mango wontons or Spam salmon pâté during the Spam recipe contest at the Alaska State Fair (p228).

We dare you to try…

Muktuk This is an Iñupiat delicacy that is made up of the outer skin of a whale and the attached blubber. It has the consistency of stale Jell-O and, needless to say, is an acquired taste. Head to Barrow if you want a sample.

tinues with hamburgers, french fries and grilled sandwiches for lunch. There is almost always halibut and salmon on the dinner menu. Sit at the counter or squeeze into a booth, and indulge in large portions and strong coffee.

Most small towns also have a hamburger hut, a small shack or trailer with picnic tables outside, serving burgers, hot dogs, wraps or fried fish; as well as a pizza parlor with a blackboard menu of pizzas, calzones, hot subs and beer and wine. All will be open well into the evening.

Cities will have bistros and upscale restaurants, many located along the waterfront with a cozy bar on one side and tables on the other. During the summer they generally serve dinner from 4pm until as late as 10pm. There will also be Asian restaurants (many with split hours – 11am to 2pm and 4pm to 9pm) that will do as much take-out as sit-down business.

Wild salmon is fast food in Alaska. After a Kodiak Subway shop first offered Alaskan salmon subs in 2006, 28 Subways have since added it to their menu.

Quick Eats

You'll find street vendors in larger cities (especially those with cruise-ship traffic) selling hot dogs, reindeer sausages and sometimes deep-fried halibut. Most large supermarkets will have ready-to-eat items, delis and even Asian food bars, for meals that are quick and affordable. And, of course, there are always fast-food chains; McDonald's, Burger King and Wendy's are present and increasing.

VEGETARIANS & VEGANS

Alaska is not the land of milk and honey – or vegetables and tofu – for vegetarians and vegans. Part of it is cultural; subsistence – living off the land by hunting and fishing – is still widely practiced in Alaska. And part of it is the fact that there is so little agriculture in the state.

While places catering to vegans are rare, you will find at least one health food store in most midsize towns and cities, as well as a number of restaurants advertising 'vegetarian options.' If fish is part of your diet, there's no need to worry. Most menus list as many salmon and halibut mains as beef and pork, if not more. Alternatively, search out Chinese and other Asian restaurants for the best selection of meatless dishes. Also keep in mind that Carrs, Safeway and other large supermarkets often have well-stocked salad bars, self-serve affairs at $6 per pound.

Check out the Alaska Division of Agriculture online chart (www.dnr.state.ak.us/ag/AKGVegetables.pdf) for when to buy Alaskan-grown vegetables, from brussel sprouts to rutabagas.

EATING WITH KIDS

Most restaurants in Alaska are low-key and casual, making them well suited for families. The number of upscale places where a fussy infant would be embarrassing are limited to only a few cities. For more on traveling with children see p39.

HABITS & CUSTOMS

Alaskans don't differ greatly from other Americans in their habits and customs when it comes to mealtime. They eat three meals a day, most of them at home, snack in between, use a fork, knife and spoon and eat kohlrabi only when someone tells them to.

Restaurants are naturally busy on Fridays and Saturdays, but reservations are not that important. The exceptions are fine restaurants in Anchorage and cruise-ship ports such as Juneau, Ketchikan and Skagway, where four boats can suddenly triple the town's population and fill every place that posts a menu.

Tipping is expected in Alaska, and it's insulting if you leave, for example, a $1 tip on a $25 meal. The tourism season is far too short for waiters to earn a living on their wages alone. Tip 15% on breakfast, lunch and café dinners; 20% at an upscale restaurant. Don't forget to tip your bartender,

In *Life's A Fish and Then You Fry* (2002), by Randy Bayliss, the author's humorous writing is paired with Ray Troll's fishy illustrations for a seafood cookbook that will have you chuckling while you're cooking.

GASTRONOMIC SHOPPING

Alaskans place a high premium on anything that is fresh and edible. Despite the state's limited agricultural sector, there are almost 20 farmers markets and countless seafood shops. Here's where to look for the freshest food in Alaska:

Aleutian Fresh Seafoods (www.aleutianfreshseafood.com) This Dutch Harbor shop is where you order fresh seafood, from red king crab to halibut cheeks, after you're home.

Anchorage Market & Festival Fresh veggies Saturday and Sunday in downtown Anchorage (p215).

Coastal Cold Storage The seafood is so fresh in this Petersburg shop it's still swimming (p148).

Haines Farmer's Market Occurs every other Saturday in summer (p185).

Tanana Valley Farmers Market Open throughout the summer on Wednesday and Saturday in Fairbanks (p388).

Friday Fling A weekly market held in summer near the visitors center in Palmer, the land of giant vegetables (p227).

Tanana Valley Farmers Market Open throughout the summer on Wednesday and Saturday in Fairbanks (p388).

even if your time at the bar didn't involve food. When a pint of beer is $5, a $1-a-drink tip is not too outrageous.

Finally, Alaska is gradually going smoke-free. Many cities, including Juneau, have already banned smoking in all restaurants and bars. Double-check before you light up after a meal.

Environment

It's one thing to be told Mt McKinley is the tallest mountain in North America. It's another to see it crowning the sky in Denali National Park; a mountain so tall, so massive and so overwhelming, it has visitors stumbling off the park buses. As a state, Alaska is the same; a place so huge, so wild and so unpopulated, it's incomprehensible to most people until they arrive. Only when they are standing on the edge of a river, watching thousands of salmon spawning upstream and being feasted upon by a pair of 1000lb brown bears, do they begin to understand that Alaska's environment – its land and its wildlife – is special, rare and irreplaceable.

The website www.arcticcircle.uconn.edu is a great introduction to the way of life, history and issues concerning Arctic Alaska, including the Arctic National Wildlife Refuge.

THE LAND

In July 2008, Okmok Caldera, the 3500ft volcano on Umnak Island in the Aleutian Islands, erupted violently sending ash more than 6 miles in the air, causing flights to be canceled at the Dutch Harbor airport, 60 miles away. Welcome to the Ring of Fire. As much as glaciers and towering mountains, belching volcanoes and trembling earthquakes are trademarks of Alaska. That's because, in geological time, the Alaskan landmass is relatively young and still very active; the result of plate tectonics, where the Pacific Plate (the ocean floor) drifts under the North American Plate.

The state represents the northern boundary of the chain of Pacific Ocean volcanoes known as the 'Ring of Fire' and is the most seismically active region of North America. Alaska claims 52% of the earthquakes that occur in the country and averages more than 13 each day. Most are mild shakes, some are deadly. Three of the six largest earthquakes in the world and seven of the 10 largest in the USA occurred in Alaska. Volcanoes are almost as numerous. Most of the state's volcanoes lie in a 1550-mile arc from the Alaska Peninsula to the tip of the Aleutian Islands. This area contains more than 65 volcanoes, 46 of them active in the last 200 years. Since 1960 Alaska has averaged more than two eruptions per year.

Ash from Katmai's Novarupta eruption in 1912, the greatest volcanic eruption in the 20th century, traveled as far as Seattle, Virginia and even to Africa.

Colliding plates also created three impressive mountain systems that arch across the state. The Coast Range, a continuation of Washington state's Olympic Range, which includes the St Elias Range and the Chugach and Kenai Mountains, sweeps along the southern edge of Alaska before dipping into the sea, southwest of Kodiak Island. The Alaska and Aleutian Ranges parallel the same arc, and the Brooks Range skirts the Arctic Circle.

In between the Alaska Range and the Brooks Range is Interior Alaska: an immense plateau rippled by foothills, low mountains and great rivers, among them the third-longest in the USA, the Yukon River, which runs for 2300 miles. North of the Brooks Range is the North Slope, a tundra that gently descends to the Arctic Ocean.

The Alaska Volcano Observatory website (www.avo.alaska.edu) has web cams and a Volcano Alert map so you can see what's shaking and where.

Southeast Alaska

Southeast Alaska is a 500-mile coastal strip extending from north of Prince Rupert to the Gulf of Alaska. In between are the hundreds of islands of the Alexander Archipelago, and a narrow strip of coast, separated from Canada's mainland by the glacier-filled Coast Mountains. Winding through the middle of the region is the Inside Passage waterway; the lifeline for isolated communities, as the rugged terrain prohibits road building. High annual rainfall and mild temperatures have turned the Southeast into rainforest, broken up by majestic mountain ranges, glaciers and fjords that surpass those in Norway.

The Southeast has many small fishing towns and Native villages, and the larger communities of Ketchikan, Sitka and the state capital, Juneau. Other highlights of the region include the wilderness areas of Glacier Bay, Admiralty Island, Misty Fiord and Tracy Arm, plus the White Pass & Yukon Route railroad, built in the days of the Klondike Gold Rush. Because the Alaska Marine Highway connects the Southeast to Bellingham (mainland USA) and Prince Rupert (Canada), this region is often the first area for travelers to visit.

The classic *Alaska Wilderness* (2005) by Robert Marshall is a fascinating account of Marshall's trips by foot, boat and dogsled in the 1930s to the then little-explored Brooks Range.

Prince William Sound & Kenai Peninsula

Like the Southeast, much of this region (also known as Southcentral Alaska) is a mixture of rugged mountains, glaciers, steep fjords and lush forests. This mix of terrain makes Kenai Peninsula a superb recreational area for backpacking, fishing and boating, and Prince William Sound, home of Columbia Glacier, a mecca for kayakers and other adventurers.

The weather along the coastline can often be rainy and stormy, but the summers are usually mild, and in August it's generally sunny. The peninsula is served by the Alaska Marine Highway, or by road from Anchorage. Highlights of the region are the historical and charming towns of Homer, Seward, Cordova and Hope; and backpackers will find many opportunities for outdoor adventure in the wilderness areas of the Chugach National Forest and Kenai National Wildlife Refuge.

Roadside Geology of Alaska (1988), by Cathy Connor & Daniel O'Haire, explores the geology you see from the road, covering everything from earthquakes to why there's gold on the beaches of Nome – not dull reading by any means.

Southwest Alaska

Stretching 1500 miles from Kodiak Island to the international date line, Southwest Alaska is an island-studded region that includes the Aleutian Islands, the Alaska Peninsula and Bristol Bay. Home to 46 active volcanoes, Southwest Alaska is also rich in wildlife. It boasts the largest bears in the world, on Kodiak Island, the richest salmon runs in Alaska at Bristol Bay and great opportunities to view marine mammals and birds on the Alaska Marine Highway ferry run to the Aleutian Islands.

The fickle weather and the high cost of traveling to the region, has limited tourism here – Unalaska receives only a handful of cruise ships in the summer – compared with areas like the Southeast and the Kenai Peninsula. Among the region's more popular destinations are Kodiak Island, Katmai National Park in the Alaska Peninsula, and the towns of Unalaska and Dutch Harbor in the Aleutians.

Denali & the Interior

Three major highways – the George Parks, Glenn and Richardson Hwys – cut across Alaska's Interior and pass numerous recreational areas, including Denali National Park, Alaska's most noted attraction.

Northern Lights: The Science, Myth, and Wonder of Aurora Borealis (2001) by George Bryson has stunning color photographs combined with the legends, myths and science surrounding this incredible polar phenomenon.

The heartland of Alaska offers warm temperatures in the summer and ample opportunities for outdoor activities in some of the state's most scenic and accessible areas. With the Alaska Range to the north, the Wrangell and Chugach Mountains to the south and the Talkeetna Mountains cutting through the middle, the Interior has a rugged appearance matching that of either Southeast or Southcentral Alaska, but without much of the rain and cloudy weather.

The Bush

This is the largest slice of Alaska and includes the Brooks Range, Arctic Alaska, and Western Alaska on the Bering Sea. The remote, hard-to-reach Bush is separated from the rest of the state by mountains, rivers and vast road-less distances, offering a glimpse of a lifestyle unaffected by the state's tourist industry. The main communities are Nome, Barrow, Kotzebue and

Bethel, while scattered between are small isolated Native villages. The climate in the summer can range from a dry and chilly 40°F in the nightless Arctic tundra, to the wet and fog of the considerably warmer Bering Sea coast, a flat landscape of lakes and slow-moving rivers.

CLIMATE

The oceans surrounding 75% of the state, the mountainous terrain and the low angle of the sun, give Alaska an extremely variable climate, and daily weather that is infamous for its unpredictability.

In the Interior and up around Fairbanks, precipitation is light, but temperatures can fluctuate by more than 100°F during the year. Fort Yukon holds the record for the state's highest temperature, at 100°F in June 1915, yet it once recorded a temperature of -78°F in winter. Fairbanks regularly has the odd summer's day that hits 90°F and always has nights during winter that drop below -60°F.

The Southeast and much of Southcentral have a temperate maritime climate; much like Seattle only wetter. Juneau averages 57in of rain or snow annually, and Ketchikan gets 154in a year, most of which is rain as the temperatures are extremely mild, even in winter.

Shielded from Southcentral Alaska's worst weather by the Kenai Mountains, the Anchorage Bowl receives only 14in of rain annually and enjoys a relatively mild climate: January averages 13°F, July about 58°F. Technically a sub-Arctic desert, Anchorage does have more than its fair share of overcast days, especially in early and late summer.

For visitors, the most spectacular part of Alaska's climate is its long days. At Point Barrow, Alaska's northernmost point, the sun doesn't set for 2½ months from May to August. In other Alaskan regions, the longest day is on June 21 (the summer solstice), when the sun sets for only two hours in Fairbanks and for five hours in the Southeast. Even after sunset in late June, daylight is replaced not by darkness, but by a dusk that still allows good visibility.

The Denali National Park web cam (www.nature.nps.gov/air/WebCams/parks/denacam/denacam.cfm) records visibility conditions from Wonder Lake, so if the day is clear Mt McKinley is stunning.

The website www.beringglacier.org has photos, video and articles on the Bering Glacier, which is the largest in North America at 1.3 million acres.

WILDLIFE

Even from the road, most people see more wildlife during their trip in Alaska than they do in a lifetime elsewhere. But to increase such sightings, you should know what you're looking for and where to look (p81). The best wildlife areas are highlighted in the boxed text, p25.

NATIONAL, STATE & REGIONAL PARKS

One of the main attractions of Alaska is public land, where you can play and roam over an area of 384,000 sq miles, more than twice the size of California. The agency with the most public land is the Bureau of Land Management (BLM; 133,594 sq miles), followed by the US Fish & Wildlife Service (USFWS; 120,312 sq miles) and the National Park Service (84,375 sq miles).

Alaska's 15 national parks are the state's crown jewels as far as most travelers are concerned. The park system attracts more than two million visitors a year, with the most popular units being **Klondike Gold Rush National Historical Park** (☎ 907-983-9221; www.nps.gov/klgo), which draws 850,000 visitors to Skagway, and **Denali National Park** (☎ 907-683-2294; www.nps.gov/dena), home of Mt McKinley. Other popular units are **Glacier Bay National Park** (☎ 907-697-2230; www.nps.gov/glba), a highlight of every cruise-ship itinerary in the Southeast, and **Kenai Fjords National Park** (☎ 907-224-7500; www.nps.gov/kefj) in Seward.

The heaviest recorded annual snowfall in Alaska was 974.5in at Thompson Pass, north of Valdez, in the winter of 1952-53.

Alaska State Parks oversees 121 units that are not nearly as renowned as most national parks, and thus far less crowded at trailheads and in campgrounds. The largest is the 1.6-million-acre **Wood-Tikchik State Park** (☎ 907-269-8698; www.alaskastateparks.org), a road-less wilderness north of Dillingham. The

ALASKA'S GLACIERS

They may be melting rapidly but Alaska's glaciers are still fascinating, and rank as one of the most popular attractions among tourists. These rivers of ice form when the snowfall in the mountains exceeds the rate of melting. As the snow builds up, it becomes a solid cap of ice that, because of gravity, flows like a frozen river, often on a layer of meltwater that is as thin as a sheet of paper. Because glacial ice absorbs all the colors of the spectrum except blue, which it reflects, glacial ice often appears blue. The more overcast the day, the bluer glacial ice appears. If it's raining on the day you are to view a glacier, rejoice; the blue will never be more intense.

Alaska is one of the few places in the world where active glaciation occurs on such a grand scale. There are an estimated 100,000 glaciers in Alaska, covering 29,000 sq miles, or 5% of the state, and containing three-quarters of all Alaska's fresh water.

The largest glacier is the Bering Glacier, which stretches 118 miles from the St Elias Range to the Gulf of Alaska. If you include the Bagley Ice Field, where the Bering Glacier begins, this glacial complex covers 2250 sq miles, making it larger than Delaware. Just to the east is the Malaspina Glacier complex, which is 60 miles long and 1200ft thick.

Tidewater glaciers extend into the sea or a lake, causing them to shed icebergs in an explosion of water. The southernmost tidewater glacier in North America is the LeConte Glacier, near Petersburg, in the Southeast. La Perouse Glacier, in Glacier Bay National Park, is the only one that discharges icebergs directly into the Pacific Ocean. The largest collection of tidewater glaciers is in Prince William Sound, where 20 of them are active.

The longest tidewater glacier is Hubbard, which begins in Canada and stretches 76 miles to Russell Fjord, near Yakutat. It might also be one of the most active. In 1986, and again in 2002, Hubbard rapidly advanced across the fjord, reaching the shoreline on the other side and turning Russell Fjord into what was dubbed 'Russell Lake,' the largest glacier-dammed lake in the world. Both times, the ice dam broke with a dramatic onslaught of water rushing back to the sea. In 2008 Hubbard surged within 170yd of the mainland, before retreating.

Active tidewater glaciers can be easily viewed from tour boats. The best places to go for such a day cruise are Glacier Bay National Park (p178), Kenai Fjords National Park (p268) or Prince William Sound (p251), out of Whittier.

The Great Kobuk Sand Dunes comprise a 25-sq-mile swath of sand, 40 miles above the Arctic Circle. Remnants of ancient glaciers, some dunes rise 100ft high.

most popular is **Chugach State Park** (☎ 907-345-5014; www.alaskastateparks.org), the 495,000-acre unit that is Anchorage's after-work playground.

Both the BLM and the USFWS oversee many refuges and preserves that are remote, hard to reach and not set up with visitor facilities such as campgrounds and trails. The major exception is the **Kenai National Wildlife Refuge** (☎ 907-262-7021; http://kenai.fws.gov), whose 14 campgrounds and great fishing are an easy drive from Anchorage, and a popular weekend destination for locals and tourists alike.

For more pretrip information, contact the **Alaska Public Lands Information Center** (☎ 907-271-2737; www.nps.gov/aplic/center), a clearinghouse for information on all of Alaska's public lands.

ENVIRONMENTAL ISSUES

Gates of the Arctic is unusual for a national park because 1500 people live within it in 10 villages, relying on subsistence hunting and gathering to survive.

Due to Alaska's size and its huge tracts of wilderness, its environmental issues are, more often than not, national debates. And the focus of most debates centers on the effects of global warming on Alaska or the push for the extraction of minerals from the wilderness.

Fewer and fewer people argue these days that global warming is not an issue. Even the Bush administration, which has otherwise steadfastly opposed mandatory cuts in emissions, acknowledged the issue when it allowed the polar bear to be listed as a threatened species due to the melting of its habitat (see the boxed text, opposite). In short, Alaska's temperatures are rising, causing Arctic sea ice and glaciers to melt at alarming rates. Some scientists now believe

Arctic sea ice could disappear entirely by 2040, or even sooner. Meanwhile, Portage Glacier has retreated so fast it can no longer be viewed from its visitor center, and famed Mendenhall Glacier is expected to retreat totally onto land and cease being a tidewater glacier as early as 2010. The warmer temperatures have also caused the treeline to move north into the North Slope tundra and an infestation of the spruce bark beetle across an area the size of Connecticut in the Kenai Peninsula. Global warming has been blamed for the Mat-Su Valley being invaded by grasshoppers, the decline of yellow cedar in the Southeast and gray whales frolicking near Barrow in the middle of the winter. In Shishmaref, a barrier island village on the Seward Peninsula, residents watched with horror as homes literally slipped into the Bering Sea due to the loss of protective sea ice that buffers them against storms.

Alaska's other environmental issue centers on development versus preservation, and is best symbolized by the debate over drilling for oil in the Arctic National Wildlife Refuge (ANWR; see the boxed text, p50). But the ANWR is hardly the only wilderness in contention. The proposed Pebble Mine would be a 2-mile-wide open pit on state land in Southwest Alaska, with copper and gold deposits estimated to be worth a staggering $362 billion. But the minerals would be extracted from near the headwaters of Bristol Bay, streams that support the world's largest run of wild salmon, and that has environmentalists,

Wrangell-St Elias, Kluane and Glacier Bay National Parks and Tatshenshini-Alsek Provincial Park form one of the largest World Heritage Sites at 24.34 million acres.

Visit www.auroraweb cam.com for live aurora webcasts from Fairbanks and a gallery of great photos and videos of spectacular northern lights in white, green and red.

SAVING THE POLAR BEAR

It took three years of wrangling with the Bush administration, a lawsuit and turning the polar bear into the symbol of the impact of global warming, but wildlife activists finally prevailed. In May 2008, the Bush administration listed polar bears as 'threatened' under the Endangered Species Act, acknowledging that the dramatic decline of Arctic sea ice, in a warming climate, could drive them to the brink of extinction.

This change in direction was historical and stunning. It was the first time the Endangered Species Act had been invoked to protect an animal principally threatened by global warming. And it was done by a government which had steadfastly opposed mandatory cuts in emissions.

Biologists estimate 20,000 to 25,000 polar bears live in the Arctic. That's a healthy population, but the bears' dependence on sea ice for survival makes them vulnerable. Polar bears hunt by waiting near holes in ice for seals, their main source of food, to come up for air. They also travel, mate and sometimes give birth, on the ice. Since 1980, the northern ice cap has been shrinking, according to the National Snow and Ice Data Center, and in 2007 there was a record melt of more than a million acres of Arctic sea ice.

The result is that polar bears are showing up on northern Alaska beaches in increasing numbers during the summer. When bears get stranded on land they can't hunt, and must live off body fat or search for washed-up sea mammal carcasses, until the frigid temperatures of autumn, when prevailing winds push the sea ice closer to shore. In 2007, the US Geological Survey released a study concluding that two-thirds of the world's polar bears could be gone by 2050, due to the loss of ice.

Environmentalists hoped the decision would require the government to protect the bears' habitat, including curbing greenhouse gas emissions and oil drilling in the Arctic, but the ruling came with provisions to prevent such measures. The Department of Interior must establish a management plan for polar bears and monitor their populations, but officials said the ruling will still allow energy exploration in Alaska, and not affect power plants in the contiguous states.

Along with the usual probusiness groups and conservatives, also opposed to the listing were Inuit tribes in Arctic Canada. These people not only hunt the bears for food and clothing, but also guide hunts, an important source of hard currency. The vast majority of their clients are from the USA, wealthy sportsmen who pay up to $30,000 for the privilege of shooting a polar bear. Listing the bear as a threatened species means those hunters can no longer bring their trophies home to the USA, and demand for hunts is expected to drop dramatically.

MAJOR PARKS OF ALASKA

Park	Features	Activities	Page
Admiralty Island National Monument	wilderness island, chain of lakes, brown bears, marine wildlife	bear watching, kayaking, canoeing, cabin rentals	p175
Chena River State Recreation Area	Chena River, alpine areas, granite tors, campgrounds, cabin rentals	backpacking, canoeing, hiking	p392
Chugach State Park	Chugach Mountains, alpine trails, Eklutna Lake	backpacking, mountain biking, paddling, hiking, campgrounds	p206
Denali National Park	Mt McKinley, brown bears, caribou, Wonder Lake, campgrounds	wildlife viewing, backpacking, hiking, park bus tours	p327
Denali State Park	alpine scenery, trails, views of Mt McKinley, campgrounds	backpacking, hiking, camping	p351
Gates of the Arctic National Park & Preserve	Brooks Range, Noatak River, treeless tundra, caribou	rafting, canoeing, backpacking, fishing	p415
Glacier Bay National Park & Preserve	tidewater glaciers, whales, Fairweather Mountains	kayaking, camping, whale watching, lodge, boat cruises	p177
Independence Mine State Historical Park	Talkeetna Mountains, alpine scenery, gold mine ruins, visitor center	mine tours, hiking	p230
Kachemak Bay State Park	glaciers, protected coves, alpine areas, cabin rentals	kayaking, backpacking, boat cruises	p293
Katmai National Park & Preserve	Valley of 10,000 Smokes, volcanoes, brown bears, lodge	fishing, bear watching, backpacking, kayaking	p311
Kenai Fjords National Park	tidewater glaciers, whales, marine wildlife, steep fjords, cabin rental	boat cruises, kayaking, hiking	p266
Kenai National Wildlife Refuge	chain of lakes, Russian River, moose, campgrounds	fishing, canoeing, wildlife watching, hiking	p271
Kodiak National Wildlife Refuge	giant bears, rich salmon runs, wilderness lodges, cabin rentals	bear watching, flightseeing, cabin rentals	p309
Misty Fiords National Monument	steep fjords, 3000ft sea cliffs, lush rainforest	boat cruises, kayaking, cabin rentals, flightseeing	p131
Tracy Arm-Fords Terror Wilderness Area	glaciers, steep fjords, a parade of icebergs, marine wildlife	boat cruises, kayaking, wildlife watching	p168
Wrangell-St Elias National Park	mountainous terrain, Kennecott mine ruins, glaciers	backpacking, flightseeing, rafting, mine tours	p369

commercial fishers and Alaska Natives up in arms. Other mining projects in Southeast Alaska are also being bitterly debated.

Glaciers of Alaska (2001), by Alaska Geographic Society, is a comprehensive look at Alaska's rivers of ice, from the Mendenhall in the Southeast to glaciers in the Brooks Range.

Issues of resources exploitation are not restricted to land. After the king crab fishery collapsed in 1982, the commercial fishing industry was rebuilt on pollack, whose mild flavor made it the choice for imitation crab, and fish sandwiches served at fast-food restaurants. Pollack has been called 'the world's largest fishery,' but since 2006, when a record 730 million lb were processed at Dutch Harbor, the fishery has been slipping backwards. Pollack is not alone. At least four times since 1997, salmon runs of Bristol Bay and Kuskokwim River have been declared economic disasters, and in 2008, the king salmon run up the Yukon River was so poor that even subsistence gatherers were restricted from catching them.

Alaska is still wild and big, but it doesn't seem as abundant as it once was.

For more information on environmental issues, contact these conservation organizations:

Alaska Sierra Club (☎ 907-276-4048; www.alaska.sierraclub.org)

No Dirty Gold (☎ 202-887-1872; www.nodirtygold.org) A campaign opposing abusive gold mining around the world, including the proposed Pebble Mine.

Southeast Alaska Conservation Council (☎ 907-586-6942; www.seacc.org)

Wilderness Society (☎ 907-272-9453; www.wilderness.org)

Outdoor Activities & Adventures

You didn't come all this way to sit in a theater watching three acts of *Hamlet*. Or to stand in a gallery staring at an impressionist painting of lord-knows-what. Or even to spend an evening consuming a six-course meal featuring more silverware and dishes than the last hostel you stayed at.

What truly unites all Alaskans, young and old, tall and small, is the overwhelming desire to be out in the wilderness. You don't have to scale Mt McKinley to enjoy the Alaskan outdoors – there are plenty of ways to leave the pavement behind because Alaska is, after all, the USA's biggest playground. Now go outside and play!

CABINS

Every agency overseeing public land in Alaska, from the Bureau of Land Management (BLM) and the National Park Service (NPS) to the Alaska Division of Parks, maintains rustic cabins in remote areas. The cabins are not expensive ($25 to $50 per night) but they are not easy to reach either. Most of them are accessed via a floatplane charter. Others can be reached on foot, by boat or by paddling. By arranging a charter and reserving a cabin in advance you can sneak away into the wilderness, with half the effort and time that backpackers or paddlers put in, and reach remote corners of Alaska.

USFS cabins can be the most affordable wilderness fishing trips in Alaska. Most of them are located near water and those beside a lake come with a rowboat.

Tongass National Forest (www.fs.fed.us/r10/tongass/cabins/cabins.shtml) and **Chugach National Forest** (www.fs.fed.us/r10/chugach/cabins/index.html) have the most cabins available, almost 190. Alaska Division of Parks has more than 40 cabins scattered from Point Bridget State Park near Juneau to Chena River State Recreation Area east of Fairbanks. You can get a list of cabins and reserve them up to six months in advance through the **DNR Public Information Center** (☎ 907-269-8400; www.alaskastateparks.org).

The BLM manages 12 cabins in the **White Mountain National Recreation Area** (☎ 907-474-2251, 800-437-7021; aurora.ak.blm.gov; per night $20-25) north of Fairbanks, and the US Fish & Wildlife Service has seven in the **Kodiak National Wildlife Refuge** (☎ 907-487-2600; kodiak.fws.gov; per night $45) on Kodiak Island. In **Kenai Fjords National Park** (☎ 907-224-3175; www.nps.gov/kefj; per night $50), the NPS maintains three cabins that are reached by floatplane or water taxi and are reserved through the **Alaska Public Lands Information Center** (☎ 907-271-2737) after January 1 for that summer.

Since 1985 Alaska has averaged only 4.5 bear attacks a year, which included 24 fatalities and 45 serious injuries.

CAMPING

Camping is not just cheap accommodations in Alaska; it's a reason to be outside, soaking up the scenery while watching that trout you just caught sizzling on an open campfire. Camping is such a popular activity that many communities have set up facilities on the edge of town; Homer's Karen Hornaday Memorial Campground (p286) and Wrangell's City Park (p142) are particularly scenic spots to pitch a tent.

The Dalton Hwy north of Coldfoot is the longest service-free stretch of road in North America – 244 miles without a gas station, McDonald's or anything else.

But the best camping experience is away from towns at one of the public campgrounds operated by the Alaska Division of Parks, the US Forest Service (USFS) or the BLM in northern Alaska. The state park system maintains the most – more than 70 rustic campgrounds scattered throughout Alaska, with fees from free to $15 a night in the more popular ones. The majority do not take reservations.

If you are planning to camp in Alaska, here are five campgrounds you should not pass up:

Blueberry Lake State Recreation Site (p375) Ten sites in a scenic alpine setting north of Valdez.

Fort Abercrombie State Historical Park (p304) Near Kodiak; wooded sites, interesting WWII artifacts and intriguing tidal pools to explore.

Marion Creek Campground (p413) Camp north of the Arctic Circle with stunning views of the Brooks Range at this BLM facility along the Dalton Hwy.

Mendenhall Lake Campground (p168) Near Juneau, a beautiful USFS campground with a glacial view from many sites.

Ninilchik View State Campground (p278) Lots of sites overlooking Cook Inlet, Old Ninilchik, and great clamming beaches.

Weather Underground (www.wunderground.com/US/AK) is the best site to check before you head into the Alaskan wilderness for a weekend of hiking or paddling.

CANOEING & KAYAKING

The paddle is a way of life in Alaska and every region has either canoeing or kayaking opportunities or both. Both the Southeast and Prince William Sound offer spectacular kayaking opportunities, while Fairbanks and Arctic Alaska are home to some of the best wilderness canoe adventures in the country. For paddling possibilities and rental locations see the regional chapters. For the best canoe and kayak trips you can do on your own see the Wilderness Hikes & Paddles chapter (p89).

CYCLING

With its long days, cool temperatures, a lack of interstate highways and a growing number of paved paths around cities such as Anchorage, Juneau and Fairbanks, Alaska can be a land of opportunity for road cyclists.

Ride with a guide! Alaskabike (www.alaskabike.com) offers a 360-mile, eight-day tour of the state for $2995 which includes your bicycle, lodging and meals.

Cyclists do have to take some extra precautions in Alaska. Other than cities and major towns, comprehensively equipped bike shops are rare, so it's wise to carry not only metric tools but also a tube-patch repair kit, brake cables, spokes and brake pads. Due to high rainfall, especially in the Southeast, waterproof saddle bags are useful, as are tire fenders. Rain gear, mittens and a woolen hat are also necessities.

Some roads do not have much of a shoulder, so cyclists should utilize the sunlight hours to pedal when traffic is light in such areas. It is not necessary to carry a lot of food, as you can easily restock on all major roads.

You can rent road bicycles in many towns. Alaska's three major bike clubs – **Arctic Bicycle Club** (☎ 907-566-0177; www.arcticbike.org) of Anchorage, **Juneau Freewheelers** (www.juneaufreewheelers.com) and **Fairbanks Cycle Club** (www.fairbankscycleclub.org) – are good sources for information and news on cycling events.

DOG SLEDDING

If Alaska is too hot or crowded for you in the summer, arrive in the winter and join a dog sled expedition. There are more than two-dozen outfitters from Bettles to Homer that will set you up with a team and then lead you into the winter wilderness.

Find all things mushing at Sled Dog Central (www.sleddogcentral.com) including outfitters, Iditarod news and interviews with mushers. Can you pass the sled dog quiz?

Some outings are only three or four hours long, others offer an eight-day journey into the Brooks Range with your own team. The best time for such an adventure is late February through early April, when the days are long, the temperatures are much more agreeable and the snow base is still deep. You do not need previous experience with dog teams or mushing but you should be comfortable with winter camping and have cold-weather clothing and gear.

One of the best places for such an adventure is Denali National Park with **Earthsong Lodge** (☎ 907-683-2863; www.earthsonglodge.com). The lodge, near Healy, features a sled dog kennel, and winter tours with your own team range from overnight ($640) to five days ($3100). **Denali West Lodge** (☎ 907-674-3112; www.denaliwest.com) has multiday trips to the base of Mt McKinley including a six-day package ($8500). Just outside of Fairbanks, **Paws For Adventure** (☎ 907-378-3630; www.pawsforadventure.com) offers mushing schools, one-day tours, and even a weeklong sled dog adventure with your own team ($2950).

Even if there's no snow around, you can still experience the thrill of the dogs. A growing number of kennels offer summer tours that includes playing with the pups, learning about mushers and the Iditarod, and short demonstration rides in wheeled carts. In Big Lake, **Happy Trails Kennel** (☎ 907-892-7899; www.buserdog.com) is operated by Martin Buser, four-time winner of the Iditarod, while in the Mat-Su area is **Plettner Sled Dog Kennels** (☎ 877-892-6945; www.plettner-kennels.com), where Lynda Plettner, an 11-time participant in the Iditarod, trains her dogs.

Top off your canine experience by visiting the **Iditarod Trail Sled Dog Headquarters** (☎ 907-376-5155; www.iditarod.com) in Wasilla or the **Knik Museum and Sled Dog Musher's Hall of Fame** (☎ 907-376-2005) located on the Iditarod Trail.

A word of caution: People for the Ethical Treatment of Animals (PETA) feel that dog sledding – especially the Iditarod and other races – is harmful to dogs. Go to www.peta.org for more information.

Minus 148 Degrees (1999) by Art Davidson is a mountaineering classic about the first successful winter ascent of Mt McKinley, when at one point the windchill factor reached -148°F.

FISHING

Many people cling to a 'fish-per-cast' vision of angling in Alaska. They expect every river, stream and lake, no matter how close to the road, to be bountiful, but often go home disappointed when their fishing efforts produce little to brag about. Serious anglers visiting Alaska carefully research the areas to be fished and are equipped with the right gear and tackle. They often pay for guides or book a room at remote camps or lodges where rivers are not fished out by every passing motorist.

If you plan to camp away from towns or, even better, undertake a wilderness trip, by all means pack a rod and reel. A backpacking rod that breaks down into five sections and has a light reel is ideal and in the Southeast and Southcentral will allow you to cast for cutthroat trout, rainbow trout and Dolly Varden (another type of trout). Further north, especially around Fairbanks, you'll get grayling, with its sail-like dorsal fin, and arctic char. In August, salmon seem to be everywhere.

Want to hook that monster halibut from a kayak? Liquid Adventures (☎ 888-325-2925; www.liquid-adventures.com) is an outfitter that will take you out for a shot at one.

An open-face spinning reel with light line, something in the 4lb to 6lb range, and a small selection of spinners and spoons will allow you to fish a wide range of waters from streams and rivers to lakes. For fly fishing, a No 5 or No 6 rod with a matching floating line or sinking tip is well suited for Dolly Vardens, rainbows and grayling. For salmon, a No 7 or No 8 rod and line are better choices. You can purchase the locally used lures and flies after you arrive.

You will also need a fishing license. A nonresident's fishing license costs $145 a year, but you can purchase a 7/14-day license for $55/80; every bait shop in the state sells them. You can also order a license online or obtain other information through the **Alaska Department of Fish & Game** (☎ 907-465-4100; www.state.ak.us/adfg).

Serious anglers should consider a fishing charter. Joining a captain on his boat is $170 to $250 per person for four to six hours on the water, but local knowledge is the best investment you can make to put a fish on your line. Communities with large fleets of charter captains include Homer, Seward, Petersburg, Kodiak and Ketchikan, with halibut most in demand among visitors. Head to Soldotna to land a 50lb king salmon in the Kenai River.

Alaska Fly Fishers (www.akflyfishers.com) has great information for visiting anglers, including what flies to bring, when to fish, and where to go to catch what.

If money is no option, fly-in fishing adventures are available from cities such as Anchorage and Fairbanks. These outings use small charter planes to reach wilderness lakes and rivers for a day of salmon and steelhead fishing. In Anchorage, **Regal Air** (☎ 907-243-8535; www.regal-air.com) will take you on a nine-hour guided fly-in fishing trip to a river in Lake Clark National Park for $409. It's an expensive day trip but the fishing is legendary, sometimes even a catch per cast.

FLIGHTSEEING

There isn't a bush pilot in Alaska who wouldn't be more than willing to take you on a flightseeing trip. Happy to, in fact. Most flightseeing is done in small planes, holding three to five passengers, with the tour lasting, on the average, one to two hours. A much smaller number are done in helicopters due to the high costs of operating the aircraft. Concerns were raised about the safety of such flights after 15 people died in four flightseeing crashes in 2007, two that occurred near Ketchikan. But considering the large number of tours that take place in Alaska every summer, flightseeing is still deemed a safe activity.

The fastest growing outdoor activity in Alaska is bear watching and now there's a guide to the best viewing sites in the state – Stephen Stringham's *Bear Viewing in Alaska* (2007).

Among the most spectacular places to book a flight is Ketchikan to view Misty Fiords National Monument (p132), Haines to view Glacier Bay National Park (p183) and Talkeetna for a flight around Mt McKinley (p348). With the rising price of fuel, expect to pay anywhere from $200 to $300 per person for a one-hour flight.

GLACIER TREKKING & ICE CLIMBING

Quick! Walk on a glacier before they melt back among the mountain peaks. Most first-time glacier trekkers envision a slick and slippery surface but in reality the ice is very rough and embedded with gravel and rocks to provide surprisingly good traction. There are several roadside-accessible glaciers, the Matanuska Glacier (p367) being the best known, where you can walk a short distance on the gravel-laced ice in just hiking boots.

For a more interesting afternoon, hook up with a guiding company that offers glacier treks. On such outings you'll be outfitted with a helmet, crampons and an ice axe and roped up for several miles of walking on the frozen surface. The beauty of the ice, sprinkled with azure pools, sliced by deep blue crevasses and surrounded by bare rock mountains, is stunning. In Juneau, **Above & Beyond Alaska** (☎ 907-364-2333; www.beyondak.com) will lead you on a six-hour trek across the Mendenhall Glacier ($150). **St Elias Alpine Guides** (☎ 888-933-5427; www.steliasguides.com) does the same for Root Glacier near McCarthy and **MICA Guides** (☎ 800-956-6422; www.micaguides.com) will do the same at the Matanuska Glacier.

During the 2008 climbing season, 1272 climbers attempted Mt McKinley and 755 reached the top of North America's highest peak for a 59% success rate.

Glaciers are also the main destination in Alaska for ice climbers in the summer. Ice falls and faces, where the glacier makes its biggest vertical descents out of the mountains, are where climbers strap on crampons and helmets and load themselves with ropes, ice screws and anchors. Inexperienced climbers should sign up for a one-day ice climbing lesson, where guides lead you to an ice fall and then teach you about cramponing, front pointing and the use of ice tools. All of the above outfitters offer such ice climbing excursions, as does the **Ascending Path** (☎ 877-783-0505; www.theascendingpath.com) of Girdwood, which uses Byron Glacier as its classroom ($189).

HIKING

Alaska Wildlands Adventures (☎ 800-334-8730; www.alaskawildland.com), an eco-friendly travel company that specializes in outdoor adventure, donates 10% of its earnings to local environmental organizations.

Even if you don't have any desire to hoist a hefty backpack, don't pass up an opportunity to spend a day hiking one of the hundreds of well-maintained and easy-to-follow trails scattered across the state. How good is the day hiking in Juneau? The trailhead for the Mt Roberts Trail (p165) is only five blocks from the state capitol, while the USFS maintains 29 other trails accessible from the Juneau road system. Anchorage is also blessed with numerous close-to-home trails. A 15-minute drive from downtown and you can be at a tree-line trailhead in Chugach State Park, where a path quickly leads into the alpine. Skagway, Girdwood, Seward and Sitka also have numerous trails close to main streets.

Keep in mind that even when day hiking you have to be prepared for Alaska's finicky weather. Too often visitors undertake a day hike with little or no equipment and then, three hours from the trailhead, get caught in

PANNING FOR A FORTUNE

With gold prices reaching an all-time high of $900 an ounce in 2008 and the economy slumping, more people are heading to Alaska in search of gold. But after all the gold rushes that have been staged, can there possibly be any gold left in Alaska for recreational gold panners? You bet! Geologists estimate that only 5% of what the state contains has been recovered.

Even short-term visitors can strike it rich. Alaska has more than 150 public prospecting sites where you can recreationally pan for gold without staking a claim. The best choices are in the Interior region of the state. They include, on Taylor Hwy, the Jack Wade Dredge at Mile 86 and American Creek at Mile 151; on Petersville Rd off the George Parks Hwy at Trapper Creek, the Petersville State Recreation Mining Area; and on Glenn Hwy, Caribou Creek at Mile 106.8 and Nelchina River at Mile 137.5.

When panning for gold, you must have one essential piece of equipment: a gravity-trap pan, which can usually be purchased at hardware stores. Those who have panned for a while also show up with rubber boots and gloves to protect feet and hands from icy waters; a garden trowel to dig up loose rock; a pair of tweezers to pick up gold flakes; and a small bottle to hold their find.

Panning techniques are based on the notion that gold is heavier than the gravel it lies in. Fill your pan with loose material from cracks and crevices in streams, where gold might have washed down and become lodged. Add water to the pan, then rinse and discard larger rocks, keeping the rinsing in the pan. Continue to shake the contents toward the bottom by swirling the pan in a circular motion, and wash off the excess sand and gravel by dipping the front into the stream.

You should be left with heavy black mud, sand and, if you're lucky, a few flakes of gold. Use tweezers or your fingernails to transfer the flakes into a bottle filled with water.

bad weather wearing only a flimsy cotton jacket. Bring a day pack with you to Alaska and for a day hike load it up with a waterproof parka, woolen mittens and hat, a knife, high-energy food (such as chocolate or a granola bar), matches, a map and compass or GPS unit, a water bottle and insect repellent. Most day hikes described in regional chapters can easily be walked in lightweight nylon hiking boots made by sporting-shoe companies like Vasque, Lowa or Merrell.

Built by Alaskan ice climbers, the new website www.alaskaiceclimbing.com has brief descriptions of climbs throughout the state, maps and an ice-conditions forum.

For the best multiday backpacking adventures in Alaska turn to the Wilderness Hikes & Paddles chapter (p89). For the state's best close-to-town day hikes hit the trail on one of these:

Crow Pass Trail (p221) From Girdwood a round-trip hike of 8 miles takes you past gold mining artifacts, an alpine lake and Raven Glacier.

Deer Mountain Trail (p102) Just arrived in Alaska? This 2.5-mile-long trail from downtown Ketchikan to the top of Deer Mountain will whet your appetite to tie up your hiking boots at every stop.

West Glacier Trail (p165) This 3.4-mile-long trail near Juneau hugs a mountainside while providing a bird's-eye view of the Mendenhall Glacier.

Williwaw Lakes Trail (p207) Within minutes of the heart of Anchorage, this easy 13-mile hike leads you to a series of alpine lakes in the Chugach State Park and offers the possibility of seeing Dall sheep.

MOUNTAIN BIKING

The mountain bike's durable design, knobby tires and suspension system may have been invented in California but it was made for Alaska. With such a bike you can explore an almost endless number of dirt roads, miner's two-tracks and even hiking trails that you would never consider with a road bike. For many, the versatile mountain bike is the key, and 4WD tracks are the avenue to escaping roads and RVers for the scenery and wildlife of the backcountry.

There isn't a statewide guidebook to off-road riding in Alaska but *Mountain Bike Anchorage* (2005) by Rosemary Austin does a fine job covering trails and two-tracks from Girdwood to Eklutna.

Just remember to pick your route carefully before heading out. Make sure the length of the route and the ruggedness of the terrain are within your capability, and that you have appropriate equipment. Always pack a lightweight, wind-and-water-resistant jacket and an insulating layer because the weather changes quickly in Alaska and so can the terrain. Even when renting a bike, make sure you can repair a flat with the proper spare tube and tools. Water, best carried in a hydration pack, is a must and so is energy food.

There is much mountain-bike activity around Anchorage, and several places to rent bikes (p206). Within the city, mountain bikers head to Kincaid Park (p206) and Far North Bicentennial Park (p206) for their fill of rugged single track. In surrounding Chugach State Park, the Powerline Pass Trail is an 11-mile round-trip adventure into the mountains, while rentals are available for the 13.5-mile Lakeside Trail (p226), a popular leisurely ride that skirts Eklutna Lake.

Southeast Alaska is loaded with wildlife and *Alaska's Inside Passage Wildlife Viewing Guide* (2006) by Riley Woodford tells you where and when to look for it.

The Resurrection Pass, Russian River and Johnson Pass Trails in the Chugach National Forest have become popular among off-road cyclists in the Kenai Peninsula. North of Anchorage, Hatcher Pass (p230) is a haven of mountain-biking activity, with riders following Archangel Rd (also known as the Archangel Valley), Craggie Creek Trail and Gold Mint Trail to glaciers and old mines in the Talkeetna Mountains.

The most popular area for riders in Fairbanks is the Chena River State Recreation Area (p392), while in Juneau mountain bikers head to Perseverance Trail (p164) near downtown, and Montana Creek Trail (p165) out Egan Dr near the Mendenhall Glacier.

If you are able to travel with equipment on your bike (sleeping bag, food and tent), you can partake in a variety of overnight trips or longer bicycle journeys. The 92-mile Denali Park Rd (p338) is off-limits to vehicles, but you can explore it on a mountain bike. Another excellent dirt road for such an adventure is the 135-mile Denali Hwy (p353) from Paxson to Cantwell.

If you need a guide and a set of wheels, **Alaska Backcountry Bike Tours** (☎ 866-354-2453; www.mountainbikealaska.com) is a great little company that offers bike adventures from Anchorage, including both day outings and multiday trips. Single-day rides include the Eklutna Lakeside Trail ($139) and a 20-mile ride along Johnson Pass Trail in the Kenai Peninsula ($139). The Alaskan Epic (camp/lodge $1195/1595) is five days and 85 miles of single track with your choice of accommodations at night either a campsite or a bed in a lodge.

PADDLING

Both white-water and expedition rafting are extremely popular in Alaska. The Nenana River just outside of Denali National Park is a mecca for white-water thrill seekers with companies like the **Denali Outdoor Center** (☎ 907-683-1925; www.denalioutdoorcenter.com) offering daily raft trips through the summer through Class IV rapids. The season climaxes on the second weekend after the Fourth of July holiday when the **Nenana River Wildwater Festival** (www.nenanawildwater.org) is staged as two days of river races and a wildwater rodeo. Other rivers that attract white-water enthusiasts include the Lowe River near Valdez, Six Mile Creek with its Class V rapids near Hope, the Matanuska River east of Palmer and the Kennicott River at McCarthy.

www.riverfacts.com – this excellent website has details, maps and links for rivers throughout the country including more than 100 in Alaska.

Expedition rafting tours are multiday floats through remote wilderness areas. While there can be some white-water activity during the trips, the raft is used primarily as transportation. Thanks in part to the controversy over drilling for oil, the Arctic National Wildlife Refuge (ANWR) is one of the most popular places for people seeking this type of wilderness experience. But it's not cheap. **Arctic Treks** (☎ 907-455-6502; www.arctictreksadventures.com) offers a 10-day float through the ANWR of the Hulahula River with a price tag of $4150 per person. The Tatshenshini-Alsek River system is another highly regarded wilderness raft trip that begins in the Yukon Territory and ends in Glacier Bay National Park (p183).

RUNNING FOR THE MOUNTAINS

Alaska has a lot of mountains and a lot of people who like to run. So running to the top of a mountain is as natural in this state as catching a salmon. Alaska's oldest and most famous mountain run is the **Mt Marathon Race** (www.sewardak.org) that dates back to 1890 when two miners wagered $100 that no man could run from downtown Seward to the top of the mountain and back in under an hour. Today so many people want to run the Mt Marathon Race on the July 4 weekend they have to hold a lottery for entries.

Mountain runners are an interesting breed that includes marathoners and cross-country skiers along with climbers, mountain bikers and even dog mushers. Iditarod musher DeeDee Jonrowe races up mountains as part of her cross-training for the famed sled dog race. Olympic cross-country skier Nina Kemppel, who has won the women's division of the Mt Marathon Race several times, uses it as part of her training, too. Hunters also get running before they head to the mountains to track alpine-loving Dall sheep.

Mountain running isn't adventure racing – you're never searching for the course – and it's not ultra-marathons, those long 50- or 60-mile events. But it is grueling and Alaskans love it so much that in 2001 **Alaska Mountain Runners** (www.alaskamountainrunners.org) was established to promote and develop the sport.

Other mountain events include the **Crow Pass Crossing** (☎ 907-276-7277; mid-July), a 24-mile race along the Cross Pass Trail from Girdwood to Eagle River, and the **Lost Lake Run** (www.lostlakerun.org; late August), a 15-mile run to the alpine along a USFS trail. If you're in Nome don't forget the **Anvil Mountain Run** (www.nomealaska.org; July 4), a 10.6-mile race from Front St to the top of the 1134ft-high peak.

ROCK CLIMBING & MOUNTAINEERING

Rock climbing has been growing in popularity in Alaska. On almost any summer weekend, you can watch climbers working bolt-protected sport routes just above Seward Hwy along Turnagain Arm. Canyons in nearby Portage are also capturing the attention of rock climbers. Off Byron Glacier, several routes grace a slab of black rock polished smooth by the glacier. Not far from Portage Lake, a short hike leads to the magnificent slate walls of Middle Canyon.

The illustrations are cartoonish but the information on glacier trekking in Andy Tyson's *Glacier Mountaineering: the Illustrated Guide to Glacier Travel and Crevasse Rescue* (2000) is solid.

Fairbanks climbers head north of town to the limestone formations known as Grapefruit Rocks, or else pack a tent and sleeping bag for the Granite Tors Trail (p393) off the Chena Hot Springs Rd. A 7-mile hike from the trailhead brings them to the tors, a series of 100ft granite spires in a wilderness setting.

For climbing equipment and more information in Anchorage, contact **Alaska Mountaineering & Hiking** (☎ 907-272-1811; www.alaskamountaineering.com). In Fairbanks, contact **Beaver Sports** (☎ 907-479-2494; www.beaversports.com) for equipment. Mt McKinley and the other high peaks in Alaska also draw the attention of mountain climbers from around the world. For information on scaling the state's loftiest peaks start with the Anchorage-based **Mountaineering Club of Alaska** (☎ 907-272-1811; www.mcak.org). Its bulletin board is loaded with mountaineering-related topics. The best mountaineering guidebook to the state is *Alaska: A Climbing Guide* by Michael Wood and Colby Coombs.

Alaska's most unusual mountain bike event is the Fat Tire Festival at the end of July, a 60-mile ride from Chitina to McCarthy on a Saturday and chainless downhill races on Sunday.

Outfitters include **Alaska Mountain Guides and Climbing School** (☎ 800-766-3396; www.alaskamountainguides.com), which runs a climbing school in Haines as well as leading high-altitude climbing expeditions from Mt McKinley to Mt Fairweather, **Alaska Mountaineering School** (☎ 907-733-1016; www.climbalaska.org) of Talkeetna, which specializes in Mt McKinley ($4500), and **St Elias Alpine Guides** (☎ 888-933-5427; www.steliasguides.com), which tackles Mt Blackburn and other peaks in Wrangell-St Elias National Park.

SKIING & SNOWBOARDING

Alaska's main downhill ski area, the home of Olympian gold medalist Tommy Moe, is **Alyeska Resort** (☎ 907-754-2111; www.alyeskaresort.com) in Girdwood. With an annual snowfall of 631in and 2500 vertical feet of terrain, Mt Alyeska can challenge the most die-hard downhillers and snowboarders with a season that often begins in early November and lasts through April. This world-class resort has 68 runs, almost 40% black diamonds, which are serviced by nine lifts including a 60-passenger aerial tram. None of the other handful of downhill areas in Alaska comes close to what Alyeska has to offer.

Some of the finest cross-country skiing in the US is in Anchorage, and the Nordic Ski Association of Anchorage (www.anchoragenordicski.com) can help you enjoy it.

The only way to achieve more exciting runs than what Alyeska has is to jump into a helicopter. **Chugach Powder Guides** (☎ 907-783-4354; www.chugachpowderguides.com) offers heli-skiing at Alyeska and in the Alaska Range. **Valdez Heli-Ski Guides** (☎ 907-835-4528; www.valdezheliskiguides.com) operates in the Chugach Mountains near Valdez, where the longest run through the deep powder is a descent of 6200 vertical feet.

SURFING

Surfin' USA? Alaska has more coastline than any other state in the USA, but the last thing most people associate with the frozen north is surfing. Until now.

Following a *Surfer* magazine cover story on surfing in Alaska, the state's first surf shop, **Icy Waves Surf Shop** (☎ 907-784-3226; www.icywaves.com), opened in Yakutat in 1999. That caught the attention of CBS News, which sent a camera crew to the remote town for three days. Yakutat's 20-minute segment on the news show *Sunday Morning* with Charles Osgood propelled it into the world limelight and made the small town 'Surf City Alaska.'

Too cold (and snowy) to climb? Head indoors with a list of all the Alaska rock gyms from www.indoorclimbing.com/alaska.html.

Due to its big waves and uncrowded beaches, Yakutat was named one of the five best surf towns in the USA by *Outside Magazine* in 2005. Today more than 100 surfers from all over the world will visit the surf capital of Alaska every summer to join 20 or so locals for 'surfing under St Elias,' the 18,000ft peak that overshadows the town. The best waves occur from mid-April to mid-June and mid-August through September and, to the surprise of non-Alaskan surfers, the water isn't all that cold. The Japanese current pushes summer water temperatures into the mid-60s, while the rest of the surfing season they range from the mid-40s to the mid-50s.

Surfers have also hit the beaches of Sitka, home of the **Cold Salt Surf Shop** (☎ 907-966-2653; www.coldsalt.com), and Kodiak. Alaska's 'Big Island' has an almost endless number of places to surf, but the majority of surfers head to the beaches clustered around Pasagshak Point, 40 miles south of town.

A surfin' safari, Alaskan style, means packing a wet suit with hood, booties and gloves, and often wearing a helmet. You'll also need to watch out for the brown bears, which often roam the beaches in search of washed-up crabs, salmon and other meals. Surfers have been known to encounter gray whales, sea otters, and even chunks of ice if they hit the waves too soon after the spring breakup.

Climbers can now register online to climb Mt McKinley or Mt Foraker at www.pay.gov/paygov/forms/formInstance.html?agencyFormId=16355280.

ZIPLINING

That new-fangled thrill, ziplining, which involves riding a metal cable through the forest, isn't yet big in Alaska, but it has arrived. In Southeast Alaska it is bound to become more popular thanks in part to the rainforest that covers much of the region and the large number of cruise ships that pass through it. At **Icy Strait Point** (www.icystraitpoint.com), a cruise-ship stop near Hoona, the ZipRider cable ride is more than a mile long and includes a 1300ft vertical drop. **Alaska Canopy Adventures** (☎ 877-947-7557; www.alaskacanopy.com) operates ziplines in Ketchikan (p126) and Juneau (p167).

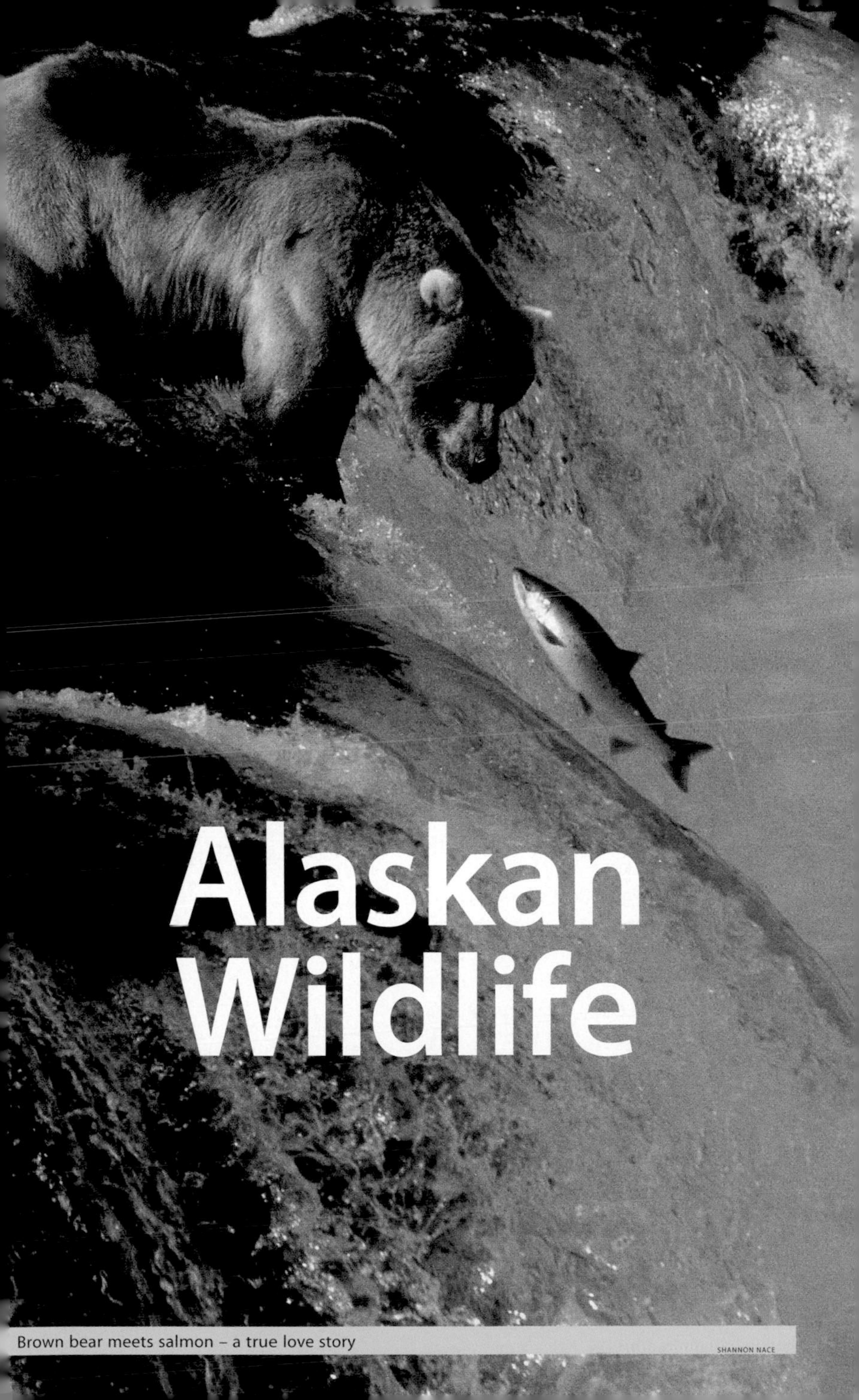

Alaskan Wildlife

Brown bear meets salmon – a true love story

SHANNON NACE

Few aspects of the Alaska wilderness are as appealing to visitors as its wildlife. With almost three-quarters of its population concentrated in three cities, Alaska is able to boast one of the largest concentrations of wildlife on earth. It's one of the few places in the USA where entire ecosystems are still intact and ancient migratory routes uninterrupted. Some species that are threatened or endangered elsewhere – brown bears and bald eagles – are thriving in the 49th state. There are almost twice as many caribou in Alaska as people, and 400 species of birds have been sighted in the state. More than 20 million shorebirds and waterfowl migrate through the Copper River Delta near Cordova every spring.

LAND MAMMALS

Bears

In 2005 a US Forest Service worker was charged by a huge brown bear and was left with no choice but to shoot it. The amazing animal stood 14ft tall, weighed more than 1600lb and was the largest brown bear recorded. Today it's displayed at Anchorage International Airport.

There are three species of bear in Alaska – brown, black and polar – but you're most likely to see brown bears, since they have the greatest range.

At one time, brown and grizzly bears were listed as separate species, but now both are classified as *Ursus arctos*. The difference isn't as much genetics as size. Browns live along the coast, where abundant salmon runs help them reach weights exceeding 800lb – with the famed Kodiak brown bear often tipping the scales at 1500lb. Grizzlies are browns found inland, away from the salmon runs. Normally a male weighs from 500lb to 700lb, and females half that.

The elusive polar bear

MARK

Alaska has more than 98% of the US population of brown bears, or an estimated 30,000. In July and August you can see brown bears fishing along rivers. By early fall, bears will often move to the tundra and to open meadows, to feed on berries.

The most common way to identify a brown bear is by the prominent shoulder hump, easily seen behind the neck when it's on all fours. Brooks Falls (p312) at Katmai National Park and Kodiak National Wildlife Refuge (see the boxed text, p310) are the best places to see large brown bears, but Southeast Alaska (see the boxed text, p120) can also be good.

Though black bears are the USA's most widely distributed bruin, their range is more limited in Alaska. They live in most forested areas of the state, but not north of the Brooks Range, on the Seward Peninsula or on many large islands, such as Kodiak and Admiralty.

The average male weighs 180lb to 250lb. A brown or cinnamon black bear often appears in Southcentral Alaska, leaving many backpackers confused about what the species is. Beyond measuring an upper rear molar, look for a straight facial profile to confirm it's a black bear.

Polar bears *(Ursus maritimus)* have always captured our interest because of their size and white color, but they're not easy to encounter. Plan on stopping at the zoo in Anchorage, or an expensive side trip to Barrow, if you want to see one. Polar bears dwell only in the northern hemisphere, and almost always in association with Arctic Sea ice.

A male weighs between 600lb and 1200lb, but occasionally it tops 1400lb. The polar bear's adaptations to a life on the sea ice include its white, water-repellent coat, dense underfur, specialized teeth for a carnivorous diet (primarily seals), and hair that almost completely covers the bottom of its feet.

Moose

The moose is long-legged to the extreme, but short-bodied, with a huge rack of antlers and a drooping nose. Standing still, they look uncoordinated until you watch them run or, better still, swim. They're the world's largest members of the deer family, and the Alaskan species is the largest of all moose. A newborn weighs 35lb and can grow to more than 300lb in five months; cows weigh 800lb to 1200lb; and bulls 1000lb to more than 1600lb, with antlers up to 70in wide.

The moose population ranges from an estimated 120,000 to 160,000, and historically moose have always been the most important game animal in Alaska.

Moose are widespread and range from the Stikine River in the Southeast to the Colville River on the North Slope. Moose are frequently sighted along the Alcan, and Denali National Park (p334) is an excellent place to watch them. But the best place to see the biggest moose is the Kenai Peninsula, especially if you take time to paddle the Swanson River or Swan Lake canoe routes in the Kenai National Wildlife Refuge (see the boxed text, p272).

top five SPECIES VISITORS WANT TO SEE

Brown Bears
Katmai National Park (p311), Anan Creek Wildlife Observatory (p139), Steep Creek (p174)

Humpback Whales
Glacier Bay National Park (p177), Kenai Fjords National Park (p266), Sitka (p149)

Moose
Kenai National Wildlife Refuge (p271), Denali National Park (p332)

Seals
Tracy Arm (p168), Leconte Glacier (p146), Prince William Sound (p232)

Puffins
St Lazaria Island National Wildlife Refuge (p154), Gull Island (p294), Aluetian Islands ferry trip (p316)

A bull moose can weigh up to 1600lb MARK NEWMAN

Caribou

Although more than a million caribou live in Alaska's 32 herds, they are difficult to view, as they travel from the Interior north to the Arctic Sea. Caribou range in weight from 150lb to more than 400lb. Some caribou have been known to migrate 3000 miles a year between their calving grounds, rutting areas and winter home.

The principal predators of caribou are wolves, and some packs on the North Slope have been known to follow caribou herds for years, picking off the young, the old and the injured. The caribou are crucial to the Iñupiat and other Alaska Natives, who hunt more than 30,000 a year to support their subsistence lifestyle.

The best place for the average visitor to see caribou is Denali National Park (p334).

Perhaps one of the greatest wildlife events left in the world is the migration of the Western Arctic herd of caribou, the largest such herd in North America, with almost 500,000 animals. The herd uses the North Slope for its calving area, and in late August many of the animals begin to cross the Noatak River on their journey southward. During that time, the few visitors lucky enough to be on the river are often rewarded with the awesome experience of watching 20,000 caribou crossing the tundra toward the Brooks Range.

Mountain Goats

Mountain goats are the only North American species in the widespread group of goat antelopes, and are characterized by a fondness for rugged alpine terrain that allows them to avoid predators. More mountain goats are killed by snow slides than by wolves or bears.

Although mountain goats are often confused with Dall sheep, they are easily identified by their longer hair, short black horns and deep chest.

There are around 80,000 Dall sheep in Alaska

MARK

npback whales can be seen from ferries and cruise boats

MARK NEWMAN

In Alaska mountain goats range through the bulk of the Southeast, fanning out north and west into the coastal mountains of Cook Inlet, as well as the Chugach and Wrangell Mountains. Good locations to see them include Glacier Bay (p177) and Wrangell-St Elias National Park (p369). Public scopes in Juneau's Marine Park (p163) allow visitors to look for goats on Mt Juneau.

Dall Sheep

These are more numerous and widespread than mountain goats – they number close to 80,000 – and live principally in the Alaska, Wrangell, Chugach and Kenai mountain ranges. Not far from Anchorage Dall sheep are often seen at Windy Corner, a natural mineral lick at Mile 107 on the Seward Hwy (p218).

It's spectacular to watch rams in a horn-clashing battle, but they're not fighting for a female, just for social dominance. Dall sheep prefer rocky, open, alpine tundra regions. In the spring and fall, however, they move to lower slopes, where the grazing is better. The best time to spot rams, and see them clash, is right before the mating period, beginning in November.

top five WILDLIFE-VIEWING FESTIVALS

Stikine River Garnet Festival (p141)
The Stikine River hosts the largest springtime concentration of bald eagles in Alaska.

Copper River Delta Shorebird Festival (p245)
Five million shorebirds rest and feed on the tidal flats of the Copper River Delta during spring migration.

Kachemak Bay Shorebird Festival (p286)
Homer stages a migration festival in early May, featuring guided birding tours by boat, bike, bus and on foot.

Sitka WhaleFest! (p155)
Visitors and locals gather in Sitka in early November to listen to world-renowned biologists talk about whales, and then to hop on a boat to look for them.

Alaska Bald Eagle Festival (p187)
More than 3000 eagles gather along a 4 mile stretch of the Chilkat River, the largest gathering of eagles in the world.

Wolves

While gray wolves are struggling throughout most of the USA – outside Alaska, only Minnesota has a substantial population – they inhabit 85% of Alaska, and their numbers are strong despite predator control programs. No animal has been more misunderstood. A pack of wolves is no match for a healthy 1200lb moose; wolves can usually only catch and kill the weak, injured or young, thus strengthening the herd they are stalking.

In total, about 8000 wolves live in packs throughout almost every region of Alaska. Most adult males average 85lb to 115lb, and their pelts can be either grey, black, off-white, brown or yellow, with some tinges approaching red. Wolves travel, hunt, feed and operate in the social unit of a pack. In the Southeast their principal food is deer, in the Interior it's moose and in Arctic Alaska it's caribou.

Beavers & River Otters

Around lakes and rivers you stand a good chance of seeing river otters and, even more likely, beavers, or at the very least, the lodges and dams beavers build. Both live throughout the state, except in the North Slope. Often larger than their relatives further south, otters range from 15lb to 35lb, and beavers weigh between 40lb and 70lb, although 100lb beavers have been recorded in Alaska.

FISH & MARINE MAMMALS

Whales

The three most common whales seen in coastal waters are the 50ft-long humpback, with its humplike dorsal fin and long flippers, the smaller bowhead whale and the gray whale. The humpback is by far the most frequently seen whale by visitors on cruise ships and on the state ferries, as they often lift their flukes (tail) out of the water to begin a dive, or blow every few seconds when resting near the surface. Biologists estimate 1000 humpbacks migrate to the Southeast and more than 100 head to Prince William Sound each year.

At one time Glacier Bay was synonymous with whale watching. But today tour boats head out of almost every Southeast Alaska port, loaded with whale-watching passengers. You can also join such wildlife trips in Kenai Fjords National Park (p268), near Seward, and in Kodiak (p305).

Seals love to bask in the sun

ERNEST MA

Seals

The most commonly seen marine mammals are seals, which often bask in the sun on an ice floe. Six species exist in Alaska,

The bald eagle has a wingspan of up to 8ft
ERNEST MANEWAL

but most visitors will encounter just the harbor seal, the only seal whose range includes the Southeast, Prince William Sound and the rest of the Gulf of Alaska. The average weight of a male is 200lb – achieved through a diet of herring, flounder, salmon, squid and small crabs.

Two other species, ringed seals and bearded seals, appear for the most part in the northern Bering, Chukchi and Beaufort Seas, where sea ice forms during winter.

Dolphins & Porpoises

Many visitors also see dolphins and harbor porpoises, even from the decks of the ferries. Occasionally, ferry travelers spot a pod of orcas (killer whales), whose high black-and-white dorsal fins make them easy to identify. Orcas, which can be more than 20ft long, are the largest members of the dolphin family, which also includes the beluga or white whale. Belugas range in length from 11ft to 16ft and often weigh more than 3000lb. The 50,000 belugas that live in Alaskan waters travel in herds of more than 100. Most visitors will spot them in Turnagain Arm, along the Seward Hwy (p218). Beluga Point, at Mile 110, is a popular observation area.

Salmon

Salmon runs are where thousands of fish swim upstream to spawn, and rank among Alaska's most amazing and easiest-to-find sights. From late July to mid-September, many coastal streams are choked with salmon. You won't see just one fish here and there, but thousands – so many, that they have to wait their turn to swim through narrow gaps of shallow water.

Five kinds of salmon populate Alaskan waters: sockeye (also referred to as red salmon), king or chinook, pink or humpie, coho or silver, and chum. And in many cases you don't have to leave the city to see a run. In the heart of Anchorage, Ship Creek supports runs of king, coho and pink, and from a viewing platform (p202) you can watch salmon spawning upriver and locals trying to catch one for dinner. In downtown Ketchikan, you can watch salmon in Ketchikan Creek (p123).

BIRDS

Bald Eagles

The most impressive bird in Alaska's wilderness is the bald eagle – with a white tail and head, and a wingspan that often reaches 8ft – and it has become the symbol of the nation. While elsewhere the bird is on the endangered species list, in Alaska it thrives. It can be sighted almost daily in most of the Southeast, is common in Prince William Sound and is impossible to miss in Dutch Harbor (p319) in the Aleutian Islands.

The bird is also responsible for a spectacle that exceeds even the salmon runs: bare trees, without a leaf remaining, supporting 80 or more white-headed eagles, with up to four or five to a branch. This occurs in November, when more than 4000 eagles migrate to the Chilkat River near Haines to feed on a late salmon run. For more information on seeing bald eagles in this area, see the boxed text, p187.

Take a wildlife cruise to see the playful horned puffin

DAVID

Ptarmigan

The state bird of Alaska is the ptarmigan, a cousin of the prairie grouse. Three species of the ptarmigan can be found throughout the state, in high treeless country.

Seabirds & Waterfowl

Alaskan seabirds include the playful horned and tufted puffins, six species of auklet and three species of albatross (which boast a wingspan of up to 7ft). The puffin, in particular, is a crowd pleaser, due to its large colorful bill, stout body and red, webbed feet. The optimum way to see puffins and a variety of seabirds is onboard a wildlife cruise to coastal islands used for breeding. Two of the best are St Lazaria Island, home to 1500 pairs of breeding tufted puffins, near Sitka (p154), and Gull Island (see the boxed text, p294), in Kachemak Bay State Park.

An amazing variety of waterfowl also migrates to Alaska, including trumpeter swans. The trumpeter swan is the world's largest member of the waterfowl family and occasionally weighs 30lb. Other waterfowl include Canada geese, of which more than 130,000 nest in Alaska; all four species of eider; the colorful harlequin duck; and five species of loon *(Gavia)*.

Wilderness Hikes & Paddles

Much of Alaska's wilderness is hard to reach for visitors with limited time or small budgets. Specialized equipment, the complicated logistics of reaching remote areas or the lack of backcountry knowledge keeps many out of the state's great wilderness tracts such as the Arctic National Wildlife Refuge (ANWR). To experience such a remote and pristine place you may need to turn to a guiding company and pay a premium price.

But that doesn't mean you can't sneak off on your own for a trek into the mountains or a paddle down an icy fjord. There are so many possible adventures in Alaska that even the most budget-conscious traveler can take time to explore what lies beyond the pavement. Do it yourself and save.

The best way to enter the state's wilderness is to begin with a day hike the minute you step off the ferry or depart from the Alcan. After the initial taste of the woods, many travelers forgo the cities and spend the rest of their trip on multiday adventures into the backcountry to enjoy Alaska's immense surroundings.

The Alaska Department of Natural Resources website – www.dnr.state.ak.us/parks/aktrails – has details on trails in every corner of the state.

There are also a range of paddling opportunities, from calm rivers and chains of lakes for novice canoeists to remote fjords and coastlines whose rugged shorelines and tidal fluctuations are an attraction for more experienced open-water paddlers. In particular, Alaska is an icy paradise for kayakers. Double bladed paddlers can easily escape into a watery wilderness, away from motor boats and cruise ships, and enjoy the unusual experience of gazing at glaciers or watching seal pups snuggle on icebergs from sea level.

This chapter covers 20 popular wilderness excursions. They are either maintained trails or natural paddling routes that backpackers can embark on as unguided journeys if they have the proper equipment and sufficient outdoor experience.

BACKPACKING

The following hikes are those trails that occur along popular and developed routes. Backpackers still require the appropriate gear and knowledge to be totally self-reliant in the wilderness, which is a foreign experience for many city dwellers.

Backpacking Gear

Double-check your equipment before leaving home. Most towns in Alaska will have at least one store with a wall full of camping supplies,

TOP PICKS: HIKES & PADDLES

- **Chilkoot Trail** (p91) – as much historical as it is adventurous
- **Tracy Arm Kayak Route** (p108) – more affordable than Glacier Bay
- **Chena Dome Trail** (p98) – views of Mt McKinley and the midnight sun
- **Iditarod National Historic Trail** (p93) – the best way to bypass Anchorage
- **Swan Lake Canoe Route** (p112) – calm water, beautiful lakes and good fishing

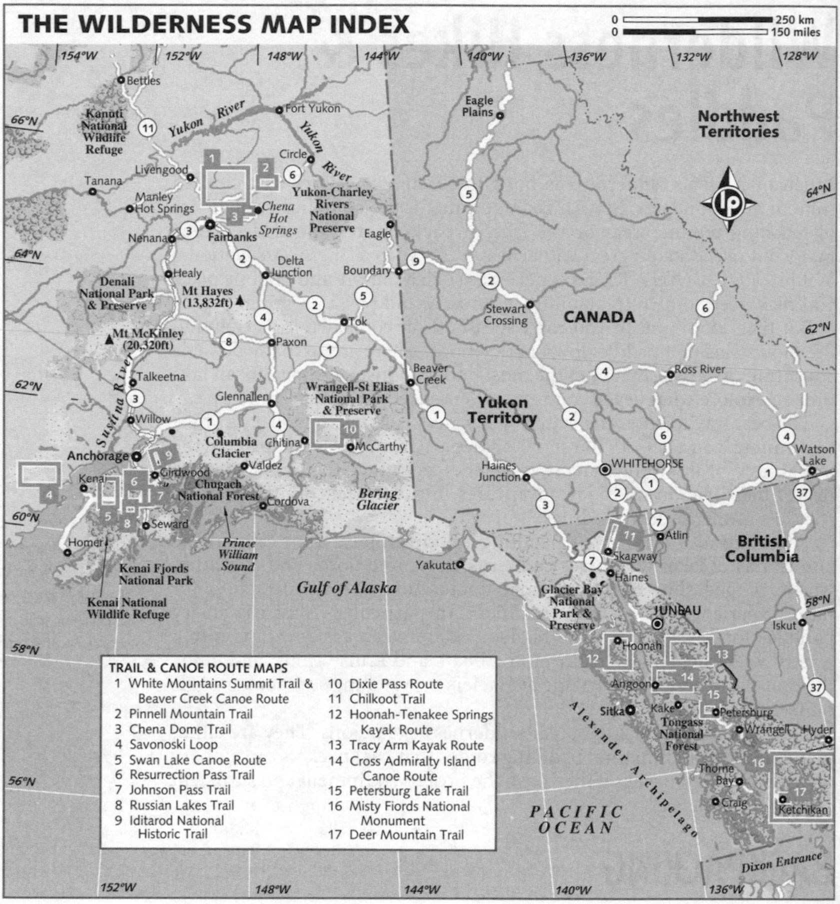

but prices will be high and by mid-to-late summer certain items will be out of stock.

For the backpacker the absolutely essential equipment, aside from a backpack, includes a lightweight tent with rain fly and bug netting, a three-season sleeping bag with a temperature range of -10°F to 40°F, hiking boots that are broken in before you arrive in Alaska, a water filter, a compass or GPS unit and the corresponding US Geological Survey (USGS) map for the area (see p427). Your clothing bag should include mittens, a hat, a fleece pullover (it can get cold at night, even in July) and rain gear, both pants and parka (because it will definitely rain).

Longtime Alaskan Ike Waits has produced *Denali National Park Guide to Hiking, Photography & Camping* (2005), the most comprehensive guide to Alaska's best-known national park.

Equipment you should consider packing includes a self-inflating sleeping pad, a reliable backpacker's stove, a small cooking kit and sports sandals for a change of footwear at night or for fording rivers and streams.

Backcountry Conduct

Behave in the backcountry! Check with the nearest US Forest Service (USFS) office or National Park Service (NPS) headquarters before entering the backcountry. By telling them your intentions, you'll get peace of mind from knowing that someone is aware you're out there.

Take time to check out the area before unpacking your gear. Avoid animal trails (whether the tracks be moose or bear), areas with bear scat, and berry patches with ripe fruit. Throughout much of Alaska, river bars and old glacier outwashes are the best places to pitch a tent. If you come along the coast stay well above the high-tide line, the last ridge of seaweed and debris on the shore, to avoid waking up with saltwater flooding your tent.

Do not harass wildlife. Avoid startling an animal, as it will most likely flee, leaving you with a short and forgettable encounter. Never attempt to feed wildlife; it is not healthy for you or the animal.

Finally, be thoughtful when in the wilderness. It is a delicate environment. Carry in your supplies and carry out your trash. Never litter or leave garbage smoldering in a fire pit. Better still, don't light a fire in heavily traveled areas because numerous fire pits are an eyesore. Use biodegradable soap and do all washing away from water sources. In short, leave no evidence of your stay. Only then can an area remain a true wilderness.

CHILKOOT TRAIL

Section	Miles
Dyea trailhead to Canyon City	7.5
Canyon City to Sheep Camp	4.3
Sheep Camp to Chilkoot Pass	3.5
Chilkoot Pass to Happy Camp	4.0
Happy Camp to Deep Lake	2.5
Deep Lake to Lindeman City	3.0
Lindeman City to Bare Loon Lake	3.0
Bare Loon Lake to the Log Cabin	6.0
Bare Loon Lake to Lake Bennett trailhead	4.0

From the legendary Chilkoot Trail to a paddle down the Yukon River, *Klondike Trail: the Complete Hiking and Paddling Guide* (2001) by Jennifer Voss will lead you on an adventure of a lifetime.

Level of difficulty: medium to hard
Information: **National Park Service** (☎ 907-983-2921; www.nps.gov/klgo)

The Chilkoot (Map p92) is unquestionably the most famous trail in Alaska. Every summer more than 3000 people spend three to four days following the historic route. It was the route used by the Klondike gold miners in the 1898 gold rush, and walking the well-developed trail is not so much a wilderness adventure as a history lesson. The trip is 32 to 34 miles long (depending on where you exit) and includes the Chilkoot Pass – a steep climb up to 3525ft, where most hikers scramble on all fours over the boulders and loose rocks.

For many, the highlight of the hike is riding the historic White Pass & Yukon Route (WP&YR) railroad from Lake Bennett to Skagway. There are cheaper ways to return, but don't pass up the train. Experiencing the Chilkoot and returning on the WP&YR is probably the ultimate Alaska trek, combining great scenery, a historical site and an incredible sense of adventure.

Getting Started

The Chilkoot Trail can be hiked from either direction (starting at Skagway or Lake Bennett), but it's actually easier and safer when you start from Dyea in the south and climb up the loose scree of the Chilkoot Pass rather than down. From Skagway, make your way 8 miles northwest to the Dyea

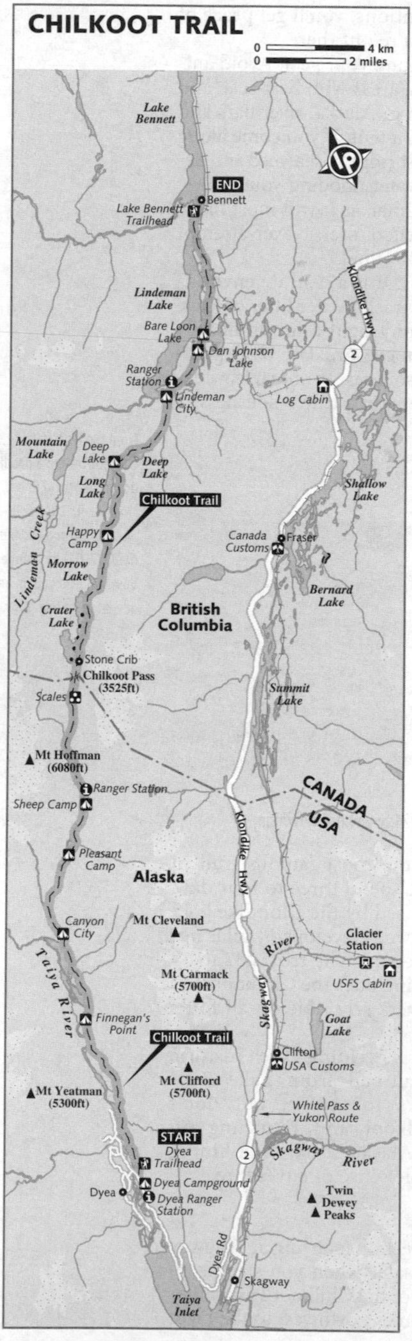
CHILKOOT TRAIL
0 4 km
0 2 miles
Lake Bennett
END
Bennett
Lake Bennett Trailhead
Lindeman Lake
Bare Loon Lake
Dan Johnson Lake
Ranger Station
Lindeman City
Klondike Hwy
2
Log Cabin
Mountain Lake
Deep Lake
Deep Lake
Long Lake
Chilkoot Trail
Shallow Lake
Happy Camp
Canada Customs
Fraser
Lindeman Creek
Morrow Lake
Bernard Lake
Crater Lake
British Columbia
Stone Crib
Chilkoot Pass (3525ft)
Scales
Summit Lake
Mt Hoffman (6080ft)
Ranger Station
Sheep Camp
CANADA
USA
Klondike Hwy
Pleasant Camp
Alaska
Canyon City
Mt Cleveland
Glacier Station
Taiya River
River
USFS Cabin
Mt Carmack (5700ft)
Skagway
Finnegan's Point
Goat Lake
Chilkoot Trail
Clifton
USA Customs
Mt Clifford (5700ft)
Mt Yeatman (5300ft)
White Pass & Yukon Route
START
Dyea Trailhead
2
Skagway River
Dyea Campground
Dyea
Dyea Ranger Station
Twin Dewey Peaks
Dyea Rd
Skagway
Taiya Inlet

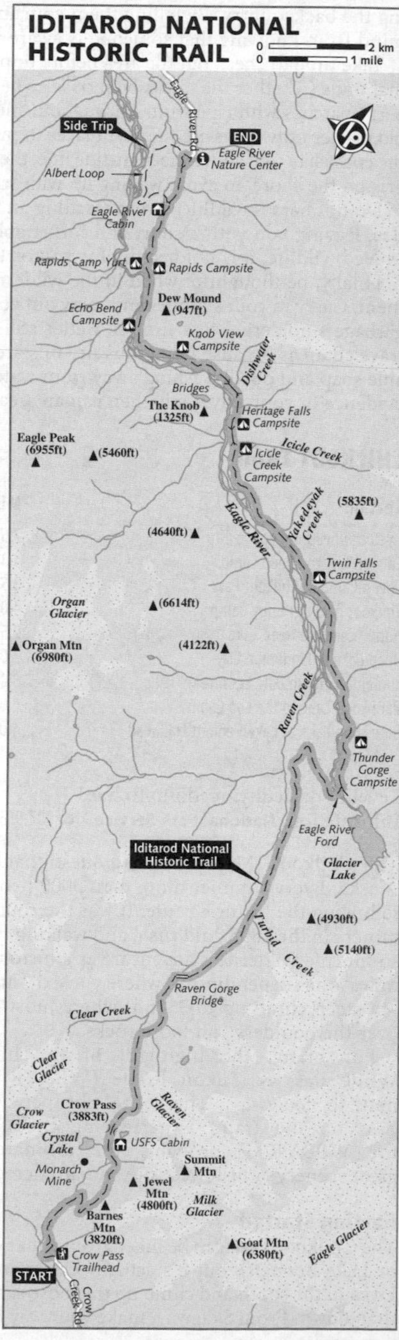
IDITAROD NATIONAL HISTORIC TRAIL
0 2 km
0 1 mile
Eagle River Rd
Side Trip
END
Eagle River Nature Center
Albert Loop
Eagle River Cabin
Rapids Camp Yurt
Rapids Campsite
Dew Mound (947ft)
Echo Bend Campsite
Knob View Campsite
Dishwater Creek
Bridges
The Knob (1325ft)
Heritage Falls Campsite
Eagle Peak (6955ft)
(5460ft)
Icicle Creek
Icicle Creek Campsite
Yakedeyak Creek
(5835ft)
(4640ft)
Eagle River
Twin Falls Campsite
Organ Glacier
(6614ft)
Organ Mtn (6980ft)
(4122ft)
Raven Creek
Thunder Gorge Campsite
Eagle River Ford
Iditarod National Historic Trail
Glacier Lake
Turbid Creek
(4930ft)
(5140ft)
Raven Gorge Bridge
Clear Creek
Clear Glacier
Raven Glacier
Crow Glacier
Crow Pass (3883ft)
Crystal Lake
USFS Cabin
Summit Mtn
Monarch Mine
Jewel Mtn (4800ft)
Milk Glacier
Barnes Mtn (3820ft)
Goat Mtn (6380ft)
Eagle Glacier
Crow Pass Trailhead
START
Crow Creek Rd

trailhead. Mile 0 of the Chilkoot is just before the Taiya River crossing. **Frontier Excursions** (☎ 877-983-2512, 907-983-2512; www.frontierexcursions.com) charges $10 for a ride to the trailhead from Skagway.

In Skagway, stop at the **Chilkoot Trail Center** (☎ 907-983-9234), across from the WP&YR depot on Broadway St, to obtain backpacking permits. A permit costs C$50/25 per adult/child, and covers both the US segment and the portion of the trail administered by Canada. Parks Canada allows only 50 hikers per day on the trail and holds only eight permits to be handed out each day at the Trail Center. It's wise to reserve your permits ($11.70 per reservation) in advance through **Parks Canada** (☎ 867-667-3910, 800-661-0486; www.pc.gc.ca/lhn-nhs/yt/chilkoot) if walking in July or early August.

The 33-mile-long Chilkoot Trail is considered the world's longest outdoor museum due to all the artifacts that the participants of the Klondike Gold Rush left behind.

Getting Back

At the northern end of the trail, hikers can catch the train on the **White Pass & Yukon Route** (☎ 800-343-7373; www.whitepassrailroad.com) from June through August. The train departs from Bennett at 2pm from Sunday to Friday. The one-way fare to Skagway is $95.

The alternative way to leave the trail at the northern end is to hike 6 miles from Bare Loon Lake Campground to the log cabin on Klondike Hwy. Frontier Excursions operates services to the log cabin and provides a drop-off and pickup ticket for $25 per person (minimum two people). It also offers combination tickets for a drop-off at Dyea and a pickup at the log cabin for $30.

IDITAROD NATIONAL HISTORIC TRAIL

Section	Miles
Crow Pass trailhead to Crow Pass	4.0
Crow Pass to Eagle River Ford	9.0
Eagle River Ford to Icicle Creek	7.3
Icicle Creek to Eagle River Nature Center	5.7

Level of difficulty: medium
Information: **Eagle River Nature Center** (☎ 907-694-2108; www.ernc.org); **USFS Glacier Ranger District** (☎ 907-783-3242; www.fs.fed.us/r10/chugach)

The best backpacking adventure near Anchorage is the Iditarod trail, a 26-mile route once used by gold miners and mushers. This classic alpine crossing begins in Chugach National Forest near Girdwood, 37 miles east of Anchorage, climbs Crow Pass and wanders past Raven Glacier. You then enter Chugach State Park and descend Eagle River Valley, ending north of Anchorage at the Eagle River Nature Center. The trail is well maintained and well marked but requires fording Eagle River, which is tricky in rain.

With a light pack and good weather you could cover this trail in one long Alaskan summer day. Heck, they stage a mountain race here every summer with the winner covering it in less than 3½ hours. But why rush? The alpine scenery is remarkable, the mining ruins along the trail interesting, and the hike reasonably challenging. Plan two days or even three because this is why you come to Alaska – to wander in the mountains.

For trails around the Kenai Peninsula, Anchorage area, and from Palmer to Valdez, check out *55 Ways to the Wilderness in Southcentral Alaska* (1994) by Helen Nienhueser and John Wolfe.

Getting Started

The Crow Pass trailhead is reached 7 miles from Mile 90 Seward Hwy via Alyeska Hwy and Crow Creek Rd. The northern trailhead is the end of Eagle River Rd, 12 miles from the Glenn Hwy. There is transportation to

Girdwood (p216). To return to Anchorage you can catch People Mover bus 79 or 102 from the Eagle River Transit Center on Glenn Hwy.

You must have a stove; campfires are not allowed in the state park. Near Mile 3 of the trail is a **USFS cabin** (☎ 877-444-6777, 518-885-3639; www.recreation.gov; $35) in a beautiful alpine setting. At the other end of the trail are yurts and a cabin ($65) rented out by the **Eagle River Nature Center** (☎ 907-694-2108; www.ernc.org).

RESURRECTION PASS TRAIL

Section	Miles
Northern trailhead to Caribou Creek Cabin	6.9
Caribou Creek Cabin to Fox Creek Cabin	4.7
Fox Creek Cabin to East Creek Cabin	2.8
East Creek Cabin to Resurrection Pass	4.9
Resurrection Pass to Devil's Pass Cabin	2.1
Devil's Pass Cabin to Swan Lake Cabin	4.4
Swan Lake Cabin to Juneau Lake Cabin	3.3
Juneau Lake Cabin to Trout Lake Cabin	2.7
Trout Lake Cabin to Juneau Creek Falls	2.3
Juneau Creek Falls to southern trailhead	4.4

By linking Resurrection Pass, Russian Lakes and Resurrection River Trails in Chugach National Forest, you can hike 71 miles from Seward to Hope and cross only one road.

Level of difficulty: easy
Information: **USFS Seward Ranger District** (☎ 907-224-3374; www.fs.fed.us/r10/chugach)

Located in the Chugach National Forest, this 39-mile trail was carved by prospectors in the late 1800s and today is the most popular hiking route on the Kenai Peninsula. It's an increasingly popular trail for mountain bikers, who can ride the entire route in one day. For those on foot, the trip can be done in three days by a strong hiker but most people prefer to do it in four to five days to make the most of the immense beauty of the region.

There are eight **USFS cabins** (☎ 877-444-6777, 518-885-3639; www.recreation.gov; $35-45) along the route but they must be reserved in advance. Most hikers take a tent and camp stove, as fallen wood is scarce during summer.

Getting Started

The northern trailhead is 20 miles from the Seward Hwy and 4 miles south of Hope on Resurrection Creek Rd. Hope, a historic mining community founded in 1896 by gold seekers, is a charming, out-of-the-way place to visit, but Hope Hwy is not an easy road for hitchhiking. (See p437 for more on hitching in Alaska.)

From Hope Hwy, go south at the Resurrection Pass trail signs onto Resurrection Creek Rd, passing the fork to Palmer Creek Rd. The southern trailhead is on the Sterling Hwy, near Cooper Landing.

RUSSIAN LAKES TRAIL

Section	Miles
Cooper Lake trailhead to junction of Resurrection River Trail	5.0
Trail junction to Upper Russian Lake Cabin	4.0
Upper Russian Lake Cabin to Aspen Flats Cabin	3.0
Aspen Flats Cabin to Lower Russian Lake	6.0
Lower Russian Lake to Russian River USFS Campground	3.0

RESURRECTION PASS TRAIL

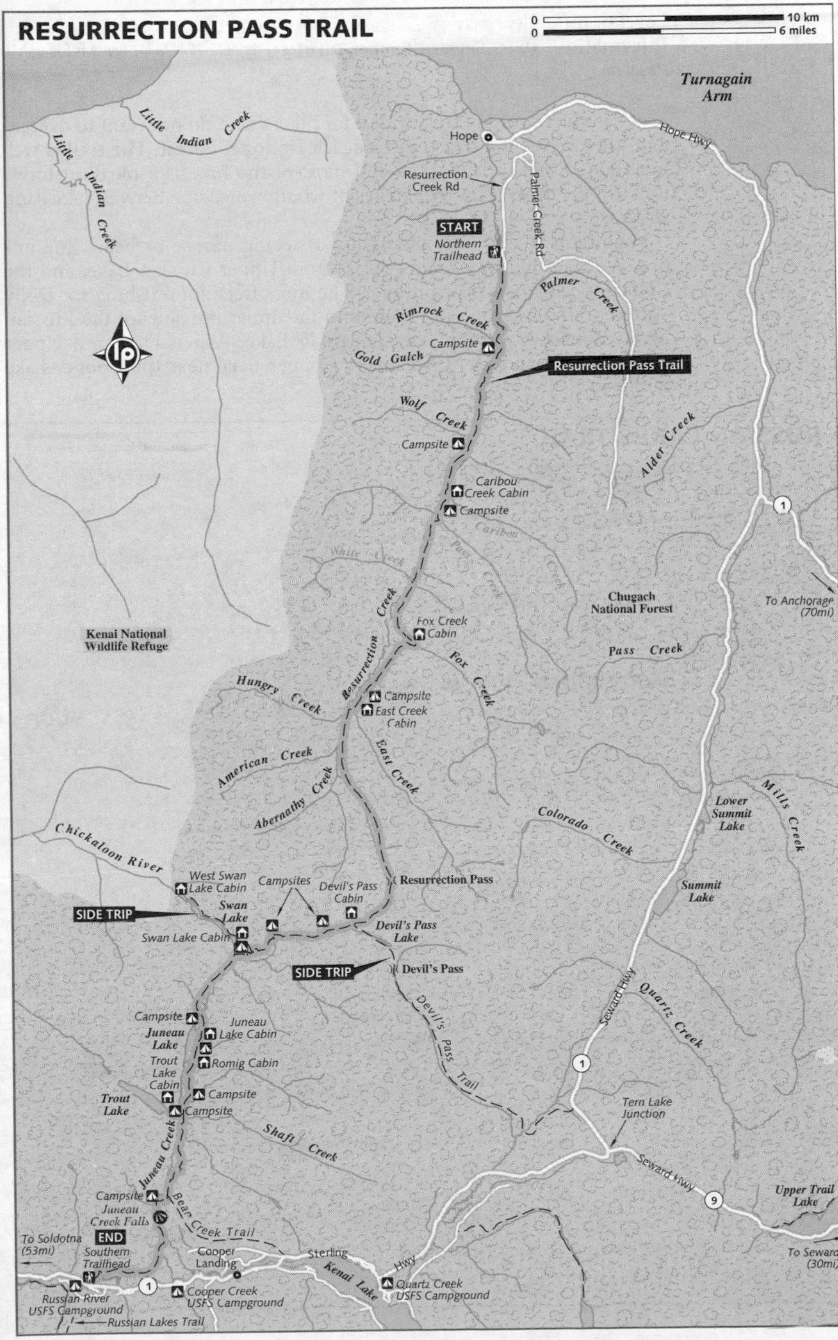

Level of difficulty: easy
Information: **USFS Seward Ranger District** (☎ 907-224-3374; www.fs.fed.us/r10/chugach)

This 21-mile, two-day trek is ideal for hikers who do not want to overextend themselves too much in Chugach National Forest. The trail is well maintained and well marked and most of the hike is a pleasant forest walk that is broken up by patches of wildflowers, ripe berries, lakes and streams.

Highlights include the possibility of seeing moose or bears, the impressive glaciated mountains across from Upper Russian Lake, and the chance to catch your own dinner. The trek offers good fishing for Dolly Varden, rainbow trout and salmon in the upper portions of the Russian River; rainbow trout in Lower Russian Lake, Aspen Flats and Upper Russian Lake; and Dolly Varden in Cooper Lake near the Cooper Lake trailhead.

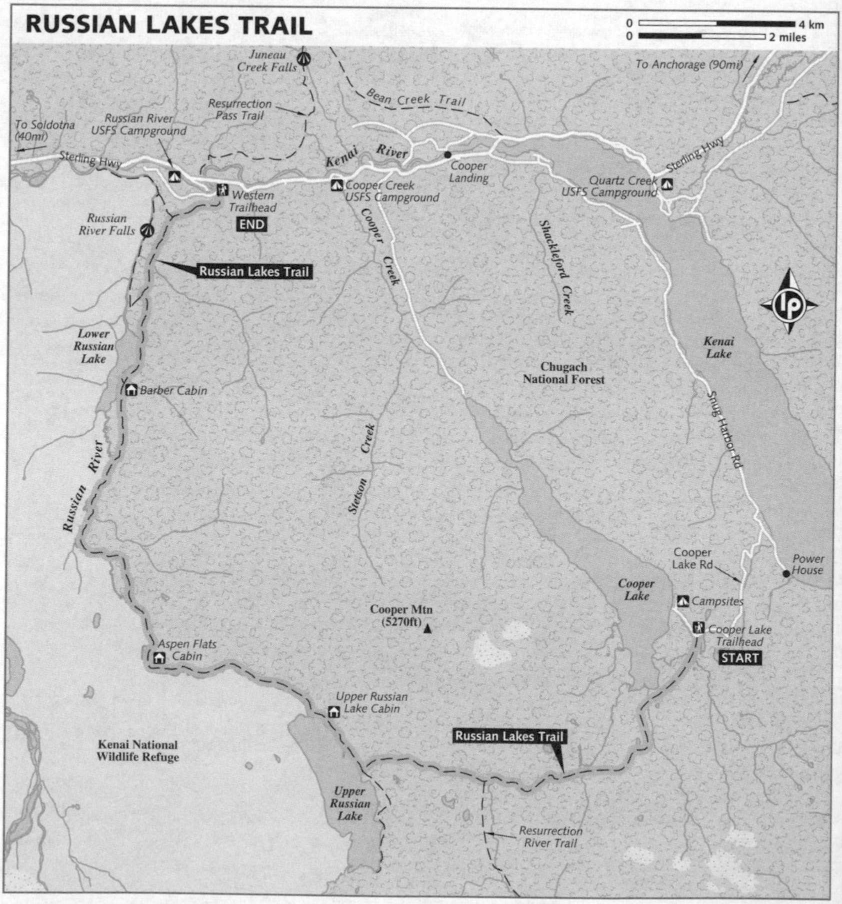

Three **USFS cabins** (☎ 877-444-6777, 518-885-3639; www.recreation.gov; $35-45) are on the trail – Upper Russian Lake Cabin (9 miles from the Cooper Lake trailhead), Aspen Flats Cabin (12 miles from the Cooper Lake trailhead) and Barber Cabin (3 miles from the western trailhead).

Getting Started

It is easiest to begin this trek from the Cooper Lake trailhead, the higher end of the trail. To get there, turn off at Mile 47.8 Sterling Hwy onto Snug Harbor Rd; the road leads south 12 miles to Cooper Lake and ends at a marked parking lot and the trailhead.

The western trailhead is on a side road marked 'Russian River USFS Campground' at Mile 52.7 Sterling Hwy. From there it's just under a mile's hike to the parking lot at the end of the campground road – the beginning of the trail. There is a small fee if you leave a car here. If you're planning to camp at Russian River the night before starting the hike, keep in mind that the camp-ground is extremely popular during the salmon season in June and July.

Shane Shepherd and Owen Wozniak's *50 Hikes in Alaska's Chugach State Park* (2001) covers the state park's best trails and routes near Anchorage.

JOHNSON PASS TRAIL

Section	Miles
Northern trailhead to Bench Creek Bridge	3.8
Bench Creek Bridge to Bench Lake	5.5
Bench Lake to Johnson Pass	0.7
Johnson Pass to Johnson Lake	0.6
Johnson Lake to Johnson Creek Bridge	5.1
Johnson Creek Bridge to Upper Trail Lake	3.7
Upper Trail Lake to Seward Hwy trailhead	3.6

Level of difficulty: medium
Information: **USFS Seward Ranger District** (☎ 907-224-3374; www.fs.fed.us/r10/chugach)

In the same area as the Resurrection Pass and Russian Lakes trails, and nearly as popular, is the Johnson Pass trail (Map p98) – a two-day, 23-mile hike over a 1550ft alpine pass. The route was originally part of the Iditarod trail blazed by prospectors on their way from Seward to the golden beaches of Nome.

Most of the trail is fairly level, which makes for easy hiking and explains its popularity with mountain bikers. Anglers will find Arctic grayling in Bench Lake and rainbow trout in Johnson Lake. Plan to camp at either Johnson Lake or Johnson Pass; these places are above the treeline, making a small stove necessary.

Getting Started

The trail can be hiked from either direction. The northern trailhead is at Mile 64 of the Seward Hwy, 63 miles south of Anchorage, and is reached from a gravel road marked 'Forest Service trail No 10.' The trail goes south over Johnson Pass and then to the shore of Upper Trail Lake before reaching the Seward Hwy again at Mile 32.5, just northwest of the small hamlet of Moose Pass. Hitchhiking from either end of the trail is easy during the summer, or arrangements can be made with Seward Bus Lines (p216).

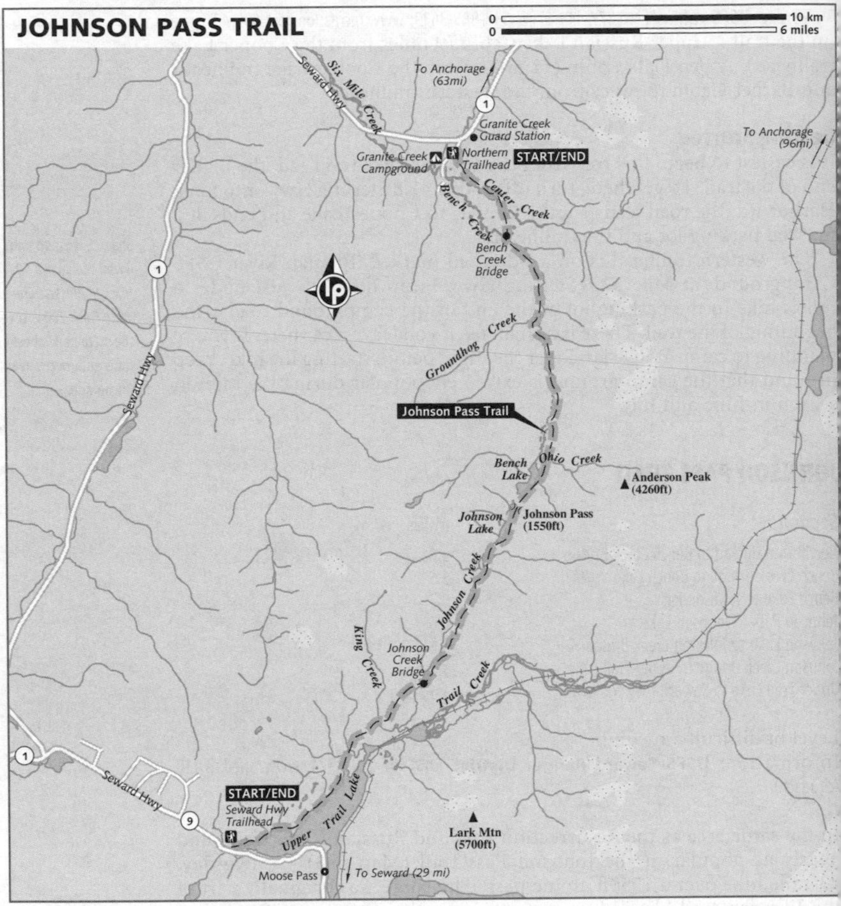

CHENA DOME TRAIL

Section	Miles
Northern trailhead to timberline	3.0
Timberline to military airplane wreck	5.5
Airplane wreck to Chena Dome summit	2.0
Chena Dome Summit to spur to free-use shelter	6.5
Free-use shelter to final descent off ridge	10.0
Final descent to southern trailhead	2.5

Level of difficulty: hard
Information: **Alaska Division of Parks** (☎ 907-451-2705; www.alaskastateparks.org)

Fifty miles east of Fairbanks in the Chena River State Recreation Area this 29.5-mile loop trail makes an ideal three- or four-day backpacking trip for people who enjoy alpine romping. The trail circles the Ange Creek drainage area, with the vast majority of it along tundra ridgetops

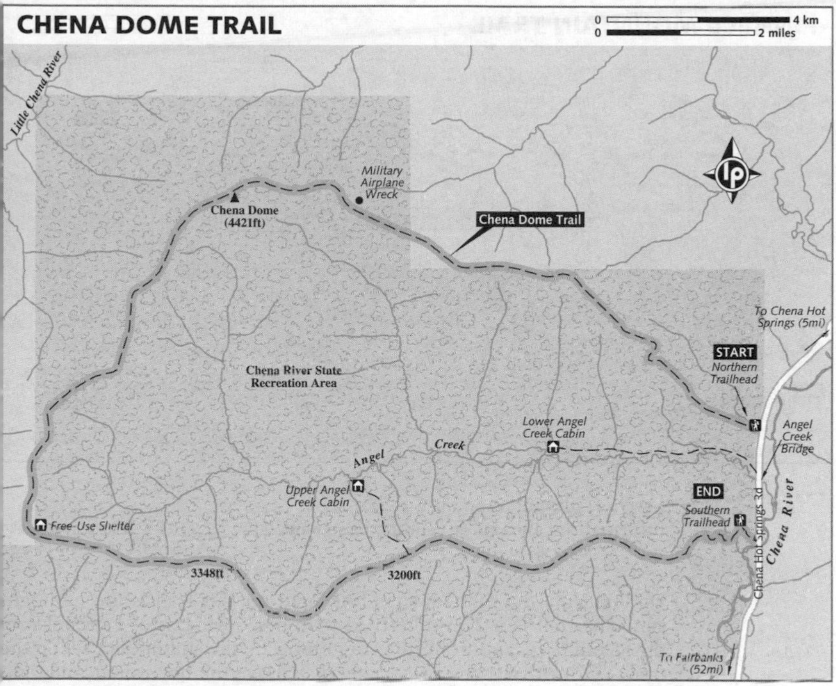

above the treeline. Highlights of the hike are views from Chena Dome, a 4421ft flat-topped ridge; picking blueberries in August; and a free-use shelter.

Getting Started

It's easier to hike the loop by beginning at the northern trailhead at Mile 50.5 Chena Hot Springs Rd. The trailhead is 0.7 miles past Angel Creek Bridge. The southern trailhead is at Mile 49. You can hitch or call **Chena Hot Springs Resort** (☎ 907-451-8104, 800-478-4681; www.chenahotsprings.com), which will provide round-trip van transportation for $45 per person (minimum two people).

Pack a stove as open fires are not permitted in the area, and carry at least 3 quarts (3L) of water per person. Replenish your water bottles from small pools in the tundra. There is a free-use shelter at Mile 17, while a 1.5-mile and 1500ft descent from the main trail will bring you to Upper Angel Creek cabin ($25 per night), which can be used as a place to stay on the third night; reserve through **Alaska Division of Parks** (☎ 907-451-2705; www.dnr.state.ak.us/parks/cabins/onlineres.htm).

PINNELL MOUNTAIN TRAIL

Section	Miles
Eagle Summit trailhead to Porcupine Dome	6.0
Porcupine Dome to Ptarmigan Creek shelter	4.0
Ptarmigan Creek shelter to North Fork shelter	8.0
North Fork shelter to Twelvemile Summit trailhead	9.5

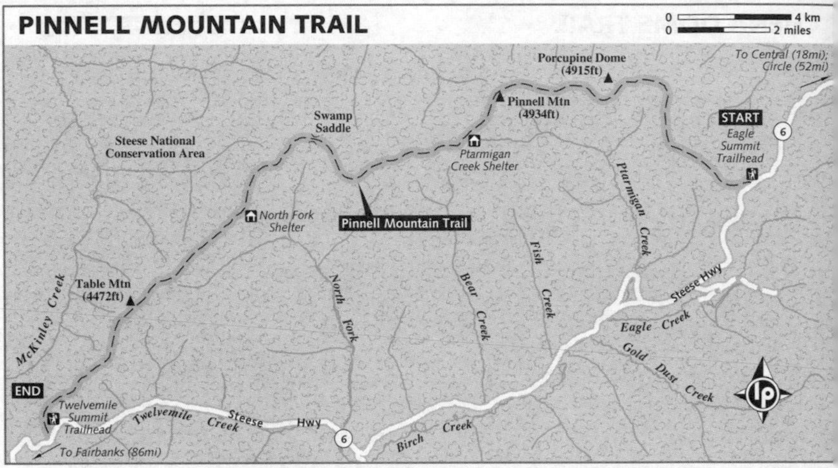

Level of difficulty: medium to hard
Information: **Bureau of Land Management** (BLM; ☎ 907-474-2200; aurora.ak.blm.gov)

Undoubtedly the most outstanding sight on this trail is the midnight sun. The trail is a 27.3-mile trek, 85 miles northeast of Fairbanks on the Steese Hwy, and from June 18 to June 25, the sun doesn't set on the trail. You can view the sun sitting just above the horizon at midnight from several high points on the trail, including at the Eagle Summit trailhead.

Hike with the locals of the Fairbanks Area Hiking Club, which organizes weekly treks throughout the summer. See www.fairbankshiking.org for more information.

The route is mostly along tundra ridge tops that lie above 3500ft and can be steep and rugged, but the tundra wildflowers are unmatched in most of the state and the views are spectacular, with the Alaska Range visible to the south and the Yukon Flats to the north. Water is scarce in the alpine sections, so bring plenty.

Getting Started

This is a three-day trek, covering 8 to 10 miles a day. Most hikers start at the Eagle Summit trailhead on Mile 107.3 Steese Hwy, the higher end of the trail. The Twelvemile Summit trailhead is closer to Fairbanks, at Mile 85 Steese Hwy. Two free-use shelters (North Fork shelter and Ptarmigan Creek shelter) along the trail are great places to wait out a storm or cook a meal, but bring a tent with good bug netting. Take at least 2 quarts (2L) of water per person and refill your supply at every opportunity at snow patches, springs or tundra pools.

Traffic on the Steese Hwy this far out of Fairbanks is a steady trickle. Hitchhiking is possible if you are willing to give up a day getting there. Even those who bring a car will end up hitchhiking back to the trailhead where they began.

Check with the **Fairbanks Visitors Bureau** (☎ 907-456-5774; www.explorefairbanks.com) to see if anyone is running a van service up the Steese Hwy. Otherwise, the best alternative to hitchhiking is to rent a car and take the opportunity to drive to Central or the wilderness town of Circle on the Yukon River. **Rent-A-Wreck** (☎ 907-452-1606, 800-478-1606) in Fairbanks has small cars for $43 a day.

WHITE MOUNTAINS SUMMIT TRAIL

Section	Miles
Summit trailhead to Wickersham Dome	6.0
Wickersham Dome to 3100ft high point	4.0
3100ft high point to Wickersham Creek Trail junction	8.0
Wickersham Creek Trail junction to Borealis-Le Fevre Cabin	2.0

Level of difficulty: hard
Information: **Bureau of Land Management** (BLM; ☎ 907-474-2200; aurora.ak.blm.gov)

The Bureau of Land Management (BLM), which maintains the Pinnell Mountain Trail, also administers the White Mountains National Recreation Area, including the Summit Trail. This 20-mile, one-way route was built for summer use and has boardwalks over the wettest areas. The trail winds through dense spruce forest, traverses scenic alpine ridgetops and Arctic tundra, and ends at Beaver Creek, in the foothills of the majestic White Mountains.

On the opposite bank of the creek from the trail is the **Borealis-Le Fevre Cabin** (☎ 800-437-7021), which can be reserved, but you must bring a tent, as Beaver Creek is rarely low enough to ford safely. The grayling fishing is outstanding here, but most parties stop short of the river, camping above the treeline so they don't have to deal with swamps near the end.

Fording rivers is common in the Alaska backcountry and the best time to do it is early morning when the water is usually the lowest.

Discover the city with the best hiking in Alaska in *Juneau Trails* (2005) by Alaska Geographic – a handy and inexpensive guide with excellent maps to 30 trails.

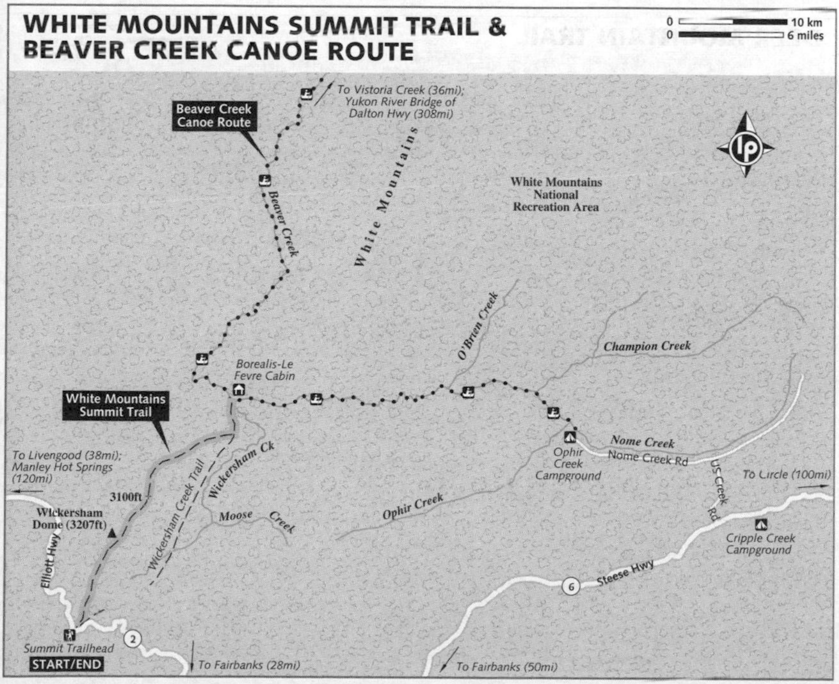

Hiking in for a day of fishing is a five-day adventure. Even if hikers stop short of Beaver Creek, they still require two or three days to camp near the highest point along the route. The Summit trailhead is at Mile 28 Elliott Hwy, 31 miles north of Fairbanks. Bring water as it is scarce in the alpine sections.

Getting Started

Hitchhiking is generally more difficult on the Elliott Hwy than the Steese Hwy. Contact **Dalton Highway Express** (☎ 907-474-3555; www.daltonhighwayexpress.com) about possible drop-off or pickup at the trailhead. The company runs vans to Prudhoe Bay and will try to accommodate a White Mountains request if possible.

Once you get there, don't confuse the White Mountains SummitT-trail (also called the summer trail), which was made for hikers, with the Wickersham Creek Trail. The Wickersham Creek, or winter trail, departs from the same trailhead but was cut primarily for snow machines, cross-country skiers and people using snowshoes.

SeaTrails provides brief descriptions and maps that can be downloaded for more than 80 trails in 19 communities in Southeast Alaska on their site at www.seatrails.org.

DEER MOUNTAIN TRAIL

Section	Miles
Deer Mountain trailhead to Deer Mountain summit	3.1
Deer Mountain summit to Blue Lake	2.2
Blue Lake to John Mountain Trail	2.0
John Mountain to Upper Silvis Lake	2.0
Upper Silvis Lake to S Tongass Hwy	2.0

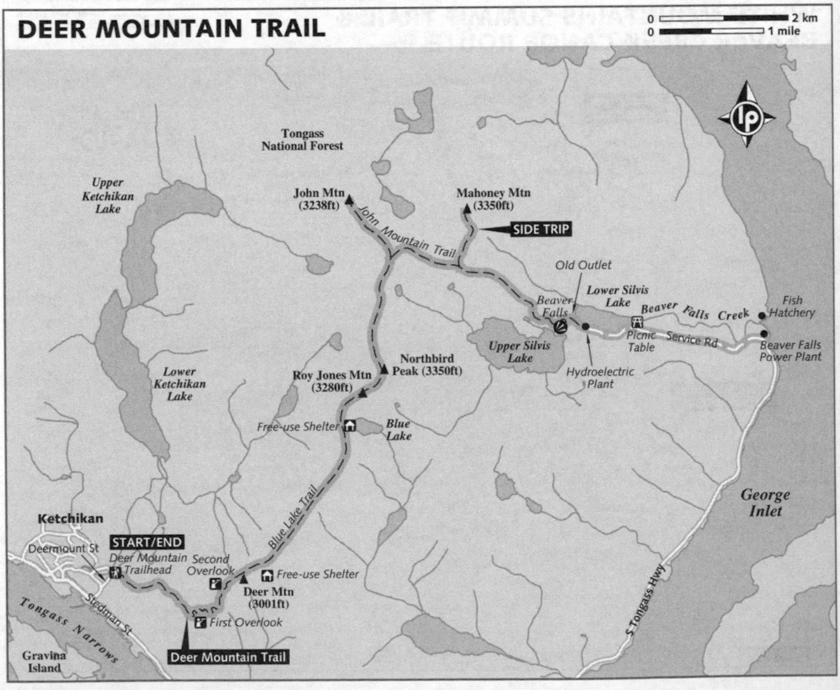

Level of difficulty: medium to hard
Information: **Southeast Alaska Visitor Center** (☎ 907-228-6220; www.fs.fed.us/r10/tongass)

Located in Ketchikan, the Deer Mountain Trail is part of a challenging, overnight alpine trail system incorporating three trails. It's an 11-mile trip, beginning with the 3-mile Deer Mountain Trail that leads into the Blue Lake Trail. This path follows a natural route along an alpine ridge that extends 4 miles north to John Mountain. From here, hikers can return to the Ketchikan road system by taking the John Mountain Trail for 2 miles to Upper Silvis Lake and then following an old service road from the hydroelectric plant on Lower Silvis Lake to a parking lot off the S Tongass Hwy.

A quarter of a mile before reaching the Deer Mountain summit, you pass the junction with Blue Lake Trail and the posted trail to the Deer Mountain cabin, a free-use shelter above the treeline. Within 2 miles the Blue Lake Trail reaches Blue Lake, a popular camping area that, at 2700ft, is above the treeline in a scenic alpine setting.

Juneau advocacy group Trail Mix offers trail updates, outings and opportunities to help repair local paths at www.juneautrails.org.

Getting Started

The trailhead for the Deer Mountain Trail can be reached by following a road from the corner of Fair and Deermount Sts in Ketchikan. Just before a landfill, a side road posted 'Deer Mountain' leads you a short distance to the trailhead.

To get to the start of the John Mountain Trail, head east on S Tongass Hwy for 12.9 miles to the Beaver Falls Power Plant. From here there is a 2-mile hike along an old access road from the power plant at the tidewater to the hydroelectric plant on the south side of Lower Silvis Lake. From the road you'll find the start of a trail that climbs steeply to the Upper Silvis Lake. The John Mountain Trail begins at the old outlet at the western end of the upper lake.

PETERSBURG LAKE TRAIL

Section	Miles
Kupreanof Island dock to Saltwater Arm	2.0
Saltwater Arm to Petersburg Creek	2.5
Petersburg Creek to Petersburg Lake Cabin	6.0
Petersburg Lake Cabin to Portage Bay	7.0
Portage Bay to Salt Chuck East Cabin	4.5

Level of difficulty: medium
Information: **USFS Petersburg Ranger District** (☎ 907-772-3871; www.fs.fed.us/r10/tongass)

Across the Wrangell Narrows from the fishing community of Petersburg is the Petersburg Lake Trail (Map p104), the first segment of a trail system collectively known as the Portage Mountain Loop. The Petersburg Lake Trail is well planked and allows backpackers access to the Petersburg Lake cabin in the wilderness without the expense of bush-plane travel. However, to hike further to Portage Bay or Salt Chuck along the Portage Mountain Loop requires wilderness experience, and map and compass skills, as the trails are not planked or maintained, and are only lightly marked.

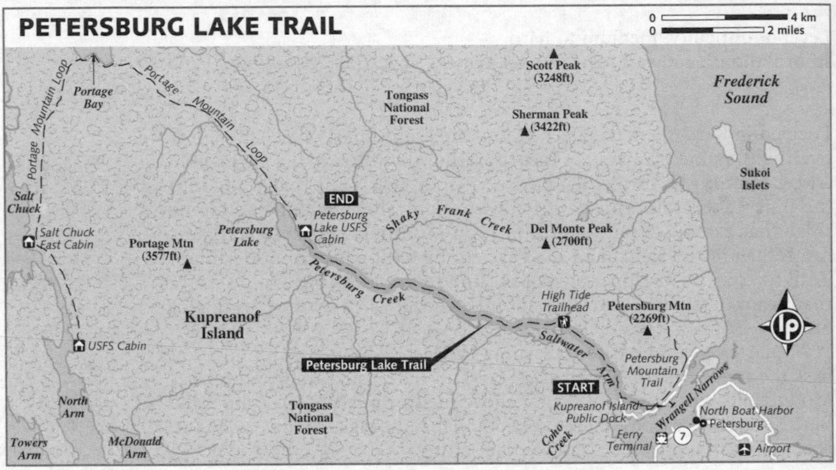

Bring a fishing rod, as there are good spots for catching Dolly Varden and rainbow trout. In August and early September there are large coho and sockeye salmon runs throughout the area, attracting anglers and bears.

The trek begins at the Kupreanof Island public dock. From the dock a partial boardwalk leads southwest for a mile past a handful of cabins, then turns northwest up the tidewater arm of the creek almost directly across Wrangell Narrows from the ferry terminal. A well-planked trail begins at the saltwater arm and continues along the northern side of Petersburg Creek to the **Petersburg Lake USFS cabin** (☎ 877-444-6777, 518-885-3639; www.recreation.gov; $35). From the cabin, Portage Mountain Loop continues north to Portage Bay.

Getting Started

The only hitch to this trip is getting across Wrangell Narrows to the public dock on Kupreanof Island. Either hitch a ride at the North Boat Harbor or call **Tongass Kayak Adventures** (☎ 907-772-4600; www.tongasskayak.com), which runs hikers across the channel for $25 per person.

You'll need good waterproof clothing as well as rubber boots. Bring a tent or plan to reserve the USFS cabin at least two months in advance.

Hiking with Grizzlies (2006) by former Denali National Park bear observer Tim Rubbert tells you how to travel into grizzly country to make sure you come back out.

DIXIE PASS ROUTE

Section	Miles
McCarthy Rd to Dixie Pass trailhead	3.8
Dixie Pass trailhead to Strelna Creek	3.0
Strelna Creek to Dixie Pass	8.5

Level of difficulty: hard
Information: **Wrangell-St Elias National Park** (☎ 907-822-5234; www.nps.gov/wrst)

Even by Alaskan standards, Wrangell-St Elias National Park is a large tract of wilderness. At 20,625 sq miles, it's the largest US national park, contains the most peaks over 14,500ft in North America, and has the greatest concentration of glaciers on the continent.

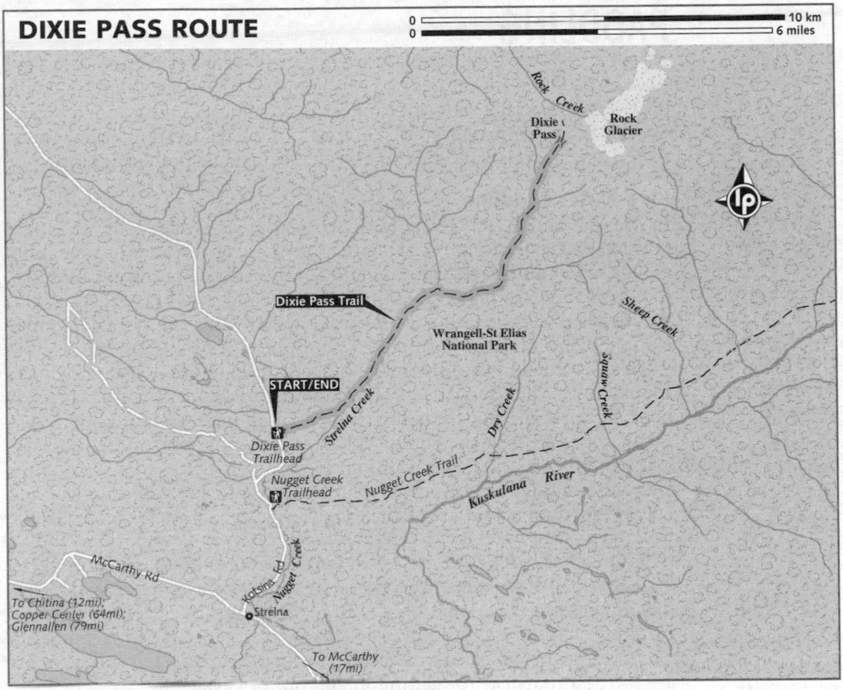

Within this huge, remote park, Dixie Pass provides the best wilderness adventure that doesn't require a bush-plane charter. The trek from the trailhead up to Dixie Pass and return is 24 miles. Plan to camp there at least one or two additional days to take in the alpine beauty and investigate the nearby ridges. Such an itinerary requires three or four days and is moderately hard.

To get to the Dixie Pass trailhead, hike 2.5 miles up Kotsina Rd from Strelna and then another 1.3 miles along Kotsina Rd after the Nugget Creek Trail splits off to the northeast. The trailhead is on the right-hand side of Kotsina Rd; look for a marker, usually a pile of rocks with a stick in it.

The route begins as a level path for 3 miles to Strelna Creek, and then continues along the west side of the creek for another 3 miles to the first major confluence. After fording the creek, it's 5 to 6 miles to the pass; along the way you'll cross two more confluences and hike through an interesting gorge. The ascent to Dixie Pass is fairly easy to spot, and once there you'll find superb scenery, and alpine ridges to explore.

Greg Fensterman will keep you from getting lost on 50 hikes and backpacking treks in *Hiking Alaska's Wrangell-St Elias National Park* (2008), which includes GPS waypoints.

Getting Started

Collect supplies in Copper Center, then stop at the park headquarters to complete a backcountry trip itinerary and get your USGS quadrangle maps (Valdez C-1 and McCarthy C-8). To arrange a drop-off from Glennallen or Chitina and a pickup at Nugget Creek/Kotsina Rd, 14.5 miles east of Chitina, call **Backcountry Connection** (☎ 907-822-5292; www.alaska-backcountry-tours.com), which runs a daily bus to McCarthy. The one-way fare from Glennallen to McCarthy, with a drop-off and pickup at Kotsina Rd, is $109.

PADDLING

Alaskan paddling adventures range from open-water sea kayaking and rafting rivers thundering with white water to portaging a canoe through a chain of calm lakes. No matter your skill level or how wild you like your water, there are many opportunities for an extended paddle in the Far North.

Blue-Water Paddling

In Alaska, 'blue water' refers to the coastal areas of the state, which are characterized by extreme tidal fluctuations, cold water, and the possibility of high winds and waves. Throughout Southeast and Southcentral Alaska, the open canoe is replaced with the kayak, and blue-water paddling is the means of escape into coastal areas such as Muir Inlet in Glacier Bay National Park or Tracy Arm Fjord, south of Juneau.

Held in mid-May in Anchorage, the annual Alaska Sea Kayaking Symposium (www.aksks.org) is a weekend of classes, product demonstrations, lectures and kayak-related activities.

Tidal fluctuations are the main concern in blue-water areas. Paddlers should always pull their boats above the high-tide mark and keep a tide book in the same pouch as their topographic map. Cold coastal water, rarely above 45°F in the summer, makes capsizing worse than unpleasant. With a life jacket, survival time in the water is less than two hours; without one there is no time. If your kayak flips, stay with the boat and attempt to right it and crawl back in. Trying to swim to shore in Arctic water is risky at best.

Framed backpacks are useless in kayaks; gear is best stowed in duffel bags or small day packs. Carry a large supply of assorted plastic bags, including several garbage bags. All gear, especially sleeping bags and clothing, should be stowed in plastic bags, as water tends to seep in even when you seal yourself in with a cockpit skirt. Over-the-calf rubber boots are the best footwear for getting in and out of kayaks.

Alaskan waters are generally too cold for sea kayakers to wear Neoprene booties. Most paddlers opt for calf-high rubber boots, often referred to as Southeast sneakers.

White-Water Paddling

Throughout Alaska's history, rivers have been the traditional travel routes through the rugged terrain. Many rivers can be paddled in canoes; others, due to extensive stretches of white water, are better handled in rafts or kayaks.

Alaska's rivers vary, but they share characteristics not found on many rivers in the Lower 48: water levels tend to change rapidly, while many rivers are heavily braided and boulder-strewn. Take care in picking out the right channel to avoid spending most of the day pulling your boat off gravel. You can survive flipping your canoe in an Alaskan river, but you'll definitely want a plan of action if you do.

Much of the equipment for white-water canoeists is the same as it is for blue-water paddlers. Tie everything into the canoe; you never know when you might hit a whirlpool or a series of standing waves. Wear a life jacket at all times. Many paddlers stock their life jacket with insect repellent, water-proof matches and other survival gear in case they flip and get separated from their boat.

The Alaska River Guide (2008) by Karen Jettmar is the complete river guide for Alaska, covering 100 trips, from the Chilkat in the Southeast to Colville on the Arctic slope.

Research the river you want to run and make sure you can handle the level of difficulty. The class categories:

Class I – easy Mostly flat water with occasional series of mild rapids.

Class II – medium Frequent stretches of rapids with waves up to 3ft high and easy chutes, ledges and falls.

Class III – difficult Features numerous rapids with high, irregular waves and difficult chutes and falls that often require scouting. These rivers are for experienced paddlers who use kayaks or rafts.

Class IV – very difficult Long stretches of irregular waves, powerful eddies and even constricted canyons. Scouting is mandatory. Suitable for rafts or white-water kayaks, and paddlers must wear helmets.

Class V – extremely difficult Continuous violent rapids, powerful rollers and high, unavoidable waves and haystacks. These rivers are only for paddlers with white-water kayaks who are proficient in the Eskimo roll.
Class VI – highest level of difficulty Rarely run except by very experienced kayakers under ideal conditions.

MISTY FIORDS NATIONAL MONUMENT

Section	Miles
Ketchikan to Thorne Arm	13.0
Thorne Arm to Point Alava	9.0
Point Alava to Winstanley Island	21.0
Winstanley Island to Rudyerd Bay	9.0
Rudyerd Bay to Walker Cove	10.0

With its tips, safety advice and contacts, the website for Knik Canoers & Kayakers (www.kck.org) is a great start for anybody thinking about a paddling adventure in Alaska.

Level of difficulty: open water
Information: **Southeast Alaska Discovery Center** (☎ 907-228-6220; www.fs.fed.us/r10/tongass)

The Misty Fiords National Monument encompasses 3594 sq miles of wilderness and lies between two impressive fjords – Behm Canal (117 miles long) and Portland Canal (72 miles long). The two natural canals give the preserve its extraordinarily deep and long fjords with sheer granite walls that rise thousands of feet out of the water. Misty Fiords is well named; annual rainfall is 14ft.

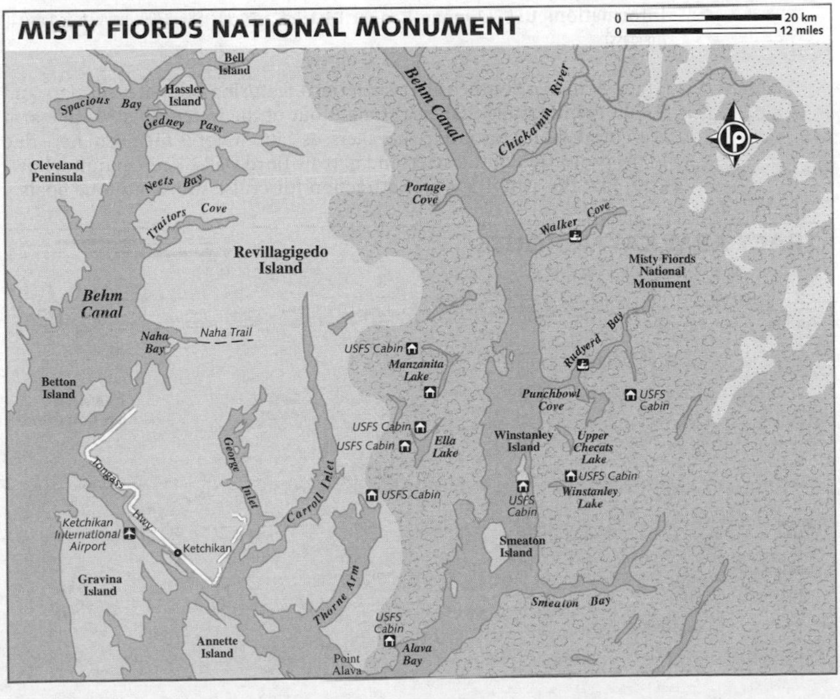

The destinations for many kayakers are the smaller but impressive fjords of Walker Cove and Punchbowl Cove in Rudyerd Bay, off Behm Canal. Dense spruce-hemlock, rain forest is the most common vegetation type throughout the monument, and sea lions, harbor seals, killer whales, brown and black bears, mountain goats, moose and bald eagles can all be seen.

Experienced kayakers can paddle out of Ketchikan (a seven- to 12-day trip) but most paddlers arrange to be dropped off deep in Behm Canal near the protected water of Rudyerd Bay.

Misty Fiords has 15 **USFS cabins** (☎ 877-444-6777, 518-885-3639; www.recreation.gov; $25-45), which should be reserved in advance. Two paddles – Alava Bay and Winstanley Island in Behm Canal – allow kayakers to end the day at the doorstep of a cabin.

Getting Started

Southeast Sea Kayaks (☎ 907-225-1258, 800-287-1607; www.kayakketchikan.com), beside the Ketchikan waterfront, has single/double kayaks for $49/59 per day and discounts apply for longer rentals. This wonderful outfitter can assist in all aspects of a self-guided trip, including boat transportation to Behm Canal. The round-trip cost is $250 to $350 per person depending on where they drop you off. It's best to reserve kayaks well before the summer season.

You can't do this trip without good rain gear and a backpacker's stove – wood in the monument is often too wet for campfires. Be prepared for extended rain periods and make sure all gear is sealed in plastic bags.

TRACY ARM KAYAK ROUTE

Level of difficulty: open water
Information: **USFS Juneau Ranger District** (☎ 907-586-8790; www.fs.fed.us/r10/tongass)

Tracy Arm is a Southeast Alaskan fjord featuring tidewater glaciers and 2000ft granite walls that rise straight out of the water. This 30-mile arm is an ideal choice for novice kayakers, as calm water is the norm here due to the protection of the steep and narrow fjord walls. Keep in mind, however, that the arm is a major attraction for cruise ships and tour boats.

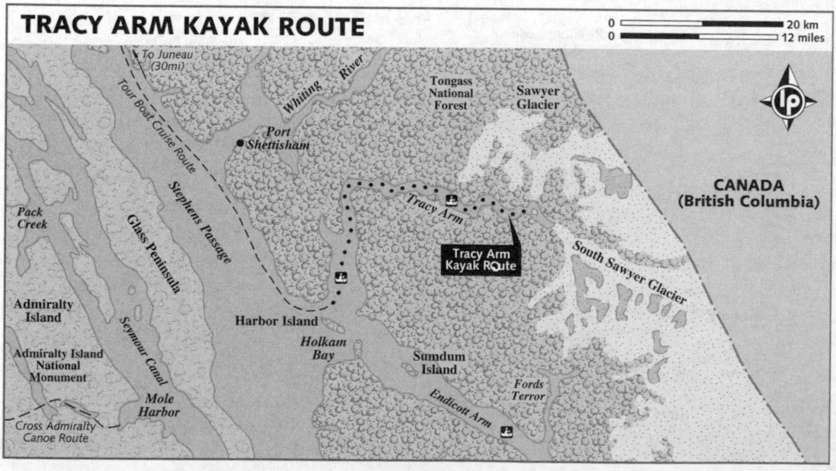

If you have more experience as a kayaker, consider exploring the other fjords that adjoin Tracy Arm at Holkam Bay. Just to the south is Endicott Arm, another 30-mile fjord that was carved by Dawes and North Dawes Glaciers. It is the icebergs from these glaciers, some as large as three-story buildings, that often make it into the main shipping lanes of Stephens Passage, delighting travelers on the state ferries. The other advantage of paddling Endicott Arm over Tracy Arm is that there are considerably more places to pitch a tent at night. The only camping spots in the first half of Tracy Arm are two valleys almost across from each other, eight miles north along the fjord, and a small island at the head of the fjord.

Before you purchase anything for your Alaskan adventure, see what the Gear Junkie thinks about it at thegearjunkie.com.

Getting Started

The departure point for Tracy Arm-Fords Terror Wilderness Area is Juneau. Kayaks can be rented in Auke Bay from **Alaska Boat & Kayak** (☎ 907-364-2333; www.juneaukayak.com) for $50/70 per day for a single/double kayak, with discounts for multiday rentals. **Adventure Bound Alaska** (☎ 907-463-2509, 800-228-3875; www.adventureboundalaska.com) charges $175 per person for drop-off and pickup in Tracy Arm. Drop-offs and pickups make the trip considerably easier; otherwise it's a two- or three-day paddle in open water.

HOONAH–TENAKEE SPRINGS KAYAK ROUTE

Level of difficulty: open water
Information: **USFS Juneau Ranger District** (☎ 907-586-8790; www.fs.fed.us/r10/tongass)

This 40-mile paddle follows Port Frederick and Tenakee Inlet from Hoonah to Tenakee Springs (Map p110) and includes a portage of 100yd or so. You pass a depressing number of clear-cuts around Hoonah and up Port Frederick, but there are few other signs of civilization once beyond the villages. The area in the Tongass National Forest consists of rugged and densely forested terrain populated by brown bears, often seen feeding along the shore.

Carry a tide book, and reach the portage at high tide. There's boot-sucking mud along the portage, but take heart, it's just a short walk over a low ridge to the next inlet. After the paddle, Tenakee Springs has natural hot springs to melt away those kayaking aches.

Getting Started

This adventure is good for those on a budget but with lots of time, as the **Alaska Marine Hwy** (☎ 800-642-0066; www.ferryalaska.com) connects both Hoonah and Tenakee Springs to Juneau. The one-way fare from Juneau to Hoonah/Tenakee Springs with a kayak is $52/57.

It's best to start the paddle from Hoonah in order to end the trip in Tenakee Springs, a charming village. However, this has to be planned carefully, as there is only one ferry every three to five days from Tenakee Springs. Kayaks can be rented in Juneau from **Alaska Boat & Kayak** (☎ 907-364-2333; www.juneaukayak.com).

GLACIER BAY – MUIR INLET

Section	Miles
Mt Wright to Wachusett Inlet	16.0
Wachusett Inlet to Riggs Glacier	9.0
Riggs Glacier to Muir Glacier	8.0
Muir Glacier to Mt Wright	33.0

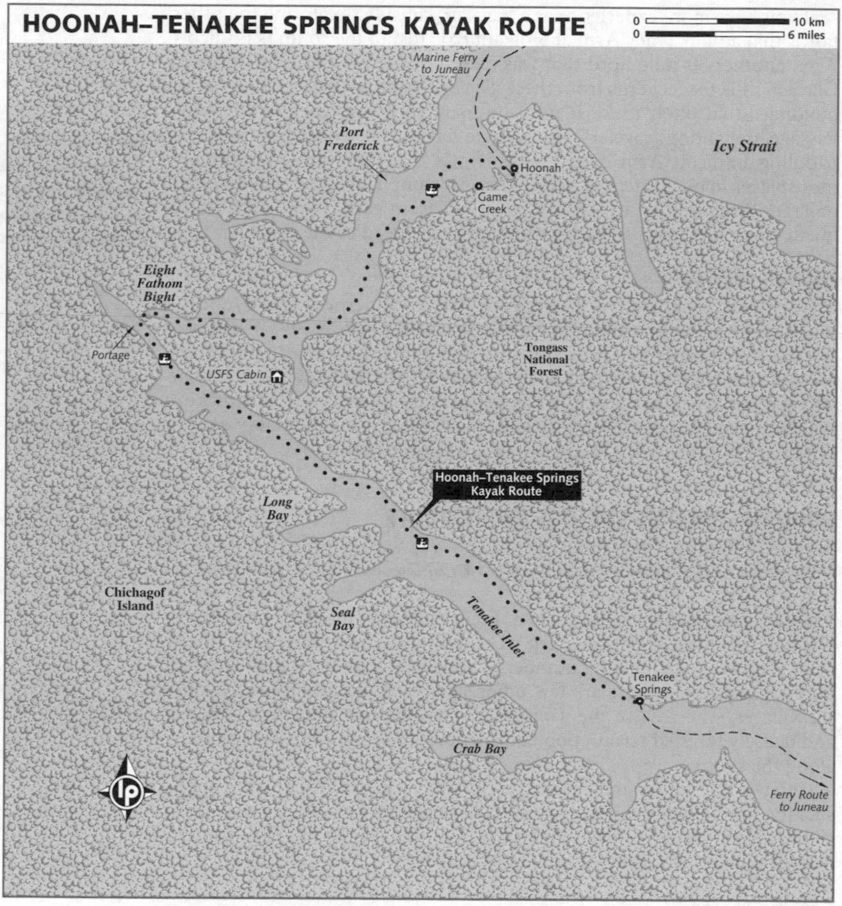

Level of difficulty: open water
Information: **Glacier Bay National Park** (☎ 907-697-2230; www.nps.gov/glba)

Glacier Bay is a kayaker's paradise. With the stunning alpine scenery of the Fairweather Mountains, views of many glaciers, and abundant marine wildlife, it's easy to understand the park's attraction to blue-water paddlers. The drawbacks are the cost of getting there, the cost of getting up the bay with a kayak and the armada of cruise ships that visit. However, by utilizing the tour boat within the park, you can put together a paddle that stays totally in Muir Inlet (East Arm), Glacier Bay's designated wilderness area where motorized vessels are banned.

The tour boat will drop you off near the entrance of the inlet, allowing you to avoid the long paddle from Bartlett Cove, the park headquarters. Many kayakers then travel the length of the inlet to McBride, Riggs and Muir Glaciers at the north end before returning for a pickup. Such a trip would require four or six days of paddling and would be roughly a $600 to $800 per person side trip from Juneau. Those with more time but less money can book just a drop-off and then paddle back to Bartlett Cove, an eight- to 10-day trip. A round-trip paddle out of Bartlett Cove to the glaciers of Muir Inlet is a two-week adventure for most people.

Getting Started

It's best to arrange both kayak rental and tour-boat passage in advance. Within the park **Glacier Bay Sea Kayaks** (☎ 907-697-2257; www.glacierbayseakayaks.com) rents single/double kayaks for $40/60 a day. The **Fairweather Express** (☎ 907-264-4600, 888-229-8687; www.visitglacierbay.com), which departs daily at 7:30am, provides drop-offs and pickups near Mt Wright at the mouth of Muir Inlet from mid-May to late September. The round-trip is $214 per person. Glacier Bay Sea Kayaks will also book the drop-off for you.

Keep in mind that the Alaska Marine Hwy does not service Gustavus. That leaves flying as the only option, with the average round-trip ticket costing around $200. See p177 for further information about Glacier Bay National Park.

In a recent study in Alaska, bear spray, when used correctly, proved to be 92% effective in deterring attacks, working equally well on brown and black bears.

CROSS ADMIRALTY ISLAND CANOE ROUTE

Section	Miles
Angoon to Salt Lake Tidal Falls	10.0
Tidal Falls to Davidson Lake portage	2.5
Portage to Davidson Lake	3.5
Davidson Lake to Hasselborg Lake portage	6.0
Portage to Hasselborg Lake	1.7
Hasselborg Lake to Beaver Lake portage	2.0
Portage to Beaver Lake	0.5
Beaver Lake to Mole Harbor portage	3.0
Portage to Mole Harbor	2.5

Level of difficulty: mostly Class I
Information: **Admiralty Island National Monument** (☎ 907-586-8800; www.fs.fed.us/r10/tongass/districts/admiralty)

Admiralty Island National Monument, 50 miles southwest of Juneau, is the site of one of the most interesting canoe routes in Alaska. This preserve is a fortress of dense coastal forest and ragged peaks, where brown bears outnumber anything else on the island, including humans. The Cross Admiralty Island Canoe Route (Map p112) is a 32-mile paddle that spans the center of the island from the village of Angoon to Mole Harbor.

Although the majority of the route consists of calm lakes connected by streams and portages, the 10-mile paddle from Angoon to Salt Lake Tidal is subject to strong tides that must be carefully timed. Avoid Kootznahoo Inlet, as its tidal currents are extremely difficult to negotiate; instead, paddle through the maze of islands south of it. Leave Angoon at low tide, just before slack tide so that the water will push you into Mitchell Bay.

The traditional route is to continue on to Mole Harbor via Davidson Lake, Lake Guerin, Hasselborg Lake, Beaver Lake and Lake Alexander, all connected by portages. Because of the logistics and cost of being picked up at Mole Harbor with a canoe, most paddlers stop in the heart of the chain and after a day or two of fishing backtrack to Angoon to utilize the Alaska Marine Hwy for a return to Juneau.

There are good camping spots at Tidal Falls on the eastern end of Salt Lake, on the islands at the south end of Hasselborg Lake and on the portage

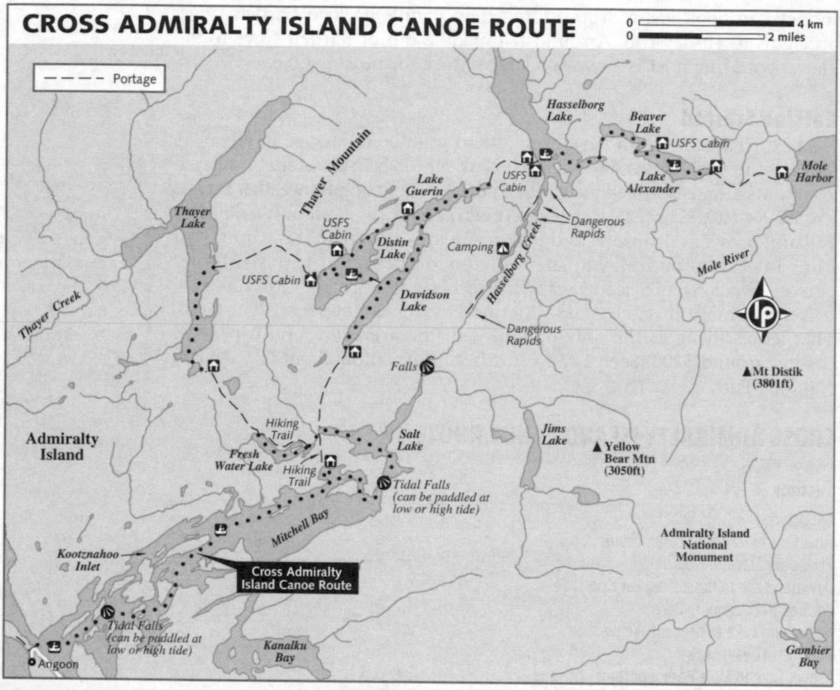

between Davidson Lake and Distin Lake. For those who can plan in advance, there are several **USFS cabins** (☎ 877-444-6777, 518-885-3639; www.recreation.gov; $35-45) along the route, including those on Hasselborg Lake, Lake Alexander and Distin Lake.

Grab *The Kenai Canoe Trails* (1995) by Daniel L Quick for a guide to the wildlife refuge's Swan Lake and Swanson River canoe routes, with maps, fishing information and photos.

Getting Started

This adventure begins with a ferry trip to the village of Angoon from Juneau where you can rent a canoe with one-way fare up to $37 plus another $22 to carry a canoe onboard. Carefully set up your trip around the ferry schedule, but a boat arrives at Angoon roughly every two to three days.

Rent your canoe in Juneau from **Alaska Boat & Kayak** (☎ 907-364-2333; www.juneaukayak.com; $50 a day), which is conveniently located near the ferry terminal in Auke Bay.

Learn to paddle in Homer at the Alaska Kayak School (☎ 907-235-2090; www.alaskakayakschool.com), which teaches sea kayaking, white-water kayaking and canoeing.

SWAN LAKE CANOE ROUTE

Level of difficulty: Class I
Information: **Kenai National Wildlife Refuge** (☎ 907-262-7021; kenai.fws.gov)

In the northern lowlands of the Kenai National Wildlife Refuge there is a chain of rivers, lakes, streams and portages that make up the Swan Lake canoe route. The trip is perfect for novice canoeists, as rough water is rarely a problem and portages do not exceed half a mile.

Fishing for rainbow trout is good in many lakes, and wildlife is plentiful; a paddle on this route could result in sightings of moose, bears, beavers or a variety of waterfowl.

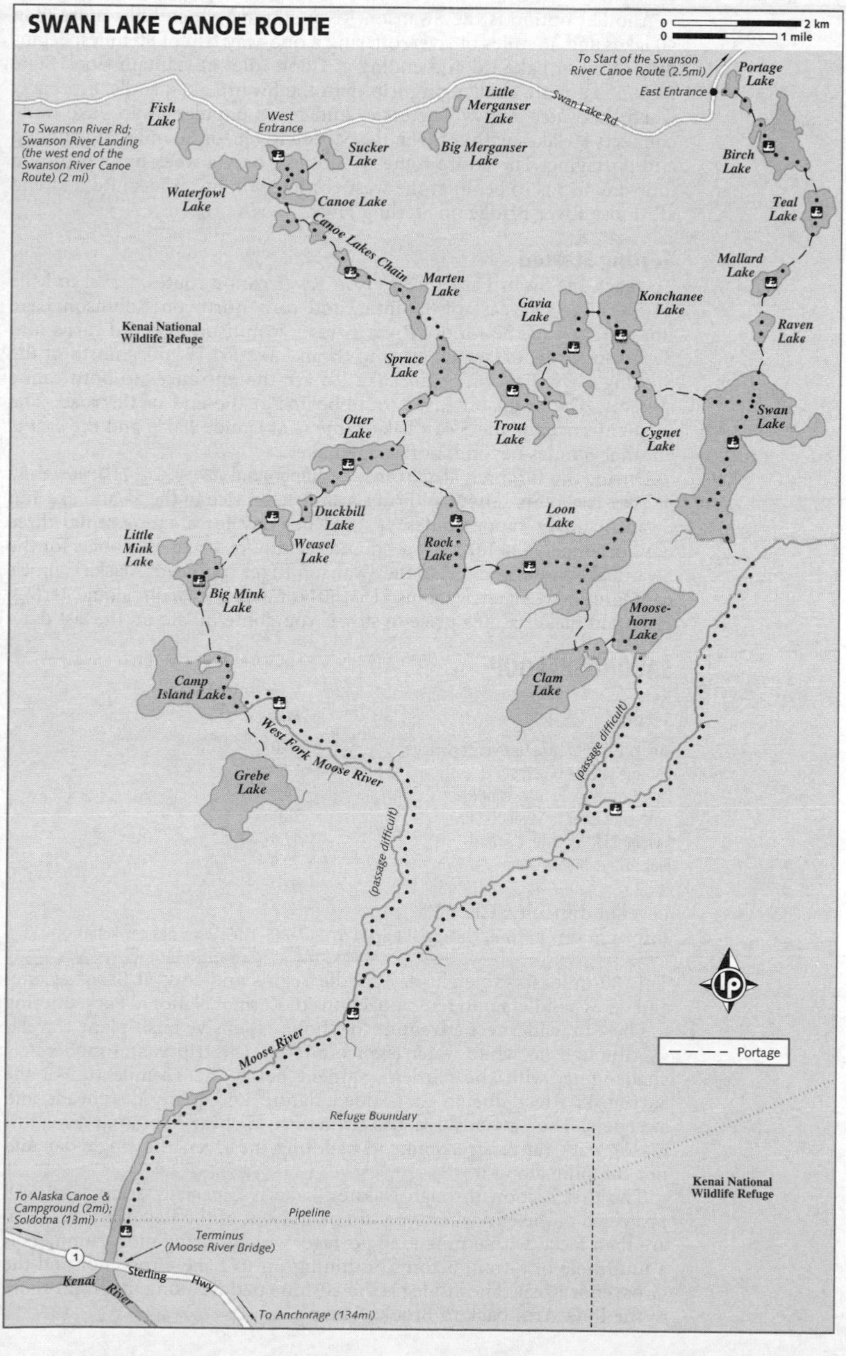
SWAN LAKE CANOE ROUTE
0 2 km
0 1 mile
To Start of the Swanson River Canoe Route (2.5mi)
Portage Lake
East Entrance
Swan Lake Rd
Little Merganser Lake
Big Merganser Lake
Fish Lake
West Entrance
To Swanson River Rd; Swanson River Landing (the west end of the Swanson River Canoe Route) (2 mi)
Sucker Lake
Waterfowl Lake
Canoe Lake
Canoe Lakes Chain
Birch Lake
Teal Lake
Mallard Lake
Raven Lake
Marten Lake
Gavia Lake
Konchanee Lake
Kenai National Wildlife Refuge
Spruce Lake
Trout Lake
Cygnet Lake
Swan Lake
Otter Lake
Duckbill Lake
Weasel Lake
Rock Lake
Loon Lake
Little Mink Lake
Big Mink Lake
Moose-horn Lake
Clam Lake
Camp Island Lake
West Fork Moose River
Grebe Lake
(passage difficult)
(passage difficult)
Moose River
Portage
Refuge Boundary
Kenai National Wildlife Refuge
To Alaska Canoe & Campground (2mi); Soldotna (13mi)
Pipeline
Terminus (Moose River Bridge)
1
Sterling Hwy
Kenai River
To Anchorage (134mi)

Another option is the Swanson River system, which links more than 40 lakes and 46 miles of river, offering a one-way trip of 80 miles, beginning at Swan Lake Rd and ending at Cook Inlet in Captain Cook State Park. It's a more challenging trip than the Swan Lake paddle, especially when the water is low. The easier and more popular Swan Lake route connects 30 lakes with forks in the Moose River for 60 miles of paddling and portaging. The entire route would take only a week but a common four-day trip is to begin at the west entrance on Swan Lake Rd and end at Moose River Bridge on Sterling Hwy.

Getting Started

To reach the Swan Lake or Swanson River canoe routes, travel to Mile 84 Sterling Hwy east of Soldotna and turn north on Robinson Lake Rd, just west of the Moose River Bridge. Robinson Lake Rd turns into Swanson River Rd, which leads to Swan Lake Rd 17 miles north of the Sterling Hwy. East on Swan Lake Rd are the entrances to both canoe systems. The Swanson River route begins at the end of the road. The west entrance for the Swan Lake route is at Canoe Lake, and the east is another 6 miles beyond, at Portage Lake.

During the summer, **Alaska Canoe & Campground** (☎ 907-262-2331; www.alaskacanoetrips.com) rents canoes and runs a shuttle service to the Swan Lake and Swanson River canoe routes. It's $42 per day for a canoe rental three days or longer, $45 for a drop-off and pickup for up to four boats for the Swan Lake route, and $50 to the Swanson River trailhead. Alaska Canoe's campground (tent sites/cabins $15/150) is near the takeout along Sterling Hwy and makes a nice place to stay if you come in late on the last day.

SAVONOSKI LOOP

Section	Miles
Brooks Camp to Lake Grosvenor portage	30.0
Portage to Lake Grosvenor	1.0
Lake Grosvenor to Grosvenor River	14.0
Grosvenor River to Savonoski River	3.0
Savonoski River to Iliuk Arm	12.0
Iliuk Arm to Brooks Camp	20.0

Level of difficulty: Class I
Information: **Katmai National Park** (☎ 907-246-3305; www.nps.gov/katm)

This 80-mile, six- to eight-day paddle begins and ends at Brooks Camp and takes paddlers into remote sections of Katmai National Park, offering the best in wilderness adventures without expensive bush-plane travel.

Although no white water is encountered, the trip is still moderately challenging, with the hardest segment being the 12-mile run of the Savonoski River due to its braided nature and many deadheads and sweepers. The Savonoski is also prime brown bear habitat and for this reason park rangers recommend paddling the river in a single day and not camping along it.

The first section through Naknek Lake is especially scenic and well protected at the end where you dip in and out of the Bay of Islands. You are then faced with a mile-long portage, which during most summers is a mud-hole of a trail, before continuing on to Lake Grosvenor and the Grosvenor River. The last leg is the 20-mile paddle along the south shore of the Iliuk Arm back to Brooks Camp.

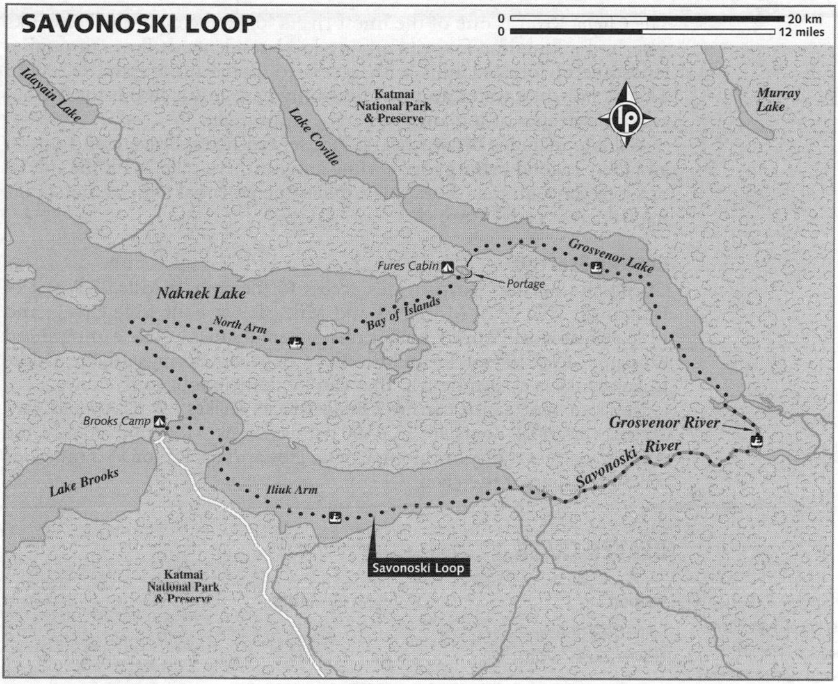

Getting Started

See p311 for information on reservations and getting to the area. Paddlers have to remember that Katmai is famous for its sudden and violent storms, some lasting for days.

The preferred mode of travel on this route is a kayak due to the sudden winds and rough nature of the big lakes. Most visitors either fly in with a folding kayak or rent a kayak from **Lifetime Adventures** (☎ 800-952-8624; www.lifetimeadventures.net) in Brooks Camp. Folding kayaks are $45/55 a day for a single/double or $245/280 per week. The Anchorage-based outfitter will also arrange an unguided trip that includes airfare from Anchorage to King Salmon, floatplane charter to Brooks Camp and folding kayaks for $875 per person per week.

CHENA RIVER

Section	Miles
Second Bridge to Hodgins Slough	15.0
Hodgins Slough to Bailey Bridge	16.0
Bailey Bridge to Chena River Dam	8.5
Chena River Dam to Badger Slough	19.0
Badger Slough to University Avenue	15.5

Level of difficulty: Class I-II
Information: **Northern Area Office** (☎ 907-451-2659; www.alaskastateparks.org)

The Chena River is one of the finest rivers for canoeing in the Fairbanks area, and a longtime favorite among local residents. It flows through a landscape of forested hills with access to alpine tundra above 2800ft. There's no white water and paddlers only have to watch out for the occasional sweeper or logjam.

Wildlife includes brown bears, moose, red foxes, beavers and otters, and there is good fishing for grayling and northern pike. With the Interior's long, hot summer days, this trip has the potential to be an outstanding wilderness adventure.

Getting Started

Chena Hot Springs Rd provides access to the river at Mile 27.9 east of Fairbanks; Mile 28.6, Mile 29.4 and Mile 33.9 at Four Mile Creek; and Mile 39.6 at North Fork Chena River, where there is a state campground (20 campsites, $10 fee). From Mile 39.6 Chena Hot Springs Rd, the paddle to Fairbanks is a 70-mile trip that can be done in four to five days.

You can rent canoes from **7 Bridges Boats & Bikes** (☎ 907-479-0751; www.7gablesinn.com/7bbb). Boats are $35/100 per day/week. More importantly, the company offers transport along Chena Hot Springs Rd for $3 a mile. See p393 for a map of the river.

For lots of great information and upcoming events visit the Fairbanks Paddlers at www.fairbankspaddlers.org. You might even be able to buy a used canoe or kayak.

BEAVER CREEK

Section	Miles
Nome Creek to Victoria Creek	127
Victoria Creek to Dalton Hwy	272

Level of Difficulty: Class I
Information: **Bureau of Land Management** (BLM; ☎ 907-474-2200; www.ak.blm.gov)

Beaver Creek is *the* adventure for budget travelers with time and a yearning to paddle through a roadless wilderness. The moderately swift stream, with long clear pools and frequent rapids, is rated Class I and can be handled by novice canoeists with expedition experience. The 111-mile creek is part of the White Mountains National Recreation Area; it flows past hills forested in white spruce and paper birch below the jagged peaks of the White Mountains. For a map of this route see p101.

The scenery is spectacular, the chances of seeing another party remote, and you'll catch so much grayling you'll never want to eat another one. You can also spend a night in the Borealis-Le Fevre cabin, a BLM cabin on the banks of Beaver Creek.

To get there, go north at Mile 57 of the Steese Hwy on US Creek Rd for 6 miles, then northwest on Nome Creek Rd to the Ophir Creek Campground. You can put in at Nome Creek and paddle to its confluence with Beaver Creek. Most paddlers plan on six to nine days to reach Victoria Creek, a 127-mile trip, where gravel bars are used by bush planes to land and pick up paddlers.

From the Nome Creek/Beaver Creek confluence, the paddle along Beaver Creek is through the White Mountains, where the scenery includes limestone towers, buttes and spires. A day's paddle beyond Victoria Creek, Beaver Creek spills out of the White Mountains into Yukon Flats National Wildlife Refuge, where it meanders through a marshy area. Eventually it flows north into the Yukon River, where, after two or three days, you'll pass under the Yukon River Bridge on the Dalton Hwy. If you arrange to be picked up here, you can avoid another airfare. This is a 399-mile paddle and a three-week expedition – the stuff great Alaskan adventures are made of.

Getting Started

Rent a canoe from **7 Bridges Boats & Bikes** (☎ 907-479-0751; www.7gablesinn.com/7bbb). They'll take you to Mile 57 of the Steese Hwy, where US Creek Rd reaches Nome Creek Rd. For pickup at Yukon River Bridge 175 miles north of Fairbanks, call **Dalton Hwy Express** (☎ 907-474-3555; www.daltonhighwayexpress.com).

Southeast Alaska

Windswept. Treeless. Permanently frozen. Not Southeast Alaska. This lush, green and wet region of Alaska, clinging by a thread to the rest of the state, stretches 540 miles from Icy Bay south to Portland Canal but only is 140 miles across at its widest point. The Panhandle is a slender piece of land, a rain forest, filled with glaciers, mountains and a thousand islands known as the Alexander Archipelago.

On public ferries or cruise ships you sail past rugged snowcapped mountains that rise steeply from the water to form sheersided fjords embellished by cascading waterfalls. Ice-blue glaciers descend from the highest peaks and fan out into valleys of dark green Sitka spruce before melting into waters filled with whales, sea lions, harbor seals and salmon.

The Southeast was once Alaska's heart and soul, and Juneau was not only the capital but the state's largest city. But WWII and the Alcan (Alaska Hwy) turned Anchorage and Fairbanks into the economic focal points of Alaska. Today Southeast is characterized by big trees and small towns. Each community here has its own history and character: from Norwegian-influenced Petersburg to Russian-tinted Sitka. You can feel the gold fever in Skagway, see almost a dozen glaciers near Juneau or go to the harbor in Haines and find a fishing boat selling live Dungeness crabs. Each town is unique and none of them should be bypassed.

HIGHLIGHTS

- **Easiest bear watching** (p125) – after zipping down a mountain, check out the bears at Ketchikan's Herring Creek
- **Best small museum** (p138) – two presidents, Hollywood and Wyatt Earp – find out who else passed through town at the Wrangell Museum
- **Best community bath** (p158) – meet everybody in Tenakee Springs at the community hot springs bathhouse
- **Most fun on ice** (p174) – strap on the crampons and take a hike across Juneau's Mendenhall Glacier
- **Best USFS Cabin** (p191) – the Laughton Glacier Cabin, near Skagway, is simple and small, the glacier around the corner is anything but

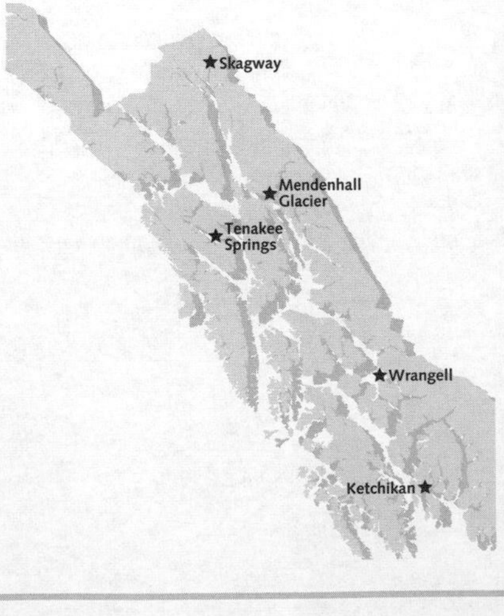

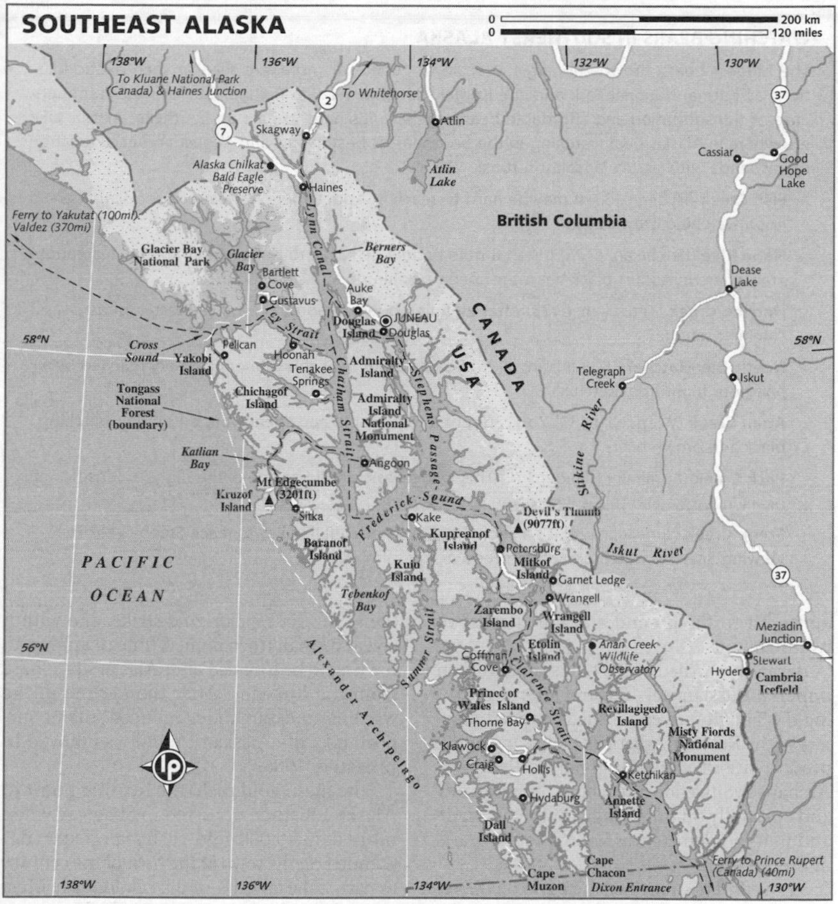

Climate

The Southeast has Alaska's most mild climate. Greatly affected by warm ocean currents, the region offers warm summer temperatures averaging 69°F, with an occasional heat wave that sends temperatures to 80°F. The winters are equally mild, and subzero days are rare. Residents, who have learned to live with an annual rainfall of 60in to 200in, call the frequent rain 'liquid sunshine.' The heavy precipitation creates the dense, lush rain forests and numerous waterfalls most travelers come to cherish.

History

Petroglyphs lying along the shoreline in Wrangell, Petersburg and other locations indicate human habitation in Southeast Alaska dates back at least 8000 to 10,000 years. The Russians arrived in 1741, entered Sitka Sound and sent two longboats ashore in search of fresh water. The boats never returned, and the Russians wisely departed.

What the unfortunate shore party encountered were members of Tlingit tribes, who over time had developed the most advanced culture of any group of Alaska Natives. The Tlingits were still there in 1799 when the Russians returned and established the Southeast's first nonindigenous settlement. Aleksandr Baranov built a Russian fort near the present ferry terminal to continue the rich sea-otter fur trade. He was in Kodiak three years later when Tlingits, armed with guns from British and American traders, overwhelmed the fort,

WATCHING BEARS IN SOUTHEAST ALASKA

The biggest bears, browns tipping the scale at 1000lb or more, are seen at such exotic locations as Katmai National Park and the Kodiak National Wildlife Refuge. But for sheer numbers, ease of transportation and affordable bear watching it's hard to pass up Southeast Alaska. Like elsewhere in Alaska, bear watching in the Southeast is best in July and August and each location corresponds with particular salmon runs:

- **Fish Creek** (Hyder; p133) It may be hard to reach but once there it's easy to spend an afternoon watching brown bears.
- **Naha Rive** (Ketchikan; p125) It's an 8-mile paddle by kayak to Naha River National Recreation Trail where in August black bears are snagging salmon at a small waterfall.
- **Herring Creek** (Ketchikan; p125) After ziplining down a mountain you can watch black bears catching salmon.
- **Neet's Bay Hatchery** (Ketchikan; p125) Bears gather near this salmon hatchery reached by a half-hour flight from Ketchikan.
- **Anan Creek** (Wrangell; p139) You can rent a USFS cabin and spend your entire day watching black and brown bears.
- **Pack Creek** (Admiralty Island; p176) This wilderness island has one of the highest densities of bears in Alaska and this is where you can see them.
- **Steep Creek** (Juneau; p174) It's a short hike in Mendenhall Valley to reach Steep Creek Fish Viewing Site and watch black bears feeding on salmon.

burned it to the ground and killed most of its inhabitants.

Baranov returned in 1804, this time with an imperial Russian warship, and after destroying the Tlingit fort, established the headquarters of the Russian-American Company at the present site of Sitka. Originally called New Archangel, Sitka flourished both economically and culturally on the strength of the fur trade and in its golden era was known as the 'Paris of the Pacific.'

In an effort to strengthen their grip on the region and protect their fur-trading interests, the Russians built a stockade near the mouth of the Stikine River in 1834. They named it Redoubt St Dionysius but in 1840 the political winds shifted and the Russians leased the entire Southeast coastline to the British, who renamed the new outpost Fort Stikine. After purchasing Alaska from the Russians, the Americans formally took control of the territory in Sitka in 1867. A year later Wrangell was renamed and raising its third national flag in less than 30 years.

In 1880, at the insistence of a Tlingit chief, Joe Juneau and Dick Harris returned to Gastineau Channel to prospect for gold again. This time they hacked their way through the thick forest to the head of Gold Creek. They found, in the words of Harris, 'little lumps as large as peas and beans.' The news spurred the state's first major gold strike, and within a year a small town named Juneau appeared, the first to be founded after Alaska's purchase from the Russians. After the decline in the whaling and fur trades reduced Sitka's importance, the Alaskan capital was moved to Juneau in 1906.

The main gold rush, the turning point in Alaska's history, occurred in Skagway when more than 40,000 gold-rush stampeders descended on the town at the turn of the century as part of the fabled Klondike Gold Rush. Most made their way to the Yukon goldfields by way of the Chilkoot Trail until the White Pass & Yukon Railroad was completed in 1900.

In 1887 the population of Skagway was two; 10 years later, 20,000 people lived there and the gold-rush town was Alaska's largest city. A center for saloons, hotels and brothels, Skagway became infamous for its lawlessness. For a time, the town was held under the tight control of Jefferson Randolph 'Soapy' Smith and his gang, who conned and swindled naive newcomers out of their money and stampeders out of their gold dust. Soapy Smith was finally removed from power by a mob of angry citizens. In a gunfight between Smith and city engineer Frank Reid, both men died, and Smith's reign as the 'uncrowned prince of Skagway' ended after only nine months.

At the time Wrangell was also booming as the supply point for prospectors heading up the Stikine River to the Cassiar Gold District of British Columbia in 1861 and 1874, and then using the river again to reach the Klondike fields in 1897. Wrangell was as ruthless and lawless as Skagway. With miners holding their own court, it was said 'that a man would be tried at 9am, found guilty of murder at 11:30am and hung by 2pm.'

Just as gold fever was dying out, the salmon industry was taking hold. One of the first canneries in Alaska was built in Klawock on Prince of Wales Island in 1878. Ketchikan was begun in 1885 as a cannery and in 1897 Peter Buschmann arrived from Norway and established Petersburg as a cannery site because of the fine harbor and a ready supply of ice from nearby LeConte Glacier.

After WWII, with the construction of the Alcan (Alaska Hwy) and large military bases around Anchorage and Fairbanks, Alaska's sphere of influence shifted from the Southeast to the mainland further north. In 1974 Alaskans voted to move the state capital again, this time to the small town of Willow, an hour's drive from Anchorage. The so-called 'capital move' issue hung over Juneau like a dark cloud, threatening to turn the place into a ghost town. The issue became a political tug-of-war between Anchorage and the Southeast, until voters, faced with a billion-dollar price tag to construct a new capital, defeated the funding in 1982.

Today Juneau is still the capital and the Panhandle a road-less, lightly populated area where residents make a living fishing and catering to tourists and cruise ships.

Getting There & Around

Most of the Southeast may be roadless but getting there and getting around is easy. Ketchikan is only 1½ hours away from Seattle by air on **Alaska Airlines** (☎ 800-426-0333; www.alaskaair.com) or 37 hours on the **Alaska Marine Highway** (☎ 800-642-0066; www.ferryalaska.com) from Bellingham, WA. The state ferries, North America's longest public ferry system, also provide transportation between the regions, cities, towns and little fishing ports. Separate ferries link Prince of Wales Island with Ketchikan, Wrangell and Petersburg (p137), Haines with Skagway (p187), and Juneau and Glacier Bay (p173).

SOUTHERN PANHANDLE

Residents like to call this region of Alaska 'rain forest islands;' lush, green, watery, remote and roadless to the outside world. This is the heart of Southeast Alaska's fishing industry, and the region's best wilderness fishing lodges are scattered in the small coves of these islands. Cruise ships pass through, but only inundate Ketchikan; the other communities receive few if any vessels. Best of all, two ferry systems, the Alaska State Marine Highway and the Inter-Island Ferry Authority, serve the area so island hopping, even in this remote rain forest, is easy.

KETCHIKAN

pop 13,166

Once known as the 'Canned Salmon Capital of the World,' today Ketchikan settles for 'First City', the initial port for Alaska Marine ferries and cruise ships coming from the south. It could also be called the 'Thin City.' Just 90 miles north of Prince Rupert, Ketchikan hugs the bluffs that form the shoreline along the southwest corner of Revillagigedo Island. Space is so scarce here, the airport had to be built on another island.

Founded as a cannery site in 1885, Ketchikan's mainstay for most of its existence was salmon, and then timber when the huge Ketchikan Pulp Mill was constructed at Ward Cove in 1954. But in the 1970s, strikes and changes in public policy began to mar the logging industry. Louisiana-Pacific closed the sawmill in the city center after a strike in 1983 and the pulp mill in 1997, resulting in hundreds of workers losing their high-paying jobs.

There is still commercial fishing in Ketchikan, and the industry accounts for 30% of the local economy. What rings the local cash registers now is tourism. Beginning in the mid-1990s Ketchikan transformed itself into a cruise-ship capital with up to 10 ships visiting a day. Many Alaskans were appalled by the commercialism that took over downtown, where many shops are owned by the cruise-ship companies and open only from May to October.

If you stay in Ketchikan longer than an hour, chances are good that it will rain at least once. The average annual rainfall is 162in, but in some years it has been known to be more than 200in. Local residents never use umbrellas or let the rain interfere with daily activities, even outdoor

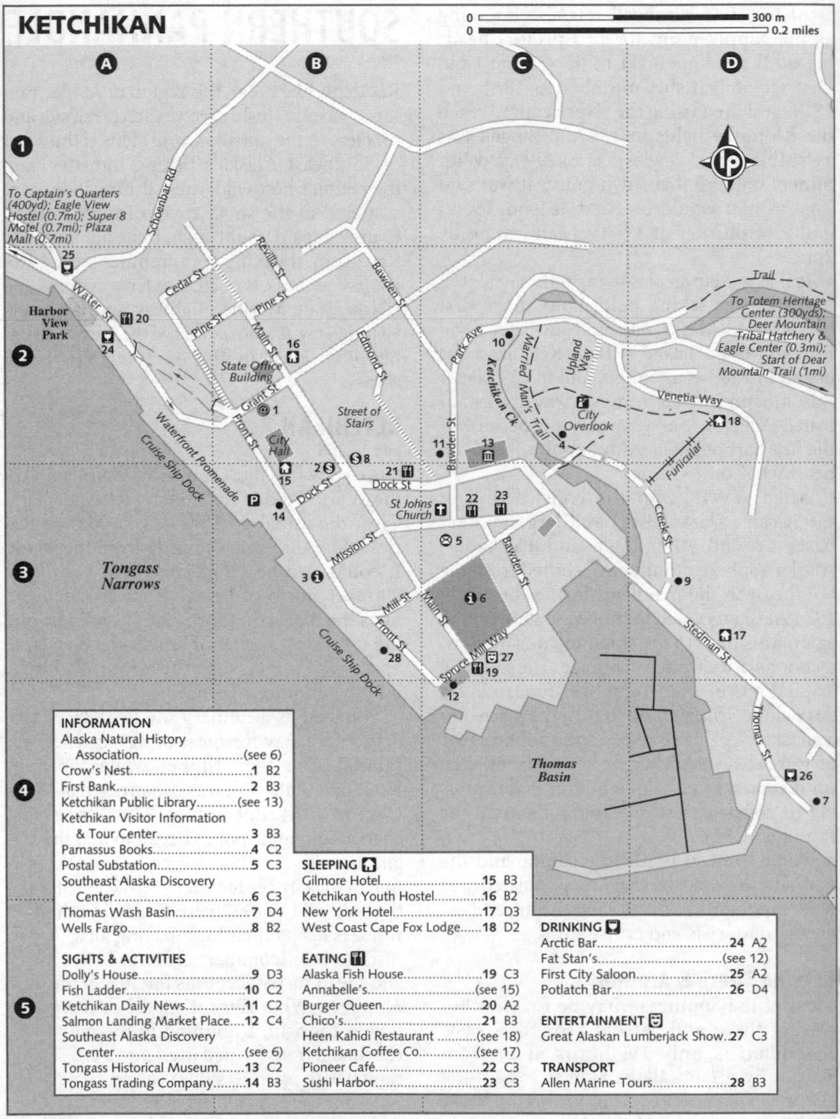

ones. If they stopped everything each time it drizzled, Ketchikan would cease to exist.

When the skies finally clear, the beauty of Ketchikan's setting becomes apparent. The town is backed by forested hills and faces a waterway humming with floatplanes, fishing boats, ferries and barges hauling freight to other Southeast ports.

Orientation

Several miles long but never more than 10 blocks wide, Ketchikan centers on the single main drag of Tongass Ave, which sticks to the shore of Tongass Narrows like a bathtub ring. On one side of Tongass, many businesses and homes are built on stilts out over the water, while on the other side they cling to the steep slopes and often have winding wooden staircases leading to their doors. North of town, Tongass Ave becomes the N Tongass Hwy. South of town it's the S Tongass Hwy.

Downtown is a two-block area for about two blocks inland from the cruise-ship docks. The area northwest of downtown along Tongass, known as the West End, has a commercial/industrial feel; here you'll find fish-processing plants and Plaza Mall. Southeast along Tongass it's more residential, and past Saxman Totem Park it's rural.

Information

BOOKSTORES

Alaska Natural History Association (Map p122; ☎ 228-6220; 50 Main St; 🕑 8am-5pm) The Southeast Alaska Discovery Center bookstore offers an extensive selection of Alaska titles and comfortable sitting areas to thumb through them.

Parnassus Books (Map p122; ☎ 225-7690; 5 Creek St; 🕑 8:30am-6pm) Half hidden on Creek St but well worth searching for is this delightful bookstore filled with Alaskan books, cards and local art.

LAUNDRY

Highliner Laundromat (Map p128; ☎ 225-5308; 2701 Tongass Ave; 🕑 7am-9pm) Out toward Plaza Mall; also has showers and storage lockers.

Thomas Wash Basin (Map p122; ☎ 247-9274; 124 Thomas St; 🕑 8am-6pm) Convenient to the Potlatch Bar (p130) is this cleverly named place, which has showers, an espresso bar, wi-fi and serves great meatloaf sandwiches.

LIBRARY & INTERNET ACCESS

Crow's Nest (Map p122; ☎ 225-6119; 308 Grant St; per 30min/hr $2.50/5; 🕑 6am-6pm) Cheapest Internet in town plus a huge espresso machine. Get wired and surf.

Ketchikan Public Library (Map p122; ☎ 225-3331; 629 Dock St; 🕑 10am-8pm Mon-Wed, to 6pm Thu-Sat, 1-5pm Sun) The library makes it impossible for short-term visitors to access the internet by requiring a library card ($10) and a $20 deposit that won't be refunded for 24 hours.

MEDICAL SERVICES

Ketchikan General Hospital (Map p128; ☎ 225-5171; 3100 Tongass Ave) Between the ferry terminal and downtown.

MONEY

First Bank (Map p122; ☎ 228-4474; 331 Dock St) Its 24-hour ATM is less than a block from the one at Wells Fargo.

Wells Fargo (Map p122; ☎ 225-2184; 306 Main St) One of a handful of banks mixed in with the gift shops downtown.

POST

Main post office (Map p128; 3609 Tongass Ave) Near the ferry terminal.

Postal substation (Map p122; 422 Mission St; 🕑 9am-5:30pm Mon-Sat, to 2pm Sun) A post office open on Sunday? Everything is open when the cruise ships are in.

TOURIST INFORMATION

Ketchikan Visitor Information & Tour Center (Map p122; ☎ 225-6166, 800-770-3300; www.visit-ketchikan.com; City Dock at 131 Front St; 🕑 7am-5pm) Pick up brochures and free maps, ask the friendly staff questions, use courtesy phones, even book tours here. A second center is near Berth 3 of the cruise ship dock and open when ships are in.

Southeast Alaska Discovery Center (Map p122; ☎ 228-6220; www.fs.fed.us/r10/ketchikan; 50 Main St; 🕑 8am-5pm) You don't need to pay the admission to seek recreation information at this Alaska Public Lands Information Center. Separate from the displays is a trip-planning room containing an information desk and computer access to reserve USFS cabins.

Sights

SOUTHEAST ALASKA DISCOVERY CENTER

Three large totems greet you in the lobby of the **center** (Map p122; ☎ 228-6220; 50 Main St; adult/child $5/free; 🕑 8am-5pm) while a school of silver salmon, suspended from the ceiling, leads you toward a slice of nicely re-created rain forest. Upstairs, the exhibit hall features sections on Southeast Alaska's ecosystems and Alaska Native traditions. You can even view wildlife here. There's a spotting scope trained on Deer Mountain for mountain goats while underwater cameras in Ketchikan Creek let you watch thousands of salmon struggling upstream to spawn.

CREEK STREET & DOLLY'S HOUSE

Departing from Stedman St is Creek St, a boardwalk built over Ketchikan Creek on pilings – a photographer's delight. This was Ketchikan's famed red-light district until prostitution became illegal in 1954. During Creek St's heyday, it supported up to 30 brothels and became known as the only place in Alaska where 'the fishermen and the fish went upstream to spawn.' The house with bright red trim is **Dolly's House** (Map p122; ☎ 225-6329; 24 Creek St; adult/child $5/free; 🕑 8am-5pm or when cruise ships are in), the parlor of the city's most famous madam, Dolly Arthur. Now it's a museum dedicated to this notorious era. You can see the brothel, including its bar, which was placed over a trapdoor to the creek for quick disposal of bootleg whiskey.

A BRIDGE TO SOMEWHERE

Ketchikan was thrust into the national limelight in 2005 when it was revealed that a $233 million appropriation was tucked into the Transportation Equity Act for a bridge to nearby Gravina Island, home to less than 50 people. Cited as a classic example of pork barrel politics, the media, from *USA Today* to the ABC news program *20/20*, had a field day with the story and the Gravina Access Project was soon dubbed the 'Bridge to Nowhere.'

As so often the case with a story like this, facts rarely matter. The Bridge to Nowhere had become the poster child for excessive government spending and Ketchikan was ridiculed by news commentators from around the country, the vast majority of whom had never been to Alaska.

The day Ketchikan International Airport opened on Gravina Island in 1976 a hard link from the city to the Southeast's second-largest airport was on the drawing board. There was almost universal agreement that a twice-an-hour ferry was not suitable transportation for the half million passengers the small vessel carries back and forth to the airport annually. Over the years 14 different options were examined, including three tunnels, but local opposition to the various plans and a state budget awash in red ink delayed the project.

In the meantime any proposed bridge continued to grow as Ketchikan's economy switched from logging to tourism. Every season cruise ships became bigger and more numerous and eventually required a span across the Tongass Narrows that was nearly as long as the Golden Gate Bridge and taller than the Brooklyn Bridge. The final price tag was $398 million, with the majority of it coming from the federal government.

Or that was the plan. But Ketchikan was the victim of rotten timing. Just after the passage of the transportation bill, Hurricane Katrina devastated New Orleans and suddenly the national media focused on the bridge appropriation as unnecessary pork in a time of need elsewhere. That whipped up public outcry which led to Congress removing the bridge earmark from the bill.

In the strange game that is Washington DC, Ketchikan lost its bridge but Alaska still received most of the federal money which was used for anything but the bridge. In 2007, the Ketchikan bridge project was finally cancelled altogether by Governor Sarah Palin.

What most commentators failed to realize is that the bridge didn't just connect a city to its airport – it was a link to flat land, which in this area of the state is almost as scarce as a way out of town. If Ketchikan is to grow its economy beyond cruise ships and provide affordable housing to its residents, it needs someplace to build. In a town that clings to a side of a mountain, Gravina Island was that place, a 95-sq-mile island with large tracts of gentle terrain suitable for small industries, warehouses and neighborhoods.

'The bottom line,' one city official said, 'you can't keep building up a mountain.'

TOTEM HERITAGE CENTER

A 15-minute walk from the cruise-ship docks is **Totem Heritage Center** (off Map p122; ☎ 225-5900; 601 Deermount St; adult/child $5/free; 8am-5pm), where totem poles salvaged from deserted Tlingit communities are restored. Inside the center 17 totems are on display in an almost spiritual setting that shows the reverence Alaska Natives attach to them. More are erected outside and the entire center is shrouded in pines and serenaded by the gurgling Ketchikan Creek.

DEER MOUNTAIN TRIBAL HATCHERY & EAGLE CENTER

A bridge across Ketchikan Creek links the Totem Heritage Center with the **Deer Mountain Tribal Hatchery & Eagle Center** (off Map p122; ☎ 225-5158, 225-6767, 800-252-5158; 1158 Salmon Rd; adult/child $9/free, combined admission with Totem Heritage Center $12/free; 8am-4:30pm). The hatchery raises 350,000 king salmon, coho salmon, steelhead and rainbow trout annually and releases them into the nearby stream. In July or later, you'll see not only the salmon fry but returning adult fish swimming upstream to spawn. The center is also home to a pair of eagles who were injured and can no longer fly.

TONGASS HISTORICAL MUSEUM

Sharing a building with the Ketchikan Public Library is the **Tongass Historical Museum** (Map p122; ☎ 225-5600; 629 Dock St; adult/child $2/free; 8am-5pm), which houses a basement collection of local historical and Alaska Native artifacts, many dealing with Ketchikan's fishing industry. More interesting is the impressive **Raven**

Stealing the Sun totem just outside and an observation platform overlooking the Ketchikan Creek falls.

THOMAS BASIN

If you thought Creek St was photogenic, cross Stedman St and be ready to burn some megapixels. **Thomas Basin** (Map p122) is home to Ketchikan's fishing fleet and the city's most picturesque harbor. When the boats come in you can photograph them unloading their catch and then follow the crews to the colorful **Potlatch Bar** (p130) nearby, a classic fisherman's pub.

STAIRWAYS & BOARDWALKS

All over Ketchikan there are stairways leading somewhere higher. Sure, they're knee-bending climbs, but the reward for your exertion is great views from the top. Heading back west along Dock St, just past the Ketchikan Daily News Building, is Edmond St, also called the **Street of Stairs** (Map p122) for obvious reasons. Heading down Park Ave from the hatchery, you'll pass the **Upland Way** stairs that climb to a viewpoint. Nearby is a bridge across Ketchikan Creek, the site of a fish ladder and one end of **Married Man's Trail** (Map p122) – a delightful series of boardwalks and stairs leading up to the **West Coast Cape Fox Lodge** (p127) or back to Creek St.

Ketchikan's newest boardwalk is the **Waterfront Promenade** (Map p122) that begins near Berth 4, passes **Harbor View Park** (Map p122), a city park that is composed entirely of decking and pilings, follows the cruise ship docks and then wraps around Thomas Basin Harbor. Along the way there are plenty of whale-tail and halibut benches to take a break and admire the maritime scenery.

Activities

BEAR WATCHING

Like much of Alaska, Ketchikan charter pilots have met the public's interest in bear watching. The most affordable bear viewing is to paddle a kayak to Nada Bay (right) to see black bears feeding on salmon in August or visit Alaska Canopy Adventures (p126) which provides access to the bears feeding in Herring Creek. Then there are the seaplane adventures:

Alaska Seaplane Tours (☎ 225-1974, 866-858-2327; www.alaskaseaplanetours.com) Flies to Prince of Wales Island to watch bruins on a two-hour tour ($339).

Promech Air (☎ 225-3845, 800-860-3845; www.promechair.com) Its three-hour tour is a flight to the Neet's Bay Hatchery with 1½ hours watching black bears ($278).

Seawind Aviation (☎ 225-1206, 877-225-1203; www.seawindaviation.com) A 2½-hour tour to Traitors Cove north of Ketchikan where a short hike brings you to a viewing spot of feeding black bears ($340).

HIKING

Most Ketchikan-area trails are either out of town or must be reached by boat. The major exception is **Deer Mountain Trail** (Map p122), a well-maintained 2.5-mile trail that begins near downtown. The trailhead is near the southeast end of Fair St and the route climbs to the 3000ft summit of Deer Mountain. Overlooks along the way provide panoramic views – the first is about a mile up the trail. Toward the top of the mountain is a free-use shelter and more trails into the alpine region. For a map, see the Wilderness Hikes & Paddles chapter (p102).

The easy 1.3-mile **Ward Lake Nature Walk** (Map p128), an interpretive loop around Ward Lake, begins near the parking area at the lake's north end. Beavers, birds and the occasional black bear might be seen. To reach the lake, follow N Tongass Hwy 7 miles from downtown to Ward Cove; turn right on Revilla Rd and continue up 1.5 miles to Ward Lake Rd.

The 2.3-mile (one way) **Perseverance Trail** (Map p128) from Ward Lake to Perseverance Lake passes through mature coastal forest and muskeg. The view of Perseverance Lake with its mountainous backdrop is spectacular, and the hiking is moderately easy. The trailhead is on Ward Lake's east side just past CCC Campground.

Ketchikan's other alpine trek is **Dude Mountain Trail** (Map p128), reached from Revilla Rd by turning right on Brown Mountain Rd, 5 miles from N Tongass Hwy. At the end of Brown Mountain Rd is the trailhead for Dude Mountain Trail, which begins as a boardwalk through stands of old-growth spruce then becomes a trail as you follow a narrow ridge to the 2848ft peak. It's a 1-mile trek and a gain of 1200ft to the top, but once there you're in open alpine and can easily ridge-walk to Diana Mountain (3014ft) or Brown Mountain (2978ft). Plan on two hours for the round-trip to Dude Mountain.

PADDLING

Ketchikan serves as the base for some of the best kayaking in the Southeast. Possibilities include anything from an easy paddle around the waterfront to a weeklong trip in Misty Fiords National Monument (p107). Pick up charts and topographic maps from the Southeast Alaska Discovery Center and outdoor supplies from **Tongass Trading Company** (Map p122; ☎ 225-5101; 201 Dock St), across from the Gilmore Hotel.

Southeast Sea Kayaks (Map p128; ☎ 225-1258, 800-287-1607; www.kayakketchikan.com; 1621 Tongass Ave; kayaks per day single/double $45/60), in the Westflight Building, also offers tours including a 2½-hour paddle of Ketchikan's waterfront (adult/child $89/69). A much better paddling experience, however, is its Orcas Cove trip (adult/child $159/129), a four-hour adventure that begins with a boat ride across the Tongass Narrows and then paddling among protected islands looking for sea lions, orcas and seals.

Betton Island

Due west of Settler's Cove State Park at the north end (Mile 18.2) of N Tongass Hwy is this island and several smaller islands nearby, making it an excellent day paddle if you're staying at the campground. Although Clover Pass is a highly trafficked area, the backside of Betton Island offers a more genuine wilderness setting. Pack a tent and sleeping bag and you can turn this into an overnight excursion by camping on the great beaches of the Tatoosh Islands on the west side of Betton Island.

Naha Bay

Also from Settler's Cove State Park, it's an 8-mile paddle to Naha Bay, the destination of an excellent three- or four-day adventure. At the head of the bay is a floating dock where you can leave your kayak and set off down the Naha River National Recreation Trail. The scenic 5.4-mile trail follows the river up to Jordan and Heckman Lakes, both of which have **USFS cabins** (Map p128; ☎ 877-444-6777, 518-885-3639; www.recreation.gov; cabins $35). The fishing here is good and black bears are plentiful – in August you might see them catching salmon at a small waterfall 2 miles up the trail from Roosevelt Lagoon.

A narrow outlet connects Naha Bay with Roosevelt Lagoon. You don't have to enter the lagoon to access the trail. Kayakers wishing to paddle into the lagoon must either portage around the outlet or enter it at high slack tide, as the narrow pass becomes a frothy, roaring chute when the tide is moving in or out.

George & Carroll Inlets

From Hole in the Wall Bar & Marina (p131), 7.5 miles southeast of Ketchikan down the S Tongass Hwy, you can start an easy one- to four-day paddle north into George or Carroll Inlets or both. Each inlet is protected from the area's prevailing southwesterlies, so the water is usually calm (although north winds occasionally whip down George Inlet). From Hole in the Wall to the top of George Inlet is a 26-mile paddle.

WILDERNESS CABINS

Some 30 **USFS cabins** (☎ 877-444-6777, 518-885-3639; www.recreation.gov; cabins $25-45) dot the Ketchikan area. It's best to reserve them in advance but often early in the summer and midweek something will be available. Some cabins can be reached by boat but most visitors fly to them. Within about 20 miles of Ketchikan are Alava Bay Cabin ($35), on the southern end of Behm Canal in Misty Fiords National Monument; Fish Creek Cabin ($45), connected by a short trail to Thorne Arm; and the two Patching Lake Cabins ($25), which offer good fishing for cutthroat trout and grayling.

ZIPLINING

Ketchikan has everything needed to be the zipline capital of Alaska: lush rain forests and elevation. There are two zipline operations now, more are bound to come. The best is **Alaska Canopy Adventures** (☎ 225-5503; www.alaskacanopy.com; 116 Wood Rd; per person $160), which uses eight lines, three suspension bridges and 4WD vehicle to transport you up a mountain so you can zip 4600ft to the bottom. Also onsite is the Alaska Rain forest Sanctuary, where visitors can view wildlife including salmon runs and bears that feast on them.

Tours

Being the cruise-ship port that it is, more tours operate in and around Ketchikan than can possibly be booked in a two-week vacation, much less a six-hour stopover. The best place to see what's available and to sign up is the **Ketchikan Visitor Information & Tour Center** (Map p122; ☎ 225-6166) building on City Dock, where a whole wing is devoted to a gauntlet of tour providers touting their services.

Alaska Amphibious Tours (☎ 225-9899, 866-341-3825; www.akduck.com; adult/child $38/24) Uses amphibian vehicles that double as a bus and a boat to provide 1½-hour tours of the downtown area and the harbor. The top-heavy vehicle puts you 8ft above anything on the road for a great view, but the time spent cruising the harbor is shorter than most passengers would like.

Alaska Undersea Tours (☎ 247-8899, 877-461-8687; www.alaskaunderseatours.com; adult/child $49/29) From top of the water to below it, this 1½-hour tour puts you in a semisubmersible vessel with underwater viewing windows so you can see the marine life and seascapes in the Ketchikan harbors.

our pick **Bering Sea Crab Fishermen's Tour** (☎ 888-239-3816; www.56degreesnorth.com; adult/child $149/99) Ketchikan is a long way from the Bering Sea and they don't catch many king crabs here, but you can experience both on the *Aleutian Ballad*. The crab boat, once featured on the TV show *Deadliest Catch*, has been modified with a 100-seat amphitheater for a 3½-hour, on-the-water tour of commercial fishing. Right in front of you Bering Sea crabbers pull up huge pots full of tanner, Dungeness and even giant king crabs as well as bait lines to catch rockfish and shark. This seemingly out-of-place tour is extremely interesting.

Classic Tours (☎ 225-3091; www.classictours.com; per person $109-139) Small, personal tours of the city and Saxman Village. Only five people at a time because a 1955 Chevy with fuzzy black dice is used to show you around. How cool is that?

Northern Tours (☎ 247-6457, 877-461-8687; www.northerntoursofalaska.com; adult/child $40/25) Offers the standard city tour and a trip to Totem Bight in a two-hour outing in a minibus.

Festivals & Events

Ketchikan's **Fourth of July** celebration includes a parade, contests, softball games, an impressive display of fireworks and a logging show. The smaller **Blueberry Festival**, held at the State Office Building and the Main Street Theater on the first weekend in August, consists of arts and crafts, singers, musicians, and food stalls serving blueberries every possible way.

Sleeping

Ketchikan charges 13% on lodging in city and bed taxes.

BUDGET

There are no public campgrounds close to town. The closest campgrounds are 4.5 miles north of the ferry terminal at Ward Lake Recreation Area (p131).

Ketchikan Youth Hostel (Map p122; ☎ 225-3319; 400 Main St; dm $15; ⏲ 7-9am & 6-11pm Jun-Aug; ⊠) Right downtown is this hostel spread out in a Methodist church complex that includes a large kitchen, three small common areas and separate-sex dorm rooms. The friendly hostel is spotlessly clean but there are chores, lockout and a curfew.

Eagle View Hostel (off Map p128; ☎ 225-5461; www.eagleviewhostel.com; 2303 Fifth Ave; dm $25; ⏲ Apr-Oct; ⊠) This hostel is well named. From the breakfast table inside you gaze down at the boat traffic in Tongass Narrows, the mountains beyond and occasionally an eagle that is almost at eye level. Keep that in mind when you first arrive in town and realize you have to carry your luggage up five steep blocks from the bus stop at Plaza Mall. The house has dorms for men and women and a couple's room. There is no curfew or lockout.

MIDRANGE

Captain's Quarters (off Map p122; ☎ 225-4912; www.ptialaska.net/~captbnb; 325 Lund St; r $100-110; ⊠) There are three rooms, one with a full kitchen, and a private entrance.

Super 8 Motel (Map p128; ☎ 225-9088; 800-800-8000; 2151 Sea Level Dr; r $109-121) Eighty-two rooms are lined along the waterfront behind Plaza Mall. Pay the token extra money for one of the Narrows-view rooms, as the area surrounding the motel is aesthetically challenged. A shuttle service to/from the ferry/airport is available.

Gilmore Hotel (Map p122; ☎ 225-9423, 800-275-9423; www.gilmorehotel.com; 326 Front St; r $115-155; ⊠ 🖳) Built in 1927 as a hotel and renovated several times since, the Gilmore has 38 rooms that still retain a historical flavor. The rooms are 'historically proportioned' (ie small) but comfortable, with cable TV, coffeemakers and hair dryers. The entire 2nd floor is nonsmoking.

our pick **New York Hotel** (Map p122; ☎ 225-0246, 866-225-0246; www.thenewyorkhotel.com; 207 Stedman St; r $129/144, ste $189-209; ⊠ 🖳) A historic, boutique hotel in a great location between Creek St and Thomas Basin. The eight rooms are filled with antiques and colorful quilts but have been updated with cable TV, small refrigerators and a private bath. The hotel also has six suites a short walk away, five of them on Creek St, which feature comfortable living rooms, small kitchen areas and sleeping accommodations for four. The 2nd-floor perch means you can watch the salmon spawn in the creek below and the seals that follow them on high tides.

Narrows Inn (Map p128; ☎ 247-2600, 888-686-2600; www.narrowsinn.com; 4871 N Tongass Hwy; s $135-150, d $140-155; ⊠ 🖳) A mile north of the airport ferry on

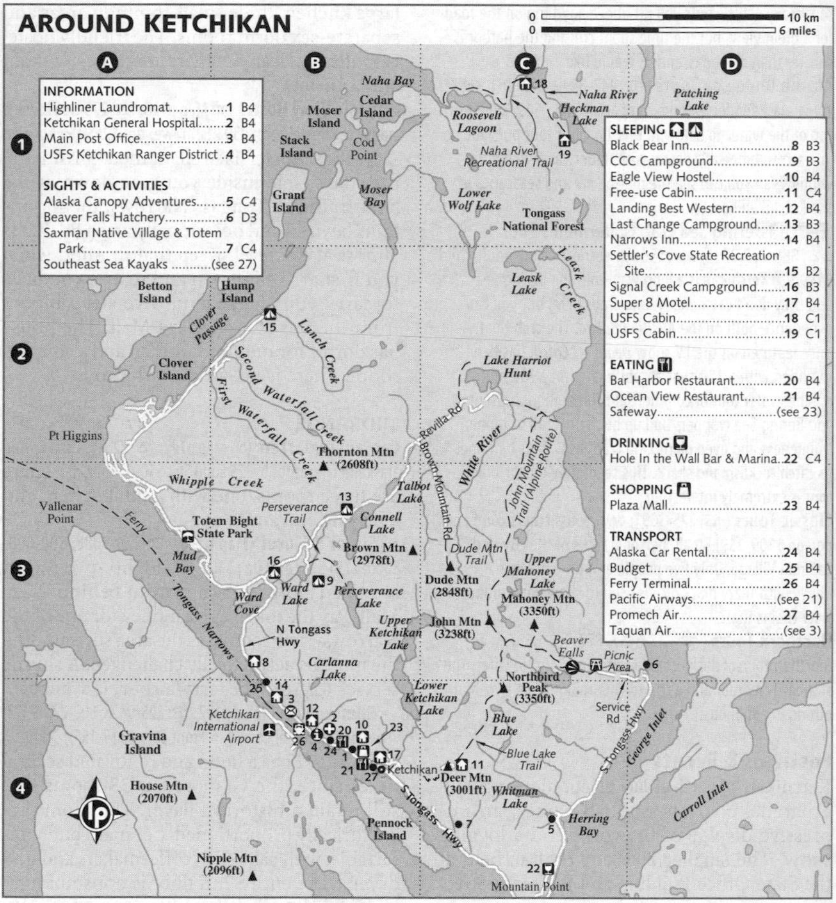

the waterfront, it offers 44 standard rooms that are well kept and very clean. You pay extra for the ocean-view rooms despite the fact that the view from most of them is the airport runway on the other side of the Narrows.

TOP END

our pick **Black Bear Inn** (Map p128; ☎ 225-4343; www.stayinalaska.com; 5528 N Tongass Hwy; r $160-230; ☒ 💻) This incredible B&B offers a range of waterfront accommodations 2.5 miles north of the downtown madness. There are four bedrooms in the home and a small apartment on the 2nd floor. Outside is a logger's bunkhouse that was floated to Ketchikan and renovated into a charming cabin. Every room in the house has been beautifully put together by the proprietor who doubles as an artist. Among the many amenities is a covered hot tub outside where you can soak while watching eagles soaring and whales swimming in the narrows.

Landing Best Western (Map p128; ☎ 225-5166, 800-428-8304; www.landinghotel.com; 3434 Tongass Ave; s/d from $193/203; 💻) Across the street from the ferry terminal is this sprawling hotel with 107 rooms and suites that feature cable TV, microwaves, coffeemakers and small refrigerators. Onsite is a pub, restaurant and a fitness center, just in case walking the 2 miles downtown isn't enough exercise for you. The location is great for late arrivals but the price is high for what you get.

West Coast Cape Fox Lodge (Map p122; ☎ 225-8001, 866-225-8001; www.westcoasthotels.com/capefox; 800 Venetia

Way; r $195-229;) This is Ketchikan's splashiest lodging. Perched atop the hill behind Creek St, it offers the best views in town and can be reached by a high-tech funicular tram from the Creek St boardwalk. The opulent lodge has 72 amenity-filled rooms and suites, and an acclaimed restaurant overlooking the city. There is so much native art in the lobby – baskets, totems, an 1880 ceremonial shirt – it's like walking through a gallery. Also on-site is a coffee shop, gift store and staff that can arrange almost any tour possible.

Eating

Ketchikan has many places to eat, but the expensive Alaskan prices usually send the newly arrived visitor into a two-day fast. If this is your first Alaskan city, don't fret – it only gets worse as you head north!

RESTAURANTS

Annabelle's (Map p122; ☎ 225-6009; 326 Front St; chowders $6-9, dinner $18-30; 10am-9:30pm) At the Gilmore Hotel, this keg and chowder house has a seafood-heavy menu, a wonderful bar and 1920s decor. The chowder is good, the keg half of the restaurant even better, with its long polished bar, brass foot rest and antique slot machine. Where are the spittoons?

Ocean View Restaurant (Map p128; ☎ 225-7566; 1831 Tongass Ave; lunch specials $7-9, dinner $13-20; 11am-11pm) Ketchikan's best Mexican restaurant offers 10 types of burritos, nine sizzling fajita dishes and, in that great Alaskan tradition, pasta, pizza and a decent veal marsala. It's all served in pleasant surroundings overlooking the Narrows.

Sushi Harbor (Map p122; ☎ 225-1233; 629 Misson St; lunch specials $9-11, rolls $7-13; 10am-10pm, to 9pm Sun). This Japanese restaurant bustles all day with locals, tourists and cruise-ship workers. Who knew sushi would be such a hit in Ketchikan? Just a bowl of udon noodles will keep you going all afternoon.

Heen Kahidi Restaurant (Map p122; ☎ 225-8001; 800 Venetia Way; breakfast $8-12, lunch $10-18, dinner $18-40; 7am-9pm Mon-Thu, to 9:30pm Fri & Sat, to 8:30pm Sun;) Generally regarded as Ketchikan's best dining experience, the West Coast Cape Fox Lodge restaurant offers hilltop dining with floor-to-ceiling windows providing a view of the world below. The dinner menu is split between seafood and steaks.

Bar Harbor Restaurant (Map p128; ☎ 225-2813; 2813 Tongass Ave; lunch $9-12, dinner $15-30; 11am-9pm Mon-Fri, 5-9pm Sat & Sun;) A small cozy place between downtown and the ferry terminal with an intriguingly eclectic menu that is constantly changing. Yeah, they serve seafood here but there's also a lot of things on the menu that didn't start life in the water, such as the signature dish, Ketchikan's best prime rib. Beer and wine are available, and so is a back deck with its covered tables and watery view.

CAFÉS

Ketchikan Coffee Co (Map p122; ☎ 225-0246; 207 Stedman St; breakfast $7-10, lunch $8-13; 7am-4pm Sat-Thu, to midnight Fri;) The historic ambience of the New York Hotel spills over into its fine coffee bar. Along with lattes and espressos, there are beers and wines on the blackboard menu and often live music on Friday evening. In the morning you can enjoy a bagel sandwich or surf the internet.

Pioneer Café (Map p122; ☎ 225-3337; 619 Mission St; breakfast $8-13, lunch $8-12, dinner $10-17; 6am-10pm Sun-Thu, 24hr Fri & Sat) One of the few downtown restaurants that was around when the lumber mills were. It serves reindeer sausage at breakfast and some of the best clam chowder in the city.

Chico's (Map p122; ☎ 225-2833; 435 Dock St; lunch $6.50-8, dinner $9.50-14, medium pizzas $14-18; 10am-11pm) A Mexican place that also serves pizza, a gyro plate and a three-piece fried chicken dinner. Hey, they're just trying to make living. The majority of the menu is Mexican and the interior definitely south of the border in this small restaurant of less than a dozen tables.

QUICK EATS

our pick **Burger Queen** (Map p122; ☎ 225-6060; 518 Tongass Ave; burgers $5-8; 11am-3pm Mon, 11am-7pm Tue-Sat) Ketchikan's favorite burger joint. Ten varieties, including one with a Polish sausage *and* a hamburger patty, plus 30 flavors of milkshakes. Order a burger and fries and it'll deliver it to the Arctic Bar across the street where you can be sipping a beer.

Alaska Fish House (Map p122; ☎ 225-4055; cnr Main St & Spruce Mill Way; sandwiches $9-15; 8am-4pm) Located at ground zero of the cruise-ship strip, this outdoor seafood stand has good salmon chowder, halibut tacos and even fish cakes, along with covered outdoor seating.

GROCERIES

Safeway (Map p128; 2417 Tongass Ave; salad bar per lb $6; 5am-midnight) A grocery store on the side of Plaza Mall; has a salad bar, Starbucks, deli and ready-to-eat items including Chinese food.

An informal inside dining area overlooks the boat traffic on Tongass Narrows.

Drinking

Arctic Bar (Map p122; ☎ 225-4709; 509 Water St) Just past the tunnel on downtown's northwest side, this local favorite has managed to survive 70 years by poking fun at itself and tourists. Inside is a sign used to promote Moose Drool Brown Ale, a real beer served there, while on the back deck overlooking the Narrows is a pair of fornicating bears. Hanging below the wooden bruins, in full view of every cruise ship that ties up in front of the bar, is the sign 'Please Don't Feed The Bears.'

Fat Stan's (Map p122; ☎ 247-9463; Salmon Landing Market) A small and surprisingly mellow place considering it's located in the touristy cruise-ship area. Maybe that's because it makes 20 different types of martinis including Key lime pie and watermelon Jolly Roger. Sip some gin and watch the crowds.

First City Saloon (Map p122; ☎ 225-1494; 830 Water St) Recently renovated, this sprawling club now has two bars, pool tables and comfortable lounge areas with sofas, ottomans and wi-fi. Its dance floor features a 1970s disco ball and a stripper's pole. This is the one place in Ketchikan that rocks, with live music at least twice a week during the summer, often impromptu when cruise-ship bands are looking to let loose.

Potlatch Bar (Map p122; ☎ 225-4855; 126 Thomas St) Just above Thomas Basin, is this longtime fisher's pub that has managed to retain the hard working spirit that Ketchikan needed to survive.

Entertainment

Great Alaskan Lumberjack Show (Map p122; ☎ 225-9050, 888-320-9049; www.lumberjacksports.com; off Spruce Way; adult/child $34/17) When the lumberjacks are at the peak of their axe-and-saw battles you can hear the crowd cheering throughout downtown. A favorite of cruise ships, the hour-long show features 'rugged woodsmen' using handsaws and axes, climbing poles, log rolling and engaging in other activities that real loggers haven't engaged in since the invention of the chainsaw. There are two to three shows daily, depending on how many cruise ships are in.

Getting There & Away

AIR

Flights to Ketchikan from Seattle, Anchorage and major Southeast communities are all possible with **Alaska Airlines** (☎ 00-252-7522; www.alaskaair.com).

Pacific Airways (Map p128; ☎ 225-3500, 877-360-3500; www.flypacificairways.com; 1935 Tongass Ave) offers scheduled floatplane flights between Ketchikan and Prince of Wales Island; Hollis (one way $115), Craig/Klawock ($130) and Thorne Bay ($115).

Ketchikan has many bush-plane operators, including **Taquan Air** (Map p128; ☎ 225-8800, 800-770-8800; www.taquanair.com; 4085 Tongass Ave) and **Promech Air** (Map p128; ☎ 225-3845, 800-860-3845; www.promechair.com; 1515 Tongass Ave).

BOAT

Northbound Alaska Marine Highway ferries leave almost daily in summer, heading north for Wrangell ($37, six hours), Petersburg ($60, nine hours), Sitka ($83, 20 hours), Juneau ($107, 29 hours) and Haines ($134, 33½ hours). Ferries leave Ketchikan twice a week (Sunday and Wednesday) and head south to Bellingham ($239, 37 hours). The MV *Lituya* provides service to Metlakatla ($21, 1½ hours) Thursday through Monday. For sailing times call the **ferry terminal** (Map p128; ☎ 225-6181; 3501 Tongass Ave).

The **Inter-Island Ferry Authority** (☎ 225-4838, 866-308-4848; www.interislandferry.com) operates the MV *Stikine,* which departs Ketchikan at 3:30pm daily and arrives at Hollis on Prince of Wales Island at 6:30pm (one way adult/child $37/18).

Getting Around

TO/FROM THE AIRPORT

The Ketchikan airport is on one side of Tongass Narrows, the city is on the other. A small car-and-passenger ferry ($5 for walk-on passengers) runs between the airport and a landing off Tongass Ave, just northwest of the main ferry terminal. The **Airporter** (☎ 225-9800) bus meets all arriving Alaska Airlines flights at the terminal and will take you to/from downtown for $25, ferry fare included. There isn't a better way to arrive at the First City than **Tongass Water Taxi** (☎ 225-8294). Richard Schuerger meets all flights at the baggage-claim area and then gives you a lift on his boat to the dock nearest to your destination. The cost downtown is $19 for the first person and $8 for every additional person.

BUS

Ketchikan's excellent public bus system is called the **Bus** (☎ 225-8726; fare $1), but don't worry, there's more than one of them. There are now three lines, with the green line circling through the heart of the city from the airport ferry to Thomas Basin, the red line heading north past Saxman Village to Rotary Beach and the blue line heading south all the way to Totem Bight State Park. The green and red buses run daily, the blues only on weekdays.

CAR

For two to four people, renting a car is a good way to spend a day seeing sights out of town. There's unlimited mileage with either of the following but a 16% tax:

Alaska Car Rental (Map p128; ☎ 225-2232, 225-5123, 800-662-0007; 2828 Tongass Ave; compacts $55)

Budget (Map p128; ☎ 225-6004, Ketchikan International Airport; ☎ 225-8383, 4950 N Tongass Hwy; compacts $57)

TAXI

Cab companies in town include **Alaska Cab** (☎ 225-2133) and **Yellow Taxi** (☎ 225-5555). The fare from the ferry terminal or the airport ferry dock to downtown is $12.

AROUND KETCHIKAN

South Tongass Highway

On S Tongass Hwy 2.5 miles south of Ketchikan, is **Saxman Native Village & Totem Park** (Map p128; ☎ 225-4421; www.capefoxtours.com; village tour adult/child $35/17; ⌚ 8am-5pm), an incorporated Tlingit village of 430 residents. The village is best known for its **Saxman Totem Park**, which holds 24 totem poles brought here from abandoned villages around the Southeast and restored or recarved in the 1930s. Among the collection is a replica of the Lincoln Pole (the original is in the Alaska State Museum in Juneau), which was carved in 1883, using a picture of Abraham Lincoln, to commemorate the first sighting of white people.

You can wander around the Totem Park at no charge, but most visitors take an Alaska Native–led two-hour village tour that includes a Tlingit language lesson, traditional drum-and-dance performance, narrated tour of the totems and a visit to the carving shed. Independent travelers can join this tour by prebooking at the Ketchikan visitors bureau or by calling the village a day in advance.

From Saxman, S Tongass Hwy continues another 12 miles, bending around Mountain Point and heading back north to George Inlet. This route is more scenic than N Tongass Hwy, but holds little in the way of stores, restaurants or campgrounds. One exception is **Hole in the Wall Bar & Marina** (Map p128; ☎ 247-2296; 7500 S Tongass Hwy; ⌚ noon-2am), a funky little hangout that feels light years away from the tourist madness of Ketchikan in summer. There's not much inside other than a handful of stools, a woodstove, a pool table and a lot of friendly conversation usually centered on fishing. But the bar is in a beautiful location, perched above a small marina in a narrow cove off George Inlet.

In Herring Bay there is a hatchery and Alaska Canopy Adventures (p126), a zipline operation. The S Tongass Hwy then ends at Beaver Falls Hatchery, where the Silvis Lake Trail begins nearby.

North Tongass Highway

The closest campgrounds to Ketchikan are in Ward Lake Recreation Area; take N Tongass Hwy 4.5 miles north of the ferry terminal and turn right onto Revilla Rd, then continue 1.5 miles to Ward Lake Rd. **CCC Campground** (Map p128; sites $10), basically an overflow area, is on Ward Lake's east shore while **Signal Creek Campground** (Map p128; sites $10) has 24 sites on the south shore. **Last Chance Campground** (Map p128; Revilla Rd; sites $10) is in a beautiful area with four scenic lakes, 19 sites and three trails that depart into the lush rain forest.

Ten miles northwest of Ketchikan is **Totem Bight State Park** (Map p128; ☎ 247-8574; 9883 N Tongass Hwy; sites free), which contains 14 restored or recarved totems and a colorful community house. Just as impressive as the totems are the park's coastline and wooded setting. A viewing deck overlooks Tongass Narrows.

Tongass Hwy ends 18 miles north of Ketchikan at **Settler's Cove State Recreation Area** (Map p128; sites $10), a scenic coastal area with a lush rain forest bordering a gravel beach and rocky coastline. Its campground has 14 sites, a quarter-mile trail to a waterfall and observation deck, and is rarely overflowing like those at Ward Lake.

MISTY FIORDS NATIONAL MONUMENT

This spectacular, 3570-sq-mile national **monument** (Map p107), just 22 miles east of Ketchikan, is a natural mosaic of sea cliffs, steep fjords and rock walls jutting 3000ft straight out of the ocean. Brown and black bears, mountain goats, Sitka deer, bald eagles and a multitude of marine mammals inhabit this drizzly realm. The monument receives

150in of rainfall annually, but many people think Misty Fiords is at its most beautiful when the granite walls and tumbling waterfalls are veiled in fog and mist. Walker Cove, Rudyerd Bay and Punchbowl Cove – the preserve's most picturesque areas – are reached via Behm Canal, the long inlet separating Revillagigedo Island from the mainland.

Kayaking is *the* best way to experience the preserve (see p107). Ketchikan's **Southeast Sea Kayaks** (☎ 225-1258, 800-287-1607; www.kayakketchikan.com; 1621 Tongass Ave) offers a one-day guided paddle in which small groups and their kayaks are transported by boat to the fjords and back (adult/child $399/369). It also has a three-day weekender guided tour ($899) and rents kayaks (see Paddling, p125).

You can also view the area on sightseeing flights or day cruises. Flightseeing may be the only option if you're in a hurry, and most tours include landing on a lake and a short walk in the rain forest. But keep in mind that this is a big seller on the cruise ships and when the weather is nice it is an endless stream of floatplanes flying to the same area: Rudyerd Bay and Walker Cove. Throw in the tour boats and one local likened such days to 'the Allie invasion of Omaha Beach.'

For more on the monument, contact the **USFS Ketchikan Ranger District** (Map p128; ☎ 225-2148; www.fs.fed.us/r10/tongass; 3031 Tongass Ave).

Sleeping

If you plan ahead, you can rent one of 13 **USFS cabins** (☎ 877-444-6777, 515-885-3639; www.recreation.gov; cabins $25-45) in the area. The cabins must be reserved in advance, usually several months. A 14th cabin, at Big Goat Lake, is free and available on a first-come, first-served basis, as are four Adirondack shelters (three-sided free-use shelters) in the preserve.

Getting There & Around

There isn't an air charter in Ketchikan that doesn't do Misty Fiords. The standard offering is a 1½-hour flight with a lake landing for $220 to $250, and it's easily booked at the visitors center. The following air charters offer tours and cabin drop-offs:

Alaska Seaplane Tours (☎ 225-1974, 866-858-2327; www.alaskaseaplanetours.com)

our pick **Family Air Tours** (☎ 247-1305, 800-380-1305; www.familyairtours.com)

Seawind Aviation (☎ 225-1206, 877-225-1203; www.seawindaviation.com)

Southeast Aviation (☎ 225-2900, 888-359-6478; www.southeastaviation.com)

Cruises on a speedy catamaran are another option. **Allen Marine Tours** (Map p122; ☎ 225-8100, 877-686-8100; www.allenmarinetours.com; 50 Front St) is the main operator, using an 80ft catamaran to offer a four-hour tour through the monument, which includes a narration, snacks and use of binoculars to look at wildlife (adult/child $153/95).

PRINCE OF WALES ISLAND

pop 3536

For some tourists, the Alaska they come looking for is only a three-hour ferry ride away from the crowds of cruise-ship tourists they encounter in Ketchikan. At 140 miles long and covering more than 2230 sq miles, Prince of Wales Island (POW) is the USA's third-largest island, after Alaska's Kodiak and Hawaii's Big Island.

This vast, rugged island is a destination for the adventurous at heart, loaded with hiking trails and canoe routes, Forest Service cabins and fishing opportunities. The 990-mile coastline of POW meanders around numerous bays, coves, saltwater straits and protective islands, making it a kayaker's delight. And for someone carrying a mountain bike through Alaska, a week on the island is worth all the trouble of bringing the two-wheeler north. The island has the most extensive road system in the Southeast, 1300 miles of paved or maintained gravel roads that lead to small villages and several hundred miles more of shot-rock logging roads that lead to who-knows-where.

Presently tourism is relatively light but is bound to increase due to the expanding service of the Inter-Island Ferry Authority. The Authority launched its first vessel, MV *Prince of Wales,* in 2002 replacing the Alaska Marine Highway service between Ketchikan and Hollis. Four years later the Authority launched MV *Stikine* and opened a second route from Coffman Cove to Wrangell and South Mitkof Island, eliminating the need to backtrack to Ketchikan if you want to visit POW.

There are no cruise ships on POW but there are clear-cuts and you must be prepared for them. Blanketing the island is a patchwork quilt of lush spruce-hemlock forest and fields of stumps where a forest used to be. They are a sign that you have reached real Alaska, a

DETOUR: HYDER

On the eastern fringe of Misty Fiords National Monument, at the head of Portland Canal, is Hyder (Map p119; pop 83), a misplaced town if there ever was one. It was founded in 1896 when Captain DD Gailland explored Portland Canal for the US Army Corps of Engineers and built four stone storehouses, the first masonry buildings erected in Alaska, which still stand today. Hyder and its British Columbian neighbor Stewart boomed after major gold and silver mines were opened in 1919. Hyder became the supply center for more than 10,000 residents. It's been going downhill ever since, the reason it now calls itself 'the friendliest ghost town in Alaska.'

A floatplane or a long drive from Prince Rupert are the only options for getting here. Because of Hyder's isolation from the rest of the state it's almost totally dependent on larger Stewart (pop 700), just across the Canadian border. Hyder's residents use Canadian money, set their watches to Pacific time (not Alaska time), use Stewart's area code and send their children to Canadian schools. When there's trouble, the famed Canadian Mounties step in. All this can make a sidetrip here a little confusing.

The most famous thing to do in Hyder is drink at one of its 'friendly saloons.' The historic **Glacier Inn** (☎ 250-636-9092) is the best known and features an interior papered in signed bills, creating the '$20,000 Walls' of Hyder. Next door is First and Last Chance Saloon, and both bars hop at night. There's also the **Toastworks** (☎ 250-636-2344; 306 5th Ave; breakfast $5-8; 🕑 7-11am) in Stewart, a restaurant that doubles up as a toaster museum. No kidding.

But the best reason to find your way to this out-of-the-way place is for bear watching. From late July to September, you can head 6 miles north of town to Fish Creek Bridge and watch brown and black bears feed on chum salmon runs. The USFS has constructed a viewing platform here and there are interpreters on-site during summer. Continue along the road and you cross back into British Columbia at Mile 11. At Mile 23 is a point from which to view the impressive **Bear River Glacier**, Canada's fifth largest. If you don't have wheels **Seaport Limousine** (☎ 250-636-2622; www.seaportnorthwest.com; 516 Railway St) picks up at Stewart hotels every evening for a trip out to the observation area (per person C$12).

For lodging there is the **Hyder Base Camp Hostel** (www.hyderhostel.com; dm $25; ⊠ 💻), a rustic facility that is open from mid-May through mid-September and accepts reservations only through email. A quarter-mile from downtown Hyder is the venerable family-run **Grandview Inn** (☎ 250-636-9174; www.grandviewinn.net; s/d $70/75) with 10 rooms, private baths and TV. The nicest accommodations are on the Canadian side at **Ripley Creek Inn** (☎ 250-636-2344; www.ripleycreekinn.com; 306 5th Ave; r $50-$120; ⊠ 💻) which has 11 rooms in its main lodge and 21 more in a handful of historical buildings nearby, one a former brothel. A mile from Stewart is **Bear River RV Park** (☎ 250-636-9205; www.stewartbc.com/rvpark; Hwy 37A, Stewart; sites camp/RV C$14/23) with 55 sites along the Bear River. In Stewart your room rate will be jacked skyward by Canada's 7.5% Goods & Services Tax (GST) and another 10% in BC provincial taxes.

Unfortunately if you're in Ketchikan, the only way to reach Hyder is to fly with **Taquan Air** (Map p122; ☎ 225-8800, 800-770-8800; www.taquanair.com), which makes the run twice a week on Monday and Thursday ($370 round-trip). That may seem expensive but consider that a day trip to Admiralty Island's Pack Creek to see brown bears is around $500. If you're in Terrace, BC, with nowhere to go, Seaport Limousine in Stewart offers scheduled buses to Stewart that depart at 6:45am Monday to Friday (one way C$55).

For information on either town, contact the **Stewart/Hyder International Chamber of Commerce** (☎ 250-636-9224, 888-366-5999; www.stewart-hyder.com; 222 5th Ave, Stewart).

resource-based state where people make a living from fishing, mining and cutting down trees.

Orientation & Information

Hollis (pop 186), where the ferry from Ketchikan lands, has few visitor facilities and no stores or restaurants. The towns best set up for tourism are Craig (pop 1054) and Klawock (pop 743), only 7 miles apart and a 31-mile drive across the island along the paved Hollis-Klawock Hwy. Founded as a salmon-canning and cold-storage site in 1907, Craig is the island's largest and most interesting community, with its mix of commercial fishermen and loggers.

PRINCE OF WALES ISLAND

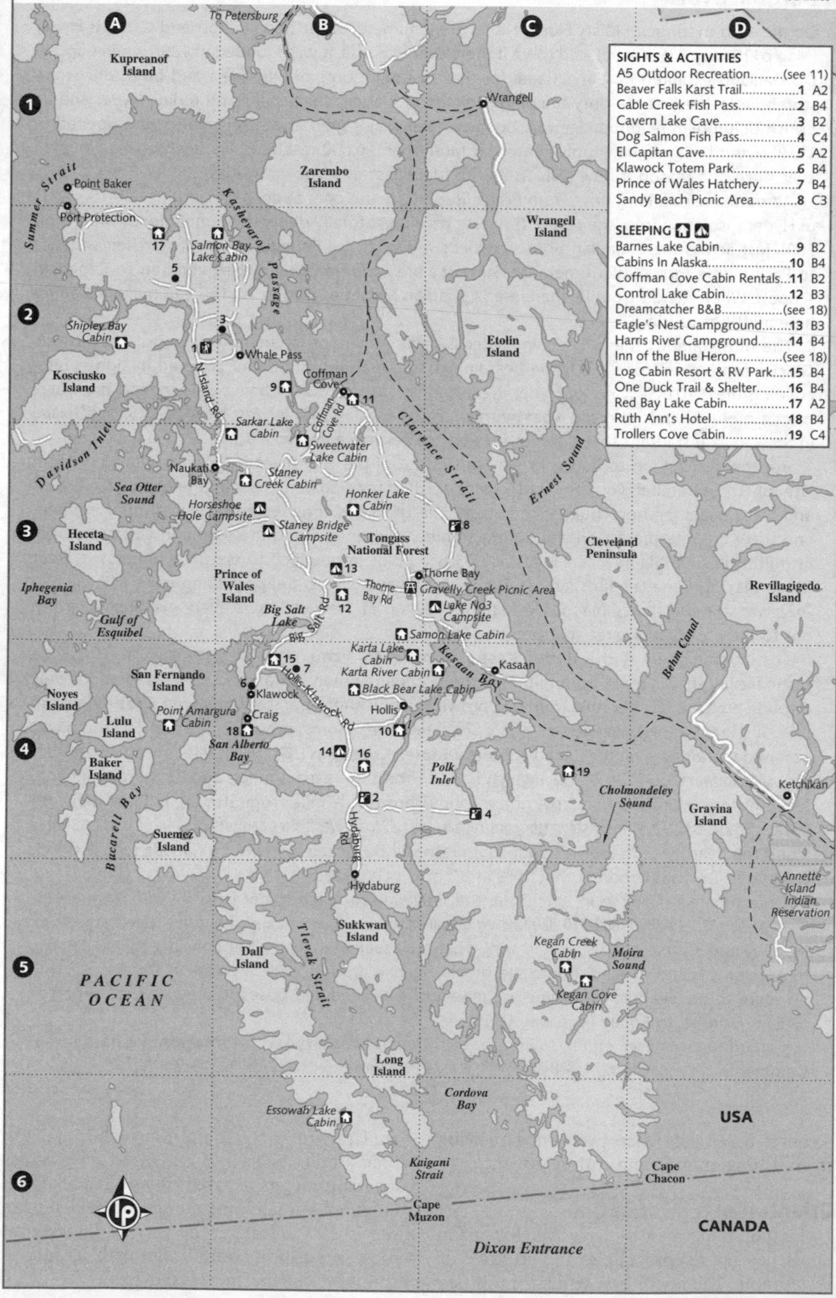

Also supporting lodging, restaurants, small grocery stores and other visitor amenities are Thorne Bay (pop 467), 38 miles northeast from Klawock, and Coffman Cove (pop 147), 55 miles north of Klawock. POW now has 150 miles of paved roads that connect all of these towns, with the exception of Coffman Cove.

For a quick visit, the map found inside the free *Prince of Wales Island Guide* is sufficient. For an extended stay or if you're planning to explore the logging roads, purchase the *Prince of Wales Island Road Guide* ($10) published by the USFS. Either is available at the POW Chamber of Commerce or USFS Ranger Station.

Alicia Roberts Medical Center (☎ 755-4800; Hollis-Klawock Hwy, Klawock) Main medical facility on the island.

Craig Library (☎ 826-3281; 504 3rd St, Craig; ⌚ 10am-noon & 1-5pm Tue-Fri, 7-9pm Mon-Thu, noon-4pm Sat) Has used books for sale and free internet access.

Prince of Wales Chamber of Commerce (☎ 755-2626; www.princeofwalescoc.org; Klawock Bell Tower Mall, Hollis-Klawock Hwy; ⌚ 10am-3pm Mon-Fri) Operates a visitors center in Klawock with internet and wi-fi.

Post office (Craig-Klawock Hwy, Craig) Next to Thompson House Supermarket.

USFS office (⌚ 8am-5pm Mon-Fri) Craig (☎ 826-3271; 900 9th St); Thorne Bay (☎ 828-3304; 1312 Federal Way) In Craig, head here for information on trails, cabins and paddling adventures.

Voyageur Bookstore & Coffee Company (☎ 826-2333; 801 Water St; ⌚ 7am-5pm Mon-Fri, from 8am Sat, 10am-4pm Sun) A wonderful bookstore in Craig with an espresso bar. There's free wi-fi with a coffee purchase.

Wells Fargo (☎ 826-3040; 301 Thompson Rd, Craig) Next to the post office and equipped with a 24-hour ATM.

Sights & Activities

Of the three totem parks on POW, the **Klawock Totem Park** (Bayview Blvd) is by far the most impressive and obviously a great source of community pride. Situated on a hill overlooking the town's cannery and harbor, Klawock's 21 totems are the largest collection in Alaska and make for a scenic, almost dramatic setting. The totems are either originals from the former village of Tukekan or replicas.

The **Prince of Wales Hatchery** (☎ 755-2231; Mile 9 Hollis-Klawock Hwy; ⌚ 8am-noon & 1-4pm) was established in 1897 and today is the second-oldest one in Alaska. The present facility was built in 1976 and raises coho, king and sockeye salmon with many released into the adjacent Klawock River. Inside the visitors center is an aquarium and gift shop where fresh coho is often for sale; outside you can occasionally see black bears feeding across the river.

On the island's southern half, you can watch salmon attempt to negotiate a couple of **fish ladders** during the summer spawning season. Both **Cable Creek Fish Pass** and **Dog Salmon Fish Pass** have viewing platforms, from which you might also see hungry black bears.

The USFS maintains more than 20 hiking trails on POW, with the majority of them being short walks to rental cabins, rivers or lakes. In the south, a good hike can be made to **One Duck Shelter** from a trailhead on the road to Hydaburg, 2 miles south of Hollis junction. The trail is steep, climbing 1400ft in 1.2 miles, but it ends at a three-sided free-use shelter that sleeps four. To spend the night in the open alpine area with panoramic views of the Klawock Mountains is worth the knee-bending climb. To the north the **Balls Lake Trail** begins in the Balls Lake Picnic Area just east of Eagle's Nest Campground and winds 2.2 miles around the lake.

Mountain bikers have even more opportunities than hikers. Bikes can be rented in Coffman Cove from **A5 Outdoor Recreation** (☎ 329-2399; www.a5outdoorrec.com; 103A Sea Otter Dr; per day $25) and then taken on any road to explore the island. One of the most scenic roads to bike is South Beach Rd (also known as Forest Rd 30) from Coffman Cove to Thorne Bay. It's a 37-mile ride along the narrow, winding dirt road that is often skirting Clarence Strait. Along the way is **Sandy Beach Picnic Area** (Mile 6 Sandy Beach Rd), an excellent place to see humpback whales, orcas and harbor seals offshore or examine intriguing tidal pools at low tides.

Opportunities for paddlers are almost as limitless as they are for mountain bikers. At the north end of POW off Forest Rd 20 is the **Sarkar Lakes Canoe Route**, a 15-mile loop of five major lakes and portages along with a USFS cabin and excellent fishing. For a day of kayaking depart from Klawock and paddle into **Big Salt Lake**, where the water is calm and the birding is excellent. A5 Outdoor Recreation also rents kayaks (single/double $50/60 per day) as well as canoes ($55 per day) and will provide transportation for an additional fee.

Sleeping

Log Cabin Resort & RV Park (☎ 755-2205, 800-544-2205; www.logcabinresortandrvpark.com; Big Salt Lake Rd; sites per person $10, cabins $95-170) Located a half-mile up Big Salt Rd in Klawock, it offers condos, three

CAVING ON PRINCE OF WALES ISLAND

One of the most unusual aspects of POW's geology is the broad cave system found in the north end of the island. The karst formation is an area of eroded limestone concealing underground streams and caverns, and it includes more than 850 grottos and caves. The caves received national attention in the mid-1990s when paleontologists from the University of South Dakota discovered the remains of a man dating back 9500 years in one cave, and the almost perfect remains of a brown bear that dated 45,000 years in another. Both let scientists speculate how the last ice age affected animal and human migration from Asia.

The two most popular caves are northwest of Thorne Bay, a 94-mile drive from Hollis, and can be easily viewed even if you've never worn a headlamp. At **El Capitan Cave** (Forest Rd 15), 11 miles west of Whale Pass, you can take a free, two-hour, ranger-led cave tour offered daily in summer at 9am, noon and 2:30pm. Tours are limited to six people and involve a 370-step stairway trail. Contact the USFS **Thorne Bay Ranger Station** (☎ 828-3304) for reservations (required at least two days in advance; no children under seven). Nearby **Cavern Lake Cave**, on the road to Whale Pass, features an observation deck allowing visitors to peer into the cave's mouth at the gushing stream inside.

Also in the area is the short, wheelchair-accessible **Beaver Falls Karst Trail**, on the main road between the two turnoffs for Whale Pass, which offers an above-ground experience as its boardwalk leads past sinkholes, pits, underground rivers and other typical karst features.

rustic beachfront cabins and tent space with showers and a community kitchen. It also rents canoes (per day $25) for use on Big Salt Lake or Klawock Lake.

Coffman Cove Cabin Rentals (☎ 329-2251; per person $40) A pair of self-contained cabins with fully equipped kitchens and within walking distance of the ferry terminal.

Inn of the Blue Heron (☎ 826-3608; www.littleblueheroninn.com; 406 9th St; s $79-99, d $99-115; ⊠ 💻) A delightful B&B overlooking a boat harbor in Craig with three upstairs rooms featuring TVs, small refrigerators and microwaves.

Cabins in Alaska (☎ 888-648-7277; www.cabinsinalaska.com; Hollis-Craig Rd; bunkhouses/cabins $100/200) Less than 6 miles west of the Hollis Ferry Terminal is this resort with cabins that sleep four and bunkhouses that sleep two. Both have kitchens while nearby is a bathhouse with showers and laundry facilities.

Dreamcatcher B&B (☎ 826-2238; www.dreamcatcherbedandbreakfast.com; 1405 Hamilton Dr; r $105; ⊠ 💻) Three guestrooms in a beautiful seaside home in Craig. Big picture windows and a wraparound deck give way to a wonderful view of water, islands, mountains and, of course, clear-cuts.

Ruth Ann's Hotel (☎ 826-3378; cnr Main & Water Sts; r $110-136; ⊠) Across the street, Ruth Ann's renowned restaurant is her hotel which has 14 rooms in two buildings.

CABINS & CAMPING

There are 18 **USFS cabins** (☎ 877-444-6777, 518-885-3639; www.recreation.gov; $35-45), one Adirondack shelter and two campgrounds on the island. Two cabins can be reached by rowing across a lake, thus eliminating the floatplane expense required with many others. **Control Lake Cabin** is reached from State Hwy 929, where a dock and rowboat are kept on the west end of the lake. **Red Bay Lake Cabin** is at the north end of the POW, off Forest Rd 20, and reached with a half-mile hike to a boat and then a 1.5-mile row across the lake.

Harris River Campground (sites $8) This is near the Hollis Rd junction. The 14-site USFS campground has fire rings, BBQ grills and picnic tables; seven sites have tent pads.

Eagle's Nest Campground (sites $8) This 11-site campground, 18 miles west of Thorne Bay, overlooks a pair of lakes. It has a canoe-launching site and a half-mile shoreline boardwalk.

Eating

Dave's Dine (☎ 755-2986; 6648 Big Salt Rd; breakfast $5-9, lunch $6-11, dinner $11-20; 🕑 11am-7pm Mon-Thu, to 8pm Fri, 8am-8pm Sat, to 7pm Sun) A rambling diner in Klawock with a sloping floor and an attached bus that serves as the kitchen. The burgers are good and the onion rings are great; don't let them roll off the table.

Dockside Restaurant (☎ 826-5544; Front St, Craig; breakfast $6-13, lunch $9-12; 🕑 5:30am-3pm) New owners took over this wonderful breakfast place but its legendary pies ($3.75 per slice) are just as good as before, only now Ellen's making them.

Ruth Ann's Restaurant (☎ 826-3377; 300 Front St, Craig; dinner $16-49; 🕑 7am-9pm; ⊠) This would be a favorite no matter what Alaskan city it was located in, but in Craig it becomes one of those unexpected joys. The small restaurant with an even smaller bar offers quaint waterfront dining with views of the bay, weathered wharfs and fishing boats returning with their catch that often ends up on your plate: salmon, oysters, steamer clams and giant prawns stuffed with crab.

Getting There & Away

The **Inter-Island Ferry Authority** (☎ 866-308-4848, Coffman Cove 329-2345, Hollis 530-4848, Ketchikan 225-4838; www.interislandferry.com) operates a pair of vessels, with the MV *Stikine* departing daily from Hollis at 8am and from Ketchikan at 3:30pm (one way adult/child $37/18). The MV *Prince of Wales* departs Coffman Cove at 7am Friday, Saturday and Monday for Wrangell ($37/18) and then the south end of Mitkof Island ($49/27), where there is road access to Petersburg.

Getting Around

For lengthy stays it's best to rent a car in Ketchikan and take it over on the ferry. Rates for the ferry are based on vehicle length; a subcompact one way is $50. You can also rent a Ford Escort (pavement only) or a 4WD Kia Sportage in Craig through **Wilderness Rent-A-Car** (☎ 800-949-2205; www.wildernesscarrental.com) for $70 per day with unlimited mileage.

Indian Time Taxi (☎ 401-0800; 401-0700) connects with ferries in Hollis but you will want to give them a call from Ketchikan to reserve a seat. The one-way fare to Craig is $35.

WRANGELL & AROUND

pop 2023

Strategically located near the mouth of the Stikine River, Wrangell is one of the oldest towns in Alaska and the only one to have existed under three flags and ruled by four nations – Tlingit, Russia, Britain and America.

Wrangell's heyday was as a jumping-off point for three major gold rushes up the Stikine River from 1861 to the late 1890s. Back then Wrangell was as lawless and ruthless as Skagway and at one point Wyatt Earp, the famous Arizona lawman, filled in as a volunteer marshal for 10 days before moving on to Nome. Wrangell's most famous visitor, however, was John Muir, who came in 1879 and again in 1880. Muir wrote that 'Wrangell village was a rough place. It was a lawless draggle of wooden huts and houses, built in crooked lines, wrangling around the boggy shore of the island for a mile or so.'

Eventually Wrangell became a fishing and lumber town typical of Southeast Alaska, and when the timber industry crashed in the early 1990s the town was hit harder than most. Some pin a brighter future on an emerging dive fishery as more than 60 divers already harvest sea urchins, sea cucumbers and geoducks. Others see Wrangell's salvation in the proposed Bradfield Rd and ferry, which would connect the town to Canada's mainland roads.

Of all the Alaska Marine Hwy's major stops, Wrangell is the least gentrified. Cruise ships are only a once-a-week occurrence here, so the town is rarely inundated and isn't ritzy. You don't come to Wrangell for posh luxury hotels or well-developed tourist attractions. Instead, use Wrangell as a home base for exploring the surrounding wilds.

The island offers great mountain-biking and bike-camping opportunities; kayakers can explore the Stikine River or myriad islands and waterways around the river's mouth; and local guides lead boat trips to Anan Creek bear observatory and other places of interest.

Orientation & Information

Wrangell is blessed with a ferry terminal downtown, so even if you're not planning to spend the night here, you can still disembark for a brief look around or a (quick!) hike to the petroglyphs.

Churchill Laundromat (Shakes St; 🕒 7am-9pm) Next to the Marine Bar (how convenient!) with showers and a sign that reads 'No Pets Allowed In Showers!'

First Bank (☎ 874-3363; 224 Brueger St) Across from IGA Supermarket, it also maintains a 24-hour ATM on Front St.

Irene Ingle Public Library (☎ 874-3535; 124 2nd St; 🕒 10am-noon & 1-5pm Mon & Fri, 1-5pm & 7-9pm Tue-Thu, 9am-5pm Sat) A wonderful facility for such a small town; includes free internet access on four computers and a paperback exchange.

Post office (112 Federal Way) At the town's north end.

USFS Office (☎ 874-2323; 525 Bennett St; 🕒 8am-4:30pm Mon-Fri) Located three-quarters of a mile north of town; has information on regional USFS cabins, trails and campgrounds.

Wrangell Medical Center (☎ 874-7000; 310 Bennett St) For anything from Aspirin to Zoloft.

Wrangell Museum (☎ 874-3770; 296 Outer Dr; 🕒 10am-5pm Mon-Sat) The gift shop in this fine museum has the best selection of Alaskan books in town.

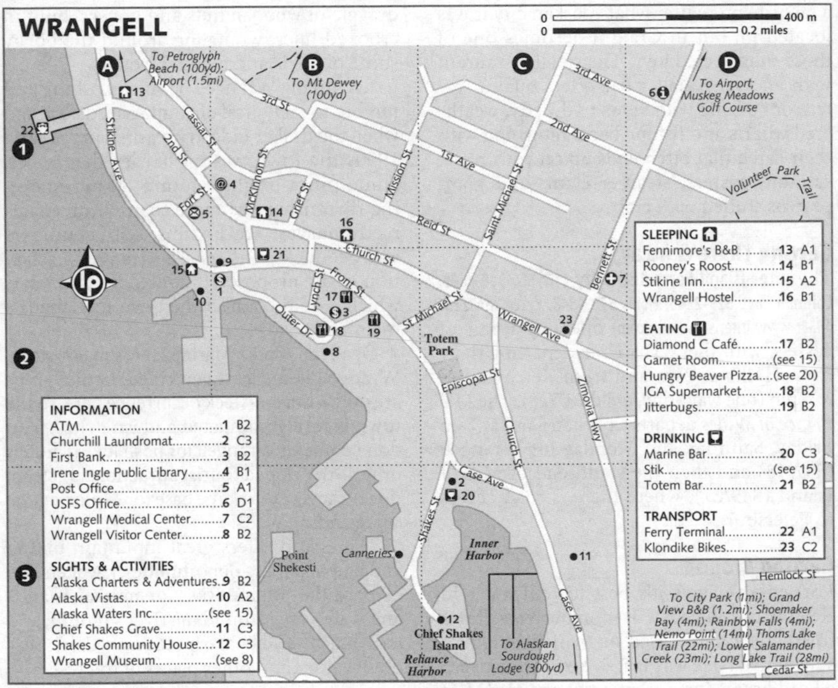

Wrangell Visitor Center (☎ 874-3699, 800-367-9745; www.wrangell.com; 296 Outer Dr; 🕑 10am-5pm Mon-Sat) In the Nolan Center, stocks the free *Wrangell Guide* and shows a 10-minute film on the area in a small theater. It also offers internet access ($5/10 per 20 minutes/hour).

Sights

WRANGELL MUSEUM

This impressive **museum** (☎ 874-3770; 296 Outer Dr; adult/child/family $5/3/12; 🕑 10am-5pm Mon-Sat) in the Nolan Center is what the colorful history and characters of Wrangell deserves. As you stroll through the many rooms an audio narration automatically comes on and explains that chapter of Wrangell's history, from Tlingit culture and the gold-rush era to the time Hollywood arrived in 1972 to film the movie *Timber Tramps*. You can marvel at a collection of Alaskan art that includes a Sidney Laurence painting or be amused that this rugged little town has had two presidential visits (Warren Harding and Ronald Reagan).

CHIEF SHAKES ISLAND

This **island** (Shakes St) is the most enchanting spot in Wrangell. The small grassy islet is in the middle of the boat harbor and reached by a pedestrian bridge. The tiny island, with its totems, tall pines and the half-dozen eagles usually perched in the branches, is a quiet oasis compared to the hum of the fishing fleet that surrounds it. In the middle is **Shakes Community House**, an excellent example of a high-caste tribal house that contains tools, blankets and other cultural items. It's open only to accommodate cruise ships (call the Wrangell Museum for times). Just as impressive are the six totems surrounding the tribal house, all duplicates of originals carved in the late 1930s.

PETROGLYPH BEACH

Located on the town's north side is a state historic park where you can see primitive rock carvings believed to be at least 1000 years old. The best set is located three-quarters of a mile from the ferry terminal and can be reached by heading north on Evergreen Ave where a sign marks the boardwalk that leads to a viewing deck with interpretive displays and petroglyph replicas. Follow the stairway to the beach and then turn right and walk north about 50yd. Before you reach the wrecked fishing vessel (photographers will love it), look for the carvings on the large rocks, many of them resembling spirals and faces. There are almost 50 in the area and you need to hunt around to find most of them. The majority are submerged at high tide so check a tide book before you leave and bring a bottle of water. The carvings are easier to see when wet.

TOTEMS

For its size, Wrangell has an impressive collection of totems, more than a dozen scattered through town. Pick-up the free *Wrangell Guide* at the visitor center and spend an afternoon locating them all. Make sure you stop at **Chief Shakes Grave** to see the killer-whale totems.

Activities

BEAR WATCHING

Thirty miles southeast of Wrangell on the mainland, Anan Creek is the site of one of the largest pink salmon runs in Southeast Alaska. From the platforms at Anan Creek Wildlife Observatory (Map p119) you can watch eagles, harbor seals, black bears and a few brown bears chowing down gluttonously on the spawning humpies. This is one of the few places in Alaska where black and brown bears coexist – or at least put up with each other – at the same run. Permits ($10) are required from early July through August, or basically when the bears are there, and are reserved online (www.fs.fed.us/r10/tongass/recreation/wildlife_viewing/ananobservatory) or by calling the USFS Office (p137) in Wrangell. Almost half of the daily 60 permits go to local tour operators. Another 18 are available from March 1 for that particular year and 12 permits are issued three days in advance.

Anan Creek is a 20-minute floatplane flight or an hour boat ride, and almost every tour operator in town offers a trip there. **Alaska Charters & Adventures** (☎ 874-4157, 888-993-2750; www.alaskaupclose.com; 7 Front St) offers a eight-hour trip to the observatory ($198) and **Alaska Waters Inc** (☎ 874-2378, 800-347-4462; www.alaskawaters.com), at the Stikine Inn, has a six-hour boat tour ($245). **Sunrise Aviation** (☎ 874-2319; www.sunriseflights.com; Wrangell Airport) will provide permits and fly you in and out for $375 each way for up to four passengers.

The best way to see the bears, if you can plan ahead, is to reserve the USFS **Anan Bay Cabin** (☎ 877-444-6777; www.recreation.gov; $35), which comes with four permits and is a mile hike from the observation area. This cabin can be reserved six months in advance and during the bear-watching season it pretty much has to be.

HIKING

Other than the climb up Mt Dewey and walking the Volunteer Park Trail, all of Wrangell's trails are off the road and often include muskeg. You'll need a car for the roads and a pair of rubber boots for the trails.

Mt Dewey Trail is a half-mile climb up a hill to a small clearing in the trees, overlooking Wrangell and the surrounding waterways. From Mission St, walk a block and turn left at 3rd St. Follow the street past the houses to the posted stairway on the right. The hike to the top takes 15 minutes or so, but the trail is often muddy. John Muir fanatics will appreciate the fact that the great naturalist climbed the mountain in 1879 and built a bonfire on top, alarming the Tlingit people living in the village below. Ironically, the only signs on top now say 'No Campfires.' The other hike in town is the half-mile **Volunteer Park Trail**, a pleasant forested walk that begins near the park's ball field off 2nd Ave.

Signposted 4.7 miles south of the ferry terminal on the Zimovia Hwy is the **Rainbow Falls Trail**. The trail begins directly across from Shoemaker Bay Recreation Area. It's less than a mile to the waterfalls and then another 2.7 miles along **Institute Creek Trail** to the Shoemaker Bay Overlook Shelter. The lower section of the trail can be soggy at times, the upper section steep. The views are worth the hike, and a pleasant evening can be spent on the ridge. A round-trip takes four to six hours.

A 1.4-mile path to the lake, **Thoms Lake Trail** is reached by following Zimovia Hwy to its paved end and then turning east on Forest Rd 6267. About halfway across the island, just before crossing Upper Salamander Creek, turn right on Forest Rd 6290 and follow it 4 miles to the trailhead. The first half-mile of the trail is planked, but the rest cuts through muskeg and can get extremely muddy during wet weather. There's an old ragged, but still usable, cabin on the lake.

Long Lake Trail begins 28 miles southeast of Wrangell on Forest Rd 6270 and is a pleasant 0.6-mile hike. The planked trail leads to a shelter, skiffs and outhouses on the shores of the lake. Plan on an hour round-trip for the trek.

MUSKEG MEADOWS

Completed in 1998 atop the sawdust and wood chips left behind by local sawmill operations, Wrangell's nine-hole **Muskeg Meadows Golf Course** (☎ 874-4653; www.wrangellalaskagolf.com; Ishiyama Dr; per round $20), half a mile east of Bennet Dr, may be the first certified course in the Southeast, but it's uniquely Alaskan. Surrounded by wilderness, members are rarely alarmed when a bear comes bounding across a fairway. Then there is the club's Raven Rule: if a raven steals your ball you may replace it with no penalty provided you have a witness. Finally, the course's narrow fairways and tangled roughs of spruce and muskeg have resulted in this warning posted in the clubhouse: 'You got to have a lot of balls to play Muskeg Meadows.'

PADDLING

One look at a nautical chart of Wrangell will have kayakers drooling and dreaming. Islands and protected waterways abound, though many are across the vast Stikine River flats, where experience is a prerequisite due to strong tides and currents. Novices can enjoy paddling around the harbor, over to Petroglyph Beach or to Dead Man's Island.

Alaska Vistas (☎ 874-2997, 866-874-3006; www.alaskavistas.com; 106 Front St; 🕑 7am-6pm), inside the Java Junkies espresso shed, a wi-fi hot spot at City Dock, rents kayaks (per day single/double $55/65). The company also runs guided kayak tours including a full-day East West Cove paddle ($210) on the well-protected east side of Wrangell Island. Vans are used to transport you to the east shore and a jet boat returns you to Wrangell at the end of the day.

Rainwalker Expeditions (☎ 874-2549; www.rainwalkerexpeditions.com) also rents kayaks (single/double $40/60 per day) and offers a kayaker drop-off service to the easy-to-explore back side of the island. The company also has Hike-Bike-Kayak tour ($99) that includes paddling to Shoemaker Bay, hiking the Rainbow Falls Trail and biking back to town.

Stikine River

A narrow, rugged shoreline and surrounding mountains and glaciers characterize the beautiful, wild Stikine River, which begins in the high peaks of interior British Columbia and ends some 400 miles later in a delta called the Stikine Flats, just north of Wrangell. The Stikine is North America's fastest navigable river, and its most spectacular sight is the Grand Canyon of the Stikine, a steep-walled gorge where violently churning white water makes river travel impossible. John Muir called this stretch of the Stikine 'a Yosemite 100 miles long.'

Trips from below the canyon are common among rafters and kayakers. They begin with a charter flight to Telegraph Creek in British Columbia and end with a 160-mile float back to Wrangell.

Travelers arriving in Wrangell with a kayak but insufficient funds to charter a bush plane can paddle from the town's harbor across the Stikine Flats (where there are several USFS cabins) and up one of the Stikine River's three arms. By keeping close to shore and taking advantage of eddies and sloughs, experienced paddlers can make their way 30 miles up the river to the Canadian border, or even farther, passing 12 **USFS cabins** (☎ 877-444-6777; www.recreation.gov), the two bathing huts at **Chief Shakes Hot Springs** and **Shakes Glacier** inside Shakes Lake along the way. But you must know how to line a boat upstream and navigate a highly braided river and, while in the lower reaches, accept the fact that you'll encounter a lot of jet-boat traffic.

Wrangell's USFS office can provide information on the Stikine River, including two helpful publications: *Stikine River Canoe/Kayak Routes* ($5) and *Lower Stikine River Map* ($5), the latter covering the river up to Telegraph Creek.

Several Wrangell guide services run trips on the Stikine or offer drop-off services for kayakers. **Breakaway Adventures** (☎ 874-2488, 888-385-2488; www.breakawayadventures.com) uses a jet boat for a day trip up the river that includes Shakes Glacier and the hot springs ($170). **Stikeen Wilderness Adventures** (☎ 800-874-2085; www.akgetaway.com) provides a water-taxi service for kayakers and rafters, charging $225 per hour for up to six passengers or $205 if you rent kayaks from Alaska Vistas. Also providing tours or transport up the Stikine River is **Alaska Charters & Adventures** (☎ 874-4157, 888-993-2750; www.alaskaupclose.com).

Festivals & Events

The summer's biggest event is the **Fourth of July** celebration. All of Wrangell gets involved in the festival, which features a parade, fireworks, live music, a logging show, street games, food booths and a salmon bake.

In the third week of April, Wrangell hosts its **Stikine River Garnet Festival**, where boat tours head up the river to gather green crystallized stones known as garnets and witness the largest springtime concentration of bald eagles in Alaska.

Sleeping

Wrangell levies a 7% sales tax and a flat $4 per room bed tax on all lodging.

Wrangell Hostel (☎ 874-3534; 220 Church St; dm $18; ☒) In the First Presbyterian Church, this basic place has separate-sex dorm rooms with foam-rubber pads and inflatable mattresses, showers and a large kitchen and dining room. It has no lockout hours, graciously letting you hang out there during an all-day rain, but an 11pm curfew is requested.

Fennimore's B&B (☎ 874-3012; www.fennimoresbbb.com; 321 Stikine Ave; r $90; ☒) The easiest lodging for late-night ferry passengers to reach, as it's a five-minute walk, if that, across the street from the ferry terminal. Four rooms, basic but clean, on the 1st floor have private bath and private entrances. All have cable TV, a refrigerator, microwave and queen-size bed. It's pleasant to sit on the wrap-around deck, and there are bikes for guests to tool around town on.

Alaskan Sourdough Lodge (☎ 874-3613, 800-874-3613; www.akgetaway.com; 1104 Peninsula St; s/d $104/114; ☒ 💻) This family-owned lodge was hosting visitors when there were still lumber mills in Wrangell. It offers 16 rooms, a sauna, steam bath, free transportation to/from the ferry or airport and a front deck full of wicker furniture with a view of the harbor.

Rooney's Roost (☎ 874-2026; www.rooneysroost.com; 206 McKinnon St; r $110-130; ☒ 💻) Within easy walking distance from the ferry, just a short way up 2nd St, is this antique-filled B&B. There are four guestrooms with queen-size beds, TV and private baths. In the morning you enjoy a full breakfast, and in the afternoon you can relax on the deck with view of Wrangell.

Grand View B&B (☎ 874-3225; www.grandviewbnb.com; Mile 1.9 Zimovia Hwy; r $115-135; ☒ 💻) Just beyond City Park is this seaside B&B with its entire ground devoted to guests. That includes three spacious rooms, a large kitchen and outdoor covered patio. The best part is the living room that features four comfy recliners positioned in front of a row of picture windows looking out at Zimovia Strait.

WHEN AN ARTIST IS A CHARTER CAPTAIN

At **Alaska Charters & Adventures** (☎ 874-4157, 888-993-2750; www.alaskaupclose.com; 7 Front St) you can book a cruise to LeConte Glacier or purchase a painting. You can meet a well-known artist or hire her to take you up the Stikine River. They're all the same. Brenda Schwartz-Yeager is an artist whose distinct maritime-theme watercolors are seen throughout the Southeast. She's also a licensed charter captain and in her Wrangell shop you can book a cruise or watch her paint.

The unusual combination is the result of growing up on fishing boats in Wrangell. 'There's not much else to pass the time on a boat than either work or soak up the amazing scenery,' Schwartz-Yeager said. 'So I drew everything I saw the way some people would write a journal every day.'

Eventually Schwartz-Yeager developed her trademark style; classic watercolor techniques combining the creativity of wispy backgrounds with accurately detailed vessels and lighthouses. Then in the early 1980s while sailing in Prince William Sound she discovered she was out of paper in her sketch book. She was about to draw a scene on the back of a maritime navigational chart but everybody on the boat encouraged her to do it on the front. 'I thought it was a crazy idea at first but afterwards loved the concept of 'this is where I was and this is what I saw',' Schwartz-Yeager said.

Today, that unique style, vessels painted on the brown navigation charts, can be seen in West Coast galleries from California to Alaska. But in Wrangell the artist is often working in her shop if she's not out a running a boat-load of visitors to watch brown bears on Anan Creek or baiting their hooks so they can catch a 80lb halibut.

Which begs the question, is she an artist or a charter captain? 'I found out they go hand-in-hand. I quit running boats for a season while my kids were little but I quickly discovered that I get my inspiration to paint from all the beautiful things I see on the water.'

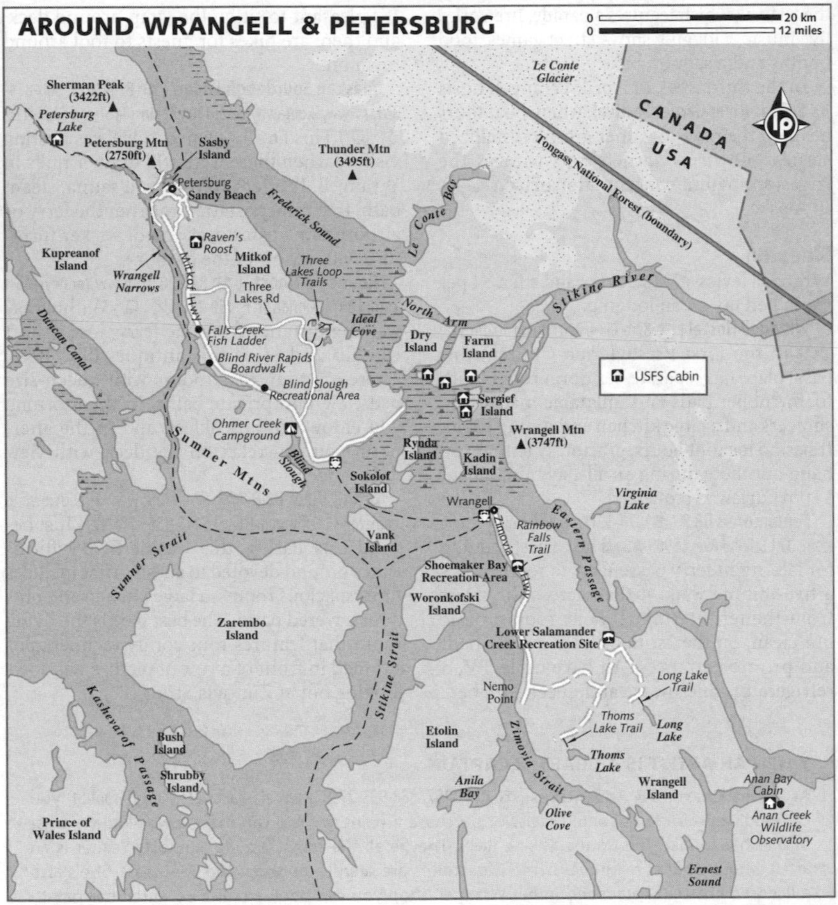

Stikine Inn (☎ 874-3388; www.stikineinn.com; 107 Stikine Ave; s/d $130/160; 💻) Wrangell's largest motel is on the waterfront near the ferry dock and underwent a major renovation in 2008 that included its bar, lobby and many of the 33 rooms. The waterside rooms are now among the best in town while there's also an onsite restaurant, saloon and gift shops.

CAMPING

City Park (☎ 874-2444, Mile 1.7 Zimovia Hwy) For those with a tent, the closest campground is this delightful waterfront park, 1 mile south of town and immediately south of a historic cemetery. Within the pleasant wooded setting are eight sites, shelters and rest rooms. Camping is free, but for tents only. There's a one-night limit if you have a car, but that's overlooked if you arrive on foot.

Shoemaker Bay Recreation Area (☎ 874-2444; Mile 4.5 Zimovia Hwy; sites limited to 5 days free, RV sites limited to 10 days $15-25) This is across from the Rainbow Falls trailhead in a wooded area near a creek. There are 25 sites, 15 with hook-ups for RVers, and a tent-camping area for everybody sleeping in ripstop nylon. All sites have a good view of Zimovia Strait.

Nemo Point (☎ 874-2323; Forest Rd 6267; sites free) This offers the best camping on Wrangell Island, but unfortunately it is 14 miles from town. Each of the six free wheelchair-accessible sites has a picnic table, outhouse and a stunning view of Zimovia Strait. Take

Zimovia Hwy/Forest Hwy 16 south to Forest Rd 6267. The sites stretch along 4 miles of Forest Rd 6267.

Lower Salamander Creek Recreation Site (☎ 874-2323; Forest Rd 50050; sites free) East of Nemo Point, you're allowed three free campsites along beautiful Salamander Creek. Take Zimovia Hwy 23 miles south of town to Forest Rds 6265 and 50050.

Eating

Jitterbugs (☎ 874-3350; 309 Front St; 5:30am-2pm Mon-Sat) An early-morning espresso stand proffering lattes, cappuccinos and Italian sodas with an attitude and a dash of humor. Signs above the outside tables range from 'Friends Don't Let Friends Drink Starbucks' to 'Jitterbugs parking only. Violators will be decaffeinated.'

Diamond C Café (☎ 874-3322; 223 Front St; breakfast $6-12, lunch $8-14; 6am-3pm) Eat what the locals eat; eggs and hash browns, biscuits and gravy, deep-fried fish and chips, and listen to the conservative pulse of the community from the tables around you.

Garnet Room (☎ 874-3388; 107 Stikine Ave; breakfast $8-13, dinner $12-25; 6am-9pm) Located on the ground floor, Stikine Inn's restaurant features a menu dominated not by fish but 21 types of burgers ($9 to $15). Every one of them is served with excellent harbor views.

Hungry Beaver Pizza (☎ 874-3005; Shakes St; pizzas $17-23; 4-10pm) Adjoining the Marine Bar, this Beaver serves up Wrangell's favorite pie: a taco pizza with seasoned hamburger, refried beans and cheese, baked and then loaded with lettuce, tomatoes, salsa and sour cream. It comes with the fantasy of spending the winter in Mexico.

Alaskan Sourdough Lodge (☎ 874-3613; 1104 Peninsula St; dinner $19-24) If you call ahead, it allows you to join its guests for home-style meals that include a salad bar and often crab, halibut and salmon during the summer.

IGA Supermarket (223 Brueger St; 8am-6pm Mon-Sat) It has an in-store bakery, espresso and a deli with some ready-to-eat items and sandwiches.

Drinking

Stik (☎ 874-3388; 107 Stikine Ave) The Stikine Inn's new lounge is the classiest place to have a drink and watch the fishing boats slip into the harbor.

Totem Bar (☎ 874-3533; Front St) On Wednesday this is the biggest scene in town because it's karaoke night in Wrangell.

Marine Bar (☎ 874-3005; Shakes St) Fishing industry folks hang out at this place, near the harbor.

Getting There & Around

Daily northbound and southbound flights are available with **Alaska Airlines** (☎ 874-3308, 800-426-0333). Many claim the flight north to Petersburg is the 'world's shortest jet flight,' since the six- to 11-minute trip is little more than a takeoff and landing.

Alaska Marine Highway (☎ 874-3711) services run almost daily both northbound and southbound from Wrangell in summer. To the north is Petersburg ($33, three hours) via the scenic, winding Wrangell Narrows, to the south Ketchikan ($37, six hours). The **Inter-Island Ferry Authority** (☎ 866-308-4848; www.interislandferry.com) operates the new MV *Stikine* between Coffman Cove on Prince of Wales Island and Wrangell ($37, three hours) on Friday, Saturday and Sunday. On the same days the boat connects Wrangell with the south end of Mitkof Island ($26, one hour), where Petersburg is 25 miles away by road.

Practical Rent-A-Car (☎ 874-3975), at the airport, rents compacts for $47 per day plus a 17% rental tax. **Klondike Bikes** (☎ 874-2549; 502 Wrangell Ave) rents bikes for $25/75 per day/week.

PETERSBURG

pop 3123

From Wrangell, the Alaska Marine Highway ferry heads north to begin one of the Inside Passage's most scenic sections. After crossing over from Wrangell Island to Mitkof Island, the vessel threads through the 46 turns of Wrangell Narrows, a 22-mile channel that is only 300ft wide and 19ft deep in places. So winding and narrow is the channel that locals call it 'pinball alley.' Others refer to it as 'Christmas tree lane' because of the abundance of red and green navigational lights.

At the other end of this breathtaking journey lies Norwegian-influenced Petersburg, one of Southeast Alaska's hidden gems. Peter Buschmann arrived in 1897 and found a fine harbor, abundant fish and a ready supply of ice from nearby LeConte Glacier. He built a cannery in the area, enticed his Norwegian friends to follow him here, and gave his first name to the resulting town. Today, a peek into the local phone book reveals the strong Norwegian heritage that unifies Petersburg.

The waterfront of this busy little fishing port is decorated with working boats and weathered boathouses, while tidy homes and businesses – many done up with distinctive Norwegian rosemaling, a flowery Norwegian art form – line the quiet streets. Petersburg boasts the largest home-based halibut fleet in Alaska and processes more than $32 million worth of seafood annually in its four canneries and two cold-storage plants. The canneries sit above the water on pilings, overlooking boat harbors bulging with vessels, barges, ferries and seaplanes. Even at night, you can see small boats trolling the nearby waters for somebody's dinner.

The town lies across Frederick Sound from a spectacular glaciated wall of alpine peaks – including the distinctive Devil's Thumb – that form a skyline of jagged snowcapped summits. Nearby LeConte Glacier discharges icebergs to the delight of visitors.

Without a heavy dependency on timber, Petersburg enjoys a healthier economy than Wrangell or Ketchikan, so it doesn't need to pander to tourists. That makes Petersburg a joy for independent travelers, who will quickly discover the locals are friendly and their stories interesting.

Orientation

The ferry terminal is a mile north from downtown Petersburg; the airport is a mile east. Either is an enjoyable walk, unless you're hauling too many bags or it's the middle of the night. The main road out of town is the Mitkof Hwy, which heads 34 miles south to Sumner Strait, with the first half paved to Blind Slough. The best map for downtown and the road system is the free Petersburg Chamber of Commerce's *Petersburg Map*.

Information

First Bank (☎ 772-4277; 103 N Nordic Dr) Has a 24-hour ATM.

Glacier Laundry (☎ 772-4144; 313 Nordic Dr; 🕓 6am-9pm Sat-Thu, 24hr Fri) This place doesn't close on Friday so all the cannery workers can jump in the shower ($2) and be ready for the weekend.

Petersburg Medical Center (☎ 772-4299; 103 Fram St; 🕓 9am-5pm Mon-Fri, to 1pm Sat) Has a 24-hour

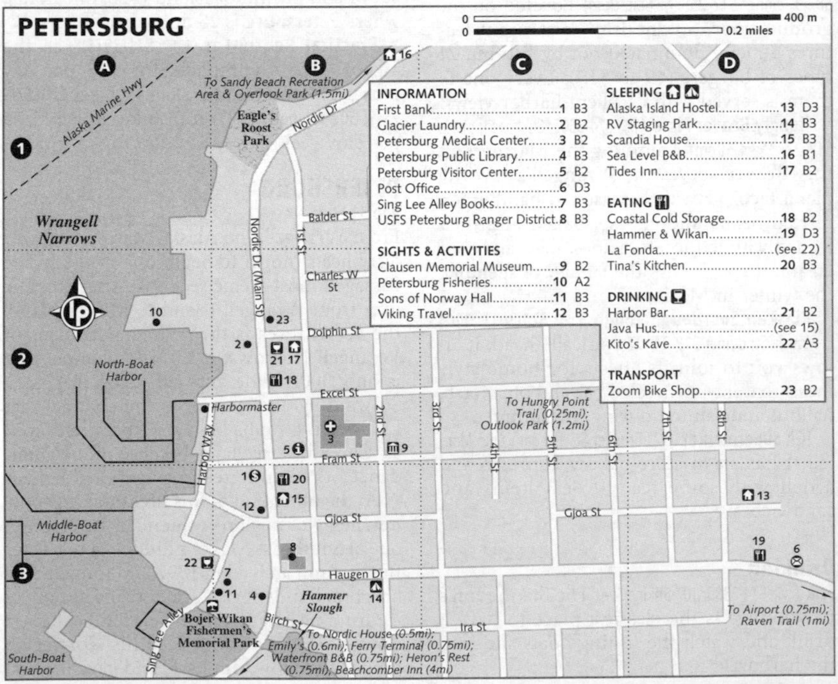

emergency room, while on Saturday operates as a drop-in health clinic.

Petersburg Public Library (☎ 772-3349; 12 S Nordic Dr at Haugen; noon-9pm Mon-Thu, 10am-5pm Fri & Sat) Upstairs in the Municipal Building. There's free, no-hassle internet and wi-fi.

Petersburg Visitor Center (☎ 772-4636, 772-3646; www.petersburg.org; cnr Fram & 1st Sts; 9am-5pm Mon-Sat, noon-4pm Sun) A good first stop, with both tourist and USFS information.

Post office (1201 Haugen Dr; 9am-5:30pm Mon-Fri, 11am-2pm Sat) Located half a mile east of downtown on the way to the airport.

Sing Lee Alley Books (☎ 772-4440; 11 Sing Lee Alley; 9:30am-5:30pm Mon-Sat, 1-3pm Sun) In a former 1929 boardinghouse, this delightful bookstore has five rooms of books and a well-read proprietor .

USFS Petersburg Ranger District (☎ 772-3871; 12 N Nordic Dr; 8am-5pm Mon-Fri) For information about hiking trails, paddling, camping or reserving cabins.

Sights

Clausen Memorial Museum (☎ 772-3598; 203 Fram St; adult/child $3/free; 10am-5pm Mon-Sat) holds an interesting collection of artifacts and relics, mostly related to local fishing history. Exhibits include the largest king salmon ever caught (126lb), a giant lens from the old Cape Decision lighthouse, a Tlingit dugout canoe and the 30-minute film, *Petersburg; The Town Fish Built*. Outside is *Fisk*, the intriguing fish sculpture that was commissioned in 1967 to honor the Alaska Centennial.

Heading south, Harbor Way passes Middle Boat Harbor and turns into **Sing Lee Alley**. This was the center of old Petersburg, and much of the street is built on pilings over Hammer Slough. On the alley, **Sons of Norway Hall** is the large white building with the colorful rosemaling built in 1912 and the center for Petersburg's Norwegian culture. Come on down and play bingo at 7pm on Saturday; 'O-32,' ja shore you betcha.

Also along Sing Lee Alley is **Bojer Wikan Fishermen's Memorial Park**. This deck of a park is built on pilings over Hammer Slough and features an impressive statue of a fisher that honors all his fellow crew members lost at sea. Also on display is the *Valhalla*, a replica of a Viking ship that was built in 1976 and purchased by Petersburg two years later.

The **North-Boat Harbor** (Excel St at Harbor Way), is the best one for wandering the docks, talking to crews and possibly even scoring some fresh fish. Begin at the Harbormaster Office where a wooden deck provides a picturesque overview of the commercial fleet and has a series of interpretive panels that will teach you the difference between purse seine and a long-liner. Continue north along the waterfront to see **Petersburg Fisheries** (Dolphin St at Nordic Dr), the original outfit founded by Peter Buschmann in 1900; today it's a subsidiary of Seattle's Icicle Seafoods.

From downtown, Nordic Dr heads north on a scenic route that ends at **Sandy Beach Recreation Area**, a beautiful day-use area 2 miles from downtown. There are 2000 year-old Tlingit fish traps snaking the mud flats and a rock with petroglyphs carved on it. Both the traps and the carvings are hard to spot but the Petersburg Ranger District (left) organizes guided interpretive walks to them during the summer here. Call for times.

Activities

HIKING

Within town is the 0.7-mile **Hungry Point Trail** that begins at the ball field at the end of Excel St and cuts across muskeg. The gravel path keeps your feet dry, but surrounding you are stunted trees so short you have a clear view of Petersburg's mountainous skyline. The trail ends at Sandy Beach Rd and by heading right a quarter-mile you reach **Outlook Park**, a marine wildlife observatory with free binoculars to search Frederick Sound for humpbacks, orcas and sea lions.

The 4-mile **Raven Trail** begins at the water tower on the airport's southeast side (accessible from Haugen Dr). It crosses muskeg areas on a boardwalk, then climbs to beautiful open alpine areas at 2000ft. Some sections are steep and require a little scrambling. The trail eventually leads to the USFS **Raven's Roost Cabin** (☎ 877-444-6777, 515-885-3639; www.recreation.gov; cabins $35). The cabin is above the treeline, providing easy access to good alpine hiking and spectacular views of Petersburg, Frederick Sound and Wrangell Narrows.

On Kupreanof Island, the 3.5-mile **Petersburg Mountain Trail** climbs to the top of Petersburg Mountain (2750ft), which offers views of Petersburg, the Coast Mountains, glaciers and Wrangell Narrows. Plan on five hours for the round-trip. To get across the channel, go to the skiff float at the North Boat Harbor and hitch a ride with somebody who lives on Kupreanof Island. On the Kupreanof side, head right on the overgrown road toward Sasby Island. You can also call **Tongass**

Kayak Adventures (☎ 772-4600; www.tongasskayak.com), which runs hikers across the channel for $25 per person.

Petersburg Lake Trail is a 10.5-mile trail in the Petersburg Creek-Duncan Salt Chuck Wilderness on Kupreanof Island leading to the USFS **Petersburg Lake Cabin** (☎ 877-444-6777, 515-885-3639; www.recreation.gov; cabins $35). See p102 for details.

At Mile 14.5 of the Mitkof Hwy is the mile-long **Blind River Rapids Boardwalk** that winds through muskeg to the rapids, a scenic area and busy in June for king salmon fishing.

Along Three Lakes Rd, a USFS road heading east off Mitkof Hwy at Mile 13.6 and returning at Mile 23.8, are **Three Lakes Loop Trails**, a series of four short trails that total 4.5 miles. At Mile 14.2 is a 3-mile loop with boardwalks leading to Sand, Crane and Hill Lakes, all known for good trout fishing. Sand Lake has a free-use shelter. From the Sand Lake Trail, a 1.5-mile trail leads to Ideal Cove on Frederick Sound.

PADDLING

Petersburg offers interesting possibilities for kayakers, LeConte Glacier and Tebenkof Bay Wilderness among them, but many of the trips require a week or more. Kayak rentals are available from **Tongass Kayak Adventures** (☎ 772-4600; www.tongasskayak.com; s/d $55/65), which also offers kayak transfers and guided tours, including a four-hour paddle up Petersburg Creek ($85). Its best outing, however, begins with boat transport to LeConte Glacier for a day spent whale watching and paddling among the icebergs ($225).Week-long discounts are available.

LeConte Glacier

The most spectacular paddle in the region is to LeConte Glacier, 25 miles east of Petersburg. It's North America's southernmost tidewater glacier. From town, it takes one to two days to reach the frozen monument, including crossing Frederick Sound north of Coney Island. The crossing should be done at slack tide, as winds and tides can cause choppy conditions. If the tides are judged right, and the ice is not too thick, it's possible to paddle far enough into LeConte Bay to camp within view of the glacier.

Thomas Bay

Almost as impressive as LeConte Glacier is Thomas Bay, 20 miles from Petersburg and north of LeConte Bay on Frederick Sound's east side. The bay has a pair of glaciers, including Baird Glacier, where many paddlers go for day hikes. The mountain scenery around the bay is spectacular, and the area has three USFS cabins: **Swan Lake Cabin** (per night $35), **Spurt Cove Cabin** (per night $25) and **Cascade Creek Cabin** (per night $35). All need reservations. Paddlers should allow four to seven days for the round-trip out of Petersburg.

Kake to Petersburg

Kayakers can take the ferry to the Alaska Native village of Kake and paddle back to Petersburg. This 90-mile route follows Kupreanof Island's west side through Keku Strait, Sumner Strait and up the Wrangell Narrows to Petersburg. The highlight of the trip is Rocky Pass, a remote and narrow winding waterway in Keku Strait that has almost no boat traffic other than the occasional kayaker. Caution has to be used in Sumner Strait, which lies only 40 miles away from open ocean and has its share of strong winds and waves. Plan on seven to 10 days for the trip.

WHALE WATCHING

In recent years, whale watching has become a popular trip out of Petersburg. From mid-May to mid-September humpback whales migrate through, and feed in, Frederick Sound 45 miles northwest of Petersburg with the peak feeding period in July and August. Other wildlife that can be spotted includes Steller's sea lions, orcas and seals.

A handful of charter-boat operators offer six- to eight-hour whale-watching tours that range from $275 to $325 per person. Among them are **Kaleidoscope Cruises** (☎ 772-3736, 800-868-4373; www.petersburglodgingandtours.com), run by Barry Bracken, a marine biologist who focuses on eco-education, and **Whale Song Cruises** (☎ 772-9393, 772-3724; http://whalesongcruises.com), which is equipped with a hydrophone so you can listen to the whales as well as see them.

Tours

For a large selection of area tours, head to **Viking Travel** (☎ 772-3818, 800-327-2571; 101 N Nordic Dr), which acts as a clearinghouse for just about every tour in town. Possibilities include a four-hour boat tour to LeConte Glacier ($170), an eight-hour whale-watching tour ($270) and a helicopter flightseeing tour with a glacier walk ($305).

Most of the charter operators that do whale watching also have sightseeing trips to view LeConte Glacier, and that includes Kaleidoscope Cruises (see opposite), whose five-hour tour is $190 per person. **Pacific Wing Air Charters** (☎ 772-4258; www.pacificwing.com) offers a 45-minute flightseeing trip to the glacier ($165).

Also available, either through Viking or directly, is a combination rain-forest hike and LeConte Glacier cruise with **Tongass Kayak Adventures** (☎ 772-4600; www.tongasskayak.com; per person $180). The full-day outing begins with a hike along Three Lakes Loop Rd and then another to Ideal Cove where a charter boat picks you up for an afternoon at the glacier.

Festivals & Events

The community's best event, famous around the Southeast, is the **Little Norway Festival**, held the third full weekend in May. The festival celebrates Norwegian Independence Day (May 17). The locals dress in old costumes, there's a foot race in the morning, Nordic Dr is filled with a string of booths, games and beer tents in the afternoon, and several dances are staged in the evenings. Best of all are the fish and shrimp feeds, all-you-can-manage-to-eat affairs that are held on various nights.

Sleeping

The city adds 10% sales and bed tax on accommodations.

BUDGET

RV Staging Park (☎ 772-3392, 772-4430; 2nd St at Haugen Dr; sites $6) There's a small RV park right in town but seriously think twice before staying at this depressing mud hole. For those who arrive in a RV or van the city maintains RV Staging Park, a gravel parking area where you can park for the night before moving on. No amenities and unfortunately no place to pitch a tent.

Ohmer Creek Campground (☎ information 772-3871; Mile 22 Mitkof Hwy; sites $6) The USFS campground is 21 miles southeast of town, but it's cheap. It has 15 sites (for tents or RVs), an interpretive trail, fishing in the creek and a scenic setting.

our pick **Alaska Island Hostel** (☎ 772-3632; 877-772-3632; www.alaskaislandhostel.com; 805 Gjoa St; dm $25; May-Sep;) This is Petersburg's excellent and only budget-lodging alternative. The nine-bunk hostel, a short walk from downtown, is clean, comfortable, casual and fun. Amenities include internet access, coffee and tea, laundry facilities, kitchen and a BBQ outside. The proprietor is very accommodating to late night ferry arrivals.

MIDRANGE

Heron's Rest (☎ 772-3373; www.heronsrestalaska.com; 613 Rambler St; d $70-120;) Reached from a private road and tucked away in a personal forest, this elegant B&B is closer to the ferry terminal than downtown. Separated from the main house are three spacious bedrooms and a comfortable living room featuring a flat panel TV, wet bar and a full breakfast in the morning served to a view of the mountains. Completing this Southeast Alaska setting are stacks of crab pots outside (the couple fish commercially) and herons occasionally resting in the surrounding trees.

Nordic House (☎ 772-3620; www.nordichouse.net; 806 S Nordic Dr; without bath s/d $79/89, with bath r $99;) Within an easy walk of the ferry terminal, this place offers five basic rooms that are large and clean. Guests have use of a kitchen/common area that overlooks the boat harbor.

Waterfront B&B (☎ 772-9300, 866-772-9301; www.waterfrontbedandbreakfast.com; 1004 S Nordic Dr; r $95-105;) The closest place to the ferry terminal – it's practically next door. It has an outdoor hot tub where you can soak while watching the ferry depart. Five bright and comfortable rooms have private bath and share a living room that overlooks the Petersburg Shipwrights. For many guests, watching a boat being repaired on dry dock is far more interesting than whatever is on TV.

Sea Level B&B (☎ 772-3240; www.sealevelbnb.com; 913 N Nordic Dr; r $95-125;) A B&B built on pilings over the Wrangell Narrows, making it look more like a boathouse than a home. Two guestrooms have private bath and large picture windows filled with the boat traffic cruising past Mt Petersburg. On the outside deck there are chairs and rod holders so you can catch your dinner when the tides are in.

Tides Inn (☎ 772-4288, 800-665-8433; www.tidesinnalaska.com; 307 1st St; s/d $100/110;) The largest motel in town, with 45 rooms, some with kitchenettes. Rates include a light (very light) continental breakfast.

Scandia House (☎ 772-4281, 800-722-5006; www.scandiahousehotel.com; 110 Nordic Dr; s/d $110/120, ste $195;)

The most impressive place in town, this hotel has 33 bright and modern rooms, some with kitchenettes, and a main-street location. Rates include courtesy shuttle service from the airport/ferry and muffins and coffee in the morning, though it's hard to pass up the jolting espresso in the adjoining Java Hus.

Eating

Emily's (☎ 772-4555; 1000 S Nordic Dr; 🕑 7am-5pm Mon-Fri) If you're catching a morning ferry, stop by Petersburg's best bakery for a cup of coffee and something that just came out of the oven. Even the day-old bread is better than anything else in town.

our pick **Coastal Cold Storage** (☎ 772-4177; 306 N Nordic Dr; breakfast $4-6, lunch $9-12; 🕑 7am-3pm) You're in Petersburg, you have to indulge in what they catch. At the very least, stop at this processor/seafood store/carryout restaurant for a shrimp burger, salmon-halibut chowder or the local specialty, halibut beer bits. Or purchase whatever is swimming in the tanks; steamer clams, oysters or Dungeness crab. Need a beer with those bits? It'll deliver your order next door to the Harbor Bar.

Tina's Kitchen (☎ 772-2090; Nordic Dr next to Scandia House; sandwiches $7-9, dinner $8-12; 🕑 10am-8pm Mon-Sat, 11am-7pm Sun) From this parking lot shack comes good food and great prices. Tina's Korean beef sticks are wonderful: marinated, grilled slices of steak served with steamed rice and kimchi. She also serves good Mexican and local seafood and there's a large tent with heaters where you can mingle with locals while staying dry and warm.

La Fonda (☎ 772-4918; Sing Lee Alley in Kino's Kave; mains $8-12; 🕑 11am-9pm Mon-Sat, noon to 7pm Sun) You may be eating in a bar, but this is good Mexican. Enjoy *camarones a la diabla* (shrimp marinated in Habanero sauce) at night or *huevos rancheros* (ranch eggs) anytime during the day.

Beachcomber Inn (☎ 772-3888; 384 Mitkof Hwy; dinner $15-30; 🕑 bar 5-11pm Sun-Thu, to midnight Fri & Sat, restaurant 5:30-9pm) Built on pilings over the sea, this rambling inn is all restaurant and bar. Every seat has a fabulous maritime-and-mountain view but the small tables on the covered outdoor deck are an especially nice place to kick back. The inn is 4 miles south of town but runs a free shuttle van. So even if you don't want to feast on smoked black cod or a bowl of halibut ceviche, come for a drink as an excuse to gather in the view while chatting up the locals.

Hammer & Wikan (1300 Howkan; 🕑 7am-8pm Mon-Sat, 8am-7pm Sun) Off Haugen Dr on the way to the airport, this is Petersburg's main supermarket.

Drinking

Java Hus (☎ 772-2626; Nordic Dr next to Scandia House; 🕑 6am-6pm Mon-Sat, 7am-4pm Sun; ⊠) This is where Petersburg gets buzzed first thing in the morning.

Harbor Bar (☎ 772-4526; 310 Nordic Dr) The classic place of fishers and cannery workers, with pool tables and an excellent beer selection.

Kito's Kave (☎ 772-3207; Sing Lee Alley) This has regular live music and dancing and when the cruise ships are in, it can be a rowdy place that hops until well after midnight.

Getting There & Around

There are daily northbound and southbound flights with **Alaska Airlines** (☎ 772-4255, 800-426-0333). The airport is on Haugen Dr, a quarter mile east of the post office.

The Alaska Marine Highway **ferry terminal** (☎ 772-3855) is a mile south of downtown. Like the tides, the ferry schedule seems to be in a constant state of fluctuation but in 2008 the high-speed MV *Fairweather* was making a straight run between Juneau and Petersburg ($66, 4½ hours) on Tuesday and Friday.

The new MV *Stikine* of the **Inter-Island Ferry Authority** (IFA; ☎ 866-308-4848; www.interislandferry.com) departs from the south end of Mitkof Island for Wrangell ($26, one hour) and Coffman Cove on Prince of Wales Island ($49, five hours) on Friday, Saturday and Sunday. The IFA terminal is 25 miles from Petersburg but **South Mitkof Express** (☎ 772-3818; $25) provides transport. Call to reserve a seat in advance.

Scandia House (☎ 772-4281, 800-722-5006; www.scandiahousehotel.com; 110 Nordic Dr) rents midsize cars for $58 a day and boats for $140. **Zoom Bike Shop** (☎ 772-2546; www.zoombikeshop.com; 400 N Nordic Dr; 🕑 10am-5:30pm Tue-Sat) is a bike shop downtown that rents mountain and road bicycles for $25 a day. For the 24-hour taxi service there's **Midnight Rides Cab** (☎ 772-2222).

NORTHERN PANHANDLE

Southeast Alaska gets serious when you enter the northern half of the Panhandle. The mountains get higher, the glaciers are more numerous, fiords seem steeper, there's more snow in the winter that lingers on the mountains longer into the summer. You have the current capital and a former one. You have Alaska's most famous gold rush and two roads that actually go somewhere else. Most of all, the dramatic scenery you witness in the Northern Panhandle leads to great wilderness adventures, whether it's canoeing across Admiralty Island, kayaking in Glacier Bay or hiking on Mendenhall Glacier.

SITKA

pop 8805

Fronting the Pacific Ocean on Baranof Island's west shore, Sitka is a gem in a beautiful setting. Looming on the western horizon, across Sitka Sound, is the impressive Mt Edgecumbe, an extinct volcano with a graceful cone similar to Japan's Mt Fuji. Closer in, a myriad of small, forested islands out in the Sound turns into beautiful ragged silhouettes at sunset, competing for attention with the snowcapped mountains and sharp granite peaks flanking Sitka on the east. And in town, picturesque remnants of the Sitka's Russian heritage lurk around every corner.

Sitka is the heart of the Russian influence in Southeast Alaska. The Russians may have landed here as early as 1741 and stayed for more than a century until the Americans finally arrived in 1867 after purchasing Alaska from them. Today Sitka's Russian history, the main attraction for tourists, is as interesting and as well preserved as the Klondike Gold Rush era is in Skagway.

Orientation

The heart of Sitka's downtown is St Michael's Cathedral, the city's beloved Russian Orthodox church, with Lincoln St serving as Main St. From here you're within easy walking distance of almost all of Sitka's attractions. To head out the road, follow either Halibut Point Rd north to the ferry terminal and Starrigavan Campground or Sawmill Creek Rd southeast. Harbor Dr will lead you across O'Connell Bridge and to the airport.

Information

BOOKSTORES

Old Harbor Books (☎ 747-8808; 201 Lincoln St; 9am-6pm Mon-Fri, 10am-5pm Sat, to 3pm Sun) A fine bookstore with a large Alaska section.

LAUNDRY

Sitka Laundry Center (☎ 747-7284; 906 Halibut Point Rd; 6:30am-9pm) Conveniently located across from a McDonald's so you can have a McBurger while waiting for your clothes to dry.

LIBRARY & INTERNET ACCESS

Highliner Coffee (327 Seward St, Seward Square Mall; per 30 min $4.25; 5:30am-5pm Mon-Sat, 8am-4pm Sun;) Two computers for internet access and free wi-fi if you purchase a drink.

Kettleson Memorial Library (☎ 747-8708; 320 Harbor Dr; 10am-9pm Mon-Fri, 1-9pm Sat & Sun) Next door to the Centennial Building and overlooking the harbor is the city's impressive library with free internet access.

MEDICAL SERVICES

Sitka Community Hospital (☎ 747-3241; 209 Moller Dr) By the intersection of Halibut Point Rd and Brady St.

MONEY

First National Bank of Anchorage (☎ 747-3272; 318 Lincoln St) Downtown with a 24-hour ATM.

POST

Pioneer substation (336 Lincoln St; 8:30am-5:30pm Mon-Sat) Conveniently located downtown.

Post office (1207 Sawmill Creek Rd) Main center is 1 mile east of town.

TOURIST INFORMATION

Sitka Convention & Visitors Bureau (☎ 747-5940; www.sitka.org; 303 Lincoln St, Suite 4; 8am-5pm Mon-Fri) Across the street from the cathedral. The bureau also staffs a visitor-information desk in the Centennial Building next to Crescent Harbor.

USFS Sitka Ranger District Office (☎ 747-6671, recorded information 747-6685; 204 Siginaka Way at Katlian St; 8am-4:30pm Mon-Fri) Has information about local trails, camping and USFS cabins.

Sights

ISABEL MILLER MUSEUM

Within the Centennial Building is this **museum** (☎ 747-6455; 330 Harbor Dr; admission by donation; 8am-5pm Mon-Sat), which is one room with a good portion of it a gift shop. The rest is crammed with a collection of relics, a model of the town as it appeared in 1867 and displays on Russian Alaska. Outside between the museum and the library is an impressive handcarved Tlingit canoe, made from a single log.

ST MICHAEL'S CATHEDRAL

Two blocks west of the Centennial Building is the **cathedral** (☎ 747-8120; Lincoln St; donation $2; 9am-4pm Mon-Fri). Built between 1844 and 1848, the church stood for more than 100

years as Alaska's finest Russian Orthodox cathedral. When a fire destroyed it in 1966, the church was the oldest religious structure from the Russian era in Alaska. Luckily the priceless treasures and icons inside were saved by Sitka's residents, who immediately built a replica of their beloved church.

CASTLE HILL & TOTEM SQUARE

Continue west on Lincoln St for the walkway to Castle Hill. Kiksadi clan houses once covered the hilltop site, but in 1836 the Russians built 'Baranov's Castle' atop the hill to house the governor of Russian America. It was here, on October 18, 1867, that the official transfer of Alaska from Russia to the USA took place. The castle burned down in 1894.

More Russian cannons and a totem pole can be seen in **Totem Square**, near the end of Lincoln St. Across Katlian St from the square is the prominent, yellow **Alaska Pioneers Home**. Built in 1934 on the old Russian Parade Ground, the home is for elderly Alaskans. The 13ft-tall bronze prospector statue in front of the state home is modeled on longtime Alaska resident William 'Skagway Bill' Fonda.

BLOCKHOUSE & PRINCESS MAKSOUTOFF'S GRAVE

Still more of Sitka's Russian background guards the hill north of the Alaska Pioneers Home. The **blockhouse** (cnr Kogwanton & Marine Sts) is a replica of what the Russians used to protect their stockade from the Indian village.

Across Marine St, at the top of Princess St, is **Princess Maksoutoff's Grave**, marking the spot where the wife of Alaska's last Russian governor is buried. But for a strategically placed chain-link fence, the grave would be in the Russian Cemetery. But a bright and shiny sign proclaims this tiny three-grave site as the **Lutheran Cemetery**. Cynics might postulate that the princess probably lost her status as a bona fide Lutheran when she married the Russian Orthodox governor, but now that she's a bona fide tourist attraction, the Lutherans want her back.

More old headstones and Russian Orthodox crosses can be found in the overgrown and quintessentially creepy **Russian Cemetery** (located at the north end of Observatory St, or just squeak through the gap in the chain-link fence behind the princess' grave), where the drippy verdure seems poised to swallow up the decaying graves, like something out of a Stephen King novel.

RUSSIAN BISHOP'S HOUSE

East of downtown along Lincoln St, the **Russian Bishop's House** (☎ 747-6281; Lincoln St at Monastery St; adult/child $4/free; 🕑 9am-5pm) is the oldest intact Russian building in Sitka. Built in 1843 out of Sitka spruce, the two-story log house is one of the few surviving examples of Russian colonial architecture in North America. The National Park Service (NPS) has renovated the building to its condition in 1853, when it served as a school, Bishop's residence and chapel. Tours are on the hour and half-hour until 4:30pm.

SHELDON JACKSON MUSEUM

Farther east along Lincoln St on the former campus of Sheldon Jackson College is **Sheldon Jackson Museum** (☎ 747-8981; 104 College Dr; adult/child $4/free; 🕑 9am-5pm). The college may be gone but this fine museum survived because the state of Alaska purchased it in 1983. The unusual building, built to look like a tribal community house, is home to a small but excellent collection of indigenous artifacts gathered from 1888 to 1898 by Dr Sheldon Jackson, a minister and federal education agent in Alaska. Among the artifacts are Alaska Native masks, hunting tools and baskets, and a collection of boats and sleds used in Alaska – from reindeer sleds and dogsleds to kayaks and umiaks.

SHELDON JACKSON AQUARIUM

Just past the campus on Lincoln St is the **Sheldon Jackson Aquarium** (☎ 747-3824; 801 Lincoln St; admission by donation; 🕑 8:30am-5:30pm when volunteers

THE END OF SHELDON JACKSON COLLEGE

In 1878, Presbyterian missionary Sheldon Jackson arrived from New York and opened a school in Sitka on the upper floor of an old soldiers barracks. It originally served as a training school for Tlingit Indians before becoming a boarding school, a junior college and finally a fully accredited four-year liberal-arts institution. Along the way Sheldon Jackson College earned the honor of being Alaska's oldest educational institution in continuous existence.

That is, until June 2007 when the school's Board of Trustees suddenly suspended academic operations due to a financial crisis that included a $6 million debt. A year later most buildings on campus were deserted and boarded-up and the prospect that the property would be subdivided for sale in parcels appear more likely with every passing day.

In Sitka most residents were shocked at the sudden turn of events, some angry with the Board of Trustees for mishandling the school's finances, almost everybody was sad for the loss of this cultural institution. Although Sheldon Jackson College had only 300 full- and part-time students, it had a long history that was closely tied to Sitka and was a source of community pride. It was on the campus that James Michener stayed for the three summers he spent in Alaska working on his epic novel, *Alaska*. In 2003 *Outside Magazine* listed the college as one of the best for hitting the books and the backcountry due to its mountainous surrounding and its unique outdoor leadership program.

It also had a beautiful 17-acre campus that served as a green belt separating the shops of downtown Sitka from the magnificent totem poles of Sitka National Historical Park. Sheldon Jackson College was not only scenic – it overlooked bustling Crescent Harbor and Mount Edgecumbe – but historical, having received National Historic Landmark status in 2001.

If subdivided it's anybody's guess what the campus will be turned into. One thing's for sure, Alaska's oldest college will never again be a place of higher learning.

are available). The aquarium, a working hatchery, was once the home of the college's hatchery program and a was saved from closure by volunteers. Hopefully it will remain a summer attraction where children come to view an 800-gallon 'Wall of Water' aquarium filled with sea anemones, rockfish and starfish or get their hands wet in three touch tanks examining huge starfish or the coarse shell of an abalone.

SITKA NATIONAL HISTORICAL PARK

To the east Lincoln St ends at this 113-acre park, Alaska's smallest national park, at the mouth of Indian River. The park preserves the site where the Tlingits were finally defeated by the Russians in 1804 after defending their wooden fort for a week. The Russians had arrived with four ships to revenge a Tlingit raid on a nearby outpost two years earlier. The Russians' cannons did little damage to the walls of the Tlingit fort and, when the Russian soldiers stormed the structure with the help of Aleuts, they were repulsed in a bloody battle. It was only when the Tlingits ran out of gunpowder and flint, and slipped away at night, that the Russians were able to enter the deserted fort.

Begin at the park's **visitors center** (☎ 747-0110; adult/child $4/free; ⏰ 8am-5pm), where Russian and indigenous artifacts are displayed and a 12-minute video in the theater will provide an overview of the battle. Outside carvers will be working on a totem while nearby is Totem Trail, a mile-long path that leads you past 18 totems first displayed at the 1904 Louisiana Exposition in St Louis and then moved to the newly created park. It is these intriguing totems, standing in a beautiful rain forest setting by the sea and often enveloped in mist, that have become synonymous with the national park and even the city itself. Eventually you arrive at the site of the Tlingit fort near Indian River, where its outline can still be seen. You can either explore the trail as a self-guided tour or join a ranger-led 'Battle Walk.'

ALASKA RAPTOR CENTER

For an eye-to-eye encounter with an eagle, head to this **raptor center** (☎ 747-8662, 800-643-9425; www.alaskaraptor.org; 1101 Sawmill Creek Rd; adult/child $12/6; ⏰ 8am-4pm Mon-Fri), reached by turning right on the first gravel road after crossing Indian River. The 17-acre center treats 200 injured birds a year, with its most impressive facility being a 20,000-sq-ft flight-training center that helps injured eagles, owls, falcons and hawks regain their ability to fly. In the center eagles literary fly past you only 2ft or 3ft away at eye level, so close you can feel the wind from their beating wings – amazing.

Activities

HIKING

Sitka offers superb hiking in the beautiful but tangled forest surrounding the city. A complete hiking guide is available from the USFS Sitka Ranger District office (p149). **Sitka Trail Works** (☎ 747-7244; www.sitkatrailworks.org), a nonprofit group that raises money for trail improvements, arranges hikes throughout the summer and **Shore to Summit** (☎ 747-7244; www.shoretosummit.org; per person $50) offers two guided walks daily that includes transportation.

Indian River Trail

This easy trail is a 5.5-mile walk along a clear salmon stream to Indian River Falls, an 80ft cascade at the base of the Three Sisters Mountains. The hike takes you through typical Southeast rain forest, and offers the opportunity to view brown bears, deer and bald eagles. The trailhead, a short walk from the town center, is off Sawmill Creek Rd, just east of Sitka National Cemetery. Pass the driveway leading to the Public Safety Academy parking lot and turn up the gated dirt road. This leads back to the city water plant, where the trail begins left of the pump house. Plan on four to five hours round-trip to the falls.

Gavan Hill Trail

Also close to town is this trail, which ascends almost 2500ft over 3 miles to Gavan Hill peak. The trail offers excellent views of Sitka and the surrounding area. From the trail's end, the adventurous hiker can continue to the peaks of the Three Sisters Mountains.

Gavan Hill is also linked to Harbor Mountain Trail. Halfway across the alpine ridge is a free-use USFS shelter available on a first-come, first-served basis; it's 3.5 miles from the Gavan Hill trailhead, a hike of three to four hours.

From Lincoln St, head north up Baranof St for six blocks. The trailhead and a small parking area is reached just before the cemetery gate at the end of Baranof St. Camping is good in the trail's alpine regions, but bring drinking water as it is unavailable above the treeline.

Sitka Cross Trail

Rather than leading up out of town, this easy, well-used 2.2-mile trail runs roughly parallel to civilization, from one end of town to the other. The west end starts by the water tower at the intersection of Charteris St and Georgeson Loop, but you can pick it up behind the baseball field at the end of Kimsham St, beside the hostel. The trail leads east from there, crossing Gavan Hill Trail and ending at Indian River Trail. Along the way you'll pass peat bogs and old-growth forests.

Harbor Mountain Trail

This trail is reached from Harbor Mountain Rd, one of the few roads in the Southeast providing access to a subalpine area. Head 4 miles northwest from Sitka on Halibut Point Rd to the junction with Harbor Mountain Rd. A parking area and picnic shelter are 4.5 miles up the rough dirt road.

Another half-mile further is the parking lot at road's end, where an unmarked trail begins on the lot's east side. The trail ascends 1.5 miles to alpine meadows, knobs and ridges with spectacular views. From here a trail follows the tundra ridge to the free-use shelter on the saddle between Harbor Mountain and Gavan Hill, where you can pick up Gavan Hill Trail. Plan on spending two to four hours if you are just scrambling through the alpine area above Harbor Mountain Rd.

Mosquito Cove Trail

At the northwest end of Halibut Point Rd, 0.7 miles past the ferry terminal, Starrigavan Recreation Area offers a number of short but scenic trails. One of them, Mosquito Cove Trail, is an easy and scenic 1.25-mile loop over gravel and boardwalk.

Mt Verstovia Trail

This 2.5-mile trail is a challenging climb of 2550ft to the 'shoulder,' a compact summit that is the final destination for most hikers, although it is possible to continue climbing to the peak of Mt Verstovia (3349ft). The panorama from the shoulder on clear days is spectacular, undoubtedly the area's best.

The trailhead is 2 miles east of Sitka, along Sawmill Creek Rd; look for a large sign for the trailhead near a lone restaurant (which changes names so frequently that it shall here remain nameless). The Russian charcoal pits (signposted) are reached within a quarter-mile, and shortly after that the trail begins a series of switchbacks. It's a four-hour round-trip to the shoulder, from where a ridgeline leads north to the peak (another hour each way).

Beaver Lake Trail

This short trail starts from Sawmill Creek Campground, which is reached from Sawmill Creek Rd, 5.5 miles east of Sitka. Across from the former pulp mill on Sawmill Creek Rd, turn left onto Blue Lake Rd for the campground; the trailhead is on the campground's south side.

Although initially steep, the 0.8-mile trail levels out and ends up as a scenic walk through open forest, muskeg and marsh areas to Beaver Lake, which is surrounded by mountains. Plan on an hour round-trip.

Mt Edgecumbe Trail

The 6.7-mile trail begins at the USFS **Fred's Creek Cabin** (☎ 877-444-6777, 518-885-3639; www.recreation.gov; cabins $35), reservations required, and ascends to the crater of this extinct volcano. Views from the summit are spectacular on a clear day. About 3 miles up the trail is a free-use shelter (no reservations required).

Mt Edgecumbe (3201ft) is on Kruzof Island, 10 miles west of Sitka, and can only be reached by boat because large swells from the ocean prevent floatplanes from landing. See Getting Around (p158) for local operators who will drop off and pick up hikers. Actual hiking time is five to six hours one-way, but by securing Fred's Creek Cabin, you can turn the walk into a three-day adventure with two nights spent in shelters. That would be Sitka's best backpacking adventure by far but, due to the rising cost of fuel, a drop-off and pick-up will run to $400 per party.

PADDLING

Sitka also serves as the departure point for numerous blue-water trips along the protected shorelines of Sitka Sound, Baranof and Chichagof Islands. You can rent kayaks in town at **Sitka Sound Ocean Adventures** (☎ 747-6375; www.ssoceanadventures.com), which operates from a blue bus in the parking lot near the main harbor. Kayaks are available (single/double $55/65 per day) with discounts for multiday rentals. Guided trips are also available, indicated by the company motto on the side of the bus, 'Tip Your Guide, Not Your Kayak!'

Katlian Bay

This 45-mile round-trip from Sitka Harbor to scenic Katlian Bay (on Kruzof Island's north end) and back is one of the area's most popular paddles. The route follows narrow straits and well-protected shorelines in marine traffic channels, making it an ideal trip for less experienced blue-water paddlers, who will never be far from help.

A scenic sidetrip is to hike the sandy beach from Katlian Bay around Cape Georgiana to Sea Lion Cove on the Pacific Ocean. Catch the tides to paddle the Olga and Neva Straits on the way north and return along Sukot Inlet, staying overnight at the USFS **Brent's Beach Cabin** (☎ 877-444-6777, 518-885-3639; www.recreation.gov; cabins $35). Plan on four to six days for the paddle.

Shelikof Bay

You can combine a 10-mile paddle to Kruzof Island with a 6-mile hike across the island from Mud Bay to Shelikof Bay along an old logging road and trail. Once on the Pacific Ocean side, you'll find a beautiful sandy beach for beachcombing and the USFS **Shelikof Cabin** (☎ 877-444-6777, 518-885-3639; www.recreation.gov; cabins $35).

West Chichagof

Chichagof Island's western shoreline is one of Southeast Alaska's best blue-water destinations for experienced kayakers. Unfortunately, the trip often requires other transportation, because few paddlers have the experience necessary to paddle the open ocean around Khaz Peninsula (which forms a barrier between Kruzof Island's north end and Slocum Arm, the south end of the West Chichagof-Yakobi Wilderness). For most paddlers that means a water-taxi service to take you there.

The arm is the southern end of a series of straits, coves and protected waterways that shield paddlers from the ocean's swells and extend over 30 miles north to Lisianski Strait. With all its hidden coves and inlets, the trip is a good two-week paddle. Travelers with even more time and a sense of adventure could continue another 25 miles through Lisianski Strait to the fishing village of Pelican, where the ferry stops twice a month in summer. Such an expedition would require at least two to three weeks.

SNORKELING & SURFING

Island Fever Diving & Adventures (☎ 747-7871; www.islandfeverdiving.com; 805 Halibut Point Rd) is a full-service dive shop but its most popular offerings are snorkeling trips. It provides all the gear, including dry suits, and transportation for either a 2½-hour adventure to Magic Island ($118) or a four-hour trip to No Thorofare Bay ($150). The water may be cold but the giant kelp forests and colorful sea stars, anemones and fish are stunning.

They catch a few waves in Sitka, big ones actually, and the friendly staff at **Cold Salt Surf Shop** (☎ 966-2653; www.coldsalt.com; 236 Lincoln St) can show you where and assist in arranging an outing.

WHALE WATCHING

More than a dozen companies in Sitka offer boat tours to view whales and other marine wildlife and most of them swing past St Lazaria Island National Wildlife Refuge, home to 1500 pairs of breeding tufted puffins.

Sea Life Discovery Tours (☎ 966-2301, 877-966-2301; www.sealifediscoverytours.com) operates a glass-bottomed boat that gives visitors views of the area's underwater marine life from 10ft below the surface. The narrated two-hour tours (adult/child $86/63) includes a touch tank onboard making it an excellent choice for children.

our pick **Sitka's Secrets** (☎ 747-5089; www.sitkasecret.com) runs its 27ft boat to St Lazaria Island that carries only six passengers for a far more personal adventure. It's three-hour cruise ($120 per person) to view seabirds and whales is operated by a married couple, both degreed biologists and former national wildlife refuge managers.

Sitka Wildlife Quest/Allen Marine Tours (☎ 747-8100, 888-747-8101; www.allenmarinetours.com) offers a two-hour cruise (adult/child $59/39) on Tuesday and Thursday at 6pm to view whales, sea otters, puffins and other wildlife and a three-hour tour (adult/child $79/49) on Saturday at 8:30am. All tours depart from Crescent Harbor dock and reservations are not needed.

If you can't afford a wildlife cruise, try **Whale Park** (Sawmill Creek Rd), 4 miles south of town, which has a boardwalk and spotting scopes overlooking the ocean. Fall is the best time to sight cetaceans; as many as 80 whales – mostly humpbacks – have been known to gather in the waters off Sitka from mid-September to the end of the year.

WILDERNESS CABINS

A number of USFS cabins lie within 30 minutes flying time of Sitka. Among the most popular cabins are **Redoubt Lake Cabin**, at the northern end of Redoubt Lake, about 10 miles south of Sitka; **Baranof Lake Cabin**, which enjoys a scenic (though reportedly buggy) mountainous setting on the island's east side; barrier-free **Lake Eva Cabin**, also on Baranof Island's east shore, north of the Baranof Lake Cabin; and **White Sulphur Springs Cabin**, on the west shore of Chichagof Island, which is popular with locals because of the adjacent hot-springs bathhouse.

All cost $35 per night and should be reserved in advance through ☎ 877-444-6777, 518-885-3639 or www.recreation.gov. For air-taxi service, try **Harris Aircraft Services** (☎ 966 3050; www.harrisaircraft.com).

Tours

Sitka Tours (☎ 747-8443) If you're only in Sitka for as long as the ferry stopover, don't despair: Sitka Tours runs a bus tour (two hours, adult/child $12/6) just for you. The tour picks up and returns passengers to the ferry terminal, making brief visits to Sitka National Historical Park and St Michael's Cathedral. Time is allotted for the obligatory T-shirt-shopping experience.

Sitka Wildlife Tours (☎ 752-0006; http://sitkawildlifetours.com) offers two-hour van tours ($50 per person), which includes stopping at Sitka National Historical Park and Fortress of the Bears, where a pair of brown bears reside near Blue Lake.

Tribal Tours (☎ 747-7290, 888-270-8687; www.sitkatribe.org) A wide array of local tours with a Native Alaskan perspective. Its 2½-hour bus tour (adult/child $44/34) includes Sitka National Historical Park, Sheldon Jackson College and a Tlingit Native dance performance. It also has a 2½-hour coach and hiking tour that includes driving out to Old Historic Sitka and hiking Starrigavan Trail (per person $50).

Festivals & Events

Sitka Summer Music Festival (☎ 747-6774; www.sitkamusicfestival.org) extends Sitka's reputation as the Southeast's cultural center at this three-week event in June which brings together professional musicians for chamber-music concerts and workshops. The evening concerts are truly a treat to the senses; classical music filling Centennial Hall where the glass backdrop of the stage gives way to views of the harbor, snow-covered mountains and eagles soaring in the air. The highly acclaimed event is so popular you should purchase tickets in advance of your trip.

On the weekend nearest October 18, **Alaska Day Festival** sees the city re-enact, in costumes (and even beard styles) of the 1860s, the transfer of the state from Russia to the USA.

The city stages the **WhaleFest!** (☎ 747-7964; www.sitkawhalefest.org) during the first weekend of November to celebrate the large fall gathering of humpbacks with whale-watching cruises, lectures, craft shows and more.

Sleeping

Sitka levies a 12% city and bed tax on all lodging.

BUDGET

Sitka International Youth Hostel (☎ 747-8661; 109 Jeff Davis St) Sitka's United Methodist Church hostel closed in 2006 but one is planned for the historic Tillie Paul Manor, which once served as the Sitka Hospital. The new hostel will be downtown less than a block from Crescent Harbor and is expected to be open by 2009.

Camping

Two USFS campgrounds are in the area, but neither is close to town.

Sawmill Creek Campground (Blue Lake Rd; sites free) In the opposite direction from town from Starrigavan Bay, via Sawmill Creek Rd and Blue Lake Rd, is this free 11-site campground that features mountain scenery, the Beaver Lake Trail and fishing opportunities in nearby lakes.

Starrigavan Recreation Area (Mile 7.8 Halibut Point Rd; sites $12-30) Sitka's finest campground has 35 sites spread along three loops for three types of campers: RVers, car-and-tent campers, and backpackers and cyclists' walk-in sites. You're 7 miles from town but the coastal scenery is beautiful and nearby is Old Sitka State Historic Site, which features trails and interpretive displays dedicated to the site of the original Russian settlement. Most of the new amenities – bird- and salmon-viewing decks, boardwalks and vault toilets – are wheelchair accessible and departing from the campground are several hiking trails and Nelson Logging Rd for mountain bikers.

MIDRANGE

Karras Day Rental (☎ 747-3978; 230 Kogwanton St; s/d $55/85) Nothing fancy but reasonably price and only a few blocks from the downtown area. There are four rooms with shared bath, common area and their own entrance in a private home overlooking the colorful Katlian St harbor area.

our pick Ann's Gavan Hill B&B (☎ 747-8023; www.annsgavanhill.com; 415 Arrowhead St; s/d $75/95; ⊠ 🖳) An easy walk from downtown is this lovely Alaskan home with a wrap-around deck that includes two hot tubs. The three bedrooms are spacious, comfortable and equipped with a TVs and VCRs. The delightful proprietor is a former commercial fisherwomen and still an avid hunter, the reason for the bear skin and marine charts on the walls.

Sitka Hotel (☎ 747-3288; www.sitkahotel.com; 118 Lincoln St; s/d $99/105; 🖳) A fire in 2005 resulted in Sitka's oldest hotel being extensively renovated and now the new backside rooms are large and comfortable, and many feature views of Sitka Sound. The rest of the rooms are smaller but well kept and all have cable TV and a few even have kitchenettes. The renovation also spelt the end of the affordable shared-bathroom accommodations. Still, the location and services (laundry, luggage storage, wi-fi) makes the Sitka Hotel a good value.

Cascade Inn (☎ 747-6804, 800-532-0908; www.cascadeinnsitka.com; 2035 Halibut Point Rd; r $115-140; ⊠ 🖳) Perched right above the shoreline, all 10 rooms in this inn face the ocean and have private balcony overlooking it. Sure you're 2.5 miles north of town but the inn's oceanfront deck with its sauna and BBQ is worth waiting for a downtown bus.

Super 8 Motel (☎ 747-8804, 800-800-8000; 404 Sawmill Creek Rd; s/d $124/132) This is a Super 8 Motel so you know what you're getting: large, clean, utilitarian rooms. The rate is higher but its downtown location, indoor hot tub, free continental breakfast and 24-hour Laundromat make it a popular choice.

TOP END

our pick Shee Atiká Totem Square Inn (☎ 747-3693; 866-300-1353; www.totemsquareinn.com; 201 Katlian St; r $140-179; ⊠ 🖳) Extensively renovated, this is Sitka's finest hotel with 68 large, comfortable rooms featuring the traditional (Native Alaskan art and prints on the walls) and the modern (flat panel TVs, hairdryers and wi-fi). There's work-out facility, breakfast room, laundry, business center and free airport shuttle. Its best feature, however, is still the views from the rooms, overlooking either the historic square or a harbor bustling with boats bringing in the day's catch.

Fly-in Fish Inn (☎ 747-7910; www.flyinfishinn.com; 485 Katlian St; r $159-179; ⊠ 🖳) In the middle of the bustling harbors and canneries of Katlian is Sitka's newest and most unusual inn. Fly-in Fish Inn is gracious luxury with 10 large rooms featuring refrigerators, wet bars, microwaves, cable TV, you name it. There's also a dining room that serves a full breakfast, a small bar and a seaplane dock, so arranging a flightseeing or fly-in fishing trip is as easy as calling the front desk.

Westmark Sitka Hotel (☎ 747-6241, 800-544-0970; www.westmarkhotels.com; 330 Seward St; r $169, ste $259; ⊠ 🖳) The business traveler's favorite. It has 101 rooms and suites, a central location, a fine restaurant and bar with views of the harbor and room service.

Eating

RESTAURANTS

Little Tokyo (☎ 747-5699; 315 Lincoln St; lunch $8-10; fish & tempura rolls $6-12; ⊠) Even crewmembers from the commercial fleet, who know a thing or two about raw fish, say this sushi bar is a good catch.

Twin Dragon (☎ 747-747-5711; 201 Katlian St; lunch $7-10, dinner $11-17; ⊠) Located in the back of the Totem Square Inn, the Chinese dishes – Mandarin, Szechwan and Cantonese – are good; the view of the bustling boat harbor is outstanding. Hungry? The family specials begin at $14 and include four mains.

Victoria's (☎ 747-9301; 118 Lincoln St; breakfast $8-13, lunch $9-14, dinner $15-24; 🕑 4:30am-10pm; ⊠) Sitka's early morning breakfast joint. If you're a late riser come back in the evening for good selection of seafood, from cedar plank salmon and steamed clams to pan fried oysters.

Level II (☎ 747-3900; 407 Lincoln St; breakfast $11-16, lunch $11-17, dinner $19-23; ⊠) An upstairs location in the MacDonald Bayview Trading Company Building allows every table at this long, narrow restaurant a view of the boat traffic in the harbor. The menu is basic, but the portions are generous.

our pick Ludvig's Bistro (☎ 966-3663; 256 Katlian St; dinner $20-32; 🕑 2-10pm; ⊠) Sitka's boldest restaurant is steadily becoming known as the Southeast's best. Too bad it's so quaint. Ludvig's is as colorful as the commercial fishing district that surrounds it but there are only seven tables and a handful of stools at its brass-and-blue-tile bar. But an evening here is well worth the wait or even a reservation. The menu is described as 'rustic Mediterranean fare' and almost everything is local, even the sea salt. The Katlian Special is whatever the local boats catch that day then pan-seared with a hint of smoke from Sitka alder.

CAFÉS

Back Door Café (☎ 747-8856; 104 Barracks St; light fare less than $5; 6:30am-5pm Mon-Sat, 9am-2pm Sun;) Accessed through either Old Harbor Books on Lincoln St or through the…you guessed it… which is off Barracks St is this small coffeehouse. The cruise-ship hordes parading endlessly down Lincoln St can't immediately see it so they go elsewhere. As a result, this café is as local as it gets. You'll find an eclectic clientele here and a menu that includes bagel sandwiches and excellent high-octane espresso drinks.

Highliner Coffee (☎ 747-4924; 327 Seward St, Seward Square Mall; light fare less than $5; 5:30am-5pm Mon-Sat, 8am-4pm Sun;) At the Highliner they like their coffee black and their salmon wild, which explains why the walls are covered with photos of local fishing boats and articles on the dangers of eating farm-raised fish. Come here to catch the buzz from a latte and the local issues. Indulge in some homebaked goodies.

Galley Deli (☎ 747-9997; 2A Lincoln St; sandwiches $7-8; 10am-3pm Mon-Fri, 11am-3pm Sat;) If you can find this deli in the back of the Raven Radio Building then you can create your own sandwich on homemade breads like Kalamata olive and feta or buttermilk dill and enjoy it on a pleasant outdoor porch.

Café Mellow Days (☎ 747-6000; 315 Lincoln St; breakfast $6-10, lunch $7-12; 6:30am-6:30pm;) Brightly colored walls, splashy art and new age music will mellow you out here and put you in the mood for the just-baked breads, muffins and quiches. For lunch be healthy and start with a salad or veggie wrap and finish with a strawberry and cream smoothie.

GROCERIES

Sea Mart (1867 Halibut Point Rd) Sitka's main supermarket is northwest of town and features an ATM, bakery, deli, ready-to-eat items and a dining area overlooking Mt Edgecumbe.

Lakeside Grocery (705 Halibut Point Rd) Sea Mart is Sitka's finest supermarket but if that's too much walking for a package of Raman noodles head to Lakeside, which still has sandwiches, soups and a salad bar.

Drinking

Pioneer Bar (☎ 747-3456; 212 Katlian St) The 'P-Bar' is Alaska's classic maritime watering hole. The walls are covered with photos of fishing boats, their crews and big fish and a blackboard with messages like 'Tendering job wanted.' Don't ring the ship's bell over the bar unless you're ready to buy every crewmember a round.

our pick **Fly-in Fish Inn Bar** (☎ 747-7910; 485 Katlian St) A delightfully little six-stool bar on the backside of the inn. On the covered deck outside you can watch deckhands unload the day's catch.

Victoria's Pourhouse (☎ 747-5451; 118 Lincoln St) A friendly pub inside the Sitka Hotel with the largest TV screen in Sitka.

Entertainment

New Archangel Russian Dancers (☎ 747-5516; adult/child $8/4) Whenever a cruise ship is in port, this troupe of more than 30 dancers in Russian costumes takes the stage at Centennial Hall for a half-hour show. A schedule is posted at the hall.

Sheet'ka Kwaan Naa Kahidi Dancers (☎ 747-7290; www.sitkatribe.com; 200 Katlian St; adult/child $8/4) Not to be outdone, these dancers perform traditional Tlingit dances at the eponymous Tlingit Clan House, next to the Pioneers' Home.

Getting There & Away

AIR

Sitka is served by **Alaska Airlines** (☎ 966-2926, 800-426-0333; www.alaskaair.com) and its airport is on Japonski Island, 1.8 miles west, or a 20-minute walk, of downtown. The white **Airport Shuttle** (☎ 747-8443) minibus meets all jet flights in summer and (one way/round-trip $8/10).

Floatplane air-taxi service to small communities and USFS cabins is provided by **Harris Aircraft Services** (☎ 966-3050, within Alaska 877-966-3050; www.harrisaircraft.com).

BOAT

The Alaska Marine Highway **ferry terminal** (☎ 747-8737) is 6.5 miles northwest of town; ferries depart in both directions almost daily to Juneau ($39, nine hours), Angoon ($31, six hours), Petersburg ($39, 11 hours) and Tenakee Springs ($31, nine hours).

Ferry Transit Bus (☎ 747-8443; one way/round-trip $8/10), operated by Sitka Tours, meets all ferries year-round for the trip to and from town. You can also catch a Community Ride bus Monday through Friday.

DETOUR: TEBENKOF BAY WILDERNESS

Kake is the departure point for blue-water kayak trips into Tebenkof Bay Wilderness, a remote bay system composed of hundreds of islands, small inner bays and coves. The return paddle is a scenic 10-day adventure that can offer sightings of bald eagles, black bears and various marine mammals. Paddlers should have ocean-touring experience and be prepared to handle a number of portages. Kayaks can be rented in Juneau, Sitka or Petersburg and then carried on the ferry to Kake.

The most common route is to paddle south from Kake through Keku Strait into Port Camden, at the western end of which is a 1.3-mile portage trail to the Bay of Pillars. From the Bay of Pillars, you encounter the only stretch of open water, a 3-mile paddle around Point Ellis into Tebenkof Bay. The return east follows Alecks Creek from Tebenkof Bay into Alecks Lake, where a 2.3-mile portage trail leads to No Name Bay. From here paddlers can reach Keku Strait and paddle north to Kake via scenic Rocky Pass.

Getting Around

BICYCLE

Yellow Jersey Cycle Shop (☎ 747-6317; 329 Harbor Dr; per 2hr/day $15/25), across the street from the library, rents quality mountain bikes.

BUS

Sitka's public bus system, **Community Ride** (☎ 747-7103; adult/child $2/1; 🕑 6:30am-6:30pm Mon-Fri), has expanded significantly in recent years and now offers hourly service from downtown to as far south as Whale Park and as far north as the ferry terminal.

CAR

At the airport, **Northstar Rent-A-Car** (☎ 966-2552, 800-722-6927) rents compacts for $55 per day but there is a 20% tax. Hey, you get unlimited mileage (like you need that in Sitka).

TAXI

For a ride around Sitka, try **More's Taxi Service** (☎ 738-3210).

WATER-TAXI

The going rate for water-taxi service from **Esther G Sea Taxi** (☎ 747-6481, 738-6481) or **EZC Transfer Co** (☎ 747-5044) is $150 per hour.

SECONDARY PORTS

On the ferry runs between Sitka and Juneau, you can stop at a few of secondary ports to escape the cruise ships and tourists at the larger towns. Some stops are scenic, others are not; all are a cultural experience in rural Alaska.

Kake

pop 536

Kake is an Indian beachfront community on the northwest coast of Kupreanof Island, the traditional home of the Kake tribe of the Tlingit Indians. Today the community maintains subsistence rights and also runs commercial fishing and fish processing to supplement its economy. Kake is known for having the tallest totem pole in Alaska (and some say the world), a 132ft carving that was first raised at Alaska's pavilion in the 1970 World's Fair in Osaka, Japan.

Within town, 1.5 miles from the ferry terminal, are three general stores, a Laundromat, restaurant and **Waterfront Lodge** (☎ 785-3472; 222 Keku Rd; s/d $85/125; 💻 ⊠).

The Alaska Marine Highway ferry MV *Le Conte* stops twice weekly at Kake on its run between Petersburg ($35, four hours) and Sitka ($37, 10 hours). **Wings of Alaska** (☎ 789-0790; www.wingsofalaska.com) will fly you back to Juneau for $156.

Tenakee Springs

pop 102

Since its period in the late 19th century as a winter retreat for fishers and prospectors, Tenakee Springs has evolved into a rustic village known for its slow and relaxed pace. On the east side of Tenakee Inlet, the settlement is basically a ferry dock, a row of houses on pilings and the hot springs – the main attraction – which bubble out of the ground at 108°F.

Tenakee's alternative lifestyle centers around the free public bathhouse at the end of the ferry dock. The building encloses the principal spring, which flows through the concrete bath at seven gallons per minute. Bath hours, separate for men and women, are posted, and most locals take at least one good soak per day, if not two.

While you're in the area, always keep an eye out for marine mammals, such as humpback whales (commonly seen in Tenakee Inlet), killer whales and harbor porpoises. You may also see brown bears, as Chichagof Island is second only to Admiralty Island in the Southeast for the density of its bear population.

SLEEPING & EATING

Opposite the bathhouse, at the foot of the ferry dock, is **Snyder Mercantile Co** (☎ 736-2205; ⏲ 9am-4pm Wed-Mon). Founded by Ed Snyder, who arrived in a rowboat full of groceries in 1899, the store has been in business ever since and sells limited supplies and groceries. For food, there's **Rosie's Blue Moon Café** (⏲ 10am-6pm) and the **Bakery & Giftshop** (☎ 736-2262; ⏲ 8am-2pm Tue-Sat), both on Tenakee Ave.

Finding lodging is a little more challenging than finding a meal in Tenakee Springs. **Tenakee Hot Springs Lodge** (☎ 736-2400; 364-3640; s/d $90/150; ⊠ 💻) features six rooms, a communal kitchen and a great view from its deck. Or you can pitch a tent at the rustic campground a mile east of town, at the mouth of the Indian River.

GETTING THERE & AWAY

The ferry MV *Le Conte* stops at Tenakee Springs roughly once a week, connecting it to Hoonah and Juneau northbound and to Angoon and Sitka (and occasionally Kake and Petersburg) southbound. Study the ferry schedule carefully to make sure you don't have to stay in town longer than you want. The one-way fare from Tenakee Springs to Juneau or Sitka is $35.

Alaska Seaplane Service (☎ 888-350-8277, in Juneau 789-3331; www.akseaplanes.com) has scheduled service charging $125 one way.

Hoonah

pop 852

Hoonah is the largest Tlingit village in Southeast Alaska and the start of the 40-mile kayak route to Tenakee Springs (p109). The Huna, a Tlingit tribe, have lived in the Icy Strait area for hundreds of years, and legend tells of them being forced out of Glacier Bay by an advancing glacier. A store was built on the site of Hoonah in 1883, and an established community has been here ever since.

The town lacks the charm of Tenakee Springs, and even much coastal beauty due to intense logging of Port Frederick, but there is excellent whale watching which can be arranged with **Fishes** (☎ 945-3327; www.visithoonah.com/fishes), a Hoonah-based charter boat offering three-hour trips daily ($150). Nearby is **Icy Strait Point Cannery** (☎ 789-8018; www.icystraitpoint.com). Restored in 2004 as strictly a cruise-ship attraction, the cannery halls are filled with gift shops, restaurants, a museum and a mid-1930s cannery line display. Outside is the world's longest zipline at 5330ft, which includes a 1300ft vertical drop.

GETTING THERE & AWAY

Alaska Marine Highway's MV *Le Conte* docks in Hoonah three days a week from Sitka ($37, seven hours) and Juneau ($33, four hours). The **ferry terminal** (☎ 945-3292) is half a mile from town. **Wings of Alaska** (☎ 789-0790; www.wingsofalaska.com) has regularly scheduled flights for $69/138 one way/roundtrip.

Pelican

pop 110

If you time it right, you can catch the twice-a-month state ferry to Pelican, a lively little fishing town on Chichagof Island's northwest coast. The cruise through Icy Straits is scenic, with a good possibility of seeing humpback whales, and the two hours in port is more than enough time to walk the length of town, and even have a beer, in one of Southeast Alaska's last true boardwalk communities.

The town was established in 1938 by a fish packer and named after his boat. Fishing is Pelican's raison d'être. It has the closest harbor to Fairweather's salmon grounds; the reason its population swells with commercial fishers and cold-storage workers for the June to mid-September trolling season.

INFORMATION

The website of the **Pelican Visitors Association** (www.pelican.net) has lodging and charter fishing information. Pelican has a small library, several bars, a café, Laundromat/internet café, general store, and a liquor store with adjoining steam baths and showers.

SIGHTS & ACTIVITIES

Pelican is a photographer's delight. Most of it is built on pilings over tidelands, and its main street, dubbed Salmon Way, is a mile-long wooden boardwalk. Only a very short gravel road runs beyond that.

The kayaking is excellent out of Pelican and at **Highliner Lodge** (☎ 735-2476) you can rent singles/doubles for $50/75 per day. For kayak drop-offs, fishing, or whale watching, contact **Lisianaki Inlet Charters** (☎ 735-2282).

SLEEPING & EATING

Highliner Lodge (☎ 735-2476, 877-386-0397; www.highlinerlodge.com; Boat Harbor; s/d $175/225; 💻) Even if this wasn't Pelican, this lodge would still a great place to stay, featuring not only rooms and suites but a café and sauna.

Rose's Bar & Grill (☎ 735-2288) A classic Alaskan fishermen's bar where you can mingle with trollers, long-liners and Pelican Seafood workers.

GETTING THERE & AWAY

Alaska Marine Highway's MV *Le Conte* runs from Juneau to Pelican and back twice a month, providing a unique day trip for $100 round-trip.

If you miss the ferry, call **Alaska Seaplane Service** (☎ in Juneau 735-2244, in Pelican 789-3331, 888-350-8277; www.akseaplanes.com), which offers scheduled flights to/from Juneau (one way $165).

JUNEAU

pop 30,966

Juneau is a capital of contrasts and conflicts. It borders a waterway that never freezes but lies beneath an ice field that never melts. It was the first community in the Southeast to slap a head tax on cruise-ship passengers but draws more of them, almost a million, than any other town. It's the state capital but since the 1980s Alaskans have been trying to move it. It doesn't have any roads that go anywhere but half its residents and its mayor are opposed to a plan to build one that would.

Welcome to America's strangest state capital. In the winter it's a beehive of legislators, their loyal aides and lobbyists locked in political struggles. They no more leave, then in May the cruise ships arrive with swarms of passengers. It's the most geographically secluded state capital in the country, the only one that cannot be reached by car – only boat or plane.

But Juneau is also the most beautiful city in Alaska and arguably the nation's most scenic capital. The city center, which hugs the side of Mt Juneau and Mt Roberts, is a maze of narrow streets running past a mix of new structures, old storefronts and slanted houses, all held together by a network of staircases. The waterfront is bustling with cruise ships, fishing boats and floatplanes buzzing in and out. High above the city is the Juneau Ice Field, covering the Coastal Range and sending glaciers down between the mountains like marshmallow syrup on a sundae.

The state's first major gold strike and the first town to be founded after Alaska's purchase from the Russians, Juneau became the territorial capital in 1906. Juneau's darkest hour occurred in the late 1970s after Alaskans voted to move the state capital again. The so-called 'capital move' issue became a political tug-of-war between Anchorage and the Southeast, until voters, faced with a billion-dollar price tag of a new capital, defeated the funding in 1982. The statewide vote gave Juneau new life, and the town burst at its seams, booming in typical Alaskan fashion.

Considering it's still a state capital, Juneau isn't the hive of cultural activity you might expect. Entertainment venues are minimal and good restaurants are rare. But many find it a refreshing haven of liberalism in a state that is steadily marching to the right. Spend a morning eavesdropping in cafés and coffeehouses and you'll hear the environmental and social conscience of Alaska.

For visitors who come to Alaska for outdoor adventure, what really distinguishes the state capital from other Alaskan towns – and certainly other state capitals – is the superb hiking. Dozens of great trails surround the city; some begin downtown, just blocks from the capitol. Juneau also serves as the departure point for several wilderness attractions, including paddling paradises such as Glacier Bay National Park, Tracy Arm-Fords Terror Wilderness and Admiralty Island National Monument.

Orientation

While the downtown area clings to a mountainside, the rest of the city 'officially' sprawls over 3100 sq miles to the Canadian border, making it one of the largest cities (in area) in the USA.

The city center is the busiest and most popular area among visitors in summer. From there, Egan Dr, the Southeast's only four-lane highway, heads northwest to Mendenhall Valley. Known to locals as simply 'the Valley,' this area contains a growing residential section, much of Juneau's business district and world-famous Mendenhall Glacier. In the Valley, Egan Dr

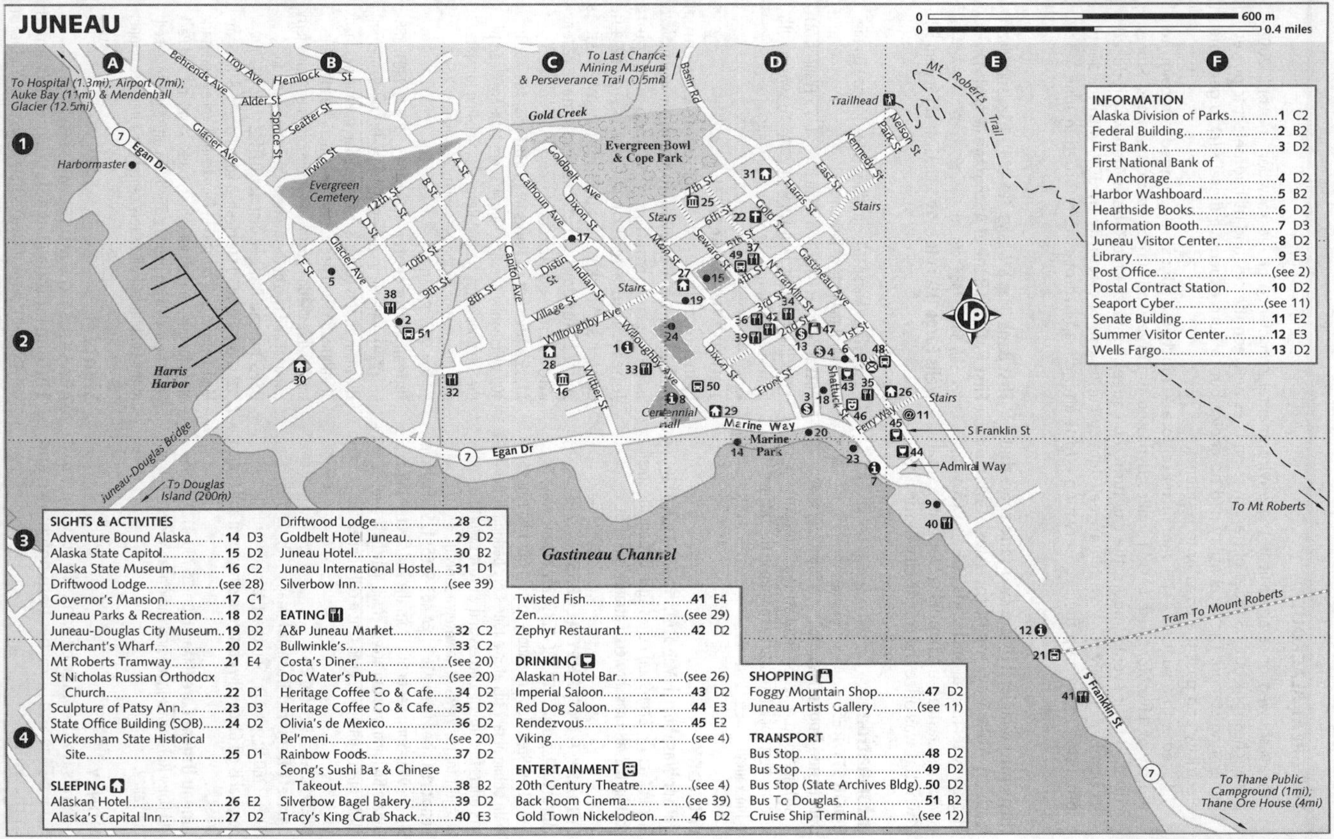

INFORMATION
- Alaska Division of Parks ... 1 C2
- Federal Building ... 2 B2
- First Bank ... 3 D2
- First National Bank of Anchorage ... 4 D2
- Harbor Washboard ... 5 B2
- Hearthside Books ... 6 D2
- Information Booth ... 7 D3
- Juneau Visitor Center ... 8 D2
- Library ... 9 E3
- Post Office ... (see 2)
- Postal Contract Station ... 10 D2
- Seaport Cyber ... (see 11)
- Senate Building ... 11 E2
- Summer Visitor Center ... 12 E3
- Wells Fargo ... 13 D2

SIGHTS & ACTIVITIES
- Adventure Bound Alaska ... 14 D3
- Alaska State Capitol ... 15 D2
- Alaska State Museum ... 16 C2
- Driftwood Lodge ... (see 28)
- Governor's Mansion ... 17 C1
- Juneau Parks & Recreation ... 18 D2
- Juneau-Douglas City Museum ... 19 D2
- Merchant's Wharf ... 20 D2
- Mt Roberts Tramway ... 21 E4
- St Nicholas Russian Orthodox Church ... 22 D1
- Sculpture of Patsy Ann ... 23 D3
- State Office Building (SOB) ... 24 D2
- Wickersham State Historical Site ... 25 D1

SLEEPING
- Alaskan Hotel ... 26 E2
- Alaska's Capital Inn ... 27 D2
- Driftwood Lodge ... 28 C2
- Goldbelt Hotel Juneau ... 29 D2
- Juneau Hotel ... 30 B2
- Juneau International Hostel ... 31 D1
- Silverbow Inn ... (see 39)

EATING
- A&P Juneau Market ... 32 C2
- Bullwinkle's ... 33 C2
- Costa's Diner ... (see 20)
- Doc Water's Pub ... (see 20)
- Heritage Coffee Co & Cafe ... 34 D2
- Heritage Coffee Co & Cafe ... 35 D2
- Olivia's de Mexico ... 36 D2
- Pel'meni ... (see 20)
- Rainbow Foods ... 37 D2
- Seong's Sushi Bar & Chinese Takeout ... 38 B2
- Silverbow Bagel Bakery ... 39 D2
- Tracy's King Crab Shack ... 40 E3
- Twisted Fish ... 41 E4
- Zen ... (see 29)
- Zephyr Restaurant ... 42 D2

DRINKING
- Alaskan Hotel Bar ... (see 26)
- Imperial Saloon ... 43 D2
- Red Dog Saloon ... 44 E3
- Rendezvous ... 45 E2
- Viking ... (see 4)

ENTERTAINMENT
- 20th Century Theatre ... (see 4)
- Back Room Cinema ... (see 39)
- Gold Town Nickelodeon ... 46 D2

SHOPPING
- Foggy Mountain Shop ... 47 D2
- Juneau Artists Gallery ... (see 11)

TRANSPORT
- Bus Stop ... 48 D2
- Bus Stop ... 49 D2
- Bus Stop (State Archives Bldg) ... 50 D2
- Bus To Douglas ... 51 B2
- Cruise Ship Terminal ... (see 12)

THE GREAT BLACKOUT

Juneau showed once again it is the environmental conscience of Alaska when in April, 2008 avalanches took out 1.5 miles of transmission lines between the city and its hydroelectric power-generating station. The local utility had no choice but to burn expensive diesel fuel to generate electricity and pass the costs onto residents.

Faced with a sudden 447% rate increase, locals launched a Juneau Unplugged campaign to the cry of 'Live More, Use Less.' Families bypassed the dryer and turned to clothes lines. Stores curtailed their evening hours, the city turned off street lights, the Mt Roberts Tramway reduced its number of daily runs. Within a week Juneau cut its use of electricity by 30% with residents promising to keep up their conservation efforts after cheap hydropower returned in June.

turns into Glacier Hwy, a two-lane road that leads to Auke Bay, site of the Alaska Marine Highway terminal, and ends at Echo Cove.

Across Gastineau Channel is Douglas, a small town that was once the major city in the area.

Information

BOOKSTORES

Hearthside Books (Map p161; ☎ 586-1726; www.hearthsidebooks.com; 254 Front St; 🕑 9am-8pm) Juneau's best bookstore also has a store in the Nugget Mall in the Valley.

LAUNDRY

Harbor Washboard (Map p161; ☎ 586-1133; 1114 Glacier Ave; 🕑 8am-9pm) Across Egan Dr from the small boat harbor; also has showers. Entrance is on F St.

LIBRARY & INTERNET ACCESS

Library (Map p161; ☎ 586-5249; 292 Marine Way; 🕑 11am-9pm Mon-Thu, noon-5pm Fri-Sun) Juneau's main public library sits atop a four-story parking structure and offers free internet access and wi-fi. It's worth a stop here just for the views of downtown Juneau.

Seaport Cyber (Map p161; ☎ 463-9865; 175 S Franklin St; 🕑 9am-5pm; per hr $6) From the 2nd floor of the Senate Building, you can access email, purchase phonecards, burn a photo CD, even rent a cell phone.

MEDICAL SERVICES

Bartlett Regional Hospital (Map p170; ☎ 796-8900; 3260 Hospital Dr) Southeast Alaska's largest hospital is off Glacier Hwy between downtown and Lemon Creek.

Juneau Urgent Care (Map p170; ☎ 790-4111; 8505 Old Dairy Rd) A walk-in medical clinic near Nugget Mall in the Valley.

MONEY

There's no shortage of banks in Juneau. Most have ATMs and branches both downtown and in the Valley.

First Bank (Map p161; ☎ 586-8801; 1 Sealaska Plaza)

First National Bank of Anchorage (Map p161; ☎ 586-5400; 238 Front St)

Wells Fargo (Map p161; ☎ 586-3324; 123 Seward St)

POST

Post office (Map p161; cnr 9th St & Glacier Ave) On the 1st floor of the Federal Building.

Postal contract station (Map p161; 145 S Franklin St; 🕑 8:30am-4:30pm Mon-Fri, 9am-2pm Sat) Conveniently located downtown in the Seward Building.

TOURIST INFORMATION

Conveniently lumped together in Centennial Hall, Juneau's convention center complex, is all the information you need to explore Juneau, find a trail or get out of town. The center's Alaska Marine Highway desk is staffed Monday to Friday and can make reservations and sell tickets.

Alaska Division of Parks (Map p161; ☎ 465-4563; 400 Willoughby Ave; 🕑 8am-4:30pm Mon-Fri) Head to the 5th floor of the Natural Resources Building for state park information or the availability of cabins at Point Bridget State Park (p175).

Juneau Visitor Center (Map p161; ☎ 586-2201, 888-581-2201; www.juneau.com; 101 Egan Dr; 🕑 9am-5pm) The main visitors center is in Centennial Hall and has loads of information and free maps. The center also maintains smaller information booths at the airport, the marine ferry terminal and two of them where the cruise ships dock.

USFS Juneau Ranger District Office (Map p170; ☎ 586-8800; 8510 Mendenhall Loop Rd; 🕑 8am-5pm Mon-Fri) The new office is in Mendenhall Valley and is the place for questions about cabins, trails, kayaking and Pack Creek bear viewing permits. The USFS office is also linked to the Centennial Hall visitors center via a free-use phone.

Sights

ALASKA STATE MUSEUM

The outstanding **Alaska State Museum** (Map p161; ☎ 465-2901; www.museums.state.ak.us; 395 Whittier St;

adult/child $5/free; ⌚ 8:30am-5:30pm) is near Centennial Hall and on its 1st floor features artifacts from Alaska's six major indigenous groups. The most intriguing exhibit, 'Art of Survival,' shows how Native Alaskans have turned living in a hostile land into an art form with a display of items ranging from waterproof gut parkas and a century-old umiaq skin boat to tom cod fishing rods. Beautifully effective. The top floor is devoted to the state's Russian period and major gold strikes, and connecting the two is a circular ramp that winds around the museum's most popular exhibit; an impressive diorama of a full-size eagle's nest in a two-story high tree.

JUNEAU-DOUGLAS CITY MUSEUM

This **museum** (Map p161; ☎ 586-3572; 114 W 4th St; adult/child $4/free; ⌚ 9am-5pm Mon-Fri, from 10am Sat & Sun) focuses on gold with interesting mining displays and the video *Juneau: City Built On Gold*. If you love to hike in the mountains, the museum's 7ft-long relief map is the best overview of the area's rugged terrain other than a helicopter ride. If not, then on Tuesday, Thursday and Saturday, the staff leads a historical walking tour (adult/child $10/7) of the downtown area beginning at 1:30pm at the museum.

ALASKA STATE CAPITOL

Next to the City Museum is the **Alaska State Capitol** (Map p161; ☎ 465-3800; 120 4th St; ⌚ 8am-5pm Mon-Fri, from 9am Sat). Built in 1929–31 as the territorial Federal Building, the capitol looks like an overgrown high school. Stuffed inside are legislative chambers, the governor's office, and offices for the hundreds of staff members who arrive in Juneau for the winter legislative session. Free 30-minute tours are held every half-hour and start from the visitor desk in the lobby; a self-guided tour pamphlet is also available.

LAST CHANCE MINING MUSEUM

Amble out to the end of Basin Rd, a beautiful half-mile walk from the north end of Gastineau Ave, to the intriguing **Last Chance Mining Museum** (off Map p161; ☎ 586-5338; 1001 Basin Rd; adult/child $4/free; ⌚ 9:30am-12:30pm & 3:30-6:30pm). The former Alaska-Juneau Gold Mining Company complex is now a museum where you can view the remains of the compressor house and examine tools of what was once the world's largest hard-rock goldmine. There is also a re-created mining tunnel and a 3D glass map of shafts that shows just how large it was. Nearby is the Perseverance Trail (p164), and combining the museum with a hike to more mining ruins is a great way to spend an afternoon.

MT ROBERTS TRAMWAY

As far as trams go this **tramway** (Map p161; ☎ 463-3412, 888-461-8726; www.goldbelttours.com; 490 S Franklin St; adult/child $25/13.50; ⌚ 9am-9pm) is rather expensive for a relatively short five-minute ride. But from a marketing point of view, its location couldn't be better. It whisks passengers right from the cruise-ship dock up 1800ft to the treeline of Mt Roberts, where they'll find a restaurant, gift shops and a small theater with a film on Tlingit culture. Or skip all that and just use the tram for access to day hikes in the alpine area (p164).

WATERFRONT AREA & S FRANKLIN ST

Between the cruise ships and Willoughby Ave, **Marine Park** (Map p161) is an open space where kids practice their skateboard tricks, state workers enjoy a sack lunch and tired tourists occasionally take a nap in the sun. Spotting scopes let you search Mt Juneau for mountain goats while on the dock is a **sculpture of Patsy Ann** (Map p161), the late faithful Fido who became known as the 'Official Greeter of Juneau' for her tendency to rush down to the docks to meet arriving cruise ships. A block inland from the waterfront is **S Franklin St**, a refurbished historical district where many buildings date from the early 1900s and have since been turned into bars, gift shops and restaurants.

OTHER MUSEUMS & HISTORICAL SITES

Overlooking downtown Juneau is **Wickersham State Historical Site** (Map p161; ☎ 586-9001; 213 7th St), which preserves the 1898 home of pioneer judge and statesman James Wickersham. In 2008, the museum was closed due to budget problems of a planned renovation. Call to see if it has re-opened.

Two blocks downhill is **St Nicholas Russian Orthodox Church** (Map p161; ☎ 586-1023; 326 5th St; admission by donation; ⌚ noon-5pm Mon-Fri, 9am-2pm Sat, 1-5pm Sun). Built in 1893 against the backdrop of Mt Juneau, the onion-domed church is the oldest original one in Alaska. From a small gift shop filled with *matreshkas* (nestling dolls) and other handcrafted items from

Russia, you enter the church where, among the original vestments and religious relics, a row of painted saints stare down at you. Playing softly in the background are the chants from a service. If you weren't spiritual before, you are now.

Across from the Juneau-Douglas City Museum is the **State Office Building** (Map p161; 400 Willoughby Ave), known locally as the SOB. From the outdoor court on the 8th floor there is a spectacular view of the channel and Douglas Island, while in the lobby is a massive Kimball organ dating back to 1928. Every Friday at noon a performance is given, a good reason to join state workers for a brown-bag lunch. West of the SOB along 4th Ave is the pillared **Governor's Mansion** (Map p161; 716 Calhoun Ave). Built and furnished in 1912 at a cost of $44,000, the mansion is not open to the public.

Activities

CYCLING

Bike paths run between Auke Bay, Mendenhall Glacier and downtown, and from the Juneau-Douglas Bridge to Douglas. Pick up a route guide at the Centennial Hall's main visitors center. Because most of Juneau's trails are steep, mountain biking is limited, but the Windfall Lake and Peterson Lake trails are popular with off-road cyclists.

Cycle Alaska (Map p170; ☎ 321-2453; 3172 Pioneer Ave; per 4/8hr $25/35) rents quality road and mountain bikes along with children's bikes and tandems, and will deliver them. The company offers a Bike & Brew, a four-hour bicycle tour that includes Auke Bay, Mendenhall Glacier and finishes off at the Alaskan Brewing Co.

Driftwood Lodge (Map p161; ☎ 586-2280; 435 W Willoughby Ave; incl helmet & lock per 8hr/day$15/30) rents basic mountain bikes.

GOLD PANNING

Juneau was built on gold, or more realistically, the tailings from its gold mines, and for many visitors that's the most fascinating part of its history. Two of the Juneau area's most successful historic mines were the **Alaska-Juneau Mine**, on the side of Mt Roberts, and the **Treadwell Mine**, across Gastineau Channel near Douglas. The Alaska-Juneau Mine closed in 1944 after producing more than $80 million in gold, then valued at $20 to $35 per ounce. The Treadwell Mine closed in 1922 after a 1917 cave-in caused the company's financial collapse. During its heyday at the turn of the 20th century, the Treadwell made Douglas the channel's major city, with a population of 15,000. For more information about these mines and what you can see of them today, stop by the Juneau-Douglas City Museum (p163).

Alaska Travel Adventures (☎ 789-0052, 800-791-2673; www.bestofalaskatravel.com; adult/child $49/33) offers a 1½-hour gold panning tour with a local prospector showing you color in Gold Creek. But you don't have to join a tour to pan, because recreational panning is easy and any hardware store in Juneau will sell you a gold pan for far less (black plastic ones are the cheapest and easiest to see the flecks of gold). The best public creeks to pan are Bullion Creek in the Treadwell Mine area, Gold Creek up by the Last Chance Basin, Sheep Creek on Thane Rd, and Salmon, Nugget and Eagle Creeks off Egan Dr and Glacier Hwy north of downtown.

HIKING

Few cities in Alaska have such a diversity of hiking trails as Juneau. A handful of these trails are near the city centre, the rest are out the road and shown on the Around Juneau map (Map p170) in this chapter. All five hike-in **USFS cabins** (☎ 877-444-6777, 518-885-3639; www.recreation.gov; cabins $35) should be reserved.

Guided Walks

Gastineau Guiding (☎ 586-2666; www.stepintoalaska.com) offers a number of guided hikes (adult/child $79/49) that include snacks, ponchos if needed and transportation. Most hikes last four hours and trails used include West and East Glacier Trail and the Perseverance Trail.

our pick **Juneau Parks & Recreation** (☎ 586-5226, recorded information 586-0428; www.juneau.org/parksrec; 155 S Seward St) offers volunteer-led hikes every Wednesday (adults) and Saturday (kids OK) in 'rain, shine or snow.' Call or check the website for a schedule and the trails.

City Center Trails

Perseverance Trail (off Map p161) off Basin Rd is Juneau's most popular and in 2008 received a $890,000 facelift. The trail is a path into Juneau's mining history but also provides access to two other popular treks, **Mt Juneau Trail** (Map p170) and **Granite Creek Trail** (Map p170), and together the routes can be combined into a rugged 10-hour walk for hardy hikers, or an overnight excursion into the mountains surrounding Alaska's capital city.

To reach Perseverance Trail, take 6th St one block southwest to Gold St, which turns into Basin Rd, a dirt road that curves away from the city into the mountains as it follows Gold Creek. The trailhead is at the road's end, at the parking lot for Last Chance Mining Museum. The trail leads into Silverbow Basin, an old mining area that still has many hidden and unmarked adits and mine shafts; be safe and stay on the trail.

From the Perseverance Trail, you can pick up Granite Creek Trail and follow it to the creek's headwaters basin, a beautiful spot to spend the night. From there, you can reach Mt Juneau by climbing the ridge and staying left of Mt Olds, the huge rocky mountain. Once atop Mt Juneau, you can complete the loop by descending along the Mt Juneau Trail, which joins Perseverance Trail a mile from its beginning. The hike to the 3576ft peak of Mt Juneau along the ridge from Granite Creek is an easier but longer trek than the ascent from the Mt Juneau Trail. The alpine sections of the ridge are serene, and on a clear summer day you'll have outstanding views. From the trailhead for the Perseverance Trail to the upper basin of Granite Creek is 3.3 miles one way. Then it's another 3 miles along the ridge to reach Mt Juneau.

Mt Roberts Trail (Map p161) is a 4-mile climb up Mt Roberts that begins at a marked wooden staircase at the northeast end of 6th St. It starts with a series of switchbacks, then breaks out of the trees at Gastineau Peak and comes to the tram station. From here it's a half-mile to the Cross, where you'll have good views of Juneau and Douglas. The Mt Roberts summit (3819ft) is still a steep climb away through the alpine brush. If you hike up, you can ride down the Mt Roberts Tramway to S Franklin St for only $5. And if you purchase $5 worth of food or drink at the visitors center on top, like a beer that you well deserve, the ride down is free.

Dan Moller Trail is a 3.3-mile trail leading to an alpine bowl at the crest of Douglas Island, where you'll find the Dan Moller Cabin. Just across the channel in West Juneau, the public bus conveniently stops at Cordova St and from there, you turn left onto Pioneer Ave and follow it to the end of the pavement to the trailhead. Plan on six hours for the round-trip.

Mendenhall Glacier Trails

East Glacier Loop (Map p170) is one of many trails near Mendenhall Glacier, a 3-mile round-trip providing good views of the glacier from a scenic lookout at the halfway point. Pick up the loop along the **Trail of Time**, a half-mile nature walk that starts at the Mendenhall Glacier Visitor Center.

Nugget Creek Trail (Map p170) begins just beyond the East Glacier Loop's scenic lookout. The 2.5-mile trail climbs 500ft to Vista Creek Shelter, a free-use shelter that doesn't require reservations, making the round-trip to the shelter from the Mendenhall Glacier Visitor Center an 8-mile trek. Hikers who plan to spend the night at the shelter can continue along the creek toward Nugget Glacier, though the route is hard to follow at times.

West Glacier Trail (Map p170) is one of the most spectacular hikes in the Juneau area. The 3.4-mile trail begins off Montana Creek Rd past Mendenhall Lake Campground and hugs the mountainside along the glacier, providing exceptional views of the icefalls and other glacial features. It ends at a rocky outcropping, but a rough route continues from there to the summit of Mt McGinnis (4228ft), another 2 miles away. Allow five hours for the West Glacier Trail, or plan on a long day if you want to tackle the difficult Mt McGinnis route.

Juneau Area Trails

Point Bishop Trail (Map p170) is at the end of Thane Rd, 7.5 miles southeast of Juneau. This 8-mile trail leads to Point Bishop, a scenic spot overlooking the junction of Stephens Passage and Taku Inlet. The trail is flat but can be wet in many spots, making waterproof boots the preferred footwear. The hike makes for an ideal overnight trip, as there is good camping at Point Bishop.

Montana Creek Trail (Map p170) and **Windfall Lake Trail** (Map p170) connect at Windfall Lake and can be combined for an interesting 11.5-mile overnight hiking trip. It is easier to begin at the trailhead at Montana Creek and follow the Windfall Lake Trail out to the Glacier Hwy.

The 8-mile Montana Creek Trail, known for its high concentration of bears, begins near the end of Montana Creek Rd, 2 miles from its junction with Mendenhall Loop Rd. The 3.5-mile Windfall Lake Trail begins off a gravel spur that leaves the Glacier Hwy just before it crosses Herbert River, 27 miles northwest of Juneau. The trail has been improved considerably in recent years and now features the newest USFS cabin in the Juneau area. Windfall Lake Cabin sleeps six and is open as a warming shelter during the day.

Spaulding Trail (Map p170) is primarily used for cross-country skiing, but can be hiked in summer. The 3-mile route provides access to the Auke Nu Trail, which leads to the John Muir Cabin. The trailhead is off Glacier Hwy just past and opposite Auke Bay Post Office, 12.3 miles northwest of Juneau.

Peterson Lake Trail (Map p170) is a 4-mile route along Peterson Creek to its namesake lake, a favorite among hike-in anglers for the good Dolly Varden fishing. The trailhead is 20ft before the Mile 24 marker on Glacier Hwy, north of the Shrine of St Terese. Wear rubber boots, as it can be muddy during summer. The Peterson Lake Cabin turns this trail into a delightful overnight adventure.

Herbert Glacier Trail (Map p170) extends 4.6 miles along the Herbert River to Herbert Glacier, a round-trip of four to five hours. The trail is easy with little climbing, though wet in places, and begins just past the bridge over Herbert River at Mile 28 of Glacier Hwy.

Amalga Trail (Map p170), also known as the Eagle Glacier Trail, is a level route that winds 7.5 miles to the lake formed by Eagle Glacier and the Eagle Glacier Cabin. Less than a mile from the glacier's face, the view from the cabin is well worth the effort of reserving it in advance. The trailhead is beyond the Glacier Hwy bridge, across Eagle River, 0.4 miles past the trailhead for the Herbert Glacier Trail. Plan on a round-trip of seven to eight hours to reach the impressive Eagle Glacier and return to the trailhead, a round-trip of 15 miles.

PADDLING

Day trips and extended paddles are possible out of the Juneau area in sea kayaks. Rentals are available from **Alaska Boat & Kayak** (Map p170; 789-6886, 364-2333; www.juneaukayak.com; 11521 Glacier Hwy; single/double $50/70; 9am-6pm), which is based in the Auke Bay Harbor and offers transport service and multiday discounts. The company also offers half-day and full-day guided paddles.

Mendenhall Lake

This lake at the foot of Mendenhall Glacier is an excellent destination for a paddle. Alaska Boat & Kayak offers a self-guided package to Mendenhall Lake ($95) which includes kayaks, transportation and a waterproof map that leads you on a route among the icebergs in this relatively clam body of water. It also shows you where to land for a short hike to view the glacier up close.

Auke Bay

The easiest trip is to paddle out and around the islands of Auke Bay. You can even camp on the islands to turn the adventure into an overnight trip.

Taku Inlet

This waterway is an excellent four- to five-day trip with close views of Taku Glacier. Total paddling distance is 30 to 40 miles, depending on how far you travel up the inlet. It does not require any major crossing, though rounding Point Bishop can be rough at times. It is possible to camp at Point Bishop and along the grassy area southwest of the glacier, where brown bears are occasionally seen.

Berners Bay

At the western end of Glacier Hwy, 40 miles from Juneau, is Echo Cove, where kayakers put in for paddles in the protected waters of Berners Bay. The bay, which extends 12 miles north to the outlets of the Antler, Lace and Berners Rivers, is ideal for an overnight trip or longer excursions up Berners River. The delightful USFS **Berners Bay Cabin** (877-444-6777, 518-885-3639; www.recreation.gov; cabins $35) is an 8-mile paddle from Echo Cove. Alaska Boat & Kayak (left) charges $150 roundtrip for transporting two kayaks to Echo Cove.

WHALE WATCHING

The whale watching in nearby Stephens Passage is so good that some tour operators will refund your money if you don't see at least one. The boats depart from Auke Bay and most tours last three to four hours. Some operators offer courtesy transport from downtown.

Allen Marine Tours (Map p170; 789-0081, 888-289-0081; www.allenmarinetours.com; per person $123) Combines whale watching with a stop at its remote Orca Point Lodge for a salmon feast.

Harv & Marv's (Map p170; 209-7288, 866-909-7288; www.harvandmarvs.com; per person $135) Small, personalized tours with never more than six passengers in the boat.

our pick **Orca Enterprises** (Map p170; 789-6801, 888-733-6722; www.alaskawhalewatching.com; adult/child $114/84) Uses a 42ft jet boat, that is fully disabled-accessible, to look at sea lions, orcas and harbor seals as well as humpback whales.

WILDERNESS CABINS

Numerous **USFS cabins** (877-444-6777, 518-885-3639; www.recreation.gov) are accessible from Juneau, but all are heavily used, requiring advance reservations. If you're just passing through, check with the **USFS Juneau Ranger District Office** (Map p170; ☎ 586-8790; 8510 Mendenhall Loop Rd; 8am-5pm Mon-Fri) for a list of what's available.

The following cabins are within 30 minutes' flying time from Juneau; air charters will cost around $500 to $600 round-trip from Juneau, split among a planeload of up to five passengers. **Alaska Seaplane Service** (Map p170; ☎ 789-3331; www.flyalaskaseaplanes.com) and **Wings of Alaska** (Map p170; ☎ 789-0790; www.wingsofalaska.com) can provide flights on short notice.

West Turner Lake Cabin (cabins $35) is one of the most scenic and is by far the Juneau area's most popular cabin. It's 18 miles east of Juneau on the west end of Turner Lake, where the fishing is good for trout, Dolly Varden and salmon. A skiff is provided.

Admiralty Island's north end has three popular cabins, all $35 a night. **Admiralty Cove Cabin** is on a scenic bay and has access to Young Lake along a rough 4.5-mile trail. Brown bears frequent the area. The two **Young Lake Cabins** have skiffs to access a lake with good fishing for cutthroat trout and landlocked salmon. A lakeshore trail connects the two cabins.

There are also three rental cabins in Point Bridget State Park that rent for $35 a night. **Cowee Meadow Cabin** is a 2.5-mile hike into the park, **Blue Mussel Cabin** is a 3.4-mile walk and **Camping Cove Cabin** a 4-mile trek. Both Blue Mussel and Camping Cove overlook the shoreline and would make a great destination for kayakers. Reserve them through the **DNR Public Information Center** (☎ 269-8400; www.dnr.state.ak.us/parks/cabins).

ZIPLINING

Juneau has a pair of ziplines where you can harness up and fly through 100ft trees like an eagle on the prowl.

Alaska Canopy Adventures (Map p170; ☎ 523-0947; www.alaskacanopy.com; per person $169) At the other end of Douglas Island is this zipline course reached by boat from downtown Juneau. The course includes nine lines, two sky bridges and a 40ft repel down a Sitka spruce at the end.

our pick **Alaska Zipline Adventures** (Map p170; ☎ 321-0947; www.alaskazip.com; adult/child $139/99) Located at beautiful Eaglecrest Ski Area on Douglas Island, this course includes five ziplines and a sky bridge that zigzag across Fish Creek Valley. Transportation is included.

Juneau for Children

The best attraction for kids visiting Juneau is the **Macauley Salmon Hatchery** (Map p170; ☎ 463-4810, 877-463-2486; www.dipac.net; 2697 Channel Dr; adult/child $3.25/1.75; 10am-6pm), 3 miles northwest of downtown. The hatchery has huge seawater aquariums loaded with local marine life, from tanner crabs to octopus, while the interpretive displays explaining the life cycle of salmon are museum quality. Underwater viewing windows and a 450ft fish ladder allow children to witness, from July to September, the amazing the sight of thousands of salmon fighting their way upstream to spawn. You can also wander the outside grounds and pier to watch people catching lunker salmon. Or rent a rod and reel at the adjacent Go Fish Grill ($10 per hour) and try your luck.

The City of Juneau maintains a wonderful system of parks including **Twin Lakes Park** (Map p170; Old Glacier Hwy), just past the hospital, which is stocked with king salmon and equipped with a fishing pier. There's also a solar-system trail around the lake that provides a realistic idea of how far each planet is from the sun. And don't forget the **Alaska State Museum** (p162) has a children's room where your young explorers can dress up in customes and then take over the wheel of Captain Cook's ship, *Discovery*.

Tours

The easiest way to book a tour in Juneau is to head to the cruise ship terminal, near the Mt Roberts Tram, where most of the operators will be hawking their wares from a line of booths like sideshow barkers at a carnival.

CITY & GLACIER

Gray Line (☎ 586-3773, 800-544-2206; www.graylineofalaska.com) Has several tours including the standard city-Macauley Salmon Hatchery-Mendenhall Glacier tour. The daily three-hour tour is adult/child $44/22.

Mendenhall Glacier Transport/Mighty Great Trips (☎ 789-5460; www.mightygreattrips.com) Offers a city-and-glacier tour for only $27.

Juneau Steamboat Co (☎ 723-0372; www.juneausteamboat.com) Uses a unique 30ft, 16-passenger steamboat to give you a view of Juneau and the surrounding gold mines from the middle of the Gastineau Channel on this hour-long tour (per person $49).

JUNEAU ICE FIELD

The hottest tour in Juneau is a helicopter ride to the Juneau Ice Field for a 20-minute ride in the basket of a dogsled. These tours last less than two hours and are $400 a pop but when the weather is nice, people (primarily cruise-ship passengers) are waiting to hand over their money.

Era Helicopters (Map p170; ☎ 586-2030, 800-843-1947; www.era-aviation.com) You spend an hour on Middle Branch Glacier as part of its glacier dogsled adventure ($465). For something more affordable, book its hour-long, four-glacier tour ($265) that includes a 20-minute glacier landing.

our pick **NorthStar Trekking** (☎ 790-4530; www.glaciertrekking.com) Skip the dogsled and strap on the crampons. NorthStar offers several glacier treks that first begin with a helicopter ride and includes all equipment and training. On its two-hour glacier trek ($379) you cross two miles of frozen landscape riddled with crevasses for a hike that is as stunning as it is pricy.

Temsco Helicopters (☎ 789-9501, 877-789-9501; www.temscoair.com) Its mushing and glacier flightseeing tour ($469) lasts 1½ hours and lands at a dog camp on Denver Glacier. The company also has a 55-minute Mendenhall Glacier tour ($249) that includes 25 minutes' walking around high up on the glacier.

Wings of Alaska (☎ 586-6275; www.wingsofalaska.com) Its 40-minute glacier flightseeing adventure (adult/child $170/140) is the most affordable way to get into the air for a peek at the ice field.

TRACY ARM

This steepsided fjord, 50 miles southeast of Juneau, has a pair of tidewater glaciers and a gallery of icebergs floating down its length. Tracy Arm makes an interesting day trip, far less expensive and perhaps even more satisfying than a visit to Glacier Bay. You're almost guaranteed to see seals inside the arm, and you might spot whales on the way there. **Adventure Bound Alaska** (☎ 463-2509, 800-228-3875; www.adventureboundalaska.com; adult/child $140/90) is the longtime tour operator to Tracy Arm and uses a pair of boats that leave daily from the Juneau waterfront. Reserve a seat in advance if you can, the full-day tour is popular with cruise ships, and pack a lunch along with your binoculars. Alternatively, get there under your own steam – see p108.

Festivals & Events

Alaska Folk Festival (☎ 463-3316; www.alaskafolkfestival.org) attracts musicians from around the state for a week of performances, workshops and dances at Centennial Hall in mid-April.

Juneau Jazz & Classics festival (☎ 463-3378; www.jazzandclassics.org; tickets $20-60) brings jazz and classical music concerts and workshops during the third week in May. Similar to the Alaska Folk Festival.

Gold Rush Days is a late-June festival of logging and mining events.

Fourth of July celebrations include a parade, carnival, fireworks and a lot of outdoor meals – from Sandy Beach in Douglas to Juneau's city center.

Sleeping

Juneau tacks on 12% in bed and sales taxes to the price of lodging.

BUDGET

Juneau International Hostel (Map p161; ☎ 586-9559; www.juneauhostel.org; 614 Harris St; dm $10; ⊠ 💻) Alaska's best hostel and certainly its most affordable. One of the eight bunkrooms is a family room while amenities include laundry, storage and free internet access and wi-fi. In the lounge area, the overstuffed sofas are strategically placed around a large bay window with a view of snowy peaks and Douglas Island. Best of all is the downtown location. You're only a few blocks from the Mt Roberts Trail. The only gripes are a strict lockout (9am to 5pm) and chores.

Camping

Thane Public Campground (off Map p161; ☎ 586-5252; 1585 Thane Rd; sites $5) Located about a mile south of downtown on Thane Rd is the city-operated basic place for tents only.

Auke Village Campground (Map p170; Glacier Hwy; sites $10) Located 2 miles from the ferry terminal on Glacier Hwy, this is a 11-site USFS campground with shelters, tables, firewood and a nice beach. It's first-come, first-served.

Eagle Beach State Recreation Area (Map p170; ☎ 586-2506; Mile 28 Glacier Hwy; sites $10) This is 15 miles from the ferry terminal and 28 miles from downtown Juneau. Recently renovated, the state recreation area now includes a ranger station and day-use parking area and 17 wooded campsites with fire rings and vault toilets; ideal for tenters.

Mendenhall Lake Campground (Map p170; Montana Creek Rd; campsites $10, RV sites $26-29) One of Alaska's most beautiful USFS campgrounds. The 69-site area (18 sites with hookups) is on Montana Creek Rd, off Mendenhall Loop Rd, and has a separate seven-site walk-in backpacking unit. The campsites are alongside Mendenhall Lake, and many have spectacular views of the icebergs or even the glacier that discharges them. Twenty sites can be reserved in advance (☎ 877-444-6777, 518-885-3639; www.recreation.gov).

Spruce Meadow RV Park (Map p170; ☎ 789-1990; www.juneaurv.com; 10200 Mendenhall Loop Rd; campsites $20, RV sites $28-30) If Mendenhall Lake Campground is full, this full-service campground is practically next door. Spruce Meadows has all the amenities, from a Laundromat and cable TV to a modem station to check email, plus it's right on the city bus route.

MIDRANGE

Alaskan Hotel (Map p161; ☎ 586-1000, 800-327-9347; www.thealaskanhotel.com; 167 S Franklin St; r without/with bath $60/90, ste $120) The smallish rooms in this historical hotel are a little worn but you accept that for the gold rush ambience this place breathes and the price. Most rooms have small refrigerators, sinks and cable TV but avoid the ones overlooking Franklin St unless you plan to join the revelry below.

Driftwood Lodge (Map p161; ☎ 586-2280, 800-544-2239; www.driftwoodalaska.com; 435 Willoughby Ave; r $94-100, ste $125; ⊠ 💻) Near the Alaska State Museum, this lodge is the best value in accommodations downtown. The 63 rooms are clean and updated regularly, the motel offers 24-hour courtesy transportation to the airport and the ferry and it's hard to top the location unless you're willing to spend twice as much.

Super 8 Motel (Map p170; ☎ 789-4858, 800-800-8000; 2295 Trout St; s/d $110/120; 💻) Your run-of-the-mill Super 8 but of the handful of chain motels clustered around the airport it's by far the most affordable. It offers free airport and ferry shuttle and a fish freezer big enough to hold that trophy halibut you landed.

Auke Lake B&B (Map p170; ☎ 790-3253, 800-790-3253; www.admiraltytours.com; 11595 Mendenhall Loop Rd; r $125-165; ⊠ 💻) Located 10 minutes from Mendenhall Glacier, this Valley B&B has three rooms, a huge deck and a hot tub that overlooks Auke Lake. Each room has a private bath, phone, TV/VCR, refrigerator and coffeemaker while guests have use of a paddleboat, canoes or kayak.

our pick Silverbow Inn (Map p161; ☎ 586-4146, 800-586-4146; www.silverbowinn.com; 120 2nd St; r $138-228; ⊠) A boutique inn on top of the best (and only) bagel shop downtown. The 11 rooms as well as the inn itself are filled with antiques but come with private bath, king and queen beds and flat panel TVs. A 2nd-floor deck features a hot tub with a view of the mountains of Douglas Island. Breakfast is served in the morning, wine-and-cheese in the evening.

Juneau Hotel (Map p161; ☎ 586-5666; www.juneauhotels.net; 1200 W 9th St; ste $169; ⊠ 💻) New, freshly painted and located within easy walking distance of downtown attractions, this all-suites hotel is Juneau's best deal in accommodations. The 73 suites have full kitchens, sitting areas, two TVs each and even washers and dryers.

TOP END

Alaska's Capital Inn (Map p161; ☎ 907-586-6507, 888-588-6507; www.alaskacapitalinn.com; 113 W 5th St; r $175-$305; ⊠ 💻) Political junkies will love this place, it's across the street from the state capitol. In the gorgeously restored home of a wealthy goldrush-era miner, who obviously found color, the inn has seven rooms with private bath, phone and TV/VCR, and feature hardwood floors covered by colorful Persian rugs. The backyard doesn't have a blade of grass; rather multiple decks, gardens and a secluded hot tub that even the governor can't spy on. In the morning there's a full breakfast, in the evening wine and cheese is served on the back deck, which overlooks the city.

Goldbelt Hotel Juneau (Map p161; ☎ 586-6900, 888-478-6909; www.goldbelttours.com; 51 Egan Dr; r $179-189; 💻) Alaska Native–owned and centrally located downtown, the hotel has big rooms and big, comfortable beds with such amenities as room service, cable TV and courtesy pickup from the airport. The waterfront rooms are $10 extra but face a view of the cruise ships sailing in and the floatplanes taking off.

Pearson's Pond (Map p170; ☎ 789-3772, 888-658-6328; www.pearsonspond.com; 4541 Sawa Cr; r $399-499; ⊠ 💻) The ultimate in luxury and pampering in Southeast Alaska. This inn offers five suites and two larger condos that are surrounded by the rain forest and perched above a pond dotted with wildlife. Pearson's has not one but two hot tubs, viewing decks everywhere, including one on the pond, robes and slippers in the closet, wine and cheese every evening. Need we say more?

Eating

We miss the Fiddlehead already. Juneau's best restaurant for almost 30 years closed in 2006, taking this city down yet another rung on the gastronomic ladder of adventurous eating and fine cuisine. Juneau struggles to serve up a restaurant scene worthy of a state capital. Even fast-food fanatics find a limited menu here; basically a McDonald's and a Taco Bell.

SALMON BAKES

Juneau has several salmon bakes. Though aimed primarily at tourists, they provide great food (hard to go wrong with wild salmon)

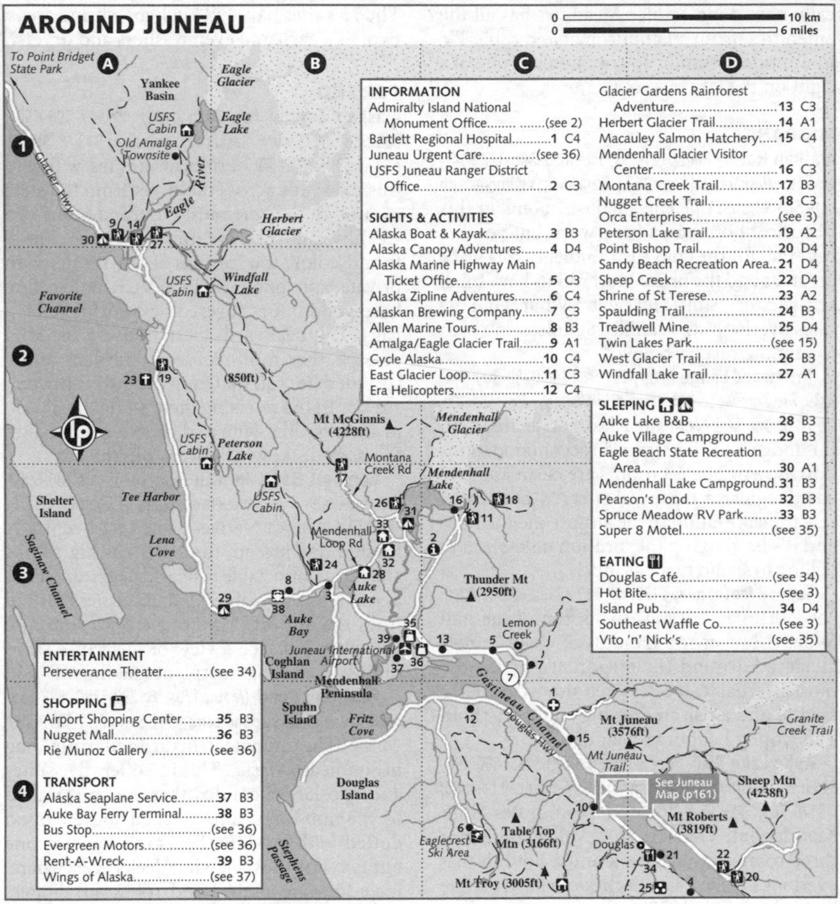

with an experience conveying the flavor of frontier Alaska.

Thane Ore House (off Map p161; ☎ 586-3442; 4400 Thane Rd; dinner $21; ⊠) Found 4 miles south of town, this is the best. The all-you-can-eat dinner of grilled salmon, halibut and ribs includes a salad bar, corn, baked beans and more. There is a courtesy bus that departs nightly from the downtown area.

Taku Glacier Lodge (☎ 586-6275, 789-0790; www.takuglacierlodge.com; adult/child $240/200) Reached via a floatplane flight up nearby Taku Inlet, a trip to the lodge allows you to combine flightseeing, glacier viewing and a salmon bake in one evening. The tour lasts three hours and includes 45 minutes of flying, making it a much better experience and cheaper than taking a helicopter to the ice field. Sign up at the lodge's booth behind Merchant's Wharf on Juneau's waterfront.

RESTAURANTS

Seong's Sushi Bar & Chinese Takeout (Map p161; ☎ 586-4778; 740 W 9th St; sushi $4-6, Chinese lunch $7-9, dinner $11-13; ⊠) Across from the Federal Building, this little hole-in-the-wall is bright, airy and at lunchtime it's filled with government workers who know how to save a buck. The sushi menu is extensive and loved by locals.

Olivia's de Mexico (Map p161; ☎ 586-6870; 222 Seward St; lunch $7-10, dinner $9-17; 🕒 11am-9pm Mon-Fri, from 5pm Sat; ⊠) A friendly family-run *cocina,* whose spicey aroma and Mexican music spills onto the street enticing you into its brightly colored restaurant downstairs. Hungry? Two people can feast on its Burrito Ranchero.

Doc Water's Pub (Map p161; ☎ 586-3627; Merchant's Wharf on Marine Way; sandwiches $8-12, dinner $13-27; 🕑 10:30-1am Sun-Thu, to 3am Fri & Sat; ⊠) If the midnight munchies attack, you can head here for a wild salmon burger or even a regular one. But this is a better place to linger in the late afternoon sun at an outdoor table overlooking the harbor, drinking beer and nibbling on a plate of seafood ceviche while being entertained by the tourists and the seagulls converging on the wharf.

Zephyr Restaurant (Map p161; ☎ 780-2221; 200 Seward St; lunch $10-14, dinner $14-29; 🕑 11:30am-2pm & 5-9:30pm Mon-Sat; ⊠) Juneau's newest restaurant is easily one of its best. The Italian restaurant ladens its Mediterranean menu with fresh Alaskan seafood (who doesn't?), but also offers such classic mains like veal scallopini and adventurous dishes like polenta lasagna. Its interior of muted colors and hardwood floors is soothing and its wine list is extensive enough to complement the menu.

Bullwinkle's (Map p161; ☎ 586-2400; 318 Willoughby Ave; med pizza $12-18; 🕑 11am-11pm Mon-Thu, to midnight Fri & Sat, noon-11pm Sun) There's been a moose and a flying squirrel pitching pizza in Juneau for 35 years. The beerhall-like restaurant has changed little in that time and neither has the pizza, it's as tasty as ever. Bullwinkle's also has good sandwiches and a decent little salad bar for the veggie deprived. Enjoy a pitcher of beer and free popcorn while waiting for your garlic chicken pizza.

our pick **Island Pub** (Map p170; ☎ 364-1595; 1102 2nd St; pizza $13-18; 🕑 4-10pm) Across the channel from the Capital City, this relaxing, unhurried restaurant serves firebrick-oven focaccia and gourmet pizza to a mountainous view. Don't worry about a Red Dog Saloon mob scene. You're on Douglas Island.

Twisted Fish (Map p161; ☎ 463-5033; 550 S Franklin St; dinner $15-22; ⊠) Beef be gone. Located between Taku Smokeries and a wharf where commercial fishermen unload their catch, this restaurant is about local seafood, from its menu to the large colorful salmon hanging from the ceiling. Indulge yourself by ordering salmon grilled on a cedar plank or Alaskan rockfish cooked with mango and lime. If you have to have a burger, at the very least order a halibut burger.

Zen (Map p161; ☎ 586-5074; Goldbelt Hotel, 51 Egan Dr; breakfast $5-12, dinner $20-30) Zen calls itself an Asian fusion restaurant, taking what's readily available, Alaska seafood, and infusing it with a touch of the Oriental. You end up with entrees like ginger halibut, black-cod stir fry or shrimp Alfredo made with jumbo udon noodles. If the prices are too upscale for you then come before 3pm – many of the $9 lunch specials are the same dishes.

CAFÉS

Southeast Waffle Co (Map p170; ☎ 789-2030; 11806 Glacier Hwy; waffles $4-6; 🕑 6am-midnight Mon-Fri, 7am-midnight Sat, 7am-10pm Sun; 💻) All you campers in the Mendenhall Valley and out the road, here's where you come in Auke Bay for a latte, free wi-fi and a blackboard menu of great waffles, from some stuffed with ham and cheese to chocolate chip waffles served with peanut butter.

Silverbow Bagel Bakery (Map p161; ☎ 586-4146; 120 2nd St; bagel sandwiches $5-8; 🕑 7am-6pm; ⊠) Downtown, this place bakes bagels daily, serving them au natural, with a variety of spreads and toppings, or using them as bookends for breakfast and lunch sandwiches.

Costa's Diner (Map p161; Merchant's Wharf on Marine Way; breakfast $6-8; 🕑 8am-3pm Wed-Mon; ⊠) Juneau's lunch counter, literally. There's only stools and a corner table inside and three tables in the hallway of the Merchant's Wharf. You write down your order on a sticky note and then call out 'order in.' There's no cash register, you merely toss your money into a brass pot on the counter. Strange? Maybe, but the food – like White Trash Eggs Benedict or curry-and-potatoes crepes – is good and the portions huge.

our pick **Hot Bite** (Map p170; ☎ 790-2483; 11465 Auke Bay Harbor Dr; hamburgers $8-13; 🕑 11am-7pm; ⊠) You have to drive out to the Auke Bay Harbor for the best milkshakes and burgers in Juneau. The small café is housed is the one-time ticket office of Pan American Airways but has seating outside where you can watch the state ferry sail out of Auke Bay. As if three scoops of ice cream wasn't enough, the cheesecake shake also has cream cheese and graham cracker crumbs mixed in.

Douglas Café (Map p170; ☎ 364-3307; 916 3rd St; breakfast $8-11, burgers $9-11, dinner $18-21; 🕑 11am-2:30pm Mon, 11am-8:30pm Tue-Fri, 9am-8:30pm Sat, to 12:30pm Sun; ⊠) Douglas' other fine eatery, well worth making your way over the bridge. It serves 14 different types of burgers, each weighing in at a third of a pound, and for dinner it offers up mains such as jambalaya, tarragon-lime chicken and apple-brandy pork.

Heritage Coffee Co & Café (Map p161; ☎ 586-1087; 174 S Franklin; 6:30am-7pm Mon-Fri, 7am-6pm Sat-Sun; ☒) Juneau's most popular coffeehouse, for good reason. The coffee is great, the sofas comfortable and with the purchase of an espresso drink you get free internet. The company also has a café at 216 2nd St that is a bit quieter and features outdoor seating.

QUICK EATS

Pel'Meni (Map p161; Merchant's Wharf on Marine Way; dumplings $5; 11:30am-1:30am Sun-Thu, to 3:30am Fri & Sat) The only thing on the menu, well there is no menu, are authentic homemade Russian dumplings, filled with either potato or sirloin, spiced with hot sauce, curry and cilantro and served with a piece of bread to clean the bowl afterwards. The perfect end to a night of drinking, the reason Pel'Meni is open to the wee hours. Record buffs will be amazed by the wallful of LPs and the turntable that provides the proper late-night atmosphere.

Tracy's King Crab Shack (Map p161; Cruise Ship Dock; crab $8-17; 11am-6pm) Squeezed between the Library Parking Garage and the Cruise Ship Dock is a row of food booths with the best being Tracy's shack. From this little hut she serves up crab bisque, crab rolls and mini crab-cakes. If there are two of you, split a bucket of king crab ($49), almost three pounds of the sweetest seafood you'll ever have.

GROCERIES

Rainbow Foods (Map p161; ☎ 586-6476; 224 4th St; 9am-7pm Mon-Fri, 10am-6pm Sat-Sun) Practically right next door to the conservative, dig-and-drill politicians in the state capitol is this natural food store, a hangout for liberals and environmentalists. Along with a large selection of fresh produce and bulk goods, the store has a hot-and-cold food bar ($7.50 per pound) for lunch, espresso and a bulletin board with the latest cultural happenings.

A&P Juneau Market (Map p161; ☎ 586-3101; 615 W Willoughby Ave) Near the Federal Building, this supermarket has a good selection of local seafood, an espresso counter, salad bar ($5 per pound), deli and small seating area.

Drinking

Nightlife centers on S Franklin and Front Sts, a historic, quaint (but not quiet) main drag attracting locals and tourists alike.

Red Dog Saloon (Map p161; ☎ 463-3658; 200 Admiral Way at S Franklin St) A sign at the door says it all – Booze, Antiques, Sawdust Floor, Community Singing – and the cruise-ship passengers love it! Most don't realize, much less care, that this Red Dog is but a replica of the original, a famous Alaskan drinking hole that was across the street until 1987. Now that was a bar. The duplicate is interesting, but the fact that it has a gift shop should tell you who the clientele is during summer.

Alaskan Hotel Bar (Map p161; ☎ 586-1000; 167 S Franklin St) In keeping with the gold-rush atmosphere of the hotel, this low-key, half-hidden bar has red velvet sofas, Tiffany lamps, an impressive back bar, even a cigar room.

Viking (Map p161; ☎ 586-2159; 218 Front St) In this classic tin-ceiling building are actually three bars. At street level is a sports pub with four giant TV screens and almost 20 beers on tap, while in the back is a cozy martini lounge complete with sofas and easy chairs along with a dance floor. Upstairs is a billiards hall with seven tables and free internet. Surf while drinking a pint.

Imperial Saloon (Map p161; ☎ 586-1960; 241 Front St) This is where the local softball teams come after the game. Inside are pool tables, darts and a dance floor with a DJ Thursday to Saturday. There's free wi-fi and some tables open up to busy Front St, making them prime pickings for people-watchers.

Rendezvous (Map p161; ☎ 586-1270; 184 S Franklin St) Another bar offering free wi-fi and cheap pitchers of beer but also Karaoke once a week, local bands frequently and even an occasional live burlesque show.

Entertainment

Perseverance Theater (Map p170; ☎ 364-2421; www.perseverancetheatre.org; 914 3rd St, Douglas) Founded in 1979, this is Alaska's only genuine full-time professional theater company. Sadly the theatre season begins in September and ends in May.

Back Room Cinema (Map p161; ☎ 586-4146; 120 2nd St) Located in the Silverbow Inn, it screens art films and classics three nights a week. The movies are free and the seating is at tables where you can enjoy a beer, dessert or even dinner while watching the silver screen.

our pick **Gold Town Nickelodeon** (☎ 586-2876; www.goldtownnick.110mb.com; 171 Shattuck St; Thu-Sun) This delightful art house theater presents small budget, foreign films and documentaries. On Thursday the popcorn is free.

20th Century Theatre (☎ 463-3549; www.juneaumovies.com; 222 Front St) Shows two current releases (or current by Alaskan standards) a night.

Shopping

Like most cruise-ship ports, Juneau is overrun with many of the same gift shops and jewelry stores that you'll see in Ketchikan or Skagway, begging the question, 'Who comes to Alaska to shop at a Caribbean jewelers?' The situation between the cruise-ship stores and local shops has become tense in recent years, the reason you see signs like 'Open All Year' or 'An Alaskan Family Owns This Store.'

Thanks to such signs finding a local shop is not hard and once inside you'll see some truly unique artwork. One of the best downtown is the **Juneau Artists Gallery** (Map p161; ☎ 586-9891; www.juneauartistsgallery.com; Senate Bldg at 175 S Franklin St; 9am-9pm), a co-op of 26 local artists who have filled the store with paintings, etchings, glass work, jewelry, pottery and quilts. The person behind the counter ready to help you is that day's 'Artist On Duty.' Out in the Valley, near Nugget Mall, is the **Rie Munoz Gallery** (Map p170; ☎ 789-7449; 2101 Jordan Ave; 9am-5:30pm) featuring a large selection of Rie Munoz prints as well as Dale DeArmond, Byron Birdsall and several other noted Alaskan artists.

For packs, outdoorwear, USGS topo maps and anything else you need for backcountry trips stop at **Foggy Mountain Shop** (Map p161; ☎ 586-6780; www.foggymountainshop.com; 134 N Franklin St; 9:30am-6pm Mon-Fri, 10am-5:30pm Sat). This is the only outdoor shop in town with top-of-the-line equipment and the prices reflect that.

Getting There & Away

AIR

Alaska Airlines (☎ 800-252-7522; www.alaskaair.com) offers scheduled jet service to Seattle, all major Southeast cities, Glacier Bay, Anchorage and Cordova daily in summer.

Alaska Seaplane Service (Map p170; ☎ 789-3331, 888-350-8277; www.flyalaskaseaplanes.com), at the airport, flies floatplanes from Juneau to Angoon ($125), Elfin Cove ($165), Pelican ($165) and Tenakee Springs ($125).

Wings of Alaska (Map p170; ☎ 789-0790; www.wingsofalaska.com; 8421 Livingston Way) flies to Angoon ($90), Gustavus ($93), Haines ($105), Hoonah ($69) and Skagway ($114).

BOAT

Alaska Marine Highway (☎ 465-3941, 800-642-0066; www.ferryalaska.com) ferries dock at Auke Bay Ferry Terminal, 14 miles from downtown. In summer, the mainline ferries traversing the Inside Passage depart daily southbound for Sitka ($45, nine hours), Petersburg ($66, eight hours) and Ketchikan ($107, 18 hours). You can shorten the sailing times on the high-speed MV *Fairweather*, which connects Juneau and Petersburg twice a week and Juneau and Sitka five times a week. There are also daily northbound sailings for Haines ($37, 4½ hours) and Skagway ($50, 5 ½ hours).

Several shorter routes also operate in summer. The smaller MV *Le Conte* regularly connects Juneau to the secondary ports of Hoonah ($33, four hours), Tenakee Springs ($35, eight hours) and Angoon ($37, 12 hours). Two times a month, the MV *Kennicott* departs Juneau for a trip to Yakutat ($85, 15½ hours) then across the Gulf of Alaska to Whittier ($221, 39 hours); reservations are strongly suggested.

Getting Around

Good luck.

TO/FROM THE AIRPORT & FERRY

A taxi to/from the airport costs around $25. The city bus express route runs to the airport, but only from 7:30am to 5:30pm Monday to Friday. On weekends and in the evening, if you want a bus you'll need to walk 10 minutes to the nearest 'regular route' stop on the backside of Nugget Mall. The regular route headed downtown stops here regularly from 7:15am until 10:45pm Monday to Saturday, and from 9:15am until 5:45pm Sunday. The fare on either route is $1.50/1 per adult/child.

Unbelievable but true: no buses or regularly scheduled shuttles go to the ferry terminal in Auke Bay; an ungodly long 14 mile distance from downtown. Some of the hotels and B&Bs offer courtesy transportation by prebooking – try to line up one of these if possible, as it will make your life much easier. A few taxis, including **Glacier Taxi** (☎ 796-2300), show up for most ferry arrivals, charging $35 to downtown. You can stick out your thumb (hitchhiking is commonplace) or take the city bus to/from the end of the line, which is almost 2 miles south of the ferry terminal at DeHart's Store in Auke Bay. One way to save a few dollars out to the ferry is to take the bus to the airport, where there are usually cabs stationed, and then catch a taxi the rest of the way.

BUS

Juneau's sadistic public bus system, **Capital Transit** (☎ 789-6901), stops well short of the ferry terminal and a mile short of the Mendenhall Glacier Visitor Center. Even getting to/from the airport can be problematic: only the 'express' route goes right to the terminal, and it only runs during business hours on weekdays. At other times, you'll have to schlep your bags between the airport and the 'regular' route's stop at Nugget Mall, a 10-minute walk.

The 'regular' route buses start around 7am and stop just before midnight, running every half-hour after 8am and before 6:30pm. The main route circles downtown then heads out to the Valley and Auke Bay Boat Harbor via Mendenhall Loop Rd, where it travels close to Mendenhall Lake Campground. Routes 3 and 4 make stops in the Mendenhall Valley either from downtown or Auke Bay while a bus runs every hour from city stops to Douglas. Fares are $1.50/1 each way per adult/child, and exact change is required. Major stops downtown include the Federal Building and on Main St, a block from Egan Hwy.

CAR

Juneau has many car-rental places, and renting a car is a great way for two or three people to see the sights out of the city or to reach a trailhead. For a $45 special, call **Rent-A-Wreck** (Map p170; ☎ 789-4111; 2450 Industrial Blvd), a mile from the airport, which provides pickup and drop-off service between 6am to 6pm. **Evergreen Motors** (Map p170; ☎ 789-9386; 8895 Mallard St) has compacts for around $54 a day. It offers pickups and drop-offs in the Valley and out to the ferry, but not downtown. You can also rent a car at the airport, but will have to stomach a 26% tax as opposed to a 15% tax elsewhere.

AROUND JUNEAU

Alaskan Brewing Company

Alaska's largest **brewery** (Map p170; ☎ 780-5866; www.alaskanbeer.com; 5429 Shaune Dr; 🕑 11am-7pm) also makes some of its best beer. Established in 1986, the brewery is in the Lemon Creek area and reached from Anka St, where the city bus will drop you off, by turning right on Shaune Dr. The tour includes viewing the small brewery, free sampling of lagers and ales plus an opportunity to purchase beer in the gift shop, even five-gallon party kegs ($55). The brewery's beer-bottle collection from around the world is amazing. So many beers, so little time to drink them.

Glacier Gardens Rain Forest Adventure

This 50-acre **garden** (Map p170; ☎ 790-3377; 7600 Glacier Hwy; www.glaciergardens.com; adult/child $22/16; 🕑 9am-6pm), near the brewery, includes ponds, waterfalls and lots of ferns and flowers on the side of Thunder Mountain. You hop on electric carts for a guided tour of the gardens that ends at a viewing point almost 600ft up the mountain.

Mendenhall Glacier

The most famous of Juneau's ice floes, and the city's most popular attraction, is Mendenhall Glacier, Alaska's famous drive-in glacier. The river of ice is 13 miles from downtown, at the end of Glacier Spur Rd. From Egan Dr at Mile 9 turn right onto Mendenhall Loop Rd, staying on Glacier Spur Rd when the loop curves back toward Auke Bay.

The Mendenhall Glacier flows 12 miles from its source, the Juneau Ice Field, and has a 1.5-mile-wide face. On a sunny day it's beautiful, with blue skies and snowcapped mountains in the background. On a cloudy and drizzly afternoon it can be even more impressive, as the ice turns shades of deep blue.

Near the face of the glacier is the USFS **Mendenhall Glacier Visitor Center** (Map p170; ☎ 789-0097; adult/child $3/free; 🕑 8am-7:30pm), which houses various glaciology exhibits, a large relief map of the ice field, an observatory with telescopes and a theater that shows the film *Magnificent Mendenhall*.

Outside you'll find six hiking trails, ranging from a 0.3-mile photo-overlook trail to a trek of several miles up the glacier's west side (p164). For many the most interesting path is the mile-long Moraine Ecology Trail, which leads to a salmon-viewing platform overlooking **Steep Creek**. From July through September you'll not only see salmon spawning in the stream but also brown and black bears feasting on them. This is Southeast Alaska's most affordable bear-viewing site.

The cheapest way to see the glacier is to hop on a Capital Transit bus (left) but that leaves you a mile short of it. It's easier to jump on a bus from **Mendenhall Glacier Transport** (MGT; ☎ 789-5460; www.mightygreatrips.com; one way/round-trip $7/10). MGT picks up from the cruise-ship docks downtown for the glacier, making a run every 30 minutes. The last bus of the day depends on the cruise ship schedule.

GLACIER TREKKING

One of the most unusual outdoor activities in Juneau is glacier trekking: stepping into crampons, grabbing an ice axe and roping up to walk on ice 1000 years or older. The scenery and the adventure is like nothing you've experienced before as a hiker. The most affordable outing is offered by **Above & Beyond Alaska** (☎ 364-2333; www.beyondak.com). Utilizing a trail to access Mendenhall Glacier, it avoids expensive helicopter fees on its guided six-hour outing. The cost is $185 per person and includes all mountaineering equipment and transportation.

Shrine of St Terese

At Mile 23.3 Glacier Hwy is the Shrine of St Terese (Map p170), a natural stone chapel on an island connected to the shore by a stone causeway. As well as being the site of numerous weddings, the island lies along the Breadline, a well-known salmon-fishing area in Juneau. The island is perhaps the best place to fish for salmon from the shore.

Point Bridget State Park

Juneau's only state park is 2850-acre **Point Bridget State Park** (off Map p170; Mile 39 Glacier Hwy), which overlooks Berners Bay and Lynn Canal; salmon fishing is excellent off the Berners Bay beaches and in Cowee Creek. Hiking trails wander through rain forest, along the park's rugged shoreline and past three rental cabins (p166). The most popular hike is Point Bridget Trail, a 3.5-mile, one-way walk from the trailhead on Glacier Hwy to Blue Mussel Cabin at the point, where often you can spot sea lions and seals playing the surf. Plan on six to seven hours for a round-trip with lunch at the cabin.

ADMIRALTY ISLAND

Only 15 miles southeast of Juneau is Admiralty Island National Monument, a 1493-sq-mile preserve, of which 90% is designated wilderness. The Tlingit Indians, who know Admiralty Island as Kootznoowoo, 'the Fortress of Bears,' have lived on the 96-mile-long island for more than 1000 years.

Admiralty Island has a wide variety of wildlife. Bays such as Mitchell, Hood, Whitewater and Chaik contain harbor seals, porpoises and sea lions. Seymour Canal, the island's largest inlet, has one of the highest densities of nesting eagles in the world, and humpback whales often feed in the waterway. Sitka black-tailed deer are plentiful, and the streams choke with spawning salmon during August.

But more than anything else, Admiralty Island is known for its bears. The island has one of the highest populations of bears in Alaska, with an estimated 1500 to 1700 living there, enjoying a good life roaming the drainages for sedges, roots and berries much of the year, but feasting on salmon in August before settling into dens on the upper slopes to sleep away most of the winter.

Admiralty is a rugged island, with mountains that rise to 4650ft and covered by tundra and even permanent ice fields. Numerous lakes, rivers and open areas of muskeg break up the coastal rain forest of Sitka spruce and western hemlock.

You can fly in for a stay at a USFS cabin, spend time kayaking Seymour Inlet and Mitchell Bay or arrange a bear-watching trip to Pack Creek. The most unusual adventure on the island is the **Cross Admiralty Island canoe route** (p111), a 32-mile paddle that spans the center of the island from the village of Angoon to Mole Harbor. Although the majority of the route consists of calm lakes connected by streams and portages, the 10-mile paddle from Angoon to Mitchell Bay is subject to strong tides that challenge even experienced paddlers.

Most visitors arrive from Juneau where they secure supplies and obtain information from the **Admiralty Island National Monument office** (Map p170; ☎ 586-8800; www.fs.fed.us/r10/tongass/districts/admiralty; 8510 Mendenhall Loop Rd) in Mendenhall Valley.

Angoon

pop 478

The lone settlement on Admiralty Island is Angoon, a predominantly Tlingit community. Tlingit tribes occupied the site for centuries, but the original village was wiped out in 1882 when the US Navy, sailing out of Sitka, bombarded the indigenous people after they staged an uprising against a local whaling company. In 1973 Angoon won a $90,000 out-of-court settlement from the federal government for the bombardment.

Today the economy is a mixture of commercial fishing and subsistence, and in town the strong indigenous heritage is evident in the painted fronts of the 16 tribal community houses. The old lifestyle is still apparent in this remote community, and time in Angoon can be spent observing and gaining some understanding of the Tlingit culture. Tourism seems to be tolerated only because the village is a port of call for the ferry. It's also a dry community, so you'll find no bars.

The village is perched on a strip of land between Chatham Strait on Admiralty Island's west coast and turbulent Kootznahoo Inlet, which leads into the national monument's interior. The community serves as the departure point for many kayak and canoe trips into the heart of the monument, including the 32-mile Cross Admiralty canoe.

Many people are content to just spend a few days paddling and fishing Mitchell Bay and Salt Lake. To rent a canoe or kayak in Angoon, call **Favorite Bay Inn** (☎ 788-3234), which charges $60 a day, less for a rental of six days or longer. The tides here are among the strongest in the world; the walk between the airport and the town allows you to view the turbulent waters at mid-tide.

SLEEPING

Lodging is limited in Angoon. By far the best place to stay is **Favorite Bay Inn** (☎ 788-3234; s/d $119/139; ☒), a large, rambling log home 2 miles from the ferry terminal where you can get a bed and a hearty breakfast.

GETTING THERE & AWAY

Approximately three southbound and two northbound ferries a week stop at Angoon on the run from Sitka to Juneau in summer. The one-way fare to Angoon is $33 from Juneau, $31 from Sitka. The ferry terminal is 3 miles from town.

Wings of Alaska (☎ in Angoon 788-3530; www.wingsofalaska.com) and **Alaska Seaplane Service** (☎ 789-3331, 888-350-8277; www.akseaplanes.com) offer scheduled flights between Juneau and Angoon (around $90 one way).

Pack Creek

From 4000ft in the mountains, Pack Creek flows down Admiralty Island's east side before spilling into Seymour Canal. The extensive tide flats at the mouth of the creek draw a large number of bears to feed on salmon, making the spot a favorite for observing and photographing the animals.

Within this area is **Stan Price State Wildlife Sanctuary**, named for an Alaskan woodsman who lived on a float house here for almost 40 years. The sanctuary includes an area that has been closed to hunting since the mid-1930s, and, due largely to the former presence of Price and his visitors, the bears here have become used to humans. The bears are most abundant in July and August, when the salmon are running.

Most visitors to Pack Creek are day-trippers who arrive and depart on floatplanes. Upon arrival, all visitors are met by a ranger who explains the rules. You must leave all food in a cache provided near the south sand spit. You may not leave the viewing sand spit to get closer to the bears, although you may use a small observation tower – reached by a mile-long trail – that overlooks the creek. No camping is allowed at Pack Creek. The only nearby camping is on the east side of Windfall Island (permit required), a half-mile away and accessible only by boat.

Pack Creek has become so popular that the area buzzes with planes and boats every morning from early July to late August. Anticipating this daily rush hour, most resident bears escape into the forest, but a few bears hang around to feed on salmon, having long since been habituated to the human visitors. Seeing five or six bears would be a good viewing day at Pack Creek. You might see big boars during the mating season from May to mid-June, otherwise it's sows and cubs the rest of the summer.

PERMITS

From June to mid-September, the USFS and Alaska Department of Fish and Game operate a permit system to limit visitors. Only 24 people are allowed per day from July to the end of August. One- to three-day permits should be reserved in advance and cost $50 per adult per day. Guiding and tour companies receive half the permits, leaving 12 for individuals who want to visit Pack Creek on their own. Note that only one tour company has permits for any given day, so if your schedule is critical, you'll need to shop around and find out who has the guide permits for the day you need to go; a complete list of guide companies is on the USFS website.

Permits are available starting March 1, and most are snapped up quickly. But four permits per day are available on a walk-in basis, up to three days in advance at the **USFS Juneau Ranger District Office** (Map p170; ☎ 586-8800; 8510 Mendenhall Loop Rd).

GETTING THERE & AWAY

Experienced kayakers can rent a boat in Juneau and paddle to the refuge – a two-day trip (30 to 35 miles) that uses a tram at Oliver Inlet to portage into Seymour Canal. The run down Gastineau Channel and around Douglas Island isn't bad, but the Stephens Passage crossing to reach Oliver Inlet has to be done with extreme care and a close eye on the weather. **Alaska Boat & Kayak** (☎ 789-6886, 364-2333; www.juneaukayak.com; 11521 Glacier Hwy; single/double $50/70) will rent you a kayak and also arrange a drop-off at Oliver Inlet.

Alaska Discovery/Mt Sobek (☎ 888-687-6235; www.mtsobek.com) offers a three-day tour ($1295 per person) that includes a flight from Juneau, two nights camping and kayaking to Pack Creek to watch bears. **Alaska Fly 'N' Fish** (☎ 790-2120; www.alaskabyair.com) also holds permits and offers a five-hour, fly-in tour ($600) or will transport you if you're lucky enough to snare a permit.

GLACIER BAY NATIONAL PARK & PRESERVE

Eleven tidewater glaciers that spill out of the mountains and fill the sea with icebergs of all shapes, sizes and shades of blue have made Glacier Bay National Park and Preserve an icy wilderness renowned worldwide.

When Captain George Vancouver sailed through the ice-choked waters of Icy Strait in 1794, Glacier Bay was little more than a dent in a mountain of ice. In 1879 John Muir made his legendary discovery of Glacier Bay and found that the end of the bay had retreated 20 miles from Icy Strait. Today, the glacier that bears his name is more than 60 miles from Icy Strait, and its rapid retreat has revealed plants and animals that continue to fascinate modern-day naturalists.

Apart from its high concentration of tidewater glaciers, Glacier Bay is the habitat for a variety of marine life, including whales. The humpbacks are by far the most impressive and acrobatic, as they heave their massive bodies in spectacular leaps (called 'breaching') from the water. Adult humpbacks often grow to 50ft and weigh up to 40 tons. Other marine life seen at Glacier Bay includes harbor seals, porpoises, killer whales and sea otters, and other wildlife includes brown and black bears, wolves, moose, mountain goats and more than 200 bird species.

Glacier Bay is also where the cruise-ship industry and environmentalists have squared off. After the number of whales seen in the park dropped dramatically in 1978, the NPS reduced ship visits to 79 during the three-month season. But the cruise-ship industry lobbied the US Congress and in 1996 Alaska's Republican senators pushed through a 30% increase in vessels allowed in the bay – almost 200 cruise ships a season – based on a NPS environmental assessment. Environmentalists sued the park service, calling the assessment flawed, and eventually a compromise of two large cruise ships per day was hammered out.

But the whales aren't the only area of concern here. Glacier Bay's ice, like glaciers all over Alaska, is rapidly melting. This is particularly true in Muir Inlet, or the East Arm as it's commonly called. Twenty years ago it was home to three active tidewater glaciers, but now there is only one, McBride. Only two glaciers in the park are advancing; Johns Hopkins and Lamplugh. The rest are receding and thinning.

Still, Glacier Bay is the crowning jewel in the itinerary of most cruise ships and the dreamy destination for anybody who has ever paddled a kayak. The park is an expensive sidetrip, even by Alaskan standards. Plan on spending at least $400 for a trip from Juneau, but remember that the cost per day drops quickly after you've arrived. Of the more than 300,000 annual visitors, more than 90% arrive aboard a ship and never leave the boat. The rest are a mixture of tour-group members who head straight for the lodge and backpackers who wander toward the free campground.

Orientation & Information

'Civilization' around the park is focused in two areas. **Bartlett Cove** is the park headquarters and the site of visitors centers, hiking trails and Glacier Bay Lodge. This is where the ferry from Juneau ties up, paddlers rent kayaks and visitors hop on the tour boat for a cruise to the glaciers 40 miles up the bay.

About 9 miles away is the small settlement of **Gustavus** (gus-*tay*-vus), an interesting backcountry community. The town's 400 citizens include a mix of professional people – doctors, lawyers, former government workers and artists – who decided to drop out of the rat race and live on their own in the middle of the woods. Electricity only arrived in the early 1980s and internet service for most homes is dial-up. Gustavus has no downtown. It's little more than an airstrip left over from WWII and a road to Bartlett Cove.

The best source of information is from the NPS in Bartlett Cove. Campers, kayakers and boaters can stop at the park's **Visitor Information Station** (☎ 697-2627; 🕓 6am-10:30pm) at the foot of the public dock for backcountry permits, logistical information and a 20-minute orientation video. The **Glacier Bay Visitor Center** (☎ 697-2661; www.nps.gov/glba; 🕓 noon-8:45pm) is on the 2nd floor of Glacier Bay Lodge and has exhibits, a bookshop and an information deck. The **Gustavus Visitors Association** (☎ 697-2454; www.gustavusak.com) has loads of information on its website.

Sights & Activities

GLACIERS

The glaciers are 40 miles up the bay from Bartlett Cove. If you're not on a cruise ship or don't want to spend a week or two kayaking, the only way to see them is onboard a tour boat. The *Fairweather Express* operated by **Glacier Bay Lodge & Tours** (☎ 264-4600, 888-229-8687; www.visitglacierbay.com) is a high-speed catamaran that departs at 7:30am for an eight-hour tour into the West Arm and returns by 4pm, in time for the Alaska Airlines flight back to Juneau. The tour costs $182/85 per adult/child and includes lunch and narration by an onboard park naturalist.

For a more personal and leisurely experience there's the *Kahsteen,* operated by **Gustavus Marine Charters** (☎ 697-2233; www.gustavusmarinecharters.com). The 42ft yacht heads up with four to six passengers, a pair of kayaks, a skiff for shore excursions and Mike Nigro, a former backcountry ranger, as your captain. A two-/three-day trip to the glaciers, which includes gourmet meals, is $900/1350.

HIKING

Glacier Bay has few trails, and in the backcountry, foot travel is done along riverbanks, on ridges or across ice remnants of glaciers. The only developed trails are in Bartlett Cove.

The mile-long **Forest Trail** is a nature walk that begins and ends near the Bartlett Cove dock and winds through the pond-studded spruce and hemlock forest near the campground. Rangers lead walks on this trail daily in summer; inquire at the Glacier Bay Visitor Center.

Bartlett River Trail, a 1.5-mile trail, begins just up the road to Gustavus, where there is a posted trailhead, and ends at the Bartlett River estuary. On the way, it meanders along a tidal lagoon and passes through a few wet spots. Plan on two to four hours for the 3-mile round-trip.

The **Point Gustavus Beach Walk**, along the shoreline south of Bartlett Cove to Point Gustavus and Gustavus, provides the only overnight trek from the park headquarters. The total distance is 12 miles, and the walk to Point Gustavus, an excellent spot to camp, is 6 miles. Plan on hiking the stretch from Point Gustavus to Gustavus at low tide, which will allow you to ford the Salmon River, as opposed to swimming across it. Point Gustavus is an excellent place to sight orcas in Icy Strait.

PADDLING

Glacier Bay offers an excellent opportunity for people who have some experience on the water but not necessarily as kayakers, because the *Fairweather Express* drops off and picks up paddlers at several spots deep in the bay. By using the tour boat, you can skip the long and open paddle up the bay and enjoy only the well-protected arms and inlets where the glaciers are located. The most dramatic glaciers are in the West Arm, but the upper areas of the arm are often closed to campers and kayakers due to seal-pupping and brown-bear activity. For more detailed information on kayaking the bay, see p109.

Paddlers who want to avoid the tour-boat fares but still long for a kayak adventure should try the Beardslee Islands. While there are no glaciers to view, the islands is a day's paddle from Bartlett Cove and offers calm water, protected channels and pleasant beach camping. Wildlife includes black bears, seals and bald eagles, and the tidal pools burst with activity at low tide.

our pick **Glacier Bay Sea Kayaks** (☎ 697-2257; www.glacierbayseakayaks.com; per day single/double $45/50) rents kayaks as well as leads guided trips to the Beardslee Islands (half/full day $90/140).

Alaska Mountain Guides (☎ 800-766-3396; www.alaskamountainguides.com) has a field office in Gustavus to run several guided kayak trips into Glacier Bay. A seven-day paddle to the

West Arm, which includes tour transportation as well as all equipment and food, is $1950 per person, and an eight-day paddle up the East Arm that begins from Bartlett Cove is $2200.

Spirit Walker Expeditions (☎ 697-2266, 800-529-2537; www.seakayakalaska.com) has paddling trips to Point Adolphus where humpback whales congregate during the summer. Trips begin with a short boat ride with the kayaks across Icy Strait to Point Adolphus and run $435 for a day paddle and $1040 for a three-day paddle.

WHALE WATCHING

Cross Sound Express (☎ 697-2726, 888-698-2726; www.taz.gustavus.com) operates the 47ft MV *Taz*, which carries up to 23 passengers and departs the Gustavus dock daily during the summer at 8:30am and 1:30pm for a 3½-hour whale-watching tour. The cost is $110/55 per adult/child.

our pick **Woodwind Sailing Adventures** (☎ 697-2282; http://sailglacierbay.homestead.com) is a spacious 40ft sailing catamaran that offers a whale-watching trip to Icy Point ($160) and an excellent kayaking with-the-whales day trip to Pt Adolphus ($260).

Tours

You can see Glacier Bay in a hurry, though you have to ask yourself if that is a wise use of your travel funds. For a quickie flightseeing tour, Haines is the closest community and thus offers cheaper flights (see p183).

Glacier Bay Lodge & Tours (☎ 264-4600, 888-229-8687; www.visitglacierbay.com) Has a Weekend Kayak Package that includes round-trip ferry transport Auke Bay-Bartlett Cove, a night at Glacier Bay Lodge and kayak drop-off and pick-up for a night up the bay. The cost is $400 per person but does not include kayak rental.

Gray Line (☎ 586-3773, 800-544-2206; www.grayline ofalaska.com) Offers a three-day package from Juneau that includes round-trip flight to Gustavus, two nights at Glacier Bay Lodge and a boat tour of the West Arm ($875 per person).

Sleeping & Eating

Most of the accommodations are in Gustavus, which has a 4% bed tax.

BARTLETT COVE

NPS campground (0.25 miles south of Glacier Bay Lodge) This is set in a lush forest just off the shoreline, and camping is free. There's no need for reservations, there always seems to be space for another tent. It provides a bear cache, eating shelter and pleasant surroundings. Coin-operated showers are available in the park, but there aren't any places selling groceries or camping supplies.

Glacier Bay Lodge (☎ 697-2225, 888-229-8687; www.visitglacierbay.com; 199 Bartlett Cove Rd; r $160-185; ⊠) This is the only hotel and restaurant in Bartlett Cove. The lodge has 55 rooms, a crackling fire in a huge stone fireplace and a dining room that usually hums in the evening with an interesting mixture of park employees, backpackers and locals from Gustavus. Nightly slide presentations, ranger talks and movies held upstairs cover the park's natural history.

GUSTAVUS

Aimee's Guest House (☎ 697-2330; www.glacierbay alaska.net; Gustavus Rd; ste $100-150; ⊠) A former smokehouse on the Salmon River (the reason for the colorful fish mural outside) has been converted into a pair of bright, airy and comfortable vacation rentals featuring one or two bedrooms, full kitchens and everything you would need to spend a few days in Gustavus. The upper level deck, with its hammock, wicker furniture and bed outside, is classic Alaska.

Good River B&B (☎ 697-2241; www.glacier-bay.us; Good River Rd; s/d/cabins $105/110/120; ⊠) A three-story log home with three guestrooms, shared bath, free bicycles and homebaked treats for breakfast. Tucked away in the woods is the Honeymoon Cabin, with no running water and only an outhouse but cute and very cozy. It's the ideal Alaskan honeymoon.

Bear's Nest Café & Cabin Rentals (☎ 697-2440; 2 White Dr; cabins $110-139, r $135 ⏲ noon-8pm; ⊠) This small restaurant off of Wilson Rd features organic produce and local seafood with daily vegetarian offerings but is best known for its live music on Friday and Saturday. It's so packed with locals and park workers some evenings, people are sitting on the floor.

Annie Mae Lodge (☎ 697-2346, 800-478-2346; www.anniemae.com; Grandpa's Farm Rd; s $115-145, d $160-190; ⊠ 💻) A large rambling lodge with wraparound porches and 11 rooms, most with private bath. On the 2nd level all seven rooms have a private entrance off the porch, while a large dining room and common area is where a continental breakfast is served in the morning and dinners are available in the evening for an additional charge.

Blue Heron B&B (☎ 697-2337; www.blueheronbnb.net; State Dock Rd; r/cottages $145/185) Surrounded by 10 acres of fields and gardens is this B&B with two rooms and two cottages with kitchenettes. All are modern, bright and clean, and each has a TV/VCR and private bath. In the morning everybody meets in the sun room for a full breakfast ranging from organic rolled oats with blueberries to omelets. Everything you need to enjoy Gustavus – rubber boots, rain pants, bikes, transportation anywhere – is provided.

Homeshore Café (☎ 697-2822; Gustavus Rd at Wilson Rd; pizza $10-14; 11:30am-2pm & 5-8pm Tue-Sat) Salads, sandwiches and surprisingly good pizza with beer to wash it down.

Beartrack Mercantile (State Dock Rd; 9am-7pm Mon-Sat, 10:30am-6pm Sun) On the way to the dock, Gustavus' only market has limited groceries and makes good deli sandwiches.

Getting There & Around

Alaska Airlines (☎ 800-252-7522; www.alaaskaair.com) offers the only jet service but its rarely the cheapest airfare, with a round-trip ticket running $225 for the daily 25-minute trip from Juneau to Gustavus. **Wings of Alaska** (☎ Juneau 789-0790; Gustavus 697-2201; www.wingsofalaska.com) offers scheduled flights for $93/186 one way/round-trip, as does **Air Excursions** (☎ 697-2375; www.airexcursions.com), which is usually a few dollars cheaper. Both maintain a counter at Juneau Airport.

Glacier Bay Lodge & Tours operates the **Glacier Bay Ferry** (☎ 264-4600, 888-229-8687; www.visitglacierbay.com; one way adult/child $75/38) on Friday and Sunday with the boat departing Bartlett Cove at 4pm and Auke Bay at 7:30pm for the return trip.

If you arrive at the Gustavus airport, you're still 9 miles from Bartlett Cove. The Glacier Bay Lodge bus meets all Alaska Airline flights and charges $12 for the ride. So does **TLC Taxi** (☎ 697-2239).

HAINES

pop 2257

Heading north of Juneau on the state ferry takes you up Lynn Canal, North America's longest and deepest fjord. Along the way, Eldred Rock Lighthouse stands as a picturesque sentinel, waterfalls pour down off the Chilkoot Range to the east, and the Davidson and Rainbow Glaciers draw 'oohs' and 'aahs' as they snake down out of the jagged Chilkat Mountains to the west. You end up in Haines, a scenic departure point for Southeast Alaska and a crucial link to the Alaska Hwy. Every summer thousands of travelers, particularly RVers, pass through this slice in the mountains on their way to Canada's Yukon Territory and Interior Alaska.

Haines is 75 miles north of Juneau on a wooded peninsula between the Chilkat and Chilkoot Inlets. Originally a stronghold of the wealthy Chilkat Tlingit Indians, it was a gun-toting entrepreneur named Jack Dalton who put Haines on the map. In 1897 Dalton turned an old Indian trade route into a toll road for miners seeking an easier way to reach the Klondike. The Dalton Trail quickly became such a heavily used pack route to mining districts north of Whitehorse that the army arrived in 1903 and established Fort William H Seward, Alaska's first permanent post. For the next 20 years it was Alaska's only army post and then was used as a rest camp during WWII.

WWII led to the construction of the Haines Hwy, the 159-mile link between the Southeast and the Alcan. Built in 1942 as a possible evacuation route in case of a Japanese invasion, the route followed the Dalton Trail and was so rugged it would be 20 years before US and Canadian crews even attempted to keep it open in winter. By the 1980s, the 'Haines Cut-off Rd' had become the paved Haines Hwy and now more than 50,000 travelers in cars and RVs follow it annually.

After logging fell on hard times in the 1970s, Haines swung its economy towards tourism and it's still surviving. And it should. Haines has spectacular scenery, quick access to the rivers and mountains where people like to play and is comparatively dry (only 53in of rain annually). All of this prompted *Outside* magazine to plaster a photo of Haines on its cover in 2004 and call it one of the country's '20 best places to live and play.'

You'll immediately notice that this town is different from what you've experienced elsewhere in the Southeast. Maybe it's the relative lack of cruise-ship traffic, which gives Haines a tangible sense of peace and tranquility. As a port Haines receives less than 40,000 cruise-ship passengers in a season – it is lucky to reach the number that Juneau sees in a good weekend. Or maybe it's the fact that there isn't a restaurant, gift shop or tour operator along Main St that is owned by a corporate conglomerate. Haines' businesses are uniquely Haines, and most likely the person behind the counter is one who owns the store. The town isn't especially well developed for tourism: you won't find a salmon bake here and, no doubt for many travelers, that's part of its charm.

Information

BOOKSTORES

Babbling Book (☎ 766-3356; 223 Main St; ⏲ 11am-5pm Mon-Sat) Stocks a great selection of Alaska books, cards and calendars, while its walls serve as the notice board for Haines' cultural scene.

MEDICAL SERVICES

Haines Medical Clinic (☎ 766-6300; 131 1st Ave S) For whatever ails you.

LAUNDRY

Haines Quick Laundry (☎ 766-2330; Mile 0 Haines Hwy; ⏲ 7am-9pm) At the foot of Mud Bay Rd, behind the Quick Mart. Showers are 25¢ a minute – wash fast.

LIBRARY & INTERNET ACCESS

Haines Borough Public Library (☎ 766-2545; 111 S 3rd Ave; ⏲ 10am-9pm Mon-Tue, from noon Wed & Thu, 10am-6:30pm Fri, 12:30-4:30pm Sat & Sun) The cultural jewel of the community. This impressive facility has a book exchange, six computers for internet access (donation), a beautiful reading area with rocking chairs and a two-story window overlooking the mountains. Curl up and read before the majestic view.

MONEY

First National Bank of Anchorage (☎ 766-6100; 123 Main St) For all your presidential-portrait needs.

POST

Post office (near cnr Haines Hwy & Mud Bay Rd) Close to Fort Seward.

TOURIST INFORMATION

Alaska Division of Parks (☎ 766-2292; Ste 25, 219 Main St; ⏲ 8am-5pm Mon-Fri) For information on state parks and hiking.

Haines Convention & Visitors Bureau (☎ 766-2234, 800-458-3579; www.haines.ak.us; 122 2nd Ave; ⏲ 8am-5pm Mon-Fri, 9am-5pm Sat & Sun) Has rest rooms, free coffee and racks of free information for tourists. There is also a lot of information on Canada's Yukon for those heading up the Alcan.

Sights

The **Sheldon Museum** (☎ 766-2366; 11 Main St; adult/child $3/free; ⏲ 10am-5pm Mon-Fri, 1-4pm Sat & Sun) houses a collection of indigenous artifacts upstairs with an interesting display on Chilkat blankets. Downstairs is devoted to Haines' pioneer and gold-rush days and includes the sawn-off shotgun that Jack Dalton used to convince travelers to pay his toll.

The **Hammer Museum** (☎ 766-2374; 108 Main St; adult/child $3/free; ⏲ 10am-5pm Mon-Fri) is a monument to Dave Pahl's obsession with hammers. He's got a zillion of them (well, actually 1500 on display) and several hundred more in storage. In Pahl's museum you learn world history through the development of the hammer, from one less than one-quarter of an ounce to another weighing more than 40lb. You can't miss the museum, there is a 20ft-high hammer outside.

An impressive wildlife diorama is featured at the **American Bald Eagle Foundation** (☎ 766-3094; www.baldeagles.org; 113 Haines Hwy; adult/child $3/1; ⏲ 10am-5pm Mon-Fri, 1-5pm Sat & Sun) – it displays more than 180 specimens and almost two dozen eagles. A highlight is the live video feed from a remote camera trained on an active eagle's nest.

Fort Seward, reached by heading uphill (east) at the Front St–Haines Hwy junction, was Alaska's first permanent army post. Built in 1903 and decommissioned after WWII, the fort is now a national historical site with a handful of restaurants, lodges and art galleries utilizing the original buildings. A walking-tour map of the fort is available at the visitors center, or you can just read the historical panels that have been erected there. Within the parade ground is **Totem Village**. Although not part of the original fort, it includes two tribal houses and totem poles and is the home of the **Chilkat Dancers Storytelling Theater Show** (☎ 766-2540; adult/child $12/6; ⏲ 4:30pm Mon-Fri), an hour-long performance of Alaska Native dramatization.

More indigenous culture can be seen in Fort Seward in the former post hospital at the **Alaska Indian Arts Center** (☎ 766-2160; www.alaskaindianarts.com; 24 Fort Seward Dr; ⏲ 9am-5pm Mon-Fri), where indigenous artists carve totems or weave Chilkat blankets.

Dalton City, the movie set for *White Fang* that was relocated to the Southeast Alaska State Fairgrounds, is a beacon for beer lovers. Among the false-front buildings and wooden sidewalks is the **Haines Brewing Company** (☎ 766-3823; Fair Dr; ⏲ 1-7pm Mon-Sat), the maker of such beer as Dalton Trail Ale, Elder Rock Red and Black Fang. Tours are short – hey this is a

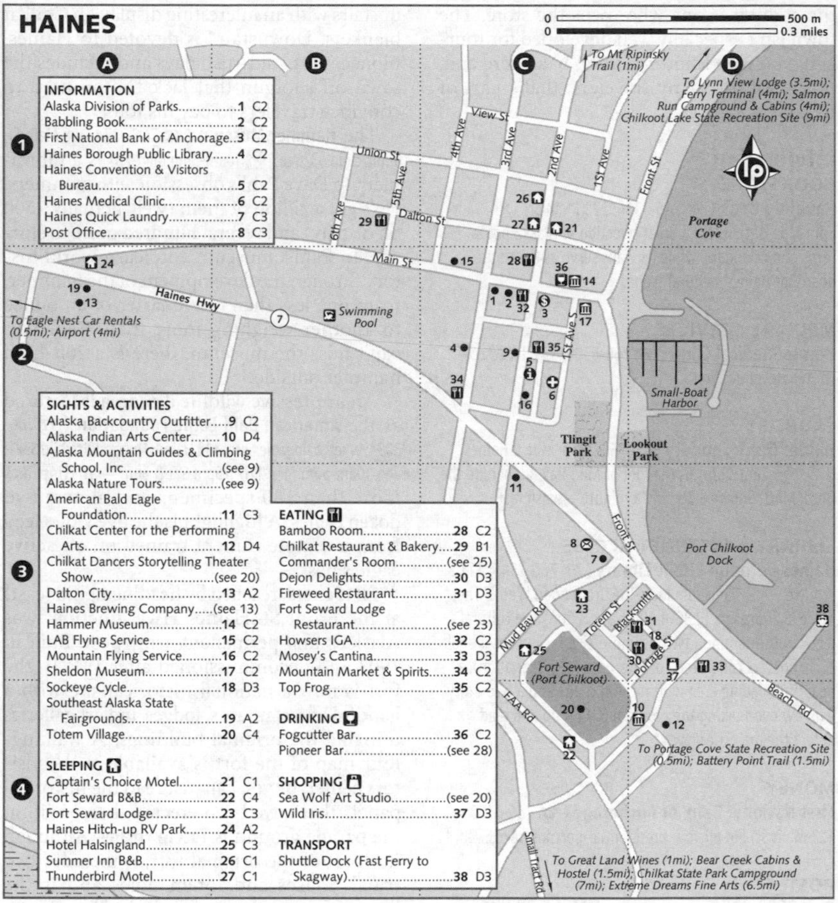

one-room brewery – but pints are available or you can have a half-gallon growler ($9) filled for later. Most of the restaurants in town also serve the local brew and, frankly, why drink anything else? As local author Heather Lende says on a sign in the brewery, 'Life is too short to waste my alcohol consumption on cheap beer.'

Activities

CYCLING

You can discover some great road trips or what little single-track mountain biking there is in Haines by visiting **Sockeye Cycle** (☎ 766-2869, 877-292-4154; www.cyclealaska.com; 24 Portage St; ⌚ 9am-1pm & 2-5pm Mon-Sat), which rents a variety of top-of-the-line bicycles ($14/25/35 per two/four/eight hours). The most popular road trip is the scenic 22-mile ride out to Chilkoot Lake. The shop also offers bike tours, with its best being an eight-hour ride on dirt roads through the alpine of the newly created Tatshenshini/Alsek Provincial Park. The cost is $175 per person and includes mountain bikes, guide, transport and lunch.

HIKING

Two major trail systems are within walking distance of Haines. South of town are the Chilkat Peninsula trails, including the climb to Mt Riley. North of Haines is the path to the summit of Mt Ripinsky. Stop at the visitors bureau and pick up the brochure *Haines is for Hikers*, which describes the trails in more detail. For outdoor gear or a guided hike, stop by **Alaska Backcountry Outfitter** (☎ 766-2876; 111 2nd Ave; ⏰ 10am-5pm).

Mt Ripinsky Trail

The trip to the 3563ft summit of Mt Ripinsky (also known as the South Summit) offers a sweeping view of the land from Juneau to Skagway. The route, which includes Peak 3920 and a descent from 7 Mile Saddle to Haines Hwy, is either a strenuous 10-hour journey for experienced hikers or an overnight trip.

To reach the trailhead, follow 2nd Ave north to Lutak Rd (the road to the ferry terminal) and past the fire station. Leave Lutak Rd when it curves right and head up the hill on Young St. Turn right along an old, buried pipeline and follow it for a mile to the start of the trail, just as the pipeline heads downhill to the tank farm.

The North Summit has a benchmark and a high wooden surveyor's platform. You can camp in the alpine area between the two peaks and then continue the next day by descending the North Summit and hiking west along the ridge to Peak 3920. From here you can descend to 7 Mile Saddle and then to the Haines Hwy, putting you 7 miles northwest of town. This is a 10 mile loop and a challenging overnight hike; the trail is steep in places and easily lost. The views, however, are spectacular.

Battery Point Trail

This 2-mile trail is a flat walk along the shore to Kelgaya Point, where you can cut across to a pebble beach and follow it to Battery Point for excellent views of Lynn Canal. The trail begins a mile beyond Portage Cove Recreation Site at the end of Beach Rd. Plan on a two-hour round-trip.

Mt Riley Trails

This climb to a 1760ft summit is considerably easier than the one to Mt Ripinsky, but it still provides good views in all directions, including vistas of Rainbow and Davidson Glaciers. One trail up the mountain begins at a junction 2.2 miles up the Battery Point Trail out of Portage Cove Recreation Site. From here, you hike 3 miles over Half Dome and up Mt Riley.

Another route, closer to town, begins at the end of FAA Rd, which runs behind Officers' Row in Fort Seward. From the road's end, follow the water-supply access route for 2 miles to a short spur that branches off to the right and connects with the trail from Mud Bay Rd. The hike is 3.9 miles one way and eliminates having to find a ride out to the third trailhead to Mt Riley, 3 miles out on Mud Bay Rd. The trailhead off Mud Bay Rd is posted and this 2.8-mile route is the steepest but easiest to follow and most direct to the summit. Plan on a five- to six-hour round-trip.

Seduction Point Trail

This trail begins at Chilkat State Park Campground and is a 6.5-mile, one-way hike to the point separating Chilkoot and Chilkat Inlets. The trail swings between forest and beaches, and provides excellent views of Davidson Glacier.

If you have the equipment, this trail can be turned into an excellent overnight hike by setting up camp at the cove east of Seduction Point. Carry in water and check the tides before departing, as the final stretch along the beach after David's Cove should be walked at low- or midtide. The entire round-trip takes nine to 10 hours.

RIVER RUNNING

Haines is also a departure point for numerous raft trips. **Chilkat Guides** (☎ 766-2491, 888-292-7789; www.raftalaska.com; adult/child $89/62) offers a four-hour float daily down the Chilkat River through the bald-eagle preserve, with opportunities to view eagles and possibly brown bears; there is little or no white water.

On a much grander scale of adventure is the exciting nine- to 10-day raft trip down the Tatshenshini-Alsek River system, from Yukon Territory to the coast of Glacier Bay. This river trip is unmatched for its scenic mix of rugged mountain ranges and dozens of glaciers. Chilkat Guides and **Alaska Discovery/Mt Sobek** (☎ 888-687-6235; www.mtsobek.com) both run the trip, which costs between $3000 and $3300 per person.

Both outfits will pick you up from your accommodations.

Tours

Other than Gustavus, Haines is the closest community to Glacier Bay National Park, making flightseeing tours much more reasonable than Skagway or Juneau.

our pick **Alaska Nature Tours** (☎ 766-2876; www.alaskanaturetours.net; 109 2nd Ave) Offers excellent environmentally focused tours with knowledgeable guides for activities that range from birding and bear watching to

THE HELI-SKIING CAPITAL OF ALASKA

On the wall in the small lounge at Fort Seward Lodge is a huge ski, while on the TV over the bar are usually videos of daredevil downhillers flying, and sometimes tumbling, down incredibly steep mountains. Welcome to Haines, the heli-skiing capital of Alaska. Or it should be.

That title usually goes to Valdez or even Girdwood, home of Alyeska Ski Resort. But the bartender and patrons at Fort Seward Lodge will tell you their community is much better suited for the extreme sport. Haines is tucked further inland than the other two, with a mountain range shielding it from the warm, moist weather of the Pacific. That gives Haines colder, drier and thus more powdery snow, what heli-skiers thrive on. Nor is Haines lacking for vertical drop. It's surrounded by steep, high mountains that often allow skiers to descend more than 4000ft on a single run.

There are now two heli-skiing companies based in Haines: **Southeast Alaska Backcountry Adventures** (Seaba; ☎ 877-617-3418; www.skiseaba.com) and **Alaska Heliskiing** (☎ 767-5745; www.alaskaheliskiing.com). The best skiing is February through April and both companies offer packages then. Alaska Heliskiing's seven-day package includes six runs a day, accommodations and equipment rental ($3950). The accommodations are at the Fort Seward Lodge, naturally.

easy hikes to Battery Point. Its Twilight Wildlife Watch is a 2½-hour tour (adult/child $65/50) that departs at 6:15pm and heads up the Chilkoot River, stopping along the way to look for eagles, mountain goats and brown bears who emerge at dusk to feed on spawning salmon.

Haines-Skagway Fast Ferry (☎ 766-2100, 888-766-2103; www.hainesskagwayfastferry.com; Beach Rd) If you don't have time for Skagway, the Fast Ferry has a Rail & Sail Tour (adult/child $155/78) that includes round-trip transport to the Klondike city and the Summit Excursion on the White Pass & Yukon Railroad.

Mountain Flying Service (☎ 766-3007, 800-954-8747; www.flyglacierbay.com; 132 2nd Ave) Offers an hour-long tour of the Glacier Bay's East Arm for $159 per person and an 80-minute tour of the more dramatic West Arm for $199. On a clear day, it's money well spent.

Festivals & Events

Haines stages the **Great Alaska Craft Beer & Home Brew Festival** in the third week of May when most of the state's microbrews compete for the honors of being named top suds.

Like every other Alaskan town, Haines has a festive celebration for **Fourth of July**.

Haines' biggest festival, the **Southeast Alaska State Fair**, is at the end of July with five days of live music, parades, logging and livestock shows and the famous pig races that draw participants from all Southeast communities.

Sleeping

Haines tacks 9.5% tax onto the price of lodging.

BUDGET

Salmon Run Campground & Cabins (☎ 766-3240; www.salmonrunadventures.com; 6.5 Mile Lutak Rd; sites $15, cabins $65-75) Situated near the campground are two small cabins that come with heating and bunks but no indoor plumbing or kitchen facilities.

Bear Creek Cabins & Hostel (☎ 766-2259; www.bearcreekcabinsalaska.com; 1.5 Small Tract Rd; dm/d cabins $20/48) A 20-minute walk outside town – follow Mud Bay Rd near Fort Seward and when it veers right, continue straight onto Small Tract Rd for 1½ miles – this hostel has no lockout or curfew. A number of cabins surround a well-kept, grassy common area. Two of the cabins are used as the hostel dorms. A rest-room/shower building also has laundry facilities and there is a common kitchen area.

Camping

Portage Cove State Recreation Site (Beach Rd; sites $5) Half a mile southeast of Fort Seward or a 2-mile walk from downtown, this scenic campground overlooks the water and has nine sites that are for backpackers and cyclists only. Follow Front St south; it becomes Beach Rd near Fort Seward.

Chilkoot Lake State Recreation Site (Lutak Rd; sites $10) Five miles north of the ferry terminal. The campground has 32 sites and picnic shelters. The fishing for Dolly Varden is good on Chilkoot Lake, a turquoise blue body of water surrounded by mountains.

Chilkat State Park Campground (Mud Bay Rd; sites $10) Found 7 miles southeast of Haines toward the end of Chilkat Peninsula; this campground has good views of Davidson and Rainbow Glaciers spilling out of the mountains into the Lynn canal. There are 15 woodsy campsites and a beach to explore at low tide.

Haines Hitch-up RV Park (☎ 766-2882; www.hitchuprv.com; 851 Main St; RV sites $29-40; 💻) Wedged between two major roads, this open but beautifully tended park is for RVs only, no tents. It has 92 sites with hookups, some with cable TV, as well as laundry and shower facilities.

MIDRANGE

Hotel Halsingland (☎ 766-2000, 800-542-6363; www.hotelhalsingland.com; 13 Fort Seward Dr; r $69-119; ⊠) The grand dame of Haines hotels is the former bachelor officers' quarters and overlooks the Fort Seward's parade ground. A National Historic Landmark, the hotel is a little worn around the edges but some rooms still have fireplaces and classic claw-foot bathtubs. Four economy rooms with shared bath are $69 a night.

Summer Inn B&B (☎ 766-2970; www.summerinnbnb.com; 117 2nd Ave; s/d $75/90; ⊠) Built in 1912 in the heart of town by Tim Vogel, a member of Soapy Smith's gang in Skagway, this B&B has five bedrooms with shared bath along with an enclosed porch where you can watch life in Haines come and go. Rates include a full breakfast, while Soapy Smith fanatics can still take a soak in Vogel's original bathtub.

our pick **Fort Seward Lodge** (☎ 766-2009, 877-617-3418; www.ftsewardlodge.com; 39 Mud Bay Rd; s/d $95/110, without bath $75; ⊠) Under new ownership, the former Post Exchange of Fort Seward is now one of Haines' best places to spend a night. The updated rooms are simple but clean and feature TVs and coffeemakers. Along with affordable accommodations the lodge offers free shuttle service from the ferry terminal.

Lynn View Lodge (☎ 766-3713; www.lynnviewlodge.com; 6.5 Mile Lutak Rd; r $95-125, cabins $85; ⊠) A mile from the ferry terminal, this B&B has a great view of Lynn Canal and a long, covered porch to relax on and soak up the scenery. Accommodations range from two rooms with shared bath and two suites with private bath to two small cabins. Cars are also available for $69 a day.

Fort Seward B&B (☎ 766-2856, 800-615-6676; r $95-145; ⊠) Haines' first B&B occupies the restored former home of the army's surgeon; a mammoth three-story Victorian house with seven guestrooms, five with shared bath, two with private bath. A wide porch overlooks the parade grounds and Lynn Canal beyond. If the view alone isn't worth the room rate then innkeeper Norm Smith's wonderful sourdough pancakes are. Guests also enjoy free use of bikes and kites.

Thunderbird Motel (☎ 766-2131, 800-327-2556; www.thunderbird-motel.com; 216 Dalton St; s/d $100/110) Somehow a TV, microwave and refrigerator are squeezed into tiny rooms. What, no dishwasher!

Captain's Choice Motel (☎ 766-3111, 800-478-2345; www.capchoice.com; 108 2nd Ave N; s/d $113/123; ⊠ 💻) Haines' nicest lodging has the best view of the Chilkat Mountains and Lynn Canal and a big flower-ringed sundeck to enjoy it. Rooms are spacious enough to include a microwave, small refrigerator, coffeemaker and TV. A light breakfast if offered in the morning and courtesy transportation to the ferries is available.

Eating

If you're craving fresh seafood, check the bulletin boards around town as there are often notices from commercial fishers selling fish or Dungeness crab off their boats in the harbor for a fraction of what you pay in a restaurant. For fresh veggies, there's the **Haines Farmer's Market** held every other Saturday during the summer at the Southeast Alaska State Fairground from 10am to 1pm.

RESTAURANTS

our pick **Mosey's Cantina** (☎ 766-2320; 31 Tower Rd; lunch $8-15, dinner $14-18; 🕑 11:30am-2:30pm & 5:30-8:30pm Mon-Sat; ⊠) A cute and cozy Mexican restaurant with only seven tables inside and a few more outside. The tamales, halibut-stuffed burritos and enchiladas are very goods. Best of all it serves the local beer.

Fireweed Restaurant (☎ 766-3838; 37 Blacksmith St; sandwiches $12-15, pastas $11-15, pizza $11-21; 🕑 4:30-9pm Tue, 11:30am-3pm and 4:30-9pm Wed-Sat; ⊠) This clean, bright and laid-back bistro looks like it belongs in California not Haines. On its menu are words like 'organic', 'veggie' and 'grilled' as oppose to 'deep fried' and 'captain's special'. Vegetarians actually have a choice here (try the veggie baked ziti); everybody else can indulge in sandwiches, burgers and the town's best pizza, all washed down with beer served in icy mugs.

Fort Seward Lodge Restaurant (☎ 766-2009; 39 Mud Bay Rd; dinner $17-28; 🕑 5-9:30pm Wed-Mon; ⊠) In what used to be Fort Seward's Post Exchange is now one of Haines' best restaurants. The two-level restaurant has a small bar that's a refreshing break from the smoky, main-street watering holes and a menu that includes the standards of halibut, crab and salmon but also some diversions from the sea like the excellent bourbon baby back ribs. Dangling from the ceiling in the middle is the original red velvet swing that ladies swung to the delight of the soldiers.

Commander's Room (☎ 766-2000; 13 Fort Seward Dr; dinner $22-28; 5:30-9pm; ☒) Located in Hotel Halsingland is Haines' most upscale restaurant. Begin the evening with a drink in its cozy Officer's Club Lounge and then venture into Commander's Room where you'll find white tablecloths, a fine wine list and a chef who has a herb garden out back. Try the Moroccan spiced braised lamb shank or seared salmon that's topped with a rhubarb-ginger chutney.

CAFÉS

Chilkat Restaurant & Bakery (☎ 766-3653; Dalton St at 5th Ave; breakfast $5-8, sandwiches $6-8; 7am-3pm Mon-Sat; ☒) A local favorite that has been baking goodies and serving breakfast for 25 years. For a nice break from eggs and potatoes, try the homemade granola with blueberries…but first you have to get past that display case filled with the daily offering of muffins and pastries. Heck with the granola, have a slice of rhubarb-strawberry pie for breakfast.

Bamboo Room (☎ 766-2800; 2nd Ave; breakfast $7-12, lunch $8-14, dinner $13-25; 6am-10pm) CBS newsman Charles Kuralt once ate breakfast at this café and loved it. No doubt he had the blueberry pancakes with whipped cream. Attached to the Pioneer Bar (how convenient), the Bamboo likes to claim it has the best halibut fish and chips in the Southeast but it's hard to pass up a plate of steamed Dungeness crabs served whole.

QUICK EATS & GROCERIES

Top Frog (2nd Ave; breakfast $2.50-5; 6am-8pm) Next to the visitor center is this bright-green latte shed with outdoor tables and the most affordable breakfast sandwiches and burgers in town.

Mountain Market & Spirits (☎ 766-3340; 3rd Ave at Haines Hwy; breakfast $3-8, sandwiches $6-8; 7am-7pm Mon-Fri, 8am-7pm Sat, 8am-6pm Sun) The center of Haines hipness and healthy eating. The market stocks health foods and local specialties like Birch Boy syrup, made by tapping birch instead of maple trees. Its deli is loaded with vegetarian options, espresso drinks and indoor seating. Adjoining the store is Mountain Spirits, the best wine shop in town.

Dejon Delights (☎ 766-2505; 37 Portage St; 10am-6pm) A shop in Fort Seward that turns out some of the best smoked fish in the Southeast, such as salmon that is first marinated in stout beer or lemon peppered halibut. If camping at Portage Bay, pick up a fillet of just-caught salmon and grill it on your campfire to the view of mountainous Lynn Canal. That is Alaska.

Howsers IGA (211 Main St) The main supermarket in Haines.

Drinking

Fogcutter Bar (☎ 766-2555; Main St) Haines is a hard-drinking town and this is where a lot of them belly up to the bar and spout off.

Pioneer Bar (☎ 766-3443; 2nd Ave) This longtime favorite went smokeless in 2007 and it's business *increased!* Next thing you know the gang at the Pioneer will be munching carrot sticks with their beer.

Shopping

Despite a lack of cruise-ship traffic, or maybe because of it, Haines supports an impressive number of artists and has enough galleries to fill an afternoon.

Sea Wolf Art Studio (☎ 766-2558; www.tresham.com; Ft Seward Parade Ground; 10am-4:30pm) Housed in a log cabin is Tresham Gregg's gallery. Gregg is one of Haines' best-known indigenous artists and he combines spiritism, animism and shamanism of Northwest Coast Indians to create woodcarvings, totems, masks, bronze sculpture and talismanic silver jewelry.

our pick **Extreme Dreams Fine Arts** (☎ 766-2097; www.extremedreams.com; Mile 6.5 Mud Bay Rd; 10am-6pm) Near the entrance of Chilkat State Park is this wonderful gallery packed with the work of 20 local artists, from watercolors and weaving to handblown glass, cast silver and beautiful beads. The gallery also has a climbing wall because it's the studio of artist John Svenson, a renowned mountain climber who has scaled the highest peak on every continent except Mt Everest.

Wild Iris (☎ 766-2300; 22 Tower Rd; 9am-7pm) The mayor of Haines is the man behind the counter of this gallery, just one of a growing number on the edge of Fort Seward. Outside the home is a beautiful Alaskan garden, inside a fine selection of original jewelry, silkscreen prints, cards, pastels and other local art.

Getting There & Around

AIR

There is no jet service to Haines, but **Wings of Alaska** (☎ 766-2030; www.wingsofalaska.com) has daily flights to Juneau ($110) and Skagway ($60).

A VALLEY FULL OF EAGLES

The **Alaska Chilkat Bald Eagle Preserve** was created in 1982 when the state reserved 48,000 acres along the Chilkat, Klehini and Tsirku Rivers to protect the largest known gathering of bald eagles in the world. Each year from October to February, more than 4000 eagles congregate here to feed on spawning salmon. They come because an upwelling of warm water prevents the river from freezing, thus encouraging the late salmon run. It's a remarkable sight – hundreds of birds sitting in the bare trees lining the river, often six or more birds to a branch.

The best time to see this wildlife phenomenon is during the **Alaska Bald Eagle Festival**. The five-day event attracts hundreds of visitors from around the country to Haines in the second week of November for speakers and presentations at the Sheldon Museum and the American Bald Eagle Foundation Center. But the basis of the festival is trooping out to the Chilkat River on 'expedition buses' with noted naturalists on board and encountering eagles that you cannot see anywhere else in the country at anytime of the year.

If the rain, snow and sleet of November is not on your Alaskan agenda then you can still see many eagles during the summer from the Haines Hwy, where there are turnouts for motorists to park and look for birds. The best view is between Mile 18 and Mile 22, where you'll find spotting scopes, interpretive displays and viewing platforms along the river. The numbers are not as mind-boggling as in early winter but 400 eagles live here year-round and more than 80 nests line the rivers.

Among guides who conduct preserve tours is **Alaska Nature Tours** (☎ 766-2876; www.alaskanaturetours.net; 109 2nd Ave), which conducts three-hour tours (adult/child $65/50) daily in summer. The tours cover much of the scenery around the Haines area but often concentrate on the river flats and river mouths, where you usually see up to 40 eagles, many of them nesting.

There is also **River Adventures** (☎ 766-2050, 800-478-9827; www.jetboatalaska.com), which uses jet boats for its Eagle Preserve River Adventure. The tour includes bus transportation 24 miles up the river to the jet boats and then a 1½-hour boat ride to look for eagles and other wildlife. The price is $100 per person.

BOAT

State ferries, including the high-speed catamaran MV *Fairweather*, depart daily from the **ferry terminal** (☎ 766-2111; 2012 Lutak Rd) north of town heading for Skagway ($31, one hour) and Juneau ($37, 5½ hours). **Haines Shuttle** (☎ 766-3138) meets all the ferries and charges $20 for the 4-mile trip into town. It also departs Haines 30 minutes before each ferry arrival, after stopping at various hotels around town.

Haines-Skagway Fast Ferry (☎ 766-2100, 888-766-2103; www.hainesskagwayfastferry.com; Beach Rd) uses a speedy catamaran to cruise down Taiya Inlet to Skagway in 35 minutes. The 80ft cat departs Haines from the Fast Ferry shuttle dock at 6am, 11am and 5pm and more often if cruise ships are packing Skagway. One-way fares are adult/child $31/16, round trip $62/32.

BUS

Amazingly no buses serve Haines. You'll need to either thumb it north or take the ferry to Skagway and get a bus north from there.

CAR

To visit Alaska Chilkat Bald Eagle Preserve on your own, you can rent a car at **Captain's Choice Motel** (☎ 766-3111, 800-478-2345), which has compacts for $69 a day with unlimited mileage. There is also **Eagle Nest Car Rentals** (☎ 766-2891, 800-354-6009; 1183 Haines Hwy), in the Eagle Nest Motel, which has cars for $49 a day with 100 miles included.

SKAGWAY

pop 846

Situated at the head of Lynn Canal is Skagway, one of the driest places in an otherwise soggy Southeast. While Petersburg averages more than 100in of rain a year and Ketchikan a drenching 154in, Skagway gets only 26in annually.

Much of Skagway is within Klondike Gold Rush National Historical Park, which comprises downtown Skagway, the Chilkoot Trail, the White Pass Trail corridor and a Seattle visitors center. Beginning in 1897, Skagway and the nearby ghost town of Dyea were the starting places for more than 40,000

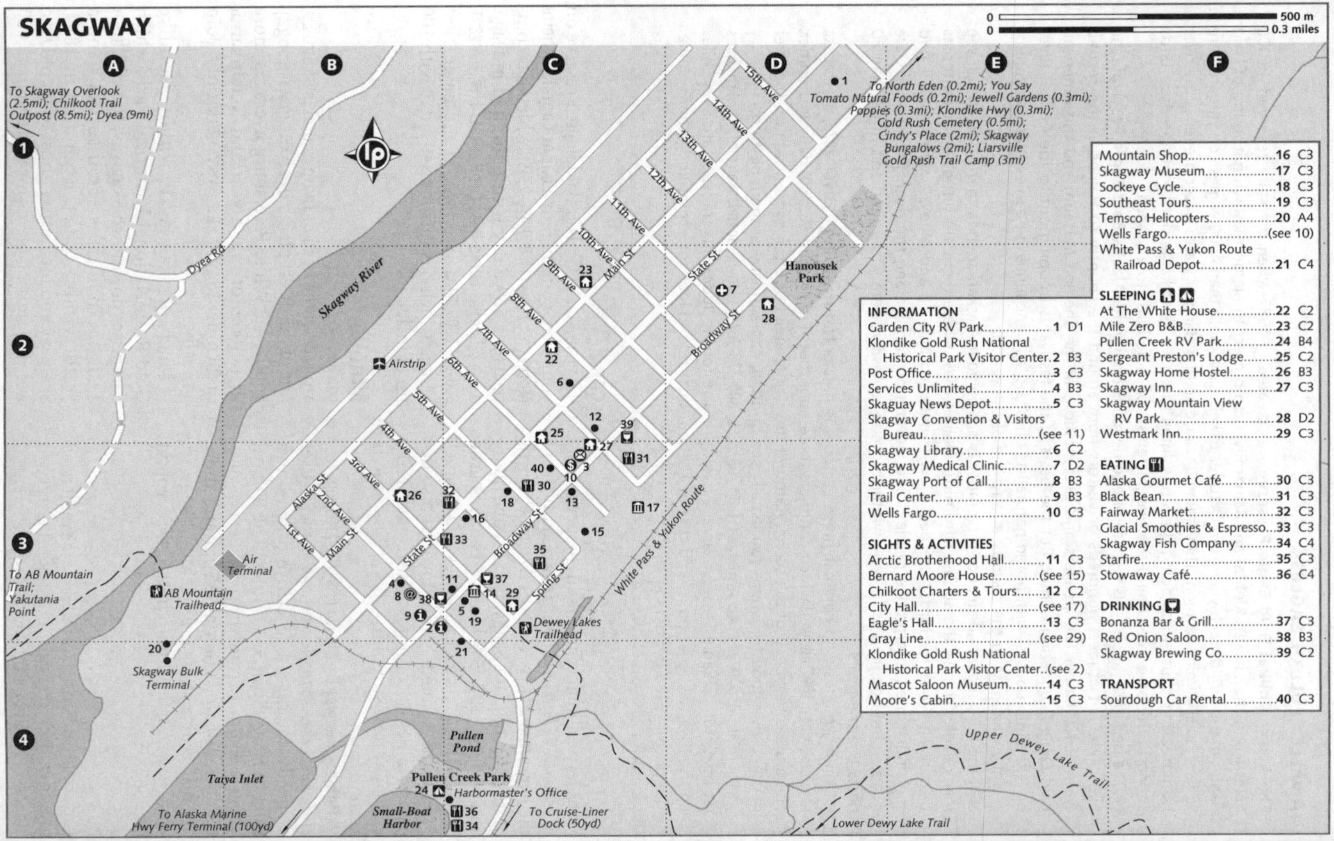
SKAGWAY
0 500 m
0 0.3 miles
A
B
C
D
E
F
1
2
3
4
To Skagway Overlook (2.5mi); Chilkoot Trail Outpost (8.5mi); Dyea (9mi)
To North Eden (0.2mi); You Say Tomato Natural Foods (0.2mi); Jewell Gardens (0.3mi); Poppies (0.3mi); Klondike Hwy (0.3mi); Gold Rush Cemetery (0.5mi); Cindy's Place (2mi); Skagway Bungalows (2mi); Liarsville Gold Rush Trail Camp (3mi)
Dyea Rd
Skagway River
Airstrip
Air Terminal
AB Mountain Trailhead
To AB Mountain Trail; Yakutania Point
Skagway Bulk Terminal
Hanousek Park
White Pass & Yukon Route
Dewey Lakes Trailhead
Upper Dewey Lake Trail
Lower Dewy Lake Trail
Pullen Pond
Pullen Creek Park
Harbormaster's Office
Small-Boat Harbor
Taiya Inlet
To Alaska Marine Hwy Ferry Terminal (100yd)
To Cruise-Liner Dock (50yd)
1st Ave
2nd Ave
3rd Ave
4th Ave
5th Ave
6th Ave
7th Ave
8th Ave
9th Ave
10th Ave
11th Ave
12th Ave
13th Ave
14th Ave
15th Ave
Alaska St
Main St
State St
Broadway St
Spring St
INFORMATION
Garden City RV Park....1 D1
Klondike Gold Rush National Historical Park Visitor Center....2 B3
Post Office....3 C3
Services Unlimited....4 B3
Skaguay News Depot....5 C3
Skagway Convention & Visitors Bureau....(see 11)
Skagway Library....6 C2
Skagway Medical Clinic....7 D2
Skagway Port of Call....8 B3
Trail Center....9 B3
Wells Fargo....10 C3
SIGHTS & ACTIVITIES
Arctic Brotherhood Hall....11 C3
Bernard Moore House....(see 15)
Chilkoot Charters & Tours....12 C2
City Hall....(see 17)
Eagle's Hall....13 C3
Gray Line....(see 29)
Klondike Gold Rush National Historical Park Visitor Center....(see 2)
Mascot Saloon Museum....14 C3
Moore's Cabin....15 C3
Mountain Shop....16 C3
Skagway Museum....17 C3
Sockeye Cycle....18 C3
Southeast Tours....19 C3
Temsco Helicopters....20 A4
Wells Fargo....(see 10)
White Pass & Yukon Route Railroad Depot....21 C4
SLEEPING
At The White House....22 C2
Mile Zero B&B....23 C2
Pullen Creek RV Park....24 B4
Sergeant Preston's Lodge....25 C2
Skagway Home Hostel....26 B3
Skagway Inn....27 C3
Skagway Mountain View RV Park....28 D2
Westmark Inn....29 C3
EATING
Alaska Gourmet Café....30 C3
Black Bean....31 C3
Fairway Market....32 C3
Glacial Smoothies & Espresso....33 C3
Skagway Fish Company....34 C4
Starfire....35 C3
Stowaway Café....36 C4
DRINKING
Bonanza Bar & Grill....37 C3
Red Onion Saloon....38 B3
Skagway Brewing Co....39 C2
TRANSPORT
Sourdough Car Rental....40 C3

gold-rush stampeders who headed to the Yukon primarily by way of the Chilkoot Trail. The actual stampede lasted only a few years but it produced one of the most colorful periods in Alaskan history, that of a lawless frontier town controlled by villainous 'Soapy' Smith who was finally removed from power in a gun fight by town hero Frank Reid.

At the height of the gold rush, Michael J Heney, an Irish contractor, convinced a group of English investors that he could build a railroad over the White Pass Trail to Whitehorse. The construction of the White Pass & Yukon Route was nothing short of a superhuman feat, and the railroad became the focal point of the town's economy after the gold rush and during the military buildup of WWII.

The line was shut down in 1982 but was revived in 1988, to the delight of cruise-ship tourists and backpackers walking the Chilkoot Trail. Although the train hauls no freight, its rebirth was important to Skagway as a tourist attraction. Today Skagway survives almost entirely on tourism, as bus tours and more than 400 cruise ships a year turn this village into a boomtown again every summer. Up to five ships a day stop here and, on the busiest days, more than 8000 tourists – 10 times the town's resident population – march off the ships and turn Broadway into something of an anthill. It's the modern-day version of the Klondike Gold Rush and the fact that one gift shop is called the 'Alaska Fleece Company' probably has Soapy Smith smiling in his grave.

The best day to be here is Saturday, when only one cruise ship is in port. But even if there are 2000 tourists in town (two ships' worth), Skagway can still be a pleasant place. To totally escape these crowds you have to skip Skagway and depart the Southeast through much quieter Haines.

Orientation & Information

Unlike most Southeast towns, Skagway is a delightful place to arrive by sea. Cruise-ship and state-ferry passengers alike step off their boats and are funneled to Broadway St, Skagway's main avenue and the heart of Klondike Gold Rush National Park Historic District. Suddenly you're in a bustling town, where many people are dressed as if they are trying to relive the gold-rush days and the rest are obviously tourists from the luxury liners.

BOOKSTORES

Skaguay News Depot (☎ 983-3354; 264 Broadway St; 🕑 8:30am-7pm Mon-Thu, 9am-6pm Fri & Sat, 9am-5pm Sun) A small bookstore with an excellent selection on the Klondike Gold Rush.

LAUNDRY

Garden City RV Park (☎ 983-2378; 15th Ave at State St; 🕑 7am-9pm) Has a Laundromat with showers at the campground.

Services Unlimited (☎ 983-2595; 170 State St; 🕑 7am-7pm) Has a Laundromat.

LIBRARY & INTERNET ACCESS

Skagway Library (☎ 983-2665; 8th Ave at State St; 🕑 noon-9pm Mon-Fri, 1-5pm Sat & Sun) Internet access is free but its three computers are so heavily used, people sign up for them the night before.

Skagway Port of Call (☎ 983-9503; 221 2nd Ave; per 15 min/hr $1.25/5; 🕑 9:30am-7:30pm Mon-Thu, 10am-5pm Fri & Sat, 10am-4pm Sun) Makes a living, and probably a decent one, selling cruise-ship workers high-speed internet access on 20 computers, phone cards and every brand of instant noodles made in Asia.

MEDICAL SERVICES

Skagway Medical Clinic (☎ 983-2255; 340 11th Ave; 🕑 9am-5pm) If gold fever strikes, head to this clinic.

MONEY

Wells Fargo (☎ 983-2264; Broadway St at 6th Ave) Occupies the original office of National Bank of Alaska.

POST

Post office (☎ 983-2330; 641 Broadway St) Next door to Wells Fargo bank.

TOURIST INFORMATION

Klondike Gold Rush National Historical Park Visitor Center (☎ 983-9223; www.nps.gov/klgo; Broadway St at 2nd Ave; 🕑 8am-6pm) For everything outdoors – local trails, public campgrounds, NPS programs – head to the NPS' center.

Skagway Convention & Visitors Bureau (☎ 983-2854, 888-762-1898; www.skagway.com; Broadway St at 2nd Ave; 🕑 8am-6pm Mon-Fri, 9am-6pm Sat & Sun) For information on lodging, tours or what's new, visit this bureau housed in the can't-miss Arctic Brotherhood Hall (think driftwood).

Trail Center (☎ 983-9234, 800-661-0486; Broadway at 2nd Ave; 🕑 8am-5pm) If you're stampeding to the Chilkoot Trail, first stop here in the restored Martin Itjen House at the foot of Broadway. The center is a clearinghouse for information on permits and transportation. The Chilkoot Trail hike is covered in detail on p91.

Sights

KLONDIKE GOLD RUSH NATIONAL HISTORICAL PARK VISITOR CENTER

The first stop of the day should be this **NPS center** (☎ 983-9223; www.nps.gov/klgo; Broadway St at 2nd Ave; 8am-6pm) in the original 1898 White Pass & Yukon Route depot. The center features displays – the most impressive being a replica of the ton of supplies every miner had to carry over the Chilkoot Pass – ranger programs and a small bookstore. The 30-minute film *Days of Adventure, Dreams of Gold,* an excellent introduction to the gold rush, is shown on the hour. Rangers also lead a 45-minute walking tour of the historic district five times a day. Everything is free.

SKAGWAY MUSEUM

Skagway Museum (☎ 983-2420; 7th Ave at Spring St; adult/child $2/1; 9am-5pm Mon-Fri, 10am-5pm Sat, 10am-4pm & Sun) is not only one of the finest in a town filled with museums but one of the finest in the Southeast. It occupies the entire 1st floor of the venerable century-old McCabe Building, a former college, and is devoted to various aspects of local history, including Alaska Native baskets, beadwork and carvings, and, of course, the Klondike Gold Rush. The display that draws the most looks is the small pistol Soapy Smith kept up his sleeve.

MASCOT SALOON MUSEUM

This is the only saloon in Alaska that doesn't serve beer, wine or a drop of whiskey – but it did during the gold rush, and plenty of it. Built in 1898, the **Mascot** (Broadway St at 3rd Ave; admission free; 8am-6pm) was one of 70 saloons during Skagway's heyday as 'the roughest place in the world.' The park service has since turned it into a museum that looks into the vices – gambling, drinking, prostitution – that followed the stampeders to the goldfields, encouraging visitors to belly up to the bar for a shot of sinful history.

MOORE'S CABIN & BERNARD MOORE HOUSE

A block southeast of the city museum is **Moore's Cabin** (5th Ave at Spring St; admission free; 10am-5pm), Skagway's oldest building. Captain William Moore and his son, Bernard, built the cabin in 1887, when they staked out their homestead as the founders of the town. Moore had to move his home to its present location when gold-rush stampeders overran his homestead. The NPS has since renovated the building and, in doing so, discovered that the famous Dead Horse Trail that was used by so many stampeders actually began in the large lawn next to the cabin. Adjacent to the cabin is the restored **Bernard Moore House**, which features exhibits and furnishings depicting family life during the gold rush.

WELLS FARGO BANK

This **bank** (Broadway St at 6th Ave; admission free; 9:30am-5pm Mon-Fri) dates back to 1916 when a group of East Coast businessmen founded the National Bank of Alaska and built the bank a year later. In 1981 the bank underwent an extensive historic renovation and today it is an interesting place to visit even if you're not short on cash yet. Two of the five brass teller gates are originals, there are spittoons in case you're chewing tobacco and on display everywhere are banking artifacts, from a classic 'Cannonball' safe to an old coin machine.

ARCTIC BROTHERHOOD HALL

The most outlandish building of the seven-block historical corridor along Broadway St, and possibly the most photographed building in Alaska, is this defunct **fraternal hall**, now home of the Skagway Convention & Visitors Bureau. The original driftwood, 8833 pieces of it, that covers the facade were attached in 1899 and extensively renovated, piece-by-piece, in 2005.

GOLD RUSH CEMETERY & REID FALLS

Visitors who become infatuated with Smith and Reid can walk out to **Gold Rush Cemetery**, a 1.5-mile stroll northeast on State St. Follow State until it curves into 23rd Ave and just before crossing the bridge over the Skagway River look for the 'Gold Rush Cemetery' signs. They'll lead you to Soapy's grave across the railroad tracks and the rest of the cemetery, the site of many stampeders' graves as well as the plots of Reid and Smith. From Reid's gravestone, it's a short hike uphill to lovely **Reid Falls**, which cascades 300ft down the mountainside.

JEWELL GARDENS

If the crowds are overwhelming you, cross the Skagway River to **Jewell Gardens** (☎ 983-2111; Klondike Hwy; adult/child $12/6; 9am-5pm). Located where Henry Clark started the first truck farm in Alaska, the garden is a quiet spot of flowerbeds, ponds, giant vegetables and a miniature train. There is also a pair of glassblowing studios where artists give fascinating demonstrations while making beautiful glassware. Call for times of the glassblowing and then hop on a SMART bus that will drop you off at the entrance.

DYEA

In 1898 Skagway's rival city, **Dyea** (*die*-yee), at the foot of the Chilkoot Trail, was the trailhead for the shortest route to Lake Bennett, where stampeders began their float to Dawson City. After the White Pass & Yukon Route was completed in 1900, Dyea quickly died. Today the town is little more than a few old crumbling cabins, the pilings of Dyea Wharf and Slide Cemetery, where 47 men and women were buried after perishing in an avalanche on the Chilkoot Trail in April 1898.

To explore the ghost town, you can pick up the *Dyea Townsite Self-Guided Walking Tour* brochure from the NPS center. The guide will lead your along a mile loop from the townsite parking area past what few ruins remain. Or join a ranger-led walk which meets at the parking area at 10am and 2pm daily.

Dyea is a 9-mile drive along winding Dyea Rd, whose numerous hairpin turns are not for timid RVers. But it's a very scenic drive especially at **Skagway Overlook**, a turnoff with a viewing platform 2½ miles from Skagway. The overlook offers an excellent view of Skagway, its waterfront and the peaks above the town. Just before crossing the bridge over the Taiya River, you pass the Dyea Campground (p193).

Activities

HIKING

The 33-mile Chilkoot Trail (p91) is Southeast Alaska's most popular hike, but other good trails surround Skagway. There is no USFS office in Skagway, but the NPS Visitor Center has a free brochure entitled *Skagway Trail Map*. You can also get backcountry information and any outdoor gear you need (including rentals) at the excellent **Mountain Shop** (☎ 983-2544; www.packerexpeditions.com; 355 4th Ave).

Dewey Lakes Trail System

This series of trails leads east of Skagway to a handful of alpine and subalpine lakes, waterfalls and historic sites. From Broadway, follow 3rd Ave southeast to the railroad tracks. On the east side of the tracks are the trailheads to Lower Dewey Lake (0.7 miles), Icy Lake (2.5 miles), Upper Reid Falls (3.5 miles) and Sturgill's Landing (4.5 miles).

Plan on taking an hour round-trip for the hike to Lower Dewey Lake, where there are picnic tables, camping spots and a trail circling the lake. At the lake's north end is an alpine trail that ascends steeply to Upper Dewey Lake, 3.5 miles from town, and Devil's Punchbowl, another 1.25 miles south of the upper lake.

The hike to Devil's Punchbowl is an all-day trip or an ideal overnight excursion, as the views are excellent and there is a free-use shelter on Upper Dewey Lake that is in rough condition but does not require reservations. There are also campsites at Sturgill's Landing.

Yakutania Point & AB Mountain Trails

The Skagway River footbridge, reached by following 1st Ave west around the airport runway, leads to two trails of opposite caliber. For an easy hike to escape the cruise-ship crowds turn left from the bridge and follow the mile-long trail to picnic areas and lovely views at Yakutania Point and Smugglers Cove.

Nearby on Dyea Rd is AB Mountain Trail, also known as the Skyline Trail. This route ascends 5.5 miles to the 5100ft summit of AB Mountain, named for the 'AB' that appears on its south side when the snow melts every spring. The first 30 minutes is along a well-defined trail through a hemlock forest to a view of Skagway. After that the trail is considerably more challenging, especially above the treeline, and requires a full day to reach the summit.

Denver Glacier Trail

This trail begins at Mile 6 of the White Pass & Yukon Route, where the USFS has renovated a White Pass & Yukon Route caboose into the **Denver Caboose** (☎ 877-444-6777; www.recreation.gov; cabin $35), a rental cabin of sorts. Hikers need to make arrangements with the White Pass & Yukon Route to be dropped off at the caboose. The trail heads up the east fork of Skagway River for 2 miles, then swings south and continues another 1.5 miles up the glacial outwash to Denver Glacier. Most of the trail is overgrown with brush, and the second half is particularly tough hiking.

Laughton Glacier Trail

At Mile 14 of the White Pass & Yukon Route is a 1.5-mile hike to the USFS **Laughton Glacier**

Cabin (☎ 877-444-6777; www.recreation.gov; cabins $35). The cabin overlooks the river from Warm Pass but is only a mile from Laughton Glacier, an impressive hanging glacier between the 3000ft walls of the Sawtooth Range. The alpine scenery and ridge walks in this area are worth the $60 ticket the White Pass & Yukon Route charges to drop off and pick up hikers. There are two excursion trains from Skagway, so this could be a possible day hike. But it's far better to carry a tent and spend a night in the area.

CYCLING

Sockeye Cycle (☎ 983-2851; 381 5th Ave; bikes per 2/4/8hr $14/25/35) rents hybrids and mountain bikes and offers several bike tours out of Skagway that include all equipment. Its 2½-hour Klondike Tour ($75) begins with van transportation to Klondike Pass (elevation 3295ft) on the Klondike Hwy. From there it's a 15-mile downhill ride back to town, with plenty of stops to view waterfalls and the White Pass & Yukon Route.

RAFTING

Skagway Float Tours (☎ 983-3688; www.skagwayfloat.com) offers a three-hour tour of Dyea that includes a 45-minute float down the placid Taiya River (adult/child $75/55). Its Hike & Float Tour ($85/65) is a four-hour outing that includes hiking 1.8 miles of the Chilkoot Trail then some floating back.

Tours

WHITE PASS & YUKON ROUTE RAILROAD

Without a doubt the most spectacular tour from Skagway is a ride aboard the historic railway of the **White Pass & Yukon Route** (☎ 983-2217, 800-343-7373; www.whitepassrailroad.com; depot on 2nd Ave). Two different narrated sightseeing tours are available; reservations are required for both.

The premier trip is the Yukon Adventure (8½ hours, 135 miles round-trip). At Skagway's railroad depot you board parlor cars for the trip to White Pass on the narrow-gauge line built during the 1898 Klondike Gold Rush. This segment is only a small portion of the 110-mile route to Whitehorse, but it contains the most spectacular scenery, including crossing Glacier Gorge and Dead Horse Gulch, viewing Bridal Veil Falls and then making the steep 2885ft climb to White Pass, only 20 miles from Skagway. You make a whistle stop at the historic 1903 Lake Bennett Railroad Depot for lunch and then board the train to follow the shoreline of stunning Lake Bennett to Carcross. At this small Yukon town, buses take you back to Skagway. The Yukon Adventure departs from Skagway Sunday through Friday and the fare is $229/115 per adult/child. Note that Lake Bennett is across the border in British Columbia, Canada, so passengers will need to carry passports or other proof of citizenship.

The Summit Excursion (three to 3½ hours, 40 miles round-trip) is a shorter tour to White Pass Summit and back. The tour is offered at 8:15am and 12:45pm daily mid-May to mid-September, and also at 4:30pm Monday through Thursday until early September. Tickets are $103/52 per adult/child and can be purchased at the depot.

SUMMIT & CITY TOUR

This is the standard tour in Skagway and includes Gold Rush Cemetery, White Pass Summit and Skagway Overlook, including a lively narration that might be historically accurate. The cost ranges from around $35 to $50 per person for a two- to three-hour outing. Companies offering such a tour and others:

Frontier Excursions (☎ 983-2512, 877-983-2512; www.frontierexcursions.com)

Gray Line (☎ 983-2241, 800-544-2206) At the Westmark Inn.

Skagway Tour Co (☎ 983-2168, 866-983-2168; www.skagwaytourco.com)

our pick **Southeast Tours** (☎ 983-2990; www.southeasttours.com; 2990 French Alley)

OTHER TOURS

A couple of cruise tourist-oriented attractions are located a short way out the Klondike Hwy.

Red Onion Saloon (☎ 983-2222; cnr Broadway St & 2nd Ave) Skagway's beloved saloon was once a house of sin, the reason for its tours of the upstairs bedrooms, now a brothel museum. Tours are '$5 for 15 minutes just like in 1898' and are offered throughout the day.

Alaska Fjordlines (☎ 800-320-0146; www.alaskafjordlines.com) Offers a day cruise to Juneau aboard the fast *Fjordland*, a 65ft catamaran. Continental breakfast is served on the way down, and on arrival in Juneau, passengers transfer to a bus for a tour of Mendenhall Glacier and the city. You're on your own there for lunch, then a light dinner is served onboard during the return trip. The tour is $155.

Klondike Gold Dredge Tours (☎ 983-3175, 877-983-3175; www.klondikegolddredge.com; Mile 1.7 Klondike Hwy; adult/child $45/35) Runs two-hour tours of a former working gold dredge that was in Dawson before being moved to Skagway where it has hit the mother lode. Tours include trying your hand at gold panning.

Liarsville Gold Rush Trail Camp (☎ 983-3000; Mile 3 Klondike Hwy; adult/child $39/27) Offers a miner's show, a turn at gold panning and Skagway's salmon bake. You book it and pick up the bus at Skagway Mountain View RV Park (below)

Festivals & Events

Skagway's **Fourth of July** celebrations feature a footrace, parade, street dance and the Ducky Derby, when a thousand plastic ducks are raced down a stream. But the town's most unusual celebration is **Soapy Smith's Wake**, on July 8. Locals and the cast of the *Days of '98 Show* celebrate with a hike out to the grave and a champagne toast, with champagne often sent up from California by Smith's great-grandson.

Sleeping

Skagway levies an 8% sales and bed tax on all lodging.

BUDGET & CAMPING

Dyea Campground (☎ 983-2921; sites $6) Located near the Chilkoot trailhead in Dyea, about 9 miles north of Skagway, this 22-site campground is operated by the NPS on a first-come, first-served basis. There are vault toilets and tables but no drinking water.

Pullen Creek RV Park (☎ 983-2768, 800-936-3731; www.pullencreekrv.com; sites/with car/with electricity & water $14/18/25) Located in a busy location near the ferry terminal and cruise ships. It has 46 sites with hookups and some tent sites.

Skagway Home Hostel (☎ 983-2131; www.skagwayhostel.com; 456 3rd Ave; dm $15-20; ⊠ 💻) A home in a quiet residential neighborhood a half-mile from the ferry terminal. It's a relaxed, if somewhat cluttered, hostel with kitchen and laundry facilities and pleasant gardens and a BBQ outside. Dinner is often available ($5). During July and August it's best to reserve one of the 22 bunks online.

Skagway Mountain View RV Park (☎ 983-3333, 888-778-7700; 12th Ave at Broadway St; campsites $15, RV sites $18-26) The town's best campground for tenters. It has 60 RV sites and a limited number of campsites. Amenities include firepits, laundry facilities, coin-operated showers, and dump stations for both humans and RVs. It's easy walking distance from downtown, but you won't feel trampled by tourists.

MIDRANGE

Cindy's Place (☎ 983-2674, 800-831-8095; www.alaska.net/~croland; Mile 1 Dyea Rd; cabins s $50-115, d $65-125) Two miles from town are two large log units with private baths and a small, cozy one without a shower. Each of them have refrigerator, microwave and coffeemaker, and are tucked away into the forested ridge. In the morning fresh-baked goods magically appear on your doorstep.

our pick **Sergeant Preston's Lodge** (☎ 983-2521, 866-983-2521; www.sgt-prestonslodgeskagway.com; 370 6th Ave; s $75-110, d $90-120; ⊠ 💻) Recently updated, this motel is the best bargain in Skagway. All 38 rooms are modern, clean and equipped with TVs, small refrigerators, microwaves and private bath. Other amenities include free internet access, courtesy transportation and very accommodating proprietors.

Skagway Bungalows (☎ 983-2986; www.aptalaska.net/~saldi; Mile 1 Dyea Rd; cabins $125, $99 for 3 nights or longer) Right next door to Cindy's Place are two more classic log cabins, situated among the trees on top of rock outcroppings as if Frank Lloyd Wright was here for the summer. Each cabin has a bath, a kitchenette and a small covered deck with a view of Reid Falls across the Skagway River.

Skagway Inn (☎ 983-2289, 888-752-4929; www.skagwayinn.com; Broadway St at 7th Ave; r $119-189; ⊠ 💻) In a restored 1897 Victorian that was originally one of the town's brothels – what building still standing in Skagway wasn't? – the inn is downtown and features 10 rooms with or without baths. All are small but filled with antique dressers, iron beds and chests, and a full breakfast is included.

Westmark Inn (☎ 983-6000, 800-544-0970; 3rd Ave at Spring St; r $129; 💻) Skagway's largest hotel is more of a sprawling complex with 250 rooms on both sides of 3rd Ave.

TOP END

At the White House (☎ 983-9000; www.atthewhitehouse.com; 475 8th Ave at Main St; r $120-160; ⊠ 💻) A very comfortable 10-room inn filled with antiques, remembrances of the Klondike and colorful comforters on every bed. Rooms are spacious and bright even on a rainy day and feature private bath, cable TV and phone. In the morning you wake up to a breakfast of

SOUTHEAST ALASKA

fresh-baked goods and fruit served in a sun-drenched dining room.

Mile Zero B&B (☎ 983-3045; www.mile-zero.com; 901 Main St; r $145; ⊠ 💻) This B&B is a like a motel with the comforts of home, as the six large rooms have their own bath and a private entrance on the wraparound porch. If you hook the fish of your dreams there's a BBQ area where you can grill it for dinner.

Chilkoot Trail Outpost (☎ 983-3799; www.chilkoottrailoutpost.com; Mile 8.5 Dyea Rd; cabins $145-175; ⊠ 💻) Hitting the 'Koot? Start the big adventure with a good night's sleep at this resort located a half-mile from the trailhead. The cabins are very comfortable and equipped with microwaves, refrigerators and coffeemakers. In the morning you can fuel up on a buffet breakfast at the main lodge. There are bicycles available, and the screened-in gazebo is strategically located at a waterfall.

Eating

Skagway has more than 20 restaurants operating during the summer and some would say better ones than what you find in that capital city just to the south. You decide.

RESTAURANTS

Skagway Fish Company (☎ 983-3474; Congress Way; salad & sandwiches $10-16, dinner $18-36; 🕑 11am-10pm) Located next to the Stowaway Café is this restaurant overlooking the harbor, with a horseshoe bar in the middle and crab traps on the ceiling. You can certainly feast on fish, like halibut stuffed with cream cheese, shrimp and veggies or coconut-curry prawns, but surprisingly, what many locals rave about are its baby back ribs.

our pick Starfire (☎ 983-3663; 4th Ave at Spring St; lunch $12-15, dinner $14-19; 🕑 11am-10pm Mon-Fri, 4-10pm Sat & Sun; ⊠) Skagway's restaurants are among the best in the Southeast, so why wouldn't its Thai be authentic and good? Order pad thai or spicy drunken noodle and enjoy it with a beer on the outdoor patio, so pleasant and secluded you would never know Skagway's largest hotel is across the street.

Poppies (☎ 983-2012; Klondike Hwy; dinner $15-23; 🕑 5:30-9:30pm Thu-Sun; ⊠) Located within Jewell Gardens (p190), this restaurant has the best salads in town because the greens are grown just outside and probably picked that afternoon. Mains range from boneless Colorado lamb leg to marinated chicken breast stuffed with sun-dried tomatoes, pine nuts and feta cheese. All served to a view of the gardens in full bloom with AB Mountain looming overhead.

Stowaway Café (☎ 983-3463; 205 Congress Way; dinner $18-27; 🕑 4-10pm; ⊠) Just past the harbormaster's office, this place is fun, funky and fantastic. Outside, is a beautiful mermaid and the restaurant's artfully cluttered front and back yards. The small café has a handful of tables, a view of the boat harbor, and excellent fish and Cajun-style steak dinners. Skagway's best dish is Stowaway's wasabi salmon.

CAFÉS

Glacial Smoothies & Espresso (☎ 983-3223; 336 3rd Ave; breakfast $4-7, sandwiches $7-9; 🕑 6am-6pm; ⊠) For healthy sandwiches, smoothies named Gold Rush (peaches, pineapple, banana) and Cabin Fever (peanut butter, chocolate, banana) or to sip a latte while surfing the internet ($3/5 per 20 minutes/hour).

Alaska Gourmet Café (☎ 983-2448; 344 5th Ave; breakfast $6-12, sandwiches $10-11, dinner $17-25; 🕑 6am-9pm; ⊠) A trendy café with a wide-ranging menu loaded with vegetarian dishes. For breakfast there's veggie eggs benedict or homemade granola with yogurt; for lunch how about curried vegetables baked in a puff pastry? A little pricy perhaps but Juneau would die for a café this creative.

QUICK EATS & GROCERIES

North Eden (☎ 983-2784; 21st Ave at State St; breakfast $4-6, lunch $5-6; 🕑 6:30am-2pm; ⊠) Not much dust in your gold poke? This is Skagway's most affordable espresso bar, with cheap breakfasts and lunch bowls heaped with spicy red beans, lentils or rice for $5 or less. You know it's healthy, the eatery is paired up with a natural food store.

Black Bean (☎ 983-3225; cnr 7th Ave & Broadway; breakfast $5-7, burritos $9; 🕑 7am-5pm) If you're headed for the Chilkoot, stop here. The giant breakfast or chicken burrito will motor you halfway down the trail. The homemade salsas are excellent.

You Say Tomato Natural Foods (☎ 983-2784; 21st Ave at State St) Located in a replica of the Whitehorse Railroad Depot is this natural foods store with organic produce.

Fairway Market (4th Ave at State St) This is Skagway's grocer, a place where a gallon of milk costs more than $6.

Drinking & Entertainment

Red Onion Saloon (☎ 983-2200; Broadway St at 2nd Ave) Skagway's beloved brothel at the turn of

DETOUR: YAKUTAT

Isolated on the strand that connects the Southeast to the rest of Alaska, Yakutat – of all places – is now something of a tourist destination, admittedly a minor one. The main reason is improved transportation. You still can't drive to the most northern Southeast town but in the late 1990s it became a port for the **Alaska Marine Highway** (☎ 800-642-0066; www.ferryalaska.com) when the MV *Kennicott* began its cross-Gulf trips. Now the ferry stops twice a month during the summer, headed to either Juneau or Whittier, while **Alaska Airlines** (☎ 800-252-7522; www.alaskaair.com) stops daily both northbound and southbound.

What does Yakutat have to offer curious tourists? Big waves, a big and very active glacier and a lot of USFS cabins next to rivers with big salmon.

The waves rolling in from the Gulf of Alaska have made Yakutat the surf capital of the Far North (p154). This town of 621 even has its own surf shop, the **Icy Waves Surf Shop** (☎ 907-784-3226; www.icywaves.com).

Just 30 miles north of Yakutat is **Hubbard Glacier**, the longest tidewater glacier in the world. The 76-mile-long glacier captured national attention by galloping across Russell Fjord in the mid-1980s, turning the long inlet into a lake. Eventually Hubbard receded to re-open the fjord, but did it again in 2002 and came within 170 yards in 2008, its latest gallop across the fjord. The 8-mile-wide glacier is easily Alaska's most active. The rip tides and currents that flow between Gilberts Point and the face of the glacier, a mere 1000ft away, are so strong that they cause Hubbard to calve almost continuously at peak tides. The entire area, part of the 545-sq-mile Russell Fjord Wilderness, is one of the most interesting places in Alaska and usually visited through flightseeing or boat tours. The **Yakutat Charter Boat Co** (☎ 888-317-4987; www.alaska-charter.com) runs a four-hour tour of the area for $140 per person. **Alaska Discovery/Mt Sobeck** (☎ 888-687-6235; www.mtsobek.com), which used to run week-long kayaking trips to the glacier, has plans to resume the guided outings in 2009.

There are also 12 **USFS cabins** (☎ 877-444-6777, 518-885-3639; www.recreation.gov; per night $25-35) in the area, five of them accessible via Forest Hwy 10, which extends east from Yakutat. Many are near rivers and lakes that are renowned, even by Alaskan standards, for sport fishing of salmon, steelhead trout and Dolly Varden.

Yakutat has a dozen lodges and B&Bs. The **Mooring Lodge** (☎ 888-551-2836; www.mooringlodge.com; 1-4 persons $350) has a cedar sauna, while the **Glacier Bear Lodge** (☎ 784-3202, 866-425-6343; www.glacierbearlodge.com; r $170; 💻) has a restaurant and bar. Do you want to sweat or swill? For more information contact the **Yakutat Chamber of Commerce** (www.yakutatalaska.com) or the USFS **Yakutat Ranger Station** (☎ 784-3359).

the century is now its most famous saloon. The 'RO' is done up as a gold-rush saloon, complete with mannequins leering down at you from the 2nd story to depict pioneer-era working girls. When bands are playing here, it'll be packed, noisy and rowdy.

Bonanza Bar & Grill (☎ 983-6214; Broadway St) With Guinness, Newcastle and many other excellent beers on tap and TVs on the wall, this is the closest thing Skagway has to a sports bar.

Skagway Brewing Co (☎ 983-2739; Broadway St at 7th Ave) Skagway's microbrew offers you Klondike Gold (a wheat ale) and Chilkoot Trail IPA among others. In the fine spirit of Juneau's Red Dog Saloon there's a Brewpub Gift Shop next door.

our pick **Days of '98 Show** (☎ 983-2545; Eagle's Hall; 598 Broadway at 6th Ave; adult/child $18/9) is Southeast Alaska's best and longest-running melodrama. The evening show begins with 'mock gambling,' moves onto Robert Service poetry and then climaxes with an entertaining show covering the town's gold-rush days and focusing on Soapy and his gang. Up to four shows are offered daily but call as it is heavily dependent on the cruise ships.

Getting There & Away

AIR

Regularly scheduled flights from Skagway to Juneau, Haines and Glacier Bay are available from **Wings of Alaska** (☎ 983-2442; www.wingsofalaska.com). Expect to pay $120 to $130 one way to Juneau, $65 to Haines and $205 to Gustavus.

BOAT

There is a daily run of the **Alaska Marine Highway** (☎ 983-2229, 800-642-0066; www.ferryalaska.com) from

Skagway to Haines ($31, one hour) and Juneau ($50, 6½ hours) and back again. In Skagway, the ferry departs from the terminal and dock at the southwest end of Broadway St.

Haines-Skagway Fast Ferry (☎ 888-766-2103; www.hainesskagwayfastferry.com) provides speedy transport on a catamaran to Haines. The boat departs from the Skagway small boat harbor at 8am, noon and 6pm Monday through Thursday in summer with additional trips if needed by the cruise ships. The round-trip/one-way fare is $61/31.

BUS

Yukon-Alaska Tourist Tours (☎ 866-626-7383, in Whitehorse 867-668-5944; www.yukonalaskatouristtours.com) offers a minibus service three times daily to Whitehouse, departing the train depot in Skagway at 8:45pm, 1:30pm and 3pm. One way is $55 for the first two runs and $40 for the 3pm departure.

Alaska Direct Bus Line (☎ 800-770-6652, in Whitehorse 867-668-4833; www.alaskadirectbusline.com) runs a bus on Sunday, Wednesday and Friday from Whitehorse for either Anchorage ($220) or Fairbanks ($190).

HITCHHIKING

Hitchhiking is possible along the Klondike Hwy just after a ferry pulls in. But backpackers thumbing north would do better buying a $27 ferry ticket to Haines and trying the Haines Hwy instead, as it has considerably more traffic.

TRAIN

It's possible to travel part-way to Whitehorse, Yukon Territory, on the trains of the **White Pass & Yukon Route** (☎ 983-2217, 800-343-7373; www.whitepassrailroad.com) then complete the trip with a bus connection at Fraser, British Columbia. The northbound train departs from the Skagway depot at 8am and 12:30pm daily in summer, and passengers arrive in Whitehorse by bus at 1pm and 4:30pm Yukon time. The one-way fare is adult/child $110/55; twice what the Yukon-Alaska Tourist Tours bus costs but the ride on the historic, narrow-gauge railroad is worth it.

Getting Around

BICYCLE

Several places in town rent bikes but Sockeye Cycle (p192) has the best bikes.

BUS

From May 1 to September 30, the city runs the SMART bus on two different routes. The regular route ($1.50) runs from the docks up to 8th Ave; the long route ($2.50) runs from 8th Ave to Jewell Gardens. Buses run whenever there are cruise ships in town, which in Skagway is almost always.

CAR

Sourdough Car Rental (☎ 983-2523; 6th Ave at Broadway St) has compacts for $69 a day with unlimited miles. In Skagway, there's a 14% tax on rental cars.

TAXI

Just about every taxi and tour company in Skagway will run you out to Dyea and the trailhead for the Chilkoot Trail, and the price hasn't gone up in years – $10 per person. **Frontier Excursions** (☎ 983-2512, 877-983-2512; www.frontierexcursions.com; Broadway St at 7th Ave) has trips daily.

Anchorage & Around

Once you realize that Anchorage isn't simply a big city on the edge of the wilderness but rather a big city *in* the wilderness, it starts to make sense. The town manages to mingle hiking trails and traffic jams, small art galleries and Big Oil, like no other city. At first, the minimalls and busy streets can be off-putting, but look behind its seemingly soulless sprawl and you'll find independent businesses thriving. Between streets, more than 100 miles of city trails meander in hidden greenbelts. Anchorage may be the only major city where you can watch urban moose munch on neighborhood shrubs and fisherman pull salmon from a downtown creek.

And Anchorage is not just the city – the municipality stretches across 1955 sq miles, all the way past the mountain-ringed ski community of Girdwood to the residential suburbs of Eagle River. Traveling from one end to the other is a day's road trip, but it's one where you might spot beluga whales, Dall sheep, or even a black bear or two.

Towering behind the municipality is the nation's third-largest state park, the half-million acre Chugach. The wilderness is never far, which is why Anchorage's young population (the average age is 32) is an active one. Stay for a few days, explore the bike trails, patronize the art galleries and dine in a few restaurants, and you'll see the reasons why half the state's population chooses to live here.

HIGHLIGHTS

- **Best way to space out** (p203) – following the speed-of-light planet walk along the coastal trail from downtown Anchorage to Kincaid Park
- **Most urbane place to hook a salmon** (p202) – backed by office buildings in downtown's Ship Creek
- **Best place to catch a wave** (p218) – watching the bore tide fill Turnagain Arm near Beluga Point in one swoop
- **Biggest leap of faith** (p220) – propelling yourself across Girdwood's Winner Creek Gorge's handtram
- **Best place to eat your veggies** (p228) – taking in 100lb kale and 70lb cabbage at the Alaska State Fair in Palmer

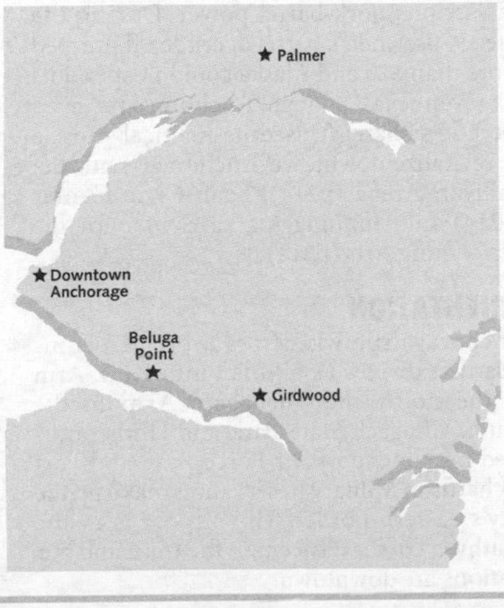

ANCHORAGE

pop 283,938

HISTORY

Though British explorer Captain James Cook sailed past the site in 1779 in search of the elusive Northwest Passage, and hopeful gold prospectors had been visiting Ship Creek since the 1880s, Anchorage wasn't founded until 1915. That was the year the Alaska Railroad called the area home and the 'Great Anchorage Lot Sale' was held. A tent city of 2000 people popped up in no time.

Anchorage soon became the epicenter for Alaska's fledgling rail, air and highway systems. The Depression-era colonizing of the Matanuska Valley, WWII, and the discovery of Cook Inlet oil in the 1950s all added to the explosive growth of these years. Anchorage's population, 8000 before WWII, then jumped to 43,000. After the 1964 Good Friday Earthquake, which dumped more than 100 homes into Knik Arm, the city was rebuilding itself when another opportunity arose: the discovery of a $10 billion oil reserve in Prudhoe Bay.

Although the Trans-Alaska Pipeline doesn't come within 300 miles of Anchorage, the city took its share of the wealth, growing a further 47% between 1970 and 1976. As headquarters of various petroleum and service companies, Anchorage still manages to gush with oil money.

This city of stage plays and snowy peaks has serious pork-barrel power. During the late 1970s, when a barrel of crude oil jumped more than $20 and Alaska couldn't spend its tax revenue fast enough, Anchorage received the lion's share. It used its political muscle to revitalize downtown Anchorage with the Sullivan Arena (p214), Egan Civic Center (p214) and stunning Alaska Center for the Performing Arts (p214).

ORIENTATION

Anchorage sprawls across a broad peninsula that divides Cook Inlet into Knik Arm to the north and Turnagain Arm to the south. Chugach State Park and lands occupied by Elmendorf Air Force Base and Fort Richardson Military Reservation make up the city's eastern border. The airport is in the southwest of the city center; the train and bus stations are downtown.

The pedestrian-friendly downtown is arranged in a regular grid: numbered avenues run east–west and lettered streets north–south. East of A St, street names continue alphabetically, beginning with Barrow. The grid begins to break down as you leave downtown, but numbered streets remain reliable.

As it heads northeast from downtown, 5th Ave becomes Glenn Hwy, the route to Fairbanks and Valdez; south from the city center, C St becomes New Seward Hwy, with service to the Kenai Peninsula. Heading due south, L St becomes Spenard Rd, which runs through Midtown and Spenard en route to the airport.

Maps

At the start of the tourist season, free city maps pop up in Anchorage like wildflowers in July. The Anchorage Convention & Visitors Bureau has one, but the best is the *Alaska Activities Map,* published by Alaska Channel. Any of them are more than adequate to navigate you through the downtown area. For something more detailed, where all the streets have a name, there's Rand McNally's *Anchorage* ($4). The best map for hikers interested in area trails is *Chugach State Park,* published by Imus Geographics ($8).

The best place to purchase maps is the Title Wave Books (below) or the Alaska Publics Land Information Center (Aplic, p201). The Aplic has a National Geographic Map Machine where you can create your own custom, waterproof topographic maps for $8 per sheet.

INFORMATION

Bookstores

Title Wave Books (Map p200; ☎ 278-9283; 1360 W Northern Lights Blvd; ⏲ 9am-9pm Mon-Thu, to 10pm Fri & Sat, 11am-7pm Sun) A huge, fabulous, (mostly) used bookstore, with lots of books on Alaska and everything else. It also runs the new Title Wave Books Downtown (Map pp204-5; ☎ 258-9283; 415 W 5th Ave; ⏲ 9am-10pm), where you can find a smaller but excellent collection of new and used books.

Laundry

Cole's Coin Op Laundromat (Map p200; ☎ 276-9114; 413 W Fireweed Ave; ⏲ 7am-11pm) Charges $1.75 per load.

K-Speed Wash (Map pp204-5; ☎ 279-0731; 600 E 6th Ave; ⏲ 7am-8pm Mon-Sat) To clean your clothes at the speed of 'K,' whatever that means, try this place.

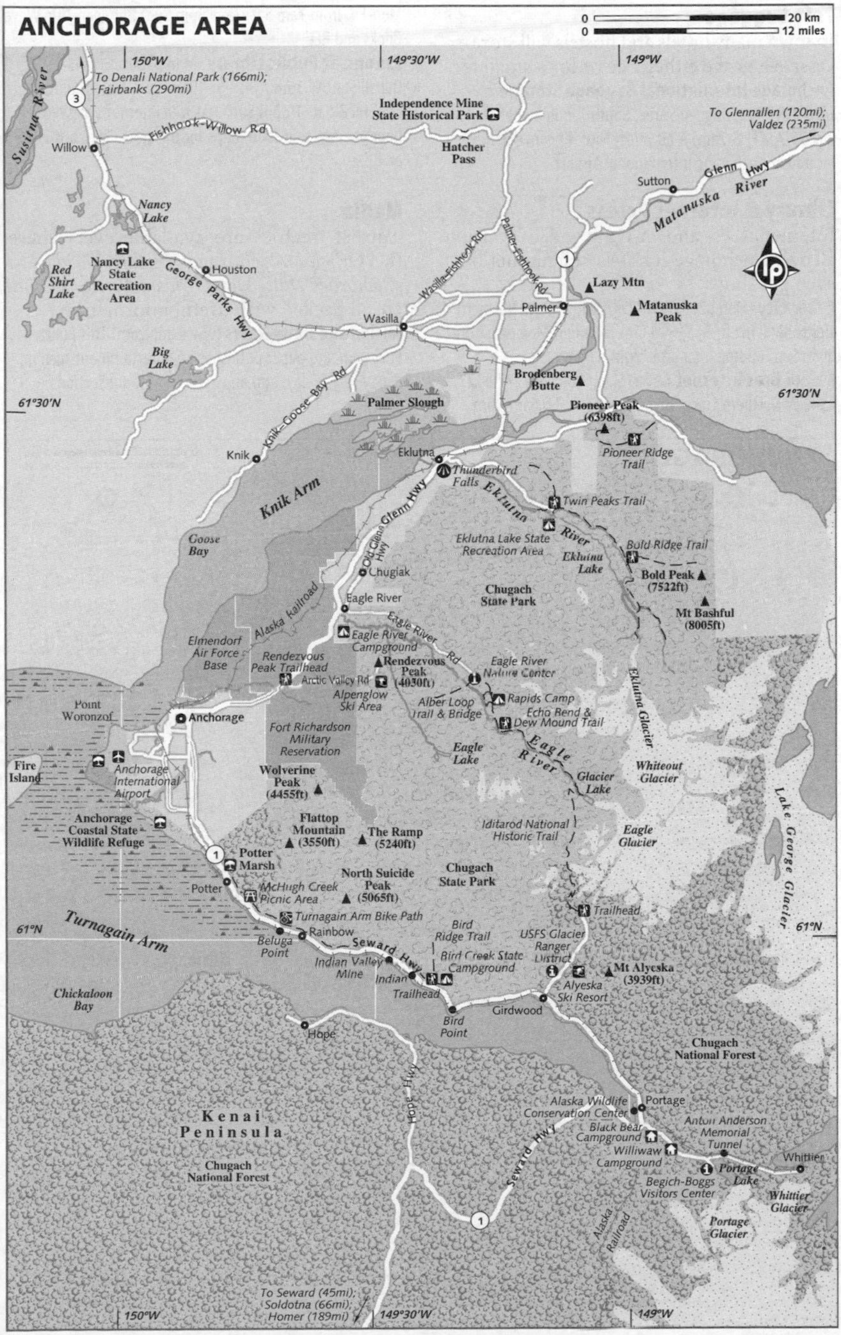
ANCHORAGE AREA
0 20 km
0 12 miles
150°W
149°30'W
149°W
61°30'N
61°N
To Denali National Park (166mi); Fairbanks (290mi)
Susitna River
Willow
Fishhook-Willow Rd
Independence Mine State Historical Park
Hatcher Pass
To Glennallen (120mi); Valdez (235mi)
Sutton
Glenn Hwy
Matanuska River
Nancy Lake
Red Shirt Lake
Nancy Lake State Recreation Area
Houston
George Parks Hwy
Wasilla-Fishhook Rd
Palmer-Fishhook Rd
Lazy Mtn
Matanuska Peak
Palmer
Wasilla
Big Lake
Knik-Goose Bay Rd
Brodenberg Butte
Palmer Slough
Pioneer Peak (6398ft)
Pioneer Ridge Trail
Knik
Eklutna
Thunderbird Falls
Knik Arm
Eklutna River
Twin Peaks Trail
Old Glenn Hwy
Glenn Hwy
Goose Bay
Eklutna Lake State Recreation Area
Eklutna Lake
Bold Ridge Trail
Bold Peak (7522ft)
Mt Bashful (8005ft)
Chugiak
Chugach State Park
Eagle River
Alaska Railroad
Eagle River Rd
Eagle River Campground
Elmendorf Air Force Base
Rendezvous Peak Trailhead
Rendezvous Peak (4030ft)
Arctic Valley Rd
Alpenglow Ski Area
Eagle River Nature Center
Rapids Camp
Albert Loop Trail & Bridge
Echo Bend & Dew Mound Trail
Eklutna Glacier
Point Woronzof
Anchorage
Fort Richardson Military Reservation
Eagle Lake
Eagle River
Glacier Lake
Whiteout Glacier
Fire Island
Anchorage International Airport
Wolverine Peak (4455ft)
Lake George Glacier
Anchorage Coastal State Wildlife Refuge
Flattop Mountain (3550ft)
The Ramp (5240ft)
Iditarod National Historic Trail
Eagle Glacier
Potter Marsh
Potter
North Suicide Peak (5065ft)
McHugh Creek Picnic Area
Chugach State Park
Trailhead
Turnagain Arm
Turnagain Arm Bike Path
Beluga Point
Rainbow
Bird Ridge Trail
USFS Glacier Ranger District
Seward Hwy
Indian Valley Mine
Indian
Bird Creek State Campground
Trailhead
Mt Alyeska (3939ft)
Alyeska Ski Resort
Chickaloon Bay
Girdwood
Bird Point
Hope
Chugach National Forest
Hope Hwy
Portage
Alaska Wildlife Conservation Center
Anton Anderson Memorial Tunnel
Kenai Peninsula
Black Bear Campground
Williwaw Campground
Whittier
Seward Hwy
Begich-Boggs Visitors Center
Portage Lake
Chugach National Forest
Whittier Glacier
Portage Glacier
Alaska Railroad
To Seward (45mi); Soldotna (66mi); Homer (189mi)

Left Luggage

In town many hotels and hostels will store excessive luggage either free or for a small fee.

Anchorage International Baggage Storage (☎ 248-0373; Baggage Area, South Terminal; per bag per day $5-7; ⌚ 5-2am) A bit pricey, but it's conveniently located at Anchorage International Airport.

Library & Internet Access

Internet access and wi-fi are widely available all over Anchorage at hotels, restaurants, bars, even gift shops.

Cyber City (Map p200; ☎ 277-7601; 1441 W Northern Lights Blvd; per hr $4; ⌚ 11am-midnight Mon-Sat, from noon Sun) Midtown for late-night gamers.

Kaladi Bros Internet Café (Map p200; ☎ 277-5127; 1340 W Northern Lights Blvd; per hr $7; ⌚ 6am-9pm Mon-Fri, from 7am Sat, 7am-8pm Sun) Between Title Wave Books and REI.

ZJ Loussac Public Library (Map p200; ☎ 343-2975; Denali St at W 36th Ave; ⌚ 10am-9pm Mon-Thu, to 6pm Fri & Sat, 1-5pm Sun) Has free internet access (one hour per day) and topo maps for the state. Take bus 2, 36 or 102.

Media

Tourist freebies are available everywhere: the *Official Anchorage Visitors Guide* and *Anchorage Daily News' Alaska Visitor's Guide* are all packed with useful information.

Anchorage Daily News (www.adn.com) This Pulitzer Prize-winning paper publishes an entertainment section, *Play*, every Friday, and an excellent outdoor section on Sunday.

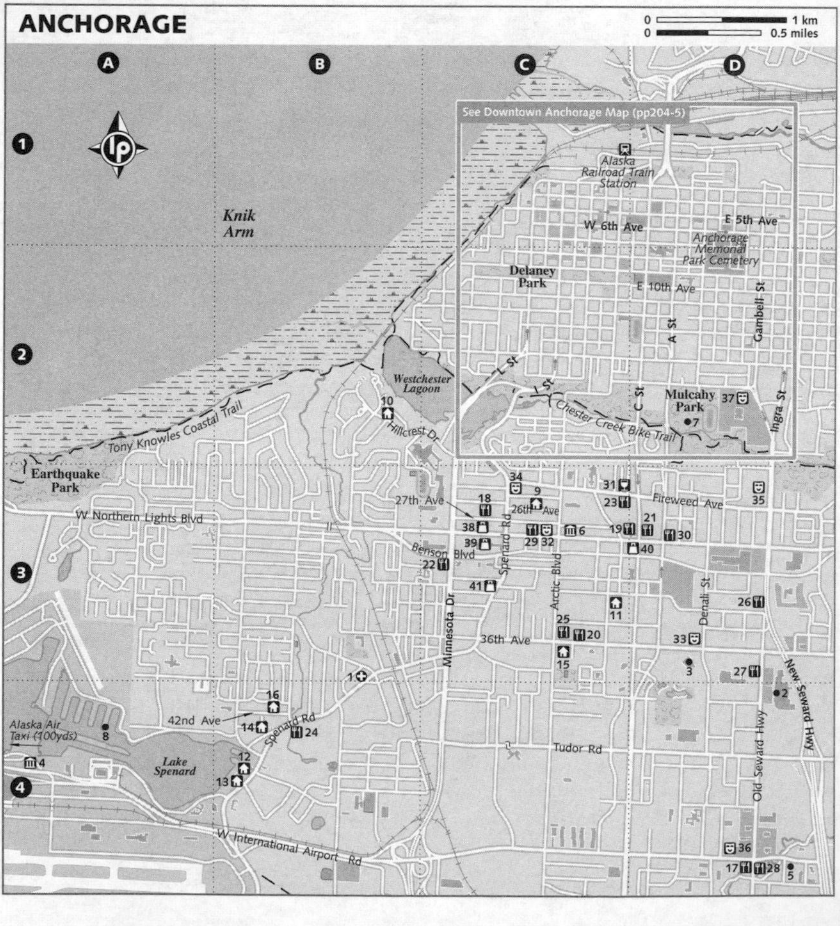

Anchorage Press (www.anchoragepress.com) A hip, free weekly with events listings and social commentary.

Medical Services

Alaska Regional Hospital (Map p219; ☎ 276-1131; 2801 DeBarr Rd; ⏲ 24-hr emergency service) Near Merrill Field. Take buses 13 and 15 there.

First Care Medical Center (Map p200; ☎ 248-1122; 3710 Woodland Dr, ste 1100; ⏲ 7am-midnight) Walk-in clinic just off Spenard Rd in Midtown. Bus 7 stops there.

Providence Alaska Medical Center (Map p219; ☎ 562-2211; 3200 Providence Dr) The largest in the state. Buses 1, 3, 13, 36, 45 and 102 go there.

Money

Key Bank (Map pp204-5; ☎ 257-5500, 800-539-2968; 601 W 5th Ave)

Wells Fargo (Map p200; ☎ 800-869-3557; 301 W Northern Lights Blvd) The main bank is in Midtown and one of 12 in the city.

Post

Post office (Map pp204-5; 344 W 4th Ave) This one's downtown in the Village at Ship Creek Center, but there are nearly a dozen more in town.

Tourist Information

Alaska Public Lands Information Center (APLIC; Map pp204-5; ☎ 644-3661; www.nps.gov/aplic; 605 W 4th Ave; ⏲ 9am-5pm) In the Federal Building (you'll need photo ID to get in). The center has handouts for hikers, bikers, kayakers, fossil hunters and just about everyone else, on almost every wilderness area of the state. Start here, go there. There are also excellent wildlife displays, free movies, fun dioramas, and at 11am and 2:30pm daily a guided Captain Cook walk to Resolution Park, covering the sea captain's travels in Alaska.

Log Cabin Visitor Center (Map pp204-5; ☎ 257-2342; www.anchorage.net; 524 W 4th Ave; ⏲ 7:30am-7pm Jun-Aug, 8am-6pm May & Sep) Has pamphlets, maps, bus schedules, city guides in several languages and a lawn growing on its roof.

Visitors center (☎ 266-2437; Anchorage International Airport) Several are located in the baggage-claim areas of both terminals; the south-terminal desk is staffed 9am to 4pm daily in summer.

Travel Agencies

New World Travel (Map p200; ☎ 276-7071; 3901 Old Seward Hwy) In the University Center a few blocks from the ZJ Loussac Public Library.

Dangers & Annoyances

When you're negotiating rush-hour traffic or squeezing into a crowded parking lot, it's easy to forget that Anchorage is truly on the edge of the wilderness. And spotting a bear or moose in this decidedly urban setting is naturally exciting – but don't let your guard down. While very, very few people are killed or even injured by bears, in 2008 a series of (nonfatal) grizzly attacks in Far North Bicentennial Park (see p206) prompted officials to close the Rover's Run trail. In general, steer clear of salmon

INFORMATION
Cole's Coin-Op Laundry.........(see 31)
Cyber City.........(see 38)
First Care Medical Center.........1 B3
Kaladi Bros Internet Café.........(see 39)
New World Travel.........2 D4
Title Wave Books.........(see 39)
Wells Fargo.........(see 6)
ZJ Loussac Public Library.........3 D3

SIGHTS & ACTIVITIES
Alaska Aviation Heritage Museum.........4 A4
Alaska Wild Berry Products.........5 D4
Heritage Library Museum.........6 C3
Mulcahy Ball Park.........7 D2
Regal Air.........8 A4
Rust's Flying Service.........(see 4)

SLEEPING
26th St Hostel.........9 C3
Anchorage Guest House.........10 B2
Arctic Adventure Hostel.........11 C3
Jason's International Hostel.........(see 11)
Lake Hood Inn.........12 B4
Millennium Hotel.........13 B4
Puffin Inn.........14 B4
Qupqugiaq Inn.........15 C3
Spenard Hostel.........16 B4

EATING
Arctic Roadrunner.........17 D4
Bear Tooth Grill.........18 C3
Bombay Deluxe.........19 C3
Café Europa.........20 C3
Central Market.........(see 19)
Charlie's Bakery.........21 D3
City Diner.........22 C3
Greek Corner.........23 C3
Gwennie's Old Alaska Restaurant.........24 B4
Jen's Restaurant.........25 C3
Middle Way Café.........(see 39)
Moose's Tooth Brewpub.........26 D3
New Sagaya's Midtown Market.........27 D3
Organic Oasis.........(see 18)
Peanut Farm.........28 D4
Ray's Place.........(see 18)
Salmon Express.........(see 6)
Sweet Basil Café.........29 C3
Taco King.........30 D3

DRINKING
Reilly's.........31 C3

ENTERTAINMENT
Bear Tooth Theatrepub.........(see 18)
Blues Central at the Chef's Inn.........32 C3
Century 16 Theatre.........33 D3
Chilkoot Charlie's.........34 C3
Fireweed Theatre.........35 D3
Great Alaskan Bush Company.........36 D4
Sullivan Arena.........37 D2

SHOPPING
Alaska Mountaineering & Hiking.........(see 34)
Dos Manos.........38 C3
Great Outdoor Clothing Company.........(see 39)
REI.........39 C3
Salvation Army.........40 D3
Second Chance.........41 C3

TRANSPORT
Advantage Car & Van Rental.........(see 24)
Alaska Rider Motorcycle Tours.........(see 16)

streams while the fish are spawning, especially during twilight hours. For more information on bear safety, see p424.

SIGHTS

Downtown Anchorage

ANCHORAGE MUSEUM OF HISTORY & ART

Pardon the dust. At the time of writing this **museum** (Map pp204-5; ☎ 343-4326; www.anchoragemuseum.org; 121 W 7th Ave; adult/child $6.50/2; 🕑 9am-6pm Fri-Wed, to 9pm Thu) was undergoing a $75 million renovation, due to finish in 2009, that will almost double its size. Even without the renovation, the Anchorage Museum is Alaska's best cultural jewel in this rough-and-tumble state. The 1st floor is dedicated to the arts and has the Art of the North Gallery, with entire rooms of Alaskan masters Eustace Ziegler and Sydney Laurence. The Alaska Gallery on the 2nd floor – the best way to learn your Alaskan history – is filled with life-size dioramas that trace 10,000 years of human settlement from early subsistence villages to modern oil dependency. Guided tours of the Alaska Gallery are offered throughout summer at 10am, 11am and noon daily.

The spacious atrium **Marx Bros Café** (☎ 343-6190; lunch $8-14) serves a selection of lunches, desserts and espresso.

SHIP CREEK VIEWING PLATFORM

From mid- to late summer, king, coho and pink salmon spawn up Ship Creek, the historical site of Tanaina Indian fish camps. The overlook (Map pp204–5) is where you can cheer on those love-starved fish humping their way toward destiny. Follow C St north as it crosses Ship Creek Bridge and then turn right on Whitney Rd.

OSCAR ANDERSON HOUSE

Housed in the city's oldest wooden-framed home, this little **museum** (Map pp204-5; ☎ 274-2336; www.anchoragehistoric.org; 420 M St; adult/child $3/1; 🕑 1-5pm Mon-Fri) overlooks the delightful Elderberry Park and is open June to mid-September. Anderson was the 18th person to set foot in Anchorage and built his house in 1915. Today it's the only home museum in Anchorage.

4TH AVENUE MARKET PLACE/VILLAGE OF SHIP CREEK CENTER

This **shopping mall** (Map pp204-5; ☎ 278-3263; 333 W 4th Ave; admission free; 🕑 10am-7pm Mon-Sat, 11am-6pm Sun) contains the usual gift shops, but also a lot of history. Painted on the walls outside is a historic timeline of Anchorage, while inside are displays devoted to the 1964 Good Friday Earthquake. An Alaska Native dance show is staged at 1pm daily and, if you're intrigued by the dancing, there's a shuttle-van service to the Alaska Native Heritage Center.

RESOLUTION PARK

At the west end of 3rd Ave, this small park is home to the Captain Cook Monument (Map p200), built to mark the 200th anniversary of the English captain's 'discovery' of Cook Inlet. If not overrun by tour-bus passengers, this observation deck has an excellent view of the surrounding mountains. Nearby, on 2nd Ave, is the Alaska Statehood Monument, marking the original 1915 town site with a bust of oft-ignored President Ike Eisenhower.

DELANEY PARK

Known locally as the Park Strip (Map pp204–5), this narrow slice of well-tended

GAY & LESBIAN ANCHORAGE

It's not West Hollywood, but Anchorage does have a handful of gay- and lesbian-friendly bars (see p214) and lodgings (see p210). The city is becoming more gay- and lesbian-friendly, but consider the situation carefully before revealing your sexual orientation.

The weeklong **Pridefest** (mid-June) is a gay-pride celebration that includes a Queer Film Festival, Drag Queen Bingo, a parade through downtown and a party at Delaney Park.

The **Gay & Lesbian Community Center of Anchorage** (GLCCA; Map pp204-5; ☎ 929-4528; www.identityinc.org; 336 E 5th Ave; 🕑 3-9pm Mon-Fri, noon-6pm Sat & Sun) has a community bulletin board and lots of info, including gay-friendly doctor recommendations. It also helps organize Anchorage Pridefest and carries a newsletter, *North View*.

Alaska GLBT News (alaskaglbtnews@yahoo.com) and **Anchorage Pride** (www.egroups.com/subscribe/anchoragepride) both provide news and events listings via email.

You can also call the **Gay & Lesbian Helpline** (☎ 258-4777, toll-free across Alaska 888-901-9876; 🕑 6-11pm) for information or help.

OFFBEAT ANCHORAGE

The wildest salmon in Anchorage are nowhere near Ship Creek. They're found spawning along downtown streets as part of the **Wild Salmon on Parade**, an annual event in which local artists turn fiberglass fish into anything but fish. The art competition has resulted in an 'Alaska Sarah Salmon'; a fish with boxing gloves titled 'Socked Eye Salmon'; and 'Marilyn MonROE.' The 30 or so colorful fish appear on the streets in early June and stick around until September. To see them all, pick up a fish tour map at the Log Cabin Visitors Center (p201).

A massive sun sits at the corner of 5th Ave and G St, marking the start of the **Anchorage Lightspeed Planet Walk**. This built-to-scale model of the solar system extends from the sun all the way out to Kincaid Park. The scale is set so that walking pace mimics the speed of light, but it'll take you all day to reach marble-sized Pluto at that pace. Travel faster than the speed of light by renting a bike.

Most of us would rather avoid the police. But who can resist the **Alaska State Trooper Museum** (Map pp204-5; ☎ 279-5050; www.alaskatroopermuseum.com; 245 W 5th Ave; admission free; ⏰ 10am-4pm Mon-Fri, from noon Sun)? Dedicated to displaying law enforcement starting from when Alaska was a territory, the storefront museum has a 1952 Hudson Hornet cop car and state-issued sealskin cop boots.

grass stretches from A to P Sts between W 9th and W 10th Aves; there's an impressive playground near the corner of E St. It was the site of the 50-ton bonfire celebrating statehood in 1959 and Pope John Paul II's 1981 outdoor mass. Today it hosts festivals like Summer Solstice and Pridefest, not to mention Frisbee games any time the weather's nice.

Midtown Anchorage & Spenard

HERITAGE LIBRARY MUSEUM

Inside the Midtown Wells Fargo bank, this **museum** (Map p200; ☎ 265-2834; 301 W Northern Lights Blvd; admission free; ⏰ noon-5pm Mon-Fri) is home to one of the largest collections of Alaska Native artifacts in the city and includes costumes, baskets and hunting weapons. There are also original paintings covering walls, including several by Sydney Laurence and lots of scrimshaw. The museum's collection is so large that there are displays in the elevator lobbies throughout the bank.

ALASKA AVIATION HERITAGE MUSEUM

Ideally located on the south shore of Lake Hood, the world's busiest floatplane lake, is this **museum** (Map p200; ☎ 248-5325; www.alaskaairmuseum.org; 4721 Aircraft Dr; adult/child $10/6; ⏰ 9am-5pm), a tribute to Alaska's colorful bush pilots and their faithful planes. Housed within are 25 planes along with historic photos and displays of pilots' achievements, from the first flight to Fairbanks (1913) to the early history of Alaska Airlines. You can view early footage of bush planes in the museum's theater or step outside to its large observation deck and watch today's pilots begin their own quest for adventure with a roar on Lake Hood.

Greater Anchorage

ALASKA NATIVE HERITAGE CENTER

Experiencing Alaska Native culture firsthand in the Bush is logistically complicated and expensive. Instead, come to this 26-acre **center** (Map p219; ☎ 330-8000, 800-315-6608; www.alaskanative.net; 8800 Heritage Center Dr; adult/child $23.50/16; ⏰ 9am-5pm) and see how humans survived – and thrived – before central heating.

The main building houses meandering exhibits on traditional arts and sciences – including kayaks and rain gear that rival outdoors department store REI's best offerings. It also features various performances, among them the staccato Alaghanak song, lost for 50 years: the center collected bits and pieces of the traditional song from different tribal elders and reconstructed it. Outside, examples of typical structures from the Aleut, Yupik, Tlingit and other tribes are arranged around a picturesque lake. Docents explain the ancient architects' cunning technology: check out wooden panels that shrink in the dry summers (allowing light and air inside) but expand to seal out the cold during the wet winter.

This is much more than just a museum; it represents a knowledge bank of language, art and culture that will survive no matter how many sitcoms are crackling through the Alaskan stratosphere. It's a labor of love, and of incalculable value.

The center runs a free shuttle bus that picks up from five places downtown, including the

DOWNTOWN ANCHORAGE

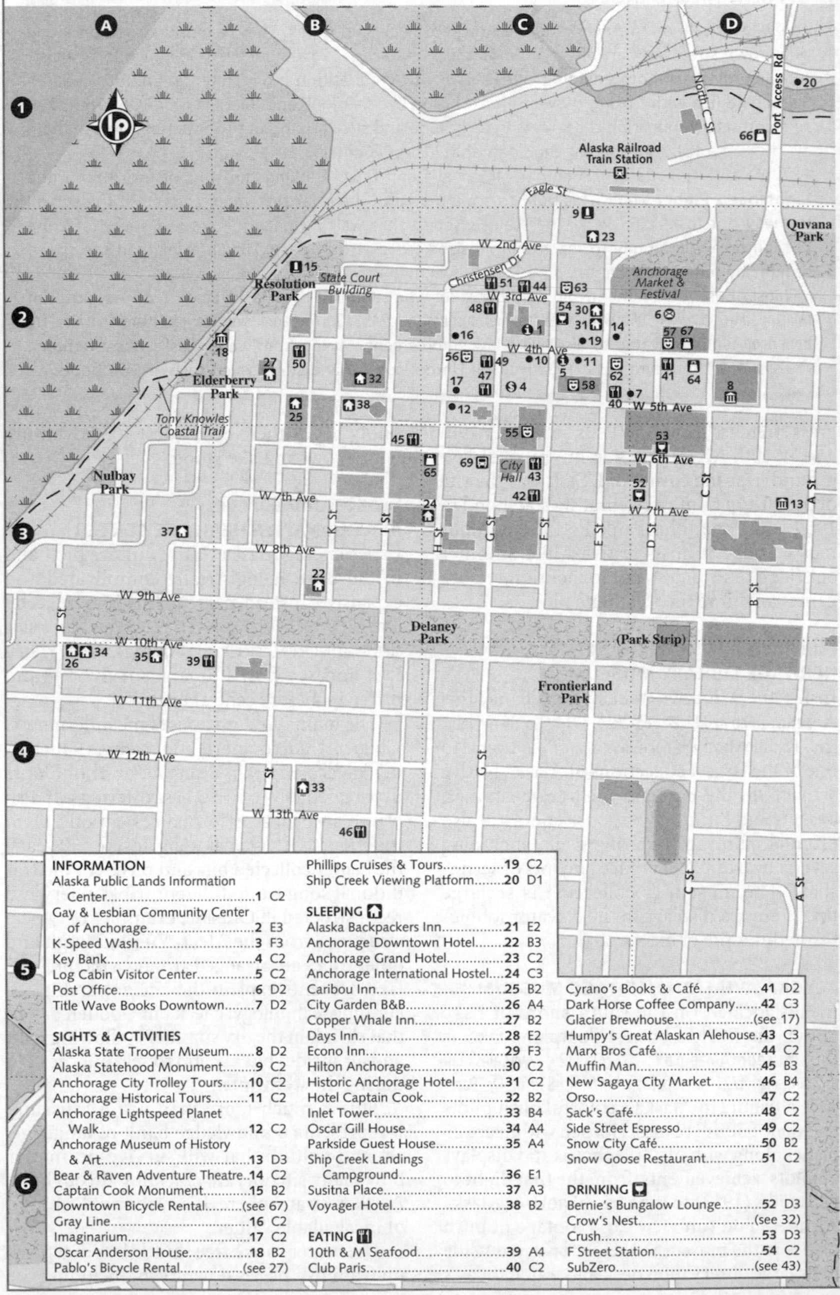

INFORMATION
Alaska Public Lands Information Center 1 C2
Gay & Lesbian Community Center of Anchorage 2 E3
K-Speed Wash 3 F3
Key Bank 4 C2
Log Cabin Visitor Center 5 C2
Post Office 6 D2
Title Wave Books Downtown 7 D2

SIGHTS & ACTIVITIES
Alaska State Trooper Museum 8 D2
Alaska Statehood Monument 9 C2
Anchorage City Trolley Tours 10 C2
Anchorage Historical Tours 11 C2
Anchorage Lightspeed Planet Walk 12 C2
Anchorage Museum of History & Art 13 D3
Bear & Raven Adventure Theatre 14 C2
Captain Cook Monument 15 B2
Downtown Bicycle Rental (see 67)
Gray Line 16 C2
Imaginarium 17 C2
Oscar Anderson House 18 B2
Pablo's Bicycle Rental (see 27)
Phillips Cruises & Tours 19 C2
Ship Creek Viewing Platform 20 D1

SLEEPING
Alaska Backpackers Inn 21 E2
Anchorage Downtown Hotel 22 B3
Anchorage Grand Hotel 23 C2
Anchorage International Hostel 24 C3
Caribou Inn 25 B2
City Garden B&B 26 A4
Copper Whale Inn 27 B2
Days Inn 28 E2
Econo Inn 29 F3
Hilton Anchorage 30 C2
Historic Anchorage Hotel 31 C2
Hotel Captain Cook 32 B2
Inlet Tower 33 B4
Oscar Gill House 34 A4
Parkside Guest House 35 A4
Ship Creek Landings Campground 36 E1
Susitna Place 37 A3
Voyager Hotel 38 B2

EATING
10th & M Seafood 39 A4
Club Paris 40 C2
Cyrano's Books & Café 41 D2
Dark Horse Coffee Company 42 C3
Glacier Brewhouse (see 17)
Humpy's Great Alaskan Alehouse 43 C3
Marx Bros Café 44 C2
Muffin Man 45 B3
New Sagaya City Market 46 B4
Orso 47 C2
Sack's Café 48 C2
Side Street Espresso 49 C2
Snow City Café 50 B2
Snow Goose Restaurant 51 C2

DRINKING
Bernie's Bungalow Lounge 52 D3
Crow's Nest (see 32)
Crush 53 D3
F Street Station 54 C2
SubZero (see 43)

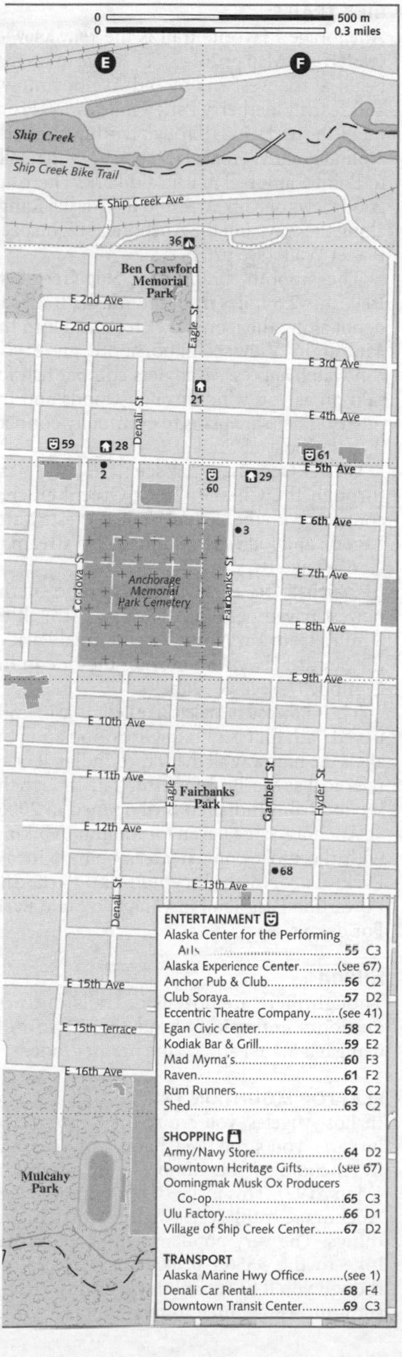

Log Cabin Visitors Center (p201) and the Anchorage Museum of History & Art (p202).

ALASKA BOTANICAL GARDEN

The **garden** (Map p219; ☎ 770-3692; 4601 Campbell Airstrip Rd; adult/family $5/10; ⏲ daylight hr) is a colorful showcase for native species, where gentle paths lead you through groomed herb, rock and perennial gardens in a wooded setting. The mile-long Lowenfels Family Nature Trail, built for tanks during WWII, is a great place to learn your basic Alaskan botany or just watch the bald eagles pluck salmon from Campbell Creek.

ALASKA NATIVE MEDICAL CENTER

This **hospital** (Map p219; ☎ 800-478-1636; 4315 Diplomacy Dr; admission free) has a fantastic collection of Alaska Native art and artifacts: take the elevator to the top floor and wind down the staircase past dolls, basketry and tools from all over Alaska.

EARTHQUAKE PARK

For decades after the 1964 earthquake, this park (Map p200) remained a barren moonscape revealing the tectonic power that destroyed nearby Turnagain Heights. Today Earthquake Park, at the west end of Northern Lights Blvd on the Knik Arm, is being reclaimed by nature; you'll have to poke around the bushes to see evidence of tectonic upheaval.

UNIVERSITY OF ALASKA ANCHORAGE

UA-Anchorage (Map p219; ☎ 786-1800; www.uaa.alaska.edu; Providence Dr) is the largest college campus in the state, but there is far less to do here than at its sister school UA Fairbanks. The Campus Center is home to a small art gallery and the bookstore, which has a good selection of Alaskana, clothing that says 'Alaska' on it and used microbiology texts. Take buses 1, 3, 13, 36, 45 or 102. There are trails from the campus that connect UA to Goose Lake, Chester Creek Greenbelt and Earthquake Park.

GOOSE LAKE

You'll stop complaining about global warming once you experience an 85°F Anchorage afternoon at **Goose Lake** (Map p219; UA Dr). Just off Northern Lights Blvd (buses 3 and 45), this is the city's most developed lake for swimming, with lifeguards, paddleboat rentals and a small café, which serves fresh-baked pizza.

RUSSIAN JACK SPRINGS PARK

Named after the original homesteader of the site, this 300-acre park (Map p219) is south of Glenn Hwy on Boniface Parkway and can be reached by buses 8, 45, and 15. The park has tennis courts, hiking and biking trails, and a picnic area. Near the DeBarr Rd entrance you'll find the **Mann Leiser Memorial Greenhouses** (☎ 343-4717; ⌚ 8am-3pm), a toasty oasis of tropical plants, exotic birds and fish.

FAR NORTH BICENTENNIAL PARK

Comprising 4000 acres of forest and muskeg in east central Anchorage, this park (Map p219) features 20 miles of trails. In the center of the park is Bureau of Land Management's (BLM's) Campbell Tract, a 700-acre wildlife preserve where it's possible to see moose and bears in the spring and brilliant fall colors in mid-September. Take O'Malley Rd east to Hillside Dr and follow the signs. There is an active grizzly population (see p201), and it's wise to steer clear of salmon streams during the twilight hours.

KINCAID PARK

At the western 'nose' of the peninsula and southern terminus of the Tony Knowles Coastal Trail is a beloved 1400-acre park (off Map p219) populated by hikers and cyclists all summer long. Trails wind through a rolling terrain of forested hills where there are views of Mt Susitna, Mt McKinley on a clear day and fiery sunsets in the evening. From certain spots on the Coastal Trail you can stand directly under incoming jets. Follow Raspberry Rd west to the parking lot and trailheads.

ACTIVITIES

Cycling

Anchorage has 122 miles of paved paths that parallel major roads or wind through the greenbelts, making a bicycle the easiest and cheapest way to explore the city. If you run out of gas before the end of the ride, all People Mover buses (p217) are equipped with bike racks.

Downtown Bicycle Rental (Map pp204-5; ☎ 279-5293; www.alaska-bike-rentals.com; 333 W 4th Ave; per 3/24hr $16/32; ⌚ 8am-8pm) has road, hybrid and mountain bikes as well as tandems, trailers and even clip-in pedals and shoes. Locks, helmets and bike maps are free.

Pablo's Bicycle Rental (Map pp204-5; ☎ 250-2871; 5th & L St; per 3/24hr $15/30; ⌚ 7am-7pm) is next to Copper Whale Inn downtown.

BIKE TRAILS

Anchorage's favorite trail is the **Tony Knowles Coastal Trail** (Map pp204–5), 11 scenic miles that begin at the west end of 2nd Ave downtown and reach Elderberry Park a mile away. From there, the trail winds through Earthquake Park, around Point Woronzof (Map p199) and finally to Point Campbell in Kincaid Park. There are good views of Knik Arm and the Alaska Range along the way, and the Anchorage Lightspeed Planet Walk (see p203).

The smooth, brand-new **Ship Creek Bike Trail** runs 2.6 miles from the Alaska Railroad depot along the namesake creek and into the Mountain View neighborhood. Here you can watch aggressive anglers combat fish for salmon as you wind through woods and industry. There are plans to eventually connect it to the Coastal Trail.

Chester Creek Trail is a scenic 6-mile path through the Chester Creek Greenbelt that connects with the Coastal Trail at Westchester Lagoon and follows a mountain-fed stream to Goose Lake Park.

Campbell Creek Trail features some of the newest paved path in Anchorage, stretching 8 miles from Far North Bicentennial Park to the Seward Hwy with most of the ride in the Campbell Creek Greenbelt.

The **Girdwood to Indian Bike Path** is a 13-mile paved path that begins in Girdwood and parallels the highway all the way to Indian. Locals refer to it as the 'Bird-to-Gird' trail, though the section from Indian to Bird opened in 2006.

Anchorage is a haven for mountain biking, with the most popular areas being Kincaid Park, Far North Bicentennial Park and Powerline Pass Trail in Chugach State Park. For details see p77.

Hiking

Though there are dozens of trails in town, outdoors enthusiasts head to 773-sq-mile Chugach State Park for the mother lode.

FLATTOP MOUNTAIN TRAIL

In Los Angeles, you cruise the Sunset Strip; in Paris, you stroll the Champs-Elysées; and in Anchorage, you climb Flattop Mountain (Map p199). This is the first mountain every Anchorage youth scales on the way to higher things. The very popular 3-mile round-trip hike to the 3550ft peak is easy to follow, though you'll be scrambling a bit toward the summit. Allow three to five hours. Another trail continues 3 more miles along the ridgeline to Flaketop Peak. From the same parking area, you can also access the 2-mile Blueberry Loop (perfect for kids) and 11-mile Powerline Trail, popular with cyclists.

From Seward Hwy, head 4 miles east on O'Malley Dr and make a right on Hillside Rd; after 1 mile make a left on Upper Huffman Rd and follow the signs to the Glen Alps park entrance. Parking is $5. For transportation there's **Flattop Mountain Shuttle** (☎ 279-3334; round-trip adult/child $22/15) which leaves various locations downtown at 1 and 7pm daily.

THE RAMP

This 14-mile round-trip hike (Map p199) starts close to the Flattop Mountain trailhead and it takes you past alpine summits and through tranquil tundra. Rather than following the upper trail to Flattop Mountain, hike half a mile to Powerline Trail. Turn right and follow the power line for 2 miles, where an old jeep trail crosses over from the left and heads downhill to the south fork of Campbell Creek.

The trail then crosses the creek and continues to a valley on the other side. Hike up the alpine valley to Ship Lake Pass, which lies between the 5240ft Ramp and the 4660ft Wedge, with great camping and climbing. Allow eight to 10 hours.

WILLIWAW LAKES TRAIL

This easy 13-mile hike (Map p199) also begins close to the Flattop Mountain trailhead, leading to the handful of alpine lakes at the base of Mt Williwaw. The trail makes a pleasant overnight hike and many consider it the most scenic outing in the Hillside area of Chugach State Park.

Walk half a mile to the Powerline Pass Trail and then turn right, continuing 300yd to Middle Fork Loop Trail. Follow it down and across the south fork of Campbell Creek, then north for 1.5 miles to the middle fork of the creek. Here you reach a junction; make a right on Williwaw Lakes Trail. You can make this an overnight trek or a seven- to nine-hour day hike.

WOLVERINE PEAK TRAIL

This strenuous but rewarding 14-mile round-trip ascends the 4455ft triangular peak, visible from Anchorage. The marked trail begins at an old homesteader road that crosses the south fork of Campbell Creek. Keep heading east and the road will become a footpath that ascends above the tree line and eventually fades out (mark it for the return trip). From there, it's 3 miles to Wolverine Peak.

From Seward Hwy, head 4 miles east on O'Malley Rd and make a left on Hillside Dr and follow the signs to the Prospect Heights entrance of Chugach State Park. Parking costs $5.

RENDEZVOUS PEAK ROUTE

The 4-mile trek to this 4050ft peak is an easy three- to five-hour trip, rewarding hikers with incredible views of Mt McKinley, Cook Inlet, Turnagain and Knik Arms, and the city far below. From the parking lot, a short trail leads along the right-hand side of the stream up the valley to the northwest. It ends at a pass where a short ascent to Rendezvous Peak is easily seen and climbed.

From Glenn Hwy, exit Arctic Valley Rd (Fort Richardson) and follow signs to Arctic Valley; a 7-mile gravel road leads to the Alpenglow Ski Area parking lot. Parking costs $5.

MCHUGH LAKE TRAIL

This 13-mile trail originates at McHugh Creek Picnic Area, 15 miles south of Anchorage at Mile 111.8 of the Seward Hwy. The route follows the McHugh Creek valley, and in 7 miles reaches Rabbit and McHugh Lakes, two beautiful alpine pools reflecting the 5000ft Suicide Peaks.

The first 3 miles feature some good climbs, and the round-trip trek makes for a long day. It's better to haul in a tent and then spend the afternoon exploring the open tundra country and nearby ridges.

ANCHORAGE FOR KIDS

Anchorage is exceptionally kid-friendly – more than 40 city parks boast playscapes. Close to downtown, **Frontierland Park** (Map pp204-5; 10th Ave & E St) is a local favorite, while **Valley of the Moon Park** (Arctic Blvd & W 17th St) makes a delightful picnic spot. Entice your family to the Anchorage Museum of History & Art (p202) by promising to first explore the hands-on exhibits of its Children's Gallery.

Alaska Zoo

The unique wildlife of the Arctic is on display at this **zoo** (Map p219; ☎ 346-3242; 4731 O'Malley Rd;

ANCHORAGE & AROUND

adult/child $9/5; 9am-6pm Wed, Thu & Sat-Mon, to 9pm Tue & Fri), the only one in North America that specializes in northern animals, including snow leopards, Amur tigers and Tibetan yaks. Alaska native species, from wolverines and moose to caribou and Dall sheep, are abundant. What kids will love watching, however, are the bears. The zoo has all four Alaskan species (brown, black, glacier and polar) but Ahpun, the polar bear, is clearly the star attraction.

Imaginarium

Whoever thought science could be so much fun? At the **Imaginarium Science Discovery Center** (Map pp204-5; ☎ 276-3179; 725 W 5th Ave; adult/child $5.50/5; 10am-6pm Mon-Sat, noon-5pm Sun) kids can hug a life-size *Tyrannosaurus rex*, stand inside a giant bubble, pick up a sea star from a touch tank or become a human gyroscope.

H²Oasis

Qualifying as surreal, Anchorage's original **waterpark** (Map pp204-5; ☎ 344-8610; www.h2oasiswaterpark.com; 1520 O'Malley Rd; adult/child $22/17; 10am-10pm) is a $7 million, three-level amusement zone with palm trees, water slides, a wave pool and the 505ft Master Blaster, one very wet roller coaster. Feel free to just watch from the grown-ups-only hot tubs.

Alaska Wild Berry Products

If the Flattop Mountain hike is overly ambitious for your kids, head to this giant jam and gift shop with **chocolate falls** (Map p200; ☎ 907-562-8858; 5525 Juneau St; admission free; 10am-11pm). It's definitely a tourist trap, but who can resist a chocolate waterfall? Outside there's a short nature trail that leads to a handful of reindeer that kids can feed and pet.

Bear & Raven Adventure Theatre

This **mini-amusement park** (Map pp204-5; ☎ 277-4545; 315 E St; adult/child $10.50/8.50; 10am-8:30pm) is a cheesy but easy downtown break from shopping. The littlest ones will likely be bored with the 30-minute video, but the virtual 'rides' (reeling in a salmon, for example) ought to satiate them.

TOURS

City Tours

Anchorage City Trolley Tours (Map pp204-5; ☎ 775-5603; 612 W 4th Ave; rides $15; tours on the hr 9am-5pm) One-hour rides in a bright red trolley past Lake Hood, Earthquake Park and Cook Inlet, among other sights.

Anchorage Historical Tours (Map pp204-5; ☎ 274-3600; 524 W 4th Ave; adult/child $5/1) Starting at the Old City Hall, its hour-long downtown walking tour begins at 1pm Monday to Friday.

Gray Line (Map pp204-5; ☎ 277-5581, 800-544-2206; www.graylineofalaska.com; 745 W 4th Ave) A three-hour bus tour covers downtown plus the Alaska Native Heritage Center (adult/child $51/26).

Flightseeing Tours

They're costly and never as long as you wish, but they're a stunning way to spend an hour or two. If you've got the cash – lots of it – flightseeing tours provide an eagle-eye view of the wilderness and mountains, imparting a sense of scale that's difficult to appreciate from the ground.

Alaska Air Taxi (off Map p200; ☎ 243-3944, 800-789-5232; www.alaskaairtaxi.com) Has a 1½-hour tour over the Chugach Mountains to Knik Glacier ($229) and another the same length and price to Blackstone Glacier in Prince William Sound.

Regal Air (Map p200; ☎ 243-8535; www.regal-air.com) Flying out of Lake Hood, this has some of the best rates for flightseeing. Its three-hour Mt McKinley tour is only $329, a 1½-hour tour of Knik Glacier is $199.

Rust's Flying Service (Map p200; ☎ 243-1595, 800-544-2299; www.flyrusts.com) Offers a three-hour Mt McKinley flight that includes flying the length of Ruth Glacier ($345) and a three-hour Columbia Glacier tour ($340).

Day Tours

Have a leftover day? Have an adventure. There are few places in Alaska that somebody in Anchorage isn't willing to whisk you off to in a day. Gray Line (above) offers a one-day trip to Barrow ($643) with four hours in the village itself and the rest of the day spent flying. Pray for clear weather.

Alaska Railroad (Map pp204-5; ☎ 265-2494, 800-544-0552; www.akrr.com; 411 W 1st Ave) Has a number of one-day tours from Anchorage that begin with a train ride. Its nine-hour Spencer Glacier Float Tour (per person $185) includes a ride to Spencer Lake and a gentle raft trip among the glacier's icebergs. The Resurrection Bay Park Ranger Cruise ($200) is a train ride to Seward and a five-hour wildlife cruise.

Phillips Cruises & Tours (Map pp204-5; ☎ 276-8023, 800-544-0529; www.26glaciers.com; 519 W 4th Ave) Takes you by bus to Whittier and then on a boat past 26 glaciers in Prince William Sound. The eight-hour tour (adult/child $138/78) is offered daily and includes lunch.

Rust's Flying Service (Map p200; ☎ 243-1595, 800-544-2299; www.flyrusts.com) One of many air charters that will zip you off to Katmai National Park to view brown bears feeding on salmon at Brooks Falls. The 10-hour tour is $750 per person.

FESTIVALS & EVENTS

These are just a few of Anchorage's more popular events; contact the **Anchorage Convention & Visitors Bureau** (☎ 276-3200; www.anchorage.net) to see what's on while you're here.

Anchorage Fur Rendezvous (☎ 274-1177; www.furrondy.net) The place to get fresh-trapped furs is still the 'Rondy,' but most folks prefer to sculpt ice, ride the Ferris wheel in freezing temperatures in February or March, or watch the 'Running of the Reindeer.' When the Rondy ends the famed 1100-mile National Historic Iditarod Trail begins. Better stay another week.

Blues on the Green Is there a better way to spend a mid-June day than listening to blues and jazz at Kincaid Park? Musicians range from locals to bigger acts like John Lee Hooker Jr.

Mayor's Midnight Sun Marathon (☎ 786-1230; www.mayorsmarathon.com) You know it's going to be a long day when you start this on the Summer Solstice in late June.

SLEEPING

Several new hostels in town are helping bring the cost of sleeping down, but Anchorage is expensive. Tack on the city's 12% sales-and-bed tax to the prices given here.

Budget

CAMPING

Chugach State Park has several public campgrounds, but none is close to town.

Ship Creek Landings (Map pp204-5; ☎ 277-0877; www.alaskarv.com; 150 Ingra St; sites camp/RV $15/30; 💻) It isn't exactly pristine wilderness and there's the train rumbling by, but it does provide laundry facilities, internet access and a convenient location.

Centennial Park Campground (Map p219; ☎ 343-6986; 8300 Glenn Hwy; sites $20) It's 5 miles from downtown but is pleasant, with 'the hottest showers in town.' People Mover buses 3 or 75 stop nearby.

HOSTELS

26th Street Hostel (Map p200; ☎ 274-1252; 1037 W 26th St; site/dm/r $15/25/67; ⊠ 💻) This hostel is close to all the midtown action, plus has free internet, continental breakfast, and luggage storage. Campsites are in the grassy backyard. Buses 3 and 7 stop on Spenard Rd, a block away.

Spenard Hostel (Map p200; ☎ 248-5036; www.alaskahostel.org; 2845 W 42nd Pl; sites/dm/r $20/21/88; ⊠ 💻) Two blocks from Spenard Rd is this relaxed hostel, with laundry, no lockout and three kitchens to avoid mealtime madness. Campsites are a little cramped on the side of the house, but you can even rent one of its tents if you don't have your own. Guests can rent mountain bikes ($3 per hour) and store bags ($1/15 per day/month). Reservations are highly recommended for July and August. Take buses 7 or 36.

Arctic Adventure Hostel (Map p200; ☎ 562-5700; www.arcticadventurehostel.com; 337 W 33rd Pl; dm/r $21/42; ⊠ 💻) The rooms in this Midtown joint are minuscule and somewhat institutional, but tidy, and there's a max of three beds in each dorm. All rooms share bathrooms, but the private ones come with TVs and are great value. The kitchen is huge – a great place to cook a big spread. The friendly owner will rent you bikes and camping gear, and internet is free. Take bus 9.

Alaska Backpackers Inn (Map pp204-5; ☎ 277-2770; www.alaskabackpackers.com; 327 Eagle St; dm/s/d $22/50/60; ⊠ 💻) Anchorage's newest hostel is roomy, comfortable and professional, and has a different painting on every dorm room floor. There are never more than four beds in a room, which are generally single-sex. A bit east of central downtown, it's still within walking distance to restaurants and bars.

our pick **Qupqugiaq Inn** (Map p200; ☎ 563-5633; www.qupq.com; 640 W 36th Ave; dm $24, s/d with bath $87/104, without bath $69/90; ⊠ 💻) This colorful establishment has curved hallways, tiled floors, granite windowsills and a continental breakfast that includes French-pressed coffee and roll-your-own oats. The large dorms sleep eight, and the private rooms are bright and clean. Bus 36 stops right outside.

Jason's International Hostel (Map p200; ☎ 562-0263; 3324 Eide St; dm $25; ⊠ 💻) Though it feels like the bunk beds have been thrown haphazardly into any space available and a huge flat-screen TV dominates the common area, Jason's actually has quite a few amenities, including breakfast, airport pick-up, and free top ramen. The amazing garden – with bistro tables on the landscaped terrace – is great place to hang out and try to forget that the neighborhood isn't too scenic.

Anchorage International Hostel (Map pp204-5; ☎ 276-3635; www.anchoragehostel.org; 700 H St; dm/r $25/65; ⊠) Though somewhat regimented with lockout times (10am to 4pm) and curfews (1am), this hostel's location is hard to beat; it's downtown, practically across from the bus terminal. It also has laundry facilities, common areas, and luggage storage.

Anchorage Guest House (Map p200; ☎ 907-274-0408; www.akhouse.com; 2001 Hillcrest Dr; dm $35, r from $89; ⊠ 💻) This spacious suburban home feels more like a B&B than a hostel, which is why it costs a bit more. Owner and singer/songwriter Andy Baker offers laundry ($2), bag storage ($1 per day), and bike rentals ($5 per hour) for the nearby coastal trail. Buses 3, 7 and 36 cruise within easy walking distance; exit at West High School.

MOTELS

John's Motel & RV Park (Map p219; ☎ 277-4332, 800-478-4332; www.johnsmotel.com; 3543 Mountain View Dr; RV sites $25, s/d $55/60) It's more RV park than motel. Only thing smaller than the 18 rooms is the price.

Caribou Inn (Map pp204-5; ☎ 272-0444, 800-272-5878; www.cariboubnb.com; 501 L St; s/d with bath $119/129, without bath $99/109; ⊠) The downtown location is perfect and the 14 rooms, though stuffy and a bit run-down, are acceptable and come with a full breakfast. Among the amenities are free bikes and airport/train shuttle service.

Midrange

B&BS

City Garden B&B (Map pp204-5; ☎ 276-8686; www.citygarden.biz; 1352 W 10th Ave; r $100-150; ⊠ 💻) One of several B&Bs located on a two-block stretch of 10th Ave, this is an open, sunny, gay- and lesbian-friendly place with more cutting-edge art than antiques. The nicest of the three rooms has a private bath.

Oscar Gill House (Map pp204-5; ☎ 279-1344; www.oscargill.com; 1344 W 10th Ave; r $115-135; ⊠) This historic clapboard home was built in 1913 in Knik and later moved to its Midtown location. The B&B offers three guest rooms (two that share a bath), a fantastic breakfast and free bikes.

Lake Hood Inn (Map p200; ☎ 258-9321; www.lakehoodinn.com; 4702 Lake Spenard Dr; r $119-139; ⊠ 💻) If you're infatuated with floatplanes and bush pilots, book a room here. This spotless upscale home, with four guest rooms, is adorned with airplane artifacts, from a Piper propeller that doubles as a ceiling fan to a row of seats from a Russian airline. Outside are two decks where you can watch a parade of floatplanes lift off the lake.

MOTELS

Econo Inn (Map pp204-5; ☎ 274-1515; 642 E 5th Ave; s/d/ste $90/95/160; ⊠ 💻) Shabby but adequate, with a free airport shuttle to sweeten the deal.

Anchorage Downtown Hotel (Map pp204-5; ☎ 258-7669; www.anchoragedowntownhotel.com; 826 K St; r $100-150; ⊠ 💻) This small hotel located on the outskirts of downtown is a pleasant place to stay with 16 rooms that feature private baths, coffeemakers, small refrigerators and microwaves.

Puffin Inn (Map p200; ☎ 243-4044, 800-478-3346; www.puffininn.net; 4400 Spenard Rd; s $110-190, d $140-235; ⊠ 💻) It has three tiers of fine rooms, from 26 sardine-can, economy rooms to full suites, all accessible via free 24-hour airport shuttle.

Days Inn (Map pp204-5; ☎ 276-7226; www.daysinnalaska.com; 321 E 5th Ave; r $169; 💻) Clean, utilitarian and small, with a 24-hour restaurant and a free shuttle to the train station or airport.

HOTELS

Voyager Hotel (Map pp204-5; ☎ 277-9501, 800-247-9070; www.voyagerhotel.com; 501 K St; r $189; 💻 ⊠) A 40-room hotel with a great location downtown. Each room comes with a kitchenette, and some have peek-a-boo inlet views.

Inlet Tower (Map pp204-5; ☎ 276-0110, 800-544-0786; www.inlettower.com; 1200 L St; r $229-269; ⊠ 💻) Fifteen floors of spacious suites with kitchenettes, gourmet coffee for the coffeemaker and large TVs with in-room movies. The views are amazing.

Top End

B&BS

Susitna Place (Map pp204-5; ☎ 274-3344; www.susitnaplace.com; 727 N St; r $100-140, ste $155-185; 💻 ⊠) On the edge of downtown, this 4000-sq-ft home sits on a bluff overlooking Cook Inlet and Mt Susitna in the distance. Four rooms have shared baths while the Susitna suite comes with a fireplace, Jacuzzi and a private deck.

Parkside Guest House (Map pp204-5; ☎ 278-2290; www.campdenali.com; 1302 W 10 Ave; r $160-185; ⊠ 💻) This elegant B&B has four large rooms that lead out to a spacious 2nd-floor sitting area with a fireplace, rocking chairs and a view of the city skyline and Cook Inlet. Relax in a Jacuzzi tub, do your laundry or store your luggage here.

Copper Whale Inn (Map pp204-5; ☎ 258-7999; www.copperwhale.com; W 5th Ave & L St; r $185-210; ⊠ 💻) Recently remodeled rooms make this city-center place both elegant and bright. There's a relaxing waterfall pond, and breakfast is served with a view in the living room. It's also gay and lesbian friendly.

HOTELS

Anchorage Grand Hotel (Map pp204-5; ☎ 929-8888, 888-800-0640; www.anchoragegrandhotel.com; 505 W 2nd Ave; r $199; ⊠ 💻) This converted apartment building rests on a quiet street with 31 spacious suites that include full kitchens and separate living and bedroom areas. Many overlook Ship Creek and Cook Inlet and its downtown location is convenient to everything.

our pick **Historic Anchorage Hotel** (Map pp204-5; ☎ 272-4533, 800-544-0988; www.anchoragehistorichotel.com; 330 E St r from $249; ⊠ 💻) This boutique hotel was established only a year after the city was, in 1916, though the current building is from 1936. It's luxurious, and you're sure to receive lots of personal attention.

Hotel Captain Cook (Map pp204-5; ☎ 276-6000, 800-843-1950; www.captaincook.com; cnr 4th Ave & K St; r from $250; ⊠ 💻 🏊) The grand dame of Anchorage accommodations still has an air of an Alaskan aristocrat right down to the doormen with top hats. There are plenty of plush services and upscale shops: Jacuzzis, fitness clubs, beauty salon, jewelry store, and four restaurants including the famed Crow's Nest Bar on the top floor.

Millennium Hotel (Map p200; ☎ 243-2300, 800-544-0553; 4800 Spenard Rd; r $259; ⊠ 💻) A large, 248-room resort with a woodsy lodge feel overlooking Lake Spenard. PETA members take note; there are stuffed animals, trophy mounts and large fish everywhere. All rooms have been recently renovated, and are large with king or queen beds.

Hilton Anchorage (Map pp204-5; ☎ 272-7411, 800-245-2527; www.hiltonanchorage.com; 500 W 3rd Ave; r $300; ⊠ 💻) The Hilton has the best location of any of the luxury hotels, right in the heart of the downtown scene. Three restaurants, a fitness center with a pool, two 1000lb bears in the lobby, and lots of elegance. If you're going to pay this much, ask for a room with a view of Cook Inlet.

EATING

Anchorage has lots of fast food, espresso stands and, of course, more fried halibut and smoked salmon than you can shake a rod and reel at. But the bustling city also boasts a variety of international cuisines, from Polynesian to Mexican to Vietnamese, that you'll be hard-pressed to find in the Bush. Take advantage of this savory melting pot while you can.

In 2007, all restaurants and bars went smoke-free.

Downtown

RESTAURANTS

Club Paris (Map pp204-5; ☎ 277-6332; 417 W 5th Ave; lunch $7-20, dinner $17-56; 🕑 11am-2:30pm Mon-Sat, 5-10pm daily) This longtime restaurant – it survived the 1964 earthquake – serves the best steaks in Anchorage. If there's room on your credit card try the 4in-thick filet mignon.

Glacier Brewhouse (Map pp204-5; ☎ 274-2739; 737 W 5th Ave; lunch $8-16, dinner $10-34; 🕑 11am-11pm) Grab a table overlooking the three giant copper brewing tanks and enjoy wood-fired pizzas and rotisserie-grilled ribs and chops with a pint of oatmeal stout.

Orso (Map pp204-5; ☎ 222-3232; 737 W 5th Ave; lunch $9-16, dinner $16-27; 🕑 11am-10:30pm) The walls are smoked salmon and the wooden floors are covered with oriental rugs, and there's modern art all around and soft jazz floating into both dining levels and the bar. Its mains consist of Mediterranean grill with an Alaskan twist.

Sack's Café (Map pp204-5; ☎ 274-4022; 328 G St; lunch $9-12, dinner $18-35; 🕑 11am-2:30pm & 5-9:30pm Mon-Thu, 11am-2:30pm & 5-10pm Fri & Sat, 10:30am-2:30pm & 5-9:30pm Sun) A bright, colorful restaurant serving elegant fare that is consistently creative. It is always bustling (reservations recommended) and has the best weekend brunch in town.

Humpy's Great Alaskan Alehouse (Map pp204-5; ☎ 276-2337; 610 W 6th Ave; dinner $12-30; 🕑 11-2am) Anchorage's most beloved beer place, with 44 draughts on tap. There's also ale-battered halibut, gourmet pizzas, outdoor table, and live music most nights.

Snow Goose Restaurant (Map pp204-5; ☎ 277-7727; 717 W 3rd Ave; medium pizza $13-14; 🕑 11:30am-11:30pm) The outdoor deck on the 2nd floor is positioned to look onto Cook Inlet, Mt Susitna and the sunsets whenever they occur. There are few things nicer than enjoying an Urban Wilderness Pale Ale on a sunny evening.

our pick **Marx Bros Café** (Map pp204-5; ☎ 278-2133; 627 W 3rd Ave; dinner $34-50; 🕑 5:30-10pm Tue-Sat) They woo you into this historic (1916) home promising views of Cook Inlet but let's face it, you're looking at fuel tanks along Ship Creek. Some of Anchorage's most innovative cooking and a 500-bottle wine list are the real reasons this 14-table restaurant is so popular. The menu changes nightly, but the beloved halibut macadamia always stays put. In the summer book your table a week in advance.

CAFÉS

Cyrano's Books & Café (Map pp204-5; ☎ 274-2599; 413 D St; light meals $5-8; noon-10pm Tue-Sun) An offbeat bookstore where you can lose yourself in a paperback over tempting sweets, soups and salads.

Muffin Man (Map pp204-5; ☎ 279-6836; 817 W 6th Ave; dishes $5-11; 7:30am-3pm Mon-Fri, 8am-2pm Sat) In a funky tiled building, this café serves breakfast and lunch. Try the Sockeye Salmon Scramble.

our pick **Snow City Café** (Map pp204-5; ☎ 272-2489; 1034 W 4th Ave; breakfast $7-12, lunch $7-9; 7am-4pm) Consistently voted best breakfast by *Anchorage Press* readers, this busy café serves healthy grub to a mix of clientele that ranges from the tattooed to the up-and-coming. For breakfast skip the usual eggs-and-toast and try a bowl of Snow City granola with dried fruit, honey and nuts.

QUICK EATS

Scattered among the gift shops on 4th Ave downtown are hot-dog vendors where $3 to $4 gets you a dog or a reindeer sausage smothered in sauerkraut.

Side Street Espresso (Map pp204-5; ☎ 258-9055; 412 G St; 7am-3pm Mon-Sat; ☒) It serves espresso, bagels and muffins within walls covered in art.

Dark Horse Coffee Company (Map pp204-5; ☎ 279-0647; 646 F St; 6:45am-6pm Mon-Fri, 8am-4pm Sat, 9am-4pm Sun; ☒) It has lots of lattes, big pastries, even bigger waffles, and savory quiches and sandwiches. Internet is $2 for 15 minutes; wireless is free. Surf and sip.

GROCERIES

New Sagaya City Market (Map pp204-5; ☎ 274-6173; 3900 W 13th Ave; 6am-10pm Mon-Sat, 8am-9pm Sun) Eclectic and upscale, this is a grocery store with lots of organic goodies, a great deli specializing in Asian fare and seating indoors and outdoors.

10th & M Seafood (Map pp204-5; ☎ 272-3474; 1020 M St; 8am-6pm Mon-Fri, from 9am Sat) This market sells the freshest seafood in a city that loves its seafood fresh. Staff will also butcher and ship your freshly killed moose or 200lb halibut.

Midtown

RESTAURANTS

Greek Corner (Map p200; ☎ 276-2820; 302 W Fireweed; lunch $6-10, dinner $11-20; 11am-10pm Mon-Fri, from noon Sat, from 4pm Sun) Best moussaka and stuffed grape leaves in Alaska. So what are they doing serving pizza and pasta? Trying to make a living.

Ray's Place (Map p200; ☎ 279-2932; 32412 Spenard Rd; dinner $7-13; 10am-3pm & 5-8pm Mon-Fri, 10am-3pm & 5-9pm Sat & Sun) Leave Chilkoot Charlies (p214) early and cross the street to this Vietnamese restaurant that does great soups and stirfries and stocks Vietnamese beer.

City Diner (Map p200; ☎ 277-2489; 3000 Minnesota Dr; breakfast $7-13, lunch or dinner $8-19; 7am-10pm) You can't miss the gleaming silver facade of this nouveau diner. It tries hard and manages to succeed with all-day breakfast and giant milkshakes. Just like the good old days.

Thai Kitchen (Map p219; ☎ 907-561-0082; 3405 Tudor Rd; dinner $8-12; 11am-3pm & 5pm-9pm; ☒) This kid-friendly place comes highly recommended, with more than 100 items on the menu, dozens of which are vegetarian.

our pick **Bear Tooth Grill** (Map p200; ☎ 276-4200; 1230 W 27th St; burgers $8-12, dinner $10-20; 4-11pm; ☒) A popular hangout with an adjacent theater (p214) that serves excellent burgers and seafood as well as Mexican and Asian fusion dishes. The microbrews are fresh and the cocktails are the best in town – if you're up for a splurge, lash out on the *el Cielo* (the sky) margarita.

Moose's Tooth Brewpub (Map p200; ☎ 258-2537; 3300 Old Seward Hwy; medium pizza $12-21; 11am-11pm Mon-Thu, to midnight Fri & Sat, noon-11pm Sun) An Anchorage institution serving 18 custom-brewed beers including monthly specials. There are also 50 gourmet pizzas on the menu, and it's *the* place refuel after a long day in the Chugach.

Bombay Deluxe (Map p200; ☎ 277-1200; 555 W Northern Lights Blvd; mains $15-20; 11am-2pm & 5-10pm) Skip the mediocre lunch buffet and order straight off the menu. Don't forget to try the samosas.

Jen's Restaurant (Map p200; ☎ 561-5367; 701 W 36th Ave; lunch $10-22, dinner $18-37; 11am-2pm Mon, 11am-2pm & 6-10pm Tue-Fri, 6-10pm Sat) This fine restaurant in Midtown has dazzled the critics with innovative, Scandinavian-accented cuisine emphasizing fresh ingredients and elaborate presentation. There's also a wine bar that stays open to midnight with music and a menu of tapas.

CAFÉS

Middle Way Café (Map p200; ☎ 272-6433; 1200 W Northern Lights Blvd; breakfast $4-9, lunch $6-11; 8am-5:30pm Mon-Fri, 10:30am-4:30pm Sat & Sun) This veggie-friendly café serves healthy breakfasts (try the huevos rancheros) and organic salads, soups and sandwiches.

Gwennie's Old Alaska Restaurant (Map p200; ☎ 243-2090; 4333 Spenard Rd; breakfast $6-11, dinner $15-25; 6am-10pm Mon-Sat, from 8am Sun) Alaska at its best; lots to look at – totems, stuffed bears and a gurgling stream – and big portions. Non-Alaskans can probably share a reindeer sausage omelet and not be hungry for two days.

Organic Oasis (Map p200; ☎ 277-7882; 2610 Spenard Rd; mains $7-12; 11am-8pm Mon & Sat, to 9pm Tue-Thu, 1-6pm Sun) Anchorage's hippest juice bar. Not into puréed carrots? It also serves beer, wine, wraps, pasta and burgers with loads of veggie choices.

Café Europa (Map p200; ☎ 563-5704; 601 W 36th Ave; lunch $8; 6am-6pm Mon-Fri, from 7am Sat, 8am-5pm Sun) Come here for the soup-and-sandwich lunch, but don't leave without a fresh-baked French pastry.

Sweet Basil Café (Map p200; ☎ 274-0070; 1201 E Northern Lights Bvld; sandwiches $8; 10:30am-6:30pm Mon-Fri, 11am-4pm Sat) It does inexpensive, healthy cuisine (and decidedly unhealthy, but recommended, desserts), fruit smoothies and coffee.

QUICK EATS

Salmon Express (Map p200; ☎ 345-1598; 606 W Northern Lights Blvd; fast food $4-8; 10:30am-6pm Mon-Fri) It serves salmon chowder, salmon kebabs and the recommended salmon quesadillas from the most ramshackle little drive-through stand imaginable.

Charlie's Bakery (Map p200; ☎ 677-7777; 2729 C St; mains $6-12; 11am-8:30pm Mon-Sat) The most authentic Chinese food you'll find in Anchorage, sold next to French baguettes.

Taco King (Map p200; ☎ 276-7387; 113 W Northern Lights Blvd; dinner $7-8; 10:30am-11pm Mon-Sat, noon-10pm Sun) It does authentic street-style Mexican cuisine, including chicken enchiladas and *carne asada* (grilled steak). The five salsas are made fresh daily.

GROCERIES

New Sagaya Midtown Market (Map p200; ☎ 561-5173; 3700 Old Seward Hwy; 6am-10pm Mon-Sat, 8am-9pm Sun) Near the library, this market has Asian food to go, upscale groceries that include fresh seafood, and an excellent bakery.

Central Market (Map p200; ☎ 277-1170; 555 W Northern Lights Blvd; 9am-9pm) A touch of Asia in the heart of Anchorage.

South Anchorage

Arctic Roadrunner (Map p200; ☎ 561-1245; 5300 Old Seward Hwy; burgers $4-5; 10:30am-9pm Mon-Sat; ⊠) Since 1964 this place has been turning out beefy burgers and great onion pieces and rings. If your timing is right you can eat outdoors while watching salmon spawn up Campbell Creek.

Tap Root (Map p219; ☎ 345-0282; 1330 Huffman Rd; breakfast $5-11, lunch or dinner $10-16; 8am-10:30pm Tue-Sat, 9am-3pm Sun; ⊠) A busy and casual café with live music (occasional $5 cover), Belgian beers, homemade hummus and very relaxed service.

Peanut Farm (Map p200; ☎ 523-3683; 5227 Old Seward Hwy; breakfast $7-11, sandwiches $7-9; 6-2am) What was once a small, funky bar is now a shockingly large restaurant and sports bar complex, complete with TVs at every table. The food is mediocre, but when the salmon are running the creekside deck is the best place in town to relax and watch your future dinner swim by.

Southside Bistro (Map p219; ☎ 348-0088; 1320 Huffman Park Dr; dinner $11-36; 11:30am-10pm Tue-Thu, to 11pm Fri & Sat) Upscale dining on the south side of town, this bistro is well worth the splurge. We can't get enough of the chevre salad.

DRINKING

With its young and lively population, Anchorage has a lot to do after the midnight sun finally sets. The free *Anchorage Press* and Friday *Anchorage Daily News* both have events listings.

Bernie's Bungalow Lounge (Map pp204-5; 626 D St) Pretty people, pretty drinks: this is the place to see and be seen. On Thursdays bands play on the tiki torch-lit patio, on the weekends it's DJs.

Crush (Map pp204-5; 343 W 6th Ave) This swanky wine bar serves 'bistro bites,' a menu of appetizers and salads. It's great for a nibble and a glass (or bottle) of reasonably priced wine.

SubZero (Map pp204-5; 610 6th Ave) Slick and silver, this wi-fi hot spot around the corner from Humpy's has an ice bar and upscale drinks, including more than 100 Belgian beers.

Reilly's (Map p200; 317 W Fireweed) A friendly pub with the goodness of Ireland on tap: Guinness Extra Stout, Murphy's Irish Stout and Harp Irish Ale.

F Street Station (Map pp204-5; 325 F St) This is the place where everybody knows your name. The only thing missing in this friendly, music-free drinking hole is Norm sitting at the end of the bar.

There's upscale dining at the **Crow's Nest** (Map pp204-5; 5th Ave & K St), at the top of the Hotel

Captain Cook, but most come for a drink and a million-dollar view of Cook Inlet.

ENTERTAINMENT

Clubs

our pick **Chilkoot Charlie's** (Map p200; ☎ 272-1010; www.koots.com; 2435 Spenard Rd) More than just Anchorage's favorite meat market, 'Koots', as the locals call it, is a landmark. The sprawling, wooden edifice has 22 beers on tap, 10 bars, four dancefloors and a couple of stages where basically every band touring Alaska ends up. Its newest addition is a replica of the legendary Bird House. The original was a log-cabin bar on Seward Hwy that was still standing but drunkenly slanted after the 1964 earthquake before burning down in 2002.

Anchor Pub & Club (Map pp204-5; 712 4th Ave) This clean new joint serves soups and sandwiches, has a dance floor and a lounge, and proudly displays the largest Blue Ocean TV screen on the west coast.

Shed (Map pp204-5; 535 W 3rd Ave; Fri & Sat cover $5) It's karaoke seven days a week and they'll cut a CD of your performance. DJs take over in the basement after 10pm Thursday through Saturday.

Rum Runners (Map pp204-5; 415 W E St) Is packed when DJs are spinning after 10pm Friday and Saturday, and it now boasts a mojito bar.

Club Soraya (Map pp204-5; 333 W 4th Ave; cover $3-10) A huge Latin dance place. If you can't shake it or swing it, dance lessons are on offer most nights of the week, including salsa from 9pm to 10pm on Friday followed by live music, tango on Wednesday, and swing on Thursday.

Gay & Lesbian Venues

Several straight bars are regarded as gay and lesbian friendly: try Bernie's Bungalow Lounge (see p213) and the Moose's Tooth Brewpub (p212).

Mad Myrna's (Map pp204-5; 530 E 5th Ave; cover Sat & Sun $5-10) A fun, cruisy bar with line dancing on Thursday, Drag Divas shows on Friday and dance music most nights after 9pm.

Kodiak Bar & Grill (Map pp204-5; 225 E 5th Ave) Charges a $3 cover until 2am, serves alcohol until 3am, and after that this club is open to minglers 18 years and up.

Raven (Map pp204-5; 708 E 4th Ave) The other gay and lesbian bar in town.

Live Music

There's plenty of jazz and blues to be found in Anchorage: **Blues Central at the Chef's Inn** (Map p200; ☎ 272-1341; 825 W Northern Lights Blvd) is an intimate venue with live blues and jazz nightly. Anchorage Museum of History & Art (p202) offers Jazz After Hours at 7pm on Thursday, free with the cost of museum admission ($6.50). For free jazz head to Cyrano's Books & Café (p212).

For other music, check out Humpy's Great Alaskan Alehouse (p211), which features live music Monday to Saturday at around 9pm with a mix of acoustic, bluegrass and blues throughout the summer. If you're packing your six-string, Monday is open-mic night. The Snow Goose Restaurant (p211) also offers an open mic as well as local acoustic artists, and its small theatre often hosts musicians from out of state. Organic Oasis (p213) has live jazz, bluegrass or acoustic alternative music most evenings.

If line dancing is your thing, mosey down to the **Long Branch Saloon** (Map p219; 1737 E Dimond Blvd). It has pool tables, stiff drinks and live country and western music almost nightly.

Cinemas

Bear Tooth Theatrepub (Map p200; ☎ 276-4200; www.beartooththeatre.net; 1230 W 27th Ave) Cruise into this very cool venue (check out the mural on the lobby ceiling) where you can enjoy great microbrews, wine or even dinner while watching first-run movies ($3) – Monday night is 'art house' night, and features foreign and independent films.

Alaska Experience Center (Map pp204-5; ☎ 272-9076; 333 W 4th Ave; adult/child movie $10/6, earthquake exhibit $7/6, combined ticket $13/10; 🕑 10am-9pm) More a tourist trap than movie house, with IMAX nature films and a theatrical simulation of the 1964 Good Friday Earthquake.

Fireweed Theatre (Map p200; ☎ 800-326-3264, ext 101; cnr Fireweed & Gambell Rd) and **Century 16 Theatre** (Map p200; ☎ 770-2602; 301 E 36th Ave), across from the library, are both fine places for a flick.

Theater & Performing Arts

Anchorage had an orchestra before it had paved roads, which says a lot about priorities around here.

Alaska Center for the Performing Arts (Map pp204-5; ☎ 263-2900, tickets 263-2787; www.alaskapac.org; 621 W 6th Ave) impresses tourists with the film *Aurora: Alaska's Great Northern Lights* (adult/child $8.75/$6.75; 🕑 on the hour 9am to 9pm) during summer in its Sydney Laurence Theatre. It's also home to the **Anchorage Opera** (☎ 279-

2557; www.anchorageopera.org), **Anchorage Symphony Orchestra** (☎ 274-8668; www.anchoragesymphony.org), **Anchorage Concert Association** (☎ 272-1471; www.anchorageconcerts.org)and **Alaska Dance Theatre** (☎ 277-9501; www.alaska danc etheatre.org).

Egan Civic Center (Map pp204-5; ☎ 263-2800; www.egancenter.com; 555 W 5th Ave) Try this place for top-drawer musical groups and other big events.

Sullivan Arena (Map p200; ☎ 279-0618; www.sullivanarena.com; 1600 Gambell St) It also hosts musical events.

Eccentric Theatre Company (Map pp204-5; ☎ 274-2599; 413 D St; tickets $12-15) Adjacent to Cyrano's Books & Café, this may be the best live theater in town, staging everything from *Hamlet* to *Archy and Mehitabel* (comic characters of a cockroach and a cat), Mel Brooks' jazz musical based on the poetry of Don Marquis. Only in Anchorage....

Other Entertainment

Anchorage Bucs (☎ 561-2827; www.anchoragebucs.com) and **Anchorage Glacier Pilots** (☎ 274-3627; www.glacierpilots.com) play semipro baseball at Mulcahy Ball Park, where living legend Mark McGuire slammed a few homers. General admission is around $5.

Great Alaskan Bush Company (Map p200; ☎ 561-2609; 631 E International Airport Rd) It's about as beloved as a strip club gets. The cozy landmark is woman-owned and -operated, and everyone agrees that the truly moral thing to do is tip well.

SHOPPING

Outdoor Gear

With so much wilderness at its doorstep you'd expect Anchorage to have a wide variety of outdoor shops – and it does.

REI (Map p200; ☎ 272-4565; 1200 Northern Lights Blvd; 🕑 10am-9pm Mon-Fri, to 8pm Sat, 11am-7pm Sun) Anchorage's largest outdoor store has everything you might ever need, from wool socks to backpacks to kayaks to camp chairs. Besides being able to repair your camp stove or bike tire, it will also rent canoes, bear containers, tents, and bikes.

Alaska Mountaineering & Hiking (Map p200; ☎ 272-1181; www.alaskamountaineering.com; 2633 Spenard Rd; 🕑 9am-7pm Mon-Fri, to 6pm Sat, noon-5pm Sun) Staffed by experts and stocked with high-end gear, AMH is the place for serious adventurers.

Great Outdoor Clothing Company (Map p200; ☎ 277-6665; 1200 W Northern Lights Blvd; 🕑 10am-8pm Mon-Sat, to 6pm Sun) Next door to REI, this place is a manufacturer's outlet with better prices on clothing, Gore-Tex parkas and hiking boots.

Army/Navy Store (Map pp204-5; ☎ 279-2401; 320 W 4th Ave; 🕑 9:30am-6:30pm Mon-Fri, 9am-5:30 Sat) One of the cheapest places in town to buy hardy military gear.

Secondhand stores are also a great place to find fleece jackets and woolen caps. Try the **Second Chance** (Map p200; ☎ 277-2748; 3106 Spenard Rd; 🕑 noon-7pm Mon-Sat, to 6pm Sun) for old-school toasty Bunny Boots, or the **Salvation Army** (Map p200; ☎ 561-5544; 300 W Northern Lights Blvd; 🕑 10am-8pm Mon-Sat) for everything else.

Souvenirs

Moose-dropping jewelry and thin T-shirts are available downtown at a variety of cheesy tourist shops.

Anchorage Market & Festival (Map pp204-5; ☎ 272-5634; www.anchoragemarkets.com; W 3rd Ave & E St; 🕑 10am-6pm Sat & Sun) This was called the 'Saturday Market' until it became so popular they opened it on Sundays. A fantastic open market with live music and almost 100 booths stocked with cheap food, Mat-Su Valley veggies and souvenirs from birch steins to birch syrup.

Ulu Factory (Map pp204-5; ☎ 276-3119; 211 W Ship Creek Ave; 🕑 8am-7pm) The *ulu* (oo-loo) is to Alaska what the rubber alligator is to Florida: everybody sells them. Still, this shop is interesting, with demonstrations that will teach you how to use the cutting tool.

Dos Manos (Map p200; ☎ 569-6800; 1317 W Northern Lights Blvd; 🕑 11am-6pm Mon-Sat) Across from Title Wave Books, they sell locally crafted art and jewelry, and very cool Alaska-themed T-shirts.

Northway Mall Wednesday Market (Map p219; 3101 Penland Parkway; 🕑 9am-4pm Wed) Many vendors head to this market on Wednesday; take buses 8 or 45.

Alaska Native Arts & Crafts

Alaska Native Heritage Center (Map p219; ☎ 330-8000, 800-315-6608; www.alaskanative.net; 8800 Heritage Center Dr; 🕑 9am-5pm) Stocks a gift shop with artifacts of questionable authenticity, but also features booths where craftspeople make fresh knick-knacks while you watch.

Downtown Heritage Gifts (Map pp204-5; ☎ 330-8008; 333 4th Ave; 🕑 9am-6pm) The Alaska Native Heritage Center also has a downtown store in the Ship Creek Center with a larger selection and longer hours than its gift shop.

Alaska Native Arts Foundation Gallery (☎ 258-2623; www.alaskanativearts.org; 500 W 6th Ave; 🕑 10am-6pm Mon, Wed & Fri, to 7pm Tue & Thu, 11am-5pm Sat) The gallery showcases Native art in a bright, open space.

ANC Auxiliary Craft Shop (Map p219; ☎ 729-1122; 4315 Diplomacy Dr; 🕑 10am-2pm Mon-Fri, from 11am 1st & 3rd Sat of month) Located on the 1st floor of the Alaska Native Medical Center, it has some of the finest Alaska Native arts and crafts available to the public. It does not accept credit cards.

Oomingmak Musk Ox Producers Co-op (Map pp204-5; ☎ 272-9225; www.qiviut.com; 604 H St; 🕑 9am-9pm Mon-Fri, to 6pm Sat & Sun) Handles a variety of very soft, very warm and very expensive garments made of Arctic musk-ox wool, hand-knitted in isolated Inupiaq villages.

GETTING THERE & AWAY

Air

Ted Stevens Anchorage International Airport, 6.5 miles west of the city center, is the largest airport in the state, handling 130 domestic and international flights daily from more than a dozen major airlines.

Alaska Airlines (☎ 800-252-7522; www.alaskaair.com) provides the most intrastate routes to travelers, generally through its contract carrier, ERA Aviation, which operates services to Valdez, Homer, Cordova, Kenai, Iliamna and Kodiak. You can book tickets either online or at the airport.

PenAir (☎ 800-448-4226; www.penair.com) flies smaller planes to 27 difficult-to-pronounce destinations in Southwest Alaska, including Unalakleet, Aniak and Igiugig.

Boat

The **Alaska Marine Highway** (Map pp204-5; ☎ 272-4482; 605 W 4th Ave; 🕑 8am-5pm Mon-Fri) doesn't service Anchorage but does have an office in the Old Federal Courthouse.

Bus

Anchorage is a hub for various small passenger and freight lines that make daily runs between specific cities. Always call first; the turnover in Alaska's volatile bus industry is unbelievable.

Alaska Direct Busline, Inc (☎ 277-6652, 800-770-6652; www.alaskadirectbusline.com) has regular services between Anchorage and Glennallen ($65), Tok ($95), Fairbanks ($105) and Whitehorse ($210) and points in-between.

Homer Stage Line (☎ 868-3914; www.homerstageline.com) runs daily in the summer between Anchorage and Cooper Landing ($45), Soldotna ($55), Homer ($65) and Seward ($50).

Seward Bus Line (☎ 563-0800; www.sewardbuslines.net) runs between Anchorage and Seward ($50) twice daily in summer.

Talkeetna Shuttle Service (☎ 733-1725, 888-288-6008; www.denalicentral.com) runs a service between Anchorage and Talkeetna ($65) twice daily in summer.

Alaska Yukon Trails (☎ 800-770-7275; www.alaskashuttle.com) runs a bus up the George Parks Hwy to Talkeetna ($59), Denali National Park ($65) and Fairbanks ($91). The next day it will transport you from Fairbanks to Dawson City, Canada ($162), via the Top of the World highway.

Alaska Park Connection (☎ 800-266-8625; www.alaskacoach.com) offers daily service from Anchorage to Denali National Park ($79) and Seward ($56) as well as between Seward and Denali ($135).

Train

From its downtown depot, the **Alaska Railroad** (Map pp204-5; ☎ 265-2494, 800-544-0552; www.akrr.com; 411 W 1st Ave) sends its *Denali Star* north daily to Talkeetna (adult/child $80/40), Denali National Park ($129/65) and Fairbanks ($179/90). The *Coastal Classic* stops in Girdwood ($49/25) and Seward ($59/30) while the *Glacial Discovery* connects to Whittier ($52/26). You can save 20% to 30% traveling in May and September.

GETTING AROUND

To/From the Airport

People Mover bus 7 offers hourly service between downtown and the airport ($1.75, 6:15am to 10:55pm Monday to Friday, 8:35am to 8:35pm Saturday, 10:35am to 6:14pm Sunday). Pick-up is at both the international and domestic terminals.

You can call **Alaska Shuttle Service** (☎ 338-8888, 694-8888; www.alaskashuttle.net) for door-to-door service to downtown and South Anchorage ($30) or Eagle River ($45). These fares are for one to three passengers, so it's cheaper if you can share. Plenty of the hotels and B&Bs also provide a courtesy-van service. Finally, an endless line of taxis will be eager to take your bags and your money. Plan on a $20 to $25 fare to the downtown area.

RIDING THE ALASKA RAILROAD

In a remote corner of the Alaskan wilderness, you stand along a railroad track when suddenly a small train appears. You wave a white flag in the air – actually yesterday's dirty T-shirt – and the engineer acknowledges you with a sound of his whistle and then stops. You hop onboard to join others fresh from the Bush; fly fishermen, backpackers, a hunter with his dead moose, locals whose homestead cabin can be reached only after a ride on the *Hurricane Turn*, one of America's last flag-stop trains.

This unusual service between Talkeetna and Hurricane along the Susitna River is only one aspect that makes the Alaska Railroad so unique. At the other end of the rainbow of luxury is the railroad's Gold Star Service, two lavishly appointed cars that in 2005 joined the *Denali Star* train as part of the Anchorage–Fairbanks run. The 89ft double-decked dome cars include a glass observation area on the 2nd level with 360-degree views and a bartender in the back serving your favorite libations. Sit back, sip a chardonnay and soak in the grandeur of Mt McKinley.

Take your pick, rustic or relaxing, but don't pass up the Alaska Railroad. There's not another train like it.

The railroad was born on March 12, 1914, when the US Congress passed the Alaska Railroad Act, authorizing the US president to construct and operate the line. With the exception of the train used at the Panama Canal, the US government had never before owned and operated a railroad.

It took eight years and 4500 men to build a 470-mile railroad from the ice-free port of Seward to the boomtown of Fairbanks, a wilderness line that was cut over what was thought to be impenetrable mountains and across raging rivers. On a warm Sunday afternoon in 1923, President Warren Harding – the first US president to visit Alaska – tapped in the golden spike at Nenana.

The Alaska Railroad has been running ever since. The classic trip is to ride the railroad from Anchorage to Fairbanks, with a stop at Denali National Park. Many believe the most scenic portion, however, is the 114-mile run from Anchorage to Seward, which begins by skirting the 60-mile-long Turnagain Arm, climbs an alpine pass and then comes within a half-mile of three glaciers. There are cheaper ways to reach Seward, Fairbanks or points in-between. But in the spirit of adventure, which is why many of us come to Alaska, a van or bus pales in comparison to riding the Alaska Railroad.

Bus

Anchorage's excellent bus system, **People Mover** (☎ 343-6543; www.peoplemover.org; Downtown Transit Center, 700 W 6th Ave; 8am-5pm Mon-Fri), runs from 6am to midnight Monday to Friday, 8am to 9pm Saturday and 9:30am to 7pm Sunday. Pick up a schedule at the Downtown Transit Center ($1) or call for specific route information. One-way fares are adult/child $1.75/1.00 and an unlimited day pass ($4) is available at the transit center.

Mascot (☎ 376-5000; www.matsutransit.com), the Mat-Su Community Transit, has service between Anchorage and Wasilla and Palmer, with three runs a day that depart from the Downtown Transit Center Monday through Friday (one way/day pass $2.50/6).

Car & Motorcycle

If at all possible, rent your car in the city where you'll be hit with an 18% rental tax. At the airport they'll also add an airport tax that pushes it up to 32% on all rentals. Ouch! That's highway robbery before you even get to the highway. All the national concerns (Avis, Budget, Hertz, Payless, National etc) have counters in the airport's south terminal.

Denali Car Rental (Map pp204-5; ☎ 276-1230, 800-757-1230; 1209 Gambell St) has subcompacts for $65/390 per day/week with 150 daily miles included.

Advantage Car & Van Rental (Map p200; ☎ 243-8806, 888-877-3585; 4211 Spenard Rd) is another Spenard cheapie, with compacts for $70/420 per day/week.

Alaska Rider Motorcycle Tours (Map p200; ☎ 272-2777, 800-756-1990; www.akrider.com; 4346 Spenard Rd) rents Harley Davidsons (per day $250) and Kawasakis (per day $150) and offers both guided and self-guided tours. It's pricey, but still much better value than traditional psychotherapy.

Taxi

If you need to call a cab, try either **Anchorage Yellow Cab** (☎ 272-2422) or **Anchorage Checker Cab** (☎ 276-1234).

ANCHORAGE & AROUND

SOUTH OF ANCHORAGE

The trip out of Anchorage along Turnagain Arm is well worth the price of a train ticket or rental car. Sure, it might be quicker (and probably cheaper) to fly, but staying on the ground will make you appreciate just how close to the wilderness Anchorage really is.

SEWARD HIGHWAY

Starting at the corner of Gambell St and 10th Ave in Anchorage, Seward Hwy parallels the Alaska Railroad south 127 miles to Seward. Once it leaves Anchorage proper, the highway winds along massive peaks dropping straight into Turnagain Arm. Expect lots of traffic, a frightening percentage of which involves folks who have (1) never seen a Dall sheep before and (2) never driven an RV before; it's a frustrating and sometimes deadly combination. Mile markers measure the distance from Seward.

If you're lucky (or a planner), you'll catch the bore tide (see boxed text below), which rushes along Turnagain Arm in varying sizes daily.

Potter Marsh (Mile 117) was created in 1916, when railroad construction dammed several streams; at the time of writing it was in the process of being filled with eroded earth. You can stretch your legs along the 1500ft boardwalk while spying on ducks, songbirds, grebes and gulls.

Chugach State Park Headquarters (☎ 345-5014; Mile 115; ⏲ 10am-4:30pm Mon-Fri) is housed in the Potter Section House, a historic railroad workers' dorm that also includes a free museum with a snowplow train and other era artifacts.

Turnagain Arm Trail, an easy 11-mile, hike, begins at Mile 115. Originally used by Alaska Natives, the convenient route has since been used by Russian trappers, gold miners and happy hikers. The trail, with a mountain goat's view of Turnagain Arm, alpine meadows and beluga whales, can also be accessed at the McHugh Creek Picnic Area (Mile 112), Rainbow (Mile 108) and Windy Corner (Mile 107).

Indian Valley Mine (☎ 653-1120; www.indianvalleymine.com; Mile 104; admission $1; ⏲ 9am-9pm Jun-Aug), a lode mine originally blasted out in 1901, still produces gold. You can buy bags of ore ($3 to $50) and see for yourself. The wonderful proprietors are extremely knowledgeable on the history and science of Alaskan gold mining; ask about the potato retort.

Indian Valley Trail (Mile 103) is a mellow 6-mile path that starts 1.3 miles along the gravel road behind Turnagain House. You can also access Powerline Trail for a much longer hiking or biking. Nearby is the **Brown Bear Motel** (☎ 653-7000; www.brownbearmotel.com; Mile 103 Seward Hwy; s/d $52/57) with clean rooms and cheap beer in the adjoining Brown Bear Saloon that can get hopping at night.

Bird Ridge Trail (Mile 102) starts with a wheelchair-accessible loop, then continues with a steep, popular and well-marked path that reaches a 3500ft overlook at Mile 2; this is a traditional turnaround point for folks in a hurry. Or you can continue another 4 miles to higher peaks and even better views from sunny Bird Ridge, a top spot for rock climbing.

Bird Creek State Campground (Mile 101; sites $10) is popular for fishing, hiking and, best of all, the sound of the bore tide rushing by your tent. Remind children and morons to stay off the deadly mud flats.

CATCHING THE BORE TIDE

One attraction along the Turnagain Arm stretch of Seward Highway is unique among sights already original: the bore tide. The bore tide is a neat trick of geography that requires a combination of narrow, shallow waters and rapidly rising tides. Swooping as a wave sometimes 6ft in height (and satisfyingly loud), the tide fills the Arm in one go. It travels speeds of up to 15mph, and every now and then you'll catch a brave surfer or kayaker riding it into the Arm.

So, how to catch this dramatic rush?

First, consult a tide table, or grab a schedule, available at any Anchorage visitors center. The most extreme bore tides occur during days with minus tides between -2.0ft and -5.5ft, but if your timing doesn't hit a huge minus, aim for a new or full moon period. Once you've determined your day, pick your spot. The most popular is Beluga Point (Mile 110), and a wise choice. If you miss the tide, you can always drive further up the Arm and catch it at Bird Point (Mile 96).

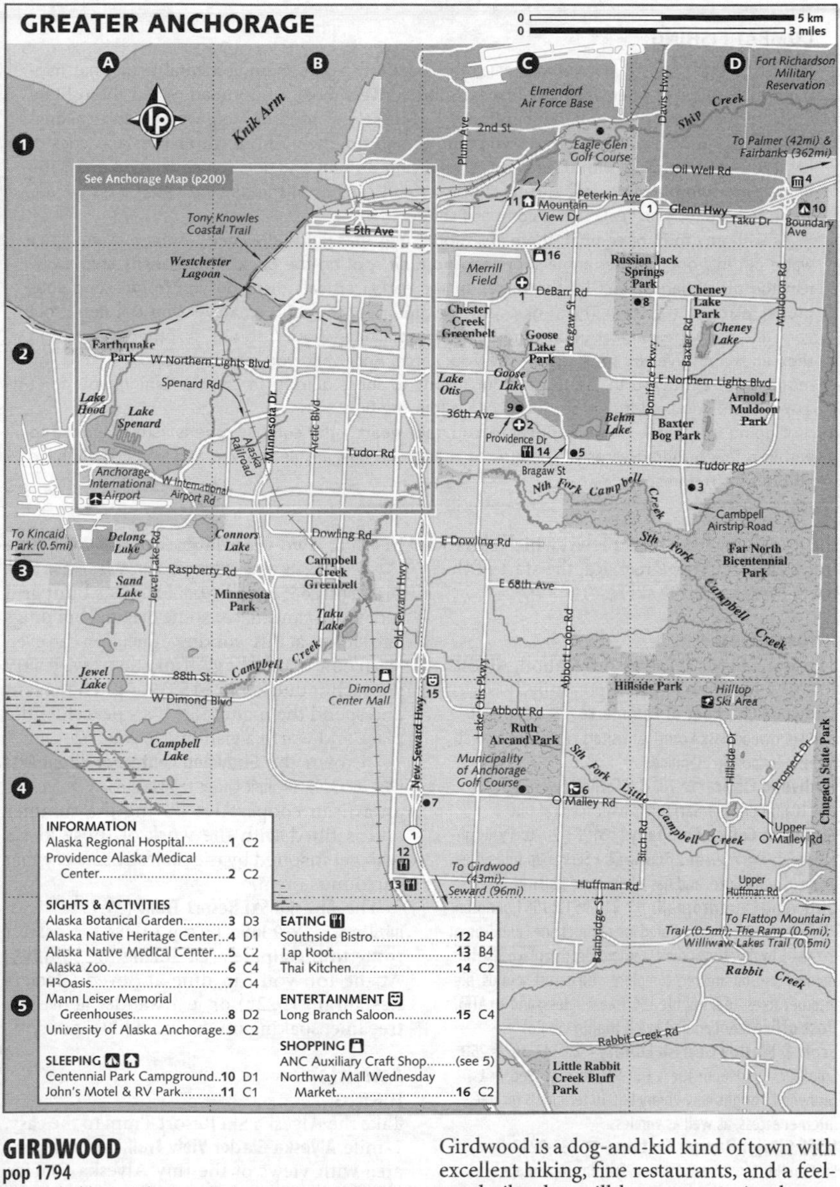

GIRDWOOD

pop 1794

Encircled by mighty peaks brimming with glaciers, Girdwood is a laid-back antidote to the bustle of Anchorage. Home to the luxurious Alyeska Ski Resort and the fabled Girdwood Forest Fair (cancelled in 2008 – check www.girdwoodforestfair.com for future events), Girdwood is a dog-and-kid kind of town with excellent hiking, fine restaurants, and a feel-good vibe that will have you staying longer than anticipated.

Orientation

Girdwood lies 37 miles south of Anchorage at Mile 90 Seward Hwy. There's a strip mall at

COMBAT FISHING

In a place that's mostly natural and wild, there are few sights more unnatural than what happens each summer wherever Alaska's best salmon rivers meet a busy road. When the fish are running, the banks become a human frenzy – a ceaseless string of men, women and children hip-to-hip, hundreds of fishing rods whipping to and fro, the air filled with curses and cries of joy, the waters rippling with dozens of fish dancing on taut and sometimes tangled lines. The banks are a jumble of coolers and tackle boxes and catches-of-the-day. Rub your eyes all you want: the scene is for real. This is combat fishing.

As with any form of combat, there are subtle rules that guide the chaos. Among them: don't wade out in front of other anglers, or snap up their spot on the bank if they briefly step away. (On the other hand, don't let the glares of the earlier arrivals dissuade you from taking your proper place in the fray.) Try to give your neighbor space – and whatever you do, don't foul your line with theirs. Most importantly, if you get a bite, shout 'fish on!' so others can reel in their lines and give you room to wrestle your catch. And while you may be tempted to milk the moment for all it's worth, try to get your trophy to shore quickly. In combat fishing, you don't 'play' a fish; you land it fast, so others can rejoin the fight.

If going into battle doesn't appeal to you, take heart – the combat zone is usually limited to within a few hundred yards of the closest road. Hike half a mile upriver, and you'll likely have all the fish to yourself.

the junction with Alyeska Hwy, which runs 3 miles east to Crow Creek Rd, the start of the town center and the ski resort.

Information

There are ATMs at the Tesoro Station, Alyeska Resort and Crow Creek Mercantile.

Girdwood Chamber of Commerce (☎ 222-7682; www.girdwoodalaska.com) No visitors center but a great website for pretrip planning.

Girdwood Clinic (☎ 783-1355; Hightower Rd; 🕑 10am-6pm Tue-Sat) Offers basic medical care.

Girdwood Coffee Company (☎ 783-2020; 🕑 Hightower Rd; 🕑 7:30am-2:30pm; 💻) Serves up free wireless with your latte, and has a bookstore in back.

Girdwood Laundromall (☎ 317-0512; 158 Holmgren Pl; 🕑 7am-9pm; 💻) Voted the number one Laundromat in the US by *American Coin-Op Magazine*, this place also has themed coin-op showers complete with nature sounds, plus internet access (per minute 15¢, free wireless) and an ATM.

Post office (cnr Limblad Ave & Hightower Rd)

Scott & Wesley Gerrish Library (☎ 343-4024; 250 Egloff Dr; 🕑 1-6pm Tue & Thu-Sat, to 8pm Wed; 💻) Girdwood's bright new library has 10 terminals for free internet access, as well as wireless.

USFS Glacier Ranger Station (☎ 783-3242; Ranger Station Rd; 🕑 8am-5pm Mon-Fri) Has topo maps, a viewing scope, and information on area hikes, campgrounds and public-use cabins.

Sights

Girdwood was named for James Girdwood, who staked the first claim on Crow Creek in 1896. Two years later the **Crow Creek Mine** (☎ 229-3105; www.crowcreekmine.com; Mile 3.5 Crow Creek Rd; adult/child $5/free; 🕑 9am-6pm) was built and today you can still see some original buildings and sluices at this working mine. You can even learn how to pan for gold and then give it a try yourself (adult/child $15/5) or pitch the tent and spend the night ($5). It's a peaceful little place and worth a visit just to walk around.

In town the **Girdwood Center for Visual Arts** (☎ 783-3209; Olympic Circle; 🕑 11am-6pm) serves as an artisan cooperative during the summer and is filled with the work of those locals who get inspired by the majestic scenery that surrounds them.

The **Alyeska Ski Resort Tram** (☎ 754-1111; admission $18; 🕑 9:30am-9:30pm) offers the easiest route to the alpine area during the summer. At the top you can dine at Seven Glaciers Restaurant (p222) or just wander above the tree line, soaking up the incredible views.

Activities

HIKING

Take the Alyeska Ski Resort Tram to the easy, 1-mile **Alyeska Glacier View Trail**, in an alpine area with views of the tiny Alyeska Glacier. You can continue up the ridge to climb the so-called summit of Mt Alyeska, a high point of 3939ft. The true summit lies farther to the south, but is not a climb for casual hikers.

Winner Creek Gorge is an easy and pleasant hike that winds 5.5 miles through lush forest, ending in the gorge itself, where Winner Creek becomes a series of cascades. The first half of the trail is a boardwalk superhighway, but towards the end it can get quite muddy. From the gorge you can connect to the **National Historic Iditarod Trail** for a 7.7-mile loop. Either way, you'll cross the gorge on an ultrafun hand-tram. The most popular trailhead is near Arlberg Rd: walk along the bike path past the Alyeska Prince Hotel, toward the bottom of the tram. Look for the footpath heading into the forest.

The highly recommended **Crow Pass Trail** is a short but beautiful alpine hike that has gold-mining relics, an alpine lake, and often there are Dall sheep on the slopes above. It's 4 miles to Raven Glacier, the traditional turnaround point of the trail, and 3 miles to a **USFS cabin** (☎ 877-444-6777, 518-885-3639; www.recreation.gov; cabins $35). Or you can continue on the three-day, 26-mile route along the Iditarod Trail to the Eagle River Nature Center (p93). The trailhead is 5.8 miles north of Alyeska Hwy on Crow Creek Rd.

CYCLING

The most scenic ride is the Indian-Girdwood Trail – dubbed Bird-to-Gird – a paved path that leads out of the valley and along the Seward Hwy above Turnagain Arm. The fabulously scenic route extends to Mile 103 of the highway, linking Alyeska Resort with Indian Creek 17 miles away. **Girdwood Ski & Cyclery** (☎ 783-2453; www.girdwoodskicyclery.com; bikes per 3hr/day $15/30; 10am-7pm) will rent you the bikes to enjoy it.

The **Alyeska Resort** (☎ 754-1111; www.alyeska.com; mountain bike rentals per day $55) has been working on extensive mountain bike trails suitable for beginners as well as adrenaline addicts. The excellent elevated tread single-tracks are accessible on Chair 7 ($29) or on ascending trails from the main lodge (free). Though there are plans for more trails, when we visited there was a beginner, an intermediate and two expert routes.

Tours

Girdwood is a small speck in a large wilderness, and there's plenty on offer for anyone wanting to explore.

Alpine Air (☎ 783-2360; www.alpineairalaska.com; Girdwood airport) Has a one-hour glacier tour that includes a helicopter landing on the ice ($299).

Ascending Path (☎ 783-0505; www.theascendingpath.com) A climbing-guide service that has a three-hour

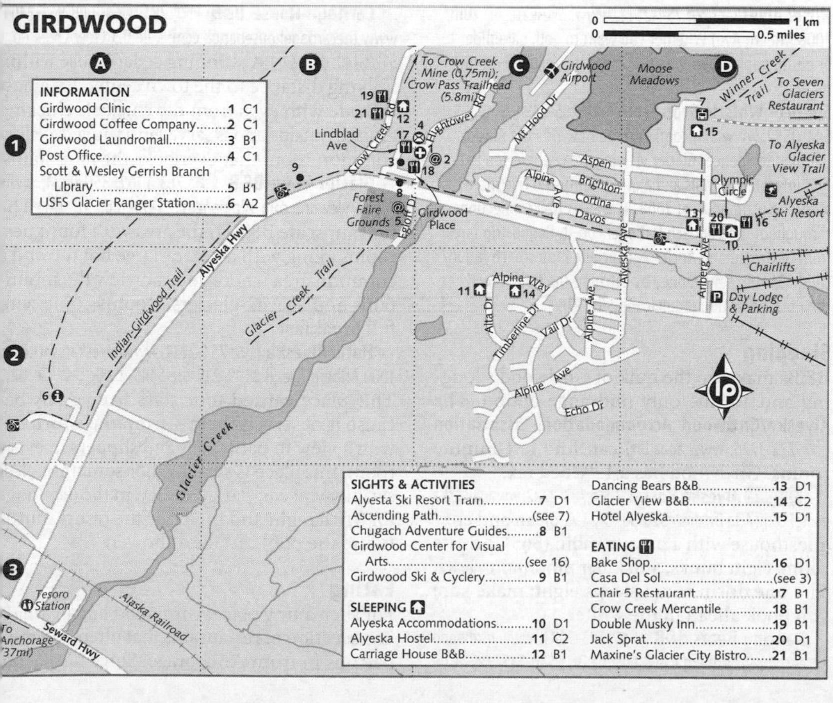

BERRY PICKING

Come late August, bears, birds and human bellies all begin hankering for a seasonal treat: wild berries. If you time it right, you can fill buckets full of several kinds of juicy berries – Southcentral grows 'em big and tasty.

Any mountainside should yield bushes full of plump blueberries, but most popular (and accessible) areas around Anchorage include the aptly named Blueberry Hill on Flattop Mountain (see p206) and the Mount Alyeska in Girdwood (see p220).

Other berries to look for:

Salmonberries These resemble raspberries in shape, but are generally a brighter color. They like moist, sunny slopes, and grow in thickets.

High- and low-bush cranberries These taste better after a frost, and you can find them on lower slopes.

Crowberries Also called 'bearberries,' this black berry grows on an evergreen mat. They're a bit seedy and tart, but good as fillers for pies or in jam.

glacier hike on Alyeska Glacier ($139), including a midnight-sun glacier trek from mid-June to mid-July that begins at 8pm. The company also offers a three-hour rock-climbing outing designed for beginners ($129).

Chugach Adventure Guides (☎ 783-4354; www.alaskanrafting.com) Offers guided raft trips through some of the whitest water in Alaska, the class V canyons of Sixmile River ($135). If you can't handle that icy roller coaster, trips through Class III rapids ($75 to $95) are available. The Guides also connect with the Spencer Whistle Stop Train (see p221).

Hotel Alyeska (☎ 754-2111, www.alyeskaresort.com; 1000 Arlberg Ave) Whether you want to golf, paraglide or photograph brown bears, this has the (expensive) tour for you.

Spencer Whistle Stop Train (☎ 265-2494, 800-544-0552; www.akrr.com) You can now ride the Alaska Railroad to Spencer Glacier viewing area, where you'll find interpretive trails and a group campsite. Five more stops are planned as of 2008, as well as trail connections throughout the Chugach National Forest. Round-trip fares from Girdwood and Anchorage include motorcoach (adult/child $95/48); save money by catching the train directly at the Portage station (adult/child $59/30).

Sleeping

B&Bs make up the bulk of Girdwood's lodging and are the only midrange option. The **Alyeska/Girdwood Accommodations Association** (☎ 222-3226; www.agaa.biz) can find last-minute rooms. Girdwood has a 12% bed tax.

our pick **Alyeska Hostel** (☎ 783-2222; www.alyeskahostel.com; Alta Dr; dm/r $20/50; ⊠) A clean and cozy guesthouse with a private cabin ($65), private room, eight bunks, and killer mountain views. The one dorm room sleeps eight; make sure you book ahead in the winter.

Dancing Bears B&B (☎ 783-3083; www.girdwoodhotel.com; cnr Arlberg Ave & Cortina Dr; r $80-115; ⊠ 💻) Operated by one of the local artists, this B&B was recently remodeled with bamboo floors. Your stay includes a guest kitchen and a hot tub, as well as a full breakfast.

Alyeska Accommodations (☎ 783-2000, 888-783-2001; www.alyeskaaccommodations.com; r $110-450) At the Alyeska Ski Area; sublets massive, privately owned (and decorated) condos, many with full kitchens, hot tubs and saunas. If you need something smaller, it also rents rooms and cabins.

Carriage House B&B (☎ 783-9464, 888-961-9464; www.thecarriagehousebandb.com; Mile 0.3 Crow Creek Rd; r $120-140; ⊠ 💻) A stunning cedar house within walking distance to the town center. Breakfast is made with eggs from the chickens clucking around outside and is served in a vaulted-ceiling common room that overlooks the mountains.

Glacier View B&B (☎ 783-1160, 350-0674; www.glacierviewbnb.com; Alpina Way; r $130-180; ⊠ 💻) The most upscale B&B in the area with four guest rooms along with an extra-large hot tub and a common area where you can view the mountains and see six glaciers. Rooms come with full breakfast.

Hotel Alyeska (☎ 754-2111, www.alyeskaresort.com, 1000 Arlberg Ave; d $199-239, ste $440-2200; ⊠ 💻 🏊) This place earned four stars from AAA because it deserved them – from the whirlpool with a view to bathrobes and slippers in every room, this place is swanky. For something less swanky you can park your RV in the day lodge for $10 a night and then ride the resort shuttle to use the pool or take a shower.

Eating

For such a tiny place, Girdwood has an amazing selection of restaurants that often pull their patrons in from Anchorage. Since it's part of the municipality of Anchorage, all restaurants and bars are refreshingly smoke-free.

Crow Creek Mercantile (☎ 783-3900; Nightower Rd; 🕑 8am-midnight Mon-Fri, from 9am Sat & Sun) Girdwood's tiny grocery store also has some ready-to-eat items.

Bake Shop (☎ 783-2831; Olympic Circle; mains $3.50-10; 🕑 7am-7pm Sun-Fri, to 8pm Sat) Always busy, this bright place serves wholesome omelets with fresh-baked breads, all of which you can enjoy at one of the large wooden tables. One of the giant cinnamon rolls is big enough to share with a friend – or not.

Casa Del Sol (☎ 783-0088; 158 Holmgren Pl; mains $7-12; 🕑 11am-10pm) Attached to the Laundromall, this small joint serves up fresh Mexican food while your laundry spins. When we visited it was in the process of getting a beer and wine license.

Jack Sprat (☎ 783-5225; Olympic Circle Dr; brunch $9-13, dinner $12-33; 🕑 4-9pm Mon-Fri, 10am-10pm Sat & Sun) Creative, fresh cuisine at the base of the ski hill. Many dishes are vegetarian-friendly, and you can enjoy your meal on the enclosed sun porch. The yam fries are massive and highly recommended.

our pick **Maxine's Glacier City Bistro** (☎ 783-1234; Crow Creek Rd; dinner $12-22; 🕑 5pm-midnight Wed-Mon) Maxine's is a Mediterranean bistro with a Girdwood feel (friendly dogs congregate outside while their owners eat). Share the *meze* or lamb *shwarma*, as they're huge, but keep the wonton tacos for yourself. Live music livens up the already colorful place on Friday and Saturday nights.

Chair 5 Restaurant (☎ 283-2500; 5 Lindblad Ave; medium pizza $13-17, dinner $15-26; 🕑 11-2am, food served to 10pm) The kind of bar and restaurant skiers love after a long day on the slopes. It features more than 60 beers, including a dozen on tap, gourmet pizzas, big burgers and a lot of blackened halibut.

Double Musky Inn (☎ 783-2822; Crow Creek Rd; dinner $20-44; 🕑 5-10pm Tue-Thu, 4:30-10pm Fri-Sun) Folks drive down from Anchorage for the New York strip encrusted in cracked peppercorn, the reason you have to wait (reservations are not accepted) two hours on weekends. The cuisine is Cajun accented, hence the masks and mardi-gras beads hanging from the ceiling. The desserts are divine.

Seven Glaciers Restaurant (☎ 754-2237; dinner $28-52; 🕑 5-9:30pm) Sitting on top of Mt Alyeska, 2300ft above sea level, is the best of Alyeska Resort's six restaurants and bars. The hotel tram will take you to an evening of gourmet dining and absolutely stunning views that include Turnagain Arm and, yes, seven glaciers. The menu is dominated by seafood; even the meat mains are offered with a side of king crab.

Getting There & Away

Although the fare is steep, you could hop on the **Alaska Railroad** (☎ 265-2494; www.akrr.com) in Anchorage for a day trip to Girdwood (one way adult/child $55/28). On its way to Seward, the *Coastal Classic* train arrives at Girdwood at 8am daily during the summer and again at 9pm for the return journey to Anchorage.

The **Girdwood Shuttle** (☎ 783-1900; www.girdwoodshuttle.com) will take you from several spots in Girdwood to Ted Stevens International Airport, downtown Anchorage, or south to Whittier ($40). **Seward Bus Lines** (☎ 563-0800; www.sewardbuslines.net) can arrange transport to Seward and Anchorage, while **Homer Stage Line** (☎ 868-3914; www.homerstageline.com) can arrange transportation throughout the Kenai Peninsula. **Magic Bus** (☎ 230-6773; www.themagicbus.com) is an accommodating charter-bus service that leaves Anchorage at 10:30am and departs Girdwood for the return trip at 6:30pm (one way/round-trip $30/50).

SOUTH OF GIRDWOOD

Seward Hwy continues southeast past Girdwood and a few nifty tourist attractions to what's left of Portage, which was destroyed by the 1964 Good Friday Earthquake and is basically a few structures sinking into the nearby mud flats.

The Wetland Observation Platform (Mile 81) features interpretive plaques on the ducks, Arctic terns, bald eagles and other wildlife inhabiting the area.

Alaska Wildlife Conservation Center (☎ 783-2025; www.awcc.org; Mile 79; adult/child $7.50/5; 🕑 8am-8pm May-Sep) is a nonprofit wildlife center where injured and rescued animals are on display. If you haven't seen a bear or moose on your trip yet, swing through.

PORTAGE GLACIER

Portage Glacier Access Rd leaves Seward Hwy at Mile 79, continuing 5.4 miles to the **Begich-Boggs Visitors Center** (☎ 783-2326; 🕑 9am-6pm) en route to Whittier (see p247), on the other side of the Anton Memorial Tunnel.

The building, with its observation decks and telescopes, was designed to provide great views of Portage Glacier. But ironically (and to the dismay of thousands of tourists) the glacier has retreated so fast you can no longer see it from the center. Still, inside are neat high-tech wildlife displays and the excellent movie, *Voices from the Ice* (admission $1, shown every 30 minutes).

Most people view the glacier through **Gray Line** (☎ 277-5581), whose cruise boat MV *Ptarmigan* departs from a dock near the Begich-Boggs Center five times daily in June to September for a trip to the face of it. It's a costly one-hour cruise; adult/child $29/14.50 or $69/34.50 with transportation from Anchorage. If you have a pair of hiking boots, Portage Pass Trail, a mile-long trek to the pass, will provide a good view of Portage Glacier. The trail begins near the tunnel on the Whittier side, so it's a $12-per-car fare to drive through and then return.

The brand-new multi-use Trail of Blue Ice parallels Portage Glacier Access Rd and meanders through forest on a wide gravel (and occasionally boardwalk) trail. When we visited in 2008 sections were still being constructed, though eventually the trail will connect Portage Lake to the Seward Highway.

Another interesting hike is Byron Glacier View Trail, a single, flat mile to an unusually ice worm-infested snowfield and grand glacier views.

There are two USFS campgrounds. **Black Bear Campground** (Mile 3.7 Portage Glacier Access Rd; sites $14) is beautiful and woodsy – and caters more to tent campers – while **Williwaw Campground** (Mile 4.3 Portage Glacier Access Rd; s/d $28) is stunningly located beneath Explorer Glacier and receives more of an RV crowd. Both campgrounds are extremely popular, although sites at Williwaw can be reserved in advance through **Recreation.gov** (☎ 877-444-6777, 518-885-3639; www.recreation.gov).

NORTH OF ANCHORAGE

As you drive out of Anchorage, you'll soon parallel Knik Arm, while the Chugach Mountains stay to your right. Small communities dot either side of the road, but Eagle River and Eklutna offer the best access to the mountains. Both communities are worthy of a day trip from Anchorage, but to escape the hustle of the city, use these small towns as a base for exploring both Anchorage and the wilds around it.

GLENN HIGHWAY

In Anchorage, 5th Ave becomes Glenn Hwy, running 189 miles through Palmer, where it makes a junction with the George Parks Hwy, to Glennallen and the Richardson Hwy. Milepost distances are measured from Anchorage.

At Mile 11.5 of Glenn Hwy is **Eagle River Campground** (☎ 694-7982; Hiland Rd exit; sites $15), with beautiful walk-in sites. The river runs closest to the shady sites in the 'Rapids' section. Keep in mind this is one of the most popular campsites in the state and half the sites can be reserved up to a year in advance.

Eagle River

pop 30,000

At Mile 13.4 of Glenn Hwy is the exit to Old Glenn Hwy, which takes you through the bedroom communities of Eagle River and Chugiak. Eagle River has a couple of plazas and just about every business you'll need. The Bear Paw Festival, held here in July, is worth the trip just for the 'Slippery Salmon Olympics,' which involves racing with a hula hoop, serving tray and, of course, a large dead fish. Most people, however, come here for the drive down Eagle River Rd.

INFORMATION

Acute Family Medicine Clinic (☎ 622-4325; 11470 Business Blvd; 🕒 9am-7pm Mon-Fri, 9am-5pm Sat & Sun) Offers walk-in service.

Chugiak-Eagle River Chamber of Commerce (☎ 694-4702; www.cer.org; 11401 Old Glenn Hwy; 🕒 9am-4pm) Is located in the Eagle River Shopping Mall and has lots of pamphlets and free maps of town.

Key Bank (☎ 694-4464; 10928 Eagle River Rd) Also has an ATM.

Laundry Basket (☎ 694-8670; 12110 Business Blvd; 🕒 7am-10pm Mon-Sat, 8am-9pm Sun) Located in the Regional Park Plaza.

SIGHTS & ACTIVITIES

Eagle River Road

This stunning sidetrip into the heart of the Chugach Mountains follows the Eagle River for 13 miles. The road is paved and winding, and at Mile 7.4 there is a put-in for rafts to float the Class I and II section of the river. Class III and IV rapids are located upstream: put in at Echo Bend, which is accessed by the 3-mile footpath from the Eagle River Nature Center. The traditional pullout point is at Eagle Creek Loop Bridge. **Lifetime Adventures** (☎ 746-4644, 694-7982;

Eagle River Campground) guides rafts down the Class III portions of Eagle River (per person $30).

The road ends at the **Eagle River Nature Center** (☎ 694-2108; www.ernc.org; 32750 Eagle River Rd; admission per vehicle $5; 🕑 10am-5pm Sun-Thu, to 7pm Fri & Sat). The log-cabin center offers wildlife displays, telescopes for finding Dall sheep, guided hikes on most Saturday and Sundays, and heaps of programs for kids.

Hiking

Several trails depart from the Eagle River Nature Center, with **Rodak Nature Trail** being the easiest. Kids will love the mile-long interpretive path, as it swings by an impressive overlook straddling a salmon stream and a huge beaver dam. Albert Loop Trail is a slightly more challenging 3-mile hike through boreal forest and along Eagle River.

The **National Historic Iditarod Trail** is a 26-mile trek used by gold miners and sled-dog teams until 1918, when the Alaska Railroad was finished. It's a three-day hike through superb mountain scenery to Girdwood and the region's best backpack adventure. For details see Wilderness Hikes & Paddles (p93).

For a shorter outing you can turn around at the Perch, a very large rock in the middle of wonderland, then backtrack to the Dew Mound Trail at Echo Bend and loop back to the Nature Center, making this a scenic 8-mile trip. Pitch a tent at Rapids Camp (Mile 1.7) or Echo Bend (Mile 3), or rent one of two yurts ($65 per night) close by.

Thunderbird Falls, closer to Eklutna, is a rewarding 2-mile walk with a gorgeous little waterfall for the grand finale. Anchorage's People Mover buses 76 and 102 stop at the trailhead, off Thunderbird Falls exit of Glenn Hwy.

SLEEPING & EATING

Eagle River has a 12% bed tax, and all restaurants are smoke-free.

Eagle River Motel (☎ 694-5000, 866-256-6835; www.eaglerivermotel.com; 11111 Old Eagle River Rd; s $89-139, d $94-143; 💻) Rooms are equipped with microwaves and refrigerators, and it's a better deal than you'd find in Anchorage.

Alaska Chalet B&B (☎ 694-1528, 877-694-1528; www.alaskachaletbb.com; 11031 Gulkana Cr; r/ste $90/135; ⊠ 💻) In a small neighborhood within walking distance of downtown Eagle River, this is a European-style B&B. The clean guest quarters are separate from the main house and include kitchenettes, and the host speaks German.

Falling Water Creek B&B (☎ 696-4726; 2947 Misty Mountain Rd; r $100-125; ⊠ 💻) In a spacious log home with sweeping views of Eagle River valley and the Chugach. One room has the view, the other has sounds of the nearby creek.

Jitters (☎ 694-5487; 11401 Old Glenn Hwy; quick eats $3-8; 🕑 5:30am-9pm Mon-Fri, 6:30am-7pm Sat, from 8am Sun) The best place to stop after a rainy hike. It serves up soup, sandwiches and pastries in a warm environment; live music is often playing throughout the day.

Haute Quarter Grill (☎ 622-4745; 11221 Old Glenn Hwy; dinner $16-30; 🕑 5-9:30pm Tue-Sat) A highly recommended splurge, it offers a lot of gourmet for your dollar – try the giant scallops that are grilled in a roasted walnut marinade.

Eklutna

pop 335

This 350-year-old Alaska Native village is just west of the Eklutna Lake Rd exit, Mile 26.5 of Glenn Hwy. One of the most interesting anthropological sites in the region is preserved at **Eklutna Village Historical Park** (☎ 688-6026; tour $3; 🕑 10am-4pm), where the uneasy marriage of the Athabascan and Russian Orthodox cultures is enshrined. The interior of St Nicholas Church is modeled after Noah's arc while outside, outdoor altars abound, including a heartfelt lean-to for St Herman, patron saint of Alaska. The most revealing structures, however, are the 80 brightly colored spirit boxes in the nearby Denáina Athabascan cemetery. Invest your time in one of the half-hour tours.

Eklutna Lake State Recreation Area (sites $10) is 10 long, bumpy miles east on Eklutna Lake Rd. It's worth every minute once the sky suddenly opens, unveiling a stunning valley with glacier-and-peak-ringed Eklutna Lake, the largest body of water in Chugach State Park, at its center.

Rochelle's Ice Cream & Cheely's General Store (☎ 688-6201, 800-764-6201; www.goalaskan.com; Eklutna Lake Rd; cabin/r $50/70; 🕑 9am-9pm Sun-Thu, to 10pm Fri & Sat) has laundry, showers, and groceries. The Eklutna room is cozy and has a lake view, while the cabins are extremely basic, without electricity or running water.

ACTIVITIES

Eklutna Lake State Recreation Area in Chugach State Park is a recreational paradise, including more than 27 miles of hiking and mountain-biking trails that can be accessed from the campground.

Lakeside Trail is a flat 13-miles to the other end of the lake, with two excellent free campsites: Eklutna Alex Campground (Mile 9) and Kanchee Campground (Mile 11). East Fork Trail diverts from the main trail at Mile 10.5 and it runs another 5.5 miles to a great view of Mt Bashful, the tallest mountain (8005ft) in the park. Keep going an easy 1 mile past the Lakeside Trail terminus to view the receding Eklutna Glacier. ATVs can use the trails Sunday through Wednesday, hikers and bikers anytime.

Bold Ridge Trail is a steep 3.5-mile spur hike that begins 5 miles along the Lakeshore Trail and continues to the alpine area below Bold Peak (7522ft) for views of the valley, Eklutna Glacier and even Knik Arm. People with the energy can scramble up nearby ridges. Plan on two hours to climb the trail and an hour for the return. To actually climb Bold Peak requires serious equipment.

Twin Peaks Trail is shorter (3.5 miles from the parking lot), but just as steep. It takes you through lush forest into alpine meadows presided over by the imposing eponymous peaks. Berries, wildlife and great lake views make scrambling toward the top downright enjoyable.

The lake makes for great paddling. **Lifetime Adventures** (☎ 746-4644; www.lifetimeadventures.net; Eklutna Lake State Recreation Area; 10am-6pm Sun-Fri, to 8pm Sat) rents single kayaks (half-/full day $30/50) and doubles for $5 more. It also rents mountain bikes (half-/full day $25/35) and offers a fun Paddle & Pedal rental where you kayak down the lake and then ride a mountain bike back ($75 per person).

PALMER

pop 5500

Filled with old farming-related buildings, Palmer at times feels more like the Midwest than Alaska, except that it's ringed by mountains. Many downtown venues exude 1930s ambience, with antique furniture and wood floors. Sure, Palmer is subjected to the same suburban sprawl as anywhere else, but its charm lies in its unique history and living agricultural community. For those who want to skip the city hassles and high prices of Anchorage, Palmer is an excellent option with just enough choices in lodging, restaurants and sights to keep you satisfied for a day or two.

From Eklutna Lake Rd, Glenn Hwy continues north, crossing Knik and Matanuska Rivers at the northern end of Cook Inlet, and at Mile 35.3 reaching a major junction with the George Parks Hwy. At this point, Glenn Hwy curves sharply to the east and heads into Palmer, 7 miles away. If you're driving, a much more scenic way to reach Palmer is to leave Glenn Hwy just before it crosses Knik River and follow Old Glenn Hwy into town.

History

Born during President Roosevelt's New Deal, Palmer was one of the great social experiments in an era when human nature was believed infinitely flexible. The mission was to transplant 200 farming families, who were refugees from the Depression-era dustbowl (the worst agricultural disaster in US history), to Alaska, where they would cultivate a new agricultural economy.

Trainloads of Midwesterners and their Sears & Roebuck furniture were deposited in the Matanuska and Susitna valleys, both deemed suitable by the government for such endeavors. Nearly everything was imported, from building materials (and plans) to teachers. Soil rich by Alaskan standards enjoyed a growing season just long enough for cool-weather grains and certain vegetables. There was little margin for error, however, and any unexpected frost could destroy an entire year of seed and sweat.

Original buildings stand throughout Palmer, many of which have been refurbished and maintain their hearty wooden farm feel. Descendents of the original colonists, who refer to themselves as Colony children or grandchildren, still inhabit Palmer and have wonderful stories to tell. Stop in at the Colony House Museum (opposite) for an idea of what the big move was like for the families transplanted here.

Information

Alaskana Bookstore (☎ 745-8695; 564 S Denali St; noon-5:30pm Fri-Sun) Huge selection of used and rare, state-related tomes.

Fireside Books (☎ 745-2665; 720 S Alaska St; 10am-7pm Mon-Sat, noon-4pm Sun;) New and used books, many locally oriented, and a good selection of maps.

Laundry Depot (☎ 745-3008; 127 S Alaska St; 8am-10pm;) Shower ($4.50 per 20 minutes) or access the internet ($4 per 30 minutes) while you launder.

Mat-Su Regional Hospital (☎ 861-6000; 2500 S Woodworth Loop) Gleaming and new, near the intersection of the Parks and Glenn Hwys.

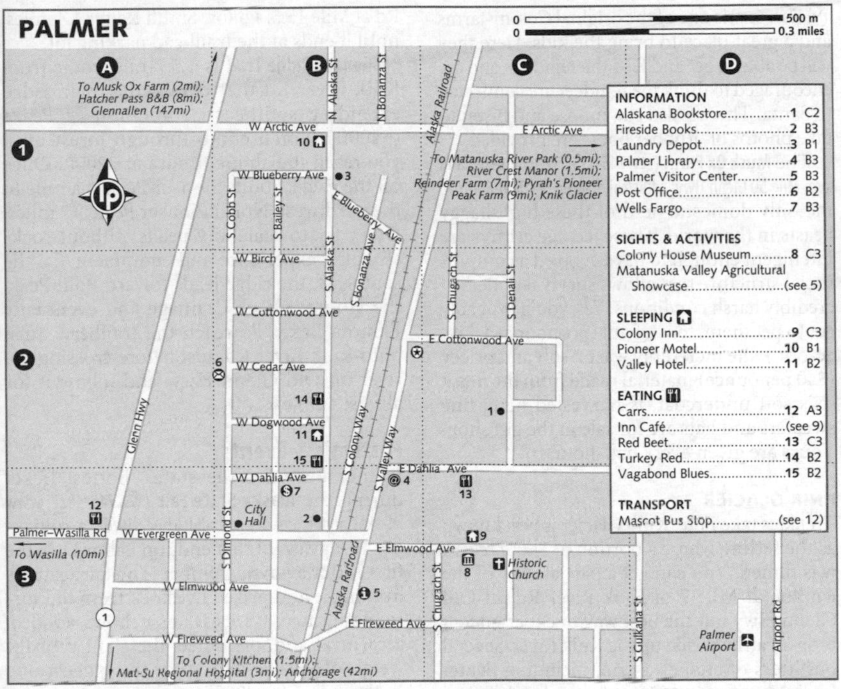

Palmer Library (☎ 745-4690; 655 S Valley Way; ⏰ noon-6pm Mon-Fri, 10am-2pm Sat; 💻) An excellent library with free internet access.

Palmer Visitor Center (☎ 745-2880; www.palmerchamber.org; 723 S Valley Way; ⏰ 9am-6pm) In the log cabin downtown; has pamphlets, maps of the town, free coffee, a booking phone, and a small collection of colonial-era tools and other artifacts.

Post office (cnr S Cobb St & W Cedar Ave)

Wells Fargo (☎ 745-2161; 705 S Bailey St) Lets you drain that account.

Sights & Activities

Outside the visitors center is **Matanuska Valley Agricultural Showcase** (⏰ 8am-7pm Jun-Aug), a garden featuring flowers and the area's famous oversized vegetables. But you have to be passing through in August if you want to see a cabbage bigger than a basketball. Every Friday during summer is **Friday Fling** (⏰ 11am-6pm Jun-Aug), an open-air market with local produce, art, crafts, food and live music.

The friendly **Colony House Museum** (☎ 745-1935; 316 E Elmwood Ave; adult/child $2/1; ⏰ 10am-4pm Tue-Sun) is run by Colony children, and their enthusiasm for Palmer's history is evident. Take the time for a guided tour, and you'll leave with an appreciation of the enormity of the colonizing project. The museum itself was a 'Colony Farm House' built during the original settlement of Palmer, and its eight rooms are still furnished with artifacts and stories from that era. To bring the living-room piano to Alaska, members of one pioneer family left behind their luggage and stuffed their clothes in it, the only way to make their weight allotment.

FARMS

If you have a vehicle, cruise through Palmer's back roads past original Colony farms. Go northeast 9 miles on Glenn Hwy and hop on Farm Loop Rd; look for vegetable stands if you're passing through here from mid- to late summer. South of Palmer, Pyrah's **Pioneer Peak Farm** (☎ 745-4511; Mile 2.8 Bodenberg Loop Rd; ⏰ 9am-5pm Mon, to 9pm Tue-Sat) is the largest pick-your-own-vegetables place in the Mat-Su Valley, with would-be farmers in the fields from July to early October picking everything from peas and potatoes to carrots and cabbages.

The **Reindeer Farm** (☎ 745-4000; www.reindeerfarm.com; Mile 11.5 Old Glenn Hwy; adult/child $6/4;

(⏰ 10am-6pm) is one of the original Colony farms and a great place to bring the kids. Here they will be able to pet and feed the reindeer, and are encouraged to think the reindeer are connected to Santa. There's also elk, moose and bison to take photos of. Rubber boots are provided.

The **Musk Ox Farm** (☎ 745-4151; www.muskoxfarm.org; Mile 50 Glenn Hwy; adult/child $8/6; ⏰ 9am-6pm) is the only domestic herd of these big, shaggy beasts in the world. These ice-age critters are intelligent enough to have evolved a complex social structure that allows survival under incredibly harsh conditions. Yes, you'll probably get to pet them, too. Qiviut (pronounced 'kiv-ee-oot'), the incredibly warm, soft and pricey ($40 per ounce) material made from the musk ox's soft undercoat, is harvested here; fine sweaters and hats are for sale in the gift shop. Tours are given every half-hour.

KNIK GLACIER

Trekkies take note: Knik Glacier is best known as the setting where a portion of *Star Trek VI* was filmed. You can get a partial view of the ice floe at Mile 7 of Knik River Rd off Old Glenn Hwy but the best way to experience it is on an airboat ride up the Knik River. Several outfitters offer such a trip, including **Hunter Creek Adventures** (☎ 746-1577; www.knikglacier.com; 4hr tour $99), which has tours departing at 10am and 2pm daily and include a cookout within view of the ice.

HIKING

The best hike near Palmer is the berry-lined climb to the top of 3720ft Lazy Mountain. The 2.5-mile trail is steep at times, but makes for a pleasant trek that ends in an alpine setting with good views of Matanuska Valley farms. Take Old Glenn Hwy across the Matanuska River, turn left onto Clark-Wolverine Rd and then right onto Huntly Rd; follow it to the Equestrian Center parking lot and trailhead, marked 'Foot Trail.' Plan on three to five hours for the round-trip.

The 8-mile **Matanuska Peak Trail** is also often steep. It traverses the south slope of Lazy Mountain, above the McRoberts Creek Valley. As you ascend Matanuska Peak, you'll climb 5670ft in 4 miles – be prepared for a long day. You'll be richly rewarded for your hard work, however, by the views of the Knik and Matanuska Rivers, as well as Cook Inlet. To reach the trailhead, take Old Glenn Hwy from Palmer toward Butte and turn left onto Smith Rd at Mile 15.5. Follow Smith Rd for 1.4 miles, until it ends at the trailhead parking lot.

Pioneer Ridge Trail is a 5.7-mile route from Knik River Rd that climbs the main ridge extending southeast from Pioneer Peaks (6400ft). You'll climb through forest until you reach the alpine tundra at 3200ft. Once on the ridge, South Pioneer Peak is a mile to the northwest, North Pioneer Peak is 2 miles. Don't try to scale any peaks without rock-climbing experience and equipment. To the southeast, the ridge leads toward Bold Peak, the Hunter Creek drainage and eventually Eklutna Lake. To reach the trailhead, turn onto Knik River Rd, just before crossing the river on Old Glenn Hwy, and follow it for almost 4 miles.

Festivals & Events

Palmer becomes the state's hottest ticket during the **Alaska State Fair** (☎ 745-4827; www.alaskastatefair.org; per day adult/child $10/6), a rollicking 12-day event that ends on Labor Day, the first Monday in September. The fair features live music and prized livestock from the surrounding area, as well as horse shows, a rodeo, a carnival and, of course, the giant cabbage weigh-off to see who grew the biggest one in the valley (the 2008 winner weighed in at 73.4lb – small by Palmer standards). If greased pigs, Spam-sponsored recipe contests and the Great Alaskan Husband Holler contest aren't enough to get you here, try this: berry pie cook-offs.

The fairground is also home to the **Mat-Su Miners** (☎ 745-6401; www.matsuminers.org; adult/child $4/2), another semipro team of the Alaska Baseball League that plays against clubs like Fairbanks Goldpanners and the Anchorage Bucs. Until 1980 the Palmer players were the Valley Green Giants but changed their name for obvious reasons.

Sleeping

If you arrive late, the Palmer Visitor Center has a courtesy phone outside with direct lines connected to area accommodations. Add 8% tax to the prices here.

Matanuska River Park (☎ 745-9631; Mile 17.5 Old Glenn Hwy; sites camp/RV $10/15) Run by Parks & Rec and less than a half-mile east of town, this place lets you pitch a tent or park a trailer. Some sites are wooded and there is a series of trails that winds around ponds and along the Matanuska River.

Pioneer Motel (☎ 745-3425; 124 W Arctic Ave; r $73-84) Your best budget option. The rooms are nicer than the outside appearance indicates and come with microwaves, coffeemakers and refrigerators. Quilt-like comforters brighten the rooms.

Hatcher Pass B&B (☎ 745-6788; www.hatcherpassbb.com; Mile 6.6 Palmer-Fishhook Rd; cabin s/d $79/89; ☒ ☐) If you have wheels you can rent a cabin at several places on the way to Hatcher Pass. This B&B, 6 miles from Palmer, offers five button-cute log cabins with bath, kitchenette and TV. It's also pet-friendly.

River Crest Manor (☎ 746-6214; www.rivercrestmanor.com; 2655 Old Glenn Hwy; r $85-95; ☒ ☐) A beautiful, expansive home that provides three guest rooms across the road from the Matanuska River. It's about 1.5 miles from downtown Palmer.

Valley Hotel (☎ 745-3330, Alaska only 800-478-7666; 606 S Alaska St; r $90-120; ☒ ☐) With small rooms and thin walls, this isn't the best deal in town but it's certainly adequate. Its Caboose Lounge is a friendly pub to end a day, and the 24-hour café is a great place to start or end one.

our pick **Colony Inn** (☎ 745-3330; 325 E Elmwood; s/d $100/130; ☒ ☐) What was constructed in 1935 as the Matanuska Colony Teacher's Dorm is now Palmer's nicest lodge. The 12 rooms are spacious, especially the corner rooms, well-kept and equipped with TVs, pedestal sinks, and whirlpool tubs. There's an inviting parlor for reading, furnished with antiques. Register at the Valley Hotel.

Eating

Hearty cuisine is growing like cabbage in Palmer, and it's no longer necessary to drive to Anchorage for an upscale meal.

Carrs (☎ 745-7505; 535 W Evergreen; 24hr) Stock up for your day hike here – they've got groceries, a deli, and a salad bar stocked in late summer with Mat-Su's finest.

Vagabond Blues (☎ 745-2233; 642 S Alaska St; light meals $4-7; 7am-9pm Mon-Sat, 8am-6pm Sun) A cozy, gay-friendly coffee shop, with local art on the walls and often live music at night. It has healthy, homemade quiches, soups and salads.

Colony Kitchen (☎ 746-4600; 1890 Glenn Hwy; breakfast $6-12, dinner $11-20; 6am-10pm) If you like your breakfast big, you'll be stoked: not only is your most important meal huge, but they serve it all day. Diner dinners include fried chicken, meat loaf and chicken fried steak. You'll eat beneath stuffed birds suspended from the ceiling (hence its other name, the Noisy Goose Café).

Inn Café (☎ 746-6118; 325 E Elmwood; sandwiches $6-10, brunch $15; 11am-2pm Mon-Fri, 9am-2pm Sun) This former teacher's dorm now houses a pleasant restaurant with the kind of creaky wood-floored ambience expected in Palmer. Sandwiches and salads are served on weekdays, and brunch is on Sunday.

Turkey Red (☎ 746-5544; 550 S Alaska St; lunch $7-11, dinner $11-27; 8am-9pm Mon-Sat, to 10pm Sat) Palmer's classiest – and its most expensive – joint is an upscale café serving fresh dishes made from scratch, homemade dessert, and beer and wine. Vegetarians won't be disappointed, and much of the produce is organic and locally grown.

our pick **Red Beet** (☎ 745-4050; 320 E Dahlia; lunch $11; 11:30am-late afternoon) Housed in the renovated Palmer Trading Post, this excellent restaurant serves a daily three-course set menu with a dessert option. The food is organic and/or locally grown, and the coffee French-pressed. It's worth it alone just to sit in the wide, wood building, which smells like baking bread and has a view into the open kitchen.

Getting There & Around

The Mat-Su Community Transit system, **Mascot** (☎ 376-5000; www.matsutransit.com; single ride/day pass $2.50/6), makes six trips daily between Wasilla and Palmer and three commuter runs from the Valley to the Transit Center in Anchorage. If staying in Anchorage you can use the bus for a cheap day trip to Palmer, or vice versa. All buses stop at Carrs.

Alaska Cab (☎ 746-2727) and **Mat-Su Taxi** (☎ 373-5861) both provide service around town, as well as to Wasilla ($25 to $35) and Anchorage ($65 to $75).

WASILLA

pop 7028

Just 7 miles north of the Glenn Hwy/George Parks Hwy junction, Wasilla was a sleepy little town in the 1970s that served local farmers. Today it's best known to outsiders as the hometown of 2008 Republican Vice Presidential candidate Sarah Palin, who served as its mayor from 1996 to 2002. Though the major news networks have disappeared from Wasilla's street, Palin still serves as Governor of Alaska and bounces between here and Juneau.

DETOUR: HATCHER PASS

A side-trip from Palmer (or even a base) is the photogenic Hatcher Pass. This alpine passage cuts through the Talkeetna Mountains and leads to meadows, ridges and glaciers. Gold was the first treasure people found here; today it's footpaths, abandoned mines and popular climbs that outshine the precious metal.

The main attraction of Hatcher Pass is 272-acre **Independence Mine State Historical Park** (Mile 18 Hatcher Pass Rd; admission per vehicle $5), a huge, abandoned gold mine sprawled out in an alpine valley. The 1930s facility, built by the Alaska-Pacific Mining Company (APC), was for 10 years the second-most-productive hardrock goldmine in Alaska. At its peak, in 1941, APC employed 204 workers here, blasted almost 12 miles of tunnels and recovered 34,416oz of gold, today worth almost $18 million. The mine was finally abandoned in 1955.

Today you can explore the structures, hike several trails and take in the stunning views at Hatcher Pass. The **visitors center** (☎ 745-2827; ⌚ 11am-7pm) has a map of the park, a simulated mining tunnel, displays on the ways to mine gold (panning, placer mining and hardrock) and guided tours ($5 per person, 1pm and 3pm). From the center, follow Hardrock Trail past the dilapidated buildings, which include bunkhouses and a mill complex that is built into the side of the mountain and looks like an avalanche of falling timber. Make an effort to climb up the trail to the water tunnel portal, where there is a great view of the entire complex and a blast of cold air pouring out of the mountain.

Hatcher Pass also offers some of the best alpine hiking in the Mat-Su areas. The easy, beautiful **Gold Mint Trail** begins at a parking lot across from Motherlode Lodge, at Mile 14 Fishhook-Willow Rd. The trail follows the Little Susitna River into a gently sloping mountain valley and within 3 miles you spot the ruins of Lonesome Mine. Keep hiking and you'll eventually reach Mint Glacier.

With two alpine lakes, lots of waterfalls, glaciers and towering walls of granite, the 7-mile **Reed Lakes Trail** (9 miles to the upper lake) is worth the climb, which includes some serious scrambling. Once you reach upper Reed Lake continue for a mile to **Bomber Glacier**, where the ruin of a B-29 bomber lies in memorial to six men who perished there in a 1957 crash. A mile past Motherlode Lodge, a road to Archangel Valley splits off from Fishhook-Willow Rd and leads to the Reed Lakes trailhead, a wide road. If you've got a 4WD, you can (theoretically) drive the first 3 miles of the **Craigie Creek Trail**, posted along the Fishhook-Willow Rd just west of Hatcher Pass. It's better, however, to walk the gently climbing old road up a valley and past several abandoned mining operations to the head of the creek. It then becomes a very steep trail for 3 miles to Dogsled Pass, where you can access several wilderness trails into the Talkeetna Mountains.

If the weather is nice and you have the funds it's hard to pass up spending the night at the pass. **Motherlode Lodge** (☎ 688-4051, 866-369-4050; www.motherlodelodge.com; Mile 14 Hatcher Pass Rd; r $135; ⊠) was originally built in the 1930s as part of the local mining operation. It has since been renovated into an inn with a restaurant and bar where every stool gives way to views of the mountains. **Hatcher Pass Lodge** (☎ 745-5897; www.hatcherpasslodge.com; Mile 17.5 Hatcher Pass Rd; r/cabins $95/165; ⊠), inside the state park, is a highly recommended splurge. Aside from spectacular views at 3000ft, the lodge has seven cabins, three rooms, a (pricey) restaurant and bar, and a sauna built over a rushing mountain stream.

But before Wasilla made political news, it was defined by the urban sprawl that reached it in the 1980s. From 1980 to 1983 the population of Wasilla doubled as Alaskans who wanted to commute to Anchorage moved in. Today it's a full-fledged bedroom community of the big city to the south. Shopping centers and businesses – including the biggest Wal-Mart in the state – have sprouted like weeds along the highway. If you need services – banks, auto mechanics etc – you'll find them here and should take advantage of them, as things get sketchier and more expensive between here and Fairbanks.

Information

Digital Cup (☎ 373-2727; 545 S Knik-Goose Bay Rd; per 30min $2; ⌚ 9am-8pm Mon-Thu, to 10pm Fri & Sat, noon-8pm Sun; 💻) Offers free wireless and steaming-hot coffee.

Dorothy Page Museum & Visitor Center (☎ 373-9071; 323 Main St; museum adult/child $3/free; 9am-5pm Mon-Sat) In town is this three-room museum named after the woman known as 'the Mother of the Iditarod.'

Matanuska-Susitna Visitors Center (☎ 746-5000; www.alaskavisit.com; Mile 35.5 George Parks Hwy; 8:30am- 6:30pm) This large lodge sits near the junction of the Parks and Glenn Hwys and has a great view of the mountains surrounding Knik Inlet from its outdoor deck. Inside are racks of area information.

Sights & Activities

For years, Wasilla served as the official 'restart' of the Iditarod, the famous 1100-mile dogsled race to Nome. Warmer winters have moved the start further north so many times that in 2008 it was officially moved to Willow. The **Iditarod Trail Headquarters** (☎ 376-5155; www.iditarod.com; Mile 2.2 Knik Rd; admission free; 8am-7pm) is still housed near Wasilla, however. This log-cabin museum's most unusual exhibit is Togo, the famous sled dog that led his team across trackless Norton Sound to deliver serum to diphtheria-threatened Nome in 1925 – a journey that gave rise to today's Iditarod. He's been stuffed and is now on display, rather unceremoniously, in the corner. Outside, you can get a short sled-dog ride (rides $10, 9am-5pm) on a wheeled dogsled, or just hold a lovable sled-dog puppy for free. For more on the Iditarod, see p58.

Sleeping & Eating

Wasilla has a 7.5% bed and sales tax.

Lake Lucille Park (☎ 745-9631; Mile 2.4 Knik Rd; sites $10) This park is the closest campground. The 64 sites share rest rooms, a shelter, lake access, and a network of trails.

Windbreak Hotel (☎ 376-4209; 2201 E George Parks Hwy; s/d $85/95; ⊠ 💻) Right off the highway, this is Wasilla's most affordable accommodations, with 10 rooms, private baths, a friendly pub and a good café.

Alaska Kozey Cabins (☎ 376-3190; 351 E Spruce Ave; d $129; ⊠ 💻) For a night in the woods, check out these six *kozey* log cabins on five private acres. The cabins sleep up to six ($20 for each additional person) and are equipped with wi-fi, a kitchen, cable TV and a private bath.

Teeland's Mercantile (☎ 357-5633; 495 E Herning Ave; lunch $7-10; lunch) Housed in the first general store in the valley, Teeland's has soup, salads, sandwiches and coffee.

Great Bear Brewing Co (☎ 373-4782; 238 N Boundary St; burgers $8-11, dinner $16-22; 11am-midnight) Wasilla's eatery of choice with great homebrewed ales (including the 'Valley Trash Blonde'), tasty food and a dozen creative burgers. Tuesday is pasta-bar night.

Getting There & Around

BUS

Mascot (Mat-Su Community Transit; ☎ 376-5000; www.matsutransit.com; single ride/day pass $2.50/6) makes six trips daily to Palmer, with buses in Wasilla departing from both the Wal-Mart and Carrs. There are three commuter runs to Transit Center in Anchorage that depart Wasilla Wal-Mart at 5:55am, 9:30am, and 4:30pm.

CAR

A rental car in Wasilla is cheaper than Anchorage and it's the best way to reach Hatcher Pass (opposite). **Valley Car Rental** (☎ 775-2880; 435 S Knik St) is in downtown Wasilla and has compacts for $45 (plus 12.5% tax) a day with unlimited mileage.

TRAIN

The **Alaska Railroad** (☎ Anchorage 265-2494, 800-544-0552; www.alaskarailroad.com) stops at Wasilla en route from Anchorage to Denali at 9:45am daily in summer *if* there are paid reservations (otherwise it just blows on by). Fare is $135 to Denali and $194 to Fairbanks. The train from Fairbanks arrives at 6:05pm; the fare to (or from) Anchorage is $50. Any of the bus services to Denali will drop you off in town en route far cheaper than the train.

Prince William Sound

Enclosed in a jagged-edged circle and infused with fjords and glaciers, Prince William Sound is a stunner. With only three cities, the 15,000 sq mile region is mostly wilderness packed with quiet coves and rainy islands. It's a paddler's dream – as if the scenery wasn't enough, Ma Nature threw in whales, sea lions, harbor seals, eagles, Dall sheep, mountain goats and bears.

Despite sharing a similar environment, Prince William Sound's three cities couldn't be more different. Each arose from a different need and blossomed in a different manner.

Valdez is dominated by slopes, including near-vertical crags, luring outdoor extremists, and the distant North Slope, from which the Trans-Alaska Pipeline originates. The mountain-ringed waters act as a highway for oil tankers, while the Columbia Glacier beckons paddlers like a siren.

Earthy Cordova is defiant in its refusal to sell out. Isolated from roads, cruise ships and oil money, Cordovans are doing just fine. The salmon-rich ocean fuels the economy, and when they need to hit the open road they head out to the Copper River Hwy, a spectacular gravel road that spins past glaciers and over one of the largest continuous wetlands on earth.

In contrast, Whittier is a living relic of WWII: a small town created solely as a military hideout. Practically overshadowed by the mountains that kept it safe during the war, Whittier is accessible by ferry or by a 2.5-mile tunnel, from which you emerge to find yourself improbably surrounded by crashing waterfalls, lofty peaks and Soviet-style architecture.

HIGHLIGHTS

- **Ultimate calves** – watching ice tumble from the face of supergiant Columbia Glacier (p238) near Valdez, and super-active Childs Glacier (p248) near Cordova
- **Best experience on public transportation** (p234) – watching orcas and Dall porpoises from a cozy booth on an Alaska Marine Highway ferry
- **Most carefree highway** (p248) – spinning down the 50-mile Copper River Hwy across braided rivers and glowing lupine
- **Deepest drive** (p252) – steering through the Anton Anderson Memorial Tunnel to Whittier
- **Biggest vertical drop** (p238) – strapping on your skis and letting go in the Chugach Mountains around Valdez, where extreme skiing is not for the fainthearted

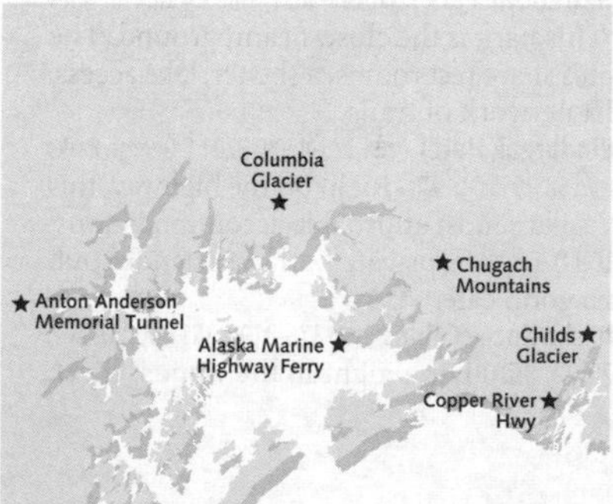

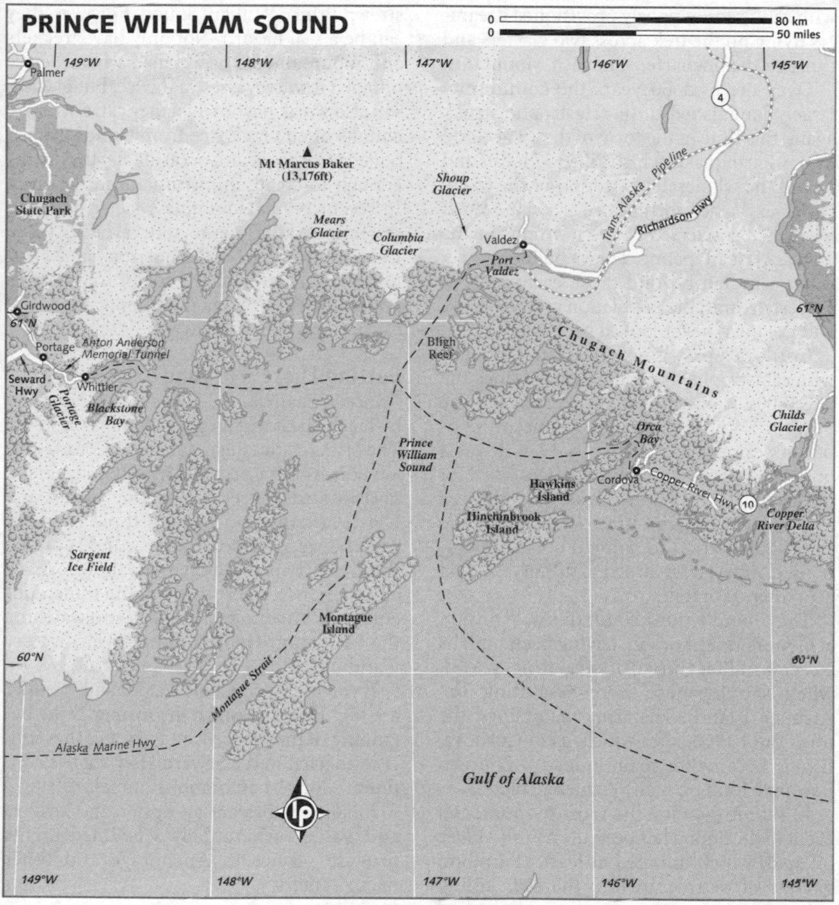

Climate

It's wet here – except in the winter, when it's snowy. That's right, precipitation is the norm in Prince William Sound, where clouds, bloated with moisture from crossing the Pacific, crash into the Chugach Mountains and dump their watery burden. In summer, Valdez is the driest of the towns; Whittier is by far the wettest. In all communities, average July daytime temperatures are barely above 60°F. So no matter what your travel plans are, pack your fleece and some bombproof wet-weather gear. And as the raindrops fall, just remember that if it wasn't for precipitation, this place wouldn't be the glacier-carved, snowcapped, forest-clad Eden that it is.

History

Prince William Sound was long a crossroads of Alaska Native cultures; the region has been inhabited at various times by coastal Chugach Inuit people, Athabascans originally from the Interior and Tlingits who traveled up from Alaska's panhandle. The first European to arrive was Vitus Bering, a Danish navigator sailing for the tsar of Russia, who anchored his ship near Kayak Island, east of Copper River, in 1741.

The Sound's three major towns have rather divergent modern histories. Valdez was settled in 1897, when 4000 gold prospectors took what had been billed as the 'All-American Route' to the Klondike goldfields. It turned out to be one of the most dangerous trails, with hundreds of poorly provisioned dreamers dying on the trek across two glaciers and through the uncharted Chugach Mountains.

Over the next 60 years the community largely languished until catastrophe struck again, this time in the form of the 1964 Good Friday Earthquake, which killed 37 locals and forced the wholesale relocation of the town. However, Valdez' fortunes turned in the 1970s when it was selected as the terminus of the Trans-Alaska Pipeline. The $9 billion project was a windfall beyond those early miners' wildest dreams; the population grew by 320% and the town never looked back.

Cordova's past is somewhat less fraught with catastrophe. A cannery village since the late 1800s, it was chosen a century ago as the port for a railway from the Kennecott copper mines near McCarthy. By 1916 it was a boomtown, with millions of dollars worth of ore passing through its docks. The railroad and town prospered until 1938, when the mine closed and the railroad ceased operations. Cordova then turned to fishing, its main economic base today.

The Sound's third community, Whittier, is of more recent origin, having been built as a secret military installation during WWII, when the Japanese were assaulting the Aleutian Islands. The army maintained the town until 1968, after which, as in Cordova, fishing became the main industry. Tourism now puts food on many residents' plates.

In recent decades, the most monumental event in the Sound has been the *Exxon Valdez* oil spill, which dumped at least 11 million gallons of petroleum into the sea, killing countless birds and marine mammals, and devastating the fishing industry for several years. Though fishing – and the environment – has largely rebounded, oil is still easy to find beneath the surface of beaches, and certain species are never expected to recover.

Parks & Protected Lands

Prince William Sound is completely enveloped by the vast Chugach National Forest, the second-largest national forest in the US. The USFS maintains an office in Cordova (p241), and information booths in both Valdez and Whittier.

Dangers & Annoyances

By definition, glaciers move at a glacial pace, so you'd think they'd be harmless. In glacier-strewn Prince William Sound, however, they can be a real hazard. Not only have trekkers and mountaineers been killed when they've plunged into crevasses in the ice, but glaciers can also wreak havoc when they calve. Massive chunks often crack free from Childs glacier, outside Cordova, and occasionally they're big enough to create mini tsunami in the river. In recent years, Columbia Glacier has been retreating rapidly (the source of all those icebergs glowing on the horizon) and giant underwater bergs have broken free only to pop to the surface in a random location. Use caution if you're in a kayak.

Getting There & Around

Prince William Sound is all about the sea, and by far the best way to get around is on water. The **Alaska Marine Highway ferry** (☎ 800-642-0066; www.ferryalaska.com) provides a fairly convenient, fairly affordable service, linking Valdez and Cordova daily and making three runs per week between Valdez, Cordova and Whittier. But the ferry is more than just transport: it's an experience. There's something transcendent about bundling up on deck and watching the mountain-riddled, fjord-riven, watery world unfold.

If you must drive, both Valdez and Whittier are highway accessible; the former is the beginning of the Richardson Hwy and the latter is connected to the Seward Hwy via the continent's longest automobile tunnel.

Finally, planes are an option in Cordova and Valdez, where daily scheduled flights provide service to Anchorage and other major centers.

VALDEZ

pop 4353

Despite its natural attractions, Valdez is not primarily a tourist mecca. Nor, despite its proximity to the Sound, is it mainly a fishing village. On August 1, 1977, when the first tanker of oil issued forth from the Trans-Alaska Pipeline Terminal across the bay, Valdez became an oil town. Though it's hard to ignore the vertical slopes surrounding Valdez (and why would you want to?), it's just as difficult to ignore the presence of Big Oil. Massive storage tanks squat across the harbor, and the drive into town along the Richardson Hwy overlooks the pipeline as it snakes its way from the northern oil fields to this (in)famous port.

Valdez is still one of Alaska's prettiest spots, with glaciers galore, wildlife running amok and a Norman Rockwell-style harbor cradled by some of the highest coastal mountains (topping 7000ft) in the world. The city offers excellent paddling, hiking and other outdoor adventures, plus some quality restaurants, accommodations and museums, as befits a city blessed by the biggest boom Alaska has ever known.

Orientation

Valdez is on a flat slip of land on the north shore of Port Valdez, a gray-green inlet ringed by glaciated peaks and linked to Prince William Sound via Valdez Narrows. To take in the view, visitors gravitate to the waterfront along Fidalgo and North Harbor Drs; from there, the town stretches about a dozen walkable blocks back toward the mountains and Mineral Creek Canyon. At the west end of the waterfront is the ferry terminal. East of town, Egan Dr turns into the Richardson Hwy, passes the airport, crests Thompson Pass and runs 366 miles to Fairbanks.

Information

Crooked Creek Information Site (☎ 835-4680; Mile 0.9 Richardson Hwy) Staffed by US Forest Service (USFS) naturalists offering great advice about outdoorsy activities. The nearby viewing platform is a good place to watch chum and pink salmon spawn in July and August.

Harbormaster's office (☎ 835-4981; 300 N Harbor Dr) Has showers ($4).

Like Home Laundromat (☎ 831-0567; 121 Egan Dr; showers per 10 min $4) In the Valdez Mall; has showers and laundry machines.

Post office (cnr Galena Dr & Tatitlek Ave)

Valdez Community Hospital (☎ 835-2249; 911 Meals Ave) Has an emergency room.

Valdez Consortium Library (☎ 835-4632; 212 Fairbanks Dr; 🕑 10am-6pm Mon & Fri, 10am-8pm Tue-Thu, to 6pm Sat; 💻) Head here for free internet access.

Valdez Medical Clinic (☎ 835-4811; 912 Meals Ave) Provides walk-in care.

Valdez Visitor Information Center (☎ 835-2984; www.valdezalaska.com; 200 Fairbanks Dr; 🕑 8am-7pm Mon-Sat, noon-7pm Sun) Has free maps and a courtesy phone for booking accommodations. There's an unstaffed information booth at the airport with a direct line to the downtown visitors center.

Wells Fargo (☎ 835-4381; 337 Egan Dr) This bank can probably handle extremely large accounts considering the presence of the local oil fields.

Sights

VALDEZ MUSEUM

This fairly gargantuan **museum** (☎ 835-2764; www.valdezmuseum.org; 217 Egan Dr; adult/child $6/free; 🕑 9am-6pm) includes an ornate, steam-powered antique fire engine, a 19th-century saloon bar and the ceremonial first barrel of oil to flow from the Trans-Alaska Pipeline. There are arresting photos of the six minutes when Valdez was shaken to pieces by the 1964 Good Friday Earthquake, and an exhibit featuring correspondence from stampeders attempting the grueling All-American Route from Valdez to the inland goldfields. Wrote one goldseeker, 'I wash at least once a month, whether I need it or not.'

'REMEMBERING OLD VALDEZ' ANNEX

Operated by the Valdez Museum, this **annex** (☎ 835-5407; 436 Hazelet Ave; admission free with Valdez Museum ticket; 🕑 9am-6pm) is dominated by a scale model of the Old Valdez township. Each home destroyed in the Good Friday Earthquake has been restored in miniature, with the family's name in front. Other exhibits on the earthquake and subsequent tsunamis and fires are moving, but none are as heartwrenching as the recordings of ham radio operators communicating across the Sound as the quake wore on. This is a fitting memorial to the lives and countless memories lost on Valdez' darkest day.

MAXINE & JESSE WHITNEY MUSEUM

This high-quality **museum** (☎ 834-1614; 303 Lowe St; adult/child $5/3; 🕑 9am-7pm) has a brand-new home at the Prince William Sound Community College. The center is devoted to Alaska Native culture and Alaskan wildlife, and features ivory and baleen artwork, moose-antler furniture, and natural-history displays, including some very creative taxidermy. Kid-delighting exhibits include fossils and arrowheads in cool pull-out drawers.

SMALL-BOAT HARBOR

Valdez' harbor is a classic: raucous with gulls and eagles, reeking of fish guts and sea salt and creosote, and home to all manner of vessels. The benches and long boardwalk are ideal for watching lucky anglers weighing in 100lb or 200lb halibut, and for taking in the fairytale mountainscape in the background. Nearby is the **civic center** (Fidalgo Dr), which has more picnic tables and panoramic vistas.

PRINCE WILLIAM SOUND

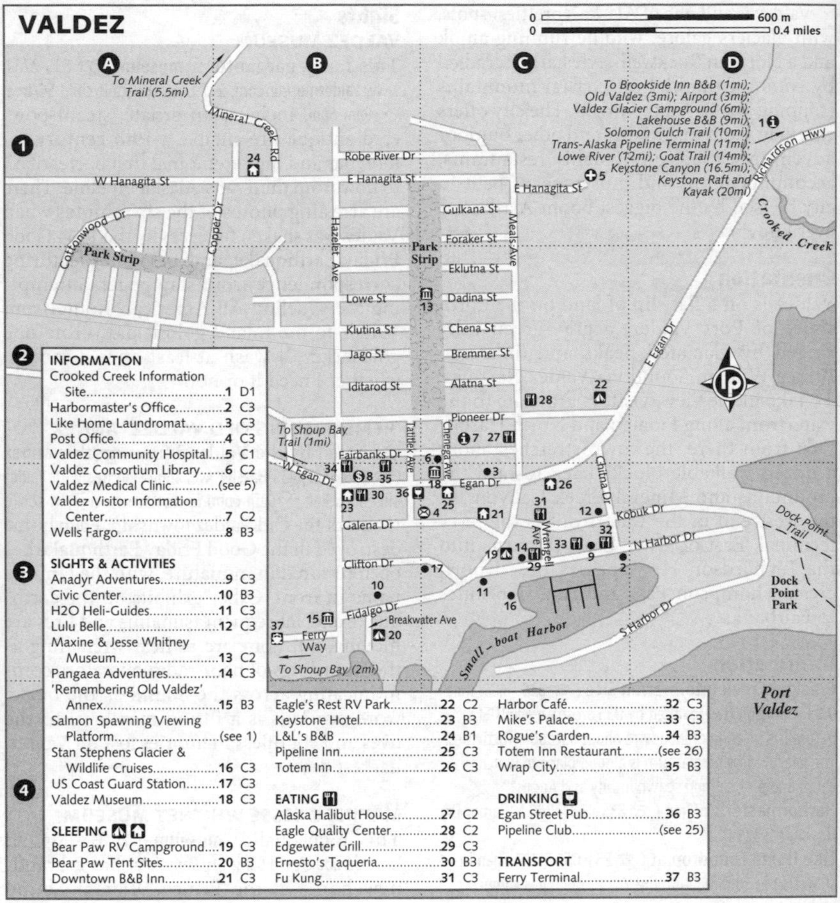

OLD VALDEZ

Valdez has been unduly blessed by nature, but 5:46pm, March 27, 1964 was payback time. Some 45 miles west of town and 14 miles underground, a fault ruptured, triggering a magnitude-9.2 earthquake – the most powerful in American history. The land rippled like water as Valdez slid into the harbor; tsunamis destroyed what was left. Thirty-seven people died.

After the quake, survivors labored to relocate and rebuild Valdez at its present site. But if you drive out the Richardson Hwy you can see the ghostly and overgrown foundations of Old Valdez. The **Earthquake Memorial**, listing the names of the dead, is reached by turning off the highway onto the unsigned gravel road just south of Mark's Repair. On the day of the quake, Valdez' post office was here; in mere moments the ground sank so far that nowadays high tides reach the spot.

TRANS-ALASKA PIPELINE TERMINAL

Across the inlet from town, Valdez' ever-pumping heart once welcomed visitors, but since September 11, 2001 stricter security protocols have closed it to the public. From the end of Dayville Rd you can still get a peek at the facility, including the storage tanks holding nine million barrels of oil apiece. But heed the dire warnings: plenty of septuagenarian RVers have been pulled over and interrogated for getting too close. Those truly interested in the terminal can learn more about it at the Maxine and Jesse Whitney Museum (p235), which offers a pipeline 'video tour,' featuring great photography and a narrative that amounts to little more than Big Oil hype.

Activities

HIKING

Valdez has a number of scenic and historic trails to get you away from town and up into the surrounding slopes.

Dock Point Trail

Not so much a hike as an enjoyable stroll through Dock Point Park beside the small-boat harbor, this 1-mile loop offers views of the peaks and the port, proximity to eagle nests, as well as salmonberry and blueberry picking.

Mineral Creek Trail

A great walk away from town is the trek to the old Smith Stamping Mill. Built by WL Smith in 1913, the mill required only two men to operate it and used mercury to remove the gold from the ore.

To reach the trailhead, turn onto Mineral Creek Rd from Hanagita St. The marginal road bumps along for 5.5 miles and then turns into a mile-long trail to the old mill. Bears and mountain goats are often visible on this hike.

Shoup Bay Trail

This verdant stunner has views of Port Valdez, Shoup Glacier and the impressive Gold Creek delta. Turn around when you reach Gold Creek Bridge at Mile 3.5 to make this a somewhat challenging day, or go another seven steep, difficult and not always perfectly maintained miles along the water (and sometimes through it), bearing right to follow Shoup Bay to its tidewater glacier. A free campsite and two reservable **public-use cabins** (in Soldotna ☎ 262-5581; www.alaskastateparks.org; $65), Kittiwake and Moraine, are at the end of the trail, near a noisy kittiwake rookery. **McAllister Creek Cabin** ($65) is accessible by boat only. The trailhead is at a parking lot at the western terminus of Egan Dr.

Solomon Gulch Trail

A mile past the Solomon Gulch Fish Hatchery on Dayville Rd, this 1.7-mile trail is a steep uphill hike that quickly leads to splendid views of Port Valdez and the city below. It ends at Solomon Lake, which is the source of 80% of Valdez' power.

Goat Trail

The oldest hike in the area is the Goat Trail, originally an Alaska Native trade route and later used by Captain Abercrombie in his search for safe passage to the Interior. Today, you can pick up the posted trailhead at Mile 13.5 of the Richardson Hwy, just past Horsetail Falls in Keystone Canyon. A few spots have been washed out; don't try to cross any rushing streams.

PADDLING

This is a kayaker's paradise, though folks sticking to the bay will be rewarded with views of seagulls fighting over cannery offal for the first hour or so. Independent kayakers

THE EXXON VALDEZ

Two decades after the *Exxon Valdez* left Valdez' Trans-Alaska Pipeline Terminal with a tippled captain, causing the worst environmental disaster in modern American history, the damage lingers. Not only can oil from the 1989 spill still be collected from just beneath the surface of beaches throughout the Sound, but, while certain fisheries have rebounded, herring stocks haven't recovered at all. The Dungeness crab population remains low and many pink-salmon runs have been eliminated. Loons, harlequin ducks, otters and seals still suffer the effects of the spill. And at the time of writing, the citizens whose lives were permanently changed have yet to receive any portion of the original $5 billion awarded by an Anchorage jury in 1994.

On June 26, 2008 the US Supreme Court reduced the punitive damage awards from a previous reduction of $2.5 billion to $507 million. The jury is still out on whether the plaintiffs will receive any interest on that amount.

Thankfully, other legacies of the disaster are more inspiring. Long-recommended security measures have finally been enacted at oil-processing facilities across the nation. Double-hulled tankers, once a pipe dream of environmentalists, will be a pipeline requirement by 2015; some are already in service. Tugs must once again escort tankers passing through Prince William Sound. And the *Exxon Valdez* itself, now renamed the *SeaRiver Mediterranean*, has been banned from ever returning to Valdez.

HELI-SKIING

To a certain set of unhinged individuals, Valdez is legendary not for its oil spill or its earthquake, but for being *the* place to strap on skis, slip from a helicopter and plunge into the snowy abyss.

Thanks to geography and climate, nowhere else do such steep slopes get so much sticky snow. At inland ski resorts in, say, Colorado, dry powder barely clings to 50-degree inclines; here in the coastal Chugach Mountains, the sopping-wet flakes glue to angles of 60-plus-degrees, creating ski slopes where elsewhere there'd be cliffs. Factor in 1000in of snow per winter and mountains that descend 7000ft from peak to sea, and you've got a ski-bum's version of Eden.

Since extreme skiing exploded here a decade ago, numerous companies have cropped up to capitalize. **Valdez Heli-Ski Guides** (☎ 835-4528; www.valdezheliskiguides.com) offers a day of heli-skiing (usually six runs) for $900; **H20 Heli-Guides** (☎ 835-8418; www.h2oguides.com; 100 N Harbor Dr) has three-day heli-skiing packages – including lodging – for $4425. Alas, the ski season lasts only from February to the end of April; after that, extremists will have to settle for H20's mellower summer offerings – for instance, spending a day with crampons and ice-axes, scaling a sheer blue-ice cliff on Worthington Glacier ($225).

should be aware of no-go zones around the pipeline terminal and moving tankers; contact the **US Coast Guard** (☎ 835-7222; 105 Clifton Dr) for current regulations.

OUR PICK **Anadyr Adventures** (☎ 835-2814, 800-865-2925; www.anadyradventures.com; 225 N Harbor Dr) rents kayaks to (very) experienced paddlers (single/double $45/65, discounts for multiple days) and offers guided trips, ranging from a day at Columbia Glacier ($199) to a week on the water aboard the 'mothership' (from $2700). The office also has internet terminals ($6 per hour) and a small book exchange.

Pangaea Adventures (☎ 835-8442, 800-660-9637; www.alaskasummer.com; 107 N Harbor Dr) has guided tours, costing from $59 for a three-hour trip on Duck Flats to $229 for a day trip to Columbia Glacier. It also does longer custom tours and rents kayaks ($45/65 per single/double).

Shoup Bay

Protected as a state marine park, this bay off Valdez Arm makes for a great overnight kayaking trip. The bay is home to a retreating glacier, which has two tidal basins and an underwater moraine that protects harbor seals and other sea life. It's about 10 miles to the bay and another 4 miles up to the glacier. You must enter the bay two hours before the incoming tide to avoid swift tidal currents.

Columbia Glacier

A mile wide and rising 300ft from the waterline at its face, this is the largest tidewater glacier in Prince William Sound, and a spectacular spot to spend a few days kayaking and watching seals and other wildlife. In recent years the glacier has been in 'catastrophic retreat,' filling its fjord with so many calved bergs that it's difficult to get within miles of the face. Only experienced paddlers should attempt to paddle the open water from Valdez Arm to the glacier, a multiday trip. Others should arrange for a drop-off and pickup; Anadyr Adventures charges $500 for up to six people one way.

Lowe River

This glacial river, 12 miles from Valdez, cuts through impressive Keystone Canyon. The popular float features Class III rapids, sheer canyon walls and cascading waterfalls. The highlight is Bridal Veil Falls, which drops 900ft from the canyon walls.

Keystone Raft & Kayak Adventures (☎ 835-2606, 800-328-8460; www.alaskawhitewater.com; Mile 16.5 Richardson Hwy) provides 1½-hour trips ($40) along 6 miles of white water past the cascading waterfalls that have made the canyon famous. It also has half-day and day trips on the Class IV Tsaina and Tonsina Rivers.

Tours

Columbia Glacier is the second-largest tidewater glacier in North America, spilling forth from the Chugach Mountains and ending with a face as high as a football field. Several tour companies can take you into Columbia Bay, west of Port Valdez, but it's difficult for any boat to get close to the face as the water is too clogged with ice. You're more likely, therefore, to see calving further west in Unakwik Inlet, where the more accessible Mears Glacier, a smaller ice-tongue, dumps bergs from a snout just half the height of Columbia's.

our pick **Lu-Lu Belle Glacier Wildlife Cruises** (☎ 835-5141, 800-411-0090; www.lulubelletours.com; Kobuk Dr) The dainty and ornately appointed MV *Lu-Lu Belle* is all polished wood, leather and oriental rugs. Cruise into Columbia Bay where, unless winds have cleared away the ice, wildlife is more the attraction than glacier-calving. The tour departs at 2pm daily, costing $100.

Stan Stephens Glacier & Wildlife Cruises (☎ 835-4731, 866-867-1297; www.stanstephenscruises.com; 112 N Harbor Dr) The biggest tour operator in town runs large vessels on seven-hour journeys to Columbia Glacier ($105) and nine-hour trips ($140) to both Columbia and Mears Glaciers. Lunch and lots of tummy-warming tea are included.

Festivals & Events

Fourth of July Valdez hosts a celebration.

Gold Rush Days A five-day festival in mid-August that includes a parade, bed races, dances, a free fish feed and a portable jailhouse that's pulled throughout town by locals, who arrest people without beards and other innocent bystanders.

Sleeping

As Valdez no longer has a hostel, devout budgeteers will have to settle for a campsite. The town does have plenty of B&Bs and most belong to the **Valdez Bed & Breakfast Association** (www.valdezbnb.com). The visitors center has a 24-hour hotline outside, where you can book last-minute rooms. Valdez' 6% bed tax is not included in the rates quoted here.

BUDGET

Valdez Glacier Campground (☎ 835-2282; Airport Rd; sites $10) Located 6 miles out of town, this spot has 101 pleasant wooded sites and a nice waterfall. Though it's privately owned, it has a noncommercial feel.

Bear Paw RV Campground (☎ 835-2530; www.bearpawrvpark.com; 101 N Harbor Dr; sites camp/RV $20/30) Conveniently located right downtown, this campground has two locations: one is for RVs, and the other (on Breakwater Ave within walking distance to the ferry) has a wooded glade just for tents.

Eagle's Rest RV Park (☎ 835-2373, 800-553-7275; www.eaglesrestrv.com; 631 E Pioneer Dr; sites $25, RV sites $33-43, cabins $125-145) Also has showers and laundry, but the tent sites are a bit open and bland.

MIDRANGE

L&L's B&B (☎ 835-4447; www.lnlalaska.com; 533 W Hanagita St; r with/without bath $80/70; ⊠ 💻) Located in a big, airy suburban home, this B&B has two bicycles at your disposal.

Keystone Hotel (☎ 835-3851, 888-835-0665; 401 W Egan Dr; s/d summer $85/95; ⊠) This modular relic of the pipeline boom years has lots of clean, cramped, prefab rooms, plus you get continental breakfast.

Pipeline Inn (☎ 835-4444; 112 Egan Dr; r $100) Here you'll find worn and aesthetically out-of-date rooms, but some hold four or five people, making this a good big-group option.

Downtown B&B Inn (☎ 835-2791, 800-478-2791; www.valdezdowntowninn.com; 113 Galena Dr; r with/without bath $110/95; ⊠ 💻) More hotel than B&B, though you do get breakfast with your clean, basic room.

TOP END

our pick **Brookside Inn B&B** (☎ 835-9130, 866-316-9130; www.brooksideinnbb.com; 1465 Richardson Hwy; r $125, ste $160; ⊠) This 100-year-old home originated in Ft Liscum, was moved to Old Valdez, and then to its present location after the earthquake. Original floors and arched windows create cozy ambience, and the homemade breakfast is served on a large sunporch.

Totem Inn (☎ 835-4443, 888-808-4431; www.toteminn.com; 144 E Egan Dr; r $129; ⊠ 💻) This large place has refrigerators and microwaves in each room. The suites are deluxe, while the older rooms are a bit small.

Lakehouse B&B (☎ 835-4752; www.lakehousevaldez.net; Mile 6 Richardson Hwy; r $130-145; ⊠ 💻) This ambling, sunny place has six rooms, all spacious and each with its own deck painted a cheerful bright red and overlooking the absurdly pretty Robe Lake. It's in a peaceful location, and if you've got your own wheels, this is a good option.

Eating

RESTAURANTS

Edgewater Grille (☎ 835-3212; 107 N Harbor Dr; breakfast $6-17, lunch & dinner $9-30; 🕒 6am-10pm, bar to 11pm) While this joint grills burgers and serves them up on homemade buns, the more creative dishes – we like the blackened salmon fajita – are quite tasty, too. The clean, comfortable bar is a refreshing change from the smoke-clogged venues elsewhere in town.

Totem Inn Restaurant (☎ 835-4443; 144 E Egan Dr; breakfast $7-12, lunch & dinner $8-20; 🕒 5am-11pm) In the morning, tourists and locals flock here for the excellent breakfasts and Alaska-sized mugs of coffee. Lunch is all about burgers and sandwiches, while dinner has decent seafood.

Mike's Palace (☎ 835-2365; 201 N Harbor Dr; mains $10-20; 🕒 11am-9pm) This locals' favorite specializes in Italian dinners, but also has a few Mexican dishes to spice things up.

Fu Kung (☎ 835-5255; 207 Kobuk Dr; lunch $7-10, dinner $12-17; 11am-11pm Mon-Sat, from 4pm Sun) In a building that wonderfully fuses Asian and Alaskan themes, this restaurant has fantastic Chinese food. Lunch specials include egg rolls and quality wonton soup.

CAFÉS, QUICK EATS & GROCERIES

Rogue's Garden (☎ 835-5880; 354 Fairbanks Dr; 7am-6pm Mon-Fri, 9am-5pm Sat;) Carries a small selection of organic groceries and brews fair-trade espresso.

Eagle Quality Center (☎ 835-2100; 185 Meals Ave; 4:30am-midnight) With its impressive sandwich and salad bar, this grocery store is among Valdez' best places for a bite.

Alaska Halibut House (☎ 835-2788; 208 Meals Ave; fish $4-10; 11am-9pm Mon-Sat, to 8pm Sun) Frying up fresh local fish, this place is what every fast-food joint should be. The halibut basket is delish.

our pick **Ernesto's Taqueria** (☎ 835-2519; 328 Egan Dr; meals $7-9; 5:30am-9:30pm) Locally loved, this place serves large portions of serviceable Mexican food on the cheap, and has a cold selection of Mexican beer.

Harbor Café (☎ 835-4776; 255 N Harbor Dr; burgers $7-10; 6am-9pm) Breakfast is overpriced, but the lunch and dinner menu has a wide selection of decent burgers and sandwiches, which you can enjoy on the bright, covered sundeck.

Wrap City (☎ 835-8383; 321 Egan Dr; wraps $8; 11am-1pm Wed-Sat or when the 'open' sign is on) Attached to a darling little art gallery, the Rose Cache, this joint has a small, rotating menu of delicious wraps – the vegetarian special is always spot on. It also packs box lunches for tours.

Drinking & Entertainment

Pipeline Club (☎ 835-2788; 112 Egan Dr) If you've ever hugged a tree in your life, this crowd may not be for you. This smoky lounge is the watering hole where Captain Hazelwood had his famous scotch-on-the-rocks before running the *Exxon Valdez* aground.

Egan Street Pub (210 Egan Dr) This pub, at Glacier Sound Inn, keeps at least three microbrews on tap at all times.

Getting There & Around

AIR

There are flight services with **ERA Aviation** (☎ 835-2636, 800-843-1947; www.flyera.com) three times daily between Anchorage and Valdez; one-way tickets cost from $165 to $197, depending on how early you make reservations. The **Valdez Airport** (Airport Rd) is 3 miles from town, off the Richardson Hwy.

BICYCLE

Bikes can be rented through **Anadyr Adventures** (☎ 835-2814, 800-865-2925; www.anadyradventures.com; 225 N Harbor Dr; per half/full day $15/25).

BOAT

Within Prince William Sound, the **Alaska Marine Highway ferry** (☎ 835-4436, 800-642-0066; www.ferryalaska.com) provides daily services from Valdez to Cordova ($50) and Whittier ($89). The new speed ferry halves the old times, but on the older, slower ferry you're more likely to see whales and sea lions as you amble along.

CORDOVA

pop 2194

Cut off from Alaska's road system (for now), Cordova is slightly inconvenient and somewhat expensive to get to. Perhaps that's why this picturesque outpost, spread thinly between Orca Inlet and Eyak Lake, and overshadowed by Mt Eccles, can still claim to be one of the Alaskan coast's truly endangered species: a fishing village that hasn't sold its soul to tourism. That's all the more reason to visit.

Though not set in the same sort of mountain-thronged kingdom as Valdez, Cordova is more appealing: a quaint cluster of rainforest-rotted homes climbing up a pretty hillside overlooking the busy harbor. Populating the place are folks who, you can't help thinking, exemplify what's best about Alaska: ruggedly independent freethinkers, clad in rubber boots and driving rusted-out Subarus, unconcerned with image or pretense, and friendly as hell. They seem to revel in their isolation. In recent years, pro-development politicians have proposed connecting the community to the state highway system. Judging from the ubiquity of 'No Road' bumper stickers in town, it's a prospect the locals abhor.

Visitors will also be enthralled by what lies beyond the town limits. Just outside the city along the Copper River Hwy is one of the largest wetlands in Alaska, with more than 40 miles of trails threading through spectacular glaciers, alpine meadows and the remarkable Copper River Delta. Into that delta run some of the world's finest salmon, and fishermen here turn them into what may be the fattest and finest fillets you'll ever enjoy.

Orientation

Cordova's main north–south drag is officially 1st St, but is often called Main St – the names are used interchangeably. 1st St becomes the Copper River Hwy as it leaves town, connecting Cordova to the airport at Mile 12, continuing another 40 miles to Childs Glacier and Million Dollar Bridge. The village itself is easy to explore on foot, but seeing the Copper River Delta will require arranging transportation for all but the hardiest explorers.

Information

Bidarki Recreation Center (☎ 424-7282; cnr 2nd St & Council Ave; 9am-9:30pm Mon-Sat) For $5 you get a shower plus all-day use of the sauna and the fitness room.
Chamber of Commerce (☎ 424-7260; www.cordovachamber.com, www.cordovaalaska.com; 404 1st St; 10am-4pm Mon-Fri) If you find it open, you can get visitor info here.
Cordova Community Medical Center (☎ 424-8000; 602 Chase Rd) Provides emergency services.
Cordova Library (☎ 424-6667; 622 1st St; 10am-8pm Tue-Fri, to 5pm Sat & Sun;) In the same building as the Cordova Museum. Has the best lowdown on town: lots of pamphlets, plus B&B listings and free city maps. Internet access is free and very popular with the cannery crew; put your name on the list and *then* check out the museum.
First National Bank (☎ 424-3258; 515 1st St) Has fresh cash; the Wells Fargo across the street serves it up from its 24-hour ATM.
Harbormaster's office (☎ 424-6400; Nicholoff Way) Has $5 showers and a small book swap.
Orca Book & Sound (☎ 424-5305; 507 1st St; internet per 1 hr $9, wi-fi $6; 6:30am-5:30pm Mon-Sat;) If you can't wait for an internet terminal at the library, head here. It's also your best source for locally oriented literature, and the owners are friendly, helpful and knowledgeable about the area.
Post office (cnr Railroad & Council Aves) Near the small-boat harbor.
USFS Visitor Center (☎ 424-7661; 612 2nd St; 8am-5pm Mon-Fri) This excellent office has the latest on trails, campsites and wildlife in the Copper River basin.

Sights

CORDOVA MUSEUM

Adjacent to the Cordova Library, this **museum** (622 1st St; admission by donation; 10am-6pm Mon-Fri, to 5pm Sat, 2-4pm Sun) is a small, grassroots collection worth seeing. Displays cover local marine life, relics from the town's early history – including a captivating lighthouse lens – and a three-seater *bidarka* (kayak) made from spruce pine and 12 sealskins.

Want your heart wrenched? Peruse the museum's coverage of the *Exxon Valdez* oil spill. The amateur photos and local newspaper headlines revive the horror more vividly than any slick documentary. Then there's the jar of oily sediment collected in 2006 – nearly 20 years after the spill.

ILANKA CULTURAL CENTER

This excellent **museum** (☎ 424-7903; 110 Nicholoff Way; admission free; 10am-5pm Mon-Fri), operated by local Alaska Natives, has a small but high-quality collection of Alaska Native art from all over the state. Don't miss the intact killer-whale skeleton – one of only five in the world – with flippers that could give you quite a slap. Also on display is artist Mike Webber's *Shame Pole*, a totem pole that tells the grim tale of the oil spill, spitting back Exxon's then–top official Don Cornett's famous words, 'We will make you whole again.' This place also has a wonderful gift shop and offers classes on such crafty subjects as scrimshaw and spruce-root weaving. Call for a schedule.

PRINCE WILLIAM SOUND SCIENCE CENTER

This dockside **research facility** (☎ 424-5800; www.pwssc.org; 300 Breakwater Ave; admission free; 8:30am-5:30pm Mon-Fri) offers themed 'Discovery Packs' for kids, which include information on the birds, flora and geology of Cordova. You can call ahead to reserve a pack, or stop by to pick one up. Inside the facility there's not much for visitors save for an impressively enormous gray-whale skull suspended from the ceiling, some oil sediments, and T-shirts.

SMALL-BOAT HARBOR

In Cordova, the standard greeting among locals is 'Been fishing?' Unsurprisingly, the harbor is the community's heart, humming throughout the season as fishers frantically try to meet their quota before the runs are closed. The fishing fleet is composed primarily of seiners and gillnetters, with the method used by the fishers determining the species of salmon they pursue. The former primarily target pink salmon, while the latter, generally one-person operations, go for kings and reds early in the season and silvers later on.

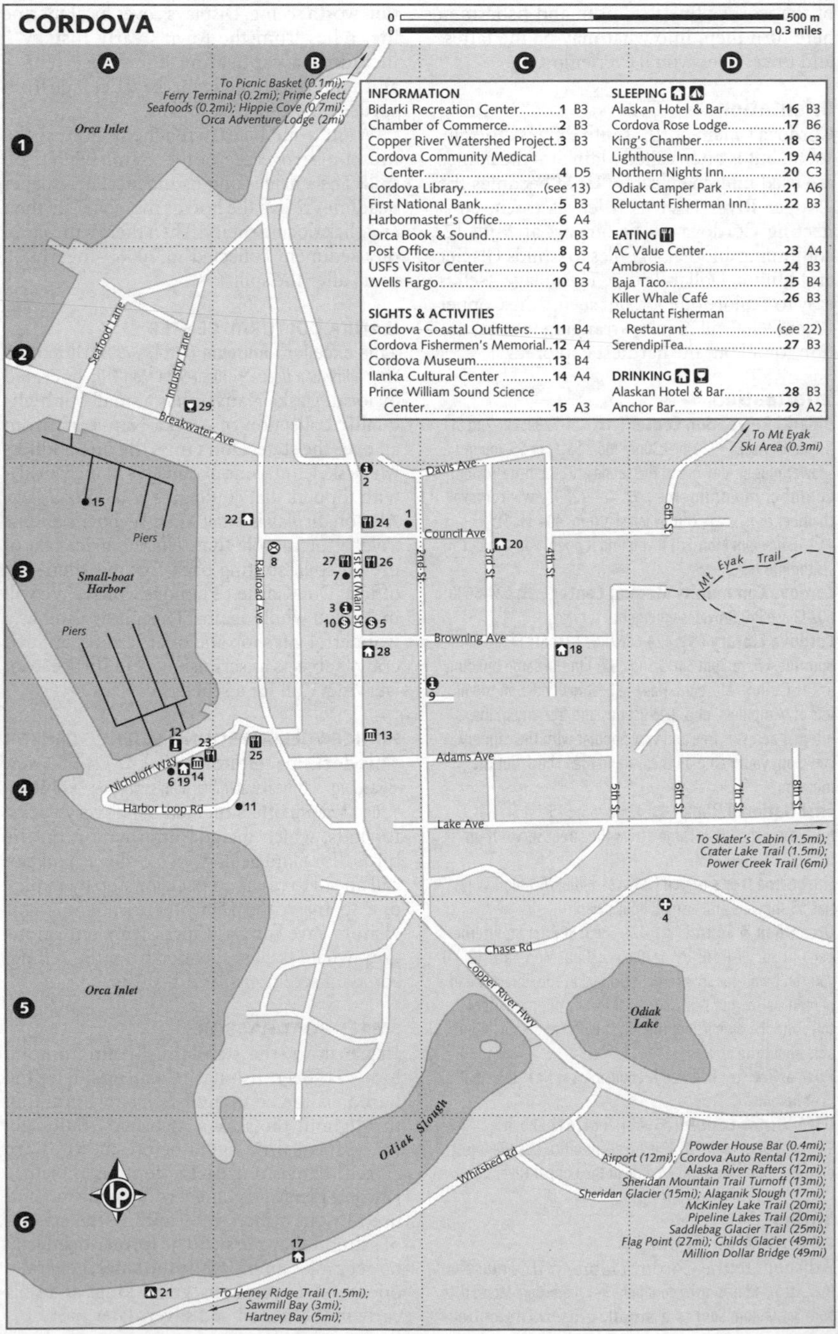
CORDOVA
0 500 m
0 0.3 miles
A
B
C
D
1
2
3
4
5
6
INFORMATION
Bidarki Recreation Center.............1 B3
Chamber of Commerce.................2 B3
Copper River Watershed Project.3 B3
Cordova Community Medical Center.....................4 D5
Cordova Library.....................(see 13)
First National Bank....................5 B3
Harbormaster's Office.................6 A4
Orca Book & Sound....................7 B3
Post Office..............................8 B3
USFS Visitor Center....................9 C4
Wells Fargo.............................10 B3
SIGHTS & ACTIVITIES
Cordova Coastal Outfitters......11 B4
Cordova Fishermen's Memorial..12 A4
Cordova Museum.....................13 B4
Ilanka Cultural Center 14 A4
Prince William Sound Science Center..........................15 A3
SLEEPING
Alaskan Hotel & Bar..................16 B3
Cordova Rose Lodge..................17 B6
King's Chamber........................18 C3
Lighthouse Inn.........................19 A4
Northern Nights Inn...................20 C3
Odiak Camper Park 21 A6
Reluctant Fisherman Inn.............22 B3
EATING
AC Value Center.......................23 A4
Ambrosia..................................24 B3
Baja Taco.................................25 B4
Killer Whale Café 26 B3
Reluctant Fisherman Restaurant.............................(see 22)
SerendipiTea............................27 B3
DRINKING
Alaskan Hotel & Bar..................28 B3
Anchor Bar...............................29 A2
To Picnic Basket (0.1mi); Ferry Terminal (0.2mi); Prime Select Seafoods (0.2mi); Hippie Cove (0.7mi); Orca Adventure Lodge (2mi)
Orca Inlet
Seafood Lane
Industry Lane
Breakwater Ave
To Mt Eyak Ski Area (0.3mi)
Davis Ave
Council Ave
Piers
Small-boat Harbor
Railroad Ave
1st St (Main St)
2nd St
3rd St
4th St
6th St
Mt Eyak Trail
Browning Ave
Nicholoff Way
Harbor Loop Rd
Adams Ave
Lake Ave
5th St
7th St
8th St
To Skater's Cabin (1.5mi); Crater Lake Trail (1.5mi); Power Creek Trail (6mi)
Chase Rd
Copper River Hwy
Odiak Lake
Odiak Slough
Whitshed Rd
Powder House Bar (0.4mi); Airport (12mi); Cordova Auto Rental (12mi); Alaska River Rafters (12mi); Sheridan Mountain Trail Turnoff (13mi); Sheridan Glacier (15mi); Alaganik Slough (17mi); McKinley Lake Trail (20mi); Pipeline Lakes Trail (20mi); Saddlebag Glacier Trail (25mi); Flag Point (27mi); Childs Glacier (49mi); Million Dollar Bridge (49mi)
To Heney Ridge Trail (1.5mi); Sawmill Bay (3mi); Hartney Bay (5mi);

Watching over the hubbub is the **Cordova Fisherman's Memorial**, a quiet place dominated by artist Joan Bugbee Jackson's sculpture *The Southeasterly* (1985), and spotted with flower bouquets.

SALMON CANNERIES

Every summer, Cordova's population swells with youths hoping to make a mint canning salmon on 30-hour shifts. Whether you're curious about the effects of sleep deprivation on adventurous teenagers or just want to see how some of the finest salmon in the world is processed, ask at the chamber of commerce about canneries offering tours. You can watch your *own* catch get processed at **Prime Select Seafoods** (☎ 424-7750, 888-870-7292; www.pssifish.com; 210 Seafood Lane), a smaller-scale operation that packs salmon and ships it to your home.

Activities

HIKING

More than 35 miles of trails are accessible from Cordova roads. Several of these paths lead to USFS cabins (p245). As in much of the Southeast, the hiking in this area is excellent, combining lush forest with alpine terrain, great views and glaciers. See p246 for transportation options.

Heney Ridge Trail

Cordova's most popular trail – as it's accessible without a car – is this scenic, fairly easy 3.7-mile route beginning at Mile 5.1 of Whitshed Rd. The first stretch winds around Hartney Bay, followed by a mellow 2-mile climb through forests and wildflowers (and, in rainy weather, lots of mud – rubber boots are recommended) to the treeline. It's another steep mile up to the ridge, where you'll enjoy a gorgeous view.

Crater Lake & Power Creek Trails

The 2.4-mile Crater Lake Trail begins on Eyak Lake, about half a mile beyond the municipal airport, across from Skater's Cabin. The trail ascends steeply but is easy to follow as it winds through lush forest. At the top it offers panoramic views of both the Copper River Delta and Prince William Sound. Plan on two to four hours for the round-trip.

Once at the lake you can continue with a 4.5-mile ridge route to Alice Smith Cutoff, which descends to the Power Creek Trail. The entire 12-mile loop makes for an ideal overnight backpacking trip. Halfway along the ridge is a free-use shelter, while at Mile 4.2 of the Power Creek Trail is the **USFS Power Creek Cabin** (☎ 877-444-6777, 518-885-3639; www.recreation.gov; $35). Arrange to be dropped off at the Power Creek trailhead and hike all the way back into town via the Mt Eyak Trail.

McKinley Lake & Pipeline Lakes Trails

The 2.5-mile McKinley Lake Trail begins at Mile 21.6 of the Copper River Hwy and leads to the head of the lake and the remains of the Lucky Strike gold mine. There are two **USFS cabins** (☎ 877-444-6777, 518-885-3639; www.recreation.gov; $35), McKinley Lake Cabin, just past the trailhead, and McKinley Trail Cabin, at Mile 2.4. The abandoned Lucky Strike mine

CORDOVA ICEWORM FESTIVAL

They're real, and every February Cordovans celebrate them. Ice worms spend their entire lives on ice, and if they warm up too much they disintegrate (read: melt). These little critters feed on snow algae, and thread through tiny cracks in the ice. Their coloring tends to mimic glacial ice: white or blue. They're just mysterious enough that not only did they became the topic of a Robert Service poem, 'Ballad of the Ice Worm Cocktail,' but they've also captured the attention of NASA, which has been studying what makes the worms such excellent survivors.

Towards the end of a Cordovan winter, it might also feel as if you, too, have spent your entire life on ice, which is why in 1961, Cordova residents got together and decided to break the monotony of the winter (and celebrate their survival of it, no doubt) with the **Iceworm Festival** (www.iceworm.org).

This tongue-in-cheek celebration includes the crowning of a Miss Iceworm, the Survival Suit Race in which participants don survival suits and plunge into the harbor, and a parade that culminates with a giant ice worm float. The festivities last a full week, which might be what it takes to snap out of a long winter.

is accessible via an unmaintained trail behind McKinley Trail Cabin.

Departing from the midway point of the McKinley Lake Trail is the Pipeline Lakes Trail, which loops back to the Copper River Hwy at Mile 21.4. Almost all of this marshy 2-mile trail has been boardwalked to provide easier access to several small lakes packed with grayling and cutthroat trout, but if it's rainy consider bringing rubber boots.

Sheridan Mountain Trail

This trail starts near the picnic tables at the end of Sheridan Glacier Rd, which runs 4.3 miles from the turnoff at Mile 13 of Copper River Hwy. Most of the 2.9-mile route is a moderate climb, which passes through mature forests before breaking out into an alpine basin. From there, the view of mountains and the Sheridan and Sherman Glaciers is stunning, and it only gets better when you start climbing the surrounding rim. This trail isn't the best maintained, putting it into the 'difficult' category.

Saddlebag Glacier Trail

You reach this trail via a firewood-cutting road at Mile 25 of Copper River Hwy. It's an easy 3-mile walk through cottonwoods and spruce, emerging at Saddlebag Lake. Outstanding views of surrounding peaks and cliffs (and maybe mountain goats) are made even more fabulous by the namesake glacier, which litters the lake with icebergs.

CYCLING

Most of Cordova's trails are too muddy and steep to ride; an exception is the **Saddlebag Glacier Trail**. However, if you have a few days, the Copper River Hwy itself is a remarkable mountain-bike route. Plan on at least three days if you ride out to the end of the road and back, or two days if you are dropped off at the end of the road and then ride the 48 miles back to town. For bicycle rentals and shuttles, see p247.

SKIING

The small but much-loved **Mt Eyak ski area** (☎ 424-7766; 6th St; ⏲ mid-Nov–mid-May), just a quick walk from town, features an 800ft drop, an average of 118in of natural snow annually, and runs that accommodate everyone from novice snowboarders to world-class skiers. The most famous attraction is the vintage ski lift from Sun Valley, Idaho.

BIRDING

The Copper River Delta and the rich waters of Prince William Sound attract an astonishing number and variety of birds. Spring migration is the busiest, and that is when the town hosts the Copper River Delta Shorebird Festival (opposite). Stop at the **USFS Visitor Center** (☎ 424-7661; 612 2nd St; ⏲ 8am-5pm Mon-Fri) for a birding checklist and advice about where to break out the binoculars.

A favorite birding area is Hartney Bay, 6 miles southwest of town along Whitshed Rd, where as many as 70,000 shorebirds congregate during spring migration. Bring rubber boots and plan to be there two hours before or after high tide for the best fall and spring viewing conditions. Sawmill Bay, at Mile 3 of Whitshed Rd, is also a prime bird-watching spot.

Another good place for bird and wildlife watching is Alaganik Slough. Turn south on Alaganik Slough Rd at Mile 17 of Copper River Hwy and travel 3 miles to the end, where a picnic area and boardwalk offer great views of dusky Canada geese, bald eagles and other feathered friends.

Also check out Odiak Lake, just southeast of town, and Eyak Lake on the Power Creek Trail.

PADDLING

The Copper River flows for 287 miles, beginning at Copper Glacier near Slana in the Interior and ending in the Gulf of Alaska, east of Cordova. Most of the river is for experienced rafters, as rapids, glaciers and narrow canyons give it a white-water rating of Class II-III much of the way. The 20-mile stretch between Million Dollar Bridge and Flag Point, at Mile 27 of the Copper River Hwy, is considerably wider and slower. Below Flag Point, the river becomes heavily braided, which inevitably means dragging your boat through shallow channels.

Alaska River Rafters (☎ 424-7238, 800-776-1864; www.alaskarafters.com; Mile 13 Copper River Hwy) operates rafting trips at Sheridan Glacier, on the Copper River and elsewhere in the area; guided half-day trips start from $95/75 per adult/child, ranging up to $1275/675 per adult/child for a six-day multi-sport adventure, which includes rafting, kayaking, and hiking.

If the ocean is more your speed, **Cordova Coastal Outfitters** (☎ 424-7424, 800-357-5145; www.cdvcoastal.com; Harbor Loop Rd; kayaks per day single/double

$35/50), in a cabin behind the AC Value Center, rents kayaks and arranges guided tours in placid, pristine Orca Inlet north of town.

WILDERNESS CABINS

There are nine **USFS cabins** (☎ 877-444-6777, 518-885-3639; www.recreation.gov; $25-45) located in the Cordova area, and they're much easier to reserve than those in other Southcentral Alaskan parts. Three are best accessible by boat or plane: Tideman Slough bunks six in the wilderness of the Copper River flats; Softuk Bar sleeps six on a remote beach 40 miles southeast of Cordova; and popular Martin Lake, 30 minutes east of town by floatplane, has a rowboat and sleeps six people. Two others are along the McKinley Lake Trail (p243) and a third is on the Power Creek Trail (p243). Hinchinbrook Island, 20 minutes from Cordova by plane and at most two hours by boat, has three more cabins: Shelter Bay, Double Bay and Hook Point.

Tours

The Copper River Delta, right in Cordova's backyard, is a can't-miss experience. Guided daylong driving tours of the delta are conducted by **Alaska River Rafters** (☎ 424-7238, 800-776-1864; www.alaskarafters.com; Mile 13, Copper River Hwy). The trips run to Million Dollar Bridge and Childs Glacier, and cost $85 per person with a six-person minimum. You can add a flightseeing excursion for another $100.

Festivals & Events

Iceworm Festival (☎ 424-3861; www.iceworm.org) Cordova's famous homegrown and tongue-in-cheek event is held on the second weekend of February. This draws mainly locals and their friends and families, who honor the miniscule glacier-dweller *Mesenchytraeus solifugus* by parading a 150ft-long puppet of him through the streets. There are also feasts, variety shows, tightly bundled-up beauty queens, and contests like the survival-suit races, in which competitors don buoyant, insulated jumpsuits and plunge into the frigid sea, racing to be the first to reach a buoy and return to shore.

Copper River Delta Shorebird Festival (☎ 424-7260) On the first weekend of May, this festival celebrates the largest migration in the USA, as some five million shorebirds throng the delta – the biggest continuous wetland on the Pacific coast – en route to their Arctic breeding grounds. The festival draws birders from the world over, and features presentations and workshops by international experts and field trips to the prime viewing areas. Nonbirders, don't scoff: this event fills every hotel room in town.

Sleeping

Cordova tacks on 12% in bed-and-sales tax to the rates listed here.

BUDGET

When we visited, the **Copper River Watershed Project** (☎ 424-3334; 511 1st St) was building campsites ($7) a half-mile north of the ferry terminal at Hippie Cove, a good option for those leaving on an early-morning ferry.

Odiak Camper Park (☎ 424-7282; Whitshed Rd; sites camp/RV $5/22) A half-mile from town, this is basically a gravel parking lot with a rest room and a view. Make reservations at the Bidarki Recreation Center.

Alaska River Rafters (☎ 424-7238, 800-776-1864; www.alaskarafters.com; Mile 13 Copper River Hwy; sites camp/RV $15/20) Has 16 wooded sites in a mossy forest across from the airport.

Skater's Cabin (☎ 424-7282; cabin 1st/2nd/3rd night $25/35/50) On Eyak Lake with a nice gravel beach and a woodstove, this place can be booked through the Bidarki Recreation Center. The escalating prices are to deter multiday use so more people can enjoy it.

Alaskan Hotel & Bar (☎ 424-3299; 600 1st St; r with/without bath $66/44) If you're looking for a good night's sleep, bring earplugs – it sounds (and smells) as if you're sleeping in the bar below you. The sheets are clean, though, and it's only a short stumble to your bed from the party down below.

MIDRANGE & TOP END

our pick **Northern Nights Inn** (☎ 424-5356; www.northernnightsinn.com; cnr 3rd St & Council Ave; r from $85; ⊠ 💻) In a 100-year-old house painted Kennecott red, rooms range from basic to suites with kitchenettes. Some have peek-a-boo views of the bay, and all are furnished with antiques and period pieces.

Cordova Rose Lodge (☎ 424-7673; www.cordovarose.com; 1315 Whitshed Rd; r $85-145; ⊠ 💻) This spot has a higgledy-piggledy assortment of structures, including rooms in a large barge docked – sort of – on Odiak Slough. The more expensive rooms include a full breakfast.

King's Chamber (☎ 424-3373; www.thekingschamber.com; cnr 4th St & Browning Ave; r from $100; ⊠) At the top of downtown, King's Chamber has several homey units that range from an efficiency unit to a four-bedroom apartment. Owner Mark King grew up in Cordova in the commercial fishing industry and tells interesting stories about the way things used to be before the oil spill. Kids under 16 stay for free.

Reluctant Fisherman Inn (☎ 424-3272, 800-770-3272; www.reluctantfisherman.com; cnr Railroad & Council Aves; r $100-130; ⊠ 💻) As close to luxurious as Cordova gets, this place overhangs Orca Inlet and has a restaurant and lounge.

Orca Adventure Lodge (☎ 424-7249, 866-424-6722; www.orcaadventurelodge.com; Railroad Ave; d from $140; ⊠ 💻) Housed in the historic Orca Cannery 2 miles north of downtown, this waterfront lodge caters to adventurers with daily adventure-tour packages, and can include meals at the café.

Lighthouse Inn (☎ 424-7080; www.cordovalighthouseinn.com; 203 Nicholoff Way; r $145; ⊠ 💻) This inn has brilliant views of the small-boat harbor from its small, plush rooms, all with baths.

Eating

Picnic Basket (☎ 424-4337; Railroad Ave; meals $3-9; 🕒 11am-8pm Tue-Sun) This spot does the cheapest (and best) halibut and chips in town, in addition to homemade desserts.

our pick **Killer Whale Café** (☎ 424-7733; 1st St; breakfast $5-10, sandwiches & burgers $8-10; 🕒 6:30am-3pm Mon-Sat, to 1pm Sun) This café serves hearty breakfasts and fresh (sometimes organic) soups, wraps and sandwiches. This is where the town's lefties hang out, plotting environmental strategy.

our pick **Baja Taco** (☎ 424-5599; Harbor Loop Rd; fast food $6-10; 🕒 8am-9pm) Graft a bus onto a cabin, add flowers, cattle skulls and nautical implements, and what do you have? The best fish-taco stand north of San Diego. It also serves beer and espressos and great Mexican-flavored breakfasts – try the migas.

Reluctant Fisherman Restaurant (☎ 424-3272, 800-770-3272; cnr Railroad & Council Aves; meals $8-35; 🕒 11:30am–midnight) At lunchtime this place fills with locals digging into hearty all-American fare and taking in the best harbor views in town.

Ambrosia (☎ 424-7175; 413 1st St; dinner $12-20, pizza $15-30; 🕒 11:30am-10pm) Nothing pretentious here, but the Italian food comes out steaming hot. Plus, wine by the glass is only $3.50.

QUICK EATS & GROCERIES

SerendipiTea (☎ 424-8327; 505 1st St; 🕒 10am-6pm Mon-Sat) Has a small selection of organic groceries.

AC Value Center (☎ 424-7141; 106 Nicholoff Way; 🕒 7:30am-10pm Mon-Sat, 8am-9pm Sun) A supermarket with a deli, espresso bar, ATM and Western Union.

Drinking & Entertainment

There's not much of a formal entertainment scene in Cordova, but with scads of young cannery workers thronging the place in the summertime, there always seems to be a jam session going on somewhere.

Powder House Bar (☎ 424-3529; Mile 2 Copper River Hwy; dinner $8-20; 🕒 10am-late Mon-Sat, from noon Sun) Overlooking Eyak Lake on the site of the original Copper River & Northwestern Railroad powder house, this is a fun place with live music, excellent beer, soup and sandwiches for lunch, and quality steak and seafood dinners. Friday is sushi day – it starts at noon and goes till the sushi's all gone.

Alaskan Hotel & Bar (☎ 424-3299; 600 1st St) This raucous fishers' bar offers wine tastings from 5pm to 7pm on Wednesday.

Anchor Bar (Breakwater Ave) Across from the small-boat harbor, this is your basic watering hole that's open 'as long as there are fish.'

Getting There & Around

Compact Cordova can be easily explored on foot, but the major problem for travelers exploring the outlying Copper River area is finding transportation. Hitchhiking along the Copper River Hwy is possible, though you might not encounter many passing motorists, even in the summer months.

AIR

ERA Aviation (☎ 800-866-8394; www.flyera.com) flies twice daily between Anchorage and Cordova's Merle K 'Mudhole' Smith Airport; an advance-purchase ticket is $166/332 one way/round-trip. **Alaska Airlines** (☎ 800-252-7522; www.alaskaair.com) comes here on a milk run from Anchorage to Yakutat and Juneau once per day. To Juneau, an advance-purchase ticket is $190/380 one way/round-trip.

BOAT

The **Alaska Marine Highway** (☎ 424-7333, 800-642-0066; www.ferryalaska.com) runs ferries daily to Valdez ($50, four hours) and Whittier ($89, 6½ hours). You can now choose to take the bright new speed ferry, which halves the time of the older ferry, but both trips are scenic and pleasant. Note that several times a week the trip to Whittier routes through Valdez, making the journey an all-day affair.

BICYCLE

Cordova Coastal Outfitters (☎ 424-7424, 800-357-5145; www.cdvcoastal.com; Harbor Loop Rd) rents mountain bikes for $18 a day, including helmet, water bottles and a rack for gear. The company also provides drop-offs at the end of Copper River Hwy for $175 per trip for up to six people with gear.

CAR

Chinook Auto Rentals (☎ 424-5279, 877-424-5279; www.chinookautorentals.com; Mile 13 Copper River Hwy) starts its cars at $55 per day. Another option is right next door at **Cordova Auto Rental** (☎ 424-5982; www.ptialaska.net/~cars) across from the airport. It hires out cars for $75 per day with unlimited mileage, and also promises to beat any price.

WHITTIER

pop 174

You can see glaciers and brown bears, even mountains taller than Denali, without once visiting Alaska. But you will never, in a lifetime of searching, find another place like Whittier.

Shortly after the Japanese attack on the Aleutian Islands during WWII, the US began looking for a spot to build a secret military installation. The proposed base needed to be not only an ice-free port, but also as inaccessible as possible, lost in visibility-reducing cloud cover and surrounded by impassable mountains. They found it all right here.

And so, in this place that would be considered uninhabitable by almost any standard, surrounded by 3500ft peaks and hung with sloppy gray clouds most of the year, Whittier was built. A supply tunnel was blasted out of solid granite, one of Alaska's true engineering marvels, and more than 1000 people were housed in a single tower, the Buckner Building. It wasn't picturesque, but it was efficient.

The army maintained Whittier until 1968, leaving behind not only the Buckner Building, now abandoned, but also the 14-story-tall Begich Towers, where, it seems, some 80% of Whittiots now reside. A labyrinth of underground tunnels connects the complex with schools and businesses, which certainly cuts down on snow-shoveling time. The structure has also given rise to a unique society, where 150-odd people, though virtually isolated from the outside world, live only a few cinder blocks away from one another. It's obviously a must-see attraction for cultural anthropologists.

The rest of us, however, come to Whittier for many of the reasons the military did. The impossibly remote location provides access to an almost unspoiled wilderness of water, ice and granite. Kayaking and scuba diving are superb, and the docks are packed with cruise ships and water-taxis waiting to take you out into the wildlife-rich waters. The town itself is rarely described as adorable, but then it's never really had the luxury of such pretensions.

But all this is changing. Until recently Whittier was accessible only by train or boat; though only 11 miles from the most traveled highway in Alaska, the hamlet was effectively isolated from the rest of the Kenai Peninsula. In 2000, however, the Anton Anderson Memorial Tunnel was overhauled for auto traffic, opening one of the most abnormal places imaginable to increased tourism and slow normalization.

Orientation & Information

Tucked in a pocket of mountains hard against the Sound, Whittier is famously compact. Still, it can be disorienting, because it doesn't so much have a streetscape as a variety of routes through its massive parking lot and rail yard. On the waterfront you'll find the Triangle, a colorful clutter of restaurants, tour operators and gift shops located between the small-boat harbor and the new ferry terminal. The **Anton Anderson Memorial Tunnel** is west of town, while Begich Towers looms to the south. Most of the hiking trails and berry patches are farther east, on Salmon Run Rd.

An information gazebo sits in the Triangle, but when we visited it wasn't being utilized. The post office is in Begich Towers, along with the police and fire stations, a medical clinic – even a church.

Anchor Inn (☎ 472-2354; 100 Whittier St; www.anchorinnwhittier.com; 🕑 9am-9pm; 💻) Has an ATM, two computers for internet, a coin-op laundry and showers.

Harbormaster's Office (Harbor View Rd) Has pay phones and showers.

Harbor Store (☎ 472-2277; Harbor View Rd; 🕑 8am-8pm) Has an ATM and sells phone cards.

Sportsman Inn (☎ 472-2354; Blackstone Rd; 🕑 10am-midnight; 💻) Beneath the looming Buckner Building ruin; has free wi-fi and internet access on several new terminals.

USFS Information Yurt (☎ 242-8539; Harbor View Rd; 🕑 9am-5pm Fri-Sun) Has the best info on the town and on hiking, camping, public-use cabins and kayaking in Chugach National Forest.

DETOUR: COPPER RIVER HWY

As if Cordova wasn't cool enough, there's something equally cool just out its back door: the Copper River Hwy. This 50-mile, mostly gravel road is the gateway to the Copper River Delta, a wildlife-rich wilderness with amazing opportunities for hiking, fishing and birding. Just as amazing are the twin wonders at the road's end: the improbable Million Dollar Bridge and the breathtaking Childs Glacier.

Constructed on the old railroad bed to the Kennecott mines, the highway was once destined to connect Cordova with Interior Alaska. Construction was interrupted after the 1964 Good Friday Earthquake knocked out the fourth span of the Million Dollar Bridge. Today, the road is gravel past Mile 13, difficult to hitchhike, pricey to arrange transportation, but worth every hassle. Before departing, visit the USFS Visitor Center in Cordova, which has maps and info on roadside attractions.

Copper River Delta

The Copper River Hwy begins as 1st St downtown. Barely 5 miles on, the mountains take a dramatic step back and you emerge, miraculously, into the open-skied 700,000-acre Copper River Delta, a 60-mile arc formed by six glacier-fed river systems.

Millions of birds and waterfowl stop here during the spring and fall, including seven million western sandpipers and the entire population of West Coast dunlins. Other species include Arctic terns, dusty Canada geese, trumpeter swans, great blue herons and bald eagles. There's also a chance you'll spot moose, brown bears, beavers and porcupines.

The delta, which crosses Chugach National Forest, has numerous hiking trails and rafting opportunities. Sockeye-salmon fishing begins in mid-June and peaks around July 4. Coho-salmon runs occur from August to September, and cutthroat trout and Dolly Varden can be caught throughout the summer and fall.

Childs Glacier

A common malaise affecting tourists in Alaska could be called 'glacier fatigue.' But no matter how jaded you've become, Childs will blow your mind.

For a warm-up, visit **Sheridan Glacier** at Mile 15 of the highway. Sheridan Glacier Access Rd leads to picnic tables with partial views of the ice floe and a 1-mile trail across the glacial moraine.

At the end of the Copper River Hwy, the 0.6-mile Copper River Trail takes you along the river to the observation deck for Childs Glacier. It's probable, however, that you'll hear the glacier before you see it. A rarity in Alaska, Childs is advancing some 500ft a year, perpetually dumping bergs into Copper River. The thunderous calvings are particularly frequent in late spring and summer, when the water's high. But heed the warnings: the glacier is a mere 1200ft away, and potentially deadly waves can reverberate quickly across the river when particularly big bergs break off the glacier.

Nearby, **Childs Glacier Recreation Area** (sites $5) has five wooded campsites that are a great place to awaken in the morning – if the calving doesn't keep you up.

Million Dollar Bridge

Just beyond the recreation area is this four-span trestle, created during the winter of 1909–10 but put out of commission by the 1964 earthquake. In 2004, fearing the damaged fourth span would fall into the river, the state spent $18 million to return the bridge to a passable condition.

You can now drive, bike or walk on to the bridge to take in the views. Downstream, close enough to hear it grumble, is Childs Glacier. Upstream, meanwhile, is the Miles Glacier – the source of those icebergs racing beneath you. In 1910, Miles' rapid advance threatened the newly constructed bridge, forcing workers to chisel at its face day and night. It stopped just feet from the struts. Now, it's 4 miles distant.

Sights

Whittier's dystopian townscape is perversely intriguing, and thus well worth a stroll. Start at **Begich Towers**, visible from anywhere in town, where the 1st, 14th and 15th floors are open to nonresidents. Watching children playing in the cinder-block corridors, you can't help contemplating how much of your private business would be common knowledge if you'd grown up here.

From the southwest corner of Begich Towers, you can look west to Whittier Creek, while above it, falling from the ridge of a glacial cirque, is picturesque **Horsetail Falls**. Locals use the cascade to gauge the weather: if the tail is whipping upwards, it's too windy to go out in a boat. There are also great views of dozens of other waterfalls streaking from the snowfields to the Sound.

Heading back toward the waterfront along Eastern Ave, you'll come to the rather extravagantly named **Prince William Sound Museum** (100 Whittier St; adult/child $3/1.50; 🕑 variable), which occupies an ill-lit room beside the Anchor Inn Grocery Store. The space has lots of tidy displays about Whittier's military history, but the most striking exhibit is about the man who engineered the town's tunnel, Anton Anderson. A Swedish-Australian immigrant, Anderson discovered he had a knack for carving holes through mountains, and then found he had a knack for politics, eventually becoming the mayor of Anchorage.

Climbing Blackstone Rd from the museum, the **Buckner Building** dominates the otherwise picture-postcard view. Once the largest structure in Alaska, the 'city under one roof' looms dismal and abandoned above town; the use of asbestos in the structure has complicated attempts to remodel or tear down the eerie edifice.

From here, walk along the **Shotgun Cove Trail** (right), which winds through blueberry and salmonberry thickets to First Salmon Run Picnic Area, and then head a quarter mile down the road to your right (northeast) to get to **Smitty's Cove**. At low tide you can comb the beach westward, following the water's edge past the ferry terminal to the Triangle.

This clutter of restaurants, tour outfits and quirkier-than-average gift shops is fun; don't miss **Log Cabin Gifts** (☎ 472-2501; The Triangle; 🕑 11am-6pm), Whittier's best stab at adorable. The knickknacks, including lots of high-quality leatherwork, are handmade by owner Brenda Tolman, but the live reindeer outside are the real crowd pleasers. If it's wet out, though, they'll be back in their pen in front of the Begich Towers. Apparently, they don't like rain – which makes it tough to live in Whittier.

Continue along the water to the small-boat harbor, where you'll find local commercial fishing boats and a whole lot of pleasure vessels owned by Anchorage-based weekenders. After checking out the fleet, finish up your tour with a meal at any of the good, inexpensive eateries lining the water.

Activities

HIKING

Portage Pass Trail

Whittier's sole USFS-maintained trail is a superb afternoon hike, providing good views of Portage Glacier, Passage Canal and the surrounding mountains and glaciers. Even better, hike up in the late afternoon and spend the evening camping at Divide Lake.

The Portage Pass Trail is along an old roadbed and is easy to follow. To reach it, head west of town toward the tunnel, then follow the signs leftward onto a road crossing the railroad tracks. You'll find a parking area at the trailhead. Proceed along the right fork as it begins to climb steeply along the flank of the mountain. There's a steady ascent for a mile, finishing at a promontory (elevation 750ft) that offers views of Portage Glacier and Passage Canal to the east.

The trail then descends for a half-mile to Divide Lake and Portage Pass. At this point the trail ends, and a route through alder trees continues to descend to a beach on Portage Lake. It's a 2-mile hike one way from the trailhead to the lake, and it's well worth bashing some brush at the end. There are great views from the shores of Portage Lake and plenty of places to set up camp on the alluvial flats.

Shotgun Cove Trail

This 0.8-mile walk along a dirt road leads to the First Salmon Run Picnic Area, so named because of the king and silver salmon runs during June and late August. The forest and mountains en route are scenic but, in true Whittier fashion, the roadsides are debris-strewn and the picnic area is in disrepair.

From the northeast corner of the Buckner Building, follow Salmon Run Rd up the

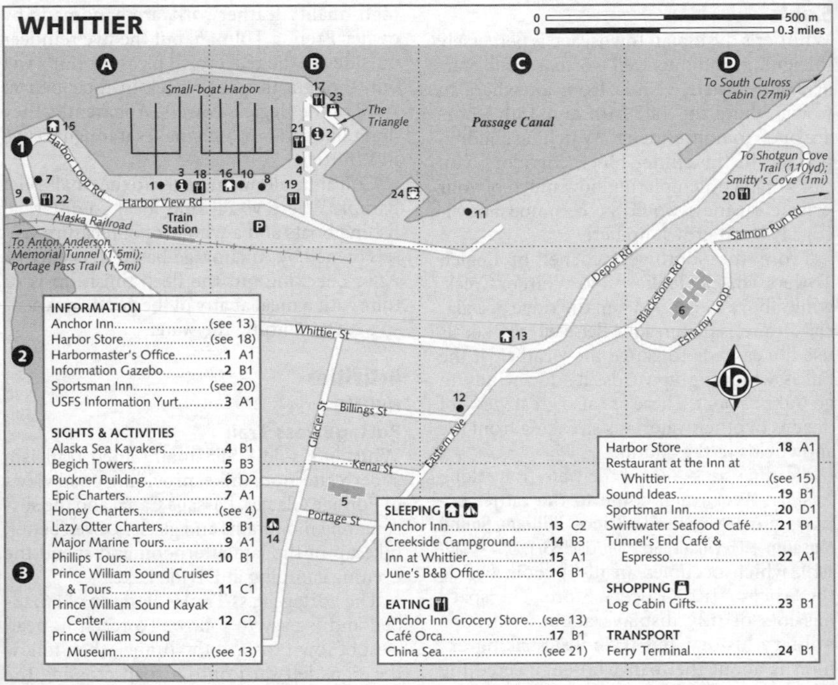

mountain, staying to the right at the first fork and to the left at the second fork.

At the picnic area you can cross a bridge over the stream and continue another 3 miles to Second Salmon Run. This walk, along what is known as Shotgun Cove Rd, is exceptionally scenic, with views of Billings Glacier most of the way.

PADDLING

Whittier is a prime location for sea kayakers, as it's practically surrounded by glaciated fjords and inlets. The most common overnight trip from Whittier is Blackstone Bay, which contains a pair of tidewater glaciers, Blackstone and Beloit. Many kayakers utilize charter boats to access the dramatic fjords to the north, including Harriman Fjord, College Fjord and Unakwik Inlet.

Prince William Sound Kayak Center (☎ 472-2452, 877-472-2452; www.pwskayakcenter.com; Eastern Ave; 🕑 7am-7pm) is a well-run organization that rents kayaks (single/double $50/80, discounted for multiple days) and runs guided tours, including three-hour paddles to the kittiwake rookery (per person $160) and day-long excursions to Blackstone Bay (for two people $425; hefty discount if you can get six folks together). It also has escorts for multiday trips. These aren't guided tours: while escorts will suggest camping spots and routes, you're in charge of your own trip, including food and gear. It's a neat option for independent-minded folks who don't have the experience to feel comfortable spending a week on the water solo. The company will also let customers 'camp' and use the climbing wall inside its cavernous (but waterproof) facility.

Lazy Otter Charters (☎ 694-6887, 800-587-6887; www.lazyotter.com; Harbor View Rd; per person $195; 🕑 6:30am-7pm) offers escorted day trips to Blackstone Bay for a minimum of four people. It also runs a water-taxi.

Alaska Sea Kayakers (☎ 472-2534, 877-472-2534; www.alaskaseakayakers.com; The Triangle; 🕑 7am-7pm) rents kayaks ($40 to $75 per day), arranges water-taxis and takes various multiday tours to places like Harriman Fjord, Nellie Juan Glacier and Whale Bay. It has two booking offices (the second at Lot 11, Harbor View Rd) and both will set you up with whatever you need.

Epic Charters (☎ 242-4339; www.epicchartersalaska.com; Harbor Loop Rd; 🕐 8am-6pm) rents kayaks for $45/55 per single/double per day, and also offers guided kayak charters and glacier viewing from $99 per person.

WILDERNESS CABINS

There are six **USFS cabins** (☎ 877-444-6777, 518-885-3639; www.recreation.gov; $35) accessible by boat from Whittier. Pigot Bay and Paulson Bay are the closest, with excellent salmon fishing and good views; Harrison Lagoon has the best access for mobility-impaired folks, plus some great tide pools; Shrode Lake comes with a boat; Coghill Lake is a scenic spot with good fishing and berry-picking; and South Culross Passage is on a picturesque cove on Culross Island.

DIVING

Whittier is a top spot for (involuntary shiver) Alaskan scuba diving – it's one of the wildest places easily accessible to human beings. The best time to dive is March through June.

Popular spots include the Dutch Group islands, known for the high visibility offshore, and the kittiwake rookery. There, a combination of steep cliffs and fresh fertilizer from the birds above has created a gently swaying rainbow of nudibranchs. Good places to view giant Pacific octopuses, wolf eels and crabs the size of manhole covers are located in Esther and Culross Passages, close to **South Culross Passage cabin** (☎ 877-444-6777, 518-885-3639; www.recreation.gov; $45). Divers also often head to Smitty's Cove, which is east of the ferry terminal and is the only dive spot accessible by foot.

Lazy Otter Charters (☎ 694-6887, 800-587-6887; www.lazyotter.com; Harbor View Rd) can provide water-taxi service to the best underwater locations. It charges a minimum of $185 for the boat plus additional fees that are based on mileage.

Tours

Various tour boats sail from the small-boat harbor into a rugged, icy world that's unbelievably rich in wildlife. On the way to Harriman Fjord, ships pass so close to a kittiwake rookery that you can see the eggs in the nests of the black-legged birds.

Honey Charters (☎ 888-477-2493; www.honeycharters.com; The Triangle) Offers tours of Blackstone Bay (per person $125) and Barry Arm ($175), both with a four-person minimum, as well as sightseeing trips to Cordova ($175) and Valdez ($175), which both have a 12-person minimum. It specializes in water-taxi transportation to public-use cabins and to remote hunting, fishing and hiking destinations. It's $12 per nautical mile for up to 30 people; rates are 40% cheaper if you can coordinate drop-offs and pickups with other groups.

Major Marine Tours (☎ 800-764-7300, 274-7300; www.majormarine.com; Harbor Loop Rd) Has a USFS ranger on every cruise. It does a five-hour tour of glacier-riddled Blackstone Bay for $107/53 (plus tax) per adult/child.

Phillips Tours (☎ 472-2416, 800-544-0529; www.26glaciers.com; Harbor View Rd) Packs in 26 glaciers on a speedy boat ride for adult/child $139/79. Don't blink.

Prince William Sound Cruises & Tours (☎ 472-2410, 800-992-1297; www.princewilliamsound.com; 1 Harbor Pier) Offers 'quality time' with the very active Surprise Glacier on its six-hour tour of Esther Passage (per adult/child $129/64.50).

Sleeping

Those wishing to stay overnight in Whittier face unappealing options: camping in puddles, flopping at a dive of a hotel or paying through the nose for something nicer. Also note that a 5% sales tax will be added to the prices listed here.

There's only one official campground in Whittier: the horrid **Creekside Campground** (Glacier St; sites $10), which is basically a mud-soaked, clear-cut gravel quarry. Ask around and locals will point you to informal spots along Salmon Run Rd.

Anchor Inn (☎ 472-2354; www.anchorinnwhittier.com; 100 Whittier St; s/d $100/131; ☒) This multipurpose venue has cinder-block walls, and overlooks a junkyard on one side and the rail yard on the other, but it'll do in a pinch. There's an attached restaurant, bar, laundry and grocery store.

June's B&B (☎ 472-2396, 888-472-2396; www.breadnbuttercharters.com; Lot 7, Harbor View Rd; condos $145-450; ☒) This business offers an insight into the local lifestyle, putting you up in comfortable, homey suites atop Begich Towers. Occasionally owner June rents out an economy suite on the ground floor.

Inn at Whittier (☎ 472-7000; www.innatwhittier.com; Harbor Loop Rd; r $219-399; 💻 ☒) Rooms are bland but the view isn't – make sure you spend the $20 extra for a water view. Rates are considerably less from mid-April to mid-May. Attached is a high-end restaurant and Whittier's best stab at a swank bar.

Eating

Sound Ideas (☎ 472-2535; Lot 1 Harbor View Rd; 9am-8pm) Has a beautiful selection of fudge made on the premises.

Tunnel's End Café & Espresso (☎ 472-3000; 12 Harbor Loop Rd; mains $4-13; 7:30am-7pm Wed-Sun, to 4pm Mon) Breakfast is nothing fancy, but it's cheap. For later, there are grilled salmon sandwiches and fried halibut.

Swiftwater Café (☎ 472-2550; The Triangle; mains $6-14; 11:30am-9pm Sun-Thu, to 10pm Fri & Sat) The fish and chips hit the spot when it's raining horizontally outside. You can peruse the photos of famous Alaskan shipwrecks over your rhubarb crisp ($4.50).

Sportsman Inn (☎ 472-2354; Blackstone Rd; mains $6-16; 10am-midnight;) Serves pub grub like hot wings and pizza.

China Sea (☎ 472-3663; The Triangle; lunch $8-10, dinner $10-19; 11am-10pm) Serving up Chinese and Korean food, this place has an $11 lunch buffet featuring fresh kung po halibut.

Café Orca (☎ 472-2549; The Triangle; light meals $8-12; 11am-7pm) The vegetable sandwiches, lattes and homemade desserts here aren't cheap, but it's a restful place with a great little waterfront deck.

Restaurant at the Inn at Whittier (☎ 472-7000; Harbor Loop Rd; breakfast & lunch $8-18, dinner $23-30; 8am-10pm) This dining room has glorious views of the Sound and cooks up steaks and seafood. Have a martini at McGrew's, the posh pub attached to the restaurant.

GROCERIES

Harbor Store (☎ 472-2277; Harbor View Rd; 8am-8pm) This store has groceries and snacks for your hike.

Anchor Inn Grocery Store (☎ 472-2354; 100 Whittier St; 9am-10pm) A bigger grocery store across town.

Getting There & Around

Whittier is one of those places where getting there is half the fun. Sometimes, leaving can be even better.

BOAT

The **Alaska Marine Highway ferry** (☎ 800-642-0066; www.ferryalaska.com) sails three times per week direct to Valdez ($89, 3½ to seven hours), and another three times per week direct to Cordova for the same price. Both trips are super-scenic – think Dall porpoises, Stellar sea lions and a kittiwake rookery. Twice per month a ferry departs Whittier, crosses the Gulf of Alaska and docks in Juneau ($221; 39 hours). The ferry terminal is beside the Triangle.

BUS

Magic Bus (☎ 230-6773; www.themagicbus.com) has a daily bus between Anchorage and Whittier (one way/round-trip $40/50, 1½ hours), which leaves Anchorage at 10:30am and departs Whittier for the return trip at 5:30pm. Note that if you're making an Alaska Ferry connection, the arrival time is too late for the 12:45pm ferry.

Whittier Shuttle (☎ 783-1900; www.whittieralaskashuttle.com) coordinates with the cruise ships' schedules, running shuttles from Whittier to Anchorage at 10am and 3pm, with one trip from Anchorage at 12:25pm (adult/child one-way $55/45).

Prince William Sound Cruises & Tours (☎ 472-2410, 877-777-2805; www.princewilliamsound.com) can book independent travelers on the shuttle between Anchorage and Whittier ($69 either one-way or round-trip, 2½ hours). The bus leaves downtown Anchorage around 8:30am, and makes the return drive from Whittier at 5pm.

Every so often, **Homer Stage Line** (☎ 235-2252; www.thestageline.net) has connections from Whittier to Seward and Homer.

CAR

Whittier Access Rd, also known as Portage Glacier Access Rd, leaves the Seward Hwy at Mile 79, continuing to Whittier through the claustrophobic Anton Anderson Memorial Tunnel, which at 2.7 miles long is the longest 'railroad-highway' tunnel in North America. Negotiating the damp one-lane shaft as you skid across the train tracks is almost worth the steep price of admission (per car/RV $12/20) which is charged only if you're entering Whittier; if you bring your car into town on the Alaska Marine Hwy you can exit through the tunnel for free. Eastbound and westbound traffic alternate every 15 minutes, with interruptions for the Alaska Railroad. Bring a magazine.

TRAIN

The **Alaska Railroad** (☎ 265-2494, 800-544-0552; www.akrr.com) operates the *Glacier Discovery* train between Anchorage and Whittier (one way/round-trip $60/74, 2½ hours) daily May through September. It departs Anchorage at 10am and Whittier at 6:55pm.

Kenai Peninsula

Set enticingly across Turnagain Arm from Anchorage, the Kenai Peninsula is a veritable jungle gym for Anchorage residents and tourists alike. With two main roads splintering across an area the size of Belgium, the peninsula is an accessible wilderness, allowing visitors to edge as far away from civilization as they feel comfortable. Here, you can gawk at Dall sheep from inside an RV, or watch grizzlies snap salmon from streams so remote you'll have to fly there.

The Kenai Mountains form the eastern two-thirds of the peninsula, and there are more hiking trails and alpine lakes here than you can explore in a summer. Glaciers are crammed into every cranny, and their retreat from the Talkeetna Mountains thousands of years ago has left the comparatively flat western side of the peninsula pocked with trout-filled lakes excellent for canoeing. Then there's the marine world: the peninsula's jagged coastline makes for some of the best kayaking you'll find, with waters full of marine mammals, birds and fish.

The towns along the Kenai Peninsula are as varied as the topography. There's Homer, swirling with artists and good vibes; and Seward, huddled in the mountains with its railroad-grid historic downtown and charming small-boat harbor. Mellow Hope hides down a spur road, waiting for you to discover its homestead buildings and gold rush relics half-overgrown with grass. Other small communities sit tucked off the two-lane roads, each boasting something different than the last, whether it's a Russian Orthodox church, a packed salmon stream, or a stretch of sandy beach.

But, no matter where you choose to stop, you are always only a few steps away from the wilderness.

HIGHLIGHTS

- **Clammiest feeling** – catching low tide and razor clams in Clam Gulch (p277) for a steamy, succulent meal
- **Most positive outlook** – gazing down at Turnagain Arm and Alaska's first Gold Rush town from the 3700ft Hope Point (p257)
- **Biggest natural stair-stepper** – the near-vertical trail up Seward's Mt Marathon (p260), where Fourth of July racers have been running to the top since 1915.
- **Blankest stare** – gazing across the vast expanse of the 900-sq-mile Harding Ice Field (p267)
- **Best hideout** – exploring the spooky WWII bunkers 6 miles outside Seward at Caines Head (p263)

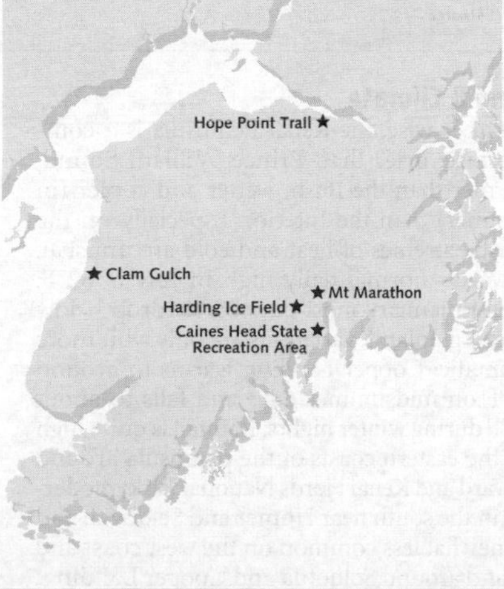

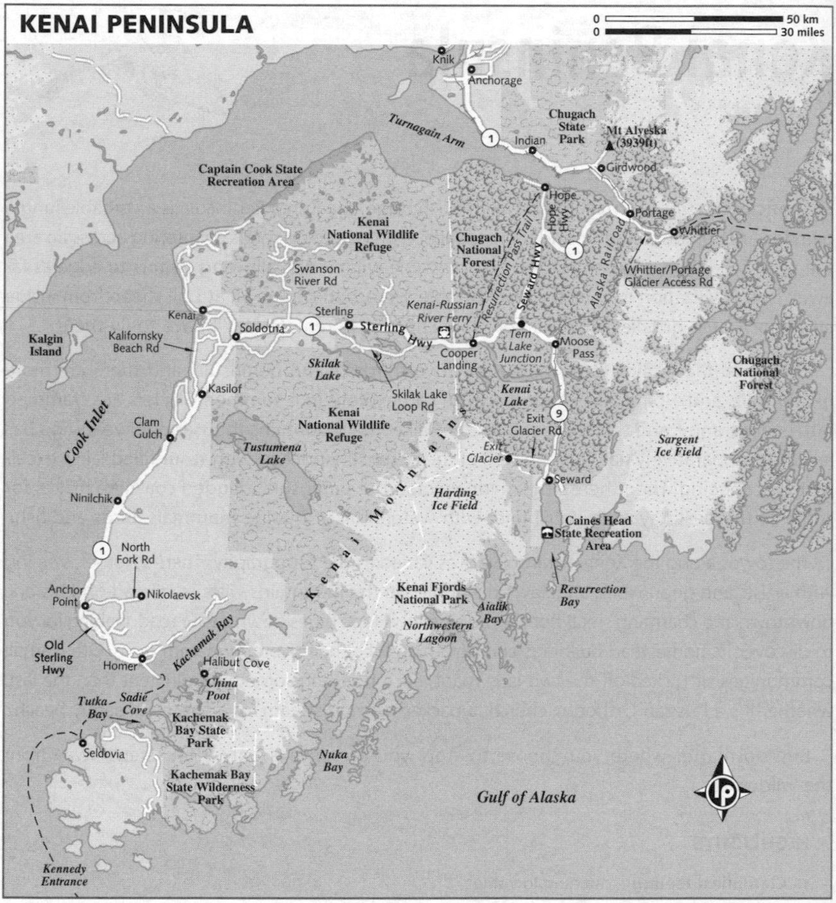

Land & Climate

Weather-wise, the Kenai Peninsula is a compromise: drier than Prince William Sound, warmer than the Bush, wetter and cooler (in summer) than the Interior. Especially on the coast, extremes of heat and cold are unusual. Seward's normal daily high in July is 62°F; even in January most days barely drop below freezing. Inland, variations are only a bit more dramatic: Cooper Landing warms to around 68°F on midsummer days and falls to about 15°F during winter nights. Rainfall is quite high on the eastern coasts of the peninsula around Seward and Kenai Fjords National Park; moderate in the south near Homer and Seldovia; and somewhat less common on the west coast and inland around Soldotna and Cooper Landing.

Geographically, the Kenai Peninsula is a grab-bag. The Chugach Range receives the most attention, but in actuality mountains only cover around two-thirds of the peninsula. On the west side, the land flattens out into a marshy, lake-pocked region excellent for canoeing and trout fishing.

History

For millennia, Dena'ina Indians made the Kenai Peninsula their home, as did Alutiiqs in the south and Chugaches in the east. They largely subsisted as many modern residents do: by pulling fish from the area's bountiful waterways. In 1741 Vitus Bering, a Dane sailing for the Russians, was the first European to lay eyes on the peninsula; in 1778 British explorer Captain James Cook sailed up the inlet that would bear his name, landing north of the present-day city of Kenai and claiming the area for England. Despite that, the first white settlement on the peninsula was Russian – St Nicholas Redoubt, founded at the mouth of the Kenai River as a fur trading post in 1791. Orthodox missionaries arrived soon thereafter, and many of the local Alaska Natives were converted to that faith.

When Alaska came under American rule in 1867 the US established Fort Kenay near where the redoubt had stood. The surrounding settlement endured as a commercial fishing village until 1957, when the nearby Swanson River became the site of the state's first major oil strike. Kenai has been an oil town ever since.

The Alaska Railroad made its start in Seward in 1903, where Resurrection Bay was the closest ice free port. The Kenai Peninsula was officially on the map as the main thoroughfare for goods to Anchorage, and eventually for coal leaving the state.

The 1964 Good Friday Earthquake hit the peninsula hard. After the earth finally stopped churning, oil tanks exploded and tsunamis rolled through Seward, ravaging the town. With the bridges, railroad and boat harbor gone, Seward was suddenly cut off from the rest of the state. Homer suffered too: the quake dropped the Spit by 6ft and leveled most of the buildings. It took six years and almost $7 million to rebuild.

Since then tourism has boomed on the Kenai Peninsula, turning the region into Alaska's premier playground for visitors and locals, and becoming a key engine of the region's economy.

Parks & Protected Lands

As developed as the Kenai Peninsula can sometimes seem, it's mostly trackless wilderness under federal and state protection. On the east side of the peninsula is glorious Kenai Fjords National Park (p266), encompassing tidewater glaciers that pour down from one of the continent's largest ice fields, as well as the steep-sided fjords those glaciers have carved. With the exception of a single road to much-visited Exit Glacier, the park is accessible only to boaters, paddlers and alpinists. Abutting the park in places, and taking in much of the most southerly part of the Kenai Peninsula, is Kachemak Bay State Park (p293) – a wondrous land of mountains, forests and fjords, all accessible by water-taxi from Homer. Like Kenai Fjords National Park, this state park is a paddler's paradise, and what it lacks in tidewater glaciers it makes up for in excellent trails. Finally, covering much of the interior of the peninsula, there's the Kenai National Wildlife Refuge (p271), with excellent canoeing and hiking routes, plus some of the world's best salmon fishing.

Getting There & Around

If you've ever been stuck in a Soldotna traffic jam or huffed fumes behind a string of Seward-bound RVs, you'll know: the Kenai Peninsula is a place of vehicles. Two busy, paved highways extend through this region. The Seward Hwy runs south from Anchorage to Seward, while the Sterling Hwy (p269) spurs westward off the Seward Hwy to Soldotna, then drops down to Homer. If you don't have your own wheels, you could rent some in Anchorage (p217). Alternatively, hop aboard a long-haul bus. **Homer Stage Line** (☎ 868-3914; www.homerstageline.com) operates daily between Anchorage, Homer and Seward; Seward is also connected to Anchorage by a couple of other operators (p266).

Another (excellent) transport possibility is rail; the southern terminus of the **Alaska Railroad** (☎ 265-2494, 800-544-0552; www.akrr.com) is at Seward, which is visited daily by trains from Anchorage.

Finally, as with everywhere in Alaska, there's always flying. Homer and the city of Kenai are served by **ERA Aviation** (☎ 235-7565, 800-426-0333; www.flyera.com); many of the peninsula's other towns also have airstrips and scheduled flights.

SEWARD HIGHWAY

The Seward Hwy is a road-trip-lovers delight, with smooth, winding turns through mountains that have you craning your neck around every corner. The 127 miles of highway is all Scenic Byway, and there are plenty of turnoffs for gawking and snapping photos. Keep in mind that the mileposts along the highway show distances from Seward (Mile 0) to Anchorage (Mile 127). The first section of this road – from Anchorage to Portage Glacier (Mile 79) – is covered in the Anchorage chapter (p218).

TURNAGAIN PASS & AROUND

After it departs Turnagain Arm, Seward Hwy heads for the hills. Near Mile 68 it begins climbing into the alpine region of **Turnagain Pass**, where there's a roadside stop with garbage cans and toilets. In early summer, this area is a kaleidoscope of wildflowers.

Bertha Creek Campground (Mile 65 Seward Hwy; sites $10), just across the Bertha Creek Bridge, is understandably popular – site No 6 even has a waterfall view. You can spend a day climbing the alpine slopes of the pass here, or head to Mile 64 and the northern trailhead of both the 23-mile **Johnson Pass Trail** (p97) and the paved **Sixmile Bike Trail**, which runs 8 miles – not six – along the highway.

Granite Creek Campground (Mile 63 Seward Hwy; sites $10) is reminiscent of Yosemite Valley: wildflower meadows, dramatic mountains…the works. Also similar to Yosemite, the sites here fill up fast.

The Hope Hwy junction and south trailhead for the Sixmile Bike Trail are both at Mile 56.7. From here, the Hope Hwy heads 16 miles north to the small hamlet of Hope (below).

The Seward Hwy continues south of this junction to Upper Summit Lake, surrounded by neck-craning peaks. The lakeside **Tenderfoot Creek Campground** (Mile 46 Seward Hwy; sites $14) has 27 sites that are open enough to catch the view but wooded enough for privacy.

Within walking distance of the campground is **Summit Lake Lodge** (☎ 244-2031; www.summitlakelodge.com; Mile 45.8 Seward Hwy; d $90; ⊠), with basic rooms, an espresso/gift shop and a bustling **restaurant** (lunch $7-14, dinner $11-23; 8am-11pm).

The **Devil's Pass Trail** (Mile 39.4 Seward Hwy) is a very well-signed, difficult, 10-mile hike over a 2400ft gap to the Resurrection Pass Trail (p94).

At **Tern Lake Junction** (Mile 37 Seward Hwy) is the turnoff for the Sterling Hwy (p269), running 143 miles to Homer.

HOPE

pop 147

Hope has beautiful views of Turnagain Arm surrounded by snowcapped mountains; a quaint and historic downtown; wonderful restaurants and gold rush–era relics; and incredible camping and hiking opportunities within easy access from Anchorage by car. With all this great stuff to distract you, it might take a minute to figure out what's missing. Give up? Here's a hint: just try to find one lame tourist trap. See? Even the gift shops around here are cool.

Somehow, the moose-nugget jewelry purveyors have passed this place by, perhaps missing the turnoff at Mile 56.7 of the Seward Hwy, or failing to follow the winding Hope Hwy the 16.5 miles necessary to reach this rustic hamlet. Don't make the same mistake.

Orientation & Information

Driving along the Hope Hwy you'll encounter a few roadside stores and lodges at Mile 15.9. Just beyond, at Mile 16.2, Palmer Rd leaves the highway heading west and then forks; you need to take the right-hand fork, Resurrection Creek Rd, which runs 5 miles to the Resurrection Pass trailhead (p94), but if you stay left you'll wind 6 miles to Cour d'Alene Campground. Hope itself lies at Mile 16.5 of the Hope Hwy. What's best described as 'downtown Hope' is just east of the highway along Old Hope Rd.

Alaska Dacha (☎ 782-3223; Mile 15.8 Hope Hwy; 9am-9pm) Has the only pay phone between here and Moose Pass, plus sundries, showers, internet, and laundry.

Hope Library (☎ 782-3121; Old Hope Rd; donation appreciated; when the neon sign says 'open';) In a one-room 1938 schoolhouse. Don't miss its gift shop next door, which sells locally made crafts to help support this grassroots facility.

Post office (Old Hope Rd) Opposite the museum, but had plans to move to Palmer Rd in early 2009.

Sights & Activities

HOPE-SUNRISE MINING MUSEUM

This small **log cabin** (☎ 782-3740; Old Hope Rd; admission free; noon-4pm) preserves relics from early miners and homesteaders with a great deal of respect. Creaky buildings give a feel for life at the turn of the 20th century; a quick guided tour is worth the tip for history buffs and anyone with a little extra time.

GOLD PANNING

There are about 125 mining claims throughout the Chugach National Forest. Some of the more serious prospectors actually make money, but most are happy to take home a bottle with a few flakes of gold in it.

The Hope area provides numerous opportunities for the amateur panner, including a 20-acre claim that the US Forest Service (USFS) has set aside near the Resurrection Pass trailhead for recreational mining. Out at the claim there are usually some regulars

KENAI PENINSULA

who don't mind showing newcomers how to swirl the pan. Other panning areas are Sixmile Creek, between Mile 1.5 and Mile 5.5 of the Hope Hwy, and many of the creeks along the Resurrection Pass Trail.

HIKING

The northern trailhead of the legendary 39-mile Resurrection Pass Trail (p94) is near the end of Resurrection Creek Rd. From Porcupine Campground (right), two fine trails lead to scenic points overlooking Turnagain Arm.

The **Gull Rock Trail** is a flat 5-mile, four- to six-hour walk to Gull Rock, a rocky point 140ft above the Turnagain shoreline. The trail follows an old wagon road built at the turn of the 19th century, and along the way you can explore the remains of a cabin and sawmill. You can camp at Gull Rock, but dead spruce trees are a serious fire hazard; stick with a stove.

Hope Point is steeper and a bit more difficult, following an alpine ridge 5 miles for incredible views of Turnagain Arm. Begin at an unmarked trail along the right-hand side of the small Porcupine Creek. After 0.3 miles, the trail leaves the side of the creek and begins to ascend an outcrop with good views. From here, you can follow the ridge above the treeline to Hope Point (elevation 3708ft). Except for an early-summer snowfield, you'll find no water after Porcupine Creek.

PADDLING

Sixmile Creek is serious white water, with thrilling – and dangerous – rapids through deep gorges that survivors describe as 'the best roller coaster in Alaska.' The first two canyons are rated Class IV; the third canyon is a big, bad Class V.

Chugach Outdoor Center (☎ 277-7238; www.chugachoutdoorcenter.com; Mile 7.5 Hope Hwy) guides trips down Sixmile twice daily during summer. The two-canyon run is $99 per person; if you want to defy death on all three canyons it's $149 per person.

Nova River Runners (☎ 800-746-5753; www.novalaska.com) also does twice-daily trips down the river, at $90 for the Class IV canyons, and $135 for the Class V.

Sleeping

Near the end of Resurrection Creek Rd, just before and just after the Resurrection Pass trailhead, are many underdeveloped camping spots beneath a verdant canopy. The nearby creek is popular with gold panners.

Coeur d'Alene Campground (Mile 6.4 Palmer Rd; sites free) This is a gorgeous informal campground at the end of a narrow, winding back road. Pick any spot next to the river that looks good.

Porcupine Campground (Mile 17.8 Hope Hwy; sites $14) Popular for a reason: it's the trailhead for Hope Point and Gull Rock (left) and has transcendent views (especially from sites 4, 6, 8 and 10) of Turnagain Arm. It's highly recommended.

Seaview Café (☎ 782-3300; B St; sites camp/RV $6/18, cabins $50) Has exposed waterfront sites for camping. The cabins have no running water – outhouses are outside – and haven't received favorable reviews.

Bowman's Bear Creek Lodge (☎ 782-3141; www.bowmansbearcreeklodge.com; Mile 15.9 Hope Hwy; cabins $150; ⊠) This place has five hand-hewn, log cabins surrounding a beautiful pond and burbling creek.

Eating

Tito's Discovery Café (☎ 782-3274; Mile 16.5 Hope Hwy; breakfast $6-10, wraps $11-12, dinners $12-16; 7am-9pm) This is a very popular eatery, that serves homemade soups, seafood wraps, and local gossip.

Seaview Café (☎ 782-3300; B St; mains $10-20; noon-9pm Sun-Wed, to 11pm Thu-Sat) Serves up good beer and chowder with views of the Arm. There's always live music on weekends.

our pick **Bowman's Bear Creek Lodge** (☎ 782-3141; Mile 15.9 Hope Hwy; Sun brunch $20, dinner $10-24; 4-10pm Tue-Sun, 10am-2pm Sun) A fabulous menu that changes daily, with homemade desserts, seafood specials, and a friendly, intimate dining room.

Getting There & Away

Hope remains idyllic in part because of its isolation. Though the **Seward Bus Line** (☎ 224-3608) and **Homer Stage Line** (☎ 224-3608; www.homerstageline.com) will drop you off at the junction of the Hope and Seward Hwys, the only way to get to the town proper is by driving, hitching, pedaling or plodding.

MOOSE PASS & AROUND

pop 201

Four miles south of Tern Lake Junction on the Seward Hwy is the trailhead for the **Carter**

TOP PICKS: KENAI PENINSULA HIKES FOR KIDS

The Kenai Peninsula is a choose-your-own-adventure kind of wilderness, so if your kids aren't the kind who'd choose to hike without some kind of instant gratification, take heart: stunning, mellow, and short hikes (yes, ones that combine all three characteristics) are available on the peninsula. Test out a few of these:

Tonsina Point (p263) An easy 3-mile round-trip gets you out of Seward and onto a beach where you can spot sea otters and sea lions, bald eagles, and if you're lucky, a whale. The trail is narrow but not too steep, and you can watch salmon swim up clear Tonsina Creek from the wooden bridge above.

Grayling Lake Trail (opposite) Wide, level paths lead not just to Grayling Lake, but also Meridian and Leech Lakes. These lakes are great for fishing grayling, and the hike shouldn't have junior too tuckered out by the end.

Ptarmigan Creek Trail (below) This one's a bit longer, but for older kids it might be just right. The hike is rewarding without making you scramble, and the postcard-perfect alpine lake makes a nice stopping place.

Glacier Lake Trail (p295) About the same distance as Ptarmigan Creek Trail, this one also leads to a spectacular lake where you can stare at Grewingk Glacier.

Lake Trail (Mile 33 Seward Hwy), a steep 1.9-mile Jeep track providing quick access to subalpine terrain and Carter Lake, where you can continue another mile to some excellent campsites and Crescent Lake. Sturdy hikers can press on another 4 miles to **Crescent Lake Cabin** (☎ 877-444-6777; www.recreation.gov; cabin $45). If you're not driving, Seward-bound buses can drop you off here (see p266).

At Mile 29.4 the village of **Moose Pass** relaxes along the banks of Upper Trail Lake. Founded during the Hope-Sunrise gold rush of the late 19th century, Moose Pass (which was named by a mail carrier who couldn't get past one of the critters) came into its own when the original Iditarod National Historic Trail was cut around the lake in 1910–11. Today the small town is known for its lively **Summer Solstice Festival**.

To get up close to those mountains, try **Scenic Mountain Air** (☎ 288-3646; www.scenicmountainair.com), which runs floatplanes into the hills above Moose Pass. Shorter trips start at $50 with a minimum of four people.

Eating options are limited here, but **Estes Brothers Grocery** (☎ 288-3151; 9am-7pm Mon-Sat, from 10am Sun) has a deli, a small information booth and a gold rush-era waterwheel. For a more leisurely meal, try the quality **Trail Lake Lodge Restaurant** (☎ 288-3103; Mile 29.5 Seward Hwy; breakfast & lunch $7-9, dinner $11-24; 8am-9pm) which serves excellent quesadillas and red chili salmon burgers.

The **Moose Pass RV Park** (☎ 288-5624; Mile 28.9 Seward Hwy; sites camp $10, RV $12-17) is a bit unkempt but the unruly alders keep the sites fairly private. Look for the chainsaw sculpture of the moose wearing Carharts coveralls at the entrance.

For a bed, try **Trail Lake Lodge** (☎ 288-3103; www.traillakelodge.com; Mile 29.5 Seward Hwy; r $99-115; ⊠), which has good, basic accommodations, some overlooking namesake Trail Lake. Call ahead as it often books to large groups.

Just South of Moose Pass are several sleeping options close enough to Seward to use as a base, but far enough out to escape the crowds.

our pick **Trail River Gardens B & B** (☎ 288-3194 or 491-1600; www.trailriver.com; 30847 Seward Hwy; with/without view $125/100; ⊠) has delicious pastries in the morning. The one river view room is about as peaceful a space you can hope for, and there are – you guessed it – some beautiful gardens outside.

Farther south is **Kenai Lake Resort** (☎ 288-5059; www.kenailakeresort.com; 27177 Seward Hwy; cabins from $115, RV sites $25; ⊠), which has mediocre RV sites but fabulous lakeside cabins, with firepits and lofts with views. When we visited it was about to open a café and gift shop with wireless internet access.

Nearby, the **Trail River Campground** (Mile 24 Seward Hwy; www.recreation.gov; sites $18) is run by the USFS and has 91 lovely sites among tall spruce trees along Kenai Lake and Lower Trail River.

After departing Moose Pass, the highway winds through National Forest. At Mile 23, the **Ptarmigan Creek Trail** leads 3.5 miles from the campground to Ptarmigan Lake. Here you'll find turquoise, trout-filled waters that reflect the mountains that cradle it. A 4-mile trail continues around the north side of the lake, which is brushy in places and wet in others; plan on five hours for the round-trip. The **Ptarmigan Creek Campground** (sites $14) has 16 sites that were once shady but now resemble a clear-cut in places due to the spruce beetle.

The **Victor Creek Trail** (Mile 19.7 Seward Hwy), on the east side of the highway, is a fairly steep path that ascends 3 miles to good views of the surrounding mountains.

If everywhere else is full, head to **Primrose Landing Campground** (Mile 17.2 Seward Hwy; sites $10), a quiet and wooded spot with wonderful views of Kenai Lake and Andy Simon Mountain. Half the sites are along a wide rushing creek, and it's also where the Primrose Trail begins. This trail leads south to Lost Lake, and traverses to Mile 5 of the Seward Hwy. About 2 miles up the path is an unmarked side trail to the right, which leads to a magnificent waterfall – the source of that roaring you can hear as you hike. See p262 for more info on the Lost Lake hike.

The **Grayling Lake Trail**, accessed from a parking lot at Mile 13.2, leads two pleasant miles to Grayling Lake, a beautiful spot with views of Snow River and (surprise!) excellent fishing for grayling. Side trails connect Grayling Lake with Meridian and Leech Lakes. This is a nice hike for kids.

SEWARD

pop 2661

Seward is an unpolished gem, rewarding visitors with small-town charm and phenomenal access to the mountains and sea. Located at the terminus of both the Alaska Railroad and the Seward Hwy, and a final stop on many cruises, the town is easily accessible from Anchorage. Its Fourth of July festival is notorious for being the biggest – and wildest – in Alaska. Seward's old-town shops, small-boat harbor and 360-degree view offer plenty to entertain you for days, but can also serve as a base for excursions into the marine and mountainous playgrounds. Travelers flock to kayak, hike, fish, whale watch and glacier-view.

History

Seward got its start in 1903, when settlers arrived plotting construction of a northbound rail line. Once the Alaska Railroad was completed two decades later, this ice-free port would become the most important shipping terminal on the Kenai Peninsula. The city also served as the southern terminus of the 1200-mile Iditarod National Historic Trail to Nome, long a major dogsled thoroughfare via the Interior and Bush. In WWII the town got another boost when the US Army built Fort McGilvray at Caines Head, just south of town.

Orientation & Information

Seward unrolls north to south between hulking Mt Marathon on the western side and Resurrection Bay to the east. The Seward Hwy approaches from the north; many businesses are along this stretch or on Herman Leirer Rd (locals still call it 'Exit Glacier Rd), which spurs off the highway at Mile 3.7. Once in town, the highway becomes the town's main drag, 3rd Ave. The body of the city is divided into two centers: the newer, touristy harbor and the historic downtown. Lowell Point stretches to the south of town, and other amenities can be found just north along the Seward Hwy.

INTERNET ACCESS

Grant Electronics (☎ 224-7015; 222 4th Ave; per hr $8; 🕑 9am-6pm; 💻) Has Internet access and burns digital photos onto CDs.

Kayak Adventures Worldwide (☎ 224-3960; 328 3rd Ave; per 15 min $2; 🕑 8am-7pm; 💻) Gets you online.

Sea Bean (☎ 224-6623; 225 4th Ave; free wireless, internet access per 15 min/1 hr $2/7; 🕑 7am-8pm; 💻) Also has printing services and burns digital photos onto CDs.

Seward Library (☎ 224-3646; 238 5th Ave; access free; 🕑 10am-9pm Mon-Fri, to 7pm Sat; 💻) Sells used books and displays what it claims is Benny Benson's first signed flag.

MONEY

First National Bank of Anchorage (☎ 224-4200; 303 4th Ave) One of two banks in town.

MEDICAL SERVICES

Providence Seward Medical Center (☎ 224-5205; 417 1st Ave) At the west end of Jefferson St.

POST

Post office (cnr 5th Ave & Madison St) The informal community gathering place.

TOURIST INFORMATION

Chamber of Commerce (☎ 224-8051; www.sewardak.org; 2001 Seward Hwy/3rd Ave; 🕑 8am-6pm Mon-Thu, to

8pm Fri, 9am-5pm Sat, 10am-3pm Sun) At the entrance to town, this helpful place provides everything from trail maps to local menus, plus lots of good advice.
Harbormaster's Office (Small-boat harbor; 8am-5pm, showers 24hr) Has showers for $2.
Kenai Fjords National Park Visitor Center (224-3175; 8am-6pm) Beside the small-boat harbor.
Seward Information Center (224-5560; www.sewardinformation.com; 1412 4th Ave; 9am-6pm Mon-Sat, to 1pm Sun) Free booking service for accommodation (helpful with last-minute bookings), transportation, and tours.
Seward Parks and Recreation (224-4054; 519 4th Ave; adult/child $4/2; 10am-10pm Mon-Fri) Has a gym and sauna as well as showers.
USFS Ranger Station (224-3378; 334 4th Ave; 8am-5pm Mon-Fri) Has maps and information about Seward's outstanding selection of trails, cabins, and campgrounds.

Sights

ALASKA SEALIFE CENTER

A fitting legacy of the *Exxon Valdez* oil spill settlement, this $56-million **marine center** (224-6300, 800-224-2525; www.alaskasealife.org; 301 Railway Ave; adult/child $20/10; 8am-7pm) is more than just one of Alaska's finest attractions. As the only coldwater marine-science facility in the Western Hemisphere, it serves as a research and educational center and provides rehabilitation for injured marine animals; for $6 more you can tour the labs at 9am and 12:30pm daily.

Amazing enough for most folks are the regular exhibits, such as oil-spill displays and the Alaska Waters Gallery, with aquariums holding colorful fish and gossamer jellyfish. Kids will love the tidepool touch tank, where you can hold sea anemones and starfish.

Without a doubt the highlight, however, is a series of two story-deep, glass-sided tanks: upstairs you get the above-water view of seabird rookeries and recuperating harbor seals, while below deck you'll be eyeball-to-eyeball with prowling sea lions and puffins diving for dinner. An outdoor observation platform offers a fabulous view of the mountains ringing Resurrection Bay and a chance to watch salmon thrash their way up a fish ladder. Plan to spend the better part of one of your best afternoons here.

BENNY BENSON MEMORIAL

This humble monument at the corner of the Seward Hwy and Dairy Hill Lane honors Seward's favorite son, Benny Benson. In 1926 the orphaned 13-year-old Alaska Native boy submitted his design for the Alaska state flag, arguably the loveliest in the Union. His stellar design (you can see one of his first at the library) includes the North Star, symbolizing the northernmost state, the Great Bear constellation for strength, and a blue background for both the sky and the forget-me-not, Alaska's state flower. Seward will never forget.

SEWARD MUSEUM

This eclectic, if a bit dusty, **museum** (224-3902; 336 3rd Ave; adult/child $3/1; 9am-5pm) has an excellent Iditarod exhibit; a rare 49-star US flag; and relics of Seward's Russian era, the 1964 Good Friday Earthquake, and the 1989 oil spill. There are also lots of amusing antiques, including an ancient electric hair-curling machine and a 'cow raincoat' designed for the oft-drenched cattle at the now-defunct Seward dairy. The staff are enthusiastic and knowledgeable, and worth engaging. The museum has eventual plans to move to a new site next to the library.

SMALL-BOAT HARBOR

The small-boat harbor, at the northern end of 4th Ave, hums during the summer with fishing boats, charter vessels, cruise ships and a number of sailboats. At its heart is the **harbormaster's office** (224-3183; 8am-5pm). Look for the huge anchors outside. Radiating outward from the docks are seasonal restaurants, espresso bars, tourist offices, hotels and almost any other service the visitor might want. There are also picnic tables and a free sighting scope overlooking the harbor and the bay. A paved bike trail leads to the (other) city center.

Activities

HIKING

Mt Marathon Trail

According to (rather suspect) local legend, grocer Gus Borgan wagered $100 in 1909 that no-one could run Mt Marathon in an hour, and the race was on. Winner James Walters clocked in at 62 minutes, losing the bet but becoming a legend. The 3.1-mile suffer-fest quickly became a celebrated Fourth of July event and today is Alaska's most famous footrace, pitting runners from all over the world against the 3022ft-high peak. In 1981 Bill Spencer set the record at 43 minutes, 23 seconds. Many runners take

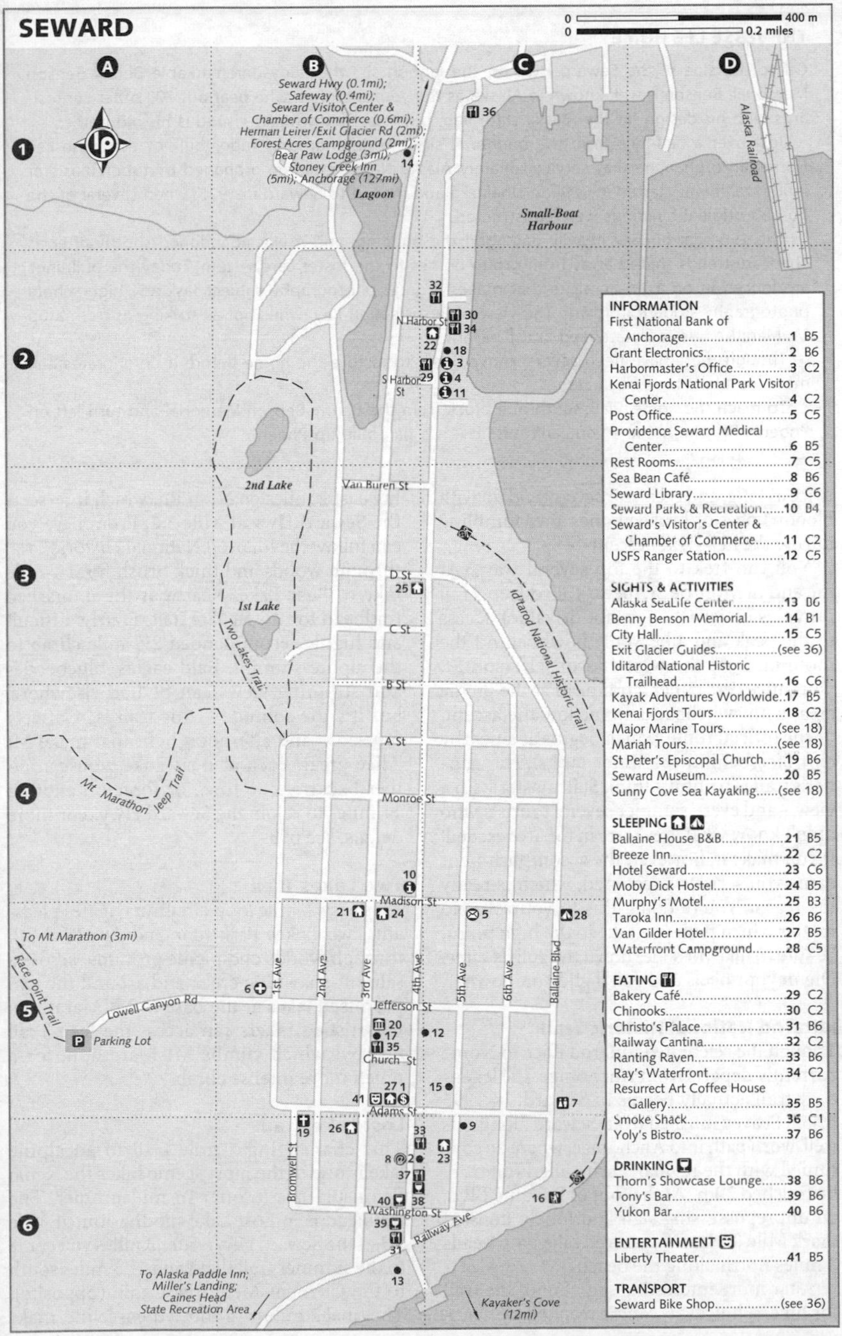
SEWARD
0 400 m
0 0.2 miles
Seward Hwy (0.1mi); Safeway (0.4mi); Seward Visitor Center & Chamber of Commerce (0.6mi); Herman Leirer/Exit Glacier Rd (2mi); Forest Acres Campground (2mi); Bear Paw Lodge (3mi); Stoney Creek Inn (5mi); Anchorage (127mi)
Lagoon
Small-Boat Harbour
Alaska Railroad
2nd Lake
1st Lake
Two Lakes Trail
Mt Marathon Jeep Trail
Iditarod National Historic Trail
To Mt Marathon (3mi)
Race Point Trail
Lowell Canyon Rd
Parking Lot
N Harbor St
S Harbor St
Van Buren St
D St
C St
B St
A St
Monroe St
Madison St
Jefferson St
Church St
Adams St
Washington St
Railway Ave
Bromwell St
1st Ave
2nd Ave
3rd Ave
4th Ave
5th Ave
6th Ave
Ballaine Blvd
To Alaska Paddle Inn; Miller's Landing; Caines Head State Recreation Area
Kayaker's Cove (12mi)
INFORMATION
First National Bank of Anchorage 1 B5
Grant Electronics 2 B6
Harbormaster's Office 3 C2
Kenai Fjords National Park Visitor Center 4 C2
Post Office 5 C5
Providence Seward Medical Center 6 B5
Rest Rooms 7 C5
Sea Bean Café 8 B6
Seward Library 9 C6
Seward Parks & Recreation 10 B4
Seward's Visitor's Center & Chamber of Commerce 11 C2
USFS Ranger Station 12 C5
SIGHTS & ACTIVITIES
Alaska SeaLife Center 13 B6
Benny Benson Memorial 14 B1
City Hall 15 C5
Exit Glacier Guides (see 36)
Iditarod National Historic Trailhead 16 C6
Kayak Adventures Worldwide 17 B5
Kenai Fjords Tours 18 C2
Major Marine Tours (see 18)
Mariah Tours (see 18)
St Peter's Episcopal Church 19 B6
Seward Museum 20 B5
Sunny Cove Sea Kayaking (see 18)
SLEEPING
Ballaine House B&B 21 B5
Breeze Inn 22 C2
Hotel Seward 23 C6
Moby Dick Hostel 24 B5
Murphy's Motel 25 B3
Taroka Inn 26 B6
Van Gilder Hotel 27 B5
Waterfront Campground 28 C5
EATING
Bakery Café 29 C2
Chinooks 30 C2
Christo's Palace 31 B6
Railway Cantina 32 C2
Ranting Raven 33 B6
Ray's Waterfront 34 C2
Resurrect Art Coffee House Gallery 35 B5
Smoke Shack 36 C1
Yoly's Bistro 37 B6
DRINKING
Thorn's Showcase Lounge 38 B6
Tony's Bar 39 B6
Yukon Bar 40 B6
ENTERTAINMENT
Liberty Theater 41 B5
TRANSPORT
Seward Bike Shop (see 36)

THE JESSE LEE HOME

Off to the side of the Seward Hwy on the lagoon sits the fairly unremarkable Benny Benson Memorial. Benson is well-known in Alaska as the young orphan who beat out 700 other contestants with his design for the Alaska state flag, but lesser known and visited is his old home.

Just over a half-mile from the memorial sits the deteriorating Tudor hulk of the Jesse Lee Home, an orphanage that serviced mainly Alaska Native children orphaned by tuberculosis or influenza. It was started in 1890 in Unalaska and moved to Seward in 1925, when several of the home's original buildings were constructed.

The 1964 earthquake heavily damaged the building, and it was abandoned shortly after as childcare trends shifted away from group homes to the foster care system. Today the buildings are fenced in on a 2½ acre site that makes a great photography subject (ask any high school photography student in town). The view of Resurrection Bay, while not as striking as from atop Mt Marathon, is easily attained and pleasant.

Though there have been several movements to restore the home before it deteriorates any more, no plans have been set.

To reach the home, walk south one block from the Benny Benson Memorial and turn left on Phoenix Rd. The home – you can't miss it – is a half-mile up Phoenix.

twice as long, and each year several end up with bloody knees or broken bones after tumbling during the hell-bent descent.

You can trek to the top several ways. At the end of Monroe St, the so-called Jeep Trail provides easier (though not drivable) access to the peak and a heavenly bowl behind the mountain. At the west end of Jefferson St, you can access either a trailhead at the picnic area, with switchbacks to mellow the ascent, or the official route, which begins at a nearby cliff face behind the water tanks. The runner's trail is painful – think Stairmaster with a view – and every summer several tourists who didn't know what they were in for are rescued. If you make it, however, the accomplishment earns you serious street cred, which is really the reason you're doing this to yourself. No matter which path you take to the high point, be sure to hike (or slide) down the gully's scree. Dig in your heels and you'll glide on down.

Iditarod National Historic Trail

Though the celebrated Iditarod Race to Nome currently departs from Anchorage, the legendary trail actually begins in Seward. In 1995 Mitch Seavey mushed from Seward along this well-worn path into Anchorage, where he continued with the regularly scheduled Iditarod; he finished 20th. At the foot of Ballaine Blvd, an unprepossessing sign and lonely dogsled mark Mile 0. Nearby, a paved bike path heads 2 miles north along the beach.

A far more interesting segment of the trail for hikers, however, can be reached by heading east 2 miles on Nash Rd, which intersects the Seward Hwy at Mile 3.2. From here you can follow the Iditarod National Historic Trail through woods and thick brush for a 4-mile hike to Bear Lake. Nearby is the unmarked trailhead for the **Mt Alice Trail**, a fairly difficult and highly recommended 2½-mile climb to the alpine summit. Bald eagles, blueberries and stunning views can be had elsewhere, but it's the solitude – this trail is relatively unused – and afternoon light that make Mt Alice great. Back at Bear Lake, you can either backtrack to town or forge on another 11 miles to rejoin the Seward Hwy. For more details, see p93.

Two Lakes Trail

This easy 1-mile loop circumnavigates pleasant Two Lakes Park (cnr 2nd Ave & C St), through woods and picnic grounds, across a salmon-spawning creek and around the two promised lakes at the base of Mt Marathon. Unsatisfied hikers can access the Jeep Trail nearby, which climbs Mt Marathon, for a much more intense climb.

Lost Lake Trail

This challenging 7-mile trail to an alpine lake is one of the most scenic hikes the Kenai Peninsula has to offer in midsummer. The trailhead is in Lost Lake subdivision, at Mile 5.3 of the Seward Hwy. After 3 miles you come to the summer trail that winds 1.5 miles south to the Clemens Memorial Cabin (opposite). The final 2 miles are above the treeline, making the shores of Lost Lake a wondrous place to pitch a tent.

If you'd rather not return the same way, continue around the east side of Lost Lake to the **Primrose Trail**, an 8-mile alpine trek ending at Primrose Campground at Mile 17.2 of the Seward Hwy (see Seward Hwy earlier, p259). Plan on seven to 10 hours for the round-trip to Lost Lake, and bring a camp stove, as wood is hard to come by.

Caines Head State Recreation Area

This 6000-acre preserve, 5.5 miles south of Seward on Resurrection Bay, contains WWII military facilities (bring a flashlight for exploring), a 650ft headland, the Coastal Trail, and two public-use cabins (p264). There's a $5 day-use fee for the recreation area, paid at the trailhead. If you're not up for an overnight backpacking excursion, the hike to Tonsina Point is an easy 3-mile round-trip. In 2006, however, floods washed out the Tonsina Creek bridge, making it necessary for hikers to trek along the creek to the shore and cross the stream where it braids. There are plans to repair the bridge in 2009. Beyond that you will need to time your passage with low tide; hikers have gotten stranded and even drowned after being caught by the rising waters.

GLACIER TREKKING

For those not satisfied with merely gazing up at Seward's backyard glacier, **our pick** **Exit Glacier Guides** (☎ 224-5569; www.exitglacierguides.com) gives you the chance to tread upon it. Its five-hour ice-hiking trip costs $120 per person, gears you up with ice-axes and crampons, ascends part-way up the Harding Ice Field Trail and then heads out onto the glacier for crevasse exploration and interpretive glaciology. It also offers custom trips, where you can do multi-day tours of the Harding Ice Field.

MOUNTAIN BIKING

Popular with hikers, the Lost Lake Trail (opposite) makes for sometimes steep and technical, but highly rewarding, single-track riding. Local cyclists say the Iditarod National Historic Trail (opposite) and the Resurrection River Trail (p267) are also good rides.

For bike rentals, see p266.

PADDLING

Though the best and most impressive paddling in the region is within Kenai Fjords National Park (p267), getting there requires a costly water-taxi. If you're looking to save money and don't mind foregoing the park's tidewater glaciers and more ample wildlife, kayaking right outside Seward in Resurrection Bay can still make for a stunning day on the water. Both **Sunny Cove Sea Kayaking** (☎ 224-8810, 800-770-9119; www.sunnycove.com; small-boat harbor) and **Kayak Adventures Worldwide** (☎ 224-3960; www.kayakak.com; 328 3rd Ave) guide half- and full-day trips in the bay. The latter, as well as **Miller's Landing** (☎ 224-5739, 866-541-5739; www.millerslandingak.com; cnr Lowell Rd & Beach St), also rents kayaks.

SLED-DOG MUSHING

Hey, this is where the Iditarod started. Why not meet the dogs?

IdidaRide (☎ 800-478-3139; www.ididaride.com; Exit Glacier Rd; adult/child $59/29) is cheesy, but it's more like Stilton than Velveeta: after touring Iditarod veteran Mitch Seavey's kennels and hearing junior mushers discuss their experiences with subzero sleep deprivation, delicate doggy feet and cutthroat competition, you'll be strapped in for a 20-minute training run in a cart hitched behind a team of huskies.

Godwin Glacier Dog Sled Tours (☎ 224-8239, 888-989-8239; www.alaskadogsled.com; adult/child $430/390) goes one better, transporting you by helicopter to an alpine glacier, where you'll be met by lots of dogs and a genuine snow-sledding adventure, even in July.

WILDERNESS CABINS

Seward is a great place for a cabin getaway in the wilderness. You can paddle, fly and even hike to a remote, rustic lodging administered by the Alaska Division of Parks, USFS and even the National Park Service as Kenai Fjords National Park has several boat-accessible public-use cabins (p269).

Orca Island Cabins (☎ 491-1988; www.orcaislandcabins.com; yurts d $275) In Humpy Cove, 9 miles southeast of Seward, this privately-owned place has a floating cabin with private bath and kitchen, plus three onshore yurts with similar facilities. All have propane-powered ranges and water-heaters but no electricity, and kayaks for rent for a one-time fee ($40). These are a great choice for those who want to rough it without roughing it *too* much. The price includes water-taxi.

Clemens Memorial Cabin (☎ 877-444-6777, 518-885-3639; www.recreation.gov; cabins $45) Located 4.5 miles up the Lost Lake Trail (opposite), sleeps eight.

The cabin is located at the treeline, providing spectacular views of Resurrection Bay.

Resurrection River Cabin (☎ 877-444-6777, 518-885-3639; www.recreation.gov; cabins $35) This is 6.5 miles from the southern trailhead of the Resurrection River Trail (p267).

Derby Cove Cabin (www.alaskastateparks.org; cabins $65) Just off the tidal trail between Tonsina Point and North Beach in Caines Head State Recreation Area, 4 miles from the Lowell Point trailhead. It can be accessed on foot at low tide, or by kayak anytime.

Callisto Canyon Cabin (www.alaskastateparks.org; cabins $65) Also located just off the tidal trail, a half-mile before you reach Derby Cove. It can be reached on foot or by kayak.

Festivals & Events

Seward knows how to party, and these are just a few of the more popular events.

Polar Bear Jumpoff Festival A favorite of costumed masochists who plunge into frigid Resurrection Bay with a smile in mid-January, all to raise money for cancer.

Mt Marathon Race This Fourth of July race attracts runners who like to test themselves by running up a near vertical peak, and fans who like to drink beer and yell.

Silver Salmon Derby An event held in mid-August that gets even bigger crowds, all vying for prizes in excess of $150,000.

Seward Music & Arts Festival Held the last weekend in September, this summer's end celebration brings together an eclectic mix of local artists and musicians, and is particularly kid-friendly, with circus training and mural-painting.

Sleeping

Above and beyond the listed rates you have to add 11% in Seward sales and bed taxes to lodging.

BUDGET

Camping

Near Exit Glacier, Kenai Fjords National Park maintains one free, drive-up campground (p269). There are lots of informal campsites along Exit Glacier Rd.

Waterfront Campground (☎ 224-3331; Ballaine Blvd; sites camp $8, RV $12-25) Perfectly situated between the city center and boat harbor. Most of it is open gravel parking for RVers, but there are grassy campsites, as well as a compact skateboard park, volleyball nets and a paved bicycle path running through.

Forest Acres Campground (☎ 224-4055; cnr Hemlock St & Seward Hwy; sites camp/RV $8/12) Located 2 miles north of town just off the Seward Hwy on Hemlock St; has quiet sites shaded by towering spruce.

Miller's Landing (☎ 224-5739, 866-541-5739; www.millerslandingak.com; cnr Lowell Rd & Beach St; sites camp $23, RV $28-30, cabins $45-250) This touristplex – offering everything from campsites to kayak rentals to fishing charters – isn't very clean or organized, but the waterfront location is hard to beat.

Hostels

Snow River Hostel (☎ 440-1907; www.snowriverhostel.org; Mile 16 Seward Hwy; dm/d/cabins $20/50/50) Nestled beside the forest and a burbling creek, this cordwood place is some distance from town, but worth the trip for the idyllic atmosphere and easy access to challenging Lost Lake Trail. The kitchen comes stocked with pancake mix.

Moby Dick Hostel (☎ 224-7072; www.mobydickhostel.com; 430 3rd Ave; dm/r $18/70) Friendly, well located and popular, though it's overdue for a fresh coat of paint and new carpeting.

Kayaker's Cove (☎ 224-8662; www.geocities.com/kayakerscove_99664; dm/cabins $20/60) Located 12 miles southeast of Seward near Fox Island; accessible by kayak or water-taxi only. There's a shared kitchen, and you'll need to bring your own food. It rents single/double kayaks for $20/30.

Ballaine House B&B (☎ 224-2362; www.superpage.com/ballaine/; 437 3rd Ave; s $50, d $65-82; ⊠) Raved about by readers, this place – one of the original Seward homes – does cook-to-order breakfasts and offers a wealth of advice on what to do around town.

MIDRANGE & TOP END

Among Seward's midrange places, dozens are B&Bs; you can book through **Alaska's Point of View** (☎ 224-2323, 800-844-2424) even at the last minute.

Stoney Creek Inn (☎ 224-3940; www.stoneycreekinn.net; Stoney Creek Ave; d $95-85) This secluded place comes with a fantastic sauna and hot tub next to a deliciously icy-cold salmon stream, as well as continental breakfast.

our pick **Alaska Paddle Inn** (☎ 362-2628; www.alaskapaddleinn.com; 13745 Beach Dr; r from $179) Two custom-built rooms overlook the beach and bay on Lowell Point. Arched ceilings, walk-in tiled showers, and gas fireplaces make this place both one of the coziest and classiest in Seward. Discounts for stays of multiple days.

Van Gilder Hotel (☎ 800-204-6835; www.vangilderhotel.com; 307 Adams St; d $109-219) Gossips say poltergeists plague the 1st floor of this landmark, which dates from 1916. If you dare to spend the night, however, you'll find elegant suites with antique furnishings, plus some affordable European pensions without baths.

Taroka Inn (☎ 224-8975; www.alaskaone.com/tarokainn; 235 3rd Ave; r $135-175) This place, which served as officers' quarters during WWII, has huge, unpretentious, kitchenette-equipped suites. If you've got a big group, this would be a great deal.

Hotel Seward (☎ 224-8001, 800-440-2444; www.hotelsewardalaska.com; 221 5th Ave; r $89-450) The 'historic' side was recently remodeled and has affordable shared-bath rooms; the new wing makes for an excellent splurge with grand views of Resurrection Bay. An old-time saloon serves up appetizers, but the lobby is definitely overdoing it in the taxidermy department.

Bear Paw Lodge (☎ 224-3960; www.kayakak.com; 10411 Bear Paw Dr; king r $155, d $100; ☒ 💻) All the logs for this warm place were locally harvested and hand-peeled, a feat so time-consuming the builders notched the last log and threw a party when it was set. The king room can sleep up to six, and the three double rooms share two baths. All have full use of the large kitchen.

Murphy's Motel (☎ 224-8090; www.murphysmotel.com; 911 4th Ave; r $129-169) You'll find nice harbor views from private decks at this clean and professional place. There are some smaller rooms without views.

Breeze Inn (☎ 224-5283; www.breezeinn.com; 1306 Seward Hwy; r $129-219) Has basic motel rooms, and for just a bit more, even nicer Jacuzzi-equipped suites in the newer annex.

Seward Windsong Lodge (☎ 224-7116; www.sewardwindsong.com; Exit Glacier Rd; d $189-239) This Alaska Native corporation-owned place is immaculate, modern and snazzy, but devoid of good views – and soul.

Eating

RESTAURANTS

Exit Glacier Salmon Bake (☎ 224-2204; Exit Glacier Rd; lunch $6-10, dinner $18-22; 🕑 5-10pm) Its motto – 'cheap beer and lousy food' – is wrong on the second count. Locals like the salmon sandwich, which you can adorn with pickles from a barrel.

Yoly's Bistro (☎ 224-3295; 220 4th Ave; lunch $7-14, dinner $12-25; 🕑 11am-10pm) The menu is a delicious blend of curries, seafood, and burgers, with a decent wine and beer selection. Listen to live music on weekends.

Resurrection Roadhouse (☎ 224-2223; Exit Glacier Rd; lunch $9-14, dinner $18-46; 🕑 6am-2pm & 5-10pm) This local favorite is home to the 'Buddha Belly' pizza, sweet potato fries worth traveling for, and the best deck in town. It also has a vast range of on-tap brews, and the bar is open until midnight.

Ray's Waterfront (☎ 224-5606; breakfast & lunch $10-16, dinner $19-31; 🕑 11am-10pm) Hands down, this is Seward's culinary high point, with attentive service, picture-postcard views and the finest seafood above water.

Chinook's Waterfront Restaurant (☎ 224-2207; 1404 4th Ave; lunch & dinner $12-25; 🕑 noon-10pm) With plywood floors, a corrugated-metal bar, and the beautiful harbor-front location, this place is hip and relaxing. It does seafood, pasta and burgers.

Christo's Palace (☎ 224-5255; 133 4th Ave; dinner $19-25; 🕑 11am-midnight) Has a huge dining room dominated by a 1950s Brunswick bar (featuring a great selection of beer on tap). The pizza gets raves.

CAFÉS & QUICK EATS

Resurrect Art Coffee House Gallery (☎ 224-7161; 320 3rd Ave; 🕑 7am-7pm) In an old high-ceilinged church; serves espressos, Italian sodas and bagels, displays great local art and hosts live jazz on Tuesday nights. The best place to read the paper and check out the view is from the airy choir loft.

Bakery Café at the Harbor (☎ 224-6091; 1210 4th Ave; breakfast & lunch $3-6, dinner $5-10; 🕑 5am-7pm) This busy joint is a bargain: breakfast is delish, and dinner includes half-pound burgers on homemade buns. Also sells box lunches for those going out on the bay for the day.

Sea Bean (☎ 224-6623; 225 4th Ave; light meals $2-7; 🕑 7am-8pm; 💻) Serves hot paninis, Belgian waffles, ice cream, and espressos, with a helping of free wireless internet.

Railway Cantina (☎ 224-8226; light meals $4-8; 🕑 11am-8pm) Near the small-boat harbor; offers unorthodox quesadillas, burritos and tacos. Try the 'black-n-blue' quesadilla, with blackened chicken and blue cheese.

Le Barn Appetit (☎ 224-3462; Eagle Lane; mains $5-16; 🕑 7am-2pm & 4-9pm) European cuisine meets ramshackle Alaska décor in this unorthodox eatery off Exit Glacier Rd. There's not really a fixed menu – except for crepes, which are so sinful that, as chef Yvon Van Driessche says, 'you must go to confession.'

our pick **Smoke Shack** (☎ 224-7427; 411 Port Ave; breakfast & lunch $6-11; 🕑 6am-8pm) Housed in a rail car, this tiny joint oozes blue collar atmosphere.

It has the best breakfast in town, with biscuits and gravy made from scratch.

GROCERIES

Safeway (☎ 224-3698; Mile 1.5 Seward Hwy; 🕑 24hr) Has sushi, espressos, a sandwich bar and all the groceries you need.

Drinking & Entertainment

Seward has no shortage of welcoming watering holes, most featuring a mix of young and old, locals and tourists. Almost all the bars are downtown.

Yukon Bar (☎ 224-3063; 201 4th Ave) There are hundreds of dollars pinned to this bar's ceiling and almost nightly live music. It's festive.

Tony's Bar (☎ 224-3045; 135 4th Ave) It's not quite as festive (there are maybe seven dollars pinned to the ceiling), but locals consider it the best place just to hang out.

Thorn's Showcase Lounge (☎ 224-3700; 208 4th St; mains $14-18) This saloon serves the strongest drinks in down – try its White Russians. The Jim Beam collection is valued at thousands of dollars; can you spot the pipeline bottle?

Pit Bar (☎ 224-3006; Mile 3.5 Seward Hwy) Just past Exit Glacier Rd; this is where the crowd heads when the bars close in town. Open until 5am.

Liberty Theatre (☎ 224-5418; 304 4th Ave; admission $7) A delightful little WWII-era cinema showing first-run flicks daily.

Getting There & Around

BICYCLE

You can rent bikes through **Seward Bike Shop** (☎ 224-2448; 411 Port Ave; per half-/full-day cruisers $14/23, mountain bikes $21/38; 🕑 9:30am-6:30pm Mon-Sat, 11am-4pm Sun), in a WWII-era railroad car, which has the latest details on local biking trails, and **Kayak Adventures Worldwide** (☎ 224-3960; www.kayakak.com; 328 3rd Ave; bikes per half/full day $10/15).

For a ride where someone else does the hard work, try **Handlebar Taxi Co** (☎ 362-2221; www.handlebartaxi.com; per mile/hr $10/25), which has been known to pedal folks out to the Pit Bar late in the evening. The rickshaw-like pedicab comes with protection from the wind and rain, as well as a driver.

BUS

The **Seward Bus Line** (☎ 224-3608; www.sewardbuslines.net) departs at 9:30am daily en route to Anchorage ($50).

Homer Stage Line (☎ 868-3914; www.homerstageline.com) runs daily from Seward to Homer ($55) and Anchorage ($55).

The **Park Connection** (☎ 800-266-8625; www.alaskacoach.com) has a daily service from Seward to Denali Park (one way $135) via Anchorage (one way $56).

TRAIN

From May to September, the **Alaska Railroad** (☎ 265-2631, 800-544-0552; www.akrr.com; 408 Port Ave; one way/round-trip $69/110) offers a daily run to Anchorage. It's more than just public transportation; it's one of the most famous rides in Alaska, complete with glaciers, steep gorges and rugged mountain scenery.

TROLLEY

The **Seward Trolley** (☎ 224-4378; one way adult/child $5/3) runs between the ferry terminal and downtown every half-hour from 10am to 7pm daily.

KENAI FJORDS NATIONAL PARK

Seward is the gateway to Kenai Fjords National Park, created in 1980 to protect 587,000 acres of Alaska's most awesome, impenetrable wilderness. Crowning the park is the massive Harding Ice Field; from it, countless tidewater glaciers pour down, carving the coast into dizzying fjords.

With such a landscape – and an abundance of marine wildlife to boot – the park is a major tourist attraction. Unfortunately, it's also an expensive one. That is why road-accessible Exit Glacier is its highlight attraction, drawing more than 100,000 tourists each summer. Hardier souls can ascend to the Harding Ice Field from the same trailhead, but only experienced mountaineers equipped with skis, ice axes and crampons can investigate the 900 sq miles of ice.

The vast majority of visitors either take a quick trip to Exit Glacier's face or splurge on a tour-boat cruise along the coast. For those who want to spend more time in the park, the coastal fjords are a blue-water kayaker's dream; to reach the area, though, you either have to paddle the sections exposed to the Gulf of Alaska or pay for a drop-off service.

Orientation & Information

Ice-bound inland areas of the park stretch west and northwest of Seward, penetrated only by a few trails and the 8.4-mile-long Exit

Glacier Rd, which spurs off the Seward Hwy at Mile 3.7. Some 20 miles south of town the park joins the coastline, taking in such sizable fjords as Aialik Bay, Northwestern Lagoon, McCarty Fjord and North Arm, as well as mountains exceeding 6000ft in height.

Exit Glacier Nature Center (9am-8pm) At the Exit Glacier trailhead; has interpretive displays, sells postcards and field guides, and is the starting point for ranger-guided hikes (below).

Kenai Fjords National Park Visitor Center (☎ 224-2125; 1212 4th Ave; 8am-7pm) In Seward's small-boat harbor; has information on hiking and camping, and issues free backcountry permits.

Sights & Activities

HIKING

Ranger-Led Hikes

At 10am, 2pm and 4pm daily, rangers at the Exit Glacier Nature Center lead free one-hour hikes to the face of the glacier, providing information on the wildlife and natural history of the area. For a more strenuous outing, show up at the nature center on a Saturday at 9am for the guided ascent of the Harding Ice Field Trail. The trek lasts eight hours; pack a lunch and rain gear.

Harding Ice Field Trail

This strenuous and extremely popular 4-mile trail follows Exit Glacier up to Harding Ice Field. The 936-sq-mile expanse remained undiscovered until the early 1900s, when a map-surveying team discovered that eight coastal glaciers flowed from the exact same system.

Today you can rediscover it via a steep, roughly cut and sometimes slippery ascent to 3500ft; for reasonably fit trekkers, that's a good three- or four-hour trip. Beware of bears; they're common here.

The trek is well worth it for those with the stamina, as it provides spectacular views of not only the ice field but of Exit Glacier and the valley below. The upper section of the route is snow-covered for much of the year; bring a jacket and watch for crevasses, which may be hidden under a thin and unstable bridge of snow. Camping up here is a great idea, but the free, tiny public-use cabin at the top is for emergencies only.

Resurrection River Trail

This 16-mile trail accesses a 72-mile trail system connecting Seward and Hope. This continuous trail is broken only by the Sterling Hwy and provides a wonderful wilderness adventure through streams, rivers, lakes, wooded lowlands and alpine areas. It's difficult and expensive to maintain, so expect to encounter natural hassles like downed trees; boggy patches and washed-out sections are common. Resurrection River Cabin (p264) is 7 miles from the trailhead.

The southern trailhead is at Mile 8 of Exit Glacier Rd. The northern trailhead joins the Russian Lakes Trail (p94) 5 miles from Cooper Lake or 16 miles from the Russian River Campground off the Sterling Hwy. The hike from the Seward Hwy to the Sterling Hwy is a 40-mile trip, including Exit Glacier.

PADDLING

Bluewater paddles out of Resurrection Bay along the coastline of the park are for experienced kayakers only; others should invest in a drop-off service. You'll be rewarded, however, with wildlife encounters and close-up views of the glaciers from a unique perspective. Most companies can arrange drop-off and pickup; it's about $250 for the round-trip to Aialik Bay and $275 to $300 for the more remote Northwestern Lagoon.

our pick **Kayak Adventures Worldwide** (☎ 224-3960; www.kayakak.com) is a highly respected, eco-oriented operation that guides educationally-based half- and full-day trips ($70 to $125). It also arranges a two-day adventure with Exit Glacier Guides (p263) for a day of kayaking and a day of glacier hiking.

Sunny Cove Sea Kayaking (☎ 224-8810, 800-770-9119; www.sunnycove.com) doesn't rent kayaks, but does arrange a multitude of different trips, including $65 three-hour paddles in Resurrection Bay, $375 full-day journeys in Aialik Bay, and $159 excursions that combine a half-day of paddling with a salmon-bake lunch on Fox Island and a Kenai Fjords cruise.

Miller's Landing (☎ 224-5739, 866-541-5739; www.millerslandingak.com) rents kayaks (single/double $45/50) and equipment, and also provides a water-taxi service as far as Aialik Bay, as does **Alaska Saltwater Lodge** (☎ 224-5271; www.alaskasaltwaterlodge.com).

Weather Permitting Water-taxi (☎ 224-6595; www.watertaxiak.com) provides pickup and drop-off service throughout the park.

Aialik Bay

This is a popular arm for kayakers, and deservedly so. With several glaciers to visit, many

DAY TRIP TO EXIT GLACIER

The marquee attraction of Kenai Fjords National Park is Exit Glacier, named by explorers crossing the Harding Ice Field who found the glacier a suitable way to 'exit' the ice and mountains. Now 3 miles long, it's believed the river of ice once extended all the way to Seward.

From the Exit Glacier Nature Center, the **Outwash Plain Trail** is an easy half-mile walk to the glacier's alluvial plain – a flat expanse of pulverized silt and gravel, cut through by braids of grey meltwater. The **Overlook Loop Trail** departs the first loop and climbs steeply to an overlook at the side of the glacier before returning; don't skip the short spur to Falls Overlook, a scenic cascade off the upper trail. Both trails make for a short hike, not much more than a mile in length; you can return along the half-mile **nature trail** through cottonwood forest, alder thickets and old glacial moraines before emerging at the ranger station. Note how the land becomes more vegetated the farther you get from the ice – the result of having had more time to recover from its glacial scouring.

For a long, steep hike and a view the likes of which you may never see elsewhere, hike up the **Harding Ice Field Trail** (see p267). Pack food and water because it's long and steep, but gazing across the vast expanse of ice – one of the last remnants of the ice age – is an experience that can't be replicated.

Despite all the warning signs, some folks still cozy up to the face of the crackling, calving glacier for photos. Please note that this glacier has removed such people from the gene pool before, by dropping large chunks of ice on their heads. It's a great spot to explain global warming *and* natural selection to the kids.

people hire water-taxis to drop them near Aialik Glacier, then take three or four days to paddle south past Pedersen Glacier and into Holgate Arm, where they're picked up. The high point of the trip is Holgate Glacier, an active tidewater glacier that's the main feature of all the boat tours.

Northwestern Lagoon

This fjord is more expensive to reach but much more isolated, with not nearly as many tour boats. The wildlife is excellent, especially the seabirds and sea otters, and more than a half-dozen glaciers can be seen. Plan on three to four days if you're being dropped inside the lagoon.

Tours

The easiest and most popular way to view the park's dramatic fjords, glaciers and abundant wildlife is from a cruise ship. Several companies offer the same basic tours: wildlife cruises (three to five hours) take in Resurrection Bay without really entering the park. Don't bother. Much better tours (eight to 10 hours) explore Holgate Arm or Northwestern Fjord. Some offer a buffet lunch on beautiful Fox Island, which basically means spending an hour picking at trays of overcooked salmon when you could instead be whale watching. Eat on the boat.

Kayak Adventures Worldwide (☎ 224-3960; www.kayakak.com) offers several joined sailing and kayaking tours, where you can paddle all day and return to a snug bed on the water.

With an office base at the small-boat harbor, **Kenai Fjords Tours** (☎ 224-8068, 877-777-2805; www.kenaifjords.com) goes the farthest into the park (Northwestern Fjord; per adult/child $159/79.50) and offers the widest variety of options, including an all-inclusive overnight on Fox Island at the Kenai Fjords Wilderness Lodge (per person $359 based on double occupancy). It also does package deals that include rail travel from Anchorage.

Although it has fewer options, **Major Marine Tours** (☎ 224-8030, 800-764-7300; www.majormarine.com) is cheaper and includes a national park ranger on every boat. It has a half-day Resurrection Bay tour (per adult/child $65/32) and a full day viewing Holgate Arm ($127/63). The latter tour is a local favorite. With both tours, you can add a prime rib and salmon buffet feast for $15.

Owned by Kenai Fjords Tours, **Mariah Tours** (☎ 877-777-2805; www.kenaifjords.com) operates smaller vessels, carries fewer passengers and offers more intimate tours, which are often adapted to the interests of the group. Its full-day outings into the park are per adult/child $145/73.

For flightseeing trips, contact **Scenic Mountain Air** (☎ 224-6607; www.sewardair.com), at Seward airport, which flies over the fjords. Prices start at $149 for 45 minutes and rise to $264 for 1½ hours.

Sleeping

Exit Glacier Campground (Exit Glacier Rd; sites free) Located 9 miles from Seward, this is the only formal campground in the park. It has great walk-in sites for tents only and a bearproof food-storage area. Other campsites are dotted along Exit Glacier Rd – look for small turn-offs in the alders.

Public-use cabins (☎ 224-3175; www.nps.gov/aplic/cabins/nps_cabins.html; cabins $50) There are three cabins along the fjords, in addition to countless other informal campsites that line the kayak-accessible beaches of Aialik Bay and Northwestern Lagoon. Aialik Cabin is on a beach perfect for hiking, beachcombing and whale watching; Holgate Arm Cabin has a spectacular view of Holgate Glacier; and North Arm is actually much closer to Homer. You'll want to reserve these well in advance through the **Alaska Public Lands Information Center** (☎ 271-2742).

Getting There & Around

To reach the coastal fjords, you'll need to take a tour (opposite) or a water-taxi (p267).

Getting to Exit Glacier is a bit easier. If you don't have a car, **Exit Glacier Guides** (☎ 224-5569) runs an hourly shuttle to the glacier in its recycled-vegetable-oil van between 9:30am and 5pm. The van departs from the Holiday Inn Express at the small-boat harbor and costs $10 round-trip. Otherwise, there are cabs: **Glacier Taxi** (☎ 224-5678) charges $50 for as many people as you can squeeze in.

STERLING HIGHWAY

At **Tern Lake Junction** (Mile 37 Seward Hwy), the paved Sterling Hwy turns off from the Seward Hwy, heading westward through the forests and mountains to Soldotna and then bending south along Cook Inlet toward Homer.

TERN LAKE JUNCTION TO COOPER LANDING

From Tern Lake Junction it's only 58 miles to Soldotna, not much more than an hour's drive. Yet this stretch contains so many hiking, camping and canoeing opportunities that it would take you a month to enjoy them all. Surrounded by the Chugach National Forest and Kenai National Wildlife Refuge, the Sterling Hwy and its side roads pass a dozen trails, 20 campgrounds and an almost endless number of lakes, rivers and streams. Mileposts along the highway show distances from Seward, making Tern Lake Junction, at Mile 37, the starting point of the Sterling Hwy.

This is one of Alaska's top playgrounds, and summer crowds (both Alaskans and tourists) can be crushing at times. Be prepared, during July and August, to stop at a handful of campgrounds before finding an available site.

For good, basic rooms, there's **Sunrise Inn & Café** (☎ 595-1222; Mile 45 Sterling Hwy; r $125, RV sites $25; gourmet grub $8-15; 7am-10pm), which also has RV spaces but no campsites. It's a grand place to stop for affordable and outstanding dishes like the vegetarian 4:20 Love Burger or the Hippie Girl breakfast. Beware, however, the Pig Vomit Omelet.

Just past Sunrise Inn, **Quartz Creek Campground** (Mile 0.3 Quartz Creek Rd; sites $13) on the shores of Kenai Lake is crazily popular with RVs and fishers during salmon runs. The campground is so developed that the sites are paved. Tenters may want to continue 3 miles more down Quartz Creek Rd to the USFS **Crescent Creek Campground** (sites $10), which is a little prettier and much more secluded.

The **Crescent Creek Trail**, about half a mile beyond the Crescent Creek Campground, leads 6.5 miles to the outlet of Crescent Lake and the USFS's **Crescent Saddle Cabin** (☎ 877-444-6777; www.recreation.gov; cabins $45). It's an easy walk or bike ride and has spectacular autumn colors in September. Anglers can fish for Arctic grayling in the lake during the summer. The **Carter Lake Trail** connects the east end of the lake to the Seward Hwy, with a rough path along the south side of the lake between the two trails.

COOPER LANDING & AROUND

pop 353

After skirting the north end of Kenai Lake, you enter scenic Cooper Landing at Mile 48.4. The picturesque outpost, named for Joseph Cooper, a miner who worked the area in the 1880s, is best known for its rich and brutal combat salmon fishing along the Russian and Kenai Rivers (see the boxed text, p220). While rustic log-cabin lodges featuring giant fish freezers are still the lifeblood of this town, the trails and whitewater rafting opportunities attract a very different sort of tourist. Businesses plying fine dining, chakra alignment and other organic amusements are finding fertile ground among the towering mountains.

Orientation & Information

Cooper Landing is largely strung along the Sterling Hwy where the Kenai River flows from Kenai Lake. A few places are on Bean Creek Rd north of the river while others are down Snug Harbor Rd beside the lake.

Cooper Landing Library (☎ 595-1241; Bean Creek Rd; 1-4pm Mon-Sat;) Close to Mile 47.7 Sterling Hwy; offers free internet access after you purchase a $5 library card. It's worth it just to enjoy the wood stove.

Post office (Mile 0.1 Snug Harbor Rd)

Wildman's (☎ 595-1456, 866-595-1456; www.wildmans.org; Mile 47.5 Sterling Hwy; 7am-11pm) Your basic backcountry superstore, with snacks, booze, espresso beverages, an ATM, laundry and showers ($4).

Sights & Activities

K'BEQ INTERPRETIVE SITE

This riverfront **site** (☎ 398-8867; Mile 52.6 Sterling Hwy; admission $5; 11am-7pm), run by the local Kenaitzie tribe, is a refreshing reminder of what this area was like before the flood of sport fishermen. A quarter-mile boardwalk winds past an ancient house pit and other archaeological relics, while interpretive panels address berry-picking, steam bath–building and more traditional methods of catching fish on the Kenai.

FISHING

Cooper Landing is littered with fishing-guide operations, so you'll have no trouble finding someone to set you up with a rod and reel, take you out in a boat, and help you catch your dinner. Most of the fishing on the Upper Kenai is for rainbow trout, Dolly Varden, and silver and sockeye salmon. Expect to pay at least $150 for a half-day on the water and more than $200 for a full day. Fishing trips are run by numerous companies including the following:

Alaska River Adventures (☎ 595-2000, 888-836-9027; www.alaskariveradventures.com; Mile 47.9 Sterling Hwy)

Alaska Rivers Company (☎ 595-1226; www.alaskariverscompany.com; Mile 49.9 Sterling Hwy)

Gwin's Lodge (☎ 595-1266; www.gwinslodge.com; Mile 52 Sterling Hwy; cabins & chalets $99-159)

HIKING

Cooper Landing is the starting point for two of the Kenai Peninsula's loveliest multiday trails: the 39-mile Resurrection Pass Trail (p94) to Hope; and the 21-mile Russian Lakes Trail p94), a favorite of fishers and families.

OTHER ACTIVITIES

Alaska River Adventures (☎ 595-2000, 888-836-9027; www.alaskariveradventures.com; Mile 48 Sterling Hwy) runs scenic three-hour floats on the Kenai (per person $49). The coolest trip, however, is the Paddle Saddle ($179), which combines a float trip with gold panning and a two-hour horseback ride.

Alaska Rivers Company (☎ 595-1226, 888-595-1226; www.alaskariverscompany.com; Mile 49.9 Sterling Hwy) runs guided raft trips down the Kenai River (per half-/full day $49/135), with the longer trip bumping over some Class III rapids.

Kenai Lake Sea Kayak Adventures (☎ 595-3441; www.kenailake.com; Mile 0.3 Quartz Creek Rd) has guided three-hour sea-kayak trips on Kenai Lake ($65) that are a good introduction to paddling, in a stunning setting to boot. It also rents mountain bikes (half/full day $35/45) and leads four-hour bike tours to Crescent Lake ($65).

our pick **Alaska Horseman Trail Adventures** (☎ 595-1806; www.alaskahorsemen.com; Mile 45 Sterling Hwy) is the place to feel like a cowboy or girl. It offers horseback rides along Quartz and Crescent Creeks (per half-/full day $130/175) and pricier guided overnight trips that include rafting and/or flightseeing. The guest ranch includes squawking peacocks, a hot tub and sauna, and a wall-tent cabin (per night $125).

Sleeping

Cooper Creek Campground (Mile 50.7 Sterling Hwy; sites $18-28) This campground has 29 sites on both sides of the highway, including some right on the Kenai River. Good luck hooking one of those.

Russian River Campground (Mile 52.6 Sterling Hwy; www.recreation.gov; s/d sites $18/28) Located where the Russian and Kenai Rivers merge, this place is beautiful and incredibly popular when red salmon are spawning; you'll want to reserve one of the 83 sites. It costs $11 just to park there.

Kenai Riverside Campground & RV Park (☎ 595-1406, 888-536-2478; www.kenairiversidecampground.com; 16918 Sterling Hwy; sites camp/RV $15/30, r $69) Has wooded campsites along the river and six shared-bath rooms that are clean and bright, if a bit small.

Hutch B&B (☎ 595-1270; www.arctic.net/~hutch; Mile 48.5 Sterling Hwy; r incl breakfast $70-99, cabins incl breakfast $225;) In a three-story, balcony-ringed lodge, the big, simple, clean rooms are the best deal in town, and its minimess hall the cutest.

Alaskan Sourdough B&B (☎ 595-1541; www.alaskansourdoughbb.com; Mile 1 Bear Creek Rd; r incl breakfast $125;) It's a bit run-down, but serves pancakes made with a century-old sourdough starter. It also has a wedding chapel where you can make it official with the sweetheart you met on the trail; traditional Yup'ik and standard Christian ceremonies are available.

Gwin's Lodge (☎ 595-1266; www.gwinslodge.com; Mile 52 Sterling Hwy; cabins & chalets $99-159) This classic 1952 log-cabin lodge is a fish-frenzied madhouse when the sockeyes are running. It's got a 24-hour restaurant, a salmon-bake, and a round-the-clock grocery store that books everything from fishing charters to flightseeing. It's a landmark.

Eating

Cooper Landing Grocery (☎ 595-1677; Mile 48.2 Sterling Hwy; 10am-8pm) Has scads of snacks and souvenirs.

Gwin's Lodge (☎ 595-1266; Mile 52 Sterling Hwy; breakfast $5-15, lunch $9-14, dinners $17-25) In addition to other hearty American fare, this jam-packed place serves salmon omelets, salmon chowder, salmon salad, grilled salmon – even salmon-stuffed halibut.

Eagle Crest Restaurant (☎ 595-1425; breakfast & lunch $8-14, dinner $17-36; 7am-2:30pm & 5:30-10pm) Located at Kenai Princess Lodge, this is rustic-chic and perhaps overpriced.

Getting There & Around

If you're without wheels, your best option for reaching Cooper Landing is **Homer Stage Line** (☎ 868-3914; www.homerstageline.com), which runs daily buses through here from both Anchorage and Homer. From either end, it's $45 per person one way.

KENAI NATIONAL WILDLIFE REFUGE

Once west of the Resurrection Pass trailhead, you enter the Kenai National Wildlife Refuge, managed by the US Fish & Wildlife Service. Originally called the Kenai National Moose Range, 1.73 million acres was set aside by President Roosevelt in 1941 and the 1980 Alaska Lands Act increased that acreage to the almost 2 million acres that it now encompasses. It supports impressive populations of Dall sheep, moose, caribou and bear, and has attracted hunters from around the world since the early 1900s.

Information

Kenai National Wildlife Refuge Visitor Contact Station (Mile 58 Sterling Hwy; 10am-4pm), near the junction of Skilak Lake Rd, has up-to-date information on camping, hiking, canoeing and fishing throughout the refuge.

Sights & Activities

The **Russian River Ferry** (Mile 55 Sterling Hwy; per passenger $9.25), west of the confluence of the Kenai and Russian Rivers, transports more than 30,000 anglers across the water every summer to some of the finest fishing anywhere. It costs $11 just to park there; the ferry fee is in addition to that.

The 3-mile **Fuller Lakes Trail** (Mile 57 Sterling Hwy) leads to Fuller Lake just above the treeline. The well-marked trail begins with a rapid ascent to Lower Fuller Lake, where you cross a stream over a beaver dam and continue over a low pass to Upper Fuller Lake. At the lake, the trail follows the east shore and then branches; the fork to the left leads up a ridge and becomes a route to the **Skyline Trail**. This route is not maintained and is unmarked above the bush line. It follows a ridge for 6.5 miles and descends via the Skyline Trail to Mile 61 of the Sterling Hwy. Those who want to hike both trails should plan to stay overnight at Upper Fuller Lake, where there are several good campsites.

Skilak Lake Road makes a scenic 19-mile loop off the Sterling Hwy, and provides access to an assortment of popular recreational opportunities. There are five campgrounds along the road. Some, like Hidden Lake and Upper Skilak, cost $10 a night for a vehicle and $5 for a walk-in site, while others are free. All these campgrounds are well-marked and, from east to west, are as follows:

Campground	Sites	Location
Hidden Lake	44	Mile 3.6
Upper Skilak Lake	25	Mile 8.4
Lower Ohmer Lake	3	Mile 8.6
Engineer Lake	4	Mile 9.7
Lower Skilak Lake	14	Mile 14.0

The eastern entrance to the **Kenai River Trail** begins at Mile 0.6 of Skilak Lake Rd. A half-mile down this trail are wonderful views of the Kenai River Canyon.

The **Skilak Lookout Trail** starts at Mile 5.5 of Skilak Lake Rd and ascends 2.6 miles to a knob (elevation 1450ft) that has a panoramic view of the mountains and lakes. Plan on four to five hours for the round-trip.

The **Seven Lakes Trail**, a 4.4-mile hike to the Sterling Hwy, begins at Engineer Lake. The

EXPLORING THE REFUGE CANOE TRAIL SYSTEM

One of only two wilderness canoe systems established in the US (the other is the Boundary Waters, Minnesota) the **Kenai National Wildlife Refuge Canoe Trail System** (www.fws.gov/) offers yet another unique experience for the Alaskan visitor. Divided into two areas, the Swan Lake and the Swanson River routes, the system connects 120 miles of lakes and water trails in an undulating landscape.

Swan Lake is the more popular area, covering 60 miles and 30 lakes and connecting to the Moose River. You could spend well over a week paddling the entire route, but shorter trips are possible. The Swanson River route requires longer portages and isn't as well marked as Swan Lake, but you'll be rewarded for effort with solitude and excellent trout fishing. This route covers 80 miles, 40 lakes, and 46 miles of the Swanson River.

Several outfitters can rent you canoes and paddles: try **Alaska Canoe & Campground** (☎ 262-2331; 35292 Sterling Hwy; per 12/24hr $37.50/52.50, 3 days or more per night $42.50)

trail is easy walking over level terrain and passes Hidden and Hikers Lakes before ending at Kelly Lake Campground on a side road off the Sterling Hwy.

If you choose to stay on the Sterling Hwy past the Skilak Lake Rd junction, a side road at Mile 69 leads south to the **Peterson Lake Campground** (sites free) and **Kelly Lake Campground** (sites free), near one end of the Seven Lakes Trail. **Watson Lake Campground** (Mile 71.3 Sterling Hwy; sites free) has 3 sites. Four miles farther down the highway is the west junction with Skilak Lake Rd.

At Mile 81, the Sterling Hwy divides into a four-lane road, and you soon arrive in the small town of **Sterling** (pop 1800), where the Moose River empties into the Kenai. Sterling meets the usual travelers' needs, with restaurants, lodges, gas stations and small grocery stores.

It also has a hostel of sorts: **Jana House** (☎ 260-4151; Swanson River Rd; campsite/RV sites/dm/r $10/16/25/60), in a vast, renovated schoolhouse. This is by no means an international backpackers hostel, but it does provide clean, affordable bunks for fishermen looking to sleep on the cheap.

Izaak Walton Recreation Site (Mile 82 Sterling Hwy; sites $13), at the confluence of the Kenai and Moose Rivers, is popular among anglers during the salmon runs and with paddlers ending their Swan Lake Route canoe trip at the Moose River Bridge (p114).

Swanson River Road, at Mile 85 of the Sterling Hwy, heads north for 18 miles, with Swan Lake Rd heading east for 12 miles at the end of Swanson River Rd. The roads offer access to the Swanson River and Swan Lake canoe routes, and three campgrounds: **Dolly Varden Lake Campground** (Mile 14 Swanson River Rd; sites free), **Rainbow Lake Campground** (Mile 16 Swanson River Rd; sites free); and **Swanson River Campground** (sites free), at the very end of the road. Even without a canoe, you'll enjoy a day or two exploring the trails that connect prized fishing holes.

Across the Sterling Hwy from Swanson River Rd is the entrance to Scout Lake Rd, where you'll find the **Scout Lake Campground** (sites $10) and **Morgans Landing State Recreation Area** (sites $13). This is a particularly scenic area on the bluffs overlooking the Kenai River, a 3½-mile drive from the Sterling Hwy.

The **Alaska Division of Parks office** (☎ 262-5581; 8am-5pm Mon-Fri) for the Kenai Peninsula offers information on both Kachemak Bay State Park to the south and Caines Head State Recreation Area in Seward.

CITY OF KENAI & AROUND

pop 6975

At first blush, Kenai is a sorry sight – an object lesson in poor city planning. It's not convenient or especially picturesque, existing primarily as a support community for the drilling operations at Cook Inlet.

It's long been a rare bird: a major Alaskan city with minimal tourism. Lately, though, this faded boomtown has taken some hesitant steps toward wooing visitors – especially those tantalized by the excellent salmon fishing that takes place at the mouth of the Kenai River.

This wealth of sustenance has made Kenai one of the oldest continuously inhabited European settlements in Alaska. When Russian fur traders arrived here in 1791, they built their 300-strong colony next to the Dena'ina Indian village of Skitok. With statehood, US troops established a fort at the strategically important site.

The first Russian Orthodox Church on mainland Alaska today presides over a replica of the 1867 fort, which hasn't fully realized its potential as adorable tourist magnet. And then there's the view: Mt Redoubt (the volcano that erupted steam and ash in December 1989) to the southwest, Mt Iliamna at the head of the Aleutian Range and the Alaska Range to the northwest. Nice.

North of town, around Mile 19 of the Kenai Spur Hwy, is Alaska's largest concentration of oil infrastructure outside Prudhoe Bay. Signs prohibit parking along the industrialized strip, but perhaps the sight of 15 oil platforms pumping out the highest-quality crude oil in Alaska is best appreciated while your car's burning the very product they work so hard to extract.

Orientation & Information

Located on the busy Kenai Spur Hwy, the city of Kenai is about 10 miles northwest of Soldotna – though with urban sprawl, the two towns almost merge. In Kenai, the highway itself is the main drag, lined with strip malls and franchise stores. The area of interest to visitors is accessed by turning south off the highway onto Main St, which runs past the visitors center to scenic and historic 'Old Town' above the waterfront.

Alaska USA Bank (☎ 800-525-9094; 230 Kenai Spur Hwy; 10am-6pm Mon-Sat) Has a 24-hour ATM.

Central Peninsula General Hospital (☎ 262-4404; Marydale Dr) Just west of the Kenai Spur Hwy.

Kenai Community Library (☎ 283-4378; 163 Main St Loop; 10am-8pm Mon-Thu, to 5pm Fri & Sat; internet) Has free internet access; bring an ID.

Kenai Visitors & Cultural Center (☎ 283-1991; www.visitkenai.com; 11471 Kenai Spur Hwy; 9am-7pm Mon-Fri, 10am-6pm Sat & Sun; internet) Has all the usual pamphlets and can get last-minute rooms in the area's B&Bs. The impressive center, built in 1991 to mark the city's 200th anniversary, has a museum (below).

Post office (140 Bidarka St) Just north of the Kenai Spur Hwy.

Wash-n-Dry (☎ 283-8473; 502 Lake St; 8am-10pm) Has a laundry and showers ($5.30).

Sights & Activities

KENAI VISITORS & CULTURAL CENTER

In a town without much of a visitor industry, this excellent **visitors center** (☎ 283-1991; www.visitkenai.com; 11471 Kenai Spur Hwy; adult/child $3/free; 9am-7pm Mon-Fri, 10am-6pm Sat & Sun) is itself among the main attractions. The museum features historical exhibits on the city's Russian heritage, offshore drilling and a room full of stuffed wildlife staring down from the rafters. It also has quality Alaska Native art from around the state. Free movies about the city's strange history are screened, and docents offer free guided tours and classes throughout the summer.

OLD TOWN KENAI

From the visitors center, follow Overland Ave west to what locals refer to as 'Old Town' – an odd amalgam of historic structures and low-rent apartments, all stupendously situated high above the mouth of the Kenai River. You can pick up a free *Walking Tour* pamphlet at the visitors center. Near Cook Inlet, the US military established **Fort Kenay** in 1867 and stationed more than 100 men here. What stands today is a replica constructed as part of the Alaska Centennial in 1967. It's not open to the public.

Across Mission St from the fort is the ornate **Russian Orthodox Church** (☎ 283-4122; 11am-4pm Mon-Fri), a white-clapboard structure topped with baby blue onion domes. Built in 1895, it's the oldest Orthodox church on mainland Alaska. West of the church overlooking the water is **St Nicholas Chapel**, built in 1906 on the burial site of Father Igumen Nicolai, Kenai's first resident priest.

Head southeast on Mission St, and you'll be traveling along the **Bluff**, a good vantage point to view the mouth of the Kenai River or the mountainous terrain on the west side of Cook Inlet. In the late spring and early summer you can often see beluga as they ride the incoming tides into the Kenai River to feed on salmon.

KENAI BEACH

Down below the bluffs is an oddity in Alaska: a sweeping, sandy beach, ideal for picnicking, Frisbee-chucking and other waterfront fun. There are stellar views of the volcanoes across the inlet, and from July 10 to 31 you can watch hundreds of frantic fishermen dip-net for sockeye salmon at the mouth of the Kenai River. (Sadly, unless you've lived in Alaska for the past year, you can't participate.) The beach can be reached by taking Spruce Dr off Mile 12 of the Kenai Spur Hwy.

CAPTAIN COOK STATE RECREATION AREA

By following the Kenai Spur Hwy north for 36 miles, you'll first pass the trailer parks and chemical plants of the North Kenai industrial district to this uncrowded state recreation area that encompasses 4000 acres of forests, lakes, rivers and beaches along Cook Inlet. The area offers swimming, camping and the beauty of the inlet in a setting that is unaffected by the stampede for salmon to the south.

The Kenai Spur Hwy ends in the park after first passing Stormy Lake, where you'll find a bathhouse and a swimming area along the water's edge. **Discovery Campground** (sites $10) has 53 sites on the bluff overlooking Cook Inlet, where some of the world's greatest tides ebb and flow. The fishing in Swanson River is great, and this is a fine place to end the Swan Lake canoe route (p112).

Sleeping

Finding a last-minute room during summer's king salmon runs can be more challenging than hauling in a 70-pounder, but log onto **Kenai Peninsula B&B Association** (www.kenaipeninsulabba.com) and it'll see what it can do. If you're on a tight budget, head north along the Kenai Spur Hwy, where several motels cater to oil workers and offer lower rates. Kenai adds 10% in bed-and-sales tax to lodging.

Beluga Lookout RV Park (☎ 283-5999; 929 Mission St; sites camp $30, RV $40-50; 💻) This is basically a parking lot with a great view and a gift shop, as well as laundry and showers. There's a nice covered sitting area for gazing at the view while you eat your dinner.

Harborside Cottages B&B (☎ 283-6162, 888-283-6162; www.harborsidecottages.com; cnr Main St & Riverview Ave; cottage $150-195; ⊠ 💻) This place has five small-but-immaculate bluffside cottages, each equipped with kitchenettes. The views here are spectacular.

Uptown Motel (☎ 283-3660; www.uptownmotel.com; 47 Spur View Dr; r $169-179; 💻) The rooms here are clean but could use some updating. The very cool lobby is full of antiques, including an old barber chair and cash register.

Eating & Drinking

our pick Veronica's Coffee House (☎ 283-2725; 604 Peterson Way; light meals $3-8; 🕑 9am-9pm Mon-Wed, to 9:30pm Thu-Sat, 10am-8pm Sun) In an Old Town log building dating from 1918; serves espressos and healthy sandwiches and hosts open mics, folk jams and live bands. There's a warm wooden sun porch filled with flowers – the best place in town to relax with a sandwich.

Little Ski-Mo's Burger-N-Brew (☎ 283-4463; 11504 Kenai Spur Hwy; $8-11; 🕑 11am-11pm Mon-Sat, to 10pm Sun) Across from the visitors center, this is a popular All-American fast-food joint with baseball on the tube and every type of burger known to man.

Charlotte's Restaurant (☎ 283-2777; 115 Willow St; 🕑 7am-3pm Mon-Sat, from 8am Sun) Grab sandwiches or just some fresh-baked goodies for your beach picnic.

Paradisos Restaurant (☎ 283-2222; 11397 Kenai Spur Hwy; dinner $13-35; 🕑 11am-11pm Sun-Fri, to midnight Sat) If you're tired of seafood, head to this longtime favorite for Italian, Greek and Mexican dishes.

Louie's Restaurant (☎ 283-3660; 47 Spur View Dr; dinner $19-29; 🕑 5am-11pm) Under stuffed moose and elk heads in the Uptown Motel, Louie's serves the best surf-and-turf in the city.

Safeway (☎ 283-6360; 10576 Kenai Spur Hwy; 🕑 24hr) Offers the usual groceries, plus it has a deli and salad bar.

Getting There & Around

AIR

Kenai has the main airport on the peninsula and is served by **ERA Aviation** (☎ 283-3168, 800-866-8394; www.flyera.com), which offers 17 daily flights between Anchorage and Kenai. The round-trip fare is $190.

BUS

The **Homer Stage Line** (☎ 868-3914; www.homerstageline.com) makes daily trips departing from Kenai to Anchorage ($55), and Seward and Homer ($40).

TAXI

Alaska Cabs (☎ 283-6000) serves Kenai and Soldotna.

SOLDOTNA

pop 3983

Blink hard and you still won't miss Soldotna, try as you might. A town whose clot of stoplights inspired the local nickname 'Slow-dotna' would be just another ugly, over-commercialized roadside-service center, interchangeable with a zillion other American towns, save for one thing: a river runs through it, filled to bursting with the biggest salmon on the planet. Indeed, the world's largest sport-caught king salmon was reeled in right here – a 97.2lb behemoth, hooked by local resident Les Anderson in

1985. Biologists believe genetics and the fact that Kenai River salmon often spend an extra year at sea account for their gargantuan size. A trophy salmon elsewhere in Alaska is a 50lb fish, while here, anglers don't get too excited until a king salmon tops 75lb. Most experts agree it's only a matter of time before the first 100lb king is landed. Until that day, and probably long after it, fast-growing Soldotna will be the most fish-crazy place in Alaska.

Orientation & Information

Situated where the Sterling Hwy crosses the Kenai River, Soldotna sprawls in every direction, including practically to the city of Kenai, some 12 miles northwest along the Kenai Spur Hwy. The intersection of the Spur Hwy and the Sterling Hwy is referred to as the 'Y.'

Central Peninsula General Hospital (☎ 262-4404; Marydale Dr) Is just west of the Kenai Spur Hwy.

Joyce Carver Memorial Library (☎ 262-4227; 235 S Binkley St; 9am-8pm Mon-Thu, noon-6pm Fri, from 9am Sat;) Near the post office; has free internet access with an ID.

Post office (175 S Binkley St) Just west of the Kenai Spur Hwy and north of the Soldotna 'Y.'

River City Books (☎ 260-7722; 43977 Sterling Hwy Ste A; 9am-7pm Mon-Sat, 11am-5pm Sun) Stocks lots of books by local authors.

Soldotna Chamber of Commerce & Visitors Center (☎ 262-1337; 44790 Sterling Hwy; www.soldotnachamber.com; 9am-7pm; per 20 min $5;) Has internet plus up-to-date fishing reports and a nice boardwalk along the river.

Wash & Dry (☎ 262-8495; 1221 Smith Way; 24hr summer;) Near the intersection of the Kenai Spur and Sterling Hwys at the Soldotna 'Y'; has showers ($5), laundry, and free wireless internet.

Wells Fargo (☎ 262-4435; 44552 Sterling Hwy) Has cash and an eclectic collection of historical exhibits.

Sights & Activities

SOLDOTNA HOMESTEAD MUSEUM

This **museum** (☎ 262-3832; 44790 Sterling Hwy; entry by donation; 10am-4pm Tue-Sat, from noon Sun) includes a wonderful collection of homesteaders' cabins spread through six wooded acres in Centennial Park. There's also a one-room schoolhouse (that probably looks a lot more fun than the school you went to), a torture-chamber collection of early dental tools and a replica of the $7.2-million check the US paid Russia for Alaska.

KENAI NATIONAL WILDLIFE REFUGE HEADQUARTERS

Opposite Kalifornsky Beach Rd near the Kenai River is the junction with Funny River Rd. Turn left (east) here and turn right (south) immediately onto Ski Hill Rd, following it for a mile to reach this excellent, kid-friendly **information center** (☎ 262-7021; admission free; 8am-5pm Mon-Fri, from 9am Sat & Sun). It features displays on the life cycles of salmon, daily slide shows and wildlife films in its theater; and naturalist-led outdoor programs in the refuge on the weekends. Two short loop trails begin at the visitors center and wind into the nearby woods or to a viewing platform on Headquarters Lake. Ask for a map.

FISHING

From mid-May through September, runs of red, silver and king salmon make the lower Kenai River among the hottest sportfishing spots in Alaska. If you're green to the scene but want to wet a line, first drop by the visitors center where staff members will assist you in determining where to fish and what to fish for. They can also hook you up with a guide, who'll charge you up to $300 a day but vastly improve your chances of catching dinner – and of not violating the river's fairly Kafkaesque regulations. Rather go it alone? From the shore, you've still got a shot at catching reds (from mid-July to early August) and silvers (late July through August). Try casting from the 'fishwalk' below the visitors center, or from city campgrounds (below). If you don't have your own rod, you can pick up inexpensive gear from **Trustworthy Hardware** (☎ 262-4655; 44370 Sterling Hwy; 8am-8pm Mon-Fri, 9am-6pm Sat, from 10am Sun), right across the highway from Sal's Klondike Diner.

Sleeping

Spending the night in Soldotna is a catch-22: outside fishing season there's no reason to stay here; in season, there's nowhere to stay – just about every campsite and room is taken. What's left will cost you dearly. Make reservations. The chamber of commerce can locate last-minute rooms, or call **Accommodations on the Kenai** (☎ 262-2139), a referral service for area B&Bs, lodges and fish camps. The **Kenai Peninsula B&B Association** (www.kenaipeninsulabba.com) has listings for the entire peninsula.

Centennial Park Campground (☎ 262-5299; www.ci.soldotna.ak.us; cnr Sterling Hwy & Kalifornsky Beach Rd;

sites $15) Maintained by the city, this campground has boardwalked fishing access to the Kenai River.

Swiftwater Park Campground (☎ 262-5299; www.ci.soldotna.ak.us; cnr E Redoubt Ave & Rinehardt; campsites $15) Also run by the city; it doesn't have a boardwalk but is still a good place for pulling in prized salmon.

Duck Inn (☎ 262-1849; 43187 Kalifornsky Beach Rd; r $90-120) Located 3.5 miles out on K-Beach Rd, this inn is a good deal, except for the rooms right above the biker bar.

Diamond M Ranch (☎ 283-9424, 866-283-9424; www.diamondmranch.com; Mile 16.5 Kalifornsky Beach Rd; sites $30-40, r $7-149, cabins $99-159; ⊠ 💻) Fifteen years ago, this was just the Martin family farm – but with fishermen constantly asking to camp in their field, the Martins converted it to a tourist megaplex, complete with kids' programs, walking tours, movie nights, and horse rides. If you get up early enough, you can help milk the cows that share the 80 acres with an extensive campground, cabins, and full B&B.

Hooligan's Lodge (☎ 262-9951; www.hooliganslodge.com; 44715 Sterling Hwy; r $119-159; ⊠ 💻) The motel rooms are fish-themed and the lobby is comfortable. If you roll into town without reservations it may be one of the few places available.

Kenai River Lodge (☎ 262-4292; www.kenairiverlodge.com; 393 Riverside Dr; r $120-170, ste $400; ⊠ 💻) Has a private fishing hole right outside and delicious river views. It was completely remodeled in 2008, and all rooms come with coffee, microwave and fridge.

Soldotna B&B Lodge (☎ 262-4779, 877-262-4779; www.soldotnalodge.com; 399 Lovers Lane; r $99-357) This is the luxury place, drawing blue-chip anglers and honeymooners. It has plush rooms, custom adventure and fishing packages, and rooms with kitchenettes and some without baths. There's breakfast in a river-front sunroom and a private fishing hole for reds.

Riverside House (☎ 262-0500, 877-262-0500; www.alaska.net/~clc1972/; 44611 Sterling Hwy; r Jul $135-150, r Aug-Jun $80-100, RV sites $20; ⊠ 💻) Never mind the unappealing exterior, this place has big and perfectly tolerable rooms, some of which overlook the river. RVs can park here, but tents aren't allowed.

Eating & Drinking

Kaladi Brothers Coffee Co (☎ 262-5115; 315 S Kobuk St; snacks $2-5; 🕑 6am-7pm Mon-Fri, 7am-9pm Sat, 8am-7pm Sun) Despite the odd location, this is a fun hangout, with good coffee, baked goodies, and art – check out the ceiling tiles.

Moose is Loose (☎ 760-7861; 44278 Sterling Hwy; snacks $2-7; 🕑 4:30am-6pm Tue-Sun) This Moose comes with coffee and goodies galore, attracting both tourists and locals.

Sal's Klondike Diner (☎ 262-2220; 44619 Sterling Hwy; breakfast & lunch $5-9, dinner $9-14; 🕑 24hr) Being Soldotna's best stab at a tourist trap, this diner is jammed with weary travelers, gabbing locals and frantic waitresses. The meals aren't as tasty as they are ample.

St Elias Brewing Company (☎ 260-7837; 434 Sharkathmi Ave; dinner $8-14; 🕑 4-10pm) Stone-fires 11-inch pizzas and bakes sandwiches in an echoing brewery. Delicious. Beer-lovers should order the sampler.

Mykel's (☎ 262-4305; www.mykels.com; dinner $15-34; 🕑 11am-3pm and 5-10pm) This is Soldotna's fanciest place, with high-backed leather booths and dishes like duck with apple shallot sauce ($24).

BJ's (cnr Sterling Hwy & Lovers Lane) Insofar as a hobo can have a home, this squat, cinderblock bar is home to the peninsula's favorite minstrel, Hobo Jim. It's a bit of a dive, but that's the way he likes it.

Safeway (10576 Kenai Spur Hwy) This supermarket, just before the Soldotna 'Y' junction, has a deli, salad bar, bakery and Starbuck's.

Getting There & Around

Homer Stage Line (☎ 868-3914; www.homerstageline.com) has buses passing through daily en route to Anchorage ($55) and Homer ($40).

SOUTH TO HOMER

After Soldotna, traffic thins out as the Sterling Hwy rambles south, hugging the coastline and opening up to grand views of Cook Inlet. This stretch is 78 miles long and passes through a handful of small villages near some great clamming areas, ending at the charming town of Homer. Take your time in this area; the coastline and Homer are worth every day you decide to spend there.

Kasilof

pop 596

The fishing village of Kasilof is at Mile 108.8 Sterling Hwy. Turn west on Kalifornsky Beach Rd and travel 3.6 miles to reach the small-boat harbor on the Kasilof River. The Sterling Hwy crosses a bridge over the Kasilof River a mile south of the Kalifornsky Beach Rd turnoff.

Kasilof River State Recreation Site (day-use $5), just across the bridge, has no campsites but is a popular day-use and boat-launch area along a productive river.

Tustumena Lodge (☎ 262-4216; Mile 111 Sterling Hwy; r per person $34), at the giant 'T,' has cheap lodging in the most rudimentary of rooms. The adjacent bar also boasts the world's largest hat collection – well over 28,000. Amid this jungle of caps it occasionally hosts live music.

At Mile 111.5 of the Sterling Hwy, the Cohoe Loop Rd heads northwest toward the ocean, passing **Cohoe Cove Campground** (☎ 262-1939; campsites $10), which is both pretty and pretty packed with anglers. Also along the road is **Crooked Creek State Recreation Area** (sites $10), another top spot for salmon fishing. The 'campground' is a gravel lot where you'll be cheek-by-jowl with your neighbor.

Southeast of the Cohoe Loop Rd intersection on the Sterling Hwy is Johnson Lake Access Rd, which quickly passes the **Johnson Lake Recreation Area** (sites $10), with somewhat boggy open-forest sites for folks who prefer rainbow trout to salmon.

Clam Gulch

pop 175

At Mile 117.4 of the Sterling Hwy, before reaching the hamlet of Clam Gulch, you pass the turnoff to a 2-mile gravel road. Just west on the road is **Clam Gulch State Recreation Area** (day-use $5, sites $10), a gorgeous bluffside spot overlooking a sandy beach renowned for its very productive razor-clam beds. The dirt lot won't tantalize tent campers, but it's a convenient place to park while rooting through the sand for succulent mollusks. If you have a reliable 4WD you can do what the Alaskans do: just motor your way straight onto the beach.

The village of Clam Gulch is less than a mile south of the gravel road on the Sterling Hwy, and it has a post office and gas station. The run-down **Clam Shell Lodge** (☎ 262-4211; r $50-80) provides rooms that are simple in the extreme. Instead, it's best to go for **Clam Gulch Lodge** (☎ 260-3778, 800-700-9555; www.clamgulch.com; Mile 119.6 Sterling Hwy; d $105), which is a delightful family-friendly B&B with stunning views.

Ninilchik

pop 778

For many travelers, Ninilchik, at Mile 135 Sterling Hwy, is merely a stop for gas and a quick look at its Russian church. But this appealing little village is well worth spending a night, either at its stellar hostel, its affordable hotels or one of its numerous campsites boasting volcanic views.

The community is among the oldest on the Kenai Peninsula, having been settled in the 1820s by employees of the Russian-American Company. Many stayed even after imperial Russia sold Alaska to the US, and their descendants form the heart of the present community.

ORIENTATION & INFORMATION

Though Ninilchik's core is found along the Sterling Hwy between the Ninilchik River and Deep Creek, several tourist services – especially RV parks and fishing-charter operations – straggle out to the east along Kingsley and Oilwell Rds. The intriguing Old Ninilchik Village and the waterfront, meanwhile, are west of the highway in a small valley, accessible via Mission Ave.

Alaskan Angler RV Resort (☎ 800-347-4114; Kingsley Rd) For a shower ($2) or laundry facilities.

Ninilchik General Store (☎ 567-3378; Mile 135.7 Sterling Hwy; 🕑 9am-10pm) Has an ATM, lots of fishing and camping gear, and a few tourist-oriented brochures posted out front.

Ninilchik Public Library (☎ 567-3333; Sterling Hwy; 🕑 11am-4pm Mon-Thu, 1-6pm Fri, 11am-2pm Sat; 💻) Just north of Oilwell Rd, has three free internet terminals.

Post office (Kingsley Rd) Is just past the Alaskan Angler.

SIGHTS & ACTIVITIES

Begin a scenic walk through Alaska's Russian history at the **Frances Rose Gift Shop** (🕑 9am-7pm Mon-Sat), a log cabin built in the late 19th century, then completely dismantled and restored, log by log, in 1984. It has Russian and Alaska Native trinkets and jewelry for sale, and you may be able to pick up a copy of the free *Tour of Ninilchik Village* brochure. **Old Ninilchik Village**, the site of the original community, is a postcard scene of faded log cabins in tall grass and beached fishing boats against the spectacular backdrop of Mt Redoubt.

The most spectacular building is the **Old Russian Church**, which received a facelift recently and is reached via a posted footpath behind the Village Cache Gift Shop. Built in 1901, the historic blufftop structure sports five golden onion-domes and commands an unbelievable view of Cook Inlet and the volcanoes on the other side. Adjoining it is a prim Russian Orthodox cemetery of white-picket cribs. Together they make for a photographer's delight on a clear day.

Clamming is Ninilchik's No 1 summer pastime (see below), however. At low tide, go to either **Ninchilik Beach State Recreation Site**, across the river from the old village, or **Deep Creek State Recreation Site**. It costs $5 to park at the state recreation areas. You can either purchase a shovel ($16) and bucket ($5) at the Ninilchik General Store or rent one from the Village Cache.

The main event in Ninilchik is the **Kenai Peninsula State Fair**, the 'biggest little fair in Alaska,' which takes place annually in mid-August.

SLEEPING

our pick **Eagle Watch** (☎ 567-3905; www.home.gci.net/~theeaglewatch; Mile 3 Oilwell Rd; dm/r $13/35) This hostel, situated on an outrageously scenic and peaceful bluff high above the Ninilchik River, lives up to its name: eagles throng here, feeding on spawned-out salmon in the waters below. The facilities are charmingly rough-hewn but immaculate, and you're free to use the friendly owners' clam shovels and buckets. There's a lockout from 10am to 5pm.

Ninilchik View State Campground (Mile 135.5 Sterling Hwy; sites $10) By far the best of Ninilchik's public

DIGGING FOR CLAMS

Almost all of the beaches on the west side of the Kenai Peninsula (Clam Gulch, Deep Creek, Ninilchik and Whiskey Gulch) have a good supply of razor clams, considered by mollusk connoisseurs to be a true delicacy. Not only do razors have the best flavor, but they're also among the largest of the mollusks. The average razor clam is 3½in long, but (in true Alaska fashion) most clammers are after clams that reach 5in, 6in or even 7in in length.

To clam, you first have to purchase a sportfishing license (a one-day visitor's license is $20, and a seven-day license is $55). The daily bag limit is 60 clams, but remember – that's an awful lot of clams to clean and eat. Two dozen per person are more than enough for a meal. While the clamming's good from April to August, the best time is July, right before spawning. And though you can dig for clams anytime the tide is out, the best clamming is during extra-low, 'minus,' tides. Consult a tide book – and count on hundreds of other clammers to do the same.

- For equipment, you'll need a narrow-bladed clam shovel that can either be purchased or, if you don't feel like hauling it around all summer, rented at many lodges and stores near the clamming areas. You'll also want rubber boots, rubber gloves, a bucket and a pair of pants to which you're not terribly attached.
- Once on the beach, you have to play detective. Look for the clam's 'footprint,' a dimple mark left behind when it withdraws its neck. That's your clue to the clam's whereabouts, but don't dig directly below the imprint or you'll break its shell. Shovel a scoop or two next to the mark and then reach into the sand for the clam. You have to be quick, as a razor clam can bury itself and be gone in seconds.
- Once you're successful, leave the clams in a bucket of seawater, or better yet, beer, for several hours to allow them to 'clean themselves.' Many locals say a handful of cornmeal helps this process. The best way to cook clams is right on the beach over an open fire while you're taking in the mountain scenery across Cook Inlet. Use a large covered pot and steam the clams in saltwater, or for more flavor, in white wine with a clove of garlic.
- Here's where to go:

Clam Gulch (p277) This is the most popular and, many say, most productive spot by far. The Clam Gulch State Recreation Area is a half-mile from Mile 118 of the Sterling Hwy, where there's a short access road to the beach from the campground.

Ninilchik (p277)The best bet is to camp at Ninilchik View State Campground, located above the old village of Ninilchik. From there, you can walk to beaches for clamming.

Deep Creek Just south of Ninilchik is the Deep Creek State Recreation Site, where there's camping and plenty of parking along the beach.

Whiskey Gulch Look for the turnoff at about Mile 154 of the Sterling Hwy. Unless you have a 4WD vehicle, park at the elbow-turn above the beach.

Mud Bay On the east side of the Homer Spit is Mud Bay, a stretch abundant with eastern soft-shells, cockles and blue mussels. Some surf clams (rednecks) and razor clams can also be found on the Cook Inlet side of the Spit.

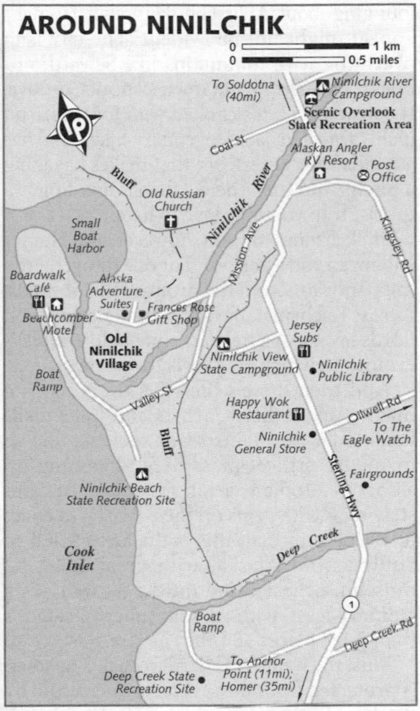

AROUND NINILCHIK

campgrounds, it's set atop a wooded bluff with a view of the old village and Cook Inlet. A stairway leads down to the beach.

Ninilchik Beach State Recreation Site (sites $10) Across the river from the old village, this windy spot is little more than a gravel parking lot beside the ocean. The clamming, however, is fantastic.

Ninilchik River Campground (Mile 134.9 Sterling Hwy; sites $10) Across the Sterling Hwy from Coal St; this campground has great river access and some pleasant trails.

Ninilchik Scenic Overlook State Recreation Area (Mile 134.6 Sterling Hwy; sites $10) It has 25 RV-oriented parking 'sites' on a bluff above the Ninilchik River.

Beachcomber Motel (☎ 567-3417; www.beachcombermotelrvpark.com; Beach Rd; r $70-125, RV sites $35) This place is right on the beach beside the old village, and has half a dozen ultra cute rooms, some with kitchenettes.

Deep Creek State Recreation Site (Mile 137.2 Sterling Hwy; sites $10) Situated on the beach near the mouth of the creek, this is another parking lot-style campground, with little to offer in the way of privacy.

Alaskan Angler RV Resort (☎ 800-347-4114; www.afishhunt.com; Kingsley Rd; sites camp/RV $15/40, cabins $129-179) A privately owned place with on-site fish processing. There's a tenting area back in the trees, and guests can rent rods and reels ($10), hip boots ($5) and clam shovels ($5).

Alaska Adventure Suites (☎ 277-1800; www.alaskaadventuresuites.com; ste $195-235) Right beside the Village Cache, has a sizable volcano-view suite and a slightly smaller village-view suite. Both are tricked out with kitchens and all the amenities.

EATING

Boardwalk Café (☎ 567-3388; breakfast $5-10, dinner $9-23; 🕘 9am-9pm) This nautically-inclined stand practically overhangs the crashing surf and serves quality espressos and very fine fish-and-chips. The homemade clam chowder ($5.25) is a must.

Jersey Subs (☎ 567-1018; sandwiches $7-11; 🕘 7am-7pm Wed-Mon) In a little red shack across from the school; this is a local fave for overstuffed subs.

Happy Wok Restaurant (☎ 567-1060; 15945 Sterling Hwy; mains $9-20; 🕘 11am-10pm) This place is near the general store, and provides quality lunch and dinner specials that draw both local fishermen and visiting clam diggers.

Ninilchik General Store (☎ 567-3378; Mile 135.7 Sterling Hwy; 🕘 7am-10pm) If you're wanting groceries, fried food, or sandwiches, this is where to find them.

Anchor Point

pop 1815

Twenty miles south of Ninilchik is Anchor Point, which is, as a monument here notes, 'the most westerly point on the North American continent accessible by a continuous road system.' Captain Cook christened the site in 1778, after the *Resolution* lost a kedge anchor to the tidal currents. Today, the town is a fishing hot spot during early summer, with Anchor River renowned for its population of king and silver salmon and steelhead trout. Be prepared for massive crowds during the king run in late May and early June; otherwise, it's a sleepy little place.

For local info, stop in at the **Anchor Point Visitor Center** (☎ 235-2600; Mile 156 Sterling Hwy; 🕘 8am-4pm) which has maps, brochures and coffee. For $3 you can pick up a certificate proving you have experienced 'North America's Most Westerly Highway Point.' For internet access, staff members will direct you to **Anchor Point Library** (☎ 235-5692; Fritz Rd; 9am-4:30pm Mon, to 4pm Wed, to 4:30pm Fri, to noon Sat;), adjacent to the VFW (look for the anti-aircraft gun).

Near the turnoff to the library on the Sterling Hwy is the **Blue Bus** (☎ 235-6285; Mile 156.7 Sterling Hwy; fast food $6-9; 11am-7pm, to 3pm Sun), which features long lines of locals waiting for burritos, sandwiches and charter lunches.

Just down the highway from the visitors center is the turnoff to the Old Sterling Hwy, where you'll find the town's main hotel, the **Anchor River Inn** (☎ 235-8531, 800-435-8531; www.anchorriverinn.com; Sterling Hwy at Old Sterling Hwy; r $59-109). It has small economy rooms called 'fisherman's specials,' plus larger, more modern rooms costing twice as much. The adjacent **Anchor River Inn Restaurant** (dinner $15-35, other meals $6-14; 8am-9pm) serves seafood, steaks and salads.

Progressing down the Old Sterling Hwy you'll come to Anchor Beach Rd and the **Anchor Angler** (☎ 235-8351; 1 Anchor Beach Rd; 6am-10pm), a tackle shop with the best fishing tips in town, as well as a nifty collection of antique rods and reels. Get hooked up here and go catch some dinner!

On the opposite side of Anchor Beach Rd is the Anchor River State Recreation Area, with five campgrounds. Four of them are on the river while the last one, **Halibut Campground** (Mile 1.5 Anchor Beach Rd; sites $10), has 20 sites and overlooks Cook Inlet Beach. The road ends at a beautiful stretch of sand with good views of Mt Redoubt and Mt Iliamna across the inlet. Almost as intriguing are the huge tractors busily launching fishing vessels into the surf.

If the campgrounds along Anchor Beach Rd seem too busy, backtrack 4 miles up the Sterling Hwy to **Stariski Creek State Recreation Site** (Mile 152 Sterling Hwy; sites $10), with 16 private and mostly-wooded sites, some right at the edge of a 100ft bluff over the ocean.

HOMER

pop 5384

Lucky is the visitor who drives into Homer on a clear day. As the Sterling Hwy descends into town, a panorama of mountains sweeps in front of you. The Homer Spit slowly comes into view, jutting into a glittering Kachemak Bay, and just when you think the view might unwind forever it ends with the dramatic Grewingk Glacier.

Hearing travelers' tales of Homer, you half expect to find lotus-eaters and mermaids lounging about. At first blush, though, Homer's appeal might not be evident. The city isn't overhung with mountains like Seward, nor does it have the quaint townscape of Cordova. It sprawls a bit, it's choked with tourists, isn't lushly forested, lacks legendary hikes, and has a windswept waterfront that makes kayaking a bitch. And then there's the Homer Spit – a tourist trap you may love to hate.

Stick around for a bit, however, and Homer will make you a believer. For one thing, there's the panorama, and the promise that it holds. Across Kachemak Bay, glaciers and peaks and fjords beckon – a trekkers' and paddlers' playground to which Homer is the portal.

And then there's the vibe: the town is a magnet for radicals, artists and folks disillusioned with mainstream society, who've formed a critical mass here, dreaming up a sort of utopian vision for their city, and striving – with grins on their faces – to enact it. Because of that, this is the arts capital of Southcentral Alaska, with great galleries, museums, theater and music. As well, it's a culinary feast, with more wonderful eateries than most places 10 times its size.

Plus, the weather is hard to beat. The town is protected from the severe northern cold by the Kenai Mountains to the north and east. Winter temperatures rarely drop below 0°F, while summer temperatures rarely rise above 70°F. The annual precipitation is only 28in, much of it snow.

History

Homer was founded, and picked up its name, when Homer Pennock, an adventurer from Michigan, landed on the Spit with a crew of gold-seekers in 1896, convinced that Kachemak Bay was the key to their riches. It wasn't, and Pennock was soon lured to the Klondike, where he also failed to find gold. Three years later the Cook Inlet Coal Field Company established the first of a succession of coalmines in the area. It was fishing, though, that would come to dominate the town's economy for most of the 1900s.

Orientation

Homer lies at the end of the Sterling Hwy, 233 road miles from Anchorage. For tourists, there are two distinct sections of town. The 'downtown' area, built on a hill between high bluffs to the north and Kachemak Bay to the south, lies along – or nearby to – busy Pioneer Ave.

DETOUR: NIKOLAEVSK

Tucked inconspicuously down a winding road from Anchor Point sits one of several Russian Old Believer Villages on the Kenai Peninsula. The Old Believers are members of a sect that split from mainstream Russian Orthodoxy in the 1650s, defending their 'old beliefs' in the face of what they considered heretical reforms. Long considered outcasts in Russia, they fled communism in 1917, ending up in Brazil, then Oregon, and then – in 1968 – Alaska, where they finally felt they could enjoy religious freedom while avoiding the corruptive influences of modernity.

Nowadays, Alaska's Old Believers number at most 3000. They're hardcore traditionalists, speaking mainly Russian, marrying in their teens, raising substantial broods of children, and living simply. The men – usually farmers or fishermen – are forbidden from trimming their beards; the women typically cover their hair and are garbed in long dresses. The Old Believers tend to keep to themselves, inhabiting a handful of isolated villages on the Kenai Peninsula, of which Nikolaevsk is the most prominent.

To get there, head 10 miles east on North Fork Rd, which departs the Sterling Hwy in the heart of Anchor Point and winds through hillbilly homesteads and open, rolling forest. Right before the pavement ends, hang a left at Nikolaevsk Rd. Two miles later, you'll enter the village.

At first, you may be disappointed. Apart from the dress and language of the inhabitants (who are often nowhere to be seen), the community appears downright Alaskan: wooden prefab homes, rusting pickup trucks, gardens with gargantuan produce. Look hard, though, and you'll notice subtle Russian touches – the ornate scrollwork on a porch railing, for instance. Impossible to miss is the village's house of worship, the Church of St Nikolas, built in 1983 and sporting an elaborately painted façade and a white-and-blue onion dome. You can look, but don't photograph the inside unless you get permission. There's a donation box located outside (hint, hint).

But to really get into the heart of Nikolaevsk, you must follow the signs to the **Samovar Café & B&B** (☎ 235-6867; www.russiangiftsnina.com; mains $5-12; r $39-79, sites camp/RV $15/29; café ⌚ 10am-10pm Mon-Fri, to 8pm Sat), which has more than simply the best Russian food on the peninsula, and more than a wonderful collection of cheap and colorful (and pretty basic) accommodations. This small restaurant is a wacky welcome mat into the world of the Old Believers. Nina, the proprietor, is an electrical engineer, writer, and force of nature. She'll offer you two dining choices: in the sun room, where she'll simply serve your meal, or inside, where you can 'dine in Russia.' This choice gets you an inside seat, borscht, cream puffs and delicious *pelimeny* (Siberian dumplings), Nina's stories, and a photo session where she'll dress you up in traditional Orthodox gear. The cost is the price of two of her hand-painted spoons ($20 to $25) and the experience is well worth the purchase. You'll stumble out the café feeling like you visited another country, in another time. After it's finished, Nina will tell you exactly how much to tip. However much it is, it will be well worth one of the most unique dining and cultural experiences that you'll have in Alaska.

Heading eastward, Pioneer Ave becomes rural East End Rd, with a number of other lodging and eating options. The second section of Homer, and certainly the most notorious, is the Homer Spit, a skinny tongue of sand licking halfway across Kachemak Bay. In summer, the Spit is a madhouse of fishing charters and tourist traps; in winter it all but shuts down. Many locals say they assiduously avoid the Spit; many tourists make a beeline there, unaware that there's another side to Homer.

Information

BOOKSTORES

Homer Bookstore (Map p282; ☎ 235-7496; 332 E Pioneer Ave; ⌚ 10am-7pm Mon-Sat, noon-5pm Sun) Sells new books to what's clearly a more intellectually demanding market than most. The selection is phenomenal.

Old Inlet Bookshop (Map p282; ☎ 235-7984; 106 W Bunnell Ave; ⌚ 9am-5pm Tue-Sun) Has stacks and stacks of quality used books.

LAUNDRY

East End Laundry (Map p284; ☎ 235-2562; Mile 2.9 E End Rd; ⌚ 9am-8pm Mon-Sat, 9am-7pm Sun) Also has showers ($4) and is convenient to Seaside Farm.

Sportsman's Supply & Rental (Map p284; ☎ 235-2617; 1114 Freight Dock Rd; ⌚ 6am-11pm) Offers showers ($5.50) and laundry right on the Spit.

Washboard Laundromat (Map p282; ☎ 235-6781; 1204 Ocean Dr; ⌚ 7:30am-9pm) Sure, the showers are pricey ($6), but you can stand under them as long as you

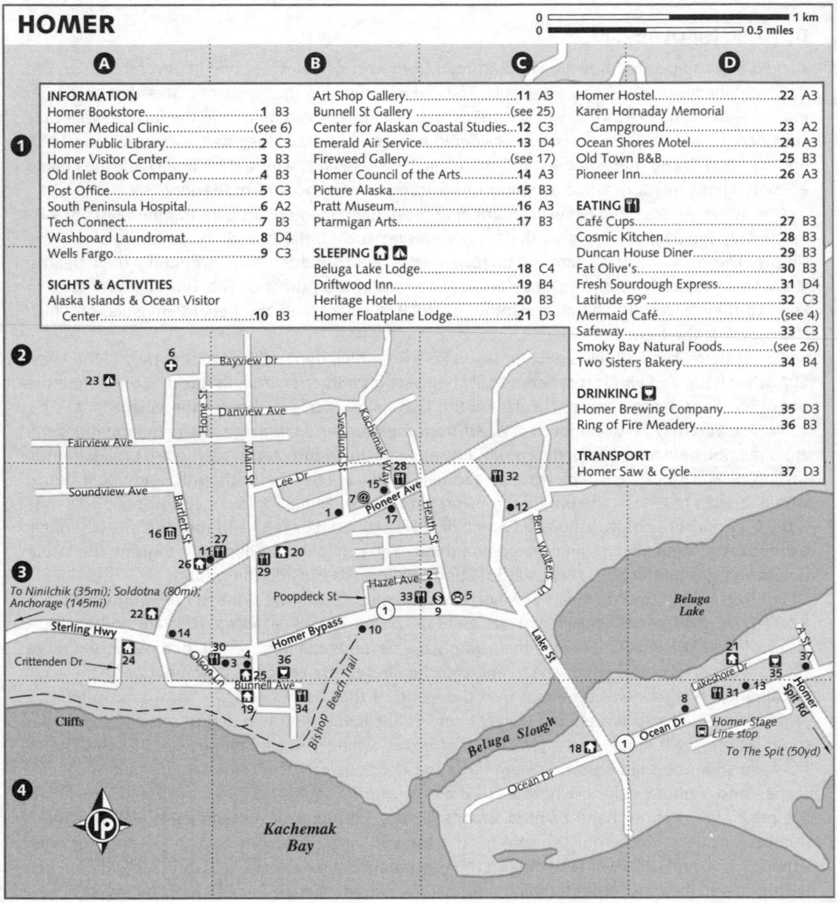

want. You can even sweat away your worries in the steam room ($6.75)

LIBRARY & INTERNET ACCESS

Homer Public Library (Map p282; ☎ 235-3180; 500 Hazel Ave; 10am-8pm Tue & Thu, 10am-6pm Mon, Wed, Fri & Sat) Homer's brand new library is arty and open. Internet access is free, and it even has laptop cubicles with a view of Kachemak Bay.

K-Bay Caffé (Map p284; ☎ 235-1551; www.kbaycaffe.com; 59415 E End Rd; 6:30am-7pm Mon-Sat, 7:30am-6pm Sun;) Has free internet access (donations appreciated) on one computer, plus wi-fi. The coffee is the best in town.

Tech Connect (Map p282; ☎ 235-5248; 432 E Pioneer Ave; per hr $6; 9am-6pm Mon-Fri, from 10am Sat;) Offers internet access.

MEDICAL SERVICES

Homer Medical Clinic (Map p282; ☎ 235-8586; 4136 Bartlett St) Next door to South Peninsula Hospital; for walk-in service.

South Peninsula Hospital (Map p282; ☎ 235-8101, 866-235-0369; Bartlett St) North of the Pratt Museum.

MONEY

Wells Fargo (Map p282; ☎ 235-8151; 88 Sterling Hwy) For cash this is as good a bank as any.

POST

Post office (Map p282; 3658 Heath St) Sells phonecards.

TOURIST INFORMATION

Halibut Derby Office (☎ 235-7740; www.homerhalibutdergy.com; Homer Spit Rd; 5:30am-8am & 3-8pm)

Has a few pamphlets and is the official weigh-in station for the Homer Halibut Derby.

Homer Visitor Center (☎ 235-7740; www.homeralaska.org; 201 Sterling Hwy; 9am-7pm Mon-Fri, 10am-6pm Sat & Sun) Has countless brochures and a funky mosaic on the floor. It's operated by the chamber of commerce, however, and only provides info on members.

Sights

HOMER SPIT

Generally known as 'the Spit' (Map p284), this long needle of land – a 4½-mile sand bar stretching into Kachemak Bay – is viewed by some folks as the most fun place in Alaska. Others wish another earthquake would come along and sink the thing. Regardless, the Spit throbs all summer with tourists who mass here in unimaginable density, gobbling fish-and-chips, quaffing specialty coffees, getting chair massages, purchasing alpaca sweaters, arranging bear-watching trips, watching theatrical performances, and – oh yeah – going fishing in search of 300lb halibut. The hub of all this activity is the **small-boat harbor**, one of the best facilities in Southcentral Alaska and home to more than 700 boats. Close by is the **Seafarer's Memorial**, which, amid all the Spit's hubbub, is a solemn monument to residents lost at sea.

Beach combing, bald-eagle watching (they seem as common here as pigeons in New York City) and watching recently docked fishermen angling for cute tourist chicks at the Salty Dawg Saloon are all favorite activities. You can also go clamming at Mud Bay, on the east side of the Spit. Blue mussels, an excellent shellfish overlooked by many people, are the most abundant.

If you'd rather catch your dinner than shovel or buy it, try your luck at the **Fishing Hole**, just before the Pier One Theater. The small lagoon is the site of a 'terminal fishery,' in which salmon are planted by the state and return three or four years later to a place where they can't spawn. Kings can be caught here from mid-May to the end of June, while silvers run in August. **Sportsman's Supply & Rental** (☎ 235-2617; 1114 Freight Dock Rd; 6am-11pm), close by, rents rods ($10) as well as rakes and shovels (each $5) for clamming.

PRATT MUSEUM

This recently renovated **museum** (Map p282; ☎ 235-8635; www.prattmuseum.org; 3779 Bartlett St; adult/child $6/3; 10am-6pm) is fantastic – so much so, it has loaned exhibits to the Smithsonian. There's lots of local art and Alaska Native artifacts, but a more impressive feature is the interactive displays on the area's wildlife, designed to mesmerize both kids and ex-kids. Particularly cool is the remote gull-cam, which you can rotate to zoom in on Gull Island's roosting birds in real time. More sobering is the Storm Warning Theater, with harrowing tales about fishing on Kachemak Bay, where making a living can end your life. A box of tissues is provided for those brought to tears. And then there's the 'Darkened Waters' exhibit, a stunning and emotional look at the Exxon oil spill.

More light-hearted and whimsical, and perhaps the coolest aspect of the museum, is the Forest Ecology Trail, where artists can contribute to the 'Facing the Elements' exhibit. Paths wind through the trees, and you'll stumble upon small exhibits, be they mirrors, rocks, or pottery. A must-do.

The Pratt also offers 1½-hour harbor tours ($5) throughout summer at 3pm Friday and Saturday, leaving from the Salty Dawg Saloon.

ALASKA ISLANDS & OCEAN VISITOR CENTER

More a research facility and **museum** (Map p282; ☎ 235-6961; www.islandsandocean.org; 95 Sterling Hwy; admission free; 9am-6pm) than a visitors center, this impressive new place has numerous cool interactive exhibits, perhaps the best of which is a room that's a replica seabird colony, complete with cacophonous bird calls and surround-view flocking. There's also a decent film about ship-based marine research, a hands-on discovery lab, and a slate of daily educational programs and guided walks. It's operated jointly by the Kachemak Bay Research Reserve and the Alaska Maritime National Wildlife Refuge, which, though headquartered in Homer, mainly takes in the distant Aleutian Islands. With the Aleutians as the main focus of the center, many visitors may come away unclear how it all relates to Homer.

CENTER FOR ALASKAN COASTAL STUDIES

This **nonprofit organization** (Map p282; ☎ 235-6667; www.akcoastalstudies.org; 708 Smokey Way; 9am-5pm Mon-Fri), devoted to promoting appreciation of Kachemak Bay's ecosystem, runs the Carl E Wynn Nature Center (p285) and the Peterson Bay Field Station (p295), both of which offer guided hikes and educational programs throughout the summer. Drop by to learn

AROUND HOMER

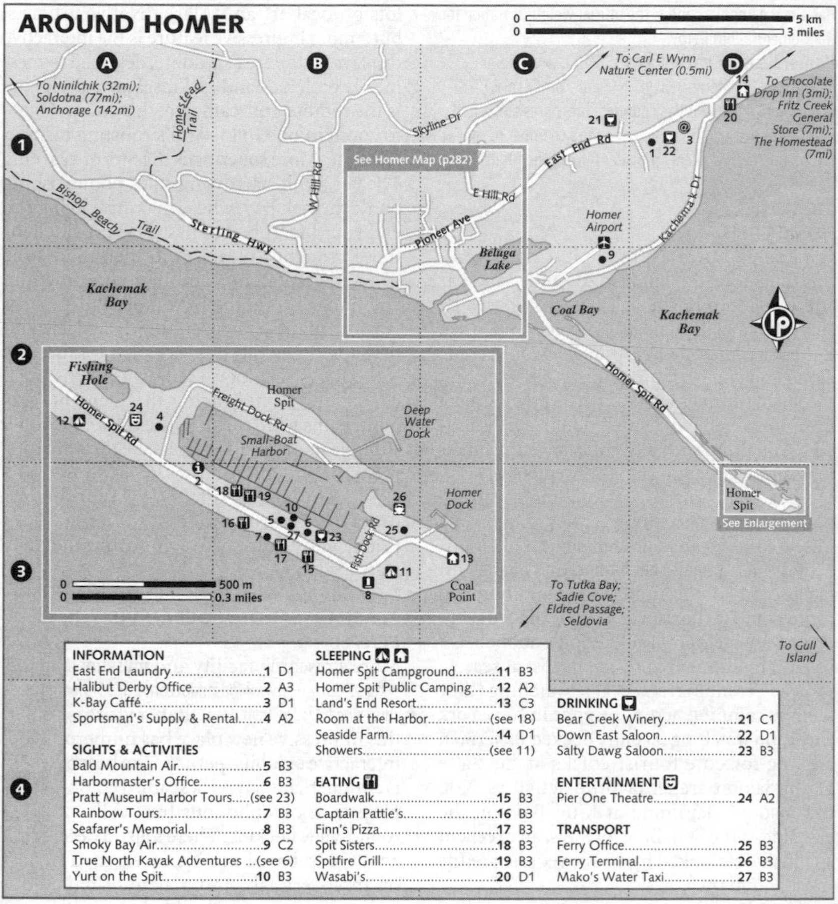

INFORMATION
East End Laundry....1 D1
Halibut Derby Office....2 A3
K-Bay Caffé....3 D1
Sportsman's Supply & Rental....4 A2

SIGHTS & ACTIVITIES
Bald Mountain Air....5 B3
Harbormaster's Office....6 B3
Pratt Museum Harbor Tours....(see 23)
Rainbow Tours....7 B3
Seafarer's Memorial....8 B3
Smoky Bay Air....9 C2
True North Kayak Adventures....(see 6)
Yurt on the Spit....10 B3

SLEEPING
Homer Spit Campground....11 B3
Homer Spit Public Camping....12 A2
Land's End Resort....13 C3
Room at the Harbor....(see 18)
Seaside Farm....14 D1
Showers....(see 11)

EATING
Boardwalk....15 B3
Captain Pattie's....16 B3
Finn's Pizza....17 B3
Spit Sisters....18 B3
Spitfire Grill....19 B3
Wasabi's....20 D1

DRINKING
Bear Creek Winery....21 C1
Down East Saloon....22 D1
Salty Dawg Saloon....23 B3

ENTERTAINMENT
Pier One Theatre....24 A2

TRANSPORT
Ferry Office....25 B3
Ferry Terminal....26 B3
Mako's Water Taxi....27 B3

more about their offerings, and to get maps and info about Kachemak Bay State Park. It also operates the **Yurt on the Spit** (Map p284; Homer Spit Rd; 11am-8pm), right behind Mako's Water-Taxi, which does a daily 'Creatures of the Dock' tour at 1pm and 4pm ($5).

Activities

HIKING

For all its natural beauty, Homer has few good public trails. For a map of short hiking routes around town, pick up the *Walking Guide to the Homer Area* at the visitor center.

Bishop's Beach Trail

This hike (Map p284) is a 7-mile waterfront trek from north of Homer back into town (you could do it in reverse, but you're likely to miss the turnoff to the highway). The views of Kachemak Bay and the Kenai Mountains are superb, while the marine life that scurries along the sand at low tide is fascinating.

The trailhead is opposite Diamond Ridge Rd, 5 miles north along the Sterling Hwy. The trail begins by descending along Diamond Creek, then hits the beach. Check a tide book, and leave before low tide and return before high tide. High tides cover most of the sand, forcing you to scramble onto the base of the nearby cliffs. Within 4 miles you'll pass a sea-otter rookery a few hundred yards offshore. The hike ends 3 miles later at Homer's Bishop Park, below the Islands & Ocean Visitor Center.

Another option is to grab a scone from Two Sisters Bakery (see p288) and wander a ways down the beach.

Homestead Trail

This 6.7-mile trek (Map p284) from Rogers Loop Rd to the City Reservoir, just off Skyline Dr on Crossman Ridge Rd, is a 2½-mile walk to Rucksack Dr, which crosses Diamond Ridge Rd. Along the way you pass through open meadows, with panoramic views of Kachemak Bay, and Mt Iliamna and Mt Redoubt on the other side of Cook Inlet. The trek continues another 4.2 miles, following Rucksack Dr and Crossman Ridge Rd to the reservoir. Cars are banned from both dirt roads.

To reach the trail, head out of town on the Sterling Hwy and turn right on Rogers Loop Rd across from the Bay View Inn. The trailhead is a half-mile farther, on your right.

Carl E Wynn Nature Center

Situated on the bluffs that are above Homer, this moose-ridden 140-acre **reserve** (Map p284; ☎ 235-6667; Skyline Dr; adult/child $7/5; ⏰ 10am-6pm) is highly recommended for families and anyone interested in the area's ethnobotany. With a few short interpretive nature trails, one of them boardwalked and wheelchair accessible, this is a grand place to learn which plants can be used to heal a cut, condition your hair or munch for lunch. Naturalist-led hikes leave at 10am and 2pm daily in summer. It also has a slate of lectures and other programs; call the center for a schedule.

HALIBUT FISHING

There are more than two dozen charter captains working out of the Spit, and they charge anywhere from $200 to $400 for a halibut trip. For a clue who to go with, peruse the board beside the Halibut Derby Office (Map p284), which lists the biggest fish caught that summer, along with who captained the boat. Other than that, the biggest distinction between the charter operations is vessel size: bigger boats bounce around less when the waves kick, meaning greater comfort and less mal de mer. Make sure you buy a derby ticket (p286).

CYCLING & MOUNTAIN BIKING

Though Homer lacks formal mountain-biking trails, the dirt roads in the hills above town lend themselves to some great rides, especially along Diamond Ridge Rd and Skyline Dr. For an easy tour, just head out E End Rd, which extends 20 miles east to the head of Kachemak Bay. There's also good biking to be had in Seldovia (p292), an easy day or overnight trip from Homer by water-taxi. To rent a bike and get more recommendations on good routes, head to Homer Saw & Cycle (p289).

PADDLING

Though, theoretically, you could spend a wavy day paddling in the vicinity of the Spit, you'll find infinitely better scenery and more varied wildlife, and far more sheltered waters, across the bay in the state park (p296). Due to fast currents and massive waves, attempting the wide-open crossing is a poor idea; you're better off taking your kayak across on a water-taxi or renting one from the various companies that maintain fleets of kayaks on the far side.

WHALE WATCHING

Whenever you're out in the bay there's a chance of spotting whales – sometimes you can even spot orcas from the tip of the Spit. But only the MV *Rainbow Connection*, operated by **Rainbow Tours** (Map p284; ☎ 235-7272; Homer Spit Rd), runs a dedicated whale watching tour. The comfortable 65ft vessel leaves Homer at 9am, cruises to Seldovia, and then spends six-plus hours seeking out humpbacks, orcas, minkes, finbacks and gray whales in Kachemak Bay and Kennedy Entrance. The $135 price includes lunch. Be sure to bundle up and bring your binocs.

BEAR WATCHING

Due largely to the density of tourists visiting Homer, the town has become a major departure point for bear-watching trips to the famed bruin haven of Katmai National Park (p311), located on the Alaska Peninsula 100-plus miles southwest by floatplane. Due to the distances involved, these trips cost a pretty penny: expect to pay between $500 and $600 per person for a day trip. However, that may be a small price to pay for the iconic Alaskan photo: a slavering brown bear, perched atop a waterfall, snapping its fangs on an airborne salmon.

Bald Mountain Air (Map p284; ☎ 235-7969; www.baldmountainair.com; Homer Spit Rd; per person $615) runs trips to the park headquarters at Brooks Camp, where countless bears converge to snag salmon ascending Brooks River – and where countless tourists converge to watch them. Once-in-a-lifetime photos are pretty much certain.

Emerald Air Service (Map p284; ☎ 235-6993; www.emeraldairservice.com; 1320 Lake Shore Dr; per person $530) is run by respected naturalists and offers a far more wilderness-oriented experience, bypassing Brooks Camp and seeking out bears along isolated Katmai beaches and lakeshores.

Festivals & Events

There's always something happening in Homer, especially in May – check to see what's on at the visitors center.

Homer Jackpot Halibut Derby (www.homerhalibutderby.com) May 1 marks the beginning of the five-month, $200,000-plus contest to catch the biggest fish (in 2008, it was a 348-pounder). Tickets cost $10, are good for one day of fishing, and can be bought at numerous places in Homer, including the derby office on the spit (p282). If you're going on a halibut charter, you may as well buy a ticket. Many a traveler has missed out on the jackpot because they didn't have a ticket.

Kachemak Bay Shorebird Festival (☎ 235-7337; www.homeralaska.org/shorebird) Brings hundreds of birders and 100,000 shorebirds to Mud Bay in early May, making it the largest bird migration site along the Alaskan road system. The tidal flats of Homer become the staging area for thousands of birds, including one-third of the world's surfbirds.

Spring Arts Festival A month-long May event that began as an outlet for local artists to display their work and has since evolved into a full-scale festival.

Kachemak Bay Kayak Festival (www.kachemakkayakfestival.com) A great time to paddle into town is at the end of May.

Sleeping

Homer has B&Bs galore. There are two reservation services with many, many more listings: **Cabins & Cottages Network** (☎ 235-0191; www.cabinsinhomer.com) and **Homer's Finest Bed & Breakfast Network** (☎ 235-4938, 800-764-3211; www.homeraccommodations.com). Homer adds a 7.5% sales tax to lodging.

BUDGET

Homer Spit Public Camping (Map p284; Homer Spit Rd; sites camp/RV $8/15) On the west beach of Homer Spit a catch-as-catch-can tent city springs up every night of the summer. It's a beautiful spot, though often windy (make sure you add weight to your tent if you leave), crowded, and sometimes rowdy. The self-registration stand is right across the road from Sportsman's Supply.

Karen Hornaday Memorial Campground (Map p282; sites camp/RV $8/15) Below the bluffs just north of downtown, this is the best camping option in Homer. It has private, wooded sites with impressive views and is probably a better choice for families with small children than the campgrounds on the Spit: unlike those, it has a playground instead of the Salty Dawg Saloon.

Homer Hostel (Map p282; ☎ 235-1463; www.homerhostel.com; 304 W Pioneer Ave; dm $22, s/d $47/56) This hostel is a bit cluttered, but it's perfectly located downtown. You can rent bikes and fishing poles and store your backpacks for $1.

Seaside Farm (☎ 235-7850; www.xyz.net/~seaside; E End Rd; sites/dm/r/cabins $10/25/65/75) Located 5 miles from the city center, this is more like Burning Man than a regulation youth hostel. The dorm rooms are dark and a bit dingy but camping in the grassy field overlooking Grewingk Glacier is excellent. The outdoor cooking pavilion is patrolled by roosters and impromptu jam sessions often spark up around the campfire. The several cabins scattered around the grounds are basic, but travelers do recommended them.

Homer Spit Campground (Map p284; ☎ 235-8206; Homer Spit Rd; sites camp/RV $29/31) Catering more to the RV crowd, this Spit-end place has coin-operated laundry facilities, showers ($5) and about 150 bald eagles, which 'the Eagle Lady' has been feeding every winter since 1979. They hang around all summer to keep her company.

MIDRANGE

Driftwood Inn (Map p282; ☎ 235-8019, 800-478-8019; www.thedriftwoodinn.com; 135 W Bunnell Ave; RV sites $32-48, r $69-165, cottages $275; 💻) This has a variety of accommodations, including European-style rooms with without baths, snug, cedar-finished 'ships quarters,' and a house with a deck affording some stunning oceanfront views.

Room at the Harbor (Map p284; ☎ 299-6767, 299-6868; Homer Spit Rd; s/d $85/100; ⊠) This establishment has one beautiful room upstairs from Spit Sisters. Though the shower is in the room one of the beds is in its own nook overlooking the boat harbor.

our pick **Old Town B&B** (Map p282; ☎ 235-7558; www.oldtownbeadandbreakfast.com; 106 W Bunnell Ave; d $95-115; ⊠ 💻) There are beautiful rooms with wood floors, great views, fresh flowers and cookies, and lots of antiques. Breakfast is served in a lovely little sitting room.

KENAI PENINSULA

HOMER ART GALLERIES

The cold, dark season of unemployment has inspired a saying in these parts: 'If you're starving, you might as well be an artist.' Just browsing these great galleries is a treat, and on the first Friday of the month, many break out the wine and cheese, and stay open late for a series of openings all over town. This is just the tip of the iceberg – grab a free *Downtown Homer Art Galleries* flyer at the visitors center with many more gallery listings, or stop by the **Homer Council of the Arts** (Map p282; ☎ 235-4288; www.homerart.org; 355 W Pioneer Ave; 9am-6pm Mon-Fri), with its own awesome gallery and information on various tours.

Art Shop Gallery (Map p282; ☎ 235-7076; 202 W Pioneer Ave; 10am-7pm Mon-Sat, 11am-5pm Sun) Does framing and features a fairly tourist-centric selection of Alaska-wide art and souvenirs.

Bunnell Street Gallery (Map p282; ☎ 235-2662; www.bunnellstreetgallery.org; 106 W Bunnell Ave; 10am-6pm Mon-Sat, noon-4pm Sun) An avant-garde place with the priciest and most experimental offerings – definitely the star of the show.

Fireweed Gallery (Map p282; ☎ 235-3411; 475 E Pioneer Ave; 10am-6pm Mon-Sat, 11am-5pm Sun) Has a more statewide representation than most of the other galleries. It's got photography, metalwork, oil paintings, jewelry, and is also home to the Kachemak Bay Watercolor Society.

Picture Alaska (Map p282; ☎ 235-2300; 448 E Pioneer Ave; 9:30am-6:30pm Mon-Sat, 11am-5pm Sun) Specializes in affordable prints and neat little knick-knacks.

Ptarmigan Arts (Map p282; ☎ 235-5345; 471 E Pioneer Ave; 10am-7pm Mon-Sat, 10am-6pm Sun) An artist-owned and operated co-op featuring mostly works from the Kenai Peninsula, including jewelry, textiles, Alaska Native pieces, and Homer spruce ash-glaze pottery.

Pioneer Inn (Map p282; ☎ 235-5670, 800-782-9655; www.pioneerinnhomerak.com; 244 W Pioneer Ave; r $89-119; ⊠ 💻) Has a couple of smaller (and thus cheaper) rooms, along with a number of near-luxurious larger suites with kitchenettes. The owners are super friendly and the location is great.

Heritage Hotel (Map p282; ☎ 235-7787, 800-380-7787; 147 E Pioneer Ave; r $119-165; ⊠ 💻) Housed in a 1948 log cabin, has an older section with small, rustically decorated rooms, plus a newer wing with rooms that are larger but less charming. Light sleepers take note: the Heritage is right next door to a nightclub, so you should try to reserve a room on the opposite side.

Chocolate Drop Inn (Map p284; ☎ 235-3668, 800-530-6015; www.chocolatedropinn.com; 57745 Taku; r from $175, ste $200; ⊠ 💻) This is a stunning log inn overlooking the bay, with an outdoor hot tub and indoor sauna, as well as a great room and a video room. Though anyone is welcome, hunters and fishermen will feel especially at home.

Homer Floatplane Lodge (Map p282; ☎ 877-235-9600, 235-4160; www.floatplanelodge.com; 1244 Lakeshore Dr; r from $150; ⊠ 💻) There are three slips for floatplanes and a variety of all-inclusive packages on offer, such as a three-night stay covering lodging, meals and halibut fishing for $1500 (plus 7.5% tax). Cabins and rooms come with kitchenettes and are cozy as can be.

Ocean Shores Motel (Map p282; ☎ 235-7775, 800-770-7775; www.akoceanshores.com; 451 Sterling Hwy; d $119-199) This has clean and spacious rooms, most with pleasant decks. Those down by the ocean cost the most; the cheaper ones are up on the hill and lack good views. The owner is a serious kayak buff and worth talking to if you're planning to paddle.

TOP END

Beluga Lake Lodge (Map p282; ☎ 235-5995; 204 Ocean Dr Loop; d $125-255; ⊠ 💻) This lodge overlooks its namesake lake and is pleasant and clean; the smallest rooms are cozy while the biggest ones sleep eight and have full kitchens.

Bear Creek Lodging (Map p284; ☎ 235-8484; www.bearcreekwineryalaska.com; Bear Creek Dr; d $225; ⊠) On a stunning hillside at the Bear Creek Winery, this place has two posh, romantic suites (each with a kitchenette), a hot tub overlooking the fruit vineyard and koi pond, and a complimentary bottle of vino beside each bed.

Land's End Resort (Map p284; ☎ 800-478-0400; www.lands-end-resort.com; r $140-245; ⊠) Located at the end of the Spit; it's considered a luxury hotel for its grand views and storied ambience, but only the pricier rooms really fit that description. New privately-owned 'lodges' (luxury condos) crowd the Spit's beach like a city skyline; you can rent a room in one for $150 to $225 or an entire place for $375 to $450.

Eating

Loosen your belt, because bite for bite, no place in Alaska has the culinary variety of Homer. There are great coffee shops on nearly every corner, an unfair share of eclectic gourmet sandwich joints, and several urbane dining rooms that'll make you forget you're in the boonies. Though there are some good options on the Spit, you'll pay substantially more than for dining in town.

RESTAURANTS

Captain Pattie's (Map p284; ☎ 226-3663; Homer Spit Rd; lunch $7-18, dinner $20-29; 🕑 11am-10pm) This oceanfront eatery has become a Spit institution by selling overpriced seafood to a constant stream of landlubbers. It claims its halibut is Alaska's best, but those in the know always order crab.

Café Cups (Map p282; ☎ 235-8330; 162 W Pioneer Ave; dinner $11-30; 🕑 4:30-9:30pm Tue-Sat) In a charming little building (you'll know it by the cups outside) with a menu that includes excellent curries and hand-cut rib-eyes. Though the food is delicious, the service can be quite harried.

our pick **Fat Olives** (Map p282; ☎ 235-8488; 276 Olson Lane; dinner $16-29; 🕑 11am-9:30pm) Housed in the old 'bus barn,' this chic and hyper-popular pizza joint/wine bar serves affordable appetizers like prosciutto-wrapped Alaska scallops and delicious mains like wood oven-roasted rack of lamb. You can also grab a huge slice of pizza to go ($4).

Wasabi's (Map p284; ☎ 235-3662; East End Rd; sushi rolls $6-32; 🕑 5-10pm) This swanky sushi bar, with views of Kachemak Bay, is almost anti-Homer in its sleekness. The bar infuses its own rum and vodka with pineapples or strawberries, and there's an extensive sake list. For those afraid of raw fish, it also serves standards such as halibut, but with a twist – sake cream sauce ($26).

Homestead (Map p284; ☎ 235-8723; Mile 8.2 E End Rd; dinner $26-32; 🕑 5-9pm) Considered the best – and perhaps the most delicious – restaurant in Homer, with mains such as cranberry duck ($28) and teriyaki rockfish ($29). Though the waiters wear black ties, patrons can come as they are (hey, this is Homer, after all). Reservations are recommended.

CAFÉS

Cosmic Kitchen (Map p282; ☎ 235-6355; 510 E Pioneer Ave; burritos & sandwiches $6-11; 🕑 9am-8pm Mon-Sat, to 3pm Sun; 💻) With excellent burritos, burgers and a salsa bar, this joint has is the place to go for a filling meal on the cheap. It also serves breakfast until 3pm.

Duncan House Diner (Map p282; ☎ 235-5344; 125 E Pioneer Ave; breakfast & lunch $6-11; 🕑 6am-3pm) This busy downtown place fries up home-style breakfast among home-style decor.

Fresh Sourdough Express (Map p282; ☎ 235-7571; 1316 Ocean Dr; breakfast $6-10, lunch & dinner $6-11; 🕑 7am-9pm) This is the first official 'green' restaurant in Alaska, and you can taste it. Almost everything is organic and as much as possible locally raised or grown. Come here for breakfast – you'll be served a small bakery sweet while you wait for your 'howling hotcakes.' Box lunches are also available.

Spitfire Grill (Map p284; ☎ 235-9379; Homer Spit Rd; mains $8-14; 🕑 noon-9:30pm) With a unique menu that includes local sausage, a chicken apple sandwich, and raved-about brisket, this small eatery actually gets locals down to the Spit.

QUICK EATS

Latitude 59° (Map p282; ☎ 235-5574; 3858 Lake St; light meals $2-5; 🕑 7am-6pm Mon-Sat; 💻) A wonderfully relaxed coffee shop and art gallery serving bagels, pastries, smoothies and espressos.

Spit Sisters (Map p284; ☎ 235-4921; Homer Spit Rd; pastries $2-5; 🕑 7am-7pm) If you're after a feisty girl-power vibe, you've come to the right place. There's a great view overlooking the small-boat harbor, and delicacies to enjoy – apricot scones, blackberry muffins, sticky buns – made by the revered Two Sisters Bakery in town.

Two Sisters Bakery (Map p282; ☎ 235-2280; 233 E Bunnell Ave; light meals $3-8; 🕑 7am-8pm Mon-Sat, 9am-4pm Sun) A beloved Homer institution with espresso and great fresh-baked bread, plus quiche, soups, salads and pizza by the slice.

Fritz Creek General Store (Map p284; ☎ 235-6521; Mile 8.2 East End Rd; quick eats $3-8; 🕑 7am-9pm Mon-Sat, 10am-6pm Sun) What is an excellent deli doing all the way out on East End Rd? Serving some of the best take-out food in Homer. It's worth the drive for the veggie burritos alone, but you shouldn't leave without dessert. It also does pizza, tamales, hoagies (sandwiches) and espresso.

Mermaid Café (Map p282; ☎ 235-7649; 3487 Main St; breakfast & lunch $5-12; 🕑 9am-3pm Tue-Fri, to 2pm Sat, to 1pm Sun) This sunny spot has all the basics such as soups, salad and sandwiches, and all the bread is house-baked. Don't miss the French toast.

Boardwalk (Map p284; ☎ 235-7749; Homer Spit Rd; fast food $5-15; 11am-9pm) Widely viewed as the best place on the Spit for halibut – tempura-battered, fried and served kabob-style. Notice, however, that fishermen, unlike the tourists, go for the burgers.

Finn's Pizza (Map p284; ☎ 235-2878; Homer Spit Rd; pizza $10-20) Finn's wood-fired pizzas are best enjoyed with a pint of ale in the sunny upstairs solarium. Is there anything better than an excellent pizza and unobstructed views of the bay? We didn't think so.

GROCERIES

Safeway (Map p282; Mile 90 Sterling Hwy; 24hr) On the way to the Spit, this is the best place in town for groceries, fresh baked breads, deli sandwiches and salads.

Smoky Bay Natural Foods (Map p282; ☎ 235-7252; 248 W Pioneer Ave; 10am-6:30pm Mon-Fri, 10am-6pm Sat, noon-5pm Sun) Sells organic veggies, groceries, and herbs, and has a great bulk foods selection. The deli counter is open from 11am to 2pm on weekdays.

Drinking & Entertainment

The bumper sticker says it all: 'Homer, Alaska: A quaint drinking village with a fishing problem.'

Salty Dawg Saloon (Map p284; Homer Spit Rd) Maybe the most storied bar on the Kenai Peninsula, the Salty Dawg is one of those places that's famous for being famous. In the evenings every square foot of its wood shaving-laden floor is packed with tourists singing along to sea shanties, rubbing elbows with the occasional fisherman and paying 50% more for beer than they would elsewhere in town. The lighthouse tower atop the whole party, visible from anywhere in town, stays lit during opening hours.

Homer Brewing Company (Map p282; ☎ 399-8060; 1411 Lakeshore Dr; noon-7pm Mon-Sat, to 5pm Sun) Isn't a bar, but it does offer 'tours' with free samples of fresh beer – try the broken birch bitter ale, and then grab a growler to go.

Ring of Fire Meadery (Map p282; ☎ 235-2656; 178 E Bunnell Ave; noon-6pm) Like the brewery, this isn't a bar, but there's a tasting room where you can sample the excellent mead, made with locally grown berries and fruit. It's unique and highly recommended.

Bear Creek Winery (Map p284; ☎ 235-8484; Bear Creek Dr; www.bearcreekwineryalaska.com; 10am-6pm) Wineries are scarcer than vineyards in Alaska, but this impressive family-run operation bottles some fine berry-based wines, plus fireweed mead and rhubarb vino. It conducts tours and tastings daily in the summer, and sells its product on-site.

Down East Saloon (Map p284; ☎ 235-6002; 3125 E End Rd) This spacious bar is where locals head to listen to live music. The view is killer, but you'll likely be paying more attention to whichever Homer talent is on stage.

Pier One Theater (Map p284; ☎ 235-7333; Homer Spit Rd; admission $16) Live drama and comedy is performed in a 'come-as-you-are' warehouse next to the Fishing Hole on the Spit. Shows start at 8:15pm Friday and Saturday, and 7:30pm Sunday during summer.

Homer Theater (Map p282; ☎ 235-6728; cnr Main St & Pioneer Ave) First-run movies are shown here.

Getting There & Around

AIR

The contract carrier for Alaska Airlines, **ERA Aviation** (☎ 235-7565, 800-426-0333; www.flyera.com) provides daily flights between Homer and Anchorage from Homer's airport, 1.7 miles east of town on Kachemak Dr. The advance-purchase fare runs about $140 one way, $250 round-trip.

Smokey Bay Air (Map p284; ☎ 235-1511; www.smokeybayair.com; 2100 Kachemak Dr) offers flights to Seldovia for $47 each way.

BICYCLE

Homer Saw & Cycle (Map p282; ☎ 235-8406; www.homersaw.com; 1532 Ocean Dr; 9am-5:30pm Mon-Fri, 11am-5pm Sat) rents mountain bikes ($25 per day).

BOAT

The Alaska Marine Highway provides thrice-weekly service from Homer to Seldovia (each way $33, 1½ hours) and Kodiak (each way $74, 9½ hours), with connecting service to Seward as well as the Aleutians. The **ferry terminal** (Map p284; ☎ 235-8449; www.ferryalaska.com) is at the end of Homer Spit.

Rainbow Tours (Map p284; ☎ 235-7272; Homer Spit Rd; one way/round-trip $30/45) offers the inexpensive Rainbow Connection shuttle from Homer to Seldovia. It departs at 9am, gets to Seldovia an hour later, and then returns to take you back to Homer at 5pm. It'll transport your bike for $5 and your kayak for $10.

Many water-taxi operations shuttle campers and kayakers between Homer and points across Kachemak Bay. Though the companies are good and work closely together, the most respected by far is **Mako's Water-taxi** (Map p284; ☎ 235-9055; www.makoswatertaxi.com; Homer Spit Rd). It usually charges $75 (includes state park fee) per person round-trip with a two-person minimum.

BUS

The **Homer Stage Line** (☎ 868-3914; www.homerstageline.com) runs daily from Homer to Anchorage (one way/round-trip $65/120), Seward ($55/100) and all points in between.

CAR

To obtain an affordable rental car, stop at **Polar Car Rental** (☎ 235-5998; airport). The small dealer has subcompacts for $62 a day.

Kostas Taxi (☎ 399-8008, 399-8115) and **Kachecab** (☎ 235-1950) are fierce rivals, and can get you anywhere around town for a reasonable fare.

SELDOVIA

pop 284

If the tourist-thronged towns of the Kenai Peninsula have left you frazzled, catch a boat to Seldovia, on the south side of Kachemak Bay and in a world of its own. Living up to the nickname 'City of Secluded Charm,' the community has managed to retain much of its old Alaskan character, and can be a restful (and inexpensive) day, or overnight, trip from Homer.

History

One of the oldest settlements on Cook Inlet, Russians founded the town in the late 18th century and named it after their word *seldevoy*, meaning 'herring bay.' By the 1890s Seldovia had become an important shipping and supply center for the region, and the town boomed right into the 1920s with salmon canning, fur farming and, of course, a (short-lived) herring industry.

But then the highway came, stretching only as far as the tip of the Homer Spit. After it was completed in the 1950s Seldovia's importance as a supply center began to dwindle. Today it relies primarily on fishing but is making its best stab at becoming a tourist destination. It's a process that's happening in fits and starts: the hiking and biking possibilities here are excellent and the accommodations are plush, but the culinary offerings are limited and the galleries feel a bit like desperate rummage sales. All in all you'll find a village with quaintness to spare, but little tourist infrastructure, which may be the best thing about the place.

Orientation & Information

As the crow flies, Seldovia is about 15 miles southwest of Homer. located on the far side of Kachemak Bay. The community, oriented toward Seldovia Bay and flanked by Seldovia Slough to the west, is compact: a sprinter could tour the downtown in 30 seconds, while the airport is a mere half-mile walk. For a real road trip, head out Jakolof Bay Rd, which runs for 10 or so miles.

The post office is near the corner of Main St and Seldovia St. There's an ATM at Linwood Bar & Grill (p293) but no banks in town.

When we visited in 2008, there were no public showers in town, but there were rumors of a new Laundromat, with showers, opening in 2009.

Harbormaster's Office (☎ 234-7886; 🕒 8am-9pm) Has toilets.

Information stand (Main St) Close to the small-boat harbor, with a few flyers tacked up; several more flyers are available in the Harbormaster's Office.

Library (☎ 234-7662; 250 Seldovia St; 🕒 afternoon Tue, Thu & Sat; 💻) Has one terminal for internet access.

Seldovia Chamber of Commerce (www.xyz.net/~seldovia) Its website is great for pre-trip planning.

Seldovia Medical Clinic (☎ 234-7825; 250 Seldovia St) Not far off Main St.

Seldovia Village Tribe Visitor Center (☎ 234-7898; www.svt.org; cnr Airport Ave & Main St; per 15min $2; 🕒 10am-5pm; 💻) Has internet access.

Sights & Activities

SELDOVIA VILLAGE TRIBE VISITOR CENTER

This **visitors center** (☎ 234-7898; www.svt.org; cnr Airport Ave & Main St; 🕒 10am-5pm; 💻), opened in 2005, attempts to showcase Seldovia's Alaska Native heritage – a unique blend of Alutiiq (Eskimo) and Tanaina (Indian) cultures. Though enjoyable (especially on a rainy day), the displays are a hodge-podge, featuring artifacts like arrowheads and stone knives dredged up from nearby waters, a series of old photos of Seldovia, and an exhibit about the intricacies of seal hunting. You can buy souvenirs here, and pay to use the public-use internet terminal ($2 per 15 minutes).

Run by the Seldovia Native Association is the **Alaska Tribal Cache** (☎ 234-7898; www.alaskatribalcache.com; 234 Main St; 🕒 10am-6pm Mon-Sat, noon-5pm Sun), across town, which sells jams, jellies and marmalade, all made on-site with fresh wild berries picked by local kids – and shoestring travelers (see opposite).

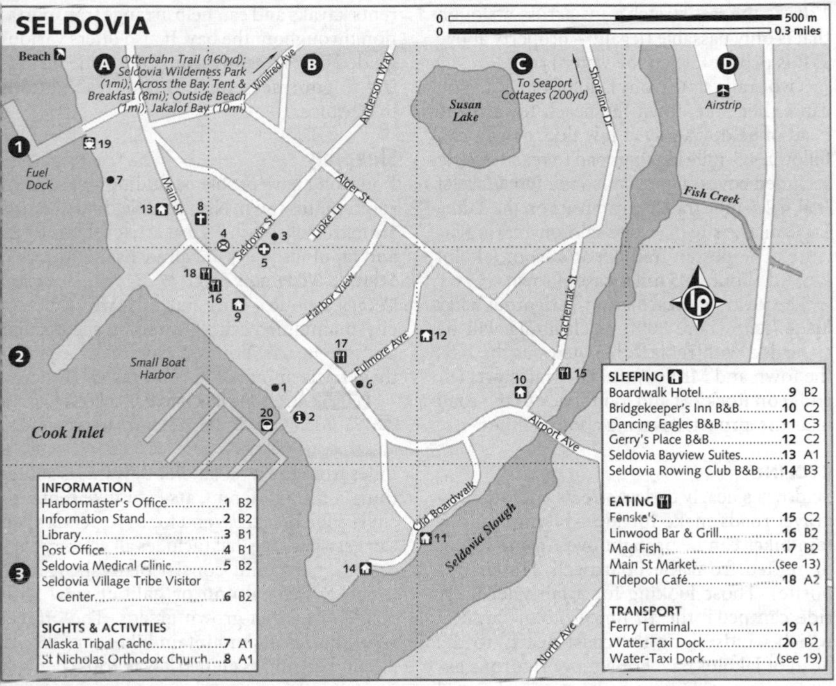

ST NICHOLAS ORTHODOX CHURCH

Seldovia's most popular attraction is this onion-domed **church** (1:30-3:30pm Mon-Sat), which overlooks the town from a hill just off Main St. Built in 1891 and restored in the 1970s, the church is open on weekday afternoons, when you can see the exquisite icons inside. Note the chandelier, made from old barrel staves. Though there is no resident clergyman, occasionally the priest from Nanwalek travels here to conduct services.

OUTSIDE BEACH

This beach is an excellent place for wildlife sightings and a little beachcombing. To reach it, follow Anderson Way (Jakolof Bay Rd) out of town for a mile, then head left at the first fork to reach the picnic area at Outside Beach Park. You stand a good chance of spotting eagles, seabirds and possibly even otters here. At low tide, you can explore the sea life among the rocks, and on a clear day the views of Mt Redoubt and Mt Iliamna are stunning.

BERRY PICKING

Seldovia is known best for its blueberries, which grow so thick just outside town that from late August to mid-September you often can rake your fingers through the bushes and fill a two-quart bucket in minutes. You'll also come across plenty of low-bush cranberries and salmonberries, a species not found around Homer. Be aware, however, that many of the best berry areas are on tribal land; before setting out, stop at the **Seldovia Native Association** (☎ 234-7898; 234 Main St) in the same building as the Alaska Tribal Cache, which will sell you a berry-picking permit for a nominal fee. If you're feeling light in the wallet, you may even be able to sell your harvest to the Cache for about $2 per pound – and you can keep as many as you want for personal use.

HIKING

The **Otterbahn Trail** was famously created by local high school students, who dubbed it the 'we-worked-hard-so-you-better-like-it trail.' The trailhead lies behind Susan B English School, off Winfred Ave. Lined with salmonberries and affording great views of Graduation Peak, it skirts the coastline most of the way and reaches Outside Beach in 1.5 miles. Make sure you hike it at tides below

17ft, as the last stretch runs across a slough that is only passable (legally – property above 17ft is private) when the water is out.

Two trails start from Jakolof Bay Rd. You can either hike down the beach toward the head of Seldovia Bay at low tide, or you can follow a 4.5-mile logging road to reach several secluded coves. There is also the **Tutka/Jakolof Trail**, a 2.5-mile trail to a campsite on the Tutka Lagoon, the site of a state salmon-rearing facility. The posted trail departs from Jakolof Bay Rd about 10.5 miles east of town.

The town's newest hike is the rigorous **Rocky Ridge Trail**, where 800ft of climbing will be rewarded with remarkable views of the bay, the town and Mt Iliamna. The trail starts (or ends) on Rocky St and loops back to the road near the airport, covering about 3 miles.

CYCLING

Seldovia's nearly carless streets and outlying gravel roads make for ideal biking; mountain bikes can be brought over from Homer or rented from the Boardwalk Hotel (opposite). Those looking for a fairly leisurely ride can pedal the 10-mile Jakolof Bay Rd, which winds along the coast nearly to the head of Jakolof Bay. For a more rigorous experience, continue on another 6 miles beyond the end of the maintained road, climbing 1200ft into the alpine country at the base of Red Mountain.

In the past, fit cyclists could also depart from Jakolof Bay Rd for an epic 30-mile round-trip ride along the rough Rocky River Rd, which cuts across the tip of the Kenai Peninsula to Windy Bay. In recent years washouts have made the road largely impassable; inquire about current conditions.

PADDLING

There are some excellent kayaking opportunities in the Seldovia area. Just north, Eldred Passage and the three islands (Cohen, Yukon and Hesketh) that mark its entrance are prime spots for viewing otters, sea lions and seals, while the northern shore of Yukon Island features caves and tunnels that can be explored at high tide. Even closer are Sadie Cove, and Tutka and Jakolof Bays, where you can paddle in protected water amid interesting geological features, and near numerous camping areas along the beaches.

Kayak'Atak (☎ 234-7425; www.alaska.net/~kayaks/; kayaks 1st day single/double $50/80, subsequent days $35/50) rents kayaks and can help arrange transportation throughout the bay. It also offers various guided tours starting from $80, some including a 'gourmet lunch.' Make reservations in advance.

Sleeping

You won't have problems finding an excellent room in this town. Note that Seldovian B&Bs are extremely plush – great art, lovely antiques and fabulous views are almost standard.

Seldovia Wilderness Park (☎ 234-7643; sites camp/RV $5/8) About a mile out of town; this is a city-maintained campground on spectacular Outside Beach. You can pay for your site at the ferry terminal or harbormaster's office.

our pick **Across the Bay Tent & Breakfast** (summer ☎ 235-3633, winter ☎ 345-2571; www.tentandbreakfastalaska.com; tent cabins per person $75; ☒) Located 8 miles from town on Jakolof Bay, this is something a little different. Its cabinlike tents include a full breakfast, and for $110 per day you can get a package that includes all your meals – and dinner could consist of fresh oysters, beach-grilled salmon or halibut stew with a side of garden-grown greens. The offbeat resort also rents mountain bikes for $25 per day and organizes guided kayak trips (per half day $85). Bring your sleeping bag.

Seaport Cottages (☎ 243-7471; cabins $125) These cottages are up from the slough and cozied up in the woods. There's also a three-bedroom apartment in town, which is a screamin' deal at $150/night.

Bridgekeeper's Inn B&B (☎ 234-7535; www.thebridgekeepersinn.com; r $125-135) A cozy place with private baths and full breakfasts; one room has a balcony overlooking the salmon-filled slough.

Boardwalk Hotel (☎ 234-7816, 800-238-7862; www.alaskaone.com/boardwalkhotel/; 234 Main St; r $109-139) Has big, beautiful rooms with lots of wicker; the pricier ones have huge windows overlooking the bay and small-boat harbor. It also rents bikes (opposite) and fishing poles ($10).

Seldovia Rowing Club B&B (☎ 234-7614; www.seldoviarowingclub.net; 343 Bay St; r $135) Also located on the Old Boardwalk, this place – the first B&B in Southcentral Alaska – has homey suites decorated with quilts, antiques and owner Susan Mumma's outstanding watercolors. She serves big breakfasts and often hosts in-house music concerts.

Dancing Eagles B&B (☎ 234-7627; www.dancingeagles.com; s/d $85/135, cabins $210) On the Old

Boardwalk; this rambling collection of rustic yet upscale structures is as close to the ocean as you can be without getting wet. It serves full breakfasts that you can eat on a marvelous outcrop rising from the harbor.

Seldovia Bayview Suites (☎ 234-7631, 800-478-7898; 381 Main St; r with/without view $149/119) Though the rooms here are sterile and charmless, they're spacious and blessed with beautiful views; enjoy them from the waterside hot tub. The $275 suite will sleep eight comfortably, plus perhaps 30 on the floor.

Eating

Perhaps the most frustrating thing about Seldovia is that it can sleep far more people than it can feed. The situation is improving – slightly – and at least there are a couple of good options for eating.

Fenske's Warehouse Books & Coffee (☎ 234-7850; 230 Kachemak St; snacks $2-5; 🕒 9am-5pm) This incredibly cozy place is tucked in the forest above the slough like a juicy secret. Stacks of books fill the small space, and you can get coffee, hot chocolate, and birdseed cookies to nibble on while you read away a rainy day.

Tidepool Café (☎ 234-7502; 267 Main St; breakfast $6-11, lunch $9-16, dinner $16-30; 🕒 7am-3pm daily, plus 5:30-9pm Wed-Sun) In a sunny space overlooking the harbor, this eclectic eatery serves great wraps, sandwiches and espressos, and has dinner offerings like drunken mussels ($13) and sweet-chili salmon ($23). You'll need reservations for dinner.

Mad Fish (☎ 234-7676; 221 Main St; lunch $9-11, dinner $13-29; 🕒 11:30am-9pm) The only white-tablecloth venue in Seldovia is a bit overpriced but serves adequate croissant sandwiches and chowder. Its bread is fresh-baked.

Linwood Bar & Grill (☎ 234-7674; 257 Main St; burgers $11-13, pizzas $12-25; 🕒 grill 6-10pm) A dark harborfront saloon which has plenty of cigarette smoke to go with your meal.

Main Street Market (☎ 234-7633; 381 Main St; 🕒 9am-7pm) This is where to go for groceries, liquor, espressos and T-shirts.

Getting There & Around

BICYCLE

If you didn't bring your two-wheeler over from Homer, the Boardwalk Hotel rents **mountain bikes** (per hr guests/nonguests $20/30). All-day rates are also available. These are best for tooling around town, however, rather than biking out Jakalof Bay Rd.

BOAT

Alaska Marine Highway ferries provide twice-weekly service between Homer and Seldovia ($33, 1½ hours) with connecting service throughout the peninsula and the Aleutians. The **Seldovia ferry terminal** (☎ 234-7886, www.ferryalaska.com) is at the north end of Main St.

Rainbow Tours (☎ 235-7272; drop-off at Homer Spit Rd; one way/round-trip $30/45) offers the inexpensive Rainbow Connection shuttle from Homer to Seldovia. It departs at 9am, gets to Seldovia an hour later, and then returns to take you back to Homer at 5pm. It'll transport your bike for $5 and your kayak for $10.

Mako's Water-taxi (☎ 235-9055; www.makoswatertaxi.com; drop-off at Homer Spit Rd; round-trip $135) offers an excellent tour that takes you by boat, car, and plane. Mako's drops you off at Jakolof Bay, from which you'll be driven to Seldovia. You return to Homer via a short flightseeing trip.

Central Charters (☎ 235-7847, 800-478-7847; www.centralcharter.com; drop-off at Homer Spit Rd, one way/round-trip $30/50) does a daily six-hour tour from Homer, leaving at 11am, circling Gull Island, and deboarding you in Seldovia to enjoy the village for the afternoon.

PLANE

Smokey Bay Air (☎ 235-1511; www.smokeybayair.com; 2100 Kachemak Dr; one way $47) offers a scenic 12-minute flight from Homer, over the Kenai Mountains and Kachemak Bay to Seldovia.

Homer Air (☎ 235-8591; www.homerair.com; one way/round-trip $45/90) flies to Seldovia hourly.

Great Northern Air Guides (☎ 800-243-1968, 243-1968; www.gnair.com; one way about $190) can fly you to Anchorage.

TAXI

For rides out to Jakolof Bay Rd or to the airport, try **Jim's Shuttle Service** (☎ 234-7848, 399-8159) or **Seldovia Cab & Limousine** (☎ 234-7830, 399-0469).

KACHEMAK BAY STATE PARK

Stand on Homer Spit and look south, and an alluring wonderland sprawls before you: a luxuriantly green coastline, sliced by fjords and topped by sparkling glaciers and rugged peaks. This is Kachemak Bay State Park, which, along with Kachemak Bay State Wilderness Park to the south, includes 350,000 acres of idyllic wilderness accessible only by bush plane or boat. It was Alaska's first state park. According to locals, it remains the best.

DETOUR: ACROSS THE BAY

Opposite Homer but outside Kachemak Bay State Park is a handful of compelling destinations easily accessible by water-taxi.

Gull Island

Halfway between the Spit and Halibut Cove, the 40ft-high Gull Island attracts some 16,000 nesting seabirds: puffins, kittiwakes, murres, cormorants and many more species. If you can cope with the stench, you'll enjoy photographing the birds up close, even if you don't have a 300mm lens.

Mako's Water-taxi (☎ 235-9055; www.makoswatertaxi.com; Homer Spit Rd) has a one-hour island tour (per person $40, three-person minimum) and a two-hour tour that includes adorable sea otters (per person $75, four-person minimum). Several other companies do Gull Island tours as well.

Halibut Cove

Halibut Cove, an absurdly quaint village of 30 permanent residents, is a place you'll wish you grew up in. In the early 1920s the cove had 42 herring salteries and had more than 1000 residents. Today it's home to the noted Saltry restaurant, several art galleries, and a warren of boardwalks – but no roads.

The *Danny J* travels to the cove twice daily. It departs Homer at noon, swings past Gull Island and arrives at 1:30pm. There, you have 2½ hours to explore and have lunch. The ferry returns to the Spit by 5pm and then makes an evening run to the cove for dinner, returning to Homer at 10pm. The noon tour costs $50 per person, while the evening trip costs $30. Make reservations through **Central Charters** (☎ 235-7847, 800-478-7847; www.centralcharter.com), which has an office on the Spit.

For many couples, dining at the **Saltry** (☎ 296-2223; lunch $11-22, dinner $14-25) makes for the ultimate date, with an outdoor deck over the aquamarine inlet and excellent seafood and vegetarian cuisine. Its lunch seatings are at 1:30pm and 3pm; for dinner it's 6pm or 7:30pm.

After eating, check out the galleries. **Halibut Cove Experience** (☎ 296-2215) displays the paintings, pottery and sculpture of more than a dozen local artisans – a significant percentage of the adult population. **Cove Gallery** (☎ 269-2207), just up the steps from where the *Danny J* docks, is where Diana Tillion sells her octopus-ink watercolors. The art's okay, but it's worth the visit just to learn how she gets the ink out of the octopi.

To make Halibut Cove an even more interesting sidetrip, spend the night. **Quiet Place Lodge** (☎ 296-2212 Jun-Aug, 235-1800 Sep-May; www.quietplace.com) has luxurious facilities and all-inclusive packages that cover transport and meals, while at the more basic **Country Cove Cabins** (☎ 888-353-2683, 296-2257; www.xyz.net/~ctjones/home.htm; d $90), you get kitchen facilities where you cook for yourself.

North of Seldovia

In Tutka Bay, Sadie Cove and Eldred Passage are a selection of quality lodges accessed only by water-taxi.

Otter Cove Resort (☎ 235-7770; www.ottercoveresort.com; cabins $80), located on Eldred Passage, has affordable camping-style cabins (but with electricity) near the Sadie Knob Trail, rents kayaks (per single/double $40/70) and guides single- and multiday paddling trips. It is also home to the **Rookery** (lunch $8-13, dinner $12-25; ⏲ noon-9pm), serving seafood and steak in a beautiful seaside setting. Round-trip transportation is $45.

Tutka Bay Wilderness Lodge (☎ 235-3905, 800-606-3909; www.tutkabaylodge.com; r per person from $790) is an all-inclusive resort with chalets, cottages and rooms surrounding the lodge house, where guests enjoy meals with a sweeping view of the inlet and Jakolof Mountain. The accommodations are very comfortable, the food is excellent and the amenities include a sauna, deepwater dock, boathouse and hiking trails. Activities range from clamming to sea kayaking. There's a two-night minimum stay.

Sadie Cove Wilderness Lodge (☎ 888-283-7234, 235-2350; www.sadiecove.com; r per person $400) is just to the north of Tutka Bay in Sadie Cove. This wilderness lodge offers similar amenities – cabins, sauna, outdoor hot tub, Alaskan seafood dinners – but it's not quite as elegant or pricey.

The most popular attraction is Grewingk Glacier, which can be seen across the bay from Homer. Viewing the glacier at closer range means a boat trip to the park and a very popular one-way hike of 3.5 miles. Outside the glacier, however, you can easily escape into the wilds by either hiking or kayaking. With more than 40 miles of trails, plenty of sheltered waterways, numerous campsites and a few enclosed accommodation options, this is a highly recommended outing for a day or three.

Orientation

The park takes in much of Kachemak Bay's south side, extending from Chugachik Island in the northeast to Tutka Bay, east of Seldovia, in the southwest. In places it crosses the peninsula to the Gulf of Alaska; elsewhere, it abuts Kenai National Wildlife Refuge and Kenai Fjords National Park.

Center for Alaskan Coastal Studies (☎ 235-6667; www.akcoastalstudies.org; 708 Smokey Way; 9am-5pm Mon-Fri) Has maps and information about the park, both at its downtown Homer headquarters off Lake St and at its yurt on the Spit behind Mako's Water-taxi. National Geographic's *Trails Illustrated* map of the park is an excellent resource, depicting hiking routes, public-use cabins, docks and campsites, and it's available here. The Center also operates the Peterson Bay Field Station across the bay (below).

Mako's Water-taxi (☎ 235-9055; www.makoswatertaxi.com; Homer Spit Rd) Can give you the lowdown on possible hikes and paddles in the park – and about the logistics of getting over and back.

Sights & Activities

PETERSON BAY FIELD STATION

Though technically it's outside the park, this **field station** (☎ 235-2778), operated by the Center for Alaskan Coastal Studies, provides an excellent introduction to the ecology and natural history of the area. In summer, staff members lead day-long educational tours of the coastal forest and waterfront tide pools; the best intertidal beasties are seen during extremely low, or 'minus,' tides. Inside the station, too, you can get up close and personal with a touch tank full of squishy sea creatures. It costs $105, which includes the boat ride over from the Spit. For $155 you can combine a morning natural history tour with an afternoon of guided paddling in Peterson and China Poot Bays. If you want to overnight here, the station has bunks and yurts (p296).

HIKING

Glacier Lake Trail

The most popular hike in Kachemak Bay State Park is this 3½-mile, one-way trail that begins at the Glacier Spit trailhead, near the small Rusty Lagoon Campground. The level, easy-to-follow trek proceeds across the glacial outwash and ends at a lake with superb views of Grewingk Glacier. Camping on the lake is spectacular, and often the shoreline is littered with icebergs (and day-trippers). At Mile 1.4 you can connect to the 6½-mile **Grewingk Glacier Trail**, with a hand-tram and access to the face of the glacier. If you don't have time for the entire hike, there are excellent views less than a mile from the tram.

Alpine Ridge Trail

At the high point of the mile-long Saddle Trail, an offshoot of the Glacier Lake Trail, you will reach the posted junction for this 2-mile climb to an alpine ridge above the glacier. The climb can be steep at times but manageable for most hikers with day packs. On a nice day, the views of the ice and Kachemak Bay are stunning.

Lagoon Trail

Also departing from the Saddle Trail is this 5½-mile route that leads to the ranger station at the head of Halibut Cove Lagoon. Along the way it passes the Goat Rope Spur Trail, a steep 1-mile climb to the alpine tundra. You also pass the posted junction of Halibut Creek Trail. If Grewingk Glacier is too crowded for you, follow this trail a half-mile to Halibut Creek to spend the night in a beautiful, but much more remote, valley.

The Lagoon Trail is considered a moderately difficult hike and involves fording Halibut Creek, which should be done at low tide. At the ranger station, more trails extend south to several lakes, as well as Poot Peak and the Wosnesenski River.

Poot Peak

This is a difficult, slick, rocky ascent of 2600ft Poot Peak. The trailhead begins at the Halibut Cove Lagoon, where a moderate 2.6-mile climb along the China Poot Lake Trail takes you to a campsite on the lake. From there, the trail to the peak diverges after the Wosnesenski River Trail junction. For a little over a mile you'll clamber upward through thinning forest until you reach the Summit

Spur, where the route climbs even more precipitously to the mountain's lower summit, 2100ft in elevation. From here, reaching the very top involves scaling a shifting wall of scree, a feat that should be attempted only by those who have some rock-climbing experience. In wet weather, it should be avoided altogether. Getting from the lake to the summit and back will likely take the better part of a day.

Grace Ridge Trail

This is a 7-mile trail that stretches from a campsite at Kayak Beach trailhead to deep inside Tutka Bay in the state park. Much of the hike runs above the treeline along the crest of Grace Ridge, where, needless to say, the views are stunning. There's also access from Sea Star Cove public-use cabin (see p269). You could hike the trail in a day, but it makes a great two-day trek with an overnight camp in the alpine.

Emerald Lake Trail

This steep, difficult 6.4-mile trail begins at Grewingk Glacial Lake and leads to Portlock Plateau. You'll witness firsthand the reclamation of the wasted forest (due to spruce bark beetle damage) by brushy alder and birch, considered delicacies by local wildlife. At Mile 2.1 a spur trail reaches the scenic Emerald Lake, and there are great views of the bay from the plateau. In spring, stream crossings can be challenging.

PADDLING

You can also spend three or four days paddling the many fjords of the park, departing from Homer and making overnight stops at Glacier Spit or Halibut Cove. Think twice before crossing Kachemak Bay from the Spit, however. Although it's only 3.5 miles to the eastern shore, the currents and tides are powerful and can cause serious problems for inexperienced paddlers.

A tiny family-run outfit, **Seaside Adventures** (☎ 235-6672; www.seasideadventure.com; trips incl water-taxi half-/full day $110/140) will show you the bay on kayak complete with running commentary about local flora and fauna.

St Augustine Charters (☎ 299-1894; www.homerkayaking.com; paddles incl water-taxi half-/full-day $95/135) offers rentals from its Peterson Bay Kayak Center, as well as guided paddles. It does multiday excursions, too, involving paddling, trekking along state park trails, and camping at seaside sites.

True North Kayak Adventures (☎ 235-0708; www.truenorthkayak.com), based on Yukon Island, runs half-day paddles amid the eagles overhead and otters for $99, water-taxi included. Once you've spent all that time crossing the bay, however, it makes more sense to spring for the full-day paddle ($145). There are also several multiday options that cross Eldred Passage into Tutka Bay or Sadie Cove. For experienced kayakers, it rents rigid single/double kayaks for $45/65 per day.

Glacier Lake Kayaking & Hiking (☎ 888-777-0930, 235-0755; www.threemoose.com) offers kayaking on Glacier Lake, inside Kachemak Bay State Park, combined with guided hikes ($175).

Sleeping

Camping is permitted throughout Kachemak Bay State Park. Moreover, numerous free, primitive camping areas have been developed, usually at waterfront trailheads or along trails. Consult the Alaska Division of Parks for the locations and facilities.

Center for Alaskan Coastal Studies (☎ 235-6667; www.akcoastalstudies.org; Heath St; 🕑 9am-5pm Mon-Fri) This organization reserves bunks ($25) or yurts ($80) close to its Peterson Bay Field Station, just outside the park. Add a $25 membership fee to the lodging cost. Lodgers can use the kitchen at the field station.

Public-use cabins (☎ 269-8400; 262-5581; www.alaskastateparks.org; cabins $65) There are five cabins, which can be reserved in the park. Three are in Halibut Cove: Lagoon Overlook, with a pair of bunk-beds; Lagoon East Cabin, which has disabled access; and Lagoon West Cabin, a half-mile west of the public dock. Moose Valley Cabin is about 2.5 miles from the Halibut Cove Lagoon Ranger Station and only sleeps two ($35). Sea Star Cove Cabin, on the south shore of Tutka Bay, is convenient to the Tutka Lake Trail. China Poot Cabin is accessible by kayak or water-taxi. Make reservations for any of them months in advance.

Yurts (☎ 299-1680; www.nomadshelter.com; yurts $65) There are eight of these for rent in the park, maintained by a private operator. All are near the ocean and equipped with bunks and woodstoves. They're located at the mouth of Humpy Creek, at the mouth of Halibut Cove, in China Poot Bay, near the North Eldred Passage Trailhead, near the northwest and southeast Grace Ridge Trailheads, in Tutka

Bay and on Quarry Beach at the mouth of Sadie Cove.

Getting There & Around

The state park makes an excellent sidetrip for anybody who has a tent, a spare day and the desire to escape the overflow of RVers on Homer Spit. A number of water-taxis offer drop-off and pickup service (round-trip $50 to $80). Because boat access to some of the trailheads is tidally dependent, you'll need to work with them to establish a precise rendezvous time and location – and then be sure to stick to it.

Mako's Water-taxi (☎ 235-9055; www.makoswatertaxi.com) is the most respected of Homer's water-taxi services, famed for making timely pickups even in foul weather – and for dropping off beer to unsuspecting campers. For most cross-bay destinations it charges $70 with a two-person minimum. To Seldovia, the boat costs $250, so grab all your friends and fill 'er up.

Other good outfits include **Smoke Wagon Water-taxi & Charter** (☎ 235-2947, 888-205-2947; www.homerwatertaxi.com) and **Tutka Bay Taxi** (☎ 399-1723; www.tutkabaytaxi.com).

Southwest Alaska

Southwest Alaska stretches 1500 miles into oblivion. For travelers heading north it's by far the most overlooked and forgotten region of the state. Partly because what it offers – wilderness, great sportfishing, unparalleled bear viewing – is also available in easier-to-reach areas of Alaska.

But mostly because Southwest Alaska is as remote as you can get in a state that prides itself on hard-to-reach places. Southwest is spread out over more than 1500 miles, in four areas: the Kodiak Archipelago with Kodiak Island, the Alaska Peninsula, the Aleutian Islands and Bristol Bay. For the most part it is an island-studded region with stormy weather and violent volcanoes. This is the northern rim of the Ring of Fire. Along the Alaska Peninsula and the Aleutian Islands are 46 active volcanoes – the greatest concentration anywhere in North America.

Despite the harsh weather and volcanic activity – or maybe because of it – Southwest Alaska is rich in wildlife. It boasts the world's largest bears, on Kodiak Island; Alaska's richest salmon runs, in Bristol Bay; and the largest gathering of nesting seabirds in the world, on the tiny Pribilof Islands. Few places on earth have such abundant wildlife.

But you can't drive or take a train to Southwest, making the region hard to reach, expensive to visit and easy to bypass. However, the adventurous do find their way here, because even in Alaska there are few experiences quite like riding a state ferry across the North Pacific or watching 1000lb bears gorge themselves on salmon, only 60ft away from you.

HIGHLIGHTS

- **Hardest lottery to win** (p316) – put in for the McNeil River lottery and cross your fingers to see the world's greatest concentration of brown bears
- **Best (and cheapest!) nature tour** (p304) – join a ranger at Fort Abercrombie State Historical Park for an afternoon of tidal-pool snooping
- **Most adventurous boat trip** (p308) – there's no cruise like the trip on the 'Trusty Tusty' along the Alaska Peninsula to the Aleutian Islands
- **Best historic site** (p319) – head to Dutch Harbor's Mt Ballyhoo for amazing views and to explore gun turrets, Quonset huts and other WWII military remains
- **Best bear camp** (p313) – spend two days or even a week watching big brownies at remote Hallo Bay Bear Camp in Katmai National Park & Preserve

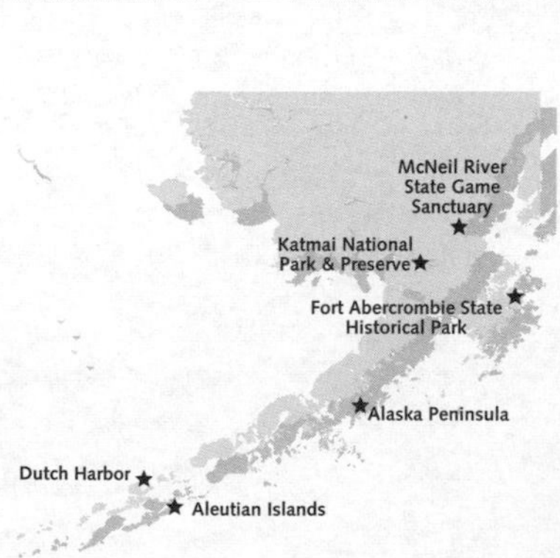

Climate

With little to protect it from the high winds and storms that sweep across the North Pacific, Southwest is home to the worst weather in Alaska. Kodiak is greatly affected by the turbulent Gulf of Alaska and receives 80in of rain per year, along with regular blankets of pea-soup fog and occasional blustery winds. On the northern edge of the Pacific, Unalaska and the Alaskan Peninsula receive less rain (annual precipitation ranges from 60in to 70in), but are renowned for unpredictable and stormy weather. Rain, fog and high winds are common. Summer temperatures range from 45°F to 65°F, with the clearest weather often occurring in early summer and fall.

History

More than any other region of the state, Southwest Alaska has the most turbulent history, marked by massacres, violent eruptions and WWII bombings.

When Stepan Glotov and his Russian fur-trading party landed at present-day Dutch Harbor in 1759, there were more than 30,000 Aleuts living on Unalaska and Amaknak Islands. After the Aleuts destroyed four ships and killed 175 fur hunters in 1763, the Russians returned and began a systematic elimination of Aleuts, massacring or enslaving them. It's estimated that by 1830 only 200 to 400 Aleuts were living on Unalaska.

The Russians first landed on Kodiak Island in 1763 and returned 20 years later when Siberian fur trader Gregorii Shelikof established a settlement at Three Saints Bay. Shelikof's attempts to 'subdue' the indigenous people resulted in another bloodbath where more than 1000 Alutiiqs were massacred, or drowned during their efforts to escape.

The czar recalled Shelikof and in 1791 sent Aleksandr Baranov to manage the Russian-American Company. After an earthquake nearly destroyed the settlement at Three Saints Bay, Baranov moved his operations to more stable ground at present-day Kodiak. It became a bustling port and was the capital of Russian America until 1804 when Baranov moved again, this time to Sitka.

Some violence in Southwest Alaska was caused by nature. In 1912 Mt Katmai on the nearby Alaska Peninsula erupted, blotting out the sun for three days and blanketing Kodiak with 18in of ash. Kodiak's 400 residents escaped to sea on a ship but soon returned to find buildings collapsed, ash drifts several feet high and spawning salmon choking in ash-filled streams.

The town was a struggling fishing port until WWII when it became the major staging area for the North Pacific operations. At one point Kodiak's population topped 25,000, with a submarine base at Women's Bay, an army outpost at Buskin River and gun emplacements protecting Fort Abercrombie.

Kodiak was spared from attack during WWII, but the Japanese bombed Unalaska only six months after bombing Pearl Harbor and then invaded Attu and Kiska Islands (see p48). More hardship followed: the Good Friday Earthquake of 1964 leveled downtown Kodiak and wiped out its fishing fleet; the king-crab fishery crashed in the early 1980s; and the *Exxon Valdez* oil spill soiled the coastline at the end of the decade. But this region rebounded after each disaster, and today Unalaska and Kodiak are among the top three fishing ports in the country.

National Parks & Refuges

Southwest Alaska is home to some of the state's largest and most intriguing national parks and refuges. Unfortunately all of them are isolated and expensive to visit. Katmai National Park & Preserve (p311), on the Alaska Peninsula, and Kodiak National Wildlife Refuge (p309) are renowned for bear watching. Lake Clark National Park & Preserve (p314), across Cook Inlet from Anchorage, is a wilderness playground for rafters, anglers and hikers.

Most of the Aleutian Islands and part of the Alaska Peninsula form the huge Alaska Maritime National Wildlife Refuge, headquartered in Homer (p283). The refuge encompasses 3.5 million acres and more than 2500 islands, and is home to 80% of the 50 million seabirds that nest in Alaska.

Getting There & Away

Alaska Airlines (☎ 800-252-7522; www.alaskaair.com) and **PenAir** (☎ 800-448-4226; www.penair.com) service the region and one or the other provides daily flights to Kodiak, King Salmon, Unalaska, Dillingham and Bethel. **Era Aviation** (☎ 800-866-8394; www.eraaviation.com) also flies to Kodiak from a number of destinations throughout Alaska.

The most affordable way to reach the region is via the **Alaska Marine Highway** (☎ 800-642-0066;

SOUTHWEST ALASKA

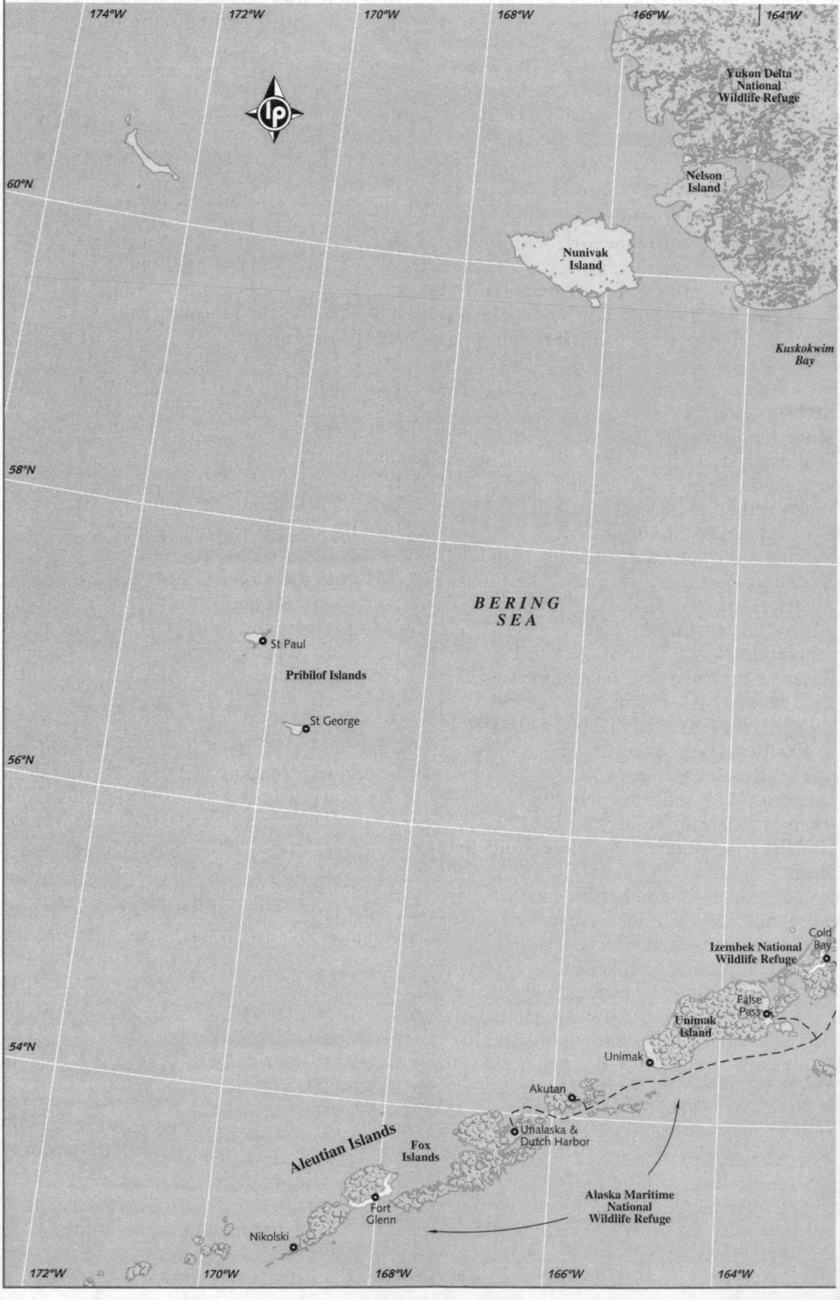

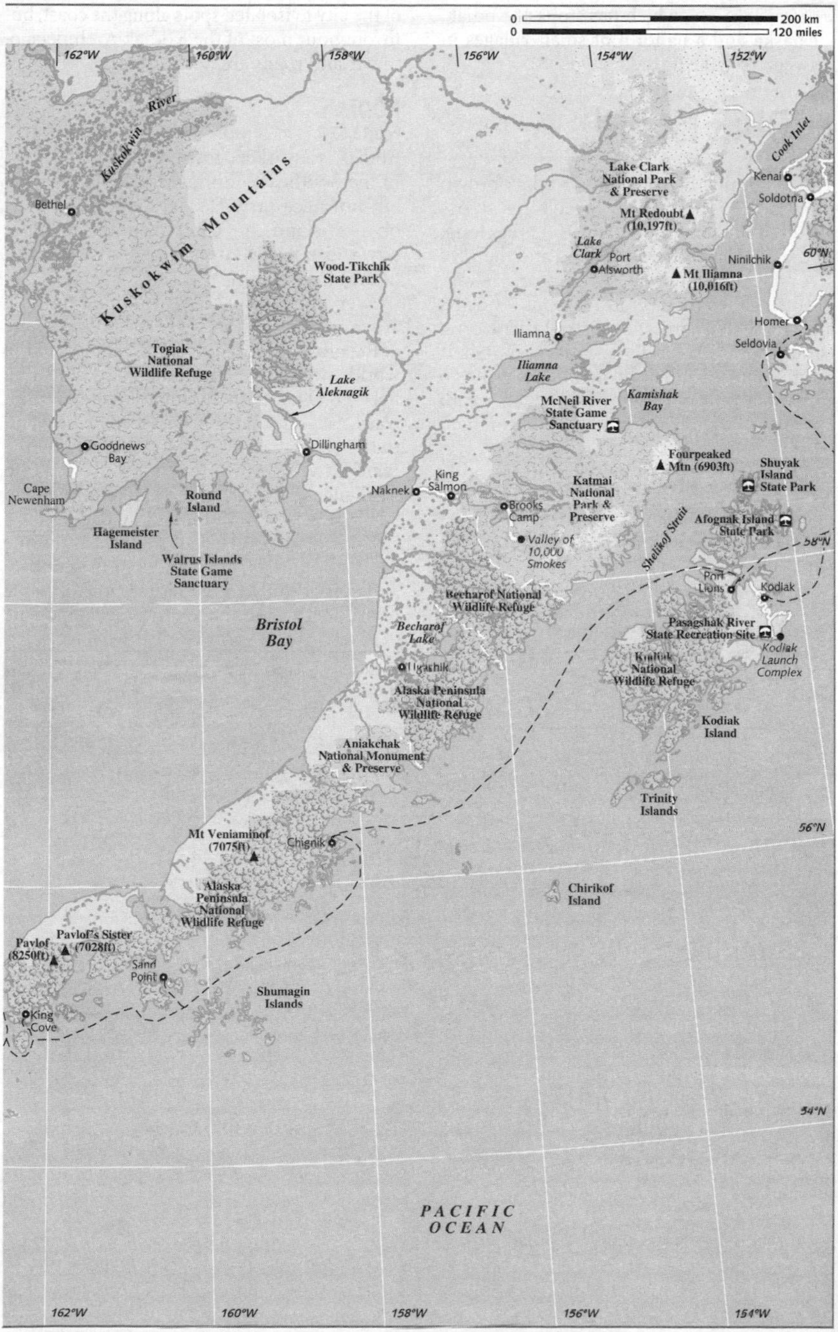
0 200 km
0 120 miles
162°W
160°W
158°W
156°W
154°W
152°W
Kuskokwin River
Kuskokwim Mountains
Bethel
Lake Clark National Park & Preserve
Mt Redoubt (10,197ft)
Lake Clark
Port Alsworth
Mt Iliamna (10,016ft)
Cook Inlet
Kenai
Soldotna
Ninilchik
60°N
Homer
Seldovia
Wood-Tikchik State Park
Togiak National Wildlife Refuge
Lake Aleknagik
Iliamna
Iliamna Lake
Kamishak Bay
McNeil River State Game Sanctuary
Goodnews Bay
Dillingham
Fourpeaked Mtn (6903ft)
Shuyak Island State Park
Cape Newenham
Round Island
Hagemeister Island
Walrus Islands State Game Sanctuary
Naknek
King Salmon
Brooks Camp
Katmai National Park & Preserve
Valley of 10,000 Smokes
Shelikof Strait
Afognak Island State Park
58°N
Port Lions
Kodiak
Becharof National Wildlife Refuge
Bristol Bay
Becharof Lake
Pasagshak River State Recreation Site
Kodiak Launch Complex
Kodiak National Wildlife Refuge
Ugashik
Alaska Peninsula National Wildlife Refuge
Kodiak Island
Aniakchak National Monument & Preserve
Trinity Islands
56°N
Mt Veniaminof (7075ft)
Chignik
Chirikof Island
Alaska Peninsula National Wildlife Refuge
Pavlof (8250ft)
Pavlof's Sister (7028ft)
Sand Point
Shumagin Islands
King Cove
54°N
PACIFIC OCEAN
162°W
160°W
158°W
156°W
154°W

www.ferryalaska.com), which has stops at Kodiak, Unalaska and a handful of small villages in between (see the boxed text, p308).

KODIAK ISLAND

The only thing bigger than a Kodiak brown bear is the island itself. Stretching across 3670 sq miles and more than 100 miles long, Kodiak is Alaska's largest island and the US's second largest, after the Big Island of Hawaii. It's fitting then that its most famous residents are the world's largest terrestrial carnivores. Fattened by the island's legendary, abundant salmon runs, Kodiak brown bears grow to gargantuan proportions – males can weigh up to 1500lb – and an estimated 3000 of them live in the Kodiak Archipelago.

There are also people on the island – roughly 14,000 – but for the most part they're tucked away in the northeast corner. The vast majority of this island is a green and jagged wilderness that was so deeply carved by glaciers, no point on land is more than 15 miles from the ocean. A few roads will lead you out of the city to isolated spots along the coast, but throughout most of the Kodiak Archipelago, towns and roads are nonexistent.

KODIAK

pop 13,574

Kodiak is a workers' town. Unlike many ports in the Southeast, tourism in Kodiak is nice, but not necessary. Hence, there's no hostel on the island, no campgrounds near the city and nobody running a shuttle service to the airport.

Everybody is too busy working, primarily at sea. Kodiak sits at the crossroads of some of the most productive fishing grounds in the world and is home to Alaska's largest fishing fleet – 650 boats, including the state's largest trawl, longline and crab vessels. The fleet and the 12 shore-based processors, including the *Star of Kodiak*, a WWII vessel converted into a fish plant downtown, account for more than 50% of employment on the island.

Kodiak works hard. It's consistently one of the top three fishing ports in the country and second only to Dutch Harbor for value of product and tonnage processed. Since the

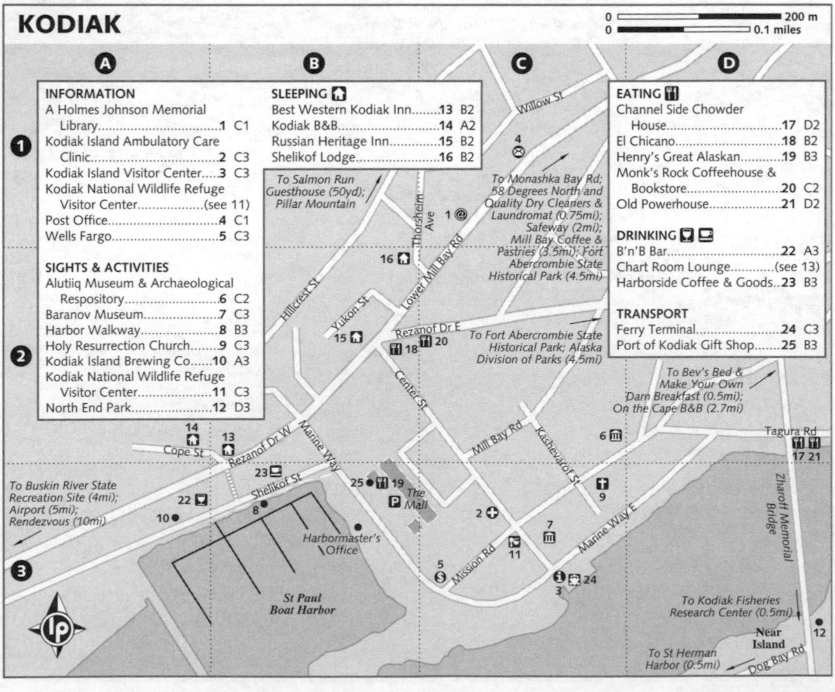

king-crab moratorium in 1983, Kodiak has diversified to catch everything from salmon, pollack and cod to sea cucumbers. In 1995 Kodiak set a record when 49 million lb of salmon crossed its docks.

It is also home to the largest US coastguard station, while at Cape Narrow, at the south end of the island, is the Kodiak Launch Complex (KLC), a $38 million low-Earth orbit launch facility.

You'll find residents friendly: lively at night in the bars, and often stopping to offer you a lift even without a thumb being extended. But in the morning they go to work. This is the real Alaska: unaltered, unassuming and not inundated by tourism. Arrive for the scenery, stay to enjoy outdoor adventures that range from kayaking to photographing a 1000lb bear. But most of all, come to Kodiak to meet people who struggle at sea to earn a living on the stormy edge of the Pacific Ocean. This is a lesson in life worth the price of an airline ticket from Anchorage.

Orientation

Lucky you if you're arriving in Kodiak on the state ferry. The vessel ties up downtown right next to the Kodiak Island Visitor Center. How convenient is that? There are three main roads in Kodiak that will lead you through downtown and beyond. In town, Rezanof Dr heads east and then north to Fort Abercrombie State Historical Park. Lower Mill Bay Rd is roughly parallel to the north; Mission Rd to the south. Everything in between is basically a cross street. Rezanof Dr also heads west from the city, becomes Chiniak Hwy and reaches the airport in 5 miles, after which it heads south.

Information

A Holmes Johnson Memorial Library (☎ 486-8686; 319 Lower Mill Bay Rd; 🕓 10am-9pm Mon-Fri, 10am-5pm Sat, 1-5pm Sun) Offers free internet access on 10 computers and is a great place to hole up and read.

Alaska Division of Parks (☎ 486-6339; 1400 Abercrombie Dr; 🕓 8:30am-5pm Mon-Fri, 9am-3pm Sat & Sun) Maintains an office at Fort Abercrombie State Historical Park, 4.5 miles northeast of the city off Monashka Bay Rd, and is the place for information on trails, campgrounds and recreation cabins.

Kodiak Island Ambulatory Care Clinic (☎ 486-6188; Suite 102,1202 Center St; 🕓 9am-8pm Mon-Fri, 10am-6pm Sat) For emergency and walk-in medical care.

Kodiak Island Visitor Center (☎ 486-4782, 800-789-4782; www.kodiak.org; 100 Marine Way; 🕓 8am-7pm Mon & Tue, 9am-5pm Wed & Thu, 8am-7pm Fri,10am-2pm & 5-9pm Sat, noon-5pm Sun) Next to the ferry terminal, with brochures and maps of the city.

Kodiak National Wildlife Refuge Visitor Center (☎ 487-2626; http://kodiak.fws.gov; 402 Center St; 🕓 9am-5pm) This new visitor center is downtown and loaded with information.

Post office (419 Lower Mill Bay Rd) The main post office is just northeast of the library.

Quality Dry Cleaners & Laundromat (☎ 486-2638; Ole Johnson Ave & Mill Bay Rd; 🕓 8am-8pm) Also has showers for $5.

Wells Fargo (☎ 486-3126; 202 Marine Way) Has an ATM and a king-crab display in its lobby.

Sights

BARANOV MUSEUM

Housed in the oldest Russian structure in Alaska is **Baranov Museum** (☎ 486-5920; 101 Marine Way; adult/child $3/free; 🕓 10am-4pm Mon-Sat, from noon Sun), across the street from the visitor center. The museum fills the Erskine House, which the Russians built in 1808 as a storehouse for precious sea-otter pelts. Today it holds many items from the Russian period of Kodiak's history, along with fine examples of Alutiiq basketry and carvings. The gift shop is particularly interesting, offering a wide selection of *matreshkas* (nesting dolls), brass samovars and other Russian crafts.

HOLY RESURRECTION CHURCH

Near the Alutiiq museum on Mission Rd is **Holy Resurrection Church** (☎ 486-5532; 385 Kashevarof St), which serves the oldest Russian Orthodox parish in the New World, established in 1794. The present church, marked by its beautiful blue onion domes, was built in 1945 and is the third one to occupy this site. You are free to join tours that are staged when a cruise ship is in. The adjacent small gift shop (open 10am to 2pm Monday to Thursday, and 9am to 4pm Friday) is stocked with *matreshkas*, religious books and icons.

KODIAK NATIONAL WILDLIFE REFUGE VISITOR CENTER

This new **visitor center** (☎ 487-2600; 402 Center St; 🕓 9am-5pm) focuses on the Kodiak brown bear, the most famous resident of the refuge, with an exhibit room that's especially well suited for children, a short film on the bears and a bookstore. Interested in seeing a big bruin? Stop here first.

ALUTIIQ MUSEUM & ARCHAEOLOGICAL REPOSITORY

Preserving the 7500-year heritage of Kodiak's indigenous Alutiiq people is the **Alutiiq Museum & Archaeological Repository** (☎ 486-7004; www.alutiiqmuseum.com; 215 Mission Rd; adult/child $5/free; ⏲ 9am-5pm Mon-Fri, from 10am Sat). The exhibits display one of the largest collections of Alutiiq artifacts in the state, ranging from a kayaker in his waterproof parka of seal gut to a 19th-century spruce-root hat and the corner of a sod house. Take time to explore 'Sharing Words,' an intriguing interactive computer program that uses village elders to teach Alutiiq words and songs in an attempt to save the indigenous language.

ST PAUL BOAT HARBOR

The pulse of this city can be found in its boat harbors. St Paul Boat Harbor is downtown, and the larger of the two. Begin with the **Harbor Walkway** (Shelikof St), where a series of interesting interpretive displays lines the boardwalk above the docks. Then descend to the rows of vessels, where you can talk to the crews or even look for a job.

FORT ABERCROMBIE STATE HISTORICAL PARK

This military fort, 4.5 miles northeast of Kodiak, off Monashka Bay Rd, and its pair of 8in guns, were built by the US Army during WWII for a Japanese invasion that never came. In the end, Kodiak's lousy weather kept the Japanese bombers away from the island. The fort is now a 186-acre state historical park, sitting majestically on the cliffs above scenic Monashka Bay. Between the guns is Ready Ammunition Bunker, which stored 400 rounds of ammunition during the war. Today it contains the small **Kodiak Military History Museum** (☎ 486-7015; adult/child $3/free; ⏲ 1-4pm Fri-Mon).

Just as interesting as the gun emplacements are the tidal pools found along the park's rocky shorelines, where an afternoon of searching for sea creatures can be spent. Park naturalists lead exploration walks when there are significant low tides and tidal-pool snooping is at its best. Call the **Alaska Division of Parks** (☎ 486-6339) for exact days and times.

PILLAR MOUNTAIN

From the top of this 1270ft mountain behind the city you'll have excellent views of the surrounding mountains, ocean, beaches and islands. One side seems to plunge directly down to the harbor below, and the other overlooks the green interior of Kodiak Island. Pick up the bumpy dirt road to the top by walking or driving north up Thorsheim Ave and turning left on Maple Ave, which runs into Pillar Mountain Rd.

KODIAK ISLAND BREWING CO

This is another one of Alaska's great one-man breweries. Behind the counter, pouring the suds, at **Kodiak Island Brewing Co** (☎ 486-2537; 338 Shelikof St; ⏲ noon-7pm) is brewmaster/owner/tour guide Ben Millstein. He'll be more than happy to give you a short tour (it's only a one-room operation) or simply let you taste the five beers he brews. His Liquid Sunshine is so good you might walk out with a half-gallon growler for $8, or even a case-sized party pig for $34.

Activities

HIKING

The Kodiak area has dozens of hiking trails, but few are maintained, and trailheads are not always marked. Windfall can make following the track difficult, or even totally conceal it. Still, hiking trails are the best avenues to the natural beauty of Kodiak Island.

The best source of hiking information is the **Alaska Division of Parks** (☎ 486-6339) or the excellent *Kodiak Audubon's Hiking & Birding Guide* (sold at various places around town including the Kodiak National Wildlife Refuge Visitor Center for $13), a large waterproof topographical map with notes on the trails and birds.

For transportation and company on the trail, the local Audubon Society offers group hikes almost every Saturday and Sunday from May to October, meeting at 9:30am at the ferry terminal. You can get a list of the hikes and the contact person from the Kodiak Island Visitor Center or the Kodiak National Wildlife Refuge Visitor Center (p303). Plant-lovers might consider **Backwoods Botany** (☎ 486-5712, ext 201; tours $25; ⏲ 1pm Mon-Fri) and its 3-hour plant-identification hiking tour of the island.

Barometer Mountain

This popular hiking trail is a steep climb and a 4-mile round-trip to the 2452ft summit. To reach the trailhead, follow Chiniak Rd south of Buskin River State Recreation Site (p306) and turn right on Burma Rd, the first road immediately after passing the end of the airport's runway. Look for a well-worn trail on the left. The trek, which begins in thick alder before climbing the hogback ridge of the mountain, provides spectacular views of Kodiak and the bays south of the city.

Termination Point

Another popular hike, this 5-mile loop starts at the end of Monashka Bay Rd and branches into several trails near Termination Point, a spectacular peninsula that juts out into Narrow Strait. Most hiking is done in a lush Sitka spruce forest that shelters you even on the most blustery of days. If you're nervous about your navigational skills, simply hike the coastal half of the loop and then backtrack.

North Sister Mountain

Starting 150ft up a creek bed a mile before the end of Monashka Bay Rd, this trail (find it on the left side of the creek bed) first leads up steeply through dense brush, but then levels off on alpine tundra. The summit of North Sister (2100ft) is the first peak seen (to your left), about a mile from the trailhead. The other two sisters are also accessible from here.

Pyramid Mountain

Two trails, both starting on Anton Larsen Bay Rd, lead to the top of Pyramid Mountain (2401ft). Avoid the easternmost trail, accessed off the golf course, which is brush-choked and hard going. Instead, continue west to Anton Larsen Pass, where the other trail begins in the parking area on the right. It's a steep but easy-to-follow 2-mile climb to the top.

Anton Larsen Pass

This 5-mile loop is a scenic ridge walk and a far easier alpine hike than Barometer Mountain. The trail begins just north of the gravel parking lot, at the pass on the left side of Anton Larsen Bay Rd. A well-defined trail leads you through meadows; at a fork, the trail heads right to cross a bridge and climbs to a broad alpine ridge. Once on top, use the rolling ridge to skirt a distinctive, glacial valley before descending back to the fork in the trail.

CYCLING

Mountain bikers will find Kodiak's gravel roads interesting to ride on, especially 12-mile Anton Larsen Bay Rd. Leading northwest from near Buskin River State Recreation Site, the road crosses a mountain pass and leads to the island's west side, where you will find quiet coves and shorelines to explore. Plan on two hours for the ride to Anton Larsen Bay. Another favorite is Burma Rd, picked up near the airport (see Barometer Mountain, opposite). It can be combined with a stretch of Chiniak Rd for a 12-mile, two- to three-hour loop.

58 Degrees North (☎ 486-6249; 1231 Mill Bay Rd; per 24hr $35; 🕑 10am-6pm Mon-Sat) is an outdoor shop that rents out mountain bikes. If you are planning to do a lot of bike exploration, purchase the *Kodiak Island Mountain Bike Guide* for $9.

PADDLING

With its many bays and protected inlets, scenic coastline and offshore rookeries, much of Kodiak is a kayaker's dream. Unfortunately, there is nowhere in Kodiak to rent a kayak. A number of outfitters do offer fully equipped tours.

our pick **Orcas Unlimited** (☎ 539-1979; www.orcasunlimited.com; 1 day $200-240, 2 day $720-860) has a full-day paddle looking for marine wildlife around islands near Kodiak, utilizing a mother ship with a dive platform to make this outing ideal for beginner kayakers. It also has a two-day kayak adventure in which you spend the night onboard.

Alaska Wilderness Adventures (☎ 487-2397; www.akwildadventures.com; full day $145-160) specializes in whale watching, along with seeing other marine wildlife like sea otters and puffins, from kayaks. Destinations depend on where the wildlife is.

Kodiak for Children

If the kids are tagging along in Kodiak, cross the Zharoff Memorial Bridge to Near Island, where you'll find several attractions well-suited to families. Best of all, they're free.

Kodiak Fisheries Research Center (☎ 481-1800; Trident Way; 🕑 8am-4:30pm Mon-Fri) Opened in 1998 to house the fisheries research being conducted by various agencies, it has an interesting lobby that includes displays, touch tanks and a large aquarium.

North End Park (Trident Way) Reached as soon as you cross the bridge. The small park is laced with forested trails that converge at a stairway to the shoreline. At low tide you can search the tidal pools here for starfish, sea anemones and other marine life.

St Herman Harbor (Dog Bay Rd) A great place to look for sea lions, which often use the Dog Bay Breakwall as a haul-out, while eagles are usually perched in the trees onshore.

Tours

Several companies provide either a city tour of Kodiak or a daylong scenery-viewing tour that includes Baranov Museum, Pillar Mountain and Fort Abercrombie State Historical Park. But Kodiak is one place where you should skip the ground tour and hit the water.

Galley Gourmet (☎ 486-5079, 800-253-6331; www.kodiak-alaska-dinner-cruises.com; brunch/dinner $110/135) Along with whale watching and harbor cruises, Marty and Marion Owen offer a delightful dinner cruise onboard their 42ft yacht. Marty navigates the boat while Marion whips up meals, like salmon Kiev stuffed with crab, and serves them on white table linen, to views of coastal scenery. The nightly dinner cruise is 3½ hours; brunch is a two-hour cruise and is offered only on the weekends.

Helios Sea Tours (☎ 486-5310; www.kodiakriver camps.com; 5hr tours $178-290) Offers three-, five- and seven-hour whale-watching tours on a smaller 27ft vessel.

Kodiak Tours (☎ 486-3920; www.kodiaktours.com; half-/full-day $55/95) The best operator of tours on land. Uses a mini-bus.

Festivals & Events

Kodiak Crab Festival The town's best event, it was first held in 1958 to celebrate the end of crabbing season. Today the week-long event in late May features parades, a blessing of the fleet, foot and kayak races, fishing-skills contests (such as a survival-suit race) and a lot of cooked king crab.

Fourth of July Kodiak celebrates with fireworks that begin at midnight.

Bear Country Music Festival Features country, bluegrass and Alaskan music in mid-July.

State Fair & Rodeo Held on Labor Day weekend at the Bell Flats rodeo grounds.

Sleeping

Lodging is expensive in Kodiak and there's an 11% sales and bed tax on top of all tariffs. The most current list of B&Bs is on the website of the **visitor center** (www.kodiak.org).

Budget

Buskin River State Recreation Site (Mile 4.5, W Rezanof Dr; sites $10) Four miles southwest of the city, this 168-acre park includes a pleasant, 15-site rustic campground, the closest to the city, along with a self-guided nature trail and good salmon fishing in the Buskin River.

Fort Abercrombie State Historical Park (Mile 4, E Rezanof Dr; sites $10) The other camping option, has 13 wooded sites northeast of Kodiak.

Midrange

Russian Heritage Inn (☎ 486-5657; www.russianherit ageinn.com; 119 Yukon St; r $80-90, ste $110-120; 💻) You pick this motel for location and price. Past patrons have been hard on the 25 rooms but they do have microwaves, coffeemakers and small refrigerators.

our pick **Bev's Bed & Make Your Own Darn Breakfast** (☎ 486-8217; www.bevsbedandbreakfast .com; 1510 Mission Rd; r $85-110; ⊠ 💻) The name of this B&B is misleading. Bev no longer runs it and the new host often brings down muffins and fresh-baked breads for breakfast. But you still can't beat the price for what you get; four comfortable bedrooms with queen-size beds, a fully stocked kitchen that you can use anytime, laundry and cable TV, all within a 15-minute walk of downtown.

Kodiak B&B (☎ 486-5367; home.gci.net/~mmonroe; 308 Cope St; s/d $98/148; ⊠ 💻) Kodiak's oldest B&B is the most convenient to downtown. It's just up the hill from the boat harbor, with two rooms, a private sitting room, a friendly owner and nice views.

Shelikof Lodge (☎ 486-4141; www.shelikoflodge.com; 211 Thorsheim Ave; s/d $100/111; ⊠ 💻) Nicest rooms downtown for what you pay, plus a good restaurant and a lounge that's not the smokiest in town. A bonus is the airport shuttle service.

Salmon Run Guesthouse (☎ 486-0091; www.salmon runguesthouse.com; 410 Hillside Dr; r with/without bath $110/150; ⊠) It's a bit of a climb to this downtown B&B, but worth every uphill step. The three guestrooms are like small apartments with fully equipped kitchens, eating areas, baths and private entrances. TV, laundry facilities and fresh-baked goodies in the morning make this a very pleasant place to spend a night or two.

Top End

On the Cape B&B (☎ 486-4185; www.onthecape.net; 3476 Spruce Cape Rd; r $135-160; ⊠ 💻) A beautiful home between downtown and Fort Abercrombie, with three large rooms whose windows are filled with the ocean and any fishing boat motoring by. The Grande Suite includes king bed with private deck and Jacuzzi tub. The others don't have a Jacuzzi, but that's okay: there's a large deck outside with a hot tub and a seaside view.

Best Western Kodiak Inn (☎ 486-5712, 888-563-4254; www.kodiakinn.com; 236 W Rezanof Dr; r $169-184; 💻) Kodiak's largest and most upscale motel is situated downtown and has 81 rooms along with a fine restaurant, outdoor hot tub and airport-shuttle service.

Eating

Monk's Rock Coffeehouse & Bookstore (☎ 486-0905; 202 W Rezanof Dr; sandwiches $5-7; 10am-6pm Mon-Fri, to 5pm Sat) A relaxing place with lots of Alaskan titles, Russian Orthodox books and icons, and comfortable sofas. The lattes are potent and the soups and sandwiches very affordable.

our pick **Mill Bay Coffee & Pastries** (☎ 486-4411; 3833 E Rezanof Dr; breakfast $5-7, lunch $8-10; 7am-6pm Mon-Sat, 8am-5pm Sun; ☒) What's a French chef doing in Kodiak? Joel Chenet's love of hunting is the reason this city is blessed with the best pastries in Alaska, hands down. Get there early: the case is empty of tortes, éclairs and apple pies by midafternoon. For a seafood treat, try the Kodiak sea burger: a salmon patty topped with crab, shrimp and cream cheese, and served on a toasted brioche bun.

Old Powerhouse (☎ 481-1088; 516 Marine Way; lunch special $8-10, dinner $15-22; 11:30am-2pm & 5-9pm Tue-Thu, 11:30am-2pm & 5-10pm Fri & Sat, 5-9pm Sun; ☒) Kodiak's best dining experience is this historic power plant that has been beautifully renovated into a Japanese seafood restaurant. The waterfront location means you can sit on an outdoor deck, or in a solarium, watching fishing boats glide right past you, while feasting on sushi, seafood or excellent *udon*, *soba* and *yakisoba* noodles.

El Chicano (☎ 486-6116; 103 Center St; lunch $8-11, dinner $11-17; 11am-9:30pm Sun-Thu, to 10:30pm Fri & Sat) A sprawling restaurant and bar that serves big portions of Mexican food and 'grande' margaritas. It isn't the most authentic Mexican in Alaska but it has the local beer on tap and there is an outdoor deck for the three days in summer the sun's out.

Henry's Great Alaskan (☎ 486-8844; 512 Marine Way; sandwiches $9-13, dinner $16-33; 11:25am-10pm Mon-Thu, to 10:30pm Fri & Sat, noon-9:30pm Sun) Located on the mall in front of the small-boat harbor, Henry's is more bar than restaurant at night, but its menu is interesting. Where else in Kodiak can you order crawfish pie or Henry's bouillabaisse: a bowl of clams, mussels, halibut and Cajun sausage in a rich seafood broth?

Channel Side Chowder House (☎ 486-4478; 450 E Marine Way; fish 'n' chips $9-15; 7am-7:30pm Mon-Thu, 7am-8pm Fri, 8am-8pm Sat, 9am-6pm Sun; ☒) You know the fish is fresh at this bright and busy chowder house located right in the middle of a boat harbor. The chowder is the finest in Kodiak and if you're really hungry, order it in a bread bowl.

Safeway (2685 Mill Bay Rd; 6am-midnight) Kodiak's largest and best grocery store has ready-to-eat items, an espresso counter and a seating area.

Drinking & Entertainment

Clustered around the city waterfront and small-boat harbor are a handful of bars that cater to Kodiak's fishing industry. If you visit these at night you'll find them interesting places, overflowing with skippers, deckhands and cannery workers drinking hard and talking lively.

Harborside Coffee & Goods (☎ 486-5862; 216 Shelikof St; 6:30am-7pm Mon-Sat, from 7am Sun; ☒) An espresso bar overlooking the harbor, with a bulletin board listing deckhand jobs.

Chart Room Lounge (☎ 486-5712; 236 W Rezanof Dr) Situated in the Kodiak Inn, the 2nd-floor location allows you to sip a glass of wine with a nice view of the harbor and mountains. An acoustic guitarist on Fridays makes the setting even more mellow.

B'n'B Bar (☎ 486-3575; 326 Shelikof St) Across from the harbor, B'n'B claims to be Alaska's oldest bar, having served its first beer in 1899. It's a fishermen's bar with a giant king crab on the wall, and the most level pool table in a town that feels an earthquake now and then.

Rendezvous (☎ 487-2233; 11653 Chiniak Hwy) This bar and restaurant is a 15-minute drive out of town, past the Coast Guard base, but its atmosphere is worth the gas (even at $5 a gallon). It hosts the best live music in Kodiak with singers taking the stage several times a month.

Getting There & Away

Both **Alaska Airlines** (☎ 487-4363, 800-252-7522) and its contract carrier **ERA Aviation** (☎ 487-4363, 800-866-8394; www.eraaviation.com) fly to Kodiak daily. Fares range between $300 and $350. The airport is 5 miles south of Kodiak on Chiniak Rd. Other than the offerings from a few motels, there is no shuttle service into town. **A&B Taxi** (☎ 486-4343) charges $20 for the ride.

Alaska Marine Highway's MV *Tustumena* (see the boxed text, p308) stops at **Kodiak Ferry Terminal** (☎ 486-3800; 100 Marine Way) several times a week, coming from Homer (one way $74, 9½ hours), and stopping twice a week at Port Lions, a nearby village on Kodiak Island. Once

THE TRUSTY TUSTY

The easiest way to see 'Bush Alaska' without flying is to hop onto the Alaska Marine Highway ferry when it makes its special runs to the eastern end of the Aleutian Islands. The MV *Tustumena,* a 290ft vessel that holds 220 passengers, is one of only two ferries in the Alaska Marine Highway fleet rated as an oceangoing ship; hence its nickname, the 'Trusty Tusty.' It is also one of the oldest vessels in the fleet, thus its other nickname the 'Rusty Tusty.'

Once a month from May through September, the *Tustumena* leaves Kodiak on a Wednesday, and continues west to Chignik, Sand Point, King Cove, Cold Bay and False Pass, docking at each village for two hours, which is plenty of time to get off for a quick look around. It reaches Unalaska and Dutch Harbor by Saturday morning, and stays put for five hours before backtracking, returning to Kodiak on Monday evening and Homer later that night.

This is truly one of the best bargains in public transportation. The scenery and wildlife are spectacular. You'll pass the perfect cones of several volcanoes, the treeless but lush green mountains of the Aleutians and distinctive rock formations and cliffs. Whales, sea lions, otters and porpoises are commonly sighted, and bird life abounds. Occasionally a brown bear is seen rambling along the beach. More than 250 species of birds migrate through the Aleutians and if you don't know a puffin from a kittiwake, you can attend daily presentations by naturalists from the US Fish & Wildlife Service (USFWS).

Viewing wildlife and scenery depends, however, on the weather. It can be an extremely rough trip at times, deserving its title 'the cruise through the cradle of the storms.' The smoothest runs are from June to August, while in the fall 40ft waves and 80-knot winds are the norm. That's the reason for barf bags near the cabins and Dramamine in the vending machines, right above the Reese's Peanut Butter Cups. Its tiny bar – three stools, two tables – is called the Pitch And Roll Cocktail Lounge.

Cabins are available and are a worthwhile expense if you can manage to reserve well in advance (double $311 each way). The trip is long, and the Tusty's solarium isn't as comfortable as most of the Southeast ferries for cabinless sleeping. Bring a good sleeping pad, and loads of Cup-of-Noodles, instant oatmeal and tea (there's free hot water) if you want to avoid the restaurant onboard. Also bring a good book. On days when the fog surrounds the boat, there is little to look at but the waves lapping along the side.

a month the 'Trusty Tusty' continues west to Unalaska and Dutch Harbor ($293 one way from Kodiak). Several times a month the MV *Kennicott* sails to Kodiak from Homer and Whittier (one way $91, 10 hours).

Getting Around

The cheapest car rental in Kodiak is **Rent-A-Heap** (☎ 487-4001; airport terminal) with used, two-door compacts for $37 a day plus 37¢ per mile. If you're planning to drive around the island, that mileage rate will quickly drain your funds. **Budget Rent-A-Car** (☎ 487-2261; airport terminal) offers compacts for $60 a day with unlimited mileage. You can rent either in town at **Port of Kodiak Gift Shop** (☎ 486-8550; 508 Marine Way).

AROUND KODIAK

More than 100 miles of paved and gravel roads head from the city into the wilderness that surrounds Kodiak. Some of the roads are rough jeep tracks, manageable only by 4WD vehicles, but others can be driven or hitched along to reach isolated stretches of beach, great fishing spots and superb coastal scenery.

South of Kodiak, Chiniak Rd winds 48 miles to Cape Greville, following the edge of three splendid bays. The road provides access to some of Alaska's best coastal scenery and there are opportunities to view sea lions and puffins offshore, especially at Cape Chiniak near the road's southern end.

Just past Mile 30 of Chiniak Rd is the junction with Pasagshak Bay Rd, which continues another 16.5 miles due south. Along its way it passes **Pasagshak River State Recreation Site** (Mile 8.7, Pasagshak River Rd) which has 12 free campsites near a beautiful stretch of rugged coastline, 45 miles from town. This small, riverside campground is famous for its silver and king-salmon fishing and for a river that reverses its flow four times a day with the tides. These scenic areas, not the city, are the true attractions of Kodiak Island.

Kodiak National Wildlife Refuge

This 2812-sq-mile preserve, which covers the southern two-thirds of Kodiak Island, all of Ban and Uganik Islands and a small section of Afognak Island, is the chief stronghold of the Alaska brown bear. An estimated 2300 bears reside in the refuge and the surrounding area, which is known worldwide for brown-bear hunting and to a lesser degree for salmon and steelhead fishing. Bird life is plentiful: more than 200 species have been recorded, and there are 600 breeding pairs of eagles that nest within the refuge. Flowing out of the steep fjords and deep glacial valleys and into the sea are 117 salmon-bearing streams that account for 65% of the total commercial salmon harvest in Kodiak.

The refuge's diverse habitat ranges from rugged mountains and alpine meadows to wetlands, spruce forest and grassland. No roads enter the refuge, and no maintained trails lie within it. Access into the park is by charter plane or boat out of Kodiak, and most of the refuge lies at least 25 air miles away.

Like most wilderness areas in Alaska, an extensive trip into the refuge is something that requires advance planning and some money. Begin before you arrive in Alaska by contacting the **Kodiak National Wildlife Refuge Headquarters** (☎ 487-2600; kodiak.fws.gov; 1390 Buskin River Rd, Kodiak, AK 99615).

If you're looking for somewhere to sleep, the Kodiak office of the US Fish & Wildlife Service (USFWS) administers eight cabins in the refuge, none accessible by road. The closest to Kodiak are Uganik Lake Cabin and Veikoda Bay Cabin. The rate is $30 a night and the cabins are reserved through four lotteries throughout the year. If all dates are not booked in the lottery, the open dates are booked by phone on a first-come, first-served basis. Contact the refuge visitor center (p303) for more information.

Afognak Island State Park

Afognak Island lies just north of Kodiak Island in the archipelago. Some 75,000 acres of Afognak are protected in the pristine Afognak Island State Park, which has two public-use cabins: Laura Lake Cabin and Pillar Lake Cabin. The cabin at Pillar Lake is a short walk from a beautiful mile-long beach. Both cabins are accessed by floatplane, cost $35 a night, and are reserved through **Alaska Division of Parks** (☎ 486 6339; www.alaskastateparks.org). You can check the cabin availability and make reservations online six months in advance.

Shuyak Island State Park

The northernmost island in the Kodiak Archipelago, remote and undeveloped Shuyak is 54 air miles north of Kodiak. It's only 12 miles long and 11 miles wide, but almost all of the island's 47,000 acres are taken up by Shuyak Island State Park, featuring forests of virgin Sitka spruce and a rugged shoreline dotted with secluded beaches. Otters, sea lions and Dall porpoises inhabit offshore waters, while black-tailed deer and a modest population of the famous Kodiak brown bear roam the interior.

Kayakers enjoy superb paddling in the numerous sheltered inlets, coves and channels – the area boasts more protected waterways than anywhere else in the archipelago. Most of the kayaking takes place in and around Big Bay, the heart of the state park. From the bay you can paddle and portage to four public cabins and other protected bays. Rental kayaks on the island are available through **Mythos Expeditions Kodiak** (☎ 486-5536; www.thewildcoast.com; s/d 4-day rentals $181/221).

The park's four cabins are on Big Bay, Neketa Bay and Carry Inlet. The cabins ($75 per night) are cedar structures with bunks for eight, woodstoves, propane lights and cooking stoves but no running water. Shuyak Island cabins are also reserved through **Alaska Division of Parks & Outdoor Recreation** (☎ 486-6339; www.alaskastateparks.org), and can be reserved six months in advance online.

ALASKA PENINSULA

The Alaska Range doesn't suddenly stop at Mt McKinley. It marches southwest to merge with the Aleutian Range and form the backbone of the Alaska Peninsula, Alaska's rugged arm that reaches out for the Aleutian Islands. This volcanic peninsula stretches 550 miles from Cook Inlet to its tip at Isanotski Strait and includes Alaska's largest lakes – Lake Clark, Iliamna Lake and Becharof Lake – and some of the state's most active volcanoes, with Mt Redoubt and Mt Iliamna topping more than 10,000ft. Wildlife abounds, communities do not.

The peninsula's most popular attraction, Katmai National Park & Preserve, has turned King Salmon into the main access point. Two

THE BEARS OF KODIAK

There is a wide variety of wildlife in Kodiak National Wildlife Refuge but almost everybody arrives hoping to catch a glimpse of just one animal – the Kodiak bear. This subspecies of the brown bear, *Ursus arctos middendorffi*, is the largest land carnivore in the world. Males normally weigh in at more than 800lb but have been known to exceed 1500lb. Females usually weigh in at 400lb to 600lb. Biologists estimate there are 3000 brown bears living in the archipelago, or one bear per 1.5 sq miles, with more than 2300 on Kodiak Island itself. That's three times the number of brown bears in the rest of the USA. From mid-July to mid-September the bears congregate at streams to gorge themselves on spawning salmon. The runs are so heavy that the bears often become selective, and many feast only on females and then eat only the belly portion containing the eggs.

That's the best time to see the bears, and the most common way to do it is with a bear-sighting flight. Just about every air-charter company in town offers a bear-watching flight, in which you often land at Frazer Lake, home of a huge sockeye salmon run, to watch a half-dozen bears feed. After August the air charters head to the Katmai Coast. The average tour is a four-hour trip that includes two hours on the ground photographing bears, and costs $450 to $550 per person.

Among the many air services offering bear tours are **Andrew Airways** (☎ 487-2566; www.andrewairways.com), **Harvey Flying Service** (☎ 487-2621; www.harveyflyingservice.com), **Kingfisher Aviation** (☎ 486-5155, 866-5155; www.kingfisheraviation.com) and **Sea Hawk Air** (☎ 486-8282, 800-770-4295; www.seahawkair.com).

A much more adventurous way of seeing the bears is through **Kodiak Treks** (☎ 487-2122; www.kodiaktreks.com), which offers low-impact, small-group bear-watching trips from its remote lodge on an island in Uyak Bay. Harry Dodge, a noted bear biologist, leads guests from the lodge, by boat and boot, to various viewing spots to view up to two dozen bears. The cost is $300 per person per day and covers lodging, meals and equipment but not your charter flight to Uyak Bay.

other preserves – McNeil River State Game Area and Lake Clark National Park & Preserve – also attract the interest of travelers; while the Alaska Marine Highway also stops at four small communities along the peninsula on its way to the Aleutians.

KING SALMON

pop 426

A former WWII airbase, King Salmon is now a service center with a healthy percentage of government and transportation employees living on the banks of the beautiful Naknek River. The town is a little rough around the edges and, along with its wide, open landscape, this gives King Salmon a quiet, edge-of-the-world appeal.

Just under 300 air miles from Anchorage, King Salmon is the air-transport hub for Katmai National Park & Preserve (opposite). Most visitors see little more than the airport terminal and the float dock where they catch a flight into the park.

Information

King Salmon's post office is about a mile west of the airport, but you can purchase stamps, and mail letters, at the visitor center.

AC Value Center (☎ 246-6109; 100 Eskimo St; ⌚ 7am-10pm Mon-Sat, to 8pm Sun) By King Salmon Mall; sells some camping gear and supplies.

Camai Medical Center (☎ 246-6155; 211 School Rd; ⌚ 9am-5pm Mon-Fri) For anything routine, get yourself to Naknek's medical center. Also on call for emergencies.

Katmai National Park Headquarters (☎ 246-3305; ⌚ 8am-4:30pm Mon-Fri) A block from the terminal, in King Salmon Mall; turn right as you exit the terminal.

King Ko Inn (☎ 246-3377; 100 Airport Rd; ⌚ 8am-6pm) Has laundry facilities with showers. At $10 for a shower, think twice about how clean you want to be.

King Salmon Visitor Center (☎ 246-4250; ⌚ 8am-5pm) The National Park Service (NPS) and the two area boroughs operate this center, next door to the airport terminal. The center has natural-history displays and videos, and sells an excellent selection of books and maps (including topographic maps).

Wells Fargo (☎ 246-3306; King Salmon Mall) Has an ATM.

Sleeping & Eating

Lodging, already scarce and expensive in King Salmon, became even more so in 2006 when the town's largest hotel, Quinnat Landing Hotel, burnt down. Best to avoid spending the night here if you can, by planning your trip – including having prebooked accommodations in Katmai (p313) – so that you fly out the day you arrive. The bed tax is 10% on top of the prices listed here.

Dave's World/R&G Boat Rental (☎ 246-3353, 246-8651; rgbrakna@bristolbay.com; Municipal Dock 1; campsites $10, 4-person cabins $85) Has a 160-acre spread you can camp on, with most of it across the Naknek River from King Salmon, a $5 (round-trip) skiff ride away. Dave has another small camping area by the office, on the town side, and if you need lodging in King Salmon, his three rustic cabins are the best deal in town.

Antlers Inn (☎ 246-8525, 888-735-8525; antlers@bristolbay.com; s/d $190/210, ste s/d $240/260) Another option is this friendly, family-run inn just behind the King Salmon Mall. Rooms share bathrooms, while the suites have kitchenettes and their own baths. Amazingly, it's free to camp outside, and there is even a shower building, if you can handle an occasional bear wandering through.

King Ko Inn (☎ 246-3377, 866-234-3474; www.kingko.com; 100 Airport Rd; cabin s/d $195/215; 💻) Friendly, comfortable and adjacent to the airport terminal. It offers 16 cabins with private baths; eight of them also have kitchenettes. The King Ko is also home to the liveliest bar in town.

The King Ko Inn has a full-service restaurant, or you might try **Eddie's Fireplace Inn** (☎ 246-3435; Airport Rd; breakfast $11-14, dinner $20-32; 🕑 7am-10pm), across the street, with an atmospheric bar and a kitchen that is open all day.

Getting There & Away

Alaska Airlines (☎ 800-252-7522; www.alaskaair.com) flies up to six times daily between Anchorage and King Salmon during the summer. Round-trip fare is $500 to $600.

KATMAI NATIONAL PARK & PRESERVE

In June 1912 Novarupta Volcano erupted violently and, with the preceding earthquakes, rocked the area now known as Katmai National Park & Preserve. The wilderness was turned into a dynamic landscape of smoking valleys, ash-covered mountains and small holes and cracks fuming with steam and gas. Only one other eruption in documented historic times, on the Greek island of Santorini in 1500 BC, displaced more ash and pumice.

If the eruption had happened in New York City, people living in Chicago would have heard the explosion; the force of the eruption was 10 times greater than the 1980 eruption of Mt St Helens, in the state of Washington. For two days, people in Kodiak could not see a lantern held at arm's length, and the pumice, which reached half the world, lowered the average temperature in the northern hemisphere that year by 2°F. In history books, 1912 is remembered as the year without a summer, but the most amazing aspect of this eruption, the most dramatic natural event in the 20th century, was that no-one was killed. Katmai is that remote.

In 1916 the National Geographic Society sent Robert Grigg to explore the locality. Standing at Katmai Pass, the explorer saw for the first time the valley floor with its thousands of steam vents. He named it the Valley of 10,000 Smokes, and the name stuck. Grigg's adventures revealed the eruption's spectacular results to the world, and two years later, the area was turned into a national monument. In 1980 the monument was enlarged to 4.2 million acres and designated a national park and preserve.

The fumaroles no longer smoke and hiss and today the park is best known for bears. In July, at the peak of bear viewing, throngs of visitors arrive to watch brown bears, snagging salmon in midair, just 30yd away. Those who can plan months in advance can arrive during that peak and stay in an affordable campground. Those who can't, often end up taking expensive daytrips into the park. Neither is cheap but, no matter what the costs, for many people the bears and fishing at Katmai end up being the highlight of their Alaskan trip.

Information

Katmai National Park & Preserve (☎ 246-3305; www.nps.gov/katm; King Salmon) is not a place to visit on a whim. Because of the cost of reaching the park, it's best to spend at least four days, or more, here to justify the expense.

The park's summer headquarters is Brooks Camp, on the shores of Naknek Lake, 35 miles from King Salmon. The camp is best known for Brooks Falls, which thousands of bright-red sockeye salmon attempt to jump every July, much to the interest of bears and tourists. In the middle of the wilderness, this place crawls with visitors (and bears) during July, when as many as 300 people will be in Brooks Camp and the surrounding area in a single day.

When you reach the camp on a floatplane, take a good look; bears are usually seen lumbering along the beach between the lodge

THE GRIZZLY MAN

A self-described 'ecowarrior' from New York, Timothy Treadwell spent 13 summers in Katmai National Park & Preserve living and filming brown bears in the backcountry. Eventually he came to believe that the bears trusted him – at times allowing him to touch them or even play with their cubs. Treadwell used his films to raise public awareness of the problems faced by bears in North America, and by 2001 he was notable enough to appear on the Discovery Channel, the *Late Show with David Letterman* and *Dateline NBC*. His tragic end came in 2003 when he and his girlfriend were killed, and partially ingested, by a bear – the first such incident in the 85-year history of the park.

Using Treadwell's more than 100 hours of footage of his interactions with grizzly bears, German director Werner Herzog produced the documentary *Grizzly Man*, which premiered at the 2005 Sundance Film Festival to critical acclaim. Several books have also been written about Treadwell, including *The Grizzly Maze* in 2006 by Alaskan author Nick Jans.

and the planes pulled up on the sand. If the coast is clear, you're directed to go to the NPS Visitor Center, where you are enrolled in the 'Brooks Camp School of Bear Etiquette,' a mandatory 20-minute bear orientation. Among the things you learn is that bears have the right-of-way here; if a brownie lies down right on the trail and takes a nap, no visitors use the trail until it wakes up and moves on. These 'bear jams' have been known to last hours.

Rangers at the center also answer questions, help you fill out backcountry permits, stage a variety of interpretive programs and sell books and maps.

Most visitors come in July, when the salmon and brown bears are at their peak. Unfortunately, mosquitoes, always heavy in this area, are also at their peak. The best time for hiking and backpacking trips is from mid-August to early September, when the fall colors are brilliant, the berries ripe and juicy and the insects scarce. Be prepared for frequent storms. In fact, be ready for rain and foul weather at any time in Katmai, and always pack warm clothing.

Activities

BEAR WATCHING

Katmai has the world's largest population of protected brown bears (more than 2000). At Brooks Camp they congregate around Brooks River to benefit from the easy fishing for sockeye salmon. Most of this occurs from late June through July, when 40 to 60 bears gather along a half-mile stretch of the Brooks River. In that period it is near impossible to get a campsite, a cabin or even a spot on the observation decks, without planning months in advance. The bear activity then tapers off in late July and August, when the animals follow the salmon up into the streams feeding into Brooks Lake. It increases again in September as the bears return to the lower rivers to feed on spawned-out fish. That said, a few brown bears can be seen in the Brooks Camp area during summer; a couple of younger ones always seem to be hanging around.

Brooks Camp has three established viewing areas. From the lodge, a dirt road leads to a floating bridge over the river and the first observation deck – a large platform dubbed 'Fort Stevens' by rangers, for the Alaskan senator who secured the funding for it. From here you can see the bears feeding in the mouth of the river or swimming in the bay.

Continue on the road to the Valley of 10,000 Smokes, and in half a mile a marked trail winds to Brooks Falls. Two more viewing platforms lie along this half-mile trail. The first sits above some riffles that occasionally draw sows trying to keep their cubs away from aggressive males at the falls.

The last deck, at the falls, is the prime viewing area, where you can photograph the salmon making spectacular leaps or a big brownie at the top of the cascade waiting with open jaws to catch a fish. At the peak of the salmon run, there might be eight to 12 bears here, two or three of them atop the falls themselves. The observation deck holds 40 people, and in early to mid-July it will be crammed with photographers, forcing rangers to rotate people on and off.

HIKING

Hiking and backpacking are the best ways to see the park's unusual backcountry. Like

Denali National Park, in Alaska's Interior, Katmai has few formal trails; backpackers follow river bars, lake shores, gravel ridges and other natural routes. Many hiking trips begin with a ride on the park bus along the dirt road to Three Forks Overlook, in the Valley of 10,000 Smokes. The bus will also drop off and pick up hikers and backpackers along the road. The one-way fare is $51.

The only developed trail from Brooks Camp is a half-day trek to the top of **Dumpling Mountain** (2520ft). The trail leaves the ranger station and heads north past the campground, climbing 1.5 miles to a scenic overlook. It then continues another 2 miles to the mountain's summit, where there are superb views of the surrounding lakes.

PADDLING

The area has some excellent paddling including the Savonoski Loop, a five- to seven-day adventure; see p114 for details. Other popular trips include a 30-mile paddle from Brooks Camp to the **Bay of Islands** and a 10-mile paddle to Margot Creek, which has good fishing and lots of bears.

Kayaks are the overwhelming choice for most paddlers due to high winds blowing across big lakes, and possible rough water. Accomplished paddlers should have no problem, but the conditions can sometimes get dicey for novices.

Lifetime Adventures (☎ 746-4644, 800-952-8624; www.lifetimeadventures.net; folding kayaks daily single/double $45/55, weekly single/double $245/280), in Brooks Camp, rents folding kayaks.

Tours

INDEPENDENT TOURS

The only road in Katmai is 23 miles long. It's a scenic traverse of the park that leads from the lodge, past wildlife-inhabited meadows and river valleys and ends at Three Forks Overlook, which has a sweeping view of the Valley of 10,000 Smokes. **Katmailand** (☎ 243-5448, 800-544-0551; www.katmailand.com) runs the lodge at Brooks Camp. It has a daily bus to Three Forks Overlook and back, which leaves at 9am, with three hours at the cabin, and returns to the lodge at 4:30pm.

Each bus carries a ranger who talks during the bus trip and leads a short hike from the cabin into the valley below. Views from the cabin include almost 12 miles of barren, moonlike valley where the lava oozed down, with snowcapped peaks beyond. It's an amazing sight.

The fare for the tour is a steep $88 per person (with a packed lunch $96), but if the weather isn't too bad most people feel it's money well spent. Sign up for the tour at the Katmailand office across from the lodge as soon as you arrive at Brooks Camp. The bus is filled most of the summer, and you often can't get a seat without making a reservation a day or two in advance.

Brooks Lodge also offers an hour-long flightseeing tour around the park for $150 per person (two people minimum).

PACKAGE TOURS

Because of the logistics of getting there and the need to plan and reserve so much in advance, many visitors arrive in Katmai as part of a one-call-does-it-all package tour. A shockingly large number are part of a one-day visit, spending large sums of money for what is basically an hour or two of bear watching. At the height of the season, in July, there can easily be 20 floatplanes or more lined up on the beach at Brooks Camp.

our pick **Hallo Bay Bear Camp** (☎ 235-2237, 888-535-2237; www.hallobay.com) This ecofriendly camp is on the outside coast of Katmai National Park and is designed exclusively for bear viewing. The cabins are simple but comfortable and the camp can handle only 12 guests at a time. In such an intimate setting, the bear watching can be surreal at times. Packages include airfare from Homer, lodging, meals and guides and begin at $1200 per person for two nights.

Katmailand (☎ 243-5448, 800-544-0551; www.katmailand.com) Offers packages that are geared for either anglers or bear watchers. Its one-day tour to see the bears of Brooks Falls is $589 per person. A three-night angler's package which includes all transportation, lodging and meals is $1542 to $1849 per person based on double-occupancy.

Lifetime Adventures (☎ 746-4644, 800-952-8624; www.lifetimeadventures.net) If you have the time, this outfit offers a seven-day camping adventure that includes hiking in the Valley of 10,000 Smokes and kayaking near Margot River. The cost is $2450 per person and includes the flight from Anchorage, charters into the park, all equipment and guides.

Sleeping & Eating

If you plan to stay at Brooks Camp, either at the lodge or in the campground, you must make reservations. No walk-ins are accepted, so if you don't have reservations, you're limited to staying in King Salmon and visiting the park on day trips.

Campground (reservations ☎ 877-444-6777, 518-885-3639; www.recreation.gov) Reservations for the campground are accepted from the first Monday of January, for that year. It might be easier to win the New York lottery than to obtain a campground reservation for prime bear-watching in July, as often the campsites are completely booked before the end of the first week of January. Camping is $8 per person per night and limited to a maximum of seven nights. If you don't have a reservation, you don't get a site.

Important: the 18-site campground holds a maximum of 60 people, and reservations are made by person, not by site. If you don't provide the names of everyone in your party when you make your reservation, space will be held for just one person. Woe to the reservation-maker who gave only his or her name, then found on arrival that the campground had no room for the other members of the party. It's happened.

Brooks Lodge (Katmailand; ☎ 243-5448, 800-544-0551; www.katmailand.com) The lodge has 16 basic, but modernized, cabin-style rooms, each with two bunk beds and a private bath with shower. Cabins are rented as part of package tours that include transportation from Anchorage, and in July there is a three-night maximum stay. A three-night package is $1497 per person, a three-night stay outside of the prime bear-viewing period is $920 to $1190.

A store at Brooks Camp sells limited supplies of freeze-dried food, white gas (for camp stoves), fishing equipment, flies, and other odds and ends…such as beer. You can also sign up for the all-you-can-eat meals at Brooks Lodge without renting a cabin (renters pay too): for adults and children respectively, breakfasts are $15 and $10, lunches $19 and $14 and dinners $32 and $23. Also in the lodge is a lounge with a huge stone fireplace, soft chairs and bar service in the evening.

Getting There & Away

Most visitors to Katmai fly into King Salmon on **Alaska Airlines** (☎ 800-252-7522; www.alaskaair.com). Once you're in King Salmon, a number of air-taxi companies offer the 20-minute floatplane flight out to Brooks Camp. **Katmai Air** (☎ 243-5448, 800-544-0551; www.katmailand.com/air-services), the Katmailand-affiliated company, charges $176 for a round-trip.

LAKE CLARK NATIONAL PARK & PRESERVE

Situated only 100 miles southwest of Anchorage, Lake Clark National Park & Preserve features spectacular scenery that is a composite of Alaska; an awesome array of tundra-covered hills, mountains, glaciers, coastline, the largest lakes in the state and two active volcanoes. The centerpiece of the park is spectacular Lake Clark, a 42-mile-long turquoise body of water ringed by mountains. But the park is also where the Alaska Range merges into the Aleutian Range to form the Chigmit Mountains, and is home to Mt Iliamna and Mt Redoubt: two volcanoes that in 1990 were seen, from as far afield as Anchorage, tossing ash into the air. Despite its overwhelming scenery and close proximity to Alaska's largest city, less than 5000 visitors a year make it to this 5625-sq-mile preserve. So close, yet so far away.

Those who do arrange a trip here are usually a mix of anglers, river runners and experienced backpackers. There are no roads and few trails in the park but there are three designated National Wild Rivers that have long been havens for rafters and paddlers in inflatable canoes and kayaks. The park's watershed is one of the world's most important producers of red salmon, contributing 33% of the US catch, and anglers arrive from around the world, often on daytrips from Anchorage. Lake Clark also has a scattering of remote, isolated lodges and if you're willing to pay the price, you can truly escape into a pristine wilderness for a few days without having to sleep on the ground.

Information

NPS Park Headquarters (☎ 644-3626; www.nps.gov/lacl; 240 West 5th Ave, Ste 236, Anchorage; 🕒 8am-5pm Mon-Fri) For any pretrip planning.

Ranger Station (☎ 781-2218; 🕒 8am-4:30pm Mon-Fri) In Port Alsworth; has displays and videos on the park; sells a limited selection of maps and books.

Activities

HIKING

Lake Clark is best suited to the experienced backpacker. Most extended treks take place in the western foothills north of Lake Clark, where the open and relatively dry tundra provides ideal conditions for hiking.

The 50-mile historic **Telaquana Trail**, first used by indigenous Dena'ina Athabascans, and later by fur trappers and miners, is the park's best cross-country route. It begins on Lake Clark's north shore, near the Athabascan village of Kijik, and ends near Telaquana Lake. In between, you pass through boreal forests, ford glacial rivers and cross the fragile alpine tundra along the western flank of the Alaska Range.

Less-experienced backpackers can be dropped off at the shores of the many lakes in the area to camp and undertake day hikes. Among the more popular are **Twin Lakes**, where dry tundra slopes provide for easy travel to ridges and great views. Along the lower lake there is a backcountry patrol cabin that is usually staffed during the summer, and there is good fishing throughout the area. You will most likely encounter fly-in, day-use fishing parties from Anchorage, a few rafters and other backpackers.

PADDLING

Float trips down any of the three designated wild rivers are spectacular and exciting, with waterways rated from Class III to Class IV. The best way to handle a boat rental is through **Alaska Raft & Kayak** (☎ 561-7238, 800-606-5950; www.alaskaraftandkayak.com; 401 W Tudor Rd, Anchorage; ⏲ 10am-6pm Mon-Sat), which rents inflatable kayaks and canoes (per day $75) and 14ft to 16ft rafts (per day $100) in Anchorage. The shop will also deliver the boat to **Lake Clark Air** (☎ 781-2208, 888-440-2281; www.lakeclarkair.com) in Anchorage for your flight into the national park and pick it up when you return.

Chilikadrotna River begins at Twin Lakes and offers good water for intermediate rafters. Its steady current and narrow course winds through upland spruce and hardwood forest, draining the west flank of the Alaska Range. From the lakes to a pre-arranged pickup on the Mulchatna River is a 60-mile, four-day float with some Class III stretches.

The fast, but small, glacial **Tlikakila River** flows from Summit Lake to upper Lake Clark through a narrow, deep valley within the Alaska Range. The 46-mile trip takes three days and hits a few stretches of Class III water. The hiking in tundra around Summit Lake is excellent, and from there you make a portage to the river.

Above Bonanza Hills is the **Mulchatna River**, a shallow, rocky channel from its headwaters at Turquoise Lake, with stretches of Class III rapids. Below the hills, the Mulchatna River is an easy and leisurely float. Plan on two days to float from the lake to the end of Bonanza Hills. The entire river is a 220-mile run to the Nushagak River.

Sleeping

Port Alsworth is on Lake Clark's southeastern shore and serves as the main entry point into the park.

Farm Lodge (☎ 781-2208, 888-440-2281; www.thefarmlodge.com; r per person with/without meals $185/125) With 13 rooms, this is the largest inn of the handful in town. It also offers meals, outfitting service and has a plane for backpacking drop-offs and river trips.

Island Lodge (☎ 877-349-3195; islandlodge.com) Among the wilderness lodges within the park, this is the best. Reached only by floatplane, the resort is on an island in the northeast end of Lake Clark and features the main lodge, cabins and a delightful lakeside sauna. Activities range from kayaking and rafting to fishing and wildlife viewing and packages begin at $1932 per person for three days and four nights.

Getting There & Away

PenAir no longer flies into Iliamna, a small village located 30 miles south of the park. The best bet is to fly into Port Alsworth or arrange with an Anchorage charter pilot for drop off at the start of your backcountry adventure. **Lake Clark Air** (☎ 781-2208, 888-440-2281; www.lakeclarkair.com) offers daily flights to Port Alsworth from Anchorage for a round-trip fare of $400.

THE LOWER PENINSULA

Most visitors to the little fishing villages on the western peninsula arrive on the Alaska Marine Highway's MV *Tustumena,* which goes from Kodiak to Unalaska and Dutch Harbor (see the boxed text, p308). The ferry usually stops for two hours: long enough to get out and walk from one end of the village to the other, and for most people, that's ample. If you decide to stay over at any village, you'll be able to find food and shelter, and then return to Anchorage through **PenAir** (☎ 800-448-4226; www.penair.com). A one-way flight from the peninsula communities to Anchorage ranges from $475 to $525.

The first stop after departing Kodiak is **Chignik** (☎ 749-2280), where everybody piles off the Tusty. Passengers follow the boardwalk to

DETOUR: MCNEIL RIVER STATE GAME SANCTUARY

The McNeil River State Game Sanctuary, just north of Katmai National Park & Preserve on the Alaska Peninsula and 250 miles southwest of Anchorage, was created in 1967 to protect the world's largest concentration of brown bears. This spot is renowned among wildlife photographers, and just about every great bear-catches-salmon shot was taken either here or on the Brooks River. Often, 20 brown bears will feed together at McNeil River Falls, and up to 72 have congregated here at one time.

The Alaska Department of Fish & Game has set up a viewing area and runs a lottery to allow 10 visitors per day for a four-day period, to watch the bears feed. From a camp, park guides lead a 2-mile hike across sedge flats and through the thigh-deep Mikfik Creek to the viewing area, on a bluff. There you can watch the bears feed less than 60ft away, in the pools where the salmon gather between leaps. Though an expensive sidetrip for most visitors, watching and photographing giant brown bears at such close range is a once-in-a-lifetime experience. In other words, if you win this lottery, go!

Visits to the game sanctuary are on a permit basis only – by lottery – and your odds of drawing a permit from the lottery are less than one in five; applications are received from around the world. You can apply for the lottery draw online at the **Alaska Department of Fish & Game – Division of Wildlife Conservation** (☎ 267-2182; www.wildlife.alaska.gov/index.cfm?adfg=mcneil_river.main), or download an application and return it by mail, with a $25-per-person nonrefundable fee, by March 1. The user fee for the sanctuary is $350 for non-Alaskans.

July is the prime month for bear watching. Most visitors depart for McNeil River from Homer with a round-trip air charter that costs around $400 per person. Among the Homer-based air services offering flights to McNeil River is **Bald Mountain Air Service** (☎ 235-7969, 800-478-7969; www.baldmountainair.com).

the **Donut Hole** (☎ 749-2285) to indulge in blueberry-filled donuts, cinnamon rolls and other sweet treats and often bring boxes of them back to the ship. It's the only time this tiny bakery has a line of people out the door.

The next port is on the northwest coast of Popof Island, **Sand Point** (☎ 383-2696; sptcity@arctic.net), the largest commercial fishing base in the Aleutians, with a population of 992. It was founded in 1898 by a San Francisco fishing company as a trading post and cod-fishing station, but also bears traces of Aleut, Scandinavian and Russian heritage. The town's **St Nicholas Chapel**, a Russian Orthodox church, was built in 1933 and is now on the National Register of Historical Places.

At the Alaska Peninsula's western end, near the entrance to Cold Bay, is **King Cove** (☎ 497-2340; amscity@arctic.net), founded in 1911, when a salmon cannery was built. Today, with a population of 756, it is a commercial fishing base and home to Peter Pan Seafoods, whose salmon cannery is the largest operation under one roof in Alaska.

On the west shore of the same bay is **Cold Bay** (☎ 532-2401; coldbayak@arctic.net), with a population of 72. A huge airstrip was built here during WWII – today it's the third-longest in the state, making Cold Bay the transport center for the entire Aleutian chain. You can still see Quonset huts and other remains from the WWII military buildup.

ALEUTIAN ISLANDS

Where the Alaska Peninsula ends, the Aleutian Islands begin: a jagged 1100-mile arc that stretches across the north Pacific, to within 500 miles of Russia's Kamchatka Peninsula. This is a barren, windswept and violent place, as 27 of the 46 most active volcanoes in the US form islands here.

For most visitors, the Aleutians is limited to three stops aboard the Alaska Marine Highway's MV *Tustumena* (p308). The first is a two-hour stop at **False Pass** (☎ 548-2319; cityoffalsepass@ak.net). That is more than enough time to wander the length of this small, but picturesque, fishing village (pop 46) on the tip of Unimak Island, looking across a narrow passage at the Alaska Peninsula. The second is a very brief stop at **Akutan** (☎ 698-2228; akutan@gci.net), another village (pop 859), that the ferry reaches at 5:30am, before continuing on to Unalaska and Dutch Harbor.

UNALASKA & DUTCH HARBOR

pop 3678

On the road from the ferry terminal to Unalaska and Dutch Harbor, two things catch your eye: concrete pillboxes and crab pots. In a nutshell, that's the story of these twin towns on Unalaska and Amaknak Islands: the pillboxes are a violent WWII reminder of the past, while the crab pots acknowledge the important role of commercial fishing in the towns' future.

Located at the confluence of the Pacific Ocean and the Bering Sea, the world's richest fishery, Dutch Harbor, is the only natural deepwater port in the Aleutians. More than 400 vessels call here each year from as many as 14 countries. From this industrialized port of canneries and fish-processing plants, the newly rebuilt Bridge to the Other Side arches over to the residential community of Unalaska.

The area, and Dutch Harbor in particular, shot into the limelight in 2007, when Discovery Channel's *The Deadliest Catch* emerged as one of the most popular reality shows on TV. Each week viewers tune in to watch crab boats and their crews battle four-story high waves, icy temperatures and paralyzing fatigue, to fill their holds with a gold mine of king crab, before heading back to Dutch Harbor.

Ironically, since the dramatic crash of the king crab fishery, in 1982, it has been pollack, an unglamorous bottom fish, that has been the backbone of Unalaska and Dutch Harbor's economy. Pollack accounts for more than 80% of all seafood processed, and is the reason the towns have been the country's number one commercial fishing port for the past 20 years. In 2006, Dutch Harbor set a record when 911 million lb of seafood, at an export value of $165 million, crossed its docks. The impact of so much fish is an influx of cannery workers, who arrive from around the world to temporarily double the area's population as they turn pollack into fish sticks or imitation crab.

During the 1970s Unalaska and Dutch Harbor were Alaska's version of the Wild West, with drinks, money and profanity flowing freely at every bar in town. With the crash of the king crab, the towns became more community-oriented, and with the recent drop of the pollack fishery, residents are now trying to survive another downturn in the boom-and-bust cycle of fishing. Unfortunately, short-time visitors returning on the ferry don't have an opportunity to soak in the color and unique character of these towns. To stay longer, you need to splurge on an expensive airline ticket, something budget travelers find hard to justify. But those who do will discover a few days in Unalaska and Dutch Harbor can be a refreshing cure from an overdose of RVers, cruise ships and tour buses.

Information

Iliuliuk Family & Health Clinic (☎ 581-1202; 34 LaVelle Ct; ⏰ walk-in 8:30am-6pm Mon-Fri, 7am-5pm

THE COLD BAY LOTTERY

The most interesting attraction during the long run of the MV *Tustumena* from Kodiak to Dutch Harbor is **Izembek National Wildlife Refuge** (☎ 532-2445, 877-836-6332; www.r7.fws.gov/nwr/izembek), just outside Cold Bay. At 417,533 acres Izembek is the smallest Alaskan refuge, but still half the size of Rhode Island. It was created in 1960 to protect 142 bird species, mainly the black brant (a type of goose). Almost the entire North American brant population of 135,000 birds arrives in spring and fall during the annual migration, to feed on the large eelgrass beds in Izembek Lagoon. When the salmon are running, brown-bear densities in the refuge can be among Alaska's highest: as many as six bears per mile along some streams. The lagoon is also home to seals and sea otters. In other words, a wildlife paradise.

The lagoon lies 11 miles from Cold Bay and is almost impossible to visit during the typical two-hour layover of the ferry, unless you're lucky. Do you feel lucky? If so, drop your name in the lottery for the US Fish & Wildlife Service (USF&WS) tour that heads out to the lagoon every time the ferry is in port. The USF&WS naturalist onboard the MV *Tustumena* organizes the drawing because there are only 16 seats on the bus and usually 100 passengers who want to be in one of them. If you do draw a ticket you'll be treated to a narrated ride out to Grant Point Wildlife Overlook, where you'll see thousands of birds, sea otters, red fox and possibly even brown bears. The 1½-hour tour is free and, best of all, the Tusty won't leave without you. Or at least, not without its naturalist.

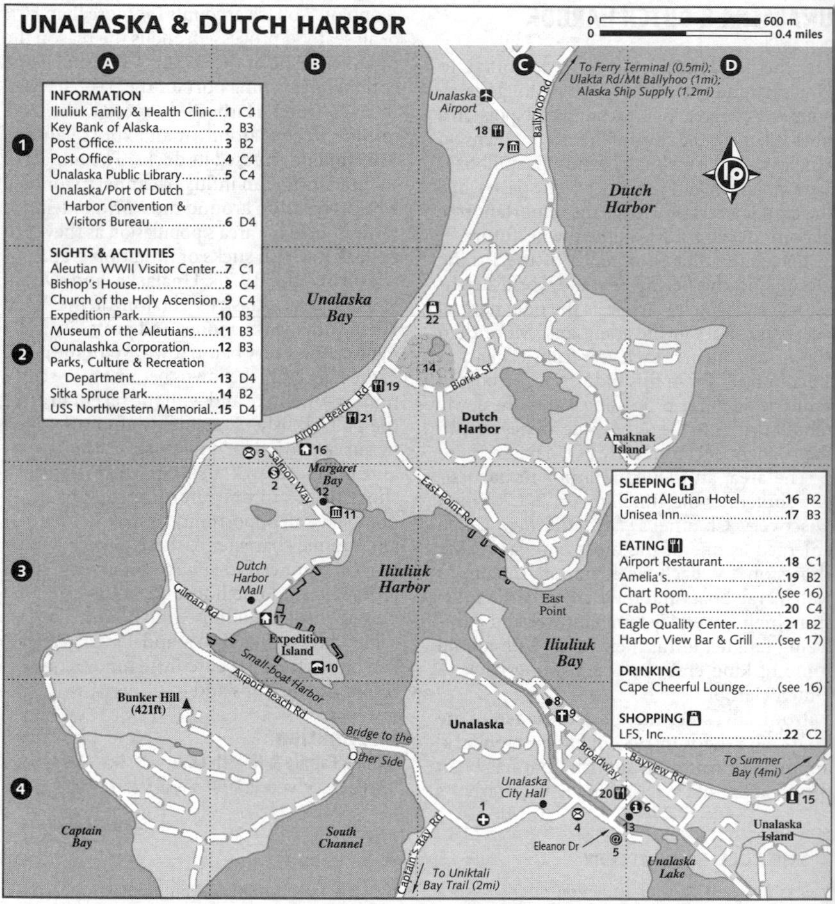

Sat) Just off Airport Beach Rd near Unalaska City Hall; has walk-in and 24-hour emergency service.

Key Bank of Alaska (☎ 581-1300; 100 Salmon Way) Across from Grand Aleutian Hotel in Dutch Harbor; has a 24-hour ATM.

Post office Dutch Harbor (Airport Beach Rd); Unalaska (82 Airport Beach Rd) The Dutch Harbor post office is near Grand Aleutian Hotel.

Unalaska Public Library (☎ 581-5060; 64 Eleanor Dr; 🕒 10am-9pm Mon-Fri, noon-6pm Sat & Sun) Near the 5th St Bridge, offers free internet access on 14 computers.

Unalaska/Port of Dutch Harbor Convention & Visitors Bureau (☎ 581-2612, 877-581-2612; www.unalaska.info; cnr 5th & Broadway, Unalaska; 🕒 8am-5pm Mon-Fri or when the ferry is in) Located in the Burma Street Russian Church, originally a military chapel built during WWII.

Sights

MUSEUM OF THE ALEUTIANS

The small but impressive **Museum of the Aleutians** (☎ 581-5150; www.aleutians.org; 314 Salmon Way; adult/child $5/free; 🕒 9am-5pm Tue-Sat, from noon Sun) is one of the best native cultural centers in Alaska. A short walk from the Grand Aleutian Hotel, the museum relives the Aleutian story from prehistory through the Russian America period to WWII and the present. Many of the exhibits focus on the enduring relationship between the Aleuts and the Russian Orthodox Church, but, for many, the most fascinating displays are the tools, boats and grass baskets that allowed these clever and creative people to live in such a harsh environment.

CHURCH OF THE HOLY ASCENSION

Unalaska is dominated by the Church of the Holy Ascension, the oldest Russian-built church still standing in Alaska. It was built in 1825 and then enlarged in 1894, when its floor plan was changed to a *pekov* (the shape of a crucifix). On Broadway Ave, overlooking the bay, the church and its onion domes are a photographer's delight. The church contains almost 700 pieces of art, ranging from Russian Orthodox icons and books to the largest collection of 19th-century paintings in Alaska. The best time to view the interior of the church is after services, 6:30pm on Saturday and 11am Sunday morning.

Outside the church is a small graveyard, where the largest grave marker belongs to Baron Nicholas Zass. Born in 1825 in Archangel, Russia, he eventually became bishop of the Aleutian Islands, and all of Alaska, before his death in 1882. Next door to the graveyard is the **Bishop's House**.

ALEUTIAN WWII NATIONAL HISTORIC AREA

In 1996 the US Congress created this 134-acre national historic area to preserve the bloody history of the WWII battles on the Aleutian Islands. The park is unique because the Alaska Native Ounalashka Corporation (p320), not the Federal Government, owns and manages it.

To learn about the 'Forgotten War,' begin at the **Aleutian WWII Visitor Center** (☎ 581-9944; 2716 Airport Beach Rd; adult/child $4/free; 🕒 10am-6pm Fri-Mon, from 1pm Tue-Thu), near the airport, in the original air control tower the military built in 1942. Downstairs, exhibits relive the Aleutian campaign, including the bombing of Dutch Harbor by the Japanese for two days and the Battle of Attu, the first battle on American soil since the War of 1812. Upstairs is the re-created air control tower, while in a theater you can watch documentaries about the war effort in Alaska.

Most of the park preserves Fort Schwatka, on **Mt Ballyhoo**, the highest coastal battery ever constructed in the US. Looming nearly 1000ft above the storm-tossed waters of the Bering Sea, the Army fort encompassed more than 100 concrete observation posts, command stations and other structures built to withstand earthquakes and 100mph winds. The gun mounts here are still among the best preserved in the country and include tunnels and bunkers that allowed gunners to cart ammunition from one side of the mountain to the other.

The 1634ft mountain of military artifacts is behind the airport and can be reached on foot or by vehicle via Ulakta Road, picked up half a mile north of the ferry terminal, along Ballyhoo Rd. If on foot, the gravel road is an hour's climb to the top, but the views of Unalaska Island on the way up, and on top, are excellent. Pick up the free *Fort Schwatka Self-Guided Tour* brochure at the museum.

An easier climb is **Bunker Hill**, also part of the national historic area. This coastal battery was known to the military as Hill 400, and was fortified with 155mm guns, ammunition magazines, water tanks, 22 Quonset huts and a concrete command post at the top. You can hike to the peak of Bunker Hill along a gravel road picked up just after crossing the bridge to Amaknak Island.

More war history can be found in Unalaska by following Bayview Rd to the southeast end of town. In a picturesque hillside graveyard along the bay is the **USS Northwestern Memorial**. Launched in 1889, the passenger and freight ship was retired in 1937, then repaired by the military in 1940 to serve as a floating bunkhouse. It was bombed during the attack on Dutch Harbor and burned for five days. In 1992, for the 50th anniversary of the event, the propeller was salvaged by divers and is now part of the memorial.

SITKA SPRUCE PARK

Within Dutch Harbor is this national historical landmark, along Biorka Drive, where the Russians planted Sitka Spruce in 1805. It's the oldest recorded afforestation project in North America. Three of the gnarly spruce are said to be the originals. The park also features interpretive displays and a short trail to an edge-of-the-cliff overlook.

EXPEDITION PARK

The number of bald eagles in and around Unalaska and Dutch Harbor is mind-boggling. There's so many birds that locals view them as scavengers, which they are by nature, rather than the majestic symbol of the USA. And because the islands are treeless, you can see them on the roofs of houses, on streetlights and even picking through dumpsters behind stores. The best place to photograph them up close and in a somewhat natural setting is Expedition Park, at the end of Bobby Storrs

Boat Harbor, off Gilman Rd. Because the park is perched above the harbor there are always a few birds resting in the stand of dead pines, and sometimes more than a dozen.

Activities

HIKING

Because of the treeless environment, hiking is easy here. And don't worry about bears – there aren't any.

Before hiking anywhere, even Mt Ballyhoo or Bunker Hill, you must obtain a permit (daily $6 per person and weekly $15) from the **Ounalashka Corporation** (☎ 581-1276; www.ounalashka.com; 400 Salmon Way; 8am-5pm Mon-Fri), in Dutch Harbor. Also call Unalaska's **Parks, Culture & Recreation Department** (PCR; ☎ 581-1297; 37 S 5th St; 9am-5pm Mon-Fri), which organizes hikes in summer for locals and visitors.

The area has few developed trails, but an enjoyable day can be spent hiking to **Uniktali Bay**, a round-trip of 8 to 10 miles. From Captains Bay Rd, turn east on a gravel road just before you pass Westward Cannery. Follow the road for a mile to its end; a foot trail continues along a stream. In 2 miles, the trail runs out, and you'll reach a lake in a pass between a pair of 2000ft peaks. Continue southeast to pick up a second stream, which empties into Uniktali Bay. The bay is an undeveloped stretch of shoreline and a great place to look for glass floats from Japanese fishing nets that wash ashore.

PADDLING

The many protected harbors, bays and islets of Unalaska Island make for ideal sea-kayaking conditions. The scenery is stunning and the wildlife plentiful. It is possible to encounter Steller's sea lions, sea otters and harbor porpoises. **Aleutian Adventure Sports** (☎ 581-4489; www.aleutianadventure.com) has kayak rentals for $69 and $89 per day for single and double kayaks respectively, as well as an introductory kayak class, for $75, and guided trips.

Tours

If you're planning to return with the ferry, a van tour is the best way to see a lot in your short stay. But book in advance if you can. The few tour operators in town are always overwhelmed when the ferry pulls in. The length, and thus the cost, of such tours depends on the ferry departure and the weather, but generally they last four hours and range from $60 to $75 per person.

Aleut Tours (☎ 581-1747) Tours with an emphasis on native culture.

our pick **Extra Mile Tours** (☎ 581-6171; www.unalaskadutchharbortour.com) The best of the bunch, operator Bobbie Lekanoff is also a very knowledgeable birder.

Mr Kab Tours (☎ 581-2000) Locals who talk more about themselves than what you're looking at.

Sleeping

Rooms are scarce in Dutch Harbor and nonexistent in Unalaska. It might pay to call the visitors center to see if any locals have started a B&B or are simply taking in travelers. On top of the prices listed following you have to add an 8% tax.

Ounalashka Corporation (☎ 581-1276; www.ounalashka.com; 400 Salmon Way; permits daily/weekly per person $6/15) This native corporation owns most of the land out of town and allows camping if you obtain a permit. A flat patch shielded from the strong winds is at a premium on the island, so the best places to pitch a tent tend to be along the beach. The closest to town is on the southwest corner of Bunker Hill (p319). Even better, but further away, is Summer Bay, 4 miles from Unalaska.

Unisea Inn (☎ 581-3844; 88 Salmon Way; s/d $99/110) Across the street from Dutch Harbor Mall, this 25-room inn is sandwiched between a shipyard and a fish-processing plant. Guests check in at the Grand Aleutian and are shuttled over, but be forewarned: it can get loud at times.

Grand Aleutian Hotel (☎ 581-3844, 866-581-3844; www.grandaleutian.com; 498 Salmon Way; s/d $164/184;) Crabbers have been hard on this 105-room hotel, the reason its rooms will be updated beginning in 2009. This is the only full-service, tourist-class place in town and the uninterested staff knows it. Still, the rooms are large and feature queen- or king-size beds, cable TV and coffeemakers.

Eating & Drinking

Amelia's (☎ 581-2800; Airport Beach Rd; breakfast $7-13, burgers $9-12, dinner $14-29; 6am-10pm) This Dutch Harbor restaurant does a little of everything, from breakfast and burgers to seafood and pasta, but the majority of its menu is Mexican, including almost a dozen types of burritos. Amazingly, none of them is stuffed with crab or halibut.

Crab Pot (☎ 581-3663; 5th St & Broadway Ave; sandwiches $8-13; 10am-10pm Mon-Fri) It's your choice at this delightful Unalaska deli; a landwich or a seawich. Go local and have a crab-and-avocado seawich.

Airport Restaurant (☎ 581-6007; breakfast & lunch $9-14, dinner $15-27; 9am-10:30pm Mon-Sat, to 10pm Sun) This restaurant would be popular even if it wasn't at an airport notorious for bad weather. For dinner you can go American, Asian or something from the sea, like king crab or sautéed mussels. It also has a bar if your plane is really late.

our pick **Harbor View Bar & Grill** (☎ 581-7246; 88 Salmon Way; pizza $18-29; 11am-10pm) Dutch Harbor's newest restaurant, in the Unisea Inn, has pizza, salads, pasta and the best sushi bar in a town that knows its sushi. All enjoyed to a view of the boat harbor.

Chart Room (☎ 866-581-3844; 498 Salmon Way; dinner $20-40; 6am-11pm, to 9:30pm Sun;) This is the best restaurant in the Aleutian Islands, and certainly the most expensive. It's on the 2nd floor of the Grand Aleutian Hotel and, surprisingly, has more meat on its menu than seafood. But it's best known for its Wednesday seafood buffet, featuring local halibut, salmon, shrimp and king crab, and great sushi. It's hard to imagine a $32 meal being a bargain, but for seafood lovers this one is.

Eagle Quality Center (2029 Airport Beach Rd; 7am-11pm) Dutch Harbor's best supermarket, with fresh produce, a bakery, a hot food bar and even a seating area.

Cape Cheerful Lounge (☎ 581-3844; 498 Salmon Way) The Grand Aleutian Hotel bar hops at night, and when the sun is out drinkers move to an outdoor deck.

Shopping

It's amazing how many *Deadliest Catch* buffs show up in Dutch Harbor looking for the Alaska Ship Supply hoodies that the fishing crews wear on the popular Discovery Channel show. You'll find them upstairs at **Alaska Ship Supply** (☎ 581-1284; www.alaskashipsupply.com; 1362 Ballyhoo Rd; 8am-8pm), just past the ferry terminal. An even better selection of Dutch Harbor logo clothing, raingear and other related commercial fishing gear can be seen at **LFS, Inc** (☎ 581-2178; 2315 Airport Beach Rd; 8am-8pm Mon-Sat, to 4pm Sun).

Getting There & Around

The airport is on Amaknak Island, 3 miles from Unalaska. The ferry terminal is even further north, off Ballyhoo Rd. Cab fare to downtown Unalaska costs $10 to $12 from the airport, or $14 to $16 from the ferry. There are a zillion cabs running all over Unalaska and Dutch Harbor, including **Aleutian Taxi** (☎ 581-1866).

To get out and see the island there are a couple of car rental companies, including **North Port Car Rental** (☎ 581-3880), which is located at the airport and has vehicles for $75 a day. A mountain bike is another way to get around as the extensive, lightly used dirt roads left over from the WWII buildup make for great riding. You can hire a mountain bike from **Aleutian Adventure Sports** (☎ 581-4489; daily/weekly $35/125).

Other than the once-a-month ferry, the only way of getting out of Unalaska and Dutch Harbor is flying. The town is serviced by **PenAir** (☎ 800-448-4226; www.penair.com) but you book the ticket through **Alaska Airlines** (☎ 800-252-7522; www.alaskaair.com). There are three to four flights daily and a one-way ticket is $500 to $600.

BRISTOL BAY

This is fish country. Bristol Bay is home to the world's largest run of red salmon, as well as the other four Pacific species – king, silver, chum and pink. During the summer, the spawning runs turn Dillingham into the world's salmon capital, and the departure point into a paradise of sportfishing. From June through September, anglers from around the world shell out several thousand dollars each to stay at exclusive fly-in fishing lodges scattered throughout the region.

For wilderness adventurers, the attraction is Wood-Tikchik State Park, the largest state park in the country and a great destination for a raft or kayak trip.

DILLINGHAM

pop 2405

Commercial fishing has made Dillingham the largest community in the Bristol Bay region. The first cannery was built in 1884 and today Icicle, Peter Pan, Trident and Unisea all operate fish-processing plants in the city, handling mostly salmon.

Dillingham serves as the jumping-off point for trips to Wood-Tikchik State Park and the region's numerous fishing lodges. The airport is located 2.5 miles west of town and the only place you can drive to is Lake Aleknagik, the southernmost lake in the Wood River chain, connected to Dillingham by a 23-mile gravel road that was built in 1960. At the end of the road you'll find **Lake Aleknagik State Recreation Site**, which has a free seven-site campground.

Information

Bristol Bay Area Health Corporation (☎ 842-5201; 6000 Kanakanak Rd; walk-in 8am-5pm Mon-Fri) Has walk-in and 24-hour emergency care.

Dillingham Library (☎ 842-5610; 348 D St; 10am-6pm Mon-Fri, to 2pm Sat) Offering free internet access in the same building as the Dillingham Museum and visitor center.

Dillingham Visitor Center (☎ 842-5115; 348 D St; 10am-6pm Mon-Fri, to 2pm Sat)

Wells Fargo (☎ 842-5284; 512 Seward St) Has an ATM.

Sleeping & Eating

Dillingham has a number of hotels and lodges, but the price of accommodations here is on the high side, partly because of the 10% bed tax.

Beaver Creek B&B (☎ 842-7335, 866-252-7335; www.dillinghamalaska.com; 1800 Birch Cr; per person per night $80; ☒) Four miles from town, this B&B has three rooms in a house and several cottages and cabins nearby.

Bristol Inn (☎ 842-2240, within Alaska 800-764-9704; 104 Main St; s/d $151/165) This place is pricey for what you get. Better to book a room at a B&B, which will throw in breakfast and free transport from the airport.

Besides the Bristol Inn, there are a handful of other restaurants including the **Muddy Rudder** (☎ 842-2634; 100 Main St; breakfast $9-17, dinner $19-37; 7am-9pm), the local favorite for breakfast.

Getting There & Away

Dillingham is serviced by **PenAir** (☎ 800-448-4226; www.penair.com) with four flights daily in the summer from Anchorage. A round-trip ticket costs from $450 to $550.

WOOD-TIKCHIK STATE PARK

At 2500 sq miles, Wood-Tikchik is the country's largest state park. Thirty miles north of Dillingham, the park preserves two large systems of interconnecting lakes that are the

DETOUR: PRIBILOF ISLANDS

The Pribilofs are a five-island archipelago marooned in the Bering Sea, 300 miles from Alaska's mainland and 750 miles from Anchorage. They're desolate, foggy and windswept but overrun with wildlife, making them a far-flung tourist attraction. The two tiny communities – St Paul (pop 447) and St George (pop 114) – are the world's largest indigenous Aleut villages, but the human numbers here pale in comparison to the staggering quantity of seals and birds.

The Pribilofs' charcoal-colored beaches host a mad scene each summer as a million fur seals, having spent the year at sea between California and Japan, swim ashore to breed and raise their young. The barking throng is the largest gathering of sea mammals in the world. Meanwhile, the islands' dizzying ocean-cliffs become home to extensive bird rookeries. More than 2.5 million seabirds, ranging from common murres and crested auklets to tufted puffins and cormorants, nest here, making the Pribilofs the largest seabird colony in the Northern Hemisphere. It's easy to reach the cliffs to photograph the birds, and blinds have been erected on beaches to observe wildlife. This is hard-core birding as more than 230 species of birds are sighted during the summer.

Because of the strict regulations and limited facilities, most travelers take package tours here. **St Paul Island Tours** (☎ 877-424-5637; www.alaskabirding.com) offers a variety of packages from Anchorage, including a three-day tour for $1456, which covers airfare, accommodations and transportation to the beaches and rookeries (but not meals).

The alternative, though not a whole lot cheaper, is to travel to the island on your own. **PenAir** (☎ 243-2323, 800-448-4426; www.penair.com) flies from Anchorage to St Paul for $946 (round-trip). The **King Eider Hotel** (☎ 546-2477; r per person $175), a series of converted trailer homes, has Spartan accommodations and shared baths, but will arrange for a tour guide if you request one.

Perhaps a more unique experience, which still allows you to see an immense amount of wildlife, is to travel independently to St George, the smaller and much less visited island. Since St George isn't that big (only 5 miles wide) you can hike to within view of the wildlife. Accommodations are available at the 10-room, shared-bath **St George Hotel** (☎ 272-9886; www.stgeorgetanaq.com; r per person $169), a designated national historical landmark, and PenAir will fly you there for $1029 round-trip. The **Aleutian Pribilof Islands Association** (www.stgeorgeaalaska.com) is a great resource for traveling to St George.

important spawning grounds for Bristol Bay's salmon. Wildlife in the park includes brown and black bears, beavers, moose, foxes and wolves. The fishing for arctic char, rainbow trout, dolly varden, grayling, salmon and northern pike is excellent.

With the exception of the 11 expensive fishing lodges in or just outside the park, Wood-Tikchik is almost totally undeveloped. You'll find some well-used campsites here and there, but no formal campgrounds and no trails. Even the park's ranger station is outside the park, at Lake Aleknagik.

For park information, contact **Wood-Tikchik State Park** (in Anchorage year-round ☎ 269-8698, in Dillingham late May-late Sep 842-2641; www.dnr.state.ak.us/parks/units/woodtik.htm).

Activities

The park is an ideal place for a wilderness canoe or kayak trip. **Fresh Water Adventures** (☎ 842-5060; www.freshwateradventure.com) rents out inflatable kayaks and canoes for $25 a day, or catarafts for $120 a day.

Wood River Lakes, in the park's southern half, are connected by shallow, swiftly moving rivers. For that reason, most parties are flown in and paddle out, returning to Dillingham via the Wood River. A popular spot to put in is at Lake Kulik. From there the paddle toward Dillingham is a trip of close to 140 miles requiring from 10 to 14 days. A drop-off at Lake Kulik costs around $1600 for the average party plus gear.

This route eliminates the need for a pick-up flight and is an easy paddle for most intermediate canoeists. However, the eight fishing lodges on these lakes all use powerboats in certain locations.

In the park's northern half, and much more remote than the Wood River Lakes, are **Tikchik Lakes**, a chain of six lakes. Flat-water kayaking is popular on these lakes, and those interested in river floating can get dropped off on Nishlik or Upnuk Lake and travel along the Tikchik River into Tikchik Lake. You can be picked up there or continue your journey by floating the Nuyakuk and Nushagak Rivers to one of several Alaska Native villages, where air-charter flights are available back to Dillingham. A per-party drop-off costs around $3100 to Nishlik Lake and $2800 to Upnuk Lake.

The upper lakes are more challenging and more costly to experience. But the scenery – mountains, pinnacle peaks and hanging valleys surrounding the lakes – is impressive, and there will be far less motorboat activity, if any at all.

The paddling season is from mid-June, when the lakes are finally free of ice and snow, until early October, when they begin to freeze up again. Be prepared for cool and rainy weather and pack plenty of mosquito repellent. Be cautious; sudden winds on the open lakes can create whitecap conditions, and white water may exist on many of the connecting streams.

Getting There & Away

To reach Wood-Tikchik State Park, contact any of the floatplane charter companies in Dillingham, including **Fresh Water Adventures** (☎ 842-5060; www.freshwateradventure.com), based at the Dillingham Airport.

Denali & the Interior

Mt McKinley, known to the native Athabascans as Denali or the Great One, presides regally over Alaska's vast and diverse interior. Her dominion stretches from lowland forests – sliced open by the numerous braided rivers that crisscross the region – to the towering snowcapped peaks and glaciers of the Alaska, Talkeetna and Wrangell ranges.

From her massive shoulders at more than 20,000ft, she weighs her strategy, sending her bishops and knights – the grizzly bear, wolf, coyote and fox – down past backpackers on a two-day trek through the gigantic national park that protects her flanks; past white-water paddlers challenging the rapids on the Susitna, Nenana, Yukon and Tanana Rivers; past modern-day gold prospectors, hard-line greenies, hunters, fishermen and about five billion mosquitoes. Beneath Denali's ever-watching eyes, these subjects live in constant counterpoint, constant flux: the cycle of life swirling like a violent gale through this massive stretch of earth.

For the traveler, things here are so big that getting started can be a bit daunting. But the triangular road system provides easy access to every corner – even for travelers on threadbare shoestring budgets.

HIGHLIGHTS

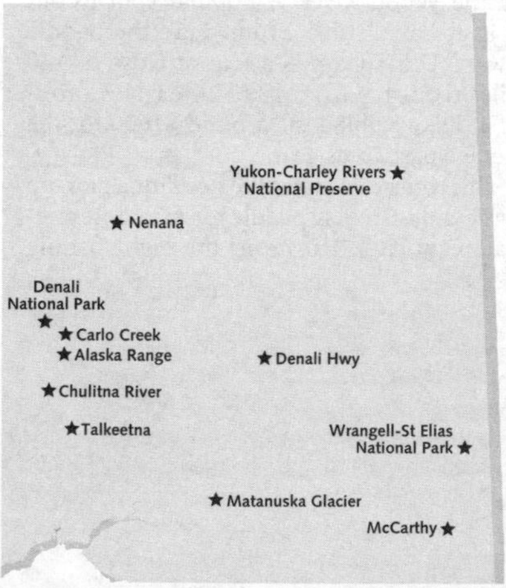

- **Greatest chance of seeing wildlife** – taking 'the tour' on the Denali National Park road (p332) before getting dropped off for a fly-by-the-seat-of-your-pants backcountry adventure (p337)
- **Smartest place to get a flat** – driving the Denali Hwy (p353), ideally just a few hundred feet from the campgrounds at Tangle Lakes (p356)
- **Biggest challenge, most solitude** – leaving the off-beat 200yd *past*-the-end-of-the-road community of McCarthy (p370) as you head into the backcountry of Wrangell-St Elias National Park (p369)
- **Best way to go with the flow** – paddling a canoe through Yukon-Charley Rivers National Preserve (p363)
- **Easiest way to get 'loaded'** – picking a date for the Nenana Ice Classic (p353), finding gold on the Chulitna River (p348), playing 'cornhole' at Carlo Creek's Panorama Pizza Pub (p342), getting blitzed at Talkeetna's Fairview Inn (p350)
- **Most righteous reason to get high** – swerving madly in a tiny Cessna as you take a flight-seeing tour of Denali National Park (p348), strapping on crampons to explore the Matanuska Glacier (p367), or groovin' out at one of the region's numerous folk festivals (p352)

Land & Climate

In this region of mountains and spacious valleys, the climate varies greatly and the weather can change on a dime.

In January temperatures can sink to -60°F for days at a time; in July they often soar above 90°F. The norm for the summer is long days with temperatures of 60°F to 70°F. However, it's common for Denali National Park to experience at least one snowfall in the lowlands between June and August.

Here, more than anywhere else in the state, it's important to have warm clothes while still being able to strip down to a T-shirt and hiking shorts. Most of the area's 10in to 15in of annual precipitation comes in the form of summer showers, with cloudy conditions common, especially north of Mt McKinley. In Denali National Park, Mt McKinley tends to be hidden by clouds more often than not.

Mountains are everywhere. The formidable Alaska Range creates a jaggy spine through the interior's midsection, while smaller ranges – the Chugach, Talkeetna and Wrangell to the south and the White Mountains to the north – sit on the flanks. From each of these mountain ranges run major river systems. Spruce and birch predominate in the lowland valleys with their tidy lakes. It is here and up on the broad tundra meadows that spectacular wildflowers show their wares during summer months. Wildfire also plays its role here, wiping out vast swaths of forest nearly every summer.

History

If archaeologists are correct, Interior Alaska was the corridor through which the rest of the continent was peopled, as waves of hunter-gatherers migrated across the Bering Land Bridge to points south. Ancestors of the region's present Native group, the Athabascans, are thought to have been here at least 6000 years.

It wasn't until the 1800s that the first white people began to trickle in. At first, the newcomers were mainly traders: Russians, who established posts along the lower Yukon and Kuskokwim Rivers, and Britons, who began trading at Fort Yukon, on the upper Yukon River, in the 1840s. Next came prospectors, whose discoveries transformed this region. The first major gold rush in the Interior was in the Fortymile district in the 1880s; similar rushes subsequently gave rise to many Interior communities. At the turn of the 20th century Talkeetna began as a supply center for gold miners working the Susitna River region. Miners took up permanent residence in Eagle, on the Canadian border, in 1898, and in nearby Chicken around the same time. Kantishna, in Denali National Park, got its start from a gold rush in 1905. Copper originally drew settlers to what is now the Interior's other major national park, Wrangell-St Elias: in 1900 some of the world's richest veins led to the birth of Kennecott and McCarthy.

Transportation projects brought the next wave of growth. In 1914 Congress agreed to fund the building of the USA's northernmost railroad, from Seward to Fairbanks. At the peak of construction, 4500 workers labored along the route, and their base camps became boomtowns. In 1915 Talkeetna was made the headquarters of the Alaska Engineering Commission, which was responsible for pushing the line north to the Tanana River. From there, Nenana – previously just a trading post – became the base for the anchor leg to Fairbanks.

Two decades later, during WWII, the building of the Alcan had the same effect on the eastern Interior: both Tok and Delta Junction got their start as highway construction camps. Another three decades after *that* came the biggest undertaking the Interior has ever seen: the laying of the $8 billion Trans-Alaska Pipeline, which transects Alaska, paralleling Richardson Hwy before running northward to the Arctic Ocean.

Parks & Protected Lands

Alaska's Interior holds two marquee national parks and one impressive national preserve. See www.nps.gov/state/ak for more information on the region's national parks.

The big name here, of course, is Denali National Park (p327), which is blessed with the continent's mightiest mountain, abundant megafauna such as moose and bear, and enough untrammeled backcountry to flee the gazillions of tourists who flock here aboard RVs, trains and tour buses. Crowding is less a problem in gargantuan Wrangell-St Elias National Park (p369), as it is less accessible and there are no trails into the park. To access it, you'll need to hike for a day or two, or get dropped off by bush plane. Located in the region's southeast corner, this preserve has even more peaks, glaciers and

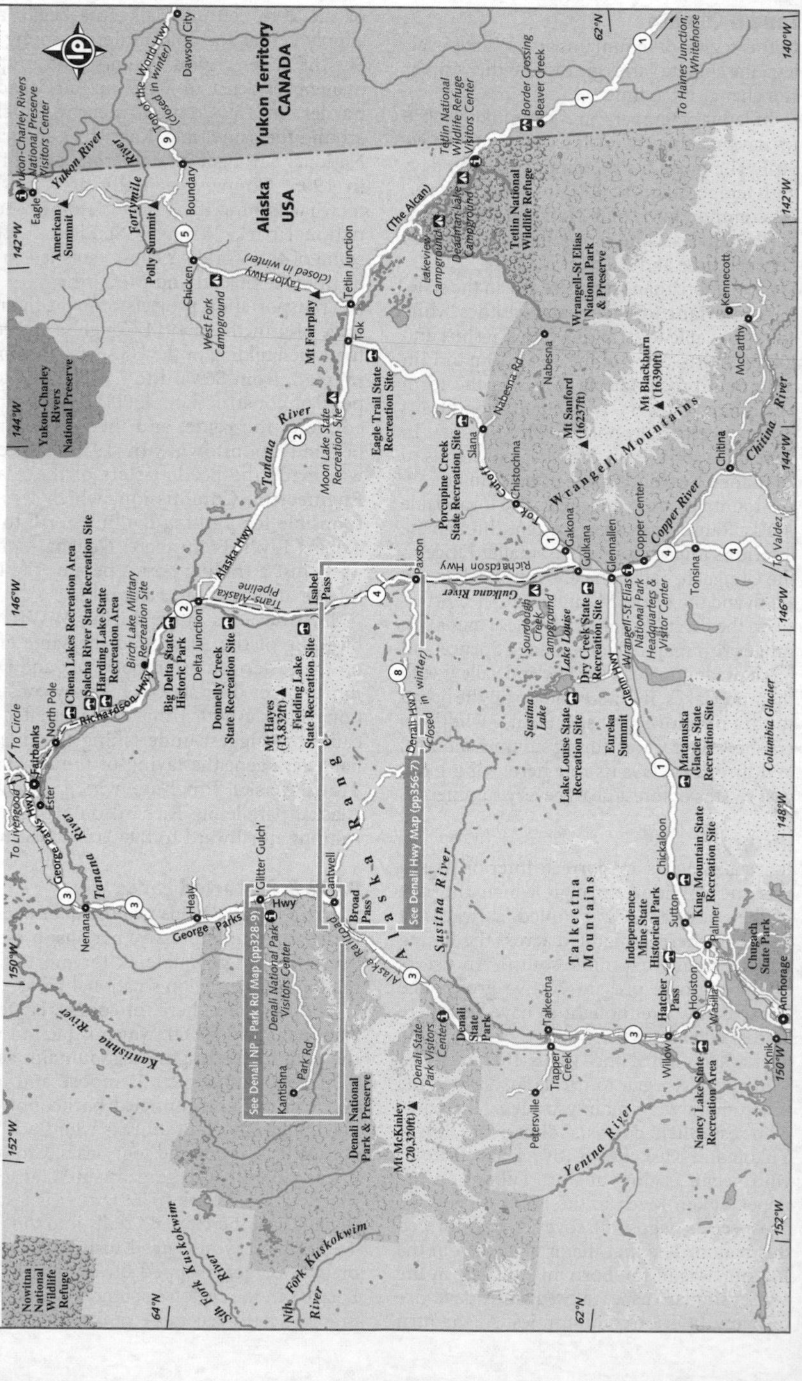
THE INTERIOR
Yukon Territory
CANADA
Alaska
USA
Dawson City
Top of the World Hwy (closed in winter)
Boundary
Eagle
Yukon-Charley Rivers National Preserve Visitors Center
Yukon River
American Summit
Fortymile River
Polly Summit
Chicken
West Fork Campground
Taylor Hwy (closed in winter)
Mt Fairplay
Tetlin Junction
Tok
Yukon-Charley Rivers National Preserve
(The Alcan)
Lakeview Campground
Deadman Lake Campground
Tetlin National Wildlife Refuge Visitors Center
Tetlin National Wildlife Refuge
Border Crossing
Beaver Creek
To Haines Junction; Whitehorse
Eagle Trail State Recreation Site
Moon Lake State Recreation Site
Tanana River
Nabesna Rd
Nabesna
Slana
Wrangell-St Elias National Park & Preserve
Mt Sanford (16237ft)
Mt Blackburn (16390ft)
Wrangell Mountains
Kennecott
McCarthy
Chitina
Chitina River
Porcupine Creek State Recreation Site
Tok Cutoff
Chistochina
Gakona
Gulkana
Glennallen
Copper Center
Copper River
Tonsina
To Valdez
Paxson
Richardson Hwy
Gulkana River
Sourdough Creek Campground
Lake Louise
Dry Creek State Recreation Site
Wrangell-St Elias National Park Headquarters & Visitor Center
Glenn Hwy
Alaska Hwy
Isabel Pass
Trans-Alaska Pipeline
Delta Junction
Big Delta State Historic Park
Donnelly Creek State Recreation Site
Fielding Lake State Recreation Site
Mt Hayes (13,832ft)
Birch Lake Military Recreation Site
Richardson Hwy
Chena Lakes Recreation Area
Salcha River State Recreation Site
Harding Lake State Recreation Area
North Pole
To Circle
Fairbanks
Ester
To Livengood
George Parks Hwy
Tanana River
Nenana
Healy
Glitter Gulch
Cantwell
Broad Pass
Alaska Range
Denali Hwy (closed in winter)
See Denali Hwy Map (pp356-7)
Susitna Lake
Lake Louise State Recreation Site
Eureka Summit
Matanuska Glacier State Recreation Site
Columbia Glacier
Talkeetna Mountains
Chickaloon
King Mountain State Recreation Site
Independence Mine State Historical Park
Sutton
Palmer
Chugach State Park
Anchorage
Hatcher Pass
Houston
Wasilla
Willow
Knik
Nancy Lake State Recreation Area
Susitna River
Alaska Railroad
Denali National Park Visitors Center
See Denali NP - Park Rd Map (pp328-9)
Park Rd
Kantishna
Denali National Park & Preserve
Denali State Park Visitors Center
Denali State Park
Talkeetna
Trapper Creek
Petersville
Mt McKinley (20,320ft)
Kantishna River
Yentna River
Sth Fork Kuskokwim River
Nth Fork Kuskokwim River
Nowitna National Wildlife Refuge
150 km
90 miles
64°N
62°N
140°W
142°W
144°W
146°W
148°W
150°W
152°W

wild creatures than Denali, with a fraction of the visitors and infrastructure.

Finally, up in the Interior's northeast is Yukon-Charley Rivers National Preserve (p362), located at the nexus of two of the state's legendary waterways, and experienced mainly by folks paddling the Yukon River.

But this is Alaska, and you don't need to go to a national park to experience nature: it's simply everywhere. There are numerous state parks (www.dnr.state.ak.us/parks) and recreation areas – like Denali State Park (p351) and the Matanuska Glacier (p367) – as well as the vast untrammeled lands controlled by the **Bureau of Land Management** (BLM; www.blm.gov/ak) and the **US Forest Service** (USFS; www.fs.fed.us/r10).

Dangers & Annoyances

Getting lost in the backcountry is a real possibility – especially in the national parks, national forest and BLM areas where there are few trails – so come prepared: carry a compass, topographic map, GPS (optional) and enough food and water to get you by for a few extra days. More important than these tools are the skills to use them. Wildlife encounters are also a concern. Long sleeves and light pants will help fend off the Alaskan state bird, the mosquito, and backcountry travelers should follow our bear tips (p424). Glacier travel and mountaineering are dangerous endeavors. If you don't know how to self-arrest and perform a crevasse rescue (or don't know what these things are) you should go with a qualified guide.

Getting There & Around

Compared to most places in the developed world, the Interior is a trackless hinterland; for Alaska, however, it's got roads galore. Highways such as George Parks, the Alcan, Richardson, Tok Cutoff & Glenn, Denali and Taylor crisscross the place, making it a good area to own or rent an auto. Both the road to Eagle and the Denali Hwy are closed during winter months.

A few long-haul bus companies keep busy here, most notably **Alaska Direct Bus Line** (☎ 800-770-6652; www.alaskadirectbusline.com), traveling the Alcan and Tok Cutoff & Glenn Hwy, and **Alaska/Yukon Trails** (☎ 800-770-7275, 800-770-2267; www.alaskashuttle.com), covering George Parks and Taylor Hwys, and the Alcan.

The corridor from Anchorage to Fairbanks is, in Alaskan parlance, the Railbelt, traversed daily in summer by the **Alaska Railroad** (☎ 265-2494, 800-544-0552; www.alaskarailroad.com). The train is a mellow, scenic alternative to driving, with depots at two of the Interior's most-visited destinations: Talkeetna and Denali National Park.

Of course, much of Alaska's heartland *isn't* accessible by road or rail – and for that, there's the old Great Land standby: the bush plane. Even small Interior towns usually have airstrips and scheduled flights, and the region's national parks are normally abuzz with flightseeing excursions. Beyond this, there's snowmachines, canoes, rafts, dogsleds, bicycles, hitchhiking (surprisingly easy and common throughout the state), and the good old two-legged trot.

DENALI NATIONAL PARK

For many travelers, Denali National Park is the beginning and end of their Alaskan adventure. And why shouldn't it be? This is probably your best chance in the Interior (if not in the entire state) of seeing a grizzly bear, a moose, a caribou, and maybe even a fox or wolf. Plus, you get the massive arching landscape of the sub-Arctic wilderness, which drops down reverentially below Mt McKinley (known to most Alaskans as Denali) – North America's highest peak and an overwhelming sight when caught on a clear day. At 20,320ft, the peak of this massif is almost 4 miles high, but what makes it stunning is that it rises from an elevation of just 2000ft – that's over 18,000 feet of rock, glacier, ice and snow. It's no wonder the native Athabascans dubbed the peak Denali (the Great One).

But it's not just this signature mountain that makes Denali National Park special. The park is also home to three-dozen species of mammal, ranging from brown (grizzly) bear, lynx, marmot and Dall sheep to fox and snowshoe hare, and 167 different bird species, including the impressive golden eagle, tundra swan, rock ptarmigan, jaeger and great horned owl. The best thing is that here in Denali, unlike most wilderness areas in the country, you don't have to be a backpacker to view this wildlife – people who never sleep in a tent have excellent, once-in-a-lifetime opportunities to get a close look at these magnificent creatures roaming free in their natural habitat.

And, for those with a bit more time and the desire to get further into the wild, there are vast expanses of untracked wilderness to explore – more than six million acres of it to be exact. That's more landmass than the US state of Massachusetts.

HISTORY

The Athabascan people used what is now called Denali National Park primarily as hunting grounds, but there were just a few temporary camps here, and it wasn't until gold was found near Kantishna in 1905 that the area really began to see development. With the gold stampede came the big-game hunters. Things weren't looking very good for this amazing stretch of wilderness until a noted hunter and naturalist, Charles Sheldon, came to town.

Sheldon, stunned by the destruction, mounted a campaign to protect the area. The result was Mt McKinley National Park. In 1923, when the railroad arrived, 36 visitors enjoyed the splendor of the new park. Later, as a result of the 1980 Alaska National Interest Lands Conservation Act, the park was enlarged by 4 million acres, and renamed Denali National Park and Preserve.

Nowadays visitors come here in droves; the park receives around 400,000 of them annually. The National Park Service (NPS) has a never-ending job trying to keep all those people from overrunning the park and destroying its wilderness character, while still ensuring that each is able to get some kind of quality experience.

Unique visitor-management strategies have been created at the park, and generally they've been successful. As a result, Denali National Park is still the great wilderness it was 10 or 20 years ago. The entrance area has changed but the park itself hasn't, and a brown bear meandering on a tundra ridge still gives the same quiet thrill as it did when the park first opened nine decades ago.

ORIENTATION

The park encompasses both the north and south flanks of the Alaska Range, 237 miles from Anchorage and about half that distance from Fairbanks. The George Parks Hwy forms its eastern boundary from just north of

DENALI NATIONAL PARK – PARK ROAD

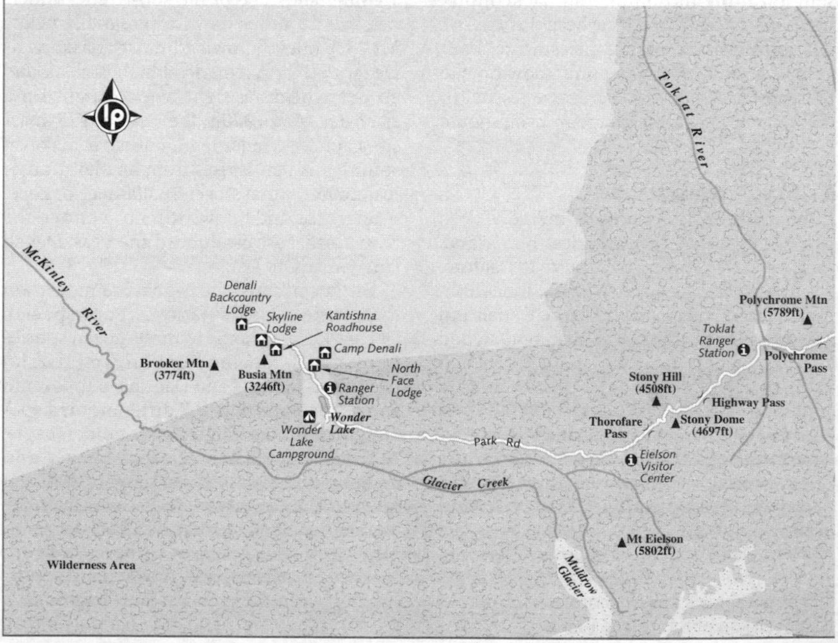

Talkeetna clear to Healy. It sprawls westward to the headwaters of the Kuskokwim River.

In all this wilderness there's only one road: the 92-mile Park Rd – note that only the first 14 miles are open to private vehicles, after that, you'll need to take a bus, bike or walk. To get to the park, exit west at Mile 237 of George Parks Hwy, a mile south of Denali Park's main lodging and business district, known locally as Glitter Gulch. The park entrance area, where most visitors congregate, extends a scant 4 miles up Park Rd. The shuttle and tour buses taking visitors into the park depart from this area, and the park headquarters, visitor center and main campground are all here.

Almost immediately on Park Rd you'll come to Riley Creek Campground, the park's largest, most developed campground. Also here is Riley Creek Mercantile, a small store and shower-house serving the campground. Across Park Rd from the store is one end of Jonesville Trail, a handy shortcut for pedestrians heading toward Glitter Gulch.

Heading west a few hundred yards on Park Rd brings you to the Wilderness Access Center (WAC, p331), at Mile 0.5. Here you'll pay your park entrance fee, arrange campground and bus bookings and join the buses that lead into the park center. In a trailer across the parking lot is the Backcountry Information Center (BIC, p331), where backpackers get backcountry permits and bear-proof food containers.

Past the WAC, Park Rd crosses the Alaska Railroad tracks and reaches a traffic circle at Mile 1.5. Arc right from the circle and you'll come to the Murie Science and Learning Center, where you can learn about ongoing research in the park; follow the circle left for the Denali Visitor Center, which has extensive displays and where the rangers will field every question imaginable.

Just next door is the extensive, cafeteria-style restaurant Morino Grill, and the adjoining Denali Bookstore. Also nearby is the train station, where the Alaska Railroad stops on its run between Anchorage and Fairbanks.

Another 2 miles beyond the traffic circle, Park Rd comes to Park Headquarters, the NPS administration office. It's of interest to visitors because it is the site of the park's sled-dog kennels.

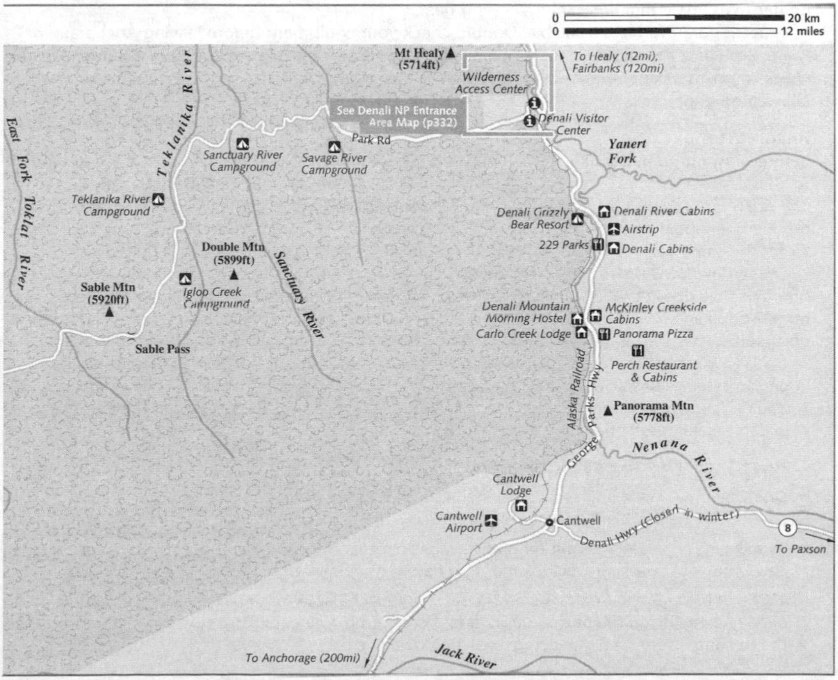

DENALI PLANNING GUIDE

Much of Alaska can be experienced by the seat of your pants, but due to Denali National Park's fleeting summer season, overwhelming popularity and the consequent regulations instituted to protect it, it pays to be prepared before coming here. And you should probably begin making your reservations at least six months in advance if you plan on staying in a park campsite, and at least three months in advance for accommodation outside the park.

When to Come

From late June to late August, despite cool, cloudy conditions and drizzle, Denali's campgrounds are full, its road is busy with shuttle buses and its entrance area is fist-to-jowl with tourists.

The hordes disappear once you're in the backcountry, and aren't an issue in the 'frontcountry' in early June and September. The latter month can be pleasant; not only are the visitors thinning out but so are the bugs. This is also when there are the clearest skies and most brilliant autumn foliage. However, shuttle buses (your ticket into the backcountry) stop running in the second week of September – bike it baby! The winners of a four-day vehicle lottery (held the previous July) follow, when 400 private cars a day are allowed entry. Then the road closes to all traffic until the following May. By late September the snow has usually arrived and another backpacking season has come and gone.

Winter visitation is the lowest of the year, so if you can handle -40°F and 4½ hours of daylight you'll have the place almost to yourself. Riley Creek Campground stays open in winter and camping is free, though the water and sewage facilities don't operate. Most area lodges are closed, but you might try Healy. You can use the unplowed Park Rd and the rest of the park for cross-country skiing and snowshoeing (bring your own equipment, as rentals are unavailable) or dogsledding. EarthSong Lodge (p343) offers several different dogsled adventures in winter.

What to Bring

Don't arrive in Denali expecting to outfit an expedition once you get there. Save for one small shop in Glitter Gulch (Denali Mountain Works, p331) and a tiny nook in the Wilderness Access Center (WAC, p331), nobody sells camping gear.

Groceries are even less available. Double-check your equipment before leaving Anchorage or Fairbanks. For a list of suggested backpacking items, see p89, or peruse the backcountry-gear checklist on the Denali National Park website. And, you shouldn't bring Rover, as dogs aren't allowed on park trails.

Reservations

Before showing up in Denali it's worthwhile to secure advanced reservations for campsites and, to a lesser degree, shuttle buses. Do so through the **Denali National Park Reservation Service** (☎ 272-7275, in the USA 800-622-7275; www.reservedenali.com). Payment is by credit card. You can reserve online for the following year beginning December 1; phone reservations start February 15 for the same year.

Sites in five of Denali's six campgrounds can be reserved in advance. Sanctuary River is the only site that doesn't take advance reservations – check in at the WAC. The campgrounds are hugely popular, so visitors without advance reservations will likely have difficulty getting a site on a walk-in basis.

Up to 65% of bus seats are available through advance reservation; the other 35% are set aside for in-person reservations at the WAC. The latter can be made no more than two days in advance.

You can only reserve backcountry permits 24 hours in advance (p337). For the itinerant souls who don't make reservations in advance, this may be your best bet for staying in the park.

A Few Itineraries to get you Started

- **One Day** If you have only a day in Denali National Park, there's only one option: taking the park bus to Eielson Visitor Center (eight hours round-trip).
- **Two Days** Try to get a permit for an overnight backpacking trip. If you don't want to backpack, you could certainly day hike for two days (or two months!).
- **Three or More Days** With this amount of time you'll be able to go backpacking or get in a lot of day hiking. If you tire of the tundra and can afford it, you could also take a raft trip down the Nenana River or a flightseeing excursion over the park.

Past Park Headquarters, Park Rd leads another 80-odd miles west into the heart of the park. It ends at a privately owned island of land called Kantishna, an old gold-mining enclave that was outside the park's original boundary but was enveloped by park additions in 1980.

WHERE TO STAY

Back out on George Parks Hwy and heading north, you'll almost immediately cross the Nenana River into **Glitter Gulch** (p342) a rather unattractive road-front strip accommodating packaged-vacation folk.

But for accommodations, you are better staying in a **park campground** (p340), anywhere in the **backcountry** (p337), **McKinley Village** (p341) – five miles south of Park Rd on George Parks Hwy – or 12 miles south in the ever-so-funky **Carlo Creek** area (p341). This is a great area to escape the crowds, but you'll need a vehicle unless you stay at the hostel, which runs four shuttles per day to the WAC.

Four very expensive lodges can be found in **Kantishna** (p340), or the budget minded can stay 12 miles north of the park entrance in **Healy** (p343).

INFORMATION

BOOKSTORES

Denali Bookstore (Mile 1.5 Park Rd; ⌚ 8am-8pm) Across from the Denali Visitor Center. It has field guides, topographic maps, coffee-table books and Alaskan literature.

INTERNET ACCESS

Black Bear Coffee House (☎ 683-1656; Mile 238.5 George Parks Hwy; per 15 min $3; ⌚ 6:30am-10pm) In Glitter Gulch.

LAUNDRY

Riley Creek Mercantile (☎ 683-9246; Mile 0.2 Park Rd; ⌚ 7am-11pm) Showers ($4) and coin-op laundry facilities.

MEDICAL SERVICES

Healy Clinic (☎ 683-2211; Healy Spur Rd) In the Tri-Valley Community Center, 13 miles north of the park and a half mile east of George Parks Hwy.

Canyon Clinic (☎ 683-4433; Mile 238.8 George Parks Hwy) Only open during summer months.

MONEY

Park Mart Store (☎ 683-2548; ⌚ 7:30am-10:30pm) In the heart of Glitter Gulch, this gas-station-cum-grocery-store-cum-liquor-store has an ATM. The closest full-service banks are in Fairbanks and on George Parks Hwy at Talkeetna Spur Rd junction.

OUTDOOR GEAR & SUPPLIES

Denali Mountain Works (☎ 683-1542; Mile 239 George Parks Hwy; ⌚ 9am-9pm) Affiliated with Too-loó-uk River Guides, this jam-packed Glitter Gulch store can sell you just about anything you'd need for the backcountry. It also rents tents, stoves and other outdoor gear.

POST & COMMUNICATIONS

As of 2008 the post office was still housed in a trailer next to Riley Creek Campground. It may end up elsewhere when all the new construction dust settles.

TOURIST INFORMATION

Backcountry Information Center (BIC; ☎ 683-9510; Mile 0.5 Park Rd; ⌚ 9am-6pm) If you want to overnight in Denali's backcountry you'll need to come to the BIC, just across the parking lot from the WAC. Here, rangers can explain the backcountry quota system, help you find an available backcountry 'unit' that matches your interests and skills, and issue you with the free backcountry permit.

Denali Visitor Center (☎ 683-2294; www.nps.gov/dena; Mile 1.5 Park Rd; ⌚ 8am-6pm) Officially opened in 2005, this 14,000 sq ft, $5 million facility is the place to come for an executive summary of Denali National Park. Upstairs there's a giant table-top relief map giving you the lay of the land; downstairs there are museum-quality displays on the area's natural and human history; and every half hour in the theater the beautifully photographed, unnarrated film *Heartbeats of Denali* provides a peek at the park's wildlife and scenery. Near the building's entrance is a streamlined selection of park literature, including the NPS' indispensable *Alpenglow* booklet, which functions as a user's manual to Denali. At peak times, the two staffers at the info desk are swamped with queries, but if you're willing to wait they can answer any question you dream up.

Murie Science & Learning Center (☎ 683-1269; Mile 1.5 Park Rd; ⌚ 9am-5pm) With some fascinating hands-on exhibits in its front lobby, this is the place to come for information on research taking place in the park. It also serves as Denali's winter visitor center. There are science talks at 10 and 11am every Tuesday, Wednesday, Saturday and Sunday.

Wilderness Access Center (WAC; ☎ 683-9274; Mile 0.5 Park Rd; ⌚ 5am-8pm) This place, which used to be Denali's main visitor center, still maintains a general-purpose info desk. The WAC's main function, however, is as the park's transport hub and campground-reservation center. You'll also pay the park-entrance fee here: $10/20 per person/family, which is good for seven days. Finally, there are espressos, muffins and other last-minute snacks,

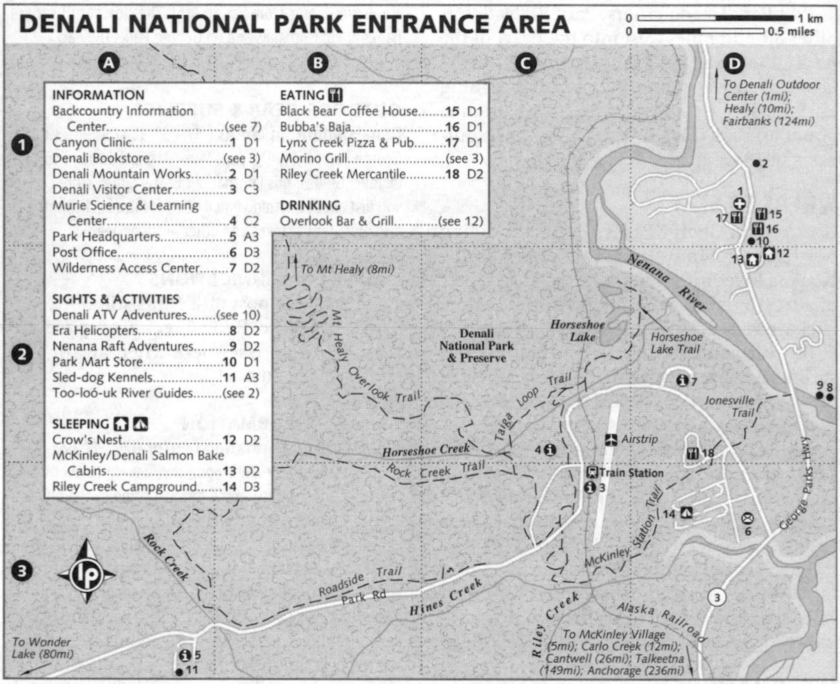

and a tiny gear store with freeze-dried meals, mosquito repellent, camping gas and so on.

DANGERS & ANNOYANCES

Be bear conscious, but remember that in the park's history, no visitor has ever been killed by a bear. Rather, most tourist fatalities here are at the hands of frigid, snowmelt-swollen waterways. If your hiking route intersects a river that's thigh-high or deeper, scout for a broad, braided, shallow place to ford, or time your crossing for early morning, when meltwaters typically subside. Undo the waistbelt on your pack so it won't pin you underwater, face upstream, and, if possible, use a walking stick to help you stagger across. Getting lost is also an issue. When traveling in the backcountry, bring along a compass and topo map, and, for God's sake, know how to use them.

SIGHTS & ACTIVITIES

Park Road

The Park Road begins at George Parks Hwy and winds 92 miles through the heart of the park, ending at Kantishna, an old mining settlement and the site of several wilderness lodges. Early on, park officials envisaged the onset of bumper-to-bumper traffic jams along this road and wisely closed almost all of it to private vehicles. With few exceptions, motorists can drive only to a parking area along the Savage River at Mile 14, a mile beyond the Savage River Campground. To venture further along the road you must walk, bike, be part of a concessionaire-run tour, or, most popularly, take a park shuttle or camper bus.

If you're planning to spend the day riding the buses (it's an eight-hour round-trip to the Eielson Visitor Center – the most popular day trip in the park), pack plenty of food and drink. It can be a long, dusty ride, and in the park there are only services at the Toklat Ranger Station and Eielson Visitor Center. Carry a park map so you know where you are and what ridges or riverbeds appeal to you for hiking.

SHUTTLE BUSES

Shuttle buses are aimed at wildlife watchers and day hikers. They aren't fancy, comfortable, high-tech wonders but big, clunky school-bus-style affairs. On board, passengers armed with binoculars and cameras scour the terrain for animals, most of which are so accustomed to the rambling buses that they rarely run and hide. When someone spots something and yells 'stop!' the driver pulls over for viewing and picture taking. The drivers are concessionaire employees, not NPS naturalists, but they provide unofficial natural history information en route. Some are better at this than others. The best wildlife and landscape viewing is from the bus's east side (on passengers' left on your way into the park, and on the passengers' right side on your way back).

Day hikers don't need a backcountry permit and can get off shuttle buses anywhere along Park Rd. After hiking, produce your bus-ticket stub and flag down the next bus that comes along. (Due to space considerations, you might have to wait a bus or two during peak season.) Many park visitors hop on and off buses several times in one day.

Certain buses head into the park as early as 5:30am; the last ones are back by around 10:35pm. It's wise to reserve a seat as far in advance as possible (see p330). The best wildlife watching is on the first morning bus. The cost varies based on how far you're riding: free to Savage River (Mile 14), $22.75 as far as Polychrome Pass (Mile 47) and Toklat River (Mile 53), $29.25 to the Eielson Visitor Center (Mile 66), $40 to Wonder Lake (Mile 85) and $43.75 to Kantishna. There's also a three-for-two pass, allowing three days of travel for the price of two. Children 14 and under ride the bus free, and 15 to17 year olds get it for half price.

CAMPER BUSES

The alternative to the shuttle buses are the less crowded, informal camper buses, aimed at ferrying overnight campers, backpackers and cyclists, and offering ample space to stow gear. To take these buses you must have a campsite or backcountry unit reserved along Park Rd, or be toting a bicycle. If you don't have a campground booking, you can't ride *in* on the camper bus, but you can probably hitch a ride *back* on one (a recommended course of action). The buses cost $29.25 to anywhere along the road. As with shuttles, it's good to reserve as far ahead as possible. Children 14 and under ride free, while 15 to 17 year olds get it for half price.

POINTS OF INTEREST

Mt McKinley is not visible from the park entrance or the nearby campgrounds and hotel. Your first glimpse of it comes between Mile 9 and Mile 11 of Park Rd, if you're blessed with a clear day. (The rule of thumb stressed by the NPS rangers is that Mt McKinley is hidden two out of every three days, but that's a random example – it could be clear for a week and then hidden for the next month.) While the 'Great One' might not be visible for most of the first 15 miles, this is the best stretch to spot moose because of the proliferation of spruce and especially willow, the animal's favorite food.

From **Savage River** (Mile 14) – which has an established trail alongside the river – the road dips into the **Sanctuary and Teklanika River valleys**, and Mt McKinley disappears behind the foothills. Both these rivers are in excellent hiking areas, and three of the five backcountry campgrounds lie along them. **Sanctuary River Campground** (Mile 22) is the most scenic, and it's a good base camp for hiking up Primrose Ridge.

The **Igloo Creek Campground** (Mile 34; see p340) lies among some spruce woods along the creek, and is the unofficial beginning of 'bear country.' From here you can make an easy day hike into the Igloo and Cathedral Mountains to spot Dall sheep, and maybe even wolves.

After passing through the canyon formed by the Igloo and Cathedral Mountains, the road ascends to 3880ft **Sable Pass** (Mile 38.5). The canyon and surrounding mountains are excellent places to view Dall sheep, while the pass is known as a prime habitat for Toklat brown bears. Given the prevalence of brown bear, the area around Sable Pass was closed to hikers and backpackers when this book went to press. From here, the road drops to the bridge over the **East Fork Toklat River** (Mile 44). Hikers can trek from the bridge along the riverbanks both north and south.

Polychrome Pass Overlook (Mile 47) is a rest stop for the shuttle buses. This scenic area, at 3500ft, has views of the Toklat River to the south. The alpine tundra above the road is good for hiking, as you can scramble up ridges that lead north and south of the rest-stop shelter.

Folks on the shuttle bus normally stop at the **Toklat River Contact Station** (Mile 53; 9am-7pm) on the way back. There are a few displays and some books for sale, as well as scopes to check out Dall sheep on the neighboring hills.

On the far side of Thorofare Pass (3900ft), **Eielson Visitor Center** (Mile 66; 9am-7pm) is the most common turning-around point for day-trippers taking the shuttle or tour bus to visit the park by wheel (an eight-hour round-trip affair). The 7400-sq-ft facility cost around $9.2 million to build, and features several 'green' design elements – solar and hydroelectric power, transplanted tundra mats on the roof deck and a low-slung architectural profile that blends well with the landscape. Finished in 2008, this remote outpost has some interesting exhibits on natural history of the region, a massive panorama of Mt McKinley to give you an idea of the mountain's topography, and ginormous windows for viewing the mountain herself. There are toilets here, but no food. Plans are in the works to have ranger-led hikes from the center, and as of press time a short nature trail had already been completed. Several day and overnight hikes are possible from the Eielson area, including one around Mt Eielson and another to Muldrow Glacier.

Past Eielson, Park Rd drops to the valley below, passing a sign for **Muldrow Glacier** (Mile 74.4). At this point, the glacier lies about a mile to the south, and the terminus of the 32-mile ice floe is clearly visible, though you might not recognize it because the ice is covered with a mat of plant life. If the weather is cloudy and Mt McKinley and the surrounding peaks are hidden, the final 20 miles of the bus trip will be a ride through rolling tundra and past numerous small lakes known as kettle ponds. Study the pools of water carefully to spot beavers or waterfowl.

Wonder Lake Campground (Mile 84) is a place where the beauty of Mt McKinley is doubled on a clear day, with the mountain's reflection on the lake's surface.

Ironically, the heavy demand for the 28 sites at Wonder Lake and the numerous overcast days caused by Mt McKinley itself prevent the majority of visitors from ever seeing this remarkable panorama. If you do experience the reddish sunset on the summit reflecting off the still waters of the lake, cherish the moment.

The campground is on a low rise above the lake's south end and is only 26 miles from the mountain. Those who come on the early buses can gain another hour at the lake by getting off and picking up a later bus for the trip back. Keep in mind that those famous McKinley-reflected-in-the-lake photos are taken along the northeast shore, 2 miles beyond the campground, so you might want to save some time for hiking.

Kantishna (Mile 90) is mainly a destination for people staying in the area's private lodges. The buses turn around here, and begin the long trip back to the WAC.

WILDLIFE WATCHING

Because hunting has never been allowed in the park, professional photographers refer to animals in Denali as 'approachable wildlife.' That means bear, moose, Dall sheep and caribou aren't as skittish here as in other regions of the state. For this reason, and because Park Rd was built to maximize the chances of seeing wildlife by traversing high open ground, the national park is an excellent place to view a variety of animals.

Anywhere between 1000 and 1800 moose roam the north side of the Alaska Range within the park, and the most spectacular scene in Denali comes in early September, when the bulls clash their immense racks over breeding rights to the cows. Moose are almost always found in stands of spruce and willow shrubs (their favorite food), and backpackers should be wary when plowing blindly through those areas of thick groundcover.

All the park's caribou belong to the Denali herd – one of 32 herds in Alaska – which presently numbers around 2000 animals. While the herd tends to range solely within the park's boundaries, it does occasionally head out to the 'real world,' primarily visiting wilderness areas on the eastern border of the park. The best time to spot caribou is often in late summer, when the animals begin to band into groups ranging up to 500 head, in anticipation of the fall migration. Caribou are easy to spot, as the rack of a bull often stands 4ft high and appears to be out of proportion with the rest of his body.

Consider yourself lucky if you spot a wolf in the park. Denali is home to a fluctuating population of the animals, with approximately 100 wolves living in 18 packs. 'In summer, wolf packs are less likely to travel in a large group because they center their activity around a den or rendezvous site, with one or more adults often remaining there with the pups,' says Park Wildlife Biologist Tom Meier. 'Also, the young ungulates, beavers and other smaller prey that are available in summer can often be taken by a single wolf. When pups become able to travel with the pack, they resume their winter pattern of moving about their territory together.' Probably your best shot at sighting a wolf is along the Park Rd, or near Igloo Campground.

North of the Alaska Range, the park holds an estimated 350 grizzly bears, usually inhabiting tundra areas. South of here, the bear density should arguably go up, as there are more salmon streams to support a bigger population, but no hard-and-true statistics are available. The black bears tend to stick to the forested areas, and avoid the grizzlies. Park biologists estimate there to be 200 black bears within the park's boundaries. Since most of Denali's streams are fed by glaciers, the fishing is poor, and bears must rely on vegetation for 85% of their diet. This accounts for their small size. Most male grizzlies here range from only 300lb to 600lb while their cousins on the salmon-rich coasts can easily top 1000lb. While there is no guarantee of seeing a grizzly in the park, your chances are pretty darned good. Most park bus drivers say they see around five to eight grizzlies per day along the road. Mile 34 marks the unofficial beginning of bear country.

In addition to moose, caribou, wolves and bears, Denali is home to 35 other species of mammal – from wolverines to mice – as well as 167 varieties of bird, 10 types of fish, and a lone amphibian, the wood frog.

RANGER-LED ACTIVITIES

If you're hesitant about venturing into the wilds on your own, or merely looking to kill some time until your desired backcountry unit opens, Denali offers a daily slate of worthwhile ranger-led hikes and presentations.

Sled-Dog Demonstrations

Denali is the only US national park where rangers conduct winter patrols via dog team. In summer the huskies serve a different purpose: amusing and educating the legions of tourists who sign up for the park's free daily tours of the sled-dog kennels, and dog demonstrations. The 40-minute show takes place at Park Headquarters at 10am, 2pm and 4pm. Free buses head there from the visitor center, departing 40 minutes before each start time.

Campground Programs

Each evening throughout the summer, rangers converge on the Riley Creek, Savage River and Teklanika Campgrounds to present 45-minute talks on Denali's wildlife and natural history. You're welcome to show up even if you're not camping there. Talks begin at 7:30pm.

Entrance-Area Hikes

To join a ranger on an easy, guided stroll (ranging from a half hour to 2½ hours) along the park's entrance area trails, check out the schedule at the visitor center and show up ready to hike at the appointed departure time.

Discovery Hikes

These are moderate-to-strenuous, three- to five-hour hikes departing from Park Rd. The location varies from day to day; you can find out the schedule at the visitor center. Sign up there one or two days in advance to ensure a space (last-minute walk-ups are accepted if there's room), then head to the WAC to reserve a shuttle ticket to wherever the hike is happening. Be sure to pack rain gear, food and water.

DAY HIKING

Even for those who have neither the desire nor the equipment for an overnight trek, hiking is still the best way to enjoy the park and to see the land and its wildlife. You can hike virtually anywhere here that hasn't been closed due to the impact on wildlife. For a day hike (which doesn't require a permit), just ride the shuttle bus and get off at any valley, riverbed or ridge that grabs your fancy. Popular areas for cross-country day hiking off Park Rd include the Teklanika River, Cathedral Mountain, the Toklat River, the tundra areas near Eielson Visitor Center, and Polychrome Pass.

The park has few trails; most hiking is cross-country over open terrain. Nature trails exist at some of the rest stops along Park Rd, and while you won't get lost following these trails, neither will you experience the primal thrill of making your own route across the landscape. A good compromise for those unsure of entering the backcountry on their own is to take a ranger-led Discovery Hike.

Cross-country hikers should not walk in a line; rather, rangers recommend you fan-out to avoid creating trails.

Park Entrance Area

A few short, maintained trails web the park entrance area. The **Horseshoe Lake Trail**, accessed at Mile 1.2 of Park Rd by the railroad crossing, is a leisurely 1½-mile walk through the woods to an overlook of an oxbow lake, followed by a steep trail to the water. Follow the tracks north a short way to the wide gravel path. The **Taiga**

Loop Trail, also commencing from the railroad tracks, turns west from the Horseshoe Lake Trail and leads to both Mt Healy Overlook Trail and Rock Creek Trail.

The moderate 2.3-mile **Rock Creek Trail** leads west to the park headquarters and dog kennels. It's far easier hiking this trail downhill from the headquarters end, where the trail begins just before Park Rd. From here it crosses Rock Creek but doesn't stay with the stream. Instead, it climbs a gentle slope of mixed aspen and spruce forest, breaks out along a ridge with scenic views of Mt Healy and George Parks Hwy, and then begins a rapid descent to its end at the Taiga Trail.

The **Roadside Trail** parallels Park Rd and takes you 1.5 miles from the Visitor Center to Park Headquarters. It's not the prettiest of trails, but it sure beats walking on the road. The new **McKinley Station Trail** is a 2.6-mile loop that takes you from the visitor center to the WAC and back again, and provides an easy route to Glitter Gulch.

Mt Healy Overlook Trail

This is the longest maintained trail in the entrance area, and the only one in the vicinity that truly lets you escape the crowds. It's a popular trail among day hikers as it provides a good workout and the reward of fine views over the Nenana River valley, Healy Ridge and other ridgelines. The trail veers off the Taiga Trail and makes a steep climb up Mt Healy, ascending 1700ft in 2.5 miles. Plan on three to five hours for the hike.

Once on the trail, you soon cross a bridge over **Horseshoe Creek**, after which there's a moderately steep climb through a forest of spruce mixed with aspen and alder. After a mile you reach a scenic viewpoint where you can gaze upon Mt Fellows to the east and the Alaska Range to the south. At this point, the trail moves from stunted spruce into thickets of alder, and at the base of a ridge begins a series of switchbacks. You reach **Halfway Rock**, a 12ft boulder, at 1.2 miles. The steep climb continues, with the switchbacks becoming shorter, and at 1.6 miles you move from a taiga zone of alder to the alpine tundra: a world of moss, lichen, wildflowers and incredible views. Keep an eye out for the large hoary marmots (a northern cousin of the groundhog), and the pika, a small relative of the rabbit.

In the final 0.4 miles the trail emerges below **Mt Healy Overlook**. You then curve steeply around the ridge to emerge at the rocky bench that is the overlook. Views from here are excellent. Sugar Loaf Mountain, at 4450ft, dominates the eastern horizon, and above the overlook to the northwest is the actual summit of Mt Healy. If you have binoculars, search the slopes to the north for Dall sheep. If the weather is clear, look to the southwest for the Mt McKinley massif, some 80 miles away. From the overlook (3425ft), hardy hikers can climb another mile to the high point of Healy Ridge (4217ft), or another 2 miles to the summit of Mt Healy (5714ft).

Savage River Loop Trail

You can get to this trailhead by car (Mile 14), but you are better off taking the Savage River Shuttle Bus as the small parking lot here often fills up. The 2-mile loop is wheelchair accessible for the first half mile and runs north from the Park Rd on either side of the river. People looking for a longer hike can continue past the bridge that marks the 'official' turn-around point along an informal trail paralleling the river's west bank.

Polychrome Pass Circuit

One cross-country route you might consider off Park Rd is Polychrome Pass Circuit, an 8-mile trek that will challenge fit, experienced day hikers. (Less studly souls might want to do it as an overnight, which requires a permit.) This hike traverses one of the park's most scenic areas.

The brilliantly colored rocks of Polychrome Pass are the result of volcanic action some 60 million years ago. Today the multicolored hills and mountains, including Polychrome Mountain (5789ft) and Cain Peak (4961ft), are a stunning sight in the low-angle light of a clear Alaskan summer day.

The route begins on the west side of Park Rd's bridge across East Fork Toklat River (Mile 42.7). Downstream, or north from the bridge, the East Fork flows as a braided river across a wide gravel bar for almost 8 miles until it enters a 7-mile-long canyon. During periods of low to medium water levels the river is braided enough for a safe crossing. If the water is high, you might run into problems; while you follow the river along its west bank, deep channels may force you to climb up and around the bordering cliffs.

It's 1.5 miles along the gravel bars from Park Rd to the first major tributary flowing from the hills south of Polychrome Mountain. Go upstream (south) along the unnamed tributary for another 1.5 miles, fording its west side at the best possible crossing. Just before the stream enters a mile-long canyon, a low pass appears to the west. It's a 200ft ascent to the pass.

From the top of the pass, it's an easy stroll down into the next valley where two streams converge. Keep in mind that the valley forms a natural travel corridor for wildlife, including brown bears. As you hike down the valley, the scenery is dominated by the northern slopes of **Polychrome Mountain**, whose colors justify its name. In early summer search the slopes for Dall sheep.

Within half a mile upstream from the confluence the stream enters a narrow canyon filled with willow, birch and alder. You'll probably have to ford the stream a few times. Be wary as you travel through the canyon. Your visibility will be limited by the brush, and bears often pass through here. Clap your hands, sing songs, argue loudly about politics. Do anything to make noise.

After a mile of bushwhacking through the canyon the stream breaks out into a wide area of the valley, where travel is far easier (though at times boggy and wet). Within another mile you arrive at the source of the stream, a small lake frequented by waterfowl. The lake is less than a quarter mile north of Park Rd.

The easiest way to return to Polychrome Pass rest area is to hike along the road, enjoying the views to the south of Toklat River, other valleys and, if you're lucky, Mt McKinley. Those who want one last climb can skip the easy road route and climb the 4000ft ridge due east of the lake. Toward the end it becomes steep and the earth underfoot is loose. Eventually you reach the 4200ft high point and from there follow the ridgeline to a low saddle at its north end. Head east from this pass, cross the bushy ravine and then climb a final hill opposite the Polychrome Pass rest area. You'll probably see people on top of the hill, viewing Polychrome Mountain during their short bus stop.

BACKPACKING

For many, the reason to come to Denali is to escape into the backcountry for a truly Alaskan experience. Unlike many parks in the Lower 48, Denali's rigid restrictions ensure you can trek and camp in a piece of wilderness all your own, even if it's just for a few days.

The park is divided into 87 backcountry units, and in 43 only a regulated number of backpackers (usually four to six) are allowed at a time. You have to obtain a free permit for the unit you want to overnight. You may spend a maximum of seven nights in any one unit, and a maximum of 30 consecutive nights in the backcountry. If you have internet access, download the national park's backcountry guide beforehand at www.nps.gov/dena/planyourvisit/upload/bcguide.pdf.

Obtain permits at the BIC, where you'll find wall maps with the unit outlines and a quota board indicating the number of vacancies in each unit. Permits are issued only a day in advance, and the most popular units fill up fast. It pays to be flexible: decide what area you're aiming for, and be prepared to take any zone in that area. If you're picky, you might have to wait several days until your choice opens up.

After you decide where you want to go among the open units, the next step is to watch the required backcountry orientation video, followed by a brief safety talk that covers, among other things, proper use of the bear-resistant food containers (BRFCs) you'll receive free of charge with your permit. The containers are bulky, but they work – they've reduced bear encounters dramatically since 1986. It's also worth noting that you're required to pack-out dirty TP, so be sure to pack at least a dozen ziplock bags. You'll then be given your permit and can buy topographic maps – topo maps are $6 and waterproof 'Trails Illustrated' maps run $9.95. From there, head over to the WAC to buy a ticket for the camper bus ($29.25) to get you out to the starting point of your trip.

Units 1, 2, 3 and 24 surround the park entrance and are often available. You could spend a night or two here, checking in at the BIC each morning awaiting a more favorable place deeper in the park.

For an overview of the different units in the park, check out the BIC's copy of *Backcountry Companion for Denali National Park* by Jon Nierenberg (Alaska National History Association), which is now out of print.

It's important to realize that Denali is a trailless park, and the key to successful backcountry travel is being able to read a topographic map. Riverbeds are easy to follow and make excellent avenues for the backpacker, but they always involve fording water.

A MOUNTAIN BY ANY OTHER NAME

The Athabascans called it Denali or the 'Great One'; their brethren to the south in the Susitna Valley called it Doleika, the 'Big Mountain'; and the Aleuts referred to it as Traleika. So why do we largely know North America's highest peak by the name McKinley?

This white-washed moniker was not even the first European name to be bestowed upon the mountain. While McKinley was first sighted by European eyes in 1794 by explorer George Vancouver, it remained unnamed until a prominent Russian administrator, Ferdinand von Wrangell, marked it on a map as Tenada. Later, during the gold rush days, it would change names again, first to Densmore's Mountain in honor of a local prospector, and soon thereafter to Mt McKinley after William McKinley, an Ohioan who would soon become president of the United States. And so the name remained for many years, at least on our maps.

But the name 'Denali' slowly began creeping back into people's minds, and finally made the maps in 1980 when the park was re-designated as Denali National Park and Preserve and the Alaskan Geographic Board officially renamed the mountain Denali. Despite these statewide changes, US mapmakers still refer to Denali as McKinley. While it serves as an easy way to differentiate between park and mountain (the reason we left it in this book), it's mainly one stalwart congressman from Ohio, Ralph Regula, who keeps the name from changing. Every time Denali – we mean, um, McKinley – comes up for a name change, the congressman blocks it. But the blocking won't go on for long. Across the US – and the world for that matter – many colonial and European names are being replaced by their original, aboriginal equivalents. Given that William McKinley never even visited Alaska, and Europeans lagged behind the first native 'explorers' by thousands of years, it seems like a good idea.

Pack a pair of tennis shoes or rafters' sandals for this.

Ridges are also good routes to hike along if the weather isn't foul. The treeline in Denali is at 2700ft, and above that you'll usually find tussock or moist tundra – humps of watery grass that make for sloppy hiking. In extensive stretches of tussock, the hiking has been best described as 'walking on basketballs.' Above 3400ft you'll encounter alpine or dry tundra, which generally makes for excellent trekking.

Regardless of where you're headed, remember that 5 miles is a full-day trip for the average backpacker in Denali's backcountry.

BIKING

No special permit is needed to cycle on Park Rd, but biking off-road is prohibited. Camper buses will carry bikes, but only two at a time and only if you have a reservation. Many cyclists ride the bus in and bike back out, carrying their gear and staying at campsites they've reserved along the way. It's also possible to take an early-morning bus in, ride for several hours and catch a bus back the same day.

You can rent bikes at **Denali Outdoor Center** (☎ 683-1925, 888-303-1925; www.denalioutdoorcenter.com; Mile 240.5 and Mile 247 George Parks Hwy). Each location charges $8 per hour (minimum two-hour rental) or $40 for a full day. Rates include a helmet, water bottle, tools and lock.

TOURS

Park Road

The park shuttle buses are the most common 'tours' along Park Rd, but there are others. None of these are especially noteworthy, and you're probably better off saving some money by simply taking the park bus. This said, unlike the shuttle buses, the tours below do include narration by a certified guide.

Park co-concessionaire **Aramark** (☎ 272-7275, 800-622-7275; www.reservedenali.com) offers a five-hour Natural History Tour ($55.95 for adults, $28 for children 14 and under) to Primrose Ridge, a four- to five-hour Teklanika Tundra Wilderness Tour ($60.50 for adults, $30.25 children 14 and under) to the Teklanika River Overlook, and a six- to eight-hour Tundra Wildlife Tour ($93.50 for adults, $46.75 for children 14 and under) to Toklat River. All include narration, hot drinks and a snack or box lunch.

The other co-concessionaire, Doyon, runs **Kantishna Roadhouse** (☎ 800-230-7275; www.seedenali.com), which offers a one-day bus tour ($139 for adults, $69.50 for children 14 and under) along Park Rd to Kantishna (p341). There you get an interpretive tour of the area, lunch in the dining hall and either gold panning or a sled-dog demo before returning on the bus. Or you can return on a sightseeing flight for an extra charge.

ATVs

If you feel the need for speed – and for ripping up the environment and wasting fuel wantonly (not to judge) – you should rent an ATV.

Denali ATV Adventures (☎ 683-4288; www.denaliatv.com; Mile 247 George Parks Hwy) offers two- and four-hour butt-busters for $85-165.

Flightseeing

Most flightseeing around Denali leaves from Talkeetna, but some companies also operate out of the park area.

Denali Air (☎ 683-2261; www.denaliair.com) charges around $325/$165 per adult/child for a narrated flight of about an hour around the mountain. Flights leave from the company's airstrip at Mile 229.5 of George Parks Hwy.

Era Helicopters (☎ 550-8625, 800-843-1947; www.eraflightseeing.com; Mile 238 George Parks Hwy) will take you up on a 50-minute Mt McKinley tour ($320) or a 75-minute flight that includes a glacier landing ($415). Heli-hiking trips are also available. The helipad is on the north side of the Nenana River bridge, at the south end of Glitter Gulch.

Fly Denali (☎ 683-2899, 866-733-7768; www.flydenali.com) is based in Healy and has tours of various durations and routes. Its 2½-hour flight includes the only glacier landing available from the park entrance ($439).

Kantishna Air Taxi (☎ 683-1223; www.katair.com) flies out of Kantishna, the McKinley park strip and Healy. The company offers hour-long flightseeing excursions around Mt McKinley ($185 per person from Kantishna, $230 from Healy); direct flights between Kantishna and the park entrance ($160); and flights from Kantishna to the park entrance with a 20-minute detour by Mt McKinley ($205). Two versions of a bus-out/fly-back day tour are also available ($223).

Atkins Guiding & Flying Service (☎ 768-2143; Cantwell) is a small-time operation that does 75-minute McKinley flybys for $360.

River Rafting

Thanks to Denali Park tourists, the Nenana River is the most popular white-water rafting area in Alaska. The river's main white-water stretch begins near the park entrance and ends 10 miles north, near Healy. It's rated Class III (see p106) and involves standing waves, rapids and holes with names such as 'Coffee Grinder' in sheer-sided canyons. South of the park entrance the river is much milder, but to many it's just as interesting as it veers away from both the highway and the railroad, increasing your chances of sighting wildlife. Raft companies offer guided trips on both stretches.

Denali Outdoor Center (☎ 683-1925, 888-303-1925; www.denalioutdoorcenter.com; Mile 240.5 & Mile 247 George Parks Hwy), with two locations, is universally considered the finest rafting outfit, with good equipment, a safety-first philosophy and friendly guides. Its canyon and scenic runs each last two hours and cost $79; you can combine the two for a half-day, $110 excursion, or take a 2½-hour inflatable kayak tour for $85.

Nenana Raft Adventures (☎ 800-789-7238; www.raftdenali.com; Mile 238 George Parks Hwy) offers trips and dips on the upper Nenana ($85), Nenana Gorge ($85) and a short afternoon 4th-class paddle ($70), as well as pricier oar-boat trips for families with young ones.

Too-loó-uk River Guides (☎ 683-1542; www.akrivers.com; Mile 239 George Parks Hwy) is affiliated with Denali Mountain Works (p331) and runs guided multiday wilderness raft trips across the state. The trips range from five to 10 days and start at $1475 per person.

COURSES

The Murie Science & Learning Center (p331) offers occasional ranger-led scientific lectures.

Alaska Geographic (☎ 866-257-2751; www.alaskageographic.org; 750 W Second Av, Suite 100, Anchorage) Offers two- and three-day courses through the Murie Science Center. Subjects range from dinosaurs to Dall sheep. Prices range from $200 to $480, and often include meals and lodging.

Denali Education Center (☎ 683-2597; www.denali.org) Offers extended educational programs with a focus on programs for seniors and youth. Prices often include meals and lodging, and begin at around $150.

SLEEPING & EATING

Denali Park occasionally stuns visitors who arrive in late afternoon or early evening seeking lodging: the cruise-ship companies book vast numbers of rooms here for their package tourists. You definitely want something reserved – even if it's just a campsite – before you show up. And expect to pay more than you'd expect. The Denali Borough charges a

7% accommodations tax on top of the prices listed below.

Groceries are extremely limited and expensive in the Denali Park area, so stock up in Fairbanks, Anchorage or Wasilla before coming here. Inside the park itself there are no restaurants except the Morino Grill. Luckily, the neighboring towns are not far apart, so there's a good variety of eating and drinking options to choose from.

Inside the Park

SLEEPING

Kantishna (an inholding) excepted, lodgings are not available inside park boundaries, so if you want overnight shelter within the park you'll need a tent or RV.

For information on reserving campsites, see p330. If you don't have a reservation, you'll probably have to find lodging outside the park for the first night or two before you can secure a campsite.

Riley Creek Campground (Mile 0.2 Park Rd; walk-in/drive-in sites $12/19) At the park's main entrance and within earshot of George Parks Hwy, this is Denali's largest and most developed campground and is the only one open year-round. It has 146 sites, piped-in water, flush toilets and evening interpretive programs. As the park's main campground, it's favored by RVers. But it's also spacious, so campers shouldn't feel overwhelmed, and the location is convenient to Riley Creek Mercantile, the WAC and Glitter Gulch.

Savage River Campground (Mile 13 Park Rd; sites $20) Despite its name, this is a mile short of the actual river. It's one of only two campgrounds with a view of Mt McKinley. The 33 sites can accommodate both RVs and tents, with such amenities as flush toilets, piped-in water and evening presentations.

Sanctuary River Campground (Mile 23 Park Rd; sites $9) This is the next campground down the road from Savage River. On the banks of a large glacial river, the seven sites are for tents only and can't be reserved in advance. While there's no piped-in water, Sanctuary River is a great area for day hiking. You can either head south to trek along the river or climb Mt Wright or Primrose Ridge to the north for an opportunity to photograph Dall sheep.

Teklanika River Campground (Mile 29 Park Rd; sites $16) There are 53 sites, flush toilets, piped-in water and evening programs at this campground, popular with tenters, RVers and the occasional wolf or two. You can drive to this campground, but once here you must park your vehicle until you're ready to return to Riley Creek.

Igloo Creek Campground (Mile 34 Park Rd; sites $9) This small waterless tent-camping area is a great jumping off point for day hikes, and marks the beginning of true bear country. The day hiking around here is excellent, especially the numerous ridges around Igloo Mountain, Cathedral Mountain and Sable Pass (currently closed) that provide good routes into alpine areas.

Wonder Lake Campground (Mile 85 Park Rd; sites $16) This is the jewel of Denali campgrounds, thanks to its eye-popping views of Mt McKinley. The facility has 28 sites for tents only but does offer flush toilets and piped-in water. If you're lucky enough to reserve a site, book it for three nights and then pray that the mountain appears during one of the days you're there. Also, pack plenty of insect repellent and maybe even a headnet: the bugs are vicious in midsummer.

EATING & DRINKING

Young seasonal workers hang out at the 'Spike' – but threatened us with pain of death if we published its location, so by all means, go ahead and try to find it on your own. The pubs in Glitter Gulch are a bit more tourist friendly.

Morino Grill (Mile 1.5 Park Rd; mains $8-9; 🕑 11am-7pm) This cafeteria-style establishment in a barnlike structure beside the visitor center is the only eatery within the park. It has burgers, paninis and small pizzas, as well as seafood chowder and reindeer stew.

Riley Creek Mercantile (☎ 683-9246; Mile 0.2 Park Rd; 🕑 7am-11pm) Next to the Riley Creek Campground, it has a few groceries, as well as espressos, deli sandwiches and wraps.

Wilderness Access Center (☎ 683-9274; Mile 0.5 Park Rd; 🕑 5am-8pm) The center has an extremely limited array of backpacker-oriented foods.

Kantishna

Located on private property at the end of Park Rd, Kantishna provides the ultimate lodging location. Here, surrounded by parkland, you'll feel as close to nature as you can get without taking rubber off your Vibram soles. Many options include meals and round-trip transportation from the park entrance.

Skyline Lodge (☎ 683-1223; www.katair.com; r with continental breakfast $195, full meal plan $33 per person) This small, solar-powered, three-room place serves as Kantishna Air Taxi's base of operations. Guests have use of a common kitchen, dining area, bath, shower and decks overlooking the Kantishna Valley.

Kantishna Roadhouse (☎ 800-942-7420; www.kantishnaroadhouse.com; per person per night $385) Owned by park co-concessionaire Doyon, Kantishna Roadhouse has clean modern cabins, a beautiful dining room, a bar and guided activities. It has a nice location on Moose Creek, but of all the Kantishna lodgings it feels the most sterile.

Denali Backcountry Lodge (☎ 376-1992, 877-233-6254; www.denalilodge.com; per person per night $390) The last lodge on this end of the road, this is a great-looking place on the banks of Moose Creek with comfortable modern cabins and common areas. Transport, meals and guided activities are included, and you can save some duckets by coming here in the 'shoulder' season.

Camp Denali (☎ 683-2290; www.campdenali.com; cabins per minimum 3-night stay per person $1425) Verging on legendary, Camp Denali has been the gold standard among Kantishna lodges for the last half-century. Widely spread across the ridgeline, the camp's simple, comfortable cabins elegantly complement the backcountry experience while minimizing impact on the natural world. Think of it as luxury camping, with gourmet meals, guided hikes, killer views of the mountain, and staff so devoted to Denali that you'll come away feeling like the beneficiary of a precious gift. You can only arrive or depart on Monday or Friday, so you'll need to plan accordingly.

North Face Lodge (☎ 683-2290; www.campdenali.com; r per minimum 3-night stay per person $1425) Affiliated with Camp Denali and just down the hill, this is a more traditionally appointed lodge complete with en suite bath and all the comforts of home. You gain amenities here, but you lose that extra intimacy with the land that Camp Denali provides. Like Camp Denali, you can only get here or leave on Mondays and Friday. Keep your fingers crossed there's no madmen worrying about 'All work and no play making Jack a dull boy.'

McKinley Village

Six miles south of the park entrance is McKinley Village (Mile 229). This tourist area is less commercialized than Glitter Gulch and sits at a cozy bend of the Nenana River. It is served by the park shuttle bus.

Denali Grizzly Bear Resort (☎ 683-2696, 866-583-2696; www.denaligrizzlybear.com; Mile 231.1 George Parks Hwy; sites $22, tent cabins from $29, cabins $61-254) This place offers wooded campsites, platform tent cabins, and 23 well-spaced wood-frame cabins in various configurations – some have a private bath and river views, some have a kitchen, some have both, and some are old historical cabins with tons of Alaskan character. The big cabins sleep six. Communal amenities include hot showers and laundry facilities.

Denali River Cabins (☎ 800-230 7275; www.seedenali.com; Mile 231 George Parks Hwy; cabins $159-209) The river-front cabins are definitely worth the extra money, as they get you out into the wilderness and away from the maze of propane-and-cedar-scented cabins on the interior of the property. There's also a sauna and some hotel-style rooms (not worth your time or money) here.

Denali Cabins (☎ 376-1992, 800-808-8068; www.denalilodges.com; Mile 229 George Parks Hwy; cabins d $212-266; 💻) Two miles south of McKinley Village, this run-of-the-mill clutch of cabins offers private baths and two outdoor hot tubs.

229 Parks (☎ 683-2567; www.229parks.com; Mile 229 George Parks Hwy; dinner $24-34; 🕒 8-11am, 5-10pm Tue-Sun) South of McKinley Village on George Parks Hwy, this is one of the best restaurants in the area. It manages to be both epicurean and ardently environmental at the same time, emphasizing organic and locally grown foods. The menu changes daily, but often features local game dishes accompanied by a veritable cornucopia of vegetarian options.

Carlo Creek

Located 12 miles south of the park entrance (Mile 224), this is one of the best places to stay near Denali Park, especially for independent travelers looking for a chilled out experience. There's good hiking nearby (stop in at the youth hostel to get the low-down on area tromps). Perhaps most importantly, you can stay here without having to cash in your retirement savings. Both the Denali Mountain Morning Hostel and Panorama Pizza Pub offer shuttle service, but it's definitely nice to have wheels if you decide to stay here.

our pick **Denali Mountain Morning Hostel** (☎ 683-7503; www.hostelalaska.com; dm $25, d $75-95; 💻) Perched lovingly beside the gurgling Carlo Creek, this is the area's only true hostel. And, lucky for indie travelers, it is one of the best in all Alaska. Only open during the summer months, the hostel features a hotchpotch of tent-cabins, log cabins and platform tents. Of course, there's a fire pit, and visitors can cook meals and swap tales in the 'octagon' – the hostel's common area. The hostel rents out backpacking gear, sells organic and bulk foods, and offers shuttle service ($5 round-trip) to the park.

Carlo Creek Lodge (☎ 683-2576; www.ccldenaliparkalaska.com; cabins with/without bath $140/85, sites $16, RV sites with/without hookups $23/18, all sites per person plus $4;) In a nice setting on the opposite bank of Carlo Creek, this lodge has a couple of affordable shared-bath cabins and a nice wooded campground. Each site has a picnic table, a fire pit with barbecue grill, and a shelter under which you could pitch a tent in bad weather. Communal amenities include a laundry room and showers.

Perch Restaurant & Cabins (☎ 683-2523, 888-322-2523; www.denaliperchresort.com; cabins with/without bath incl breakfast buffet $125/85; 🕑 6am-9am, 5-9pm;) The rooms sit way too close to each other in this woodsy Carlo Creek 'cabin ghetto.' The shared-bath cabins are right on the creek, however – nice! – and the Perch Restaurant (dinner $19 t0 $30) is one of the best in the area.

McKinley Creekside Cabins (☎ 683-1558, 888-533-6254; www.mckinleycabins.com; cabins $139-199;) Ask ahead of time for a creekside cabin at this well-maintained spot across from the hostel. The cabins aren't right on the water, but you'd be able to hear the burbling creek as you loll off to dreamland. The breakfasts here are also dreamy!

Panorama Pizza Pub (☎ 683-2623; Mile 224 George Parks Hwy; pizzas $6-20; 🕑 noon-midnight) This Carlo Creek eatery offers good beer, burgers, and pizza pies with names like the Vegghead and the Runnin' Chicken. You get a discount if you're staying across the road at the Denali Mountain Morning Hostel. Later at night it becomes more 'pub' than 'pizzeria' with locals and travelers congregating on the deck for homegrown 'cornhole' tourneys. They offer a free shuttle, so you can get here even if you aren't staying in Carlo Creek.

Glitter Gulch

Glitter Gulch (Mile 238.5) contains the mangy lion's share of park lodgings. This area's only redeeming feature is convenience, and that can't begin to make up for its total lack of compatibility with the spectacular natural world surrounding it.

SLEEPING

McKinley/Denali Salmon Bake Cabins (☎ 683-7283; www.thebakerocks.com; Mile 238.5 George Parks Hwy; cabins with/without bath $130/74;) 'The Bake's' beds are a bit concave, but this is by far the cheapest option in the Gulch. Deluxe cabins come with boob tubes, heaters and baths, and are on the dingy side of clean. The restaurant caters to a packaged tourist crowd, but heats up late night when the tourists go to bed and the local wildlife begins to howl.

Crow's Nest (☎ 683-2723, 888-917-8130; www.denalicrowsnest.com; Mile 238.5 George Parks Hwy; cabins $199;) Old pictures add a welcome touch of home to these modern log cabins up on the hill behind the gas station. The rooms are pleasant enough with TVs and private baths, and, if you can ignore the highway noise, you actually have pretty good views of the surrounding wilderness.

EATING & DRINKING

Black Bear Coffee House (☎ 683-1656; Mile 238.5 George Parks Hwy; sandwiches $9; 🕑 6:30am-10pm) Situated on the Glitter Gulch boardwalk, this place has good coffee, plus bagels, pastries and deli sandwiches.

Lynx Creek Pizza & Pub (☎ 683-2547; Mile 238.6 George Parks Hwy; pizza slices $4.50; 🕑 11am-midnight) Owned by Princess, this Glitter Gulch fixture has a small pub with log-cabin atmosphere and a nice outdoor patio. The pizza wedges are sizable and the taste is tolerable.

Bubba's Baja (☎ 683-7827; Mile 238.5 George Parks Hwy; burritos and tacos $5-10; 🕑 11am-9pm) This popular spot offers damn good burritos that will keep you farting up the trails all day long.

Overlook Bar & Grill (☎ 683-2641; Mile 238.5 George Parks Hwy; sandwiches & burgers $9-18; 🕑 11am-11pm) Way up on the hill over Glitter Gulch, the 'Big O' gets raves for its view and beer list, but razzes for slow and haphazard service. It does steak, seafood, pasta and poultry, and is a good nightlife spot.

GROCERIES

Park Mart Store (☎ 683-2548; Mile 238.4 George Parks Hwy; 🕑 7:30am-10:30pm) Situated in Glitter Gulch, this gas-station-cum-convenience-store-cum-liquor-store has the widest range of groceries in the park area. Seriously. Good luck finding fresh produce.

Healy

Healy (Mile 249.5) is 12 miles north of the park entrance and has a range of lodging options. It doesn't sit nestled into the mountains like the other towns in the area.

Ridgetop Cabins (☎ 683-2448, 866-680-2448; Mile 253.3 George Parks Hwy, about 1 mile up a dirt road to the west; www.alaskaone.com/ridgetop; 2-person/4-person cabins $120/165) Just north of Healy, this a good bet for families, offering large cabins at good prices. The friendly owners built all the cabins by hand – talk about frontiersmanship.

EarthSong Lodge (☎ 683-2863; www.earthsonglodge.com; Mile 4 Stampede Rd; r $155-195) North of Healy, off Mile 251 George Parks Hwy, this place rents out private-bath cabins above the treeline at 1900ft – just a short climb away from stunning views of Mt McKinley. In the evening you can help feed the 30 sled dogs. Proprietor Jon Nierenberg, a former Denali ranger, quite literally wrote the book (see p337) on hiking in the park's backcountry. Light meals are available here.

Denali Dome Home B&B (☎ 683-1239, 800-983-1239; www.denalidomehome.com; Mile 0.5 Healy Spur Rd; r with breakfast $165; 💻) In a huge, intriguing geodesic house, this is the best B&B in Healy. And, despite what you may think, the digs are not hippie at all. The owners are absolute oracles of wisdom when it comes to Denali Park, and do a bang-up job with breakfast.

Rose's Café (☎ 683-7673; Mile 249.5 George Parks Hwy; mains $8-17; 🕑 6:30am-10pm) This burger-and-pie joint is your best bet in town. The covered outdoor seating area outback and authentic diner-style counter seating adds to its *Nighthawks*-meets-*Easy Rider* appeal.

GETTING THERE & AROUND

Located on George Parks Hwy about four hours north of Anchorage and two hours south of Fairbanks, Denali is easily accessible. Once here, you'll find the area between Glitter Gulch and McKinley Village well served by public transport. North or south of there you may need your own car, though Denali Mountain Morning Hostel in Carlo Creek now provides limited transport to the WAC, as does Panorama Pizza Pub.

Bus

Both northbound and southbound bus services are available from Denali National Park.

Alaska/Yukon Trails (☎ 479-2277; 800-770-7275; www.alaskashuttle.com) has southbound buses that pick up at the Park Mart Store, Visitor Center and WAC around noon, reaching Anchorage ($65 one way) by 6:30pm. It makes drops at several locales in Anchorage, including the youth hostels, and charges $7 more to the airport. Northbound buses leaving Denali around noon as well and arrive in Fairbanks ($46 one way) at 4pm ($7 extra will get you to the airport).

Park Connection (☎ 800-266-8625; www.alaskacoach.com) runs to and from Fairbanks ($56 one way) and to and from points south, including Anchorage ($79 one way) and Seward ($135 one way). It leaves Anchorage at 7am and 3pm for Denali; Fairbanks at 9am down to Denali; and from Denali north to Fairbanks at 2pm and south to Anchorage at 2pm.

Denali Transportation (☎ 683-4765) offers shuttle service in and around Denali. From the park visitor center or Glitter Gulch, it goes to Healy ($26), Carlo Creek ($30) and Fairbanks ($175). Prices are per person, based on four people per vehicle.

Train

The most enjoyable way to arrive or depart from the park is aboard the **Alaska Railroad** (☎ 265-2494, 800-544-0552; www.alaskarailroad.com), with its viewing-dome cars that provide sweeping views of Mt McKinley and the Susitna and Nenana River valleys along the way. All trains arrive at the depot beside the new visitor center, only staying long enough for passengers to board. The northbound train arrives in Denali at 4:10pm and reaches Fairbanks at 8pm. The southbound train arrives in Denali at 12:40pm and gets in to Anchorage at 8pm. Tickets aren't cheap: the one-way fare from Denali National Park to Anchorage starts at $135; from Denali to Fairbanks it's $59. Children 11 and under get substantial discounts.

Plane

Talkeetna Aero Services (☎ 683-2899, 888-733-2899; www.talkeetnaaero.com), based in Talkeetna, offers air transportation to/from Talkeetna.

Kantishna Air Taxi (☎ 683-1223; www.katair.com) offers high-priced charters (around $1495 for up to five people) to and from Anchorage.

Courtesy Buses & Shuttles

The free Riley Creek Loop Bus makes a circuit through the park entrance area, picking up at the visitor center every half hour and stopping at the Horseshoe Lake trailhead, WAC and Riley Creek Campground.

BACK INTO THE WILD

Heading into the wild is nothing new in Alaska. In fact, folks have been doing it ever since the first travelers came here by foot over the Land Bridge some 30,000 years ago. So what's the big deal with 'Alexander Supertramp,' the city boy of Into the Wild fame that disappeared into the Alaska wilderness and never came back?

Well, Chris McCandless, aka Alexander Supertramp, has had a book, movie and endless articles written about him. And to many, he's become a cultural icon, the poster boy of the hard-to-classify transcendental, drop-out, fend-for-your-own-damned-self philosophy that permeates so many portions of Alaska's collective consciousness. But, to most Alaskans, McCandless was nothing more than a greenhorn that should have had more respect for the power of the Alaskan Bush, an unfortunate piece of collateral damage in the battle between Man and Wild that continues to spark in this vast wilderness.

The story begins just north of Healy, where the Stampede Trail turns off George Parks Hwy and heads west into the Bush. On April 28, 1992, 24-year-old McCandless hiked 20 miles along this road, intending to live off the land for an indefinite length of time. Less than four months later, he was dead.

Author Jon Krakauer, who chronicled McCandless' story in his book *Into the Wild* (New York: Doubleday, 1996) believes McCandless died of starvation after relying too heavily on the seed pods of the otherwise edible wild potato for a food source. The seeds, Krakauer hypothesizes, may have been moldy, and thus toxic.

Since the publication of Krakauer's book, and the subsequent release of the movie directed by Sean Penn in 2007, the bus where McCandless lived and died has become a shrine. Like visitors to Jim Morrison's grave, pilgrims by the hundred have come to pay homage to someone who, they maintain, lived life strictly on his own terms. They scratch their initials into the bus, leave flowers and survival equipment, and write reflective comments in a register at the site. Of course, there are numerous Alaskans who live a subsistence lifestyle year-on-year, spending months (or years) on end in secret camps out in the Bush, hunting, fishing and foraging for their survival. These are the true men and women that have gone 'Into the Wild.' And McCandless's story, though tragic, is but a preface to the fascinating tales found somewhere out in the wild in Alaska's vast uncharted spaces.

If you want to make your own pilgrimage to Alaska's most famous bus, you'd be wisest to do it in winter, when the Teklanika is stilled by cold and when EarthSong Lodge (p343) runs dogsled trips along the Stampede Trail. Otherwise, aim for spring or fall, when the water crossings are less hazardous. And no matter when you go, ask advice from locals, pack a map and respect Ma Nature – you don't want Chris McCandless' journey to be your own.

The park also has a free Dog Sled Demo Bus, which departs the visitor center en route to the Park Headquarters 40 minutes before each show (p335).

If you want to head north along George Parks Hwy to Glitter Gulch or south as far as McKinley Village, you can catch Aramark's courtesy shuttles. From 6:30am until 11:30pm they make a circuit between the McKinley Village Lodge, WAC, visitor center and McKinley Chalet Resort.

Many other lodgings run buses to and from the WAC and visitor center. From Carlo Creek the **Denali Mountain Morning Hostel shuttle** (☎ 683-7503; $5) takes visitors to the WAC, as does **Panorama Pizza Pub's Free Shuttle** (☎ 683-2623), although this one's for dining customers only.

Taxi

If the bus won't work for you, try one of the Healy-based taxi companies. **Caribou Cab** (☎ 683-5000) charges around $30 for a ride between Healy and the park entrance, so you'll want some fellow travelers to help split the cost.

GEORGE PARKS HIGHWAY

This ribbon of highway – drizzled ever so lovingly by vast stretches of wilderness, the reach-for-the-sky Alaska Range, funked-out towns and sprawling state and national parks – offers up the quintessential Alaskan road trip. Heading up from Anchorage to Alaska's second-biggest city, Fairbanks, the George Parks Hwy, or simply the Parks Hwy, takes you to Denali National Park (p327), and its little Alaskan-run sisters, Denali State Park (p351) and Nancy Lake State Recreation Area (below). On your way up, it's worth the time to take a break in Talkeetna (p346), an ideal spot to take a flight-seeing tour of Denali National Park.

The highway begins at the junction with Glenn Hwy 35 miles north of Anchorage and ends 327 miles away in Fairbanks. Mileposts indicate distances from Anchorage. Wasilla, at Mile 42.2, is covered in the Anchorage chapter (p229).

NANCY LAKE STATE RECREATION AREA

Located along the Nancy Lake Pkwy at Mile 67.3 of George Parks Hwy, this **state recreation area** (☎ 495-6273; day-use $5, sites $10) is one of Alaska's few flat, lake-studded parks, offering camping, fishing, canoeing and hiking. Although it lacks the dramatic scenery of the country to the north, the 22,685-acre area can be peaceful on weekdays – and thronging with Anchorage and Mat-Su residents on weekends. Pick up a map at the fee station at Mile 1.3 of Nancy Lake Pkwy, as the area can be confusing.

Activities

PADDLING

The **Lynx Lake Loop** is the most popular canoe trail in the park. This two-day, 16-mile trip takes you to 14 lakes and over an equal number of portages. The route begins and ends at the posted trailhead for the Tanaina Lake Canoe Trail at Mile 4.5 of the parkway. The portages are well marked, and many of them are planked where they cross wet sections. The route includes 12 backcountry campsites, accessible only by canoe, but bring a camp stove because campfires are prohibited in the backcountry.

The largest lake on the route is Lynx Lake. You can extend your trip by paddling south on the lake to the point where a portage leads off to six other lakes and two more primitive campsites on Skeetna Lake.

Rent canoes through the long-established **Tippecanoe Rentals** (☎ 495-6688; www.paddlealaska.com), which has a rental shed at South Rolly Lake Campground. Rates begin at $20 for an eight-hour day, $50 for two days, $65 for three days and $75 for four to seven days.

HIKING

The park's major hiking route is the **Red Shirt Lake Trail** (Mile 6.5 Nancy Lake Pkwy), which begins at the entrance of the South Rolly Lake Campground at the end of the parkway. It leads 3 miles south, primarily on high ground, and ends at Red Shirt Lake's north end. Along the way you'll pass Red Shirt Overlook, offering scenic views of the surrounding lake country, and the Chugach Mountains on the horizon.

The trail ends at a group of backcountry campsites along the lake. Tippecanoe Rentals (see left) keeps canoes at the lake; if you want to use one you must pay and pick up your paddles and life vests before hiking in.

Sleeping

Nancy Lake State Recreation Area offers two road-accessible campgrounds, numerous backcountry campsites and 13 public-use cabins. The backcountry campsites are first-come-first-served, while the cabins can be rented for up to five nights. They cost between $30 and $60 per night and come in various sizes, sleeping from four to eight people.

Four of the cabins are on Nancy Lake; three of these can be reached via a short hike from the Nancy Lake Pkwy. Four more cabins are on Red Shirt Lake, but these require a 3-mile hike in and then a short canoe paddle. The cabin on Bald Lake is accessed by a quarter-mile hike. The other four cabins are on the Lynx Lake canoe route, with three on Lynx Lake and one on James Lake. The cabins are popular. Reserve them through the **Alaska Division of Parks** (☎ 745-3975; www.alaskastateparks.org; Mile 0.7 Bogard Rd), either online or in person at its Wasilla office.

South Rolly Lake Campground (sites $10), a drive-in campground, has 98 secluded sites; it's so large that you stand a good chance of finding an open site even on the weekend. It also has a canoe-rental shed.

Nancy Lake State Recreation Site (sites $10), just off George Parks Hwy south of the entrance to the parkway, is the only other vehicle-accessible campground. It's not nearly as nice as South Rolly Lake, though. The campground has 30 sites.

WILLOW

pop 2048

In the 1970s Willow, at Mile 69 of George Parks Hwy, was a sleepy little village that became famous for its controversial selection as the new Alaskan capital, which was to be moved from Juneau. The move was put on the back burner in 1982, however, when funding for the immense project was defeated in a general state election. But little Willow will not be forgotten. Its 2000 residents – mostly part-timers who keep a vacation cabin here – are finally getting the little slice of fame they were after, with the Iditarod dogsled race moving its official re-start – it has a short ceremonial start in downtown Anchorage – from Wasilla up to Willow. The race starts in early March, and it's an exciting time to be around.

Despite this history, there's nothing too exciting about this Lilliputian village. For many travelers heading north, Willow offers the first overwhelming view of Mt McKinley. If the day is clear, the 'Great One' dominates the skyline. Actually, just about anything would dominate the skyline of this sparse little town.

There's a nice bike trail paralleling the road between Wasilla and Willow. This could either be the departure point of a grand peddle up to Fairbanks or a short day trip.

In a pinch, sardine-style camping is available at **Willow Creek State Recreation Area** (sites $10), where the 140-site 'campground' – really just a parking lot near the Susitna River – caters to king-salmon fishers unconcerned about the lack of privacy. To get there, follow the signs a few miles west from Mile 70.8 of George Parks Hwy.

TALKEETNA

pop 848

This peppery little town at the end of the road (and at times toward the edge of reality) was once the quintessential off-the-grid Alaskan community. But now, thanks to the loads of cruise-ship visitors that flood onto main street every day, Talkeetna – reached from Mile 98.7 of George Parks Hwy, where a spur road heads 14.5 miles north to town – is not much more than an over-hyped tourist trap.

But despite all this, Talkeetna (pronounced towl-*keet*-nuh) still has enough to it to keep an independent traveler engaged for a day or two, with cool old buildings, some fun hikes and paddles nearby, flightseeing tours (worth the splurge), and a bevy of interesting local characters that only seem to surface at night (or during the winter) when the cruise-shippers head back to port. After all, you can't turn back time, and the Talkeetna of today still retains some of that local flavor that made it such an interesting place to visit 20 years ago when the signature bluegrass festival was just taking flight. So drop by and stay the night (that's when the packaged tourists return to their lodge and the local wildlife begins to howl), and dive into the syncopated cultural landscape that still makes this town unique.

Once a gold-mining center, Talkeetna's biggest draw today is its proximity (at least by air) to the Alaska Range. Among alpinists, the community is famed as the staging area for ascents of Mt McKinley, Mt Foraker, the Moose's Tooth and other dizzying summits, the very names of which jump-start the saliva glands of mountaineers the world over. In late spring and early summer an international coterie of climbers fills every bed in town. On their way to or from grand successes or humbling failures (which occasionally include death), they cut loose at the bars and eat mass quantities of non-freeze-dried food in every restaurant in town.

Orientation & Information

Though famed for its proximity to the mountains, Talkeetna sits in flat, lushly wooded country near the confluence of the Susitna, Talkeetna and Chulitna Rivers (the town gets its name from a Tanaina word meaning 'river of plenty').

A few visitor services are strung along the Talkeetna Spur Rd into town, but almost everything you'll need is within a stone's throw of Main St, which begins with a 'Welcome to Beautiful Downtown Talkeetna' sign at the town park and ends a few blocks later at the riverbank.

Alaska Mountain Shop (☎ 733-1016; 22131 South F St, just north of the cemetery; vary) Buy your climbing and camping gear here.

Library (☎ 733-2359; Mile 13.5, Talkeetna Spur Rd; 11am-6pm Mon-Wed & Fri, 11am-7pm Thu, noon-5pm Sat;) Just south of town. Offers free internet access.

Matanuska Valley Federal Credit Union (☎ 733-4891; 0.3 Mile Talkeetna Spur Rd) Just up from George Parks Hwy. Has the area's only full-service bank.

Post office (Spur Rd near Main St; 9am-5pm Mon-Fri)

Sunshine Community Health Center (☎ 733-2273; Mile 4.4 Talkeetna Spur Rd) Will get that grizzly-bear tooth out of your tush.

Talkeetna-Denali Visitors Center (☎ 733-2688, 800-660-2688; www.alaskan.com/talkeetnadenali) At the junction of George Parks Hwy and Talkeetna Spur Rd, provides remarkably frank recommendations and is far more helpful than the privately owned places in town that call themselves visitor centers.

Tanner's Trading Post (☎ 733-2621; Main St; 7am-9pm) Has an ATM, a Laundromat, some grocery items and showers.

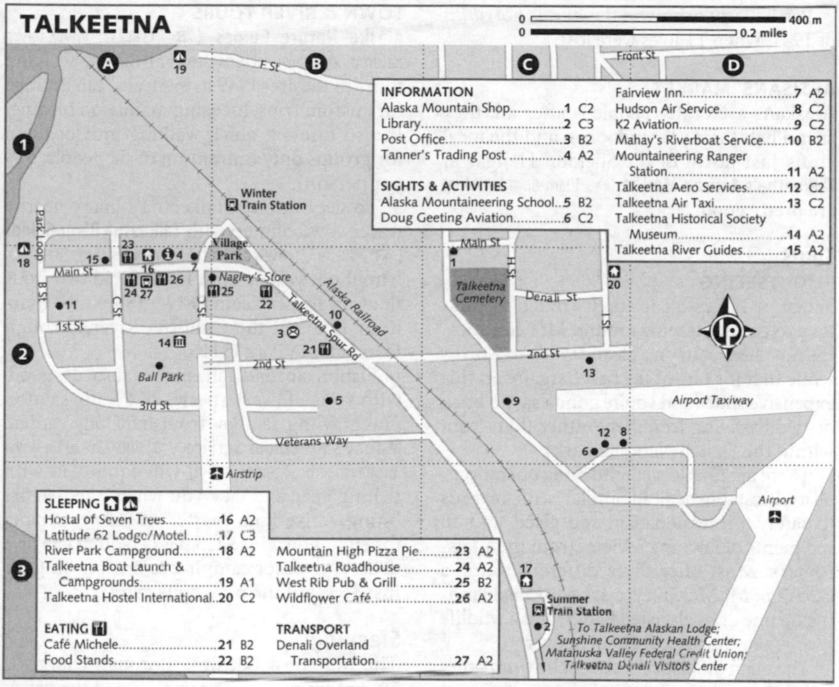

Sights

TALKEETNA HISTORICAL SOCIETY MUSEUM

A block south of Main St is this **museum** (☎ 733-2487; adult/child $3/free; 🕑 10am-6pm), a small complex of restored buildings. The town's 1936 schoolhouse features an exhibit devoted to Don Sheldon (the bush pilot who pioneered landing climbers high on Mt McKinley's glaciers for a better shot at the peak), as well as trapping and mining artifacts. The complex also includes a fully furnished trapper's cabin and a train depot. But the most fascinating building by far is the Section House. Inside you will discover a 12ft by 12ft relief model of Mt McKinley surrounded by Bradford Washburn's famous mural-like photos of the mountain. An exhibit devoted to the town's best-known climber, Ray 'the Pirate' Genet, is also on display here.

MOUNTAINEERING RANGER STATION

Whether you're intrigued by high-altitude alpinism or boggled by it, this **ranger station** (☎ 733-2231; cnr 1st & B Sts; 🕑 8am-6pm) provides an excellent window into that rarefied world. In addition to coordinating the numerous expeditions to Mt McKinley during the spring and summer, the station functions as a visitor center, with maps, books, photos and video presentations about the Alaska Range, as well as climbing-club flags from around the world and signed ice axes from successful ascents. Rangers offer presentations daily; a full calendar is posted.

TALKEETNA CEMETERY

The most solemn way to appreciate the effect of the mountain on Talkeetna is to visit the **cemetery**, a restful spot set among tall trees on 2nd St, just off Talkeetna Spur Rd near the airport.

Don Sheldon's grave is the most prominent, with the epitaph 'He wagered with the wind and won.' The Mt McKinley Climber's Memorial includes a stone for Ray Genet, despite the fact that his body was never removed from the slopes of Mt Everest. The most touching sight, however, is a memorial with the names and ages of all the climbers who've died on Mt McKinley and neighboring peaks.

Particularly grim was the *annus horribilis* of 1991, when 11 lives were lost.

ARTISANS' MARKET

Alaskans are crafty people – after all, they spend half their year indoors – and the local crafts just north of the Sheldon Hangar at **Talkeetna's Artisan Market** (10am-6pm Sat-Mon) are pretty good.

Tours

FLIGHTSEEING

When in Talkeetna, it's pretty much mandatory to go flightseeing around Mt McKinley. It's not cheap, but on a clear day it's so worthwhile that it's one of the best bargains in this expensive state (and you're gonna save a buck or two by flying from here rather than from within the Denali National Park).

There are four local flightseeing operations, all well established, all similar with regards to safety, professionalism and price, and all recipients of fawning reviews from their customers. Most offer three different tours: a circuit of Mt McKinley, a ski-equipped landing on one of its glaciated flanks, and a wildlife tour when the peak is clouded over.

The main difference between the companies is the planes they use: some have small aircraft that stay below 12,000ft but can weave in and out of canyons like gnats on steroids, while others fly higher, taking you into the thin air around the 20,320ft summit, where from April to mid-July you might even be able to spy climbing parties slogging toward the top. Also, some planes have above-window wings, meaning you get a less obstructed view of the scenery.

Decide what sort of trip works best for you and ask the right questions before you sign up. Plan on spending anywhere from around $180 to $300 per person for a flight, depending on flight length (usually between one and two hours) and whether you want to land on a glacier or circle the summit.

The companies all have their offices near the airstrip, a short jaunt across the railroad tracks from downtown.

Hudson Air Service (733-2321, 800-478-2321; www.hudsonair.com)
K2 Aviation (733-2291, 800-764-2291; www.flyk2.com)
Talkeetna Aero Services (733-2899, 888-733-2899; www.talkeetnaaero.com)
Talkeetna Air Taxi (733-2218, 800-533-2219; www.talkeetnaair.com)

TOWN & RIVER TOURS

Alaska Nature Guides (733-1237; www.alaskanatureguides.com) offers several nature walking tours in the area ($49 to $94), and can arrange for custom trips, focusing mainly on birding. It also offers a quick walking tour of town for groups only (minimum of six people, $19 per person).

To get out onto Talkeetna's many nearby waterways, sign up with **Talkeetna River Guides** (733-2477; www.talkeetnariverguides.com; Main St), who'll put you in a raft for a placid two-hour float on the Talkeetna River ($69) or a four-hour float on the Chulitna River, through Denali State Park ($115).

Fishing around Talkeetna is absurdly good, with runs of every species of Pacific salmon plus grayling, rainbow trout and Dolly Varden. **Mahay's Riverboat Service** (800-736-2210; www.mahaysriverboat.com; Spur Rd) will equip you with fishing gear and take you where the fish are biting. A five-hour charter is $165 per person; for eight hours it's $215 per person. It can also drop you off for camping or bush fishing for just $55 (but the pick-up is extra).

Sleeping

The Matanuska-Susitna Borough charges a 5% accommodations tax on top of the prices listed below.

BUDGET

River Park Campground (sites $10) This informal place at the end of Main St is a bit scruffy, but close to the river and the action. No RVs.

Talkeetna Hostel International (733-4678; www.talkeetnahostel.com; I St; sites/dm/s/d/tr $12/22/50/65/75;) This well-loved hostel even has a converted VW van ($35) you can sleep in – you can't get much more hippie than that. Popular with climbers and backpackers alike, this is the best hostel in town, with a cool host, large common area and kitchen, laundry, free internet, and the occasional fire for swapping tales and fighting the mossies. To get here, take 2nd St (the airport road) off Talkeetna Spur Rd; you'll pass I St on the way to the runway at the end of the road.

Talkeetna Boat Launch & Campgrounds (733-2604; sites $13) East of the tracks at the north end of F St, this tree-shrouded campground offers sites near the Talkeetna River and has restrooms, showers ($4) and a small store. If it seems off the beaten path, ask about the shortcut through the woods to downtown.

SCALING THE MOUNTAIN

So, has gazing up at lordly Mt McKinley infected you with summit fever?

If so, you're suffering from a century-old sickness. James Wickersham, the US district judge in Alaska, made the first documented attempt to scale Denali, reaching the 7500ft mark of the 20,320ft peak in 1903. His effort inspired a rash of ensuing bids, including Dr Frederick Cook's 1906 effort (which he falsely claimed was a success) and the 1910 Sourdough Expedition, where four Fairbanks miners, carrying only hot chocolate, donuts and a 14ft spruce pole, topped out on the North Peak only to realize it was 850ft lower than the true, more southerly summit.

Success finally came in 1913 when Hudson Stuck, Henry Karstens, Robert Tatum and Walter Harper reached the top on June 7. From there they saw the spruce pole on the North Peak to verify the claims of the Sourdough Expedition.

The most important date for many climbers, however, is 1951. That year, Bradford Washburn arrived and pioneered the West Buttress route, by far the preferred avenue to the top. Not long after, Talkeetna's two most famous characters – Ray 'the Pirate' Genet and Don Sheldon – began to have an impact on the climbing world. Genet was an Alaskan mountaineer who made a record 25 climbs up Mt McKinley, while Sheldon was a legendary glacier pilot. The two worked closely in guiding climbers to the top and, more importantly, rescuing those who failed. Sadly, the town lost both in quick succession, with Sheldon dying of cancer in 1975 and Genet freezing to death on Mt Everest four years later.

Nowadays, Denali's storied mountaineering history adds considerably to the mythic business of scaling the peak. Between 1000 and 1300 climbers attempt it each year, spending an average of three weeks on the slopes. About 85% use the West Buttress route, which involves flying in a ski plane from Talkeetna to the 7200ft Kahiltna Glacier and from there climbing for the South Peak, passing a medical/rescue camp maintained by mountaineering clubs and the National Park Service (NPS) at 14,220ft.

In a good season, when storms are not constantly sweeping across the range, more than 50% will be successful. In a bad year that rate falls below 40%, and several climbers may die.

If you're a seasoned alpinist you can mount an expedition yourself, or be among the 25% of Mt McKinley climbers who are part of guided ascents. Of the licensed guiding companies, only one is local: **Alaska Mountaineering School** (☎ 733-1016; www.climbalaska.org; Third St), which charges $5800 to lead you up the mountain.

Folks without high-altitude credentials would be better off opting for one of the company's one-, two- or three-day glacier treks on the shoulders of the mountain – a fine way to get a taste of what the mountaineers endure, but at an altitude that isn't life-threatening. These excursions cost from $1090, which covers the glacier flight and all the gear you'll need for the experience of a lifetime.

The school also offers mountaineering and glacier-travel courses ranging from $350 for a two-day glacier-travel seminar at Matanuska Glacier to $2650 for an intensive 12-day course.

Hostal of Seven Trees (☎ 733-7733; Main St; dm $20-25, r with without bath $75) While it's definitely less lively than the 'International,' this is a good bet if things are booked there, or if you are looking for a bit more comfort and quiet. Warning for you *borrachos* out there: there will be no booze in this hostel.

Talkeetna Roadhouse (☎ 733-1351; www.talkeetnaroadhouse.com; Main St; dm $21, s/d from $57/68, cabins $110) This place is the real Alaskan deal. It dates from 1917 and hosts scores of climbers in season. It has seven small private rooms without bath, a bunkroom and cute cabins out back, also without baths.

MIDRANGE & TOP END

Latitude 62 Lodge/Motel (☎ 733-2262; Mile 13.5 Talkeetna Spur Rd; s/d $68/79) If downtown Talkeetna is just too hippie-dippy for you, there's always this place, with hunting-lodge decor that includes plenty of pelts and skulls, as well as a fairly friendly bar and beer garden.

Talkeetna Alaskan Lodge (☎ 733-9500, 888-959-9590; www.talkeetnalodge.com; Mile 12.5 Talkeetna Spur Rd; r $69-399) This is a newish and luxurious Alaska Native Corporation-owned place with 153 rooms/suites, a restaurant and lounge. The hillside setting offers great views of Mt

McKinley. Prices drop dramatically before June and after August.

Eating & Drinking

If you plan on cooking for yourself, it's best to bring food in from Wasilla or Anchorage. There are a couple of cheap **food stands** on the corner of Talkeetna Spur Rd and Main St at the entrance to town.

RESTAURANTS

Talkeetna Roadhouse (☎ 733-1351; Main St; breakfast $7-13, sandwiches $7; ⏰ 7am-9pm) This venerable, colorful establishment has the best breakfast in town. Half-orders are adequate; fulls are mountain-sized. The restaurant also doubles as a bakery, cooking up giant cinnamon rolls in the morning.

Café Michele (☎ 733-5300; cnr Talkeetna Spur Rd & 2nd St; lunch $13-17, dinner $18-35; ⏰ 11am-4pm, 5:30-10pm) There's a Pacific Rim influence to the high-falluting food served at Talkeetna's fanciest restaurant. But despite the pretence – and we all enjoy a genuine cloth napkin on occasion – Café Michelle really does deliver. The international cuisine takes off in Asia with dishes like coconut-curry rice, then suddenly jets down to the US south for a romping jambalaya. Fine wines and good imported/craft beers are also available.

Wildflower Café (☎ 733-2694; Main St; sandwiches $14, mains $22-32; ⏰ 11am-9pm) Despite the circumspect service, this new entrant to the Talkeetna culinary scene is doing well for itself. The yummy burgers and large wholesome mains are served on the large deck, a perfect perch for people watching. Unfortunately, when the rain hits, things can get a bit cramped inside.

CAFÉS & QUICK EATS

Mountain High Pizza Pie (☎ 733-1234; Main St; pizza slices $3.50, sandwiches $5-11; ⏰ 11:30am-11pm) This arty, airy downtown establishment makes fabulous pizzas with names such as 'the Yentna' and 'the Grizzly.' It's also got lots of microbrews available.

West Rib Pub & Grill (☎ 733-3354; Main St; burgers & sandwiches $9-13; ⏰ 11:30-2am) Located at the back of Nagley's Store, this is a terrific place to soak in Talkeetna's live-and-let-live vibe, rubbing shoulders with visitors and locals alike. It's got burgers, salmon and halibut, plenty of craft brews, and, if it's sunny, outdoor seating.

Getting There & Around

AIR

You can stay in Talkeetna and get a ride up to Denali National Park with **Talkeetna Aero Services** (☎ 733-2899, 888-733-2899; www.talkeetnaaero.com). The company offers a day-trip package from Talkeetna to Denali National Park ($395) that includes round-trip flights, a McKinley tour (not to the summit), lunch and a bus tour in the park. If you just want a ride to the park and back, it's $225 each way, but this service is not always available.

BUS

There are a couple of options for busing between Talkeetna and points up and down George Parks Hwy. In the climbing (which starts in spring) and summer season, **Denali Overland Transportation** (☎ 733-2384, 800-651-5221; www.denalioverland.com; Main St in the Denali Dry Goods Store) runs shuttles to Denali ($75 per person, based on four person minimum) and Anchorage ($75 per person, based on four person minimum).

Alaska/Yukon Trails (☎ 479-2277, 800-770-7275; www.alaskashuttle.com) plies the whole George Parks Hwy, leaving Anchorage daily at around 7am, getting to downtown Talkeetna around 10:15am and continuing northbound through Denali Park to Fairbanks. The reverse trip departs Fairbanks around 8:45am daily, leaves downtown Talkeetna at 4:15pm and reaches Anchorage around 6:15pm. The one-way fare between Talkeetna and Denali is $52; to and from Anchorage is $59, or to or from Fairbanks it's $81.

TRAIN

The **Alaska Railroad** (☎ 265-2494, 800-544-0552; www.alaskarailroad.com) runs a couple of trains that stop in Talkeetna. From mid-May to mid-September, the *Denali Star* stops daily on its run between Anchorage and Fairbanks. The one-way adult fares are: Anchorage to Talkeetna $82; Talkeetna to Denali $79; Talkeetna to Fairbanks $115.

America's Last Flagstop Train, sometimes called the 'Local' or the 'Bud Car,' provides a local rural service from Thursday through Sunday in the summertime. It's a flag-stop train, departing Talkeetna at 12:15pm for the trip north to Hurricane Gulch, where it turns around and heads back the same day. This 'milk run' takes you within view of Mt McKinley and into some remote areas

POISON YOURSELF AT THE FAIRVIEW INN

Though not an official museum, the **Fairview Inn** (☎ 733-2423; Main St; ⏰ noon-late) might as well be. Founded in 1923 to serve as the overnight stop between Seward and Fairbanks on the newly constructed Alaska Railroad, the inn is listed on the National Register of Historic Places. Its old plank-floored saloon is classic Alaska: its walls are covered with racks of antlers, various furry critters (including a grizzly on the ceiling) and lots of local memorabilia. One corner holds Talkeetna's only slot machine; another is devoted to President Warren G Harding. When the railroad was finished in 1923, Harding arrived in Alaska and rode the rails to the Nenana River, where he hammered in the golden spike. Talkeetna locals swear (with grins on their faces) that he stopped at the Fairview Inn on the way home, was poisoned, and wound up dying in San Francisco less than a week later. Ever since, the Fairview has remained a fine place to be poisoned.

It also allows you to mingle with local residents, something not as easy to do on the express train *(Denali Star)*. Round-trip adult fare is $90.

DENALI STATE PARK

At 325,240 acres, Denali State Park is the fourth-largest state park in Alaska and is roughly half the size of Rhode Island. The entrance is at Mile 132.2 of George Parks Hwy. The park covers the transition zone between the coastal region and the spine of the Alaska Range, and provides numerous views of towering peaks, including Mt McKinley and the glaciers on its southern slopes.

Some say on a clear day the panorama of Mt McKinley here is the most spectacular view in North America. The park is largely undeveloped but does offer a handful of turnoffs, trails, three rental cabins and three campgrounds that can be reached from George Parks Hwy, which runs through the park.

It may share the same name and a border with the renowned national park to the north, but Denali State Park is an entirely different experience. Because of its lack of facilities you need to be better prepared for your hiking and backpacking adventures. But this may be the park's blessing, for it also lacks the crowds, long waits and tight regulations of Denali National Park.

At the height of the summer season, experienced backpackers may want to consider the state park as a hassle-free and cheaper alternative.

Information

The **Denali State Park Visitors Center** (☎ 745-3975; www.dnr.state.ak.us; Mile 147 George Parks Hwy; ⏰ 9am-6pm) is at the Alaska Veterans Memorial, just north of Byers Lake Campground. It has a few maps and brochures, for a price, but due to budget cuts it mostly sells candy bars and pop to the tour-bus crowd.

Activities

There are several excellent hiking trails and alpine routes in the park. Keep in mind that in the backcountry, open fires are allowed only on the gravel bars of major rivers. Pack a stove if you plan to camp overnight.

Troublesome Creek Trail was closed at the time of research do to flood damage. But when it re-opens, it's a worthwhile endeavor. The trail begins at a posted trailhead in the parking area at Mile 137.6 of George Parks Hwy and ascends along the creek until it reaches the treeline, where you enter an open area with alpine lakes and mountain views. From here the route is marked only by rock cairns as it heads north to Byers Lake. The 15-mile backpacking trip to Byers Lake Campground is of moderate difficulty, but if you're more adventurous, you can continue to Little Coal Creek Trail, a 36-mile trek above the treeline. Views from the ridges are spectacular. Numerous black bears feeding on salmon gave the creek its name. Because of them, the trail is usually closed to hikers from July to September.

Byers Lake Loop Trail is an easy 4.8-mile trek around the lake. It begins at Byers Lake Campground and passes six hike-in campsites on the other side, 1.8 miles from the posted trailhead. You can also rent canoes ($15 per hour, $45 full day) or kayaks ($10 per hour, $40 full day) at the Byers Lake Campground through **Southside River Guides** (☎ 733-7238).

Kesugi Ridge Traverse is a difficult route that departs from Byers Lake Trail and ascends its namesake ridge. Once on the ridge, you follow a route north to Little Coal Creek Trail

A GROOVABLE FEAST: ALASKA'S SUMMER FOLK FESTIVALS

Bust out the patchouli and hula-hoops, Alaska's folk festival circuit is bigger than ever. In fact, you could probably travel around this fair state doing nothing but groove. Here's some of our favorites in the interior. For a statewide listing, check out www.mosquitonet.com/~gcn/summfest.htm.

- **Trapper Creek Bluegrass Festival** (www.myspace.com/trappercreekbluegrass; Boots Bison Ranch, Mile 114 George Parks Hwy) Happens in the end of May, and actually has bluegrass performances. There's another music and arts festival here in the beginning of August.
- **Alaska Midnight Sun Song Camp** (www.songcamp.com; Alaska State Fairground, Palmer) A mid-June songwriter's gathering.
- **Fairbanks Summer Folk Fest** (www.alaskasbest.com/fiarbanksfolkfest; Pioneer Park, Fairbanks) This mid-June festival is a good family-oriented event.
- **Anderson Bluegrass Festival** (Anderson Riverside Park, Mile 283 George Parks Hwy) No bongos are allowed in the campgrounds at this mid-July bluegrass brawl, a locals' favorite.
- **Dawson City Music Festival** (www.dcmf.com; Dawson City, Canada) A mid-July freakfest in a tiny Yukon community.
- **Talkeetna Bluegrass Festival** (www.talkeetnabluegrass.com; admission $35, Suny-only $10) A four-day party coinciding with the first weekend in August. Called 'Alaska's greatest campout' and likened to Woodstock itself, the event has been an annual ritual for over 20 years. Now too big for downtown Talkeetna (attendance in past years has reportedly approached 5000 people), it takes place on a 142-acre site at Mile 102 of George Parks Hwy. Don't expect hour-upon-hour of banjo-pickin' here either, you're more likely to find yourself slam-dancing in a mud-soaked mosh-pit or gyrating to strobe-lit techno.
- **Acoustic Alaska Guitar Camp** (www.acousticalaska.com; Wasilla) BYOG (Bring Your Own Guitar) to this August jam session.

at the park's north end. Little Coal Creek Trail leads back to George Parks Hwy. The 27.4-mile route is well marked with cairns and flags.

If you're contemplating this trek, remember that it's far easier for hikers to access the ridge along Little Coal Creek Trail than it is to hike from Byers Lake Trail, which is a much steeper climb.

Little Coal Creek Trail departs from Mile 163.8 of George Parks Hwy, ascending to the alpine areas of Kesugi Ridge. From there you continue to the summit of Indian Mountain, an ascent of about 3300ft, or continue along the ridge to either Byers Lake or Troublesome Creek. Within 3 miles Little Coal Creek Trail climbs above the treeline at a spot known as the North Fork Birdhouse, a great place to set up an alpine camp for the night. It's a 9-mile round-trip to Indian Peak and 27.4 miles to Byers Lake.

Ermine Hill Trail is a short day-hike (3 miles one-way) accessed from the trailhead at Mile 156.5 George Parks Hwy.

The **Chulitna River** runs through the park. Floats can be arranged in Talkeetna (p348).

Sleeping

Lower Troublesome Creek Campground (Mile 137.2 George Parks Hwy; sites $10) This place has toilets, drinking water and 20 walk-in sites just yards from the parking lot.

Byers Lake Campground (Mile 147 George Parks Hwy; sites $10) As well as 73 sites, this campground offers access to walk-in sites along the loop trail around the lake, and to the state park's Byers Lake Cabins 1, 2 and 3. You can drive to Cabin 1, Cabin 2 is a half-mile hike from there, and Numero Tres is 70 yards beyond that. Each is $60 a night and must be reserved in advance, online at the **Alaska Division of Parks** (☎ 745-3975; www.alaskastateparks.org; Mile 0.7 Bogard Rd) in Wasilla.

Denali Viewpoint North Campground (Mile 162.7 George Parks Hwy; sites $10) This place has 20 sites and with the exception of some charming walk-in sites, it is basically a parking lot. However, the views are stunning. You overlook the Chulitna River while Mt McKinley overwhelms you from above. Interpretive displays and a spotting scope help you enjoy the panorama.

Byers Creek Lodge (☎ 733-7707; www.byerscreeklodge.com; Mile 144 George Parks Hwy; dm/r $50/150) With great views of the Alaska Range, this roadside attraction is a good bet if you prefer creature comforts to tent life.

CANTWELL & BROAD PASS

The northern boundary of Denali State Park is at Mile 168.5 George Parks Hwy. Situated at Mile 203.6, **Broad Pass** (2300ft) is a dividing line: rivers to the south drain into Cook Inlet, while waters to the north flow to the Yukon River. The area is at the treeline and worth a stop for some hiking. The mountain valley, surrounded by tall white peaks, is unquestionably one of the most beautiful spots along George Parks Hwy or the Alaska Railroad – both use the low gap to cross the Alaska Range.

North from the pass, George Parks Hwy descends 6 miles to **Cantwell** (pop 183), at the junction with Denali Hwy. At the junction you'll find gas pumps, and convenience stores. The 'town' itself is 2 miles west of here on the extension of the Denali Hwy. There's not much to see, but if you are tired, stop into 'town' and head over to the **Cantwell Lodge** (☎ 768-2300, 800-768-5522; www.cantwelllodge.ak.com; 2 miles west of George Parks Hwy on the Denali Hwy western extension; s/d $40/75) which has rundown rooms that may or may not be for rent – depending on the whim of the owner – and a cool locals' bar.

NENANA

pop 553

The only significant town between Denali National Park and Fairbanks is Nenana (nee-*na*-nuh, like 'banana') at Mile 305 of George Parks Hwy, which lies at the confluence of the Nenana and Tanana (*tan*-uh-naw, not like 'banana') Rivers. Though the big industry here is barging freight downstream, for visitors and northerners alike the community is most famous for the Nenana Ice Classic, an eminently Alaskan game of chance in which prognosticators attempt to profit by guessing when the ice will break up on the Nenana River (p355).

There's lots of info on the Ice Classic at the very helpful **Nenana Visitor Center** (☎ 832-5435; Mile 304.5 George Parks Hwy; 8am-6pm), located at the entrance to town in a one-room log cabin (note the sod roof abloom with wildflowers). Outside you'll find the *Taku Chief* river tug, which once pushed barges along the Tanana River.

Historically, Nenana was little more than a roadhouse until it was chosen as the base for building the northern portion of the Alaska Railroad in 1916. The construction camp quickly became a boomtown that made history on July 15, 1923, when President Warren G Harding arrived to hammer in the golden spike on the north side of the Tanana. The sickly Harding, the first president ever to visit Alaska, missed the golden spike the first two times, or so the story goes, but finally drove it in to complete the railroad.

In preparation for the president's arrival, the Nenana train station was built in 1922 at the north end of A St. Extensively restored in 1988 it's now on the National Register of Historic Places. The building includes the jumbled **Alaska Railroad Museum** (☎ 832-5500; admission free; 9:30am-6pm), which displays not just railroad memorabilia but local artifacts ranging from ice tongs to animal traps. East of the station, a monument commemorates Harding's visit. On Front and Market Sts, **St Mark's Episcopal Church** dates from 1905. The interior has many beautiful handcrafted features including an altar with traditional Athabascan beadwork.

Down on the river you might see some **fish wheels** at work during the late-summer salmon runs. These traditional traps scoop fish out of the water as they swim upstream to spawn. The riverfront is also home to the **Alfred Starr Nenana Cultural Center** (☎ 832-5527; 10am-6pm), which informs visitors about local culture and history.

Sleeping & Eating

Nenana RV Park & Campground (☎ 832-5230; nenanarv@gmail.com; cnr 4th & B Sts; sites camp $6, RV $15-27) Has spots for tenters in a grassy expanse near the visitor center. Showers and laundry are available.

Rough Woods Inn & Café (☎ 832-5299; www.roughwoodsinn.biz; 623 N A St; r $75-130; breakfast & lunch $2-12, dinner $8-20; 💻) Right on A St, this isn't the cleanest place on the planet, but when in Nenana… Some rooms do have kitchenettes, and they can sleep up to four people, a boon for budgeters. The wholesome family breakfasts are quite filling.

Moocher's Bar (across from Railroad Museum) is the locals' favorite.

DENALI HIGHWAY

Considered one of Alaska's most stunning drives, this 135-mile route was opened in 1957 as the only road to the national park. It became a secondary route after George Parks Hwy was completed in 1972. Now it's open only from mid-May to October, when it sees just a trickle of tourists, hunters and anglers. A highway in only the titular sense, the Denali Hwy is basically a gravel road from Cantwell, just south of Denali National Park on George Parks Hwy, to Paxson on Richardson Hwy.

Most of the highway is at or near the treeline, running along the foothills of the Alaska Range and through glacial valleys where you can see stretches of alpine tundra, enormous glaciers and braided rivers. All that scenery is a blessing, because the road itself, though perfectly passable in a standard auto, is slow going. Due to washboarding and hairpin curves you'll likely average just 35mph, taking six hours from end to end. Better yet, make fat-tire fun out of it; the highway in its rough-and-tumble state has become a favorite for mountain-bikers.

Hikers can reach the surrounding backcountry via numerous trails off the highway, though few are marked and most are trafficked by ATVs.

There are also several popular paddling routes in the area. Ask locals at the roadhouses for information and take along topographic maps that cover the areas you intend to trek or paddle.

There are no established communities along the way, but the roadhouses provide food, beds and sometimes gas. Most of the development is at the Paxson end of the highway. If you're driving, fill up with gas at Paxson or Cantwell. The following descriptions follow the route from east to west.

CANTWELL TO TANGLE LAKES

The junction at Cantwell is at Mile 133.8 of the Denali Hwy. Within 3 miles the pavement ends, rough gravel takes over, and the road ascends into the sort of big-sky territory that will dominate it for the duration.

Fifteen miles along, at Mile 118, you'll reach a put-in for the silt-choked **Nenana River**, which can be paddled in Class I to II conditions from here to George Parks Hwy, 18 river miles distant. Novices will want to pull out there; after George Parks Hwy it gets way hairier.

At Mile 104, just before a bridge over the Brushkana Creek, is the BLM's Brushkana Creek Campground (see opposite). If you've brought your rod you can try your hand at catching grayling and Dolly Varden in the fast-flowing waters.

Another fishing possibility is Butte Lake, at the end of the **Butte Lake Trail** (Mile 94 Denali Hwy), a willow-lined, 5-mile ATV track. Nearly opposite the trailhead is a pull-off with excellent mesa-top views of the Alaska Range.

Several potential hiking trails, none signposted, branch off the highway in the dozen or so miles after Gracious House Lodge, a roadhouse at Mile 82. One of them is the **Snodgrass Lake Trail**, which begins from a parking area between Mile 80 and Mile 81 and leads 2 miles south to Snodgrass Lake, known for its good grayling fishing.

Just over the Susitna River is the **Denali Trail** (Mile 79 Denali Hwy), more of a gravel road, which begins on the highway's north side at the 'Clearwater Creek Controlled Use Area' sign. The 6-mile route winds to the old mining camp of Denali, first established in 1907.

A few old buildings still remain. Several mining trails branch off the trail, including an 18-mile route to Roosevelt Lake from Denali Camp. The area can provide experienced hikers with a good two- to three-day trip.

At Mile 56 a bridge crosses **Clearwater Creek**; outhouses and informal campsites are nearby. Another 14 miles on is the MacLaren River Lodge, just before you cross the MacLaren River.

On the river's far side is **Crazy Dog Kennels** (☎ 347-9013; www.denalihighwaytours.com), the summer operation of Yukon Quest champ John Schandelmeier and his wife, Zoya DeNure, who recently finished the Iditarod. Impassioned about their pups, they run the only dog-yard in Alaska that rescues unwanted sled dogs and turns them into racers. A tour of the kennel is $20 for adults and $12 for children 12 and under; it's nice if you call ahead.

From here, the highway ascends **MacLaren Summit** (Mile 37 Denali Hwy), at 4086ft one of the highest highway passes in the state. The summit offers great views of Mt Hayes, Hess Mountain and Mt Deborah to the west and MacLaren Glacier to the north.

At Mile 32, at a parking lot on the highway's north side, signage marks the trailhead of the 2-mile **Glacier Lake Trail**. Another 7 miles down the highway you'll cross Rock Creek Bridge, where the signposted **Landmark Gap Trail** leads north 3 miles to Landmark Gap Lake, at an elevation of 3217ft. You can't see the lake from the highway, but you can spot the noticeable gap between the Amphitheater Mountains.

BREAKING THE ICE IN NENANA

For stir-crazy Alaskans, nothing heralds the end of winter like the break-up of ice on the nearest river. It's a subject of much anticipation everywhere in the state – but nowhere more than in Nenana, where this seasonal guessing game has become the state's preeminent gamble.

The **Nenana Ice Classic** (www.nenanaakiceclassic.com) began in 1917 when cabin-feverish Alaska Railroad surveyors pooled $800 and bet on when the ice would disintegrate on the frozen Tanana River. Eight decades later the wager is the same, but the stakes are much higher, with a 2008 jackpot of $303,895.

Anyone can play: just shell out $2.50 for a ticket and register your guess, down to the month, day, hour and minute. Though tickets are on sale throughout Alaska from February 1 to April 5, in the summer they can be purchased only in Nenana. Most tourist-oriented places in town sell them, including the Rough Woods Inn and the Tripod Gift Shop across from the visitor center.

Come next spring, the first movement of the ice will be determined by a 'tripod' which stands guard on the Tanana, 300ft from shore. Any surge will dislodge the tripod, which tugs on a cord, which in turn stops a clock on shore. The exact time on the clock will determine the winner.

And when will it happen? Your prediction is as good as anybody's. The earliest break-up came at 3:27pm on April 20, 1940. (Al Gore's guess is some 10 days before that; he's already booked his Lear Jet to retrieve his prize money!) The latest was 11:41am, May 20, 1964. (George W Bush predicts the ice will never melt, after years of 'misunderestimations'). The vast majority were between April 29 and May 12. And it almost never happens between midnight and 9am.

But don't get too excited: no matter what time you guess, many others will likely guess the same – meaning that if you win, your payout will likely be just a fraction of the jackpot.

You can view a replica of the Ice Classic tripod and past books of guesses – vast tomes some 4in thick – at the Nenana Visitor Center. You can usually see the next Nenana Ice Classic tripod even if you're not getting off the train. During the summer, it's on the banks of the Tanana River near the depot, ready to be positioned on the ice in February during the town's Tripod Raising Festival.

Sleeping & Eating

The Denali Hwy between Cantwell and Tangle Lakes features scores of pull-offs ideal for informal camping.

Brushkana Creek Campground (Mile 104.3 Denali Hwy; sites $8) This place offers 22 not-very-private sites, a picnic shelter, drinking water and a meat rack for the hunters who invade the area in late summer and fall.

Crazy Dog Cabins (☎ 347-9013; www.denalihighwaytours.com; Mile 42 Denali Hwy; cabins $95-110) The hospitable owners of the Crazy Dog Kennels decided to expand their offering recently, and now offer a couple of hand-hewn log cabins. None of the cabins have running water, but they have outhouse toilets and private decks that look onto a little pond: a great spot to geek out for the afternoon.

Gracious House Lodge (☎ 259-1111; www.alaskaone.com/gracious; Mile 82 Denali Hwy; r with bath $137, s/d without bath $84/105; café 8am-8pm) This half-century-old establishment is a collection of cabins, trailers and Quonset huts with killer views of the mountains. The proprietors are considering selling, but still offer flightseeing, lodging and meals.

MacLaren River Lodge (☎ 822-5444; www.maclarenlodge.com; Mile 42 Denali Hwy; dm $25, cabins $120; café 7am-10pm;) On the edge of the MacLaren River, this lodge has a bar, restaurant and pool table.

TANGLE LAKES TO PAXSON

After several miles of lonely road, the Denali Hwy suddenly gets busier and better maintained as it descends into the Tangle Lakes area, a magnet for birders, anglers and paddlers. Pavement begins around Mile 21. Most of the lakes – as many as 40 in spring – can be seen from the Wrangell Mountain Viewpoint at Mile 13.

Activities

PADDLING

The **Delta River Canoe Route** is a 35-mile paddle that starts at Tangle Lakes Campground (p356) and ends a few hundred yards from Mile 212.5 of Richardson Hwy. Cross Round Tangle Lake and continue to Lower Tangle Lake, where you must make a portage around a waterfall. Below it is a set of Class III rapids that you must either line for 2 miles or paddle if you

DENALI HIGHWAY

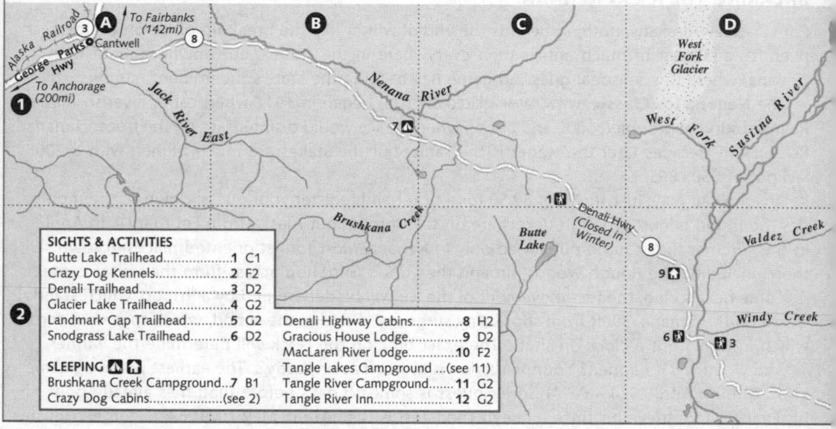

have an experienced hand. Every year many canoeists damage their boats beyond repair on these rapids and then have to hike 15 miles back out to the Denali Hwy. The remainder of the route is a much milder trip.

The **Upper Tangle Lakes Canoe Route** is easier and shorter than the Delta River route but needs four portages, which aren't marked but are easy to work out in the low-bush tundra. All paddlers trying this route must have topo maps. The route starts where the Denali Hwy crosses the Tangle River, passing through Upper Tangle Lake before ending at Dickey Lake, 9 miles to the south. There is a 1.2-mile portage into Dickey Lake.

From here, experienced paddlers can continue by following Dickey Lake's outlet to the southeast into the Middle Fork of the Gulkana River. For the first 3 miles the river is shallow and mild, but then it plunges into a steep canyon where canoeists have to contend with Class III and IV rapids. Most canoeists choose to line their boats carefully or make a portage. Allow seven days for the 76-mile trip from Tangle Lakes to Sourdough Creek Campground on the Gulkana River off Richardson Hwy.

HIKING

The unsignposted **Swede Lake Trail** (Mile 15 Denali Hwy) leads south 3 miles to Swede Lake, passing Little Swede Lake at the 2-mile mark. Beyond here it continues to the Middle Fork of the Gulkana River, but the trail is extremely wet at times and suitable only for off-road vehicles. Anglers fish the lakes for trout and grayling. Inquire at the Tangle River Inn (below) for directions to the trail and an update on its condition.

Sleeping

The Denali Highway Cabins (p369) near Paxson offer some of the nicest lodging options in the area, but they aren't all that close to the beauty that surrounds the Tangle Lakes region.

Tangle River Campground (Mile 21.7 Denali Hwy; sites free) Located right at the put-in for the Delta River canoe route, this seven-site campground is extremely popular; good luck finding a spot.

Tangle Lakes Campground (Mile 21.5 Denali Hwy; sites free) On the shores of Round Tangle Lake, this 22-site campground is still free despite its popularity.

Tangle River Inn (☎ 822-3970; www.tangleriverinn.com; Mile 20 Denali Hwy; r with/without bath $95-75, cabins $130; 💻) This is a popular stop for anglers, with a quality café in a log building overlooking the lakes. The folks running the place are friendly, but you can probably score nicer digs, with equally good views, elsewhere along the road.

THE ALCAN/ALASKA HIGHWAY

One of the most impressive engineering feats of the 20th century, the Alaska Hwy reaches 1390 miles from Dawson Creek, British Columbia to Delta Junction, Alaska. A drive up (or down) the Alcan is one of those once-

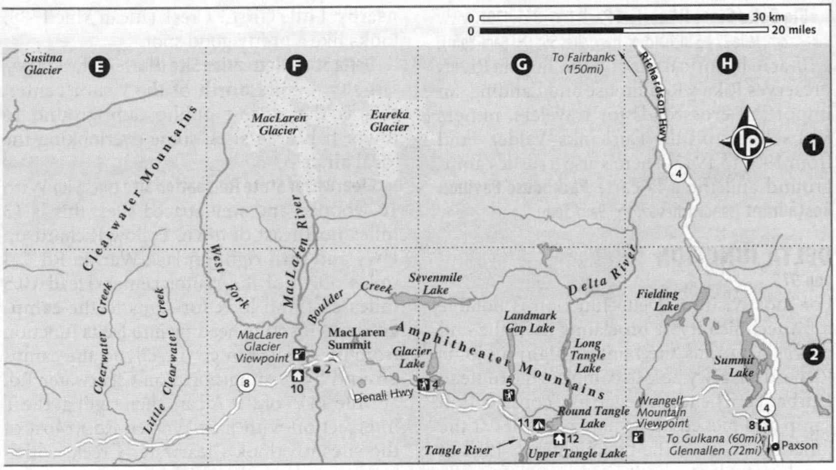

in-a-lifetime road trips that many folks dream of and few seldom actually accomplish.

The 98-mile stretch from Delta Junction to Fairbanks is 'technically' considered the Richardson Hwy, but most figure this to be the final leg of the Alcan. We, too, treat it as such.

The Alaska Hwy was famously punched through the wilderness in a mere eight months in 1942, which was part of a WWII effort to protect Alaska from expansionist Japan (p48). Commonly known as the Alcan, short for 'Alaska–Canada Military Highway,' it remains the only year-round overland route that links the 49th state to the Lower 48.

Approximately 300 of its miles, paved and well maintained, are within Alaska, between Fairbanks and the Yukon Territory border.

FAIRBANKS TO DELTA JUNCTION

From Fairbanks, Richardson Hwy runs 98 relatively unscenic miles to Delta Junction. From there, the Richardson continues to the south via Glennallen to Valdez, while the Alcan branches off and passes through Tok en route to Canada.

Chena Lakes Recreation Area (Mile 346.7 Richardson Hwy; day-use parking $5, sites $10) was the last phase of an Army Corps of Engineers flood-control project prompted by the Chena River's flooding of Fairbanks in 1967.

Two separate parks make up the area, offering nature paths, paved trails and swimming, as well as canoe, sailboat and paddleboat rentals. Three campground loops provide access to about 80 sites.

Unless you're really keen on in-line skating, the whole thing feels a bit overdeveloped for Alaska.

Salcha River State Recreation Site (Mile 323.3 Richardson Hwy; sites $10) offers access to the Salcha and Tanana Rivers for fishing and boating ($10 boat launch). It has a basic camping area on a gravel bar, plus the reservable **Salcha River Public-Use Cabin** (☎ 451-2705; www.dnr.state.ak.us/parks/cabins; per night $25) right by the boat dock. To reach the state recreation site, turn in at the Salcha Marine boat dealership.

Harding Lake State Recreation Area (Mile 321.5 Richardson Hwy; sites $10, day-use parking $5, boat launch $10) is 43 miles from Fairbanks and 1.5 miles northeast of the Alcan, and has a highly developed campground with over 90 sites, a ranger office, picnic shelters, horseshoes, volleyball, swimming, canoeing, and fishing (Arctic char and pike) in the natural lake. Five group walk-in sites are on the water.

Birch Lake Military Recreation Site (Mile 305.5 Richardson Hwy; sites $10, day-use parking $5; boat launch $10) is jam-packed on weekends, when the lake is abuzz with personal watercraft and the parking lot is filled with noisy kids on tricycles. The **Birch Lake Cabin** (☎ 269-8400; www.dnr.state.ak.us/parks/cabins; $25) is available September through May – that's right, that's the winter, Frosty.

At Mile 277.7 you'll come to Quartz Lake State Recreation Area, a large camping area (p358).

Big Delta State Historical Park (☎ 895-4201; www.rikas.com; Mile 274.5 Richardson Hwy; sites $5; 🕑 8am-8pm), a 10-acre historical park on the Tanana River, preserves Rika's Roadhouse and Landing, an important crossroads for travelers, miners and soldiers on the Fairbanks–Valdez Trail from 1909 to 1947. There's also a rustic campground and the à la carte **Packhouse Pavilion Restaurant** (sandwiches $7; 🕑 9am-5pm).

DELTA JUNCTION

pop 975

For most visitors, Delta Junction is notable for a technicality: it proclaims itself the end of the Alcan, as the famous highway joins Richardson Hwy here to complete the route to Fairbanks. The town began as a construction camp and picked up its name as it lies at the junction between the two highways. It's not much to look at, and it can be an unfriendly place, but as long as you're here, might as well stop to enjoy what the town does have to offer. The big DeltanaFair, with giant vegetables, livestock shows and parades, is on the last weekend of July.

Information

Delta Community Library (☎ 895-4102; 2291 Deborah St; 🕑 10am-6pm Mon-Thu, 10am-7pm Fri, 10am-5pm Sat, 1-5pm Sun; 💻) The best place in town to check your email. It shares a building with City Hall.

Delta Junction Visitor Center (☎ 895-5063; www.deltachamber.org; Mile 1422 the Alcan; 🕑 8am-8pm summer) More of a gift shop than a visitor center, this place is usually jammed with RVers clamoring to purchase 'End-of-the-Alaska-Highway' certificates ($1).

Sights

Across the parking lot from the visitor center is **Sullivan Roadhouse** (admission free; 🕑 9am-6pm). The classic log structure was built in 1906 and served travelers along the Fairbanks–Valdez Trail until 1927. It was placed on the National Register of Historic Places in 1979 and in 1997 was moved, log by log, from Fort Greely to its present location in the Triangle. Now a museum, the roadhouse displays historic photographs and excavated artifacts in several exhibits dedicated to travel in Alaska in the early 1900s, the so-called 'roadhouse era.'

Sleeping

Delta Junction is blessed with scads of nearby campgrounds and no bed tax. And the bold and broke may consider guerrilla camping nearby; Little Girstie Creek (Alcan Mile 1388) looks like a pretty good spot.

Delta State Recreation Site (Mile 267 Richardson Hwy; sites $10) A mile north of the visitor center, this is the closest public campground to town. It has 24 sites, some overlooking the local airstrip.

Clearwater State Recreation Site (sites $10) With 16 wooded and well-spaced sites, this is 13 miles northeast of town. Follow Richardson Hwy and turn right on Jack Warren Rd, 2.4 miles north of the visitor center. Head 10.5 miles east and look for signs to the campground. (If you're heading into Delta Junction from Tok, you can go directly to the campground by turning north on Clearwater Rd, at Mile 1415 of the Alcan, then right at the T intersection with Jack Warren Rd.) Most of the sites overlook Clearwater Creek, which has a good grayling fishery and some fun paddling opps.

Quartz Lake State Recreation Area (Mile 277.8 Richardson Hwy; sites $10) Covering 600 acres north of town (3 miles from the Richardson Hwy), this area has 16 campsites in the loop and many more RV sites in an overflow parking area. A trail from the campground leads over to nearby Lost Lake, where there are 12 more campsites. The Alaska Department of Natural Resources' reservable Glatfelder and Quartz Lake public-use **cabins** (www.dnr.state.ak.us/parks/cabins/north; per night $25) are other options.

Kelly's Alaska Country Inn (☎ 895-4667; www.kellysalaskacountryinn.com; 1616 Richardson Hwy; s/d/tr $109/119/124; 💻) Two blocks north of the visitor center, this recently remodeled place has spacious, clean rooms, some with kitchenettes. This is the best hotel in town, and some rooms even have mirrors on the domed ceilings. You know what we're talking about…Bum-chicka-bum-bum!

Eating

Buffalo Center Diner (☎ 895-5089; 1680 Richardson Hwy; breakfast $6-12, lunch $8-12, dinner $16-25; 🕑 6am-9pm) Across from the IGA, this is certainly the town's busiest restaurant and would be your standard roadside diner save for the emphasis on local buffalo products. Try a bowl of buffalo black-bean chili ($4.75).

IGA Food Cache (Mile 266 Richardson Hwy; 🕑 6:30am-9pm Mon-Sat, 9am-8pm Sun) A half-mile north of the visitor center, this is a market with a bakery, deli and an espresso cart, plus homemade soup and other ready-to-eat items to go. It's the place to go in the morning for coffee, a pastry and a bit of local news.

Getting There & Away

Alaska Direct Bus Line (☎ 800-770-6652; www.alaskadirectbusline.com) stops in Delta Junction Sundays, Wednesdays and Fridays on its run between Fairbanks ($45) and Tok ($25). From Tok you can continue to Whitehorse, Glennallen or Anchorage.

TOK

pop 1353

Tok, 92 miles up the Alcan from the Canadian border, is the first Alaskan town motorists on multiweek pilgrimages from the Lower 48 will encounter. Thus, this hodgepodge of gas stations, motels and RV parks is viewed with a strange, out-of-proportion reverence, like a sort of pearly gates opening onto heavenly Alaska. The town was born in 1942 as a construction camp for the highway, and was originally called Tokyo Camp until anti-Japanese sentiment caused locals to shorten it to Tok. From here, the rest of the state beckons: the Alcan heads 206 miles northwest to Fairbanks; Tok Cutoff & Glenn Hwy reaches 328 miles southwest to Anchorage; and the Taylor Hwy curls back 161 miles to Eagle. Good thing there's so many ways out of town, as the best thing about Tok is generally leaving Tok.

Information

Alaska Public Lands Information Center (☎ 883-5667; www.nps.gov/aplic; Mile 1314 The Alcan; 8am-7pm)

Tok Mainstreet Visitors Center (☎ 883-5775; 8am-7pm Mon-Sat, 9am-7pm Sun) Near the corner of the Tok Cutoff and the Alcan.

Sleeping

There are several B&Bs of varying quality just west of town. Check with the visitor center for listings.

Tok River State Recreation Site (Mile 1309 The Alcan; sites $15) On the Tok River's east bank, this is 4.5 miles east of Tok and has 27 campsites, a boat launch, picnic shelter, water, toilets and a telephone.

Moon Lake State Recreation Site (Mile 1331 The Alcan; sites $15) Fourteen sites sit next to placid Moon Lake, 17 miles west of Tok on the Alcan.

Burnt Paw Cabins (☎ 883-4121; www.burntpawcabins.com; r $119;) Just west of the cut-off junction, this is the best spot in the town proper, offering four modern sod-roof cabins, each with private bath and decorated with a different Alaskan theme.

Mooseberry Inn (☎ 883-5496; www.amooseberryinn.com; Mile 1316 The Alcan; r $129-149;) Just 2.5 miles west of Tok, this new B&B has cute and comfy rooms, private balconies and a big breakfast in a homey family atmosphere, making it one of the best options outside of town. The friendly owner speaks German. To get here, head south of the Alcan at Mile 1316 on Scooby Road, then take a quick right on Maes Way.

Eating & Drinking

Fast Eddy's (☎ 883-4411; Mile 1313.3 The Alcan; burgers $7-11, pizza $14-22; 6am-11pm) Perhaps the most famous eatery on the Alcan, big and bustling Fast Eddy's is a step above your average diner, with a massive salad bar and more grey-hairs than you can scare off with a rattling bottle of Geritol.

Grumpy Grizz Café (☎ 883-2233; 1314 The Alcan; sandwiches $9, mains $10-13; 6am-9pm) Next to the Chevron station, this roadside café offers several varieties of fried food: fried fish, fried chicken, fried halibut, and of course French fries. It seems only the salad bar lacks a requisite fried item, but you can always add some fried chicken to top off your greens.

Three Bears Grocery (☎ 883-5195; 1314 The Alcan; 7am-10pm) Across the Alcan from the Alaska Public Lands Information Center. It has a decent selection of groceries and a few baked goods.

Tok Lodge Bar (half mile south of the Tok cutoff) This bar has shuffle-puck, pool and jäger bombs: 'these are a few of our favorite things.'

Getting There & Away

BUS

The buses of **Alaska Direct Bus Line** (☎ 800-770-6652; www.alaskadirectbusline.com) all pass through Tok on Sunday, Wednesday and Friday, stopping at the village Texaco a short distance southeast of the highway junction down the Alcan. From there they head northwest to Fairbanks ($70), southwest to Anchorage ($92), and southeast to Whitehorse ($125), where you can transfer to a bus to Skagway.

Alaska/Yukon Trails (☎ 800-770-7275; www.alaskashuttle.com) runs tours between Fairbanks and Dawson City ($162 one way with a two-person minimum).

HITCHHIKING

For many backpackers, the most important item at the Tok Mainstreet Visitors Center is the message board. Check out the board or display your own message if you're trying to hitch a ride through Canada along the Alcan. It's best to arrange a ride in Tok and not wait until you reach the international border. In recent years, the Canadian customs post at the border has developed a reputation as one of the toughest anywhere in the world. It's not unusual to see hitchhikers, especially Americans, turned back at the border for having insufficient funds.

TAYLOR HIGHWAY

The Taylor Hwy runs 161 miles north from Tetlin Junction, 13 miles east of Tok on the Alcan, through the lovable tourist trap of Chicken and on to the sleepy, historic community of Eagle on the Yukon River. Massive wildfires in 2004 and 2005 have scarred many sections of the scenic drive, including the areas around Mt Fairplay, Polly Summit and American Summit. But the large swaths of burnt spruce forest create an interesting 'Suessical' landscape, making it still worth the drive. Until recent years the route was infamously rough, though these days the only white-knuckle stretch is the last 65 miles from Jack Wade Junction to Eagle. The highway remains closed during winter months (generally from October to May), when you can get to Eagle by plane, snowmachine or dog sled.

The highway takes paddlers to both the Fortymile River and the Yukon-Charley Rivers National Preserve, and also offers much off-road hiking. As on the Denali Hwy, many of the trailheads are unmarked, making it necessary to have the appropriate topographic maps. Many trails are off-road-vehicle tracks that hunters use heavily in late summer and fall.

By Alaskan standards summer traffic is light to moderate until you reach Jack Wade Junction, where the majority of vehicles continue east to Dawson City, Yukon, via the Top of the World Hwy (p362). Hitchhikers aiming for Eagle from the junction will have to be patient. If you're driving, leave Tok or Dawson with a full tank of gasoline, because roadside services are limited.

The first section of the Taylor, from Tetlin Junction (Mile 0) to just shy of Chicken, is now paved. Within 9 miles of Tetlin Junction you'll begin to climb Mt Fairplay (5541ft). At Mile 35 a lookout near the summit is marked by trash cans and an interpretive sign describing the history of Taylor Hwy. From here you should see superb views of Mt Fairplay and the valleys and forks of Fortymile River to the north. The surrounding alpine area offers good hiking for those wanting to stretch their legs.

The first state campground is the 25-site **West Fork Campground** (Mile 49 Taylor Hwy; sites $8), which recent forest fires nearly incinerated. There are guerrilla camping spots all along the road. Travelers packing gold pans can try their luck in West Fork River, which is the first access point for a canoe trip down Fortymile River.

Chicken

pop 6

After crossing a bridge over Fortymile River's Mosquito Fork at Mile 64.4, Taylor Hwy enters dusty Chicken, once a thriving mining center and now more of a punchline than an actual community. The town's name allegedly originated at a meeting of resident miners in the late 1800s. As the story goes, they voted to dub their new tent-city 'Ptarmigan,' since that chickenlike bird was rampant in the area. Trouble is, no-one could spell it. The town's name has been Chicken ever since.

In retrospect, it was a savvy move: Nowadays, folks flock here for 'Go peckers!' coffee mugs and 'I got laid in Chicken' ballcaps. Profiting the most seems to be the **Chicken Creek Café, Liquor Store & Saloon** (breakfast $5-11, lunch & dinner $4-12; café 7am-9pm), on a spur road 300 yards north of the bridge. Their gift shop is extensive, the saloon has hats from every corner of the world, and the café, unsurprisingly, features lots of chicken on the menu. There are plans to rent cozy, and surprisingly secluded, cabins here for $90 to $150.

Just across the road is **Chicken Gold Camp** (☎ 235-6396; www.chickengold.com; sites camp/RV $10/18, cabins $90; café 7:30am-7:30pm;), where you can pitch a tent and consume paninis, ice cream and espressos in Chicken's toniest setting. For $10 there's also gold panning or tours of the Pedro Gold Dredge ($8), which worked creeks in the area from 1959 to 1967. For $35 it also has recreational kayaks available for half-day floats on the Fortymile River; and you can arrange for 'advanced' recreational mining trips – these take you out to a working claim, where you can sluice your way to riches.

Slightly further along on Taylor Hwy is Chicken's final tourist lure, the **Goldpanner** (www.townofchicken.com.com; Mile 66.8 Taylor Hwy; sites camp/RV $10/20; 8am-10pm), with more camping and gold panning (free), plus a three-hole golf course (free). For $5 you can tour Chicken's historic cabins across the road. With Chicken getting bigger and badder every year, the Goldpanner is looking to add hostel-style rooms.

Just north of Chicken is **Chicken Creek Bridge**, built on tailing piles from the mining era. The creek, and most other tributaries of the Fortymile River, are covered from one end to the other by active mining claims, and often from the highway you can see suction from dredges looking for gold. The bridge over South Fork (Mile 75.3) marks the most popular access point for the Fortymile River canoe route.

Fortymile River

Historic Fortymile River, designated as Fortymile National Wild River, offers an excellent escape into scenic wilderness for paddlers experienced in lining their canoes around rapids. It's also a step back into Alaska's gold-rush era; the river passes abandoned mining communities, including Franklin, Steele Creek and Fortymile, as well as some present-day mining operations. The best place to start paddling is at the bridge over South Fork, because the access points south of here on Taylor Hwy are often too shallow for an enjoyable trip.

Many canoeists paddle the 40 miles from South Fork bridge to the bridge over O'Brien Creek, at Mile 113 of Taylor Hwy, where you'll see the Forty-Mile Riverboat Tours complex. This two- to three-day trip involves three sets of Class III rapids. For a greater adventure, continue past O'Brien Creek and paddle the Fortymile into the Yukon River; from here, head north to Eagle at the end of the Taylor Hwy. This trip is 140 miles long and takes seven to 10 days. You'll need to line several sets of rapids in Fortymile River. Such an expedition requires careful planning.

Eagle Canoe Rentals (☎ 547-2203; www.aptalaska.net/~paddleak), in Eagle, is the closest place to get an expedition-worthy canoe or raft.

Forty-Mile Riverboat Tours (larryjune@starband.net; Taylor Hwy Mile 113.2; sites $5, cabins $80-125) arranges riverboat tours for $85 per hour, with a minimum of four people. The standard trip takes travelers to Steele Creek. While it's nicer to sleep in Eagle, if you get road weary, they have passable cabins and a sauna here.

South Fork Bridge to Eagle

Shortly after the South Fork put-in for Fortymile River, Taylor Hwy reaches **Walker Fork Campground** (Mile 82 Taylor Hwy; sites $8), which lies on both sides of the highway and has 18 sites, tables, firewood and a short trail to a limestone bluff overlook.

On the roadside at Mile 86 is the decaying **Jack Wade Dredge**, which operated from 1900 to 1942. When we were there you could climb inside the guts of it, but safety fears may soon put an end to this.

The Top of the World Hwy meets Taylor Hwy at **Jack Wade Junction** (Mile 95.7 Taylor Hwy). From here, the route north to Eagle isn't for the faint of heart. It's the worst stretch of highway in Alaska, requires at least two hours to safely negotiate, and should be avoided by RVs – though cruise-ship tour buses manage to make it to town nearly every day.

Soon after the junction you'll climb to **Polly Summit** (3550ft) and then begin a very steep descent to the bridge over O'Brien Creek (Mile 113 Taylor Hwy), a common take-out for Fortymile River trips.

Primitive camping is possible at Mile 135, on the south side of a bridge over North Fork Solomon Creek. This is a former BLM campground that has not been maintained in years. Eight miles on is **American Summit** (3650ft), with excellent alpine views and hiking possibilities. Eagle is reached 18 miles later, after a long descent to the Yukon River.

Eagle

pop 110

One of the better-preserved boomtowns of the Alaskan mining era, Eagle is a quaint hamlet of log cabins and clapboard houses, inhabited by folks who seem disarmingly cosmopolitan. The original settlement, today called Eagle Village, was established by the Athabascans long before Francois Mercier arrived in the early 1880s and built a trading post in the area. A permanent community of miners took up residence in 1898. A year later, the US Army decided to move in and build a fort as part of its effort to maintain law and order in the Alaskan Interior. Judge Wickersham established a federal court at Eagle in 1900, and the next year President Theodore Roosevelt issued a charter that

DETOUR: TOP OF THE WORLD HIGHWAY

From Jack Wade Junction, Dawson City, one of the North's most intriguing, fun-drunk towns is just 79 miles – and almost all downhill. You reach this grail of the Klondike Gold Rush – now an irreverent tourist mecca – via the Top of the World Hwy. The route begins with a 13-mile dirt stretch sometimes called the Boundary Spur Rd, which heads to the one-horse community of Boundary (where there's gas, gifts and food, if anyone's home) and then 4 miles beyond to the international border – the continent's northernmost roadcrossing. Be forewarned: Canadian customs is open only from 8am to 8pm Alaska time; arrive too late and you'll be camping in the parking lot until morning. And these days even US citizens will be required to show a passport. Beyond the border the highway – mainly paved now, but with lots of gravel patches under repair – lives up to its name, twisting along high-country ridgetops with flabbergasting views and all sorts of offroad hiking options. There's significant wildfire damage around this area, but you'll still get some lovely views. After 66 miles of this you'll wind your way down to the Yukon River, where for now a wonderful car ferry (but soon, lamentably, an efficient, modern bridge) will convey you across the water to Dawson.

If you're without wheels, you can ride along the Top of the World Hwy with **Alaska/Yukon Trails** (☎ 800-770-7275; www.alaskashuttle.com), whose buses come this way each day in summer from Fairbanks ($162 one way). For more on Dawson City, consult Lonely Planet's *British Columbia*, which covers the Yukon Territory.

made Eagle the first incorporated city of the Interior.

Eagle reached its peak at the turn of the 20th century, when it boasted a population of more than 1500 residents, some of whom went so far as to call their town the 'Paris of the North,' though that was hardly the case. The overland telegraph wire from Valdez arrived here in 1903. This new technology proved particularly useful to the famous Norwegian explorer Roald Amundsen, who hiked overland to Eagle in 1905 after his ship froze in the Arctic Sea off Canada. From the town's telegraph office, he sent word to the world that he had just navigated the Northwest Passage. Amundsen stayed two weeks in Eagle and then mushed back to his sloop. Nine months later, the ship reached Nome, completing the first successful voyage from the Atlantic to the Pacific Ocean across the Arctic Ocean.

The gold strikes of the early 1900s, most notably at Fairbanks, began drawing residents away from Eagle and caused the removal of Judge Wickersham's court to the new city in the west. The army fort was abandoned in 1911, and at one point, it is said, the population of Eagle dipped to nine residents, seven of whom served on the city council. When the Taylor Hwy was completed in the 1950s, however, the town's population increased to its present level. In the late 1970s, noted author John McPhee arrived, rented a cabin for part of a year and worked on his bestseller *Coming into the Country*, which immortalized life in Eagle.

INFORMATION

Yukon-Charley Rivers National Preserve Visitor Center (☎ 547-2233; www.nps.gov/yuch; ⌚ 8am-5pm) The headquarters for the Yukon-Charley Rivers National Preserve is the best place for info, not just on the 3906-sq-mile preserve but on Eagle proper. It's on the banks of the Yukon River, off 1st Ave beside the downtown airstrip.

Eagle Trading Company Motel (☎ 547-2220; www.eagletrading.com; 3 Front St) The place to get pricey gas, food, cash (from the ATM) and even take a shower.

SIGHTS & ACTIVITIES

Tours

Residents say Eagle has the state's largest 'museum system,' boasting five restored turn-of-the-20th-century buildings. If you're spending a day here, the best way to see the buildings and learn the town's history is to head to **Judge Wickersham's Courthouse** (cnr Berry St & 1st Ave) at 9am, when the **Eagle Historical Society** (☎ 547-2325; www.eagleak.org) commences its three-hour town walking tour. For $5 (children 12 and under free) you'll see the Courthouse, **Eagle City Hall**, the **Log Church**, **Fort Egbert**, **Redmen Hall**, the **Customs Building Museum** and **Amundsen Park**, where a plaque commemorates explorer Roald Amundsen's visit. Tours may be available at other times through special arrangement.

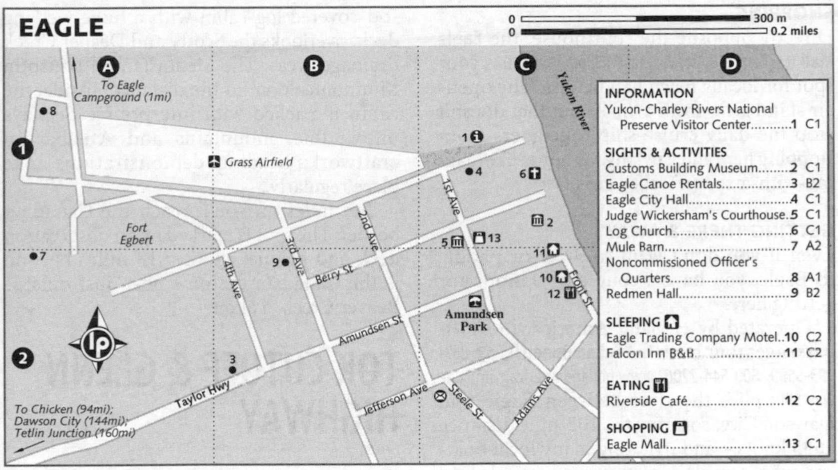

To the north of town is **Fort Egbert**, which can be reached from the Taylor Hwy via 4th Ave. The BLM has restored the old army fort, which once contained 37 buildings; among the structures are the restored mule barn, carriage house, doghouse and officers' quarters, which are clustered together in one section of the fort. You can wander past it on your own but the Eagle Historical Society tour is the only way to go inside.

Paddling

During its heyday, Eagle was an important riverboat landing for traffic moving up and down the Yukon.

Today it's a departure point for the many paddlers who float along the river through the Yukon-Charley Rivers National Preserve. The 150-mile trip extends from Eagle to Circle, at the end of the Steese Hwy northeast of Fairbanks; most paddlers take six to 10 days, though some require as few as three.

It's not a difficult paddle, but it must be planned carefully. Kayakers and canoeists should come prepared for insects, but can usually camp either in public-use cabins or on open beaches and river bars, where winds keep the bugs at bay. They also need to be prepared for extremes in weather; freezing nights can be followed by daytime temperatures of 90°F.

Eagle Canoe Rentals (☎ 547-2203; www.aptalaska.net/~paddleak; Taylor Hwy), as you enter town, provides canoes for travel between Dawson City, Eagle and Circle. Pick up the boat at either the **Dawson City River Hostel** (☎ 867-993-6823; www.yukonhostels.com) or at the shop in Eagle and then leave it in Circle. A four-day rental between Dawson City and Eagle is $120; a five-day rental between Eagle and Circle is $195. **Everts Air Alaska** (☎ 450-2350) may be able to make a flag stop in Circle to get you back to Eagle for around $165 one way; otherwise you're looking at a two-stage flight through Fairbanks or a very long drive.

For information in advance, contact the Yukon-Charley Rivers National Preserve Visitor Center (opposite).

SLEEPING & EATING

Eagle Campground (☎ 883-5121; sites $8) This BLM-operated campground has 16 sites in a well-treed area accessible by following 4th Ave 1.5 miles north through Fort Egbert. If you come by boat rather than car it's an annoyingly long hike from the river.

Eagle Trading Company Motel (☎ 547-2220; www.eagletrading.com; 3 Front St; s/d $60/70) This motel has impressively affordable rooms with pine paneling and riverfront views. Rooms one through five have the best views of the Yukon River.

Falcon Inn B&B (☎ 547-2254; http://falconinn.mystarband.net 220 Front St; s/d $75/85) The town's best B&B features its own deck overlooking Eagle Bluff, an escarpment on the Yukon River where peregrine falcons like to hang out.

Riverside Café (☎ 547-2220; breakfast $5-8, sandwiches $5-9; 🕑 7am-7pm) Right beside the motel and a stone's throw from the Yukon, this log-hewn, sunny place is where locals gather to eat and gab.

SHOPPING

Directly opposite the courthouse, the **Eagle Mall** (cnr Berry St & 1st Ave; 11am-1:30pm Mon-Sat) is your spot for locally hewn handicrafts. The open-air stand is far from a 'mall,' but that doesn't stop the daily cruise-ship tour-goers from stopping here and gawking for hours like 'gag-me-with-a-spoon' valley girls.

GETTING THERE & AWAY

Even if you don't want to drive or paddle to Eagle, you have a couple of options for getting here.

Operated by Holland America, the 110-passenger tour boat, the **Yukon Queen II** (☎ 867-993-5599, 800-544-2206; www.hollandamerica.com; one way $90) plies the river between Eagle and Dawson City, covering the 102-mile distance at 35 knots – and irritating many local boaters, who complain of swamped vessels and disturbed fishing nets. You'll need to buy your return ticket to Dawson in Eagle ($105 Canadian dollars).

Everts Air Alaska (☎ 450-2350) Flies to Eagle most days of the week from Fairbanks.

TOK TO CANADA

The journey from Tok (Mile 1314) to the Canadian border comprises 92 winding miles of the Alcan: paved but often frost-heaved, and weaving through low-slung mountains and vast wetlands. Thirteen miles east of Tok is Tetlin Junction, where Taylor Hwy branches off toward Eagle, with connections via the Top of the World Hwy to Dawson City (p362).

Shortly after the junction you'll reach the 730,000-acre **Tetlin National Wildlife Refuge** (☎ 883-5312; tetlin.fws.gov), which skirts the highway's south side all the way to the border. Waterlogged by countless lakes, marshes, streams and rivers, the refuge is a home or migratory pit-stop for nearly 200 kinds of bird. The best viewing is typically from mid-May to early June.

Two USFWS campgrounds are in the refuge. **Lakeview Campground** (Mile 1256.7 The Alcan; sites free) features 11 sites on a hillside overlooking beautiful Yager Lake, where you can see the St Elias Range to the south on a nice day. **Deadman Lake Campground** (Mile 1249.4 The Alcan; sites free) has 15 sites, a boat ramp on the lake, a short nature trail, and nightly presentations by rangers.

The **Tetlin National Wildlife Refuge Visitor Center** (☎ 774-2245; Mile 1229 The Alcan; 🕑 8am-4:30pm), a sod-covered log cabin with a huge viewing deck, overlooks the Scotty and Desper Creek drainage areas. The Mentasta and Nutsotin Mountains loom in the distance. Inside, the cabin is packed with interpretive displays on wildlife, mountains and Athabascan craftwork; beading demonstrations take place regularly.

Ten miles on you'll reach the Canadian border. The spot is marked by an observation deck and plaque; another 18 miles beyond is the Canadian customs post, just outside Beaver Creek, Yukon.

TOK CUTOFF & GLENN HIGHWAY

The quickest path from the Alcan to Anchorage, the paved Tok Cutoff & Glenn Hwy offers some of the best hiking, boating and scenery-gawking in the state. The rugged 328-mile route is graced by both the Wrangell and Chugach Mountains. Glennallen and Palmer are significant-sized communities along the way.

TOK CUTOFF

Narrow and forest-flanked, the Tok Cutoff runs 125 miles from Tok to Gakona Junction. There it meets Richardson Hwy, which heads 14 miles south to Glennallen, the eastern terminus of Glenn Hwy.

The first of only two public campgrounds on Tok Cutoff pops up at Mile 109.5 as you drive south from Tok. **Eagle Trail State Recreation Site** (sites $15), near Clearwater Creek, has 35 sites, drinking water and toilets. The historic **Valdez–Eagle Trail**, which at one time extended clear to Eagle on the Yukon River, now provides just a leisurely 20-minute stroll in the vicinity of the campground. Look for the posted trailhead near the covered picnic shelters.

Another 45 miles southwest along the highway, just north of the Nabesna Rd junction, is the 240-acre **Porcupine Creek State Recreation Site** (Mile 64.2 Tok Cutoff; sites $15), offering 12 wooded sites in a scenic spot along the creek. A mile north along the highway you'll find a historical marker and splendid views of Mt Sanford (16,237ft), a dormant volcano.

Officially, the Tok Cutoff ends at Gakona Junction, 125 miles southwest of Tok, where it merges with Richardson Hwy. Nearby is

Gakona Lodge (☎ 822-3482; www.gakonalodge.com; Mile 2 Tok Cutoff; r $95, cabins $115-150, tepee $35), a lovely log roadhouse dating from 1905 that's listed on the National Register of Historic Places. It has a dining room, a bar, nine lodge rooms, tepees with cots and a firepit, and three cabins.

From Gakona Junction, follow the Richardson Hwy 14 miles south to Glenn Hwy junction.

GLENN HIGHWAY

Among Alaska's most jaw-dropping drives, the Glenn runs 189 miles from Richardson Hwy at Glennallen through the Chugach Range to Anchorage, merging with George Parks Hwy just after Palmer. Appropriately, most of this corridor was declared a National Scenic Byway. Along the route, outdoor opportunities abound: there's great alpine hiking around Eureka Summit, easy access to the humbling Matanuska Glacier, and some of the state's best white water in the nearby Matanuska River.

Glennallen

pop 518

Glennallen is referred to by its civic fathers as 'the hub' of Alaska's road system, which is appropriate, because despite the impressive vistas (which include several peaks over 12,000ft) most travelers will find little to do here but leave. Located at the axis of the Glenn and Richardson Hwys, the town is a supply center for those going to Wrangell-St Elias National Park. The town is dry, so don't expect a whooping good nightlife.

The **Greater Copper River Valley Visitor Center** (☎ 822-5555; 9am-7pm) is at the junction of the Glenn and Richardson Hwys. West along the Glenn is the only full-service bank in the Copper Valley region, a **Wells Fargo** (☎ 822-3214; Mile 187.5 Glenn Hwy), which has an ATM.

For camping, your best bet is the very peaceful, spruce-shrouded **Dry Creek State Recreation Site** (Mile 117.5 Richardson Hwy; sites $12), 5 miles northeast of town on Richardson Hwy. In town, you can camp at **Northern Nights Campground** (☎ 822-3199; www.alaska-rv-campground-glennallen-northrnnights.net; Mile 188.7 Glenn Hwy; sites camp/RV $12/20; 8am-8pm), where showers are $3.

Otherwise, there's Glennallen's only hotel, the **Caribou Hotel** (☎ 822-3302, 800-478-3302; www.caribouhotel.com; Mile 186.9 Glenn Hwy; main hotel r $143-168, annex s/d $69/79). The lack of competition shows. Rooms in the main building are nice but overpriced; the work-camp-style annex, however, would be OK for budget travelers. At the adjoining **Caribou Hotel Restaurant** (breakfast $5-11, lunch $5-9, dinner $11-20; 7am-10pm) you can dine on meals geared to Middle American retirees: among the offerings is 'tender beef liver.'

For hitchhikers, Glennallen is notorious as a place for getting stuck (especially at Glenn Hwy junction) when trying to thumb a ride north to the Alcan. Luckily, buses are available. **Alaska Direct Bus Lines** (☎ 800-770-6652; www.alaskadirectbusline.com) passes through town every Sunday, Wednesday and Friday en route to Anchorage ($65) and Tok ($27). Call for departure times and pick-up locations.

The vans of **Backcountry Connection** (☎ 822-5292; www.alaska-backcountry-tours.com) go to and from McCarthy in Wrangell-St Elias National Park daily in summer for $99 round-trip (see p374). You'll need to make a reservation.

Tolsona Creek to Matanuska Glacier

West of Glennallen, Glenn Hwy slowly ascends through woodland into wide-open high country, affording drop-dead views of the Chugach and Talkeetna Mountains, and limitless hiking opportunities.

The first campground west of Glennallen is **Tolsona Wilderness Campground** (☎ 822-3865; www.tolsona.com; Mile 173 Glenn Hwy; sites camp/RV $20/34), a private facility with more than 90 sites bordering Tolsona Creek. Water is available, along with coin-operated showers and laundry facilities.

A lookout marks the trailhead for the **Mae West Lake Trail**, a short hike away from Mile 169.3 of Glenn Hwy. This mile-long trail leads to a long, narrow lake fed by Little Woods Creek. The trailhead for the **Lost Cabin Lake Trail** is at another pull-out on the south side of the highway at Mile 165.8. The trail winds 2 miles to the lake and is a berry-picker's delight from late summer to early fall.

At Mile 160 a 19-mile spur road runs north to scenic **Lake Louise State Recreation Area** (sites $15), which has 52 campsites in two campgrounds and is popular among Alaskans keen on swimming, boating and angling for grayling and trout. A few lodges and numerous private cabins are on the lake as well.

Little Nelchina State Recreation Site (Mile 137.4 Glenn Hwy; sites free), just off Glenn Hwy, has 11 campsites but, due to state budget cuts, no services.

DETOUR: NABESNA ROAD

For connoisseurs of roads less traveled, Alaska offers few lonelier motorways than the Nabesna Rd, jutting 42 miles south from the Tok Cutoff into the northern reaches of Wrangell-St Elias National Park.

Turning onto the Nabesna Rd from the Cutoff you'll find yourself in a place the signs call Slana (pop 108). Somewhere back through the trees there's an Alaska Native settlement on the north banks of the Slana River, where fish wheels still scoop salmon during the summer run. Also in the area are more recent settlers: in the early 1980s this was one of the last places in the USA to be opened to homesteading.

Before continuing, stop in at the NPS **Slana Ranger Station** (☎ 822-7401; Mile 0.2 Nabesna Rd; 🕑 8am-5pm), where you can get info about road conditions and possible hikes, purchase USGS maps, peruse displays and collect the free *Nabesna Road Guide*.

In the 4 miles between the ranger station and the park entrance you'll pass a handful of accommodations. More offbeat is **Huck Hobbit's Homestead** (☎ 822-3196; sites per person $5, cabins per person $20, breakfast $10, dinner $15), a wind-and-solar-powered wilderness retreat off Mile 4 of Nabesna Rd. The three cabins include beds, sheets and a cooking area. There's even an onsite greenhouse where vegetables are grown. Stay an extra day here – the scenery is beautiful – and splurge on a canoe trip down the Slana River for $50 per canoe.

Upon entering the park proper the Nabesna Rd turns to gravel. It's manageable in a 2WD vehicle for the first 29 miles, but after that several streams flow over it, making it impassable in high water (call the ranger station for the latest on road conditions). Although there are no formal campgrounds along the road, primitive sites, often with picnic tables and outhouses, exist at several waysides. Maintenance ends at Mile 42, though a rough track continues 4 miles to the private Nabesna Gold Mine, a National Historic Site.

For a comparatively easy hike, try the 4-mile **Caribou Creek Trail** (Mile 19.2 Nabesna Rd), which ascends 800ft from the road to a dilapidated cabin with unbeatable views of the surrounding peaks. A tougher day trek is the 5-mile **Skookum Volcano Trail** (Mile 36.2 Nabesna Rd), which climbs 2800ft through a deeply eroded volcanic system, ending at a high alpine pass frequented by Dall sheep. From there you can either retrace your steps or follow the rocky streambed another 3 miles back down to the road.

From Little Nelchina River, Glenn Hwy begins to ascend, and Gunsight Mountain comes into view (you have to look hard to see the origin of its name). From Eureka Summit you can see both Gunsight Mountain and the Chugach Mountains to the south, the Nelchina Glacier spilling down in the middle and the Talkeetna Mountains to the northwest. This impressive, unobstructed view extends to the west, where the highway drops into the river valley that separates the two mountain chains. **Eureka Summit** (Mile 129.3 Glenn Hwy) is the highway's highest point (3322ft).

Just after the summit, at Mile 126.4, lies one of numerous trailheads for the old **Chickaloon-Knik-Nelchina Trail**, a gold miner's route used before the Glenn Hwy was built. Today it's an extensive trail system extending to Palmer and beyond. The system is not maintained regularly, and hikers attempting any part of it should have extensive outdoor experience and the appropriate topographic maps. You will have to share the trail with off-road vehicles.

The trailhead for the **Belanger Pass Trail** (Martin Rd at Mile 123.3 of Glenn Hwy), is signposted. Usually miners and hunters in off-road vehicles use it to travel into the Talkeetna Mountains. The views from Belanger Pass, a 3-mile hike, are excellent and well worth the climb. From the 4350ft pass, off-road-vehicle trails continue another 3.5 miles north to Alfred Creek, then eventually lead around the north side of Syncline Mountain past active mining operations.

Two miles west of the Belanger Pass trailhead at Mile 121 is **Tahneta Pass**. Half a mile further on you can view the 3000ft pass at a scenic turnoff. East of the turnoff lies Lake Liela, with Lake Tahneta beyond it.

Squaw Creek Trail is another miners' and hunters' trail that begins at Mile 117.6 of Glenn Hwy and merges into the Chickaloon-Knik-Nelchina Trail. It begins as an off-road-vehicle trail, then extends 3.5 miles to Squaw Creek and 9.5 miles to Caribou Creek after ascending a low pass between the two. Although the trail can be confusing at times, the hike is a scenic one, with the Gunsight, Sheep and Syncline Mountains as a backdrop.

From here Glenn Hwy begins to descend, and the surrounding scenery becomes stunning as the road heads toward the Talkeetna Mountains, passing a Sphinx-like rock formation known as the Lion's Head at Mile 114. A half mile beyond it the highway reaches the first view of Matanuska Glacier. To the north is Sheep Mountain – aptly named, as you can often spot Dall sheep on its slopes.

Sheep Mountain Lodge (☎ 745-5121, 877-645-5121; www.sheepmountain.com; Mile 113.5 Glenn Hwy; cabins $149-189) is among the finest and most scenically situated lodges along Glenn Hwy, featuring a café, a bar, a sauna, cabins and bunkrooms without bath. The restaurant has the area's best eating.

Four miles down the road are the idyllic **Tundra Rose Guest Cottages** (☎ 745-5865, in Alaska 800-315-5865; www.tundrarosebnb.com; Mile 109.5 Glenn Hwy; cottages $128-138), in a glacier-view setting that's as pretty as the name implies. The owners serve quality meals at their nearby Grandview RV Park.

Matanuska Glacier to Palmer

One of Alaska's most accessible ice tongues, **Matanuska Glacier** nearly licks Glenn Hwy, stretching 27 miles from its source in the Chugach Mountains. Some 18,000 years ago it was way bigger, covering the area where the city of Palmer is today.

You can get to the glacier via **Glacier Park Resort** (☎ 745-2534; Mile 102 Glenn Hwy; sites $15), which charges $15 (children six and under free) to follow its private road to a parking lot at the terminal moraine. From there, a self-guided trail will take you a couple of hundred yards onto the gravel-laced ice itself; to go further, duck into the nearby office of **MICA Guides** (☎ 800-956-6422; www.micaguides.com), where you'll be outfitted with a helmet, crampons and trekking poles, and led on a 1½-hour glacier tour ($45), a three-hour trek ($70) or a six-hour ice-climbing excursion ($130). If you haven't been ice-climbing it's worth the splurge: it is both terrifying and intoxicating at the same time.

If you want to pitch your tent hereabouts you can either camp at Glacier Park's rough campsites, or head back up the hill to **Matanuska Glacier State Recreation Site** (Mile 101 Glenn Hwy; sites $15), where there are 12 tree-shrouded campsites just steps away from outrageous glacier vistas.

The **Purinton Creek Trail** starts at Mile 91 of Glenn Hwy, leading 12 miles to the foot of Boulder Creek (most of the final 7 miles is a trek along the river's gravel bars). The Chugach Mountains scenery is excellent, and you'll find good camping spots along Boulder Creek.

There's good camping, too, at the 22-site **King Mountain State Recreation Site** (Mile 76 Glenn Hwy; sites $15), a scenic campground on the banks of the Matanuska River with views of King Mountain to the southeast.

Across the highway from the campground is the headquarters of **Nova** (☎ 800-746-5753; www.novalaska.com; Mile 76 Glenn Hwy, Chickaloon), one of Alaska's pioneering rafting companies, which runs the Matanuska River daily. It offers a mild 2½-hour float at 10:30am (adult $75) and a wilder one, which features Class IV rapids around Lion's Head Wall, at 9:30am and 2pm ($80 to $90 per person). From early June to mid-July there's also the extremely popular evening Lion's Head trip, departing at 7pm and including a riverside cookout. Nova also guides glacier hikes and extended river trips on the Matanuska, Talkeetna, Copper, Chickaloon and Tana Rivers for anywhere from $350 to $3000.

For lower-key fun – perhaps a picnic and a stroll through the clovers – try the **Alpine Historical Park** (☎ 745-7000; Mile 61 Glenn Hwy; admission free; 🕑 9am-7pm), encountered just before passing through Sutton. The park contains several buildings, including the Chickaloon Bunkhouse and the original Sutton post office, which now houses a museum.

Almost 12 miles beyond Sutton is the junction with the Fishhook–Willow Rd, which provides access to Independence Mine State Historical Park (p230). The highway then descends into the agricultural center of Palmer.

From Palmer, Glenn Hwy merges with George Parks Hwy and continues south to Anchorage, 43 miles away.

RICHARDSON HIGHWAY

This is about as postcard perfect as you can get without leaving the cozy confines of your vehicle. Sprinkles of wildflower shimmer in the wind along the roadside, while off in the distance the sheltering shoulders of the Alaska and Chugach Mountains stand guard. To the south, you get access to the vast wilderness of Wrangell-St Elias National Park. And on every step of the way there are chances to hike, bike (many bikers go ahead and do the entire route) and stop for photos.

Alaska's first highway, the Richardson runs 266 miles from Fairbanks to Valdez. However, the 98-mile stretch between Fairbanks and Delta Junction is popularly considered part of the Alcan, and our coverage of the Richardson thus begins at Delta Junction, where the Alcan branches away to the east. Because the mile markers on the Richardson start in Valdez, drivers traveling from north to south will find the numbers descending.

The Richardson was originally scouted in 1919 by US Army Captain WR Abercrombie, who was looking for a way to link the gold town of Eagle with the warm-water port of Valdez. At first it was a telegraph line and footpath, but it quickly turned into a wagon trail following the turn-of-the-20th-century gold strikes at Fairbanks. Along the way it passes waterfalls, glaciers, five major rivers and the Trans-Alaska Pipeline, which parallels the road most of the way.

DELTA JUNCTION TO GLENNALLEN

Richardson Hwy runs 151 relatively untrafficked miles from Delta Junction to Glennallen, first ascending the Delta River drainage, crossing Isabel Pass over the Alaska Range, then paralleling the Gulkana and Gakona Rivers to Gakona Junction. Here, the road joins the Tok Cutoff for the final 14 miles to Glenn Hwy junction at Glennallen. This route has plenty of curves, hills and frost-heaves, but is otherwise in fine condition.

Donnelly Creek & Around

After departing Delta Junction's 'Triangle,' where the Alcan merges with Richardson Hwy at Mile 266, the highway soon passes Fort Greely (Mile 261) and, a few minutes later, the Alaska Pipeline's Pump Station No 9.

A turnoff at Mile 243.5 offers one of the best views you'll get of the pipeline, as it plunges beneath the highway. Interpretive signage provides an overview of the pipeline's history and engineering, including a fascinating explanation of how 'thermal siphons' protect the permafrost by sucking heat from areas where the pipeline is buried. There are also spectacular panoramas to the southwest of three of the highest peaks in the Alaska Range. From south to west, you can see Mt Deborah (12,339ft), Hess Mountain (11,940ft) and Mt Hayes (13,832ft).

Another interesting turnoff, at Mile 241.3, overlooks the calving grounds of the Delta buffalo herd to the west. In 1928, 23 bison were relocated here from Montana for the pleasure of sportsmen and today they number more than 400. The animals have established a migratory pattern that includes summering and calving along the Delta River. If you have binoculars you may be able to spot dozens of the beasts.

The first public campground between Delta Junction and Glennallen is just after Mile 238, where a short loop road leads west of the highway to **Donnelly Creek State Recreation Site** (sites $10), which has 12 sites. This is a great place to camp, as it's seldom crowded and is extremely scenic, with good views of the towering Alaska Range. Occasionally the Delta bison herd can be seen from the campground.

At Mile 225.4 you'll find a viewpoint with picnic tables and a historical marker pointing out what little ice remains of **Black Rapids Glacier** to the west. The glacier became known as the 'Galloping Glacier' after its famous 3-mile advance in the winter of 1936, when it almost engulfed the highway. Across from the marker, the easy **Rapids Lake Trail**, 0.3-miles long, winds through wildflowers to Black Rapids Lake.

From here, the highway ascends into alpine country and the scenery turns gonzo, with the road snaking under sweeping, scree-sided peaks. At Mile 200.5, a gravel spur leads 2 miles to the west to **Fielding Lake State Recreation Site** (sites free), where a willow-riddled 17-site campground sits in a lovely area above the treeline at 2973ft. The state's **Fielding Lake Cabin** (www.dnr.state.ak.us/parks/cabins; per night $35) is also available here by online reservation.

In another 3 miles the highway crests its highest point, **Isabel Pass** (3000ft). The pass is marked by a historical sign dedicated to Captain Wilds Richardson, after whom the highway is named. From this point you can view Gulkana Glacier to the northeast and the Isabel Pass pipeline camp below it.

For much of the next 12 miles the highway parallels the frothing headwaters of the Gulkana River as it pours toward Paxson.

Paxson & Around

At Mile 185.5 of Richardson Hwy, the junction with the Denali Hwy, you'll find the small service center of Paxson (pop 40).

You can gas up and even grab a snack at the hulking Paxson Inn, but a better place to spend the night is **Denali Highway Cabins** (Map pp356-7; ☎ 822-5972; www.denalihwy.com; r $150-175), a couple of hundred feet up the Denali Hwy, where you'll find modern log cabins, each with a private balcony, along the Gulkana River. This is one of the best cabins around, but there's one catch: it only accommodates multiday stays. It also arranges nature tours ($40), evening float trips ($45), kayak and canoe rentals ($40 to $50) and bike rentals ($35 to $45).

Ten miles south on Richardson Hwy, a gravel spur leads 1.5 miles west to **Paxson Lake BLM Campground** (sites $4-8). With 50 sites around the lakeshore, this is the best public campsite on the highway. For experienced boaters, this is also a potential put-in for white-water trips on the Gulkana River.

Over the next 20 miles, Richardson Hwy descends from the Alaska Range, presenting sweeping views of the Wrangell Mountains to the southeast and the Chugach Mountains to the southwest.

Sourdough Creek & Gulkana River

At Mile 147.5 of Richardson Hwy, the BLM's 42-site **Sourdough Creek Campground** (sites $8) provides canoeists and rafters access to the popular Gulkana River. Located in scrubby forestland that bugs seem to love, the campground has a boat launch, a fishing deck, and trails leading to a river observation shelter.

From here, you can take a **river float** down 35 placid miles to the highway bridge at Gulkana (Mile 126.8), making for a pleasant one- or two-day paddle. Harder-core canoeists can put in up the highway at Paxson Lake, turning the trip into an 80-mile excursion. Those first 45 miles, however, involve several challenging rapids, including the Class IV Canyon Rapids. Although there's a short portage around these rapids, rough Class III waters follow.

All the land from Sourdough Creek Campground south belongs to the Ahtna Native Corporation, which charges boaters to camp. The exceptions – three single-acre sites – are signposted along the riverbanks and have short trails leading back to the highway. Raft rentals and shuttle services for many of the area's rivers, including the Gulkana, can be arranged through **River Wrangellers** (☎ 822-3967, 888-822-3967; www.alaskariverwrangellers.com) in Gakona.

From the take-out at the Gulkana River Bridge you are 3 miles south of Gakona Junction, where Tok Cutoff heads northeast to Tok; and 11 miles north of Glennallen, where Richardson Hwy intersects with Glenn Hwy.

WRANGELL-ST ELIAS NATIONAL PARK

One of the world's few remaining stands of 'absolute wilderness,' Wrangell-St Elias National Park is the closest you're going to get to 'the wild as God imagined it' in all of Alaska.

Formed in 1980, this is the United State's largest national park. It stretches north 170 miles from the Gulf of Alaska and encompasses 13.2 million acres of mountains, foothills and river valleys. It is bounded by the Copper River to the west and Canada's Kluane National Park to the east. Together, Kluane and Wrangell-St Elias National Parks make up almost 20 million acres and encompass the greatest expanse of valleys, canyons and towering mountains in North America, including the continent's second- and third-highest peaks (and nine of the 16 highest peaks in the US).

Wildlife in the park is more diverse and plentiful than in any other Alaskan park. Species include moose, black and brown bear, Dall sheep, mountain goat, wolf, wolverine, beaver and three of Alaska's 32 caribou herds.

This area is a veritable crossroads of mountain ranges. To the north are the Wrangell Mountains; to the south, the Chugach Mountains; and thrusting from the Gulf of Alaska and clashing with the Wrangell Mountains are the St Elias Mountains.

Spilling out from the peaks are extensive ice fields and more than 100 major glaciers, including some of the world's largest and most active.

The Bagley Ice Field, near the coast, is 127 miles long, making it the largest subpolar mass of ice in North America. The Malaspina Glacier, which pours out of the St

Elias Mountains between Icy Bay and Yakutat Bay, is larger than Rhode Island. While the jury is still out (we're waiting for Al Gore to make another movie), the majority consensus among park rangers and naturalists is that many of these glaciers are retreating. They've been retreating for about 10,000 years now, but the current rate is alarming. With this change comes a new geography – retreating glaciers leave fjords, terminal moraines and new lakes in their wake – and essentially a new environment.

Despite these challenges, Wrangell-St Elias remains a true wilderness park, with few visitor facilities or services of any kind. See 'Wrangell-St Elias Planning Guide' (opposite) for information on accessing the park.

SIGHTS & ACTIVITIES

McCarthy Road

Edgerton Hwy and McCarthy Rd combine to provide a 92-mile route into the heart of Wrangell-St Elias National Park, ending at the footbridge across the Kennicott River to McCarthy.

The 32-mile Edgerton Hwy, fully paved, begins at Mile 82.6 of Richardson Hwy. If you want to camp before reaching the park, the best bet is lovely **Liberty Falls State Recreation Site** (Mile 24 Edgerton Hwy; sites $10), where the eponymous cascade sends its waters rushing past several tent platforms.

The end of Edgerton Hwy is 10 miles beyond, at little **Chitina** (pop 118), the last place you can purchase gas. There's a grocery store here too, and a café, an art gallery and a ranger station. Backpackers can camp along the 3-mile road south to O'Brien Creek or beside Town Lake. If it's getting late, you can crash at **Gilpatrick's Hotel Chitina** (☎ 832-2244; www.hotelchitina.com; Mile 33 Edgerton Hwy; r $159), which has simple rooms, and a restaurant and saloon.

At Chitina, the McCarthy Rd begins, auspiciously enough, by passing through a single-lane notch blasted through a granite outcrop. From here 60 miles eastward you'll be tracing the abandoned Copper River & Northwest Railroad bed that was used to transport copper from the mines to Cordova. The route is a rump-shaker: expect max speeds of 35mph.

The first few miles offer spectacular views of the Chugach Mountains, the east–west range that separates the Chitina Valley lowlands from the Gulf of Alaska. Peaks average 7000ft to 8000ft. You'll also cross the mighty Copper River, where it's possible to see a dozen fish wheels or, if your timing is right, hordes of dipnetters who descend in July and August to scoop up red and king salmon.

To accommodate these hordes, a small, free **campground** with eight sites sits next to the east side of the Copper River Bridge. There are countless informal campsites on the riverbanks.

At Mile 14.5 you'll reach the access road to the trailheads for the **Dixie Pass** (p104), **Nugget** and **Kotsina Trails**, across from the Strelna airstrip.

At Mile 17 of McCarthy Rd sits the one-lane, 525ft-long **Kuskulana River Bridge**, long known as 'the biggest thrill on the road to McCarthy.' Built in 1910, this historic railroad span is a vertigo-inducing 238ft above the bottom of the gorge. Though the state has added guard rails and new planks and thus taken some of the thrill out of the crossing, the view of the steep-sided canyon and rushing river from the bridge is awesome, and well worth the time to park at one end and walk back across it.

After rattling through another 43 miles of scrubby brush and thick forest – with few good mountain vistas and not many diversions en route – the road ends at the **Kennicott River**. If you're driving in, that's as far as you can go; to get into McCarthy, you cross the river on a footbridge and walk a short distance into the tiny town. If you're staying at a lodge or campground on the road side of the river, you can leave your car there; otherwise, you can park at a private parking lot right by the bridge for $10 a day.

Built in 1996, the footbridge replaced the hand-pulled trams the state erected when the original bridge was washed out in 1981. The footbridge has another salubrious effect: no cars means no cruise-ship tour groups. On the other side, a **shuttle** (☎ 554-4411; $5 one-way; 🕑 9am-8:30pm) can take you to McCarthy (half a mile) or Kennecott (4.5 miles), or you can hoof or bike it.

McCarthy & Kennecott

pop 54

A funky renegade mountain hamlet just half a mile past the end of the road, **McCarthy** exudes the spirit of the Alaskan frontier like few can. Facing the Kennicott Glacier's terminal moraine and just a stone's throw from the river, the tiny community is a car-free

WRANGELL-ST ELIAS PLANNING GUIDE

This is not an easy park to access. The Richardson Hwy borders the park's northwest corner, and two rough dirt roads penetrate its interior. The Nabesna Rd (p366), cuts into the park's northern reaches, but is seldom traveled and provides fewer accommodations. The most popular access by far is McCarthy Rd, which provides access to the historic mining towns of McCarthy and Kennecott (opposite). The park itself begins just after the small town of Chitina (opposite), but most will drive on to the Kennicott River, where you'll need to park your car ($10 overnight), cross a pedestrian bridge and take a shuttle (☎ 554-4111, $5 one-way) or walk on to McCarthy (0.5 miles) or Kennecott (4½ miles). The road to McCarthy is rough, but even a regular car can make it if you go slow (35 mph max). RVs will have a tougher time making it here – call ahead to check on the conditions. McCarthy provides lodging, food and other services to park visitors; Kennecott has fewer lodging and dining choices, and is largely a living museum, owned and maintained by the National Park Service.

From these jumping-off points, you'll need to backpack or fly by bush plane to see more of the park. Organized treks are available in McCarthy and Kennecott. Unlike Denali, you do not need a backcountry permit to backpack here, but it's best to leave a backpacking itinerary at any of the ranger stations, where you can also get advice and a bear canister ($80 refundable deposit) for your trip. There is no fee to enter the park.

With few visitors, you can come here even in the height of summer and still have some alone time. The winters see a lot of snow – the road is still open, though most of the hotels are closed. The winter skiing in the park is not very good; you're better off heading out of Valdez or Girdwood.

There are few places to buy groceries in the area, so it's best to bring your own food and gear. **McCarthy Mercantile** (McCarthy Main St; ⏲ 9am-7pm) has overpriced grocery items.

Wrangell-St Elias National Park Headquarters & Visitor Center (☎ 822-5234; www.nps.gov/wrst; Mile 106.8 Richardson Hwy; ⏲ 8am-6pm), outside Copper Center, 10 miles south of Glenn Hwy-Richardson Hwy junction, is the best place for info and trip suggestions. You can also pick up topographic maps, view displays and videos on the park, and leave your backpacking itinerary.

Other park offices include the **Chitina Ranger Station** (☎ 823-2205; ⏲ 10am-4:30pm Wed-Mon) at the end of the Edgerton Hwy the **McCarthy Visitor Contact Station** (☎ 554-4417; ⏲ 9:30am-4:30pm), in a kiosk just before the end of McCarthy Rd, the **Kennecott Visitor Contact Station** (☎ 554-1105; ⏲ 9am-5:30pm) on the main road in Kennecott, the **Slana Ranger Station** (☎ 822-5234; ⏲ 8am-5pm), for visitors heading down the Nabesna Rd, and the **Yakutat Ranger Station** (☎ 784-3295; ⏲ 8am-5pm Mon-Sat), if you're exploring the park's southeastern coastal regions.

A great way to visit these parks is by volunteering for the National Park Service. Visit www.volunteer.gov/gov for more information.

idyll, where the handful of gravel roads wind past rotting cabins and lovingly restored boomtown-era buildings.

Once you've crossed the Kennicott River on the footbridge, follow the road across another footbridge and about half a mile further to the unstaffed **McCarthy-Kennecott Historical Museum**, an old railroad depot featuring historical photographs, a few mining artifacts and a model of McCarthy in its heyday (donations are appreciated). At the museum, the road bends back 500ft into downtown (such as it is) McCarthy, or continues toward Kennecott, 4.5 miles up the road.

Historically, the two towns have always been different. **Kennecott** was a company town, self-contained and serious. McCarthy, on the other hand, was created in the early 1900s for miners as a place of 'wine, women and song.' In other words, it had several saloons, restaurants and a red-light district. The spirit remains lively today, and McCarthy is definitely the best spot to stay for indie travelers.

You can reach Kennecott from McCarthy on foot by walking or cycling up the main road (the old railroad grade), a 4.5-mile trek or better yet, by the Old Wagon Road (follow the signs), which does not allow traffic. There's also van service to and from McCarthy ($5 one-way), or you can hitch a ride in summer when a trickle of traffic runs between the two towns. There are limited accommodations available in town.

Hiking & Biking

You can buy US Geological Society (USGS) topographic maps at **Fireweed Arts & Crafts**

(☎ 554-4500; 9:30am-6:30pm), on the main drag in Kennecott. If you just want to wander through Kennecott on your own, stop at the visitor center and pick up a copy of the *Walking Tour of Kennecott* ($3).

Beginning from Kennicott Glacier Lodge, the **Root Glacier Trail** is a 3-mile round-trip route past the mine ruins to the sparkling white-and-blue ice. Hike northwest of town and continue past an unmarked junction to Bonanza Mine, less than a quarter mile away. Along the way you cross Jumbo Creek; a plank upstream makes fording this creek easy in normal water conditions. Another half mile further on campsites overlook the end of Root Glacier; nearby you'll find an outhouse and a storage bin (to keep bears out of your food).

You can climb the glacier, but use extreme caution if you're inexperienced or lack proper equipment (crampons, ice ax etc). A safer alternative is to follow the rough trail up the lateral moraine. The path continues another 2.5 miles, providing excellent views of the ice. For this trek, you'll need the USGS topographic maps *McCarthy B-6* and *McCarthy C-6*.

Another excellent hike from Kennecott is the alpine **Bonanza Mine Trail**. It's a round-trip of almost 8 miles and a steep uphill walk all the way. Plan on three to five hours to hike up if the weather is good and half that time to return. The trail is actually a rough dirt road to the treeline and starts just north of town at a junction that makes a sharp 180-degree turn up the mountain. Once above the treeline the view is stunning, and you can clearly see the mountain where the mine still sits. To reach the mine you have to trek up a rocky slope to the remaining bunkhouse, shafts and tram platform. Water is available at the top, but carry at least a quart (1L) if the day is hot.

One of the best ways to get in the backcountry is to get dropped off by plane. Both McCarthy Air and Wrangell Mountain Air (right) can arrange trips.

It's fun just to bike around town, but you can also bike 12 miles south of town to the **Nizina River**, a nice spot for an afternoon picnic. You can rent bikes through many of the campgrounds you'll find before the pedestrian bridge.

TOURS

Hiking

St Elias Alpine Guides (☎ 554-4445, 888-933-5427; www.steliasguides.com), with offices in McCarthy (before the river) and on Kennecott's main road, runs the only tours that go inside Kennecott's mine buildings ($25). It can also equip you with crampons for half-day hikes on Root Glacier ($60) or take you on a full-day alpine hike to the mining ruins at the base of Castle Mountain ($95). There's free day parking and cheap overnight parking ($5) at its McCarthy branch.

The other local guiding firm, also extremely experienced, is **Kennicott Wilderness Guides** (☎ 554-4444, 800-664-4537; www.kennicottguides.com), whose offerings include full-day ice-climbing and glacier excursions from $95, summer skiing tours and fly-in hiking trips

River Running

Where there are mountains and melting glaciers, there's sure to be white water. **Copper Oar** (☎ 554-4453, 800-523-4453; www.copperoar.com) has offices in the St Elias Alpine Guides Kennecott location. For a full-day float, it combines the Kennicott with the Nizina and a portion of the Chitina River and returns you to McCarthy by bush plane. The high point is going through the vertical-walled Nizina Canyon. This trip costs $275 per person (two person minimum). It also offers multiday paddles.

Kennicott Wilderness Guides (☎ 554-4444, 800-664-4537; www.kennicottguides.com) also does guided tours, including a three-day float from McCarthy to Chitina.

Flightseeing

If the day is clear, splurge on a flightseeing tour of the surrounding mountains and glaciers. Both **McCarthy Air** (☎ 554-4440; www.mccarthyair.com) and **Wrangell Mountain Air** (☎ 554-4400, 800-478-1160; www.wrangellmountainair.com), with offices on McCarthy's main drag, have a fantastic reputation, offering a wide range of scenic flights and charging around $95 to $210 per person (two person minimum) for around 35 to 90 minutes. It can also arrange flights to Chitina ($106 round-trip) and backcountry drops ($135 and up).

SLEEPING

Mccarthy

There are camping and lodging options on either side of the Kennicott River. Seeing as this is in a national park, you can camp just about anywhere that's not private property. East of the Kennicott River you are out of luck. But cross the footbridge, head out of

KENNECOTT'S COPPER BOOM (OR IS IT KENNICOTT?)

In 1900 miners 'Tarantula Jack' Smith and Clarence Warner reconnoitered Kennicott Glacier's east side until they arrived at a creek and found traces of copper. They named the creek Bonanza, and was it ever – the entire mountainside turned out to hold some of the richest copper deposits ever uncovered.

Eventually, a group of investors bought the existing stakes and formed the Kennecott Copper Corporation, named when a clerical worker misspelled Kennicott (which is why, nowadays, the town is spelled with an 'e' while the river, glacier, and other natural features get an 'i'). First the syndicate built its railroad: 196 miles of track through the wilderness, including the leg that's now McCarthy Rd and Cordova's famous Million Dollar Bridge. The line cost $23 million before it even reached the mines in 1911.

From 1911 until 1938 the mines operated around the clock and reported a net profit of more than $100 million. By 1938 most of the rich ore had been exhausted, and in November that year the mine closed permanently. With the exception of a steam turbine and two large diesel engines, everything was left behind, and Kennecott became a perfectly preserved slice of US mining history.

Unfortunately, when the railroad bed was converted to a road in 1974, Kennecott also became the country's biggest help-yourself hardware store. Locals were taking windows, doors and wiring, while tourists were picking the town clean of tools, railroad spikes and anything else they could haul away as souvenirs.

In 1998 the NPS purchased the mill, power plant and many of the buildings from private owners as the first step to restoring them. For more information, stop in at the small **NPS Visitor Center** (☎ 554-1105; 9am-5:30pm) on Kennecott's main drag, where rangers give regular talks on the area, show films and lead nature walks.

town along the Old Wagon Trail and set up your renegade campsite wherever takes your fancy. There's also good camping at the foot of the Root Glacier. It's important to camp away from the road and be bear savvy, as many human-habituated bears have been reported in the area.

Glacier View Campground (☎ 554-4490; www.glacierviewcampground.com; road's end; sites/cabins $20/85) A half mile back from the river, this place has stony sites, hot showers ($7), mountain bikes (full day $25), and the best reputation of the bunch.

our pick **Kennicott River Lodge & Hostel** (☎ 554-4441 or 590-8753; www.kennicottriverlodge.com; road's end; dm/cabins $28/100) A short walk from road's end is this beautiful two-story log lodge with outlying private and dormitory cabins offering glacier views. There's a great communal kitchen and common room, a bright outhouse and a Finnish sauna.

Lancaster's Backpackers Hotel (☎ 554-4402; www.mccarthylodge.com; McCarthy Main St; s/d $48/68) The most affordable place in McCarthy proper, this rather run-down joint has flophouse-style rooms without baths. Despite the name, there's no shared kitchen or common area here.

Currant Ridge Cabins (☎ 554-4424, 877-647-2442; www.currantridgecabins.com; Mile 56.7 McCarthy Road; cabins $169) On a little mountainside not far from the 'end of the road,' these upscale cabins are the nicest in the area with hardwood floors and hand-sewn quilts. Ask for a cabin toward the top for better views.

Kennecott

Kennecott B&B (☎ 554-4500; www.kennecottbb.com; r $199) A new entrant to town, this B&B has just one room, but it can sleep up to five people, and, as the name implies, you get breakfast.

Kennicott Glacier Lodge (☎ 258-2350, 800-582-5128; www.kennicottlodge.com; s/d from $155/195;) Built in 1987, this sprawling lodge has a 'Grande Dame' feel, kind of like Stephen King's Stanley Hotel, only without the crazy girls blurting out 'Redrum, redrum.' Glacier-view rooms don't have in-room baths (a drawback considering you're forking out so much money), but you can get private baths with some rooms, and complete meal plans are available.

EATING & DRINKING

For middle-of-nowhere mining towns, McCarthy and Kennecott offer surprisingly good grub.

McCarthy Mercantile (McCarthy Main St; sandwiches $11-12; 9am-7pm) This grocery stores sells everything from shovels to home-made power bars.

Roadside Potatohead (hotdogs, burgers, burritos $8-12; 10am-7pm Mon-Wed, 9am-8pm Thurs-Sun) Deck out your own Mr Potatohead doll as you dine is this screened-in snack shack just off McCarthy's Main St.

McCarthy Lodge (554-4402; www.mccarthylodge.com; McCarthy Main St; dinner $20-45; 7am-10am and 6-10pm) In the heart of McCarthy, this eatery has a surprisingly good wine list. Many of the greens come from the restaurant's greenhouse (ask if you can get a tour) and the rotating menu features everything from halibut to elk.

Kennicott Glacier Lodge (258-2350, 800-582-5128; www.kennicottlodge.com; Kennecott; breakfast $10-16, lunch $7-15, dinner $29-34; 7am-10am, noon-3pm, 7pm-10pm) This may be the area's most upscale dining options. You'll need a reservation for the family-style dinners, and there's only one seating: at 7pm. Bag lunches are available for day hikers.

Golden Saloon (554-4402; McCarthy Main St) Beside the McCarthy Lodge, this is the area's only true bar, with pool, frequent live music and an always intriguing cast of drinkers. There's bar food until 10pm. Thursday night open-mics are a locals' favorite.

GETTING THERE & AROUND

Air

Ellis Air (822-3368, 800-478-3368; www.ellisair.com) departs from Anchorage via Gulkana at 8:30am Wednesdays and Fridays, arriving in McCarthy at 11am and then returning. Fares are $300/600 one-way/round-trip from Anchorage or $222/444 from Gulkana.

Wrangell Mountain Air (554-4400, 800-478-1160; www.wrangellmountainair.com) offers daily scheduled flights between McCarthy and Chitina for around $106 round-trip, as well as flightseeing trips.

Bus

Backcountry Connection (822-5292, 866-582-5292; www.alaska-backcountry-tours.com) departs Glennallen at 7am daily in summer, reaching Chitina at 8:30am and the McCarthy footbridge at 11:00am. After a four-hour layover – enough time to see McCarthy and the ruins at Kennecott – the van returns to Glennallen, arriving at 8:30pm. The round-trip fare for the same day is $99; one way costs $79. You'll need to make a reservation.

McCarthy-Kennicott Community Shuttle (554-4411; one way $5) runs vans between McCarthy and Kennecott from 9am to 8:30pm daily. Pick-up at the footbridge is on the hour; in downtown Kennecott it's on the half-hour.

Bicycle

You can rent a mountain bike at Glacier View Campground.

GLENNALLEN TO VALDEZ

One of Alaska's most spectacular drives, the 115 miles of Richardson Hwy between Glennallen and Valdez lead through a paradise of snowy summits, panoramic passes, and gorgeous gorges.

Nine miles south of Glennallen is a turnoff to the Wrangell-St Elias National Park Visitor Center (p371).

Just south of the visitor center, at Mile 106, Old Richardson Hwy loops off the main highway, offering access to Copper Center (opposite). Old Richardson Hwy rejoins the Richardson Hwy at Mile 100.2.

You'll reach a lookout over **Willow Lake** at Mile 87.6. The lake can be stunning on a clear day, with the water reflecting the Wrangell Mountains, a 100-mile chain that includes 11 peaks over 10,000ft. The two most prominent peaks visible from the lookout are Mt Drum, 28 miles to the northeast, and Mt Wrangell, Alaska's largest active volcano, to the east. Mt Wrangell is 14,163ft, and on some days you can see a plume of steam rising from its crater.

Squirrel Creek State Campground (Mile 79.6 Richardson Hwy; sites $10) is a scenic 25-site camping area on the banks of the creek. You can fish for grayling and rainbow trout in Squirrel Creek.

Fourteen miles further along you'll reach what used to be the Little Tonsina River State Recreation Site. Though it's closed, a path leads down to the water, where anglers can fish for Dolly Varden most of the summer.

At Mile 28.6, the turnoff to **Worthington Glacier State Recreation Area** leads you to the glacier's face via a short access road. The recreation area includes outhouses, picnic tables and a large, covered viewing area. The mile-long **Worthington Glacier Ridge Trail** begins at the parking lot and follows the crest of the moraine. It's a scenic hike that follows the

DETOUR: COPPER CENTER

The Richardson Hwy bypasses Copper Center, but don't you do the same. This quaint village of 445 residents, reached by detouring a few miles down Old Richardson Hwy, is prettily situated on the sockeye salmon–rich Klutina River and offers a handful of worthwhile sights, including the mining exhibits at the **George Ashby Museum** (☎ 822-5285; Mile 101 Old Richardson Hwy; admission by donation; 🕑 11am-5pm), and the **Chapel on the Hill** (admission free), a log chapel built in 1942 located half-mile north of the Klutina Bridge. Overpriced and under-cloroxed, the **Copper Center Lodge** (☎ 822-3245; www.coppercenterlodge.com; Mile 101 Old Richardson Hwy; s/d $130/160) is your best lodging and dining option in town.

edge of the glacier, but exercise caution: never hike on the glacier itself due to its unstable crevasses. Thompson Pass and the surrounding area above the treeline are ideal for tramping; hikers will have few problems climbing through the heather.

Above the treeline the weather can be windy and foul as the highway ascends toward **Thompson Pass** (Mile 26 Richardson Hwy). Several scenic turnoffs near the pass (2678ft) allow lucky early summer visitors to ooh and aah at a riot of wildflowers.

Blueberry Lake State Recreation Site (Mile 24.1 Richardson Hwy; sites $15) offers 15 sites and several covered picnic shelters in a beautiful alpine setting surrounded by lofty peaks. Often during summer all the sites will be taken by RVs, but it's easy for backpackers to find a spot near the trails to pitch their tents. There's good fishing for rainbow trout in the nearby lakes.

At Mile 14.8, you'll reach the northern end of **Keystone Canyon**, which holds an abandoned hand-drilled tunnel that residents of Valdez began but never finished when they were competing with Cordova for the railroad to the Kennecott copper mines. A historical marker briefly describes how nine companies fought to develop the short route from the coast to the mines, leading to the 'shootout in Keystone Canyon.'

For the next 2 miles you'll pass through the canyon, where the smooth dark rock walls contrast extravagantly with the pure foamy white waterfalls pouring over them. Two magnificent waterfalls are here: spectacular **Bridal Veil Falls** and, half a mile further, **Horsetail Falls**. Large turnouts at both allow you to get out and fill your lungs with the pure ionized air.

Leaving the canyon at Mile 12.8 the road begins a long, gradual descent into Valdez (p234).

Fairbanks & Around

It may not be pretty, but Fairbanks is certainly evocative – and the key is in the people. While Fairbanks and its surrounding areas do have some interesting sights and activities – from paddling the mighty Chena River through the bordering-on-bleak downtown area, to heading out to remote hot springs – it's really the frontiersman persona of the locals that makes it a worthwhile stop.

Here you have back-to-landers, businesspeople and bureaucrats, gun-toting conspiracy-theorists and freaked-out survivalists, professors and hygienically challenged students at Alaska's flagship university and, last but not least, the rugged individuals who chose to build their own cabin and grow their own food, living their lives on their own terms 'out there' in log-cabin communities like Fox, Manley and Ester. It's a place where some escape the strictures of society, never to be found again.

But unfortunately for visitors, the landscape here is simply not as dramatic as other spots in the state. Sure, you have views of the Alaska Range to the south and the White Mountains to the north. But the area around here is hot and buggy in the summer, and freezing cold in the winter, a slightly wrinkled hill country covered with the soft fuzz of birch, spruce, arctic meadows and the occasional granite dome. But there is drama to be found here. It's found in the classrooms and saloons, in the far-out log cabins and in the stories and lore of the local characters that have managed to become the region's most formidable attraction.

HIGHLIGHTS

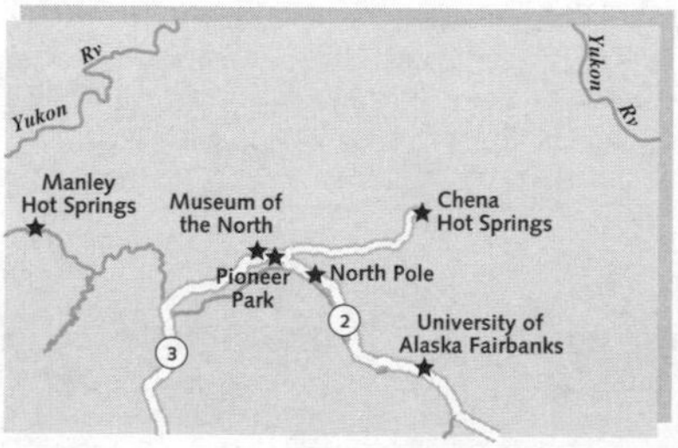

- **Best place to get naked** (p397) – soaking in the Manley Hot Springs; another fun trip takes you to the Chena Hot Springs (p392), but you'll have to wear your suit there: bummer
- **Dumbest way to drown** (p385) – getting too drunk before you paddle on to the next pub in the Great Fairbanks Pub Paddle, starting in Pioneer Park; we suggest wearing a life jacket
- **Best way to meet locals** (p389 and p383) – kicking up your heels at a rowdy local saloon or sitting in on a lecture at the University
- **Most liberating way to feel insignificant** (see the boxed text, p391) – gazing skyward at the northern lights; or you could take a backcountry trek from the Elliot Hwy (p396) or stare into the cold eyes of the Museum of the North's 36,000-year-old bison (see the boxed text, p383)
- **Guiltiest pleasures** (p382 and the boxed text, p394) – forsaking art galleries and alpine trails for a day at Alaska's own Disneyland, Pioneer Park; or taking a day trip to the North Pole

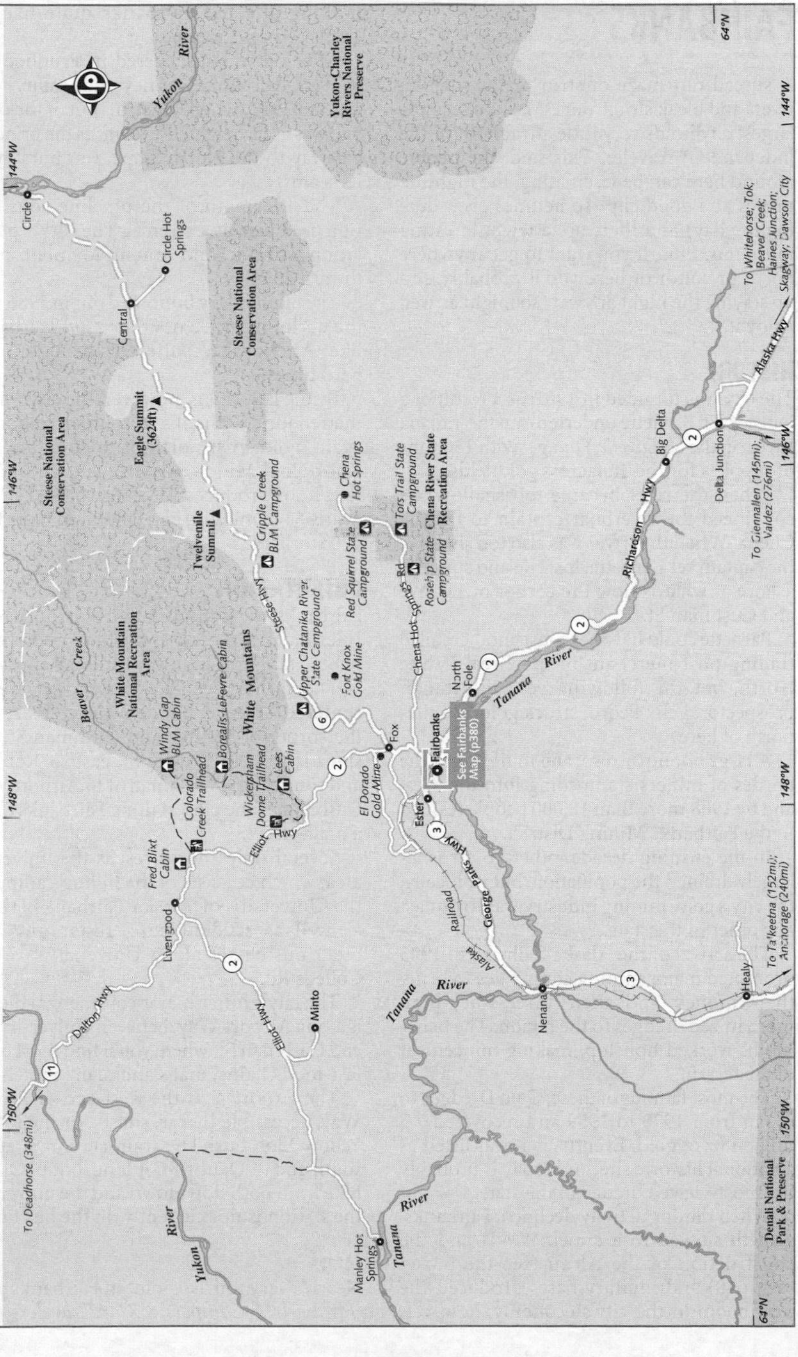
FAIRBANKS AREA
0 50 km
0 30 miles
Yukon River
Yukon-Charley Rivers National Preserve
Circle
Circle Hot Springs
Central
Steese National Conservation Area
Steese National Conservation Area
Eagle Summit (3624ft)
Twelvemile Summit
White Mountain National Recreation Area
Beaver Creek
Windy Gap BLM Cabin
Borealis-LeFevre Cabin
White Mountains
Colorado Creek Trailhead
Wickersham Dome Trailhead
Lees Cabin
Fred Blixt Cabin
Cripple Creek BLM Campground
Upper Chatanika River State Campground
Steese Hwy
Fort Knox Gold Mine
Red Squirrel State Campground
Chena Hot Springs
Tors Trail State Campground
Chena River State Recreation Area
Rosehip State Campground
Chena Hot Springs Rd
Fox
El Dorado Gold Mine
Fairbanks
See Fairbanks Map (p380)
North Pole
Ester
Tanana River
Richardson Hwy
Big Delta
Delta Junction
Alaska Hwy
To Whitehorse; Tok; Beaver Creek; Haines Junction; Skagway; Dawson City
To Glennallen (145mi); Valdez (276mi)
Livengood
Elliot Hwy
Dalton Hwy
To Deadhorse (348mi)
Minto
George Parks Hwy
Alaska Railroad
Nenana
Tanana River
Healy
To Talkeetna (152mi); Anchorage (240mi)
Manley Hot Springs
Yukon River
Denali National Park & Preserve
64°N
144°W
146°W
148°W
150°W

FAIRBANKS

A spread-out maze of strip malls, snaking rivers and bleak storefronts, Alaska's second-largest city holds very little attraction for the independent traveler. This said, the people around here can be fascinating, the nightlife moves at a good clip (sometimes even during the day) and there are a few interesting museums. Plus, if you want to get anywhere north or south of here you'll probably end up staying the night anyway, so might as well enjoy it.

HISTORY

The city was founded in 1901, as a result of a journey ET Barnette undertook up the Tanana River on the SS *Lavelle Young* – with 130 tons of supplies for the Tanacross goldfields.

When the river became too shallow, he convinced the riverboat captain to try the Chena. When that river was also too shallow, the captain set Barnette, his wife and supplies ashore at what is now the corner of 1st Ave and Cushman St.

Barnette could have been just another failed trading-post merchant in the Great White North, but the following year the Italian prospector, Felix Pedro, struck gold 12 miles north of here.

A large boomtown sprang to life amid the hordes of miners stampeding into the area, and by 1908 more than 18,000 people resided in the Fairbanks Mining District.

In the ensuing decade, other gold rushes largely drained the population, but ironically, the city's gold-mining industry was to outlast any other in the state.

The arrival of the Alaska Railroad in 1923 prompted major mining companies to bring their money and their three-story-high mechanized dredges to the region. The behemoths worked nonstop, making mincemeat of the terrain.

The most famous of these, Gold Dredge No 8, ran from 1928 to 1959 and recovered 7.5 million oz of gold. Eventually it was listed as a national historic site, and today is probably the most-viewed dredge in the state.

When mining activity declined, Fairbanks' growth slowed to a crawl. WWII and the construction of the Alcan (see the boxed text, p48) and military bases produced the next boom in the city's economy; however, nothing affected Fairbanks quite like the Trans-Alaska Pipeline.

After oil was discovered in Prudhoe Bay in 1968, Fairbanks was never the same. From 1973 to 1977, when construction of the pipeline was at its height, the town, as the principal gateway to the North Slope, was bursting at its seams.

The aftermath of the pipeline construction was just as extreme. The city's population shrank and unemployment crept toward 25%.

The oil industry bottomed out in 1986 with the declining price of crude, and Fairbanks, like Anchorage, suffered through more hard times.

By the late 1990s, however, the city was on the rebound – thanks to tourism and, once again, gold. Just north of town is the Fort Knox Gold Mine – Alaska's largest. In 2004 Fort Knox produced 338,000oz of gold (worth nearly $140 million) and employed more than 420 workers.

ORIENTATION

Fairbanks, the transportation hub for Alaska's Interior, is a messy, sprawling, pedestrian-phobic tangle of highways and rail yards.

The rather desolate downtown area is centered around Golden Heart Plaza, on the corner of 1st Ave and Cushman St, and spreads west to Cowles St, east to Noble St and south along Cushman St to Airport Way. Cushman is the closest thing Fairbanks has to a main street.

Several miles northwest is the university area, which consists of the hilltop campus of the University of Alaska Fairbanks (UAF), as well as student bars, restaurants and other businesses along University Ave and College Rd.

The city's other major commercial district is along Airport Way, between University Ave and Cushman St, where you'll find most of the fast-food chains, malls and many motels.

The airport is at the west end of Airport Way, accessible by car, shuttle or the MACS Yellow Line bus. The train station is at the south end of Danby St. A long, but plausible, hike from both downtown and the university, the station is not currently on the bus line.

Maps

Nearly every touristy joint in Fairbanks gives out the free *Campers & Car Travelers' City*

Map, which does a good job simplifying the town's knotty streetscape. For topo maps, try the new Morris Thomson Cultural & Visitor Center (right). Also, UAF's **Geophysical Institute Map Office** (Map p380; ☎ 474-6960; www.gi.alaska.edu; 930 Koyukuk Dr; 8am-5pm Mon-Fri), at the west end of campus, has a vast range of topo maps, nautical charts and Arctic maps.

INFORMATION

Bookstores

Gulliver's Books (Map p380; ☎ 474-9574; www.gullivers-books.com; 3525 College Rd; 9am-9pm Mon-Fri, 9am-8pm Sat, 11am-6pm Sun) Next to Campus Corner Mall, near UAF, this is by far the best bookstore in town, selling new and used books and Alaskan titles.

UAF Bookstore (Map p380; ☎ 474-6858; 504 Tok Lane; 8am-5pm Mon-Fri, noon-5pm Sat) In Constitution Hall on campus, has highbrow texts plus Alaskan titles.

Emergency

Police station (Map p382; nonemergency ☎ 450-6500; 911 Cushman St)

Internet Access & Libraries

College Coffeehouse (Map p380; 3677 College Rd at University Ave; 7am-midnight Mon-Fri, 8am-midnight Sat & Sun) In Campus Corner Mall; 15 minutes of internet time free with any drink purchase, or $2 per 15 minutes.

Noel Wien Library (Map p380; ☎ 459-1020; 1215 E Cowles St at Airport Way; 10am-9pm Mon-Thu, to 6pm Fri, to 5pm Sat) Take the MACS Blue Line from the Yukon Quest Headquarters to this out-of-the-way library. Along with free internet and a large Alaskan section, it has an impressive collection of paintings and prints, many by Alaskan artists. Get your library card here, and you can have access to the massive UAF library.

Second Story Café (Map p380; ☎ 474-9574; 3525 College Rd; 9am-7pm Mon-Sat, 11am-5pm Sun) Near University Ave; above Gulliver's Books by Campus Corner Mall. It has free internet access and wi-fi. There's a 30-minute limit for the one terminal.

Laundry & Showers

B&C Laundromat (Map p380; ☎ 479-2696; 7am-9:30pm) In Campus Corner Mall; has coin-operated laundry (around $5.50 per load) and $4.50 showers.

ES Laundromat (Map p382; ☎ 456-7256; 314 Wendell St; 9am-8pm) Near the new visitor center downtown, this 'washeteria' has coin-operated laundry (around $4.50 per load) and $4.50 showers.

Media

Ester Republic (www.esterrepublic.com) This fun monthly is better than *Mother Jones* on crack.

Fairbanks Daily News-Miner (www.news-miner.com) Covers the city, the Interior and the Bush.

Medical Services

Fairbanks Memorial Hospital (Map p380; ☎ 452-8181; 1650 W Cowles St) Emergency care; south of Airport Way. Word on the street is that the cafeteria here is excellent.

Tanana Valley Clinic (Map p382; 24hr ☎ 459-3500; 1001 Noble St; 8am-8pm Mon-Sat) For minor problems.

Money

Key Bank of Alaska (Map p382; ☎ 459-3362; 100 Cushman St) Downtown; has an impressive gold nugget display and an ATM.

Wells Fargo Bank (Map p382; ☎ 459-4300; 613 Cushman St; 10am-5pm Mon-Thu, to 6pm Fri) Between 6th and 7th Aves; has an ATM.

Post

Main post office (Map p382; 315 Barnette St; 10am-6pm Mon-Fri) Downtown, between 3rd and 4th Aves.

Tourist Information

Morris Thomson Cultural & Visitor Center (Map p382; ☎ 456-5774, 800-327-5774; www.nps.gov/aplic/; 101 Dunkel St; 8am-7pm) Work was not yet completed on this $29-million center when we passed through, but it should be opened by press time. The massive modern building on the edge of Griffin Park combines the maps and exhibits of the former Alaska Public Lands Information

THE YUKON QUEST: ALASKA'S 'TOUGH' DOG RACE

Like a handful of other Alaskan towns, Fairbanks bills itself as the dog-mushing capital of the world. The **Yukon Quest**, taking place each February, covers 1023 miles between here and Whitehorse along many of the early trails used by trappers, miners and the postal service. Though less famous than the Iditarod (see the boxed text, p58), mushers will attest that the Quest is tougher, forcing teams to climb four mountains more than 3000ft high and run along hundreds of miles of the frozen Yukon River. While the Iditarod has 25 rest stops, the Quest has only six. The Yukon Quest plans to set up its new headquarters (p381) in the old Log Cabin Visitor Center on the corner of 1st Ave and Cushman St.

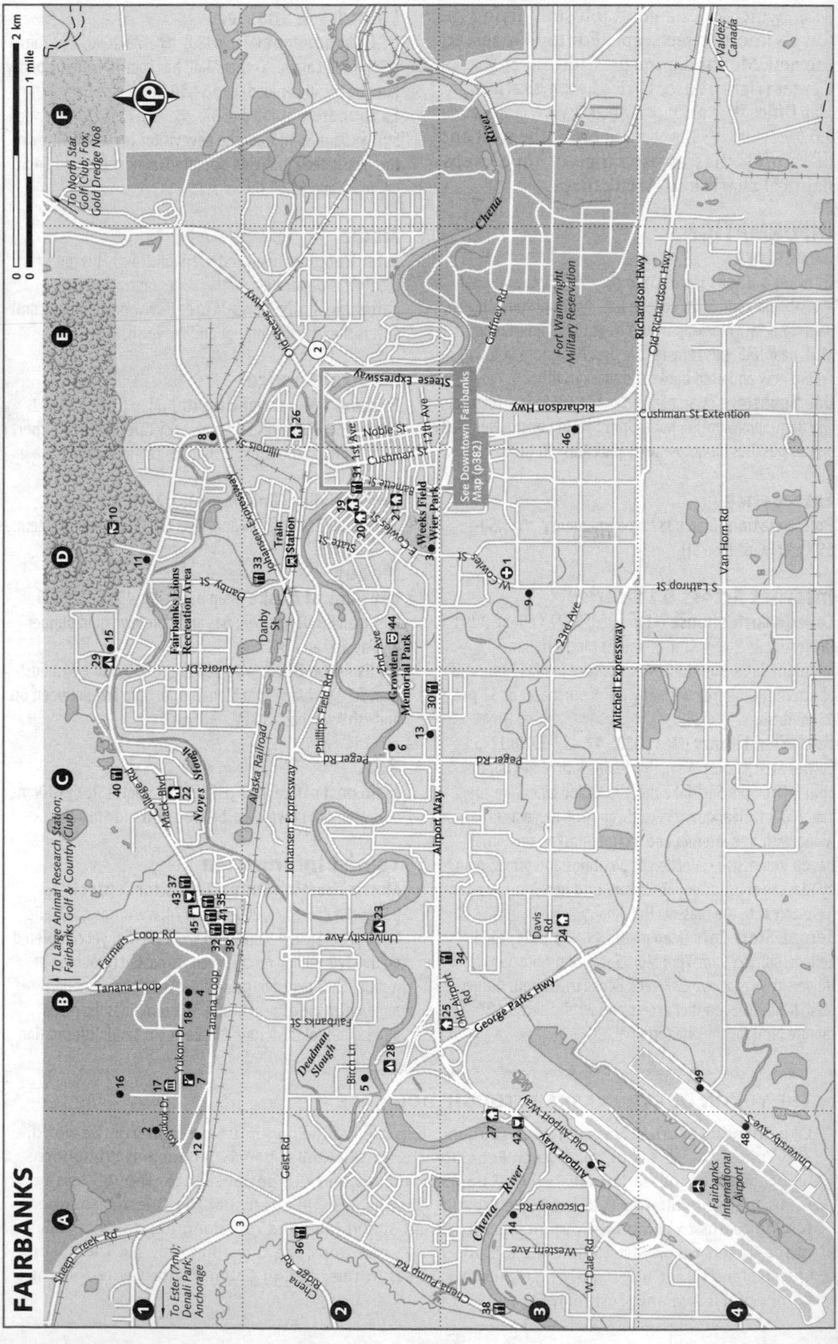
FAIRBANKS
To Ester (7mi); Denali Park; Anchorage
To Large Animal Research Station; Fairbanks Golf & Country Club
To North Star Golf Club; Fox; Gold Dredge No8
To Valdez; Canada
See Downtown Fairbanks Map (p382)
0 1 mile
0 2 km
Sheep Creek Rd
Chena Ridge Rd
Chena Pump Rd
Geist Rd
Farmers Loop Rd
Tanana Loop
Yukon Dr
Koyukuk Dr
College Rd
Mack Blvd
Noyes Slough
Deadman Slough
Fairbanks St
Birch Ln
University Ave
Johansen Expressway
Alaska Railroad
Phillips Field Rd
Peger Rd
Airport Way
Old Airport Rd
Old Airport Way
George Parks Hwy
Davis Rd
Discovery Rd
Western Ave
W Dale Rd
University Ave S
Fairbanks International Airport
Chena River
Growden Memorial Park
2nd Ave
Aurora Dr
Fairbanks Lions Recreation Area
Danby St
Train Station
Weeks Field
Wier Park
State St
E Cowles St
W Cowles St
Barnette St
1st Ave
Cushman St
Noble St
12th Ave
Illinois St
Steese Expressway
Old Steese Hwy
Gaffney Rd
Fort Wainwright Military Reservation
Richardson Hwy
Old Richardson Hwy
Cushman St Extention
23rd Ave
S Lathrop St
Van Horn Rd
Mitchell Expressway

INFORMATION
B&C Laundromat....................(see 32)
College Coffeehouse..............(see 32)
Fairbanks Memorial Hospital.......1 D3
Farmhouse Visitor Center.........(see 11)
Geophysical Institute Map Office..2 A1
Gulliver's Books.......................(see 41)
Noel Wien Library....................3 D2
Second Story Café...................(see 41)
UAF Bookstore.........................4 B1

SIGHTS & ACTIVITIES
7 Bridges Boats & Bikes..............5 B2
Alaska Outdoor Rentals & Guides.....6 C2
Alaska Range Viewpoint..............7 B1
Alaskan Prospectors & Geologists Supply.....8 E1
Big Dipper Ice Arena..................9 D3
Creamer's Field Migratory Water Fowl Refuge..............10 D1
Department of Fish & Game Office..........11 D1
Georgeson Botanical Garden.....12 A1
Go North Hostel.....................(see 24)
Pike's Landing.........................(see 27)
Pioneer Park...........................13 C2
Riverboat Discovery.................14 A3
Tanana Valley Fairgrounds........15 D1
University of Alaska Fairbanks...16 B1
University of Alaska Museum of the North.........17 B1
Wood Center...........................18 B1

SLEEPING
7 Gables Inn & Suites..................(see 5)
Ah, Rose Marie B&B...............19 D2
Alaska Heritage House B&B......20 D2
All Seasons B&B Inn..................21 D2
Billie's Backpackers Hostel.........22 C1
Chena River State Recreation Site..........23 B2
Go North Hostel.......................24 B3
Golden North Motel..................25 B3
Minnie Street B&B Inn.............26 E2
Pike's Waterfront Lodge...........27 A3
Pioneer Park...........................(see 13)
River's Edge RV Park & Campground..........28 B2
Tanana Valley Campground......29 D1

EATING
Airport Way Family Restaurant.............30 C2
Alaska Salmon Bake...............(see 13)
Big Daddy's Barbecue..............31 D2
Bun on the Run.......................(see 45)
College Coffeehouse................32 B1
Cookie Jar...............................33 D2
Fred Meyer..............................34 B3
Hot Licks.................................35 B1
Lemongrass..............................36 A2
Lulu's......................................(see 36)
Pad Thai..................................37 C1
Pump House Restaurant..........38 A3
Sam & Sharon's Sourdough Café.........39 B1
Second Story Café.................(see 41)
Tanana Valley Farmers Market..........40 C1
Wok 'n' Roll.............................41 B1

DRINKING
Boatel......................................42 A3
Marlin.....................................43 B1
Pump House Saloon...............(see 38)

ENTERTAINMENT
Growden Memorial Park..........44 D2
Palace Theatre & Saloon.........(see 13)

SHOPPING
Artworks..................................(see 32)
Bear Galley & Gift Shop..........(see 13)
Beaver Sports..........................45 B1

TRANSPORT
Air North................................(see 49)
Alaska Airlines........................(see 49)
Alaska/Yukon Trails.................46 E3
Arctic Rent-A-Car....................47 A3
Condor (Thomas Cook)..........(see 49)
Dalton Highway Auto Rentals..........48 A4
Frontier Alaska........................49 B4
Go North Hostel.....................(see 24)
Larry's Flying Service.............(see 49)
Warbelow's Air Adventures.........(see 49)
Wright Air Service..................(see 49)

Center (an excellent resource if you are planning on visiting any state or national parks and reserves in the region) with a visitors center and Tanana Elders Center. There's a historic cabin out front, and on the inside, visitors will eventually find a theater, cultural exhibits, information kiosks, internet booths and even backpacker lockers (for a small fee). While they have yet to work out all the details, the center may have classes, dance expos, films and possibly seminars. The Tanana Elders Center is off-limits to the public and is designed as a spot for these Athabascan elders to get together and pass on their stories to younger generations.

Travel Agencies

Santa's Vagabond Travel (Map p382; ☎ 452-3636; 909 Cushman St) It doesn't sell tickets to the North Pole, but it can get you just about anywhere else.

DANGERS & ANNOYANCES

Downtown Fairbanks is fairly seedy. Use the same precautions here you would use in any major city.

SIGHTS

Downtown Fairbanks

Much has been done recently to beautify and revitalize Fairbanks' downtown area. While it can still seem a bit of a wasteland – especially on weekends – it's well worth a wander.

Begin your downtown tramp at the old Log Cabin Visitor Center, which is the slated location for the **Old Log Cabin Visitor Center** (Map p382; ☎ 452-7954; www.yukonquest.com; 550 1st Ave at Cushman St; admission free; 10am-6pm Tue-Sat). If the Yukon Quest (see the boxed text, p379) really follows through with its plans to move its headquarters from the community museum to set up shop here, this should be an interesting spot, with exhibits on the grueling race. Then head out the door into **Golden Heart Plaza** (Map p382), a pleasant riverside park in the city center. In the middle of the plaza is an impressive bronze statue, *The Unknown First Family,* which depicts an Athabascan family braving the elements. You can follow a river walkway along the Chena River east from here to Griffin Park and the new Morris Thomson Cultural & Visitor Center (p379).

Heading west along 1st Ave's pretty waterfront promenade, you'll see a half dozen old log cabins and several historic buildings, including **St Matthew's Episcopal Church** (off Map p382), a beautiful log structure built in 1905 and rebuilt in 1948 after it burned down. **Immaculate Conception Church** (Map p382), just across the Chena River Bridge from Golden

Heart Plaza, was built in 1904 and moved to its present location in 1911. It's a national historic monument and features beautiful painted-glass windows.

Fairbanks Community Museum (Map p382; ☎ 457-3669; 410 Cushman St; admission free; 🕑 10am-4pm Mon-Fri), though not thrilling, merits a visit on a rainy day. This homespun place traces the city's history, mainly through old photos and newspaper clippings.

Fairbanks Ice Museum (Map p382; ☎ 451-8224; www.icemuseum.com; 500 2nd Ave; adult/child $12/6; 🕑 10am-8pm) is certainly the most bemusing sight in the city's downtown. This hour-long experience takes place in the historic, musty-smelling Lacey Street Theater, which you'll likely have largely to yourself.

Pioneer Park

Fairbanks' guiltiest pleasure is this 44-acre **theme park** (Map p380; ☎ 459-1087; Airport Way at Peger Rd; 🕑 stores noon-8pm, park 24hr), formerly known as Alaskaland. It may sound corny, but suspend your cynicism and you'll dig this vacation from your vacation. Best of all: entry is free.

The most prominent sight in the park is the **SS Nenana** (admission free), a hulking stern-wheeler that once plied the Yukon River, and now sits dry-docked in the middle of the complex. Amble through its guts and you'll learn more than you can imagine about Alaska's river-travel heyday. The park's other historical relics include the railroad car that carried President Warren Harding to the golden-spike ceremony in 1923 and a century-old

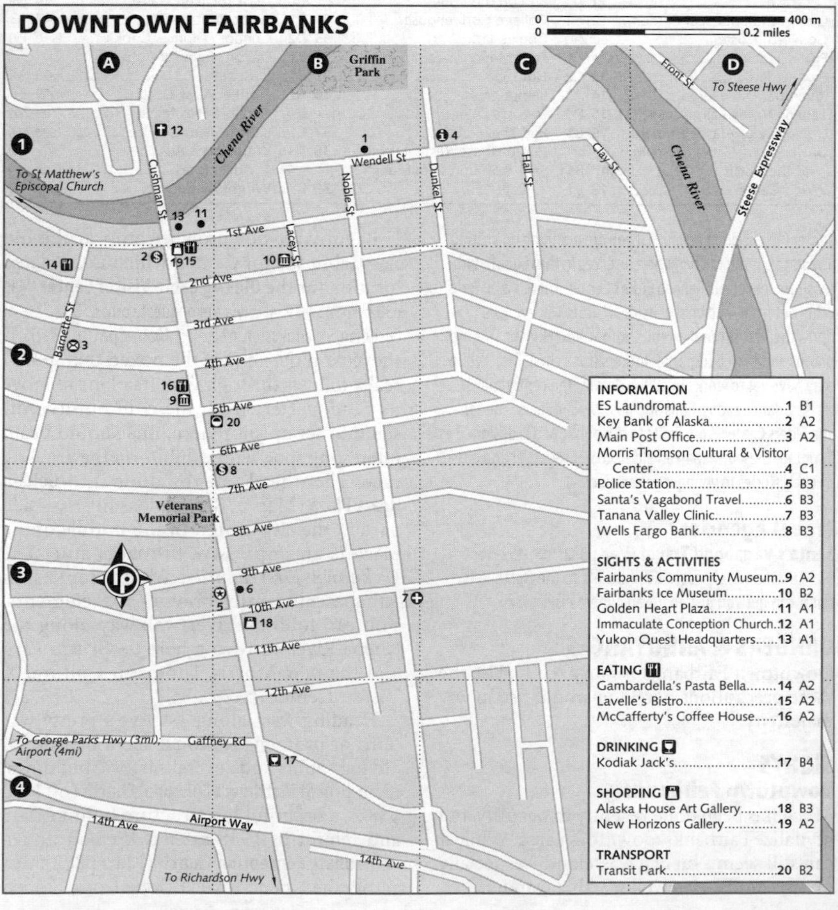

UNIVERSITY OF ALASKA MUSEUM OF THE NORTH

In an architecturally abstract igloo-and-aurora-inspired edifice near the west end of the campus is one of Alaska's finest museums, the **University of Alaska Museum of the North** (Map p380; ☎ 474-7505; www.uaf.edu/museum; 907 Yukon Dr; adult/child $10/free; 9am-9pm). A recent $42-million overhaul has doubled the facility's size and further amplified its impact. Inside, you'll find the Gallery of Alaska, which examines the geology, history and unusual aspects of each region of the state, and is where you can view the museum's most famous exhibit, Blue Babe: a 36,000-year-old bison found, by Fairbanks-area miners, preserved in the permafrost. In the new wing is a temporary-exhibit space, as well as the permanent Rose Berry Alaska Art Gallery, where northern works, ranging from ancient ivory carvings to contemporary photographs, are intermixed in an egalitarian fashion. In the museum's auditorium, two programs run several times daily (admission $5): *Dynamic Aurora* is a multimedia look at the northern lights; while *Winter* talks about, you guessed it, winter. Along with the standard museum schlock – gift shops, cafeterias and sittings rooms – there's also a viewing deck with to-infinity-and-beyond views of the Alaska Range.

carousel that still offers rides to the young and young-at-heart.

Near Peger Rd is the Alaska Salmon Bake (p389), while the park's Gold Rush Town – a street of relocated cabin-cum-gift shops – has the Palace Theatre and Saloon (p389). Nearby is the **Pioneer Museum** (admission free), mainly a jumble of antiques ostensibly chronicling the history of Fairbanks. This is also where, six times daily, you can catch the 40-minute **Big Stampede Show** (admission $4), re-enacting gold-rush days.

Across the park, the geodesic **Pioneer Air Transportation Museum** (admission $2) is chock-full of exhibits on the state's groundbreaking aviation history – there's even an experimental gyroplane and a 'flying saucer.' The **Native Village Museum** offers a perfunctory look at traditional Athabascan life, while the **Mining Valley** displays gold-mining equipment. A miniature train, the **Crooked Creek & Whiskey Island Railroad**, gives free rides around the park.

To get to Pioneer Park, take the MACS Blue Line bus.

University of Alaska Fairbanks

UAF (Map p380; ☎ 474-7581; www.uaf.edu) is the original campus of the state's university system and an interesting place to spend an afternoon. Incorporated in 1917 as the Alaska Agricultural College and School of Mines, the school began its first year with six students. Today it has more than 8000, and hundreds of degree and certificate programs.

The beautiful campus is 4 miles west of downtown, on a hilltop from which you can see Mt McKinley on a clear day. An **Alaska Range viewpoint** (p380) on Yukon Dr, near the University of Alaska Museum of the North, provides a turnout and a marker detailing the mountainous horizon.

Guided campus tours are offered at 10am weekdays; meet at the museum. The tours are free and last two hours.

Some of the campus highlights are described following. For more information on any UAF tour or attraction, call University Relations or visit UAF's website. To reach the campus, take MACS Red or Blue Line buses to UAF's Wood Center.

WOOD CENTER & CONSTITUTION HALL

A good place to start exploring the campus is **Wood Center** (Map p380; ☎ 474-7037; 505 Yukon Dr; 7:30am-5:30pm Mon-Fri), where the information desk provides the *UAF Campus Map & Visitors' Guide*, and the latest scoop on university events. This student center and general meeting place also holds a cafeteria, espresso stand, pizza parlor, pub and outdoor patio. Next door is Constitution Hall, where territorial delegates drafted the constitution for statehood. Now it houses the UAF Bookstore (p379). From here, it's always fun to head out to random classes for a bit of guerrilla learning – you never know, you may learn something new.

GEORGESON BOTANICAL GARDEN

On the edge of campus is the Agricultural and Forestry Experiment Station, where the university dabbles in growing vegetables of mythical proportions, and small grains like barley, wheat and oats that seem best suited for the short Alaskan growing seasons. Ironically, the station's grain fields are an ideal place to spot sandhill cranes, an endangered species in the rest of the country.

On the station grounds is the 5-acre **Georgeson Botanical Garden** (Map p380; ☎ 474-1944; www.uaf.edu/salrm/gbg; W Tanana Dr; admission $2, guided tours $5; 8am-8pm), a perfect picnicking spot that's a riot of wildflowers, herbs, fruits and gigantic vegetables. You can look around independently anytime during opening hours, and free guided tours are offered on Fridays at 2pm.

To reach the station take Tanana Loop west from the lower campus, bear left at the fork onto W Tanana Dr and continue for a mile.

LARGE ANIMAL RESEARCH STATION

UAF's **Large Animal Research Station** (off Map p380; ☎ 474-5724; www.uaf.edu/lars) keeps herds of musk oxen, reindeer and caribou to study their unique adaptations to a sub-Arctic climate. Viewing areas outside the fenced pastures allow a free look at the herds anytime, but bring binoculars as the animals don't always cooperatively graze nearby. The facility itself can only be seen on guided walks.

The hour-long tours (adult $10, child free) take place daily at 1:30pm and 3:30pm, while half-hour walks (adult $6) occur throughout the day. A gift shop sells, among other things, raw *qiviut* (musk-ox wool). To reach the station, head north from campus on Farmers Loop Rd, bear left onto Ballaine Rd, and then turn left again on Yankovich Rd and continue 1.2 miles to the site.

ACTIVITIES

Fairbanks has plenty to keep outdoor enthusiasts enthusiastic. Much of the best trekking and paddling, however, is well out of town, meaning those without wheels will need transportation. In winter the rivers freeze up, making ideal ski touring trails.

Hiking

Unlike Anchorage or Juneau, Fairbanks doesn't have outstanding hiking on its doorstep. The best trail for an extended hiking trip is the impressive Pinnell Mountain Trail (p99) at Mile 85.5 and Mile 107.3 of the Steese Hwy. For a variety of long and short hikes, you'll need to head to the Chena River State Recreation Area.

For more information, stop at the visitor center or at UAF's Geophysical Institute Map Office.

CREAMER'S FIELD

A handful of trails, each less than 2 miles round-trip, wind through the farmlands and forests of **Creamer's Field Migratory Waterfowl Refuge** (Map p380), an old dairy farm that's become a birders' paradise. The Alaska Department of Fish & Game seeds the area with bird-luring plants, attracting more than 100 species annually, including sandhill cranes. The **Farmhouse Visitor Center** (Map p380; ☎ 459-7307; 1300 College Rd at Danby St; 10am-5pm), adjacent to the Department of Fish & Game office and reached by the MACS Red Line, has trail guides, bug spray and a list of recent sightings.

Volunteers lead one-hour nature walks at 7pm Monday through Friday and 9am Wednesday.

UNIVERSITY OF ALASKA FAIRBANKS

UAF's backyard is laced with peaceful walking and biking trails, some several miles in length. Along the way you may find evidence of ongoing research projects; be sure not to touch them.

For a rough overview of the trails, consult the *UAF Campus Map* – free at the Wood Center.

Cycling

Fairbanks has a fine network of bike routes in and around the city. Bike paths begin at 1st Ave and Cushman St, and extend all the way past Pioneer Park, across the Chena River, to UAF and the George Parks Hwy. Shoulder bikeways lead you out of town. One of the more popular rides is to head north on Illinois St from downtown, and then loop around on College Rd and Farmers Loop Rd–University Ave, for a 17-mile ride. Pick up a free *Bikeways Map* at the Morris Thomson C&V Center.

Alaska Outdoor Rentals & Guides (Map p380; ☎ 457-2453; www.2paddle1.com; Pioneer Park; 10am-7pm) is located on the river behind Pioneer Park and rents mountain bikes for $27 per day. **Go North Hostel** (Map p380; ☎ 479-7272, 866-236-7272; www.gonorthalaska.com; 3500 Davis Rd) also has mountain bikes for $25 to $35 per day. **7 Bridges Boats & Bikes** (Map p380; ☎ 479-0751; www.7gablesinn.com; 4312 Birch Lane), at the 7 Gables Inn & Suites, rents bikes for $20 per day.

Paddling

The Fairbanks area offers a wide variety of canoeing and kayaking opportunities, from leisurely day to overnight trips, into the surrounding area; for extended backcountry expeditions, see p115 and p116, or head over to the visitor center.

Several local places rent boats and run shuttles to put-ins and take-outs: Alaska Outdoor Rentals & Guides will set you up with a canoe for $52 per day and, for another $15, pick you up at downstream locations like Pike's Landing or the Pump House Restaurant; Go North Hostel has canoes for $32 per day, can help with trip planning and will transport you to and from rivers throughout the Interior. 7 Bridges Boats & Bikes provides canoes and a shuttle service: canoes are $35 per day and transport costs $2.50 per mile, with a $20 minimum.

AROUND TOWN

An afternoon can be spent paddling the Chena River; its mild currents let you paddle upstream as well as down. You can launch a canoe from almost any bridge crossing the river, including Graehl Landing near the north side of Steese Hwy, where locals like to paddle upstream and then float back down.

From 7 Bridges Boats & Bikes you can drop a canoe in the Chena River, head downstream and into the quiet Noyes Slough, and complete the loop by paddling east back into the river, a 13-mile round-trip journey.

The best journey around town is the **Great Fairbanks Pub Paddle**. Start at Alaska Outdoor Rentals & Guides in Pioneer Park and paddle or float down river. Along the way, you can stop for brews, pub grub, horseshoes and games at the Boatel, Pike's Landing and the Pump House. Of course, it's dangerous to paddle while inebriated, so exercise restraint and caution.

CHENA & TANANA RIVERS

Those looking for an overnight – or even longer – paddle, should try a float down the Chena River from Chena Hot Springs Rd, east of Fairbanks, or a pleasant two-day trip down the Tanana River. The popular Tanana trip usually begins from the end of Chena Pump Rd and finishes in the town of Nenana, where you can return with your canoe to Fairbanks on the Alaska Railroad. This 60-mile trip can be done in a single day, but would require 10 to 12 hours of serious paddling.

CHATANIKA RIVER

For a one-day trip, the Chatanika River can be paddled for 28 miles west from Cripple Creek BLM Campground at Mile 60 of the Steese Hwy (see Map p377). The route parallels the road until the Upper Chatanika River State Campground at Mile 39. Many local paddlers avoid the complexities of shuttling this stretch by leaving a bicycle chained at the take-out, and pedaling back to their car. Extended trips on the Chatanika River are possible; you can paddle another 17 miles to a bridge at Mile 11 of the Elliot Hwy.

Gold Panning

If you've been bitten by the gold bug, Fairbanks is an ideal area to try your hand at gold panning. Start at **Alaskan Prospectors & Geologists Supply** (Map p380; ☎ 452-7398; 504 College Rd), which sells all the necessary equipment for recreational prospecting.

The next stop should be the visitor center, which distributes a helpful sheet entitled 'Where Can I Pan for Gold Without Getting Shot?' Popular places in the area include the Discovery Claim on Pedro Creek, off the Steese Hwy, across from the Felix Pedro Monument (Map p393), and several other locations further up the Steese Hwy.

TOURS

Flightseeing Tours

The Arctic Circle may be an imaginary line, but it's become one of Fairbanks' biggest draws, with small air-charter companies doing booming business flying travelers on sightseeing excursions across it. If you're gonna splurge on flightseeing – it's about $300 per person – you are better off doing it out of Talkeetna or McCarthy. Companies offering Arctic Circle 'flightseeing' trips:

Larry's Flying Service (Map p380; ☎ 474-9169; www.larrysflying.com) Offers a 1¾-hour air-only tour, or a three-hour trip with an hour-long ground tour of Fort Yukon, just north of the circle.

Northern Alaska Tour Co (☎ 474-8600, 800-474-1986; www.northernalaska.com)

Trans Arctic Circle Treks Ltd (☎ 479-5451, 800-336-8735; www.arctictreks.com)

Gold Panning & Mine Tours

El Dorado Gold Mine (Map p377; ☎ 479-6673, 866-479-6673; www.eldoradogoldmine.com; Mile 1.3 Elliot Hwy; adult/child $35/23) This daily two-hour train tour, on a mile-long narrow-gauge track, winds through a reconstructed mining camp and culminates with visitors panning gold-laden dirt.

Gold Dredge No 8 (Map p393; ☎ 457-6058; www.golddredgeno8.com; 1755 Old Steese Hwy N; adult/child

FAIRBANKS MIDNIGHT SPORTS

Tourists aren't the only folks made manic by Alaska's endless summer days. Fairbanksans, all too aware that darkness and cold are just around the corner, go into overdrive from May to September playing outdoors at all hours of the night.

The most revered of the city's wee-hour athletic activities is the **Midnight Sun Baseball Game**, held every solstice since 1906, without artificial light and, thus far, never canceled due to darkness. For the past four decades the game has pitted the local Goldpanners against an Alaska Baseball League rival. The contest is invariably the most popular of the season, and when the first pitch is hurled, at 10:30pm, the sun is still well above the horizon. By midnight – when play pauses for the traditional singing of the Alaska Flag Song – the sun is low, and at the end of nine innings it's gone. Its glow, however, lights the sky until sunrise, two hours later.

If you're more a fan of links than diamonds, Fairbanks also has a couple of golf courses where you can tee up well past your normal bedtime. **North Star Golf Club** (off Map p380; ☎ 457-4653; www.northstargolf.com; 330 Golf Club Dr; 18 holes $30) is an 18-hole course where visitors can start a round as late as 10pm. Also in the area is the venerable nine-hole **Fairbanks Golf & Country Club** (off Map p380; ☎ 479-6555; 1735 Farmers Loop Rd; 9 holes $20). Hazards at the courses include moose, marmot and sandhill crane.

$25/13) Off the old Steese Hwy at Mile 10 Goldstream Rd, this five-deck, 250ft dredge was built in 1928, operated until 1959, and was named a national historic site in 1984. Today perhaps Alaska's most visited dredge, No 8 is still making money. There are on-the-hour one-hour tours from 9:30am to 3:30pm daily; for an additional fee you can also indulge in gold panning and the all-you-can-eat Miner's Lunch.

Organized Tours

Alaska Yukon Trails (☎ 800-770-2267; www.alaskashuttle.com; tours $15-40) Offers fairly reasonable tours of area museums and the pipeline.

Fairbanks Historical City Tour (☎ 474-0286, 800-770-3343; www.riversedge.net; 4140 Boat St; adult/child $27/10) Departing from River's Edge RV Park & Campground, this four-hour motorcoach tour leaves daily at 8:30am and visits downtown, the Trans-Alaska Pipeline, and the UAF Museum and Botanical Gardens.

Gray Line (☎ 451-6835; 1980 S Cushman St; adult/child $60/30) From Transit Park, offers an overpriced four-hour 'Discover the Gold Tour' that departs at 9am and 1pm, and includes Gold Dredge No 8, the Trans-Alaska Pipeline and lunch.

Riverboat Discovery (Map p380; ☎ 479-6673, 866-479-6673; www.riverboatdiscovery.com; 1975 Discovery Dr, Mile 4.5 Airport Way; adult/child $50/35) Departing at 8:45am and 2pm daily, this 3½-hour tour navigates the Chena River via historic stern-wheeler, stopping at a replica of an Athabascan village as well as the riverfront home and kennels of Susan Butcher, four-time winner of the Iditarod.

FESTIVALS & EVENTS

There are a ton of summer music fests around here. See the boxed text, p352 for the skinny.

Summer solstice celebrations Taking place on June 21, when the sun shines for almost 23 hours, events include footraces, arts and crafts booths, and the traditional Midnight Sun Baseball Game.

Fairbanks Summer Arts Festival (☎ 474-8869; www.fsaf.org) In the last two weeks of July on the UAF campus, this festival features numerous concerts and workshops in the performing and visual arts.

Golden Days Fairbanks' largest summer happening, staged the third week of July, commemorates Felix Pedro's discovery of gold, with games and events ranging from rubber-ducky races to horse-and-rider shootouts. If you show up without a Golden Days button or garter, you risk being locked up in the mobile jail.

World Eskimo-Indian Olympics (☎ 452-6646; www.weio.org) Held annually on the second-to-last weekend in July at the Big Dipper Ice Arena (Map p380), this four-day event attracts indigenous people from across the North, who display their athletic prowess in contests like the Alaska High Kick, and test their pain thresholds in games such as the Knuckle Hop. There's also dancing, cultural performances and plenty of traditional regalia.

Tanana Valley State Fair (www.tananavalleyfair.org) In early to mid-August at the Tanana Valley Fairgrounds on College Rd (Map p380), Alaska's oldest fair has sideshows, entertainment and livestock contests.

SLEEPING

Fairbanks offers all manner of lodging options, from tents to tony resorts. Most of the campgrounds are along Airport Way, University Ave and College Rd, while hostels are scattered throughout the city. There are more than 100 B&Bs, many of which are in the downtown area; visit the visitor center for brochures. Fairbanks has an 8% bed tax that is not included in the prices following.

Budget

CAMPING

Chena River State Recreation Site (Map p380; walk-in/drive-up campsites $17/10, RV sites $25) This 29-acre park is on the Chena River, off University Ave just north of Airport Way (not to be confused with the Chena River State Recreation Area, east of Fairbanks). The lushly wooded campground has 61 sites, tables, toilets, fireplaces, water and a boat launch. It's served by the MACS Blue Line.

Pioneer Park (Map p380; ☎ 459-1095; Airport Way at Peger Rd; sites $10, 4 night maximum) If you just want to park the van or RV and don't need facilities or a hook-up, you can spend the night in the parking lot here.

Tanana Valley Campground (Map p380; ☎ 456-7956; www.tananavalleyfair.org/campground.shtml; 1800 College Rd; campsites $16, RV sites $18-20) This campground has lots of trees, plus showers and laundry facilities. It's open 24 hours.

River's Edge RV Park & Campground (Map p380; ☎ 474-0286; www.riversedge.com; 4140 Boat St; rustic campsites $20, RV sites $30-36; 💻) Near the corner of Airport Way and George Parks Hwy, people literally line up to camp 2ft from each other 'in their van down by the river.'

HOSTELS & HOTELS

Go North Hostel (Map p380; ☎ 479-7272; www.gonorthalaska.com; 3500 Davis Rd; sites $6 plus per person $6, tepee dm $20, dm $23; 💻) Fairbanks' best hostel houses backpackers in wall tents, a tepee with two beds (that makes for a great semiprivate room) and a chilled-out camping area. The friendly hostel offers nearly everything you could imagine: bike, car and canoe rental, guided backcountry trips, book exchange, internet ($3 per hour), foosball and a common kitchen area. There are a few drawbacks, like the bugs, and their audacity to charge travelers 50¢ a minute for a shower. It's also a long walk from town – get here on the MACS Yellow Line bus route or call ahead for a shuttle pickup (one way $15).

Billie's Backpackers Hostel (Map p380; ☎ 479-2034; www.alaskahostel.com; 2895 Mack Blvd; sites/dm $15/35; 💻) Right off the MACS Red Line and not far from the university, Billie's is a bit down-at-heel. But there's an easy-breezy international scene here, and plans are in the works to build a sauna. It offers the typical amenities, plus free use of bikes. Make reservations, as this place is regularly full in summer.

our pick **Ah, Rose Marie B&B** (Map p380; ☎ 456-2040; www.akpub.com/akbbrv/ahrose.html; 302 Cowles St; s/d $65/90; 💻) Just west of downtown, this highly recommended B&B has cozy rooms at an amazingly affordable rate. There aren't many rooms in this 80-year-old cottage, so call ahead. The talkative and superfriendly owner prides himself on his breakfasts.

Golden North Motel (Map p380; ☎ 479-6201, 800-447-1910; www.goldennorthmotel.com; 4888 Old Airport Rd; s/d $79/89; 💻) Strategically located between the strip club and the airport, this family-owned place is actually legit ('2 legit 2 quit' as Hammer would say). While rooms are a bit scraggly, it's affordable, convenient and offers a free shuttle to the airport or train.

Midrange

7 Gables Inn & Suites (Map p380; ☎ 479-0751; www.7gablesinn.com; 4312 Birch Lane; r $90-130, apt $120-200) This B&B, just off the Chena River, is entered via a hothouse garden and offers plush rooms, some with Jacuzzis, as well as private apartments. Full breakfasts have an international theme, like eggs in curry sauce or Norwegian farmers' omelettes.

All Seasons B&B Inn (Map p380; ☎ 451-6649, 888-451-6649; www.allseasonsinn.com; 763 7th Ave; r $139-179; 💻) On a quiet residential street downtown, the All Seasons is a bit more commercial feeling than the other B&Bs in the area, with country decor that will have you dreaming of Omaha. There's a great sun porch and the breakfasts are big and beefy.

Minnie Street B&B Inn (Map p380; ☎ 456-1802; www.minniestreetbandb.com; 345 Minnie St; r with/without bath $179/139, apt $189-239; 💻) North of the river from downtown, this spacious B&B provides full breakfasts and bountiful advice on what to do around Fairbanks, and is the nicest midrange spot in town. There's a hot tub here and the condolike suites are perfect for families.

Top End

Alaska Heritage House B&B (Map p380; ☎ 456-4100; www.alaskaheritagehouse.com; 410 Cowles St; r $189-220; 💻) Probably the fanciest B&B in town, Heritage House was built in 1916 by Arthur Williams as a way to lure his future wife up to the Great White North to marry him. The well-restored home is on the national historic register, and each room has its own flair, but the Georgia Lee boudoir is by far our favorite, with a big soaking tub and fun and frilly antiques.

Pike's Waterfront Lodge (Map p380; ☎ 456-4500, 877-774-2400; www.pikeslodge.com; 1850 Hoselton Rd; r from $220; 💻) An upscale place on the banks of the Chena River, amenities at this lodge include a steam room and sauna, exercise facilities and a deck on the river. Look for internet specials on weekends.

EATING

University Area

College Coffeehouse (Map p380; ☎ 374-0468; 3677 College Rd; coffee $2-4; 🕒 7am-midnight Mon-Fri, from 8am Sat & Sun; 💻) In Campus Corner Mall, this is one of the best spots in Fairbanks to pick up on the city's offbeat vibe. It often has live music.

Bun on the Run (Map p380; 3480 College Rd; pastries $2-5; 🕒 7am-5pm Mon-Fri, to 3pm Sat) In a pink trailer in the Beaver Sports parking lot, 'The Bun' cranks out delicious pastries and has quite a following.

Hot Licks (Map p380; ☎ 479-7813; www.hotlicks.net; 3453 College Rd; cones $2, sundaes $5-7; 🕒 noon-11pm) On warm days, the line for the homemade ice cream here is insane. Find out why with a double-scoop cone of the fresh Alaska blueberry.

Sam & Sharon's Sourdough Café (Map p380; ☎ 479-0523; University Ave at Cameron St; breakfast $6-11, burgers & sandwiches $7-11; 🕒 6am-10pm) Considered by many to be the town's best diner, this place, just down University Ave from campus, serves up sourdough pancakes all day long.

Second Story Café (Map p380; ☎ 474-9574; 3525 College Rd; wraps & sandwiches $7; 🕒 9am-7pm Mon-Sat, 11am-5pm Sun; 💻) Above Gulliver's Books, this place whips up espressos, chai and smoothies, as well as killer wraps and sandwiches.

our pick **Tanana Valley Farmers Market** (Map p380; ☎ 456-3276; www.tvfmarket.com; College Rd at Caribou Dr; 🕒 11am-4pm Wed, from 9am Sat, occasionally open Sun) The market sells fresh produce, baked goods, local handicrafts and more. Come in late August and you can buy a 20lb cabbage. Try the scrumptious falafel at Pita Place; the line's worth it.

Wok 'n' Roll (Map p380; ☎ 455-4848; 3535 College Rd; dishes $8-13; 🕒 11am-9pm Mon-Sat) Adjacent to Campus Corner Mall, this is good for quick, cheap Chinese food.

Pad Thai (Map p380; ☎ 479-1251; 3400 College Rd; mains $9; 🕒 11am-10pm Mon-Fri, from 3pm Sat & Sun) In a sunny shack next to the Marlin bar, this is among the most popular of Fairbanks' many Thai restaurants. It's not as good as Lemongrass, but it ain't bad.

Downtown

McCafferty's Coffee House (Map p382; ☎ 456-6853; 408 Cushman St; soups $5; 🕒 7am-6pm Mon-Thu, 7am-11pm Fri, 10am-11pm Sat, 10am-4pm Sun) Arty without being pretentious, this espresso emporium also serves soups and baked goods. Live music adds atmosphere on Friday and Saturday nights.

Big Daddy's Barbecue (Map p380; ☎ 452-2501; 107 Wickersham St; sandwiches $8-10, mains $13-30; 🕒 11am-10pm Mon-Sat, noon-9pm Sun) There is a great lunch buffet for $14, with beef brisket, ribs, mac-n-cheese and all the down-home fixin's at this downtown barbecue joint and bar. There's live music Thursday through Saturday.

Gambardella's Pasta Bella (Map p382; ☎ 457-4992; 706 2nd Ave; mains $12-28; 🕒 11am-10pm Mon-Sat, from 4pm Sun) *The* place for Italian food in Fairbanks, with luscious pasta dishes, gourmet subs, pizzas and homemade bread. There's an outdoor café that's a delight during Fairbanks' long summer days.

Lavelle's Bistro (Map p382; ☎ 450-0555; 575 1st Ave; mains $16-33; 🕒 4:30-9pm Sun & Mon, to 10pm Tue-Sat) Chic, urbane and blessedly devoid of 'Last Frontier' kitsch, Lavelle's has a wine list as long as your arm and mains that include potato-crusted salmon and 'the best meatloaf you've ever had.'

Airport Way & Other Areas

Lulu's (Map p380; ☎ 374-3804; 364 Chena Pump Plaza; bagels & sandwiches $2-9; 🕒 6:30am-6pm Tue-Fri, 7am-5pm Sat & Sun) This locals' fave offers good morning sledge and breakfast bagels in a little strip mall on the edge of town.

Fred Meyer (Map p380; ☎ 474-1400; cnr Old Airport Rd & Airport Way; deli meals $4-10; 🕒 7am-11pm) This airplane hangar–sized store has every grocery imaginable, plus bulk foods, an extensive salad bar and all sorts of ready-to-eat fare. A sister store is at the intersection of the Old Steese Hwy and Johansen Expressway.

Cookie Jar (Map p380; ☎ 479-8319; 1006 Cadillac Ct; breakfast $8-10; 🕒 6:30am-8pm Mon-Thu, 6:30am-9pm Fri & Sat, 8am-4pm Sun) Bizarrely situated behind a pair of car dealerships off Danby St, locals flock here for the all-day breakfast.

Lemongrass (Map p380; ☎ 456-2200; 388 Old Chena Pump Rd; mains $9-11; 🕒 11am-4pm & 5-10pm) Ignore the out-of-the-way, strip-mall setting – Fairbanks' best Thai food and most gracious service is found here.

Airport Way Family Restaurant (Map p380; ☎ 457-5182; 1704 Airport Way; mains $11-20; ⏰ 24hr) As American as you can get with big meatloaf and chicken-fried steak meals – and spectacularly kind waitresses that call you 'hon' and 'sweetie' – this family restaurant is a good bet if you're in the neighborhood.

Pump House Restaurant (Map p377; ☎ 479-8452; Mile 1.3 Chena Pump Rd; www.pumphouse.com; dinner $18-36; ⏰ 11:30am-2pm & 5-11pm) Located 4 miles from downtown, this is the best place to turn dinner into an evening, or to enjoy a great Sunday brunch. A pump house during the gold-mining era, the building is now a national historic site. The MACS Blue Line goes by here.

Alaska Salmon Bake (Map p380; ☎ 452-7274, 800-354-7274; www.akvisit.com; adult/child $31/15; ⏰ 5-9pm) Hungry souls should take in the touristy, tasty, tongue-in-cheek salmon bake at Pioneer Park. All-you-can-eat grilled salmon, halibut, cod, prime rib and countless sides. A $5 shuttle bus is available from major hotels.

DRINKING & ENTERTAINMENT

As Alaska's second-biggest city, Fairbanks always has something on the go. For a low-down on live music, movies and such, check the listings in *FBX Square*, printed each Thursday in the *Fairbanks Daily News-Miner*. Other publications with the skinny on events include *AK This Month* and the *Anchorage Press*, both available for free around town.

Bars & Live Music

If you're here in September after classes begin, head to University Pub in the Wood Center at UAF, for live music and a college atmosphere. There are fun pubs and roadhouses in the close-by communities of Ester (p392) and Fox (p395).

Marlin (Map p380; 3412 College Rd) This subterranean dive hosts Fairbanks' edgiest musical acts, most nights of the week. It's located opposite Gulliver's Books, a stone's throw from campus. There's a flophouse hostel upstairs if you absolutely can't make it home.

Kodiak Jack's (Map p382; 537 Gaffney Rd) At the south end of downtown, this is a kick-up-yer-heels country-dance spot attracting a sizable military crowd.

Pump House Saloon (Map p380; Mile 1.3 Chena Pump Rd) Enjoys the riverfront ambience of the Pump House Restaurant (above), but with a bar menu that won't break the bank.

Theater & Saloon Shows

Fairbanks Shakespeare Theatre (☎ 457-7638; www.fairbanks-shakespeare.org) Performs Shakespeare classics at various times and in different venues around Fairbanks. Check the website for a complete schedule of upcoming shows.

Palace Theatre & Saloon (Map p380; ☎ 452-7274; www.akvisit.com; adult/child $18/9) At Pioneer Park, this saloon comes alive at night with honky-tonk piano, cancan dancers and other acts in the *Golden Heart Revue*. Showtime is 8:15pm nightly. Dinner at the park's nearby Alaska Salmon Bake (left) takes place before the show.

Spectator Sports

The **Goldpanners** (www.goldpanners.com) are Fairbanks' entry in the collegiate-level Alaska Baseball League, which also includes teams from Anchorage, Mat-Su Valley and Kenai Peninsula. Games are played mid-June through July at **Growden Memorial Park** (Map p380; cnr Wilbur St & 2nd Ave; tickets $10), starting at 7pm. Don't miss the Midnight Sun Baseball Game (see the boxed text, p386) on June 21 – it's a century-old tradition.

SHOPPING

Artworks (Map p380; ☎ 479-2563; Campus Corner Mall; ⏰ 10am-6pm Mon-Fri, to 5pm Sat) Next to the College Coffeehouse, this place has lots of glass, ceramics and oil paintings, plus a limited quantity of aboriginal carvings and musk ox-wool weavings.

Alaska House Art Gallery (Map p382; ☎ 456-6449; cnr 10th Ave & Cushman St; ⏰ 11am-7pm Mon-Sat) In a log building at the south end of downtown, the gallery specializes in indigenous and native-themed creations. Artists can often be found on the premises demonstrating their talents or telling stories.

Bear Gallery & Gift Shop (Map p380; ☎ 456-6485; Pioneer Park; ⏰ 11am-9pm) Run by the Fairbanks Arts Association and located upstairs in the Alaska Centennial Center for the Arts in Pioneer Park, this gallery showcases an ever-changing array of local artists.

New Horizons Gallery (Map p382; ☎ 456-2063; 509 1st Ave; ⏰ 10am-7pm Mon-Fri, 10am-6pm Sat, noon-5pm Sun) Just across from the Yukon Quest Headquarters, this gallery focuses on jewelry.

Beaver Sports (Map p380; ☎ 479-2494; www.beaversports.com; 3480 College Rd; ⏰ 10am-8pm Mon-Fri, 10am-7pm Sat, 11am-6pm Sun) This is *the* place for outdoor gear in Fairbanks, with mountain bikes, mountaineering boots and mountains of every other species of wilderness equipment. Also, there's a handy message board for exchanging info with fellow adventurers or securing used gear.

GETTING THERE & AWAY

Air

Alaska Airlines (☎ 800-252-7522; www.alaskaair.com) flies direct to Anchorage (where there are connections to the rest of Alaska, the Lower 48 and overseas), Barrow and Seattle. The round-trip advance-purchase fare to Anchorage is around $280; to Seattle it's upwards of $650. **Frontier Alaska** (Map p380; ☎ 450-7200, 800-478-6779; www.frontierflying.com) is your best way into the Bush. It also visits Anchorage daily, charging $158 (one way) or $209 (round trip). **Air North** (in USA or Canada ☎ 800-661-0407; www.flyairnorth.com) flies to Whitehorse and other Canadian destinations.

In summer, **Condor (Thomas Cook)** (in USA & Canada ☎ 800-524-6975, in Germany 01-805-707 202; www.condor.com) operates a weekly service direct to and from Frankfurt, Germany, for about $1900 return.

For travel into the Bush, try Frontier Alaska, **Larry's Flying Service** (☎ 474-9169; www.larrysflying.com) or **Wright Air Service** (Map p380; ☎ 474-0502; www.wrightair.net). Both have offices off University Ave on the airport's east side, and together they provide scheduled flights to more than 50 communities, including Bettles (Gates of the Arctic National Park), Fort Yukon, Kotzebue, Galena and Nome.

Bus

Long-distance bus services are available from **Alaska Direct Bus Line** (☎ 800-770-6652; www.alaskadirectbusline.com), which leaves from the Downtown Transit Park, and makes a Fairbanks–Whitehorse run (one way $180) on Sunday, Wednesday and Friday. Along the way it stops at Delta Junction (one way $45), Tok (one way $70), Beaver Creek (one way $95) and Haines Junction (one way $155). At Tok, you can transfer to a bus for Glennallen and Anchorage. At Whitehorse you can catch the company's bus to Skagway.

Travel down the George Parks Hwy to Denali National Park, Talkeetna and Anchorage with **Alaska/Yukon Trails** (☎ 800-770-7275; www.alaskashuttle.com). It departs from 23rd and Cushman Sts in Fairbanks at 8:30am, arriving at Denali National Park's Murie Science Center at 11:45am, downtown Talkeetna around 2pm and Anchorage around 4pm. The company also has a daily service to Dawson City, Yukon Territory, via the Taylor Hwy, leaving at 8:30am and arriving at 6:45pm.

Car & Motorcycle

If you're driving to Fairbanks from Canada, you'll likely be coming up the Alaska Hwy (p356). It's a good 12 hours from Whitehorse to Fairbanks, with little save for Tok and a few other highway-service communities en route. From Anchorage, it's six hours to Fairbanks up George Parks Hwy.

Train

The **Alaska Railroad** (☎ 458-6025, 800-544-0552; www.alaskarailroad.com) leaves Fairbanks daily at 8:15am from mid-May to mid-September. The train gets to Denali National Park at noon and Anchorage at 8:15pm. The new **train station** (🕑 6:30am-3pm) is at the south end of Danby St. The one-way fare to Denali National Park is $47, and $155 to Anchorage.

GETTING AROUND

To/From the Airport

Fairbanks International Airport (☎ 474-2500; www.dot.state.ak.us/faiiap/) is at the west end of Airport Way, 4 miles from town and beyond walking distance of anywhere you'll want to get to.

MACS Yellow Line (☎ 459-1011) bus swings by here eight times a day between 6:30am and 8pm, charging $1.50 and taking you past some Airport Way motels and the Go North Hostel en route to Transit Park, the downtown transfer station.

Alaska Shuttle(☎ 800-770-2267; www.alaskashuttle.com) has a shuttle service to the airport to anywhere in town, for $7, and one-way shuttles within the city limits for $5.

Or grab a cab, for which you'll have to pay around $18 to go downtown.

Car

Considering Fairbanks' noncentralized streetscape, as well as the worthwhile drives beyond town, you'll likely want a vehicle while you're here. If you don't have your own there are lots of rental options to choose from, including the national franchises at the airport. Of the companies listed here, the last two are probably the only ones in town that will allow their cars on gravel highways, such as the Steese, Elliot and Dalton.

Arctic Rent-A-Car (Map p380; ☎ 479-8044; www.arcticrentacar.com; 4500 Dale Rd), near the airport, rents out compacts for around $50 per day with 200 free miles.

Dalton Highway Auto Rentals (☎ 474-3530; www.artic-outfitters.com; 3820 University Ave, east ramp of Fairbanks International Airport) rents vehicles tricked out for trips on Alaska's roughest roads. Cars and SUVs are anywhere from $149 to $239 per day, with 250 free miles a day and 35¢ per mile after that.

Go North Hostel (Map p380; ☎ 479-7272, 866-236-7272; www.gonorthalaska.com; 3500 Davis Rd) has gravel-road-ready SUVs for $100 per day with unlimited miles (with a two-day minimum).

Public Transportation

The **Metropolitan Area Commuter Service** (MACS; ☎ 459-1011; www.co.fairbanks.ak.us/transportation) provides a local bus service in the Fairbanks area from around 6:15am to 7:30pm Monday to Friday, with limited service on Saturday and to noon Sunday. **Transit Park** (Map p382; cnr Cushman St & 5th Ave) is the system's central hub – all six bus routes stop here. The three lines of most interest to travelers are the Yellow Line, which goes to the airport; the Blue Line, which runs to the library, Pioneer Park and the university; and the Red Line, which goes from the hospital on the south side of Airport Way to downtown, then out to the university via College Rd. The fare on all routes is $1.50, or you can purchase an unlimited day pass for $3.

Taxi

Cabs charge $3.10 per mile, adding up in 10¢ increments. Try **Alaska Cab** (☎ 455-7777) or **Eagle Cab** (☎ 455-5555).

AROUND FAIRBANKS

The best part of Fairbanks is generally leaving Fairbanks. And there are a number of day trips and longer adventures to be had in the outlying areas. Small communities, like Ester, Fox and Manley Hot Springs, make for good day trips, while further afield along the

THE NORTHERN LIGHTS

Fairbanks' best attraction is also its furthest-flung: the aurora borealis, better known as the northern lights. The aurora is a phenomenon of physics taking place 50 to 200 miles above the Earth. As solar winds flow across the upper atmosphere, they hit gas molecules, which light up much like the high-vacuum electrical discharge of a neon sign. The result is a solar-powered lightshow of ghostly, undulating colors streaming across the sky. In the dead of winter, the aurora often illuminates the night for hours. Other evenings 'the event', as many call it, lasts less than 10 minutes, with the aurora spinning into a giant green ball and then fading. Milky green and white are the most common colors; red auroras are the rarest. In 1958 the northern sky was so 'bloody' with brilliant red auroras that fire trucks rushed out to the hills surrounding Fairbanks, expecting to find massive forest fires.

This polar phenomenon has been seen as far south as Mexico, but Fairbanks is the undisputed aurora capital. Somebody in northern Minnesota might witness fewer than 20 'events' a year and in Anchorage around 150, but in Fairbanks you can see the lights an average of 240 nights a year. North of Fairbanks, the number begins to decrease, and at the North Pole the lights are visible for fewer than 100 nights a year.

Regrettably, from May to mid-August there's too much daylight in Alaska to see an 'event', but generally in late summer the aurora begins to appear in the Interior and can be enjoyed if you're willing to be awake at 2am. By mid-September the lights are dazzling, and people are already asking, 'did you see the lights last night?'

The 'roaring Aurora' has also given rise to another phenomenon: procreation tourism. Many Asian cultures say being conceived under the Northern Lights will lead to great things, and they've been flocking to Fairbanks in the winter to try their luck. One thing's for sure, even if you don't make a baby, it's sure fun trying.

The best viewing in Fairbanks is in the outlying hills, away from city lights. The University of Alaska Fairbanks is also a good spot.

Steese and Elliot Hwys there's good hiking and paddling, and some splendiferous hot springs resorts.

ESTER

pop 2041

Seven miles northwest of Fairbanks, on the George Parks Hwy, is the so-called 'Peoples Republic of Ester' – a scattering of back-road cabins that are home to professors, artists and other offbeat folks all united, it seems, in their desire to live 'close to other people that don't like other people, too.' While the esoteric Esterians are nice enough, there really isn't much to do here, except hit the saloon and maybe take some hikes along the back roads.

Ester was established in 1906, when miners made a sizable gold strike at Ester Creek. Soon this was a thriving community of 15,000, with three hotels and five saloons. The town came back to life in the 1920s when the Fairbanks Exploration Company began a large-scale mining operation. Most of Ester's historical buildings date from that era and were either built by the company or moved from Fox, just a few miles north of Fairbanks. Gold mining still takes place in the hills surrounding Ester. The town's only attraction, Ester Gold Camp, was closed when we passed by. Word on the street is that it won't be opening up, but you may want to stop by to check out the old tourist trap.

There are no hotels in Ester, but you can stay out late at the **Blue Loon** (☎ 457-5666; www.theblueloon.com; Mile 352.5 George Parks Hwy), one of the Fairbanks area's most popular nightspots, with live bands and DJs, dancing, food and lots of good beer. This place is so popular that it even gets some older big-name acts like the Violent Femmes and Third Eye Blind.

You can grill your own burgers and sit out on the porch at the **Golden Eagle Saloon** (cnr Main & E St), where locals rule, and girls occasionally go topless (not for money of course, just for the fun of it).

CHENA HOT SPRINGS ROAD

This fireweed-lined, forest-flanked corridor parallels the languid Chena River 56 miles east off the Steese Hwy, to the Chena Hot Springs Resort, the closest hot springs to Fairbanks and also the most developed. The road is paved and in good condition. From Mile 26 to Mile 51 it passes through **Chena River State Recreation Area**, a 397-sq-mile preserve encompassing the river valley and nearby alpine areas, which is home to some of the Fairbanks area's best hiking, canoeing and fishing.

Activities

HOT SPRINGS

At the heart of a 40-sq-mile geothermal area, the **Chena Hot Springs**, at Chena Hot Springs Resort (opposite), produce a steady stream of water that, at 156°F, must be cooled before you can even think about bathing in it. The facility has several indoor and outdoor tubs, Jacuzzis and pools, including what amounts to a boulder-ringed artificial lake with a fountain at its center. If you've just come to soak it costs $10 (adult) or $7 (child), and is open 7am to midnight. Other activities include a visit to the ice museum (adult $15, child $7.50), ice-sculpting classes, mountain biking, hiking, horseback riding, and fishing the local streams for grayling. Guided activities are available. In winter, this is one of the best places in the world to view the aurora.

PADDLING

With no whitewater and comparatively few other hazards, the peaceful Chena River offers a variety of day and multiday canoeing pos-

HOT SPRINGS NEAR FAIRBANKS

Back when Alaskan gold prospectors were stooping in the near-freezing creeks panning for gold, the Fairbanks area had one saving grace – the hot springs. There are several around Fairbanks, and all were quickly discovered and used by the miners as a brief escape from Alaska's ice and cold. Today, the same mineral water, ranging in temperature from 120°F to 150°F, soothes the aches and pains of freezing travelers and sore hikers passing through.

The hot springs include Chena Hot Springs (above), 56 miles east of Fairbanks; Tolovana Hot Springs (p397), 100 miles west of Fairbanks on the Elliot Hwy; Hutlinana Warm Springs (p397), 129 miles west of Fairbanks on the Elliot Hwy; and Manley Hot Springs (p397), at the end of the Elliot Hwy.

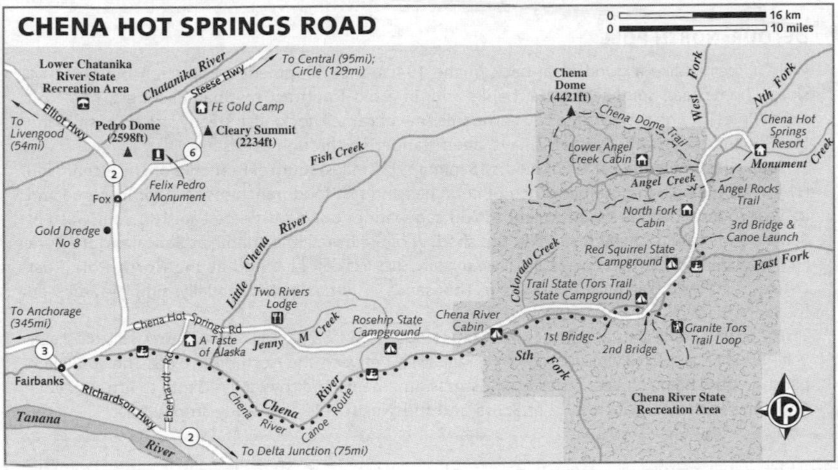

sibilities, with access points all along Chena Hot Springs Rd. For more details on paddling here, see p115.

HIKING

The 15-mile **Granite Tors Trail Loop** – accessed from the Tors Trail State Campground, at Mile 39 of the Chena Hot Springs Rd – provides access into an alpine area with unusual tors: isolated pinnacles of granite rising out of the tundra.

The first set is 6 miles from the trailhead but the best group lies 2 miles further along the trail. The entire trail is a five- to eight-hour trek gaining 2700ft in elevation, with a free-use shelter midway.

Angel Rocks Trail is a 3.5-mile loop trail that leads to Angel Rocks: large granite outcroppings near the north boundary of Chena River State Recreation Area. It's a moderate dayhike; the elevation gain is 900ft and the rocks are less than 2 miles from the road. The trail is also the first leg of the **Angel Rocks–Chena Hot Springs Traverse**, a more difficult 8.3-mile trek that ends at the Chena Hot Springs Resort, at the end of Chena Hot Springs Rd. Roughly halfway along the traverse is a free-use shelter.

The posted trailhead for Angel Rocks is just south of a rest area at Mile 49 of the Chena Hot Springs Rd. The lower trailhead for the Chena Dome Trail is practically across the street.

The upper trailhead for the most popular hike in the area, **Chena Dome Trail** (p98), is at Mile 50.5 of Chena Hot Springs Rd. The trail follows the ridge for almost 30 miles in a loop around the Angel Creek drainage area; the first 3 miles to the treeline make an excellent day hike.

Sleeping & Eating

Chena Hot Springs Rd offers a number of sleeping options, including three popular state-run campgrounds and seven public-use cabins. Two of the cabins are on the road, while the rest are accessible via (often very wet) hikes. The cabins vary in size, sleeping between four and nine people, and can be reserved via the **Alaska Division of Parks and Outdoor Recreation** (☎ 451-2695; www.alaskastateparks.org).

Rosehip State Campground (Mile 27 Chena Hot Springs Rd; sites $10) Has a nature trail and 36 well-treed, well-spaced sites, some right on the riverbank.

Tors Trail State Campground (Mile 39.5 Chena Hot Springs Rd; sites $10) Twenty-four sites in a stand of spruce, with a canoe launch on the Chena River. Across the highway is the trailhead for the Granite Tors Trail Loop.

Red Squirrel State Campground (Mile 42.8 Chena Hot Springs Rd; sites $10) With ad-hoc sites in a grassy area overlooking a placid pond, this is the least appealing of the area's campgrounds.

Chena Hot Springs Resort (☎ 451-8104; www.chenahotsprings.com; Mile 56.6 Chena Hot Springs Rd; campsites & RV sites $20, r $179, cabins & yurts with outhouse $65-249, pool $10) This come-as-you-are complex at the end of Chena Hot Springs Rd is a great spot to unwind for the weekend. Its burbling waters were discovered by gold miners in 1905,

DETOUR: NORTH POLE

Well, it *seemed* like a good idea: back in the 1940s, a development corporation bought up a sleepy homestead southeast of Fairbanks and, in a bid to attract toy manufacturers, named it North Pole. Though the Fortune 500 companies never came knocking, a steady stream of smirking tourists and their starry-eyed kids have been wandering through ever since.

Today this community of 1900 souls is 15 minutes (12 miles) south of Fairbanks on the Richardson Hwy. It would be a forgettable clutch of churches and fast-food franchises save for its name and its year-round devotion to the Yuletide. You can wander down Mistletoe Lane, do your wash at Santa's Suds Laundromat, or sleep in the shadow of a 45ft-tall Kris Kringle at **Santaland RV Park** (☎ 488-9123, 888-488-9123; www.santalandrv.com; RV sites $25-35; 💻). And at the **North Pole Post Office** (325 S Santa Claus Lane) hundreds of thousands of letters arrive annually, simply addressed to 'Santa Claus, North Pole, Alaska.'

The town's biggest attraction is **Santa Claus House** (☎ 488-2200, 800-588-4078; www.santaclaushouse.com; 101 St Nicholas Dr off Richardson Hwy; 🕓 8am-8pm), between the North Pole exits. The sprawling barnlike store holds endless aisles of Christmas ornaments and toys, a live Santa to listen to your Christmas wishes, a giant statue of Santa and the 'North Pole' – a candy-striped post.

quickly making it the premier place to soak for residents from booming Fairbanks. Over a century later the place offers something for everyone, from quick dips to multiple days of lodging, meals and amusement. The rooms feel very much like mainstream motel rooms, but there's a pretty good restaurant (with sandwiches $10 to $12, dinner $16 to $25, open 7am to 10pm) and a bar decorated with Yukon Quest memorabilia. Nearly 80% of the hotel's energy is geothermal energy, and you can take 'green and gassy' tours daily at 6pm. See p392 for more on the springs.

Lower Angel Creek Cabin (per night $25) This place is 3.6 miles along an ATV trail from Mile 50.5 of Chena Hot Springs Rd.

Chena River Cabin (Mile 32.2 Chena Hot Springs Rd; per night $40) A newer, road-accessible cabin in a stand of spruce and birch overlooking the river.

North Fork Cabin (Mile 47.7 Chena Hot Springs Rd; per night $40) Further down the road, it also has access to the river.

A Taste of Alaska (☎ 488-7855; www.atasteofalaska.com; exit on Eberhardt Rd from Mile 5.3 Chena Hot Springs Rd; d $185, cabins $205-235; 💻) Just a few miles down Chena Hot Springs Rd, this B&B has great views of the valley down below, rather dowdy rooms and a couple of private cabins complete with kitchens and plenty of space for the whole family.

Two Rivers Lodge (☎ 488-6815; Mile 16 Chena Hot Springs Rd; burgers & pub grub $10-17, dinner $14-35; 🕓 5-10pm Mon-Fri, 3-10pm Sat & Sun) The rustic decor at this friendly lodge, complete with bearskin rugs, is in keeping with the natural setting. Steak, seafood and poultry are the focus, but you can also grab some roadhouse food (burgers, ribs and such) at the friendly lounge.

Getting There & Away

Call the Chena Hot Springs Resort to book its shuttle-van service; round-trip transportation from Fairbanks is $90 for one person, or $45 per person for two or more. Hitchhiking is not the grand effort it is on the Elliot Hwy, because of the heavy summer usage of the Chena River State Recreation Area.

STEESE HIGHWAY

The scenic but severely lonely Steese Hwy follows an old miners' trail 162 miles from Fairbanks to the Athabascan village of Circle, on the Yukon River. This hilly and winding road is paved for the first 53 miles, and then has a good gravel base to the mining settlement of Central. In the final 30 miles it narrows and becomes considerably rougher and more twisty. While an interesting drive, the route's main attraction – Circle Hot Springs – has been closed for several years. If it doesn't reopen, which seems likely, this trip is not worth the trouble; inquire at the Fairbanks visitor center (p379).

The Steese Hwy starts at the junction of Airport Way and the Richardson Hwy. From there it passes the beginning of Chena Hot Springs Rd at Mile 4.6, and then the Elliot Hwy at Mile 11, near Fox.

GETTING THERE & AWAY

Hitchhiking is more difficult on the Steese Hwy than on Chena Hot Springs Rd, though people this far north are good about stopping. Still, you have to consider your time schedule and patience level before attempting it.

You can try renting a vehicle in Fairbanks, but you'll have to go with a company that permits driving on gravel roads (see p390).

If you want to fly, **Warbelow's Air Ventures** (☎ 474-0518, 800-478-0812; www.warbelows.com), in Fairbanks, has regular flights to Circle for $198 round trip.

Fox

Pop 354

The center of Fairbanks Mining District, Fox has a few worthwhile watering holes, eateries and attractions, but it's essentially a Fairbanks bedroom community, and therefore has about the same appeal as any suburb in America.

Howling Dog Saloon (Mile 11 Old Steese Hwy) serves ales and lagers from the Silver Gulch Brewery (across the road), and hosts local and out-of-town bands.

Silver Gulch Brewery (☎ 452-2739; Mile 11 Old Steese Hwy; burgers $11, mains $15-34; 🕑 4-10pm Mon-Fri, from 11am Sat & Sun) is a slightly overdone brewpub making the best beer in the region – the new restaurant and bar are certainly worth the stop. There are free brewery tours Monday, Wednesday and Friday at 3pm.

Turtle Club (☎ 457-3883; Mile 10 Old Steese Hwy; dinner $24-33; 🕑 6-10pm Mon-Sat, 5-9pm Sun) has a roadhouse atmosphere and is reputed for its prime rib.

For information on the Gold Dredge No 8, see p385.

Fox to Central

On the Steese Hwy, the **Felix Pedro Monument** (Map p393; Mile 16.6 Steese Hwy) commemorates the miner whose gold strike gave birth to Fairbanks. The stream across the highway – now known as Pedro Creek – is where it all happened. You'll likely see amateur goldpanners there 'looking for color.'

At Mile 27.9 take a sharp turn up a hill to reach the **FE Gold Camp** (Map p393; ☎ 389-2414; Mile 27.9 Steese Hwy; sandwiches $7-11, dinner $12-24, dm/r $25/55; 🕑 6am-9pm), a national historic site with a charmingly rustic bar and restaurant. There are also hostel-style accommodations, with quaint shared bathrooms. The camp was built in 1925 for the dredging that went on from 1927 to 1957 and removed an estimated $70 million in gold (at yesterday's prices).

A few miles beyond, the landscape opens up, revealing expansive vistas as well as evidence of recent forest-fire activity. **Upper Chatanika River State Campground** (Mile 39 Steese Hwy; sites $10) is the first public campground along the Steese Hwy and has 24 sites, some right on the riverbank. Have your bug dope handy – this is mosquito country. People with canoes can launch their boats here, and the fishing for grayling is good.

Cripple Creek BLM Campground (Mile 60 Steese Hwy; walk-in/drive-up sites $3/6), the next campground along, has 18 sites (including six walk-in sites with no vehicle access), tables, water and a nearby nature trail. It's the uppermost access point to the Chatanika River canoe route.

Access points for the **Pinnell Mountain Trail** are at Mile 85.6 and Mile 107 of the Steese Hwy. The first trailhead is Twelvemile Summit, which offers remarkable alpine views and is often snowy well into June. Even if you have no desire to undertake the three-day trek, the first 2 miles is an easy climb past unusual rock formations.

The **Birch Creek canoe route** begins at Mile 94 of the Steese Hwy, where a short road leads down to a canoe launch on the creek. The wilderness trip is a 140-mile paddle to the exit point, at Mile 147 of the highway. The overall rating of the river is Class II, but there are some Class III and Class IV parts that require lining your canoe.

Eagle Summit (Mile 107 Steese Hwy), 3624ft in elevation, has a parking area for the second trailhead of the Pinnell Mountain Trail. A climb of less than a mile leads to the mountaintop, the highest point along the Steese Hwy and a place where the midnight sun can be observed skimming the horizon around the summer solstice. On a clear day, summiting here can feel like ascending to heaven. The peak is also near a caribou migration route.

Central

pop 95

At Mile 127.5 the Steese Hwy reaches Central, where pavement briefly takes over. Though the settlement once offered a range of visitor services, the closure of the hot springs down the road has resulted in fewer tourist options here. Locals are keeping their fingers crossed the springs will reopen – but it seems pretty unlikely.

HISTORY

Originally referred to on maps as Central House, the town began as a supply stop on the trail from Circle City to the surrounding creeks of the Circle Mining District. Central became a town in the 1930s, thanks largely to the Steese Hwy, which was built in 1927. It's experienced a few more gold booms over the years. And today, with gold going for anywhere from $800 to $1000 an ounce, the rush is back on.

One miner alone, Jim Regan, recovered 26,000oz of gold from the Crooked Creek area between 1979 and 1986. Even more interesting was a diamond unearthed by miners in 1982. Nicknamed Arctic Ice, it was the first discovered in Alaska.

Mining is mainly done by small family operations nowadays, and the miners' distrust of anybody or any agency threatening their right to make a living is still evident throughout town, especially at the bars.

Also, if you're keen to try some panning yourself, avoid claim-jumping at all costs. The safest places are wherever the Steese Hwy crosses a creek or stream, since the road is public land.

SIGHTS & ACTIVITIES

One of the best museums of any small Alaskan town is the **Circle District Historical Society Museum** (☎ 520-1893; www.cdhs.us/Fset.htm; Mile 127.5 Steese Hwy; admission $1; 🕑 noon-5pm) in Central. Established in 1984, the main portion of the museum is a large log lodge that houses a miner's cabin, exhibits on early mining equipment and dog-team freight and mail hauling, and the Yukon Press – the first printing press north of Juneau, which produced Interior Alaska's first newspaper.

EATING & DRINKING

At the time of writing, just about the only culinary option in Central was the unappealing **Steese Roadhouse** (☎ 520-5800; breakfast $10-11, lunch $5-13, dinner $15-25; 🕑 8am-10pm), where, despite half-hearted service, locals crowd the bar to bad-mouth the government.

Circle

pop 102

Beyond Central, in what may be Alaska's *least* scenic stretch of road, the Steese Hwy passes the exit point of the Birch Creek canoe route at Mile 147 and heads to Circle (Mile 162). Much of this area is low-lying, burned-over, muddy and mosquito-ridden. Also, the road is almost humorously circuitous: at times, you'll be driving through your own dust.

Today Circle has zero attractions, but that's OK: you can spend an hour or two wandering past the shacks and shanties, appreciating the fish wheels in folks' backyards and the distinctive flat-bottomed river skiffs used to negotiate the Yukon.

Though 50 miles south of the Arctic Circle, miners who established the town in 1896 thought they were near the imaginary line and gave Circle its present name. After gold was discovered in Birch Creek, Circle became a bustling town of 1200 with two theaters, a music hall, eight dance halls and 28 saloons. It was known as the 'largest log-cabin city in the world' until the Klondike Gold Rush (1897–98) reduced its population and the river gobbled up much of the original townscape.

At the boat ramp where the Steese Hwy meets the river there's ostensibly a public **campground** (sites $5), but it's overgrown and, worse, a party spot for people from downriver villages. Basic groceries, snacks and gas for your return trip can be bought just up the road at the **HC Company Store** (☎ 773-1222).

ELLIOT HIGHWAY

From the crossroad with the Steese Hwy at Fox, just north of Fairbanks, the Elliot Hwy extends 152 miles north and then west to Manley Hot Springs, a small settlement near the Tanana River. The hot springs were open at press time, but there were rumors circulating that it might close, so call Manley Roadhouse (p398) to check before you head out.

The first half is paved, the rest is gravel, and there's no gas and few services until you reach the end. Diversions along the way are comparatively few, but the leisurely, scenic drive, coupled with the disarming charms of Manley Hot Springs, make it a worthwhile one- or two-day road trip.

Lower Chatanika River State Recreation Area (Mile 11 Elliot Hwy) is a 570-acre park offering fishing, boating and camping opportunities along the Chatanika River. The area has two free, informal campgrounds: Whitefish and Olnes Pond.

At Mile 28 of the Elliot Hwy is the Wickersham Dome Trailhead parking lot and an information box. From here, trails lead to Borealis-Le Fevre's and Lee's cabins. **Lee's Cabin** (Sun-Thu $20, Fri & Sat $25) is a 7-mile hike in and has a large picture window overlooking the

White Mountains and a loft that comfortably sleeps eight. **Borealis-Le Fevre Cabin** (Sun-Thu $20, Fri & Sat $25) is a 19-mile hike over the White Mountains Summit Trail (p101). Reserve through the **Bureau of Land Management office** (BLM; ☎ 474-2251) in Fairbanks.

At Mile 57, where a bridge crosses the Tolovana River, there's an old BLM campground that's no longer maintained, but there's still a turnoff here. The fishing here is good for grayling and northern pike, though the mosquitoes are of legendary proportions. Nearby is the start of the **Colorado Creek Trail** to Windy Gap BLM Cabin. Check with the BLM office in Fairbanks about use of the cabin during the summer.

Off Mile 62, 10 miles before the junction with the Dalton Hwy, a 500ft spur leads from the road to **Fred Blixt Cabin** (Sun-Thu $20, Fri & Sat $25). This public-use cabin should be reserved in advance through the BLM office in Fairbanks.

Livengood (*lye*-ven-good), 2 miles east of the highway at Mile 71, has no services and is little more than a scattering of log shanties. Here, the Elliot Hwy swings west and in 2 miles, at the junction of the Dalton Hwy, pavement ends and the road becomes a rutted, rocky lane. Traffic evaporates and until Manley Hot Springs you may not see another vehicle.

In short order the Elliot Hwy ascends to a high subalpine ridge, which it follows for miles, and on clear days affords views of Mt McKinley to the south.

The open country invites off-road hiking, and the breeze is often strong enough to keep mosquitoes at bay.

The rustic, privately managed **Tolovana Hot Springs** (☎ 455-6706; www.mosquitonet.com/~tolovana; cabins $30-120) can be accessed via a taxing 11-mile overland hike south from Mile 93. Facilities consist of two plastic tubs bubbling with 125°F to 145°F water, plus, a quarter mile up the valley, two cedar cabins that must be reserved in advance. The trailhead isn't signposted; contact the managers for directions.

At Mile 110 is the paved 11-mile road to the small Athabascan village of **Minto** (pop 180), which isn't known for welcoming strangers.

Beyond Minto, the Elliot Hwy briefly becomes winding and hilly, and then suddenly, at Mile 120, there's chip-sealing for the next 17 miles. Hutlinana Creek is reached at Mile 129, and a quarter mile east of the bridge is an 8-mile creekside trail to **Hutlinana Warm Springs**, an undeveloped thermal area with a 3ft-deep pool.

The springs are visited mainly in winter; in summer, the buggy bushwhack seems uninviting.

From the bridge it's another 23 miles southwest to Manley Hot Springs.

GETTING THERE & AWAY

With so little traffic on Elliot Hwy, hitching is ill-advised – though if someone *does* come along, they'll likely take pity on you. Alternatively, you can rent a vehicle in Fairbanks (p390), but you'll have to go with a company that permits driving on gravel roads. Finally, **Warbelow's Air Ventures** (☎ 474-0518, 800-478-0812; www.warbelows.com), in Fairbanks, has regular flights to Manley Hot Springs for $140 round trip.

Manley Hot Springs

pop 72

The town of Manley Hot Springs may be one of the loveliest discoveries you'll make around the Fairbanks area, that is if they keep the hot springs open (rumors were spreading as of press time that the springs might be closing). At the end of a long, lonely road, this well-kept town is full of friendly folks, tidy log homes and luxuriant gardens. Located between Hot Springs Slough and the Tanana River, the community was first homesteaded in 1902 by JF Karshner, just as the US Army Signal Corps arrived to put in a telegraph station. A few years later, as the place boomed with miners from the nearby Eureka and Tofty districts, Frank Manley arrived and built a four-story hotel. Most of the miners are gone now, but Manley's name – and the spirit of an earlier era – remains. In modern times the town has been a hotbed of high-level dog-mushing: champs like Charlie Boulding, Joe Redington Jr and four-time Iditarod champ Susan Butcher have all lived here.

Just before crossing the slough you pass the town's namesake **hot springs** (☎ 672-3231, or at the roadhouse 672-3161; admission $5; 24hr). Privately owned by famously hospitable Chuck and Gladys Dart, bathing happens within a huge, thermal-heated greenhouse that's a veritable Babylonian garden of grapes, Asian pears and hibiscus flowers.

Deep in this jungle are three spring-fed concrete tubs, each burbling at different temperatures. Pay your money, hose yourself down and soak away in this deliriously un-Alaskan setting. Heed the signs to not pick the fruit.

Across the slough and 3 miles beyond the village is the broad Tanana River, just upstream from its confluence with the Yukon. Frank Gurtler of **Manley Boat Charters** (☎ 672-3271; fishing charters per hr $65, tours per person per hr $70) can take you to catch salmon, char and grayling, or just show you the sights along the waterway.

If you get cut up or want to clean up, there's a clinic and washeteria at Mile 149.5.

SLEEPING & EATING

Public campground (sites $5) The town has a slough-front campground just past the bridge. Pay at the roadhouse.

Manley Roadhouse (☎ 672-3161; r with/without bath $120/70, sandwiches $9-11, dinner mains $22-30; 8am-10pm) Facing the slough, this antique-strewn, century-old establishment has clean, uncomplicated rooms and is the social center of town. The bar boasts an impressive array of beers while the restaurant offers locally caught king salmon. Aside from the historical rooms, it also offers simple cabins across the way.

Manley Trading Post (☎ 762-3221; 10am-5pm) You will find groceries, gas, liquor and the post office here.

The Bush

At the end of the road, and the beginning of our most hard-fought dreams, lies 'the Bush.' Mythical in its proportions and untenable vastness, this untamed region is difficult to define, but most Alaskans will tell you that it is comprised of small, isolated native villages and sweeping stretches of untracked wilderness.

For the purposes of this book, we separate the Bush geographically and include places that are essentially off the road system in the northern half of the state (including large 'commuter' cities like Barrow, Nome and Kotzebue) and the Dalton Hwy, which stretches north from Fairbanks all the way to the oil fields of Prudhoe Bay. But ask any Alaskan where the Bush lies, and they are likely to point to the woods, and simply say: 'out there.'

Traveling in these areas is not easy (or cheap) – you'll need to fly, float or walk a long way to get there – but it's a once-in-a-lifetime chance, and may be worth the extra expense.

In Western Alaska, visitors can head out on long backpacks or wilderness paddles, swagger their way through gold-rush saloons or head off the map to remote villages and natural wonders few eyes will ever see. Up north, in what we label Arctic Alaska, the land gets bigger, with the formidable Brooks Range forming a spine across the state. Nature still rules supreme in huge nature preserves like Gates of the Arctic National Park and the Arctic National Wildlife Refuge, and the adventure opportunities are truly only limited by your imagination.

HIGHLIGHTS

- **Easiest way to break an axel** (p411) – driving along the jarring Dalton Hwy; Alaska's most scenic and surreal roadway takes you up through the Brooks Range and down the desolate North Slope to the edge of the Arctic Sea
- **Coolest 'adventure light' expedition** (p407) – rolling through the countryside near the gold-rush village of Nome, spotting musk ox and reindeer along the way
- **Best place to really rough It** (p415) – tackling an adventure in the Gates of the Arctic National Park & Preserve, where there are no visitor facilities or trails

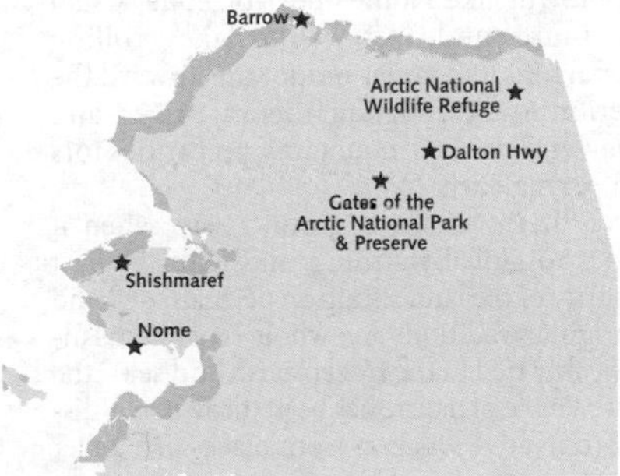

- **Best reason to visit today** (p420, p418 and p417) – visiting remote outposts like Shishmaref, the Arctic National Wildlife Refuge and Barrow may be impossible in 20 years – thanks to global warming – so what are you waiting for?
- **Smartest way to travel** (p420) – leaving the guidebook behind and heading out on your own Alaskan Bush expedition

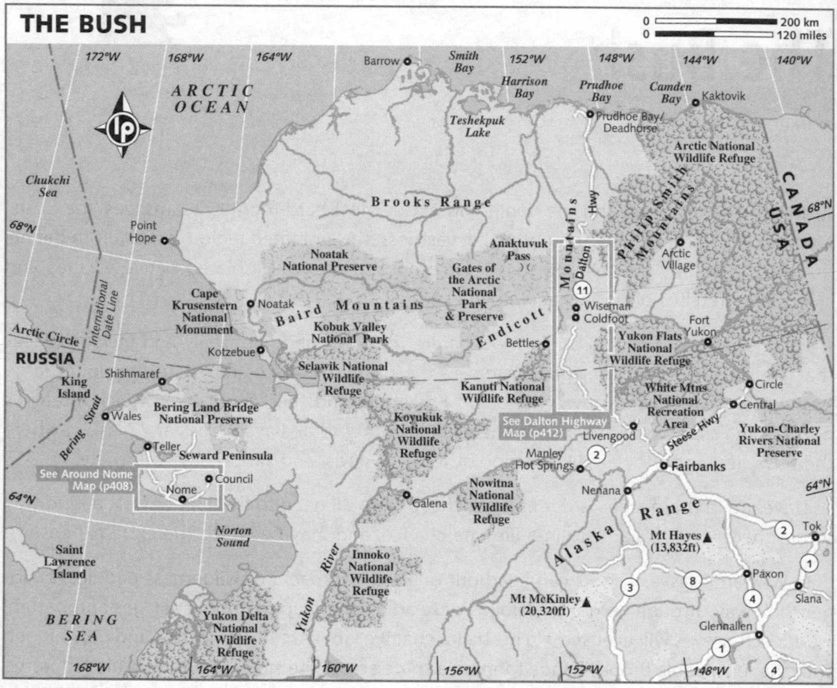

Land & Climate

The mighty Brooks Range slices this region in two. To the north, a vast plain of barren tundra sweeps down to the frozen wasteland of the Arctic Ocean. In the Western reaches, near towns like Nome and Kotzebue, you'll find more tundra, as well as lakes, rolling coastal hills and larger mountains toward the interior. And throughout there are rivers and valleys, monstrous mountains, precarious tors and permafrost.

Northern Alaska is ground zero when it comes to global warming, and with the vast majority of the land sitting on permafrost – and aboriginal traditions and whole ecosystems inextricably tied to the frozen earth and sea – the very balance of nature has been thrown into discord. Native villagers from places like Teller and Shishmaref are being forced to relocate as their houses literally fall into the sea. The highly adapted creatures that call this place home – the caribou, polar bear and musk ox – need to further adapt to their new environment or they'll perish, yet another casualty in Darwin's dark little war and man's avaricious quest for bigger cars, bigger homes and bigger horizons.

Due to its geographical diversity, the Bush is a land of many climates. In inland areas, winter holds sway from mid-September to early May, with ceaseless weeks of clear skies, negligible humidity and temperatures colder than anywhere else in America. Alaska's all-time low, –80°F, happened at Prospect Creek Camp, just off the Dalton Hwy. Closer to the ocean, winter lingers even longer but is incrementally less chilly.

During the brief summer visitors to the Bush should be prepared for anything. Barrow and Prudhoe Bay may demand a parka: July highs there often don't hit 40°F. Along the Dalton Hwy and around Nome, the weather is famously variable. Intense heat (stoked by the unsetting sun) can be as much a concern as cold.

History

The history of the Bush is largely the history of Alaska Natives. By their own accounts, they've been here since the beginning. Archaeologists say it's not been as long as that: perhaps 6000 years for the ancestors of today's Athabascans, and about 3000 years for the Iñupiat, Yupiks and Aleuts. Either way, they displayed remarkable ingenuity and endurance, thriving as fishermen, hunters and gatherers until Europeans arrived.

That happened in the 1800s, with traders and missionaries setting up shop in numerous communities along the Western Alaska coast. Whalers then entered the Bering Sea midcentury, expanding into the Arctic Ocean, and virtually decimating the bowhead whale population by 1912.

The most climactic event in the Bush, however, was the gold rush at Nome, triggered in 1898 by the 'Three Lucky Swedes' (p404). The stampede drew 20,000 people to the Seward Peninsula, giving the region, ever so briefly, the most populous town in Alaska. Nome remains the only significant non-Native community in the Bush.

Over the past century, progress in transportation, communications and social services further transformed the region. 'Bush planes' made the area relatively accessible, and towns like Barrow, Kotzebue, Nome and Bethel became commercial hubs, giving services to the smaller villages in their orbit. Political and legal battles brought more schools and better health care, and the 1971 Alaska Native Claims Settlement Act provided the region with some jobs. Today, anywhere you go in the Bush you'll find residents engaged in a fine balancing act – coping with the challenges of the 21st century, while at the same time struggling to keep their millennia-old values, practices and links to the land alive.

Parks & Protected Lands

The Bush has several national parks and preserves, but generally they cannot be reached by car, are devoid of visitor services and are for hearty adventurers only. Most famous is Gates of the Arctic National Park & Preserve (p415), spanning the spires of the Brooks Range and offering spectacular hiking and paddling. Near Kotzebue is Kobuk Valley National Park, known for the Great Kobuk Sand Dunes and the oft-paddled Kobuk River (see p410). The mountain-ringed Noatak National Preserve is just to the north of there, with the quite popular Noatak River (see p410). And to the southwest, between Nome and Kotzebue, is Bering Land Bridge National Preserve, which commemorates the peopling of the Americas and is experienced largely by visitors to Serpentine Hot Springs (p409). To the east is the massive 19.6-million acre ANWR (p418). While it's extremely costly and difficult to mount an expedition here, it may just offer the best wilderness experience of your life, with no people, massive herds of migrating caribou and one of North America's last stands of untrammeled wilderness.

Getting There & Around

The Bush is, almost by definition, road-less. You can drive (or be driven) up the Dalton Highway (see p415), but everywhere else is fly-in only, in the summer at least. Winter ice roads can take you to Bettles and some intrepid souls even make it by 4WD to Barrow during the winter. Alaska Airlines and Frontier Alaska are the main carriers (see p407) connecting urban Alaska to Bush hubs like Nome, Kotzebue and Barrow; from these, regional airlines fly to smaller villages or provide air-taxi services into the wilderness. In Nome, an insular road network also reaches out to a few surrounding destinations.

WESTERN ALASKA

A wild region in an already wild state, Western Alaska is home to the Inupiat, wild-eyed prospectors and some of Alaska's least-seen wilderness. Highlights of the area are regional hubs, like Nome and Kotzebue, and the vast tracks of undiscovered wilderness of the Noatak and Bering Land Bridge National Preserves. Here you can hike, bike and paddle your way through high-latitude tundra. But don't expect a forested wonderland: this is too far north (and too close to the Arctic and Bering Seas) for trees. Instead, you have a naked, harsh landscape carpeted with coral-like tundra grasses and flowers, herds of reindeer and, of course, the region's star Pleistocene-era ungulate, the musk ox.

NOME

pop 3497

Nome is, in so many ways, the Alaskan archetype: a rough-hewn, fun-loving, undying Wild West town, thriving at the utmost edge of the planet. It's even the finish line of that most Alaskan of races, the Iditarod (p58), and during its gold-rush heyday, Wyatt Earp and some 30,000 stampeders called the town home. With America's biggest concentration of non-Natives north of the treeline, the town

QUICK TIPS FOR SUSTAINABLE TRAVEL IN THE BUSH

Truly green travel is nearly impossible in Alaska's Bush. After all, you had to fly to get here. And once you're here, if you are staying in a town, it's likely you'll be running all your heat and electricity on diesel generators. But there are ways to travel smarter here, making a positive impact on both the ecosystems and cultures you will encounter along the way.

- **Know your cultures** There are an estimated 380 native villages in the Bush. As more people visit these villages and the villagers look increasingly to 'white' nonsubsistence economies, their cultural traditions, language and lifestyle are beginning to morph and die out. Make an effort to learn about the traditional way of life, buy locally made crafts and respect local laws and customs.
- **Keep it dry** Alcoholism and drug abuse are rampant among both whites and natives living in the Bush. Many towns are 'dry,' while others are 'damp' (alcoholic consumption is allowed but heavily restricted) or 'wet.' Respect the local laws.
- **Pack it out** You know this one: leave no trace but footsteps. Also, consider offsetting your carbon footprint (see p23).
- **Write your congressman** The fate of Alaska's environment may lie with the leaders of the US. Let them know what you think.
- **Leave your judgments behind** Many Alaska Natives still practice subsistence hunting, heading out by seal-skin boat in search of whale, seal, walrus and even polar bear. While these endangered species are protected by law – especially thanks to the 1972 Marine Mammal Protection Act – the natives are allowed to legally hunt them under the Alaska Native Land Claims Settlement Act. They use every part of the animal, and leave nothing to waste. What's more, most biologists agree that this type of hunting has little or no effect on the populations of these endangered species. Likewise, most Alaskans are in favor of drilling in ANWR (after all, it'll create more jobs in a volatile boom-and-bust economy). Engage in the conversation, but respect the rights of the locals to voice their opinions and live their lives on their own terms – it's the Alaskan way.
- **To buy or not to buy** They make a great memento, but should you buy ivory carvings or whale baleen etchings? On the one hand, Pacific walrus and the bowhead whale (the most commonly hunted whale in the region) are a protected species in the US (though each year Russians and Alaska Natives kill about 4000 Pacific walrus), but on the other hand, the Alaska Natives use every part of these mammals, and are able to supplement their subsistence earnings with the sale of walrus ivory carvings and whale baleen crafts. There's no easy answer to these questions, but most anthropologists and sustainability experts say you should make sure the material was in fact cultivated by Alaska Natives, ensuring the money goes back to native communities and not to profiteers in Japan. Visit www.alaskanativearts.org for more on Alaska Native crafts.

is both comfortably familiar and spectacularly exotic, with paved streets, grassy public squares, many saloons (more than in the rest of Bush Alaska combined) and a palpable gold-rush history.

On the flipside, there's the setting: hard against the ice-choked Bering Sea, cut off from the continental road system and patrolled by polar creatures like musk oxen and reindeer.

Of the three major towns in the Bush – Nome, Kotzebue and Barrow – Nome is the most affordable and best set up for travelers. It has a range of accommodations, from top-notch hotels to free camping on the beach, a fine visitors center, great birding and wildlife watching nearby, and friendly watering holes. It lacks the vibrant aboriginal culture of Kotzebue and Barrow, but Nome has something else the other two don't: roads. No trip to Nome would be complete without renting a pickup truck to see the remarkable outlying region.

Summer comes late here, and it's best to visit in late June for bright green tundra and decent weather. May 15 to June 15 is the best season for birders, who can expect to see arctic terns, the bristle-thighed curlew and the Siberian blue throat. The road system is closed from October or November to mid-May or early June.

Orientation & Information

Watched over by 1062ft Anvil Mountain and washed – sometimes battered – by the Bering Sea, Nome is among the most scenically situated of Alaska's Bush communities. The streetscape is a compact, orderly, walkable grid, stretching six blocks from the boulder-reinforced waterfront back into the tundra, and reaching about 18 blocks from the harbor at the western edge of town to the famed Golden Sands Beach in the east. Most visitor-oriented businesses are concentrated along a half-dozen blocks of the remarkably broad Front St, overlooking the cold, grey ocean.

Arctic Trading Post (☎ 443-2686; 67 Front St; 🕓 7:30am-10pm) Has a good selection of books on the region and the Iditarod.

Bering Land Bridge Interpretive Center (☎ 443-2522, 800-471-2352; www.nps.gov/bela; 179 Front St; 🕓 8am-5pm Mon-Fri) Diagonally across from the visitors center, in the Sitnasuak Native Corporation Building, this National Park Service center is the best place to go for information on hiking, fishing and wildlife in the area. There's also a small collection of native crafts.

Chukotka Alaska (☎ 800-416-4128; 514 Lomen Ave) Sells indigenous crafts and has a good book collection. The friendly owner will talk your ear off if you give him the chance.

Kegoayah Kozga Public Library (☎ 443-6627; 223 Front St; 🕓 noon-8pm Mon-Thu, to 6pm Fri & Sat) Has been in operation since 1902 and offers free internet access and includes a section of rare and 1st-edition books.

Nome Visitor Center (☎ 443-6624; www.nomealaska.org; 301 Front St; 🕓 9am-9pm) Make this your first stop in Nome; the extremely helpful staff will load you with brochures and coffee.

Norton Sound Hospital (☎ 443-3311; cnr W 5th Ave & Bering St) There is a 19-bed facility with a 24-hour emergency medical service as well as a pharmacy.

Police (nonemergency ☎ 443-5262; 500 Bering St)

Post office (240 E Front St) Next to Wells Fargo.

Wells Fargo (☎ 443-7688; 109A Front St) In the historic Miner's and Merchant's Bank Building (dating from 1904); has a 24-hour ATM.

Sights & Activities

CENTRAL NOME

Begin at the Nome Visitor Center and pick up a copy of its walking-tour brochure. The center has a dozen albums with historic photos, and a few exhibits, including a mounted musk ox. Outside, overlooking the seawall, is

THE BUSH

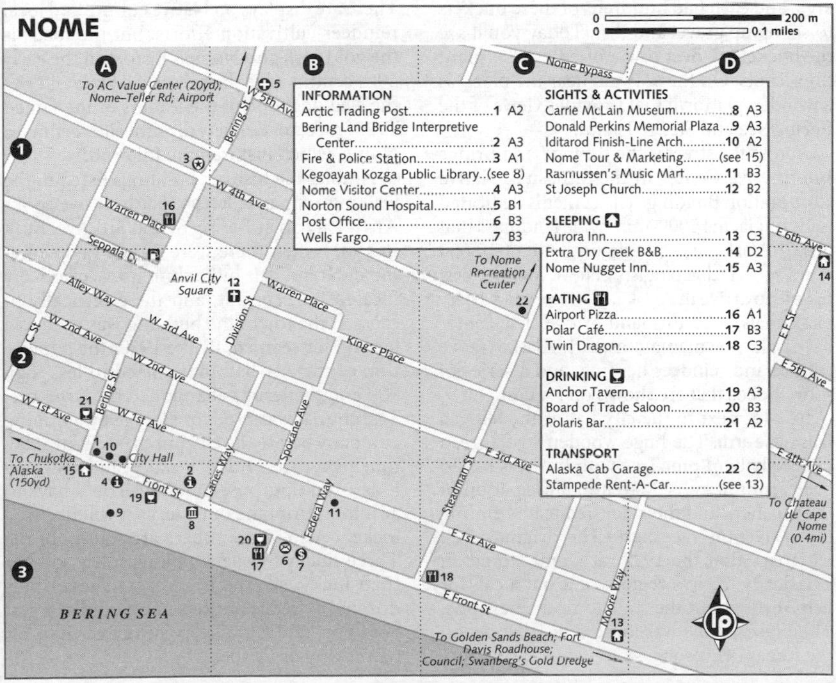

THREE LUCKY SWEDES

If it weren't for the 'Three Lucky Swedes,' Nome would probably have fallen off the map. In September 1898 Jafet Lindeberg, Erik Lindblom and John Brynteson hit the jackpot. Although newcomers from Scandinavia, with only eight weeks' mining experience between them, they found gold in Anvil Creek, just a few miles outside present-day Nome. Though one of them – Lindeberg – was Norwegian, they were dubbed the 'Three Lucky Swedes.' Their discovery triggered the greatest stampede on Alaskan soil, a 'poor man's gold rush' in which digging for gold was said to be easier than stealing it.

By the following year, 'Anvil City' was a tent metropolis of 10,000 people. Among them was John Hummel, a prospector from Idaho. Too sick to head inland to search the tundra creeks, he stayed near the ocean and, in July 1899, discovered gold on the beaches. News of the 'golden sands' resulted in 2000 stampeders working the shoreline that summer, panning more than $1 million in gold dust. It was a banner year, with each man recovering $20 to $100 of gold per day on the edge of the Bering Sea. When the news finally reached Seattle in 1900, it set off yet another stampede of hopeful miners. By the end of that year there were 20,000 people in the town that is now called Nome, making it Alaska's largest city.

Over the ensuing century, mining slowed, the population fizzled and the township suffered numerous disasters. Fires all but destroyed Nome in 1905 and 1934, and a violent Bering Sea storm overpowered the sea walls in 1974. Though little of the community's gold-rush architecture remains, the character of the city has survived.

the **Donald Perkins Memorial Plaza**, featuring a collection of old mining detritus, including dredge buckets. During Nome's golden heyday there were more than 100 gold dredges in the area, and each had hundreds of these buckets to scoop up gravel and dirt. Today you'll see the buckets all over town, often used as giant flowerpots. On the seawall, near the plaza, is a wooden platform that provides views of the Bering Sea and Sledge Island.

Across the street is the Bering Land Bridge Interpretive Center in the Sitnasuak Native Corporation Building. The center is dedicated to Beringia, the 1000-mile-wide landmass that linked Alaska and Siberia until about 10,000 years ago. Archaeologists believe that the first people to arrive in Alaska, along with a variety of animals, used this land bridge. The center has displays on mammoths, early Alaska Native culture and reindeer herding, and a series of short videos that are shown on request.

In a lot next to the city hall is the **Iditarod finish-line arch**. The huge wooden structure, a distinctly bent pine tree with burls, is raised over Front St every March in anticipation of the mushers and their dogsled teams ending the 1049-mile race here. The original arch fell apart after the 1999 race, and Nome, in a basically treeless region, sent out a call for help throughout the state to find a new one. The present pine was located near Hope, on the Kenai Peninsula.

To the east of the visitors center, on Front St, is **Carrie McLain Museum** (☎ 443-6630; 223 Front St; adult/child $1/0.50; 🕒 9:30am-5:30pm), in the basement of the Kegoayah Kozga Public Library. There are displays on Native culture and local reindeer-cultivation efforts, but the focus is the gold rush and Nome's history in the early 20th century. See the preserved body of Fritz the sled dog, one of the leaders of the famed 1925 race to deliver diphtheria serum to Nome, which inspired the Iditarod.

Among the historic buildings listed in the walking tour is **St Joseph Church**. It overlooks Anvil City Sq at Bering St and 3rd Ave. Built in 1901, when there were 30,000 people living in Nome, this huge church was originally located on Front St, and the electrically lit cross at the top of the building was used as a beacon for seamen. By the 1920s the population of the city had plummeted to less than 900 and the Jesuits abandoned the structure. The church was used for storage by a mining company before the city purchased it in 1996, moving it to its present location and restoring it as a multipurpose building. You'll have to admire it from the outside, as it will likely be locked. Also in the square are statues of the Three Lucky Swedes (looking more somber than lucky, see the boxed text above) plus dozens of dredge buckets, the 'world's largest gold pan' and a grassy expanse just right for picnicking or Frisbee.

The **University of Alaska's Northwest Campus** is located next to the Aurora Inn. You may be able to sit in on classes or attend lectures here. There's also a good library.

GOLDEN SANDS BEACH

A very interesting afternoon can be spent at Nome's Golden Sands Beach, stretching a mile east of town along Front St. At the height of summer a few local children may be seen playing in the 45°F water, and on Memorial Day (in May), more than 100 masochistic residents plunge into the ice-choked waters for the annual **Polar Bear Swim**.

Usually more numerous than swimmers here are gold prospectors, as the beach is open to recreational mining. Miners will set up camp along the shore and work the sands throughout the summer. The serious miners rig their sluice and dredging equipment on a small pontoon boat that looks more like a Rube Goldberg contraption than a seaworthy vessel, and anchor it 100yd offshore. Out at sea, they will spend up to four hours underwater in wetsuits (pumped with hot air from the engine), essentially vacuuming the ocean floor. Others set up sluice boxes at the edge of the water. Miners are generally friendly, and occasionally you can even coax one to show you his gold dust and nuggets. If you catch the fever, practically every gift shop and hardware store in town sells black plastic gold pans. As you're panning, think about the visitor who was simply beachcombing in 1984 and found a 3.5in nugget that weighed 1.29oz at the east end of the seawall, and remember that gold's now worth anywhere from $800 to $1000 per ounce.

Right outside of town, after the Tesoro Gas Station, there is a **Mine Machinery Graveyard** with a few informative placards. With no roads leading to Nome, once a piece of equipment makes the barge-ride here, it stays until it turns to dust.

After walking along the beach to Fort Davis Roadhouse (which, sadly, seems to be closed for good now) return along Front St to see **Swanberg's Gold Dredge**, near the Nome Bypass junction. The dredge was in operation until the 1950s, before being passed on to the city for its historic value.

HIKING

If you're well prepared and the weather holds, the backcountry surrounding Nome can be a hiker's heaven. Though there are no marked trails in the region, the area's three highways offer perfect access into the tundra and mountains. What's more, the lack of trees and big, rolling topography make route-finding fairly simple: just pick a point and go for it. For those who'd like a little more direction, a seven-page list of suggested day hikes is available from the Nome Visitor Center (p403). If you're setting off on anything more than a stroll up the nearest ridgeline, a map is a good idea; topo maps can be purchased at **Rasmussen's Music Mart** (☎ 443-2798; 103 Federal Way; ⏲ noon-6pm Mon-Sat), operated by avid local hiker (and former mayor) Leo Rasmussen.

Also providing great info on local trekking is the Bering Land Bridge Interpretive Center (p403). At time of research, the center was leading very popular free **guided day hikes** as well as **birding tours** on most Saturdays throughout the summer.

The climb up 1062ft **Anvil Mountain** is the closest hike to Nome and the only one that can be easily pulled off without a car. Follow the Teller Hwy 3.5 miles from town to Glacier Creek Rd, which takes you directly onto the mountain. After the road veers left, look for a smooth route up the slope and commence your climb. It's about 1 mile round-trip to the summit, ascending through wonderful wildflower patches. At the top you'll find the giant parabolic antennae of the Cold War–era White Alice Communications System, plus great views of town and the ocean, as well as the Kigluaik Mountains further inland.

Tours

Bering Air (☎ 443-5464) Offers helicopter tours of the area for around $200 per person (three person minimum). It may even be able to take you heliskiing.

our pick **Nome Discovery Tours** (☎ 443-2814; discover@cgi.net; tours $125-185) The most intimate, highly recommended tours are run by Richard Beneville, an old song-and-dance man who decided to hang up his tap shoes to live out in the Alaska wilds. He offers everything from two-hour evening tundra-exploration drives to full-day excursions to Teller, where you'll drop in on an Iñupiat family, or to Council, with fishing along the way.

Nome Tour & Marketing (☎ 304-1038; www.nomenuggetinnhotel.com; tours $75) Based out of the Nugget Inn this caters mainly to larger package-deal groups, though independents are welcome. It operates four tours daily in the summer. The four-hour history-oriented tour includes gold panning at the Little Creek Mine and a hands-on dog-mushing demonstration.

WYATT EARP IN ALASKA

A bit of the Old West found its way to Nome when Wyatt Earp and his wife arrived at the end of the 1890s. Earp was a former marshal and noted gunslinger who teamed up with Doc Holiday to win the famous shootout at the OK Corral in Tombstone, Arizona.

But when Earp heard about the Klondike Gold Rush in 1899, he packed his bags and left Arizona to seek his fortune, though not as a prospector – Earp was above working a rocker box or getting his suits dirty. Rather, he headed to Alaska to do what one friend had suggested to him: 'mine the miners.'

While on the road, Earp read about Alaska's new boomtown and quickly switched his destination; after the spring thaw of 1899 he arrived at Nome, on a steamer with his wife, Josie. Teaming up with a partner, Earp immediately built the Dexter – the first two-story, wooden structure in what was basically still a tent city full of prospectors. It was Nome's largest and most luxurious saloon, with 12ft ceilings and 12 plush clubrooms upstairs, and was located only a block from 'the Stockade,' the city's red-light district.

Earp's timing was amazing. By July of that year John Hummel had discovered gold on the beaches, and the 2000 men who stampeded to the city that summer had, by early fall, recovered $1 million in gold dust and nuggets.

Wyatt Earp managed to fleece his share of that gold. By October 1901, having already endured two winters on the Bering Sea, the Earps left Nome with, as legend has it, $80,000 – a fortune at that time. You can see pictures of Earp on the streets of Nome, and on some of the turn-of-the-century gambling devices used in town, at the Carrie McLain Museum on Front St.

Nome Visitor Center Can help you arrange dog-mushing trips in winter; see p403.
Wilderness Birding Adventures (☎ 694-7442; www.wildernessbirding.com) Runs high-priced birding trips in the area.

Sleeping

Nome tacks on 9% bed and sales taxes to its accommodations. Book rooms well in advance in summer and during Iditarod.

If the weather's good, sleeping out may be the way to go in Nome. There's free waterfront camping on Golden Sands Beach in a mile-long stretch running east from town to the Fort Davis Roadhouse; pitch your tent beside those of miners sifting the sands for glittering nuggets. Try to pitch your tent a bit down the beach as the street sweepers dump debris here daily.

Across the road is an outhouse and pavilion in the small public park at Nome Bypass. Showers are available at the **Nome Recreation Center** (☎ 443-5431; cnr D St & 6th Ave; showers $5; 5:30am-10pm Mon-Fri).

Further from town it's unofficially permissible to camp just about anywhere: simply hike away from the road corridor, avoid private property and active mining claims and clean up after yourself. Also, on Kougarok Rd is the Bureau of Land Management's (BLM) lovely, free Salmon Lake Campground (p409).

If you want a roof over your head the options are all comparatively expensive. There are a few B&Bs in town plus hotels ranging from seedy (the Polaris) to semiluxurious.

Chateau de Cape Nome (☎ 443-2083; cussy@nome.net; 1105 E 4th Ave; r from $100) Spectacularly situated overlooking the tundra on the far eastern edge of town, this is Nome's most colorful inn. The owner 'Cussy' Kauer is a descendant of gold rush–era pioneers and her place is a trove of local history. Ask for a room with a view or head upstairs to the patio, which offers great views of the Bering Sea.

Nome Nugget Inn (☎ 443-4189, 877-443-2323; www.nomenuggetinnhotel.com; 315 Front St; r $110-120) In the thick of things downtown, the Nugget has 45 smallish rooms, about half with ocean views. A couple of kitsch items like snowshoes and a pair of 'Iñupiat ice-skates' add a bit of charm to the lobby.

Extra Dry Creek B&B (☎ 443-7615; sbabcock@gci.net; 607 E F St; s/d $115/125) More like a rental apartment than a B&B, this pristine suite (named for an apparently desiccated waterway outside of town) has a full kitchen stocked with breakfast fixings that you prepare yourself.

Aurora Inn (☎ 443-3838, 800-354-4606; www.aurorainnome.com; E Front St at Moore Way; d $154-245) Probably the nicest rooms in town – 'rivaling that found in Anchorage' as one employee put it – the Aurora has simple motel-style rooms and all the amenities (but none of the charm) you could ask for.

Eating

AC Value Center (☎ 443-2243; cnr Bering St & Nome Bypass; 7:30am-9pm Mon-Sat, 10am-7pm Sun) This is the cheap-eats option. The supermarket has a bakery, espresso counter and a deli with ready-to-eat items.

Polar Café (☎ 443-5191; Front St; breakfast $7-13, lunch $7-14, dinner $14-24; 6am-10pm) Nome's only waterfront eating option, this popular eatery serves straightforward food that delivers. It has remarkable views of the Bering Sea, a down-and-out interior and a $9 salad bar that veggies will love.

our pick **Airport Pizza** (☎ 443-7992; 406 Bering St; pub grub $10-17, pizza $20-29; 7am-10pm) Hands down the best restaurant in town, this pub-tastic joint has the feeling of an airport hangar with corrugated metal walls and propeller ceiling fans. The simple pub grub will send you into the stratosphere with everything from chicken tacos to reindeer-sausage pizza.

Twin Dragon (☎ 443-5552; cnr E Front & Steadman Sts; lunch $11; 11am-11pm Mon-Sat, from noon Sun) This has good Chinese food. There's a two-person dinner special for $20 that may be the best-priced meal in town (after Subway of course).

Drinking & Entertainment

Even by Alaskan standards, drinking in Nome is legendary. All but two of the bars are clustered around one another on Front St. The **Board of Trade Saloon** (212 Front St), dating back to 1900, claims to be the oldest bar on the Bering Sea and is certainly the most notorious. For a quieter hangout where you can sit and chat with locals, try **Anchor Tavern** (114 Front St), which has a good selection of beer on tap. **Polaris Bar** (cnr Bering St & W 1st Ave) has dancing, surprisingly decent pub food and pool tables.

Getting There & Around

Nome is serviced by **Alaska Airlines** (☎ 443-2288, 800-468-2248; www.alaskaair.com), which offers at least three daily flights from Anchorage for about $500. Two of those flights also route through Kotzebue; visiting both Bush communities will cost you around $600. If you want to fly to Nome from Fairbanks you can go direct aboard **Frontier Alaska** (☎ 450-7200, 800-478-6779; www.frontierflying.com) for about $440. Flights operate six days a week.

Many people see Nome on package tours. Alaska Airlines runs day trips out of Anchorage from $499 (including airfare and a Nome Tour & Marketing excursion) and overnight stays from $600 (including airfare, tour and lodging at the Nugget Inn).

Once on the ground Nome's airport is a little more than a mile from town. If the day is nice it's a pleasant walk. If not, a cab ride is $5 per person ($8 to Golden Sands Beach).

Only two places in Nome rent cars and you'll need to book well ahead of time. Both offer unlimited mileage in an area of the state where there is very limited mileage. **Stampede Rent-A-Car** (☎ 443-3838, 800-354-4606; cnr Front St & Moore Way) is in the Aurora Inn and offers SUVs and pickups for $95 a day. **Alaska Cab Garage** (☎ 443-2939; at 4th Ave & Steadman St) has pickups, 4WD pickups and Suburbans for $85 to $100 a day. When budgeting for a rental, keep in mind that gas in Nome is extremely expensive.

Hitchhiking is possible and locals are really good about picking people up. But you must be patient – and willing to sit in the back of an open pickup on very dusty roads.

AROUND NOME

Radiating east, north and northwest from Nome are its finest features: three gravel roads, each offering passage into very different worlds and each providing a full-day adventure at minimum. While Nome can seem dirty and rundown, the surrounding country is stunning – think sweeping tundra, crystal-clear rivers, rugged mountains and some of the best chances in Alaska to see waterfowl, caribou, bears and musk oxen. But be prepared: there's no gas and few other services along Nome's highways; instead, you'll encounter road-shrouding dust and rocks determined to ravage your tires. Going slow is key. Take twice as long as you would on pavement.

Nome–Council Road

This 73-mile route, which heads northeast to the old mining village of Council, is perhaps the best excursion if you have time for only one of Nome's roads. For the first 30 miles it hugs the glimmering Bering Sea coastline and passes an outstanding, motley array of shacks, cabins, tepees and Quonset huts used by Nome residents as summer cottages and fish camps. On sunny days miles of beaches

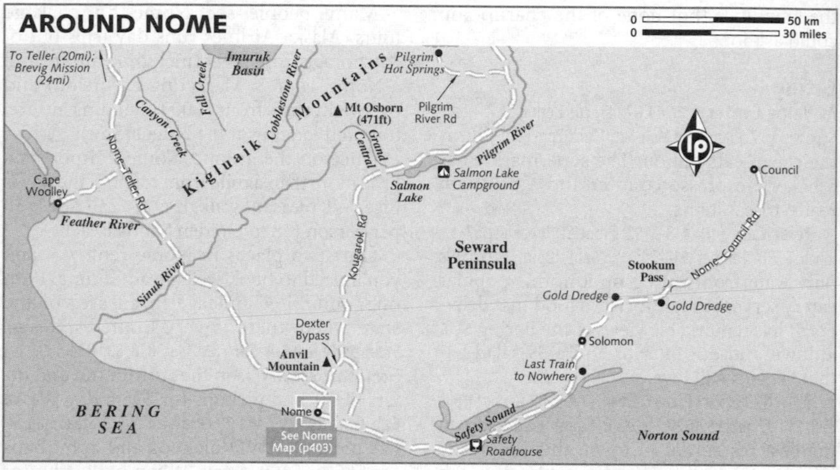

beckon – but note how far inland autumn storms have tossed driftwood. At Mile 22 the road passes **Safety Roadhouse** (☎ 443-2368; ⏰ summer only), a dollar-bill-bedecked dive of a watering hole, and then crosses the birders' wonderland of **Safety Sound**. Ten miles further along is Bonanza Crossing, on the far side of which is the Last Train to Nowhere (see the boxed text, opposite), a series of locomotives abandoned in the tundra in 1907 by the Council City & Solomon River Railroad. Just to the north is the ghost town of **Solomon**, which was originally established in 1900 and once boasted a population of 1000 and seven saloons. The town was destroyed by a storm in 1913, relocated to higher ground and then further decimated by the 1918 flu epidemic. There are occasional rumors that a B&B is coming to Solomon. Check with the Nome Visitor Center (p403).

Near Mile 40 you pass the first of two **gold dredges** within a couple of miles of each other. By 1912 almost 40 dredges worked the Seward Peninsula, and today many are still visible from the Nome road system. The two on this road are in the best shape and are the most picturesque. Nome–Council Rd begins climbing after passing the second dredge and reaches **Stookum Pass** at Mile 53. There's a parking area at the pass, so you can pull off and admire the views or take a hike on the nearby ridges.

The road ends at Mile 73 at **Council**. Actually, the road ends at the banks of the Niukluk River and Council is on the other side. Most of the houses here are weekend getaways for people living in Nome, and there are currently

FLIGHT OF THE KIND ISLANDERS

The King Islanders no longer live on their little island 40 miles out to sea from Cape Douglas. They called this precipitous land Ukivok and called themselves the Aseuluk. Anthropologists knew them as Iñupiat Eskimos and the government, unfortunately, knew them only as a burden.

In the 1950s and '60s the government basically cut off infrastructure for the island, which the King Islanders used as their winter hunting grounds, essentially severing their lifeline and forcibly relocating them to their summer lands located near Nome. The King Islanders of today mostly live in Nome though some still practice a subsistence lifestyle, heading northwest of town to Cape Woolley in the summer to fish and out to sea in their seal-skin *umiaks* in winter to hunt for whale and walrus. They are still renowned for their dancing and ivory carving and if you are lucky you may see a performance while staying in Nome. It's very difficult to visit King Island – though some top-end cruise ships are making the journey (p35) – but you can learn more about the people at the Nome Visitor Center or by checking in with the **King Island Native Community** (☎ 443-3620; www.kawerak.org/tribalHomePages/kingIsland/index.html).

THE LAST TRAIN TO NOWHERE

In all of Bush Alaska, it's almost certainly the most-photographed landmark: a set of steam locomotives, utterly out of place and out of time, moldering on the Arctic tundra at the continent's edge, hundreds of miles from the nearest functioning railway. Dubbed the Last Train to Nowhere, the three engines first plied the elevated lines of New York City in the 1880s, until Manhattan switched from steam to electric-driven trains. In 1903 the upstart Council City & Solomon River Railroad purchased the locomotives and transported them north, hoping to profit by servicing inland mines from the coast. Though the company surveyed some 50 miles of potential track, only half of that was built. By 1907 the operation went belly up. Six years later a powerful storm sealed the Last Train's fate, destroying the Solomon River railroad bridge and stranding the engines on the tundra forever. Truly, it was the end of the line.

no year-round residents. Locals drive across the river – with the water often reaching their running boards. Tourists with rental vehicles should stay put. There are no services or shops in Council, but the Niukluk is an excellent place to fish for grayling.

Kougarok Road

Also known as Nome-Taylor Rd, Kougarok Rd leads 86 miles north from Nome through the heart of the Kigluaik Mountains. There are a few artifacts from the gold-rush days, and the best mountain scenery and hiking in the Nome area, along the way. You can access the highway two ways: from its juncture off the Nome–Council Rd just east of town, or via the Dexter Bypass, which spurs off the Nome–Teller Rd a few miles northeast of Nome.

The Kigluaiks spring up almost immediately, flanking the road until around Mile 40 where the free, BLM-operated Salmon Lake Campground is beautifully situated at the north end of the large Salmon Lake. The facility features nine willow-girdled sites with tables, fire rings and an outhouse. The outlet for the Pilgrim River, where you can watch sockeye salmon spawn in August, is nearby.

Just before Mile 54 is Pilgrim River Rd, a rocky lane that heads northwest. The road climbs a pass where there's great ridge walking, then descends into a valley dotted with small tundra lakes. Less than 8 miles from Kougarok Rd, Pilgrim River Rd ends at the gate of **Pilgrim Hot Springs**. A roadhouse and saloon was located here during the gold rush, but burnt down in 1908. Later there was an orphanage for children who lost their parents in the 1918 influenza epidemic. The Catholic Church managed the orphanage until 1942. Today the hot springs are privately owned and somewhat dilapidated, but if you contact caretaker Louie Green (☎ 443-5583) ahead of time you'll likely get permission to walk inside for a soak.

Kougarok Rd crosses Pilgrim River at Mile 60, the Kuzitrin River at Mile 68 and the Kougarok Bridge at Mile 86. This is one of the best areas to look for herds of musk oxen. At all three bridges you can fish for grayling, Dolly Varden and salmon, among other species.

After the Kougarok Bridge the road becomes a rough track impassable to cars. The extremely determined, however, can shoulder a pack and continue overland for a very challenging, boggy, unmarked 30-plus miles to **Serpentine Hot Springs**, inside the Bering Land Bridge National Preserve. A free, first come, first served bunkhouse-style cabin there sleeps 15 to 20, and there's a bathhouse for slipping into the 140°F to 170°F waters. Almost no-one hikes both ways; consider chartering in or out. Check around to see who's currently making the flight; in recent years it's been variable.

Nome–Teller Road

This road leads 73 miles (a one-way drive of at least two hours) to Teller, a year-round, subsistence Iñupiat village of 256 people. The landscape en route is vast and undulating, with steep climbs across spectacular rolling tundra. Hiking opportunities are numerous, as are chances to view musk oxen and a portion of the reindeer herd communally owned by families in Teller. The huge **Alaska Gold Company dredge**, which operated until the mid-1990s, lies just north of Nome on the Nome–Teller Rd.

The road also crosses a number of rivers that drain the south side of the Kigluaik Mountains, all of them offering fishing opportunities. The Snake (spanned near Mile

DETOUR: KOTZEBUE & THE AMAZING RIVER PADDLES THAT'LL GET YOU THERE

Situated 26 miles above the Arctic Circle on the shores of the Chukchi Sea, Kotzebue – named after Polish explorer Otto von Kotzebue, who arrived here in 1816 – is one of Alaska's northernmost hubs. It's not worth the trip here unless you are planning on staging an expedition to the neighboring wilderness.

While this sounds exotic, take heed: it's a hard place for visitors to penetrate. There's no Alaska Native food at local restaurants, local hotels are sterile and costly, and there are few easy ways to meet people and get out on the land or water.

Information

Innaigvik Public Lands Information & Education Center (☎ 442-3890; cnr 2nd Ave & Lakes St) is maintained by the National Park Service (NPS), this is the best visitor resource in Kotzebue with ample info on the region's 9 million acres of parklands and on Kotzebue in general. It has displays on the area's natural history, plus topo maps and a small gift shop.

Paddling

Kotzebue provides access to some of the finest river running in Arctic Alaska. Popular trips include the Noatak, the Kobuk, the Salmon (which flows into the Kobuk) and the Selawik (which originates in the Kobuk lowlands and flows west into Selawik Lake). Trips along the Kobuk National Wild River often consist of floats from Walker Lake traveling 140 miles downstream to the villages of Kobuk or Ambler. From these villages there are scheduled flights to both Kotzebue and Bettles, another departure point for this river. **Bering Air Service** (☎ 443-5464; www.beringair.com) can transport you and your gear from either Kobuk or Ambler to Kotzebue. Most of the river is rated Class I, but some lining of boats may be required just below Walker Lake and for a mile through Lower Kobuk Canyon. Paddlers usually plan on six to eight days for the float.

The **Noatak National Wild River** is a 16-day, 350-mile float from Lake Matcharak to the village of Noatak, where Bering Air has scheduled flights to Kotzebue. However, the numerous access lakes on the river allow it to be broken down into shorter paddles. The entire river is rated from Class I to II. The upper portion, in the Brooks Range, offers much more dramatic scenery and is usually accessed from Bettles (p417). The lower half, accessed through Kotzebue, flows through a broad, gently sloping valley where hills replace the sharp peaks of the Brooks Range. The most common trip here is to put in at Nimiuktuk River where, within an hour of paddling, you enter the 65-mile-long Grand Canyon of the Noatak, followed by the 7-mile-long Noatak Canyon. Most paddlers pull out at Kelly River, where there's a ranger station with a radio. Below the confluence with the Kelly the Noatak becomes heavily braided.

For more information before you depart for Alaska, contact the Innaigvik Public Lands Information & Education Center (above).

Sleeping

In theory, you can camp south of town along the gravel beach. **Arctic Circle Education Adventures** (☎ 276-0976; www.fishcamp.org) offers custom tours and accommodation at its nearby Fish Camp facility. **Nullagvik Hotel** (☎ 442-3331; www.nullagvik.com; 308 Shore Ave) and **Bayside Hotel** (☎ 442-3600; 303 Shore Ave) also have simple rooms.

Getting There & Away

Alaska Airlines (☎ 800-426-0333; www.alaskaair.com) and **Frontier Alaska** (☎ 450-7200, 800-478-6779; www.frontierflying.com) fly here.

8), Sinuk (Mile 26.7) and Feather rivers (Mile 37.4) are three of the more productive waterways for Arctic grayling, Dolly Varden and salmon. Ten miles from Teller you'll crest a ridge that affords sublime views of Port Clarence, with the village of Brevig Mission on the far side.

Teller lies at the westernmost end of the westernmost road in North America. This wind-wracked community overlooks the slate waters of the Bering Sea and stretches along a tapering gravel spit near the mouth of Grantley Harbor. Roald Amundsen, one of the greatest figures in polar exploration, returned to earth here after his legendary 70-hour airship flight over the North Pole on May 14, 1926. In 1985 Teller again made the headlines when Libby Riddles, then a Teller resident, became the first woman to win the Iditarod.

Though Teller is a scenic place – witness the fishnets set just offshore and the salmon hanging from racks on the beach – there's little for a visitor to do.

Still, out of respect for the residents (who are likely tired of drive-by gawkers from Nome), park your car and ask one of the village kids for directions to the tiny community store. There you can buy a snack and perhaps a handmade craft, supporting the Teller economy and facilitating interaction with the locals.

With rising sea levels and melting permafrost, there are plans to move Teller, but the move, if it happens, will take several years.

ARCTIC ALASKA

Perhaps the least-visited portion of the state, Alaska's Arctic region is tough and expensive to visit. But for those looking for adventure, and strange moonlike dystopian towns, you might have just hit the jackpot. There's also plenty of outdoor stuff to do: paddling the numerous rivers, backpacking in national parks and preserves like Gates of the Arctic and ANWR, or driving the precarious and prodigious Dalton Highway. There are few cities in Arctic Alaska, but 'hubs' like Bettles, Barrow and Coldfoot will get you started.

DALTON HIGHWAY

There are precious few adventures to be had while sitting down – but then, most road trips aren't on the legendary Dalton Highway. Also known as Haul Rd, this punishing truck route rambles 414 miles from Alaska's Interior to the North Slope, paralleling the Trans Alaska Pipeline to its source at the Prudhoe Bay Oil Field. The highway reaches further north than any other on the continent and is the only way to motor through the stunning Brooks Range and the Arctic without a behemoth 4WD. If you're steeled for multiple days aboard a gravel roller-coaster – dodging hell-on-wheels big-rigs, risking bankruptcy if you need a tow, and (almost) reaching the edge of the Earth – it's a helluva trip.

Fueled by crude-oil fever, the Dalton was built in a whirlwind five months in 1974. For the ensuing two decades, however, it was effectively a private driveway for the gas companies, until a bitter battle in the state legislature opened it to the public. Even now, though, you can't drive clear to the Arctic Ocean: due to security concerns the road ends just shy of the oilfields, at the sprawling industrial camp of Deadhorse. From there the 'beach' is 8 miles distant, accessible only via a corporate tour (see p415).

Orientation & Information

Though the Dalton is slowly being tamed – since 2000 around 130 miles have been paved – it's still not a road that suffers fools. In summer the 28ft-wide corridor is a dusty minefield of potholes and frost heaves, its embankments littered with blown tires. Paint scratches and window chips are inevitable, which is why most car-rental companies don't allow their vehicles here. There are few services, such as telephones, tire repair, fuel and restaurants, and none for the final 225 miles from Wiseman to Deadhorse.

The road is open year-round but you should only tackle it between late May and early September when there's virtually endless light and little snow and ice. Drive with headlights on, carry two spares, extra water and fuel, and always slow down and swing wide for oncoming trucks. Only the reckless exceed 55mph; expect a 40mph average and two hard days to reach Deadhorse. Other alternatives are to join one of the various van tours up the highway (see p415) or drive halfway – to the Coldfoot truck stop – and from there catch a Prudhoe-bound shuttle-bus (see p415), letting the pros negotiate the roughest stretch while you gawk at the best scenery.

BLM Central Yukon Field Office (☎ 474-2200, 800-437-7021; www.blm.gov/ak/st/en/prog/recreation/dalton_hwy.htm; 1150 University Ave, Fairbanks) This office manages the campsites along the highway and has excellent information on the hikes, paddles and road conditions. Check out the website for an In-depth highway guide.

Morris Thomson Cultural & Visitor Center (Map p382; ☎ 456-5774, 800-327-5774; www.nps.gov/aplic/; 101 Dunkel St, Fairbanks; 8am-7pm) This Fairbanks visitor center has a bunch of information on the national parks in the region and can help you outfit yourself for the drive.

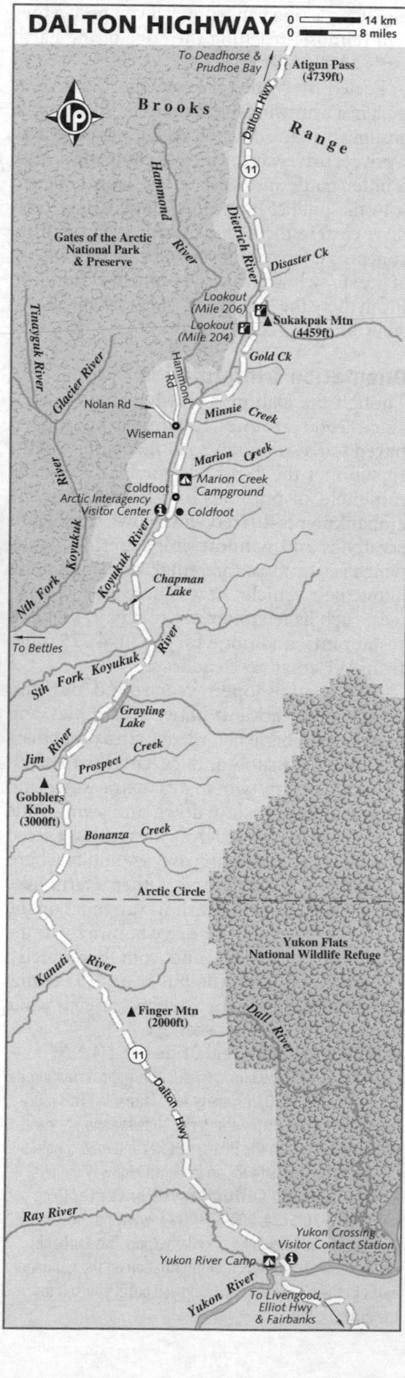

Mile 0 to 175

Mile 0 of the Dalton is at the junction with the Elliot Hwy, 84 miles from Fairbanks. Immediately, the Haul Rd announces itself: the pavement ends and the blind curves and technical pitches begin. At Mile 25 there's a lookout with good views of the pipeline crossing **Hess Creek**. Near the Hess Creek Bridge are serviceable campsites among the trees.

The highway begins descending toward the Yukon River at Mile 47, and the silvery ribbon of pipeline can be seen reaching into the distance. At Mile 56 the 2290ft-long, wooden-decked **Yukon River Bridge** carries you and the pipeline across the silty, broad river – the only place where the legendary waterway is spanned in Alaska. On the far bank, turn right and pass under the pipeline to reach the BLM's **Yukon Crossing Visitor Contact Station** (www.blm.gov/ak/st/en/prog/recreation/dalton_hwy.html; 9am-6pm Jun-Aug), featuring displays on the road and the terrain you're about to enter. It also has copies of the handy 24-page *Dalton Highway Visitor Guide* (also available on its website) and a short nature walk to a deck overlooking the Yukon.

On the opposite side of the highway is a vast muddy lot and **Yukon River Camp** (474-3557; www.yukonrivercamp.com; r with shared bath $199; breakfast $9-12, lunch $8-10, dinner $19-22; 9am-9pm), a utilitarian truck stop with work-camp–style rooms, showers for $10, costly gas, a gift shop and not-half-bad food.

Around Mile 70, as the road clambers back out of the river valley, burned-over patches of forest appear, a legacy of the wildfires that scorched the majority of the Interior in 2004 and 2005. Pavement starts at Mile 90 – a mixed blessing given its potholed, frost-heaved state. Soon the highway ascends to an alpine area with the 40ft-high granite tor of Finger Mountain beckoning to the east. At Mile 98 a windy BLM wayside offers great cross-tundra hiking to other tors, plus berry picking and views of the sprawling flats of the Kanuti National Wildlife Refuge to the west. You pass the imaginary line of the **Arctic Circle** at Mile 115. For good 24-7 views of the sun continue to **Gobblers Knob**, a hilltop lookout at Mile 132 where there's a pullover, an outhouse and, if you scale the hill to the east on the first night of summer, perpetual sun.

From Gobbler's Knob northward, the pyramids of the Brooks Range begin to dominate the scene. In the next 50 miles you'll cross several grayling-rich streams, including Prospect Creek, which, in January 1971, experienced America's lowest-ever temperature: -80°F.

Coldfoot

At Mile 175, in a mountain-rimmed hollow, you'll arrive in Coldfoot. Originally named Slate Creek, the area was first settled by miners in 1898 when a group of greenhorns got 'cold feet' at the thought of wintering in the district and headed south, and the community was renamed accordingly. It was a ghost town by 1912 but its moniker, at least, was revived in 1981 when Iditarod musher Dick Mackey set up an old school bus here and began selling hamburgers to Prudhoe Bay–bound truck drivers.

Nowadays, with an airstrip, post office and trooper detachment, you might expect Coldfoot to be a quaint Arctic hamlet. No such luck. The place consists mainly of **Coldfoot Camp** (☎ 474-3500, 866-474-3400; www.coldfootcamp.com), a pugly truck stop with the last **gas** (24hr) until Deadhorse, plus spartan rooms in the **Slate Creek Inn** (r $199) and a **restaurant** (breakfast $6-13, lunch & dinner $8-14; 6am-midnight) with passable diner-style fare and a photo collection of jackknifed 18-wheelers. At **Frozen Foot Saloon** (6-10pm) – Alaska's northernmost bar – you can sip microbrews on a deck overlooking (and oversmelling) idling trucks. The exhaust, it seems, keeps the bugs down.

A world apart is the **Arctic Interagency Visitor Center** (☎ 678-5209; 10am-10pm Jun-Aug), on the opposite side of the highway. This impressive $5-million structure opened in 2004 and features museum-quality displays about the Arctic and its denizens. It has ultrahelpful staff, a schlock-free gift shop and nightly nature presentations – the best show in town.

As the visitor-center employees will tell you, the area's best lodging is down the highway. Campers should proceed 5 miles north to **Marion Creek Campground** (Mile 180; sites $8). This 27-site campground almost always has space and is situated in an open spruce forest with stunning views of the Brooks Range.

Wiseman

pop 18

Those seeking a bed – or wanting an antidote to Coldfoot's culture of the quick-and-dirty – should push on to Wiseman, a century-old log-cabin village accessible via a short dirt spur road at Mile 189. The only authentic town on the Dalton, Wiseman occupies an enviable spot, overhung by peaks and fronting the Middle Fork of the Koyukuk River. Its heyday was 1910, when it replaced the original Coldfoot as a hub for area gold miners. Many buildings from that era still stand, including those of **Arctic Getaway Cabin & Breakfast** (☎ 678-4456; www.arcticgetaway.com), which offers a sunny, two-person cabin for $95 and antique-laden four-person cabins for $175 to $195. Next door, cheaper but more institutional, are the rooms at **Boreal Lodge** (☎ 678-4556; www.boreallodge.com; s/d without bath $60/80). It also offers a private log cabin with its own bath for $130. Once upon a time the **Wiseman Historical Museum**, near the entrance to town, was open to the public but Northern Alaska Tour Company (p415) has purchased it and admits only its own clients.

Those wanting erudition should instead follow the signs to the cabin of Wiseman's wise man, Jack Reakoff, an engaging and surprisingly urbane trapper who sells crafts and will discourse at length about local history and wildlife.

Mile 190 to 414

North from Wiseman the Dalton skirts the east edge of Gates of the Arctic National Park (p415). Dall sheep are often visible on the mountain slopes, and the scenery goes into overdrive. By Mile 194 the first views appear of the massive wall of **Sukakpak Mountain** (4459ft) looming dead ahead. Just before Mile 204 is a lookout with a half-mile trail to Sukakpak's face, while soon after, even taller promontories arise – imposing black talus cones, 7000ft high, riven by glacier-carved valleys. At Mile 235 you kiss the woods goodbye: the famed **Last Spruce**, though recently girdled by a vandal's ax, stands stately even in death near a turnout on the highway's east side.

The ascent of **Atigun Pass** (Mile 242) is where the real fun begins. At an elevation of 4739ft this is the highest highway pass in Alaska and marks the continental divide. The view from the top – with the Philip Smith Mountains to the east and the Endicotts to the west – will steal your breath away.

The Brooks Range is largely behind you once you reach the turnoff for the undeveloped Galbraith Lake Campground at Mile 275. From here on it's all rolling tundra, where hiking and camping options are limitless,

THE ALASKA PIPELINE

Love it or loathe it, if you're driving Alaska's Richardson or Dalton Hwys the Trans-Alaska Pipeline will be your traveling companion. The steely tube, 4ft wide and 800 miles long, parallels the highways from Prudhoe Bay on the Arctic Ocean down to Valdez, Alaska's northernmost ice-free port. En route, it spans 800-odd waterways and three mountain ranges, transporting about 700,000 barrels of crude oil per day – 17% of US domestic production – to tankers waiting in Prince William Sound. Back in its heyday, the pipeline was carrying around 2.1 million barrels per day, but with dwindling reserves (an estimated 2 billion barrels remain in the greater Prudhoe Bay area) they've cut down the flow. However, there's always the chance that the US will begin drilling in Arctic National Wildlife Refuge (ANWR), which would put Alaskan oil – and the pipeline – back on the map.

Before construction began in 1975, the debate over the pipeline was among America's hardest-fought conservation battles. Both sides viewed themselves as defenders of the Last Frontier; boosters viewed the project as a grand act of Alaskan pioneering and opponents called it an affront to all that's wild and wonderful about the 49th state. Since the pipeline's completion – two years and $8 billion later – the late University of Alaska president William R Wood likened it to 'a silken thread, half-hidden across the palace carpet.' Many have had less kind words for it. And after a large oil spill in 2006 it came to light that the pipeline might be corroding faster than most engineers had hoped, with some sources saying that 70% to 80% of the pipeline's three-eighth-inch walls are gone.

For about 380 of its miles, the Trans-Alaska Pipeline – like most pipelines elsewhere – runs underground. Elsewhere it can't, because the 150°F to 180°F oil it carries would melt the permafrost. It's in those places – particularly where it crosses the highway – that you'll get your best look at the line. Especially good views can be had at Mile 243.5 of the Richardson Hwy south of Delta Junction, on the Dalton at the Yukon River crossing and at the spur road to Wiseman.

Be forewarned, however: it's a bad move to get too close to the pipeline, much less to fold, bend, spindle or mutilate it. After September 11, 2001, officials identified the pipe as Alaska's number one terrorist target, ramping up security and for a while even operating a checkpoint on the Dalton Hwy. Their fears weren't entirely unfounded: in 1978 a mystery bomber near Fairbanks damaged the pipeline with explosives, spilling some 670,000 gallons of oil. Then, in 2001, a drunken hunter shot it with a .338-caliber rifle and 285,000 gallons spewed out. Officials say the pipeline has been shot – with no spillage caused – at least 50 other times.

wildflowers and berries grow in profusion and wildlife is far easier to spot. Especially at the beginning and end of summer, migrating waterbirds throng roadside ponds and caribou – members of the 31,000-head Central Arctic herd – often graze nearby. Also, keep an eye out for weird polar phenomena such as pingos – protuberant hills with a frozen center – and ice-wedge polygons, which shape the tundra into bizarre geometric patterns.

Deadhorse

You'll know the coast draws near when the weather turns dire. The gloom sets the mood for your arrival at the dystopia of Deadhorse, the world's northernmost anticlimax. Centered around Lake Colleen, this is no town – nobody lives here permanently – but a sad expanse of aluminum-clad warehouses, machinery-laden lots and workmen counting the moments until they return south.

Don't even think about camping: the tundra is a quagmire and the gravel pads are plied by speeding pickups. Having come all this way you can either turn around (after gassing up with what is, ironically, some of America's costliest petrol) or do what locals do: hole up in a hotel and watch cable TV.

Prudhoe Bay Hotel (☎ 659-2449; www.prudhoebayhotel.com; dm/d with bath $110/200) and the **Arctic Caribou Inn** (☎ 866-659-2368; www.arcticcaribouinn.com; r $185), both near the airport, aren't froufrou but are a shockingly good deal because the price includes quality café-style meals – the only food service in Deadhorse. What differentiates the two places is that, because the Caribou is more tourist-oriented, its gift shop has espressos rather than porno mags. Souvenirs and sundries can also be bought at the **Prudhoe Bay General Store** (☎ 659-2412; 🕐 7am-9pm), located on the town's east edge and containing the **post office** (☎ 659-

2669). Send Mom a postcard from the top of the world!

Tours

Various companies run similar tours:

Arctic Caribou Inn Oilfield Tour (☎ 866-659-2368; www.arcticcaribouinn.com; tours $38) This two-hour ordeal is the only way to gain access to the oil fields and the ocean. You must sign up for this tour a day in advance in order to clear security.

Northern Alaska Tour Company (☎ 800-474-1986, 474-8600; www.northernalaska.com) This is the granddaddy of the Dalton Hwy tour companies, offering all sorts of packages, including a three-day van trip to Prudhoe Bay for $889 with lodging.

Trans Arctic Circle Treks (☎ 800-336-8735, 479-5451; www.arctictreks.com) Charges $889 for a similar tour.

Getting There & Around

BUS

There's a scheduled van service between Fairbanks and Prudhoe Bay that, among other things, drops off backpackers along the way. **Dalton Highway Express** (☎ 474-3555; www.daltonhighwayexpress.com) makes the run daily during the summer, stopping overnight at Deadhorse and giving you time to take an early-morning oil-field tour before returning the next day. The round-trip fare to the Arctic Circle is $154, Wiseman and Coldfoot $194, Galbraith Lake $304 and Deadhorse $428. If you drive to Coldfoot and catch the shuttle northward it's a $234 round-trip.

CAR

Finding somebody to rent you a car in Fairbanks for travel on the Dalton is a major challenge. See p390 for more information.

GATES OF THE ARCTIC NATIONAL PARK & PRESERVE

The Gates of the Arctic National Park & Preserve is one of the world's finest wilderness areas. Covering 13,125 sq miles, it straddles the ragged spine of the Brooks Range, America's northernmost chain of mountains, and sprawls 800 miles from east to west. The sparse vegetation is mainly shrubbery and tundra; animals include grizzlies, wolves, Dall sheep, moose, caribou and wolverines. There's great fishing for grayling and Arctic char in the clear streams, and for lake trout in the larger, deeper lakes.

Within the park are dozens of rivers to run, miles of valleys and tundra slopes to hike and, of course, the 'gates' themselves: Mt Boreal and Frigid Crags, which flank the north fork of the Koyukuk River. In 1929 Robert Marshall found an unobstructed path northward to the Arctic through these landmark peaks and his name for the passage has stuck ever since.

The park contains no visitor facilities, campgrounds or trails, and the NPS is intent upon maintaining its virgin quality. Therefore, rangers urge a six-person limit on trekking parties and they've also begun strongly encouraging visitors to get off the (literally) beaten path, possibly avoiding such increasingly busy corridors as the Noatak River.

Unguided trekkers, paddlers and climbers entering the park should be well versed in wilderness travel; they should also check in at one of the ranger stations for a backcountry orientation and updates on river hazards and bear activity. To avoid confrontations with bears, campers are required to carry bearproof food canisters, checked out free-of-charge from the ranger stations.

Orientation & Information

Bettles (p417) is the main gateway to Gates of the Arctic, offering meals, lodging and transport into the backcountry. Other visitors fly in from Coldfoot (p413) on the Dalton Hwy, or hike in from nearby Wiseman (p413). You can access the northern portions of the park from Anaktuvuk (p420).

Anaktuvuk Ranger Station (☎ 661-3520; www.nps.gov/gaar) Can help you plan your trip from Anaktuvuk.

Arctic Interagency Visitors Center In Coldfoot; has info for those accessing the park from the Dalton Hwy. See p413 .

Bettles Ranger Station (☎ 692-5494; www.nps.gov/gaar; 🕑 8am-6pm Jun-Sep, 8am-noon winter) In a log building less than a quarter mile from the airstrip, it also serves as a visitors center and has displays depicting the flora and fauna of the Brooks Range, a small library and books and maps for sale.

Sights & Activities

HIKING

Most backpackers enter the park by way of charter air-taxi, which can land on lakes, rivers or river bars, and which are usually caught from Bettles. Once on the ground you can follow the long, open valleys for extended treks or work your way to higher elevations where open tundra and sparse shrubs provide good hiking terrain. One of the more popular long-distance treks is the four- to five-day hike from Summit Lake through the Gates to Redstar Lake. Less-experienced backpackers often choose to be dropped off and picked up at one lake and explore the surrounding region on day hikes from there. Lakes ideal for this include Summit Lake, the Karupa lakes region, Redstar Lake, Hunt Fork Lake or Chimney Lake.

The only treks that don't require chartering a plane are those beginning from the Dalton Hwy; these lead into several different areas along the eastern border of the park. Stop at the Arctic Interagency Visitor Center in Coldfoot (p413) for advice and assistance in trip planning. Then drive north to your access point into the park. Many backpackers stop at Wiseman, which provides access to several routes, including the following trails.

Nolan/Wiseman Creek Area

Head west at the Wiseman exit just before Mile 189 of the Dalton Hwy, and hike along Nolan Rd, which passes through Nolan – a hamlet of a few families – and ends at Nolan Creek. You can then reach Wiseman Creek and Nolan Creek Lake, which lies in the valley through which Wiseman and Nolan Creeks run, at the foot of three passes: Glacier, Pasco and Snowshoes. You can hike from any of these passes to Glacier River, which can be followed to the north fork of the Koyukuk for a longer hike.

Lower Hammond River Area

From Wiseman, go north by hiking along Hammond Rd, which can be followed for quite a way along the Hammond River. From the river you can explore the park by following one of several drainage areas, including Vermont, Canyon and Jenny Creeks. The latter heads east to Jenny Creek Lake.

PADDLING

Floatable rivers in the park include the John, the north fork of the Koyukuk, the Tinayguk, the Alatna and the middle fork of the Koyukuk River from Wiseman to Bettles. The headwaters for the Noatak and Kobuk are in the park.

The waterways range in difficulty from Class I to III. Of the rivers, the Koyukuk's north fork is especially popular because of the location and challenge – the float starts in the Gates' shadow and goes downstream 100 miles to Bettles through Class I and II waters. Canoes and rafts can be rented in Bettles and then floated downstream to the village.

Upper Noatak

The best-known river, and the most popular for paddlers, is the upper portion of the Noatak, due to the spectacular scenery as you float by the sharp peaks of the Brooks Range and because it's a mild river that many canoeists can handle on an unguided journey.

The most common trip is a 60-mile float that begins near Portage Creek and ends at a riverside lake near Kacachurak Creek, just outside the park boundary. This float is usually completed in five to seven days. It involves some Class II and possible Class III stretches of rapids toward the end. During the busy summer season, from about mid-July to the end of August, other parties may be encountered on the river and aircraft may be heard delivering visitors to the area.

Guided Tours

A few guide companies run extremely spendy trips through the Gates of the Arctic National Park & Preserve. These include **ABEC's Alaska Adventures** (☎ 457-8907, 877-424-8907; www.abecalaska.com), **Too-loó-uk River Guides** (☎ 683-1542; www.akrivers.com) and **Arctic Wild** (☎ 479-8203, 888-577-8203; www.arcticwild.com).

The best way to create an independent trip is to arrange for a float plane either in or out of the park through either Bettles Air Service (below) or Brooks Range Aviation (below). You can rent a canoe or raft from **Bettles Lodge** (☎ 692-5111, 800-770-5111; www.bettleslodge.com; per week canoe/raft $270/400).

Getting There & Away

Access to the park's backcountry is usually accomplished in two steps, with the first being a scheduled flight from Fairbanks to Bettles. There are no summer roads to Bettles, but during the winter an ice road provides access. Check out **Bettles Air Service** (☎ 800-770-5111, 692-5111), which makes regular flights to Bettles for $335 round-trip. The second step is to charter an air-taxi from Bettles to your destination within the park. A Cessna 185 on floats holds three passengers and costs around $540 per hour. Most areas in the park can be reached in under two hours. If you're in Bettles, check with **Brooks Range Aviation** (☎ 692-5444, 800-692-5443; www.brooksrange-alaska-wilderness-trips.com) or Bettles Air Service for air charters.

Alternatively, you can drive up the Dalton Highway (p411) to the Coldfoot/Wiseman area, and access the park from there, either hiking in or chartering with **Coyote Air Service** (☎ 678-5995, 800-252-0603; www.flycoyote.com).

BETTLES

pop 28

This small village serves as the major departure point to the Gates of the Arctic National Park & Preserve. If you find yourself with an unexpected day in Bettles, which can easily happen in August, take a hike up to **Birch Hill Lake**. The trailhead is unmarked, but is just to the right of the small, brown house next door to the Evansville Health Clinic. It's a 3-mile trek to the lake and can get swampy.

Sleeping & Eating

Camping is allowed behind the Bettles Flight Service building off the runway at the north edge of the aircraft parking area, where you'll find BBQ grills. It would be just as easy to pitch a tent on the gravel bars along the middle fork of the Koyukuk River.

Bettles Lodge (☎ 692-5111, 800-770-5111; www.bettleslodge.com; dm $35, r $175-195; ⊠ 💻) This is a classic Alaskan log lodge with a restaurant, a small tavern and bush pilots constantly wandering through in their hip boots.

Aurora Lodge (dm $35, r $175-195; ⊠ 💻) Part of the Bettles Lodge complex; it has eight rooms and a bunkhouse hostel.

Spirit Lights Lodge (☎ 692-5252, 888-692-2857; www.spiritlightslodge.com; dm/cabin $50/100; 💻) This lodge has three basic cabins, a bunkhouse and restaurant.

Getting There & Around

There's no summer road to Bettles – in winter they enjoy an ice road – so you'll need to fly or float here for the most part. See opposite for more information on getting to Bettles.

BARROW

pop 4054

Barrow is the northernmost settlement in the USA, the largest Iñupiat community in Alaska and one of the most distinctive places you're ever likely to visit. Originally called Ukpeagvik, which means 'place to hunt snowy owls,' the town is situated 330 miles above the Arctic Circle. It's a flat, bleak, fogbound and strangely evocative place patrolled by polar bears and locked in almost perpetual winter. It's also a town of surprising contradictions.

On one hand, Barrow's wealth is famous: due to the spoils of North Slope petroleum it boasts facilities, such as its Iñupiat Heritage Center, which are totally unexpected in a town this size. On the flipside, it's an Arctic slum packed with ramshackle structures wallowing in frozen mud.

It's also at once ancient and modern. Iñupiat have dwelled here for at least two millennia and still run the place. Barrow, as the seat of the North Slope Borough (a countylike government covering an area larger than Nebraska), is the administrative and commercial hub of Alaska's Far North. Yet locals have retained much of their traditional culture: best symbolized by the spring whale harvests, and seen during the Nalukataq Festival staged in June to celebrate successful hunts.

For tourists, however, Barrow's appeal isn't so much its Iñupiat culture as its novel latitude. They come to see the midnight sun (which doesn't set for 82 days from May to early August) and say they've been at the top of the world.

The vast majority of the 7000-plus visitors who arrive every summer are traveling as part of a package tour. Barrow is an expensive (and not really worthwhile) side trip for independent travelers.

Orientation & Information

Barrow lies along the northeasterly trending shore of the icebound Chukchi Sea, and is divided into two distinct sections. Directly north of the airport is Barrow proper: home to most of the hotels and restaurants and interlaced with a warren of gravel streets, including Stevenson St, which runs along the water. North of Isatquaq, or Middle Lagoon, is Browerville: a more residential area but also where the heritage center, post office and grocery store are located.

Barrow Arctic Science Consortium (☎ 852-4881; www.arcticscience.org) Hosts free scientific lectures most Saturdays at 1:30pm. It is located at the Ilisagvik College, about 3 miles outside of town on the Beach Road.

North Slope Borough Public Information Office (☎ 852-0215; PO Box 60, Barrow, AK 99723) You can contact this place for information in advance of your trip.

Police (nonemergency ☎ 852-6111)

Post office (cnr Eben Hobson & Tahak Sts) To send your postcards from the top of the world.

DETOUR: ARCTIC NATIONAL WILDLIFE REFUGE

Seldom has so much furor involved a place so few have ever been. The Arctic National Wildlife Refuge (ANWR, *an*-wahr) is a 19.6-million-acre wilderness in Alaska's upper-right-hand corner, straddling the eastern Brooks Range from the treeless Arctic Coast to the taiga of the Porcupine River Valley. For years the refuge has been at the core of a white-hot debate over whether to drill for oil beneath its coastal plain, which is thought to contain 10.4 billion barrels of crude oil.

Advocates, including a sizable majority of Alaskans, say drilling will create jobs, reduce gas prices and heighten America's energy security – and with modern technology, they say, it can be done with nearly zero environmental impact. Opponents – environmentalists and, most famously, the Gwich'in Athabascans who've long frequented the refuge's southern reaches – argue ANWR should remain pristine, particularly for the sake of the 150,000-head porcupine caribou herd which calves on the coastal plain. Moreover, they say, the amount of oil in ANWR is a drop in the bucket considering the US consumes 20.6 million barrels of oil per day.

Visiting ANWR is easier said than done. There are no visitor facilities of any sort and even reaching the refuge can be a trick (requiring quite a bit of gas, unless you travel like a caribou). There's only one place ANWR can be accessed by car: just north of Atigun Pass on the Dalton Highway, where the road and the refuge briefly touch. You could hike in from there, but you'll still be nowhere near the coastal plain and unlikely to see the embattled caribou.

To get deeper into ANWR, you will need to fly there. Numerous charter companies can be hired; for a list, consult the **refuge's website** (www.arctic.fws.gov). A few, like Coldfoot-based **Coyote Air Service** (☎ 678-5995, 800-252-0603; www.flycoyote.com), operate organized flightseeing trips, such as its three-hour caribou-spotting excursion. There are also plenty of outfitters who operate trips in the refuge. Most, including excellent **Alaska Discovery/Mt Sobek** (☎ 888-867-6235; www.mtsobek.com), float the Kongakut, Sheenjek, Hulahula or other rivers; some, such as **ABEC's Alaska Adventures** (☎ 457-8907, 877-424-8907; www.abecalaska.com), lead multiday backpacking excursions along the Porcupine Caribou Migration Route. Several companies have even more unorthodox offerings: for instance, **Arctic Wild** (☎ 888-577-8203; www.arcticwild.com) conducts a nine-day yoga course in the refuge.

No matter what you choose to do in ANWR, though, you'd be wise to come soon. By the time you read this drilling may already have begun; see p50.

Samuel Simmonds Memorial Hospital (☎ 852-4611; 1296 Agvik St) Will either fix you up or arrange a medevac flight to Fairbanks.
Tuzzy Consortium Library (☎ 852-1720; 5421 North Star St; 🕑 noon-9pm Mon-Thu, to 5pm Fri & Sat) In the same building as the Iñupiat Heritage Center, has free internet and lots to read when the weather's bad.
Wells Fargo (☎ 852-6200; cnr Agvik & Kiogak Sts) Has a 24-hour ATM.

Sights

The main thing to do at the top of the world is bundle up and stand on the shore of the Arctic Ocean gazing toward the North Pole. You can stroll the gravel roads that parallel the sea to view *umiaks* (Iñupiat skin boats), giant jawbones of bowhead whales, fish-drying racks and the jumbled Arctic pack ice that even in July spans the horizon. On the waterfront opposite Apayauk St at the south end of town is **Ukpiagvik**, the site of an ancient Iñupiat village marked by the remains of semisubterranean sod huts.

Follow the shore 12 miles northeast of the city and you'll come to **Point Barrow**, a narrow spit of land that's the northernmost extremity of the US (though not, as locals sometimes claim, North America). In the winter and spring this is where polar bears den; in the summer it's the featured stop of organized tours. While you can walk out to the point, it's best to go with an organized tour considering the prevalence of polar bears in the area.

Among Barrow's artificial attractions, by far the most impressive is the **Iñupiaq Heritage Center** (☎ 852-0422; Ahkovak St; admission $5; 🕑 8:30am-5pm Mon-Fri, 12:30-4pm Sat & Sun). This 24,000-sq-ft facility houses a museum, gift shop and a large multipurpose room where traditional dancing-and-drumming performances take place each afternoon. The show is worth the additional $15, and afterwards local craftspeople assemble in the lobby to sell masks, whalebone carvings and fur garments. In the center's galleries, well-curated displays include everything from poster-sized B&W portraits of local elders to a 35ft-long replica of a bowhead skeleton.

Opposite Barrow's airport is the **Will Rogers & Wiley Post Monument**, a six-sided cenotaph memorializing the famous comedian and his legendary pilot, who died together in 1935 when their plane stalled and crashed into a river 15 miles south of here. At the time Rogers was on a comedy tour en route from Fairbanks to Siberia.

Birding & Wildlife Watching

Barrow is a birder's paradise. At least 185 distinct avian species visit during the summer months. Head west of town to **Freshwater Lake** for some good birding. Along the way you pass the cemetery and are likely to see jaegers, arctic terns, snowy owls and snow buntings. East of Bowerville along the **Cakeater Rd** is another excellent birding spot.

To spot polar bear, you are best taking a tour. But don't get your hopes up too high: they're tough to spot.

Festivals & Events

The **Nalukataq Festival** is held in late June, when the spring whaling hunt has been completed. Depending on how successful the whaling captains have been, the festival lasts from a few days to more than a week. It's a rare cultural experience if you're lucky enough to be in Barrow when it happens. One Iñupiat tradition calls for whaling crews to share their bounty with the village, and during the festival you'll see families carry off platters and plastic bags full of raw whale meat. Dishes served include *muktuk*, the pink blubbery part of the whale, which is boiled, pickled or even eaten raw with hot mustard or soy sauce.

The main event of the festival is the blanket toss, in which locals gather around a sealskin tarp and pull it tight to toss people into the air – the effect is much like bouncing on a trampoline. The object is to jump as high as possible (supposedly replicating ancient efforts to spot game in the distance) and inevitably there are a number of sprains and fractures.

Tours

Arctic Adventure Tours (☎ 852-4512) Offers an intimate two-hour wildlife tour to Point Barrow to look for polar bears, marine life such as walrus and a variety of migrating birds.

Northernmost Tours (☎ 852-5893; www.northernmosttoursbarrow.com; tours $60-100) Daniel Lum, a knowledgeable Iñupiat guide, takes people all the way out to the point. He's a wealth of knowledge when it comes to local cultural and natural history, and this is the best tour in town.

Tundra Tours (☎ 852-3900, 800-882-8478; www.tundratoursinc.com) The major package-tour operator, using buses to show sightseers the town and tundra. A blanket toss and Alaska Native dance performance is included in the six-hour excursion, which costs $95 per person.

Sleeping

Camping is ill advised around Barrow due to curious, carnivorous polar bears. That means you'll be paying a pretty penny to put a roof over your head. There's a 5% bed tax in town.

UIC-NARL Hostel (☎ 852-7800; r per person $80) These shared-facility rooms, used mainly by the local community college, are the cheapest around but, inconveniently, they're several miles north of town.

Barrow Airport Inn (☎ 852-2525; airportinn@barrow.com; 1815 Momegana St; r $125; ⊠) It has 14 somewhat worn but quite tolerable rooms. Some have kitchenettes and, inexplicably, portable fans.

Top of the World Hotel (☎ 852-3900, 800-882-8478; www.tundratoursinc.com; 1200 Agvik St; s/d from $170/190) Large, soulless, but centrally located, the Top of the World is where most package-tour visitors stay. It's only $10 extra to upgrade to an ocean-view room – well worth the money.

King Eider Inn (☎ 852-4700, 888-303-4337; www.kingeider.net; 1752 Ahkovak St; r $185-315; ⊠ 💻) With a cozy log-cabin feel, wood-post beds and an inviting fireplace in the lobby, the Eider has the nicest rooms in town but none of the views you'll get from the Top of the World.

Eating

Barrow is a 'damp' town, so don't expect to be throwing back margs at the local Mexican restaurant.

Brower's Café (☎ 852-3456; 3220 Brower Hill; burgers $8-12; 🕑 11am-11pm Mon-Sat, noon-10pm Sun) This beachfront structure was built in the late 19th century by Charles Brower, an American whaler, and has whaling antiques inside and a whale-jawbone arch out front. Nowadays it's Barrow's best burger joint (with about 10 varieties) and hosts what's almost certainly America's northernmost karaoke night.

Pepe's North of the Border (☎ 852-8200; 1204 Agvik St; mains $8-22; 🕑 6am-10pm Mon-Sat, to 9pm Sun) Attached to the Top of the World Hotel, this

EXPLORE MORE OF THE BUSH

Here's a few places not covered in this book that might be worth checking out.

- **Shishmaref** On the north edge of the Seward Peninsula, this Iñupiat community will not be there for long. It's literally falling into the ocean thanks to melting permafrost, rising sea levels and global warming. Blame it on Bush, blame it on Gore, blame it on whomever you like, but visit the town before it's gone. You can also kick off adventures in Bering Land Bridge National Preserve from here. A ton of articles have been written about the 'sea change' in Shishmaref. Check out the town's Wikipedia page for a bit more info.
- **St Lawrence Island** Way out there in the Bering Sea this island, inhabited primarily by Alaskan and Siberian Yupik, is a good place for birding and watching sea mammals. There are hotels in both Gamble and Savoonga, and the natives are renowned for their ivory carvings. For more information on birding, check out www.alaskabird.org.
- **Brevig Mission** Intrepid travelers won't even need to fly to get to this small native village. You can arrange a skiff from Teller (p410).
- **Anaktuvuk Pass** Located within the Gates of the Arctic National Park, this small native village was established in the 1950s by the last remaining group of seminomadic Nunamiut. Kick off Gates of the Arctic backpacks from this North Slope town. Call the **Anaktuvuk Ranger Station** (☎ 661-3520; www.nps.gov/gaar) for more information on visiting the park from here.
- **Kaktovik** This Iñupiat enclave has tourist services such as hotels and guides, but sees a fraction of the visitation Barrow does. Visit www.kaktovik.com for some information.

'northernmost Mexican restaurant in the world' has achieved renown thanks to the tireless Barrow-boosting efforts of owner Fran Tate. The food is decent and eclectic, including lobster, flautas and big burritos.

Osaka (☎ 852-4100; 980 Stevenson St; breakfast $10-14, lunch & dinner $8-23; ⏰ 8am-midnight) Located diagonally across from the Top of the World Hotel, this place has pretty good all-American breakfasts. The $12 lunch special has everything from sashimi to plain old fish 'n' chips.

AC Store (☎ 852-6711; cnr Stuaqpak & Agvik Sts; ⏰ 8am-10pm Mon-Sat, 9am-9pm Sun) It has quick eats and groceries at diet-inducing prices.

Getting There & Around

While you can get to Barrow in the winter by ice road (you'll need a GPS, extra gas, survival gear and some big-ass *cajones*), it's best to fly. **Alaska Airlines** (☎ 852-4653, 800-468-2248; www.alaskaair.com) charges about $500 for a round-trip, advance-purchase ticket from Fairbanks and about $600 from Anchorage.

Such fares make package tours attractive. A same-day excursion, which includes airfare from Fairbanks and a town tour but not meals, is around $520 through Alaska Airlines, or $625 if you want to stay overnight.

Once on the ground the airport is an easy stroll from all three hotels, and most other points of interest can also be reached by walking. If bad weather blows in, however, cabs are available for $6. Try **Arctic Cab** (☎ 852-2227) or **Barrow Taxi** (☎ 852-2222). Cars can be rented through **UIC Auto Rental** (☎ 852-2700).

Directory

CONTENTS

ACCOMMODATIONS

Alaska offers typical US accommodations along with many atypical options such as a cabin in the mountains or a lodge in the middle of the wilderness. This guide includes recommendations for all types and budgets but it emphasizes midrange accommodations. In the regional chapters the accommodations are listed with budget first (under $100 a night) followed by midrange ($100 to $200) and top end ($200 and up).

Advance bookings are wise as the Alaskan tourist season is short, and in places such as Juneau, Skagway and Denali National Park rooms fill quickly. You will receive better accommodation rates during the shoulder seasons of April through May and September through October.

The rates listed in this book are all for high season: June through August. The listed rates do not include local taxes, which are covered for each town at the start of the Sleeping sections. In most towns you will be hit with a local sales tax *and* a bed tax, with the combination ranging from 5% up to 12% for cities such as Anchorage and Juneau.

The most affordable accommodations are hostels, campsites (bring your tent!) and campground cabins. Motels, both individually owned and national chains, are well scattered in cities and most towns. Even small rural hamlets will have a motel. The larger centers will also have a number of B&Bs housing the peak-of-summer tourists, which will range from basic rooms to plush accommodations.

As to be expected Alaska is the land of wilderness lodges. Many of them are geared towards anglers and remote fishing opportunities, must be booked well in advance, and require floatplane transport to reach. Tribal companies and the cruise ship industry (for the land portions of their tours) are also responsible for a growing number of luxurious hotels popping up across the state.

> **BOOK YOUR STAY ONLINE**
>
> For more accommodation reviews and recommendations by Lonely Planet authors, check out www.lonelyplanet.com/hotels. You'll find the lowdown on the best places to stay. Reviews are thorough and independent. Best of all, you can book online.

B&Bs

For travelers who want nothing to do with a tent, B&Bs can be an acceptable compromise between sleeping on the ground and sleeping in high-priced lodges. Some B&Bs are bargains, and most are cheaper than major hotels, but plan on spending $70 to $120 per night for a double room.

Many visitor centers have sections devoted to the B&Bs in their area, and courtesy booking

PRACTICALITIES

- Alaska has more than 30 daily, weekly and trade newspapers with the *Anchorage Daily News* being the largest and the closest thing to a statewide newspaper.
- The largest cities have local TV stations while radio stations are found all over Alaska. Voltage in Alaska is 110V – the same as everywhere else in the USA.
- There is no national sales tax in the USA and no state sales tax in Alaska, but towns have a city sales tax plus a bed tax.
- Almost every town in Alaska has a Laundromat, the place to go to clean your clothes ($3 per load) or take a shower ($3 to $5).
- US distances are in feet, yards and miles. Dry weights are in ounces (oz), pounds (lb) and tons, and liquids are in pints, quarts and gallons (4 quarts). The US gallon is about 20% less than the imperial gallon. See the conversion chart on the inside front cover of this book.
- NTSC is the standard video system (not compatible with PAL or SECAM).

phones. Details about specific B&Bs are in the regional chapters. You can also contact the following B&B reservation services to book rooms in advance of your trip:

Alaska Private Lodgings (☎ 907-235-2148; www.alaskabandb.com) Statewide.
Anchorage Alaska Bed & Breakfast Association (☎ 907-272-5909, 888-584-5147; www.anchorage-bnb.com)
Bed and Breakfast Association of Alaska (www.alaskabba.com) Statewide.
Fairbanks Association of Bed & Breakfasts (www.ptialaska.net/~fabb)
Homer Bed & Breakfast Association (☎ 877-296-1114; www.homerbedbreakfast.com)
Kenai Peninsula Bed & Breakfast Association (☎ 866-436-2266; www.kenaipeninsulabba.com)
Ketchikan Reservation Service (☎ 800-987-5337; www.ketchikan-lodging.com)
Mat-Su Bed & Breakfast Association (www.alaskabnbhosts.com)

Camping & Caravan Parks

Camping is king in Alaska and with a tent you'll always have cheap accommodations in the Far North. There are state, federal and private campgrounds from Ketchikan to Fairbanks. Nightly fees range from free to $10 for rustic public campgrounds and from $25 to $40 to park your recreation vehicle in a deluxe private campground with a full hook-up and heated restrooms with showers. Many towns that cater to tourists will have a municipal campground and several commercial campgrounds. See p73.

Hostels

Thanks to an influx of backpackers and foreign travelers each summer, the number of hostels offering budget accommodations in Alaska increases almost annually. There are now more than 40, with eight in Anchorage, nine in the Southeast and even one in tiny McCarthy. What isn't increasing is the **Hostel International-American Youth Hostels** (www.hiayh.org) in Alaska; there is now only one HI property in Anchorage.

The rest of Alaska's hostels are for backpackers, offering budget bunkrooms without all the rules of a Hostel International member. Nightly fees are from $10 at Juneau International Hostel (p168) to $35 for the Anchorage Guest House (p210). Most are around $25 a night. When you consider the access to a kitchen for cheap eats, hostels are the first step in making Alaska affordable. For more information on Alaska's hostels see the website of the **Alaska Hostel Association** (www.alaskahostelassociation.org) before your trip.

Hotels & Motels

Hotels and motels are often the most expensive lodgings you can book. Although there are bargains, the average double room in a budget hotel costs $70 to $90, a midrange motel is $100 to $200 and a top-end hotel $200 and above a night.

The drawback with hotels and motels is that they tend to be full during summer. Without being part of a tour or having advance reservations, you may have trouble finding a bed available in some towns.

Resorts

Resorts – upscale hotels that have rooms, restaurants, pools and on-site activities – are not as common in Alaska as elsewhere in the USA but are increasing due to the patronage of large companies, such as Princess Tours. The finest is Girdwood's Alyeska Resort (p222), with a four-star hotel at the base of its ski runs. If you're near Fairbanks, head to Chena Hot Springs Rd to spend some time at the Chena Hot Springs Resort (p393) for good food, log cabins and a soak in an outdoor hot tub.

ACTIVITIES

Backpacking, kayaking and canoeing are covered in the Wilderness Hikes & Paddles chapter (p89), which has 20 trips that most travelers can arrange themselves. Details on mountain biking, fishing, rock climbing, dog sledding and surfing can be found in the Outdoor Activities & Adventures chapter (p73). For companies that offer activity tours see p440.

BUSINESS HOURS

Banks and post offices in Alaska are generally open from 9am to 5pm Monday to Friday and sometimes on Saturday mornings. Other business hours vary, but many stores are open 10am to 8pm Monday to Saturday with shorter hours on Sunday. For restaurant opening hours see p64. Keep in mind that reviews in the regional chapters won't list business hours unless they differ from these standards.

CHILDREN

The Final Frontier is a great place for families. Though expensive overall, Alaska can be much more affordable if your family enjoys outdoor adventures such as camping, hiking and wildlife viewing. For more on family travel, including five great Alaskan outdoor adventures for children, see the Alaska for Families chapter (p39).

CLIMATE

From the north to the south, Alaska's climate changes drastically. The following climate charts extend from Barrow to Juneau and will provide a glimpse of temperatures and precipitation for whenever you plan to visit. For more on climate see p22 or p69.

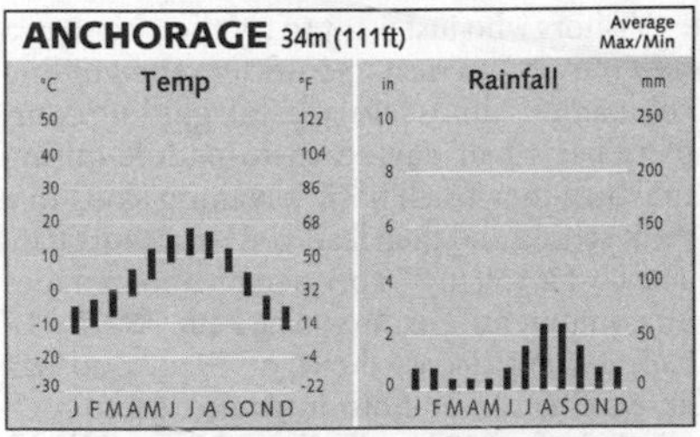

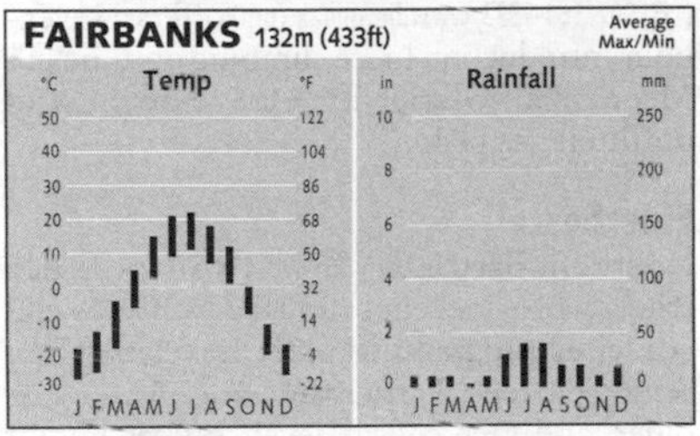

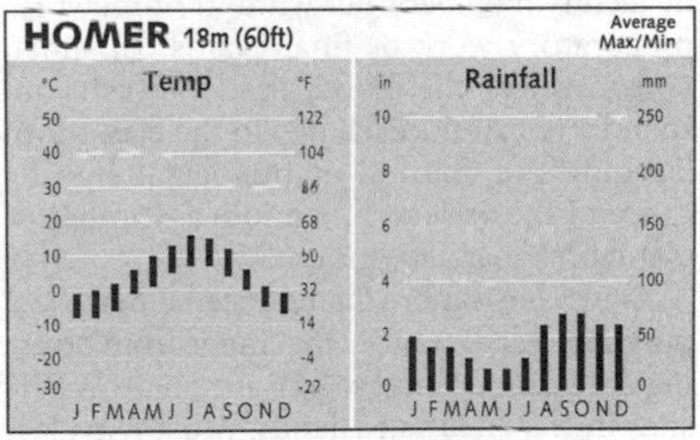

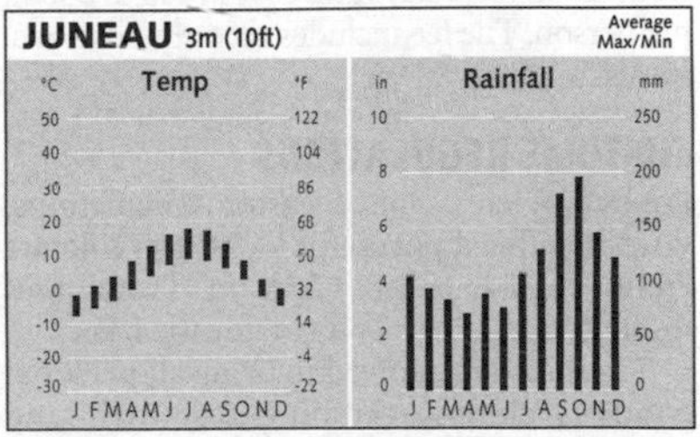

COURSES

Alaska is an outdoor classroom and outdoor leadership schools hold class there regularly. The **International Wilderness Leadership School** (☎ 800-985-4957; www.iwls.com) offers a half dozen courses including mountaineering, rock and ice climbing and sea kayaking. Courses last from 12 to 26 days and range in price from $2000 to $3500. The **National Outdoor Leadership School** (☎ 800-710-6657; www.nols.edu) has an equal number of programs that include sea kayaking, mountaineering and backpacking. Both schools can arrange for you to earn college credits while you're trekking through the wilderness.

Visitors who just want to try their hand at a new activity can turn to outfitters and guiding companies. Almost every kayak guiding company has a half-day, learn-to-paddle outing in which they teach basic kayaking skills in a calm setting and then lead you on a short trip. The cost is $50 to $70 per person and includes all equipment. The **Ascending Path** (☎ 907-783-0505; www.theascendingpath.com) of Girdwood has an excellent three-hour introduction to rock climbing for $129 while **Above & Beyond Alaska** (☎ 907-364-2333; www.beyondak.com) offers a seven-hour introduction to ice climbing on Juneau's Mendenhall Glacier for $189. For a list of outfitters see p440.

Elderhostel

Nonprofit **Elderhostel** (☎ 800-454-5768; www.elderhostel.org) provides educational adventures and academic programs to older travelers, often senior citizens. Participants are 55 years or older, and take college-level courses taught by faculty members, but without homework, preparatory work or final exams. In short, you travel to the places that interest you, spend a few hours each day in the classroom learning the cultural or biological significance of the area and then join a number of extracurricular activities.

Alaska hosts more than a dozen Elderhostel programs each summer that range from cruising the Inside Passage to ferrying out to WWII sites in the Aleutian Islands. Most trips last from seven to 14 days and cost $1000 to $3000 per person. The fee includes accommodations, meals and classes.

CUSTOMS REGULATIONS

For a complete list of US customs regulations, visit the official portal for **US Customs & Border Protection** (www.cbp.gov). Click on 'Travel' and then 'Know Before You Go' for the basics.

Travelers are allowed to bring all personal goods (including camping gear or hiking equipment) into the USA and Canada free of duty, along with food for two days and up to 100 cigars, 200 cigarettes and 1L of liquor or wine.

There are no forms to fill out if you are a foreign visitor bringing a vehicle into Alaska, whether it is a bicycle, motorcycle or car, nor are there forms for hunting rifles or fishing gear. Hunting rifles – handguns and automatic weapons are prohibited – must be registered in your own country, and you should bring proof of registration. There is no limit to the amount of money you can bring into Alaska, but anything over $10,000 must be registered with customs officials.

Keep in mind that endangered-species laws prohibit transporting products made of bone, skin, fur, ivory etc, through Canada without a permit. Importing and exporting such items into the USA is also prohibited. If you have any doubt about a gift or item you want to purchase, call the **US Fish & Wildlife Service** (USFWS; ☎ 271-6198) in Anchorage or check the USFWS website (www.fws.gov).

Hunters and anglers who want to ship home their salmon, halibut or rack of caribou can do so easily. Most outfitters and guides will make the arrangements for you, including properly packaging the game. In the case of fish, most towns have a storage company that will hold your salmon or halibut in a freezer until you are ready to leave Alaska. When frozen, seafood can usually make the trip to any city in the Lower 48 without thawing.

DANGERS & ANNOYANCES

Alaska is a relatively safe place with most of its dangers and annoyances occurring not in the cities but out in the woods. For how to deal with insects and paralytic shellfish poisoning (PSP), which affects some shellfish, see the Health chapter (p443).

Bears

Too often travelers decide to skip a wilderness trip because they hear too many bear stories. Your own equipment and outdoor experience should determine whether you take a trek into the woods, not the possibility of meeting a bear on the trail.

The **Alaska Department of Fish & Game** (ADF&G; www.adfg.state.ak.us) emphasizes that the probability of being injured by a bear is one-fiftieth the chance of being injured in a car accident on any Alaskan highway. For an extensive review of bears and safety procedures go to the ADF&G website.

The best way to avoid bears is to follow a few commonsense rules. Bears charge only when they feel trapped, when a hiker comes between a sow and her cubs or when enticed by food. Sing or clap when traveling through thick bush, so you don't surprise a bear. Don't camp near bear food sources or in the middle of an obvious bear path.

Stay away from thick berry patches, streams choked with salmon or beaches littered with bear droppings.

Leave your pet at home; a frightened dog only runs back to its owner, and most dogs are no match for a bear. Set up the spot where you will cook and eat at least 30 to 50 yards away from your tent. In coastal areas, many backpackers eat in the tidal zone, knowing that when the high tide comes in all evidence of food will be washed away.

At night try to place your food sacks 10ft or more off the ground by hanging them in a tree, placing them on top of a tall boulder or putting them on the edge of a rock cliff. In a treeless, flat area, cover up food sacks with rocks, or consider investing in a lightweight bear-resistant container. A bear usually finds a food bag using its great sense of smell. By packaging all food items in resealable plastic bags, you greatly reduce the animal's chances of getting a whiff of your next meal. Avoid odorous foods, such as bacon or sardines, in areas with high concentrations of bears. Avoid wearing scented cosmetics, including deodorant, as the smell attracts bears. Women who are menstruating should place used tampons/sanitary napkins in plastic bags and store them in bear-resistant containers up with the suspended food bag.

And please, don't take food into the tent at night. Don't even take toothpaste, hand lotion, suntan oils or anything with a smell. If a bear smells a human, it will leave; anything else might encourage it to investigate.

ENCOUNTERING A BEAR

If you do meet a bear on the trail, *do not* turn and run, it will outrun you. Stop, make no sudden moves and begin talking calmly to the animal. Speaking to a bear helps it understand that you are there. If it doesn't take off right away, back up slowly before turning around and leaving the area. A bear standing on its hind legs is not on the verge of charging; it's only trying to see you better. When a bear turns sideways or begins making a series of woofing sounds, it is only challenging you for space – just back away slowly and leave. If the animal follows you, *stop* and hold your ground.

Most bear charges are bluffs, with the animal veering off at the last minute. Experienced backpackers handle a charge in different ways. Some people throw their packs 3ft in front of them, which will often distract the bear long enough for the person to back away. Other backpackers fire a handheld signal flare over the bear's head (but never at it) in an attempt to use the noise and sudden light to scare the bear away. If an encounter is imminent, drop into a fetal position, place your hands behind your neck and play dead. If a bear continues biting you after you have assumed a defensive posture, then you must fight back vigorously.

Some people carry guns to fend off bear charges, but firearms should never be used as an alternative to common-sense approaches to bear encounters. Shooting a charging bear is a skilled operation if you are a good shot, a foolish one if you are not. You must drop the bear with one or two shots, as a wounded bear is extremely dangerous.

Other people are turning to defensive aerosol sprays that contain red pepper extract. These sprays cost $40 to $50 each and have been used with some success for protection against bears. They are effective at a range of 6 to 8 yards but must be discharged downwind. If not, you will just disable yourself.

Security

Due to a lack of large cities, Alaska is basically a safe place to carry your money, credit cards and traveler's checks. Employ common sense and be careful when moving through normally busy places like airport terminals. Don't flaunt your money when making a purchase and avoid placing a wallet in your back pocket. Always keep some money stashed away in another location just in case you do lose your wallet or purse.

DISCOUNTS

There are discounts to be mined in Alaska but you have to dig a little deeper than the rest of the country. Children do the best, often receiving discounted prices for transportation, entry fees, restaurants and even lodging. For further details see the Alaska for Families chapter (p39).

Seniors citizens and, to a lesser extent, students can also find discounts. For example, most museums, parks and major attractions will offer reduced rates to seniors and students, but most accommodations, restaurants and small tour companies will not. The reason is simple economics: for most businesses the tourist season is too short and competition for rooms, tours or charters too high to be handing out discounts.

Senior Cards

The best seniors card for US travelers to carry is the one issued by the **American Association of Retired Persons** (AARP; ☎ 888-687-2277; www.aarp.org), which can be obtained for $12.50 if you're over the age of 50 (you don't even need to be retired).

Student & Youth Cards

For student discounts your university identification is the best thing to have. The demise of Hostelling International in Alaska – there is now only one sanctioned hostel – makes its HI card of little use in the far north. It's worth purchasing an ISIC card before traveling to Alaska.

EMBASSIES & CONSULATES

International travelers needing to locate the US embassy in their home country should visit the **US Department of State website** (http://usembassy.state.gov), which has links to all of them.

There are no embassies in Alaska, but there are a handful of foreign consulates in Anchorage to assist overseas travelers with unusual problems:

Denmark (☎ 907-276-1221; Ste 610, 425 G St)
Germany (☎ 907-274-6537; Ste 650, 425 G St)
Japan (☎ 907-562-8424; Ste 1300, 3601 C St)
Norway (☎ 907-279-6942; Ste 105, 203 W 15th Ave)
UK (☎ 907-786-4848; Room 362, 2311 Providence Dr)

FESTIVALS & EVENTS

The vast majority of Alaskan festivals and special events, such as fishing derbies, take place during the summer and locals welcome visitors to their parties with open arms. For an extensive list of festivals in Alaska see p26.

FOOD

Many travelers are surprised that food prices in a Fairbanks or Anchorage supermarket are not that much higher than what they're paying at home. Then they visit their first restaurant and a glance at the menu sends them into a two-day fast. Alaskan restaurants are more expensive than most other places in the country because of the short tourist season and the high labor costs for waiters and chefs.

In this book, restaurant prices usually refer to an average main dish at dinner and do not include drinks, appetizers, dessert or tips. Restaurants can be divided into budget, midrange and upscale. Dinner is an under-$10 affair in a budget café, $10 to $27 in a midrange restaurant and usually $27 and higher at an upscale place. Refer to the Food & Drink chapter (p62) for more details on eating in Alaska.

GAY & LESBIAN TRAVELERS

The gay community in Alaska is far smaller and much less open than in major US cities, and Alaskans in general are not as tolerant to diversity. In 1998 Alaska, along with Hawaii, passed a constitutional amendment banning same-sex marriages.

In Anchorage, the only city in Alaska of any real size, you have **Identity Inc** (☎ 907-929-4528; www.identityinc.org), which has a gay and lesbian helpline, and even some openly gay clubs and bars (see p202). The **Southeast Alaska Gay & Lesbian Alliance** (www.seagla.org) is based in Juneau and offers links and travel information to visitors. **Delta V** (http://dv-8.com) is also quite useful for travelers and offers, among other things, a list of gay, lesbian, bisexual and transgender organizations throughout Alaska. The list is short, however, because most towns do not have an openly active gay community. In rural Alaska, same-sex couples should exercise discretion.

HOLIDAYS

Public holidays for Alaskan residents, which may involve state and federal offices being closed, bus services curtailed, and shop and store hours reduced, include the following:

New Year's Day January 1
Martin Luther King Day Third Monday in January
Presidents' Day Third Monday in February
Seward's Day Last Monday in March
Easter Sunday in late March or early April
Memorial Day Last Monday in May
Independence Day (aka Fourth of July) July 4
Labor Day First Monday in September
Columbus Day Second Monday in October
Alaska Day October 18
Veterans' Day November 11
Thanksgiving Day Fourth Thursday in November
Christmas Day December 25

INSURANCE

A travel insurance policy to cover theft, loss and medical problems is a smart investment. Coverage depends on your insurance and type of ticket but should cover delays by striking employees or company actions, or a cancellation of a trip. Such coverage may seem expensive but it's nowhere near the price of a trip to Alaska or the cost of a medical emergency in the USA.

Some policies offer lower and higher medical-expense options; the higher ones are chiefly for countries such as the USA, which have extremely high medical costs. There is a wide variety of medical and emergency repatriation policies and it's important to talk to your health-care provider for recommendations. See the Health chapter (p442) for more information.

For insurance on car rentals see p439.

Worldwide travel insurance is available through the **Lonely Planet website** (www.lonelyplanet.com/bookings/insurance). You can buy, extend and claim online anytime – even if you're already on the road. The following companies also offer travel insurance:

Access America (☎ 800-284-8300; www.accessamerica.com)
Insuremytrip.com (800-487-4722; www.insuremytrip.com)
Travel Guard (☎ 800-826-4919; www.travelguard.com)

INTERNET ACCESS

It's easy to surf the net, make online reservations or retrieve email in Alaska. Most towns, even the smallest ones, have internet access at libraries, hotels and internet cafés. Access ranges from free at the library and from $5 to $10 an hour at internet cafés. If you are hauling around a laptop, wi-fi is common in Alaska at bookstores, motels, coffee shops, airport terminals and even bars. This guide uses the internet icon (💻) when accommodations offer either an internet terminal or wireless internet access. Ask exactly what is offered when reserving a room. If you're not from the US, remember you will need an AC adapter and a plug adapter for US sockets.

For the best websites for travelers headed for Alaska see the Getting Started chapter (p25).

LEGAL MATTERS

Despite the history of marijuana in Alaska – it was once legal for personal use – possession of small amounts is now a misdemeanor punishable by up to 90 days in jail and a $1000 fine. The use of other drugs is also against the law, resulting in severe penalties, especially for cocaine, which is heavily abused in Alaska.

The minimum drinking age in Alaska is 21 and a government-issued photo ID (passport or drivers license) will be needed if a bartender questions your age. Alcohol abuse is also a problem in Alaska, and it's a serious offence if you are caught driving under the influence of alcohol (DUI). The blood alcohol limit in Alaska is 0.08% and the penalty for a DUI is a three-month driver's license revocation, at least three days in jail and a $1500 fine.

If you are stopped by the police for any reason while driving, remember there is no system of paying on-the-spot fines and bribery is not something that works in Alaska. For traffic violations the officer will explain your options to you and violations, such as speeding, can often be handled through the mail with a credit card.

MAPS

Unlike many places in the world, Alaska has no shortage of accurate maps. There are detailed US Geological Survey (USGS) topographical maps to almost every corner of the state, even though most of it is still wilderness, while every visitor center has free city and road maps that are more than adequate to get from one town to the next. For free downloadable maps and driving directions there is **Google Maps** (maps.google.com).

For trekking in the backcountry and in wilderness areas, the USGS topographic maps are worth the $6-per-quad cost. USGS topo maps come in a variety of scales, but hikers prefer the smallest scale of 1:63,360, with each inch equal to a mile. Canoeists and other river runners can get away with the 1:250,000 map.

In Anchorage the **USGS Earth Science Information Center** (☎ 907-786-7011; Grace Bldg, Alaska Pacific University; 🕓 8:30am-4:30pm Mon-Fri) has topo maps for the entire state. You can also order maps in advance directly from **USGS** (☎ 888-275-8747; www.usgs.gov) or you can view and order custom topo maps from cartography websites such as **Trails.com** (www.trails.com) or **Mytopo** (☎ 406-294-9411, 877-587-9004; www.mytopo.com). GPS units and accompanying mapping software that includes Alaska are available from **Garmin** (www.garmin.com) and **DeLorme** (www.delorme.com).

MONEY

All prices quoted in this book are in US dollars unless otherwise stated. US coins come in denominations of 1¢ (penny), 5¢ (nickel), 10¢ (dime), 25¢ (quarter) and the seldom seen 50¢

(half dollar). Quarters are the most commonly used coins in vending machines and parking meters, so it's handy to have a stash of them. Notes, commonly called bills, come in $1, $2, $5, $10, $20, $50 and $100 denominations. Keep in mind that the Canadian system is also dollars and cents but is a separate currency. For exchange rates, see the inside front cover.

ATMs

In Alaska ATMs are everywhere: banks, gas stations, supermarkets, airports and even some visitor centers. At most ATMs you can use a credit card (Visa, MasterCard etc), a debit card or an ATM card that is linked to the Plus or Cirrus ATM networks. There is generally a fee ($1 to $3) for withdrawing cash from an ATM, but the exchange rate on transactions is usually as good if not better than what you'll get from anywhere else.

Cash

Hard cash still works. It may not be the safest way to carry funds, but nobody will hassle you when you purchase something with US dollars. Most businesses along the Alcan in Canada will also take US dollars though they might burn you on the exchange rate.

Credit Cards

There are probably some isolated stores somewhere in Alaska that don't accept credit cards, but not many. Like in the rest of the USA, Alaskan merchants are ready and willing to accept just about all major credit cards. Visa and MasterCard are the most widely accepted cards, but American Express and Discovery are also widely used.

Places that accept Visa and MasterCard are also likely to accept debit cards. If you are an overseas visitor, check with your bank at home to confirm that your debit card will be accepted in the USA.

Moneychangers

Banks are the best place to exchange foreign currencies as the exchange counters at the airports typically have poorer rates. **Wells Fargo** (☎ 800-956-4442; www.wellsfargo.com), the nation's sixth largest bank, is the dominant player in Alaska with more than 400 branches, 13 in Anchorage alone. Wells Fargo can meet the needs of most visitors, including changing currency and offering 24-hour ATMs. You can usually count on banks being open 10am to 5pm Monday to Friday, with a few open on Saturday.

Tipping

Tipping in Alaska, like in the rest of the USA, is expected. The going rate for restaurants, hotels and taxis is about 15%. It is also common for visitors to tip guides, whether it is a bus tour, a glacier trek or a white-water raft trip. If you forget, don't worry: they'll remind you.

Traveler's Checks

Although slowly becoming obsolete thanks to ATMs, the other way to carry your funds is the time-honored method of traveler's checks. The popular brands of US traveler's checks, such as American Express and Visa, are widely used around the state and will be readily cashed at any store, motel or bank in the major tourist areas of Alaska.

PHOTOGRAPHY

The most cherished items you can take home from your trip are photos of Alaska's powerful scenery. Much of the state is a photographer's dream, and your shutter finger will be set clicking by mountain and glacier panoramas, bustling waterfronts and the diverse wildlife encountered during paddling and hiking trips.

A compact, fixed-lens, point-and-shoot digital camera is OK for a summer of backpacking in the North Country, but if you want to get serious about photography, you need either a 35mm digital camera with interchangeable lenses, at least 6 megapixels and zoom capabilities. To photograph wildlife in its natural state, a 135mm or larger telephoto lens is required to make the animal the main object in the picture. Any lens larger than 135mm on a film camera will probably also require a tripod to eliminate camera shake, especially during low-light conditions. A wide-angle lens of 35mm, or better still 28mm, adds considerable dimension to scenic views, and a fast (f1.2 or f1.4) 50mm 'normal' lens will provide you with more opportunities for pictures during weak light.

If you want simplicity, check out the latest zoom lenses. They are much more compact than they have been in the past and provide a sharpness that's more than acceptable to most amateur photographers. A zoom for a digital camera from 18mm to 150mm is ideal and many camera companies, including Nikon and Canon, now offer vibration reduction (VR), which increases sharpness by reducing camera shake.

In the cities and major towns you can turn your digital photos into prints or have them burned onto a CD at self-serve photo counters in drugstores, large supermarkets and chains like Walmart and Fred Meyer. The same places usually also have one-hour film processing, charging around $9 for a roll of 24 exposures. Film is readily available in Alaska and in cities and large towns will cost $10 to $12 for a roll of 36 exposures depending on the speed and type.

For more on cameras and photography read Lonely Planet's *Travel Photography* book.

POST

The **US Postal Service** (☎ 800-275-8777; www.usps.com) is one of the world's busiest and most reliable, but even it needs another day or two to get letters and postcards to and from Alaska. With an abundance of internet cafés and the availability of internet at libraries and hostels and hotels, think email for quick notes to friends and family. For packages, especially heavy ones, it's faster to use private carriers in Alaska such as **United Parcel Service** (☎ 800-742-5877; www.ups.com) or **Federal Express** (☎ 800-463-3339; www.fedex.com).

Sending & Receiving Mail

For travelers, especially those from overseas, tripping through Canada into Alaska, it's best to wait until you're in the USA to mail home packages. Generally, you'll find the US postal service is less expensive and much faster than its Canadian counterpart.

To receive mail while traveling in Alaska, have it sent c/o General Delivery to a post office along your route. You can receive mail at any post office that has its own five-digit zip (postal) code. Mail is usually held for 30 days before it's returned to sender; you might request your correspondents to write 'hold for arrival' on their letters.

Although everybody passes through Anchorage (zip code 99501), it's probably better to have mail sent to smaller towns like Ketchikan, Seward or Delta Junction. Zip codes for any Alaskan town can be found on the US Postal Service website.

SHOPPING

Alaska is knee deep in gift shops, often selling terrifically tacky items. Moose nuggets will be seen from one end of the state to the other, but even if they are varnished, you have to wonder who is going to wear earrings or a necklace made of animal scat. Gold-nugget jewelry is another prevalent item, but more interesting and much more affordable is what is commonly called Arctic opal. This blue and greenish stone was uncovered in the Wrangell Mountains in the late 1980s, and is now set in silver in a variety of earrings, pins and other pieces.

Want a keepsake T-shirt or jacket? Avoid the gift shops in Anchorage and Fairbanks and head for the bookstores at the University of Alaska campuses, which have an interesting selection of clothing that you won't find anywhere else.

Authentic Alaska Native–carved pieces, whether in ivory, jade or soapstone, are exquisite, highly prized and expensive. A 6-in carving of soapstone, a soft stone that indigenous people in western Alaska carve and polish, costs $150 to $300, depending on the carving and the detail. Jade and ivory will cost even more, up to $100 per inch in a carving. When shopping for such artwork, be especially conscious of who you are purchasing from. Non-Native art, sometimes carved in places as far away as Bali, is often passed off and priced as Alaska Native–produced. It is legal for Alaska Natives to produce and sell ivory work, which they obtain from the tusks of walruses that they hunt for food. Before purchasing such a piece make sure your country allows it through customs.

If you're considering investing in Native art look for the Silver Hand label, guaranteeing the item was made by an Alaska Native artist. For other art and items that are made by non–Alaska Natives, the state has created a Made In Alaska logo with a polar bear on it. For more on Native art see p58.

SOLO TRAVELERS

Maybe it's that Klondike spirit of adventure or the lack of large cities, but solo travelers are common in Alaska. Such travelers will find it easy to strike up conversations with locals in small towns, with waitstaff if they grab a stool at the counter and with bartenders if they're sitting alone at the bar. Hostels receive a large influx of solo travelers during the summer and the openness of campgrounds lends itself well to meeting other travelers. Women in particular will book nights at established B&Bs, knowing they will find friendly conversation, a sense of security and a lot of local knowledge and contacts.

The main concern of most solo travelers in Alaska is how safe is hiking, backpacking or paddling alone in the wilderness. This will depend on your skill level and where you're headed. There are lots of solo hikers every summer on the popular Chilkoot Trail (p91), but not nearly as many trekking through some remote national park in the Arctic. If you do decide to go solo in the wilderness, leave a detailed itinerary with the park service or the bush pilot dropping you off and seriously consider carrying some type of communication like an emergency two-way radio. An even better plan is to hook-up with an outfitter on a guided trip (p440) where most likely you'll meet other solo travelers.

TELEPHONE

Cell Phones

Cell phones work in Alaska and Alaskans (especially teenagers) love them as much as anywhere else in the USA. When calling home or locally in cities and towns reception is excellent but overall, in a state this large, cell phone coverage can be unpredictable and sporadic at times. Many injured climbers have been plucked off mountains in the middle of nowhere after calling for help on their cell phone. But drive north of Auke Bay in Juneau and it's hard to use your cell phone to make a dinner reservation downtown. The culprits in many cases are mountains.

Most travelers still find their cell phones to be more useful than not. Before you head north, however, check your cell phone provider's roaming agreements and black-out areas.

Phone Codes

Telephone area codes are simple in Alaska: the entire state shares 907, except Hyder, which uses 250. In this guidebook, the area code is always 907, unless a different one is listed before the phone number. Phone numbers that begin with 800, 877 and 866 are toll-free numbers and there is no charge for using one to call a hotel or tour operator. If you're calling from abroad the country code for the USA is ☎ 1.

Phonecards

Every little town and village in Alaska has public pay phones that you can use to call home if you have a phone card or a stack of quarters. There's a wide range of phone cards sold in amounts of $5, $10 and $20, and they are available at airports and in many convenience stores and internet cafés. The best way to make international calls is to first purchase a phonecard.

TIME

With the exception of several Aleutian Island communities and Hyder, a small community on the Alaskan/British Columbian border, the entire state shares the same time zone, Alaska Time, which is one hour earlier than Pacific Standard Time – the zone in which Seattle, Washington, falls. When it is noon in Anchorage, it is 4pm in New York, 9pm in London and 7am the following day in Melbourne, Australia. Although there is a movement to abolish it, Alaska still has Daylight Saving Time when, like most of the country, the state sets clocks back one hour in November and forward one hour in March.

TOURIST INFORMATION

The first place to contact when planning your adventure is the **Alaska Travel Industry Association** (ATIA; ☎ 907-929-2200; www.travelalaska.com), the state's tourism marketing arm. From the ATIA you can request a copy of the *Alaska Vacation Planner*, an annually updated magazine; a state highway map; and schedules for the Alaska Marine Highway ferry service.

Travel information is easy to obtain once you are on the road, as almost every city, town and village has a tourist contact center, whether it is a visitor center, a chamber of commerce or a hut near the ferry dock. These places are good sources of free maps, information on local accommodations, and directions to the nearest campground or hiking trail.

Most trips to Alaska pass through one of the state's three largest cities. All have large visitors bureaus that will send out city guides in advance:

Anchorage Convention & Visitors Bureau (☎ 907-276-4118; www.anchorage.net)

Fairbanks Convention & Visitors Bureau (☎ 907-456-5774, 800-327-5774; www.explorefairbanks.com)

Juneau Convention & Visitors Bureau (☎ 907-586-1737, 800-587-2201; www.traveljuneau.com)

TOURS

Because of the size of the state and its distance from the rest of the country, Alaska is the land of cruise ships and packaged tours. For information on tours, including companies that handle specialized activities such as biking and wilderness trips, see the Transportation chapter (p438).

TRAVELERS WITH DISABILITIES

Thanks to the American Disabilities Act, many state and federal parks have installed wheelchair-accessible sites and rest rooms in their campgrounds. You can call the **Alaska Public Lands Information Center** (☎ 907-271-2599) to receive a map and campground guide to such facilities. The Alaska Marine Highway ferries, the Alaska Railroad, and many bus services and cruise ships are also equipped with wheelchair lifts and ramps to make their facilities easier to access. Chain motels and large hotels in cities and town often have rooms set up for disabled guests, while some wilderness guiding companies such as Alaska Discovery (p440) are experienced in handling wheelchair-bound clients on rafting and kayaking expeditions.

The following organizations may be useful when planning your trip:

Access Alaska (☎ 907-248-4777; www.accessalaska.org) Includes statewide tourist information on accessible services and sites.

Access-Able Travel Source (www.access-able.com) A national organization with an excellent website featuring travel information and links.

Challenge Alaska (☎ 907-344-7399; www.challengealaska.org) A non-profit organization dedicated to providing recreation opportunities for those with disabilities.

Flying Wheels Travel (☎ 877-451-5006; www.flyingwheelstravel.com) A full-service travel agency specializing in disabled travel.

Society for Accessible Travel & Hospitality (☎ 212-447-7284; www.sath.org) Lobbies for better facilities and publishes *Open World* magazine.

VISAS

Since 9/11, the US has continually fine-tuned its national security guidelines and entry requirements. Double-check current visa and passport regulations before arriving in the USA and apply for visas early to avoid delays. Overseas travelers may need one visa, possibly two. For citizens of many countries a US visa is required, while if you're taking the Alcan or the Alaska Marine Highway ferry from Prince Rupert in British Columbia, you may also need a Canadian visa. The Alcan begins in Canada, requiring travelers to pass from the USA into Canada and back into the USA again.

Canadians entering the USA must have proof of Canadian citizenship, such as a passport; visitors from countries in the Visa Waiver Program (see p432) may not need a visa. Visitors from all other countries need to have a US visa and a valid passport. On the website of the **US State Department** (www.travel.state.gov) there is a 'Temporary Visas to the US' page with tips on how and where to apply for a visa and what to do if you're denied.

Note that overseas travelers should be aware of the process to re-enter the USA. Sometimes visitors get stuck in Canada due to their single-entry visa into the USA, used up when passing through the Lower 48. Canadian immigration officers often caution people whom they feel might have difficulty returning to the USA. More information about visa and other requirements for entering Canada is available on the website of the **Canada Border Services Agency** (www.cbsa-asfc.gc.ca).

Visa Application

Apart from Canadians and those entering under the Visa Waiver Program, foreign visitors need to obtain a visa from a US consulate or embassy. Most applicants must now schedule a personal interview, to which you need to bring all your documentation and proof of fee payment. Wait times for interviews vary, but afterward, barring problems, visa issuance takes from a few days to a few weeks. If concerned about a delay, check the US State Department website, which provides a list of wait times calculated by country.

Your passport must be valid for at least six months longer than your intended stay in the USA. You'll need a recent photo (2in by 2in) and you must pay a $100 processing fee, plus in a few cases an additional visa issuance fee (check the State Department website for details). In addition to the main non-immigration visa application form (DS-156), all men aged 16 to 45 must complete an additional form (DS-157) that details their travel plans.

Visa applicants are required to show documentation of financial stability, a round-trip or onward ticket and 'binding obligations' that will ensure their return home, such as family ties, a home or a job.

WORKING IN ALASKA

Opportunities for astronomical wages for employment on the Trans-Alaska Pipeline and other high-paying jobs are, unfortunately, either exaggerated or nonexistent today. Alaska usually has the highest unemployment rate in the country. In 2008 unemployment was 6.9% and as high as 20% in small towns during the winter.

If you are a US citizen or have a green card, finding some kind of work during the summer is usually not a problem, but be realistic about what you will be paid and look in the right places.

If you have access to the internet, you can get a list with descriptions of job openings at the **Alaska Department of Labor & Workforce Development** (www.labor.state.ak.us). These positions are located across the state and descriptions include education requirements, salary and contract address. You'll find jobs in the online classified ads of Alaska's largest newspapers: *Anchorage Daily News* (www.adn.com), *Fairbanks News Miner* (www.news-miner.com) and the *Juneau Empire* (www.juneauempire.com).

Once in the state, you can stop at one of the **Alaska Job Centers** (☎ 877-724-2539; www.jobs.state.ak.us/offices/index.html) run by the Department of Labor. There are 22 centers in Alaska, including four in Anchorage. Check the department's website for addresses and phone numbers.

Seafood Industry

July is the month to hang around the harbors looking for a fishing boat desperate for help, and the best cities to be in are Kodiak, Cordova, Dillingham and Dutch Harbor, where boats are based that work the fish runs in Prince William Sound and Bristol Bay; or Ketchikan, Petersburg and Sitka for boats that work the Southeast. Deckhands and crewmembers usually earn a percentage of the catch. Occasionally they are paid hourly rates from $11 to $13 an hour. Keep in mind, however, that without any previous experience you're always the last to be noticed.

Finding cannery work is more probable, as most positions don't require experience and burnout is common in this trade. Seafood processors and fillers at canneries earn between $8 and $11 an hour and work eight to 12 hours a day, seven days a week, when the fish are in. On the slime line you have to endure working in cold, wet conditions and be physically able to stand on your feet for long hours. It is possible to obtain work by simply showing up at canneries and inquiring, but if this is what your heart is set on, try to land a job in advance of arriving in Alaska. Begin by contacting the seafood giants such as **Unisea** (www.unisea.com), **Trident Seafoods** (www.tridentseafoods.com) or **Icicle Seafoods** (www.icicleseafoods.com) as all of them list job opportunities in their Alaskan cold storage and processing plants.

Visa Waiver Program

The Visa Waiver Program (VWP) lets citizens of some countries go to the USA for tourism purposes for up to 90 days without having a US visa. Currently there are 27 participating countries in the VWP, including Austria, Australia, Belgium, Denmark, Finland, France, Germany, Iceland, Ireland, Italy, Japan, the Netherlands, New Zealand, Norway, Spain, Sweden, Switzerland and the UK.

Under the program you *must* have a round-trip or onward ticket that is nonrefundable in the USA, a machine-readable passport (with two lines of letters, numbers and <<< along the bottom of the passport information page) and be able to show evidence of financial solvency.

As of 2009, citizens of VWP countries must register online with the US Department of Homeland Security at https://esta.cbp.dhs.gov at least 72 hours before their visit; once travel authorization is approved, registration is valid for two years.

VOLUNTEERING

For many travelers the only way to enjoy Alaska is to volunteer. You won't get paid, but you're often given room, board and work in a spectacular setting. Most volunteer roles are with federal or state agencies. The **Bureau of Land Management** (BLM; ☎ 907-271-5960; www.ak.blm.gov) uses hundreds of volunteers annually who serve as campground hosts, staff the Arctic Interagency Visitor's Center in Coldfoot or conduct botanical inventories.

Alaska State Parks (☎ 907-269-8708; www.alaskastateparks.org) also offers a wide range of volunteer positions that include ranger assistants, natural history interpreters, and trail crew workers where you can easily spend most

Tourism

At resorts you can seek out work as a dishwasher, housekeeper, chef or janitor. Bartenders average $10 to $12 an hour, waiters $7 to $10, but both benefit from tips, which can more than double their salary during the short, intense Alaskan tourist season. There is also a need for food preparation workers ($11 to $13) and cooks ($12 to $17), as well as bus drivers ($10 to $12), tour directors ($8 to $10) and guides (anywhere from $12 per hour to $200 per day) for various outdoor activities such as hiking and rafting. At remote lodges and resorts part of the pay is cheap or even free housing.

You can arrange these positions in advance by logging on to the **Alaska Labor Exchange System** (ALEXsys; alexsys.labor.state.ak.us) and clicking on the region that you're interested in and the industry (ie Accommodation & Food Service). Or you can contact these large tour companies in advance:

Alaska Travel Adventures (☎ 907-789-0052; www.alaskaadventures.com)
Alaska Wildland Adventures (☎ 907-783-2928; www.alaskawildland.com)
Cruise West (☎ 888-851-8133; www.cruisewest.com)
Denali & Glacier Bay National Parks (☎ 907-264-4628; www.coolworks.com/aramarkak)
Gray Line of Alaska (☎ 208-281-3535; www.graylineofalaska.com)
Princess Tours (☎ 907-550-7711; www.princesslodges.com)

Government

With so much land controlled by various government agencies there are certainly seasonal job opportunities in Alaska's parks and national lands. The **US Forest Service** (www.fs.fed.us/r10), **National Park Service** (www.nps.gov/personnel), **Bureau of Land Management** (www.ak.blm.gov) and **US Fish & Wildlife Service** (www.fws.gov) offer numerous temporary positions during the summer from forestry technician to visitor information center assistants. Most are described in brief on the agency websites, but for more detail or to apply you need to log onto **USAJOBS** (www.usajobs.opm.gov), the official job site for the federal government.

There are also temporary positions available at Alaska state parks, which could range from laboring on a trail crew to working as a park assistant. Take a look at the **Alaska Department of Natural Resources** (www.dnr.state.ak.us) or **Alaska Job Center Network** (www.jobs.state.ak.us) websites.

of your vacation in the mountains repairing paths. For other volunteer opportunities contact:

Chugach National Forest (☎ 907-743-9500; www.fs.fed.us/r10/chugach)
Student Conservation Association (☎ 603-543-1700; www.thesca.org)
Tongass National Forest (☎ 907-225-3101; www.fs.fed.us/r10/tongass)

WOMEN TRAVELERS

While most violent crime rates are lower here than elsewhere in the USA, women should be careful at night in unfamiliar neighborhoods in cities like Anchorage and Fairbanks or when hitching alone. Use common sense; don't be afraid to say no to lifts. If camping alone, have pepper spray and know how to use it.

The excellent **Alaska Women's Network** (www.alaskawomensnetwork.org) has listings of women-owned B&Bs and travel agencies across the state. **Arctic Ladies** (☎ 907-783-1954, 877-783-1954; www.arcticladies.com) arranges women-only trips. The **Anchorage Planned Parenthood Clinic** (☎ 907-563-2229; 4001 Lake Otis Pkwy) offers contraceptives, medical advice and services.

Transportation

CONTENTS

GETTING THERE & AWAY

For some travelers getting to Alaska can be half their trip. By sea it would take you almost a week on the Alaska Marine Highway ferry to reach Whittier in Prince William Sound from the Lower 48. By land a motorist in the Midwest needs 10 days to drive straight to Fairbanks. Traveling to Alaska is like traveling to a foreign country.

If you're coming from the US mainland, the quickest, and least expensive, way to reach Alaska is to fly nonstop from a number of cities. If you're coming from Asia or Europe, it's almost impossible to fly directly to Alaska as few international airlines maintain a direct service to Anchorage. Today most international travelers come through the gateway cities of Seattle, Los Angeles, Minneapolis and Vancouver to Alaska.

ENTERING THE COUNTRY

Since the 9/11 terrorist attacks, air travel in the USA has changed and you can now expect vigilant baggage screening procedures and personal searches. In short, you're going to have to take your shoes off. Non-US citizens, especially residents from Middle Eastern and Asian countries, should be prepared for an exhaustive questioning process at immigration.

The process is not as time-consuming as it was in the years immediately following the attacks and once finished most visitors will be allowed into the country. Crossing the border into Alaska from Canada used to be a relaxed process – US citizens often passed across with just a driver's license. Now this process has also become more complicated, and all travelers can expect more substantial questioning and possible vehicle searches.

Passport

If you are traveling to Alaska from overseas, you need a passport. Even Canadian citizens should carry one, as a driver's license alone may not be enough to satisfy customs officials. If you are a US resident passing through Canada you will need a passport to re-enter the USA. Make sure your passport does not expire during the trip, and if you are entering the USA through the Visa Waiver Program (VWP) you *must* have a machine-readable passport. For more on VWP or visas see p431. If you are traveling with children, it's best to bring a photocopy of their birth certificates.

AIR

Airports

The vast majority of visitors to Alaska, and almost all international flights, fly into **Ted Stevens Anchorage International Airport** (ANC; ☎ 266-2526; www.dot.state.ak.us/anc). International flights arrive at the north terminal; domestic flights arrive at the south terminal and a complimentary shuttle service runs between the two every 15 minutes. You'll find bus serv-

THINGS CHANGE...

The information in this chapter is particularly vulnerable to change. Check directly with the airline or a travel agent to make sure you understand how a fare (and ticket you may buy) works and be aware of the security requirements for international travel. Shop carefully. The details given in this chapter should be regarded as pointers and are not a substitute for your own careful, up-to-date research.

CLIMATE CHANGE & TRAVEL

Climate change is a serious threat to the ecosystems that humans rely upon, and air travel is the fastest-growing contributor to the problem. Lonely Planet regards travel, overall, as a global benefit, but believes we all have a responsibility to limit our personal impact on global warming.

Flying & Climate Change

Pretty much every form of motor travel generates CO_2 (the main cause of human-induced climate change) but planes are far and away the worst offenders, not just because of the sheer distances they allow us to travel, but because they release greenhouse gases high into the atmosphere. The statistics are frightening: two people taking a return flight between Europe and the US will contribute as much to climate change as an average household's gas and electricity consumption over a whole year.

Carbon Offset Schemes

Climatecare.org and other websites use 'carbon calculators' that allow jetsetters to offset the greenhouse gases they are responsible for with contributions to energy-saving projects and other climate-friendly initiatives in the developing world – including projects in India, Honduras, Kazakhstan and Uganda.

Lonely Planet, together with Rough Guides and other concerned partners in the travel industry, supports the carbon offset scheme run by climatecare.org. Lonely Planet offsets all of its staff and author travel.

For more information check out our website: lonelyplanet.com.

ices, taxis and car-rental companies at both terminals. The airport has the usual services, including pay phones, ATMs, currency exchange and free wi-fi. For that 90lb halibut you want to take home there's **baggage and freezer storage** (☎ 248-0373; per bag per day $7) on the ground level of the south terminal.

Airlines

Rising fuel costs have had a profound effect on air travel to Alaska. In 2008 United announced it was withdrawing from the market and many industry observers expect Asian carriers such as Korea Air and China Airlines to follow suit. The recent Delta and Northwest Airlines' merger will no doubt reduce the number of flights the two airlines currently offer and eliminate the Northwest Airlines name when the merger is fully implemented in the future. Airlines providing services Alaska include the following:

Air Canada (AC; ☎ 888-247-2262; www.aircanada.com)
Alaska Airlines (AS; ☎ 800-426-0333; www.alaskaair.com)
American Airlines (AA; ☎ 800-443-7300; www.aa.com)
Asiana Airlines (OZ; ☎ 800-227-4262; http://flyasiana.com)
China Airlines (CI; ☎ 800-227-5118; www.china-airlines.com)
Condor Airlines (DE; ☎ 800-524-6975; www.condor.de, www7.condor.com)
Continental Airlines (CO; ☎ 800-525-0280; www.flycontinental.com)
Delta Air Lines (DL; ☎ 800-221-1212; www.delta.com)
ERA Aviation (7H; ☎ 800-866-8394; www.flyera.com)
Frontier Alaska (2F; ☎ 800-478-6779; www.frontierflying.com)
Korean Air (KE; ☎ 800-438-5000; www.koreanair.com)
Mavial/Magadan Airlines (H5; ☎ 907-248-2994)
Northwest Airlines (NW; ☎ 800-225-2525; www.nwa.com)
PenAir (KS; ☎ 800-448-4226; www.penair.com)
Sun Country Airlines (SY; ☎ 800-359-6786; www.suncountry.com)
US Airways (US; ☎ 800-428-4322; www.usairways.com)

Tickets

Due to its lack of direct and international flights Anchorage, and thus Alaska, is not the most competitive place for airfares. Begin any ticket search by first checking travel websites like **Expedia** (www.expedia.com), **Orbitz** (www.orbitz.com) and **Travelocity** (www.travelocity.com). Check their prices against the websites of airlines that service Alaska, particularly **Alaska Airlines** (www.alaskaair.com), as it often has internet specials offered nowhere else. While the internet is a great way to comparison shop, you should still call the airline's sales representatives as they know how to modify the ticket (and lower its price) by changing departure days or rerouting stopovers. Beware that booking a ticket with a real, live person comes with an additional $10 to $25 fee.

For a good overview of online ticket agencies and lists of travel agents worldwide, visit **Airinfo** (www.airinfo.aero).

Asia

There is a nonstop service from Seoul to Anchorage flying with Korean Airlines and Asiana Airlines. There is also a daily nonstop service between Taipei and Anchorage with China Air. Northwest Airlines has a number of one-stop flights from Tokyo to Anchorage, changing planes in either Seattle or Portland.

Agents serving Asia:

Concorde Travel Hong Kong (☎ 852-2526-3391; www.concorde-travel.com)
STA Travel Singapore (☎ 65-6737-7188; www.statravel.com.sg); Japan (☎ 03-5391-2922; www.statravel.co.jp)

Australia & New Zealand

Air Canada has one-stop flights through San Francisco and Vancouver. Qantas has flights from Sydney to Los Angeles with direct connections on Alaska Airlines to Anchorage. Air New Zealand has a similar agreement with Alaska Airlines.

AUSTRALIA

Flight Centre (☎ 1300-133-133; www.flightcentre.com.au)
STA Travel (☎ 1300-134-782; www.statravel.com.au)

NEW ZEALAND

Flight Centre (☎ 0800-2435-44; www.flightcentre.co.nz)
STA Travel (☎ 0800-474-400; www.statravel.co.nz)

Canada

During the summer Air Canada flies nonstop from Vancouver to Anchorage, as does Alaska Airlines. For most Canadians it is far cheaper to fly on a US airline, such as Northwest, changing planes at its hubs in Minneapolis or Detroit, then continuing on to Anchorage. Another option is to fly to Whitehorse and then fly **Air North** (in Canada ☎ 800-661-0407; www.flyairnorth.com) to Fairbanks.

Agents serving Canada:

Travel Cuts (☎ 866-246-9762; www.travelcuts.com)
Travelocity (☎ 877-282-2925; www.travelocity.ca)

Continental Europe

You can book a one-stop flight from Europe but often the best fares are reached by booking multi-stops on two or more carriers. From Paris, Northwest has a daily flight to Anchorage during summer, with a change of planes in Detroit. Similar flights can be arranged from Frankfurt through American Airlines and Delta, while Northwest Airlines offers a one-stop flight from Amsterdam. Check out **Condor** (☎ 180-5-707202; www7.condor.com), a charter air operation that offers a nonstop, weekly service to Anchorage and Fairbanks from Frankfurt from May to October.

FRANCE

Nouvelles Frontieres (☎ 0825-000-747; www.nouvelles-frontieres.fr)
Voyages Wasteels (☎ 01-55-82-32-33; www.wasteels.fr)

GERMANY

Just Travel (☎ 089-747-3330; www.justtravel.de)
STA Travel (☎ 069-743-032-92; www.statravel.de)

UK & Ireland

Continental Airlines has London–Anchorage flights that require you to change planes in Houston. Delta offers a similar flight, changing planes in Cincinnati.

Travel agencies serving the UK and Ireland:

Ebookers (☎ 0800-082-3000; www.ebookers.com)
STA Travel (☎ 0870-2300-040; www.statravel.co.uk)
Travel Bag (☎ 0800-804-8911; www.travelbag.co.uk)

USA

Seattle serves as the major hub for flights into Alaska. Alaska Airlines owns the lion's share of the market with 20 flights per day to Anchorage as well as direct flights to Ketchikan, Juneau and Fairbanks. United, Delta, American, Northwest and Continental all offer Seattle–Anchorage flights.

You can also book a nonstop flight to Anchorage from a number of other US cities. Northwest Airlines flies nonstop from Minneapolis and Detroit. Delta flies in from Atlanta and Salt Lake City. Continental flies nonstop from Houston. American Airlines arrives in Anchorage from San Francisco, Los Angeles, Denver and Dallas; US Airways from Chicago, Phoenix, Las Vegas and Denver; and Sun Country from Minneapolis. Alaska

Airlines, naturally, flies nonstop to numerous cities: Atlanta, Salt Lake City, San Francisco, Los Angeles, Denver, Chicago, and Portland, among others.

LAND

What began as the Alaska-Canada Military Hwy is today the Alcan (the Alaska Hwy). This amazing 1390-mile road starts at Dawson Creek in British Columbia, ends at Delta Junction and in between winds through the vast wilderness of northwest Canada and Alaska. For those with the time, the Alcan is a unique journey north. The trip is an adventure in itself: the road is a legend among highways, and completing (or surviving) the drive is a feather in anyone's cap.

There are several ways of traveling the Alcan: bus, car or a combination of Alaska Marine Highway ferry and bus. For the road's history see p48. For more on border crossings see p434 and p431.

Bus

A combination of buses will take you from Seattle via the Alcan to Anchorage, Fairbanks or Skagway, but service is limited, the ride is a very long one and a round-trip on a bus from Seattle to Anchorage is not cheaper than flying. From Seattle, **Greyhound** (☎ 800-661-8747; www.greyhound.com) goes to Whitehorse, a 47- to 52-hour ride depending on the length of transfers. A one-way/round-trip ticket is $181/361 without any discounts. From Whitehorse, **Alaska Direct** (☎ 277-6652, 800-770-6652; www.alaskadirectbusline.com) leaves three days a week for Anchorage for $220.

Car & Motorcycle

Without a doubt, driving your own car to Alaska allows you the most freedom. You can leave when you want, stop where you feel like it and plan your itinerary as you go along. It's not cheap driving to Alaska, and that's not even considering the wear and tear and the thousands of miles you'll put on your vehicle.

The Alcan is now entirely paved and, although sections of jarring potholes, frost heaves (the rippling effect of the pavement caused by freezing and thawing) and loose gravel still exist, the infamous rough conditions of 30 years ago no longer prevail. Food, gas and lodging can be found almost every 20 to 50 miles along the highway, with 100 miles being the longest stretch between fuel stops.

On the Canadian side, you'll find kilometer posts (as opposed to the mileposts found in Alaska), which are placed every 5km after the zero point in Dawson Creek. Most Alcan veterans say 300 miles a day is a good pace – one that will allow for plenty of stops to see the scenery or wildlife.

Along the way, **Tourism Yukon** (☎ 800-661-0494; www.touryukon.com) operates a number of visitor centers stocked with brochures and maps:

Beaver Creek (☎ 867-862-7321; Mile 1202 Alcan)
Haines Junction (☎ 867-634-2345; Kluane National Park Headquarters)
Watson Lake (☎ 867-536-7469; Alcan & Campbell St)
Whitehorse (☎ 867-667-3084; 2nd St & Hanson Ave)

Hitchhiking

Hitchhiking is probably more common in Alaska than it is in the rest of the USA, and more so on rural dirt roads such as the McCarthy Rd and the Denali Hwy than on the major paved routes. Hitchhiking is never entirely safe in any country and we don't recommend it. That said, if you're properly prepared and have sufficient time, thumbing the Alcan can be an easy way to see the country, meet people and save money.

The Alcan seems to inspire the pioneer spirit in travelers who drive along it. Drivers are good about picking up hitchhikers, much better than those across the Lower 48; the only problem is that there aren't enough of them. Any part of the Alcan can be slow, but some sections are notorious. The worst is probably Haines Junction, the crossroads in the Yukon where southbound hitchhikers get stranded trying to thumb a ride to Haines in Southeast Alaska.

If you'd rather not hitchhike the entire Alcan, take the Alaska Marine Highway ferry from Bellingham, WA, to Haines and start hitchhiking from there; you'll cut the journey in half but still travel along the highway's most spectacular parts.

SEA

As an alternative to the Alcan, you can travel the Southeast's Inside Passage. From that maze of a waterway, the **Alaska Marine Highway** (☎ 465-3941, 800-642-0066; www.ferryalaska.com) and cruise ships then cut across the Gulf of Alaska to towns in Prince William Sound. For more on cruising the Far North and selecting a ship see the Cruising in Alaska chapter (p35).

TRANSPORTATION

ORGANIZED TOURS

Package tours can often be the most affordable way to see a large chunk of Alaska, if your needs include the better hotels in each town and a full breakfast every morning. But they move quickly, leaving little time for an all-day hike or other activities.

Companies that offer Alaska packages include the following:

Alaska Heritage Tours (☎ 877-248-6877, 777-2800; www.ahtours.com)
Alaska Wildland Adventures (☎ 800-334-8730; www.alaskawildland.com)
Gray Line (☎ 800-478-6388; www.graylineofalaska.com)
Green Tortoise Alternative Travel (☎ 800-867-8647; www.greentortoise.com)
Knightly Tours (☎ 800-426-2123; www.knightlytours.com)

GETTING AROUND

Traveling around Alaska is unlike traveling in any other US state. The overwhelming distances between regions and the fledgling public transportation system make getting around Alaska almost as hard as it is to get there in the first place. Come with a sense of adventure and be patient!

AIR

As a general rule, if there are regularly scheduled flights to your destination, they will be far cheaper than charter flights on the small airplanes known in Alaska as 'bush planes.' This is especially true for **Alaska Airlines** (☎ 800-426-0333; www.alaskaair.com).

Other regional carriers include:

Era Aviation (☎ 800-866-8394; www.flyera.com) South-central Alaska and Kodiak.
Frontier Alaska (☎ 800-478-6779; www.frontierflying.com) Fairbanks and Arctic Alaska.
PenAir (☎ 800-448-4226; www.penair.com) Aleutian Islands, Alaska Peninsula and Bristol Bay.

Bush Planes

When you want to see more than the roadside attractions, go to a small airfield outside of town and climb into a bush plane. With 75% of the state inaccessible by road, these small, single-engine planes are the backbone of intrastate transport. They carry residents and supplies to desolate areas of the Bush, take anglers to some of the best fishing spots in the country and drop off backpackers in the middle of untouched wilderness.

In the larger cities of Anchorage, Fairbanks, Juneau and Ketchikan, it pays to compare prices before chartering a plane. In most small towns and villages, you'll be lucky if there's a choice. In the regional chapters, bush flights are listed under the town or area where they operate.

Bush aircraft include floatplanes, which land and take off on water, and beachlanders with oversized tires that can use rough gravel shorelines as air strips. Fares vary with the type of plane, its size, the number of passengers and the amount of flying time. On average, chartering a Cessna 185 that can carry three passengers and a limited amount of gear will cost up to $300 to $350 for an hour of flying time. A Cessna 206, a slightly larger plane that will hold four passengers, costs up to $350 to $400, while a Beaver, capable of hauling five passengers with gear, costs on average $450 to $500 an hour. When chartering a plane to drop you off in the wilderness, you must pay for both the air time to your drop-off point and for the return to the departure point.

Double-check all pickup times and places when flying to a wilderness area. Bush pilots fly over the pickup point and if you're not there, they usually return to base, call the authorities and still charge you for the flight. Always schedule extra days around a charter flight. It's not uncommon to be 'socked in' by weather for a day or two until a plane can fly in. Don't panic: they know you're there.

BICYCLE

For those who want to bike it, Alaska offers a variety of cycling adventures on paved roads under the Arctic sun that allows you to peddle until midnight if you want. A bike can be carried on Alaska Marine Highway ferries for an additional fee and is a great way to explore small towns without renting a car.

Most road cyclists avoid gravel, but biking the Alcan (an increasingly popular trip) does involve riding over some gravel breaks in the paved asphalt. Mountain bikers (p77), on the other hand, are in heaven on gravel roads such as Denali Hwy in the Interior.

Anchorage's **Arctic Bicycle Club** (☎ 566-0177; www.arcticbike.org) is Alaska's largest bicycle club and sponsors a wide variety of road-bike and mountain-bike tours during the summer. Its website includes a section on touring Alaska for visiting cyclists.

If you arrive in Alaska without a bike, see the regional chapters for the towns with rentals and expect to pay $30 to $50 a day. Purchasing a bike and selling it at the end of a trip is not something often done by travelers and would only be possible in Anchorage. You can take your bike on the airlines for an excessive luggage fee of $50 per flight or ship it in advance to **Chain Reaction Cycles** (☎ 336-0383; www.chainreactioncycles.us) in Anchorage, which will assemble your bike and hold it until you arrive.

BOAT

Along with the Alaska Marine Highway (p36) the Southeast is served by the **Inter-Island Ferry Authority** (☎ 866-308-4848; www.interislandferry.com), which connects Ketchikan with Prince of Wales Island ($37) and Prince of Wales with Wrangell ($37); and **Haines-Skagway Fast Ferry** (☎ 766-2100, 888-766-2103; www.haineskagwayfastferry.com) servicing Skagway and Haines ($31).

BUS

Regular bus service within Alaska is very limited, and companies come and go with alarming frequency. The following companies have been around for a number of years. All fares are adult one way and do not include a fuel surcharge:

Alaska Direct Bus Line (☎ 277-6652, 800-770-6652; www.alaskadirectbusline.com) Anchorage to Glennallen ($65), Tok ($95), Haines Junction ($195) and Fairbanks ($105).

Alaska Park Connection (☎ 800-266-8625; www.alaskacoach.com) Anchorage to Seward ($56), Denali National Park ($79) and Fairbanks ($112).

Alaska/Yukon Trails (☎ 800-770-7275; www.alaskashuttles.com) Fairbanks to Denali National Park ($46), Anchorage ($91) and Dawson City ($162).

Dalton Highway Express (☎ 474-3555; www.daltonhighwayexpress.com) Fairbanks and Prudhoe Bay ($214).

Homer Stage Line (☎ 399-4429; www.homerstageline.com) Homer with Anchorage ($65) and Seward ($55).

Seward Bus Line (☎ 563-0800; www.sewardbuslines.net) Anchorage and Seward ($50).

Talkeetna Shuttle Service (☎ 733-1725, 888-288-6008; www.denalicentral.com) Anchorage and Talkeetna ($70).

Yukon Alaska Tourist Tours (outside Whitehorse ☎ 866-626-7383, in Whitehorse ☎ 867-668-5944; www.yukonalaskatouristtours.com) Whitehorse and Skagway ($40).

CAR & MOTORCYCLE

Not a lot of roads reach a lot of Alaska but what pavement there is leads to spectacular scenery. That's the best reason to tour the state in a car or motorcycle, whether you arrive with yours or rent one. With personal wheels you can stop and go at will and sneak away from the RVers and tour buses.

Rental & Purchase

For two or more people, car rental is an affordable way to travel, far less expensive than taking a bus or a train. At most rental agencies, you'll need a valid driver's license, a major credit card and you'll also need to be at least 21 years old. It is almost always cheaper to rent in town rather than at the airport because of extra taxes levied on airport rentals. Also be conscious of the per-mile rate of a rental. Add up the mileage you aim to cover and then choose between the 100 free miles per day or the more expensive unlimited mileage plan. Affordable car rental places, such as the following, are always heavily booked during the summer. Try to reserve these vehicles at least a month in advance.

Alaska Car & Van Rentals (☎ 243-4444; www.alaskacarandvan.com; Anchorage)

Denali Car Rental (☎ 800-757-1230; Anchorage)

Rent-A-Wreck (☎ 800-478-1606; Fairbanks)

Valley Car Rental (☎ 775-2880; Wasilla)

MOTORHOME

RVers flock to the land of the midnight sun in astounding numbers. This is the reason why more than a dozen companies, almost all of them based in Anchorage, will rent you a motorhome. Renting a recreational vehicle is so popular you have to reserve them four to five months in advance.

ABC Motorhomes (☎ 800-421-7456; www.abcmotorhome.com)

Alaska Economy RVs (☎ 800-764-4625; www.goalaska.com)

Clippership Motorhome Rentals (☎ 800-421-3456; www.clippershiprv.com)

Great Alaskan Holidays (☎ 888-225-2752; www.greatalaskanholidays.com)

Automobile Associations

AAA (☎ 800-332-6119; www.aaa.com), the most widespread automobile association in the USA, has two offices in Alaska: **Anchorage South Service Center** (☎ 907-344-4310) and **Fairbanks Service Center** (☎ 907-479-4442). Both offer the usual service including maps, discounts and emergency road service.

Fuel & Spare Parts

Gas is widely available on all the main highways and tourist routes in Alaska. In Anchorage and Fairbanks the cost of gas will only be 10¢ to 15¢ per gallon higher than in the rest of the country. Along the Alcan, in Bush communities such as Nome, and at that single gas station on a remote road, they will be shockingly high.

Along heavily traveled roads, most towns will have a car mechanic, though you might have to wait a day for a part to come up from Anchorage. In some small towns, you might be out of luck. For anybody driving to and around Alaska, a full-size spare tire and replacement belts are a must.

Insurance

Liability insurance, which covers damage you may cause to another vehicle, is required when driving in Alaska but not always offered by rental agencies because most Americans are already covered by their regular car insurance. Agencies offer Collision Damage Waiver (CDW) to cover damage to the rental car in case of an accident. This can up the rental fee by $10 to $15 a day and many have deductibles as high as $1000. It's better, and far cheaper, to arrive with rental car insurance obtained through your insurance company, as a member of AAA or as a perk of many credit cards including American Express.

Road Conditions & Hazards

For road conditions, closures and other travel advisories for the Alaska highway system, even while you're driving, contact the state's **Alaska511** (in Alaska ☎ 511, outside Alaska ☎ 866-282-7577; http://511.alaska.gov).

ACTIVITY TOURS

Whether you want to climb Mt McKinley, kayak Glacier Bay or pedal from Anchorage to Fairbanks, there's a guide company willing to put an itinerary together, supply the equipment and lead the way. Guide companies are also listed in regional chapters.

ABEC's Alaska Adventures (☎ 877-424-8907; www.abecalaska.com) Rafting and backpacking the Arctic National Wildlife Refuge and Gates of the Arctic National Park.

Alaska Discovery/Mt Sobek (☎ 888-687-6235; www.mtsobek.com) Kayaking Glacier Bay, bear viewing at Pack Creek and raft trips on the spectacular Tatshenshini River.

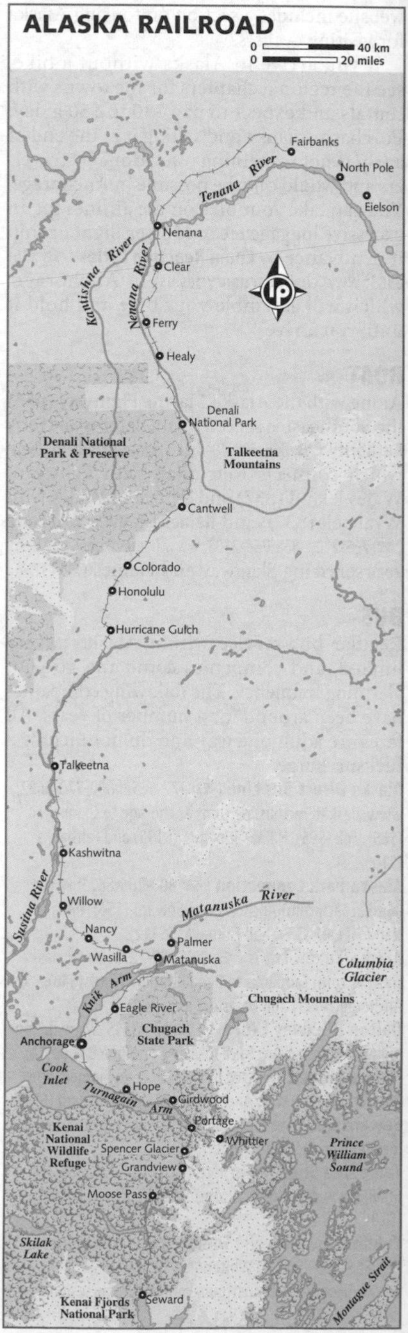

Alaska Mountain Guides (☎ 800-766-3396; www.alaskamountainguides.com) Week-long kayaking trips in Glacier Bay and mountaineering schools in Haines.
Alaskabike.com (☎ 245-2175; www.alaskabike.com) Fully supported cycle tours along the George Parks, Richardson and Glenn Hwys.
Arctic Treks (☎ 455-6502; www.arctictreksadventures.com) Treks and rafting in the Gates of the Arctic National Park and the Arctic National Wildlife Refuge.
Arctic Wild (☎ 888-577-8203; www.arcticwild.com) Floats and treks in the Brooks Range and Arctic National Wildlife Refuge.
CampAlaska (☎ 800-376-9438; www.campalaska.com) Camping tours with hiking, rafting and other activities.
St Elias Alpine Guides (☎ 888-933-5427; www.steliasguides.com) Mountaineering, rafting, trekking and glacier-skiing at Wrangell-St Elias National Park.
Tongass Kayak Adventures (☎ 907-772-4600; www.tongasskayak.com) Kayaking LeConte Glacier & Tebenkof Bay Wilderness in Southeast.

TRAIN

Alaska Railroad

It took eight years to build it (p217), but today the Alaska Railroad stretches 470 miles from Seward to Fairbanks, through spectacular scenery. You'll save more money traveling by bus down the George Parks Hwy, but few travelers regret booking the Alaska Railroad and viewing pristine wilderness from its comfortable cars.

SERVICES

The Alaska Railroad operates a year-round service between Fairbanks and Anchorage, as well as summer services (from late May to mid-September) from Anchorage to Whittier and from Anchorage to Seward.

The most popular run is the 336-mile trip from Anchorage to Fairbanks, stopping at Denali National Park. Northbound, at Mile 279 the train passes 46 miles of Mt McKinley, a stunning sight from the viewing domes on a clear day. It then slows down to cross the 918ft bridge over Hurricane Gulch.

The ride between Anchorage and Seward may be one of the most spectacular train trips in the world. From Anchorage, the 114-mile trip begins by skirting the 60-mile-long Turnagain Arm on Cook Inlet and then swings south, climbs over mountain passes, spans deep river gorges and comes within half a mile of three glaciers.

The Anchorage–Whittier service, which includes a stop in Girdwood and passes through two long tunnels, turns Whittier into a fun day trip. So does riding Alaska Railroad's *Hurricane Turn*, one of America's last flag-stop trains, which departs from Talkeetna (p217).

RESERVATIONS

You can reserve a seat and purchase tickets, even online, through **Alaska Railroad** (☎ 800-544-0552; www.akrr.com); highly recommended for the Anchorage–Denali service in July and early August. See regional chapters for prices and departures.

White Pass & Yukon Route

Built during the height of the Klondike Gold Rush, the White Pass & Yukon Railroad (p192) is still the incredible ride it must have been for the miners. The narrow gauge line is seen mostly as a tour but can be used for transport to Whitehorse and by backpackers on the Chilkoot Trail (p91).

Given all that, reservations are highly recommended anytime during the summer. Contact **White Pass & Yukon Route** (☎ 800-343-7373; www.whitepassrailroad.com) for information.

TRANSPORTATION

Health

CONTENTS

There is a high level of hygiene found in Alaska, so most common infectious diseases will not be a significant concern for travelers. Superb medical care and rapid evacuation to major hospitals are both available.

BEFORE YOU GO

INSURANCE

The cost of health care in the USA is extremely high and Alaska is no exception. Health insurance is essential in the USA, where some hospitals will refuse care without evidence of insurance. It's essential to purchase travel health insurance if your regular policy doesn't cover you when you're abroad.

A wide variety of policies are available, so check the small print. Be sure that the policy does not exclude wilderness trekking, mountaineering, kayaking, white-water rafting or any other activities you might be participating in while traveling in Alaska, or you may have a difficult time settling a claim. It is also prudent to be sure that the policy specifically covers helicopter evacuation, the most common way of reaching troubled backpackers in Alaska's wilderness areas.

Bring any medications you may need in their original containers, clearly labeled. A signed, dated letter from your physician that describes all medical conditions and medications, including generic names, is also a good idea.

If your medical insurance does not cover you for medical expenses abroad, consider getting supplemental insurance. Check the Lonely Planet website (www.lonelyplanet.com/bookings/insurance) for more information. Find out in advance if your insurance plan will make payments directly to providers or reimburse you later for overseas health expenditures.

RECOMMENDED VACCINATIONS

No special vaccines are required or recommended for travel to Alaska or the USA.

MEDICAL CHECKLIST

Recommended items for a personal medical kit:

- acetaminophen (Tylenol) or aspirin
- anti-inflammatory drugs (eg ibuprofen)
- antihistamines (for hay fever and allergic reactions)
- antibacterial ointment (eg Bactroban) for cuts and abrasions
- steroid cream or cortisone (for poison ivy and other allergic rashes)
- bandages, gauze, gauze rolls
- adhesive or paper tape
- scissors, safety pins, tweezers
- thermometer
- pocket knife
- DEET-containing insect repellent for the skin
- permethrin-containing insect spray for clothing, tents and bed nets
- sunblock

INTERNET RESOURCES

There is a wealth of travel health advice on the Internet. The World Health Organization publishes a superb book, *International Travel and Health*, which is revised annually and is available online at no cost at www.who.int/ith/en.

Another website of general interest is MD Travel Health at www.mdtravelhealth.com, which provides complete travel health recommendations for every country, updated daily, also at no cost.

It's usually a good idea to consult your government's travel-health website before departure, if one is available:

Australia (www.dfat.gov.au/travel/)
Canada (www.phac-aspc.gc.ca/tmp-pmv/index.html)

UK (www.fco.gov.uk/travelling-and-living-overseas)
USA (www.cdc.gov/travel/)

IN TRANSIT

MOTION SICKNESS

Since a great deal of travel in Alaska is done by boat and much of the overland travel is over rough, unsurfaced roads, motion sickness can be a real problem for those prone to it. Eating lightly before and during a trip will reduce the chances of motion sickness. If you are susceptible to motion sickness, try to find a place that minimizes disturbance – near the wing on aircrafts, close to midships on boats and near the center of buses. Fresh air or watching the horizon while on a boat usually helps; reading or cigarette smoke doesn't. Commercial motion-sickness preparations, which can cause drowsiness, have to be taken before the trip commences; when you're feeling sick it's too late. Ginger (available in a capsule) and peppermint (including mint-flavored sweets) are natural preventatives.

IN ALASKA

AVAILABILITY & COST OF HEALTH CARE

In general, if you have a medical emergency, the best bet is to find the nearest hospital and go to its emergency room. In many small Alaskan villages health clinics serve as hospitals but may not have 24-hour emergency services, in which case call 911 for immediate assistance. If the problem isn't urgent, you can call a nearby hospital for a referral to a local physician or a walk-in clinic. Either one would be cheaper than a trip to the emergency room.

Pharmacies are common throughout Alaska, and in small villages they are usually part of the health clinic. You may find some medications that are available over the counter in your home country will require a prescription in the USA and, as always, if you don't have insurance to cover the cost of the medication, it can be surprisingly expensive.

INFECTIOUS DISEASES

In addition to more common ailments, there are several infectious diseases that are unknown or uncommon outside North America. Most are acquired by mosquito or tick bites.

Giardiasis

Giardiasis, commonly known as giardia and sometimes called 'beaver fever,' is caused by an intestinal parasite *(Giardia lamblia)* present in contaminated water. Symptoms include stomach cramps, nausea, a bloated stomach, watery and foul-smelling diarrhea, and frequent gas. Giardia can appear several weeks after you have been exposed to the parasite. The symptoms may disappear for a few days and then return; this can go on for several weeks. Metronidazole, known as Flagyl, or tinidazole, known as Fasigyn, are the recommended drugs for treatment.

HIV & AIDS

As with most parts of the world, HIV infection occurs throughout the USA, including Alaska. You should never assume, on the basis of somebody's background or appearance, that they're free of this or any other sexually transmitted disease.

West Nile Virus

These infections were unknown in the USA until a few years ago, but have now been reported throughout the country. The exception is Alaska, which at the time of writing still had no reported cases of West Nile Virus.

For the latest update on the virus in Alaska go to the **US Geological Survey website** (http://diseasemaps.usgs.gov/).

ENVIRONMENTAL HAZARDS

Altitude Sickness

At high altitudes, acute mountain sickness (AMS) can occur and may be fatal. In the thinner atmosphere of the high mountains, lack of oxygen causes many individuals to suffer headaches, nausea, nosebleeds, shortness of breath, physical weakness and other symptoms that can have very serious consequences, especially if combined with heat exhaustion, sunburn or hypothermia. There is no hard and fast rule as to how high is too high: AMS has been fatal at altitudes of 10,000ft, although it is much more common above 11,500ft. For mild cases, everyday painkillers such as aspirin will relieve symptoms until the body adapts. Avoid smoking, drinking alcohol, eating heavily or exercising strenuously. Most people recover within a few hours or days. If the symptoms persist, it is imperative to descend to lower elevations. A number of other measures can prevent or minimize AMS:

- Ascend slowly. Have frequent rest days, spending two to three nights at each rise of 3000ft. If you reach a high altitude by trekking, acclimatization takes place gradually and you are less likely to be affected than if you fly directly to high altitude.
- It is always wise to sleep at a lower altitude than the greatest height reached during the day if possible. Also, once above 10,000ft care should be taken not to increase the sleeping altitude by more than 1000ft per day.
- Drink extra fluids. The mountain air is dry and cold, and moisture is lost as you breathe. Evaporation of sweat may occur unnoticed and result in dehydration.
- Eat light, high-carbohydrate meals for more energy.
- Avoid alcohol as it may increase the risk of dehydration.
- Avoid sedatives.

Hypothermia

Perhaps the most dangerous health threat in Alaska's Arctic regions is hypothermia. Hypothermia occurs when the body loses heat faster than it can produce it and the core temperature of the body falls. It is surprisingly easy to progress from very cold to dangerously cold due to a combination of wind, wet clothing, fatigue and hunger, even if the air temperature is above freezing point.

Dress in layers for insulation – silk, wool and some of the new artificial fibers are all good insulating materials. A hat is important as a lot of heat is lost through the head. A strong, waterproof outer layer is essential, as keeping dry is vital. Carry basic supplies, including food containing simple sugars to generate heat quickly, and lots of fluid to drink.

Symptoms of hypothermia include exhaustion, numb skin (particularly toes and fingers), shivering, slurred speech, irrational or violent behavior, lethargy, stumbling, dizzy spells, muscle cramps and violent bursts of energy. Irrationality may take the form of sufferers claiming they are warm and trying to take off their clothes.

To treat hypothermia, first get the victim out of the wind and rain, remove the victim's clothing if it's wet and replace it with dry, warm clothing. Give the victim hot liquids – not alcohol – and some high-calorie, easily digestible food like chocolate, trail mix or energy bars. This should be enough for the early stages of hypothermia, but it may be necessary to place victims in warm sleeping bags and get in with them. Do not rub victims; instead allow them to slowly warm themselves.

Insect Bites & Stings

Alaska is notorious for its biting insects. In the cities and towns you will have few problems, but out in the woods you'll have to contend with a variety of insects, including mosquitoes, black flies, white sox, no-see-ums and deer flies. Coastal areas, with their cool summers, have smaller numbers of insects than the Interior. Generally, camping on a beach where there is some breeze is better than pitching a tent in the woods. In the end, just accept the fact that you will be bitten.

Mosquitoes can often be the most bothersome pest. They emerge from hibernation before the snow has entirely melted away, peak in late June and are around until the first frost. You can combat mosquitoes by wearing light colors and a snug-fitting parka, and by tucking the legs of your pants into your socks or boots.

The most effective protection by far is a high-potency insect repellent; the best contain a high percentage of DEET (diethyltoluamide), the active ingredient. A little bottle of Musk Oil or Cutters can cost $6 or $7 (they contain 100% DEET), but it's one of the best investments you will make.

Unfortunately, repellents are less effective against black flies and no-see-ums. Their season runs from June to August, and their bite is far more annoying. The tiny no-see-um bite is a prolonged prick, after which the surrounding skin becomes inflamed and itches intermittently for up to a week or more. Unlike the mosquito, these insects will crawl into your hair and under loose clothing in search of bare skin.

Thus the best protection, and a fact of life in Alaska's backcountry, is to wear long-sleeved shirts, socks that will allow you to tuck your pants into them and a snug cap or woolen hat. You also see many backcountry travelers packing head nets. They're not something you wear a lot, as it can drive you crazy looking through mesh all day, but when you really need one a head net is a lifesaver.

Other items you might consider are bug jackets and an after-bite medication. The mesh jackets are soaked in insect repellent and kept in a re-sealable plastic bag until needed. Some people say bug jackets are the only effective way to keep no-see-ums at bay. After-bite medications contain ammonia and are rubbed on; while this might drive away your tent partner, it does soothe the craving to scratch the assortment of bites on your arms and neck.

Paralytic Shellfish Poisoning

In recent years, paralytic shellfish poisoning (PSP) has become a problem in Alaska. State officials urge people not to eat mussels, clams or snails gathered from unmonitored Alaskan beaches. PSP is possible anywhere in Alaska, and within 12 hours of consuming the infected shellfish victims experience symptoms of tingling or numbness in the lips and tongue (which can spread to the fingers or toes), loss of muscle coordination, dizziness, weakness and drowsiness. To get an update on the PSP situation, or to find out which beaches in the state are safe to clam, check the **Division of Environmental Health website** (www.dec.state.ak.us/eh/fss/seafood/psp/psp.htm).

Rabies

Rabies is a viral infection of the brain and spinal cord that is almost always fatal. The rabies virus is carried in the saliva of infected animals and is typically transmitted through an animal bite, though contamination of any break in the skin with infected saliva may result in rabies. This disease is found in Alaska, especially among small rodents such as squirrels and chipmunks in wilderness areas. Any bite, scratch or even lick from a mammal should be cleaned immediately and thoroughly. Scrub with soap and running water and then clean with an alcohol or iodine solution.

If there is any possibility, however small, that you have been exposed to rabies, you should seek preventative treatment, which consists of rabies immune globulin and rabies vaccine, and is quite safe. In particular, any contact with a bat should be discussed with health authorities, because bats have small teeth and may not leave obvious bite marks. If you wake up to find a bat in your room, or discover a bat in a room with small children, rabies prophylaxis may be necessary.

Sunburn & Windburn

Alaska has long hours of sunlight during the summer, and the sun's rays are even more intense when they are reflected off snow or water. Sunburn and windburn should be primary concerns for anyone planning to spend time trekking or paddling. The sun will burn you even if you feel cold, and the wind will cause dehydration and skin chafing. Use a good sunscreen and a moisture cream on exposed skin, even on cloudy days. A hat provides additional protection, and zinc oxide or some other barrier cream for your nose and lips is recommended for people spending any time on the ice or snow.

Reflection and glare off ice and snow can cause snow blindness so high-protection sunglasses, known by many locals as 'glacier goggles,' should be considered essential for any sort of visit on or near glaciers.

Water

Tap water in Alaska is safe to drink, but you should purify surface water taken from lakes and streams that is to be used for cooking and drinking. The simplest way to purify water is to boil it thoroughly. Remember that at high altitude, water boils at a lower temperature, so germs are less likely to be killed.

If you are trekking in the wilderness, water purification can be handled easily by investing in a high-quality filter. Filters such as Katadyn's Hiker PRO or MSR's Sweetwater are designed to take out whatever you shouldn't be drinking, including *Giardia lamblia*. They cost between $75 and $140 and are well worth it.

Glossary

Alcan or **Alaska Hwy** – the main overland route into Alaska. Although the highway is almost entirely paved now, completing a journey along this legendary road is still a special accomplishment; the Alcan begins at the Mile 0 milepost in Dawson Creek (northeastern British Columbia, Canada), heads northwest through Whitehorse, the capital of the Yukon Territory, and officially ends at Delta Junction (Mile 1390), 101 miles southeast of Fairbanks
AMS – acute mountain sickness; occurs at high altitudes and can be fatal
ANWR – Arctic National Wildlife Refuge; the 1.5-million-acre wilderness area that oil-company officials and Alaskans have been pushing hard to open up for oil and gas drilling
ATV – all-terrain vehicle
aurora borealis or **northern lights** – the mystical snakes of light that weave across the sky from the northern horizon. It's a spectacular show on clear nights and can occur at almost any time of the year. The lights are the result of gas particles colliding with solar electrons and are best viewed from the Interior, away from city lights, between late summer and winter

bidarka – a skin-covered sea kayak used by the Aleuts
blanket toss – a traditional activity of the Iñupiat, in which a large animal skin is used to toss a person into the air
BLM – Bureau of Land Management; the federal agency that maintains much of the wilderness around and north of Fairbanks, including cabins and campgrounds
blue cloud – what Southeasterners call a break in the clouds
breakup – when the ice on rivers suddenly begins to melt, breaks up and flows downstream; many residents also use this term to describe spring in Alaska, when the rain begins, the snow melts and everything turns to mud and slush
bunny boots – large, oversized and usually white plastic boots used extensively in subzero weather to prevent the feet from freezing; much to the horror of many Alaskans, the company that manufactured the boot announced in 1995 it would discontinue the style
Bush, the – any area in the state that is not connected by road to Anchorage or is not part of the Alaska Marine Hwy

cabin fever – a winter condition in which Alaskans go stir-crazy in their one-room cabins because of too little sunlight and too much time spent indoors
cache – a small hut or storage room built high off the ground to keep supplies and spare food away from roaming bears and wolves; the term, however, has found its way onto the neon signs of everything from liquor stores to pizza parlors in the cities
calve – (of an ice mass) to separate or break so that a part of the ice becomes detached
capital move – the political issue that raged in the early 1980s, concerning moving the state capital from Juneau closer to Anchorage; although residents rejected funding the move north in a 1982 state election, the issue continues to divide Alaska
cheechako – tenderfoot, greenhorn or somebody trying to survive their first year in Alaska
chum – not your mate or good buddy, but a nickname for dog salmon
clear-cut – a hated sight for environmentalists: an area where loggers have cut every tree, large and small, leaving nothing standing; the first view of a clear-cut in Alaska, often from a ferry, is a shocking sight for a traveler

d-2 – the lands issue of the late 1970s, which pitted environmentalists against developers over the federal government's preservation of 156,250 sq miles of Alaskan wilderness as wildlife reserves, forests and national parks
dividend days – the period in October when residents receive their Permanent Fund checks and Alaska goes on a spending spree

Eskimo ice cream – an Iñupiat food made of whipped animal fat, berries, seal oil and sometimes shredded caribou meat

fish wheel – a wooden trap powered by a river's current that scoops salmon or other large fish out of a river into a holding tank
freeze-up – the point in November or December when most rivers and lakes ice over, signaling to Alaskans that their long winter has started in earnest

glacier fishing – picking up flopping salmon along the Copper River in Cordova after a large calving from the Childs Glacier strands the fish during the August spawning run; practiced by both bears and people

humpie – a nickname for the humpback or pink salmon, the mainstay of the fishing industry in the Southeast

ice worm – a small, thin black worm that thrives in glacial ice and was made famous by a Robert Service poem
Iditarod – the 1049-mile sled-dog race run every March from Anchorage to Nome. The winner usually completes the course in less than 14 days and takes home $50,000

Lower 48 – an Alaskan term for continental USA

moose nuggets – hard, smooth droppings; some enterprising resident in Homer has capitalized on them by baking, varnishing and trimming them with evergreen leaves to sell during Christmas as Moostletoe
mukluks – lightweight boots of sealskin trimmed with fur, made by the Iñupiat
muktuk – whale skin and blubber; also known as *maktak,* it is a delicacy among Iñupiat and is eaten in a variety of ways, including raw, pickled and boiled
muskeg – the bogs in Alaska, where layers of matted plant life float on top of stagnant water; these are bad areas in which to hike

North Slope – the gentle plain that extends from the Brooks Range north to the Arctic Ocean
no-see-um – nickname for the tiny gnats found throughout much of the Alaskan wilderness, especially in the Interior and parts of the Brooks Range
NPS – National Park Service; administers 82,656 sq miles in Alaska and its 15 national parks include such popular units as Denali, Glacier Bay, Kenai Fjords and Klondike Gold Rush National Historical Park

Outside – to residents, any place that isn't Alaska
Outsider – to residents, anyone who isn't an Alaskan

permafrost – permanently frozen subsoil that covers two-thirds of the state but is disappearing due to global warming
petroglyphs – ancient rock carvings
portage – an area of land between waterways over which paddlers carry their boats
potlatch – a traditional gathering of indigenous people held to commemorate any memorable occasion

qiviut – the wool of the musk ox, often woven into garments

RV – recreational vehicles (motor homes)
RVers – those folks who opt to travel in an RV

scat – animal droppings; however, the term is usually used to describe bear droppings. If the scat is dark brown or bluish and somewhat square in shape, a bear has passed by; if it is steaming, the bear is eating blueberries around the next bend
scrimshaw – hand-carved ivory from walrus tusks
sourdough – any old-timer in the state who, it is said, is 'sour on the country but without enough dough to get out;' newer residents believe the term applies to anybody who has survived an Alaskan winter; the term also applies to a 'yeasty' mixture used to make bread or pancakes
Southeast sneakers – the tall, reddish-brown rubber boots that Southeast residents wear when it rains, and often when it doesn't; also known as 'Ketchikan tennis shoes,' 'Sitka slippers' and 'Petersburg pumps' among other names
squaw candy – salmon that has been dried or smoked into jerky
stinkhead – an Iñupiat 'treat' made by burying a salmon head in the sand; leave the head to ferment for up to 10 days then dig it up, wash off the sand and enjoy

taku wind – Juneau's sudden gusts of wind, which may exceed 100mph in the spring and fall; often the winds cause horizontal rain, which, as the name indicates, comes straight at you instead of falling on you; in Anchorage and throughout the Interior, these sudden rushes of air over or through mountain gaps are called 'williwaws'
tundra – vast, treeless plains

UA – University of Alaska
ulu – a fan-shaped knife that Alaska natives traditionally used to chop and scrape meat; now used by gift shops to lure tourists
umiaks – leather boats made by the Iñupiat people
USFS – US Forest Service; oversees the Tongass and Chugach National Forests, and the 190 cabins, hiking trails, kayak routes and campgrounds within them
USFWS – US Fish & Wildlife Service; administers 16 federal wildlife refuges in Alaska, more than 120,312 sq miles
USGS – US Geological Society; makes topographic maps, including those covering almost every corner of Alaska

The Authors

JIM DUFRESNE

Coordinating author, Southeast Alaska, Southwest Alaska

Jim has lived, worked and wandered across Alaska and even cashed a Permanent Fund Dividend check. As the sports and outdoors editor of the *Juneau Empire*, he was the first Alaskan sportswriter to win a national award from Associated Press. As a guide for Alaska Discovery he has witnessed Hubbard Glacier shed icebergs the size of pick-up trucks off its 8-mile-wide face. Jim now lives in Michigan but is constantly returning to the Far North to write books on Alaska including Lonely Planet's *Hiking in Alaska*.

GREG BENCHWICK

Cruising in Alaska, Denali & the Interior, Fairbanks& Around, The Bush

Greg has rumbled in the jungles of South America, walked across Spain and challenged the peaks of Alaska. He specializes in adventure and sustainable travel, and has written more than a dozen guidebooks. Greg first came to Alaska in 1996, when he dirt-bagged it at the Dragnet parking lot in Kenai and worked in a remote cannery on Bristol Bay. He has since hitchhiked from Girdwood to Haines, picked fights in Ketchikan (and lost) and, for this edition, traveled through Alaska's Bush and Interior. When he's not on the road, Greg develops his new-media company www.monjomedia.com.

CATHERINE BODRY

Anchorage & Around, Prince William Sound, Kenai Peninsula

Catherine has spent most of her adult life rebelling against her suburban upbringing. As soon as she finished college in Washington, she headed north to wilder lands, and after a few stints of summer work in Anchorage, she decided to brave an Alaskan winter. It turned out she liked it just fine, and after she completed a master's degree in English she headed to tiny Seward, where she feels right at home in hiking boots. When she's not daydreaming about traveling, Catherine is usually out on the trails. She even competed in her first Mt Marathon race while researching this book.

LONELY PLANET AUTHORS

Why is our travel information the best in the world? It's simple: our authors are passionate, dedicated travelers. They don't take freebies in exchange for positive coverage so you can be sure the advice you're given is impartial. They travel widely to all the popular spots, and off the beaten track. They don't research using just the internet or phone. They discover new places not included in any other guidebook. They personally visit thousands of hotels, restaurants, palaces, trails, galleries, temples and more. They speak with dozens of locals every day to make sure you get the kind of insider knowledge only a local could tell you. They take pride in getting all the details right, and in telling it how it is. Think you can do it? Find out how at **lonelyplanet.com**.

Behind the Scenes

THIS BOOK

This 9th edition of *Alaska* was written by Jim DuFresne (the coordinating author), Greg Benchwick and Catherine Bodry. The previous edition was written by Jim DuFresne and Aaron Spitzer. The 7th edition was written by Jim DuFresne, Paige R Penland and Don Root. This guidebook was commissioned in Lonely Planet's Oakland office, and produced by the following:

Commissioning Editors Emily K Wolman, Suki Gear
Coordinating Editor Justin Flynn
Coordinating Cartographer Andy Rojas
Coordinating Layout Designer Jacqui Saunders
Managing Editor Sasha Baskett
Managing Cartographer Alison Lyall
Managing Layout Designer Celia Wood
Assisting Editors David Andrew, Daniel Corbett, Angela Tinson, Saralinda Turner
Assisting Cartographers Ross Butler, Karen Grant
Assisting Layout Designer Jim Hsu
Cover Designer Mary Nelson Parker
Project Manager Chris Love

Thanks to Jay Cooke, Heather Dickson, Bronwyn Hicks, Rebecca Davey, Maret Sotkiewicz, Nigel Chin, Wayne Murphy, Sally Darmody, Laura Jane, Shahara Ahmed, Lucy Birchley

THANKS

JIM DUFRESNE

Twenty six years after writing the 1st edition, I'm still working on this book. That's how alluring Alaska can be once this great land gets into your blood. That's also how enduring my Alaskan friendships are. People I once lived and worked with keep beckoning me to come back: Sue and Jeff in Juneau, Bonnie and Hayden in Gustavus, Buckwheat and Jeff in Skagway, Todd and Ed in Anchorage. I also appreciate the assistance and tips passed along by visitors bureau staff, rangers at Forest Service stations, Alaska Marine Highway workers on the ferries and travelers everywhere.

GREG BENCHWICK

Besos and a big *gracias* to my partner Alejandra. I'd also like to thank my father who inspired me to adventure in Alaska and never give up. I love you, dad. There are many Alaskans to thank, including Clive S Thomas, a University of Alaska Political Science Professor who fact-checked my history sections, Philip Fitzgerald, who was kind enough to host me in his Fairbanks cabin (*gracias* Don Felipe!), Elisabeth Balster Dabney, Jay Elhard, Tom Meier and Lucy Tyrrell, and the lucky Swedes. Great work

THE LONELY PLANET STORY

Fresh from an epic journey across Europe, Asia and Australia in 1972, Tony and Maureen Wheeler sat at their kitchen table stapling together notes. The first Lonely Planet guidebook, *Across Asia on the Cheap*, was born.

Travelers snapped up the guides. Inspired by their success, the Wheelers began publishing books to Southeast Asia, India and beyond. Demand was prodigious, and the Wheelers expanded the business rapidly to keep up. Over the years, Lonely Planet extended its coverage to every country and into the virtual world via lonelyplanet.com and the Thorn Tree message board.

As Lonely Planet became a globally loved brand, Tony and Maureen received several offers for the company. But it wasn't until 2007 that they found a partner whom they trusted to remain true to the company's principles of traveling widely, treading lightly and giving sustainably. In October of that year, BBC Worldwide acquired a 75% share in the company, pledging to uphold Lonely Planet's commitment to independent travel, trustworthy advice and editorial independence.

Today, Lonely Planet has offices in Melbourne, London and Oakland, with over 500 staff members and 300 authors. Tony and Maureen are still actively involved with Lonely Planet. They're traveling more often than ever, and they're devoting their spare time to charitable projects. And the company is still driven by the philosophy of *Across Asia on the Cheap*: 'All you've got to do is decide to go and the hardest part is over. So go!'

to the editors, cartographers and authors that put this book together.

CATHERINE BODRY
First, thanks to Emily Wolman for giving me my first LP assignment. Jim DuFresne's work was my original guide and inspiration when I moved to Alaska, and Aaron Spitzer's text was a tough act to follow. I had some particularly helpful assistants: Emily, Steph, Katey, Jen, Margi, Scott, Chris – thanks for giving me beds and joining me for the ever-important bar and restaurant research. I can't thank my parents enough for always encouraging me to both write and travel, and Lael, thanks for never hesitating when I tell you I'm leaving for weeks at a time.

OUR READERS

Many thanks to the travelers who used the last edition and wrote to us with helpful hints, useful advice and interesting anecdotes:
Bakewell IV, Mark Bewsher, Tracey Brightman, Klaus Bucka-Lassen, Raniero Cerqua, Matt Chellman, Liza Chisholm, Robert Elliott, Amy Finkelstein, Nicole Gasparini, Cristina Gianotti, Brad Grossweiler, Monica Harmathy, Ya-Fang Hsiao, Emily Jamieson, Gregory Kaufmann, Bob And Kirsten Kenworthy, Tracie Kirkham, Amanda Klunder, Amaury Laporte, Susan Lehrer, Fred Lindhout, Isabelle Loo, Bob Markwell, John Mccutchan, Joseph Mckenzie, Gary Mcmichael, Maraley Mcmichael, Hans Metzler, Caroline Muller, Mike O'Brien, Anneliese Paull, Monika Pergler, Don Pirot, Jemima Robinson, Diane Spallone, Gianfranco Stanzani, Carly Szerstuk, Jochen Thorn, Pim Verver, Jan Voorhagen, Deb Woodruff, Joanne Woolever.

SEND US YOUR FEEDBACK

We love to hear from travelers – your comments keep us on our toes and help make our books better. Our well-traveled team reads every word on what you loved or loathed about this book. Although we cannot reply individually to postal submissions, we always guarantee that your feedback goes straight to the appropriate authors, in time for the next edition. Each person who sends us information is thanked in the next edition – and the most useful submissions are rewarded with a free book.

To send us your updates – and find out about Lonely Planet events, newsletters and travel news – visit our award-winning website: **lonelyplanet.com/contact**.

Note: we may edit, reproduce and incorporate your comments in Lonely Planet products such as guidebooks, websites and digital products, so let us know if you don't want your comments reproduced or your name acknowledged. For a copy of our privacy policy visit lonelyplanet.com/privacy.

ACKNOWLEDGMENTS

Many thanks to the following for the use of their content:

Globe on title page ©Mountain High Maps 1993 Digital Wisdom, Inc.

Index

INDEX

000 Map pages
000 Photograph pages

INDEX

INDEX

000 Map pages
000 Photograph pages

INDEX

000 Map pages
000 Photograph pages

GreenDex

The following attractions, activities, services, restaurants and lodgings have been selected by our authors because they demonstrate an active sustainable-tourism policy. Some are involved in conservation or environmental education, and many are locally owned and operated, thereby maintaining and preserving local identity, arts and culture.

We want to keep developing our sustainable-tourism content. If you think we've omitted somewhere that should be listed here, or if you disagree with our choices, email us at talk2us@lonelyplanet.com.au and set us straight for next time. For more information about sustainable tourism and Lonely Planet, see www.lonelyplanet.com/responsibletravel.

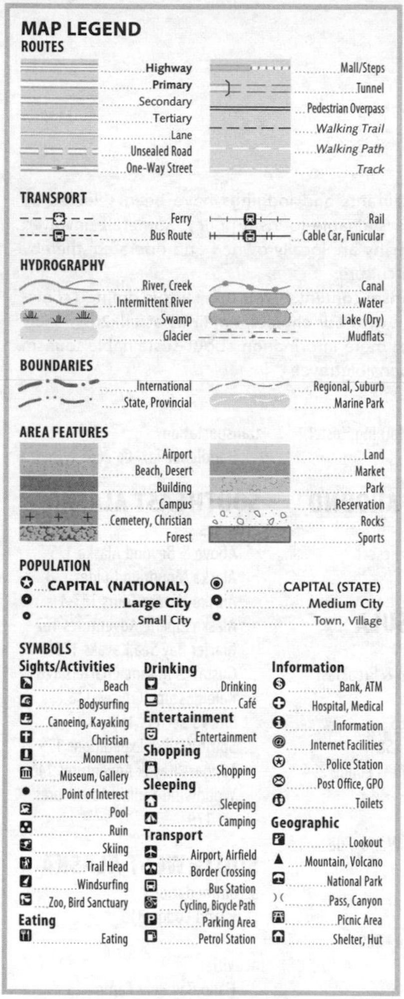

LONELY PLANET OFFICES

Australia

Head Office
Locked Bag 1, Footscray, Victoria 3011
☎ 03 8379 8000, fax 03 8379 8111
talk2us@lonelyplanet.com.au

USA

150 Linden St, Oakland, CA 94607
☎ 510 250 6400, toll free 800 275 8555
fax 510 893 8572
info@lonelyplanet.com

UK

2nd fl, 186 City Rd,
London EC1V 2NT
☎ 020 7106 2100, fax 020 7106 2101
go@lonelyplanet.co.uk

Published by Lonely Planet Publications Pty Ltd
ABN 36 005 607 983

Cover photograph: paddling past icebergs. Rob Howard/Corbis. Many of the images in this guide are available for licensing from Lonely Planet Images: www.lonelyplanetimages.com.

Printed by Fabulous Printers Pte Ltd
Printed in Singapore.